MARGARET THATCHER

THE DOWNING STREET YEARS

HarperCollins*Publishers*

HarperCollins*Publishers*
77–85 Fulham Palace Road,
Hammersmith, London W6 8JB

This paperback edition 1995
1 3 5 7 9 8 6 4 2

First published in Great Britain by
HarperCollins*Publishers* 1993

ISBN 0 00 638321 1

Photoset in Linotron Baskerville by
Rowland Phototypesetting Limited,
Bury St Edmunds, Suffolk

Printed and bound in Great Britain by
HarperCollinsManufacturing Glasgow

The Downing Street Years

LADY THATCHER was leader of the Conservative Party for fifteen years and prime minister for eleven and a half. The second volume of her memoirs, published in 1995, covers her life until her election as prime minister in 1979.

MARGARET, THE LADY THATCHER, O.M., P.C., F.R.S.
HOUSE OF LORDS
LONDON SW1A 0PW

To my husband and family without whose love and encouragement I should never have become Prime Minister.

And to all those who worked at 10 Downing Street and Chequers in whatever capacity whose unfailing support was crucial in those challenging years.

Contents

List of Illustrations

Acknowledgements

Many people assisted me in one way or another with the preparation of this book. Some I cannot name for they are still members of the civil service; others I can and do mention in what follows. But there is one person to whom I owe special thanks.

Government officials who prepare the ground for summit meetings are known in the trade as 'sherpas' after the Himalayan guides who assist people to climb Everest. My indispensable sherpa in the enterprise of writing this book has been Robin Harris. Robin has descended into the ravines of research for official papers to confirm or challenge my memory; he was a sure-footed guide through blizzards of fact and interpretation; and he ensured that the expedition reached its destination by the most direct route, in good order, and even attired with some elegance. Without his advice and help at every stage, I doubt that we could have reached the summit.

We were not alone on the journey. John O'Sullivan came skiing in occasionally, tuned up the arguments, pared the prose and pushed forward the narrative. Without him this book would have taken longer to write and it would take longer to read.

Another vital member of the team was Chris Collins, our researcher. He was meticulous, assiduous and totally committed; and to these qualities he added the valuable objectivity of the academic historian. Debbie Fletcher typed – and then retyped and typed again – the constantly evolving manuscript with impressive efficiency and unfailing cheerfulness. Tessa Gaisman brought her own special blend of good taste and common sense to the selection of the photographs. Carolyn Selman helped us sort press releases and press cuttings into manageable order. I am immensely grateful to all members of my memoirs team. Our work together has been – to borrow a phrase which appears later in this volume – 'fraught but fun'.

One of the more enjoyable aspects of memoir writing is the reliving of old times with good friends. I was able to draw on the recollections and reflections of many of those who, in different ways, were involved with the story I have told. I would like to express my special thanks to Cynthia Crawford, Sir Charles Powell, Sir Alan Walters and John Whittingdale MP, all of whose assistance was invaluable. I also had the benefit of advice on particular topics from Professor Tim Congdon, Andrew Dunlop, Lord Griffiths of Fforestfach, George Guise, Rt. Hon. the Hon. Archie Hamilton MP, Sir John Hoskyns, Sir Bernard Ingham, Dr Sheila Lawlor, John Mills, Rt. Hon. Sir Peter Morrison, Ferdinand Mount, Lord Parkinson of Carnforth, Caroline Ryder, Stephen Sherbourne, Sir Kenneth Stowe, Lady Wakeham and Lord Wolfson of Sunningdale.

Leafing through the official papers, I found them fascinating but limited: indeed, their very dryness confirmed in my mind the value of writing this book. Some stories you have to live in order to tell. But, that said, I, who never kept a diary, would have been lost without them. I am, therefore, very obliged to Sir Robin Butler and the staff of the Cabinet Office for the kind and efficient way in which they made the records of my administration available to me.

My publishers, HarperCollins, acted as publishers should – allowing the author to do her stuff but keeping her up to the mark and within the deadline. Eddie Bell was a reassuring and shrewd source of practical guidance. Stuart Proffitt worked tenaciously to ensure that jargon was removed and obscurity illumined. I am grateful to them both.

Finally, I would like to thank Julian Seymour who runs my office: without him and the members of my staff this story could not have been told.

MARGARET THATCHER
June 1993

THE
DOWNING STREET
YEARS

Introduction

'Ayes, 311. Noes, 310.' Even before the figures were announced by the tellers, we on the Opposition benches knew that Jim Callaghan's Labour Government had lost its motion of confidence and would have to call a general election. When the four tellers return to read the total of votes recorded in the lobbies, MPs can see which party has won from the positions they take up facing the Speaker. On this occasion the two Tories walked towards the Speaker's left hand in the space usually occupied by government whips. A great burst of cheering and laughter rose from the Tory benches, and our supporters in the spectators' galleries roared with out-of-order jubilation. Denis, who was watching the result from the Opposition box on the floor of the House, shouted 'hooray' and was, quite properly, reproved by one of the serjeants at arms. Through the din, however, the stentorian guards' officer tones of Spenser Le Marchant, the 6′ 6″ Tory MP for High Peak who was famous for his intake of champagne, could be heard booming out the result – the first such defeat for a British Government in more than fifty years.

We had known the figures would be close, but we had not known how close as we filed in and out of the lobbies. I looked for the unexpected faces who might decide the outcome. Labour whips had been assiduously rounding up the handful of independent MPs whose votes might put them over the top. In the end everything turned on the decision of one elusive Irish MP, Frank Maguire, who did indeed arrive at the Palace of Westminster, lifting the hopes of Labour ministers. The wait before the announcement was filled with rumour and counter-rumour across the Chamber. It seemed endless. Our Chief Whip quietly gave me his own forecast. I said nothing and tried to look inscrutable, doubtless without success. Some on the Labour benches, hearing of Mr Maguire's appearance, began to grin in anticipation of victory. But Mr Maguire had arrived only to abstain. And on

28 March 1979, James Callaghan's Labour Government, the last Labour Government and perhaps the last ever, fell from office.

The obsequies across the despatch box were brief and almost formal. Mr Callaghan told the House that he would take his case to the country and that Parliament would be dissolved once essential business had been transacted. Replying for the Opposition, I said that we would co-operate in this to ensure a dissolution of Parliament at the earliest opportunity. A slight sense of anti-climax after all the excitement took hold of MPs. On all sides we felt that the Commons was for the moment no longer the centre of events. The great questions of power and principle would be decided elsewhere. I got up to leave the Chamber for a meeting of the Shadow Cabinet in my Commons room, and Willie Whitelaw, who could often sense my mood even before I realized it myself, put an encouraging arm around my shoulder.

The Shadow Cabinet meeting was brisk and businesslike. Our main concern was to prevent the Labour Government from scoring any parliamentary runs in the limited time left to it. In particular, we were strongly of the view that there should be no budget statement, whatever limited tax changes might be needed to keep public finance on an even keel. We resolved that in office we would honour the Labour Government's pledge to increase pensions by the amounts which the Prime Minister had announced in the confidence debate. And we decided to press for an election on 26 April, the earliest possible date, knowing that Labour would wish to stretch out the timetable in the hope of restoring their party morale. (In the end we had to settle for 3 May.) Then, the business concluded, we had a celebratory drink and broke up.

Driving back to my home in Flood Street, Chelsea, with Denis, I reflected on the coming battle. We had a fight on our hands, of course; but barring accidents it was a fight we should be able to win. The Government's defeat in the confidence debate symbolized a larger defeat for the Left. It had lost the public's confidence as well as Parliament's. The 'winter of discontent', the ideological divisions in the Government, its inability to control its allies in the trade union movement, an impalpable sense that socialists everywhere had run out of steam and ideas – all these gave a *fin de siècle* atmosphere to the approaching election campaign.

The Tory Party, by contrast, had used its period in Opposition to elaborate a new approach to reviving the British economy and nation. Not only had we worked out a full programme for government; we had also taken apprenticeships in advertising and learnt how to put a complex and sophisticated case in direct, clear and simple language. We had, finally, been arguing that case for the best part of four years, so our agenda would, with luck, strike people as familiar common sense rather than as a wild radical project. On all these scores I felt a reasonable confidence.

The prospects after an election victory were another matter. Britain in 1979 was a nation that had had the stuffing knocked out of it with progressively more severe belabourings over the previous hundred years. Beginning in the 1880s, our industrial supremacy had been steadily eroding in the face of first American, then German competition. To be sure, some part of this erosion was inevitable and even welcome. As the pioneer of the industrial revolution, Britain enjoyed a head start over its competitors that was bound to diminish as nations with larger populations and more abundant natural resources entered the race. But since their rise would mean the growth of large export markets for Britain as well as fierce competition in domestic and third markets – Imperial Germany, for instance, was Britain's second largest export market in 1914 – this commercial rivalry was more blessing than curse.

What made it in the event more curse than blessing was Britain's failure to respond to the challenge effectively. We invested less; we educated and trained our people to a lower standard; and we allowed our workers and manufacturers to combine in various cartels that restricted competition and reduced efficiency. Thoughtful observers had noticed these trends by the beginning of this century. Arthur Balfour's Tory administration of 1902–5 reformed education, training and scientific research in response to a non-partisan public agitation that has come to be called the 'quest for national efficiency'. But such attempts to revive Britain's economy by social reform were battling against very profound social forces: the natural complacency of a nation grown used for more than a hundred years to 'top dog' status; the economic 'cushion' provided by Britain's vast overseas investments (equal in 1914 to 186 per cent of GNP); the deceptive might of an empire which continued to expand until 1919 but which cost more to defend than it contributed to national wealth; and, of course, the exhausting national losses of the First and Second World Wars. As a result, the Britain that woke up on the morning after 1945 was not only a nation drained by two great military efforts in defence of common civilization, but also one suffering from a prolonged bout of economic and financial anaemia.

With the election of Attlee's Labour Government, however, there began a sustained attempt, which lasted over thirty years, to halt this relative decline and kick-start a resurgence along lines which – whether we call them socialist, social democrat, statist or merely Butskellite* – represented a centralizing, managerial, bureaucratic, interventionist style of government. Already large and unwieldy after its expansion in two world wars, the British Government very soon jammed a finger in every pie. It levied high rates of tax on work, enterprise, consumption, and wealth transfer. It planned development at every level – urban, rural, industrial and scientific. It managed the economy, macro-economically by Keynesian methods of fiscal manipulation, micro-economically by granting regional and industrial subsidies on a variety of criteria. It nationalized industries, either directly by taking ownership, or indirectly by using its powers of regulation to constrain the decisions of private management in the direction the Government wanted. (As Arthur Shenfield put it, the difference between the public and private sectors was that the private sector was controlled by government, and the public sector wasn't controlled by anyone.) It made available various forms of welfare for a wide range of contingencies – poverty, unemployment, large families, old age, misfortune, ill-health, family quarrels – generally on a universal basis. And when some people preferred to rely on their own resources or on the assistance of family and friends, the Government would run advertising campaigns to persuade people of the virtues of dependence.

The rationale for such a comprehensive set of interventions was, to quote the former Labour Cabinet minister, Douglas Jay, that 'the gentleman in Whitehall really does know better what is good for the people than the people know themselves.' A disinterested civil service, with access to the best and latest information, was better able to foresee economic eventualities and to propose responses to them than were the blind forces of the so-called 'free market'.

Such a philosophy was explicitly advocated by the Labour Party. It gloried in planning, regulation, controls and subsidies. It had a vision of the future: Britain as a democratic socialist society, third way between east European collectivism and American capitalism. And there was a rough consistency between its principles and its policies – both tending towards the expansion of government – even if the pace of that change was not fast enough for its own Left.

The Tory Party was more ambivalent. At the level of principle, rhetorically and in Opposition, it opposed these doctrines and

* A political term dating from the early 1950s, denoting a consensus politician combining the moderate Conservatism of R. A. Butler with the moderate socialism of Hugh Gaitskell.

preached the gospel of free enterprise with very little qualification. Almost every post-war Tory victory had been won on slogans such as 'Britain Strong and Free' or 'Set the People Free'. But in the fine print of policy, and especially in government, the Tory Party merely pitched camp in the long march to the left. It never tried seriously to reverse it. Privatization? The Carlisle State Pubs were sold off. Taxation? Regulation? Subsidies? If these were cut down at the start of a Tory government, they gradually crept up again as its life ebbed away. The welfare state? We boasted of spending more money than Labour, not of restoring people to independence and self-reliance. The result of this style of accommodationist politics, as my colleague Keith Joseph complained, was that post-war politics became a 'socialist ratchet' – Labour moved Britain towards more statism; the Tories stood pat; and the next Labour Government moved the country a little further left. The Tories loosened the corset of socialism; they never removed it.

Indeed, Keith's formulation may have been too kind. After a reforming start, Ted Heath's Government, in which we both served, proposed and almost implemented the most radical form of socialism ever contemplated by an elected British Government. It offered state control of prices and dividends, and the joint oversight of economic policy by a tripartite body representing the Trades Union Congress, the Confederation of British Industry and the Government, in return for trade union acquiescence in an incomes policy. We were saved from this abomination by the conservatism and suspicion of the TUC which perhaps could not believe that their 'class enemy' was prepared to surrender without a fight.

No theory of government was ever given a fairer test or a more prolonged experiment in a democratic country than democratic socialism received in Britain. Yet it was a miserable failure in every respect. Far from reversing the slow relative decline of Britain *vis-à-vis* its main industrial competitors, it accelerated it. We fell further behind them, until by 1979 we were widely dismissed as 'the sick man of Europe'. The relative worsening of our economic position was disguised by the rising affluence of the West as a whole. We, among others, could hardly fail to benefit from the long economic expansion of the post-war western world led by the United States. But if we never had it so good, others – like Germany, France, Italy, Denmark – increasingly had it better. And, as the 1970s wore grimly on, we began to fail in absolute as well as relative terms.

Injections of monetary demand, which in the 1950s had produced a rise in real production and a fall in unemployment before causing a modest rise in prices, now went directly into high rates of inflation without so much as a blip on the charts for production and unemployment. State subsidies and direction of investment achieved progressively more inefficient industries and ever lower returns on capital. Laws giving protective immunity to the trade unions at the turn of the century were now abused to protect restrictive practices and overmanning, to underpin strikes, and to coerce workers into joining unions and participating in industrial action against their better judgement. Welfare benefits, distributed with little or no consideration of their effects on behaviour, encouraged illegitimacy, facilitated the breakdown of families, and replaced incentives favouring work and self-reliance with perverse encouragement for idleness and cheating. The final illusion – that state intervention would promote social harmony and solidarity or, in Tory language, 'One Nation' – collapsed in the 'winter of discontent' when the dead went unburied, critically ill patients were turned away from hospitals by pickets, and the prevailing social mood was one of snarling envy and motiveless hostility. To cure the British disease with socialism was like trying to cure leukaemia with leeches.

Another approach was needed – and for international reasons as well as domestic ones. Britain's weakened economic position meant that its international role was bound to be cramped and strained as well. Our most painful experience of the country's reduced circumstances was the failure of the Suez expedition in 1956. This was the result of political and economic weakness rather than military failure, because the Government withdrew a victorious force from the Canal Zone in response to a 'run on the pound' encouraged by the US Government. Whatever the details of this defeat, however, it entered the British soul and distorted our perspective on Britain's place in the world.

We developed what might be called the 'Suez syndrome': having previously exaggerated our power, we now exaggerated our impotence. Military and diplomatic successes such as the war in Borneo – which preserved the independence of former British colonies against Indonesian subversion, helped to topple the anti-western dictator, Sukarno, and thus altered the long-term balance of power in Asia in our interest – were either dismissed as trivial or ignored altogether. Defeats, which in reality were the results of avoidable misjudgement, such as the retreat from the Gulf in 1970, were held to be the inevitable consequences of British decline. And comic opera enterprises, such as Harold Wilson's 'invasion' of Anguilla in March 1969 (for once, 'police action' seems the right term) were gleefully seized upon to illustrate the reality of reduced British power. The truth – that Britain was a middle-ranking power, given unusual influence by virtue of its historical distinction, skilled diplomacy and versatile military forces, but greatly weakened by economic decline – seemed too complex for sophisticated people to grasp. They were determined to think themselves much weaker and more contemptible than was in fact the case, and refused all comfort to the contrary.

What made this more dangerous in the late 1970s was that the United States was undergoing a similar crisis of morale following its failure in Vietnam. In fact, the 'Vietnam Syndrome' was perhaps more debilitating than its Suez counterpart because it embodied the conviction that the United States was *fortunately* incapable of intervention abroad since such intervention would almost certainly be inimical to morality, the world's poor, or the revolutionary tides of history. Hobbled by this psychological constraint and by a Congress also deeply influenced by it, two presidents saw the Soviet Union and its surrogates expand their power and influence in Afghanistan, southern Africa and Central America by subversion and outright military invasion. In Europe, an increasingly self-confident Soviet Union was planting offensive missiles in its eastern satellites, building its conventional forces to levels far in excess of NATO equivalents. It was also constructing a navy that would give it global reach.

A theory, coined after the collapse of communism to justify the policy of 'doves' in the Cold War, holds that because the Soviet Union was comparatively weak in the late 1980s, after almost a decade of western economic and military revival, it must have been a hollow threat in the late 1970s. Quite apart from the logical absurdity of placing a cause after its effect, the history of the Soviet Union from 1917 until just the other day refutes this argument. The Soviet Union was a power which deliberately inflicted economic backwardness on itself for political and ideological reasons, but compensated for this by concentrating resources on its military sector and by using the power this gave it to obtain further resources by force or the threat of force. It would extort subsidized credits from a West anxious for peace in periods of 'thaw', and seize new territories by subversion and conquest in periods of 'chill'. By the late 1970s, the US, Britain and our European allies were faced by a Soviet Union in this second aggressive phase. We were neither psychologically, nor militarily, nor economically in shape to resist it.

Taken together, these three challenges – long-term economic decline, the debilitating effects of socialism, and the growing Soviet threat – were an intimidating inheritance for a new Prime Minister.

I ought perhaps to have been more cowed by them in my imagination than in fact I was as we drove back to Flood Street. Perhaps if I could have foreseen the great roller-coaster of events in the next eleven years, described in this volume, I would have felt greater apprehension. Perversely, however, the emotion I felt was exhilaration at the challenge. We had thought, talked, written, discussed, debated all these questions – and now, if all went well in the next few weeks, we would finally get the chance to deal with them ourselves.

Some of this exhilaration came from meeting a wide range of my fellow-countrymen in four years as Opposition Leader. They were so much better than the statistics said: more energetic, more independent, more restive at the decline of the country, and more ready than many of my parliamentary colleagues to support painful measures to reverse that decline. We would incur more odium, I believed, by reneging on our promises of radical conservatism with a U-turn than by pressing firmly ahead through whatever attacks the socialists hurled against us. I sensed, as apparently Jim Callaghan also sensed in the course of the campaign, that a sea change had occurred in the political sensibility of the British people. They had given up on socialism – the thirty-year experiment had plainly failed – and were ready to try something else. That sea change was our mandate.

And there was a more personal factor. Chatham famously remarked: 'I know that I can save this country and that no one else can.'* It would have been presumptuous of me to have compared myself to Chatham. But if I am honest, I must admit that my exhilaration came from a similar inner conviction.

My background and experience were not those of a traditional Conservative prime minister. I was less able to depend on automatic deference, but I was also perhaps less intimidated by the risks of change. My senior colleagues, growing to political maturity in the slump of the 1930s, had a more resigned and pessimistic view of political possibilities. They were perhaps too ready to accept the Labour Party and union leaders as authentic interpreters of the wishes of the people. I did not feel I needed an interpreter to address people who spoke the same language. And I felt it was a real advantage that we had lived the same sort of life.** I felt that the experiences I had lived through had fitted me curiously well for the coming struggle.

I had grown up in a household that was neither poor nor rich. We had to economize each day in order to enjoy the occasional luxury.

* The eighteenth-century statesman and prime minister, 1766–8.

** The first fifty years of my life will be related in a second volume.

My father's background as a grocer is sometimes cited as the basis for my economic philosophy. So it was – and is – but his original philosophy encompassed more than simply ensuring that incomings showed a small surplus over outgoings at the end of the week. My father was both a practical man and a man of theory. He liked to connect the progress of our corner shop with the great complex romance of international trade which recruited people all over the world to ensure that a family in Grantham could have on its table rice from India, coffee from Kenya, sugar from the West Indies and spices from five continents. Before I read a line from the great liberal economists, I knew from my father's accounts that the free market was like a vast sensitive nervous system, responding to events and signals all over the world to meet the ever-changing needs of peoples in different countries, from different classes, of different religions, with a kind of benign indifference to their status. Governments acted on a much smaller store of conscious information and, by contrast, were themselves 'blind forces' blundering about in the dark, and obstructing the operations of markets rather than improving them. The economic history of Britain for the next forty years confirmed and amplified almost every item of my father's practical economics. In effect, I had been equipped at an early age with the ideal mental outlook and tools of analysis for reconstructing an economy ravaged by state socialism.

My life, like those of most people on the planet, was transformed by the Second World War. In my case, because I was at school and university for its duration, the transformation was an intellectual rather than a physical one. I drew from the failure of appeasement the lesson that aggression must always be firmly resisted. But how? The ultimate victory of the Allies persuaded me that nations must co-operate in defence of agreed international rules if they are either to resist great evils or to achieve great benefits. That is merely a platitude, however, if political leaders lack the courage and far-sightedness, or – what is equally important – if nations lack strong bonds of common loyalty. Weak nations could not have resisted Hitler effectively – indeed, those nations that were weak did not stand up to him. So I drew from the Second World War a lesson very different from the hostility towards the nation-state evinced by some post-war European statesmen. My view was – and is – that an effective internationalism can only be built by strong nations which are able to call upon the loyalty of their citizens to defend and enforce civilized rules of international conduct. An internationalism which seeks to supersede the nation-state, however, will founder quickly upon the reality that very few people are prepared to make genuine sacrifices for it. It is likely to degenerate, therefore, into a formula for endless discussion and hand-wringing.

I held these conclusions very tentatively at the war's end. But they hardened into firm convictions in the 1940s and '50s when, in the face of the Soviet threat, those institutions like NATO which represented international co-operation between strong nation-states proved far more effective in resisting that threat than bodies like the United Nations which embodied a superficially more ambitious but in reality weaker internationalism. My concern in 1979 was that the resistance of NATO to the latest Soviet threat was less adequate than I would have liked precisely because national morale in most NATO countries, including Britain, was so depressed. To resist the Soviet Union effectively it would be necessary to restore our own self-confidence (and, of course, our military strength) beforehand.

I recalled a similar collapse of national morale from my first days in active politics as a Young Conservative fighting the 1945–51 Labour Government. Some nostalgia for the austerity period apparently lingers. That is, I believe, an exercise in vicarious sacrifice, always more palatable than the real thing. Seen from afar, or from above, whether by a socialist gentleman in Whitehall or by a High Tory, socialism has a certain nobility: equal sacrifice, fair shares, everyone pulling together. Seen from below, however, it looked very different. Fair shares somehow always turn out to be small shares. Then, someone has to enforce their fairness; someone else has to check that this fairness does not result in black markets or under-the-counter favouritism; and a third person has to watch the first two to make sure that the administrators of fairness end up with no more than their fair share. All this promotes an atmosphere of envy and tittle-tattle. No one who lived through austerity, who can remember snoek, Spam, and utility clothing, could mistake the petty jealousies, minor tyrannies, ill-neighbourliness and sheer sourness of those years for idealism and equality. Even the partial dismantling of the ration-book state in the early 1950s came as an immense psychological relief to most people.

I particularly remember the political atmosphere of those years. Although the Tory rethinking associated with Rab Butler and the Conservative Research Department was important in reviving the Tory Party's intellectual claims to office, there was a somewhat more robust and elementary rethinking going on at the grass roots. Our inspiration was less Rab Butler's Industrial Charter than books like Colm Brogan's anti-socialist satire, *Our New Masters*, which held up the moral pretensions of socialists to relentless and brilliant mockery, and Hayek's powerful *Road to Serfdom*, dedicated to 'the socialists of all parties'. Such books not only provided crisp, clear analytical arguments against socialism, demonstrating how its economic theories were connected to the then depressing shortages of our daily lives; but by their wonderful mockery of socialist follies, they also gave us the feeling that the other side simply could not win in the end. That is a vital feeling in politics; it eradicates past defeats and builds future victories. It left a permanent mark on my own political character, making me a long-term optimist for free enterprise and liberty and sustaining me through the bleak years of socialist supremacy in the 1960s and '70s.

I was elected to the House of Commons in 1959 as the Member for Finchley, and later served in the Governments of Harold Macmillan, Alec Douglas-Home and Ted Heath. I enjoyed my early ministerial career: it was an absorbing education both in the ways of Whitehall and in the technicalities of pensions policy. But I could not help noticing a curious discrepancy in the behaviour of my colleagues. What they said and what they did seemed to exist in two separate compartments. It was not that they consciously deceived anyone; they were in fact conspicuously honourable. But the language of free enterprise, anti-socialism and the national interest sprang readily to their lips, while they conducted government business on very different assumptions about the role of the state at home and of the nation-state abroad. Their rhetoric was prompted by general ideas they thought desirable, such as freedom; their actions were confined by general ideas they thought inevitable, such as equality.

At the start, as an inexperienced young minister, I had to live with this. When we went into Opposition after the 1964 and 1966 defeats, I joined with Ted Heath in a rethinking of party policy which seemed to foreshadow much of what we later came to call Thatcherism. 'Selsdon Man' won the 1970 election on a radical Conservative manifesto.* But the Party's conversion to its own philosophy proved skin-deep. After two years of struggling to put it into effect, the Heath Government changed course equally radically and adopted a programme of corporatism, intervention and reflation. I had my doubts, but as a first-time Cabinet minister I devoted myself principally to the major controversies of my own department (Education), and left more senior colleagues to get on with their own responsibilities. Yet all my instincts chafed against this. Perhaps because of my very unease, I noticed earlier than most that the very policies adopted as concessions

* The term was Harold Wilson's, derived from the name of the Selsdon Park Hotel where the Conservative Shadow Cabinet finalized its right-wing programme for the 1970 general election.

to reality were also the least successful. Incomes policy, in addition to restricting people's freedom, was invariably the prelude to a wages explosion. And that was one among many. Almost all the policies hawked about by 'practical' men on 'pragmatic' grounds turned out in the end to be highly impractical. Yet this fact never seemed to dent their enthusiasm. Indeed, Ted Heath responded to the defeat of his Government on the issue of incomes policy in the first 1974 election by proposing a still more ambitious scheme of interventionist government in the second.

While I was pondering on this mystery, Keith Joseph made a remark which reverberated powerfully in my mind. 'I have only recently become a Conservative,' he said, meaning that for his first twenty years in politics, many of them at the top, he had been a sort of moderate Fabian. I recognized both the truth of Keith's remark and also that my own case was subtly different: I had always been an instinctive Conservative, but I had failed to develop these instincts either into a coherent framework of ideas or into a set of practical policies for government. And the faster the illusions of practical men crumbled before the onrush of reality, the more necessary it was to set about developing such a framework. Keith and I established the Centre for Policy Studies to do just that.

With Keith, I had come to see ever more clearly that what appeared to be technical arguments about the relationship between the stock of money and the level of prices went right to the heart of the question of what the role of government in a free society should be. It was the job of government to establish a framework of stability – whether constitutional stability, the rule of law, or the economic stability provided by sound money – within which individual families and businesses were free to pursue their own dreams and ambitions. We had to get out of the business of telling people what their ambitions should be and how exactly to realize them. That was up to them. The conclusions I reached fitted precisely those which my own instincts and experience themselves suggested. But I was aware that all too few of my colleagues in the Shadow Cabinet and in the House of Commons saw matters like this. I knew that I would have to go carefully to persuade them of what needed to be done and why.

The years in Opposition had often been frustrating, but at least they had given me the chance to see that our policies for government reflected my priorities and had been worked out in sufficient detail. We had published the outlines of our policy in *The Right Approach* in 1976 and *The Right Approach to the Economy* the following year. We had toyed with the idea of other similar documents, but had in fact come down in favour of speeches to set out our policy proposals. Behind the public pronouncements lay years of intense work by policy groups, usually chaired by the relevant Chief Shadow Spokesmen, whose conclusions were brought before the Leader's Consultative Committee, as the Shadow Cabinet was formally known, where policies were discussed, modified, rejected or approved.

There were three points to which I had returned again and again during this period. First, everything we wished to do had to fit into the overall strategy of reversing Britain's economic decline, for without an end to that decline there was no hope of success for our other objectives. This led on to the second point: all policies had to be carefully costed, and if they could not be accommodated within our public expenditure plans they would not be approved. Geoffrey Howe and his very talented Shadow Treasury team combed through everything in great detail to ensure this was the case. Finally, we had to stress continually that, however difficult the road might be and however long it took us to reach our destination, we intended to achieve a fundamental change of direction. We stood for a new beginning, not more of the same.

I was again asking the Conservative Party to put its faith in freedom and free markets, limited government and a strong national defence; I knew that we would be able to keep the Party united around this programme for the election campaign. But in the dark days which would precede tangible success I would have to struggle to ensure that this time the Conservative Government kept its nerve. If we failed, we would never be given another chance.

I was preoccupied by these reflections as we drove home, had a small family celebration at Flood Street, and finally turned in for the night. My last thought was: the die is cast. We had made every sensible preparation for the election and for governing afterwards. If honest endeavour were the test, we would not fail. In the end, however, Man proposes and God disposes. We might deserve success, but we could not command it. It was, perversely, a comforting thought. I slept well.

CHAPTER I

Over the Shop

First days and early decisions as Prime Minister

TO THE PALACE

We knew we had won by the early hours of Friday 4 May, but it was not until the afternoon that we gained the clear majority of seats we needed – 44 as it eventually turned out. The Conservative Party would form the next government.

There were many friends with me as we waited for the results to come in during those long hours in Conservative Central Office. But I can remember an odd sense of loneliness as well as anticipation when I received the telephone call which summoned me to the Palace. I was anxious about getting the details of procedure and protocol right; it is extraordinary how on really important occasions one's mind often focuses on what in the cold light of day seem to be mere trivia. But I was haunted by tales of embarrassing episodes as one prime minister left and his successor entered office: Ted Heath's departure from No. 10 was a case in point. I now could not help feeling sorry for James Callaghan, who just a little earlier had conceded victory in a short speech, both dignified and generous. Whatever our past and indeed future disagreements, I believed him to be a patriot with the interests of Britain at heart, whose worst tribulations had been inflicted by his own party.

At about 2.45 p.m. the call came. I walked out of Central Office through a crowd of supporters and into the waiting car, which drove Denis and me to the Palace on my last journey as Leader of the Opposition.

The Audience at which one receives the Queen's authority to form a government comes to most prime ministers only once in a lifetime. The authority is unbroken when a sitting prime minister wins an election, and so it never had to be renewed throughout the years I was in office. All audiences with the Queen take place in strict confidence –

a confidentiality which is vital to the working of both government and constitution. I was to have such audiences with Her Majesty once a week, usually on a Tuesday, when she was in London and sometimes elsewhere when the royal family were at Windsor or Balmoral.

Perhaps it is permissible to make just two points about these meetings. Anyone who imagines that they are a mere formality or confined to social niceties is quite wrong; they are quietly businesslike and Her Majesty brings to bear a formidable grasp of current issues and breadth of experience. And, although the press could not resist the temptation to suggest disputes between the Palace and Downing Street, especially on Commonwealth affairs, I always found the Queen's attitude towards the work of the government absolutely correct.

Of course, under the circumstances, stories of clashes between 'two powerful women' were just too good not to make up. In general, more nonsense was written about the so-called 'feminine factor' during my time in office than about almost anything else. I was always asked how it felt to be a woman prime minister. I would reply: 'I don't know: I've never experienced the alternative.'

After the audience, Sir Philip Moore, the Queen's Secretary, took me to his office down what are called 'the Prime Minister's stairs'. I found my new principal private secretary, Ken Stowe, waiting there, ready to accompany me to Downing Street. Ken had come to the Palace with the outgoing prime minister, James Callaghan, barely an hour before. The civil service already knew a good deal about our policies because they carefully scrutinize an Opposition's manifesto with a view to the hasty preparation of a new administration's legislative programme. Of course, as I quickly learnt, some senior civil servants would need more than a conscientious reading of our manifesto and a few speeches truly to grasp the changes we firmly intended to make. Also, it takes time to build up relationships with staff which reach beyond the formal level of respect to trust and confidence. But the sheer professionalism of the British civil service, which allows governments to come and go with a minimum of dislocation and a maximum of efficiency, is something other countries with different systems have every cause to envy.

Denis and I left Buckingham Palace in the prime ministerial car: my previous car had already gone to Mr Callaghan. As we drove out through the Palace gates, Denis noticed that this time the Guards saluted me. In those innocent days before security had to become so much tighter for fear of terrorism, crowds of well-wishers, sightseers, press and camera crews were waiting for us in Downing Street itself.

The crowds extended all the way up Downing Street and out into Whitehall. Denis and I got out of the car and walked towards them. This gave me the opportunity to run through in my mind what I would say outside No. 10.

When we turned to the cameras and reporters, the cheers were so deafening that no one in the street could hear what I was saying. Fortunately, the microphones thrust in front of me picked it up and carried it over the radio and television.

I quoted a famous prayer attributed to St Francis of Assisi, beginning, 'where there is discord, may we bring harmony.' Afterwards a good deal of sarcasm was expended on this choice, but the rest of the quotation is often forgotten. St Francis prayed for more than peace; the prayer goes on: 'Where there is error, may we bring truth. Where there is doubt, may we bring faith. And where there is despair, may we bring hope'. The forces of error, doubt and despair were so firmly entrenched in British society, as the 'winter of discontent' had just powerfully illustrated, that overcoming them would not be possible without some measure of discord.

10 DOWNING STREET

Inside No. 10 all the staff had turned out to welcome us. I am assured that in the days before television there was a good practical reason for this ceremony, in that everyone in the building has to be able to recognize the prime minister personally, both for security reasons and for the smooth running of the many different services which are provided there. It is also true that within No. 10 there is almost a family atmosphere. The number of staff is relatively small – a total of between 70 or 80, though because of the shift system not all will be there at one time. That figure comprises those working in the Private Office, including the duty clerks who ensure that No. 10 is able to operate round the clock; the Press Office, where someone is also always on call; the 'garden room girls' who do the secretarial and paperwork; 'confidential filing', which sorts and files the enormous accumulations of documents; the parliamentary section which deals with Parliamentary Questions, Statements and Debates; the correspondence section where some four to seven thousand letters are received every week; the sections which deal with Church matters and with honours; the Political Office and the Policy Unit; and the messengers and other staff who keep the whole extended family supplied with tea and coffee and – above all – information from the outside world. It is an extraordinary achievement, and it requires people of unusual qualities and commitment, not least when you compare these relatively slender resources and modest surroundings with, for example, the White House with its 400 staff, or the German Chancellery with 500.

The prime minister's private secretaries, headed by the principal private secretary, are crucial to the effective conduct of government. They are the main channel of communication between the prime minister and the rest of Whitehall, and they bear a heavy burden of responsibility. I was fortunate to have a succession of superb principal private secretaries over the years. Other private secretaries, specializing in economic or foreign affairs, also quickly acquired judgement, expertise and a knowledge of my thinking which allowed me to rely on them. Bernard Ingham, my press secretary, who arrived five months after I became Prime Minister, was another indispensable member of the team. I was told that Bernard's politics had been Labour, not Conservative: but the first time we met I warmed to this tough, blunt, humorous Yorkshireman. Bernard's outstanding virtue was his total integrity. An honest man himself, he expected the same high standards from others. He never let me down.

The hours at No. 10 are long. I never minded this. There was an intensity about the job of being Prime Minister which made sleep seem a luxury. In any case, over the years I had trained myself to do with about four hours a night. The Private Office too would often be working till 11 o'clock at night. We were so few that there was no possibility of putting work on someone else's desk. This sort of atmosphere helps to produce a remarkably happy team, as well as a formidably efficient one. People are under great pressure, and there is no time for trivia. All the effort has to go into getting the work done. Mutual respect and friendly relations are often the result. This feature of No. 10 shapes people's attitudes not only towards each other but towards the prime minister whom they all directly or indirectly serve. The cheers and clapping when a new prime minister arrives may perhaps be a traditional formality. But the tears and regrets when the outgoing prime minister makes his or her final departure are usually genuine.

Of course, I had visited No. 10 when I served as Education Secretary in Ted Heath's Government of 1970–4 and, indeed, before that as a Parliamentary Secretary to the Minister of Pensions in Harold Macmillan's and Alec Douglas-Home's Governments. So I knew that the house is much larger than it looks from the outside because it is, in fact, two houses, one situated behind the other, joined by passages, with an extra wing linking the two buildings. But although familiar with the reception rooms and the Cabinet Room, I knew little of the rest of the building.

LIFE 'OVER THE SHOP'

Number Ten is more than an office: it is intended to serve as the prime minister's home. I never had any doubt that when the Callaghans had left I would move into the prime minister's small flat at the top of the building. Every practical consideration suggested it, as well as my own taste for long hours of work. As we used to say, harking back to my girlhood in Grantham, I liked living over the shop. I was not able to move out of the house in Flood Street where my family had been living for the last ten years until the first week of June. But from then, until November 1990, Downing Street and Chequers were the twin centres of my personal and professional life.

The flat at No. 10 quickly became a refuge from the rest of the world, though on occasion a good deal of business was done there too. It was right at the top of the building – up in the rafters, in fact. But that was an advantage, for the stairs provided me with about the only real exercise I got. There were plenty of cupboards and a box room in which to dump everything until it found a more permanent place and into which piles of books and papers could be pushed when visitors were due.

Denis and I decided that we would not have any living-in domestic help. No housekeeper could possibly have coped with the irregular hours. When I had no other engagement, I would go up to the flat for a quick lunch of salad or poached egg on Bovril toast. But usually it was 10 or 11 o'clock at night when I would go into the kitchen and prepare something – we knew every way in which eggs and cheese could be served and there was always something to cut at in the fridge – while Denis poured me a night-cap.

The deep freeze was always kept well stocked and the microwave, when it appeared, did sterling work when sudden meals were required because we were working late into the night on a speech, a statement or decisions required for the Falklands campaign or the Libyan raid – or Resolutions at the UN Security Council. On these occasions we used the small dining-room in the flat, which was next to the even smaller kitchen; secretaries from the Political Office, not paid by the taxpayer, would always lend a hand.

Prime Minister or not, I never forgot that I was also MP for Finchley; nor, indeed, would I have wanted to. My monthly surgeries in the constituency and the correspondence which was dealt with from within No. 10 by my secretary, Joy Robilliard (who had been Airey Neave's secretary until his death), kept me directly in touch with people's worries. I always had the benefit of a first-class constituency agent and a strongly supportive constituency chairman, which as any MP knows makes a world of difference. I also kept up my own special interests which had been developed as a result of constituency work, for example as patron of the North London Hospice.

I could never have been Prime Minister for more than eleven years without Denis at my side. Always a powerful personality, he had very definite ideas about what should and should not be done. He was a fund of shrewd advice and penetrating comment. And he very sensibly saved these for me rather than the outside world, always refusing to give interviews. He never had a secretary or public relations adviser but answered between thirty and fifty letters every week in his own hand. With the appearance of the 'Dear Bill' letters in *Private Eye* he seemed to become half the nation's favourite correspondent.

Denis shared my own fascination with politics – that, of course, is how we first met – but he also had his own outside interests, not least sport. He was passionately interested in rugby football – having indeed been a referee. He was also heavily involved in charities, an active member of the Sports Aid Foundation and of the Lord's Taverners. Denis delivered many speeches on his favourite (nonpolitical) subjects. The one which for me best summed up his character and convictions was on sport and ethics and contained these lines:

> The desire to win is born in most of us. The will to win is a matter of training. The manner of winning is a matter of honour.

Although Denis had a deep interest in everything military, and by choice would have stayed in the army at the end of the Second World War, the unexpected death of his father left him with no option but to return to run the family business, a paint and chemicals company. I am glad he did. For his industrial experience was invaluable to me. Not only was he familiar with the scientific side (something which we had in common); he was also a crack cost and management accountant. Nothing escaped his professional eye – he could see and sense trouble long before anyone else. His knowledge of the oil industry also gave me immediate access to expert advice when in 1979 the world experienced the second sudden oil price increase. Indeed, through him and our many friends I was never out of touch with industry and commerce.

Being prime minister is a lonely job. In a sense, it ought to be: you cannot lead from the crowd. But with Denis there I was never alone. What a man. What a husband. What a friend.

INSIDE DOWNING STREET

In some ways 10 Downing Street is an unusual sort of home. Portraits, busts and sculptures of one's prime ministerial predecessors remind one of the nearly 250 years of history into which one has stepped.

As prime minister one has the opportunity to make an impact on the style of No. 10. Outside the flat I had displayed my own collection of porcelain, which I had built up over the years. I also brought with me a powerful portrait of Churchill from my room in the House of Commons. It looked down on those who assembled in the antechamber to the Cabinet Room. When I arrived, this area looked rather like a down-at-heel Pall Mall club, with heavy and worn leather furniture; I changed the whole feel by bringing in bookcases, tables and chairs from elsewhere in the building. There might be some difficult times to come in the Cabinet Room itself, but there was no reason why people should be made to feel miserable while they were waiting to go in.

Although it was not until I had been there some ten years that I had the most important redecorations done, I tried from the start to make the rooms seem more lived in. The official rooms had very few ornaments and when we arrived No. 10 looked rather like a 'furnished house to let', which in a way, I suppose, it was. Downing Street had no silver. Whenever there was an official dinner the caterers had to bring in their own. Lord Brownlow, who lived just outside Grantham, lent me silver from his collection at Belton House: it sparkled and transformed the No. 10 dining-room. One particular piece had a special meaning for me – a casket containing the Freedom of the Borough of Grantham, of which both the previous Lord Brownlow and later my father had been Mayor. The gardeners who kept St James's Park brought in flowers. And happily, the flowers kept on coming, sent by friends and supporters, right until my last days at Downing Street, when you could hardly move down the corridors for a floral display which rivalled the Chelsea Flower Show. I also had the study repapered at my own expense. Its unappealing sage-green damask flock wallpaper was stripped off and replaced by a cream stripe, which was a much better background for some fine pictures.

I felt that Downing Street should have some works by contemporary British artists and sculptors, as well as those of the past. I had met Henry Moore when I was Secretary of State for Education and much admired his work. The Moore Foundation let No. 10 borrow one of his smaller sculptures which fitted perfectly in an alcove in the main hallway. Behind the sculpture was hung a Moore drawing, which was changed every three months; among my favourites were scenes of people sleeping in the London Underground during the Blitz.

I was conscious of being the first research scientist to become prime minister – almost as conscious, in fact, as I was of being the first woman prime minister. So I had portraits and busts of some of our most famous scientists placed in the small dining-room, where I often lunched with visitors and colleagues on less formal occasions.

I felt strongly that when foreign visitors came to Downing Street they should see something of Britain's cultural heritage. When I came to No. 10 all the paintings in the main dining-room were copies. They were replaced. For example, I was lent a picture of George II, who had actually given No. 10 to Sir Robert Walpole, the first prime minister. On my foreign visits I quickly found that many of our embassies had superb works of art which added greatly to the impression people had of Britain. I wanted foreign visitors to No. 10 to be similarly impressed. I knew that there were large numbers of excellent British paintings in our museums which were not on show. I was able to borrow some Turners, a Raeburn from Scotland and some pictures from the Dulwich Gallery and these were hung in the White Drawing Room and the main reception room. I also had some fine portraits hung of the nation's heroes; through them you could feel the continuity of British history. I recall on one occasion watching President Giscard d'Estaing gazing at two portraits in the dining-room – one of the young Nelson and the other of Wellington. He remarked on the irony. I replied that it was no less ironic that I should have to look at portraits of Napoleon on my visits to Paris. In retrospect, I can see that this was not quite a parallel. Napoleon lost.

On this first evening, though, I could do little more than make a brief tour of the main rooms of the building. Then I entered the Cabinet Room where I was greeted by more familiar faces – among them my daughter Carol. There was Richard Ryder who had been and would continue for a time as my political secretary, responsible for keeping me in touch with the Conservative Party in the country; David Wolfson (now Lord Wolfson) who acted as my Chief of Staff, bringing to bear his charm and business experience on the problems of running No. 10; Caroline Stephens (later to become Caroline Ryder) who became my diary secretary; Alison Ward (later Alison Wakeham) my constituency secretary; and Cynthia Crawford – known to all of us as 'Crawfie' – who acted as my personal assistant and who has stayed with me ever since. We did not waste much time in conversation. They were anxious to sort out who was to go to which office. I had exactly the same task in mind: the choice of my Cabinet.

CABINET-MAKING

Choosing a Cabinet is undoubtedly one of the most important ways in which a prime minister can exercise power over the whole conduct of government. But it is not always understood how real are the constraints under which the choices take place. By convention, all ministers must be members of either the Commons or the Lords, and there must not generally be more than three Cabinet members in the Lords, thus limiting the range of potential candidates for office. In addition one has to achieve distribution across the country – every region is easily convinced it has been left out. You must also consider the spectrum of party opinion.

Even so, the press expect the Cabinet of some twenty-two ministers to be appointed and the list to be published within about 24 hours – otherwise it is taken as a sure sign of some sort of political crisis. My American and other foreign friends are often astonished at the speed with which British Governments are formed and announced.

So I do not think that any of us at No. 10 relaxed much that day, which turned out to be a long one. (The previous night I had had no more than a couple of hours' sleep, if that.) I received the usual detailed security briefing which is given to incoming prime ministers. Then I went upstairs to the study in which I was to spend so many hours in the years which followed. I was accompanied by Willie Whitelaw and our new Chief Whip, Michael Jopling. We began to sift through the obvious and less obvious names and slowly this most perplexing of jigsaws began to take shape. While Willie, the Chief Whip and I discussed the appointments to the Cabinet, Ken Stowe sought to contact those involved to arrange for them to come in the next day.

At 8.30 p.m. we took a break for a meal. Knowing that there were no canteen facilities at No. 10, my personal staff brought in a Chinese meal from a take-away and some fifteen of us sat down to eat in the large dining-room. (That, I think, was the last take-away while I was Prime Minister.)

I knew that the hardest battles would be fought on the ground of economic policy. So I made sure that the key economic ministers would be true believers in our economic strategy. Geoffrey Howe had by now thoroughly established himself as the Party's chief economic spokesman. Geoffrey was regularly bullied in debate by Denis Healey. But by thorough mastery of his brief and an ability to marshal arguments and advice from different sources, he had shown that beneath a deceptively mild exterior he had the makings of the fine Chancellor he was to become. Some of the toughest decisions were to fall to him. He never flinched. In my view these were his best political years.

After becoming leader in 1975, I had considered appointing Keith Joseph as Shadow Chancellor. Keith had done more than anyone else to spell out in his speeches and pamphlets what had gone wrong with Britain's economic performance and how it could be transformed. He has one of the best minds in politics. He is an original thinker, the sort of man who makes you understand what Burke meant when he wrote of politics being 'philosophy in action'. He is rare in another way too: he combines humility, open-mindedness and unshakeable principle. He is deeply and genuinely sensitive to people's misfortunes. Although he had no doubt of the rightness of the decisions which we were to make, he knew that they meant unviable firms would collapse and overmanning become unemployment, and he cared about those who were affected – far more than did all our professionally compassionate critics. But such a combination of personal qualities may create difficulties in the cruel hurly-burly of political life which Chancellors above all must endure. So Keith took over at Industry, where he did the vital job that no one else could have done of altering the whole philosophy which had previously dominated the department. Keith was – and remains – my closest political friend.

John Biffen I appointed Chief Secretary to the Treasury. He had been a brilliant exponent in Opposition of the economic policies in which I believed and, before that, a courageous critic of the Heath Government's U-turn. But he proved rather less effective than I had hoped in the gruelling task of trying to control public expenditure. His later performance as Leader of the House where the qualities required were acute political sensitivity, good humour and a certain style was far happier. John Nott became Secretary of State for Trade. He, too, had a clear understanding of and commitment to our policies of monetary control, low taxes and free enterprise. But John is a mixture of gold, dross and mercury. No one was better at analysing a situation and prescribing a policy to deal with it. But he found it hard, or perhaps boring, to stick with the policy once it had been firmly decided. His vice was second thoughts.

With Geoffrey and Keith helping me to give a lead to the Cabinet, however, and with the loyalty I knew I could rely upon from Willie and some of the others, I believed we could see the economic strategy through.

Otherwise, it seemed prudent in the light of our effective performance in Opposition and the election campaign to maintain a high degree of continuity between Shadow Cabinet and Cabinet posts. Willie Whitelaw became Home Secretary, and in that capacity and later as Leader of the Lords he provided me personally and the Government as a whole with shrewd advice based on massive experience. People were often surprised that the two of us worked so well together, given our rivalry for the leadership and our different outlook on economics. But Willie is a big man in character as well as physically. He wanted the success of the Government which from the first he accepted would be guided by my general philosophy. Once he had pledged his loyalty, he never withdrew it. He supported me steadfastly when I was right and, more important, when I wasn't. He was an irreplaceable deputy prime minister – an office which has no constitutional existence but is a clear sign of political precedence – and the ballast that helped keep the Government on course.

But I felt that some changes in portfolios were required. I brought in the formidable Christopher Soames to be Leader of the House of Lords. Christopher was his own man, indeed excessively so, and thus better suited to solo performances – whether as Ambassador in Paris or the last Governor of Rhodesia – than to working in harmony with others. Peter Carrington, who had led the Lords skilfully in Opposition, became Foreign Secretary. His unrivalled experience of foreign affairs more than qualified him for the job. Peter had great panache and the ability to identify immediately the main points in any argument; and he could express himself in pungent terms. We had disagreements, but there were never any hard feelings. We were an effective combination – not least because Peter could always tell some particularly intractable foreign minister that whatever he himself might feel about a particular proposition, there was no way in which his prime minister would accept it. This generally proved convincing. I was determined, however, that at least one Foreign Office minister should have a good grounding in – and sound views on – economic policy. I had Peter bring in Nick Ridley.

Two other appointments excited more comment. To his surprise,

I asked Peter Walker to be Minister of Agriculture. Peter had never made a secret of his hostility to my economic strategy. But he was both tough and persuasive, priceless assets in dealing with the plain absurdities of the European Community's Common Agricultural Policy. His membership of the Cabinet demonstrated that I was prepared to include every strand of Conservative opinion in the new Government, and his post that I was not prepared to put the central economic strategy at risk.

That was perhaps less clear in my decision to keep Jim Prior on at Employment. I shall describe elsewhere the divergences of opinion between Jim and the rest of us during Opposition. Running on from that time there was a lively argument about trade union reform. We all agreed that trade unions had acquired far too many powers and privileges. We also agreed that these must be dealt with one step at a time. But when it came down to specific measures, there was deep disagreement about how fast and how far to move. Yet there was no doubt in my mind that we needed Jim Prior. There was still the feeling in the country, and indeed in the Conservative Party, that Britain could not be governed without the tacit consent of the trades unions. It was to be some years before that changed. If we had signalled the wholesale reform of the unions over and against their opposition at the outset, it would have undermined confidence in the Government and perhaps even provoked a challenge we were not yet ready to face. Jim was the badge of our reasonableness. He had forged good relations with a number of trade union leaders whose practical value he perhaps overestimated. But he was an experienced politician and a strong personality – qualities he subsequently demonstrated to great effect in Northern Ireland.

The law prescribes that only twenty-two people may receive the salaries of Cabinet ministers. My decision to appoint a Foreign Secretary from the House of Lords meant that we had to have an additional Foreign minister in the Cabinet to answer in the Commons. Members of the House of Commons in any case dislike seeing too many Members of the Lords in the Cabinet. They accept, of course, that the Leader of the Lords and the Lord Chancellor (in this case the distinguished and effervescent Quintin Hailsham) and possibly a third peer of obvious suitability must be in the Cabinet. But they demand that there must be a second Cabinet minister in the Commons to answer for any departmental head who is a peer. In this post I appointed Ian Gilmour. (A similar arrangement would later be necessary when David Young joined the Cabinet, first at Employment and then at Trade and Industry.) Ian remained at the Foreign Office for two years. Subsequently, he was to show me the same loyalty from the back-benches as he had in government.

I was anxious to have Angus Maude in the Cabinet to benefit from his years of political experience, his sound views, and his acid wit. He would handle government information. At the end of the day, we were short of one place. As a result, Norman Fowler, as Minister of State at Transport, was not able to be an official member of the Cabinet, although he attended all our meetings.

By about 11 p.m. the list of Cabinet was complete and had been approved by the Queen. I went upstairs to thank the No. 10 telephonists who had had a busy time arranging all the appointments for the following day. Then I was driven home.

On Saturday I saw the future Cabinet one by one. It all went smoothly enough. Those who were not already Privy Councillors were sworn in at Buckingham Palace.* By Saturday afternoon the Cabinet was appointed and the names announced to the press. That gave every new minister the weekend to draft instructions to his department to put into effect the manifesto policies. In fact there was slightly more time than usual, since Monday was a Bank Holiday.

OTHER APPOINTMENTS

On Saturday night we completed the list of junior ministers, and I saw or telephoned them on the Sunday. Many of these would later enter Cabinet, including Cecil Parkinson, Norman Tebbit, Nick Ridley and John Wakeham. The best junior ministers were always in great demand by their seniors: a really good ministerial team is of enormous importance in keeping effective political control over the work of a government department. There were some sixty posts to be filled. But the whole Government had been appointed and announced within 48 hours of my entering Downing Street.

My last and best appointment was of Ian Gow as my Parliamentary Private Secretary (or PPS). Ian's combination of loyalty, shrewdness

* The Privy Council is one of the oldest of Britain's political institutions, with the most important of the Crown's advisers among its members, including by convention all Cabinet ministers. Its meetings – usually of a few ministers in the presence of the Queen – are now purely formal, but the oath taken by new members reinforces the obligation of secrecy in conducting government business, and the issue of 'Orders in Council' is still an important procedure for enacting the legislation not requiring the approval of Parliament.

and an irrepressible sense of fun was to see us all through many difficult moments. He was an instinctive parliamentarian who loved every aspect of the House of Commons. In private conversation he had the ability to draw everyone into the political circle and make them feel theirs was the vital contribution. In public his speeches were marked by a deadpan humour which could reduce both sides of the House to tears of laughter. We remained close friends after Ian's principled resignation over the Anglo-Irish agreement which he opposed from a standpoint of undiluted Unionism. His murder by IRA terrorists in 1990 was an irreplaceable loss.

Monday was, as I have noted, a Bank Holiday. I came into No. 10 and took the opportunity to complete a number of nonministerial appointments. John Hoskyns arrived in the afternoon to become head of my Policy Unit.* John's background was in business and computers; but over and above that experience, he had strong powers of analysis and had helped formulate our economic strategy in Opposition. He propagated the theory that a 'culture of decline' was the ultimate cause of many of Britain's economic problems. In government he repeatedly compelled ministers to relate each problem to our overall strategy of reversing that decline. He kept our eye on the ball.

That same day I saw Kenneth Berrill, the head of the Central Policy Review Staff (CPRS) or 'Think-Tank'. The CPRS had originally been set up by Ted Heath as a source of long-term policy advice for the Government, at a time when there were fewer private think-tanks, fewer special advisers in government and a widespread belief that the great questions of the day could be resolved by specialized technical analysis. But a government with a firm philosophical direction was inevitably a less comfortable environment for a body with a technocratic outlook. And the Think-Tank's detached speculations, when leaked to the press and attributed to ministers, had the capacity to embarrass. The world had changed, and the CPRS could not change with it. For these and other reasons, I believe that my later decision to abolish the CPRS was right and probably inevitable. And I have to say that I never missed it.

I also asked Sir Derek Rayner to set up an Efficiency Unit that would tackle the waste and ineffectiveness of government. Derek was another successful businessman, from what everyone used to describe

* The Policy Unit was first set up by Harold Wilson in 1974 and continued by James Callaghan. The value of the Unit, whose membership I subsequently increased, lies in its flexibility and involvement in day-to-day policy matters, on the basis of close collaboration with the Prime Minister.

as my favourite company, Marks & Spencer. The two of us used to say that in politics you judge the value of a service by the amount you put in, but in business you judge it by the amount you get out. We were both convinced of the need to bring some of the attitudes of business into government. We neither of us conceived just how difficult this would prove.

On the same day I saw Sir Richard O'Brien on a matter which illustrates the extraordinary range of topics which crossed my desk in these first days. Sir Richard was not only chairman of the Manpower Services Commission, the QUANGO which supervised the nation's training schemes,* but also chairman of the committee to advise the prime minister on the appointment of a new Archbishop of Canterbury. (Donald Coggan had announced his intention to retire; his successor had to be found by the end of the year.) He informed me about the committee's work and gave me an idea of when it would be ready to make its recommendations. In view of my later relations with the hierarchy, I could wish that Sir Richard had combined his two jobs and established a decent training scheme for bishops.

It was the nation's financial and economic affairs, however, which required immediate attention. Sir John Hunt, the Cabinet Secretary, gave a reassuring impression of quiet efficiency which turned out to be entirely accurate. He had prepared a short brief on the most urgent questions, such as public sector pay and the size of the Public Sector Borrowing Requirement (PSBR), and compiled a list of imminent meetings with other heads of government. Each of these required early decisions to be made. My last appointment that Monday afternoon was with Geoffrey Howe to discuss his forthcoming budget. That night – most unusually – I managed to get back to Flood Street for dinner with the family. But there was no let-up in activity. I had a stack of papers to read on every conceivable subject.

Or so it seemed. The ceaseless flow of red despatch boxes had begun – anything up to three each evening and four at weekends. But I set to with a will. There is never another opportunity like that given to a new government with a fresh electoral mandate to place its stamp firmly on public affairs, and I was determined to take advantage of it.

* Quasi-autonomous nongovernmental organization.

EARLY DECISIONS

On Tuesday at 2.30 p.m. we held our first Cabinet meeting. It was 'informal': no agenda had been prepared by the Cabinet Secretariat and no minutes were taken. (Its conclusions were later recorded in the first 'formal' Cabinet which met on the customary Thursday morning.) Ministers reported on their departments and the preparations they had made for forthcoming legislation. We gave immediate effect to the pledges in our manifesto to see that both the police and the armed forces were properly paid. As a result of the crisis of morale in the police service, the fall in recruitment and talk of a possible police strike, the Labour Government had set up a committee on police pay under Lord Justice Edmund Davies. The committee had devised a formula to keep police pay in line with other earnings. We decided that the recommendations for pay increases due for implementation on 1 November should be brought forward. This was duly announced the following day, Wednesday. We similarly decided that the full military salary recommended by the latest Report of the Armed Forces Pay Review Body should be paid in full, as from 1 April.

At that first informal Cabinet we began the painful but necessary process of shrinking down the public sector after years in which it was assumed that it should grow at the expense of the private sector. So we imposed an immediate freeze on all civil service recruitment, though this would later be modified and specific targets for reduction set. We started a review of the controls imposed by central on local government, though here, too, we would in due course be forced down the path of applying still tougher, financial controls, as the inability or refusal of local councils to run services efficiently became increasingly apparent.

Pay and prices were an immediate concern, as they continued to be throughout those economically troubled early years. Professor Hugh Clegg's Commission on Pay Comparability had been appointed by the Labour Government as a respectable means of bribing public sector workers not to strike with postdated cheques due to be presented after the election. The Clegg Commission was a major headache, and the pain became steadily more acute as the cheques fell due.*

As regards pay bargaining in the nationalized industries, we decided that the responsible ministers should stand back from the process as

* See Chapter 2, pp. 44–5.

far as possible. Our strategy would be to apply the necessary financial discipline and then let the management and unions directly involved make their own decisions. But that would require progress in complementary areas – competition, privatization and trade union reform – before it was to show results.

There would also have to be a fundamental overhaul of the way in which prices were controlled by such interventionist measures as the Price Commission, government pressure, and subsidy. We were under no illusion: price rises were a symptom of underlying inflation, not a cause of it. Inflation was a monetary phenomenon which it would require monetary discipline to curb. Artificially holding down increases merely reduced investment and undermined profits – both already far too low for the country's economic health – while spreading a 'cost plus' mentality through British industry.

At both Cabinets, I concluded by emphasizing the need for collective responsibility and confidentiality between ministers. I said I had no intention of keeping a diary of Cabinet discussions and I hoped that others would follow my example. Inconvenient as that may be for the authors of memoirs, it is the only satisfactory rule for government. But I had to repeat this warning against leaks many times.

We were still in the first week of government, but we had to decide the content of the first Queen's Speech. This was largely the task of 'QL',* the Cabinet committee chaired by Willie Whitelaw, which was responsible for making recommendations to the Cabinet on legislation for inclusion in the Queen's Speech. We were fortunate that our manifesto commitments had been so clear; the Queen's Speech almost wrote itself.

In all this activity of government-making and policy-setting, however, I knew I could not afford to neglect the back-benchers. After twenty years in the House of Commons, through six Parliaments, I had seen how suddenly trouble could arise and the business of the House be put in jeopardy. So on Tuesday evening, before Parliament assembled the following day, I had invited the Chairman and Officers of the 1922 Committee for a talk, to celebrate our victory and discuss the work of the coming parliamentary session.** The name – which is usually abbreviated to 'the '22' – commemorates the events of that

* Queen's Speeches and Future Legislation Committee.

** The 1922 Committee consists of all Conservative Members of Parliament (other than those in office). At its meetings, and those of its sub-committees, views and policies are discussed, and the results made known to ministers by the whips and PPSs. It is also the 1922 Committee which has the decisive say in choosing the Speaker when the Conservative Party is in office.

year, when Conservative back-benchers forced the resignation of Lloyd George's coalition Government, bringing about a general election and the return of a Conservative administration under Bonar Law. It should remind anyone who is inclined to doubt it of the '22's importance to government. Even in less stormy times, a heavy legislative programme is only possible when there is a good working understanding between No. 10, the '22, the Whips' Office and the Leader of the House.

Wednesday 9 May saw the new parliament assemble for the election of the Speaker. The Speaker of the previous parliament had been George Thomas, a former Labour Cabinet minister, and he was the unanimous choice to continue in that office. My respect for George Thomas, already great, was to grow over the years. He was a deeply committed Christian with a shining integrity that gave him as Speaker a special kind of authority – but in my speech of congratulation, something else was on my mind: I had to keep remembering not to refer to Jim Callaghan as Prime Minister.

VISIT OF HELMUT SCHMIDT

On the following day Members of Parliament assembled to take the oath. But Thursday was a day of more than ceremonial importance (indeed there was one ceremony which somehow got lost in the rush – Denis's birthday). It was on that day that Helmut Schmidt, the West German Federal Chancellor, arrived in London on an official visit originally arranged with the Labour Government – the first head of a foreign government to visit me as Prime Minister.

There had been some discussion about whether this visit should go ahead. But I was particularly keen that it should. I had met Herr Schmidt in Opposition and had soon developed the highest regard for him. He had a profound understanding of the international economy on which – although he considered himself a socialist – we were to find ourselves in close agreement. In fact, he understood a good deal better than some British Conservatives the importance of financial orthodoxy – the need to control the money supply and to restrain public spending and borrowing so as to allow room for the private sector to grow. But he had to be told straight away that although Britain wanted to play a vigorous and influential role in the European Community, we could not do so until the problem of our grossly unfair budgetary contribution had been resolved.* I saw no reason to conceal our views behind a diplomatic smokescreen; indeed I wanted to convince Helmut Schmidt of both the reasonableness of our position and the strength of our determination precisely because he and West Germany exercised great influence in the Community. So I used every occasion to get the message across.

The speech which I delivered that Thursday evening at our dinner in honour of the Federal Chancellor was my first opportunity to set out my new approach towards the European Community. I rejected right from the start the idea that there was something 'un-European' in demanding that inequities be sorted out. In a passage which caught the media's attention, I said:

> It has been suggested by some people in this country that I and my Government will be a 'soft touch' in the Community. In case such a rumour may have reached your ears, Mr Chancellor, from little birds in Smith Square, Belgrave Square, or anywhere else, it is only fair that I should advise you frankly to dismiss it (as my colleagues did long ago!).** I intend to be very discriminating in judging what are British interests and I shall be resolute in defending them.

At our joint press conference the following day we were asked about our personal relations, since Helmut Schmidt was a socialist who had always referred to Mr Callaghan as 'Jim'. When I stressed the similarity of our policies, he intervened: 'Don't go too far, Prime Minister, and do not spoil my relations with my own Party, please!'

WORKING WEEKEND

On Saturday I flew to Scotland to address the Scottish Conservative Conference, something I always enjoyed. Life is not easy for Scottish Tories; nor was it to become easier. Unlike English Conservatives, they are used to being a minority party, with the Scottish media heavily slanted against them. But these circumstances gave Scottish

* For the details and course of negotiations about Britain's contribution to the European Community budget, see Chapter 3.

** No. 32 Smith Square is, of course, the home of Conservative Central Office and Belgrave Square is the address of the German Ambassador's residence.

Conservatives a degree of enthusiasm and a fighting spirit which I admired, and which also guaranteed a warm-hearted and receptive audience. Some leading Scottish Tories, though a small minority, still hankered after a kind of devolved government, but the rest of us were deeply suspicious of what that might mean to the future of the Union. While reaffirming our decision to repeal Labour's Scotland Act, I indicated that we would initiate all-party talks 'aimed at bringing government closer to the people'. In the event we did so by rolling back the state rather than by creating new institutions of government.

My main message to the conference, however, was a deliberately sombre one, intended for Britain as a whole. That same day an inflation figure of 10.1 per cent had been published. It would rise further. I noted:

> The evil of inflation is still with us. We are a long way from restoring honest money and the Treasury forecast when we took over was that inflation was on an upward trend. It will be some considerable time before our measures take effect. We should not underestimate the enormity of the task which lies ahead. But little can be achieved without sound money. It is the bedrock of sound government.

As our economic and political difficulties accumulated in the months ahead, no one could claim that they had not been warned.

We arrived back at RAF Northolt and drove to Chequers where I spent my first weekend as Prime Minister. I do not think anyone has stayed long at Chequers without falling in love with it. From the time of its first prime ministerial occupant, David Lloyd George, it has been assumed that the holders of that office would not necessarily have their own country estates. For that reason, Lord Lee's gift to the nation of his country house for the use and relaxation of prime ministers marks as much a new era as did the Reform Bills.

When I arrived as Prime Minister, the curator was Vera Thomas, who knew and loved each perfectly polished piece of furniture, each historic portrait, each glittering item of silver. Chequers itself is an Elizabethan house, but has been substantially rebuilt over the years. The centre of the house is the great hall, once a courtyard, enclosed at the end of the last century, where in winter a log fire burns, giving a slight tang of woodsmoke through every room.

Thanks to the generosity of Walter Annenberg, US Ambassador to Britain from 1969–74, Chequers has a covered swimming pool. But in the years I was there it was only used in the summer. Early on I learned that it cost £5,000 a year to heat. By saving this money we had more which could be spent on the perpetual round of necessary repairs to the house. Perhaps the most important work I had done was the cleaning of the Elizabethan panelling in the dining-room and the Great Parlour. Once the layers of varnish and dirt had gone, we discovered some beautiful marquetry beneath that had not been seen for many years.

The group which gathered for Sunday lunch just ten days after our election victory was fairly typical of a Chequers weekend. My family were there, Denis, Carol, Mark. Keith Joseph, Geoffrey and Elspeth Howe, the Pyms and Quintin Hailsham represented, as it were, the Government team. Peter Thorneycroft and Alistair McAlpine were present from Central Office – the latter having been, as Conservative Party Treasurer, one of the most effective fund raisers of all time and one of my closest and most loyal friends. David Wolfson, Brian Cartledge (my private secretary) with their wives, and our friends Sir John and Lady Tilney completed the party.

We were still in a mood to celebrate our election victory. We were away from the formality of No. 10. We had completed the initial task of getting the Government on the road. We still had that spirit of camaraderie which the inevitable disputes and disagreements of government were bound to sap. The meal was a light-hearted and convivial one. It was perhaps an instance of what a critic was later to call 'bourgeois triumphalism'.

But we were aware that there was a long road ahead. As my father used to say:

> It's easy to be a starter, but are you a sticker too?
> It's easy enough to begin a job, it's harder to see it through.

At 7 p.m. that evening Denis and I returned to London to begin my second full week as Prime Minister. Work was already piling up, with boxes coming to and from Chequers. I recall once hearing Harold Macmillan tell an eager group of young MPs, none more eager than Margaret Thatcher, that prime ministers (not having a department of their own) have plenty of spare time for reading. He recommended Disraeli and Trollope. I have sometimes wondered if he was joking.

CHAPTER II

Changing Signals

Domestic politics in the first six months – until the end of 1979

To turn from the euphoria of election victory to the problems of the British economy was to confront the morning after the night before. Inflation was speeding up; public sector pay was out of control; public spending projections were rising as revenue projections fell; and our domestic problems were aggravated by a rise in oil prices that was driving the world into recession.

The temptation in these circumstances was to retreat to a defensive redoubt, adopting a policy of false prudence: not to cut income tax when revenues were already threatening to fall; not to remove price controls when inflation was already accelerating; not to cut industrial subsidies in the teeth of a rising recession; and not to constrain the public sector when the private sector seemed too weak to create new jobs. And, indeed, these adverse economic conditions did slow down the rate at which we could hope to regenerate Britain. But I believed that was all the more reason to redouble our efforts. We were running up the 'Down' escalator, and we would have to run a great deal faster if we were ever to get to the top.

THE FIRST QUEEN'S SPEECH

Our first opportunity to demonstrate to both friends and opponents that we would not be deterred by the difficulties was the Queen's Speech. The first Loyal Address (as it is also called) of a new government sets the tone for its whole term of office. If the opportunity to set a radical new course is not taken, it will almost certainly never recur. And the world realizes that underneath all the brave new rhetoric, it is Business As Usual. I was determined to send out a clear signal of change.

By the end of the debates on the Address it was evident that the House of Commons could expect a heavy programme, designed to reverse socialism, extend choice and widen property ownership. There would be legislation to restrict the activities of Labour's National Enterprise Board and to begin the process of returning state-owned businesses and assets to the private sector. We would give council tenants the right to buy their homes at large discounts, with the possibility of 100 per cent mortgages. There would be partial deregulation of new private sector renting. (Decades of restrictive controls had steadily reduced the opportunities for those who wished to rent accommodation and thereby retarded labour mobility and economic progress.) We would repeal Labour's Community Land Act – this attempt to nationalize the gains accruing from development had created a shortage of land and pushed up prices. We removed the obligation on local authorities to replace grammar schools and announced the introduction of the Assisted Places Scheme, enabling talented children from poorer backgrounds to go to private schools. These were the first of what I hoped would be many steps to ensure that children from families like my own had the chance of self-improvement. We would, finally, curb what were often the corrupt and wasteful activities of local government direct labour organizations (usually socialist controlled).

When I spoke in the Queen's Speech debate, two points attracted particular attention: the abolition of price controls and the promise of trade union reform. Most people expected that we would keep price controls in some form, at least temporarily. After all, the regulation of prices, wages and dividends had been one of the means by which, throughout most of the western world, governments sought to extend their powers and influence and to alleviate the inflationary effects of their own financially irresponsible policies.

But there was plenty of evidence, gathered by the Confederation of British Industry (CBI), that while price controls had a minimal effect on inflation, they certainly damaged industrial profitability and investment. One of our first discussions in 'E' Committee – the economic strategy committee of the Cabinet, of which I was the chairman – was whether we should press ahead with early and total abolition of the Price Commission. Some ministers argued that with inflation accelerating, the coming rise in prices would be blamed on the Commission's abolition and therefore on the government. This argument had some force. But John Nott, the Trade Secretary, was keen to act swiftly; and he was right. It would have been still more difficult to abolish the Commission later in the year when prices were already rising faster. Perhaps the first time our opponents truly realized that the

Government's rhetorical commitment to the market would be matched by practical action was the day we announced abolition. We made public at the same time our decision to strengthen the powers of the Director-General of Fair Trading and the Monopolies and Mergers Commission to act against monopoly pricing, including prices set by nationalized industries.

I was also keen to use my speech in the debate to put an authoritative stamp on our trade union reforms. Jim Prior's preferred strategy was one of consultation with the trade unions before introducing the limited reforms of trade union law which we had proposed in Opposition. But it was vital to show that there would be no back-tracking from the clear mandate we had received to make fundamental changes. Initially, we proposed three reforms in the Queen's Speech. First, the right to picket – which had been so seriously abused in the strikes of the previous winter and for many years before – would be strictly limited to those in dispute with their employer at their own place of work; thus secondary picketing would become unlawful. Second, we were committed to changing the law on the closed shop, under which employees had effectively been compelled to join a union if they wished to obtain or keep a job, and which at that time covered some five million workers. Those who lost their jobs for this reason must in future be entitled to proper compensation. Third, public funds would be made available to finance postal ballots for union elections and other important union decisions: we wanted to discourage votes by show of hands – the notorious 'car park' votes – and the sharp practice, rigging and intimidation which had become associated with 'trade union democracy'.

In retrospect it seems extraordinary that such a relatively modest programme was represented by most trade union leaders and the Labour Party as an outright attack on trade unionism. In fact, we would have to return – and soon – to the issue of trade union reform. As time went by, it became increasingly clear to the trade union leaders and to the Labour Party that not only did we have huge public support for our policies, but that the majority of trade unionists supported them too, because their families were being damaged by strikes which many of them had not voted for and did not want. We were the ones in touch with the popular mood.

This was my first major parliamentary performance as Prime Minister, and I emerged unscathed. Nowadays, prime ministers make relatively few speeches in the House. The most important are speeches, like this, which deal with the government's legislative programme, speeches answering motions of censure, statements after international summits and debates which arise at times of international tension. This may be one reason why it is often difficult – over and above the moral blow of losing an election and leaving office – for prime ministers to revert to becoming Leaders of the Opposition, a job which demands more speech-making, but with less thorough briefing. Certainly, Jim Callaghan, who had never led his party in opposition, looked uncomfortable in that role. It was no surprise to me when he decided in October 1980 to step down from a position which his own left wing was making increasingly intolerable for him.

But it is Questions to the Prime Minister every Tuesday and Thursday which are the real test of your authority in the House, your standing with your party, your grip of policy and of the facts to justify it. No head of government anywhere in the world has to face this sort of regular pressure and many go to great lengths to avoid it; no head of government, as I would sometimes remind those at summits, is as accountable as the British prime minister.

I always briefed myself very carefully for Questions. One of the private secretaries, my political secretary, my Parliamentary Private Secretary and I would go through all the likely issues which might come up without any notice. This is because the questions on the Order Paper only ask about the prime minister's official engagements for that day. The real question is the supplementary whose subject matter may vary from some local hospital to a great international issue or to the crime statistics. Each department was, naturally, expected to provide the facts and a possible reply on points which might arise. It was a good test of the alertness and efficiency of the Cabinet minister in charge of a department whether information arrived late – or arrived at all; whether it was accurate or wrong, comprehensible or riddled with jargon. On occasion the results, judged by these criteria, were not altogether reassuring. However, little by little I came to feel more confident about these noisy ritual confrontations, and as I did so my performance became more effective. Sometimes I even enjoyed them.

THE 1979 BUDGET

The next watershed in the Government's programme was the budget. Our general approach was well known. Firm control of the money supply was necessary to bring down inflation. Cuts in public expenditure and borrowing were needed to lift the burden on the wealth-creating private sector. Lower income tax, combined with a shift from taxation on earning to taxation on spending, would increase incentives. However, these broad objectives would have to be pursued against a rapidly worsening economic background at home and abroad.

Britain's rate of inflation was running at 10 per cent when we took office, and rising. (The three-month rate was 13 per cent.) This reflected the lack of financial discipline in Labour's last years, when they broke free of the constraints imposed on them by the International Monetary Fund (IMF) in 1976. There was also a pay explosion as powerful unionized groups rode roughshod over the remains of Labour's incomes policy. And internationally, oil prices had begun to rise sharply, and were already about 30 per cent higher than six months earlier, as a result of the continuing turmoil in Iran after the fall of the Shah in 1978. This had an increasingly damaging effect on the international economy.

The oil price rise increased worldwide inflationary pressures. But it also had a perverse and, at least in the short term, damaging effect on the domestic economy because sterling was a petro-currency and it appreciated accordingly. Sterling was strong for other reasons too. Following the election there had been a general increase in confidence in the British economy. We were also pursuing a tight monetary policy, requiring high interest rates (interest rates had to go up by two percentage points at the time of the budget), and this attracted foreign capital. As a result of all these factors, sterling continued to rise.

We were perhaps better prepared for taking the required economic decisions than any previous Opposition. We had, every year, conducted our own internal public expenditure exercises, seeking to identify cuts wherever possible and putting figures on them. We had also, through the 'Stepping Stones' group of Shadow ministers and advisers of which John Hoskyns had been the main inspiration, worked out how to combine our policies to achieve the overall objective of reversing Britain's economic decline.

But no amount of advance preparation could change the unpleasant facts of finance or the budget arithmetic. The two crucial discussions on the 1979 budget took place on 22 and 24 May between me and the Chancellor. Geoffrey Howe was able to demonstrate that to reduce the top rate of income tax to 60 per cent (from 83 per cent), the basic rate to 30 per cent (from 33 per cent), and the PSBR to about £8 billion (a figure we felt we could fund and afford) would require an increase in the two rates of VAT of 8 per cent and 12.5 per cent to a unified rate of 15 per cent. (The zero rate on food and other basics would be unchanged.) I was naturally concerned that this large shift from direct to indirect taxation would add about four percentage points onto the Retail Price Index (RPI).

This would be a once and for all addition to prices (and so it would not be 'inflationary' in the correct sense of the term which means a continuing rise in prices). But it would also mean that the RPI, by which people generally measured living standards and all too frequently adjusted wage demands, would double in our first year of office.* I was also concerned that too many of the proposed public spending cuts involved higher charges for public services. These too would have a similar effect on the RPI. I recalled at my first budget meeting with Geoffrey that Rab Butler as Chancellor in 1951 had introduced his tax cuts gradually. Should we do the same? Geoffrey stuck to his guns. We went away to consider the question further.

At our second meeting we decided to go ahead. Income tax cuts were vital, even if they had to be paid for by raising VAT in this large leap. The decisive argument was that such a controversial increase in indirect taxes could only be made at the beginning of a parliament, when our mandate was fresh. If we waited, hoping that either economic growth or cuts in public expenditure would do the job for us, we might never achieve the structural shift needed to boost incentives. We must establish the direction of our strategy from the start and do it boldly. By the end of that second meeting the shape of the budget which Geoffrey Howe announced on 12 June had effectively been set.

It was generally agreed to be a dramatic reforming budget even by those opposed to us, like the *Guardian* newspaper, which described it as 'the richest political and economic gamble in post-war parliamentary history'. Its main provisions followed closely our discussions at the end of May: a cut in the basic rate of income tax from 33 to 30 per cent (with the highest rate cut from 83 to 60 per cent), tax allowances increased by 9 per cent above the rate of inflation, and the introduction of a new, unified rate of VAT at 15 per cent.

Apart from the budget's big income tax cuts, however, we were able to reduce or remove controls on a number of areas of economic life. Pay, price and dividend controls had gone. Industrial Development

* In order to try to give a better indication of the real effect of government policies on living standards, we published from 17 August 1979 a new 'Tax and Price Index' (TPI) which combined, in one figure, a measure both of the tax changes and the movements in retail prices. For those dependent on earned income, who constituted the bulk of the population, this provided a better indicator of changes in total household costs than the RPI. However, for the purposes of wage bargaining, the circumstances of an individual enterprise should determine what could be afforded.

Certificates, Office Development Permits and a range of circulars and unnecessary planning controls were also removed or modified. (Geoffrey Howe's second budget in 1980 was to announce the creation of Enterprise Zones, where businesses could benefit from tax breaks and rate exemption to attract investment and promote employment in run-down areas.)

But I took greatest personal pleasure in the removal of exchange controls – that is the abolition of the elaborate statutory restrictions on the amount of foreign exchange British citizens could acquire. These had been introduced as an 'emergency measure' at the start of the Second World War and maintained by successive governments, largely in the hope of increasing industrial investment in Britain and of resisting pressures on sterling. The overwhelming evidence was that they no longer achieved either of the objectives previously expected of them (if in fact they ever had done). With sterling buoyant and Britain beginning to enjoy the economic benefits of North Sea oil, the time had come to abolish them entirely. They were duly removed in three stages – some at the time of the Budget, a few others later in July, and the remainder in October (with the temporary exception of controls relating to Rhodesia). The legislation itself stayed on the Statute Book until 1987, but no further use was made of it. Not only did the ending of exchange controls increase the freedom of individuals and businesses; it encouraged foreign investment in Britain and British investment abroad, which has subsequently provided a valuable stream of income likely to continue long after North Sea oil runs out.

But not every capitalist had my confidence in capitalism. I remember a meeting in Opposition with City experts who were clearly taken aback at my desire to free their market. 'Steady on!', I was told. Clearly, a world without exchange controls in which markets rather than governments determined the movement of capital left them distinctly uneasy. They might have to take risks.

We had also been distracted throughout our budget discussions by the worrying level of public sector pay rises. Here we had limited freedom of manoeuvre. Hard, if distasteful, political calculations had led us to commit ourselves during the election campaign to honour the decisions of the Clegg Commission on those claims which had already been formally referred to it. The issue was now whether to refer the unsettled claims of other groups to Clegg, or to seek some new method of dealing with the problem.

It was quite clear to me that in the longer run there were only two criteria which could apply to pay in the public as in the private sector. The first was affordability: ultimately, it was the taxpayer and ratepayer who had to pay public sector wage bills, and if that burden passed beyond a certain limit, the country's economy would suffer. The second was recruitment: pay had to be sufficient to attract and retain people of the right ability and professional qualifications. However, the whole bureaucratic apparatus designed to achieve 'comparability' between public and private sector pay – not just the Clegg Commission but the Civil Service Pay Research Unit and other bodies – obscured these simple criteria.

We decided to submit evidence to the Commission about the necessity of keeping departmental budgets within reasonable limits and what that meant for public sector pay. But we also decided to keep the Commission in existence for the time being, and indeed refer new claims to it on an *ad hoc* basis. We thought at the time that the Commission might actually make lower pay awards than ministers themselves might have had to concede. But that turned out to be a highly optimistic assessment and, as a result, we underestimated the public expenditure cost of Clegg.

In retrospect, we made a mistake. Even at the time, the warning signs were evident. Geoffrey Howe told me that, allowing for some success in buying out restrictive practices, average pay could well be at least two to three percentage points higher than the recent June Forecast had assumed. In the end, it was not until August 1980 that we announced that Clegg would be abolished after its existing work had been completed. Its last report was in March 1981. The fact remains, however, that the momentum of public sector pay claims created by inflation, powerful trade unions and an over-large public sector was not going to be halted, let alone reversed, all at once.

CIVIL SERVICE REFORM

Whatever the short-term difficulties, I was determined at least to begin work on long-term reforms of government itself. If we were to channel more of the nation's talent into wealth-creating private business, this would inevitably mean reducing employment in the public sector. Since the early 1960s, the public sector had grown steadily, accounting for an increased proportion of the total workforce.* Unlike the

* The proportion of the British workforce employed in the public sector crept inexorably upwards from 24 per cent in 1961 to reach almost 30 per cent by the time we came into office. By 1990 through privatization and other measures we had brought it down again to a level below that of 1961.

private sector, it actually tended to grow during recessions while maintaining its size during periods of economic growth. In short, it was shielded from the normal economic disciplines which affect the outside world.

The size of the civil service reflected this. In 1961 the numbers in the civil service had reached a post-war low of 640,000; by 1979 they had grown to 732,000. This trend had to be reversed. Within days of taking office, as I have noted, we imposed a freeze in recruitment to help reduce the Government's pay bill by some 3 per cent. Departments came up with a range of ingenious reasons why this principle should not apply to them. But one by one they were overruled. By 13 May 1980 I was able to lay before the House our long-term targets for reducing civil service numbers. The total had already fallen to 705,000. We would seek to reduce it to around 630,000 over the next four years. Since some 80,000 left the civil service by retirement or resignation every year, it seemed likely that our target could be achieved without compulsory redundancies. We were, in fact, able to do it.

But the corollary of this was that we should reward outstanding ability within the civil service appropriately. The difficulties of introducing pay rates related to merit proved immense; we made progress, but it took several years and a great deal of pushing and shoving.

Similarly, I took a close interest in senior appointments in the civil service from the first, because they could affect the morale and efficiency of whole departments. I was determined to change the mentality exemplified in the early 1970s by a remark attributed to the then head of the civil service, that the best that the British could hope for was the 'orderly management of decline'. The country and the civil service itself were sold short by such attitudes. They also threatened a waste of scarce talent.

I was enormously impressed by the ability and energy of the members of my private office at No. 10. I usually held personal interviews with the candidates for private secretary for my own office. Those who came were some of the very brightest young men and women in the civil service, ambitious and excited to be at the heart of decision-making in government. I wanted to see people of the same calibre, with lively minds and a commitment to good administration, promoted to hold the senior posts in the departments. Indeed, during my time in government, many of my former private secretaries went on to head departments. In all these decisions, however, ability, drive and enthusiasm were what mattered; political allegiance was not something I took into account.

Over the years, finally, certain attitudes and work habits had crept in that were an obstacle to good administration. I had to overcome, for instance, the greater power of the civil service unions (which in addition were increasingly politicized). The pursuit of new and more efficient working practices – such as the application of information technology – was being held up by union obstruction. In a department like Health and Social Security where we needed to get the figures quickly to pay out benefits, these practices were disgraceful. But eventually we overcame them. There was even a problem at the very top. Some Permanent Secretaries had come to think of themselves mainly as policy advisers, forgetting that they were also responsible for the efficient management of their departments.

To see for myself, I decided to visit the main government departments to meet as many people as possible and discuss how they were tackling their priorities. I devoted most of a day to each department. In September 1979, for instance, I had a useful discussion with civil servants at the Department of Health and Social Security. I brought up the urgent need to dispose of surplus land held by the public sector. I was keen that where hospitals had land which they did not need they should be able to sell it and retain the proceeds to spend on improving patient care. There were arguments for and against this, but one argument advanced on this occasion, which was all too symptomatic of what had gone seriously wrong, was that this was somehow unfair on those hospitals which did not have the good fortune to have surplus land. We clearly had a long way to go before all the resources of the Health Service would be used efficiently for the benefit of patients. But this visit planted seeds that later grew into the Griffiths* reforms of NHS management and, later still, the internal market reforms of the Health Service in 1990.

Similarly, on 11 January the following year, I visited the Civil Service Department (CSD). This was an enlightening, if not an encouraging, experience. The CSD was set up in 1968, following publication of the Fulton Committee Report, with responsibility for the management and pay of the civil service. To the nucleus of the Pay and Management Divisions of the Treasury were added the Civil Service Commission and the newly established Civil Service College. The CSD employed 5000 people, headed by Sir Ian Bancroft, the senior Permanent Secretary. Although as Prime Minister I was in

* The Griffiths Report of 1983 was the basis for the introduction of general management in the NHS, without which the later reforms would not have been practicable. See pp. 606–17.

overall charge of the civil service, the duties were exercised by a Minister of State and the CSD had always lacked credibility and power in Whitehall.

Not without cause. When I arrived at the CSD, many of my worst fears about the civil service were confirmed. I met able and conscientious people attempting to manage and monitor the activities of civil servants in departments of which they knew little, in policy areas of which they knew even less. Because the staff of other departments were aware of the disadvantages under which the CSD worked, they took scant notice of the recommendations they received from it. After this visit, the only real question in my mind was whether responsibility for the CSD's work should be redistributed to the Treasury or the Cabinet Office.

Inevitably, my visits to government departments were not as long as I would have liked. There were other limits too on what I could learn on these occasions – particularly that senior civil servants might feel inhibited from speaking freely when their ministers were present. Consequently, after discussing the matter with Sir Ian Bancroft and having a word with Cabinet colleagues, I invited the Permanent Secretaries to dinner at No. 10 on the evening of Tuesday 6 May 1980. There were twenty-three Permanent Secretaries, Robin Ibbs (Head of the CPRS), Clive Whitmore, my principal private secretary, David Wolfson and myself around the dining-table.

This was one of the most dismal occasions of my entire time in government. I enjoy frank and open discussion, even a clash of temperaments and ideas, but such a menu of complaints and negative attitudes as was served up that evening was enough to dull any appetite I may have had for this kind of occasion in the future. The dinner took place a few days before I announced the progamme of civil service cuts to the Commons, and that was presumably the basis for complaints that ministers had damaged civil service 'morale'.

What lay still further behind this, I felt, was a desire for no change. But the idea that the civil service could be insulated from a reforming zeal that would transform Britain's public and private institutions over the next decade was a pipe-dream. I preferred disorderly resistance to decline rather than comfortable accommodation to it. And I knew that the more able of the younger generation of civil servants agreed with me. So, to be fair, did a few of the Permanent Secretaries present that night. They were as appalled as I was, and retreated into their shells. It became clear to me that it was only by encouraging or appointing individuals, rather than trying to change attitudes *en bloc*, that progress would be made. And that was to be the method I employed.*

PUBLIC SPENDING

Such an approach, however, would take years. We were dealing with crises on a weekly basis during the second half of 1979 as we scanned the figures on public spending and borrowing, against the background of an international economy slipping faster and faster into recession. Our first task was to make whatever reductions we could for the current financial year, 1979–80. Ordinarily, public spending decisions were made by government during the summer and autumn of the previous year and announced in November. Even though we were several months into the current financial year, we had to begin by reopening the public expenditure plans we had inherited from the Labour Government. We would announce our new public expenditure plans with the Budget. The scope for cuts was limited, partly because of this, partly because of our own election pledges, and partly because some changes we wanted to make required legislation.

We had promised to increase resources for defence and law and order, and not to cut spending on the National Health Service. We were also pledged to raise retirement pensions and other long-term social security benefits in line with prices – and to honour Labour's promised pension increases that year. We might have taken cash from the contingency reserve, but if there was to be any cash to take we would have to resist extra claims by government departments – no easy matter. Another possible device would be to squeeze the volume of public expenditure by holding to the existing cash limits, even though inflation had risen since they were set by the previous government. But that in turn would mean holding the line on public sector pay – again, no easy matter. Receipts from privatization might help us to balance the books. But although government-owned shares in

* It was only towards the end of my time in government that we embarked upon the radical reforms of the civil service which were contained in the 'Next Steps' programme. Under this programme much of the administrative – as opposed to policy-making – work of government departments is being transferred to agencies, staffed by civil servants and headed by chief executives appointed by open competition. The agencies operate within frameworks set by the departments, but are free of detailed departmental control. The quality of management within the public service promises to be significantly improved.

British Petroleum could be sold at once, the sale of state-owned assets on a really large scale would need legislation. Much of the work on public expenditure cuts which we had done in Opposition had been overtaken by events, the most damaging of which was the generosity of Professor Clegg. In short, we seemed to be boxed in.

But I was determined that we should make as vigorous a start as possible. I felt that the Treasury's first proposals for cuts in the current financial year, 1979–80, did not go far enough. Indeed, I had a meeting less than a fortnight after entering No. 10 with Treasury officials at which I told them so very firmly. Accordingly, John Biffen brought forward revised proposals that cut a further £500 million off the total, and I made it clear to colleagues that that was the least we could do.

In the end we were able to announce £3.5 billion of economies along with Geoffrey's Budget. In addition to the measures we were originally considering, we sought savings on industrial support, particularly regional development grants, on energy and on holding back projected spending on development land and public investment.

We also decided to raise prescription charges, which had remained at the same level for eight years during which time prices had risen two and a half times. (The wide range of exemptions would be maintained.) This had not been our first choice for savings from the DHSS budget. We had originally discussed extending the number of so-called 'waiting days' which must lapse before an applicant is entitled to sickness or unemployment benefit from three to six days. We decided not to press ahead with this, but nevertheless the idea found its way into the press in one of the leaks that were continually to bedevil our discussions of public spending.

No sooner had we agreed savings for the current year, 1979–80, than the still more difficult task was upon us of planning public expenditure for 1980–81 and subsequent years. In July 1979, when the crucial decisions were being hammered out, we had a series of particularly testing (and testy) Cabinet discussions on the issue. Our goal was what it had been in Opposition, that is to bring public expenditure back to the 1977–8 level in real terms. We hoped to achieve this by 1982–3. But, in spite of the reductions we had made, public expenditure was already threatening to run out of control. That in turn would have serious consequences for the PSBR, and thus for interest rates, in the longer term for taxation, and ultimately for our entire programme.

Nonetheless – or perhaps for that very reason – there was strong opposition from some ministers to the cuts. These were the so-called 'wets' who over the next few years took their opposition to our economic strategy to the very brink of resignation.* Some argued that the strategy had been overtaken by events; and indeed for those who had not heard that Keynes was dead, the prospect of reducing expenditure and curbing borrowing as we and the world sank into recession was undoubtedly alarming. Others put up a hundred and one reasons why any particular cut was out of the question. Defence, for instance, would not be able to achieve its sacrosanct target of 3 per cent growth a year. Or the DES would not be able to make economies in the time available (in spite of declining pupil numbers.) Or the Department of Employment would have to find money in response to the mounting jobless total. In the light of this opposition, I instructed a small group of key ministers to discuss with departments the proposals for reductions and report back to Cabinet.

Geoffrey Howe was superbly stolid in resisting this pressure. Later in July he set out for colleagues the precise implications of a failure to agree the £6.5 billion reductions he was proposing. He also dispelled some of the misunderstandings. Ministers had to recognize that we were not cutting to the bone, but merely reining in the increases planned by Labour and compensating for other increases that the deepening recession had made almost inevitable.

Labour's previously announced plans would have increased expenditure in 1979–80 by some 2 to 3 per cent over the level of 1978–9, and in 1980–81 by some 5 per cent, on the transparently erroneous assumption that the economy would grow by between 2 per cent and 3 per cent a year. Not that Labour was unique in this. The Treasury used to produce a fascinating chart, the so-called 'porcupine', in which the forecasts of economic growth in successive public spending white papers shot ever upwards, looking a little like porcupine quills, while the actual course of economic growth stubbornly remained on an only gently rising gradient. This was a literally graphic illustration of the overoptimistic assumptions on which past public expenditures plans had been based year after year. I was determined not to add another set of spikes.

In this case, Labour's plans would have involved expenditure of a further £5 billion in 1980–81 to be financed out of growth that was

* 'Wet' is a public schoolboy term meaning 'feeble' or 'timid', as in 'he is so wet you could shoot snipe off him.' The opponents of government economic policy in the early 1980s were termed 'wets' by their opponents because they were judged to be shrinking from stern and difficult action. As often happens with pejorative political labels (cf. Tory, which originally referred to Irish political bandits), 'wet' was embraced by the opponents of our economic strategy, who in turn named its supporters 'the dries'.

not happening. Moreover, this overshoot had been aggravated by a rate of pay increase in the public sector which was forecast to be 18 per cent, and which would cost another £4.5 billion. To offset these increasing obligations we had to find substantial cuts. We had to make reductions of £6.5 billion in the expenditure plans for 1980–81, just to hold the PSBR in that year down to £9 billion. That figure was in itself too high. But the 'wets' continued to oppose the cuts both in Cabinet and in the indecent obscurity of leaks to the *Guardian*.

It was not until the end of July that the Cabinet brought itself to take the necessary decisions. The conclusions were extensively leaked. Even so, we decided the wisest course was to wait for the autumn before publishing the full figures in the Autumn Statement. We had made some tough decisions in those first three months. It was, however, only a start.

Over the summer the economic situation worsened. On my return from my first Commonwealth summit in Lusaka in August, Geoffrey Howe presented me with a general survey of the economy which he rightly described as 'not very cheerful'. Unemployment was likely to begin to rise as the international recession deepened. Inflation was accelerating. Our competitiveness had worsened as a high pound and high wage costs put industry under increasing pressure. We became increasingly worried about the implications of pay rises for unemployment and bankruptcies. I asked that we should collect and circulate examples of excessive pay awards, which priced goods out of the market and destroyed jobs.

In September we again returned to public spending. We not only had to publish the conclusions we had agreed in July, but also our plans for the years up to 1983–4. And that meant more economies. We decided on a renewed drive to cut waste and reduce civil service numbers. We also agreed sharp increases in the price of electricity and gas (which had been artificially held down by Labour) that would come into effect in October 1980. Electricity would rise by 5 per cent, and gas by 10 per cent, over and above inflation.

The 1980–81 Public Expenditure white paper was duly published on 1 November. These public spending plans honoured our pledges to provide more resources for defence, law and order and social security (reflecting the year's record pensions uprating). They would also hold the public spending total for 1980–81 at the same level as 1979–80. In spite of the fact that this reduction of some £3.5 billion from Labour's plans was denounced as draconian, it really was not large enough. That was evident not only to me, but also to the financial markets, already concerned about excess monetary growth.

Here, too, we seemed to be running up the 'Down' escalator. On 5 November Geoffrey Howe came to see me. The money supply figures were well above target, principally because the PSBR and bank lending were both higher than expected. The PSBR had been affected by one strike which held up payment of telephone bills and by another which had disrupted VAT payments. Companies were borrowing to finance wage settlements they could not afford. Interest rates overseas were on the way up. And the public spending figures had also, as I suspected, proved too high for the markets. A financial crisis threatened. In the days of Denis Healey this would have elicited a fiscal package or 'mini-budget'. We had no hesitation in rejecting this approach. Higher interest rates or lower public spending, not tinkering with fiscal demand management, were the appropriate response.

On 15 November we accordingly raised Minimum Lending Rate (MLR – the successor to Bank Rate) to 17 per cent. (Measured by the RPI, inflation at this time was running at 17.4 per cent.) Other measures to help fund the PSBR were also announced.

Of course, the Opposition had a field day, attacking our whole strategy as misguided and incompetent. The fact of the matter was not that our strategy was wrong but that we had yet to apply it sufficiently rigorously and get a grip on public spending and borrowing. That in turn was increasing the pressure on the private sector through higher interest rates. Keith Joseph had warned of this in Opposition in his Stockton Lecture in 1976, which was later published as a pamphlet under the title *Monetarism is not Enough*, in which he said:

> Though, it is true, there is always talk of cutting public expenditure, it has remained almost entirely talk. Cutting public expenditure has come to mean juggling with figures . . . But whereas cuts in public expenditure rarely eventuate, squeezes on the private sector are 'for real'. The interest rate is increased, bank lending is contracted, taxes are raised, other old-fashioned deflationary measures are used. The private sector is punished for the state sector's profligacy.

I knew that we had to break this vicious spiral. We had to make further attempts to curb public spending and borrowing – no matter how difficult – because otherwise private enterprise would have to bear a crushing burden of public sector profligacy. Geoffrey and I accordingly decided that we had no alternative but to seek further spending reductions in 1980–81 and in subsequent years. He brought forward a paper, first to me and a small group of ministers and then to the full Cabinet, proposing an extra £1 billion reduction in 1980–81, and £2 billion in each of the following years. From what I had seen of departmental ministers' fierce defence of their own budgets, I knew that this would provoke trouble. But I also knew that the great majority in the Party were determined to see the strategy succeed. So I sought to take my case to them.

I had already told the Party Conference in Blackpool on 12 October:

> It is your tax which pays for public spending. The government have no money of their own. There is only taxpayers' money.

Just before the November rise in interest rates, I had used the platform of the Lord Mayor's Banquet to reaffirm that we would hold to our monetary policy in the fight against inflation:

> We shall take whatever action is necessary to contain the growth of the money supply. This government, unlike so many of its predecessors, will face up to economic realities.

I now made it clear that we would return to the attack on excessive public spending. The Party Leader's speeches to the 1922 Committee are an opportunity to appeal directly for support for the Government's policies. On Thursday 13 December, I told the '22 that we needed to 'have another go at getting expenditure down' and was well received. A little less than a month later, I agreed to be interviewed by Brian Walden on *Weekend World* and said of public spending that 'if we got a billion off, I would be quite pleased'. The atmosphere quickly became more propitious for a renewed drive against overspending.

In Cabinet on 24 January 1980 we returned to a discussion of public expenditure for 1980–81 and the years to 1983–4. Higher oil prices, almost no growth projected in industrialized countries in the coming year, and the steel strike* adding to the PSBR, formed a sombre background to our deliberations. I knew that these next two years would be crucial. We had to take the required action on inflation and public spending in that time: then as growth resumed, we would again be in a position to move towards lower taxes and lower interest rates. But the 'wets' launched a fierce attack on our policy and the theory underlying it. It was argued, for instance, that the PSBR should be allowed to rise during a recession. Our response was that it was a

* For the steel strike, see Chapter 4, pp. 108–14.

very different matter when the PSBR started out by being far too high – the legacy of a Labour Government which had doubled the national debt during its period in office. Individual ministers defended their bailiwicks. Jim Prior argued persuasively for a continuation of the special employment measures.* We agreed but decided that we would have to take another look at the the burgeoning social security budget.

A week later, Cabinet resumed its discussion – and focused closely on social security.** Both for public spending reasons and in order to deal with the 'Why Work?' problem (namely, the disincentive to work created by the small disparity between in-work and out-of-work incomes), we had already agreed to tax short-term social benefits as soon as possible. In the interim we decided to reduce these benefits – unemployment, sickness, injury, maternity and invalidity benefits – by 5 per cent. The so-called earnings related supplement (payable with certain short-term benefits) would be reduced from January 1981, and abolished in January 1982. We also decided to introduce legislation to deal with the vexed question of supplementary benefit for strikers' families. This was not only expensive to provide; it shifted the balance of power in industrial disputes against employers and responsible union leaders. In future, assessments would assume that £12 a week was provided either from the striker's own resources, or from union strike pay. We finally agreed a number of disparate savings on housing, on expenditure by the Property Services Agency, and from a rise in prescription charges to £1.

When Geoffrey Howe delivered his second budget on 26 March 1980,*** he was able to announce that we had found over £900 million in further savings in 1980–81 (though part of that was absorbed by an increase in the contingency reserve). Overall, at current prices this was over £5 billion less than Labour had planned to spend. In the circumstances, it was a formidable achievement, but also a fragile one. As the economy sank deeper into recession, there would be fresh demands, some of them difficult to resist, for higher public spending on programmes like social security and the loss-making nationalized

* These were a whole series of measures which we had inherited from the previous Labour Government and modified in various ways. They included the Youth Opportunities Programme, measures to encourage training, job release schemes, help for small firms and compensation for those in temporary, short-time work.

** Patrick Jenkin had already announced in June 1979 that we would end the statutory obligation to uprate long-term benefits in line with prices or earnings, whichever was higher: henceforth, uprating would be in line with prices.

*** For the measures in the 1980 budget see Chapter 4, pp. 95–7.

industries. In a paper he wrote for me in June 1979, John Hoskyns had used a memorable phrase about governments 'trying to pitch [their] tent in the middle of a landslide'. As we moved into the 1980–81 public expenditure round and the forecasts worsened, I could hear the canvas strain and the ground rumble.

IRISH TERRORIST OUTRAGES

The second half of 1979, though dominated by economic policy and by the intense round of diplomatic activity,* was also a time darkened by terrorism. Barely a fortnight after entering No. 10 I had delivered the address at the Memorial Service for Airey Neave.** Not long afterwards, IRA terrorists struck another blow which shocked people around the world.

I was at Chequers for the Bank Holiday Monday of 27 August when I learnt of the shocking murder of Lord Mountbatten and, that same day, of eighteen British soldiers. Lord Mountbatten was killed by an explosion on board his boat off the coast at Mullaghmore, County Sligo. Three other members of his party were killed and three injured.

In an even greater defiance of civilized custom, the murder of our soldiers was even more contemptible. Eighteen were killed and five injured in a double explosion triggered by remote controlled devices at Narrow Water, Warrenpoint, near Newry, close to the border with the Republic. The IRA had exploded the first bomb and then waited for those who came by helicopter to rescue their comrades before detonating the second. Among those murdered by the second bomb was the Commanding Officer of the Queen's Own Highlanders.

Words are always inadequate to condemn this kind of outrage: I decided immediately that I must go to Northern Ireland to show the army, police and civilians that I understood the scale of the tragedy and to demonstrate our determination to resist terrorism. Having returned to London from Chequers, I stayed there on Tuesday to allow those involved to deal with the immediate aftermath while I held two meetings with colleagues to discuss the security requirements

* For the summits I attended and the visits that I made in this period, see Chapter 3.
** See Volume II.

of the province. That evening I wrote personally to the families of the soldiers who had died; such letters are not easy to write. There were, alas, to be many more of them during my time in office.

I flew to Ulster on Wednesday morning. For security reasons, the visit was given no prior publicity. I went first to the Musgrave Park Hospital in Belfast and talked to the injured soldiers, then visited the Lord Mayor of Belfast at City Hall. I had insisted that I must meet the ordinary citizens of the city, and since the best way to do so was to walk through Belfast's shopping centre, that is where I went next. I shall never forget the reception I received. It is peculiarly moving to receive good wishes from people who are suffering. One never knows quite how to respond. But I formed then an impression I have never had reason to revise, that the people of Ulster will never bow to violence.

After a buffet lunch with soldiers of all ranks from 3 Brigade, I received a briefing from the army and then departed by helicopter to what is rightly referred to as the 'bandit country' of South Armagh. Dressed in a camouflage jacket worn by a female soldier of the Ulster Defence Regiment (a 'Greenfinch'), I saw the bomb-battered Crossmaglen RUC station – the most attacked RUC-Army post in the Province – before running back to the helicopter. It is too dangerous for either security force personnel or helicopters to remain stationary in these parts.

My final visit was to Gough barracks, the RUC base in Armagh, followed by a return flight to the mainland at six that evening. It is difficult to convey the courage of the security forces whose job it is to protect the lives of us all from terrorism. In particular, members of the UDR, who do their military duty living in the community where they and their families are always vulnerable, show a quiet, matter-of-fact heroism which I have never ceased to admire.

Back in London, we continued our urgent discussions on security. There were two major questions. How were we to improve the direction and co-ordination of our security operations in the province? And how were we to get more co-operation in security matters from the Irish Republic? On the first, we decided that the difficulties of co-ordinating intelligence gathered by the RUC and the army would be best overcome by instituting a new high-level security directorate. On the second, we agreed that I would tackle the Irish Prime Minister, Jack Lynch, when he arrived shortly for Lord Mountbatten's funeral.

Accordingly, we arranged a day's talks with Mr Lynch and his ministerial colleagues at No. 10 on the afternoon of Wednesday 5 September. The first session was a tête-à-tête between the two prime ministers; then at 4 p.m. we were joined by our respective ministers and officials.

Mr Lynch had no positive suggestions of his own to make at all. When I stressed the importance of extradition of terrorists from the Republic, he said that the Irish constitution made it very difficult. Mr Lynch pointed out that under Irish law terrorists could be tried in the Republic for offences committed in the UK. So I asked that RUC officers – who would have to amass the evidence for such prosecutions – be able to attend interrogations of terrorist suspects in the south. He said they would 'study' it. I knew what that meant: nothing doing. I asked that we extend the existing arrangements by which our helicopters could overfly the border across which terrorists seemed able to come and go almost at will. He said they would study that as well. I sought more effective liaison both between the RUC and the Garda, and between the British and Irish armies. Same response. At one point I got so exasperated that I asked whether the Irish Government was willing to do anything at all. They agreed to a further meeting between ministers and officials, but there was a fatal absence of the political will to take tough measures. I was disappointed, though not altogether surprised. However, I was determined to keep up the pressure on the Republic. I could not forget that by the time of my visit to Northern Ireland 1,152 civilians and 543 members of the security forces had been killed as a result of terrorist action.

We also lost no opportunity to use the revulsion the killings provoked in the US to inform public opinion there about the realities of life in Ulster. The emotions and loyalties of millions of decent Irish-Americans are manipulated by Irish Republican extremists, who have been able to give a romantic respectability to terrorism that its sordid reality belies. As a result, there has been a continuing flow of funds and arms which helps the IRA to continue its campaign, whereas in 1979 we were faced with the absurd situation that the purchase of 3,000 revolvers for the RUC was held up by a state department review under pressure from the Irish Republican lobby in Congress.

I visited the province again on Christmas Eve. This time I met members of the Northern Ireland prison service as well as the security forces. For the prison officers, too, faced grave danger and worked often in appalling conditions. From March 1978 they had been dealing with the consequences of the so-called 'dirty protest'* by over 350 terrorist prisoners, seeking 'special category status' and privileges.

* For the outcome of these protests and our response to the hunger strikes, see Chapter 14.

Seventeen prison officers had been murdered in the past four years, seven of them in the previous three months. It made the troubles of a political life seem very trivial.

CHAPTER III

Into the Whirlwind

Foreign affairs during the first eighteen months in 1979–1980

BRITAIN AND THE EUROPEAN COMMUNITY

I had made a number of political visits abroad before I became Prime Minister, travelling on various occasions to the Soviet Union, the United States, Germany, Israel and Australia. I enjoyed these tours – as long as there was plenty to read, interesting people to meet and we were doing useful work. But it is certainly a very different experience going abroad as Prime Minister, accompanied everywhere by a highly professional team of advisers, on what is usually a hectic schedule, and meeting heads of government on equal terms.

Familiarizing myself with this new role was not made easier by the fact that within weeks of coming into office I had to face the problem of Britain's excessive contribution to the European Community (EC) budget – something which required tough bargaining from a difficult position, and the use of diplomatic tactics which many people thought less than diplomatic. Nor was our budget contribution the only source of contention within the EC, even in those early days. It became increasingly clear to me that there were real differences of vision about Europe's future.

Shortly after I took office the first direct elections to the European Parliament were held. (In those days the Parliament was formally known as 'the European Assembly', which perhaps gives a more accurate impression of its limited role.) In the course of the campaign I made a speech in which I emphasized my vision of the Community as a force for freedom:

> We believe in a free Europe, not in a standardized Europe. Diminish that variety within the member states, and you impoverish the whole Community . . .

I went on:

> We insist that the institutions of the European Community are managed so that they increase the liberty of the individual throughout the continent. These institutions must not be permitted to dwindle into bureaucracy. Whenever they fail to enlarge freedom the institutions should be criticized and the balance restored.

There has, however, always been a contrary tendency in the Community – interventionist, protectionist, and ultimately federalist. The sharpness of the contrast between these two views of Europe would only become fully apparent as the years went by. But it was never far beneath the surface of events and I was always aware of it.

I was also very much aware of another feature of the EC, which had been apparent from its earliest days, continued to shape its development and diminished Britain's capacity to influence events – namely, the close relationship between France and Germany. Although this relationship may have seemed to depend on personal rapport – between President Giscard and Chancellor Schmidt or President Mitterrand and Chancellor Kohl – the truth is that it was explicable more in terms of history and perceptions of long-term interest. France has long feared the power of Germany and has hoped that by superior Gallic intelligence power can be directed in ways favourable to French interests. Germany, for her part, knows that although she has contributed considerably more to the EC financially and economically than any other state, she has received an enormous return in the form of international respectability and influence. The Franco-German axis would remain a factor to be reckoned with, and I shall have more to say about it later.

THE STRASBOURG EUROPEAN COUNCIL

My first European Council took place in Strasbourg on 21 and 22 June 1979. France hosted the talks. Strasbourg had been chosen as the venue in acknowledgement of the new importance of the European Parliament (which holds two-thirds of its sessions there) following the elections, in which Conservatives had won 60 of the 78 British seats.

I was confident that Chancellor Schmidt had taken away from our earlier discussions a clear impression of my determination to fight for large reductions in Britain's net budget contribution. I was hoping he would pass the message on to President Giscard, who was to chair the summit; both men were former Finance ministers and should be well able to understand Britain's point of view. (I could not help noticing too that they spoke to one another in English: but I was too tactful to remark on it.)

The background to the British budget problem is quickly described, though the precise details were extremely complicated. At the time of the negotiations for Britain's accession we had received an assurance (as I would continue to remind other member states) that:

> should an *unacceptable situation* arise within the present Community or an enlarged Community, the very survival of the Community would demand that the [Community] Institutions find equitable solutions. [my italics]

The reason why such an assurance had been necessary was that Britain's unique trading pattern made her a very large net contributor to the EC budget – so large that the situation was indeed unacceptable. We traditionally imported far more from non-EC countries than did other Community members, particularly of foodstuffs. This meant that we paid more into the Community budget in the form of tariffs than they did. By contrast, the Community budget itself is heavily biased towards supporting farmers through the Common Agricultural Policy (CAP): indeed when we came into office more than 70 per cent of the budget was spent in this way. The CAP was – and is – operated in a wasteful manner. The dumping of these surpluses outside the EC distorts the world market in foodstuffs and threatens the survival of free trade between the major economies. The British economy is less dependent on agriculture than that of most other Community countries and our farms are generally larger and more efficient than those of France and Germany; consequently we receive less in subsidy than they do. Britain traditionally received a fairer share of the receipts of the Community's non-agricultural programmes (such as the regional and social funds), but the growth of these programmes had been limited by the power of the farming lobby in Europe and by the international recession.

The previous Labour government had made a great play of 'renegotiating' the terms of Britain's original entry. In 1975 a Financial Mechanism to limit our contribution had been worked out in principle: but it had never been triggered, and never would be, unless the originally agreed conditions were changed. As a result, there was no solid agreement to which we could hold our Community partners.

One other development had worsened the overall position: Britain's prosperity, relative to that of our European neighbours, had steadily declined. In spite of North Sea oil, by 1979 Britain had become one of the least prosperous members of the Community, with only the seventh highest GDP per head of population among the member states. Yet we were expected shortly to become the largest net contributor.

So from the first my policy was to seek to limit the damage and distortions caused by the CAP and to bring financial realities to bear on Community spending. But at the Council meeting in Strasbourg I also had two short-term objectives. First, I wanted to have the budget question raised now and to gain acceptance of the need for action, though without at this stage going into too much detail. Second, I wanted to secure a firm undertaking from other heads of government that at the next Council meeting in Dublin the Commission would bring forward proposals to deal with the problem.

I sought at the start to strengthen our 'European credentials'. We Conservatives were welcomed in Strasbourg because we were seen as more pro-European than Labour: I tried to emphasize this by indicating that although we were not then in a position to join the Exchange Rate Mechanism (ERM) of the European Monetary System (EMS), we were 'minded' – an expression used so as not to offend the House of Commons to which it had not yet been announced – to swap some of our own reserves in the Bank of England for ecus (the European Currency Unit). I knew that Chancellor Schmidt was keen that we should commit sterling to the ERM; but I already had doubts about the wisdom of this course, which subsequently were reinforced. In any case, as it happened, my announcement of our intentions as regards the ecu 'swap' did not receive much visible welcome from the others: like other such concessions to the *ésprit communautaire,* it appeared simply to be pocketed and then forgotten.

If the budget issue was to concentrate minds as I wished, it had to be raised on the first day, because the communiqué is always drafted by officials overnight, ready for discussion the following morning. The draftsmen would therefore have to receive their instructions before the end of the first day. This did not prove easy. Over lunch I spoke to President Giscard about what I wanted and gained a strong impression that we would be able to deal with the budget early on. The whole group of us then set out to walk to the Hôtel de Ville through Strasbourg's narrow and attractive streets. The *bonhomie* seemed tangible.

But when we resumed, it quickly became clear that President

Giscard was intent on following his previous agenda, whatever he had given me to understand. At least I was well briefed and took an active part in the discussion about energy and the world economy. I pointed out that Britain had not flinched from the hard decisions required to ride out these difficulties and that we were making large cuts in public spending. By twenty minutes to seven that evening, we had decided, if we could, to hold Community imports of oil between 1980 and 1985 at a level no higher than that of 1978. We had agreed to stress the importance of nuclear energy. We had committed ourselves to keep up the struggle against inflation. Inevitably, I suppose, we had agreed to say something about 'convergence' between the economic performance of member states (a classic piece of Euro-jargon). In fact, we had done almost everything except what I most wanted us to do – tackle the budget issue.

Fortunately, I had been warned what might happen next. President Giscard proposed that as time was getting on and we needed to get ready for dinner, the matter of the budget should be discussed the following day. Did the Prime Minister of the United Kingdom not agree? And so at my very first European Council I had to say 'no'. As it turned out the lateness of the hour probably worked in my favour: conclusions are often easier to reach when time presses and minds are turning to the prospect of French *haute cuisine* and *grands crus*. I spelt out the facts: and the facts were undoubtedly telling. It was agreed to include in the communiqué an instruction to the Commission to prepare proposals for the next Council to deal with the matter. So, a little late, we rose for dinner. Argument always gives one an appetite.

At these gatherings, the custom was that heads of government and the President of the Commission dine together; foreign ministers formed a separate group. It was also customary to discuss foreign affairs. The plight of the Vietnamese 'boat people' was one topic which, of course, directly concerned Britain. Another was Rhodesia. It is interesting also to note that even then we were discussing the perennial problem of the Japanese trade balance.

Strasbourg had one solid result: it had put the question of Britain's unfair budget contribution squarely on the agenda. I felt that I had made an impression as someone who meant business, and afterwards I learned that this feeling was correct. It was at Strasbourg, too, that I overheard a foreign government official make a stray remark that pleased me as much as any I can remember: 'Britain is back,' he said.

THE TOKYO G7 SUMMIT

Many of the wider issues discussed at Strasbourg were raised again shortly afterwards in the still grander surroundings of the economic summit of the seven principal western industrial powers in Tokyo (the Group of Seven, or G7 for short). As soon as I had finished my report to the House of Commons on the Strasbourg Council, we drove out to Heathrow for the long flight to Japan. I knew that oil prices and their effect on the economy would again be top of the agenda. I was well briefed. Denis's knowledge of the oil industry was at my disposal and I had also had a thorough briefing by oil experts over lunch at Chequers. They knew the oil business inside out; by contrast, I was to find at Tokyo that politicians who thought they could limit oil consumption by setting out plans and targets had little practical understanding of the market.

I took the opportunity to discuss some other, equally important, matters *en route* to Tokyo. We had sought and were given permission from the Soviet Union to shorten the route to Japan by overflying Russia. In Moscow the plane landed to refuel and I was met by the Soviet Prime Minister, Alexei Kosygin, who broke off a meeting of communist prime ministers to come to the airport. To my surprise, an unscheduled dinner was laid out in the airport lounge. Hospitality in the Soviet Union was always generous for important visitors: there were two worlds, one for foreign dignitaries and the party élite, with luxuries of all kinds, and another for the ordinary people, with only the plainest of goods, and not many of them.

The motive for the Soviets' special attention was soon clear. They wanted to know more about the 'Iron Lady' – as their official news agency, Tass, had christened me following a speech I made in 1976 while Leader of the Opposition.

In East-West relations this was the lull before a huge political storm. Under the guise of *détente* the Soviets and their communist surrogates had pursued for some years a policy of covert aggression, while the West had let slip its defences. At Tokyo I was to find further evidence of the Carter Administration's overconfidence in the goodwill of the Soviet Union. The second Strategic Arms Limitation Treaty (SALT II) had been signed only days before. There was even talk of a SALT III. But the mood was about to change, for the Soviet invasion of Afghanistan was less than six months away.

Although we discussed defence, the most sensitive matter I raised with Mr Kosygin was the plight of the 'boat people', who were leaving Vietnam in their hundreds of thousands. They were the victims of appalling persecution, terrible enough to make them sell all their belongings, leave their homes and risk their lives sailing in overcrowded and dangerous ships, with no certainty of escape. A large merchant fleet sailed under the British flag and naturally our ships were picking up these tragic refugees from communism to save them from the risk of shipwreck and piracy. The rule of the sea is that survivors from shipwreck can be landed at the next port of call. But it often happened that the next port of call – in Singapore, Malaysia or Taiwan – refused to take them unless we agreed that they should be allowed to come on to Britain. At home we were still experiencing all the social and economic pressures of past mass immigration and consequently this was something we were most reluctant to agree. At Taiwan, although they would be given medical attention and food on the ship, they were not being allowed to land. The boat people themselves refused to land in Canton: they had had enough of communism. So this meant that Hong Kong became their favoured immediate destination, from where they hoped to go on to the United States or elsewhere in the West. The communists, of course, knew perfectly well that this flood of emigration was a costly embarrassment to the West and doubtless they hoped it might destabilize other countries in the region.

I put it to Mr Kosygin that Vietnam was a communist country and a close ally of the Soviet Union, and that he had considerable influence there. What was happening was a disgrace not only to the regime in Vietnam, but to communism as a whole. Could he do nothing to stop it? His words were translated to me: 'W-e-ll', he said (or the Russian equivalent), 'they are all drug-takers or criminals . . .' He got no further. 'What?', I asked. 'One million of them? Is communism so bad that a million have to take drugs or steal to live?' He immediately dropped the subject. But the point had been made and fully understood, as the nervous looks on the faces of his staff – and indeed some of mine – indicated. I could not stop the stream of persecuted refugees but I could and would always challenge the lies with which the communists sought to justify their persecution. After an hour and forty minutes we returned to the plane and resumed the flight to Tokyo. Later I referred the matter to the United Nations – it was too big for any one country to tackle.

The round of international summits makes a prime minister's life nowadays very different from what it was in the time of Anthony Eden, Harold Macmillan or Alec Douglas-Home. While in Opposition I had been sceptical of the value of much of this activity. In government I still worried that summits took up too much time and energy, particularly when there was so much to do at home: within a few months of taking office I had been to Strasbourg to represent Britain in Community matters, I was at Tokyo to represent her in the wider economic forum, and I would soon be going to Lusaka for the meeting of the Commonwealth heads of government.

The G7 had its roots in international action to counter the economic crisis of the mid-1970s. The first meeting was held in 1975 at Rambouillet in France. Since then the numbers attending and the formality of proceedings have increased year by year, and the result has not been an improvement. The principal advantages and disadvantages were well summed up by Chancellor Schmidt. The G7 summits had, he believed, helped the West to avoid what he called 'beggar my neighbour' policies – the competitive devaluations and protectionism which had inflicted such economic and political harm during the 1930s. On the other hand, he thought that too often the summits had been tempted to enter into undertakings which could not be kept; I agreed. There was always pressure, to which some governments were all too ready to bend, to come up with forms of words and ambitious commitments which everyone could accept and no one took seriously.

However, the soaring price of oil gave the 1979 Tokyo economic summit more than usual significance. Indeed, the Organization of Petroleum Exporting Countries (OPEC, the cartel of major oil producers) was meeting at the same time as the G7, its principal customers.* While we were in Tokyo the price of a barrel of Saudi oil rose from $14.54 to $18, with many OPEC crudes going higher still. Consequently, all the talk was of how to limit western dependency on oil and of deceptively specific targets to be met by particular dates. But I knew that the main way of reducing consumption was to allow the price mechanism to do its job. The danger, if we did not, was that countries would seek to accommodate higher oil prices by printing money, leading to inflation, in the hope of staving off recession and unemployment. We had seen in Britain that inflation was a cause of unemployment rather than an alternative to it, but not everyone had learned that lesson.

The previous summit had been held in Bonn in 1978 when the

* North Sea oil would soon give Britain an exceptional position among the major industrial powers, as we became a net oil exporter; but, of course, international recession would hit the markets for our industries: we were, therefore, not immune to the international consequences of the oil price rise.

doctrine of 'fine tuning demand' had still been fashionable. Germany had then been expected to act, as the jargon had it, as the 'locomotive' for growth, pulling the world out of recession. As Chancellor Schmidt was to tell the summit leaders at Tokyo, the main result had been to put up German inflation: he would not go down that path again. At Bonn there had been no new heads of government present and the old nostrums prevailed. At Tokyo, by contrast, there were three newcomers – the Japanese Prime Minister and Conference Chairman, Mr Ohira, the new Prime Minister of Canada, Joe Clark, and myself. Apart from me, the strongest advocates of free market economics were Helmut Schmidt and, to an even greater extent, Count Otto von Lambsdorff, his Finance minister.

On leaving the plane at Tokyo airport, I stepped into a huge crowd of reporters (some two thousand reporters attended these summits then, and more now). They had turned out to see that extraordinary, almost unprecedented, phenomenon – a woman prime minister. The weather was extremely hot and humid. There was very tight security. I was glad when we arrived at the hotel where the great majority of foreign delegates, with the exception of the President of the United States, were staying. Soon after my arrival, I went to see President Carter at the United States Embassy where we talked over our approach to the issues which would arise, especially energy consumption, which posed a particular problem – and one with important political implications – for the US. Mrs Carter and Amy joined us at the end of the meeting. In spite of press criticism, the Carters obviously enjoyed having their daughter travelling with them – and why not, I thought.

It was impossible not to like Jimmy Carter. He was a deeply committed Christian and a man of obvious sincerity. He was also a man of marked intellectual ability with a grasp, rare among politicians, of science and the scientific method. But he had come into office as the beneficiary of Watergate rather than because he had persuaded Americans of the rightness of his analysis of the world around them.

And, indeed, that analysis was badly flawed. He had an unsure handle on economics and was therefore inclined to drift into a futile *ad hoc* interventionism when problems arose. His windfall profits tax and controls on energy prices, for instance, only transformed the OPEC-induced price rises, which they were intended to cure, into unpopular queues at filling stations. In foreign affairs, he was over-influenced by the doctrines then gaining ground in the Democratic Party that the threat from communism had been exaggerated and that US intervention in support of right-wing dictators was almost as culpable. Hence he found himself surprised and embarrassed by such events as the Soviet invasion of Afghanistan and Iran's seizure of American diplomats as hostages. And in general he had no large vision of America's future so that, in the face of adversity, he was reduced to preaching the austere doctrine of limits to growth that was unpalatable, even alien, to the American imagination.

In addition to these political flaws, he was in some ways personally ill-suited to the presidency, agonizing over big decisions and too concerned with detail. Finally, he violated Napoleon's rule that generals should be lucky. His presidency was dogged with bad luck from OPEC to Afghanistan. What it served to demonstrate, however, was that in leading a great nation decency and assiduousness are not enough. Having said which, I repeat that I liked Jimmy Carter; he was a good friend to me and to Britain; and if he had come to power in the different circumstances of the post-Cold War world, his talents might have been more apposite.

That evening the European members of the summit met together for dinner, hosted by President Giscard. The Community had, of course, already agreed its own approach to energy at Strasbourg. The main issue now was how this would fit in with that which the three non-EC governments at the G7 wished to pursue.

The following morning, after the inevitable photographs, the first session began in the Conference Room on the second floor of the Akasaka Palace. Delegations sat around an oblong table and were arranged in alphabetical order: it was always useful that this placed us next to the United States. The precise arrangements for the arrival of the leaders reflected formal considerations of precedence, heads of state arriving after heads of government, and the order in each category determined by length of time in office. Precedence meant most to the French and least to the Americans: in fact, neither Jimmy Carter nor Ronald Reagan took much notice of it at all. As the rest of us sat there we would speculate as to who would manage to arrive last.

The meeting began, as usual, with a short general speech by each head of government. Chancellor Schmidt spoke before me in the first session, and after me in the second. We found ourselves stressing exactly the same points – the importance of the battle against inflation and the crucial role of the price mechanism in limiting energy consumption. My interventions appeared to be well received – not least by the Germans, as Count Lambsdorff subsequently told us. It was perhaps the nearest we ever came to an Anglo-German entente. I noted that many of our present difficulties stemmed from the pursuit of Keynesian policies with their emphasis on the deficit financing of public expenditure and I stressed the need to control the money supply in order to defeat inflation. There followed, after Mr Ohira and Chancellor Schmidt had taken a similar line, an extraordinary intervention by President Giscard in which he mounted a spirited defence of Lord Keynes and clearly rejected the basic free market approach as unnecessarily deflationary. Sig. Andreotti – Italy's Prime Minister then and again in my last days as Prime Minister – endorsed the French view. It was a revealing expression of the fundamental philosophical differences which divide the Community.

It was also revealing about the personalities of President Giscard and Prime Minister Andreotti. President Giscard d'Estaing was never someone to whom I warmed. I had the strong impression that the feeling was mutual. This was more surprising than it seems, for I have a soft spot for French charm and, after all, President Giscard was seen as a man of the Right. But he was a difficult interlocutor, speaking in paragraphs of perfectly crafted prose which seemed to brook no interruption. Moreover, his politics were very different from mine: though he had the manners of an aristocrat, he had the mind-set of a technocrat. He saw politics as an élite sport to be carried on for the benefit of the people but not really with their participation. There might be something to be said for this if technocrats really were cool intellectual guardians above the passions and interests of the rest of us. But President Giscard was as likely as anyone to be swept away by intellectual and political fashion; he simply expressed his passions coldly.

Prime Minister Andreotti was no more on my wavelength than the French President. Even more than the latter, this apparently indispensable participant in Italian governments represented an approach to politics which I could not share. He seemed to have a positive aversion to principle, even a conviction that a man of principle was doomed to be a figure of fun. He saw politics as an eighteenth-century general saw war: a vast and elaborate set of parade ground manoeuvres by armies that would never actually engage in conflict but instead declare victory, surrender or compromise as their apparent strength dictated in order to collaborate on the real business of sharing the spoils. A talent for striking political deals rather than a conviction of political truths might be required by Italy's system and it was certainly regarded as *de rigueur* in the Community, but I could not help but find something distasteful about those who practised it.

For all their hospitality, it would be difficult to claim too much for the quality of Japan's chairmanship of the proceedings. At one stage

I intervened to clarify for the sake of the officials – the 'sherpas' as they are known – precisely which of the two alternative draft communiqués we were discussing. While we were entertained that evening at a banquet given by the Emperor of Japan, the sherpas began their work. At about two o'clock in the morning, still in my evening dress, I went to see how the communiqué drafters were getting on with their work. I found them refining their earlier draft in the light of our discussions and setting out alternative forms of words where decisions would be required from the summit the following day. I hoped we would be as businesslike as they evidently were.

The following day we met once again at the Akasaka Palace to go through the communiqué, always a tedious and lengthy process. There was some disagreement between the Americans and the Europeans about the base year from which to set our different targets for the reduction of oil imports. But for me perhaps the most revealing discussion concerned the Japanese target. Until almost the last moment it was far from clear whether Mr Ohira's advisers would allow him to give a figure at all. Since I was quite convinced that the market itself would achieve the necessary limitation of oil consumption, regardless of what we announced, it all seemed rather academic to me. When in the end the Japanese did announce their figures no one had any idea what sort of reduction they constituted, if any; but President Carter warmly congratulated them all the same.

And so the communiqué was issued and the customary press conference held. The most important decision made had nothing to do with checking oil consumption. It was that, despite the inclinations of several G7 governments, we were not going to fall into the trap of trying to achieve a co-ordinated reflation of demand. It was a useful signal for the future.

From Tokyo I flew to Canberra, arriving the following morning. This was my third visit to Australia, though it was to be only a brief one. There was time to see my daughter, Carol, who was working as a journalist there, but my main purpose was to talk to Malcolm Fraser, the Australian Prime Minister. I briefed him on what had taken place at Tokyo. But even more important, we discussed the forthcoming Commonwealth Conference in Lusaka at which Rhodesia would inevitably be the main issue. Over the next eight months, Rhodesia was to take up a great deal of my time.

THE RHODESIAN SETTLEMENT

Rhodesia had been a long-standing source of grief to successive British governments, and an acute problem since Ian Smith's Unilateral Declaration of Independence in 1965. It had caused particular difficulties for the Conservative Party, a large section of which believed that the economic sanctions imposed against the illegal regime were futile and damaging and insisted on voting against them when they came up for annual renewal. Both the Conservative and Labour front benches had long been committed to seek a settlement on the basis of the so-called 'six principles' whose fundamental purpose was to lay down the conditions for a transition to black majority rule, while upholding the rights of the white minority and ensuring true democracy, the rule of law and an end to discrimination. But this degree of common ground between the leaders of both parties was not necessarily shared by their supporters.

The elections of April 1979 in Rhodesia fundamentally changed the whole position. Under the new constitution, worked out under the 'internal settlement' with Ian Smith, Bishop Muzorewa was elected as head of a black majority government, in a 64 per cent turn-out of a black majority electorate. The 'Patriotic Front' parties – the guerillas of Robert Mugabe and Joshua Nkomo – had not, of course, taken part in the elections. Viscount Boyd of Merton – a former Conservative Colonial Secretary – had attended as an observer and reported back to me, as Leader of the Opposition, that the elections had been fairly conducted. It was generally considered that all of the six principles had now been fulfilled and there was wide expectation that we would recognize the new government when we took office.

However, I was well aware that what the people of Rhodesia needed above all was peace and stability. It was the war, relentlessly carried on by the guerillas, which had forced the white minority government to make concessions: that war had to be ended. To bring peace we had either to win international acceptance for the new regime or bring about the changes which would win such acceptance.

The first and most immediate problem was the attitude of the neighbouring 'front line' African states. They must, if at all possible, be won over. We sent Lord Harlech, another former Conservative minister and an ex-Ambassador to Washington, for talks with the Presidents of Zambia, Tanzania, Botswana, Malawi and Angola. He also went to Mozambique and Nigeria. I was not at all keen at this stage that he should even talk to the leaders of the Patriotic Front, Mr Mugabe and Mr Nkomo: their forces had carried out atrocities which disgusted everyone and I was as keen to avoid dealings with terrorists abroad as I would be at home. However, unpleasant realities had to be faced. Peter Carrington's view was that it was essential to secure the widest possible recognition for a Rhodesian regime, since that country held the key to the whole South African region. He turned out to be right.

Accordingly, Lord Harlech did see the Patriotic Front leaders as well as Bishop Muzorewa and others. His mission at least made clear how large were the obstacles to achieving an end to the war. In July the Organization of African Unity (OAU) endorsed the Patriotic Front as the sole legitimate authentic representative of the people of Zimbabwe. Nigeria, with which Britain had important economic ties, was bitterly hostile to the Muzorewa Government. Black African states insisted on viewing Bishop Muzorewa's Government as nothing more than a façade for continued white minority rule. The fact that this greatly underrated the change which the internal settlement had effected did nothing to reduce the consequences of their attitude for Rhodesia.

Although we did not intend to continue the joint Anglo-American approach pursued by Labour, which had got nowhere, the attitude of the United States was of vital importance. President Carter was under strong political pressure from US black and liberal opinion. The Administration would soon have to say whether Bishop Muzorewa's Government met the conditions set by Congress, without which recognition and the lifting of sanctions by the US would not be possible. It was likely that the conclusion would be that it did not meet those conditions.

Yet the situation did offer opportunities, if we were able to grasp them. First, nearly everyone considered that it was Britain's responsibility to solve the problem, and even though this frequently made us the object of criticism it also gave us a relatively free hand if we knew how to use it. Second, there was a great weariness among the parties involved and not just the Rhodesians themselves. The surrounding African states were finding it costly, disruptive and dangerous to play host to the two guerilla armies, themselves the target of the well-trained and effective Rhodesian army. Nkomo's forces in Zambia were said to outnumber Zambia's own army. There was a real desire for a settlement. But how to reach it?

Our best chance of a breakthrough was likely to be at the forthcoming Commonwealth Conference in Lusaka. This would be the first regular Commonwealth Heads of Government Meeting held in Africa. Zambia adjoined the Rhodesian war zone. It was also land-locked, so that the Queen, who is traditionally present during the first days as Head of the Commonwealth (though she does not open or attend the meeting) could not use the Royal Yacht *Britannia*. There were, accordingly, some worries about Her Majesty's safety, on which it was my responsibility to advise. My feeling was that there was no reason why her visit should not go ahead, and I gave that advice shortly before the start of the Queen's African tour, from which she went on direct to Lusaka where she received an enormous welcome. I, by contrast, was far from being their favourite person, when, late in the evening of Monday 30 July, I arrived in Lusaka to face, without prior notice, a hostile and demanding press conference.

We had put the long flight out to good use, working through the precise approach we should take. I had a first-class team of advisers, and, of course, a first-class Foreign Secretary – with whom I had a lively exchange when he suggested that our mission was really a 'damage limitation exercise', at that time (as I told him) a phrase I had never even heard. I said that I wanted to do better than that; and between us in the end we managed to do so.

Our strategy was to take full responsibility ourselves for reaching a settlement. The task in Lusaka was to persuade the Commonwealth leaders to accept this, and to acknowledge that the Rhodesian problem was not the responsibility of the Commonwealth as a whole. To obtain that result we had to make it clear that Britain would be ready to resume authority in Rhodesia and to hold fresh elections. We knew also that there would have to be significant changes to the present constitution of Rhodesia if, after elections, the new government was to receive international recognition and acceptance. Those changes could only be brought about by some kind of Constitutional Conference bringing together all sides. The decision whether or not to hold such a conference would very much depend on how matters went at Lusaka.

My arrival in Zambia coincided with an announcement by the Nigerian Government that it was nationalizing BP's Nigerian oil assets. This was not a good start, but I went on to have an extremely useful day of talks with other heads of government before the conference officially began on the Tuesday. There was, in fact, a high turn out: 27 heads of government were present and all 39 full Commonwealth members were represented. Our host was President Kenneth Kaunda. At the closed session, the opening speech – one of the best of the conference – was given by Prime Minister Lee Kuan Yew of

Singapore who reviewed international political developments. But much serious business was done 'in the margins', as the diplomatic jargon has it, of the larger meetings. For example, the Prime Minister of Sri Lanka asked me whether a substantial sum of British overseas aid was still available for the construction of the massive Victoria Dam in his country. I confirmed it on a postcard – undoubtedly one of the most expensive I have ever written.

However, it was the situation in Rhodesia which had to be the real priority. In my opening public statement at the conference on the Wednesday I said that we would 'listen with the greatest attention to what is said at this meeting in Lusaka'. But on Friday, at the conference's closed session to discuss Rhodesia, I was able to be much more specific. I said that everyone should recognize just how much had changed as a result of Bishop Muzorewa's election even though 'there are those who seem to believe that the world should simply go on treating [him] as if he were Mr Smith.' I drew attention to the extensive international consultations we had undertaken to identify a solution. I acknowledged that from these we had learned the strength of the view 'that the constitution under which Bishop Muzorewa has come to power is defective in certain important respects', in particular the provisions whereby the white minority could block all unwelcome constitutional change. We had also observed that those consulted criticized the composition and powers of the various service commissions, and I noted 'it is clearly wrong that the Government of [Rhodesia/Zimbabwe] should not have adequate control over certain senior appointments.' We had been told that it was essential that the the Patriotic Front should be able to return and take a full part in politics. Finally, we had been impressed by the general conviction that any solution must derive its authority from Britain as the responsible colonial power.

I summed up our intentions:

> The British Government are wholly committed to genuine black majority rule in Rhodesia . . . We accept that our objective must be to establish . . . independence on the basis of a constitution comparable with the constitutions we have agreed with other countries . . . We will therefore present our proposals as quickly as possible to all the parties, and at the same time call on them to cease hostilities and move forward with us to a settlement.

It had been agreed to hold back the debate on southern Africa until the Friday so that after it the heads of government could go straight to their customary informal weekend retreat for private discussions on Rhodesia's future. My task was to win the support of the key figures there. A small group was set up consisting of myself and Peter Carrington, Mr (now Sir) Sonny Ramphal, Secretary-General of the Commonwealth, President Kaunda of Zambia, President Nyerere of Tanzania, Messrs Fraser and Manley, the Prime Ministers of Australia and Jamaica and Mr Adefope, the representative of Nigeria. Sir Anthony Duff, who was part of my team, drafted the heads of agreement. It all went remarkably smoothly until the very end. Our meeting ended successfully at Sunday lunch time and the full version of the agreement was to have been discussed and endorsed by the full conference on Monday morning. However, on Sunday afternoon Malcolm Fraser chose to brief the Australian press. This required some rapid and unconventional action.

That evening we all attended a Commonwealth service in Lusaka Cathedral, where we had the benefit of a long polemical sermon from the Archbishop. I had been told already that the press knew the substance of what had been decided. Sonny Ramphal and I were sitting together; he was to read the first lesson, and I the second. After he had read his I showed him a note I had received from Peter Carrington about Malcolm Fraser's intervention, suggesting that we must now brief the British press on what had taken place, subject to the Secretary-General's approval. On the back of my hymn sheet, while I was reading the second lesson, Mr Ramphal wrote an alternative suggestion. The heads of government had been invited to a barbecue that evening at Malcolm Fraser's conference villa: we could hold a meeting there and settle a communiqué to be issued at once. This seemed to me an excellent idea. I agreed to telephone Kenneth Kaunda immediately after the service to warn him of what we had in mind. And so the meeting came about. It took an hour and there were some very pointed comments. I was none too pleased with Malcolm Fraser myself. But the conclusion was satisfactory. Indeed, most of us were relieved that it had all been so amicable and that our proceedings could therefore end a day early.

I returned home on Wednesday morning. I was well pleased with what had been achieved, so much of it by Peter Carrington and Tony Duff. Many had believed that we could not come out of Lusaka with an agreement on the lines we wanted. We had proved them wrong. We had incidentally proved the Zambian press wrong too: they had so convinced themselves beforehand of the truth of their own propaganda about me that it was clearly a shock to find that they were dealing with a real person rather than a colonial cardboard cut-out. I had no illusions about the scale of the task ahead: it was never going to be easy to steer Rhodesia to independence, legitimacy and stability. But after Lusaka I believed that it could be done, and that we had won the African good will to carry it through successfully.

Britain accordingly called a Constitutional Conference for the interested parties at Lancaster House in London in September. Its purpose was emphasized as being not just to talk but to reach a settlement. Peter Carrington arranged the agenda to take the most difficult questions last, so that the first item to be agreed was the new constitution; only then would come the question of the transitional arrangements; and finally the calling of a cease-fire. We calculated that the longer the conference continued, the less any of the interested parties would be willing to take responsibility for breaking it up. We reserved to ourselves the task of putting forward final proposals in each phase and we required the parties to respond, even if these proposals did not meet all their objectives. At each stage we had to exert pressure – direct and indirect – on the two sides to reach a satisfactory compromise. Peter Carrington chaired the conference with great skill and took charge of its day-to-day work. My role lay outside it. The heads of the 'front line' states came to London in person or sent in High Commissioners to see me for a progress report. President Machel of Mozambique was especially helpful in putting pressure on Robert Mugabe. I also gave dinner for President Nyerere, another strong backer of Mr Mugabe. His concern was how to blend the three separate armies – the two guerilla armies and the Rhodesian army – into one, a task which in fact would fall to the British army to achieve. The Lancaster House proposals could not have got through without the support of the Presidents of the 'front line' states and, indeed, many other Commonwealth countries.

Just after the conference concluded, all three rival leaders – Bishop Muzorewa, Robert Mugabe and Joshua Nkomo – came to see me together at No. 10. We talked upstairs in my study. They were in contemplative mood, pondering the future. I had the clear impression that each of them expected to win. Perhaps that was just as well.

Probably the most sensitive aspect of our approach related to the transitional arrangements: it was clear to me that, both for constitutional and practical reasons, Britain must resume direct authority in Rhodesia until the elections were over, though for as short a period as possible. On 15 November a bill was introduced to provide for the appointment of a Governor and for sanctions to be removed as soon as he arrived in Rhodesia. Christopher Soames accepted the post. The decision to send him, as Governor, to Salisbury on 12 December, even before the Patriotic Front had accepted the cease-fire proposals, certainly involved some risk and was much criticized at the time. But we were clear that the momentum had to be maintained. Moreover, Christopher was an ideal appointment: not only did he have the authority of a Cabinet minister and wide diplomatic experience, he and his wife, Mary, had precisely the right style to carry off this most delicate and demanding job. Heavy pressure from the US and the 'front line' states finally led the Patriotic Front to accept the proposals for the cease-fire on 17 December, and the agreement was finally initialled on 21 December. I telephoned the Soameses in Salisbury on Christmas Day to wish them the season's greetings and ask how things were. The reply was that in spite of several severe breaches of the cease-fire and some clear intimidation by the supporters of Mr Mugabe, the situation looked increasingly hopeful.

The outcome of the elections is well known. Mr Mugabe's party, to most people's surprise, won an overwhelming victory. On 18 April Rhodesia, as the Republic of Zimbabwe, finally received its independence.

It was sad that Rhodesia/Zimbabwe finished up with a Marxist government in a continent where there were too many Marxists maladministering their countries' resources. But political and military realities were all too evidently on the side of the guerilla leaders. A government like that of Bishop Muzorewa, without international recognition, could never have brought to the people of Rhodesia the peace that they wanted and needed above all else. From the British point of view the settlement also had large benefits. With the Rhodesian question finally solved, we again played an effective role in dealing with other Commonwealth – and especially African – issues, including the pressing problem of the future of Namibia and the longer-term challenge of bringing peaceful change to South Africa. Britain had demonstrated her ability, by a combination of honest dealing and forceful diplomacy, to settle one of the most intractable disputes arising from her colonial past.

THE EC BUDGET AGREEMENT OF 1980

With the Lancaster House Conference still in progress, I had to turn my mind once again to the vexed question of how to negotiate a substantial reduction in Britain's net contribution to the European

Community budget. Figures had at long last been put on the size of that contribution and henceforth it was difficult for anyone to deny the scale of the problem. Also the European Commission had produced a report which indicated that it was indeed possible, in line with well-established Community principles, to achieve a 'broad balance' between British contributions and receipts. There were, therefore, some grounds for optimism, but I had no illusion that a settlement would be easy and I was well aware of the possibility of sharp practice. British officials had indicated to those of the presidency my concern at the procedural wrangles which had characterized the previous Strasbourg Council and my desire that the presidency should take a firm line and get the budget discussed early.

By this time, the member states of the Community knew that we were serious. On 18 October I delivered in Luxemburg the 1979 Winston Churchill Memorial Lecture, which, as the occasion required, dealt principally with foreign affairs.

I warned:

> I must be absolutely clear about this. Britain cannot accept the present situation on the Budget. It is demonstrably unjust. It is politically indefensible: I cannot play Sister Bountiful to the Community while my own electorate are being asked to forego improvements in the fields of health, education, welfare and the rest.

We had also taken every opportunity to seek wider understanding of the merits of our case. I had talks in Bonn with Helmut Schmidt at the end of October, and on 19 and 20 November there was a two-day Anglo-French summit in London. The Germans and the French knew that I meant business.

In the run up to the Dublin Council, we examined carefully the measures available to us to bring pressure on the Community. Christopher Soames, who had great experience of the ways and wiles of the Europeans, sent me a note to the effect that the Community had never been renowned for taking unpleasant decisions without long wrangling and that I should not worry too much about the cards in my hand because a major country like Britain could disrupt the Community very effectively if it chose. I noted his advice. In this spirit, we had examined quite early on – though we looked at it again later – the possibility of withholding British payments to the Community. For practical and legal reasons this always seemed a non-starter. Nevertheless, I believed that even the possibility caused satisfactory anxiety in the Commission, whose pressure to get a satisfactory settlement was vital. We also had the lever of refusing to agree agricultural price increases, which the French and German Governments – each facing elections – wanted to see. Our moral position was strengthened, too, by the fact that the French had broken the EC law by obstructing British lamb imports: the European Court of Justice found against them on 25 September – though morality counts for little in the Community.

At the next Council – in Dublin at the end of November, the Irish having now assumed the European Community Presidency – the issue of our budget contribution dominated the business. The obvious security risk from the IRA required that I be lodged overnight in splendid isolation in Dublin Castle, the former seat of British rule. The Irish press enjoyed the idea that I slept in the bed used by Queen Victoria in 1897, though I had the advantage over her of a portable shower in my room. Indeed, I was very well looked after. The hospitality was perhaps the best feature of the visit, and contrasted strongly with the atmosphere at the meetings which was extremely and increasingly hostile. I had expected something of the sort. I went to Dublin with a newly tailored suit. Ordinarily I would have enjoyed wearing something new on an occasion as important as this, but I thought twice: I didn't want to risk tainting it with unhappy memories. This was not, though, the only wise decision I made at Dublin: the principal one was to say very clearly, and with at least as much force as at Strasbourg, the word 'no'.

The Council opened amicably enough in Phoenix Park at the Irish President's official residence where he hosted lunch. Back in the Council at Dublin Castle we got down to business. My opening speech set out the facts of our case in somewhat greater detail than at Strasbourg and I elaborated on them in the vigorous debate which followed. There was a good deal of argument about the figures, at the root of which was an obscure and complex issue – how to calculate the losses and gains resulting to individual states from the operation of the CAP. But which ever way one did the sums, there was no doubt that the UK was making a huge net contribution, and unless it was mitigated it was about to become the biggest. We were not arguing that we should be net beneficiaries (though some in Britain would have wished me to); in fact, we were only asking for a 'broad balance'. It was unacceptable that at a time when we were making cuts in public spending at home we should be expected to make a net contribution of more than £1 billion a year. I emphasized Britain's commitment to the Community and our wish to avoid a crisis, but I left no one in any doubt that this is precisely what the Community would face if the problem were not resolved.

We had put forward our own proposals on the budget. But the Commission had come up with some of its own and I was prepared to accept their basic approach as a starting point. First, they proposed that action be taken to shift the weight of Community expenditure generally away from agriculture towards structural and investment programmes. The trouble was that this would take too long – if it happened at all. Second, they proposed, in addition, specific spending on UK projects to boost our receipts. But there simply were not enough suitable projects. Finally, on the contribution side, the 1975 Correction Mechanism had so far failed to cut our payments. If it were reformed on the lines the Commission was proposing, it could help reduce our net contributions – but still not by enough: we would still be contributing about the same as Germany and much more than France. Something far more radical would be required.

I made one other point which was to prove of some significance. I said that, 'the arrangement [must] last as long as the problem.' It seemed to me then, and even more so by the end of the Council, that we simply could not have these battles every year, all to establish what common sense and equity ought to have made self-evident from the beginning.

It quickly became clear that I was not going to make the other heads of government see matters like this. Some, for example the Dutch Prime Minister, Mr Andries Van Agt, were reasonable, but most were not. I had the strong feeling that they had decided to test whether I was able and willing to stand up to them. It was quite shameless: they were determined to keep as much of our money as they could. By the time the Council broke up Britain had been offered a refund of only £350 million, implying a net contribution of some £650 million. That refund was just not big enough and I was not going to accept it. I had agreed that there should be another Council to discuss the matter further, but I was not overoptimistic after what I had seen and heard in Dublin. For me it went much further than hard bargaining about money, which was inevitable. What I would not accept was the attitude that fairness as such did not seem to enter into the equation at all. I was completely sincere when I had said that Britain was asking no more than its due; and my anger when such a proposition was regarded with cynical indifference was equally genuine.

It was while reflecting on the quintessentially un-English outlook displayed by the Community at this time and later that I came across the following lines from Kipling's 'Norman and Saxon' in my old, battered collection of my favourite poet's verse. The Norman baron with large estates is warning his son about our English forefathers, the Anglo-Saxons, and says:

> The Saxon is not like us Normans. His manners are not
> so polite.
> But he never means anything serious till he talks about justice
> and right.
> When he stands like an ox in the furrow with his sullen set
> eyes on your own,
> And grumbles, 'This isn't fair dealing', My son, leave the
> Saxon alone.

At the press conference after the Council, I gave a vigorous defence of our position. I said that the other states should not have 'expected me to settle for a third of a loaf'. I also refused to accept the *communautaire* language about 'own resources'. I continued to state without apology that we were talking about Britain's money, not Europe's. I said:

> I am only talking about our money, no one else's; there should be a cash refund of our money to bring our receipts up to the average level of receipts in the Community.

Most of the other heads of government were furious. The Irish press was vitriolic. One British newspaper, *The Times*, described my performance at the press conference as 'bravura', though there was more criticism from the leader columns. The best comment, I felt, was from *Le Figaro*, which said:

> To accuse Mrs Thatcher of wishing to torpedo Europe because she defends the interests of her country with great determination is to question her underlying intentions in the same way that people used to question those of de Gaulle in regard to French interests.

I liked the comparison.

We used the period between the end of the Dublin meeting and the next European Council to press our case, both in public and through diplomatic means. On 29 and 30 January I had talks with the Italian Prime Minister (later President) Francesco Cossiga. I had already had dealings with Sig. Cossiga in 1979 when the Schild family, my constituents, were kidnapped in Sardinia. I had found him highly competent and deeply concerned. He was also a man of principle, as his earlier resignation as Minister of the Interior after the murder of the former Christian Democrat Leader Aldo Moro showed, and as I already knew him to be from my own experience. Italian politics and Italian politicians do not evoke much understanding or sympathy from the British, or indeed from the Italians, and I confess to sharing some of that disenchantment. But Francesco Cossiga was himself a sceptic about the usual Italian practices. He was the nearest thing to an independent in Italian politics; in negotiations he always played a straight hand; he could be relied upon to keep his word, as he did over the stationing of Cruise missiles in Italy; and he was an undoubted Anglophile and a strong admirer of the Glorious Revolution of 1688 as the birth of true liberal politics. I was glad that it was Sig. Cossiga who was due to host the next European Council.

On 25 February Helmut Schmidt came to London again. Our talks centred on the question of our budget contribution and on the German Chancellor's repeated wish to see sterling within the ERM, and – contrary to the usual misleading press reports – they were useful and quite jolly. On 27 and 28 March there was a full scale Anglo-German summit in London. I sought once more to stress how seriously we felt about the British contribution. Subsequently, I learned that Helmut Schmidt had been telling other Community governments that if there were no solution there was a danger that we would withhold British contributions to the Community. So I had created the desired impression. The European Council due for 31 March and 1 April had to be postponed because of a political crisis in Italy (not an unusual event), but we pressed for a new Council before the end of April and it was finally called for Sunday and Monday 27 and 28, to meet in Luxemburg.

At this time, there was a marked hardening of public opinion in Britain as the result of our treatment by the Community. In particular, there was much speculation about possible withholding of Britain's contributions, which did not displease me, though I was cautious in public on the subject. I said on *Panorama* on 25 February that we would consider withholding but would be loath to do it because it meant going against Community law. I also went on French television on 10 March and said:

> I wouldn't expect France to be the biggest contributor if she had an income below average in the Community. And I do indeed

assure you that your very distinguished French politicians would be the first to complain if that were so.

I gave an interview to *Die Welt* in which I said:

> We shall do our utmost to prevent matters coming to a crisis. But it must be realized that things cannot continue like this.

The atmosphere in Luxemburg turned out to be a good deal better than in Dublin. I was optimistic. From a discussion I had had with Sig. Cossiga, who had spoken to President Giscard, it seemed at first that the French were prepared to set a ceiling on the size of our net contributions for a period of years irrespective of the growth in the overall Community budget, subject to review at the end of the period. This would have been a step forward. On closer examination, however, it became clear that what the French really wanted was to get decisions on their most politically sensitive topics – farm prices in the CAP, lamb and fishing rights – before settling the budget. Finally, it was agreed that parallel meetings should be held over the weekend: Agriculture ministers would meet and so would a group of officials working on the budget issue.

As a result we did not get around to talking about the budget at all at our first session. Indeed, only after dinner, and the usual foreign affairs *tour de table*, did I obtain agreement that the official group should resume effective negotiation that evening. The French were the main stumbling block: the proposals their officials presented were much less helpful to us than President Giscard's had seemed to be. In the meantime, the Agriculture ministers of the other governments of the Community had agreed on a package of proposals which would have raised farm prices, increasing again the proportion of the Community budget devoted to agriculture (quite contrary to the proposals put forward in Dublin) and giving the French a sheep meat regime which was more or less all that they wanted. Against this – for us – distinctly unfavourable background, we received eventually the offer of a limit on our net contribution of about £325 million, applying only to the year 1980. Under a subsequent proposal our net contribution would have been limited to about £550 million for 1981 as well.

My reaction was that this was too little. But above all I was not prepared to have a settlement that only lasted for two years. Helmut Schmidt, Roy Jenkins (President of the Commission) and almost everyone else urged me to settle. But I was not willing to return the following year to face precisely the same problem and the attitude that went with it. So I rejected the offer. The draft communiqué, moreover, was unacceptable to us since it continued to insist on the old dogma that 'own resources are intended to provide the finance for Community policies; they are not contributions from member states.' Nor did it make reference to the assurances we had been given on our accession to the Community that action would be taken 'should an unacceptable situation arise'.

Many reacted to my decision in Luxemburg with disbelief: in some circles the very last thing expected of a British prime minister was that he or she should quite so unashamedly defend British interests. But there was, I noted, a contrast between the reaction in some of the press which was extremely hostile and the reaction in the House of Commons and the country, which was thoroughly supportive.

In fact, we were a good deal closer to a settlement than was widely recognized. Great progress had already been made in winning agreement to substantial reductions in our contribution. What remained was to secure these reductions for the first two years with a reliable undertaking for the third. We had a number of powerful levers by which we could apply pressure to this end. The French were increasingly desperate to achieve their aims in the Agriculture Council. There was even talk of overriding the British veto by abrogating the so-called Luxemburg compromise of 1966, established to accommodate de Gaulle. (This was an understanding rather than a formal agreement with the force of law, which enabled any one country to block a majority decision when its vital national interests were at stake.) In fact, precisely this did happen at the Agriculture Council in May 1982 – and this during the Falklands War. However, at this particular time it would have been a dangerous move, particularly since the French had already been found in breach of Community law over lamb imports. The Germans, too, were keen to see higher agricultural prices. Most important of all, the Community would, we thought, probably reach the limit of its financial resources in 1982. Its persistent overspending was catching up with it, and greater resources could only be made available with British agreement. Ultimately our negotiating position was a strong one.

It soon became clear that Luxemburg, following the clashes in Dublin, had had the desired effect. In spite of talk of the Luxemburg offer having now been 'withdrawn', there was evidence of a general desire to solve the budget issue before the next full European Council at Venice in June. The easiest way to achieve this appeared to be a meeting of the Community Foreign ministers.

Peter Carrington, having received his mandate from me, flew to

Brussels on Thursday 29 May with Ian Gilmour. After a marathon eighteen-hour session they came back with what they considered an acceptable agreement, arriving at lunch time on Friday to brief me at Chequers.

My immediate reaction was far from favourable. The deal involved a net budget contribution in 1980 higher than envisaged at Luxemburg. It appeared from Peter's figures that we would pay rather less under the new package in 1981, though to some extent this was sleight of hand, reflecting different assumptions about the size of that year's total budget. But the Brussels proposal had one great advantage: it now offered us a three-year solution. We were promised a major review of the budget problem by mid-1981 and if this had not been achieved (as proved to be the case) the Commission would make proposals along the lines of the formula for 1980–81 and the Council would act accordingly. The other elements of the Brussels package relating to agriculture, lamb and fisheries, were more or less acceptable. We had to agree a 5 per cent rise in farm prices. Overall, the deal marked a refund of two-thirds of our net contribution and it marked huge progress from the position the Government had inherited. I therefore decided to accept the offer.

CRISES IN THE MIDDLE EAST

Wider international affairs had not stood still while we were engaged in bringing Rhodesia to legal independence and negotiating a reduction in our Community Budget contribution. In November 1979, forty-nine American diplomatic personnel had been taken hostage in Iran, a source of deep and growing humiliation to the greatest western power. In December at the invitation of President Carter I made a short visit to the United States – the first of many as Prime Minister. In a short speech at my reception on the White House Lawn I went out of my way to reaffirm my support for American leadership of the West. Then in a speech the next day in New York I warned of the dangers of Soviet ambitions and urged the need for strong western defence:

> The immediate threat from the Soviet Union is military rather than ideological. The threat is not only to our security in Europe and North America but also, both directly and by proxy, in the Third World . . . we can argue about Soviet motives but the fact

is that the Russians have the weapons and are getting more of them. It is simple prudence for the West to respond.

I also undertook to support the United States in the UN Security Council in seeking international economic sanctions against Iran under Chapter 7 of the UN Charter. The President and I discussed defence and the situation in Ulster. I took the opportunity to thank him for all he had been doing behind the scenes in the final stages of the negotiations on Rhodesia.

Then, at the end of 1979, the world reached one of those genuine watersheds which are so often predicted, which so rarely occur – and which take almost everyone by surprise when they do: the Soviet invasion of Afghanistan. In April 1978, the Government of Afghanistan had been overthrown in a communist-inspired coup; a pro-Soviet government was established, which, however, was met by widespread opposition and eventual rebellion. In September 1979 the new President, Taraki, was himself overthrown and killed by his deputy, Hafizullah Amin. On 27 December, Amin in turn was overthrown and killed, to be replaced by Babrak Karmal, whose regime was supported by thousands of Soviet troops.

The Soviets had long considered Afghanistan to have a special strategic significance and sought to exercise influence there through so-called 'Treaties of Friendship'. It was said that they were probably concerned, in the light of events in Iran, at the possibility of anarchy in Afghanistan leading to a second fundamentalist Muslim state on their borders, which might destabilize their own subject Muslim population. The West had for some time been anxious that the Soviets would make a drive for the oil in the Gulf. And the energy crisis gave them a still stronger reason to do so.

Perhaps I was less shocked than some by the invasion of Afghanistan. I had long understood that *détente* had been ruthlessly used by the Soviets to exploit western weakness and disarray. I knew the beast.

What had happened in Afghanistan was only part of a wider pattern. The Soviets had instigated Cubans and East Germans to advance their aims and ambitions in Africa. They had been working to further communist subversion throughout the Third World, and for all the talk of international peace and friendship, they had built up armed forces far beyond their defensive needs. Whatever their precise motives now in Afghanistan, they must have known that they had threatened the stability of Pakistan and Iran – the latter unstable enough already under the Ayatollah – and were within 300 miles of the Straits of Hormuz. Moreover, bad as the situation was in itself, it could be worse as a precedent. There were other areas of the world in which the Soviets might prefer aggression to diplomacy, if they now prevailed: for example, Marshal Tito was evidently approaching the end of his life in Yugoslavia and there could be opportunities for Soviet intervention there. They clearly had to be punished for their aggression and taught, albeit belatedly, that the West would not only talk about freedom but was prepared to make sacrifices to defend it.

On Friday 28 December President Carter rang me at Chequers and we discussed at length what the Soviets were doing in Afghanistan and what our reaction should be. What had happened was a bitter blow to him. Britain had not felt able to comply with all that the Americans had wanted of us in response to the hostage crisis: in particular, we were not willing (or indeed legally able) to freeze Iranian financial assets, which would have had a devastating effect on international confidence in the City of London as a world financial centre. However, I was determined that we should follow America's lead now in taking action against the USSR and its puppet regime in Kabul. We therefore decided on a range of measures, including the curtailment of visits and contacts, non-renewal of the Anglo-Soviet credit agreement and a tightening of the rules on technology transfer. I also sought to mobilize the governments of the European Community to support the Americans. But, like President Carter, I was sure that the most effective thing we could do would be to prevent their using the forthcoming Moscow Olympics for propaganda purposes. Unfortunately, most of the British Olympic team decided to attend the Games, though we tried to persuade them otherwise: of course, unlike their equivalents in the Soviet Union, our athletes were left free to make up their own minds. At the UN our ambassador, Tony Parsons, helped to rally the 'non-aligned' countries to condemn the Soviet Union's aggression. In London, on 3 January, I saw the Soviet Ambassador to enlarge in vigorous terms on the contents of my exchanges by telegram with President Brezhnev.

From now on, the whole tone of international affairs began to change, and for the better. Hard-headed realism and strong defence became the order of the day. The Soviets had made a fatal miscalculation: they had prepared the way for the renaissance of America under Ronald Reagan.

But this was the future. America had still to go through the humiliating agony of the failed attempt to rescue the Iranian hostages. As I watched President Carter's television broadcast explaining what had happened, I felt America's wound as if it were Britain's own; and in a sense it was, for anyone who exposed American weakness increased ours. I was soon, though, in a position to demonstrate that there would be no flinching when it came to dealing with our own brand of Middle East terrorism.

I first learned of the terrorist attack on the Iranian Embassy at Prince's Gate in Knightsbridge on Wednesday 30 April during a visit I was making to the BBC. The early reports were, in fact, misleadingly anodyne. It soon became known, however, that several gunmen had forced their way into the Iranian Embassy and were holding twenty hostages – most of them Iranian staff, but also including a policeman who had been on duty outside and two BBC journalists who had been applying for visas. The gunmen were threatening to blow up both the embassy and the hostages if their demands were not met. The terrorists belonged to an organization calling itself 'the Group of the Martyr'; they were Iranian Arabs from Arabistan, Iraqi-trained and bitterly opposed to the prevailing regime in Iran. They demanded that a list of 91 prisoners be set free by the Iranian Government, that the rights of Iranian dissidents should be recognized and a special aeroplane provided to take them and the hostages out of Britain. The Iranian Government had no intention of conceding these demands; and we, for our part, had no intention of allowing terrorists to succeed in their hostage taking. I was conscious that, though the group involved was a different one, this was no less an attempt to exploit perceived western weakness than was the hostage taking of the American embassy personnel in Tehran. My policy would be to do everything possible to resolve the crisis peacefully, without unnecessarily risking the lives of the hostages, but above all to ensure that terrorism should be – and be seen to be – defeated.

Willie Whitelaw, as Home Secretary, took immediate charge of operations from the special emergency unit in the Cabinet Office. The unit is immediately activated when a security crisis occurs. On it representatives of the Cabinet Office, Home Office, Foreign Office, military, police and intelligence services advise a minister in the chair – usually, as on this occasion, the Home Secretary; I only once and briefly took this role at the time of the hijack of an aircraft from Tanzania to Stansted. Hour by hour information is gathered, sifted and analysed so that every circumstance and option can be properly evaluated. Throughout the crisis, Willie kept in regular contact with me. In turn the Metropolitan Police kept in touch with the terrorists by a specially laid telephone line. We also made contact with those who might be able to exert some influence over the gunmen. The latter wished to have an Arab country's ambassador act as intermediary. But we were extremely doubtful about this: there was a risk that the objectives of such an intermediary would be different from our own. Moreover, the Jordanians, whom we *were* prepared to trust, refused to become involved. A Muslim imam did talk to the terrorists, but without result. It was a stalemate.

Willie and I were completely agreed as to the strategy. We would try patient negotiation; but if any hostages were wounded we would consider an attack on the embassy; and if a hostage were killed we would definitely send in the Special Air Service (SAS). There had to be some flexibility. But what was ruled out from the start was to let the terrorists leave, with or without the hostages.

The position began to deteriorate on Sunday afternoon. I was called back early from Chequers and we were driving back to London when a further message came over the car-phone. There was too much interference on the line to be able to talk easily so I had my driver pull into a lay-by. Apparently, the information was that the hostages' lives were now at risk. Willie wanted my permission to send in the SAS. 'Yes, go in': I said. The car pulled back out onto the road, while I tried to visualize what was happening and waited for the outcome. Executed with the superb courage and professionalism the world now expects of the SAS, the assault took place in the full glare of the television cameras. Of the 19 hostages known to be alive at the time of the assault all were rescued. Four gunmen were killed; one was captured; none escaped. I breathed a sigh of relief when I learned that there were no police or SAS casualties. Later I went to the Regent's Park Barracks to congratulate our men. I was met by Peter de la Billière, the SAS commander, and then watched what had happened on television news, with a running commentary, punctuated by relieved laughter, from those involved in the assault. One of them turned to me and said, 'we never thought you'd let us do it.' Wherever I went over the next few days, I sensed a great wave of pride at the outcome; telegrams of congratulation poured in from abroad: we had sent a signal to terrorists everywhere that they could expect no deals and would extort no favours from Britain.

The Middle East continued to occupy my attention throughout the rest of 1980. At the European Council in Venice on 12 and 13 June the heads of government discussed Israel and the Palestinian question. The key issue was whether the Community governments were to call for the PLO to be 'associated with' the Middle East peace talks, or to 'participate in' them: I was very much against the latter course, for as long as the PLO did not reject terrorism. In fact, the final communiqué reflected what seemed to me the right balance: it reaffirmed the right of all the states in the region – including Israel – to existence and security, but also demanded justice for all peoples, which implied recognition of the Palestinians' right to self-determination. So, of course, it pleased no one.

Then the Middle East focus shifted again. In September 1980 Iraq attacked Iran and we were once again in the throes of a new crisis, with potentially dangerous political and economic implications for western interests. Saddam Hussein had decided that the chaos in Iran provided him with a good opportunity to renounce the 1975 Algiers Settlement of the two countries' disputed claims to the Shatt-al-Arab waterway and seize it by force.

Shortly after the outbreak of the war Peter Carrington came over to Chequers to discuss the situation with me. I was chiefly concerned to prevent the conflict spreading down the Gulf and involving the vulnerable oil-rich Gulf States, which had traditionally close links with Britain. I told Peter that I did not share the common view that the Iranians would quickly be beaten. They were fanatical fighters and had an effective airforce with which they could attack oil installations. I was right: by the end of the year and after initial successes, the Iraqis became bogged down and the war threatened both the stability of the Gulf and western shipping. But by this time we had put in the Armilla Patrol to protect our ships.

As I looked back on the international scene that Christmas of 1980 at Chequers, I reflected that the successes of British foreign policy had helped us through a particularly dark and difficult time in domestic, and particularly economic, affairs. But as in economic matters so in foreign affairs I knew that we were only starting the course. Tackling Britain's Community budget problem was only the first step to reforming the Community's finances. Bringing Rhodesia to legal independence was but a prelude to addressing the problem of South Africa. The West's response to the Soviet invasion of Afghanistan would have to be a fundamental rethinking of our relations with the communist bloc and this had barely begun. The renewed instability in the Gulf as a result of Iraq's attack on Iran would ultimately require a new commitment by the western powers to the security of the region. All these issues were to dominate British foreign policy in the years ahead.

CHAPTER IV

Not At All Right, Jack

The restructuring of British industry and trade union reform in 1979–1980

BRITAIN'S INDUSTRIAL PROBLEMS

In the years since the war British politics had focused, above all, on the debate about the proper role of the state in the operation of the economy. By 1979 and perhaps earlier, optimism about the beneficent effects of government intervention had largely disappeared. This change of attitude, for which I had long worked and argued, meant that many people who had not previously been Conservative supporters were now prepared to give our approach at least the benefit of the doubt. But I knew that this entirely justified lack of faith in the wisdom of the state must be matched by a renewed confidence in the creative capacity of enterprise.

A sort of cynical disdain, often disguised as black humour, had come to characterize many people's attitude to industry and unions. We all enjoyed the film *I'm All Right, Jack*, but the problem was no laughing matter.

British goods will only be attractive if they can compete with the best on offer from other countries, in respect of quality, reliability and price, or some combination of the three, and the truth is that too often British industrial products were uncompetitive. This was not simply because the strong pound was making it difficult to sell abroad, but because our industrial reputation had steadily been eroded. In the end reputation reflects reality. Nothing less than changing that reality – fundamentally and for the better – would do.

In spite of what might seem the more immediate and pressing problems of strikes, price competitiveness and international recession, the root of Britain's industrial problem was low productivity. British living standards were lower than those of our principal competitors and the number of well-paid and reasonably secure jobs was smaller because we produced less per person than they did. Some twenty-five years earlier our productivity was the highest in western Europe; by 1979 it was among the lowest. The overmanning resulting from trade union restrictive practices was concealed unemployment; and beyond a certain point – certainly beyond the point we had reached in 1979 – overmanning would bring down businesses and destroy existing jobs, and abort those which otherwise could have flourished. Outdated capacity and old jobs have to go to make the most of new opportunities. Yet the paradox which neither British trade unions nor the socialists were prepared to accept was that an increase in productivity is likely, initially, to reduce the number of jobs before creating the wealth that sustains new ones. Time and again we were asked when plants and companies closed, 'where will the new jobs come from?' As the months went by, we could point to the expansion of self-employment and to industrial successes in aerospace, chemicals and North Sea oil. Increasingly we could also look to foreign investment, for example in electronics and cars. But the fact is that in a market economy government does not – and cannot – know where jobs will come from: if it did know, all those interventionist policies for 'picking winners' and 'backing success' would not have picked losers and compounded failure.

Because our analysis of what was wrong with Britain's industrial performance centred on low productivity and its causes – rather than on levels of pay – incomes policy had no place in our economic strategy. I was determined that the Government should not become enmeshed, as previous Labour and Conservative administrations had been, in the obscure intricacies of 'norms', 'going rates' and 'special cases'. Of course, pay rises at this time were far too high in large parts of British industry where profits were small or nonexistent, investment was inadequate, or market prospects looked poor. Judged by relative labour costs, our level of competitiveness in 1980 was some 40 to 50 per cent worse than in 1978: and around three-fifths of this was due to UK unit labour costs increasing at a faster rate than those abroad, with only two-fifths the result of exchange rate appreciation. There was little, if anything, we could do to influence the exchange rate, without allowing inflation to rise still further and faster. But there was a great deal which trade union negotiators had it in their power to do if they wished to prevent their own members and others being priced out of jobs; and as the scale of union irresponsibility grew apparent, talk of the need for a pay policy began to be heard.

So it was important that from the very beginning – even before we had realized the extent of the pay explosion which was under way –

I stood firm against suggestions of pay policies. Some senior colleagues supported a return to incomes policy: shortly after we took office Jim Prior argued for early talks with the TUC and CBI about pay. We had already had vigorous disagreements on the issue in Opposition. *The Right Approach to the Economy* had gone further than I would have liked in proposing a 'forum' for discussion between employers and unions of the pay implications of government economic policy. A far weaker reference had been included in the 1979 manifesto. I had now come to feel that all such talk was at best irrelevant and at worst misguided.

Of course, it is of great importance that all those involved in wage bargaining should know and understand the economic framework in which they are operating and the facts of life confronting their particular business. Within a given money supply (provided that the government sticks to it), the more taken out in higher pay, the less available for investment, and the smaller the number of jobs.

Some people offered what they thought of as the 'German model'. We were all conscious of Germany's economic success. Indeed, we had helped create the conditions for it after the war by introducing competition and restructuring their trade unions. There were those in Britain who went further than this and said that we should copy the German corporatist tendency of making national economic decisions in consultation with business organizations and trade union leaders. However, what might work for Germany would not necessarily work for us. The German experience of hyperinflation between the wars meant that nearly everyone there was deeply conscious of the need to keep inflation down, even at the expense of a short-term rise in unemployment. German trade unions were also far more responsible than ours, and of course the German character is different, less individualistic and more regimented. So the 'German model' was inappropriate for Britain.

In any case, we already had the National Economic Development Council (NEDC) in which ministers, employers and trade unionists met from time to time. And so I was quite sure that we should not proceed further with the idea of a new 'forum'. In fact, I felt that we should do all that we could to reinforce the contrary view: the whole approach based on prices and incomes controls should be swept away. The Government would set the framework, but it was for businesses and workforces to make their own choices, and to face the consequences of their actions, good and bad. In the private sector rates of pay must be determined by what businesses could afford, depending on their profitability and productivity. In the public sector also affordability was the key – in this case meaning the scale of the burden it was right to ask the taxpayer and ratepayer to bear. Given that government was the ultimate owner and banker, however, the mechanism by which these disciplines could be made effective was bound to be less clear and direct than in the private sector.

THE 1980 BUDGET AND THE MEDIUM TERM FINANCIAL STRATEGY (MTFS)

The income tax cuts in our 1979 budget were intended to give more incentives to work. But the budget of 1980 was still more directly focused on improving our underlying economic performance. Towards the end of February Geoffrey Howe came to see me to discuss the shape of it. We were agreed entirely about the monetary and fiscal position: we would continue with the present money supply targets, which were still not being met, and keep the PSBR at the same level as the previous year.

However, I was more concerned about his tax proposals. There was no doubt about the difficulties industry was facing. Very high pay awards had left firms short of cash, though oil companies were in a better position due to the oil price rise. There was, therefore, a strong argument for a budget which helped business. On the other hand, I certainly did not want to see personal incentives diminished. It was going to be difficult to get the balance right. In any case, there was also a question of the precise means to help industry. My instinct was to go for a lower PSBR and so bring down interest rates. But many in industry wanted us to cut the National Insurance Surcharge (NIS) – a tax introduced by Labour, which had substantially raised business costs. Geoffrey had also been pressing from the previous December for a package of capital tax cuts and reliefs.

In the end we settled on a 'budget for business', but only by fairly modest and inexpensive measures. Geoffrey Howe's second budget on 26 March 1980 helped small businesses through enterprise zones,* gave tax relief to encourage the investment of venture capital, and introduced building allowances for small workshops.

* These were areas, typically around 500 acres in size, within which major tax incentives were made available to business – 100 per cent capital allowances for industrial and commercial buildings, complete relief from development land tax, exemption from local taxation, drastically simplified planning control and lighter regulation. The idea was Geoffrey's own brainchild.

As regards income tax, personal allowances generally were raised in line with inflation. But the lower rate band of 25 per cent, which we had inherited from the Labour Party and which complicated the tax system, was abolished. To balance this we raised the thresholds of the higher rate bands by about seven percentage points less than inflation. The budget also announced difficult and unpopular measures on prescription charges and social security benefits.

However, the most important aspect of the 1980 budget related to monetary policy rather than taxation. We announced in the budget our Medium Term Financial Strategy (quickly known as the MTFS), which was to remain at the heart of our economic policies throughout the period of their success and which was only relegated in importance in those final years, when Nigel Lawson's imprudence had already begun to steer us to disaster. A little historical irony is provided by the fact that Nigel himself, as Financial Secretary, signed the Financial Statement and Budget Report (FSBR), or 'Red Book', in which the MTFS first burst on an astonished world, that he had contributed much to its preparation and that he was its most brilliant and committed exponent.

The MTFS was intended to set the monetary framework for the economy over a period of years. The aim was to bring down inflation by decreasing monetary growth, while curbing borrowing to ensure that the pressure of disinflation did not fall solely on the private sector in the form of higher interest rates. The monetary figures for later years that we announced in 1980 were illustrative rather than firm targets – though this did not prevent commentators poking tiresome, if predictable, fun when the targets were altered or not met. The 1980 MTFS figures for the money supply were expressed in sterling M3 (£M3), though the Red Book noted that 'the way in which the money supply is defined for target purposes may need to be adjusted from time to time as circumstances change,' an important qualification.*

* Notes and coins are included in all the monetary measures. But since the great majority of transactions in the economy are not conducted in cash, but in transferring claims on the banking system (e.g., writing cheques), most measures also include some part of total bank deposits. Wider measures often include the deposits of other financial institutions such as building societies. £M3 comprises notes and coins in circulation with the public, together with all sterling deposits (including certificates of deposit) held by UK residents in both public and private sectors. The argument about which is the best measure continues, though a misplaced obsession with the exchange rate has since rather put such argument into the shade.

There were two important points which were forgotten by many of those who criticized the MTFS on the basis of the changes we made. First, 'monetarism' is simply the view that inflation is a monetary phenomenon and that, therefore, the reduction in the rate of growth of the money stock is essential to achieving a

Not all of those who shared our fundamental economic objectives entirely welcomed the MTFS. To some it seemed like a new version of Labour's 1965 'National Plan'. Others questioned whether it would succeed in affecting expectations in the economy as we intended, and wondered what would happen if it did not. But there was a crucial difference between the MTFS and the old style economic planning. We were seeking to secure greater financial stability, within which business and individuals could operate with confidence. We knew that we could do this only by controlling those things which government could control – namely the money supply and public borrowing. Most post-war economic planning, by contrast, sought to control such things as output and employment, which ultimately government could not control, through batteries of regulations on investment, pay and prices, that distorted the operation of the economy and threatened personal liberty. The MTFS broke with all of this. Certainly, no one could guarantee that people would adjust their behaviour to take account of the MTFS; indeed, pay bargainers, particularly in the public sector, conspicuously failed to do so, at least in the early period. The MTFS would only influence expectations in so far as people believed in our determination to stick to it: its credibility depended on that of the Government – and ultimately, therefore, on the quality of my own commitment, about which I would leave no one in doubt. I would not bow to demands to reflate: it was this which turned the MTFS from an ambitious aspiration into the cornerstone of a successful policy.

FIRST STEPS OF TRADE UNION REFORM: THE 1980 EMPLOYMENT ACT

A firm financial strategy was necessary to improve our economic performance: but we never believed that it would be sufficient, even with tax cuts and deregulation of industry. We also had to deal with the problem of trade union power, made worse by successive Labour governments and exploited by the communists and militants who had risen to key positions within the trade union movement – positions

permanent reduction in inflation. Second, there is a difference between the measurement and the control of the money supply. Our difficulty was to measure the money supply, which led to our seeking different or better measures to supplement £M3. We knew how to control the money supply, through interest rates, and did so: indeed Alan Walters was to argue persuasively that we had controlled it too much.

which they ruthlessly exploited in the callous strikes of the winter of 1978–9.

The economic effects of union power were still painfully clear. Pay rises were soaring while business prospects plummeted with the onset of recession. The engineering industry dispute in 1979 provided a good demonstration of how much poison excessive trade union power and privilege had injected into British industry – and not just the public but the private sector too. The engineering industry had every commercial reason to reduce costs so as to compete. Yet after a ten-week strike, the employers, the Engineering Employers' Federation (EEF), conceded a 39-hour week, increases of £13 a week for skilled men and an extra week's holiday phased over four years, all of this greatly increasing their costs. The EEF had crumbled and, because of the centralized system of pay bargaining, employers throughout the industry had also given in. The EEF had long accepted the closed shop as an unavoidable fact of life. So the unions' power over their members was more or less absolute. Some employers, in search of a quiet life, preferred it that way. But it meant that when a dispute did occur the trade union was able to exercise what amounted to intimidation over its members – 'lawful intimidation' in the unhappy phrase coined by Labour's former Attorney-General, Sam Silkin. Those who wanted to continue working could be threatened by the union with expulsion and the consequent loss of their job. The engineering strike was not a political strike, nor one which threatened to bring ordinary life to a halt. But it was precisely the sort of strike which no country fighting for its industrial future could afford – an object lesson in what was wrong. Its consequences damaged the whole industry for years to come.

Indeed, for the greater part of my term of office the need for new steps in trade union reform was repeatedly demonstrated by industrial disputes. The disadvantage of this was that, in a sense, we were always behind events, learning the lessons of the last strike. The advantage was, however, that we could point to recent abuses to justify reform and could therefore rely on public opinion to help us push it through.

On 14 May 1979, less than a fortnight after I formed the Government, Jim Prior wrote to me setting out his plans for trade union reform. There was a certain amount that we could do at once. We could set up our promised inquiry into the coercive recruitment practices of the printing union SLADE – which would deal also with the activities of the NGA in the advertising industry. We could also make certain changes to employment legislation by Order in Council, with the aim of reducing the heavy burden placed – on small firms in particular – by the provisions on unfair dismissal and redundancy. But we would have to consult with employers and unions quite extensively about our main proposals on secondary picketing, the closed shop and ballots. As a result, the larger changes we wanted would not be in place in time for strikes which might occur that winter. Jim Prior was optimistic that if the TUC was properly handled – and he thought that he *could* handle the TUC – they would not reject our proposals outright. The CBI was also, as usual, opposed to any 'precipitate' action. In reply I pointed out that they would be the first people to complain if secondary picketing started again. I also made it clear that I thought that a bill must be published by November, if at all possible, and should reach its committee stage in the Commons before Christmas. I had a further discussion with Jim about tactics on the afternoon of Wednesday 6 June. Jim said that for purposes of negotiation his proposals to the TUC would go somewhat further than those in our manifesto, but I insisted that our final position should not be less than the manifesto – a significantly different emphasis.

Two weeks later Jim set out his proposals in a Cabinet paper. These were very similar to those which were ultimately contained in the 1980 Act. They covered three main areas: picketing, the closed shop and ballots. We planned to limit the specific immunities for picketing, given under the legislation of 1974 and 1976, strictly to those who were themselves party to the dispute and who were picketing at the premises of their own employer. Powers would be taken to issue a statutory code on picketing. Where there was a closed shop, we proposed to give employees who might be dismissed for refusing to join a union the right to apply to an industrial tribunal for compensation. There would be a legal right of complaint for those arbitrarily expelled or excluded from union membership. We would extend the present protection for employees who objected to joining a union because of deeply held personal conviction. A new closed shop could in future only be established if an overwhelming majority of workers voted for it by secret ballot. A statutory code relating to the closed shop would be drawn up. Finally, the Secretary of State for Employment would be given power to reimburse trade unions for the postal and administrative costs of secret ballots.

These early proposals were as notable for what they did not contain as for what they did. At this stage they did not extend to the question of secondary action other than secondary picketing, nor did they deal with the wider question of trade union immunities. In particular, they left alone the crucial immunity which prevented action being taken by the courts against union funds. On the first of these points – secondary action – we were awaiting the conclusions of the House of Lords in the important case of *Express Newspapers v. MacShane*.* It is worth noting that the changes we made in all these areas, including that of picketing, were changes in the civil, not the criminal, law. In public discussion of subsequent strikes this distinction was often lost. The civil law could only change the way in which unions behaved if employers or, in some cases, workers were prepared to use it. They had to bring the case. By contrast, the criminal law on picketing, which was clarified but not substantially altered in the years ahead, had to be enforced by the police and the courts. Although the Government would make it clear that the police enjoyed its moral support and would improve police equipment and training, the constitutional limits on us in this area were real and sometimes frustrating.

As the summer wore on, it became obvious that although the TUC was prepared to talk to the Government about our proposals, it had no intention of actually co-operating with them. On 25 June at their request I met the TUC General Council. I was depressed, but not a bit surprised, to discover that there was no willingness on their side to face economic facts or to try to understand the economic strategy we were pursuing. I told the TUC that we all wanted high living standards and more jobs, but that if people wanted a German standard of living then they must achieve a German standard of output. When the TUC said that they wanted more government spending, I pointed out that there was no shortage of demand in the economy: the problem was that because of our uncompetitiveness that demand was being met by imports. I got nowhere. The TUC Conference in September was marked by unreasoning and unqualified opposition to everything we proposed – even the provision of funds for secret ballots in which no compulsion was involved, other than the moral pressure to consult their own members.

On the evening of Wednesday 12 September I held a meeting with Geoffrey Howe, Jim Prior and other colleagues to plan our strategy. I thought that it was hopeless trying to change the attitudes of most trade union leaders, who were socialist politicians first, second and third. Instead, we agreed that we must appeal over their heads to their members.

I was convinced that rank-and-file unionists felt very differently to the union bosses about the reforms. In due course, we must liberate them by breaking down the closed shop and by ensuring genuine democracy within the unions; then they themselves would bring the

* See below, pp. 102–4, 107.

extremists and union *apparatchiks* into line. But until we could make such changes – and it would take more than our present bill to do that – all we could do was to call for their support as persuasively and powerfully as we could.

So time and again I drummed home the message that it was ordinary trade unionists and their families who were hurt by the irresponsible use of trade union power. For example, in my speech to the Party Conference in Blackpool on Friday 12 October 1979, I said:

> The days when only employers suffered from a strike are long since past. Today strikes affect trade union members and their families just like the rest of us. One union can deprive us all of coal, or food, or transport easily enough. What it cannot do is defend its members against similar action by other unions . . . Recently there was a strike which prevented telephone bills from being sent. The cost of that strike to the Post Office is £110 million. It will have to be paid for by everyone who uses the telephone . . . The recent two-days-a-week strike by the Engineering Union lost industry £2 billion in sales. We may never make up those sales and we shall lose some of the jobs which depend on them.

I developed this theme again when I spoke to the Conservative Trade Unionists' (CTU) Conference in Nottingham on Saturday 17 November. Strikes were not the only problem; rather, it was the whole socialist economic approach to which the union bosses were wedded, and in particular their preference for monopoly and protection. I took the example of British Steel – which soon became all too topical – to make the point:

> British Steel would like to import coking coal to make its steel more competitive. But the NUM opposes this saying, 'Buy our coking coal, even if it is more expensive.' If British Steel agree, they must, in turn, say to the car manufacturers, 'Buy our steel, even if it is more expensive.' But then British Leyland and the other car manufacturers have to ask the consumer, 'Please buy our cars even if they are more expensive.' But we are all consumers and as consumers we all want a choice. We want to buy the best value for money. If foreign cars, or washing machines, are cheaper or better than British, the consumer wants the choice. There is a broken circuit. Producers want a protected market for their products. That is the union demand. But the same trade

unionists, as consumers, want an open market. They cannot both win. But they can both lose.

In the last part of 1979 and the early months of 1980 we continued refining the Employment Bill and spent a good deal of time on the question of secondary action and immunities. We also discussed item by item measures to deal with the burdens which past Labour legislation had placed on industry. One such burden was Schedule 11 of the Employment Protection Act, 1975. Schedule 11 was a typical case: it showed how an apparently harmless measure, introduced for the best of motives, could defeat the intentions of its originators and result in higher unemployment. Schedule 11 provided that the 'recognized terms and conditions' of employment for a particular industry should apply throughout that industry. The original aim was to deal with pockets of low pay; the principle had wartime antecedents, but in recent years it had been exploited by higher paid groups, such as those working for the BBC. In that instance the unfortunate television licence holder had to foot the bill. Generally, by forcing wage levels up to the level obtaining in the strongest firms, Schedule 11 caused jobs to be lost.

But by far the most contested issue was that of trade union immunities. Our proposals on secondary picketing had already begun to address it. But we now took a further step. We had received the report of the enquiry set up earlier into the recruitment activities of the printing union SLADE, undertaken by Mr Andrew Leggatt QC.* In response, we decided to remove the immunity where industrial disruption was called or threatened by people other than those directly working for a particular firm with the intention of coercing its employees into joining a trade union.

We decided to go further, following the House of Lords decision in the *MacShane* case on 13 December. The *MacShane* case was important because it confirmed the wide scope of existing immunities in the case of secondary action. Most of the immunities then enjoyed by trade unions had their origin in the Trade Disputes Act (1906), which Labour extended significantly after its narrow election victory in October 1974. The *MacShane* case arose from a dispute that began in 1978 between the National Union of Journalists (NUJ) and a number

* The report was damning. SLADE had been using its strength in the printing industry to recruit among freelance artists, photographic studios and advertising agencies by threatening to 'black' the printing of their work unless they joined the union. The report concluded that the campaign 'was conducted without any regard whatever to the feelings, interests, or welfare of the prospective recruits'.

of provincial newspapers. The provincial papers managed to keep going during the dispute by publishing stories supplied to them by the Press Association. The NUJ unsuccessfully attempted to prevent this, first, by direct appeal to NUJ members working for the Press Association and then, when that failed, by instructing its people on national newspapers to black Press Association material altogether. In response the *Daily Express* applied for an injunction against the NUJ. The Court of Appeal in December 1978 ruled in favour of the *Express* that the NUJ secondary action had exceeded that which could be regarded as furthering the objectives of the dispute and therefore did not enjoy immunity. As a result of this decision, injunctions could be and were granted. However, when the case went to the House of Lords, the Appeal Court's ruling was overturned. Essentially, the Lords decided that for purposes of law an industrial action was 'in furtherance of a trade dispute', and therefore immune, if trade union officials genuinely believed it to be so. This subjective test had the most disturbing implications. It meant that henceforth there would be virtually unlimited immunity for secondary industrial action.

The position was complicated by the outcome of two other court cases. One of these – *N. W. L. Limited v. Nelson & Wood*, or the 'Nawala Case' – resulted from the attempts of the International Transport Workers' Federation to prevent the employment by a British shipping company of overseas seamen in British registered ships. The Federation's action threatened the future of the British shipping industry. Still more important, however, was the second case, which widened the scope for secondary action in the steel strike. The Iron and Steel Trades Confederation (ISTC) had called out its members in the private steel sector as part of its dispute with the British Steel Corporation which had begun on 2 January 1980. Duport Steels, a private steel company, was granted an injunction by the Court of Appeal against Bill Sirs, General Secretary of the ISTC. The Court of Appeal ruled that immunity did not apply in this case because the ISTC's argument was essentially with the Government rather than BSC itself. But again, the House of Lords unanimously reversed this ruling, relying on broadly the same grounds as in the *MacShane* case. The practical result was that the strike spread once more to the private steel companies.

We were all agreed that the law as now interpreted by the Courts must be changed. In Opposition, we had opposed all of the moves Labour made to extend trade union powers and immunities and in our manifesto we had said that, 'the protection of the law should be available to those not concerned in a dispute.' We agreed that it was right now to clarify the precise limits of immunity. But we disagreed both about what immunity, if any, there should be for secondary action and about the timing of the introduction of the necessary change into the Employment Bill. Again and again, Jim Prior said that he did not want decisions about changes in the law to be linked with a particular dispute. But as the steel strike worsened, with none of our proposed legislation yet in force – let alone measures to deal with secondary strikes and blacking – the public criticism grew. I had the greatest sympathy with the critics, though I wished that some employers had earlier been rather more robust. Whenever those of us who felt that we ought to go faster put our case – and our number included Geoffrey Howe, John Nott, Keith Joseph, Angus Maude, Peter Thorneycroft and John Hoskyns – Jim Prior was always able to argue against 'hasty action' by reference to the cautious attitude of the CBI.

On the afternoon of Wednesday 30 January Jim came to see me at his request and poured out a tale of woe. Apparently the unions' mood had changed markedly for the worse since Christmas. We were facing a 'day of action' from the unions in Wales. The steel unions had managed to call out their members in private steel companies. I replied that, while I had every respect for his views, I did not share his pessimism.

In fact, by this stage I did not share Jim's analysis of the situation at all. He really believed that we had already tried to do too much and that we should go no further, whether in the area of trade union law or general economic strategy. I, for my part, had begun bitterly to regret that we had not made faster progress both in cutting public expenditure and with trade union reform.

There was, of course, a more profound and general divide between us. For all his virtues, Jim Prior was an example of a political type that had dominated and, in my view, damaged the post-war Tory Party. I call such figures 'the false squire'. They have all the outward show of a John Bull – ruddy face, white hair, bluff manner – but inwardly they are political calculators who see the task of Conservatives as one of retreating gracefully before the Left's inevitable advance. Retreat as a tactic is sometimes necessary; retreat as a settled policy eats at the soul. In order to justify the series of defeats that his philosophy entails, the false squire has to persuade rank-and-file Conservatives and indeed himself that advance is impossible. His whole political life would, after all, be a gigantic mistake if a policy of positive Tory reform turned out to be both practical and popular. Hence the passionate and obstinate resistance mounted by the 'wets' to the fiscal, economic and trade union reforms of the early 1980s. These reforms had either to fail or be stopped. For if they succeeded, a whole generation of Tory leaders had despaired unnecessarily. Ian Gilmour expressed this feeling in the clearest form; but Jim Prior was infected by it too, and it made him timid and overcautious in his trade union policy. I had to stake out a more determined approach.

Brian Walden interviewed me for *Weekend World* on Sunday 6 January. I used the occasion to say that we would be introducing a new clause in the Employment Bill to rectify the problem left by the *MacShane* judgement. I made it clear that we did not intend to remove the immunity enjoyed by trade unions as regards action intended to cause people to break their employment contracts, but would concentrate on the immunity relating to action designed to cause employers to break their commercial contracts. I also drew attention to the way in which trade union immunities had combined with nationalized monopolies to give huge power to the trade unions in these industries. We needed to restrict the immunities and to break the monopolies by introducing competition.

All my instincts told me that we would have strong public support for further action to restrict union power, and the evidence supported me. An opinion survey in *The Times* on 21 January 1980 asked people the question: 'Do you think sympathy strikes and blacking are legitimate weapons to use in an industrial dispute, or should the new law restrict their use?' Seventy-one per cent of those who replied – and 62 per cent of trade unionists who did so – said that a new law should indeed restrict their use.

It would, though, be difficult to go further without support from business leaders. On the morning of Tuesday 5 February I had two meetings with industrialists. The first was with the CBI. Some of them said that the present bill, as drafted, went as far as possible. On hearing this I did not conceal my frustration. I said that, with regard to the timing of more radical measures, there would always be a risk of confrontation with the trade unions, but that it seemed to me it would be better to accept the risk over the coming few months than wait until the autumn when the unions could cause the maximum disruption. I said that I now regretted that we had not brought forward more radical proposals when the bill was introduced. This left us with two possibilities: we could amend the existing bill or announce in the consultative document which we were planning to issue that further legislation would be introduced. The CBI went away in no doubt about my feelings.

The second meeting that day was with the private sector steel producers. There was a sharp contrast between their outlook and that of the CBI. They complained that the private steel companies had been dragged into a dispute not of their making and in which they would be the only real victims. As a result of the strike they were losing about £10 million a week. The ISTC had effectively torn up all its procedural agreements with the private companies and instructed their employees to strike. It was clear that there was no real grievance on the part of private sector steel workers: in the *Duport Steels* case, when the Court of Appeal had granted its injunction to stop secondary action, there had been a complete return to work before the Lords reversed the decision and the private sector strike resumed. The threat of losing union cards was the decisive factor in persuading private sector workers to join the strike. In these circumstances it is not surprising that the private sector steel companies wanted immediate legislation to outlaw secondary picketing. And there was nothing I was able to offer them except sympathy.

In answer to a letter from a leading industrialist urging 'caution', I replied setting out my views:

> Insofar as we do not effectively change the law we would be positively confirming what Lord Diplock said [in *Duport Steels Limited and others v. Sirs and others*]. We would be indicating that we are not prepared to protect the person who through no fault of his own has suffered damage at the hands of another. We should be telling the law-abiding citizen that we prefer to strengthen the powers of those who inflict injury rather than to help those who suffer from it.
>
> . . . You refer to moderate Trade Unionists. I have countless letters from them pleading with me to strengthen their hand against the militants, telling me that is why they voted for us and that now this Government by failing to take effective action has let them down.
>
> If we flinch from this task now, when we have public and massive Trade Union opinion with us, they are not likely to have much faith in us to do it next winter.

I finished by quoting Shakespeare's *Measure for Measure*:

> Our doubts are traitors,
> And make us lose the good we oft might win,
> By fearing to attempt.

I returned to the task of toughening up the law. Ministers now agreed to restore the law to what it had been understood to be before the *MacShane* judgement, adding further tests relating to the dispute to be applied by the Courts. There would not, however, be a total ban on secondary action. There followed a short period for consultation and the new clause was introduced into the Employment Bill at the Report Stage in the House of Commons on 17 April 1980, limiting immunity for secondary action which broke or interfered with commercial contracts. Immunity would only exist when the action was taken – by employees of suppliers or customers of the employer in dispute – with the 'sole or principal purpose' of furthering the primary dispute and when the action was reasonably likely to succeed. Of great significance for the future was the fact that we announced the publication of a green paper on trade union immunities, which would appear later in the year and would look at the whole issue from a wider perspective.

In fact, the 1980 Act did not directly affect the outcome of the steel strike. The one action open to us which could have done so would have been to accelerate the introduction of Clause 14 of the Employment Bill, which made secondary picketing unlawful. I was strongly attracted by this option. My wish to pursue it had been greatly increased by the mass picketing which had taken place at the private sector steel firm of Hadfields on Thursday 14 February. Keith Joseph telephoned me at Chequers the following Sunday morning to discuss what had happened. We had no doubt that it constituted a grave breach of the criminal law. The question was whether the use of the civil law, and in particular Clause 14, would make matters better or worse.

I telephoned Willie Whitelaw, the Home Secretary, about the public order situation and suggested that we could introduce a one-clause bill on picketing the following week. I also spoke to Michael Havers, the Attorney-General. It was clear to me that the police would need to stop large numbers of pickets arriving at their destination if picketing was to be effectively controlled and the threat of intimidation removed. The civil law, though, could not play any part in that. There was even an argument that a change in the civil law introduced directly in response to violence would make it more difficult to bring pressure on people to respect and obey the criminal law. However, I wanted all of the possibilities to be examined urgently.

After discussion with ministers on Monday (18 February) it was decided not to accelerate the clause relating to secondary picketing. But instead the Attorney-General would restate the next day in the House of Commons the criminal law as it related to picketing. Jim Prior would also write a public letter to Len Murray, the TUC General Secretary, drawing attention to the breach of all the traditionally accepted and understood codes for picketing. In these ways we sought to keep up the pressure.

THE 1980 STEEL STRIKE

The debate about trade union reform, both inside and outside government, was conducted under the shadow of industrial conflict: in particular, the issues of secondary action and immunities became inextricably entangled with the 1980 steel strike. But that strike also challenged our economic strategy directly; and it is unlikely, once the strike had begun, that our economic policies would have survived if we had suffered defeat.

The steel industry, like the motor vehicle industry, was suffering the after-effects of overambitious policies of state intervention. It was Ted Heath's Government, of which I had been a member, which had set BSC on course for huge investment in expanded capacity in the years before that first oil shock which cut so many such ambitions down to size. The following Labour Government had made some closures but, by setting up a review under Lord Beswick in 1974–5, it had largely sought to buy time. The greater the delay in taking remedial action, however, the less chance there was to make proper use of the most up-to-date plant and this, in turn, worsened the position of BSC as a whole, clouding the prospect for steelmen's jobs and increasing the burden on the taxpayer, who had to fund huge losses.

One of my first decisions about the nationalized industries was to agree to the closure of the Shotton steel works in North Wales. Measures aimed at providing new job opportunities in the area would be announced, but I knew that the closure would have a devastating effect on the steelmen and their families. A delegation from Shotton had come to see me when I was on a visit to Wales as Leader of the Opposition. I felt desperately sorry for them. They had done all that was expected. But it was not – and could not be – enough.

BSC exemplified not only the disadvantages of state ownership and intervention, but also the way that British trade unionism dragged down our industrial performance. A good example of what was wrong was to be found at the Hunterston ore terminal on the Clyde. Here BSC had built the largest deep-water jetty in Europe. It had been opened in June 1979, but could not be used until November because of a manning dispute between the Transport and General Workers' Union (TGWU) and the ISTC. For five months bulk ore carriers had to be diverted to the Continent, where their cargo was transferred to smaller vessels for shipment to Terminus Quay, Glasgow, and from there finally sent on to Ravenscraig.

As the end of 1979 approached, external factors over which we had no control made BSC's problems rapidly worsen. There was huge international overcapacity in steel as the world headed deeper into recession. Steel industries almost everywhere were facing losses and closures. But the fundamental problems of BSC were home-grown. It took BSC nearly twice as many man-hours to produce a tonne of steel as its major European competitors. We had reached the absurd position that the value added by BSC was if anything a little less than the wage bill. Over the five years to 1979–80 more than £3 billion of public money had gone into BSC, which amounted to £221 for every family in the country. Yet still the losses accumulated. Keith Joseph and I were prepared to continue for the present to fund BSC's investment and redundancy programme; what we were not prepared to do was to fund losses which arose from excessive wage costs, unearned by higher productivity.

If we were serious about turning BSC round – with all the closures, job losses, and challenges to restrictive practices that would involve – we faced the risk of a very damaging steel strike. There was only one worse alternative: to allow the present situation to continue.

BSC's cash limit for 1980–81 was first set in June 1979: the aim was for it to break even by March 1980. This objective had, in fact, been set by the previous Labour Government. But by 29 November 1979 BSC had announced a £146 million half-year loss and abandoned its break-even target for March, putting it back a further twelve months. The crisis was fast approaching.

On 6 December Keith Joseph let me know what the implications were. BSC could not afford any general wage increase from 1 January other than the consolidation of certain additional increases agreed the previous year – amounting to 2 per cent. Any further increase would be dependent on local negotiations and conditional on the equivalent improvements in productivity. The Corporation had told the unions the week before that 5 million tonnes of surplus capacity, over and above the closure of iron- and steel-making at Corby and Shotton, would have to be shut down. Already Bill Sirs was threatening a strike. I agreed with Keith that we must back the Corporation in its stand. We also agreed that BSC must win the support of public opinion and bring home to the unions the harm which a strike would do to their own members.

As the strike loomed, there was much disquiet about whether the management of BSC had properly prepared its ground for it. The figures used to justify the management's position were questioned, even by Nicholas Edwards, the Secretary of State for Wales. He might have been right. But I said that we must not attempt to substitute our judgement as politicians for that of the industry. It was up to the management of BSC – at last – to manage.

On 10 December the BSC Board confirmed that 52,000 steel jobs would have to go. The business prospects for BSC were still worsening. Indeed, when we looked at their figures for future steel demand we thought that they were, if anything, slightly optimistic. But again, there was no intention to set our judgement against that of the Board and management. Even before the strike, we had been searching for a successor to the present Chairman, Sir Charles Villiers, whose contract was due shortly to come to an end. We had already received seven or eight firm refusals from suitable candidates and it was clear that fear of government interference was one of the main deterrents.

It was difficult to be sure about the outcome of the strike. BSC, the private steel producers and the steel users all had healthy levels of stocks. The fact that the steel users and stockholders were effectively given three weeks' notice of the strike allowed them to build up stockpiles. Moreover, because of the depressed state of industry many steel-using companies were operating well below capacity. But, on the other hand, there would be serious problems for the users of tin plate, and possibly for the car industry, and the situation could, of course, rapidly worsen if dockers and transport workers took effective action to stop steel moving around the country and to halt imports. However, BSC and its workforce would suffer most. Its current prices were already above those of our European competitors and the domestic market for steel was likely to be lost permanently to foreign steel companies which could ensure a reliable supply in the future.

From the end of December I chaired regular meetings of a small group of ministers and officials to monitor the steel situation and decide what action needed to be taken. It was a frustrating and anxious time. The details of the BSC offer were not well understood either by the steel workers or by the public. BSC did little to explain its position. It would not put out broadsheets or buy newspaper space, on the ground that such actions might be seen as provocative. The hope was that other pressures could be brought to bear on the ISTC and the National Union of Boilermakers (NUB). Moreover, in a misguided attempt to canvass support for various pay offers which they had made, BSC allowed a bewildering array of different figures to gain currency, pleasing no one: to the general public the figures always seemed to be increasing, while to the unions they never seemed sufficient.

For its part, the ISTC was more conscious of pay settlements to other groups of workers – the 'going rate' – than it was of the bleak commercial realities of the industry in which its members worked. On 28 November Ford workers had voted to accept a 21.5 per cent wage increase. On 5 December coal miners had accepted a 20 per cent settlement – and been publicly praised for their moderation. All this undoubtedly added to the strength of feeling among the steelmen. On 7 January Len Murray and Bill Sirs asked for a settlement of 8 per cent plus 5 per cent 'on account' for the local productivity deals. BSC offered 8 per cent plus 4 per cent in advance for a limited period. The next day negotiations collapsed. The General and Municipal Workers' Union (GMWU) joined the strike; on the following day the craftsmen struck, and although on 10 February the craft union leaders accepted a separate settlement of 10 per cent plus 4 per cent, later that week its members rejected the offer. In the meantime, on 16 January, the ISTC had spread the strike to the private steel sector, where the uncertain legal position and the violent mass picketing added to our difficulties.

It became clear to me fairly early on, however, that the steel strike was not going to bring British industry to a halt. At my strategy meeting on 18 January the figures showed that the strike had so far had little effect on industrial production, which had fallen about 2 per cent the previous week and was perhaps marginally lower by the time we met. Even if private steel production were suspended altogether, there would be enough stocks to support normal manufacturing for another four to six weeks, with problems in some particular areas within two to three weeks. As we had foreseen, it was in the specialist area of food canning that the greatest difficulty might arise.

It was against this background that I met first the unions at their request and then the management of BSC on Monday 21 January at No. 10. The union leaders had seen Keith Joseph and Jim Prior the previous Saturday. One difficulty we had was that the unions might have drawn the wrong impression from widely reported remarks made by Jim, criticizing the BSC management. I had been angry to read this. But, when a week later I was asked about it by Robin Day on *Panorama*, my reply was sweetly dismissive: 'we all make mistakes now and then. I think it was a mistake, and Jim Prior was very, very sorry indeed for it, and very apologetic. But you don't just sack a chap for one mistake.'

In my discussion with Mr Sirs and Mr Smith (the leaders respectively of the ISTC and NUB), I said that the Government was not going to intervene in the dispute. I did not know enough about the steel industry to become involved in the negotiations though, of course, I was keen to hear their views. The unions wanted the Government to bring pressure on BSC to make an increased offer. They wanted some 'new money', but I pointed out that there is no such thing: money for the steel industry could only come from other industries which were making a profit. The real issue, I said, was productivity where – although Bill Sirs disputed the figures – it was generally accepted that BSC's performance lagged far behind. Luxemburg had reduced its steel workforce from 24,000 to 16,000 and substantially increased its productivity, with the result that it was now exporting railway lines to the UK. When I had heard this the previous autumn I had been cut to the quick, and I told him so.

That same afternoon I met Sir Charles Villiers and Bob Scholey, the Chairman and Chief Executive of BSC. They described to me precisely what was on offer and the very limited scope for flexibility. I gave them my full support.

On the following day Bob Scholey and Bill Sirs held a meeting, but to no avail. Bill Sirs continued to ask for 20 per cent, a figure which was obviously unrealistic. The only thing we could do was see the strike through. At my meeting of ministers and officials on 1 February we were told that steel was still moving from the docks. There was little or no evidence of shortages except for the deteriorating position in Metal Box, the food can producers. The report for the week ending 2 February again showed a strong position: manufacturing production was at 96 per cent of its normal level. On 12 February we received clearer evidence still about how industry was coping. Ninety per cent of steel stockholders were continuing to maintain a satisfactory level of deliveries. Limited imports were continuing and getting past the obstacles the unions put up against them. Not surprisingly, perhaps, steel users were reluctant to divulge the size of their steel stocks and potential endurance, but their morale was good. Metal Box expected to deliver 50 per cent of what customers demanded. At British Leyland full production could continue until the end of February.

The real problem was now arising in the private steel sector. The mass picketing at Hadfields raised the stakes. It had overtones of the kind of intimidation and violence which had led to the closure of the Saltley Coke Depot during the miners' strike in 1972: it was vital that we win through.

British business proved resilient and resourceful in meeting the strike: this turned out to be the decisive factor. Somehow, they got hold of the steel they needed. In the reports presented to my meetings the crunch point at which serious problems for steel users would arise never seemed to come any closer. At the meeting on 4 March all information confirmed that the strike could not succeed. The potential endurance of steel users was being increased by the continued flow of imported steel. If anything the outlook seemed slightly better than the week before. By 14 March all but one of the private sector steel companies were back in production and by the time we met on 18 March that too was working.

Although it was now obvious that the unions had lost – with the strike clearly failing to cripple industry and the strikers themselves increasingly demoralized – the precise terms on which the Government and management had won remained in the balance. On 9 March BSC had held a 'ballot about a ballot', asking workers whether they wanted a ballot on pay, which the ISTC had hitherto denied them, and this had shown strong evidence of disenchantment with the ISTC's tactics and leadership. The union wanted a way out which would save face. BSC had formally proposed arbitration on 17 February and, although rejected, the offer had remained open. There was strong pressure – which I wanted to resist – for a Court of Enquiry into the strike which would propose a settlement. I would have preferred the involvement of ACAS (the Advisory, Conciliation and Arbitration Service). It seemed to me that if ACAS had any reason for existing at all, it should surely have a role in a situation such as this. In fact, we were condemned to watch while BSC and the unions agreed to the appointment of a three-man enquiry consisting of Lords Lever and Marsh (both former Labour Cabinet ministers) and Bill Keyes of SOGAT, which on 31 March recommended a settlement well above the figure originally offered by BSC but substantially below what the ISTC had demanded. The offer was accepted.

At its final meeting on 9 April my committee was told that all the BSC plants were back in operation. Production and steel deliveries were both about 95 per cent of what they would have been without the dispute. The outcome, in spite of the size of the final settlement, was generally seen as a victory for the Government, if not for the BSC management.

The bills, however, kept on coming in. On 6 June Sir Charles Villiers wrote to Keith Joseph saying that he foresaw the need for an additional £400 million in the financial year 1980–81, over and above the £450 million already allocated. The proposals made by BSC to stay within the borrowing limit set by the Government (its EFL or External Financing Limit) involved various financial devices including the sale and lease-back of assets. The only alternative they had to suggest was that in effect BSC should go into liquidation. Clearly, whatever the pressures imposed by the strike, matters should never have been allowed to come to such a pass and it reflected badly on the management. But we had already decided what to do about that. In spite of some outcry over the terms offered, Ian MacGregor had been appointed to succeed Sir Charles Villiers. I expected him to deal with the appalling commercial and financial legacy and in due course we approved very large increases in the funding of BSC to allow him to do this. Nor were we disappointed. Another cost, which we did not begrudge, was the money made available to encourage new development in areas badly affected by redundancies, such as Llanwern, Port Talbot, Consett and Scunthorpe.

This had been a battle fought and won not simply for the Government and for our policies, but for the economic well-being of the country as a whole. It was necessary to stand up to unions which thought that because they were in the public sector they should be allowed to ignore commercial reality and the need for higher productivity. In future, pay had to depend on the state of the employing industry, and not on some notion of 'comparability' with what other people received. But it was always going to be more difficult to induce such realism where the state was owner, banker, and at times tempted to be manager as well.

BRITISH LEYLAND: 1979–1980

In many ways British Leyland presented a similar challenge to the Government as BSC, though in a still more acute and politically difficult form. Like BSC, BL was effectively state-owned and controlled, though technically it was not a nationalized industry. The company had become a symbol of Britain's industrial decline and of trade union bloody-mindedness. However, by the time I entered No. 10 it had also begun to symbolize the fightback by management. Michael Edwardes, BL's Chairman, had already demonstrated his grit in taking on the trade union militants who had brought the British car industry to its knees. I knew that whatever we decided to do about BL would have an impact on the psychology and morale of British managers as a whole, and I was determined to send the right signals. Unfortunately, unlike the case of BSC, it became increasingly clear that the action required to support BL's stand against trade union obstruction diverged from what was required on purely commercial grounds. This was a problem: but we had to back Michael Edwardes.

We had indicated in Opposition our hostility to the Ryder Plan for BL with its enormous cost, unmatched by sufficiently rigorous measures to increase productivity and earn profits.* My first direct experience as Prime Minister of BL's difficulties came in September 1979 when Keith Joseph informed me of BL's dreadful half-yearly results and of the measures the Chairman and Board intended to take. The new plan involved the closure of BL's Coventry plant. At least 25,000 jobs would be lost. Productivity would be increased. The development of BL's medium car range of models would be accelerated. The BL Board said that the Company would require additional funds beyond the £225 million remaining of the £1 billion which Labour, under the Ryder Plan, had in principle committed. In response, Keith made no financial promises. He told BL to look at the scope for raising money from its own resources – that is sales of profitable parts of the company. There was no immediate need to take decisions about funding until the Government received the new BL Corporate Plan from the National Enterprise Board (NEB) in November.

BL's workers were to be balloted on the Corporate Plan. If it received substantial majority support the Government would find it very difficult to turn down and, as quickly became apparent, the company would want a further £200 million above and beyond the final tranche of Ryder money. The ballot, of which the result would be announced on 1 November, seemed likely to go the company's way. But it might not; and that would present its own immediate problems. For if the ballot showed anything other than overwhelming support for the company's proposals there would be speculation about its future, with the prospect of BL's many small and medium-sized creditors demanding immediate payment and the large holders of loan stock adding to the pressure. BL might be forced precipitately into liquidation in circumstances which would make it impossible for us to formulate a sensible response and for an orderly disposal of its assets to take place. The economic implications of such a collapse were appalling. One hundred and fifty thousand people were employed by the company in the UK; there were perhaps an equal number of jobs in the component and other supplying industries dependent on BL. It was suggested that complete closure would mean a net loss to the

* The Ryder Plan, dating from 1975, proposed the investment by government in phases over seven years of £1.4 billion to modernize BL plant and introduce new models.

balance of trade of around £2,200 million a year and according to the NEB it might cost the Government as much as £1 billion.

There was no mistaking the political and economic gravity of the decisions required. Closure would have some awful consequences, but we must never give the impression that it was unthinkable. If ever the company and workforce came to believe that, there would be no limit to their demands on the public purse. For this reason Keith and I decided not to agree to BL's request for the Government to issue an undertaking to honour the company's debt. They had wanted us to publish a letter to this effect even before the ballot result. In fact, 87.2 per cent of those voting supported BL's plan and BL immediately sought approval from the NEB to go ahead with it. A firm request for money was made to the Government.

Our consideration of the BL Corporate Plan was delayed by two other events. First, as a result of our (unconnected) decision to remove Rolls-Royce from the purview of the NEB, Sir Leslie Murphy and his colleagues resigned and a new Board had to be appointed under Sir Arthur Knight. Second, the Amalgamated Union of Engineering Workers (AUEW) now threatened the very survival of BL by calling a strike following the dismissal on 19 November of Derek Robinson, a notorious agitator, convenor of the shop stewards at Longbridge and chairman of the so-called 'Leyland Combine Trade Union Committee'. Robinson and others had continued to campaign against the BL plan even after its approval. The management had been right to sack him, pending the outcome of an inquiry by the AUEW.

On Monday 10 December ministers, under my chairmanship, considered the Corporate Plan. The first thing I noticed was that BL's performance had deteriorated even since it had been drawn up. So I asked for up-to-date forecasts of profits and cash flow. I wanted from Michael Edwardes a proper definition of the circumstances under which the BL Board would abandon the plan. There had to be clear bench marks against which to measure future performance. I also wanted to know whether Michael Edwardes himself intended to remain as Chairman: officially, his contract had only another year to run.

We were now, though, put under pressure to approve the plan before the Christmas recess – without waiting for completion of BL's wage negotiations – in order to enable the company to sign a collaborative deal with Honda for a new middle-range car. I was not prepared to be bounced into a commitment. In any case, past experience suggested to me that the plan would not in fact be fulfilled. BL's annual plans always forecast major improvements: but every year things seemed to get worse. Its share of the UK market for cars had slumped from 33 per cent in 1974 to 20 per cent in 1979, and had fallen further, down to only 16 per cent, over the last two months. BL's productivity was only two-thirds that of its European competitors, and lower still compared with the Japanese: for the company to become competitive again productivity needed to improve by something like 50 per cent. It remained to be seen whether the Plan could transform that. The proposed new models could help. But the first of these was not due until the end of the following year, and by then all its competitors would have new models too. Meanwhile, BL was already running out of cash and would need an advance on money allocated for the next financial year.

I, therefore, asked John Nott, who brought to the problem the expertise and scepticism of a banker, to go over BL's accounts with the company's Finance Director. Keith Joseph, John Biffen and others also went over the plan in detail with Michael Edwardes. Their conclusion was that there was only a small chance of BL surviving and that it was probable that the plan would fail, followed by a run-down or liquidation of the company. About a third of BL was thought to be saleable. But the final judgement had to be based on wider considerations. We reluctantly decided that people would simply not understand liquidation of the company at the very moment when its management was standing up to the unions and talking the language of hard commercial common sense. And so, after much discussion, we agreed to endorse the Plan and to provide the necessary financial support. Keith announced our decision to the House of Commons on 20 December.

Agreeing to provide more public money was not, though, the end of the problem: it rarely is. BL's ballot on their pay offer went badly wrong, partly because the question put to the workforce – 'do you support your Negotiating Committee's rejection of the Company's wage and conditions offer?' – was confusing. Fifty-nine per cent of those taking part voted against the offer. Moreover, the AUEW enquiry found that Robinson had been unfairly dismissed by the company and an official strike was announced, to begin on 11 February. Michael Edwardes rightly refused to reinstate him or to improve on the pay offer. Contingency plans were made by the BL Board, assisted by Department of Industry and Treasury officials, to cope with the situation if the Plan had to be withdrawn and the company put into liquidation. Michael Edwardes was unwilling, even at this stage, to approach possible foreign buyers for a sell-off of BL, although he agreed to respond positively to any approaches potential buyers might make to him. Certainly, the workforce at BL could be in little doubt as to the seriousness of their position. BL's share of the market had fallen so low that in January Ford sold more of one model (the Cortina) than BL's total sales.

Michael Edwardes and the BL Board held their nerve and faced down the union threat. The strikers were told that unless they returned to work by Wednesday 23 April they would be dismissed. But much as I admired BL's tenacity, I was becoming increasingly unhappy about the Board's commercial approach. In particular, there was strong resistance from the Board to selling all or part of the company, though this took the form of obstruction rather than declared hostility.

For example, there was fierce initial resistance to my suggestion of engaging an independent financial adviser to advise on the disposal of the company's assets. It was argued that such an appointment would undermine confidence in the company's future. It was even suggested that these were matters for management, not government. I could not accept this. Government was the major shareholder in BL and it was right that the shareholder should have a say as to when and how the company's assets should be sold. In fact, such an adviser was in due course appointed, with Michael Edwardes's acquiescence.

On Wednesday 21 May Michael Edwardes and two of his colleagues came to a working dinner at No. 10. On the Government side, Geoffrey Howe and Keith Joseph, Robin Ibbs the head of the CPRS, and my private secretary were also present. Michael Edwardes said that BL faced a worse trading environment than when the 1980 Plan was prepared. It would be able to live within its agreed cash limit for 1980 but the £130 million limit provisionally decided for 1981 and the assumption that no government funding would be necessary thereafter were, he said, unrealistic. He claimed to have high hopes of collaboration with a German manufacturer, but that the prospects for selling most parts of the business in the near future were not encouraging. Only Land Rover would fetch a good price at that time, but to sell it separately would leave the rest of the business seriously weakened. Other parts of BL might be sold in a year or two as the recovery programme proceeded. It was obvious where all this was leading: BL was about to present us with yet another demand for taxpayers' money, and probably for a huge amount.

In reply, I acknowledged that BL had achieved a great deal. But I stressed my anxiety about the endless demands for extra money. I said that BL had failed to meet the targets set out in its Plan. There could be no presumption that any additional money would be provided.

As the summer wore on it became clear that the company's financial position was deteriorating even further. Michael Edwardes bombarded us with complaints. He was upset about Japanese imports. He drew attention to the (undoubtedly real) difficulties of exporting to Spain because of that country's high tariffs, while they nevertheless exported their cars freely to us. He worried about the level of sterling. But none of this could disguise the fact that things were going badly wrong at BL and that the Board seemed unable to turn things round. The company lost £93.4 million before interest and tax in the first half-year compared with a profit of £47.7 million for the same period the previous year. Michael Edwardes tried to get the Government to agree to fund the new BL medium-range car – known as the LM10 – separately and in advance of the 1981 Corporate Plan. Indeed, he wanted me to announce the Government's commitment to this at a dinner given by the Society of Motor Manufacturers and Traders (SMMT) on 6 October. I had no intention of agreeing; once again, I would not be bounced.

Instead, I delivered a rather different and possibly less welcome message to the motor industry. I acknowledged that some of the problems they faced were caused by the world recession. But that was not the real reason for the industry's difficulties. I said:

> This year we have the lowest car production for twenty years. Not because home sales are the lowest – far from it. But because people are buying foreign cars rather than our own. And some of those come from high-wage, high-exchange-rate economies. The world recession may have exacerbated our problems, but it is not the root cause in the motor industry. What has happened to the motor industry since the 1950s exemplifies what has been going wrong in too many other parts of British industry: higher pay not matched by higher productivity; low profits, so low investment; too little going into R & D and new design . . . and why haven't we had the productivity? Overmanning. Resistance to change. Too many strikes and stoppages.

The last part of that message seemed to fall on deaf ears. On 27 October BL's trade unions decided overwhelmingly to reject the company's offer of a pay increase of 6.8 per cent and recommended a strike. Michael Edwardes wrote to Keith Joseph to say that a strike would make it impossible to achieve the 1981 Corporate Plan submitted just a week before. To win support for the pay offer, he wanted to write to inform union officials of the key aspects of the 1981 Plan, including the funds required for 1981 and 1982 – a figure which he would put at £800 million. I reluctantly accepted Michael Edwardes's approach but only on the clear understanding that the Department of Industry would make it known that the Government was not committed in any way to finding these funds and that the matter had yet to be considered. In fact, on 18 November BL's union representatives backed down and finally decided to accept the company's offer. History repeated itself: almost the same thing had happened the previous year. The need to deal with an industrial relations crisis made it extremely difficult to avoid the impression that we were prepared to provide large amounts of extra public funding for the company. No matter how clear our disclaimers, inevitably people drew that conclusion.

On any rational commercial judgement, there were no good reasons for continuing to fund British Leyland. The 1980 Corporate Plan had foreseen the need for about £130 million of new government equity in the period of 1981 and beyond. In the 1981 Plan which we were now asked to approve that sum had grown by £1 billion. Meanwhile, the outlook for profits was worse. The predictions for market share in successive Plans had grown ever gloomier. Many of BL's models were uncompetitive. The Metro and the BL/Honda Bounty would help, but neither would yield much in profits. BL was still a high-cost, low-volume manufacturer of cars in a world where low cost and high volume were essential for success.

On 12 January I held a meeting at No. 10 to discuss the Corporate Plan with Keith Joseph, Geoffrey Howe, Norman Tebbit and others. I continued to argue that we should try to find some middle way between total closure and fully funding the Corporate Plan.

I knew that closure of the volume car business, with all that would mean for the West Midlands and the Oxford area, would not be politically acceptable to the Cabinet or the Party, at least in the short term. It would also be a huge cost to the Exchequer – perhaps not very different to the sort of sums BL was now seeking. I told a meeting of ministers on 16 January that the Government must get rid of its financial liability for the volume car business in a way which was both humane and politically acceptable. We might need to pay a 'dowry' to make the car business attractive to a buyer: ultimately, of course, it might mean closure – the market, not government, would ultimately determine BL's future. I said that I was in favour of supporting the BL Plan – but on condition that BL disposed of its assets rapidly or arranged mergers with other companies.

This last point was still extremely contentious. Michael Edwardes told Geoffrey Howe and Keith Joseph that the BL Board would be willing to sell Land Rover and such other parts of the business as they could and close down the volume car business: but they were not willing to sell Land Rover if they were also required to go on trying to salvage the volume car business. He said that the Board's position would be quite impossible if a public deadline were to be set for its sale.

This attitude, of course, put us in a very difficult position – as it was doubtless intended to do. It irritated one or two ministers to the point of turning them against the whole Plan. Moreover, it had not been possible for us to find the 'middle way' which I had sought and which would have involved progressive sale of the business without a total and immediate shut-down. But the political realities had to be faced. BL had to be supported. We agreed to accept BL's Corporate Plan, involving the division of the company into four more or less independent businesses. We settled the contingencies which would lead to the Plan being abandoned. We set out the objectives for further collaboration with other companies. And – most painfully – we provided £990 million.

This was not, of course, the end of the story for BL, any more than it was for BSC. In due course, it would be shown that the changes in attitude and improvements in efficiency achieved in these years were permanent.* To that extent, the account of our policy in 1979–81 towards BL is one of success – at a cost. But the huge extra sums of public money that we were forced to provide came from the taxpayer or, through higher interest rates needed to finance extra borrowing, from other businesses. And every vociferous cheer for higher public spending was matched by a silent groan from those who had to pay for it.

* See pp. 679–80.

CHAPTER V

Not for Turning

Politics and the economy in 1980–1981

NO U-TURNS

At 2.30 on the afternoon of Friday 10 October 1980 I rose to address the Conservative Party Conference in Brighton. Unemployment stood at over two million and rising; a deepening recession lay ahead; inflation was far higher than we had inherited, though falling; and we were at the end of a summer of government leaks and rifts. The Party was worried, and so was I. Our strategy was the right one, but the price of putting it into effect was proving so high, and there was such limited understanding of what we were trying to do, that we had great electoral difficulties. However, I was utterly convinced of one thing: there was no chance of achieving that fundamental change of attitudes which was required to wrench Britain out of decline if people believed that we were prepared to alter course under pressure. I made the point with a line provided by Ronnie Millar:

> To those waiting with bated breath for that favourite media catchphrase, the 'U-turn', I have only one thing to say. 'You turn if you want to. The lady's not for turning.' I say that not only to you, but to our friends overseas – and also to those who are not our friends.

The message was directed as much to some of my colleagues in the Government as it was to politicians of other parties. It was in the summer of 1980 that my critics within the Cabinet first seriously attempted to frustrate the strategy which we had been elected to carry out – an attack which reached its climax and was defeated the following year. At the time that I spoke, many people felt that this group had more or less prevailed.

ARGUMENTS ABOUT PUBLIC EXPENDITURE

Battle was to be joined over the next two years on three related issues: monetary policy, public spending and trade union reform. The 'wets' argued that because we had embraced a dogmatic monetary theory that inflation could only be brought down by a fierce monetary squeeze, we were squeezing the economy in the middle of a recession. Such dogmatism, they argued, similary prevented our using practical tools of economic policy like prices and incomes control and forced us to cut public spending when, as Keynes had argued, public spending should be increased to lift an economy suffering from lack of demand.

The most bitter Cabinet arguments were over public spending. In most cases those who dissented from the line which Geoffrey Howe and I took were not merely intent on opposing our whole economic strategy as doctrinaire monetarism; they were trying to protect their departmental budgets. It had soon become clear that the public expenditure plans announced in March 1980 had been far too optimistic. In particular, the large turn round from losses towards profitability in the nationalized industries was not going to come about; local authorities, as usual, were overspending; and the recession was proving deeper than expected, increasing spending on unemployment and other benefits. Government borrowing for the first quarter of 1980 looked like being very large. In addition, Francis Pym, Defence Secretary, was pressing for an increase in the Ministry of Defence (MoD) cash limit.

We had decided to have a general economic discussion in Cabinet on 3 July 1980, before our first collective discussion of the 1981–2 public expenditure round on 10 July. Our aim was to confront spending ministers with the full implications for taxation of a failure to control spending, and to smoke out the arguments for reflation, which were almost daily to be found in the newspapers and in the mouths of pressure groups. But I had no illusions that it would be easy to subject my colleagues' aspirations to a salutary dose of realism.

Geoffrey spelt out to Cabinet how difficult the economic situation at home and abroad had now become. Inflation in the major economies had risen sharply, oil prices had doubled, and the world was moving further into recession – led in this direction by Jimmy Carter's United States. Although output in the UK had fallen rather less than predicted in 1980, it was likely in consequence to fall faster than expected in 1981. Inflation was slowing, but less rapidly than we had hoped. The background to the public spending round and to next year's budget was, therefore, bleak. Then the discussion began. Some ministers argued for large increases in spending to stave off unemployment; others argued for prudence. I summed up by reaffirming the present strategy and noting the need to maintain public spending constraints, to reduce public sector pay increases and so to allow government borrowing and interest rates to fall – although within spending totals I was keen to see a higher priority given to dealing with unemployment, especially among young people. Round one went to Geoffrey and me.

But the debate continued inside and outside government. The 'wets'' arguments came in different forms of varying sophistication, though their central message was always the same: spend and borrow more. They used to argue that we needed extra public spending on employment and industrial schemes, over and above what we had planned and were effectively forced to spend simply as a result of the recession. But this did not escape from the fact that extra public spending – whatever it was spent on – had to come from somewhere. And 'somewhere' meant either taxes levied on private individuals and industry; or borrowing, pushing up interest rates; or printing money, setting off inflation. There was also a feeling, which I equally knew I had to resist, that the refunds which I had secured from the European Community budget should be used to finance extra spending. But why should it be assumed that public spending was better than private spending? Why should the fruits of my efforts to rein in the appetite of the European Community automatically be consumed by an almost as insatiable British public sector? I was, therefore, determined to ensure that the Cabinet endorsed the 1981–2 public expenditure total announced in the previous white paper, as reduced by the European budget receipts.

These basic differences between us came out clearly at the public spending Cabinet on 10 July. Some ministers argued that the PSBR should be allowed to increase to accommodate the huge new requirements of the loss-making nationalized industries. But the PSBR was already far too high, whatever the theoretical merits or otherwise of letting public borrowing rise in a recession. The higher it went, the greater the pressure to raise interest rates in order to persuade people to lend the Government the necessary funds. And at a certain point – if pushed too far – there would be the risk of a full-scale government funding crisis – that is, when you cannot finance your borrowing from the non-banking sector. We could not risk going further in that direction. So I emphasized once again the need to stay within the public spending plans – though within them there could be more priority given to assistance for jobs.

The defence budget was a special problem. We had already accepted the NATO commitment for annual 3 per cent real increases in our defence spending. This had the obvious merit of demonstrating to the Soviets our determination to prevent their winning the arms race on which they had embarked, but in two other respects it was unsatisfactory. First, it meant that the MoD had little incentive to get value for money in the hugely expensive equipment it purchased. Second, the 3 per cent commitment meant that Britain, spending a substantially higher proportion of its GDP on defence than other European countries and going through a peculiarly deep recession, found herself bearing an unfair and increasing burden. There were also problems relating to management of the MoD budget. By the end of 1980 the MoD had overspent its cash limit because, with the depressed state of industry, suppliers had fulfilled government orders faster than expected.

As we moved into the winter of 1980 the economic difficulties accumulated and the political pressure built up. It might have been easier to gain support in the battle for tight control of public spending if the second element of the strategy – the money supply – had been behaving predictably. But it had not. On Wednesday 3 September Geoffrey Howe and I met to discuss the monetary position. What did the figures really mean? Measured in terms of £M3, the money supply had been rising much faster than the target we had set in the MTFS at the time of the March budget. It was hard to know how much of this was the result of our removing exchange controls in 1979 and our decision in June to remove the 'corset' – a device by which the Bank of England imposed limits on bank lending. Money analysts argued that both of these liberalizations had misleadingly bloated the £M3 figures.* As I put it to Brian Walden in an interview on Sunday 1 February:

> a corset is there to conceal the underlying bulges, not to deal with them, and when you take it off you might see that the bulges are worse.

* Higher interest rates caused people to increase the amount they held in interest-bearing financial assets and to reduce cash and non-interest-bearing assets in their current accounts.

By contrast, some of the other monetary measures were undershooting their targets. The 'wets' found the wayward behaviour of £M3 a suitable subject for mockery at dinner parties. But for Geoffrey and me it was no such diversion. The arguments about which was the most accurate measure of the money supply were highly technical, but they were of great significance.

Of course, we never just looked at monetary figures to gauge what was happening. We also looked at the real world around us. And what we saw told a somewhat different tale from the high £M3 figures. Inflation had slowed down markedly, particularly prices in the shops where competition was intense. Sterling was very strong, averaging just below $2.40 during the second half of 1980. And here the crucial issue was whether the high exchange rate was more or less an independent factor bringing down inflation, or rather a result of the monetary squeeze being tighter than we intended and than the £M3 figures suggested.

Some of my closest advisers thought the latter. Professor Douglas Hague sent me a paper in which he described our policies as 'lopsided' in two respects: first, they were bearing down more heavily on the private than the public sector (which I knew to be true), and second, they were putting too much emphasis on controlling the money supply and too little on controlling the PSBR, with the result that interest rates were higher than they should have been. (I also came to share this view over the next year.) In the summer of 1980 I consulted Alan Walters, who was to join me at the beginning of 1981 as my economic policy adviser at No. 10 and upon whose judgement I came more and more to rely. Alan's view was that the monetary squeeze was too tight and that it was the narrowest definition of 'money', known as the monetary base, which was the best, indeed the only reliable, star to steer by. Certainly, during the autumn of 1980 the narrowest definitions of money suggested that we were pursuing a very severe monetary policy.

If there was uncertainty about the monetary position at this time, there was none at all about the trend in public spending, which was inexorably upwards. Public sector pay was one of the worst problems: the bills we received were largely the legacy of Labour's failed incomes policy, but they had to be paid all the same, and they set a higher base for future settlements as well. The other main culprit for the enormous increase in public spending was, as I have said, the nationalized industries. Looking at the disappointing figures emerging from the public expenditure round, I wrote at the time that they 'had undermined the Government's whole public expenditure strategy'. But there was worse to come.

In September, Geoffrey Howe sent me a note elaborating on the warning he had already given to Cabinet about public expenditure. The increases required for the nationalized industries, particularly BSC, would require larger cuts in programmes than those agreed in July in order to hold the total. To the extent that more was provided, as the Cabinet wished, for industrial support and employment, the corresponding cuts would need to be larger still. The fifth public expenditure round in sixteen months was bound to prompt squeals of indignation: and so it proved.

Indeed, a further note from Geoffrey in early October confirmed that the position was, if anything, deteriorating: the figures were worse than suggested the previous month. The latest forecast of the PSBR for 1981–2 approached £11 billion, far higher than planned. The Treasury had already begun to examine ways in which it might be reduced and were looking at the possibility of increasing taxes on the profits from North Sea oil and gas, raising employees' national insurance contributions and not fully indexing personal income tax allowances in line with inflation. All of these unpalatable tax options reinforced the necessity for further public spending cuts: we needed a cash limits squeeze on all programmes and a cut in local authority current spending, and we would have to look again at defence spending and at the even more politically sensitive social security budget. (The social security budget accounted for a quarter of total public spending, of which the cost of retirement pensions was by far the largest element. But I had pledged publicly that the latter would be raised in line with inflation during the Parliament.) We were entering perilous waters.

The tactics in handling the new public expenditure discussions were obviously very important. Geoffrey and I decided not to take the whole matter to Cabinet cold, as it were, so I called a meeting of key ministers to go into it first. The Chancellor described the position and outlined the arithmetic.

Our plan succeeded. Without too much grumbling, the Cabinet of 30 October endorsed the strategy and confirmed our objective of keeping public spending in 1981–2 and later years broadly at the levels set out in the March white paper. This meant that it would be necessary to make cuts of the order of magnitude proposed by the Treasury – though even with these reductions we would be forced to increase taxes if we were to bring the PSBR down to a level compatible with lower interest rates.

Much stronger Cabinet opposition surfaced when we began to look at the decisions required to give effect to the strategy which had been endorsed. The 'wets' now discovered a new approach. They claimed that they lacked sufficient information to judge whether the overall strategy was soundly based. Without this, they said, they were in no position to weigh the economic, political and social consequences of all the various means of achieving it, including changes in taxation and reductions in public spending. The ploy was transparent. In effect, spending ministers were trying to behave as if they were Chancellors of the Exchequer. It would be a recipe for complete absence of spending control and thus for economic chaos.

The three most important areas of discussion at our meeting on Tuesday 4 November were the Health Service and defence budgets, and the special employment measures which Jim Prior wanted. On Health, we decided that the NHS element in the National Insurance Contribution should be raised rather than the health programme itself reduced – so continuing to honour our manifesto pledge. On defence, the Cabinet accepted that the reductions would have to fall somewhere between what the Treasury demanded and the MoD was then offering. Finally, we agreed on the special employment measures, which I later announced in my speech on the Address, and which provided for 440,000 places on the Youth Opportunities Programme – 180,000 more than in the current year.

Two days later, Cabinet met again to continue the discussion. The financial position of the nationalized industries had worsened even in the short time since we had begun our spending review. Public sector pay was still a headache. If we managed to hold future public service pay increases to 6 per cent, as we wished, we could still expect a PSBR of £12 billion in 1981–2, compared with the £7.5 billion implied by the MTFS. It would not be possible to finance a PSBR of this size and reduce interest rates at the same time. Therefore, in order to avoid high interest rates substantial tax increases would be needed. In my summing up I noted that the position would be still worse, if reductions still under discussion – including defence, social security and education – were not actually agreed. In fact, Cabinet made the final decisions about the package the following week.

The Autumn Statement on 24 November 1980, therefore, contained some highly unpopular measures. Employees' National Insurance Contributions had to go up. Retirement pensions and other social security benefits would be increased by 1 per cent less than the rate of inflation next year if they turned out to have risen by 1 per cent more in the present year. There were cuts in defence and local government spending. It was announced that a new supplementary tax would be introduced on North Sea oil profits. However, there was some good news: the further employment measures – and a 2 percentage point cut in MLR.

DISSENT BY LEAKS

Few members of the public are experts in the finer matters of economics – though most have a shrewd sense when promises do not add up. By the end of 1980 I began to feel that we risked forfeiting the public's confidence in our economic strategy. Unpopularity I could live with. But loss of confidence in our capacity to deliver our economic programme was far more dangerous. We were now spending more when we believed in spending less; inflation was high when we proclaimed the primacy of bringing it down; and private industry was faltering when we had been saying for years that only successful free enterprise could make a country wealthy. Of course, we could point to factors over which we had little or no control, and above all to the world recession; and on inflation and pay settlements there was movement in the right direction. But our credibility was at stake. And the very last thing I could afford was well-publicized dissent from within the Cabinet itself. Yet this was what I now had to face.

Public dissent from the 'wets' was phrased in what was obviously intended to be a highly sophisticated code, in which each phrase had a half-hidden meaning and philosophical abstractions were woven together to condemn practical policies by innuendo. This cloaked and indirect approach has never been my style and I felt contempt for it. I thrive on honest argument. I am interested in practical options. And I prefer to debate my opponents rather than to undermine them with leaks. I do not believe that collective responsibility is an interesting fiction, but a point of principle. My experience is that a number of the men I have dealt with in politics demonstrate precisely those characteristics which they attribute to women – vanity and an inability to make tough decisions. There are also certain kinds of men who simply cannot abide working for a woman. They are quite prepared to make every allowance for 'the weaker sex': but if a woman asks no special privileges and expects to be judged solely by what she is and does, this is found gravely and unforgivably disorienting. Of course, in the eyes of the 'wet' Tory establishment I was not only a woman, but 'that woman', someone not just of a different sex, but of a different class, a person with an alarming conviction that the values and virtues of middle England should be brought to bear on the problems which the establishment consensus had created. I offended on many counts.

The economic and public expenditure discussions of 1980 repeatedly found their way into the press; decisions came to be seen as victories by one side or the other and Bernard Ingham told me that it was proving quite impossible to convey a sense of unity and purpose in this climate. During 1980 the public was treated to a series of speeches and lectures by Ian Gilmour and Norman St John Stevas on the shortcomings of monetarism, which, according to them, was deeply un-Tory, a kind of alien dogma – though they usually took care to cover themselves against charges of disloyalty by including some fulsome remarks praising me and the Government's approach. Speaking in Cambridge in November, Ian Gilmour claimed that Britain risked 'the creation of a "Clockwork Orange" society with all its attendant alienation and misery', which sounded remarkably like Britain in the 'winter of discontent'.

Industrial leaders helped worsen the general impression of disarray: in the same month the new Director-General of the CBI was promising 'a bare knuckle fight' over Government policies, though when I met the CBI shortly afterwards I am glad to say that knuckles were not in evidence. Then in December Jim Prior was reported as urging us not to use the language of the 'academic seminar'. But perhaps the most astonishing remark – not his last – was John Biffen's widely reported admission to the Conservative Party Parliamentary Finance Committee that he did not share the enthusiasm for the MTFS, which he – the Chief Secretary to the Treasury – was trying, with singularly little success, to apply in the field of public expenditure. Not surprisingly, when I met the executive of the '22 Committee later that month I found that they had a low view of ministerial efforts at presentation. I most certainly agreed. But it was not simply a question of presentation: some ministers were trying to discredit the strategy itself. This could not be allowed to continue.

I had the Christmas holiday to consider what should be done. I decided that it was time to reshuffle the Cabinet. The only question was whether a limited reshuffle would serve to change the balance sufficiently in favour of our economic strategy, or whether much more far-reaching changes were required. I decided on the former.

On Monday 5 January I made the changes, beginning with Norman St John Stevas, who left the Government. I was sorry to lose Norman but he made his own departure inevitable. He had a first-class brain and a ready wit. But he turned indiscretion into a political principle. His jokes at the expense of government policy moved smoothly from

ABOVE: On the stairs at Central Office following the 1979 general election victory, with Peter Thorneycroft, Carol, Denis and Mark

RIGHT: With Denis on the steps of Number Ten

BELOW: Speaking at the Lord Mayor's Banquet in 1981

LEFT: Presenting the deeds to one of the first tenants of the Milton Keynes Development Corporation to buy their home under the Government's new 'Right to Buy' scheme in September 1979

BELOW: With Petty Officers on HMS *Resolution* (Polaris submarine) on the Clyde, accompanied by Admiral Sir John Fieldhouse, Commander-in-Chief of the Fleet

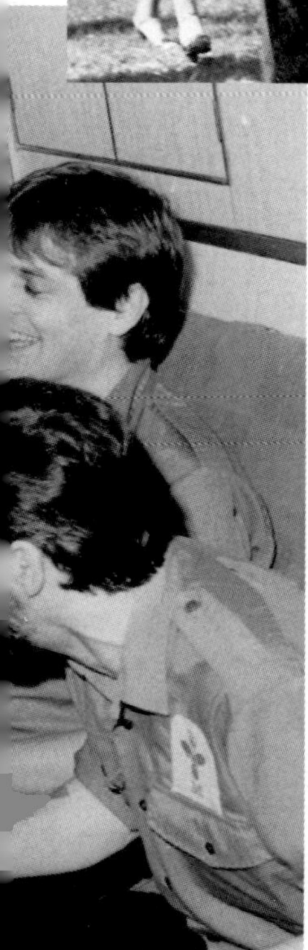

ABOVE: On my visit to Ireland after Warrenpoint in August 1979

BELOW: Inspecting the bomb-damaged coach at Chelsea Barracks, October 1981

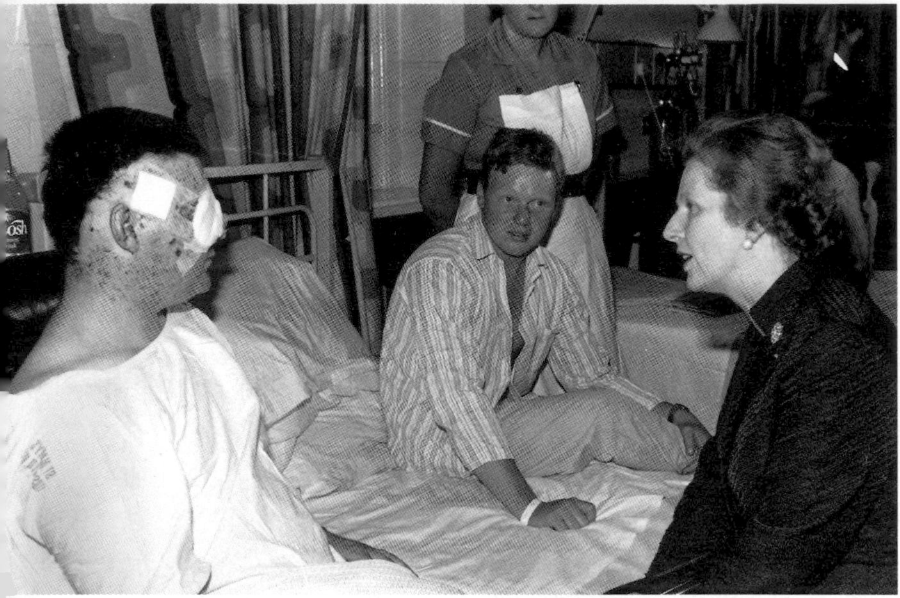

ABOVE: Visiting the injured in hospital after the Regent's Park bombing in July 1982

LEFT: Signing the Anglo-Irish Agreement at Hillsborough Castle, 15 November 1985, with Dr Garret FitzGerald, Taoiseach, and standing l-r: Peter Barry (Irish Foreign Minister), Dermot Nally (Secretary to the Irish Government), Dick Spring (Leader of the Irish Labour Party), and Tom King (Secretary of State for Northern Ireland)

OPPOSITE: The Grand Hotel, Brighton on the day after it was bombed, October 1984

GRAND

LEFT: Presenting medals on board HMS *Hermes*, 21 July 1982

LEFT: HMS *Invincible* returning to Portsmouth at the end of the Falklands War

BELOW: On the steps of St Paul's Cathedral following the Memorial Service for the Falklands War, July 1982, with Lord Lewin, Chief of Defence Staff standing beside me

RIGHT: Laying a wreath at the cemetery at San Carlos Bay in January 1983

ABOVE: Campaigning in Newbury during the 1983 general election campaign

LEFT: With Cecil Parkinson at Central Office on the night of our victory in the 1983 general election

private conversation to Commons gossip to the front page of newspapers. The other departure, Angus Maude, had employed his own sharp wit in my support but he felt that it was time to give up the job as Paymaster-General, in charge of government information, in order to return to writing. I moved John Nott to Defence to replace Francis Pym. I was convinced that someone with real understanding of finance and a commitment to efficiency was needed in this department. I moved John Biffen to replace John Nott at Trade, and at Geoffrey Howe's request appointed Leon Brittan as Chief Secretary. Leon Brittan was a close friend of Geoffrey's. He was enormously intelligent and hard-working and he had impressed me with the sharpness of his mind, particularly in Opposition when he had been one of the Party's spokesmen on the then vexed issue of Devolution. Two very talented new Ministers of State came into the Department of Industry to support Keith Joseph: Norman Tebbit and Kenneth Baker. Norman had worked closely with me in Opposition. I knew that he was totally committed to our policies, shared much of my own outlook and was a devastating Commons in-fighter. Ken was given special responsibility for Information Technology, a task in which he showed his talents as a brilliant presenter of policy. Francis Pym took over the task of disseminating government information, which he combined with the position of Leader of the House of Commons. But the first half of this appointment was to prove a source of some difficulty in the months ahead.

With this moderate Cabinet reshuffle, I had hoped that we would be able to face our economic difficulties with greater unity and determination. Certainly, both qualities were needed: the criticisms of our strategy were mounting. I counter-attacked. Both in my *Weekend World* interview on 1 February and a few days later in my speech in the Commons economic debate I replied to the arguments of those who believed that the real problem in Britain was lack of economic demand and who argued that we should remedy it by reflation. I told the House:

> As governments tried to stimulate employment by pumping money into the economy they caused inflation. The inflation led to higher costs. The higher costs meant loss of ability to compete. The few jobs that we had gained were soon lost; and so were a lot more with them. And then, from a higher level of unemployment and inflation, the process was started all over again, and each time around both inflation and unemployment rose.

But the other side had important allies in the media. A leading article in the *Sunday Times*, usually a Conservative paper, carried the headline 'Wrong, Mrs Thatcher, Wrong, Wrong, Wrong'. Indeed, the press was full of hostile comment. And that hit the morale of my supporters. On 27 February I received a memorandum from Ian Gow:

Prime Minister

1. I am sorry to say that there has been a noticeable deterioration in the morale of our back-benchers.

2. I attribute this to:-

(a) Increasing concern about the extent of the recession and unemployment.

(b) The perceived defeats for the Government on Coal and, to a lesser extent, in the pay settlement for the water workers.

(c) The size of the PSBR and the slowness with which interest rates are falling.

(d) The insatiable appetite of the Public Sector – notably BL, BSC, NCB.

(e) The Rate Support Grant.

Many of the critics inside and outside the Conservative Party felt that they had detected weakness, were determined to exploit it and saw their chance coming with the 1981 budget.

THE 1981 BUDGET

I shall never forget the weeks leading up to the 1981 budget. Hardly a day seemed to go by without the financial scene deteriorating in some way. At the end of January Geoffrey Howe was still hoping to make serious cuts in capital taxation and to provide substantial assistance for industry, but by the beginning of February the Treasury was already becoming more cautious and pessimistic about the outlook. The PSBR for the current year seemed likely to turn out between £4 and £6 billion more than the figure forecast in the 1980 budget. The current Treasury forecast, which assumed indexation of personal tax allowances and of specific duties and took account of the measures announced in November 1980, showed a PSBR for 1981–2 in the region of £11 billion (nearly 4.5 per cent of GDP), compared with a figure implied by the MTFS of around £7.5 billion (some 3 per cent of GDP). At this point the Treasury believed that we should aim for a PSBR somewhat below £10 billion. There was, therefore, a gap of £1 billion to £1.5 billion.

Personal incomes had been increasing while company profits had been shrinking, so it was clear that any extra taxation should be borne by the personal rather than the corporate sector. The Treasury were talking of raising personal allowances by a minimum of 6.5 per cent – they hoped for 9 or 10 per cent – rather than the full 15 per cent required to take account of inflation. They were planning to raise the specific duties on alcohol, tobacco and petrol by one and three-quarters or perhaps twice the rate necessary to take account of inflation. Business – especially the CBI – was pressing hard for a reduction in the National Insurance Surcharge (NIS), but there were problems with this proposal: the full year cost of each percentage point reduction was very large, the relief was indiscriminate and there was the risk that some of it might go quickly into wages. Other possible ways of helping industry – each of which had its own disadvantages – included a cut in Corporation Tax or in the Heavy Fuel Oil Duty. We had in November announced extra taxation on North Sea oil and gas profits. The question now was whether to levy a windfall tax on bank profits. Naturally, the banks strongly opposed this; but the fact remained that they had made their large profits as a result of our policy of high interest rates rather than because of increased efficiency or better service to the customer.

Yet these were essentially secondary issues – and on larger issues there were legitimate disagreements inside the 'dry' section of the Government. The main problem was to determine how tight the fiscal stance of the budget should be and the monetary policy which it would be supporting. On this question Alan Walters, who had now joined me at No. 10, had his own strong views. He argued for a larger cut in the PSBR than Geoffrey Howe was proposing. He also believed that the way in which the monetary policy was conducted was defective. But the Treasury were not prepared to move to the system of monetary base control which Alan favoured and to which I was attracted by his clear and persuasive analysis.

And this was much more than a technical disagreement. Alan Walters, John Hoskyns and Alfred Sherman had suggested that Professor Jurg Niehans, a distinguished Swiss monetary economist, should prepare a study on our monetary policy for me. Professor Niehans's report which I read in early February, though framed in highly technical language, had a clear message. It was that North Sea oil had probably not been a major factor in sterling's appreciation; rather, tight monetary policy had caused the pound to rise so high, imposing such pressure on British industry and deepening the recession. The report argued that we should use the monetary base rather than £M3 as the main monetary measure and suggested that we should allow it to rise in the first half of 1981. In short, Professor Niehans thought monetary policy was too tight and should quickly be loosened. Alan emphatically agreed with him.

My doubts at this time about the Treasury's conduct of monetary policy, however, were more than matched by the concern I felt at the steady growth in its estimates of the PSBR – the target by which we steered our fiscal policy. On 10 February 1981 Geoffrey Howe and I met to discuss the budget strategy. Geoffrey now told me that the forecast for the PSBR had been updated and showed not £11 billion but £13 billion. He was now talking about raising income tax allowances by only 6 per cent rather than the 10 per cent he had earlier envisaged – though he still wanted a substantial enterprise package. I told him that our primary concern must be to boost industry and that this meant giving priority to a reduction in interest rates, which would also help get down the exchange rate. If there were to be a choice between cutting the NIS and a lower PSBR I preferred the latter.

I was worried by the prospect of a 2 per cent addition to the RPI as a result of the indirect tax increases which were being proposed. I was sure it would be better to achieve further public expenditure cuts. But I had to agree that the chance of achieving these, given Cabinet attitudes, was very slim indeed.

At this meeting Alan Walters continued to press the view that we should allow the monetary base to grow more quickly. We also discussed the timing of any interest rate cuts which we would be able to make.

The starkness of the choices before us was now becoming clear. Later that day Alan sent me a note which summed up the problem with the PSBR. We were confronted with rapid and huge changes in the figures which made the strategic planning of the budget very difficult. But one thing was clear. The trend of PSBR forecasts was upwards. The likelihood was that we would budget for too low a reduction in the PSBR, as we had in 1980–81. To repeat that mistake would either force us to introduce an additional budget in late summer or autumn, or put great strains on the funding of government borrowing. In the last resort it might lead to a funding crisis, and it would certainly force us to increase interest rates, keeping sterling high and increasing the already severe squeeze on the private sector. We had to avoid such an outcome. We might still get things right in time – but only if we made painful decisions now, and presented them effectively, as the only possible response to the costs of the last wage round and nationalized industry losses. What we needed was a budget for employment.

On Friday 13 February I had a further meeting with Geoffrey Howe. Alan Walters was also present. The latest forecast for the PSBR was between £13.5 billion and £13.75 billion. The tax increases Geoffrey was proposing would reduce it to something between £11.25 billion and £11.5 billion, but he did not believe it was politically possible to go below £11 billion, and in his view an increase in the basic tax rate had to be ruled out. But Alan argued strongly that the PSBR should be lower still. He told us that a PSBR of, say, £10 billion would be no more deflationary than one of £11 billion because the latter would actually be worse for City expectations and for interest rates. Alan concluded by arguing that we had no alternative but to raise the basic rates of income tax by 1 or 2 per cent.

Alan was the economist. But Geoffrey and I were politicians. Geoffrey rightly observed that introducing what would be represented as a deflationary budget at the time of the deepest recession since the 1930s would be difficult enough; doing so via an increase in the basic rate would make it a political nightmare. I went along with Geoffrey's judgement about the problems of raising income tax, but I did so without much conviction and as the days went by my unease grew.

When Geoffrey and I had our next budget meeting on 17 February, he said that he too had been having second thoughts. He was now prepared to contemplate a basic rate increase. But his concern was whether it might not be better to raise the basic rate of income tax by 1 per cent and personal allowances by about 10 per cent, thus reducing the burden on people below average earnings. I confirmed that I in turn was prepared to contemplate this, but I also told him that I was coming to the view that it was essential to get the PSBR below £11 billion.

My advisers – Alan Walters, John Hoskyns and David Wolfson – continued to argue for this much lower PSBR with great passion. Keith Joseph also strongly backed this view. Alan, who knew that he could always have access to me more or less when he wished – as in my view any really close adviser should if a prime minister is not to be the prisoner of his (or her) in-tray – came in to my study to have one last attempt to get me to change my mind about the budget. He ran over again the reasons why we could never have lower interest rates – which was what the economy desperately needed – unless we had lower borrowing, which now meant higher taxes. I know today that he went away still believing that I was not persuaded. But the more I wrestled with the problem in my mind, the more accurate his analysis seemed. The budget he was arguing for would be unpopular with the public, mystifying to many of my strongest supporters in the Commons and the country and incomprehensible to those economists still stuck in post-war Keynesian orthodoxy. Its consequences for my administration were unpredictable. Yet I knew in my heart of hearts that there was only one right decision, and that it now had to be made.

Geoffrey Howe and I – without Alan who was engaged on some other business but with Douglas Wass, the Treasury's Permanent Secretary – met for a further discussion of the budget on the afternoon of Tuesday 24 February. Geoffrey still envisaged a PSBR for 1981–2 of £11.25 billion. I said that I was dismayed by such a figure and that I doubted whether it would be possible to cut interest rates, which we badly needed to do, unless government borrowing was reduced to a figure around £10.5 billion. I said that I was even prepared to accept a penny on the standard rate. In the light of all the taxpayers' money which had gone to coal and steel there would at least be a clear explanation for this.

Geoffrey argued against a penny on income tax – on which I was not too difficult to persuade for I was horrified at the thought of reversing even some of the progress we had made on bringing down Labour's tax rates. But he also argued against the need to bring down the PSBR further, and on this last point I was not persuaded at all. We had further inconclusive discussion about alternative ways to raise tax. Time was growing very short. Geoffrey was still prepared to hope for the best as regards the effect of an £11.25 billion PSBR figure on interest rates. But he knew that I just could not accept this. He went away to think further about what should be done.

Early the following morning, Alan came in to see me when I was in the flat packing my hats into boxes for my trip to the United States that afternoon. I told him that I had insisted on the lower PSBR he wanted. But I still did not know quite how Geoffrey would react. Then shortly before I left for America Geoffrey came in to see me. Having consulted his ministerial colleagues in the Treasury that morning he had accepted that we should have a smaller PSBR, below £11 billion. Rather than increase the basic rate of income tax he proposed the less unpopular course of withholding any increase in tax thresholds – though this was still an extraordinarily bold move when inflation remained at 13 per cent. This was the turning point. I was glad that Geoffrey had accepted the argument and I was pleased that he had found a way of increasing tax revenues that did not run counter to our long-term strategy of reversing Labour's high tax rates. Our budget strategy was now set. And it looked as if we would be able to announce a reduction of 2 per cent in MLR in the budget the following Tuesday.

There was one other change announced in the budget, apparently technical but of great significance: the change to planning public expenditure in cash rather than what were called 'volume' terms. Each minister would be given a cash budget within which to keep his expenditure. Since the spring of 1980 we had been considering how this should be done and I discussed it with Geoffrey Howe and others in the Treasury over lunch there on 28 January 1981. It would have seemed distinctly odd to any company finance director, or housewife for that matter, how the government in those days used to work out its annual expenditure. The Chancellor would make his assessment of government revenue in cash, but spending decisions were made in terms of the volume of services it was desired to deliver, and denominated in what commentators used to call 'funny money' – neither the prices at the time of the spending decision, nor those when the money was actually spent. The result was that the Treasury never knew until far too late in the day the cash consequences of decisions on spending. Cash limits on some government spending had already been introduced, but paradoxically, this increased the confusion as spending which had been planned in volume ran up against them. From now on everything was to be planned in cash – though, of course, departments would still have to estimate the volume of services which their cash limits would enable them to afford. This imposed the sort of financial discipline on government departments with which the private sector had to deal. The 'cash limits' approach had the valuable consequence of bearing down on real public expenditure. It also gave departments a much stronger interest in seeking out the most efficient way of delivering the services expected of them.

Unsurprisingly, however, it was not the adoption of cash planning which grabbed the budget headlines, but rather the severity of the tax increases. The budget was very unpopular. But some of the leader columns were more favourable than the headlines and no one could doubt that this was a coherent budget which had required a good deal of courage to introduce. In the eyes of our critics, of course, the strategy was fundamentally wrong. If you believed, as they did, that increased government borrowing was the way to get out of recession, then our approach was inexplicable. If, on the other hand, you thought, as we did, that the way to get industry moving again was above all to get down interest rates, then you had to reduce government borrowing. Far from being deflationary, our budget would have the reverse effect:

by cutting government borrowing and over time easing the monetary squeeze, it would allow interest rates and the exchange rate to fall, both of which had created severe difficulties for industry. I doubt that there has ever been a clearer test of two fundamentally different approaches to economic management.

The economists themselves realized that this was so. At the end of March 1981 no fewer than 364 leading members of the profession published a statement taking issue with our policy. Samuel Brittan of the *Financial Times* defended us, and so did Professor Patrick Minford from Liverpool University, who wrote to *The Times* answering the 364; I in turn wrote to congratulate him on his brilliant defence of the Government's approach. We had made our decision: the task now was to hold the political line and, where possible, to win the political argument while waiting for the strategy to work. I was confident that it would.

The dissenters in the Cabinet, meanwhile, had been stunned by the budget when they learnt its contents at the traditional morning Cabinet on budget day. The press was soon full of leaks expressing their fury and frustration. They knew that the budget gave them a political opportunity. Because it departed so radically from post-war economic orthodoxy, even some of our supporters would not wholly believe in the strategy until it started to yield results. That might not be for some time. So it was clear that the Party in the country must be mobilized in support of what we were doing. The forthcoming Central Council of the Conservative Party in Bournemouth provided an opportunity for me to do this. I had decided some time before that I would try not to go to every Central Council because the number of party political occasions I was under pressure to address each year was enormous: there were separate conferences of the English, Scottish and Welsh parties, the Women's Conference, Local Government Conference and Conferences of Young Conservatives, Conservative Students and Conservative Trade Unionists. However, I soon learnt that Central Council provided an opportunity which I could never afford to miss. Certainly that was true on this occasion. John Hoskyns and I worked late on Friday night and early into Saturday morning on my speech, which I delivered later that day. In it I threw down the challenge:

> In the past our people have made sacrifices, only to find at the eleventh hour their government had lost its nerve and the sacrifice had been in vain. It shall not be in vain this time. This Conservative Government, not yet two years in office, will hold

fast until the future of our country is assured. I do not greatly care what people say about me: I do greatly care what people think about our country. Let us, then, keep calm and strong, and let us preserve that mutual friendship in which patriotism consists. This is the road I am resolved to follow. This is the path I must go. I ask all who have the spirit – the bold, the steadfast and the young in heart – to stand and join with me as we go forward. For there is no other company in which I would travel.

I got a good reception. For the moment at least, the Party faithful were prepared to take the heat and to back the Government. But that determination might erode over the summer unless the Government stuck together.

THE COAL STRIKE WHICH NEVER WAS

Thankfully, strikes occupied far less of our time during 1981 than they had in 1980, and the number of working days lost due to strike action was only a third of that in the previous year. But two disputes – one in the coal industry, which did not in the end result in a strike, and another in the civil service, which did* – were of great importance, both to budget decisions and to the overall political climate.

A foreigner unaware of the extraordinary legacy of state socialism in Britain would probably have found the threatened miners' strike in January 1981 quite incomprehensible: £2.5 billion of taxpayers' money had been invested in the coal industry since 1974; productivity at some of the new pits was high, and a slimmed-down and competitive coal industry could have provided employees with good, well-paid jobs. But this was possible only if uneconomic pits were closed, which the National Coal Board (NCB) wished to do. Moreover, the pits which the NCB was intent on closing in a programme it put forward in early 1981 were not just uneconomic but more or less exhausted.

* The civil service strike began in March 1981 and lasted for five months. Union members struck selectively at crucial government installations, including computer staff involved in tax collection, costing the Government over £350 million in interest charges on money borrowed to cover delayed and lost tax revenue. Industrial action was also taken at GCHQ, the installation at the heart of Britain's signals intelligence, which led to our decision in January 1984 to ban trade unions there.

On 27 January the Energy Secretary, David Howell, told me about the closure plans. The following afternoon Sir Derek Ezra, NCB Chairman, visited Downing Street and briefed me in person. I agreed with him that with coal stocks piling up and the recession continuing there was no alternative to speeding up the closure of uneconomic pits. I had long regretted that past governments had made such an enormous commitment to coal: if we had spent more on nuclear power, as the French had done, our electricity would have been cheaper – and, indeed, our supplies more secure.

As in the cases of BSC and BL, it was the management which had to implement the agreed approach and, inevitably, the Government found itself dragged into a crisis we had neither sought nor predicted. The press was soon full of NCB plans to close 50 pits and a bitter conflict was predicted. The National Union of Mineworkers (NUM) was pledged to fight closures and although Joe Gormley, its President, was a moderate, the powerful left-wing faction of the union was bound to exploit the situation and it was well known that Arthur Scargill, the hard-left leader, was likely to succeed Mr Gormley as President in the near future.

At a meeting with the NUM on 11 February the NCB Board resisted pressure to publish a list of pits which it was proposing to close and denied the figure of 50. However, the Board failed to mention the idea of improved redundancy terms, which was already being discussed by the Government, and instead undertook to join the NUM in an approach to us seeking a lower level of coal imports, the maintenance of a high level of public investment and subsidies comparable to those allegedly being paid by other governments to coal industries abroad. Far from acting as management might be expected to do, the NCB Board was behaving as if it entirely shared the interests of the union representing its employees. The situation quickly deteriorated further. I was lucky to have a private, independent and knowledgeable source of advice in my press secretary, Bernard Ingham who, before working for me in Downing Street, had spent some years in the Department of Energy and was convinced from the start that the department was far too complacent about the threat posed by a strike.

On Monday 16 February I had a meeting with David Howell and others. Their tone had entirely changed. The department had suddenly been forced to look over the abyss and had recoiled. The objective had now become to avoid an all-out national strike at the minimum cost in concessions. David Howell would have to agree to a tripartite meeting with the NUM and the NCB to achieve this. The tone of the NCB Chairman had also changed in short order. I was appalled to find that we had inadvertently entered into a battle which we could not win. There had been no forward thinking in the Department of Energy about what would happen in the case of a strike. The coal stocks piled at the pit heads were largely irrelevant to the question of whether the country could endure a strike: it was the stocks at the power stations which were important, and these were simply not sufficient. I had by now even less confidence in the NCB management. It became very clear that all we could do was to cut our losses and live to fight another day, when – with adequate preparation – we might be in a position to win. When my attitude became clear one official could not prevent himself expressing disappointment and surprise. My reply was simple: there is no point in embarking on a battle unless you are reasonably confident you can win. Defeat in a coal strike would have been disastrous.

The tripartite meeting was due to take place on 23 February. In the interim, we were hoping that the NCB would be able to make a more effective presentation of their case and to prevent the NUM continuing to make all the running. Indeed, we were advised that unless we held the tripartite meeting earlier than planned the NUM Executive might vote for a strike ballot. On the morning of 18 February I met hurriedly with David Howell to agree on the concessions which would have to be offered to stave off a strike. There was still considerable confusion as to what the facts really were. Whereas the NCB had been reported to be seeking 50 or 60 pit closures, it now appeared that they were talking about 23. But the tripartite meeting achieved its immediate objective: the strike was averted. The Government undertook to reduce imports of coal to the irreducible minimum, with David Howell indicating that we were prepared to discuss the financial implications with an open mind. Sir Derek Ezra said that in the light of this undertaking to review the financial constraints under which the NCB was operating, the Board would withdraw its closure proposals and re-examine the position in consultation with the unions.

The following day David Howell made a statement to the Commons to explain the outcome of the meeting. The press reaction was that the miners had won a major victory at the expense of the Government, but that we had probably been right to surrender. This was not, however, the end of our difficulties. We agreed to improve the redundancy terms for coal miners, to finance a scheme for conversion from oil to coal in industry and to look again at NCB finances. As is always the case once corporatism takes a grip, it became extremely difficult to bring the tripartite discussions to an end without provoking a crisis and equally difficult to ensure that the whole question of government finance for the NCB did not come onto the agenda. It had already emerged at the tripartite meeting on 25 February that the NCB was in far deeper financial trouble than we had known. They were likely to overrun their external financing limit (EFL), which had already been set at some £800 million, by between £450 and £500 million and were expecting to make a loss of £350 million. We would need to challenge these figures and examine them in detail, but we could not do this – as the NCB Board undoubtedly realized – when the NUM knew almost as much about the NCB's financial position as we did. Therefore, our aim must be to draw a ring fence around the coal industry by arguing that coal was a special case rather than a precedent. We must seek to avoid any commitment for the years beyond 1981–2. Above all, we must prepare contingency plans in case the NUM sought a confrontation in the next pay round.

We confirmed these decisions at a meeting of ministers on 5 March. David Howell skilfully handled the next tripartite meeting on 11 March, at which it was understood that we would not need another tripartite meeting until the NCB's financial position had been resolved. Meanwhile, he had been instructed to prepare a memorandum on contingency plans and circulate it by Easter.

Having managed to ease the Government out of an impossible position – at what I knew to be a high political cost – I concentrated attention on limiting the financial consequences of our retreat and preparing the ground so that we would never be put in such an awful situation again. David Howell had been shaken by what had happened. He feared a repetition of the events of January. There was much argument between him and the Treasury about the new EFL for the NCB and the level of investment we ought to finance. We had to agree to an EFL of well over £1 billion. Similarly, the threat of strike action constrained what we could do immediately to increase our capacity to endure a future strike. It was clear that coal stocks at the power stations must be increased, but it was impossible to take this action without its becoming known, and the faster stocks were transferred the more visible it would be. Jim Prior advised that we should not even discuss the matter with the industries involved, on the ground that it would be provocative to do so. The Department of Energy was very slow in giving effect to the decision that 4–5 million tons should be moved by the time that the NUM pay negotiations took place in the autumn. We were told that the Central Electricity Generating Board (CEGB) would probably have to acquire extra land if higher stocks than this were to be built up. I held a meeting on 19 June to review the position. It seemed to me that the risks of moving coal stocks had been exaggerated. After all, stocks at the pits had increased from 13 million to 22 million tons over the past 12 months and it was natural that there should be some extra movement.

The real question in my mind was whether – even if we could substantially increase the rate of movement of coal to the power stations – we would in practice be able to resist a strike that winter. It was evident from the NUM Conference which took place in Jersey in July that the left wing of the union had become obsessed with the idea of taking on the Government and that Arthur Scargill, by this stage certain of the presidency, would make this his policy. Willie Whitelaw, as Home Secretary the minister in overall charge of civil contingency planning, had overseen a study of how to withstand a coal strike that winter. He sent me a report on 22 July, which concluded that a strike this year probably could not be withstood for more than 13–14 weeks. The calculations took account of the transfer of coal stocks which we had put in hand. In theory, endurance could be increased by power cuts or the use of troops to move coal to the power stations. But either option was fraught with difficulty. There would be huge political pressure to give in to a strike. The union might see what was up if we set about increasing oil stocks for power stations. In August I reluctantly concluded that no such action should be taken in advance of that year's NUM pay settlement. We would have to rely on a judicious mixture of flexibility and bluff until the Government was in a position to face down the challenge posed to the economy, and indeed potentially to the rule of law, by the combined force of monopoly and union power in the coal industry.

THE URBAN RIOTS OF 1981

Over the weekend of 10–12 April, riots broke out in Brixton, South London. Shops were looted, vehicles destroyed, and 149 police officers and 58 members of the public were injured. Two hundred and fifteen people were arrested. There were frightening scenes, reminiscent of riots in the United States during the 1960s and '70s. I accepted Willie Whitelaw's suggestion that Lord Scarman, the distinguished Law Lord, should undertake an enquiry into the causes of what had happened and make recommendations.

There was a lull; then on Friday 3 July a battle in Southall between white skinheads and Asian youths erupted into a riot in which the police quickly became the main victims, attacked with petrol bombs, bricks and anything else to hand. The mob even turned on firemen and ambulancemen. Over the weekend, Toxteth in Liverpool was also the scene of violence: once again there were outbreaks of arson, looting and savage attacks on the police. The Merseyside police reacted vigorously and dispersed the mob with CS gas.

On 8 and 9 July it was the turn of Moss Side in Manchester to experience two days of serious disorder. The police presence was initially kept deliberately low, in the hope that 'community leaders' could calm matters down. This they singularly failed to do and so the police had to move into the area in strength. Willie Whitelaw told me after his visits to Manchester and Liverpool that the Moss Side riots had taken the form of looting and hooliganism rather than direct confrontation with the police. In Liverpool, as I was to learn, racial tension and bitter hostility to the police – in my view encouraged by left-wing extremists – were more important.

The riots were, of course, a godsend to the Labour Opposition and the Government's critics in general. Here was the long-awaited evidence that our economic policy was causing social breakdown and violence. In the Commons and elsewhere I found myself countering the argument that the riots had been caused by unemployment. Behind their hands, some Conservatives echoed this criticism, complaining that the social fabric was being torn apart by the doctrinaire monetarism we had espoused. This rather overlooked the fact that riots, football hooliganism and crime generally had been on the increase since the 1960s, most of that time under the very economic policies that our critics were urging us to adopt. A third explanation – that racial minorities were reacting to police brutality and racial discrimination – we took more seriously. Indeed, it was for this reason that we had invited Lord Scarman to investigate and report on the causes of the riots immediately after the Brixton riots in April. Following his report we introduced a statutory framework for consultation between the police and local authorities, tightened the rules on stopping and searching suspects, and brought in other measures relating to police recruitment, training and discipline.

Whatever Lord Scarman might recommend, however – and whatever Michael Heseltine might achieve later by skilful public relations when he had begun to investigate the problems of Merseyside – the immediate requirement was that law and order should be restored. I told Willie on Saturday 11 July that I intended to go to Scotland Yard and wished to be shown how they handled the difficulties on the ground.

After a briefing at Scotland Yard I was taken round Brixton. At

Brixton Police Station I went into the canteen to thank the staff there – as I had thanked the police officers themselves – for all that they were doing. I also talked with the West Indian ladies in the canteen. They had gone into work throughout the disturbances, determined that the police should be supported with proper canteen facilities whenever they needed them at any hour of the day or night. They were clearly as disgusted as I was with those who were causing the trouble.

Later I returned to Scotland Yard where I had a long discussion with the Commissioner of the Metropolitan Police, Sir David McNee, his Deputy and Assistant. They had a number of worries: they told me that they wanted to see sentences administered quickly on the offenders – something which long delays at the Crown Courts often prevented; they were concerned that their powers of arrest were insufficient; and above all, they needed proper riot equipment, as a matter of urgency. I promised them every support. It was something of a shock to contemplate the kind of equipment the British police now required, which included a greater variety of riot shields, more vehicles, longer truncheons, and sufficient stocks of rubber bullets and water cannon. They had already received vital protective helmets from the MoD, but these had had to be altered because the visors provided inadequate protection against burning petrol. Afterwards I stressed to Willie the urgency of meeting these requirements.

On Monday 13 July I made a similar visit to Liverpool. Driving through Toxteth, the scene of the disturbances, I observed that for all that was said about deprivation, the housing there was by no means the worst in the city. I had been told that some of the young people involved got into trouble through boredom and not having enough to do. But you had only to look at the grounds around those houses with the grass untended, some of it almost waist high, and the litter, to see that this was a false analysis. They had plenty of constructive things to do if they wanted. Instead, I asked myself how people could live in such circumstances without trying to clear up the mess and improve their surroundings. What was clearly lacking was a sense of pride and personal responsibility – something which the state can easily remove but almost never give back.

The first people I talked to in Liverpool were the police, whose comments and requirements for equipment were similar to those in London. I also met councillors at Liverpool City Hall and then talked to a group of community leaders and young people. I was appalled by the latter's hostility to the Chief Constable and the police. But I listened carefully to what they had to say. There were two people with them who appeared to be social workers, and who began by trying to speak on their behalf. But these young people did not need anyone to speak for them: they were articulate and talked about their problems with great sincerity. The press were rather confused when, contrary to what they had been expecting, the youngsters told them that I had indeed listened. But I did more than listen: I had something to say myself. I reminded them that resources had been poured into Liverpool. I told them that I was very concerned by what they had said about the police and that while the colour of a person's skin did not matter to me at all, crime did. I urged them not to resort to violence or to try to live in separate communities from the rest of us. Before I returned to London I also talked to the Catholic Archbishop and the Anglican Bishop of Liverpool, who had jointly won national attention as great advocates for their city.

The whole visit left me in no doubt as I drove back that evening that we faced immense problems in areas like Toxteth and Brixton. People had to find once again a sense of respect for the law, for the neighbourhood, and indeed for themselves. Despite our implementation of most of Scarman's recommendations and the inner city initiatives we were to take, none of the conventional remedies relying on state action and public spending was likely to prove effective. The causes went much deeper; so must the cures.

The rioters were invariably young men, whose high animal spirits, usually kept in check by a whole range of social constraints, had on these occasions been unleashed to wreak havoc. What had become of the constraints? A sense of community – including the watchful disapproval of neighbours – is the strongest such barrier. But this sense had been lost in the inner cities for a variety of reasons. Often those neighbourhoods were the artificial creation of local authorities which had uprooted people from genuine communities and decanted them into badly designed and ill-maintained estates where they did not know their new neighbours. Some of these new 'neighbourhoods', because of large-scale immigration, were ethnically mixed; on top of the tensions which might initially arise in any event, even immigrant families with a very strong sense of traditional values found those values undermined in their own children by messages from the surrounding culture. In particular, welfare arrangements encouraged dependency and discouraged a sense of responsibility, and television undermined common moral values that would once have united working-class communities. The results were a steadily increasing rise in crime (among young men) and illegitimacy (among young women).

All that was needed for these to flower into full-scale rioting was the decline of authority and the consequent feeling among potential rioters that they could probably get away with mayhem. Authority of all kinds – in the home, the school, the churches and the state – had been in decline for most of the post-war years. Hence the rise in football hooliganism, race riots and delinquency over that period. There had even been one or two cases when the nervous indecision of the police – for instance in withdrawing officers from riots until reinforcements arrived – had both encouraged the rioters and undermined the confidence of law-abiding members of the community. What perhaps aggravated the 1981 riots into a virtual saturnalia, however, was the impression given by television that, for all these reasons, rioters could enjoy a fiesta of crime, looting and rioting in the guise of social protest. They had been absolved in advance. These are precisely the circumstances in which young men riot, and riot again – and they have nothing whatever to do with £M3.

Once we had solved the problem of the British economy, however, we would need to turn to those deeper and more intractable problems. I did so in my second and third terms with the set of policies for housing, education, local authorities and social security that my advisers, over my objections, wanted to call 'Social Thatcherism'. But we had only begun to make an impact on these by the time I left office.

MORE CABINET DISSENT AND THE SEPTEMBER 1981 RESHUFFLE

It was the 1981 budget, however, which throughout the summer continued to agitate the Cabinet. Some ministers were long-standing in their dissent. Others on whose support I had counted in the past began to fall away. The irony was that at the very time the opposition to the strategy was greatest, the trough of the recession had already been reached. Whereas in 1980 the dissenters in the Cabinet had refused to face up to the true seriousness of the economic situation and so had insisted on higher government spending than we could afford, in 1981 they made the opposite mistake by exaggerating the bleakness of the economic outlook and calling for even higher spending in a bid to reflate the economy out of recession. Surely there is something logically suspect about a solution which is always correct whatever the problem.

One of the myths perpetuated by the media at this time was that

Treasury ministers and I were obsessively secretive about economic policy, seeking always to avoid debate in Cabinet. In view of past leaks that might indeed have been an understandable approach, but it was never one we adopted. Geoffrey Howe was anxious to have three or four full economic discussions in Cabinet every year, in the belief that it would help us to win greater support for the policy; I doubted whether discussions of this sort would achieve a meeting of minds, but I went along with Geoffrey's suggestion as long as it generated practical results, and in particular greater realism about public expenditure.

At the Cabinet in mid-June there was a general discussion of the economy lasting two hours, based on several Treasury papers dealing with various elements in the debate. The main paper was a full survey of recent economic developments and the economic prospect. It showed that the public finances had been placed on a sounder basis: we had cut borrowing and repaid some international debt. Interest rates at 12 per cent in the UK were now substantially below those in the US and France, and lower than those of the major industrialized countries generally. Industrial production had ceased to fall, though unemployment – a lagging indicator, as always – was still rising. The tax burden was up; but we were at least financing that spending in a sound way – and honest money was essential to sustainable recovery.

Other ministers, however, saw little that was positive in this picture. They believed that unemployment over three million – the figure now predicted – was politically unacceptable and that higher government spending should be used to accelerate and strengthen economic recovery. My own analysis was entirely different: the way to achieve recovery was to ensure that a smaller proportion of the nation's income went to government, freeing resources for the private sector where the majority of people worked.

All these arguments came to a head at the Cabinet discussion on Thursday 23 July. I had more than an inkling of what was coming. Indeed before I went down to the Cabinet Room that morning, I had said to Denis that we had not come this far to go back now. I would not stay as Prime Minister unless we saw the strategy through. Spending ministers had submitted bids for extra expenditure of more than £6.5 billion, of which some £2.5 billion was demanded for the nationalized industries. But in view of past overspending and of the tax increases which had taken place already, the Treasury urged reduced public spending for 1982–3, below the totals derived from the March white paper. The result was one of the bitterest arguments on the economy, or any subject, that I can ever recall taking place at Cabinet during my premiership. The 'wets', of course, argued their case with redoubled vigour, strengthened by the lack of any evidence that our policies had turned things round. Some argued for extra public spending and borrowing as a better route to recovery than tax cuts. There was talk of a pay freeze. Even those, like John Nott, who had been known for their views on sound finance, attacked Geoffrey Howe's proposals as unnecessarily harsh. All at once the whole strategy was at issue. It was as if tempers suddenly broke. I too became extremely angry. I had thought that we could rely on these people when the crunch came. I just was not interested in this kind of creative accounting that enabled fair-weather monetarists to justify an about-turn. Others, though, were as loyal as ever, notably Willie, Keith and, of course, Geoffrey himself who was a tower of strength at this time. And indeed it was their loyalty that saw us through.

I had said at the beginning of the government 'give me six strong men and true, and I will get through.' Very rarely did I have as many as six. So I responded vigorously in defence of the Chancellor. I was prepared to have a further paper on the issue of tax cuts versus public spending. But I warned of the effects on international confidence of public expenditure increases or any departure from the MTFS. I was determined that the strategy should continue. But when I closed the meeting I knew that there were too many in Cabinet who did not share that view. Moreover, after what had been said it would be difficult for this group of ministers to act as a team again.

Much of this bitter disagreement found its way into the press – and not simply in reports of what had been said in Cabinet derived from nonattributable ministerial comments, but also in the form of scarcely coded public speeches and statements. There were particularly embarrassing comments from Francis Pym and Peter Thorneycroft, who between them were meant to be responsible for the public presentation of our policies. At Francis's suggestion I had authorized the recreation of the 'Liaison Committee', at which ministers and Central Office were supposed to work together to achieve a coherent message. In August it became clear that these arrangements were actually being used to undermine the strategy.

Geoffrey Howe had said in the House of Commons that the CBI's latest Industrial Trends Survey provided evidence that we were now at the end of the recession – a remark which may have been slightly imprudent, but which was strictly true. The following weekend Francis Pym in the course of a lengthy speech observed: 'there are few signs yet of when an upturn will occur. And that recovery when it comes in due course may be slower and less pronounced than in the past.'

This forecast would have been bold even from an economist; coming from Francis it verged on the visionary. For good measure he added that 'in our industrial policy we must work as partners with industry and with the trade unions to identify the key sectors of the economy and the most promising export markets' – the kind of neo-corporatist incantation which signified total rejection of the economic strategy. Even Peter Thorneycroft, who had been a superb chairman of the Party in Opposition, joined the 'wet' chorus, describing himself as suffering from 'rising damp' and saying that 'there [was] no great sign of [the economy] picking up.' Given that these comments came from the two men in charge of presenting government policy, they were extremely damaging and easily seen (in that inevitable metaphor) as 'the tip of the iceberg'.

Trade union reform was another subject of Cabinet disagreement. We had issued a green paper on trade union immunities on which comments were to be received by the end of June 1981. When they came in, these showed a desire among businessmen for further radical action to bring trade unions fully under the rule of law. But Jim Prior and I disagreed about what should be done. I wanted further action to restrict trade union immunities, which would make union funds liable to court action. Jim's proposals would not have achieved this. His analysis was, indeed, fundamentally different from mine. In his reading, history showed that the unions could defeat any legislation if they wanted to. I believed that history showed nothing of the sort, but rather that governments in the past had failed the nation through lack of nerve – drawing back when the battle was nearly won. I was also convinced that on the issue of union reform there was a great reserve of public support on which we could draw. Indeed, as I told Jim, I thought that there was a real risk that people would consider that we had done very little to tackle trade union power.

The differences between Cabinet ministers over the economic strategy – and between myself and Jim Prior over trade union reform – were not just ones of emphasis but of fundamentals. If the goals I had set out in Opposition were to be achieved they must be reaffirmed and fought for by a new Cabinet. So it was quite clear to me that a major reshuffle was needed if our economic policy were to continue, and perhaps if I were to remain Prime Minister.

I preferred to have a Cabinet reshuffle during the recess if possible, so that ministers could get used to their departments before being questioned in the House. I also believed that as matters usually got fairly difficult at the end of July, it was better for all of us to have a holiday before decisions were taken. It was not, therefore, until September that I discussed the details with my closest advisers. Willie Whitelaw, Michael Jopling (the Chief Whip) and Ian Gow came over to Chequers on the weekend of 12–13 September. For part of the time Peter Carrington and Cecil Parkinson joined us. The reshuffle itself took place on the Monday.

I always saw first those who were being asked to leave the Cabinet. I began with Ian Gilmour and told him of my decision. He was – I can find no other word for it – huffy. He left Downing Street and denounced government policy to the television cameras as 'steering full speed ahead for the rocks' – altogether a flawless imitation of a man who has resigned on principle. Christopher Soames was equally angry – but in a grander way. I got the distinct impression that he felt the natural order of things was being violated and that he was, in effect, being dismissed by his housemaid. Mark Carlisle, who had not been a very effective Education Secretary and leaned to the left, also left the Cabinet – but he did so with courtesy and good humour. Jim Prior was obviously shocked to be moved from Employment where he had come to consider himself all but indispensable. The press had been full of his threats to resign from the Government altogether if he were asked to leave his present position. I wanted this post for the formidable Norman Tebbit, and Jim could not intimidate me by threatening himself. So I called his bluff, and offered him the post of Northern Ireland Secretary. He asked for time to consider, and after some agonizing and some telephoning he accepted my offer and became Secretary of State for Northern Ireland in place of the debonair Humphrey Atkins, who succeeded Ian Gilmour as the main Foreign Office minister in the Commons.

I moved David Howell from Energy to Transport. It gave me great pleasure to promote the immensely talented Nigel Lawson, the intellectual author of the MTFS, into the Cabinet to take his place. Nigel turned out to be a highly successful Secretary of State for Energy, vigorously promoting competition, taking a real grip on his department and building up coal stocks for the inevitable struggle with the miners.

Keith Joseph had told me that he wished to move from Industry. With his belief that there was an anti-enterprise culture which had harmed Britain's economic performance over the years, it was natural that Keith should now wish to go to Education where that culture had taken deep roots. Accordingly, I sent Keith to my old department to replace Mark Carlisle. Norman Fowler returned to take up Health and Social Security, the portfolio he had held in Opposition, replacing Patrick Jenkin who took over at Industry from Keith. Janet Young, a friend for many years who had first become involved in politics as leader of Oxford City Council, became Leader of the House of Lords, the first woman to hold the post, taking over Christopher Soames's responsibility for the civil service.

Perhaps the most important change was the promotion of Norman Tebbit to replace Jim Prior at Employment. Norman had had experience of dealing with industrial relations as a trade unionist himself. He had been an official of the British Airline Pilots' Association and had no illusions about the vicious world of hard-left trade unionism, nor, by contrast, any doubt about the fundamental decency of most trade union members. As a true believer in the kind of approach Keith Joseph and I stood for, Norman understood how trade union reform fitted into our overall strategy. Norman was also one of the Party's most effective performers in Parliament and on a public platform. The fact that the Left howled disapproval confirmed that he was just the right man for the job. He was someone they feared.

I had already agreed with Peter Thorneycroft that he should cease to be Party Chairman. I had been unhappy about some of Peter's actions in recent months. But I would never forget how much he did to help win the 1979 election. He was one of an older school of political leaders – a man of force and character – and remained a friend. I appointed Cecil Parkinson to succeed him – dynamic, full of common sense, a good accountant, an excellent presenter and, no less important, on my wing of the Party.

The whole nature of the Cabinet changed as a result of these changes. After the new Cabinet's first meeting I remarked to David Wolfson and John Hoskyns what a difference it made to have most of the people in it on my side. This did not mean that we would always agree, or that there would not be the regular arguments about public spending. There would always be some dissent and Jim Prior at his own request remained a member of 'E' committee, the economic committee of the Cabinet. But it would be a number of years before there arose an issue which fundamentally divided me from the majority of my Cabinet, and by then Britain's economic recovery, so much a matter of controversy in 1981, had been accepted – perhaps all too easily accepted – as a fact of life.

The day after the reshuffle, *The Times* leader entitled *Prima Inter Pares*, summed up reaction to the changes I had made:

> the final impression . . . left by this reshuffle is the indelible stamp and style of the Prime Minister herself. She has reasserted her political dominance and restated her faith in her own policies. She has rewarded those who do, and punished some of those

who do not share that faith. If she succeeds – and by success we mean regenerating the British economy and winning the next election for the Conservative Party – it will be a remarkable personal triumph. If she fails, the fault will be laid at her door, though the damage and the casualties will spread wide through the political and economic landscape.

I could accept that.

THE 1981 CONSERVATIVE PARTY CONFERENCE

The 'wets' had been defeated, but they did not yet fully realize it, and decided to make a last assault at the 1981 Party Conference in Blackpool that October.

The circumstances on the eve of the conference were grim. Inflation, which had fallen sharply since 1980, remained stubbornly at between 11 and 12 per cent. Largely as a result of the US budget deficit, interest rates had been increased by 2 per cent in mid-September, temporarily wiping out the reduction made possible at such cost by the budget in March. Then, shortly after I arrived at Melbourne for the Commonwealth Conference on 30 September, I received a telephone call to say that we would have to make a second increase of 2 per cent. So interest rates now stood at an alarming 16 per cent.

Above all, unemployment continued its inexorable rise: it would reach the headline figure of three million in January 1982, but already in the autumn of 1981 it seemed almost inevitable that this would happen. Most people were unpersuaded, therefore, that recession was coming to an end and it was too soon for the new sense of direction in Cabinet – which I knew that the reshuffle would bring – to have had an effect on public opinion.

We were also in political difficulties for another reason. The weakness of the Labour Party, which had initially worked in our favour, had allowed the newly formed SDP to leap into political contention. In October the Liberals and SDP were standing at 40 per cent in the opinion polls: by the end of the year the figure was over 50 per cent. (At the Crosby by-election in the last week of November Shirley Williams was able to overturn a 19,000 Conservative majority to get back into the Commons.) On the eve of our Party Conference I was being described in the press as 'the most unpopular prime minister since polls began'.

Of course, the statistics were misleading at this point. Interest rates would have been higher still had we not taken the action we did in the budget. We were able to begin reducing rates again within weeks. And demographic factors were as important as the recession in explaining the rise of unemployment. The low birth rates during the First World War meant that fewer people were retiring in the early 1980s than in the early 1970s. At the same time the number of young people entering the labour market reached record levels as a result of the 1960s 'baby boom'. Between 1979 and 1981 the economy had to provide an extra 83,000 jobs a year just to stop unemployment rising.

But that was not how it seemed at the time – and the 'wets' determined to exploit our apparent difficulties to the full at Blackpool. I witnessed what seemed to be a concerted attempt to swing the Party against the Government's policies both in the Conference Hall and at the fringe meetings outside. In a speech to the Selsdon Group the critics were brilliantly answered by Nigel Lawson. Nigel pointed out that it was no argument for them to take refuge in political generalities:

> You cannot fight the war against inflation successfully unless you have economic policies that make sense. There is no point in deluding yourself that somehow politics can trump all that . . . What we are being offered [by the strategy's critics] is little more than cold feet dressed up as high principle.

In the conference economic debate no less a figure than Ted Heath spearheaded the attack. He argued that there were alternative policies available but that we just refused to adopt them. The debate was well mannered in form, well versed in content and passionate in feeling. Both sides delivered serious economic analyses at a high level – and the stakes themselves were very high. A rebuff for the platform would have emboldened back-bench 'wets' to step up their attack when Parliament resumed, with unpredictable consequences; a rebuff for the critics, which is what they received, would strengthen our moral authority. In answer to Ted Heath, Geoffrey Howe, who summed up our case with a cool, measured and persuasive speech, reminded the conference of Ted's own words in his introduction to the 1970 Conservative manifesto:

> Nothing has done Britain more harm in the world than the endless backing and filling which we have seen in recent years. Once a policy has been established, the prime minister and his colleagues should have the courage to stick with it.

'I agree with every single word of that,' said Geoffrey. His speech won over some of the doubters and ensured that we had a comfortable win. Nevertheless, in my own speech later I felt the need to fasten down our victory by taking the arguments of Ted Heath and others head on:

> Today's unemployment is partly due to the sharp increase in oil prices; it absorbed money that might otherwise have gone to increased investment or to buy in the things which British factories produce. But that is not all. Too much of our present unemployment is due to enormous past wage increases unmatched by higher output, to union restrictive practices, to overmanning, to strikes, to indifferent management, and to the basic belief that, come what may, the government would always step in to bail out companies in difficulty. No policy can succeed that shirks those basic issues.

Even though the 'wets' would continue to be sceptics for another six months, our policy had already begun to succeed. The early signs of recovery in the summer of 1981 were confirmed by statistics in the following quarter, which marked the start of a long period of sustained economic growth. Political recovery followed in the wake of these early signs of improvement, with better poll figures in the spring of 1982. We were about to find ourselves in the Falklands War, but we had already won the second Battle of Britain.

CHAPTER VI

The West and the Rest

The early reassertion of western – and British – influence in international affairs in 1981–1982

We were not to know it at the time, but 1981 was the last year of the West's retreat before the axis of convenience between the Soviet Union and the Third World. The year began with Iran's release of US hostages in a manner calculated to humiliate President Carter and ended with the crushing, albeit temporarily, of Solidarity in Poland. The post-Vietnam drift of international politics, with the Soviet Union pushing further into the Third World with the help of Cuban surrogates, and the United States reacting with a nervous defensiveness, had settled into an apparently fixed pattern. Several consequences flowed from that. The Soviet Union was increasingly arrogant; the Third World was increasingly aggressive in its demands for international redistribution of wealth; the West was increasingly apt to quarrel with itself, and to cut special deals with bodies like OPEC; and our friends in Third World countries, seeing the fate of the Shah, were increasingly inclined to hedge their bets. Such countervailing trends as had been set in motion – in particular, the 1979 decision to deploy Cruise and Pershing in Europe – had not yet been given concrete effect or persuaded people that the tide had turned. In fact it had just begun to do so.

EARLY TALKS WITH PRESIDENT REAGAN

The election of Ronald Reagan as President of the United States in November 1980 was as much of a watershed in American affairs as my own election victory in May 1979 was in those of the United Kingdom, and, of course, a greater one in world politics. As the years went by, the British example steadily influenced other countries in different continents, particularly in economic policy. But Ronald Reagan's election was of immediate and fundamental importance, because it demonstrated that the United States, the greatest force for liberty that the world has known, was about to reassert a self-confident leadership in world affairs. I never had any doubt of the importance of this change and from the first I regarded it as my duty to do everything I could to reinforce and further President Reagan's bold strategy to win the Cold War which the West had been slowly but surely losing.

I heard the news of the American election result in the early hours of Wednesday 5 November and quickly sent my warmest congratulations, inviting the President-elect to visit Britain soon. I had met Governor Reagan twice before when I was Leader of the Opposition. I had been immediately struck by his warmth, charm and complete lack of affectation – qualities which never altered in the years of leadership which lay ahead. Above all, I knew that I was talking to someone who instinctively felt and thought as I did; not just about policies but about a philosophy of government, a view of human nature, all the high ideals and values which lie – or ought to lie – beneath any politician's ambition to lead his country.

It was easy for lesser men to underrate Ronald Reagan, as many of his opponents had done in the past. His style of work and decision-making was apparently detached and broad-brush – very different from my own. This was in part the result of our two very different systems of government rather than differences of temperament. He laid down clear general directions for his Administration, and expected his subordinates to carry them out at the level of detail. These objectives were the recovery of the American economy through tax cuts, the revival of American power by means of a defence build-up, and the reassertion of American self-confidence. Ronald Reagan succeeded in attaining these objectives because he not only advocated them; in a sense, he embodied them. He was a buoyant, self-confident, good-natured American who had risen from poverty to the White House – the American dream in action – and who was not shy about using American power or exercising American leadership in the Atlantic alliance. In addition to inspiring the American people, he went on later to inspire the people behind the Iron Curtain by speaking honest words about the evil empire that oppressed them.

At this point, however, the policies of military, economic and technological competition with the Soviet Union were only beginning to be put in place; and President Reagan still had to face a largely sceptical audience at home and particularly among his allies, including most of my colleagues in the Government. I was perhaps his principal cheerleader in NATO.

So I was soon delighted to learn that the new president wished me to be the first foreign head of government to visit the United States after he took office. At 3.45 on the afternoon of Wednesday 25 February the RAF VC10 on which I travelled on such occasions took off for Washington. Peter Carrington was with me. He did not altogether share my view of the President's policies and was intent on pursuing lines which I knew would in practice be quite fruitless, given the President's unshakeable commitment to a limited number of positions. The US was already meeting opposition from its allies on a number of issues such as arms control, its support for the military government in El Salvador, and increasingly the size of the US deficit. We feared that the new Administration's plans for tax cuts might widen the deficit – though at this stage we were still hopeful that the President would succeed in achieving the large expenditure cuts he had put before Congress. With so many important things to discuss, I could see no point in raising the issue of Namibia which Peter Carrington wanted to do. I knew that the Americans would not press the South Africans to withdraw from Namibia unless the 20,000 or so Cubans also withdrew from neighbouring Angola. What is more, I privately thought that they were fully justified in asserting this linkage. In any case, there is one principle of diplomacy which diplomats ought to recognize more often: there is no point in engaging in conflict with a friend when you are not going to win and the cost of losing may be the end of the friendship.

I spent the morning of my first day in Washington in meetings with the President – first tête-à-tête, then with the US Secretary of State, Alexander Haig, and Peter Carrington present, and finally with members of the US Cabinet. Two events which occurred on the eve of our discussions had a large impact on them.

First, the Assistant Secretary for European Affairs, Lawrence Eagleburger, had come to Britain and other European capitals to show us a dossier of evidence substantiating the US claim that arms from Cuba, acting as a surrogate for the Soviet Union, were pouring into El Salvador to support the revolution against the pro-western, if undoubtedly unsavoury, government there. There was still some difference of view about whether the threat was as serious as the US claimed. But the evidence which we now saw made it easier to express support for the American objectives in the region and to resist the pressure from other lobbies. A statement was issued by the Foreign Office just before I left for America to this effect. President Reagan explained to me his determination to pursue a new policy to resist communist subversion via Cuba, which also involved closer US relations with what it saw as a vulnerable and important neighbour, Mexico. I understood all this and agreed with it: but I warned of the danger of losing the propaganda war on El Salvador – the reporting was very one-sided.

The second and much more important development was a speech by President Brezhnev, proposing an international summit and offering a moratorium on theatre nuclear forces (TNF) in Europe. Discussion about how the new Administration should respond dominated the hyperactive Washington media world. I had publicly expressed caution both about the prospect of an early summit meeting and about the Russian TNF proposals, which would have left them with overwhelming superiority since they had deployed and we had not. President Reagan turned out to be of the same mind. Both of us were well aware of Soviet tactics and of the likelihood that this was only part of their attempt to disorientate and divide their western opponents. This was the latest phase in a Soviet propaganda battle in which they proposed no further deployment of nuclear weapons just when they had completed stationing their own modernized weapon systems. This issue was to dominate alliance politics for the next six years.

When I arrived in Washington I was the centre of attention not just because of my closeness to the new president but for another less flattering reason. As I left for America, US readers were learning from a long article in *Time* entitled 'Embattled but Unbowed' that my Government was beset with difficulties. The US press and commentators suggested that given the similarity of economic approach of the British and US Governments, the economic problems we were now facing – above all high and rising unemployment – would soon be faced in the US too. This in turn prompted some members of the Administration and others close to it – but never for a moment the President himself – to explain that the alleged failures of the 'Thatcher experiment' stemmed from our failure to be sufficiently radical. Indeed, while I was in Washington Treasury Secretary Donald Regan spoke on similar lines to Congress before slipping away to join a lunch at which I was the main guest; this predictably received plenty of press coverage in Britain. I took every occasion to explain the facts of the case both to the press and to the Senators and Congressmen whom I met. Unlike the US, Britain had to cope with the poisonous legacy of socialism – nationalization, trade union power, a deeply rooted anti-enterprise culture. Labour's prices and incomes policy, combined with lax monetary policies, had greatly increased the inevitable difficulty of transition, as the public sector pay explosion forced up state spending. At one meeting, Senator Jesse Helms said that some of the US media were playing a requiem for my Government. I was able to reassure him that news of a requiem for my policies was premature. There was always a period during an illness when the medicine was more unpleasant than the disease, but you should not stop taking the medicine. I said that I felt there was a deep recognition among the British people that my policies were right.

After another short talk over coffee with the President, at which we were joined by Nancy and Denis, my party left Washington for New York. In the afternoon I had talks with Dr Waldheim, the UN Secretary-General, and then that evening spoke to an audience on the subject of 'the Defence of Freedom'. In my speech I summed up my feelings of cautious optimism about the decade now opening up before us:

> We have long known that the 1980s will be a difficult and dangerous decade. There will be crises and hardships. But I believe the tide is beginning to turn in our favour. The developing world is recognizing the realities of Soviet ambitions and Soviet life. There is a new determination in the western alliance. There is new leadership in America, which gives confidence and hope to all in the free world.

VISITS TO INDIA AND THE GULF

On 20 May 1980 I had held a meeting to consider a subject which the Russian invasion of Afghanistan had belatedly placed near the top of the western international agenda – how to prevent Soviet expansion in the developing world. With a revivified United States, the possibilities had now been transformed. But I never doubted that, over and above the role of ally and friend to the United States, there was much that Britain could achieve and that no one else could. The Left would have it that the legacy of the British empire was one of bitterness and impoverishment in the former colonies: this was a grossly distorted and inaccurate view. Nor for the most part did those with whom I dealt in these countries see Britain in that light. Sweep away some of the rhetoric and with the exception of certain issues, like relations with South Africa, you will find that no country is as trusted in every continent as Britain. In 1981 I began to make more systematic use of these relationships to promote the interests of Britain and the wider objectives of the West.

On Wednesday 15 April 1981 I began a visit to India. I had visited the country twice and met Mrs Indira Gandhi, India's Prime Minister, three times before. However, the strategic importance of India was now greater. India had been making economic progress, particularly in the crucial sector of agriculture. It was one of the leading countries in the non-aligned movement – still more so since the death of Marshal Tito. That group of nations was itself more important to us because of its attitude to the Soviet invasion of Afghanistan. India could be an even more powerful source of difficulty than benefit if she chose. Her traditionally closer relations with Russia and hostility to Pakistan, at a time when the latter was the main base for the Afghan anti-communist guerillas, meant that the West had to be sensitive to the Indian Government's feelings and needs. As regards bilateral relations, there was also the thorny question of the new and much misrepresented British Nationality Bill, which was a part of our proposals to limit future large-scale immigration to Britain – not least immigration from the Indian sub-continent.

My talks with Mrs Gandhi were interesting, but largely inconclusive. Much of the time of the Indian Cabinet seemed to be spent in allocating contracts – not perhaps too surprising in a socialist country – whereas I was more concerned with international questions. I did not manage to persuade Mrs Gandhi to condemn the Soviet invasion of Afghanistan, as I would have liked. She put up the standard excuses, but she was clearly embarrassed by it. I never succeeded in drawing Mrs Gandhi or her successors away from India's traditional alliance with the Soviet Union until the collapse of communism, or in drawing her closer to America. But we established a good Anglo-Indian working relationship in Commonwealth affairs, and on the practicalities of Third World aid, where she had a much more hard-headed grasp of what was required than most other Third World leaders. This good relationship was not soured for long by the dispute over the British Nationality Bill. She pressed strongly for amendments to it that would have permitted more Indian families to be admitted to Britain: I stood my ground in defence of the bill. My impression was that although the attack was pressed home privately and publicly – at the closing press conference I was faced with hostile questioning – Mrs Gandhi was herself largely responding to public pressure.

I liked and respected Mrs Gandhi. Her policies had been more than high-handed, but only a strong figure with a powerful personality could hope successfully to rule India. Mrs Gandhi was also – perhaps it is not just myth to see this as a female trait – immensely practical. For example, she always insisted that what India required was basic – what to some seemed primitive – means of assistance to allow its peasants to produce more food. Like me, she understood the immense benefits which science could bring and indeed was already bringing in new varieties of grain and techniques of cultivation. Her weak spot was that she never grasped the importance of the free market.

Apart from my talks with Mrs Gandhi and others, I saw three different aspects of the new India. On Thursday I addressed the Indian Parliament. On Friday I visited an Indian village where the efficiency of peasant agriculture was being transformed. On Saturday I walked around the Bombay Atomic Research Centre. The Indian visit was, I felt, not only predictably fascinating; slightly less predictably, though without any dramatic developments, it had been a success. I was sorry to leave India so soon: each visit makes me want to return for an extended stay.

On Sunday I left for Saudi Arabia and the Gulf. I had to have clothes specially made for this visit because it was important to conform to the customs of these conservative Muslim societies. Contrary to what one might have thought, they were in no way disconcerted to meet their first western woman prime minister. Later I discovered how important the wives of leading Arab figures are. Indeed, many of these women are highly cultivated, very well educated and well informed. Their influence is greatly underrated in the West and an evening's conversation with them is a highly stimulating occasion.

I was the first ever British prime minister to visit these states. But Britain's links with the area were traditionally strong, dating back to the days when we provided the defence of some of the Gulf states, long before oil was discovered. I always regretted, even at the time, the decision of Ted Heath's Government not to reverse the Wilson Government's withdrawal of our forces and the severing of many of our responsibilities east of Suez. Repeatedly, events have demonstrated that the West cannot pursue a policy of total disengagement in this strategically vital area. Britain has, however, continued to supply equipment, training and advice.

In Saudi Arabia and the Gulf states I sought to reassure my hosts that whatever decisions were made about a Rapid Deployment Force (RDF) then being discussed, which some of them feared might pave the way for direct military intervention in the Middle East, nothing of the sort would occur without their knowledge and consent. The Iraq-Iran conflict was continuing, though at a lower level of activity. No one knew how serious the threat of Islamic fundamentalism might become. Too overt a western presence might provide an excuse for it: too little support from the West might provide an opportunity. The Gulf Co-operation Council had been formed to bring together the states in the region to guarantee their mutual security: this was clearly a welcome development. It was also important that they should have the right military equipment and be trained to use it. In this our old defence links reinforced our commercial interest. Some British aeroplanes and tanks were eminently suitable for this area.

Abu Dhabi, where I arrived on Tuesday 21 April, is the largest of the members of the United Arab Emirates (UAE). Sheik Zaid, the Amir and President of the UAE, spoke for all the world like an Arab poet and was a man of great charm. He knew Pakistan well because like other Gulf Arabs he regularly went there to hunt with his hawks. The Gulf Arabs therefore learned much of interest about developments in Pakistan and Afghanistan. We supplied the UAE with a good deal of military equipment and advice, and we were keen to sell the excellent Hawk Trainer and Ground Attack aircraft throughout the Gulf.

The other main UAE state is Dubai, where I arrived on Wednesday. Its ruler was Sheik Rashid. When I arrived he was already on the airport tarmac to greet me, even though he had already seen me in Abu Dhabi. By this time he was elderly and unwell. But his powerful features, above all his eyes, still conveyed shrewdness and courage. There is a picture of the young Sheik on horseback, holding his sword aloft, marching in from the desert to claim his land: it struck me that the qualities of his generation would be difficult to repeat in the more comfortable conditions of today.

Dubai is enchanting. Like the other Gulf states that I visited, it is full of flowers, kept absolutely perfectly and tended every day. But it is also a thriving port. Like Bahrain, but unlike some other cities on the shores of the Gulf, it was established long before oil was discovered. From here Arab traders sailed to the Red Sea and to the Indian Ocean.

I also visited Muscat in Oman. Its leader, Sultan Qaboos, has always been one of Britain's closest friends in the Gulf. Historic forts guard the entrance to the port of Muscat. As elsewhere in the Gulf, development has been very carefully controlled to blend in with the traditional style of buildings. I discussed with the Sultan Oman's requirements for military equipment. Later when the price of oil fell and Oman's finances were somewhat less healthy, we suggested that they should purchase the Ground Attack Hawk and Trainer rather than the more expensive Tornado. The Sultan and I discussed the situation in the Gulf and the Iran-Iraq War. He was always a source of valuable information about events in Iran. We too were concerned that the war remained confined to those two states and to the northern end of the Gulf. We had stationed the three ships of the Armilla Patrol in the area in 1980 to keep the sea lanes open. My talks with the Sultan and other Gulf rulers laid the groundwork for later co-operation when the Iran-Iraq War threatened Gulf shipping and, subsequently, when Iraq invaded Kuwait.

My final visit on this occasion was to see Sheik Khalifa, the Emir of Qatar. Qatar has the biggest natural deposits of gas anywhere in the world and the country is very wealthy. I discussed the involvement of British firms in the development of these resources.

The pattern of the visit, combining diplomacy, commerce and private discussion would be repeated on many occasions in the years ahead. Even on this busy trip I had not been able to visit all the important players in the 'great game' of the Gulf. I would return in September to do so, visiting Bahrain and Kuwait on my way to the Commonwealth Conference in Melbourne.

THE OTTAWA G7

My second G7 summit – President Reagan's and President Mitterrand's first – took place in Montebello, just outside Ottawa, where I arrived on the afternoon of Sunday 19 July to be met by Canada's Prime Minister Pierre Trudeau. Montebello had been chosen as the site of the conference because the G7 heads of government were determined to try to avoid the relentless pressure from the media which increasingly disrupted proceedings. After each afternoon session Pierre Trudeau flew by helicopter back in to Ottawa to brief the journalists. We enjoyed a kind of splendid isolation at the Château Montebello, sometimes called the world's biggest log cabin but in fact a very luxurious hotel. It had also been decided to try to inject rather more informality into discussions. Perhaps because of the presence of Ronald Reagan, with his effortless amiability, we all called one another by our Christian names. Something I liked less was the decision that everyone should dress informally. In my experience this kind of approach always presents more rather than fewer problems in choosing what to wear. The Japanese, for example, wore the smartest white 'barbecue' suits that I have ever seen – and looked all the more formal beside the westerners in open-neck shirts and slacks. For my part, like the Japanese, I made almost no concessions to informal dress. I believe that the public really likes its leaders to look businesslike and well turned out. I was glad that in retrospect this degree of informality was not thought a success and so was not repeated.

President Reagan was subject to some criticism at Montebello about the level of US interest rates. He explained that he had inherited these from his predecessor. 'Give me time', he said; 'I want them down too.' He was as good as his word on this. He also hoped to control the US deficit by cuts in public spending, but that proved more intractable. The deficit continued to rise until about 1985. The US deficit was to be the one topic on which the President and I continued to be at odds, until the latter half of his second term when it entered a sharply declining path. My own experience of getting down deficits was that you had to keep a very firm hand on the purse strings and say 'no' to much public spending. If you are controlling public spending, you can temporarily put up taxes because in those circumstances the revenue will help to cut the deficit (and therefore interest rates). But if you are increasing spending, then a tax increase will only serve to encourage even more spending and thus may even increase the deficit. Given the separation of powers in the US Constitution, which enabled Congress to spend over and above the president's wishes, holding taxes down may be the only effective tool a president has to hold spending down. So I came to have some sympathy with Ronald Reagan's position. Where the President and I were at one was when he argued for the greatest possible international free trade. Trade also figured in others' contributions. The Japanese were, as usual, sound on the principle of free trade, but, in spite of pressure, definitely less willing to take practical measures to open up their own markets.

Helmut Schmidt, who was known to be privately critical of the policies of the new US Administration, argued for sound and orthodox public finance and open trade, and I did the same in quite a long off-the-cuff speech. My contribution was, I suspect, the more convincing because, as a result of the cuts in government borrowing in our 1981 budget, British interest rates had fallen by this time – even while we were continuing to fight inflation.*

Perhaps my most useful discussion at Ottawa was at a private meeting with President Reagan. Since we had met in Washington he had survived injuries from an assassination attempt which would have crippled many a younger man. But he looked fine. I briefed him on

* Our three-month rate was 13 per cent. By contrast, interest rates in the US stood at 18 per cent and in France, Italy and Canada between 18 and 20 per cent. German interest rates, at a nominal 13 per cent, were very high indeed in real terms – and still the deutschmark had depreciated by between 40 and 45 per cent against the US dollar in the previous twelve months.

events in Britain, putting both our economic problems and the recent inner-city riots in perspective. As regards American relations with Europe, I was becoming increasingly worried about some of the Administration's rhetoric: for example, I urged him to discourage talk about a 'rising tide of neutralism' in Europe: while I agreed with his underlying point, such warnings could all too easily prove self-fulfilling. I took this opportunity to thank him warmly for his tough stand against Irish terrorism and its NORAID supporters. It was good to know that, however powerful the Irish republican lobby in the USA might be, the Reagan Administration would not buckle before it.

MELBOURNE CHOGM AND VISIT TO PAKISTAN

Almost two months later the Commonwealth Heads of Government Meeting opened in Melbourne (on Wednesday 30 September).

The conference was overshadowed, as usual, by South African issues. Robert Mugabe, with whom I had a separate meeting, was there for the first time representing Zimbabwe. There was a good deal of hostility to the new American Administration's attitude to the problem of Namibia. I was determined to hold the line so that the so-called 'Contact Group' of five nations, including the US, should continue to be the means by which pressure for a settlement was exerted. At one point Maurice Bishop, the Marxist Prime Minister of Grenada, delivered an eloquent plea that we should send a clear message of support to our brothers in Namibia, suffering under South African rule. One of the other heads of government later suggested to me that someone should ask Maurice Bishop about the number of his own people, especially his country's professional and middle class, now held in Grenada's prisons, put there by his Government. There was also one of those arguments, which so frequently afflicted the Commonwealth, about sporting ties with South Africa. The Springboks had played in New Zealand amid scenes of disorder and Robert Muldoon was bitterly condemned for his alleged breach of the Gleneagles Agreement, by which international sporting relations with South Africa were regulated. He put up a robust defence. At least with the Rhodesian issue now settled, Britain was less the focus of international criticism by the Commonwealth than on the previous occasion, and the serious pressure for sanctions against South Africa still lay in the future.

In my interventions during the conference, I acknowledged that conditions for the developing world were undoubtedly difficult. They had been hit hard both by the rise in the oil price and by the effects of the recession on the western markets on which they relied. However, I emphasized that wealth creation rather than international wealth redistribution still had to come first – indeed more so than ever. I also defended the British record on overseas aid, which was very good when you looked further than the narrowly defined aid programme and took into account both public and private sector loans and investment. With myself and the heads of government of six other Commonwealth countries due to attend the forthcoming international conference on 'North-South' issues in Cancún, I thought it would be well worth putting the facts on the record now.

While I was in Australia Ted Heath delivered a vitriolic speech in Manchester attacking my policies. Oddly, perhaps, in view of his record, Ted had become an advocate of the politics of 'consensus'; or perhaps less oddly, since these policies seemed to come down to state intervention and corporatism. I was sent an advance copy of the speech and used my Sir Robert Menzies Lecture at Monash University to deliver a reply to him and to all the critics of my style of government. It was, unbeknown to him, President Forbes Burnham of Guyana who provided the inspiration for this in the course of the weekend retreat which the heads of government spent away from Melbourne in Canberra. In the course of this we were arguing about an issue to be reported in the final communiqué which we were drafting. At one point Forbes Burnham said that we must achieve a consensus. I asked him what he meant by 'consensus' – a word of which I had heard all too much – and he replied that 'it is something you have if you cannot get agreement.' This seemed to me an excellent definition. So in my lecture I inserted a passage which read:

> To me consensus seems to be: the process of abandoning all beliefs, principles, values and policies in search of something in which no one believes, but to which no one objects; the process of avoiding the very issues that have to be solved, merely because you cannot get agreement on the way ahead. What great cause would have been fought and won under the banner 'I stand for consensus'?

On the return journey I took the opportunity to visit Pakistan. I flew to Islamabad to be met by President Zia. The war in Afghanistan was at its height and it was arranged that I should visit one of the refugee camps set up in Pakistan for fleeing Afghans. We flew to the Nasir Bagh Afghan refugee camp by helicopter. It was large, but impeccably clean, orderly and obviously well run. I spoke under a huge tent, sheltered from the burning sun, while the refugees – men, women and children – sat cross-legged on the ground. I told them of my admiration for their refusal to 'live under a godless communist system which [was] trying to destroy [their] religion and [their] independence' and promised them my help. My speech was interrupted from time to time as people rose to their feet to express the words of approval, 'Allah be praised'.

I had lunch in the garden of the beautiful old house of the Governor at Peshawar. There, in the grounds of the house, I addressed a very large meeting of tribal leaders from the surrounding areas. Then I went by helicopter up to the Khyber Pass. I had been warned in advance that, as an honoured guest, I would be presented with the traditional sheep: I patted it appreciatively on the head and asked them to keep it for me. From there I went up to the frontier with Afghanistan itself, always busy despite its new status as a kind of dividing line between communism and freedom. I gazed across into the Soviet dominated lands beyond. A line of lorries was waiting to come through from Afghanistan to Pakistan. Relations with the Russian border guards on the Afghan side at this time were friendly enough. They were taking a very close interest in everything that was happening on our side. I reflected that Pakistan's was an unsung story of heroism, taking in hundreds of thousands of refugees and bordering the world's greatest military power. Though it was not a rich country, as I later remarked to President Zia, all the Pakistani people I saw looked healthy and well dressed. He said 'no one is short of clothes or food, thank God.' Britain was already providing aid for the refugees. But if Pakistan was to stand as a bulwark against communism it would need still more help from the West.

CANCÚN NORTH-SOUTH SUMMIT

I had successfully persuaded President Reagan in the course of our discussions in Washington of the importance of attending the Cancún summit which was held that October in Mexico. I felt that, whatever our misgivings about the occasion, we should be present, both to argue for our positions and to forestall criticism that we were uninterested in the developing world. The whole concept of 'North-South' dialogue, which the Brandt Commission had made the fashionable talk of the international community, was in my view wrong-headed. Not only was it false to suggest that that there was a homogeneous rich North which confronted a homogeneous poor South: underlying the rhetoric was the idea that redistribution of world resources rather than the creation of wealth was the way to tackle poverty and hunger. Moreover, what the developing countries needed more than aid was trade: so our first responsibility was – and still is – to give them the freest possible access to our markets. Of course, 'North-South' dialogue also appealed to those socialists who wanted to play down the fundamental contrast between the free capitalist West and the unfree communist East.

The conference's joint chairmen were President López-Portillo, our Mexican host, and Pierre Trudeau who had stepped in for the Chancellor of Austria, prevented by illness from attending. Twenty-two countries were represented. We were staying in one of those almost overluxurious hotels which you so often seem to find in countries where large numbers of people are living in appalling poverty. Cancún was built in the 1970s, on a site (it is said) chosen by computer as likely to have maximum appeal to foreign tourists. The city was badly damaged by Hurricane Gilbert in 1988. So much for information technology.

There is no immodesty in saying that Mrs Gandhi and I were the two conference media 'personalities'. India had just received the largest loan yet given by the International Monetary Fund (IMF) at less than the market rate of interest. She and others naturally wanted more cheap loans in the future. This was what lay behind the pressure, which I was determined to resist, to place the IMF and the World Bank directly under United Nations control. At one point in the proceedings I engaged in a vigorous discussion with a group of heads of government who could not see why I felt so strongly that the integrity of the IMF and the World Bank would inevitably be compromised by such a move, which would do harm rather than good to those who were advocating it. In the end I put the point more bluntly: I said that there was no way in which I was going to put British deposits into a bank which was totally run by those on overdraft. They saw the point.

While I was at Cancún I also had a separate meeting with Julius Nyerere, who was, as ever, charmingly persuasive, but equally misguided and unrealistic about what was wrong with his own country and, by extension, with so much of black Africa. He told me how unfair the IMF conditions for extending credit to him were: they had told him to bring Tanzania's public finances into order, cut protection and devalue his currency to the much lower level the market reckoned it worth. Perhaps at this time the IMF's demands were somewhat too rigorous: but he did not see that changes in this direction were necessary at all and in his own country's long-term interests. He also complained of the effects of droughts and the collapse of his country's agriculture – none of which he seemed to connect with the pursuit of misguided socialist policies, including collectivizing the farms.

The process of drafting the communiqué itself was more than usually fraught. An original Canadian draft was in effect rejected; and Pierre Trudeau left it largely to the rest of us, making clear that he thought our efforts rather less good than his own. I spent much of this time seeking to sort out drafting points with the Americans, who continued until almost the last moment to have reservations about the text.

The summit was a success – though not really for any of the reasons publicly given. At its conclusion there was, of course, the expected general – and largely meaningless – talk about 'global negotiations' on North-South issues. A special 'energy affiliate' to the World Bank was to be set up. But what mattered to me was that the independence of the IMF and the World Bank were maintained. Equally valuable, this was the last of such gatherings. The intractable problems of Third World poverty, hunger and debt would not be solved by misdirected international intervention, but rather by liberating enterprise, promoting trade – and defeating socialism in all its forms.

Before I left Mexico, I had one more item of business to transact. This was to sign an agreement for the building of a huge new steel plant by the British firm of Davy Loewy. Like other socialist countries, the Mexicans wrongly thought that large prestige manufacturing projects offered the best path to economic progress. However, if that was what they wanted, then I would at least try to see that British firms benefited. The ceremony required my going to Mexico City the night before. I stayed at the residence of the British Ambassador, Crispin Tickell. While I was there at dinner the chandeliers started swinging and the floor moved; there was nowhere you could put your feet. At first I thought that I must have been affected by the altitude, even though I had had no difficulty in my earlier days on skiing holidays. But I was reassured by our ambassador who was sitting beside me: 'No', he said, 'it's just an earthquake.'

Other earthquakes were sending out tremors that year. Before I left for the international visits chronicled in this chapter, I had been all too aware of the significance for the Cold War of the stationing of

Cruise and Pershing missiles in Europe. If it went ahead as planned, the Soviet Union would suffer a real defeat; if it was abandoned in response to the Soviet sponsored 'peace offensive', there was a real danger of a decoupling of Europe and America. My meetings with President Reagan had persuaded me that the new Administration was apprised of these dangers and determined to combat them. But a combination of exaggerated American rhetoric and the perennial nervousness of European opinion threatened to undermine the good transatlantic relationship that would be needed to guarantee that deployment went ahead. I saw it as Britain's task to put the American case in Europe since we shared their analysis but tended to put it in less ideological language. And this we did in the next few years.

But there was a second front in the Cold War – that between the West and the Soviet-Third World axis. My visits to India, Pakistan, the Gulf, Mexico and Australia for the Commonwealth Conference brought home to me how badly the Soviets had been damaged by their invasion of Afghanistan. It had alienated the Islamic countries *en bloc*, and within that bloc strengthened conservative pro-western regimes against radical states like Iraq and Libya. Traditional Soviet friends like India, on the other hand, were embarrassed. Not only did this enable the West to forge its own alliance with Islamic countries against Soviet expansionism; it also divided the Third World and so weakened the pressure it could bring against the West on international economic issues. In these circumstances, countries which had long advocated their own local form of socialism, to be paid for by western aid, suddenly had to consider a more realistic approach of attracting western investment by pursuing free-market policies – a small earthquake as yet, but one that would transform the world economy over the next decade.

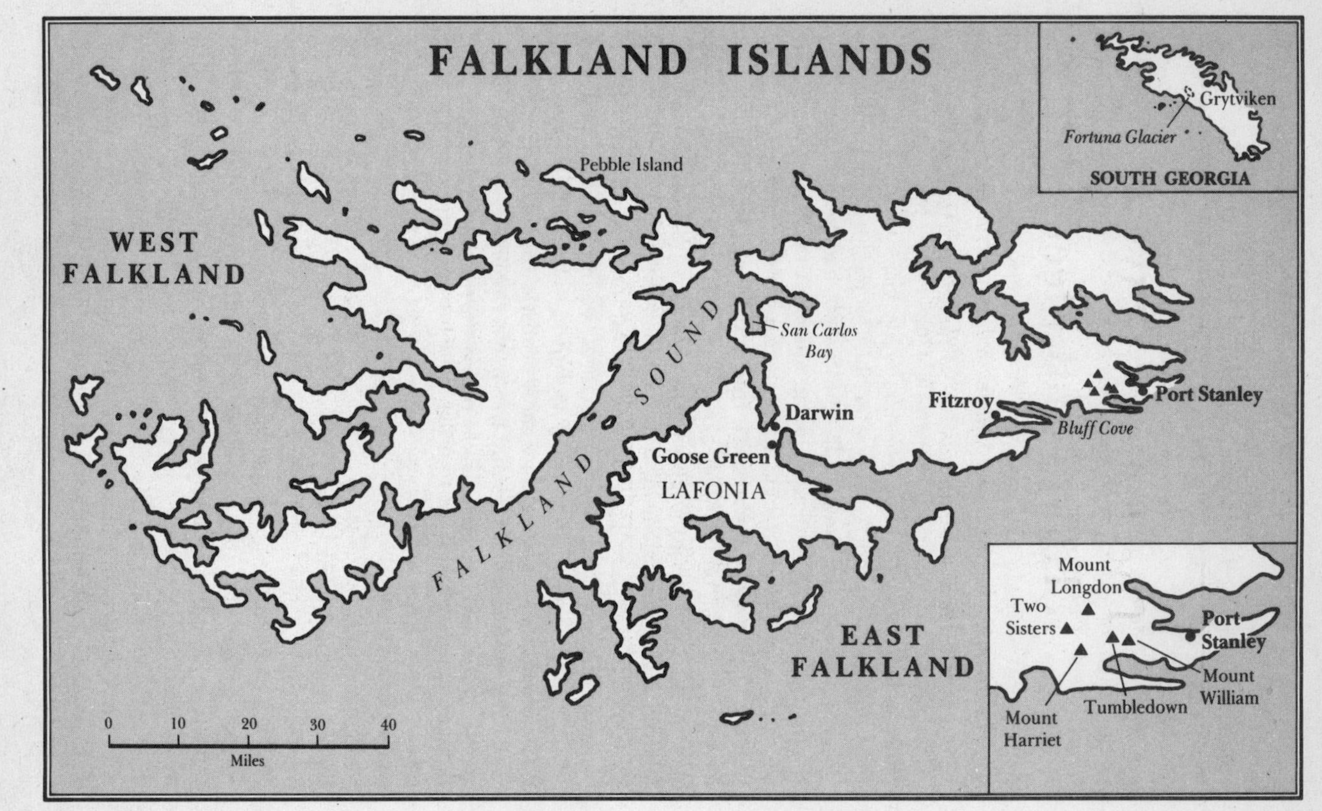
FALKLAND ISLANDS
WEST FALKLAND
Pebble Island
FALKLAND SOUND
San Carlos Bay
Darwin
Goose Green
LAFONIA
Fitzroy
Bluff Cove
Port Stanley
EAST FALKLAND
Grytviken
Fortuna Glacier
SOUTH GEORGIA
Mount Longdon
Two Sisters
Port Stanley
Mount William
Tumbledown
Mount Harriet
0
10
20
30
40
Miles

CHAPTER VII

The Falklands War: Follow the Fleet

The attempts by diplomacy and the sending of the task force to regain the Falkland Islands – to the end of April 1982

BACKGROUND

Nothing remains more vividly in my mind, looking back on my years in No. 10, than the eleven weeks in the spring of 1982 when Britain fought and won the Falklands War. Much was at stake: what we were fighting for eight thousand miles away in the South Atlantic was not only the territory and the people of the Falklands, important though they were. We were defending our honour as a nation, and principles of fundamental importance to the whole world – above all, that aggressors should never succeed and that international law should prevail over the use of force. The war was very sudden. No one predicted the Argentine invasion more than a few hours in advance, though many predicted it in retrospect. When I became Prime Minister I never thought that I would have to order British troops into combat and I do not think I have ever lived so tensely or intensely as during the whole of that time.

The significance of the Falklands War was enormous, both for Britain's self-confidence and for our standing in the world. Since the Suez fiasco in 1956, British foreign policy had been one long retreat. The tacit assumption made by British and foreign governments alike was that our world role was doomed steadily to diminish. We had come to be seen by both friends and enemies as a nation which lacked the will and the capability to defend its interests in peace, let alone in war. Victory in the Falklands changed that. Everywhere I went after the war, Britain's name meant something more than it had. The war also had real importance in relations between East and West: years later I was told by a Russian general that the Soviets had been firmly convinced that we would not fight for the Falklands, and that if we did fight we would lose. We proved them wrong on both counts, and they did not forget the fact.

Beginning in the summer of 1982, only weeks after the war, I wrote down my detailed recollection of events as I had lived through them at the centre of government. I finished the story at Chequers over Easter 1983. It was still etched in my mind, and I had all the records to hand. The task took some time to complete; it is a long and complicated story. Parts of it will have to remain secret for a considerable time to come, but it is upon my personal memoir that I have based this account.

The first recorded landing on the Falklands was made in 1690 by British sailors, who named the channel between the two principal islands 'Falkland's Sound' in honour of the Treasurer of the Navy, Viscount Falkland. Britain, France and Spain each established settlements on the islands at various times during the eighteenth century. In 1770 a quarrel with Spain caused the British Government of the day to mobilize the fleet and a naval task force was prepared, though never sent: on this occasion, a diplomatic solution was found.

The islands had obvious strategic importance, possessing several good harbours within 500 miles of Cape Horn. In the event that the Panama Canal is ever closed their significance would be considerable. But it must be admitted that the Falklands were always an improbable cause for a twentieth-century war.

The Argentine invasion of the Falklands took place 149 years after the beginning of formal British rule there, and it seems that the imminence of the 150th anniversary was an important factor in the plotting of the Argentine Junta. Since 1833 there has been a continuous and peaceful British presence on the islands. Britain's legal claim in the present day rests on that fact, and on the desire of the settled population – which is entirely of British stock – to remain British. The principle of 'self-determination' has become a fundamental component of international law, and is enshrined in the UN Charter. British sovereignty has strong legal foundations, and the Argentinians know it.

Some 800 miles to the south-east of the Falklands lies South Georgia, and 460 miles further out, the South Sandwich Islands. Here the Argentine claim is even more dubious. These islands are dependencies of the United Kingdom, though they are administered from the Falklands. Their climate is severe and they have no settled population. No state claimed them before British annexation in

1908 and there has been continuous British administration since that time.

My first involvement with the Falklands issue came very early in the life of the 1979 Parliament. It was clear that there were only two ways in which the prosperity of the Falkland Islanders could be achieved. The more obvious and attractive approach was by promoting the development of economic links with neighbouring Argentina. Yet this ran up against the Argentine claim that the Falklands and the dependencies were part of their sovereign territory. Ted Heath's Government had signed an important Communications Agreement in 1971 establishing air and sea links between the islands and the mainland, but further progress in that direction had been blocked by the Argentinians unless sovereignty was also discussed. Consequently it was argued that some kind of accommodation with Argentina would have to be reached on the question of sovereignty. Arguments of this kind led Nick Ridley (the responsible minister) and his officials at the Foreign and Commonwealth Office (FCO) to advance the so-called 'lease-back' arrangement, under which sovereignty would pass to Argentina but the way of life of the islanders would be preserved by the continuation of British administration. I disliked this proposal, but Nick and I both agreed that it should be explored, subject always to the requirement that the islanders themselves should have the final word. We could not agree to anything without their consent: their wishes must be paramount.

There was, however, another option – far more costly and, on the face of it, at least as risky. We could implement the recommendations of the long-term economic survey produced in 1976 by the former Labour minister, Lord Shackleton, and one recommendation in particular – the enlargement of the airport and lengthening of the runway. Notwithstanding the cost, such a commitment would have been seen as evidence of the British Government's determination to have no serious talks about sovereignty and it would have increased our capacity to defend the islands, since a longer runway would have allowed for rapid reinforcement by air. This in turn might have provoked a swift Argentine military response. Unsurprisingly, no government – Labour or Conservative – was prepared to act while there seemed any possibility of an acceptable solution and, accordingly, lease-back had become the favoured option.

However, as I rather expected, none of these diplomatic arguments in favour of lease-back had much appeal to the islanders themselves. They would have nothing to do with such proposals. They distrusted the Argentine dictatorship and were sceptical of its promises. But more than that, they wanted to remain British. They made this abundantly clear to Nick Ridley when he twice visited them to learn their views. The House of Commons too was noisily determined that the islanders' wishes should be respected. Lease-back was killed. I was not prepared to force the islanders into an arrangement which was intolerable to them – and which I in their position would not have tolerated either.

However, what all this meant for the future of the Falklands in the longer term was less clear. The Government found itself with very little room for manoeuvre. We were keen, if we could, to keep talking to the Argentinians, but diplomacy was becoming increasingly difficult. The Argentinians had already shown that they were not above taking direct action. In 1976 they had established and had maintained since a military presence on Southern Thule in the South Sandwich Islands, which the Labour Government did nothing to remove and which ministers did not even reveal to the House of Commons until 1978.

Then, in December 1981, there was a change of government in Buenos Aires. A new three-man military Junta replaced the previous military government, with General Leopoldo Galtieri as President. Galtieri relied on the support of the Argentine Navy, whose Commander-in-Chief, Admiral Anaya, held particularly hardline views on the Argentine claim to the 'Malvinas'.

Cynically, the new Junta continued negotiations for a few months. There were talks in New York at the end of February 1982 which seemed to go well. But then the Argentinian line hardened abruptly. With hindsight this was a turning point. But in judging our response to the new Junta it is important to remember how much aggressive rhetoric there had already been in the past, none of it coming to anything. Moreover, based on past experience our view was that Argentina was likely to follow a policy of progessively escalating the dispute, starting with diplomatic and economic pressures. Contrary to what was said at the time, we had no intelligence until almost the last moment that Argentina was about to launch a full-scale invasion. Nor did the Americans: in fact Al Haig later told me that they had known even less than we had.

A factor in all this was the American Administration's policy of strengthening ties with Argentina as part of its strategy of resisting Cuban-based communist influence in Central and South America. It later became clear that the Argentinians had gained a wildly exaggerated idea of their importance to the United States. They convinced themselves on the eve of the invasion that they need not take seriously

American warnings against military action, and became more intransigent when diplomatic pressure was applied on them afterwards to withdraw.

Could they have been deterred? It must be remembered that in order to take action to deter Argentina militarily, given the vast distance between Britain and the Falklands, we would have had to have some three weeks' notice. Further, to send down a force of insufficient size would have been to subject it to intolerable risk. Certainly, the presence of HMS *Endurance* – the lightly armed patrol vessel which was due to be withdrawn under the 1981 Defence Review proposals – was a military irrelevance. It would neither deter nor repel any planned invasion. (Indeed, when the invasion occurred I was very glad that the ship was at sea and not in Port Stanley: if she had been, she would have been captured or blown out of the water.) Most important perhaps is that nothing would have more reliably precipitated a full-scale invasion, if something less had been planned, than if we had started military preparations on the scale required to send an effective deterrent. Of course with the benefit of hindsight, we would always like to have acted differently. So would the Argentinians. The truth is that the invasion could not have been foreseen or prevented. This was the main conclusion of the Committee of Inquiry, chaired by Lord Franks, which we set up to examine the way we had handled the dispute in the run-up to the invasion. The committee had unprecedented access to government papers, including those of the intelligence services. Its report ends with the words: 'we would not be justified in attaching any criticism or blame to the present Government for the Argentine Junta's decision to commit its act of unprovoked aggression in the invasion of the Falkland Islands on 2 April 1982.'

It all began with an incident on South Georgia. On 20 December 1981 there had been an unauthorized landing on the island at Leith harbour by what were described as Argentine scrap metal dealers; we had given a firm but measured response. The Argentinians subsequently left and the Argentine Government claimed to know nothing about it. The incident was disturbing, but not especially so. I was more alarmed when, after the Anglo-Argentine talks in New York, the Argentine Government broke the procedures agreed at the meeting by publishing a unilateral communiqué disclosing the details of discussion, while simultaneously the Argentine press began to speculate on possible military action before the symbolically important date of January 1983. On 3 March 1982 I minuted on a telegram from Buenos Aires: 'we must make contingency plans' – though, in spite of my unease, I was not expecting anything like a full-scale invasion, which indeed our most recent intelligence assessment of Argentine intentions had discounted.

On 20 March we were informed that the previous day the Argentine scrap metal dealers had made a further unauthorized landing on South Georgia, again at Leith. The Argentine flag had been raised and shots fired. Again in answer to our protests the Argentine Government claimed to have no prior knowledge. We first decided that HMS *Endurance* should be instructed to remove the Argentinians, whoever they were. But we tried to negotiate with Argentina a way of resolving what still seemed to be an awkward incident rather than a precursor of conflict, so we subsequently withdrew our instructions to *Endurance* and ordered the ship to proceed instead to the British base at Grytviken, the main settlement on the island.

WEEK ONE

Yet as March drew to a close with the incident still unresolved we became increasingly concerned. On Sunday evening, 28 March, I rang Peter Carrington from Chequers to express my anxiety at the situation. He assured me that he had already made a first approach to Al Haig, the US Secretary of State, asking him to bring pressure to bear. The following morning Peter and I met at RAF Northolt on our way to the European Council at Brussels, and discussed what further steps we should take. We agreed to send a nuclear-powered submarine to reinforce HMS *Endurance* and to make preparations to send a second submarine. I was not too displeased when the following day news of the decision leaked. The submarine would take two weeks to get to the South Atlantic, but it could begin to influence events straight away. My instinct was that the time had come to show the Argentines that we meant business.

In the late afternoon of Tuesday 30 March I returned from Brussels. By that time Peter Carrington had already left on an official visit to Israel; his absence was unfortunate. The Foreign Office and the Ministry of Defence had been working to prepare up-to-date assessments and review the diplomatic and military options. The following day – Wednesday 31 March – I made my statement to the House reporting on the Brussels summit, but my mind was focused on what the Argentinians were intending and on what our response should be. The advice we received from intelligence was that the Argentine Government were exploring our reactions, but that they had not contrived the landing on South Georgia and that any escalation they might make would stop short of full-scale invasion. However, we knew that they were unpredictable and unstable, and that a dictatorship might not behave in ways we would consider rational. By now I was deeply uneasy. Yet still I do not think that any of us expected an immediate invasion of the Falklands themselves.

I shall not forget that Wednesday evening. I was working in my room at the House of Commons when I was told that John Nott wanted an immediate meeting to discuss the Falklands. I called people together. In Peter Carrington's absence Humphrey Atkins and Richard Luce attended from the Foreign Office, with FCO and MoD officials. (The Chief of Defence Staff was also away, in New Zealand.) John was alarmed. He had just received intelligence that the Argentinian Fleet, already at sea, looked as if they were going to invade the islands on Friday 2 April. There was no ground to question the intelligence. John gave the MoD's view that the Falklands could not be retaken once they were seized. This was terrible, and totally unacceptable. I could not believe it: these were our people, our islands. I said instantly: 'if they are invaded, we have got to get them back.'

At this dark moment comedy intervened. The Chief of the Naval Staff, Sir Henry Leach, was in civilian dress, and on his way to the meeting had been detained by the police in the Central Lobby of the House of Commons. He had to be rescued by a whip. When he finally arrived, I asked him what we could do. He was quiet, calm and confident: 'I can put together a task force of destroyers, frigates, landing craft, support vessels. It will be led by the aircraft carriers HMS *Hermes* and HMS *Invincible*. It can be ready to leave in forty-eight hours.' He believed such a force could retake the islands. All he needed was my authority to begin to assemble it. I gave it him, and he left immediately to set the work in hand. We reserved for Cabinet the decision as to whether and when the task force should sail.

Before this, I had been outraged and determined. Now my outrage and determination were matched by a sense of relief and confidence. Henry Leach had shown me that if it came to a fight the courage and professionalism of Britain's armed forces would win through. It was my job as Prime Minister to see that they got the political support they needed. But first we had to do everything possible to prevent the appalling tragedy, if it was still humanly possible to do so.

Our only hope now lay with the Americans – friends and allies, and people to whom Galtieri, if he was still behaving rationally, should listen. At the meeting we drafted and sent an urgent message to

President Reagan asking him to press Galtieri to draw back from the brink. This the President immediately agreed to do.

At 9.30 on Thursday morning, 1 April, I held a Cabinet, earlier than usual so that a meeting of the Overseas and Defence Committee of the Cabinet (OD) could follow it before lunch. The latest assessment was that an Argentine assault could be expected about midday our time on Friday. We thought that President Reagan might yet succeed. However, Galtieri refused altogether at first to take the President's call. He deigned to speak to the President only when it was too late to stop the invasion. I was told of this outcome in the early hours of Friday morning and I knew then that our last hope had now gone.

But how seriously did the Argentinians take American warnings anyway? On the evening of Friday 2 April as the invasion was proceeding, the US Ambassador to the United Nations, Mrs Kirkpatrick, was attending a gala dinner given by the Argentinian Ambassador in her honour. As our ambassador later asked her: how would Americans have felt if he had dined at the Iranian Embassy the night that the American hostages were seized in Tehran? Unfortunately the attitudes of Mrs Kirkpatrick and some other members of the US Administration were at this point of considerable importance.

At 9.45 on Friday morning Cabinet met again. I reported that an Argentine invasion was now imminent. We would meet later in the day to consider once more the question of sending a task force – though to my mind the issue by this stage was not so much whether we should act, but how.

Communications with the Falklands were often interrupted due to atmospheric conditions. On Friday morning the Governor of the Falklands – Rex Hunt – sent a message telling us that the invasion had begun, but it never got through. (Indeed, the first contact I had with him after the invasion was when he reached Montevideo in Uruguay, where the Argentinians flew him and a number of other senior people, on Saturday morning.) It was, in fact, the captain of a British Antarctic Survey vessel who intercepted a local Falkland Island ham radio broadcast and passed on the news to the Foreign Office. My private secretary brought me final confirmation while I was at an official lunch.

By now discussion was taking place all over Whitehall about every aspect of the campaign, including the application of economic and other sanctions against Argentina. Feverish military preparations were under way. The army was preparing its contribution. A naval task force was being formed, partly from ships currently at Gibraltar and partly from those in British ports. The Queen had already made it clear that Prince Andrew, who was serving with HMS *Invincible*, would be joining the task force: his grandfather, King George VI, had fought at the Battle of Jutland and then as now there could be no question of a member of the royal family being treated differently from other servicemen.

Cabinet met for the second time that day at 7.30 in the evening when the decision was made to send the task force. What concerned us most at this point was the time it would take to arrive in the Falklands. We believed, rightly, that the Argentinians would pile in men and material to make it as difficult as possible for us to dislodge them. And all the time the weather in the South Atlantic would be worsening as the bitter winds and violent storms of the southern winter approached.

More immediate and more manageable was the problem of how to deal with public opinion at home in the intervening period. Support for the despatch of the task force was likely to be strong, but would it fall away as time went on? In fact, we need not have worried too much about that. Ships were constantly being chartered and negotiations – above all Al Haig's shuttle diplomacy – continued. Our policy was one which people understood and endorsed. Public interest and commitment remained strong throughout.

One particular aspect of this problem, though, does rate a mention. We decided to allow defence correspondents on the ships who reported back during the long journey. This produced vivid coverage of events. But there was always a risk of disclosing information which might be useful to the enemy. I also became very unhappy at the attempted 'even-handedness' of some of the comment, and the chilling use of the third-person – talk of 'the British' and 'the Argentinians' on our news programmes.

It was also on Friday 2 April that I received advice from the Foreign Office which summed up the flexibility of principle characteristic of that department. I was presented with the dangers of a backlash against the British expatriates in Argentina, problems about getting support in the UN Security Council, the lack of reliance we could place on the European Community or the United States, the risk of the Soviets becoming involved, the disadvantage of being looked at as a colonial power. All these considerations were fair enough. But when you are at war you cannot allow the difficulties to dominate your thinking: you have to set out with an iron will to overcome them. And anyway what was the alternative? That a common or garden dictator should rule over the Queen's subjects and prevail by fraud and violence? Not while I was Prime Minister.

While military preparations were in train the focus now turned to public debate in the United Nations Security Council. At the beginning of April we had one short-term and several long-term diplomatic objectives. In the short term we needed to win our case against Argentina in the UN Security Council and to secure a resolution denouncing their aggression and demanding withdrawal. On the basis of such a resolution we would find it far easier to win the support of other nations for practical measures to pressurize Argentina. But in the longer term we knew that we had to try to keep our affairs out of the UN as much as possible. With the Cold War still under way, and given the anti-colonialist attitude of many nations at the UN, there was a real danger that the Security Council might attempt to force unsatisfactory terms upon us. If necessary we could veto such a resolution, but to do so would diminish international support for our position. This remained a vital consideration throughout the crisis. The second long-term goal was to ensure maximum support from our allies, principally the US, but also members of the EC, the Commonwealth and other important western nations. This was a task undertaken at head of government level, but an enormous burden fell on the FCO and vast numbers of telegrams crossed my desk during those weeks. No country was ever better served than Britain by our two key diplomats at this time: Sir Anthony Parsons, Britain's UN Ambassador and Sir Nicholas (Nico) Henderson, our ambassador in Washington; both possessed precisely those qualities of intelligence, toughness, style and eloquence that the situation required.

At the UN Tony Parsons, on the eve of the invasion, was busy outmanoeuvring the Argentinians. The UN Secretary-General had called on both sides to exercise restraint: we responded positively, but the Argentinians remained silent. On Saturday 3 April, Tony Parsons managed a diplomatic triumph in persuading the Security Council to pass what became Security Council Resolution (UNSCR) 502, demanding an immediate and unconditional withdrawal by the Argentinians from the Falklands. It had not been easy. The debate was bitter and complex. We knew that the old anti-colonialist bias of the UN would incline some Security Council members against us, were it not for the fact that there had been a flagrant act of aggression by the Argentinians. I was particularly grateful to President Mitterrand who, with the leaders of the Old Commonwealth, was among the staunchest of our friends and who telephoned me personally to pledge support on Saturday. (I was to have many disputes with President Mitterrand in later years, but I never forgot the debt we owed him for his personal support on this occasion and throughout the Falklands crisis.) France used her influence in the UN to swing others in our favour. I myself made a last-minute telephone call to King Hussein of Jordan, who also came down on our side. He is an old friend of Britain. I told him our difficulty; I did not have to go into lengthy explanations to persuade him to cast Jordan's vote on our side. He began the conversation by asking simply: 'what can I do for you Prime Minister?' In the end we were delighted to have the votes we needed for the Resolution and to avoid a veto from the Soviet Union. But we knew that this was a fragile achievement, and we had no illusions as to who would be left to remove the aggressor when all the talking was done: it would be us.

The debate in the House of Commons that Saturday is another very powerful memory.

I opened the debate. It was the most difficult I ever had to face. The House was rightly angry that British territory had been invaded and occupied, and many members were inclined to blame the Government for its alleged failure to foresee and forestall what had happened. My first task was to defend us against the charge of unpreparedness.

Far more difficult was my second task: convincing MPs that we would respond to Argentina's aggression forcefully and effectively. I gave an explanation of what had happened and made very clear what we intended to do. I said:

> I must tell the House that the Falkland Islands and their dependencies remain British territory. No aggression and no invasion can alter that simple fact. It is the Government's objective to see that the islands are freed from occupation and are returned to British administration at the earliest possible moment.
>
> The people of the Falklands Islands, like the people of the United Kingdom, are an island race . . . They are few in number, but they have the right to live in peace, to choose their own way of life and to determine their own allegiance. Their way of life is British: their allegiance is to the Crown. It is the wish of the British people and the duty of Her Majesty's Government to do everything that we can to uphold that right. That will be our hope and our endeavour and, I believe, the resolve of every Member of the House.

My announcement that the task force was ready and about to sail was greeted with growls of approval. But I knew that not everybody was cheering the same thing. Some saw the task force as a purely diplomatic armada that would get the Argentinians back to the negotiating table. They never intended that it should actually fight. I needed their support for as long as possible, for we needed to demonstrate a united national will both to the enemy and to our allies. But I felt in my bones that the Argentinians would never withdraw without a fight and anything less than withdrawal was unacceptable to the country, and certainly to me.

Others shared my view that the task force would have to be used, but doubted the Government's will and stamina. Enoch Powell expressed this sentiment most dramatically when he looked directly across the Chamber at me and declared sepulchrally:

> The Prime Minister, shortly after she came into office, received a soubriquet as the 'Iron Lady'. It arose in the context of remarks which she made about defence against the Soviet Union and its allies; but there was no reason to suppose that the Right Hon. Lady did not welcome and, indeed, take pride in that description. In the next week or two this House, the nation and the Right Hon. Lady herself will learn of what metal she is made.*

That morning in Parliament I could keep the support of both groups by sending the task force out and by setting down our objectives: that the islands would be freed from occupation and returned to British administration at the earliest possible moment. I obtained the almost unanimous but grudging support of a Commons that was anxious to support the Government's policy, while reserving judgement on the Government's performance.

But I realized that even this degree of backing was likely to be eroded as the campaign wore on. I knew, as most MPs could not, the full extent of the practical military problems. I foresaw that we would encounter setbacks that would cause even some of a hawkish disposition to question whether the game was worth the candle. And how long could a coalition of opinion survive that was composed of warriors, negotiators and even virtual pacifists? For the moment, however,

* Later, when the war was won, Enoch Powell returned to the subject in a Parliamentary Question: 'Is the Rt. Hon. Lady aware that the report has now been received from the public analyst on a certain substance recently subjected to analysis and that I have obtained a copy of the report? It shows that the substance under test consisted of ferrous matter of the highest quality, and that it is of exceptional tensile strength, is highly resistant to wear and tear and to stress, and may be used to advantage for all national purposes.' Ian Gow had the two quotes printed and framed for me as a Christmas present in 1982; they hang still on my office wall.

it had survived. We received the agreement of the House of Commons for the strategy of sending the task force. And that was what mattered.

I left the House, satisfied with the day's results, prepared for more difficult debates in the future, and generally in a mood of solemnity. Indeed, from the moment I heard of the invasion, deep anxiety was ever present.

Almost immediately I faced a crisis in the Government. John Nott, who was under great strain, had delivered an uncharacteristically poor performance in his winding-up speech. He had been very harshly treated in the debate. He was held responsible by many of our back-benchers for what had happened because of the Defence Review which he had pioneered. This was unfair. The budget for conventional naval forces (that is excluding the Trident programme) was £500 million higher – and also higher as a share of the defence budget – than when we took office. Though the aircraft carrier HMS *Invincible* was to be sold, this would not take place until the end of 1983, by which time she would have been replaced by HMS *Illustrious*. Similarly HMS *Hermes* was due to be replaced by HMS *Ark Royal*, ensuring that the present aircraft carrier strength of the navy was continuously maintained. But there was no doubt that the Party's blood was up: nor was it just John Nott they were after.

Peter Carrington defended the Government's position that morning in the House of Lords and had a reasonably good reception. But Peter and John then attended a packed and angry meeting of Tory back-benchers shortly after the Commons debate. Here, Peter was at a distinct disadvantage: as a peer he had struck up none of those friendships and understandings with back-benchers on which all of us have to rely when the pressure builds. As Ian Gow reported to me afterwards, it was a very difficult meeting, and feelings had boiled over.

WEEK TWO

The press over the weekend was very hostile. Peter Carrington was talking about resigning. I saw him on Saturday evening, Sunday morning and again in the evening. Both Willie Whitelaw and I did all that we could to persuade him to stay. I felt that the country needed a Foreign Secretary of his experience and international standing to see us through the crisis. But there seems always to be a visceral desire that a disaster should be paid for by a scapegoat. There is no doubt that Peter's resignation ultimately made it easier to unite the Party and concentrate on recovering the Falklands: he understood this. Having seen Monday's press, in particular the *Times* leader, he decided that he must go. Two other senior Foreign Office ministers also resigned: Humphrey Atkins and Richard Luce. In a handwritten letter he wrote to me on Tuesday 6 April, Peter said:

> I think I was right to go. There would have been continual poison and such advice as I gave you would have been questioned. The Party will now unite behind you as it should have done last Saturday.
>
> It has been a crowded and enjoyable three years and the spirited debates we have sometimes had were productive and had no rancour.
>
> Only one thing more. Though I have never pretended to agree with you about everything, my admiration for your courage and determination and resourcefulness is unbounded. You deserve to win through and if there is anything I can do to help you have only to ask.

It was a characteristically generous and encouraging letter – and these things matter when the skies are growing darker.

I also received a wonderful letter – one of a number over the years – from Laurens van der Post, who pointed out that there was one principle, more important even than sovereignty, at stake in the dispute:

> To appease aggression and evil is to connive at a greater aggression and evil later on . . . If we fail to deal with the Fascist Argentine, the Russians will be even more encouraged than they are already to nibble away with more and more acts of aggression in what is left of a free world.

Of course, he was entirely right.

John Nott also wished to resign. But I told him straight that when the fleet had put to sea he had a bounden duty to stay and see the whole thing through. He therefore withdrew his letter on the understanding that it was made public that his offer to resign had been rejected. Whatever issues might have to be faced later as a result of the full enquiry (which I announced on 8 April), now was the time to concentrate on one thing only – victory. Meanwhile, I had to find a new Foreign Secretary. The obvious choice was Francis Pym, who had had the requisite experience of Foreign Affairs in Opposition and Defence in Government. And so I appointed him, asking John Biffen to take over his former position as Leader of the House of Commons. Francis is in many ways the quintessential old style Tory: a country gentleman and a soldier, a good tactician, but no strategist. He is a proud pragmatist and an enemy of ideology; the sort of man of whom people used to say that he would be 'just right in a crisis'. I was to have reason to question that judgement. Francis's appointment undoubtedly united the Party. But it heralded serious difficulties for the conduct of the campaign itself.

It was also on Monday that I was able to talk face to face at No. 10 with Rex Hunt and the two marine commanders who had just arrived from Uruguay. I asked him whether he had been aware that an invasion was in the offing and he replied, 'No: I thought it was just another alarm of the kind we had had previously.' He told me that when he had received our message on the previous Wednesday he had contacted one of the Argentine representatives of their airline on the island who had assured him that as far as he knew nothing was afoot. However, it seemed from what I was told by one of the marines that other Argentinians had been reporting back on every detail and movement from their airline office on the Falklands. Apparently the local Argentine commander of the invasion force knew almost every one of the names of the marines reinforcements who had been there only a few days. The operation had, it seemed, been very well planned with the first wave of Argentine troops coming from the landward side. They did not, however, come out and fight but waited for overwhelming armour and other forces to arrive. Our two marine commanders were very anxious to get back to the islands. They were subsequently flown to Ascension Island – the mid-Atlantic staging post for the task force, vital to our operation – and subsequently took the surrender at Government House when Port Stanley fell.

The Governor was superb throughout, dealing effectively with the media, which was not always an easy task. He repeated again and again that I had said in the House that our objective was the restoration of British sovereignty and the return of British administration and he was sure that I meant what I said. Of course, I did. But there were many times in the coming negotiations when I wondered whether I would indeed secure Rex Hunt's return to the Falklands.

On Tuesday 6 April there was a long Cabinet discussion of the crisis. From the beginning, we were sure that the attitude of the United States would be a key element in the outcome. The Americans could do enormous damage to the Argentine economy if they wanted. I sent a message to President Reagan urging the US to take effective economic measures. But at the moment the Americans were not prepared to do this. Nico Henderson had his first discussions with Al Haig in which the main themes of their response over the next few weeks were already clear. They had stopped arms sales. But they would not 'tilt' too heavily against Argentina. To do so would deprive them of influence in Buenos Aires. They did not want Galtieri to fall and so wanted a solution that would save his face. There were clear signs that they were contemplating a mediation between the two sides. All of this was fundamentally misguided and Nico was very robust in his reply. But in practice the Haig negotiations, which flowed from all this, almost certainly worked in our favour by precluding for a time even less helpful diplomatic intervention from other directions, including the UN. In a crisis of this kind one finds any number of people lining up to act as mediators, some motivated by nothing more than a desire to cut a figure on the world stage.

That consideration lay in the future, however. At this stage the Americans were anxious to achieve a settlement that would prevent them having to choose between Britain, their natural ally, and their interests in Latin America. I should add, though, that from the first Caspar Weinberger, US Defence Secretary, was in touch with our ambassador emphasizing that America could not put a NATO ally and long-standing friend on the same level as Argentina and that he would do what he could to help. America never had a wiser patriot, nor Britain a truer friend.

It was at this Cabinet that I announced we were setting up OD(SA), which became known to the outside world as 'the War Cabinet'. Formally, this was a sub-committee of OD, though several of its members did not serve on that committee. Its exact membership and procedure were influenced by a meeting I had with Harold Macmillan, who came to see me at the House of Commons after Questions on Tuesday 6 April to offer his support and advice as the country's and the Conservative Party's senior ex-Prime Minister. His main recommendation was to keep the Treasury – that is, Geoffrey Howe – off the main committee in charge of the campaign, the diplomacy and the aftermath. This was a wise course, but understandably Geoffrey was upset. Even so I never regretted following Harold Macmillan's advice. We were never tempted to compromise the security of our forces for financial reasons. Everything we did was governed by military necessity. So the War Cabinet consisted of myself, Francis Pym, John Nott, Willie Whitelaw as my deputy and trusted adviser, and Cecil Parkinson, who not only shared my political instincts but was brilliantly effective in dealing with public relations. Sir Terence (now Lord) Lewin, Chief of Defence Staff, always attended. So did Michael Havers, the Attorney-General, as the Government's legal adviser. Of course, we were constantly advised and supported by FCO and MoD officials and by the military. It met every day, and sometimes twice a day.

By the time of our first meeting the task force had already been despatched with a speed and efficiency which astounded the world. Millions watched on television as the two carriers sailed from Portsmouth on Monday 5 April, and on that day and the following two they were joined by a force of eleven destroyers and frigates, three submarines, the amphibious assault ship HMS *Fearless* (crucial to the landings), and numerous naval auxiliaries. Merchantmen of all kinds were 'taken up from trade'. Three thousand troops were initially assigned to the operation – 3 Commando Brigade of the Royal Marines, the 3rd Battalion of the Parachute Regiment and a unit of the Air Defence Regiment. Several times in the course of the campaign we had to revise upwards our estimate of the number of troops required and send reinforcements. This first group left the UK, sailing on the cruise ship *Canberra*, on Friday 9 April. It was not always understood that to sail a large task force with troops halfway round the world, with the intention of making opposed landings, required an enormous logistical operation – both in the UK and at sea. In the end we sent over 100 ships, carrying more than 25,000 men.

The Commander-in-Chief, Fleet, was Admiral Sir John Fieldhouse; he took overall command of the task force from his base at Northwood in West London, choosing Rear Admiral Sandy Woodward as the operational commander of the surface ships in the force. (Our submarines were controlled directly from Northwood by satellite.) I have written elsewhere about Sandy Woodward: at that time I had not yet met him, but I knew of his reputation as one of the cleverest men in the navy. Admiral Fieldhouse's land deputy was Major-General Jeremy Moore of the Royal Marines. General Moore began the campaign in Northwood, departing for the South Atlantic in May. His deputy, who sailed with HMS *Fearless* in the first wave of ships, was Brigadier Julian Thompson, of 3 Commando Brigade. Brigadier Thompson was to have charge of our forces on the Falklands for a vital period after the landing until General Moore's arrival.

OD(SA) met twice on Wednesday 7 April. Throughout the war we were confronted with the problem of managing the intricate relationship between diplomatic and military requirements. I was determined that the needs of our servicemen should have priority over politics and it was on this day that we had to resolve our first problem of this kind. Our nuclear powered submarines were due in the area of the Falklands within the next few days. We would therefore shortly be in a position to set up a 200-mile Maritime Exclusion Zone (MEZ) for ships around the Falklands. Should we announce it now? Or should we postpone the announcement until after Al Haig's imminent visit the next day? In any case, for legal reasons we had to give several days' notice before the MEZ could come into effect.

In fact Al Haig's visit had to be postponed because of that day's Commons debate. At the War Cabinet which met at 7 o'clock that evening there was a classic disagreement between the MoD and the FCO on the timing of the announcement. We decided to go ahead straight away, informing Al Haig of the decision shortly in advance.

John Nott made the announcement when he wound up the debate in a speech which restored his standing and self-confidence. Not a voice was raised against the MEZ and Jim Callaghan was heard to say 'absolutely right'. It took effect in the early hours of Easter Monday morning 12 April, by which time our submarines were in place to enforce it. It is worth noting that never during the Falklands operation did we say we would take action until we were in a position to do it. I was determined that we should never allow our bluff to be called.

One other point in that day's Commons debate is worth noting. Keith Speed, the former Navy minister, argued that we could enforce a blockade against the Argentinians on the Falklands. In fact, due to the terrible weather conditions and the problems of keeping the task force supplied and maintained so far from home, there was no way that this could have been done.

All this time we were bringing as much pressure to bear on the Argentinians as we could through diplomatic methods. I had sent messages on 6 April to the heads of state and heads of government of European Community countries, the US, Japan, Canada, Australia and New Zealand. I asked them to support us against Argentina by banning arms sales, banning all or some imports, ending export credit cover for new commitments and giving no encouragement or incentive to their banks to lend to Argentina. It had been suggested at first that I should ask for a total import ban, but though that is what we wanted I thought it bad tactics to press for too much at once. The responses

* The MEZ was a circle with a 200-nautical-mile radius drawn around a point approximately at the centre of the Falkland Islands. From the time of its coming into effect any Argentine warships and naval auxiliaries found in the zone would be treated as hostile and would be liable to be attacked by British forces.

were now coming through. I have already mentioned those of the United States and of France, and our success in the UN Security Council. Helmut Schmidt assured me personally of West Germany's strong support. Not all the countries of the European Community were as positive. There were close ties between Italy and Argentina. Though opposing the use of force, the Spanish continued to support the Argentine case and – no great surprise – the Irish caused us some concern. Later it became clear that they were not to be relied upon. However, initially the EC gave us all that we asked for, imposing an embargo on Argentine imports from the middle of April for one month. When the embargo came up for renewal in mid-May there were considerable difficulties, but eventually a compromise was reached by which Italy and Ireland were able to resume links with Argentina while the other eight continued the embargo indefinitely.

The response of the Commonwealth, with the partial exception of India, had been very supportive. In particular, Malcolm Fraser in Australia banned all imports from Argentina, except those under existing contracts. Bob Muldoon and New Zealand were, if anything, even stronger in their support, later offering to lend us a frigate to replace our own guardship in the Caribbean so that we could deploy it where it was more urgently needed.

We were disappointed by Japan's somewhat equivocal attitude. Predictably, the Soviet Union increasingly leaned towards Argentina and stepped up verbal attacks on our position. If we had returned to the UN to seek a sanctions resolution we had no doubt that they would have vetoed it.

Similarly, we were subject to a stream of vitriol from a number of Latin American countries – as was the US – though, because of its own long-standing disputes with Argentina, Chile was on our side. A number of others were quietly sympathetic, whatever their public stance: Argentina had made itself none too popular by its arrogance towards the rest of Latin America. In this way action on the diplomatic front supported the objectives of our task force as it sailed further into the South Atlantic. And, of course, effective diplomacy would have been impossible without the despatch of the task force. As Frederick the Great once remarked, 'diplomacy without arms is like music without instruments.'

On Thursday 8 April Al Haig arrived in London for the first stage of his long and tiring diplomatic shuttle. I had had a concise and, as it turned out, extremely accurate account from Nico Henderson of the propositions Mr Haig was likely to advance. We made it quite clear to him – and he accepted that this was the line we would take – that he was not being received in London as a mediator but as a friend and ally, here to discuss ways in which the United States could most effectively support us in our efforts to secure Argentine withdrawal from the Falklands. Having had some initial discussions with Francis Pym, he arrived at No. 10 for talks followed by a working dinner. His team included Ed Streator from the US Embassy in London, General Vernon Walters, Mr Haig's special assistant – a powerful personality and someone I particularly liked and respected – and Thomas Enders who dealt with South American Affairs in the State Department. I was joined by Francis, John, Terry Lewin, Sir Antony Acland (head of the Foreign Office) and Clive Whitmore (my principal private secretary). The discussions were lively and direct, to use the diplomatic jargon: there was too much at stake for me to allow them to be anything else.

It was apparent from the beginning that, whatever might be said publicly, Al Haig and his colleagues had come to mediate. He sought to reassure me about the position of the United States. He said that the US was not impartial but had to be cautious about its 'profile'. The Argentine Foreign minister had indicated that they might accept Soviet assistance, which made the Americans extremely uncomfortable. In his judgement the next seventy-two hours would be the best time for negotiation as far as the Argentinians were concerned. He told us that he had decided to visit Britain first because he did not wish to go to Buenos Aires without a full understanding of our approach.

That was my cue. I told Mr Haig that the issue was far wider than a dispute between the United Kingdom and Argentina. The use of force to seize disputed territory set a dangerous precedent. In that sense, the Falklands mattered to many countries – to Germany, for example, because of West Berlin, to France because of its colonial possessions, to Guyana, a large part of whose territory was claimed by Venezuela. (Later the FCO prepared me a brief for the Versailles G7 summit listing current territorial disputes: it was a lengthy document.) We in Britain had experience of the danger of appeasing dictators. As regards the Soviet Union, I suspected that the Russians feared American involvement as much as the Americans feared the reverse. The West might be stretched, but so were the Soviets. I would be surprised if they intervened actively. I asked what pressure the Americans could bring to bear upon Galtieri? The reputation of the western world was at stake. We wished to solve the matter by diplomatic means but we would not negotiate under duress – withdrawal was a prior condition.

It became increasingly clear to me that Mr Haig was anxious not only to avoid what he described as 'a priori judgements about sovereignty' but that he was aiming at something other than the British administration which I was publicly pledged to restore. The whole of his approach rested on trying to persuade the two sides to accept some kind of neutral 'interim administration' after Argentine withdrawal to run the islands while their long-term future was decided. He talked of an American, or perhaps Canadian, presence while negotiations continued. I pointed out that this would mean that the Argentines had gained from the use of force. I told him that British sovereignty must continue and British administration be restored. Only after this had happened could there be the possibility of negotiations, and they would be subject to the overriding condition that the wishes of the islanders were paramount.

Discussion over dinner covered very much the same area. I probed what Mr Haig seemed to be proposing as regards the administration of the islands after Argentine withdrawal had been achieved. He was rather vague: but it still seemed to me that it would not be the British administration to which we were pledged.

Mr Haig would now go to Buenos Aires to assess the Argentinian position. He agreed a common line with us. We would both say to the press that we wanted UNSCR 502 to be implemented as quickly as possible and had discussed how the United States could help. He had heard the British view of the situation and knew how strongly we felt, but he should not give the slightest impression that our position had changed in any way or that we were showing any flexibility.

In fact, Mr Haig may have looked back on our friendly disagreements in London with something like nostalgia when he got to Buenos Aires and began trying to negotiate with the Argentine Junta. It became evident that the Junta itself was deeply divided and both General Galtieri and the Foreign minister Sr. Costa Mendez seemed to alter their position from hour to hour. At one stage Mr Haig thought that he had won concessions, but as he was about to leave for England on Easter Sunday, 11 April – indeed, as he was boarding the aeroplane – Sr. Costa Mendez handed him a paper which appeared to abrogate the concessions which, rightly or wrongly, he believed he had won.

I held talks at Chequers about the Falklands over the Easter weekend. On Good Friday Tony Parsons came to lunch and we discussed the negotiating strategy. The next day Francis Pym, John Nott, and Terry Lewin came down and we too had a working lunch. I am glad that Chequers played a large part in the Falklands story. Churchill had used it quite a lot during the Second World War and its atmosphere helped to get us all together.

WEEK THREE

By Easter Monday the first ships of the task force had begun arriving at Ascension Island, half way to the Falklands. The American team returned to London on the morning of that day, 12 April. The carpets were up at No. 10 for the annual spring clean and it looked a little as if someone was moving house. This was, however, a false impression.

Al Haig began by giving an oral account of his talks in Buenos Aires. He said that he had detected differences of view between the three Argentinian Armed Services. The navy were looking for a fight. However, the air force did not want a war, and the army were somewhere in between. Enthusiasm for a fight turned out to be in inverse proportion to fighting spirit. He had worked out a set of proposals which he thought the Argentinians might be brought eventually to accept. There were seven main elements:

- First, both Britain and Argentina would agree to withdraw from the islands and a specified surrounding area within a two-week period.
- Second, no further military forces were to be introduced and forces withdrawn were to return to normal duties. The Argentinians had wanted an undertaking from us to keep our task force out of the South Atlantic altogether, but Al Haig said that he had told them that this was impossible and believed that they might be satisfied if the agreement provided for British units to return to normal duties.
- Third, there would be a Commission, in place of the Governor, made up of United States, British and Argentine representatives who would act together (whether by unanimity or majority was not specified) to ensure compliance with the agreement. For that purpose they would each need to have observers. Each member of the Commission could fly his flag at headquarters.
- Fourth, economic and financial sanctions against Argentina would be lifted.
- Fifth, the traditional local administration of the islands would be restored, including the re-establishment of the Executive and Legislative Councils, to which Argentine representatives from the tiny Argentine population in the Falklands would be

added. The Argentinians were adamantly opposed to the return of our Governor.

- Sixth, the Commission would promote travel, trade and communications between the islands and Argentina, but the British Government would have a veto on its operations.
- Finally, negotiations on a lasting settlement would be pursued 'consistently with the Purposes and Principles of the United Nations Charter'. The United States had apparently insisted on this because of the references in it to the right of self-determination. It seemed that the Argentinians would only have been prepared to agree to this part of the proposals if they contained a date for the conclusion of negotiations, which was suggested as 31 December 1982.

At this time, I did not attempt to reply to Al Haig's proposals point by point: I simply restated my belief in the principle of self-determination. If the Falkland Islanders chose to join Argentina, the British Government would respect their decision. But, equally, the Argentine Government should be prepared to accept an expressed wish of the islanders to remain British. The Americans then left us for ninety minutes, as we had agreed in advance, while we discussed the proposals with the other members of the War Cabinet.

Al Haig's proposals were full of holes but they also had some attractions. If we could really get the Argentine forces off the islands by conceding what seemed a fairly powerless commission, very limited Argentine representation on each council – drawn from local residents and not nominated by the Junta – and an Argentine flag flown alongside others at Headquarters there was something to be said for these ideas. However, on closer inspection there were formidable difficulties. What security would there be for the islanders after the interim period? Clearly, the United States would have to be asked to guarantee the islands against renewed invasion. Then there were the inescapable geographical realities. The Argentinians would remain close to the Falklands; but if we had to withdraw to 'normal areas' where would our forces be? We must have the right to be at least as close as the Argentine forces. In spite of the general reference to the UN Charter, there was still nothing to make it clear that the islanders' wishes must be paramount in the final negotiations. There must also be no possibility of the Argentinians steadily increasing the number of their people on the islands during the interim period so as to become the majority – a serious worry, particularly if our people started to leave, which they might well do in those circumstances.

At this point Francis Pym, John Nott and I rejoined Al Haig. I said that I was very grateful for the tremendous amount of work which he had done but that I had a number of questions. What did the Americans envisage would happen if no final settlement had been reached by 31 December 1982? My aim in asking was to discover whether the United States was prepared to give a guarantee. The answer was not entirely clear – nor did it become clearer with the passage of time. I emphasized again the importance attached by the House of Commons to the principle of self-determination for the islanders. We would have to have some specific reference to Article 1(2) and Article 73 of the UN Charter on this matter, which enshrined the principle of self-determination. We recognized, however, that Argentina would place a different gloss upon the agreement from the British Government. Al Haig accepted this.

On the matter of their flag, I told Al Haig that wherever else it flew, it must not fly over the Governor's house. He said that for the Argentinians the governorship of the Falklands was a key issue: they wanted to keep the Governor they had appointed after the invasion on the island as a commissioner. I said that if they did that, the British Government would have to appoint Rex Hunt as our commissioner. I also raised the question of South Georgia where Britain had an absolute title, quite distinct from its claim to the Falklands. Al Haig saw no problem about this. (We regretted afterwards that we had ever put South Georgia into the first proposals. But at the time there seemed a possibility of getting the Argentines off without a battle and they had occupied the island shortly after their invasion of the Falklands themselves.)

However, the main issue was always bound to be the military one. I knew that the only reason the Argentinians were prepared to negotiate at all was because they feared our task force. I stressed that although British submarines in the proposed demilitarized zone would leave as the Argentine forces withdrew, the British task force must continue to proceed southwards, though it would not enter the demilitarized zone. This was essential: we could not afford to let the Argentinians invade a second time. One concession I might be prepared to make was that the task force could be stood off at a point no closer to the Falklands than Argentine forces were based. Anything less would be unacceptable to Parliament.

Shortly after this we adjourned for lunch and agreed to meet later in the afternoon after we had looked in detail at the proposals and, with advice from officials and the military, worked out our own detailed amendments. In the meantime the American team had made use of a direct secure line from No. 10 to the White House. As Al Haig's memoirs reveal, he had also rung the Argentine Foreign minister, on hearing that the *New York Times* had just published the terms of the document which Sr. Costa Mendez had handed him at the airport in Buenos Aires, which were utterly inconsistent with the terms presented to us. Understandably, Mr Haig now wanted to know whether this document represented the Foreign minister's suggestions or the final and official word of the Junta.

Our two teams met once more just before 6 p.m. There were a number of points to discuss; again, the single most important was the position of the task force. Al Haig said that President Galtieri would not survive if after the Argentinians had committed themselves to withdrawing from the Falkland Islands in two weeks the British newspapers continued to report that the task force was proceeding south. The Americans were not asking for our fleet to be turned around: but they were asking for it to be halted once an agreement had been reached. I replied that I would not survive in the House of Commons if I stopped the task force before Argentine withdrawal had been completed. Nor would I be prepared to do it. I was ready to let the troop ships proceed more slowly once an agreement had been signed. But the main task force must maintain its progress towards the Falklands Islands. I saw no reason to give Argentina the benefit of the doubt. I was prepared to halt the task force at the same distance from the Falklands as that between Argentina and the islands, but I could go no further than that.

We argued until late into the evening. Argentina, starting from the Communications Agreement of 1971, wanted their citizens to have the same rights to reside on the islands, own property and so on, as the Falklanders. They wanted the commission positively to promote that state of affairs and to decide upon such matters. We fought the proposal down on the grounds that the interim administration must not change the nature of life on the islands. We finally agreed that we would pursue further negotiations on a somewhat woolly text. There were, however, some conditions which had to be made absolutely clear – the withdrawal zones, the fact that the one Argentine representative per council must be local, and that Argentinians on the islands must have the same qualifying period for voting rights as the Falklanders.

This was not, however, quite the end of Easter Monday. Just before 10 o'clock that night Al Haig telephoned me to say that Sr. Costa Mendez had rung him to say that he saw no reason for the Secretary of State to go to Buenos Aires again unless any agreement about the Falkland Islands provided for the Governor to be appointed by the

Argentine Government and for the Argentine flag to continue to be flown there. And if that was not possible, the Argentinians must have assurances that at the end of negotiations with Britain there would be a recognition of Argentine sovereignty over the Falkland Islands. Al Haig was shattered. I had mixed feelings about this news, but I was certainly not going to buckle under that sort of pressure. I told Mr Haig on the telephone:

> If those are the conditions, you cannot return [direct to Buenos Aires]; but it has to be known publicly from your viewpoint that they've set those conditions and that was why you said 'we cannot have those, we cannot therefore return.' But it must be known from your viewpoint. Publicly.

Al Haig agreed; he was obviously very depressed.

Having decided not to go on to Buenos Aires, somewhat to our surprise the following morning the Americans sought another meeting with us. So our two teams met first thing. By this stage it was becoming obvious that the proposals the Americans had presented to us the previous day had no measure of Argentine approval. In fact, the status of all these proposals was doubtful. The more closely I questioned Al Haig on this point, the more uncertain it became. Since the proposals had not been agreed with the Argentinians, even if we accepted them, they might therefore not form the basis of a settlement.

This fact was made painfully clear at the meeting that morning when Mr Haig handed us a document embodying five points which he described as essential to the Argentine position. As he himself said, the practical effect of the Argentine tactics was to buy time. I always thought that this was their main purpose in negotiating.

I was becoming impatient with all this. I said that it was essentially an issue of dictatorship versus democracy. Galtieri wanted to be able to claim victory by force of arms. The question now was whether he could be diverted from his course by economic sanctions or, as I had suspected all along, only by military force. Mr Haig replied that he had made it abundantly clear to Argentina that if conflict developed the United States would side with Britain. But did we wish to bring the negotiations to an end today? He could say publicly that he was suspending his own efforts, making it clear that this was due to Argentine intransigence. But if he did so other less helpful people might try to intervene. I was keenly aware of that and I also felt that public opinion here required us not to give up on negotiations yet.

Later that day events took another bizarre turn. Al Haig told

Francis Pym of the contents of a further discussion he had had on the telephone with Sr. Costa Mendez. Apparently, the Argentinians had now dropped their five demands and moved a considerable way from their previous position. Mr Haig thought there was a chance of a settlement on the lines we had been discussing, if we would agree to language about decolonization, subject to the wishes of the islanders, with perhaps one or two small changes in addition to make the proposals more palatable still. It was to turn out that this talk of decolonization held its own particular dangers, though we agreed to look at a draft. He also urged us not to be too rigid on the question of sovereignty. He had decided to return to Washington and would decide his next step there.

It was clear from all this that Mr Haig was very anxious to keep the negotiations going. But had there been a genuine change of heart on the part of the Argentinians, or was it just wishful thinking on his part?

Wednesday 14 April was the day scheduled for a further Commons debate on the Falklands. It was an opportunity for me to spell out our objectives in the negotiations and to demonstrate to the outside world the united support of the House of Commons. I told the House:

> In any negotiations over the coming days we shall be guided by the following principles. We shall continue to insist on Argentine withdrawal from the Falkland Islands and dependencies. We shall remain ready to exercise our right to resort to force in self-defence under Article 51 of the United Nations Charter until the occupying forces leave the islands. Our naval task force sails on towards its destination. We remain fully confident of its ability to take whatever measures may be necessary. Meanwhile, its very existence and its progress towards the Falkland Islands reinforce the efforts we are making for a diplomatic solution.
>
> That solution must safeguard the principle that the wishes of the islanders shall remain paramount. There is no reason to believe that they would prefer any alternative to the resumption of the administration which they enjoyed before Argentina committed aggression. It may be that their recent experiences will have caused their views on the future to change, but until they have had the chance freely to express their views, the British Government will not assume that the islanders' wishes are different from what they were before.

There were serious concerns underlying my reference to the possibility of the islanders changing their views on the future government of the Falklands: we worried that morale might collapse and that large numbers might leave. We were able to find out a certain amount about daily life under the occupation from messages which reached London, but the picture was far from complete.

While the debate was still in progress, Al Haig was on the telephone. The Argentinians were complaining that the United States was not being even-handed between Argentina and Britain and in particular that it was supplying military aid to Britain. He wanted to make a statement which would allow him to return to Buenos Aires to continue the negotiations, ending with these three sentences:

> Since the outset of the crisis the United States has not acceded to requests that would go beyond the scope of customary patterns of co-operation. That would continue to be its stand while peace efforts were under way. Britain's use of US facilities on Ascension Island had been restricted accordingly.

While the debate continued, I discussed it with Francis Pym and, half an hour later, rang Al Haig back in Washington.

I was very unhappy about what he wanted to say and I told him so. Of course, a good deal was being done to help us. This was occurring within those 'customary patterns of co-operation' which applied between allies like the United States and Britain. But to link this with the use of Ascension Island was wrong and misleading. Moreover, to make such a statement would have a very adverse reaction on UK opinion.

I went on to point out that Ascension Island was our island, indeed the Queen's island. The Americans used it as a base – but, as the Secretary of State well knew, this was under an agreement which made it clear that sovereignty remained with us. I am glad to say that Mr Haig agreed to remove all mention of Ascension Island from his statement.

The following day Al Haig flew from Washington to Buenos Aires for further talks. Back in London, however, it was the military realities which were most on my mind. The War Cabinet met that morning not in No. 10 but in the Ministry of Defence. We had important decisions to make. More troops were needed and had to be sent to join the task force. We had to look at the new draft we had agreed the previous day to consider. (Nothing came of it in the end.) We also had to prepare a message to the United States stressing the need for them to help enforce the agreement during that period and to ensure that when it ended the Argentinians did not attempt another invasion. I am afraid that we never got very far: the Americans were not keen to accept the role of guarantor.

However, our main business at the MoD was a thorough briefing on the military realities. It was important that we all knew precisely what forces were ranged against us, their capability, the effects of the Antarctic winter and, of course, the options available. Anyone who had harboured the idea that the task force could blockade the Falklands and mount raids in the case of the negotiations being unsuccessful was soon disabused. Quite apart from the likely losses of aircraft – the two aircraft carriers had only 20 Harriers between them – the difficulties of maintaining men and equipment in those stormy seas were huge. It was clear that we had a period of some two to three weeks in May during which we might land without terrible casualties. And then there were decisions to be made about how much more equipment, aircraft and troops to send, how to deal with the resulting prisoners of war, what to do about South Georgia and when. There was to be no respite at all. And these decisions must be made quickly. I looked from the Chiefs of Staff to my colleagues. It was a lot for them to take in. With the exception of John Nott, who of course was already briefed on the difficulties, they seemed somewhat taken aback. By this stage the press had learnt that we were at the MoD and I asked that everyone look confident as we left.

Our main task on Friday 16 April was to consider and approve the rules of engagement which would apply for transit from Ascension Island, for the 200-mile zone around South Georgia and for the purposes of South Georgia's repossession. The rules of engagement are the means by which the politicians authorize the framework within which the military can be left to make the operational decisions. They have to satisfy the objectives for which a particular military operation is undertaken. They must also give the man on the spot reasonable freedom to react as is required and to make his decisions knowing that they will be supported by the politicians. So the rules have to be clear and to cover all possible eventualities. It was after very careful questioning of the Chiefs of Staff and the Attorney-General and after long discussion that they were approved. Many other rules of engagement would follow as each new phase of the operation had to be considered. This was the first time any of us had had to make such decisions.

I had received the day before a message from President Reagan who had been rung by Galtieri, who apparently said that he was anxious to avoid a conflict. There was no difficulty in replying to that. I told the President:

> I note that General Galtieri has reaffirmed to you his desire to avoid conflict. But it seems to me – and I must state this frankly to you as a friend and ally – that he fails to draw the obvious conclusion. It was not Britain who broke the peace but Argentina. The mandatory Resolution of the Security Council, to which you and we have subscribed, requires Argentina to withdraw its troops from the Falkland Islands. That is the essential first step which must be taken to avoid conflict. When it has been taken, discussions about the future of the islands can profitably take place. Any suggestion that conflict can be avoided by a device that leaves the aggressor in occupation is surely gravely misplaced. The implications for other potential areas of tension and for small countries everywhere would be of extreme seriousness. The fundamental principles for which the free world stands would be shattered.

On Friday 16 April our two vital aircraft carriers HMS *Hermes* and HMS *Invincible* reached Ascension Island.

After a week of labyrinthine negotiations, I spent the weekend at Chequers. I found time to have a private lunch with friends and an artist who was going to paint a view of the house and its surroundings. However, I had to return to No. 10 briefly on Saturday evening to receive a telephone call from President Reagan – there is a direct line from Chequers to the White House, but there were technical problems that day. I was glad to have the chance to go over the issues with the President. I was gladder still that he agreed that it would not be reasonable to ask us to move further towards the Argentine position. Al Haig had found the Argentinians even more impossible than on his first visit. The White House had instructed him to tell the Junta that if they persisted in their intransigence this would lead to a breakdown of talks and the US Administration would make clear who was to blame.

After church on Sunday morning John Nott came to lunch and we discussed the military and diplomatic situation.

Far away in the Atlantic HMS *Hermes*, *Invincible*, *Glamorgan*, *Broadsword*, *Yarmouth*, *Alacrity* and the Royal Fleet Auxiliaries *Olmeda* and *Resource* left Ascension Island for the south.

That day I also telephoned Tony Parsons at home in New York to discuss what, if anything, we should do at the United Nations. We were in the happy position of having almost perfect backing for our position, in the form of UNSCR 502. But the problem was that as the Haig initiative was manifestly stalling and as military conflict loomed there was a risk that somebody else would take an initiative and that we would be placed in a difficult and defensive position in the Security Council. We could attempt to forestall that by tabling a resolution ourselves. But then it would be amended in ways which were simply not acceptable to us. Tony Parsons and I agreed that the best we could do for the moment was to hold our ground and seek to resist the pressure, which would undoubtedly mount.

WEEK FOUR

It was on Monday that I first read the details of the proposals discussed by Al Haig and the Argentinians in Buenos Aires. In conveying them to us, the Secretary of State said that his own disappointment with this text prevented him from attempting to influence us in any way. Indeed, the proposals were quite unacceptable. The closer one looked the clearer it was that Argentina was still trying to keep what it had taken by force. The Argentinians wanted to give themselves the military advantage and have our forces redeployed far from the islands. They were intent on subverting the traditional local administration by insisting that two representatives of the Argentine Government should serve on each of the Island Councils. They wanted to flood the islands with their own people to change the nature of the population. Finally, they were not prepared to allow the islanders to choose if they wished to return to the British Administration they had enjoyed before the invasion. This latter point was shrouded in obscure language but the intention was very clear. The wording of their proposal was:

> December 31st 1982 will conclude the interim period during which the signatories shall conclude negotiations on modalities for the removal of the islands from the list of non-self-governing territories under Chapter XI of the United Nations Charter and on mutually agreed conditions for their definitive status, including due regard for the rights of the inhabitants and for the principle of territorial integrity applicable to this dispute . . .

The innocuous sounding reference to removing the islands from the list under Chapter XI ruled out a return to the *status quo ante* the invasion and so effectively denied the islanders the right to choose freely the form of government under which they were to live. A great many words to shroud the simple fact that the use of force would have succeeded, dictatorship would have prevailed and the wishes of the islanders would have been overridden. These proposals were so poor that we told Al Haig that we saw no need for him to come to London from Buenos Aires and promised to let him have detailed comments on the text when he returned to Washington.

On the same day I received a telegram from Buenos Aires which confirmed that there was no apparent let-up in the Junta's determination to secure sovereignty over the islands. Every five minutes or so Argentine Radio would play the 'Malvinas song' which ran, 'I am your fatherland and may need you to die for me.' Soon that sentiment would be put to the test: it was on this day that the War Cabinet authorized the operation to repossess South Georgia – although the recovery was somewhat delayed because our ships arrived in a Force 11 gale which lasted for several days.

Al Haig asked that Francis Pym should go to Washington to discuss our views of the Argentine text and I agreed to this. Francis sent ahead our detailed comments and essential amendments to the Buenos Aires text. We agreed that he was to be guided by these counter-proposals during his visit. He was also to seek an American guarantee for the security of the islands. Unfortunately during questions on a Commons statement the following day, Francis gave the impression that force would not be used as long as negotiations were continuing. This was an impossible position for us to take up, enabling the Argentinians to string us along indefinitely, and he had to return to the House later to make a short statement retracting the remark.

Also on Wednesday we notified Al Haig via Nico Henderson that a firm decision had been taken to recover South Georgia in the near future. Mr Haig expressed himself surprised and concerned. He asked whether our decision was final: I confirmed that it was. We were informing, not consulting him. Later he told our ambassador that he thought he would have to give the Argentine Junta advance notice of our intended operation. We were appalled. Nico Henderson persuaded him to think better of it.

Francis Pym spent Thursday in Washington discussing our proposals with Al Haig. He did not get very far in pressing the idea of an American guarantee. The Americans seemed unprepared to envisage anything going beyond the interim period. Nor, as I was shortly to learn, was he any more successful in putting across the rest of our ideas. My own thoughts, however, were elsewhere. I was desperately worried about what was happening in South Georgia.

That Thursday evening John Nott and the Chief of the Defence Staff came to Downing Street to give me urgent news. Our Special Forces had landed on the Fortuna glacier in South Georgia to carry out a reconnaissance. The first attempt to get them in had had to be abandoned because of high wind and heavy snow. During a temporary and slight improvement in conditions our men were successfully landed. But the weather then rapidly worsened with a south-west wind gusting over 70 knots. Their exposed position on the glacier became intolerable and they sent a message to HMS *Antrim* asking for helicopters to take them off. The first helicopter came in and, blinded by the snow, crashed. A second suffered the same fate. The MoD did not know whether lives had been lost. It was a terrible and disturbing start to the campaign.

My heart was heavy as I changed for a charity dinner at the Mansion House at which I was to be the main speaker. How was I to conceal my feelings? I allowed myself to wonder whether the task we had set ourselves was truly impossible. But just as I reached the foot of the stairs at No. 10 on my way out, Clive Whitmore, my principal private secretary, rushed out of his office with more news. A third helicopter had landed on the glacier and picked up all the SAS men and the other two helicopter crews. How that pilot managed it I do not know. Months later I met him – completely modest, quietly professional: his comment was that he had never seen so many people in his helicopter. As I carried on out of No. 10 and left for the dinner I walked on air. All our people had survived.

On Friday 23 April we gave a general warning to Argentina that any approach on the part of their warships, submarines or aircraft which could amount to a threat to British forces in the South Atlantic would be regarded as hostile and dealt with accordingly. Later that day I went to Northwood from where military operations and all the logistics were being directed. It was fascinating to see how the decisions were put into effect. I had lunch at the home of Admiral Fieldhouse and his wife, Midge, before returning to No. 10.

Francis Pym was now on his way back from the United States with new draft proposals.

Saturday 24 April was to be one of the most crucial days in the Falklands story and a critical one for me personally. Early that morning Francis came to my study in No. 10 to tell me the results of his efforts. I can only describe the document which he brought back as conditional surrender. Al Haig was a powerful persuader and anyone on the other side of the table had to stand up to him, not give ground. Mr Haig had clearly played upon the imminence of hostilities and the risk that Britain would lose international support if fighting broke out. I told Francis that the terms were totally unacceptable. They would rob the Falklanders of their freedom and Britain of her honour and respect. Francis disagreed. He thought that we should accept what was in the document. We were at loggerheads.

A meeting of the War Cabinet had been arranged for that evening and I spent the rest of that day comparing in detail all the different proposals which had been made up to that point in the diplomacy. The closer I looked the clearer it was that our position was being abandoned and the Falklanders betrayed. I asked for the Attorney-General to come to No. 10 and go through them with me. But the message went astray and instead he went to the Foreign Office. Less than an hour before the War Cabinet, he at last received the message and came to see me, only to confirm all my worst fears.

It is important to understand that what might appear at first glance to the untutored eye as minor variations in language between diplomatic texts can be of vital significance, as they were in this case. There were four main texts to compare. There were the proposals which Al Haig discussed with us and took to Argentina on 12 April. Our own attitude towards these had been left deliberately vague: though he had discussed them in detail with us, we had not committed ourselves to accept them. Then there were the totally impossible proposals brought back by Mr Haig after his visit to Buenos Aires on 19 April. On 22 April we amended those proposals in ways acceptable to us and it was on this basis that Francis Pym had been instructed to negotiate. Finally, there was the latest draft brought back by Francis from the United States, which now confronted me. The differences between the texts of 22 and 24 April went to the heart of why we were prepared to fight a war for the Falklands.

First, there was the question of how far and fast would our forces withdraw. Under the text Francis Pym had brought back our task force would have had to stand off even further than in the Buenos Aires proposals. Worse still, all of our forces, including the submarines, would have to leave the defined zones within seven days, depriving us of any effective military leverage over the withdrawal process. What if the Argentinians went back on the deal? Also the task force would have to disperse altogether after 15 days. Nor was there any way of ensuring that Argentine troops kept to the provision that they be 'at less than 7 days' readiness to invade again' (whatever that meant).

Second, sanctions against Argentina were to be abandoned the moment the agreement was signed, rather than as in our counter-proposals on completion of withdrawal. Thus we lost the only other means we had to ensure that Argentine withdrawal actually took place.

Third, as regards the Special Interim Authority the text reverted to the Buenos Aires proposal for two representatives of the Argentine Government on the Islands' Councils, as well as at least one representative of the local Argentine population. Moreover, there was a return to the wording relating to Argentine residence and property which would effectively have allowed them to swamp the existing population with Argentinians.

Equally important was the wording relating to the long-term negotiations after Argentine withdrawal. Like the Buenos Aires document, Francis Pym's ruled out the possibility of a return to the situation enjoyed by the islanders before the invasion. We would have gone against our commitment to the principle that the islanders' wishes were paramount and would have abandoned all possibility of their staying with us. Did Francis realize how much he had signed away?

Despite my clear views expressed that morning, Francis put in a paper to the War Cabinet recommending acceptance of these terms. Shortly before 6 o'clock that evening ministers and civil servants began assembling outside the Cabinet Room. Francis was there, busy lobbying for their support. I asked Willie Whitelaw to come upstairs to my study. I told him that I could not accept these terms and gave him my reasons. As always on crucial occasions he backed my judgement.

The meeting began and Francis Pym introduced his paper, recommending that we concur in the plan. But five hours of preparation on my part had not been wasted. I went through the text clause by clause. What did each point actually mean? How come that we had now accepted what had previously been rejected? Why had we not insisted as a minimum on self-determination? Why had we accepted almost unlimited Argentine immigration and acquisition of property on an equal basis with the existing Falkland Islanders? The rest of the committee were with me.

It was John Nott who found the procedural way forward. He proposed that we should make no comment on the draft but ask Mr Haig to put it to the Argentinians first. If they accepted it we should undoubtedly be in difficulties: but we could then put the matter to Parliament in the light of their acceptance. If the Argentinians rejected it – and we thought that they would, because it is almost impossible for any military Junta to withdraw – we could then urge the Americans to come down firmly on our side, as Al Haig had indicated they would as long as we did not break off the negotiations. This is what was decided. I sent a message to Mr Haig:

> This whole business started with an Argentine aggression. Since then our purpose together has been to ensure the early withdrawal by the Argentinians in accordance with the Security Council Resolution. We think therefore that the next step should be for you to put your latest ideas to them. I hope that you will seek the Argentine Government's view of them tomorrow and establish urgently whether they can accept them. Knowledge of their attitude will be important to the British Cabinet's consideration of your ideas.

And so a great crisis passed. I could not have stayed as Prime Minister had the War Cabinet accepted Francis Pym's proposals. I would have resigned.

That difficult and decisive argument was followed the next day by the recapture of South Georgia. At Grytviken an Argentine submarine was spotted on the surface and was successfully attacked by our helicopters and immobilized. A certain Captain Astiz had been in charge of the Argentine garrison there. His capture was to present us with problems. He was wanted for murder by both France and Sweden. He was flown to Ascension and then brought to Britain, but refused to answer questions and, due to the provisions of the Geneva Convention on Prisoners of War eventually, reluctantly, we had to return him to Argentina.

Later that afternoon I learnt of our success in South Georgia. An audience was arranged with the Queen that evening at Windsor. I was glad to be able personally to give her the news that one of her islands had been recovered. I returned to Downing Street to await confirmation of the earlier signal and the release of the news. I wanted John Nott to have the opportunity of making the announcement and so I had him come to No. 10. Together, he, the MoD press officer, and I drafted the press release and then went out to announce the good news.

A remark of mine was misinterpreted, sometimes wilfully. After John Nott had made his statement journalists tried to ask questions. 'What happens next Mr Nott? Are we going to declare war on Argentina Mrs Thatcher?' It seemed as if they preferred to press us on these issues rather than to report news that would raise the nation's spirits and give the Falklanders new heart. I was irritated and intervened to stop them: 'Just rejoice at that news and congratulate our forces and the marines . . . Rejoice'. I meant that they should rejoice in the bloodless recapture of South Georgia, not in the war itself. To me war is not a matter for rejoicing. But some pretended otherwise.

A worry for us at this point was that the press and probably some of the public began to assume that it would only be a matter of days before we retook the Falklands and that this would be as quick as the recapture of South Georgia. We knew that this was far from true. Indeed, it was only on that day that the last ships of the amphibious group necessary for the landing left Britain. Led by the assault ship HMS *Intrepid*, there were the ferries *Norland* and *Europic* carrying the 2nd Battalion of the Parachute Regiment, and – loaded with vital stores – the container ship *Atlantic Conveyor*.

WEEK FIVE

On Monday 26 April, the War Cabinet agreed the announcement of a Total Exclusion Zone (TEZ) of a 200-nautical-mile radius and the rules of engagement which were to apply to it. The military pressure on Argentina was steadily mounting. The TEZ went beyond the earlier MEZ by excluding aircraft as well as sea-going craft: the task force would shortly be close enough to the Falklands to be able to enforce it and to be at risk from air attack itself. One priority was to close down the airfield at Port Stanley.

At home the apparent imminence of full-scale military conflict began to shake the determination of those whose commitment to retaking the Falklands had always been weaker than it appeared. Some MPs seemed to want negotiations to continue indefinitely. I had to put the realities to the nation. At Prime Minister's Questions I said:

> I must point out that time is getting extremely short as the task force approaches the islands. Three weeks have elapsed since the Resolution SCR 502. One cannot have a wide range of choice and a wide range of military options with the task force in the wild and stormy weathers of that area.

I made the same point in a live interview that evening on *Panorama*:

> I have to keep in mind the interests of our boys who are on those warships and our marines. I have to watch the safety of their lives, to see that they can succeed in doing whatever it is

> we decide they have to do at the best possible time and with minimum risk to them.

I also took the opportunity to say directly just what we were fighting for:

> I'm standing up for the right of self-determination. I'm standing up for our territory. I'm standing up for our people. I'm standing up for international law. I'm standing up for all those territories – those small territories and peoples the world over – who, if someone doesn't stand up and say to an invader 'enough, stop' . . . would be at risk.

Unfortunately, the cracks now appearing in the Labour Party were likely to be widened by what was happening at the United Nations. The Secretary-General of the UN started to become more involved as the Haig mediation manifestly stalled. A low-key appeal from Sr. Perez de Cuellar to both sides – which appeared to imply that we, like Argentina, had failed to comply with UNSCR 502 – was seized upon by Denis Healey and Michael Foot. I had a serious clash with Mr Foot during Prime Minister's Questions on Tuesday 27 April on the question of our returning to the United Nations. In fact, the Secretary-General very quickly took the point, but the damage was done. We ourselves had been exploring whether an offer from President López-Portillo of Mexico to provide a venue for negotiations might be productive. But Al Haig did not wish us to pursue this and I doubt whether the Mexicans would in fact have proposed the simpler and more satisfactory formula which we wanted.

Al Haig had had his own share of diplomatic problems. His speech to a meeting of the Organization of American States justifying the United States line on the Falklands and Argentina had been greeted with stony silence. The Argentine Foreign minister, furious at the retaking of South Georgia, had publicly refused to see him, though they had been in contact privately.

Al Haig could not under these circumstances go back to Buenos Aires, which from our point of view was probably all to the good. He had again modified the proposals discussed with Francis Pym in Washington and now transmitted these to the Argentine Government. Mr Haig told the Junta that no amendments were permissible and imposed a strict time limit for their reply, though he was subsequently unwilling to stick to this. For its part, the Junta was now determined to play for time. Al Haig telephoned Francis Pym in the afternoon of

Wednesday 28 April to say that there was still no word from Buenos Aires. Both Francis and Nico Henderson continued to press him to say publicly that the Argentinians were to blame for the failure of his mediation and that the United States was openly supporting us.

At Cabinet on Thursday 29 April we discussed the continuing uncertainty. The deadline given to the Argentinians for their answer had passed, but now Mr Haig was talking of the possibility of the Argentinians amending his proposals. Where would all this end?

After Cabinet I sent a message to President Reagan saying that in our view the Argentinians must now be regarded as having rejected the American proposals. In fact, later that day the Argentinians did formally reject the American text. President Reagan now replied to my message in these terms:

> I am sure you agree that it is essential now to make clear to the world that every effort was made to achieve a fair and peaceful solution, and that the Argentine Government was offered a choice between such a solution and further hostilities. We will therefore make public a general account of the efforts we have made. While we will describe the US proposal in broad terms, we will not release it because of the difficulty that might cause you. I recognize that while you see fundamental difficulties in the proposal, you have not rejected it. We will leave no doubt that Her Majesty's Government worked with us in good faith and was left with no choice but to proceed with military action based on the right of self-defence.

This was very satisfactory. We wanted a clear statement that the Argentinians were to blame for the failure of negotiations. But we did not want to muddy the waters by revealing every detail of proposals which were in truth fundamentally unacceptable to us, nor did we want to imply that we had accepted the Haig proposals.

There was, though, one drawback. This was that once the Haig mediation had formally ended the pressure would sharply increase for us to go back to the UN where we would be faced by any number of difficulties. Indeed Tony Parsons advised us that once we were back in the Security Council there would be no way of avoiding an unacceptable call on us to halt military preparations and accept the good offices of the Secretary-General. This would mean that we would have to use our veto, which we wanted to avoid. In fact, although this assessment was correct it was not until the following month that all this came to a head. We were fortunate that it did not occur earlier.

Friday 30 April effectively marked the end of the beginning of our diplomatic and military campaign to regain the Falklands. The United States now came down clearly on our side. President Reagan told television correspondents that the Argentinians had resorted to armed aggression and that such aggression must not be allowed to succeed. Most important, the President also directed that the United States would respond positively to requests for military materiel. Unfortunately, they were not prepared to agree to place an embargo on imports from Argentina. However, the President's announcements constituted a substantial moral boost to our position.

It was on this day that the TEZ came into force. And although diplomatic and military affairs remained inextricably intertwined, it is fair to say that from now on it was the military rather than the diplomatic which increasingly commanded our attention. At that morning's War Cabinet it was the Argentine aircraft carrier, the *25 de Mayo*, which concerned us. She could cover 500 miles a day and her aircraft a further 500. Her escorts carried Exocet missiles, supplied by France in the 1970s. We were well aware that the Exocet threat should be taken seriously. It increased the danger which the Argentine carrier group posed to our ships and their supply lines. We therefore authorized an attack on the carrier, wherever she was, provided it was south of latitude 35 degrees and east of longitude 48, and outside the 12-mile limit of Argentine territorial waters. Such an attack would be based upon the right of self-defence and be within Article 51 of the UN Charter; in accordance with the notification which had been given on 23 April no further warning was required.

That evening I had to speak at a large rally in Stephen Hastings's constituency at Milton Hall in Bedfordshire. Stephen and his predecessor Alan Lennox-Boyd spoke magnificently. I was given a wonderful reception. No one present had any doubt of the justice of our cause, nor that we would eventually win through. I felt proud and exhilarated: but I felt too an almost crushing burden of responsibility. I knew that the task force would enter the waters around the Falkland Islands the following day.

* See p. 205.

CHAPTER VIII

The Falklands: Victory

The battle for the Falklands in May and June 1982

From the beginning of May through to the recapture of the Falklands in mid-June military considerations loomed ever larger in my mind. But this did not mean that the pressure for negotiations eased – far from it. I was under an almost intolerable pressure to negotiate for the sake of negotiation and because so many politicians were desperately anxious to avoid the use of force – as if the Argentinians had not already used force by invading in the first place. At such a time almost everything and everyone seems to combine to deflect you from what you know has to be done.

Yet I could never afford to ignore the diplomatic effort because on its successful conduct rested our hard-won position of UN Security Council support for Resolution 502 and, still more important, the degree of support we might receive from our allies, above all the United States. And all this time there was constant, nagging fear of the unknown. Would we have sufficient air cover? Where were the Argentine submarines? Would we be able to reach the military and diplomatic position required for a successful landing within that narrow time-frame set by the onset of intolerable winter weather in the South Atlantic?

Over breakfast at Milton Hall I received a telephone call to say that our Vulcans had bombed the runway of Port Stanley airport. Our naval task force was also bombarding Argentine positions elsewhere on the Falklands. I was told that there had so far been no British casualties but it would still be many hours before the Vulcans – after their marathon flight involving five mid-air refuellings – would be back at Ascension Island. In fact they all returned safely. The refuelling seemed a stupendous feat at the time, although such is the way of things that later performances of this kind came almost to be taken for granted.

That day the Argentine Air Force mounted a major attack on

our ships. The Argentinians were in a position to send photographs to the outside world, which we were not. They claimed that many of our aeroplanes had been shot down but in that famous broadcast Brian Hanrahan, the excellent BBC correspondent, put the record straight when he reported: 'I counted them all out and I counted them all back.' It was a great relief. But we had no illusions about the significance of the heavy attack and the vital question it raised about the sufficiency of our air cover.

The next day, Sunday, which I spent at Chequers, was one of great – though often misunderstood – significance for the outcome of the Falklands War. As often on Sundays during the crisis, the members of the War Cabinet, Chiefs of Staff and officials came to Chequers for lunch and discussions. On this occasion there was a special matter on which I needed an urgent decision.

I called together Willie Whitelaw, John Nott, Cecil Parkinson, Michael Havers, Terry Lewin, Admiral Fieldhouse and Sir Antony Acland, the Permanent Secretary at the Foreign Office. (Francis Pym was in America.) Admiral Fieldhouse told us that one of our submarines, HMS *Conqueror*, had been shadowing the Argentine cruiser, *General Belgrano*. The *Belgrano* was escorted by two destroyers. The cruiser itself had substantial fire power provided by 6 guns with a range of 13 miles and anti-aircraft missiles. We were advised that she might have been fitted with Exocet anti-ship missiles, and her two destroyer escorts were known to be carrying them. The whole group was sailing on the edge of the Exclusion Zone. We had received intelligence about the aggressive intentions of the Argentine fleet. There had been extensive air attacks on our ships the previous day and Admiral Woodward, in command of the task force, had every reason to believe that a full-scale attack was developing. The Argentine aircraft carrier, the *25 de Mayo*, had been sighted some time earlier and we had agreed to change the rules of engagement to deal with the threat she posed. However, our submarine had lost contact with the carrier, which had slipped past it to the north. There was a strong possibility that *Conqueror* might also lose contact with the *Belgrano* group. Admiral Woodward had to come to a judgement about what to do with the *Belgrano* in the light of these circumstances. From all the information available, he concluded that the carrier and the *Belgrano* group were engaged in a classic pincer movement against the task force. It was clear to me what must be done to protect our forces, in the light of Admiral Woodward's concern and Admiral Fieldhouse's advice. We therefore decided that British forces should be able to attack any Argentine naval vessel on the same basis as agreed previously for the carrier.

Later we approved reinforcements for the Falklands which would be taken there in the *QE2*. It surprised me a little that the need for reinforcements had not been clear sooner. I asked whether it was really necessary or advisable to use this great ship and to put so many people in it, but as soon as I was told that it was necessary to get them there in time I gave my agreement. I was always concerned that we would not have sufficient men and equipment when the time came for the final battle and I was repeatedly struck by the fact that even such highly qualified professionals as advised us often underestimated the requirements. We broke up still desperately worried that the aircraft carrier which could have done such damage to our vulnerable task force had not been found.

The necessary order conveying the change of rules of engagement was sent from Northwood to HMS *Conqueror* at 1.30 p.m. In fact, it was not until after 5 p.m. that *Conqueror* reported that she had received the order. The *Belgrano* was torpedoed and sunk just before 8 o'clock that evening. Our submarine headed away as quickly as possible. Wrongly believing that they would be the next targets, the *Belgrano*'s escorts seem to have engaged in anti-submarine activities rather than rescuing its crew, some 321 of whom were lost – though initially the death toll was reported to be much higher. The ship's poor state of battle readiness greatly increased the casualties. Back in London we knew that the *Belgrano* had been hit, but it was some hours before we knew that she had sunk.

A large amount of malicious and misleading nonsense was circulated at the time and long afterwards about the reasons why we sank the *Belgrano*. These allegations have been demonstrated to be without foundation. The decision to sink the *Belgrano* was taken for strictly military not political reasons: the claim that we were trying to undermine a promising peace initiative from Peru will not bear scrutiny. Those of us who took the decision at Chequers did not at that time know anything about the Peruvian proposals, which in any case closely resembled the Haig plan rejected by the Argentinians only days before. There was a clear military threat which we could not responsibly ignore. Moreover, subsequent events more than justified what was done. As a result of the devastating loss of the *Belgrano*, the Argentine Navy – above all the carrier – went back to port and stayed there. Thereafter it posed no serious threat to the success of the task force, though of course we were not to know that this would be so at the time. The sinking of the *Belgrano* turned out to be one of the most decisive military actions of the war.

However, the shocking loss of life caused us many problems because it provided a reason – or in some cases perhaps an excuse – for breaks in the ranks among the less committed of our allies: it also increased pressure on us at the UN. The Irish Government called for an immediate meeting of the Security Council, though after intense pressure from Tony Parsons and some from the UN Secretary-General, they were eventually persuaded to suspend their request – not, however, before the Irish Defence minister had described us as 'the aggressor'. There was some wavering from the French and rather more from the West Germans, who pressed for a cease-fire and UN negotiations. Moreover, by the time of the sinking of the *Belgrano*, the diplomatic scene was already becoming more difficult and complicated.

I have already mentioned the peace plan which the President of Peru had put to Al Haig and which he in turn had put to Francis Pym in Washington on 1 and 2 May, though we had no sight of it until later. With the sinking of the *Belgrano*, Mr Haig was once again bringing pressure to bear, urging on us diplomatic magnanimity and, expressing his belief that whatever the course of the military campaign there must be a negotiated outcome to avoid open-ended hostility and instability. To add to the confusion, the UN Secretary-General was now seeking to launch a peace initiative of his own, much to the irritation of Mr Haig.

WEEK SIX

Both military and diplomatic pressures now mounted. On Tuesday 4 May the destroyer HMS *Sheffield* was hit by an Argentine Exocet missile with devastating effects. The loss of the *Sheffield* was the result of a number of mishaps and mistakes, but it was a terrible demonstration of the risks our forces faced. The *Sheffield* was a relatively old ship, with outdated radar: it was transmitting via satellite to London moments before the missile struck, interfering with its capacity to detect the attack sufficiently in advance to throw up chaff as a decoy. Also the fire doors were open and, as we learnt from the raging fire that followed the missile impact, there was too much aluminium in the structure. Although the ship did not sink at first, it proved impossible due to the rough seas to bring it back home, as I had wished, and eventually she went down. At first I was told that there were 20 casualties: then 40.

It was very difficult to know how to announce this sort of news. We would have liked to inform all next of kin first, and indeed sought to do so. But meanwhile the Argentinians would be putting out statements – some true, some false but all with a deliberate purpose – before we knew the real facts. As a result, wives and families spent some agonizing days and nights. That day we also lost one of our Harriers.

By this stage Francis Pym had returned from the United States. We did not like the US/Peruvian proposals he brought with him and sought to have important changes made, above all to ensure that the wishes of the islanders were respected. Al Haig, however, would not accept our changes or pass them to the Peruvians because he believed that the Argentinians would reject them out of hand. I received a message from President Reagan urging us to make further compromise.

On the morning of Wednesday 5 May I called first the War Cabinet and then the full Cabinet to consider the US/Peruvian proposals. Francis Pym believed that in view of the battle in the South Atlantic it would be damaging to reject what were in effect Al Haig's proposals. Moreover, as I have noted, the countries of the European Community which had been very strong at first were beginning to weaken in their support. The sanctions which they had agreed were only for a month and there would be difficulty in getting everyone to approve their renewal.

I was deeply unhappy about the US/Peruvian proposals. Cabinet did not like them much either. But we had to make some response. I wanted to ensure that any interim administration would consult the islanders and that their wishes should be respected in the long-term settlement. I also wanted South Georgia and the other Falklands dependencies to be outside the scope of the proposals. Cabinet was firm about these objectives. We agreed to seek changes to meet them and in this we were successful.

I did not like this constant pressure to weaken our stance. I drafted a personal letter to President Reagan that revealed perhaps too much of my frustration, though I toned it down before it was sent. But I took comfort from the fact that I had never believed that the Argentine Junta would be prepared to withdraw on these or any other terms – and indeed the Argentinians turned down the US/Peruvian proposals. Attention now increasingly shifted to the proposals of the UN Secretary-General. The Argentinians sent their Foreign minister to New York. They hoped to capitalize on the sympathy they had gained as a result of the sinking of the *Belgrano* and their spirits had been lifted by the destruction of the *Sheffield*. There was no lack of candidates to suggest new 'initiatives' – not the least surprising or impractical of which was the suggestion of President López-Portillo that I should have a private meeting with General Galtieri in Mexico. But I was not going to sell out the islanders and I knew that the Argentine Junta could not withdraw and survive. Obviously there was little prospect of a diplomatic 'breakthrough', yet still the apparently endless negotiations continued.

Tony Parsons defended Britain's position at the UN with great force and brilliance. The Argentinians were clearly determined to get the maximum propaganda advantage in the new discussions sponsored by the UN Secretary-General. He warned Sr. Perez de Cuellar of our past experiences of trying to deal with the Junta. The Secretary-General could expect that agreements apparently satisfactory to Argentine representatives would then be disowned by the Junta and that the Argentinians were intent on establishing sovereignty as a precondition of any settlement.

I was not prepared to hold up military progress for negotiations. We were all aware that we were coming to a critical period. If we were to land and repossess the islands it would have to be done some time between 16 and 30 May. We could not leave it later because of the weather. That meant that negotiations at the UN must be completed within ten days or so. If they were successful and our principles and minimum requirements were met, well and good. If not, or they were still dragging on, then – if the Chiefs of Staff so advised – we would have to go ahead.

I had mixed feelings about the negotiations. I shared the desire to avoid a further bloody conflict. I spoke about this to Tony Parsons on the telephone on Saturday 8 May. I asked Tony to tell the Secretary-General that we would be pleased to welcome him in London. I went on:

> In the end you know we might have to go in. I say in the end – time is short. But I just feel deeply . . . first that our people there were living in self-determination and freedom before this started and one can't hand them over to anything less. But secondly that it is going to be the most awful waste of young life if we really have to go and take those islands . . . I will do everything before the final decision has to be taken to see if we can uphold the rule of international law and the liberty and justice, in which I believe passionately for our people, to see if we can stop a final battle.

However, as the negotiations with the Argentinians in Washington continued it became ever more evident that they were not prepared to make the concessions we required. They were determined to include South Georgia and the dependencies. They wanted to deny the islanders any proper means of expressing their views during the interim period. They were pressing for the complete withdrawal of the British task force to its bases in the UK – which, now that the battle for the Falklands had begun, was of course even more unacceptable than it had been before. They also wanted to be able to move in their own people and acquire property so as to change the whole terms of the argument. It was clear that the negotiations would fail. We must ensure that when they did so the Argentinians did not manage to shift the blame on to us. Ideally, we should bring them to a definite conclusion before the landings took place. An ultimatum was obviously necessary.

On Sunday afternoon at Chequers (9 May) our regular meeting reviewed the diplomatic and military scene. We discussed the state of the negotiations and where they might lead. There was also a politically sensitive military matter. Argentine civilian aircraft were flying over our supply lines and doubtless communicating their findings direct to their submarines. We had every right to act to stop this. But could we be sure that if we shot at a civilian aircraft it would turn out to be an Argentine one? The radar characteristics and the typical flight path of an aircraft on surveillance would help to identify those on such reconnaissance missions. But there was an obvious risk that something could go wrong. We also had to consider the possibility of a commando raid against Ascension Island and our forces there – unlikely perhaps, but potentially devastating.

WEEK SEVEN

We now had to stand firm against the pressure for making unacceptable compromises while avoiding the appearance of intransigence. Specific instructions went to Tony Parsons about our position on withdrawal distances, interim administration, the issue of immigration and the acquisition of property during the interim period and to ensure that the Argentinians did not get away with prejudging the issue on sovereignty: that was for the islanders to decide. There were detailed discussions on the constitutional position of a United Nations administration of the islands. Our view was that the UN representative could only administer the law, not change it. If he wished to do so he would have to act through the islands' Legislative Council. We also continued to press for a United States military guarantee of the security of the islands – but with very limited success. The UN Secretary-General was somewhat taken aback by the firmness of our stance. But Tony Parsons impressed on him the basic facts of the dispute. It was not we who had committed the aggression, though we had made a number of major concessions. Any arrangement which appeared to reward Argentine aggression would simply not be accepted in Britain.

The Argentinians could not be trusted. For example, on the issue of not prejudging sovereignty, their representative said one thing to the Secretary-General while their Foreign minister said quite the opposite in his public statements. Who was to be believed? The information we were receiving from the Americans about the attitude of the Argentine Junta confirmed our worst predictions. They were apparently not able to give way on sovereignty, even if they had wished, because of the political situation in which they now found themselves. This, however, was their problem not ours. My own views at this time were hardening because I was convinced that if anything we had already gone too far in making concessions. My feelings were echoed in the House of Commons. In the debate on Thursday 13 May Conservative back-benchers showed evidence of restlessness about our negotiations. Francis Pym continued to pursue a weaker line than I did and it was not liked.

Al Haig was now in Europe and his absence apparently gave those in the Administration who were favourable to the Argentinians an opportunity to persuade President Reagan that it was we who were being inflexible. President Reagan telephoned me at 6.40 that evening. He had gained the impression that the Argentinians and ourselves were now quite close in our negotiating positions. I had to tell him that unfortunately this was not the case. Major obstacles remained. As regards the interim arrangements, Argentina wanted greater Argentine participation than we could accept and there were substantial difficulties about ownership of property and freedom of movement. Secondly, there was the difficulty of South Georgia where our title was completely different and we were in possession. There was the added problem that we just did not know with whom we were really negotiating. The Argentinians were trying to arrange an interim administration which would lead inevitably to Argentine sovereignty. Finally, there was no guarantee that at a later stage they might not invade the islands again.

President Reagan had been talking to the President of Brazil who had been visiting Washington. There was some concern (entirely misplaced) that we were preparing an attack on the Argentine mainland: whether or not such attacks would have made any military sense, we saw from the beginning that they would cause too much political damage to our position to be anything but counter-productive. President Reagan wanted us to hold off military action. I said that Argentina had attacked our ships only yesterday. We could not delay military options simply because of negotiations. The truth was that it was only our military measures which had produced a diplomatic response, highly unsatisfactory as this was.

President Reagan was also concerned that the struggle was being portrayed as one between David and Goliath – in which the United Kingdom was cast as Goliath. I pointed out that this could hardly be true at a distance of 8000 miles. I reminded the President that he would not wish his people to live under the sort of regime offered by the military Junta and also of the length of time that many of the islanders had lived there and the strategic significance of the Falkland Islands if, for example, the Panama Canal were ever closed. I finished by seeking to persuade him – I believe successfully – that he had been misinformed about the Argentinians' alleged concessions. It was a difficult conversation but on balance probably a useful one. The fact that even our closest ally – and someone who had already proved himself one of my closest political friends – could look at things in this way demonstrated the difficulties we faced.

On the morning of Friday 14 May there were two separate meetings of the War Cabinet. One consisted of a detailed assessment of the military position and options. The other was taken up with the diplomatic situation. We decided to prepare our own terms to put to the Argentinians as an ultimatum and Tony Parsons and Nico Henderson were summoned back from the United States to Chequers to discuss these for the weekend.

Two events that day and the next gave a great boost to my morale. First, there was the welcome I received from the Scottish Conservative Party Conference in Perth – an occasion which, as I have said before, I always enjoyed. In my speech I set out precisely what we were fighting for and why. I also said:

> The Government wants a peaceful settlement. But we totally reject a peaceful sell-out.

The Leader of the Liberal Party, David Steel, accused me of 'jingoism'. How remote politicians can seem at these times of crisis: neither the audience nor the nation would fall into the same trap of characterizing determination to secure justice and the country's honour in terms like that.

Secondly, I also learned of the successful raid under cover of darkness by our SAS and Special Boat Service men on Pebble Island off the north of West Falkland, destroying all eleven Argentinian aircraft at the air strip. It was a daring venture and a significant, though unheeded, warning to the Argentinians of the professionalism of our forces.

That Sunday at Chequers was mainly spent in drafting our own final proposals, to be put to the Argentinians by the UN Secretary-General. The vital consideration was that we bring the negotiating process to an end – ideally, before the landings – but in such a way as to avoid appearing intransigent. It became clear that we would have to make a very reasonable offer. I accepted this because I was convinced that the Argentinians would reject it, and strictly on a take-it-or-leave-it basis: the Argentinians must accept the offer as a whole, or not at all, and once rejected, it would be withdrawn. We would set a time limit for their response.

Tony Parsons and Nico Henderson were both closely involved in the drafting. We went over every point in detail, working as usual around the oblong table in the Great Parlour upstairs, remodelling the draft clause by clause. At hand were voluminous reference sources on the UN and the law relating to the administration of the Falklands. We hardened our terms in respect of interim administration, ensuring something close to self-government for the islanders and denying any role to the Argentine Government. We excluded South Georgia and the other dependencies from the proposals altogether: South Georgia was back under British control and there could be no question any longer of including it in the negotiations. We made reference to Article 73 of the UN Charter, which implies self-determination, to make it clear that the wishes of the islanders would be paramount in long-term negotiations. The Argentine Government was required to give a response within 48 hours and there was to be no negotiation of the terms. This exercise also allowed me subsequently to explain each phrase to the House of Commons to allay their understandable fears that we might be prepared to yield too much.

To keep the US informed and supportive at the UN – which was crucial – I authorized Francis Pym to brief Al Haig about our proposals that evening. This was a wise decision; when Mr Haig read the text he described it as fair. The Secretary-General of the UN also seemed impressed by the flexibility which we had shown.

I myself was closely involved in our intense diplomatic effort to keep our support on the eve of what I knew would be decisive military action. It was most important that the European Community countries should continue their sanctions against Argentina, but a number of them were faltering. I telephoned the Italian Foreign minister on Sunday afternoon, though to little avail.

WEEK EIGHT

On Monday 17 May President Mitterrand was in London for talks and I was able to press the argument for sanctions with him. The same afternoon I telephoned Mr Haughey about the Irish position. I was not convinced that this would have much impact, but the effort had to be made. In fact the Community Foreign ministers, meeting in Luxemburg, decided to continue with sanctions on a 'voluntary' basis, which was less than ideal but much better than nothing.

On the morning of Tuesday 18 May the War Cabinet met with all the Chiefs of Staff. It was perhaps the crucial moment. We had to decide whether to go ahead with the landing on the Falklands; I asked each Service Chief to give his views. The discussion was very open and the difficulties were clear: we would be vulnerable on landing and, in particular, there were doubts whether we had enough air cover, given that British ships would be within easy range of Argentine attack from the mainland and their positions would be known. We had not been able to knock out as many Argentine ships or aircraft as we would have liked in the weeks before the landing. And always there was the fact that we had not been able to locate their submarines.

But it was also clear that the longer the delay, the greater the risk of losses and the worse the condition of our troops when they had to fight. The troops could not remain on board ship indefinitely. Of course, no one could quantify casualties, but the judgement was that the advantages of landing outweighed the risks of postponement. The rules of engagement had already been agreed. The attack would be by night.

None of us now doubted what must be done. We authorized the landing on the basis of the Force Commander's plan, subject to the Cabinet's final approval. It could be stopped any time until late on Thursday which would allow us thoroughly to consider any reply from the Argentinians to our proposals. The decision could thus be cancelled or reaffirmed after Cabinet on Thursday morning. Beyond that, the timing was for the Force Commander himself.

There was no lack of last-minute pressure for further diplomatic concessions. Michael Foot had written to me urging further negotiations. I replied that if we could not reach agreement with the Argentinians on terms we regarded as acceptable we would have to decide what further military action to take and we would answer for our decisions to the House of Commons. Mr Haig too had to be discouraged from bringing forward another set of proposals which would just have allowed the Argentines to go on buying time. In fact, on the next day, Wednesday, we received the Argentine response, which was in effect a comprehensive rejection of our proposals. I had never thought they would accept. Our proposals were now taken off the table. We had decided earlier – at Francis Pym's suggestion – that following Argentine rejection we would publish them, and we did so on 20 May. This was the first time during the whole of the diplomatic manoeuvring that either side had made public their actual negotiating position and our terms created a good international impression.

The Secretary-General made a last-minute attempt in messages to me and General Galtieri to put forward his own proposals. On Thursday morning (20 May) the War Cabinet met before the full Cabinet. Once again, Francis urged a compromise, and this time at the eleventh hour. He suggested that the Secretary-General's *aide-mémoire* was very similar to our own proposals and that it would not be understood if we now went ahead with military measures. But the fact was that Sr. de Cuellar's proposals were sketchy and unclear; to have accepted would have put us right back at the beginning again. I summed up very firmly. There could be no question of holding up the military timetable. It could be fatal for our forces. If the weather was right the landing would go ahead. The War Cabinet and later the full Cabinet agreed.

The Secretary-General had received no reply from the Argentinians about his *aide-mémoire* – on which we, in spite of all our reservations, had offered serious comments. He admitted the failure of his efforts to the Security Council. We published our proposals and I defended them in the House of Commons that afternoon. The debate went well and provided a good background for what now had to happen.

I had a full day of engagements in my constituency on Friday 21 May and I knew how important it was to carry on with business as usual. Before lunch I had to open a large extension of Gersons', a firm which specializes in storage, packaging and overseas removals.

There was a military band and an audience of some 1200, including many ambassadors. I was deeply moved, partly by the pride and patriotism of the people there but also, of course, because I knew (as they could not) what was due to happen at that very moment 8000 miles away. I did all that one has to do on these occasions and even rode on a fork-lift truck. Then I rushed back to the constituency office to see if there was any news. Not yet. I never telephoned Northwood on this or any other occasion to find out about operations in progress. I knew that the commanders on the spot had more important things to do than answer unnecessary enquiries from London. I returned to the Finchley office again soon after 5 p.m. and learnt by telephone and in carefully obscure language that events were taking place, but no detail.

Later that evening, while I was at a reception in Woodhouse School, still in the constituency, the news came over on the television. The Union Jack was flying in San Carlos: we had returned to the Falklands.

But I was desperately anxious about casualties. Was it really possible that we could land on that hostile coast with a fleet full of troops and equipment without being detected?

Later that night I returned to No. 10 and John Nott brought me a full report. The actual landing had been achieved without a single casualty. But now it was daytime and fierce air attacks had begun. The frigate HMS *Ardent* was lost. Another frigate – HMS *Argonaut* – and the destroyer HMS *Brilliant* were badly damaged. How the Argentine pilots missed the huge, white painted *Canberra*, acting as a troopship, I will never know. But the commanders were determined to get her out of harm's way as quickly as possible.

In fact, the main amphibious force had moved towards San Carlos Water, blessed with an overcast sky and poor visibility, while diversionary raids continued elsewhere on East Falkland. Under cover of naval gun fire, our troops had been taken ashore in landing craft, while helicopters moved equipment and stores. Five thousand men were safely landed, though we lost two helicopters and their crews. The beach-head had been established, though it would take several days for it finally to be secured.

At the Security Council, meeting in open session, Tony Parsons defended our position against predictable rhetorical attacks from Argentina's allies. At the end of the debate the Irish tabled a totally unacceptable resolution. We were able to rely on some strange allies – and not on some of those who should have been our friends. It was the Africans who amended the Irish resolution to the point at which we could accept it. This became UNSCR 505, adopted unanimously on 26 May, giving the Secretary-General a mandate to seek an end to the hostilities and full implementation of UNSCR 502.

On Saturday afternoon I visited Northwood before going on to Chequers. By now the full scale of the Argentine air attacks was all too apparent. To protect the operation at San Carlos, there had to be several levels of defence. First, there were the Sea Harriers on combat patrol flying high above the landing sites, subject to direction from the ships below. Without the Harriers, with their extraordinary manoeuvrability, flown with superb skill and courage, and using the latest version of the Sidewinder air-to-air missile supplied by Caspar Weinberger, we could not have retaken the Falklands. Second, Rapier missile batteries had been landed with the troops and placed in the hills around the bay. There were problems with the Rapiers: in particular the long journey at sea had created problems for their electronics. Then there were the air defences of the ships themselves, some based in the bay itself and others outside in Falkland Sound – principally long-range Sea Dart missiles on the Type 42 destroyers and the shorter-range Sea Wolf and Sea Cat on Type 22s and other frigates, but also anti-aircraft guns and even small arms.

At Northwood I spent some time getting up to date in the Operations Room. I did my best to seem confident, but when I left with Admiral Fieldhouse and we were out of earshot of anyone else, I could not help asking him: 'how long can we go on taking this kind of punishment?' He was no less worried. But he also had the ability of a great commander to see the other side of things. And, terrible as our losses had been and would be in the future, the fact was that we had landed our forces successfully and that serious losses were being inflicted on the Argentine airforce.

I should note here that we were assisted throughout by three important weaknesses in the Argentine air offensive, though in some ways these were the result of deliberate action on our part. First, the Argentinians concentrated their attacks – with the later tragic exception of the losses at Bluff Cove – on the naval escorts rather than the troop ships and aircraft carriers. Of course, in part that was because the escorts succeeded in shielding these units: that was their job. Second, the Argentine aircraft were forced to fly at a very low level to escape our missiles, with the result that the bombs they dropped (fused for higher altitude) frequently failed to explode. (Sadly a bomb which lodged in HMS *Antelope* did go off, sinking the ship, when a brave bomb disposal expert was trying to defuse it.) Third, the Argentinians had only a limited number of the devastating French Exocet missiles. They made desperate attempts to increase their arsenal. There was evidence that arms from Libya and Israel were finding their way through South American countries to them. We for our part were equally desperate to interdict this supply. Later, on 29 May, I was to have a telephone conversation with President Mitterrand who told me that the French had a contract to supply Exocets to Peru, which he had already held up and which both of us feared would be passed on to Argentina. As always during the conflict, he was absolutely staunch.

The Americans too, however irritating and unpredictable their public pronouncements on occasion, were providing invaluable help. I have already mentioned the Sidewinder missiles. They also provided us with 150,000 square yards of matting to create a makeshift airstrip. On 3 May Caspar Weinberger even proposed sending down the carrier USS *Eisenhower* to act as a mobile runway for us in the South Atlantic – an offer that we found more encouraging than practical.

I was working in my room at the House of Commons on the evening of Tuesday 25 May when John Nott came in to say that the destroyer HMS *Coventry* had been attacked by a wave of Argentine aircraft. Six or more had repeatedly bombed her and she was sinking. She had, in fact, been one of the two warships on 'picket duty' outside the opening of Falkland Sound, providing early warning of air attack and an air defence screen for the supply ships unloading in San Carlos Water. She later capsized and sank. Nineteen members of her crew died in the attack. John had to appear on television within half an hour. Something of what had happened was already publicly known, although not the name of the ship. It was thought better not to reveal it until we had more details about the crew. Whether the decision was right or wrong I am still not sure: the effect of not announcing the name was that every navy family was full of anxiety. In fact, the details were announced by John in the House of Commons the next day.

Later the same evening I had more bad news. I had gone into the Private Office to find out the latest about *Coventry*, but instead, the No. 10 duty clerk told me that the 18,000 ton Cunard container ship *Atlantic Conveyor* had been hit by an Exocet missile; that the ship was on fire and that orders had been given to abandon it. *Atlantic Conveyor* was loaded with vital supplies for our forces on the Falklands. Unlike the warships, she was unable to defend herself against missile attack by sending up chaff. Four of those on board were killed and the captain was drowned, though I was told later that he survived the explosion and fires, and had been seen alive in the water. Thankfully, though, the great majority were saved.

I knew that the *Atlantic Conveyor* had been carrying nineteen more Harriers, sorely needed reinforcements. Had they still been on board?

If so, would we be able to carry on? The ship was also carrying helicopters which were vital to the movement of troops and supplies in the land campaign. Their loss caused our land commanders many difficulties. Only one of the helicopters was saved. To add to our general dismay, there was also news, based on an Argentine claim, that HMS *Invincible* had been hit and damaged. And I knew that somewhere east of the Falklands was the *QE2*, carrying 3,000 troops. For me, this was one of the worst nights of the war.

Early next morning I learnt that the news was not quite so bleak. I was told of the remarkable rescue of most members of the crews of *Coventry* and the *Atlantic Conveyor*. The nineteen Harriers had previously been flown onto *Hermes* and *Invincible*. Relief flooded over me at the news: we were not fatally wounded after all, though we had lost eight helicopters and 4,500 winter tents. Moreover, the news that *Invincible* had been hit was totally false.

Stores were still being unloaded at San Carlos. Some landing and supply craft were attacked and hit and there were unexploded bombs, most of which were defused. Our hospital centre at San Carlos was also hit, but the doctors carried on.

It was, though, a frustrating time for us in London. All of us were concerned that there appeared to be little movement by our troops out of the bridgehead. It took many days to unload the stores, equipment and munitions. The loss of the helicopters meant that all of the earlier plans had to be revised.

There was another worry. Would the Argentine Navy, which had after all apparently been strongest in pressing for an invasion of our islands, really continue to skulk in Argentine ports or would they now come out to attack and disrupt our advance? Two British ships had been sunk in our territorial waters around the Falklands. Perhaps we should send our submarines to sink Argentine ships in theirs? But the Attorney-General, Michael Havers, would not have this. So our submarine commanders were left prowling up and down the Argentine twelve-mile limit.

The trouble was that we knew that their ships might break out and we might not find them quickly enough to stop them. Again, it was the Argentine aircraft carrier, *25 de Mayo*, which was the main threat. I had been told that if possible we needed to deal with their aircraft carrier before the landing, but for most of the time we had not been able to find it. We feared that it had been held in reserve to oppose the landing and that it might well appear on the Argentine national day – 25 May. Several weeks before the landing one of our submarines had found it in the middle of a bay. It was a fine point of international law to determine the limit of Argentine territorial waters: although the centre of the bay was more than twelve miles from the shore, it might be argued that the whole bay was within the limit. In the end we decided that the ship could be attacked, but by that time she had moved closer to the shore. The same issue arose regarding other Argentine vessels hugging territorial waters in the south. On this occasion Michael Havers and I had all the relevant charts laid out on the floor in the Parlour at Chequers and did the measurements ourselves. But the Argentinians were too careful and, unlike them, we were determined to stay within the constraints of international law.

Somewhat to the dismay of the UN Secretary-General and Al Haig, we made it clear that having landed we were not now prepared to negotiate. We could no longer accept the idea of an interim administration or proposals for mutual withdrawal of Argentine and British troops. The Americans were again becoming worried. They had been under ferocious verbal attacks at a meeting of the OAS on 27 May. We were put under continual pressure from Washington to avoid the final military humiliation of Argentina, which they now seemed to see as inevitable. I wish I could have been as confident. I knew, as they could not, how many risks and dangers still faced us in the campaign to recapture the islands.

This was amply demonstrated by the battle to retake Darwin and Goose Green. The Argentinians were well prepared and dug into strong defensive positions which had to be approached by our troops across the open ground of a narrow isthmus. They faced heavy enemy fire. As is well known, Colonel 'H' Jones, the commander of 2 Para, lost his life in securing the way forward for his troops. His second-in-command took over and eventually took the surrender. At one point a white flag was waved from the Argentine trenches, but when two of our soldiers advanced in response they were shot and killed. Finally, our commander sent two Argentine PoWs forward with a message to surrender, saying that they could have a parade if they liked but that they must lay down their arms. This proved acceptable. The Argentine officers harangued their men about the justice of their cause, but they surrendered all the same. The people of Goose Green, who had been imprisoned inside the community hall for three weeks, were now released. A famous battle had been won. Today there is a memorial to the Paras near Goose Green itself and a special memorial to 'H'.

The media had reported that our troops were about to take Goose Green the day before the attack. I had been furious when I learnt of this – as, I believe, had 'H'. Too much talk was giving the Argentinians warning of what we intended, though the fault did not always lie with the media themselves but also with the media management at the MoD.

On the same day that 2 Para were battling for Darwin and Goose Green I had a meeting with Cardinal Casaroli, the Pope's Secretary of State. We were all very pleased that the Pope had not postponed his visit to Britain – the first ever papal visit here – in spite of the fact that we were at war with a predominantly Catholic country. We recognized the difficulties which a visit at this time might cause him, however, and decided that it would be best if none of the Cabinet met him personally. I had, of course, already talked to the Pope on an earlier occasion and admired his principle and courage. I explained to Cardinal Casaroli what we were fighting for: I said that war was a terrible evil, but there were worse things, including the extinction of all that one believed in. We could not allow aggression to succeed. Nor could we bargain away the freedom, justice and democracy which the Falkland Islanders had enjoyed for so long and simply hand them over to Argentina, where these things were unknown. We made no public comment at the time, but I hoped that something of this message might be transmitted to the Argentinians: for the Pope was to visit Argentina after leaving Britain.

Unfortunately, the Americans now sought to revive diplomatic negotiation. Al Haig wanted to involve the Brazilians in a settlement which (contrary to what he had earlier suggested) must, he claimed, come before the final defeat of the Argentine forces on the island. These proposals were really the wrong ones at very much the wrong time. We had already made it clear that unconditional Argentine withdrawal and the return of British administration were now our goals. But I knew that we could not afford to alienate the United States, particularly at this stage. We kept in contact with Mr Haig both about the question of how to provide for and repatriate Argentine prisoners of war and more generally about our plans for the long-term future of the islands.

What would have been quite wrong was to snatch diplomatic defeat out of the jaws of military victory – as I had to tell President Reagan when he telephoned me late at night on Monday 31 May. It was not very satisfactory for either of us that I should not have had advance warning of what he was likely to say and as a result I was perhaps more forceful than friendly. The President had, it seems, again been speaking to the President of Brazil who shared his view that the best chance for peace was before the Argentinians suffered complete humiliation. As the UK now had the upper hand militarily, we should strike a deal. I could not accept this. I told him that we could not contemplate a cease-fire without Argentine withdrawal. Having lost ships and lives because for seven weeks the Argentinians refused to negotiate, we would not consider handing the islands over to a third party. I understood the President's fears. But I asked him to put himself in my position. I was sure that he would have acted in the same way as I did if Alaska – part of his own country, inhabited by his own people – had been similarly threatened. Moreover, I agreed with an excellent television interview he had given in which he had said that if the aggressor were to win, some fifty other territories, affected by similar disputes, would be at risk. This conversation was a little painful at the time but it had a worthwhile effect. The Americans now clearly understood our position and intentions. I would have a further opportunity shortly to talk to President Reagan in person during the forthcoming G7 summit at Versailles.

In the meantime, we had to deal delicately with a five-point peace plan which had been advanced by the UN Secretary-General. The pressure for a cease-fire sponsored by the UN Security Council was growing. On Wednesday 2 June after the Secretary-General had announced that he had given up his own efforts, Spain and Panama, on behalf of Argentina, sought to press to the vote an apparently innocuous Draft Resolution on a cease-fire which would have had exactly the effect we were determined to avoid. It was touch and go whether the Spanish would even now manage to obtain the necessary nine votes which would force us to veto the resolution. We ourselves lobbied as hard as possible. The vote was postponed until Friday.

At noon that day I flew to Paris for the G7. My first and most important meeting was, of course, with President Reagan who was staying at the US Embassy. We talked alone, as he preferred it. I thanked him for the great help we had received from the United States. I asked him what the Americans could do to help repatriate the Argentine PoWs. I also requested that the American vote should support us at the Security Council.

The mood at Versailles seemed very different from that which was now prevailing at the UN in New York. The heads of government were staying in the Petit Trianon. After dinner we had a long discussion about the Falklands and the response was generally sympathetic and helpful. Later the British delegation and I withdrew to the sitting-room which we had been allocated. We had been talking for about fifteen minutes when a message came through from the Foreign Office and Tony Parsons that a vote was about to be taken in the Security Council and that the Japanese were voting against us. As theirs was the ninth vote required for the resolution to pass this was particularly irritating. So much for the previous undertakings of co-operation. I tried hard to contact Mr Suzuki, the Japanese Prime Minister, to persuade him to reverse the decision and at least abstain. He could not possibly have gone to bed in such a short time. But I was told that he could not be reached.

Attention was, in fact, somewhat diverted from our problems by the extraordinary behaviour of the US Ambassador to the United Nations, Mrs Kirkpatrick. Having cast her veto alongside ours, she announced only minutes later that if the vote could be taken again she would, on instructions just received, abstain. Ironically, this rather helped us by distracting media attention from our veto. However, that had not been the intention. Apparently, succumbing to pressure from the Latin American countries, Al Haig had telephoned her from Versailles telling her to withdraw her vote of support from us but she had not received the message in time. There was a still more embarrassing sequel to this event for the United States. Just before lunch in the Palace of Versailles, the television cameras were allowed in and an American journalist asked President Reagan what had lain behind the US confusion at the United Nations the previous evening. To my amazement, he said that he did not know anything about it. He had not been told. The journalist then turned to me. I had no intention of rubbing salt into a friend's wounds, so all I said was that I did not give interviews over lunch.

That same morning the Japanese Prime Minister gave me an extremely lame explanation of Japan's vote in support of the resolution, claiming that he believed that it would lead to Argentine withdrawal. However, President Mitterrand's summing up at his press conference after the conclusion of the G7 was excellent and totally supportive.

Neither Tony Parsons nor I was particularly surprised that we had finally had to use our veto. In retrospect, we were very lucky – and it was a tribute also to Tony Parsons's skill – that we had not had to veto such a resolution much earlier.

By now, my thoughts were again on what was happening in the Falklands. Our troops had struck out against other Argentine positions. There had been no Argentine counter-attack. Major-General Moore had arrived to assume command of all land operations and the 5th Infantry Brigade (5 Brigade), reinforcing our troops on the islands, had landed on 1 June. The main problem was to transport enough equipment and ammunition forward in preparation for the final assault on the ring of mountains which protect Port Stanley.

President Reagan arrived in Britain on Monday evening on an official visit and I met him at the airport. The next day he was due to speak to Members of both Houses of Parliament. But it is the terrible losses we suffered at Bluff Cove which are etched on my mind for that day. The landing ships, *Sir Tristram* and *Sir Galahad*, full of men, equipment and munitions, had been sent round to Bluff Cove and Fitzroy in preparation for the final assault on Port Stanley. The clouds cleared while the ships were still unloading the Rapier missiles which would protect them from air attack and the Argentinians scored hits on both. *Sir Galahad* had not discharged its troops and the result was great loss of life and many survivors were left with terrible burns. The Welsh Guards took the brunt of it. As on all these occasions, the natural reaction was 'if only' – above all, if only the men had been taken off and dispersed as soon as they arrived then nothing like this number of casualties would have been suffered. But the losses would have been even greater were it not for the heroism of the helicopter pilots. They hovered close to the burning oil slicks around the ship and used the draught from their rotors to blow life rafts full of survivors away from the inferno into which they were being drawn.

Again, there were almost insuperable problems in releasing news of casualties. Rumours of very large numbers were spread by the Argentinians. Families were frantically worried. But we decided to hold up details of the numbers lost – although of course (as always) relatives were individually informed. We knew from intelligence that the Argentinians thought that our casualties were several times worse than they were and that they believed this would hold up our attack on Port Stanley. The attack on Mount Longdon, Two Sisters and Wireless Ridge was due to begin on Friday night. Surprise was vital.

I hoped against hope that our worst losses were behind us. But early on the morning of Saturday 12 June the No. 10 duty clerk came up to the flat with a note. I all but seized it from him, expecting it to say that the attack on the mountains around Port Stanley had begun. But the news was very different. I kept the note, which reads:

> HMS *Glamorgan* struck by suspected Exocet missile. Ship is in position 51/58 South. Large fire in vicinity of hangar and in gas turbine and gear room. Power still available. Ship making ten knots to the South.
>
> –MoD as yet have no details of casualties and wouldn't expect them for several hours. They will keep us informed.

Glamorgan had been bombarding the Argentine positions in Port Stanley and on the hills around before the forthcoming battle. She had in fact been hit by a land-based Exocet while on her way out of the area.

How bitterly depressed I was. At moments like this I felt almost guilty at the comfort, protection and safety in No. 10 while there was so much danger and death in the South Atlantic. That day was the Trooping of the Colour for the Queen's birthday. For the only time that I can remember the ceremony was marred by a downpour of rain. It was unpleasant for the Guards, but with the news so bad and the uncertainty so great, it seemed appropriate. I wore black, for I felt that there was much to mourn. John Nott arrived shortly before I was to take my place on the stand. He had no further news. But he thought he would have been told if the attack had not started. Afterwards, dripping wet, the guests, including Rex and Mrs Hunt, dried out before the fires in No. 10 as best we could.

Shortly before 1 o'clock we heard that all our military objectives had been achieved. But there had been a stiff battle. Two Sisters, Mount Harriet and Mount Longdon had been secured. The plan had been to press on that night to take Mount Tumbledown, still closer to Port Stanley, but the troops were tired and more time was needed to bring up ammunition, so it was decided to wait. I went up to Northwood that afternoon to hear precisely what was happening. There was better news there about *Glamorgan*; her fires were under control and she was steaming at 20 knots.

More than ever, the outcome now lay in the hands of our soldiers on the Falklands, not with the politicians. Like everyone else in Britain, I was glued to the radio for news – strictly keeping to my self-imposed rule not to telephone while the conflict was underway. On my way back from Chequers to No. 10, that Sunday (13 June), I went via Northwood to learn what I could. What was to turn out to be the final assault was bitterly fought, particularly at Mount Tumbledown where the Argentinians were well prepared. But Tumbledown, Mount William and Wireless Ridge fell to our forces, who were soon on the outskirts of Stanley.

I visited the islands seven months later and saw the terrain for myself, walking the ground at first light in driving wind and rain, wending my way around those grim outcrops of rock which made natural fortifications for the Argentine defenders. Our boys had had to cover the ground and take the positions in thick darkness. It could only have been done by the most professional and disciplined of forces.

When the War Cabinet met on Monday morning all that we knew

was that the battle was still in progress. The speed with which the end came took all of us by surprise. The Argentinians were weary, demoralized and very badly led – as ample evidence at the time and later showed. They had had enough. They threw down their arms and could be seen retreating through their own minefields into Stanley.

That evening, having learnt the news, I went to the House of Commons to announce the victory. I could not get into my own room; it was locked and the Chief Whip's assistant had to search for the key. I then wrote out on a scrap of paper which I found somewhere on my desk the short statement which, there being no other procedural means, I would have to make on a Point of Order to the House. At 10 p.m. I rose and told them that it had been reported that there were white flags flying over Port Stanley. The war was over. We all felt the same and the cheers showed it. Right had prevailed. And when I went to sleep very late that night I realized how great the burden was which had been lifted from my shoulders.

For the nation as a whole, though the daily memories, fears and even the relief would fade, pride in our country's achievement would not. In a speech I made in Cheltenham a little later, on Saturday 3 July, I tried to express what the Falklands spirit meant:

> We have ceased to be a nation in retreat. We have instead a newfound confidence – born in the economic battles at home and tested and found true 8000 miles away . . . And so today we can rejoice at our success in the Falklands and take pride in the achievement of the men and women of our task force. But we do so, not as at some flickering of a flame which must soon be dead. No – we rejoice that Britain has rekindled that spirit which has fired her for generations past and which today has begun to burn as brightly as before. Britain found herself again in the South Atlantic and will not look back from the victory she has won.

CHAPTER IX

Generals, Commissars and Mandarins

Meeting the military and political challenge of communism from the autumn of 1979 to the spring of 1983

PEACE AND ARMAMENTS

On Wednesday 23 June 1982 I travelled to New York to attend a special session of the General Assembly on disarmament, which the United Nations had called while the Falklands campaign was still in progress. The speech I made expressed my view of the role of defence and negotiations on disarmament with singular clarity. I had become increasingly unhappy about the language used on such occasions. Everyone talked about peace as if that in itself were the sole aim. But peace is not enough without freedom and justice and sometimes – as we were demonstrating in the Falklands – it was necessary to sacrifice peace if freedom and justice were to prevail. I was also convinced that much cant was spoken about the arms race, as if by slowing down the process of improving our defences we would make peace more certain. History had repeatedly demonstrated quite the opposite.

I began by quoting President Roosevelt: 'We, born to freedom and believing in freedom, would rather die on our feet than live on our knees.' I then went on to note that nuclear war was indeed a terrible threat, but conventional war a terrible reality. Since the atomic bombs dropped by the Americans on Hiroshima and Nagasaki there had been no conflicts in which nuclear weapons had been used – but some 140 conflicts fought with conventional weapons in which approaching 10 million people had died. In any case:

> The fundamental risk to peace is not the existence of weapons of particular types. It is the disposition on the part of some states to impose change on others by resorting to force against other

> nations and not in 'arms races', whether real or imaginary. Aggressors do not start wars because an adversary has built up his own strength. They start wars because they believe they can gain more by going to war than by remaining at peace . . . I do not believe that armaments cause wars [nor that] action on them alone will . . . prevent wars. It is not merely a mistaken analysis but an evasion of responsibility to suppose that we can prevent the horrors of war by focusing on its instruments. They are more often symptoms than causes.

This was the analysis which underlay the defence and security policies I intended the Government to pursue. It provided me with a view of international power politics without which we would have had no clear sense of direction. But of course it did not of itself resolve particular problems. Throughout my first years in office I repeatedly found myself trying to reconcile five different objectives. First, there could only be strictly limited resources available for defence, particularly when the economy was growing slowly or not at all. This meant that although defence expenditure was increased, it was vital that better value for money be obtained. Second, we had regularly to assess the priority we would give to the demands of NATO policy and those other areas of British interest outside the NATO area. Third, Britain had to help ensure that NATO responded effectively to the steadily increasing Soviet military threat. Fourth, as part of this, it was vital to maintain western unity behind American leadership. Britain, among European countries, and I, among European leaders, were uniquely placed to do that. Finally, nowhere more than in defence and foreign policy does what I have come to consider 'Thatcher's law' apply – in politics the unexpected happens. You have to be prepared and able to face it. There was to be no lack of examples in my years in office.

THE MILITARY BALANCE

Well before I entered Downing Street I was preoccupied with the balance of military power between the NATO alliance and the Warsaw Pact. NATO has always been a defensive alliance of western style democracies. It was founded in April 1949 in response to the growing aggression of Soviet policy, made plain by events such as the Soviet-backed communist takeover in Czechoslovakia and the Berlin blockade the previous year. Although the United States is the leading power in

NATO, ultimately it can only seek to persuade not coerce. In such a relationship the danger of dissension always exists. The Soviet aim, only thinly disguised, right up until the time when a united Germany remained in NATO, was to drive a wedge between America and her European allies. I always regarded it as one of Britain's most important roles to see that such a strategy failed.

There are other fundamental differences between NATO and its opponents. The democratic freedoms our peoples enjoy make it in practice impossible for the state to take more than a certain share of national income for military purposes. Moreover, the openness of our western societies, though they make us stronger perhaps when sacrifice is required in a manifest crisis, also make us slow to respond to insidious threats. Democracies do not, with very few exceptions, start wars. The only threat NATO ever posed to the Soviet bloc is the threat that ideas of freedom and justice pose to the masters of captive nations.

But from its foundation in May 1955 the Warsaw Pact was always an instrument of Soviet power. In 1956 in Hungary and 1968 in Czechoslovakia the Soviets had shown that any movement in eastern Europe which might threaten their own military interests would be crushed without mercy or apology. The experts might and did argue about the precise details of Soviet military doctrine. But what was clear to me and to anyone prepared to reflect on past events and present circumstances was that the Soviets and their Warsaw Pact 'allies' could not be trusted to refrain from adventurism in Europe any more than in the Third World.

Moreover, by the time we took office the Soviets were ruthlessly pressing ahead to gain military advantage. Soviet military spending, which was believed to be some five times the published figures, took between 12 and 14 per cent of the Soviet Union's GNP.* The Warsaw Pact outnumbered NATO by three-to-one in main battle tanks and artillery and by more than two-to-one in tactical aircraft. Moreover, the Soviets were rapidly improving the quality of their equipment – tanks, submarines, surface ships and aircraft. The build-up of the Soviet Navy enabled them to project their power across the world. Improvements in Soviet anti-ballistic missile defences threatened the credibility of the alliance's nuclear deterrent – not least the British independent deterrent – at the same time as the Soviets were approaching parity in strategic missiles with the United States.

* By the end of the decade 25–30 per cent of GNP was commonly estimated.

INTERMEDIATE-RANGE NUCLEAR WEAPONS (INF)

It was, however, in what in the jargon are known as 'long-range theatre nuclear forces' (LRTNF) – usually called intermediate-range nuclear forces (INF) – that the most pressing and difficult decisions were required. The so-called 'dual-track' agreement to modernize NATO's medium-range nuclear weapons, while engaging in talks with the Soviet Union on arms control, had been taken in principle by the previous Labour Government; whether they would have seen the decision through to deployment I somewhat doubt.

This agreement was needed to deal with the threat from new Soviet nuclear weapons. The Soviet SS-20 mobile ballistic missiles and their new supersonic Backfire bomber could strike western European targets from the territory of the Soviet Union. But the Americans had no equivalent weapons stationed on European soil. The only NATO weapons able to strike the USSR from Europe were those carried by the ageing UK Vulcan bombers and the F1–11s stationed in Britain. Both forces could be vulnerable to a Soviet first strike. Of course, the United States could be expected by an attacking Soviet army at some point to have recourse to its own strategic nuclear weapons. But the essence of deterrence is its credibility. Now that the Soviet Union had achieved a broad parity in strategic nuclear weapons, some thought that this reduced the likelihood of the United States taking such action. In any case, there were many in Europe who suggested that the United States would not risk its own cities in defence of Europe.

Why would the Soviets wish to acquire this new capability to win nuclear war in Europe? The answer was that they hoped ultimately to split the alliance.

For NATO, however, the possession of effective medium-range nuclear forces in Europe had a very different purpose. NATO's strategy was based on having a range of conventional and nuclear weapons so that the USSR could never be confident of overcoming NATO at one level of weaponry without triggering a response at a higher level leading ultimately to full-scale nuclear war. This strategy of 'flexible response' would not be effective if there were no Europe-based nuclear weapons as a link between the conventional and strategic nuclear response. NATO knew that the Warsaw Pact forces would never be held for more than a short time if they attacked with all the strength at their disposal in central Europe. That is why NATO repeatedly pledged that although it would never use military force first, it could not play into the Soviet hands of renouncing first use of nuclear weapons once it had been attacked. So only by modernizing its intermediate-range nuclear weapons in Europe could NATO's strategy retain its credibility. It was clear from the first that this would not be easy.

On the morning of Friday 11 May 1979 I discussed the issue with Helmut Schmidt in London. He was very concerned at the effect on German public opinion of stationing more nuclear missiles on German soil, although of course he had been one of the principal authors of the strategy. The Americans had developed a longer range equivalent of the Pershing missiles already stationed in West Germany and Cruise missiles, which could be launched from the air, sea or land. At this stage Helmut Schmidt still hankered after a sea-based system, though he later reluctantly accepted the advantages of the ground-launched Cruise missile (GLCM). He was under strong pressure from within his own party and placed equal emphasis on the second aspect of the 'dual track' approach – that is for the US to negotiate for the removal of the Soviet threat at the same time as we were preparing to deploy our own weapons. He also insisted that West Germany should not be the only recipient of these missiles which was a non-nuclear state.* In sharp contrast to future debate in Britain, the Germans were adamant that the nuclear weapons should have no 'dual key': they must be able to say to the rest of the world that they did not own or control nuclear weapons.

On the morning of Wednesday 13 June I saw Al Haig, who was at that time the outgoing Supreme Allied Commander in Europe. We discussed not only questions of nuclear policy but also what we knew of the threat posed by Soviet preparations for offensive chemical warfare, which I found deeply disquieting. I said that although my initial reaction to my first briefings on the East/West military balance had been one of concern, my considered conclusion was that the West's superiority in human and material resources would enable us to respond to any challenge. But that did not diminish my worry about our immediate problems. On the evening of Tuesday 24 July I saw General Haig's successor, General Bernard Rogers, and expressed my anxiety about the lead enjoyed by the Warsaw Pact forces in the matter of standardization of weapons and equipment and about

* Germany had forsworn nuclear, chemical and biological weapons when it joined NATO in 1955.

the vulnerability of NATO's own organization to Soviet penetration.

The deadline which NATO had set itself for achieving a firm decision on the new intermediate-range missiles was the end of that year, 1979. The longer we waited, the greater the opportunities for Soviet campaigns of propaganda and disinformation to do their work. On Wednesday 19 September the small group of ministers which I chaired to consider nuclear policy decided that the UK would accept the basing of our allotted 144 American owned GLCMs. I had received a telephone call from Helmut Schmidt asking if we could accept a further flight of 16 Cruise missiles. The Germans wished to reduce their own number and in order to prevent any further time being lost in argument I immediately agreed to the request. With Britain and West Germany remaining solid the West's strategy could be accounted a success. But would others follow our lead?

A week earlier I had already seen Prime Minister Martens of Belgium for talks in Downing Street. The Belgians were looking over their shoulder at the Dutch, whose Government's future was endangered by rifts and popular agitation against deployment of nuclear weapons. The Belgians were particularly important because if the Dutch, and possibly also the Italians, failed to go along with the decision which would soon be required, Chancellor Schmidt's own position would become perilous and it was of crucial importance to the alliance to shore up West German commitment. I told M. Martens that I wondered whether western European leaders were giving a sufficiently effective lead to public opinion. My own experience was that audiences were always quick to respond when addressed about the extent of the Soviet threat and about the need for us to have credible defences. I thought it was all a matter of resolve.

By contrast, I felt reassured – and said so – by the resolute attitude of the Italian Prime Minister, Sig. Cossiga, when I talked with him in Rome on Friday 5 October. He told me that Italy would make a positive decision on deployment. He intended to exert maximum pressure at his forthcoming meeting with the Dutch Prime Minister, Mr Van Agt, and hoped that I would do the same.

However, during this time the Soviets were at work trying to undermine NATO's unity. As I frequently pointed out in my discussions, they had been brilliantly successful in rousing popular feeling against the neutron bomb which President Carter had been considering deploying. In the months and years to come it would be clear that they had by no means lost their touch.

On Saturday 6 October, President Brezhnev made a speech in East Berlin containing a number of proposals. He announced the withdrawal of 20,000 Soviet troops and 1,000 tanks from East Germany in the next 12 months. He also offered to reduce Soviet intermediate-range nuclear systems if no 'additional' medium-range nuclear weapons were deployed in western Europe. Judged against the huge Soviet superiority in conventional forces the reductions, though of course welcome, were more cosmetic than of substance. But the proposals on theatre nuclear weapons were a good deal worse. We knew that the accuracy, ability to penetrate, mobility and the range of targets covered by these Soviet missiles and aircraft had increased enormously. Moreover, such missiles were targeted on western Europe from points beyond the Urals. Mr Brezhnev's proposals – like those which followed them – would have left the Soviets in possession of a weapon which could strike at Europe and to which we had no equivalent effective response. However, such proposals inevitably increased the temptation, in the Netherlands for example, to put all the emphasis on arms control and delay the decision on modernization and deployment.

I discussed the situation with Chancellor Schmidt again – in Bonn this time – on Wednesday 31 October. How were we to help the Dutch take the right decision at the forthcoming NATO meeting? I suggested that the whole of the Dutch Cabinet, which appeared to be split, should see the impressive NATO presentation on the military balance in Europe. Helmut Schmidt was pressing for the United States to offer to withdraw unilaterally 1,000 obsolete nuclear warheads from the Federal Republic. The Americans agreed with this and President Carter wrote to me about it. All my instincts were against unilateral gestures of this sort. But I could see the practical arguments for it and with some reluctance supported the offer – not that it had much noticeable effect on Dutch opinion or the Dutch Government. In fact, the Germans at about this time seemed to become reconciled to the prospect of the Dutch failing to agree to deployment, though it was clear that they themselves would remain firm as long as the Italians and Belgians did so. On Friday 23 November Mr Gromyko visited Bonn and gave a press conference which was evidently intended to shake European and particularly German opinion, warning that arms control negotiations could not take place if the West pursued what he described as a 'new arms race'.

On the evening of Thursday 6 December I met the Dutch Prime Minister for talks and dinner in Downing Street. I always got on well with him, but I did not envy his position. The notorious instability of coalition governments of the sort he led makes it immensely difficult to get clear decisions and stick to them. On this occasion, Mr Van

Agt explained to me in some detail the difficulties he was facing. Apparently, half the sermons in Dutch churches were now dealing with nuclear disarmament and the issue of deployment was endangering his Government's survival. I agreed with him that the fall of a NATO member government on a NATO issue would be a very serious development. But I added that NATO would have to go ahead with the decision to deploy theatre nuclear weapons or else the alliance would lose its credibility and its purpose. The Netherlands could reserve its position while waiting to see what the attitude of the Soviet Government was in arms control negotiations. The Russians were playing their traditional psychological game to discourage NATO from taking decisions and they must not be allowed to get away with it.

In fact, in an act of remarkable courage in the face of so much domestic and Soviet opposition, the NATO ministers made the required decision in Brussels on 12 December. The arms control proposals, including the American offer to withdraw 1,000 nuclear warheads from Europe, were agreed. Most important, the alliance agreed to the deployment in Europe of all the 572 new American missiles which had been envisaged. The reservations entered by the Belgian and Dutch Governments were less serious than at one time had seemed likely. The Belgians agreed to accept a share of these missiles, subject to reconsideration after six months in the light of the progress of arms control negotiations. The Dutch Government accepted the proposals as a whole but postponed the decision to take a share of the missiles in Holland until the end of 1981. The latter date was in any case well before any proposed deployment could in practice begin.

Of course, this was not the end of the matter. In June the following year we announced the sites of the Cruise missiles in Britain – Greenham Common in Berkshire and Molesworth in Cambridgeshire. From that time on Greenham was to be the focus for an increasingly strident unilateralist campaign.

The Soviet Union's own alternating bribes and threats continued to work on European public opinion. I was asked in a Dutch television interview on 4 February 1981, when I was on a return visit to see Mr Van Agt, about resistance to stationing Cruise missiles in Holland and Germany. I replied:

> I sometimes wish that those who do resist [Cruise missiles] would really turn all their effort to saying to the Soviet Union: 'Look! You have the most modern, up-to-date theatre nuclear weapons in the SS-20 . . . you have them targeted on every country in

> Europe. You increase their numbers at the rate of rather more than one a week. Do you really expect us to sit back and do nothing? If you want us not to have Cruise missiles in Europe, as a deterrent to your using yours, then dismantle yours! Take them down! Agree to be inspected so that we do know what you are doing!' . . . I know the worries. I do not like nuclear weapons either, but I value my freedom and my children's freedom, and their children's freedom and I am determined that it shall continue.

I learnt afterwards that such plain speaking as this was a rare thing in the Netherlands.

THE PURCHASE OF TRIDENT

Another early decision which we had to take, with the greatest long-term consequence for Britain, related to our independent nuclear deterrent. Britain had four nuclear-armed Polaris submarines. The previous Conservative and Labour governments had pressed ahead with a programme of improvement to our Polaris missiles. The programme, code-named Chevaline, had been paid for and managed by the United Kingdom in co-operation with the United States, using some of their facilities for trials and tests. The upgraded Polaris system would maintain the full effectiveness of our strategic deterrent into the 1990s, though at a cost which had alarmingly escalated as the development continued. However, for a variety of technical and operational reasons we could not responsibly plan for the continuance of this system much into the 1990s. If Britain was to retain its deterrent a decision would shortly have to be made about Polaris's ultimate replacement, given the time required to design or obtain new strategic nuclear forces of the sophistication necessary.

We began to look at the options from almost the first days in government. These quickly proved a good deal narrower than they at first appeared, though inevitably they seemed wider to those without access to all the information. By late September 1979 we had discarded the option of a successor force of air-launched Cruise missiles because they would be too vulnerable to attack. The possibility of co-operation with France, which retained its own independent deterrent, was rejected for technological reasons. From an early stage the American Trident looked the most promising option.

We had received firm assurances that the SALT II Agreement, reached between Presidents Carter and Brezhnev in June 1979, would not affect the situation regarding our own deterrent. But our aim was, if possible, to conclude an agreement with the Americans on purchasing Trident before the end of that year, so that it could not get caught up in the argument in the run-up to the expected ratification by the US Senate of the treaty. We also wished to have the decision made before President Carter became too preoccupied with the 1980 presidential election. The Trident missile included the advanced and very important technology of multiple nuclear warheads, each separately targeted (MIRVs). Not only was this the most up-to-date and therefore credible system – as measured against Soviet anti-submarine warfare capability and anti-ballistic missile defences – but by purchasing it from the Americans we could hope to avoid immensely expensive improvement programmes like Chevaline. On 6 December 1979 the ministers concerned agreed that the best system to replace Polaris was the Trident I (C4) MIRV system if it could be purchased from the US, less the warheads and the submarines carrying the system which would be produced in Britain. The decision was later confirmed by Cabinet.

But at this point the most troublesome and annoying complications began. Although President Carter told me that he would supply us with whatever we needed he was desperately worried that news of his decision would cause him political difficulties. He had invested great political capital in the SALT II Agreement whose chances of being ratified by the Senate were already in doubt. He was worried that the Soviets might respond to his agreement to supply Trident with some action which would result in a failure to ratify. Consequently, I was not able to speak openly about the matter when I saw him with his colleagues in Washington. The Americans were also keen to ensure that the announcement on Trident did not occur before the scheduled 12 December meeting of NATO to decide on deploying Cruise and Pershing. I could see the sense of this. But in view of the problems which SALT II was facing I began to be anxious lest the decision on Trident be postponed well into 1980.

With the Soviet invasion of Afghanistan at the end of the year the prospects of ratifying SALT II immediately sharply receded. But at this point the US Administration said that it was reluctant to announce the Trident decision because it could be seen as an overreaction to events in Afghanistan. The Americans were similarly unduly worried about the attitude of Chancellor Schmidt to the Trident decision. More hard-headedly, the Carter Administration also pressed strongly for both political and financial returns on the decision to supply us with Trident. They wanted us to agree to a form of words which would commit us to expanding our defence efforts. They were also keen to develop their defence facilities at our island of Diego Garcia in the Indian Ocean – something for which I had a good deal of sympathy. There was the matter of a substantial levy which we would be charged for American research and development costs which they were not prepared to waive.

I was not happy about some of these demands: it seemed to me that it was as much in America's interests as ours that we should have an independent strategic deterrent which would, like Polaris, be assigned to NATO and, except where the UK Government decided that supreme national interests were at stake, would be used for the purposes of international defence of the western alliance. As with the question of theatre nuclear weapons, it was the Soviet perception of the strategic threat which would ultimately determine its credibility – and whatever doubts they might have about America's willingness to launch strategic nuclear weapons in defence of Britain, they would never doubt that a British Conservative Government would do so.

On the afternoon of Monday 2 June 1980, however, I finalized the terms in discussion with Dr Harold Brown, the able US Defence Secretary, in Downing Street. I said that Britain wanted to purchase the Trident I missile on the same terms as regards research and development as Polaris, that is paying a 5 per cent levy. Dr Brown would not agree to this and said that it would have been severely criticized in Congress. But he would accept it providing the British Government bore the cost of manning the Rapier Air Defence Systems which the US intended to purchase for their bases in Britain. I agreed. I also agreed with the objective of extending and increasing US use of the base at Diego Garcia; but this made sense on its own merits and had nothing to do with the Trident decision. Dr Brown accepted this. At last the decision was effectively made and I wrote formally to President Carter requesting purchase of Trident, simultaneously informing President Giscard, Chancellor Schmidt and Prime Minister Cossiga. The decision was announced to the House by Francis Pym on 15 July and at Francis's suggestion fully debated and endorsed on 3 March 1981.

In the summer of 1980 we thought that we had made our final decision on the independent nuclear deterrent. But it was not to be. President Reagan came into office in 1981 with a programme of modernizing US strategic nuclear forces, including Trident. On

24 August the new US Defence Secretary, Caspar Weinberger, wrote to me to confirm that President Reagan had now decided to use the Trident II (D5) missile in the Trident submarines. The US Administration would make this missile available to us if we wished to buy it. On 1 October President Reagan formally told me of his decision.

I well understood and indeed supported President Reagan's decision to improve the US strategic nuclear capability. I was worried about the advances which the Soviet Union had made both in their technology and in numbers of weapons. However, we now faced a new situation. If we were still to go ahead with Trident I we risked spending huge sums on a system that would be outdated and increasingly difficult to maintain as the Americans went over to Trident II. But if we were to accept President Reagan's generous offer of the new technology represented by Trident II we risked the increasing costs of any new project. Moreover, a number of political difficulties arose.

In November 1981 a group of ministers met to discuss what we should do. We argued out all the questions between us; and all the arguments which would be raised in the outside world were discussed, including some feeble and unrealistic ones. One colleague was concerned at the impact on public opinion of choosing a still more powerful missile. Another raised the question whether it would be more difficult to keep a Trident II nuclear strategic force out of future arms control negotiations, as we had managed hitherto. A third was inclined to support the case for Trident II but with fewer missiles. Yet another, while accepting that Trident II was better than the alternatives, felt that the choice raised the more fundamental question of whether the UK could afford to continue to maintain an independent strategic nuclear deterrent at all. For my part I had two anxieties. One was, as I noted above, that the cost of a completely new missile now being developed was bound to be uncertain and on past performance was likely to escalate. The other was my unease about the implications for the strategic deterrent of Soviet developments in anti-ballistic missile defence, including particle beam and laser weapons – a possibility to which I had been alerted some years earlier but which became a matter of public debate only when President Reagan proposed his SDI initiative in March 1983.

In January 1982 we had a further and fuller discussion based on a presentation. The more we considered the question the more it seemed that if we were to maintain a credible deterrent, which I was utterly determined we should do, we must indeed have the Trident II. But we must get it on the best possible terms. The issue was put to Cabinet later that month and on 1 February I sent a message to President

Reagan saying that I would send officials to Washington to discuss terms.

Again, as with President Carter's Administration, there was plenty of hard bargaining. But I always knew that President Reagan and Caspar Weinberger would be conscious of Britain's and the alliance's long-term interests and would ultimately do what they believed to be right in defence terms, rather than just expedient or popular with the Congress. As before, the whole question of charges and levies arose. We for our part pressed hard for a fixed percentage of the work on the development of Trident to go to UK sub-contractors. The Americans who were building up their own navy were anxious to discourage us from reducing our surface fleet which we were intending to do following the Defence Review that year. We indicated the possibility of reprieving the amphibious landing ships HMS *Fearless* and HMS *Intrepid*, which pleased them. They also pressed for an extension of our armed forces' engagement in Belize, which has now become a virtually permanent commitment.

In the end, we concluded an agreement with the United States to buy Trident II on more advantageous terms than Trident I. The missile was to be purchased by us at the same price as the United States Navy's own requirements in accordance with the Polaris Sales Agreement. But the additional overheads and levies would be lower than would have been the case under the 1980 Agreement to purchase Trident I. In particular, the so-called R & D levy would be a fixed sum in real terms and there would be a complete waiver of the facilities charge which was part of the Trident I deal. The terms protected us completely from the escalation of the development cost. The United States would set up a liaison office in London to advise British industry on how to compete on equal terms with US industry for sub-contracts for the Trident II programme as a whole, including the American programme. We also decided to improve and increase the size of the submarines which would carry Trident, making them more efficient and less detectable, and by running longer between refits make them more available for patrol. The total cost of Trident II and the other changes over the whole period would be £7.5 billion, just over 3 per cent of the total defence budget over the same period. When I learnt of the terms now being offered I was delighted and I gladly authorized their acceptance.

THE DEFENCE REVIEW

It is sometimes forgotten, now that the map of Europe and indeed the world has been reshaped with the fall of communism, just how painful were the consequences of the West's efforts to strengthen its defence effort in the 1980s. The United States was as a result unable to reduce its public spending, with the consequence that the world faced higher interest rates, threatening economic recovery. We in Britain, for our part, had to match the necessary commitment to strengthen our defence with rigorous evaluation of what we could afford and where resources could be best applied. Economic, strategic and technical arguments alike pointed towards a thorough review of our defence commitments and how they should be fulfilled – and not only ours but those of the other NATO allies. Yet, at the same time, I was conscious of the danger that the wrong signals might be given to left-wing opponents of strong defence at home and to our enemies abroad.

In early November 1980 I chaired a meeting of the Overseas and Defence Committee of the Cabinet (OD) to consider a paper from Peter Carrington and Francis Pym which argued that Britain should take the initiative in proposing a wide-ranging review of NATO to make it more relevant to western defence requirements and more cost effective. In the longer term the members of the alliance should move towards greater specialization. Attractive as the idea was from our viewpoint, it quickly became clear that Chancellor Schmidt was opposed to it, on the grounds that he believed that it would weaken not strengthen NATO. Moreover, with the election of President Reagan, committed to radically different policies from his predecessor, my main emphasis came to be on keeping the alliance together, united behind American leadership. However, whether matched by international action or not, Britain was forced by pressures of circumstance to conduct its own and – as it turned out – highly controversial defence review.

I appointed John Nott to Defence in January 1981 with the remit of getting better value for money from the huge sums spent on defence. In February John, Peter Carrington and I had an initial discussion about what would be our 1981 Defence Review. John had already concluded that the defence budget was hopelessly overextended both in the short and long term. The real cost of ever more sophisticated weapons was remorselessly increasing the pressure. More sales of defence equipment could help a little – particularly if we were able to produce equipment more suited to the needs of potential overseas customers. However, defence orders were running way ahead of budget and would have to be cut back if we were to keep within any kind of financial discipline. Some fundamental strategic issues also had to be faced. There was very little scope for reducing our commitment to West Germany. A policy of forward defence was crucial to the alliance's strategy: moreover the political implications of cuts here for NATO as a whole could be very serious. Nor could savings be found in home defence: indeed the effort here would have to be increased, for example by strengthening the Territorial Army. There was no room for savings on the RAF: on the contrary, additional expenditure would probably be required. This left the navy. The navy needed more submarines and more minesweepers. But it is extremely expensive to keep up a large surface fleet and so that was plainly the area to look for cuts. None of us had any illusions about the sensitivities involved in the approach John proposed, but it was difficult to fault his analysis.

In early May I had another discussion with John about the options emerging clearly from his review. He believed that his proposals would provide the basis for a far more effective defence force for the needs of the future. But it was already clear that opposition within the armed forces and in the Conservative Party would be strong. I would have to see the Defence Chiefs of Staff to discuss with them their reactions to what was proposed. Moreover, many marginal seats would be involved, especially in dockyard closures. We would have to make every effort to explain our priorities both in the country and to our NATO allies, particularly the Americans.

What I had not expected was that the most public opposition would come from a Defence minister. On Friday 15 May Keith Speed, the Navy minister, made a speech which effectively disowned the whole strategy of the review. John Nott did not want him to resign at once and suggested that he should be moved to another department. I said that there was no question of this: if he was going to be disloyal to the Government in one department, he would in another. I saw him very late on the night of Monday 18 May and told him he must go.

In early June I met the Chiefs of the Defence Staff, at their request, with John and Peter Carrington. The press had been full of stories about my 'fury' at their lobbying against the review. But in fact I had found the behaviour of the Chiefs of Staff throughout impeccable, and I said so. No one at the meeting openly contested that the NATO central front was bound to be the decisive arena. Scenarios of conflict in the Third World might be more likely: but only on the central front could the war be lost in an afternoon. It was argued that we should again press for a full-scale NATO review. But we could not afford to postpone decisions in the hope that a NATO review might help us: moreover such a review at this time could itself destabilize the alliance.

On the morning of Monday 8 June John Nott and I met Sir Henry Leach, the First Sea Lord, who argued vigorously the importance of the surface fleet. I have the greatest respect for his judgement. He could well argue that the Falklands War proved him right. He could certainly argue today that with the end of the Cold War and events in the Gulf there is now a need for mobile forces and a strong navy. At that time I had to disagree with him because I could see no other way of meeting our NATO obligations within the financial constraints.

John announced the conclusions of the Defence Review to the House of Commons on the afternoon of Thursday 25 June. The decisions – particularly to cut the number of ships and to close the base and dockyard in Chatham – ran into fierce opposition, not least from Members of Parliament whose constituencies were affected. The closure of the dockyard went ahead. But after the Falklands campaign the following year some of the decisions of the Defence Review were altered. Certainly no one who lived through that campaign could be in any doubt about the importance of a country such as Britain with far-flung interests being able to project its military power swiftly and effectively across the globe.

THE POLISH CRISIS

No matter how effectively Britain managed its defence effort it was on the unity, strength and credibility of NATO that our security ultimately depended. It was of the utmost importance that American public opinion remained committed to western Europe. So the tensions and divisions which arose in the alliance at this time were of great concern to me. My view was that ultimately we must support American leadership: but that did not mean that the Americans could pursue their interests regardless of the opinion of their European allies.

The need to decide how to react to the imposition of martial law by General Jaruzelski's Government in Poland on 13 December 1981 highlighted problems which had been growing throughout 1981. Some European countries, most importantly the Germans, were hostile to President Reagan's economic policy and mistrustful of his rhetoric on defence and arms control. I, of course, did not share these attitudes, though I wanted tougher action to control the widening US budget deficit. What I found irritating and on occasion quite unjustified was the way in which the actions the Americans preferred inflicted a good deal more pain on their allies than on themselves and, one might argue, the communists in Poland and the Soviet Union. The first such issue was the Polish Government's crackdown on Solidarity.

I was from the first acutely aware of the importance of the Polish question. Like most people in Britain, I have always liked and admired the Poles, many of whom settled in this country during and after the war. But there was more to it than that. On 9 December 1980 I talked quite frankly to the Polish Deputy Prime Minister who visited London. I said that I was conscious of witnessing a change in a socialist state of a kind that had not occurred in the last sixty years. A new group of people – the Solidarity movement – were challenging the communists' monopoly on power on their own terms. I told him how closely we were watching events in Poland and how excited I was by what was happening. I said that the socialist system had succeeded in suppressing the human spirit for a surprisingly long time but that I had always been confident that there would be a breakthrough.

But these happy signs were not to last. The Soviets brought increasing pressure to bear on the Poles. From the end of 1980 the Americans became convinced that the Soviet Union was planning direct military intervention to crush the Polish reform movement, just as they had crushed the 'Prague Spring' of 1968.

From about the same time we began to draw up measures to punish the Soviet Union in such an eventuality. Peter Carrington and I agreed that we should respond in a measured, graduated way depending on the situation we faced. We foresaw four possibilities: a situation in which the use of force by the Polish Government against Polish workers was imminent, or had already taken place, or one in which Soviet intervention was imminent, or had already taken place. We agreed that ineffective sanctions would be worse than useless, but sanctions would have to hit the Soviets harder than they hit us. Meanwhile, we had to make a number of complex judgements about Soviet and the Polish Government's intentions. Was the present ostentatious Warsaw Pact activity the prelude to armed intervention or a means of bringing political pressure to bear on the Polish Communist Party? If we continued to provide food aid and to proceed with plans for Polish debt relief would this benefit the Polish people or play into the hands of the hardliners in Poland who were struggling to survive the consequences of their own misgovernment? These were not easy judgements to make.

Suddenly the situation changed. Martial law was declared in Poland from midnight on 12–13 December 1981 and a 'Military Council for National Salvation' consisting of military leaders was set up under the Prime Minister, General Jaruzelski. The borders were sealed, telex and telephone links severed, a curfew imposed, strikes and assemblies banned, the broadcasting system brought under tight control. There was no doubt in my mind that all of this was morally unacceptable but that did not make it easier to gauge the correct response. After all, in order to warn off Soviet intervention, we had consistently said that the Poles must be allowed to decide on their own internal affairs. Were the Soviets themselves behind it, intending to use the crackdown as a means of turning the clock back to hardline communism and subordination to Moscow? Or was this really a temporary decision, as the Jaruzelski Government claimed, forced upon them to bring some kind of order to Poland, with the implication that this would prevent a Soviet takeover? At this early stage there was a severe shortage of information not just to illuminate these questions but even as to the whereabouts and safety of leading Polish dissidents.

The more we learnt of the background to what had happened, however, the worse it appeared. President Reagan was personally outraged by what had occurred, believed that the Soviet Union was behind it and was determined to take swift action. I received a message from him on 19 December to this effect. Al Haig sent a parallel message to Peter Carrington pointing out that the Americans were not proposing that the West should now implement the far-reaching measures to meet Soviet military intervention that had already been agreed in NATO. What they wanted were some political and economic measures at once and others in reserve if the situation worsened. Without any further reference to us, the Americans would be announcing sanctions against the Soviet Union later that day. These, we were glad to note, rightly did not include abandonment of the disarmament talks going on in Geneva. But they did include measures such as the cancellation of Aeroflot landing rights, a halt to negotiations on a new long-term grain agreement (though an existing agreement would remain in place) and a halt to the export of material for the construction of the planned natural gas pipelines on which work had already begun.

It was this last point which was to be the cause of great anger in Britain and other European countries. British, German and Italian firms had legally binding contracts to provide equipment for the West Siberian Gas Pipeline, which involved components made in the United

States or under United States licence. It was not clear at this stage whether the measures announced by President Reagan against the Soviet Union applied to existing contracts as well as new ones. If the ban extended to existing contracts this would deprive British firms of over £200 million of business with the Soviet Union. Worst affected would be a contract of John Brown Engineering for pump equipment for the pipeline project on which large numbers of jobs depended.

While pressing the Americans on this particular point, I ensured that we gave them the strongest possible backing both in NATO and the European Community for the general line they wanted to take. This was by no means easy. Initially, the Germans were reluctant to take any measures against the Polish Government, let alone against the Soviet Union. The French were pressing hard for continuing the sale of food at special subsidized prices by the European Community to the Soviet Union. But I still felt that if we could persuade the Americans to take a more reasonable line over the pipeline project we would be able to demonstrate a fairly impressive western unity. The trouble was that there were those in the American Administration whose opposition to the pipeline project had nothing much to do with events in Poland. These people believed that if it went ahead the Germans and the French would be dangerously dependent on Soviet energy supplies, which would have damaging strategic implications. There was some force in this argument; but it was exaggerated. Although Russia would be providing just over a quarter of Germany's and just under a third of France's gas, this would be no more than 5 per cent of either country's total energy consumption. But in any case neither the Germans nor the French were going to accede to American pressure. Such pressure would therefore be counter-productive as well as irrelevant to the specific problem we faced in Poland. There was also American talk, which seriously worried the Bank of England, of forcing Poland to default on her international debts, which would have had severe effects on European banks.

At OD towards the end of January 1982 we discussed these possibilities. I said that there was a clear danger of the American Government's present policy damaging western interests more than those of the East and provoking a major transatlantic quarrel of precisely the sort that it had long been the main objective of Soviet policy to bring about. Britain had already offered to do more to meet American wishes than our European partners were likely to accept. This was no longer a time for concessions but for some straight talking to our American friends. I decided to approach President Reagan. I also asked other ministers to try to influence their American counterparts. An urgent invitation would be extended to Al Haig to visit London on the way back from his current visit to the Middle East.

In fact, Al Haig joined me for a late lunch at Downing Street on Friday 29 January. I told him that the single most important aim must be to keep the western alliance together. The most recent meeting of the NATO Council had gone well. But the measures now being proposed by the United States were causing concern. Anything that the West did must be designed to harm the Soviet Union more than ourselves. The reports of possible steps by the US to bring about a default on Polish debts and indeed the debts of other East European countries were worrying: although this would doubtless bring about difficulties for the countries concerned it would also create incalculable problems for the western banking system, which was so important to the reputation of the western world as a whole. I also said that whatever the Americans felt about the matter we had to face the fact that the French and the Germans were never going to abandon their contracts for the Siberian Gas Pipeline. Nearer the bone, I noted that the Americans had not included a grain embargo in their first round of measures because this would clearly hurt their own people. Indeed, few of the measures adopted by the United States would have any serious effect at home – but they would hurt Europe. To say the least there was a certain lack of symmetry.

I gained the strong impression that Mr Haig basically agreed with my analysis. I also had the sense that he was feeling increasingly isolated and powerless in the American Administration, which indeed he was to leave later in the year. He said that he thought that it would be useful if I sent a message to President Reagan about these matters, which I did later that day. I believe that the pressure I applied had some effect, but unfortunately it proved to be temporary.

Meanwhile, the West's response to events in Poland was becoming increasingly entangled with the wider question of our political and economic stance towards the Soviet Union. President Reagan sent a message to me on 8 March stressing the need to halt or at least restrict the grant of export credit to the Soviet Union, particularly credit subsidized by our Governments. The American argument was that not only was the USSR economically weak, it was suffering from an acute shortage of foreign exchange. European and other governments which provided the Soviet Union with subsidized credit were cushioning their failing system from economic realities which would otherwise have forced its reform. The Administration had a good argument here, though our assessment was that restricting credit would not have the dramatic impact which some US experts imagined. At this time we were receiving conflicting and confusing signals from the US Administration about its intentions. But I hoped that tighter controls by European governments on credit for the Soviet Union might allow us to secure the undertaking we wanted that the US restrictions on contracts for the Siberian Pipeline would not be retrospective.

Out of the blue, however, the Americans announced on 18 June that the ban on the supply of oil and gas technology to the Soviet Union was to apply not only to US companies but also to their foreign subsidiaries and to foreign companies manufacturing American-designed components under licence. I was appalled when I learnt of this decision. I condemned it in public. The reaction of the Europeans generally was still more hostile.

Britain took legislative action under the Protection of Trading Interests Act to resist what was in effect the extension of US extra-territorial authority. Then European irritation was increased still further by the news that the Americans were intending to renew grain sales to the USSR on the pretext that this would drain the USSR of hard currency – but transparently because it was in the interests of American farmers to sell their grain. The Administration was somewhat taken aback by the strength of opposition they faced and it was left to the excellent new Secretary of State, George Schultz, to find a way out of the difficulties, which he did later in the year, allowing the existing contracts for the pipeline to go ahead. But it had all been a lesson in how not to conduct alliance business.

THE VERSAILLES G7 SUMMIT

I like to think that my own relationship with President Reagan and the efforts I made to try to establish common ground between the United States and the Europeans helped to prevent disagreements over the pipeline and other trading issues from poisoning western co-operation at this critical juncture. Certainly, the summer of 1982 saw some useful international diplomacy. Between 4 and 6 June the heads of government of the G7 countries met amid the splendid opulence of Versailles. The rooms of the Palace itself were used for meetings and relaxation. There was a final banquet in the Hall of Mirrors followed by after-dinner entertainment of opera and fireworks. (In fact, I left early: it would not have been right to stay for all this while our troops were still fighting in the Falklands.)

President Mitterrand, who chaired the summit, had prepared a paper on the impact of new technology on employment. It quite often happened that the country in the chair at summit meetings felt that they must introduce some new initiatives even at the cost of extra government intervention and increased bureaucracy. This was no exception. For my part, I had no doubt about the attitude to take to technological innovation: it must be welcomed not resisted. There might be 'new' technology but technological progress itself was nothing new, and over the years it had not destroyed jobs but created them. Our task was not to make grand plans for technological innovation but rather to see how public opinion could be influenced in order to embrace not recoil from it. Fortunately, therefore, President Mitterrand's paper was kicked into touch in the form of a working group.

I had a candid bilateral discussion with Helmut Schmidt while I was at Versailles about the European Community budget – to which West Germany and Britain seemed destined to remain net contributors – and about the CAP on which so much of our money was spent. This was a particularly sore point for me, because only a few weeks before Britain had been overridden in the Agriculture Council when we had sought to invoke the Luxemburg compromise against farm price rises. Helmut Schmidt said that he wanted to maintain the Luxemburg compromise, though he doubted whether it should be applied as we wished. But he added that the CAP was a price which had to be paid, however high, to persuade members like France and Italy to come into the Community from the beginning.

As it happened, this was Chancellor Schmidt's last G7 summit. In September his governing coalition broke up when the liberal Free Democrats changed sides and put the Christian Democrat Leader, Helmut Kohl, in as Chancellor. Although I had had serious disagreements with him, I always had the highest regard for Helmut Schmidt's wisdom, straightforwardness and grasp of international economics. Sadly, I never developed quite the same relationship with Chancellor Kohl, though it was some time before the implications of this became important.

But my most vivid recollection of the proceedings at Versailles is of the impression made by President Reagan. At one point he spoke for twenty minutes or so without notes, outlining his economic vision. His quiet but powerful words provided those who did not yet know him with some insight into the qualities which made him such a remarkable political leader. After he had finished, President Mitterrand acknowledged that no one would criticize President Reagan for being true to his beliefs. Given President Mitterrand's socialist policies, that was almost a compliment.

From Paris President Reagan flew to London for an official visit where he addressed both Houses of Parliament in the Royal Gallery of the Palace of Westminster. The speech itself was a remarkable one. It marked a decisive stage in the battle of ideas which he and I wished to wage against socialism, above all the socialism of the Soviet Union. Both of us were convinced that strong defence was a necessary, but not sufficient, means of overcoming the communist threat. Instead of seeking merely to contain communism, which had been the West's doctrine in the past, we wished to put freedom on the offensive. In his speech President Reagan proposed a worldwide campaign for democracy to support 'the democratic revolution [which was] gathering new strength'. In retrospect, however, that speech had a larger significance. It marked a new direction in the West's battle against communism. It was the manifesto of the Reagan doctrine – the very obverse of the Brezhnev doctrine – under which the West would not abandon those countries which had had communism forced upon them.

I remember the speech for another reason as well. I was full of admiration that he seemed to have delivered it without a single note.

'I congratulate you on your actor's memory,' I said.

He replied, 'I read the whole speech from those two perspex screens' – referring to what we had taken to be some security device. 'Don't you know it? It's a British invention.' And so it was that I made my first acquaintance with Autocue.

THE BONN NATO SUMMIT, JUNE 1982

The NATO summit of heads of government in Bonn on 10 June was generally linked to the Versailles summit. At Versailles the G7 had demonstrated that with one or two exceptions, such as France, the major countries were committed to a return to sound economic policies. At Bonn the West was similarly able to demonstrate its commitment to strong defence.

Of course, all of us wanted both strong defence and successful negotiations with the Soviet Union to reduce the level of armaments. But there was a real question about which should come first. There continued to be a muted but important argument about the 'dual track' policy. Some countries hoped to be able to delay virtually indefinitely the implementation of the decision to deploy Cruise and Pershing missiles. For example, in the dying days of the Schmidt Government there were strong voices in Germany arguing that deployment would jeopardize the prospect of successful negotiations. By contrast, the Americans and we in Britain felt that a strong defence posture is an absolute prerequisite for any constructive relationship with the USSR and therefore deterrence is the condition for *détente*. Indeed, the original idea for the Bonn summit had come from us in Britain because we believed that it was vital to demonstrate the unity of purpose of NATO at this time. The result more or less fulfilled that intention.

But there continued to be Soviet pressure, supported by demonstrations by the so-called 'peace movement' and encouraged by the appeasement of the left-wing politicians in Europe right up to the moment when Cruise and Pershing were deployed. We were never able to rest our argument or relax our efforts.

HONG KONG AND CHINA

By the time I visited the Far East in September 1982 Britain's standing in the world, and my own, had been transformed as a result of victory in the Falklands. But one issue on which this was, if anything, a drawback was in talking to the Chinese over Hong Kong. The Chinese leaders were out to demonstrate that the Falklands was no precedent for dealing with the Colony. I was well aware of that myself, both from the military and the legal viewpoints.

On the morning of Wednesday 22 September I and my party took off from Tokyo, where I had been visiting, for Peking. Fifteen years remained of the lease to Britain of the New Territories which constitute over 90 per cent of the land of the Colony of Hong Kong. The island of Hong Kong itself is British sovereign territory, but, like the rest of the Colony, dependent on the mainland for water and other supplies. The People's Republic of China refused to recognize the Treaty of Nanking, signed in 1842, by which the island of Hong Kong had been acquired by Britain. Consequently, although my negotiating stance was founded on Britain's sovereign claim to at least part of the territory of Hong Kong, I knew that I could not ultimately rely on this as a means of ensuring the future prosperity and security of the Colony. Our negotiating aim was to exchange sovereignty over the island of Hong Kong in return for continued British administration of the entire Colony well into the future. This I knew from my many consultations with politicians and business leaders of Hong Kong was the solution which would suit them best.

The immediate danger, which had already been illustrated by reaction in Hong Kong to the provisions of our Nationality Bill and to various remarks by the Chinese communists, was that financial confidence would evaporate and that money and in due course key personnel would flee the Colony, impoverishing and destabilizing it well before the lease of the New Territories came to an end. Moreover, it was necessary to act now if new investment was to be made, since investors would be looking some fifteen years or so ahead in judging what decisions to make.

I had visited Peking in April 1977 as Leader of the Opposition. The 'Gang of Four' had been deposed a few months before and Hua Guo Feng was Chairman. Deng Xiaoping, who had suffered so much during the Cultural Revolution, had been ousted by the 'Gang of Four' the previous year and was still in detention. But on the occasion of this, my first visit as Prime Minister – indeed the first visit of any British prime minister while still in office – Deng Xiaoping was indisputably in charge.

On the afternoon of Wednesday 22 September I had my first meeting which was with the Chinese Prime Minister, Zhao Ziyang – whose moderation and reasonableness proved to be a great handicap to him in his subsequent career. We had a discussion of the world scene in which, because of the Chinese hostility to Soviet hegemony, we found much to agree about. However, the Chinese Prime Minister and I were aware that the following morning's meeting we were to have on Hong Kong would be a very different matter.

I began that meeting with a prepared statement setting out the British position. I said that Hong Kong was a unique example of successful Sino-British co-operation. I noted that the two main elements of the Chinese view concerned sovereignty and the continued prosperity of Hong Kong. Prosperity depended on confidence. If drastic changes in the administrative control of Hong Kong were to be introduced or even announced now there would certainly be a wholesale flight of capital. This was not something which Britain would prompt – far from it. But nor was it something we could prevent. A collapse of Hong Kong would be to the discredit of both our countries. Confidence and prosperity depended on British administration. If our two Governments could agree on arrangements for the future administration of Hong Kong; if those arrangements would work and command confidence among the people of the Colony; and if they satisfied the British Parliament – we would then consider the question of sovereignty.

I had hoped that this practical and realistic line of argument would prove persuasive. After all, China gained large amounts of foreign currency and investment by having a capitalist Hong Kong on her doorstep. Even at the height of the Cultural Revolution, though riots had been fomented in the Colony by the communists, the Red Guards had never been permitted to launch a full-scale attack on Hong Kong. I tried to persuade Mr Zhao that we should agree a fairly noncommittal joint public statement saying that our common objective was to maintain the prosperity of Hong Kong and that there would be early official talks between us about this.

However, it was quite clear from the Chinese Prime Minister's opening remarks that they would not compromise on sovereignty and that they intended to recover their sovereignty over the whole of Hong Kong – the island as well as the New Territories – in 1997 and no later. The fundamental position underlying the Chinese position was that the people of Hong Kong were Chinese and not British. That said, Hong Kong could become a special administrative zone administered by local people with its existing economic and social system unchanged. The capitalist system in Hong Kong would remain, as would its free port and its function as an international financial centre. The Hong Kong dollar would continue to be used and to be convertible. In answer to my vigorous intervention about the loss of confidence which such a position, if announced, would bring, he said that if it came to a choice between sovereignty on the one hand and prosperity and stability on the other China would put sovereignty first. The meeting was courteous enough. But the Chinese refused to budge an inch.

I knew that the substance of what had been said would be conveyed to Deng Xiaoping whom I met the next day. Mr Deng was known as a realist. Indeed, it was he who effectively unlocked the way to a solution in Hong Kong. He had accepted that two different economic systems could exist in one country, a fact demonstrated by the setting up of special economic zones behind Hong Kong, within China itself. On this occasion, however, he was obdurate. He reiterated that the Chinese were not prepared to discuss sovereignty. He said that the decision that Hong Kong would return to Chinese sovereignty need not be announced now, but that in one or two years' time the Chinese Government would formally announce their decision to recover it. I repeated that what I wanted was agreement in further talks that after 1997 British administration would continue with the same system of law, the same political system, and the same independent currency. If we could at a later stage reach such an agreement there would be a tremendous upsurge in confidence. I could then go to the British

Parliament and have the whole question of sovereignty dealt with to China's satisfaction.

But he was not to be persuaded. At one point he said that the Chinese could walk in and take Hong Kong later today if they wanted to. I retorted that they could indeed do so, I could not stop them. But this would bring about Hong Kong's collapse. The world would then see what followed a change from British to Chinese rule.

For the first time he seemed taken aback: his mood became more accommodating. But he had still not grasped the essential point, going on to insist that the British should stop money leaving Hong Kong. I tried to explain that as soon as you stop money going out you effectively end the prospect of new money coming in. Investors lose all confidence and that would be the end of Hong Kong. It was becoming very clear to me that the Chinese had little understanding of the legal and political conditions for capitalism. They would need to be educated slowly and thoroughly in how it worked if they were to keep Hong Kong prosperous and stable. I also felt throughout these discussions that the Chinese, believing their own slogans about the evils of colonialism, just did not realize that we in Britain considered we had a moral duty to do our best to protect the free way of life of the people of Hong Kong.

For all the difficulties, however, the talks were not the damaging failure which they might have been. Although I failed to achieve my initial objective, I managed to get Deng Xiaoping to agree to a short statement which, while not pretending that we had reached agreement, announced the beginning of talks with the common aim of maintaining the stability and prosperity of Hong Kong. It was essential that something of the sort be said to bolster the fragile confidence back in Hong Kong. Neither the people of the colony nor I had secured all that we wanted, but I felt that we had at least laid the basis for reasonable negotiations. We each knew where the other stood.

The visit had been a full and tiring one. It was not all business, however, and there was time for a little sightseeing. While I was in China I had been able to visit the extraordinarily beautiful Summer Palace on the north-western outskirts of Peking, known in Chinese as the Garden of Peaceful Easy Life. I felt that this was a less than accurate description of my own visit to the Far East.

THE BERLIN WALL

The following month I visited another monument which, unlike the Summer Palace, has now crumbled into rubble and dust. After talks with Chancellor Helmut Kohl in Bonn, I flew to Berlin and gained my first sight of the Berlin Wall and of the grey, bleak and devastated land beyond it in which dogs prowled under the gaze of armed Russian guards. Chancellor Kohl accompanied me on this visit and, whatever difficulties would arise in the future, on matters like the evils of communism and commitment to our American allies we were as one. I suspect that the German press understood, as their comments later suggested, how powerfully moved I was by Berlin. The city was vibrant and exciting, larger than I had thought, surrounded by beautiful woods – yet uniquely scarred by the two totalitarian creeds of the twentieth century.

In my speech that afternoon – Friday 29 October – I said:

> There are forces more powerful and pervasive than the apparatus of war. You may chain a man – but you cannot chain his mind. You may enslave him – but you will not conquer his spirit. In every decade since the war the Soviet leaders have been reminded that their pitiless ideology only survives because it is maintained by force. But the day comes when the anger and frustration of the people is so great that force cannot contain it. Then the edifice cracks: the mortar crumbles . . . one day, liberty will dawn on the other side of the wall.

My prophecy has been vindicated earlier than I could ever have expected.

CHAPTER X

Disarming the Left

Winning the arguments and formulating the policies for a second term – 1982–1983

THE POLITICAL SCENE, 1982–1983

It is no exaggeration to say that the outcome of the Falklands War transformed the British political scene. In fact, the Conservative Party had begun to recover its position in the opinion polls before the conflict, as people began to realize that economic recovery was underway. But the so-called 'Falklands factor', beloved of political commentators and psephologists, was real enough. I could feel the impact of the victory wherever I went. It is often said that elections are won and lost on the issue of the economy, and though there is some truth in this, it is plainly an oversimplification. In this case, without any prompting from us, people saw the connection between the resolution we had shown in economic policy and that demonstrated in the handling of the Falklands crisis. Reversing our economic decline was one part of the task of restoring Britain's reputation; demonstrating that we were not the sort of people to bow before dictators was another. As I emerged from the strain of the period in which the Falklands dominated almost every moment, I found that people were starting to appreciate what had been achieved during the last three years. I drew attention in my speeches to the record and to the fact that none of it would have happened if we had followed the policies pressed upon us by the Opposition.

The Opposition itself was divided between Labour and the new 'Alliance' of the Liberal and Social Democratic parties. Though we were not to know it at the time, Alliance support had peaked and it would never be able to recapture the heady atmosphere of late 1981 when it had led in the opinion polls and its supporters had claimed they had truly 'broken the mould' of British two-party politics. In fact, of course, the one thing you never get from parties which deliberately seek the middle way between left and right is new ideas and radical initiatives. We were the mould-breakers, they the mould. The SDP and Liberals hankered after all the failed policies of the past – incomes policies, reflation by fiscal boosts to demand, shifting more power to a European bureaucracy and away from genuinely democratic national governments. The SDP's instincts on defence were sound – as opposed to the Liberals, perpetually tempted by unilateralism – and they were contemptuous of Marxist dogma. But I always felt – and still do – that the leaders of the SDP would have done better to stay in the Labour Party and drive out the far Left. The risk was that by abandoning the Labour Party to its militant wing, while attracting support away from us, they might actually let into power the very people they were seeking to keep out.

As for Labour, the Party continued an apparently inexorable leftward shift. Michael Foot is a highly principled and cultivated man, invariably courteous in our dealings. If I did not think it would offend him, I would say he was a gentleman. In debate and on the platform he has a kind of genius. But the policies he espoused, including unilateral disarmament, withdrawal from the European Community, sweeping nationalization of industry and much greater powers for trade unions, were not only catastrophically unsuitable for Britain: they also constituted an umbrella beneath which sinister revolutionaries, intent on destroying the institutions of the state and the values of society, were able to shelter. The more the general public learned of Labour's policies and personnel the less they liked them. I was not among those many Conservatives at the time who thought that Labour would be displaced by the Alliance. Socialism represents an enduring temptation: no one should underestimate Labour's potential appeal. But there was no doubt that in the extreme form adopted under Michael Foot's leadership it was easier to beat.

The opinion polls and by-election results confirmed what my own instincts told me – that the Falklands had strengthened our standing in the country. On the eve of the war we had already moved just ahead of the Alliance parties in the polls. Between April and May our support rose ten percentage points to 41.5 per cent, well ahead of all the other parties. It rose again in the wake of the recapture of the islands and then fell back a little during the second half of the year. However, on only one occasion between then and the election did it dip below 40 per cent. I never took much notice of what the polls said about me personally. Too much concentration on this sort of thing can be a distraction. But it was also true that my own standing in the polls had gone up substantially.

The 'Falklands factor' certainly punctured the Alliance: together with mounting optimism about the economic prospect, it helped us win back those Conservative supporters who had defected to what seemed a more comfortable, moderate option. Nor was there any joy in the polls for poor Michael Foot, whether one looked at Labour support as a whole, or his personal standing as leader.

However, by-election results in the last part of the Parliament confirmed that in some constituencies there was a real danger of the Alliance splitting the centre-right vote and letting Labour in. A good Alliance result always risked setting off the bandwagon which its friends in the media longed to see rolling. In March 1982 Roy Jenkins had won a stunning victory over us in Glasgow Hillhead. Only two months later we held our vote – and the seat – in Beaconsfield and in June we actually gained Mitcham and Morden from a defector to the SDP. Yet on 28 October there were by-elections in Peckham and Birmingham (Northfield) in both of which the Conservative vote was badly squeezed by the Alliance. As a result, we lost the Birmingham seat to Labour. The risks were evident, though looking at the figures in detail, the news was not all good for Labour: we knew that they would have to do a great deal better to stand any chance of winning a general election.

The last two by-elections of the Parliament were at Bermondsey in February 1983, where a far-left Labour candidate was routed by the Liberals, and Darlington in March which was held by Labour. We did not do well, but neither of these by-elections really harmed us. Labour was the main competitor in London, so Bermondsey was not likely to do us much damage. And although Labour won at Darlington, they did not do well enough to threaten our position nationally. The commentators loved to speculate, but no one knew how much tactical voting there would be against us in a general election – that is, how many people would vote for the candidates who seemed best placed to beat those standing for the Government, rather than for their preferred party. In fact, this sort of behaviour occurs much more rarely than predicted.

I always took a close interest in by-elections. I was regularly briefed by the Party Chairman about the issues and tactics, and I also received a detailed statistical breakdown from Keith Britto, our resident psephological genius at Central Office, on swings and their implications. I myself never took part in by-election campaigns in case I caused the Government to run unacceptable political risks in the event of a bad result: and results usually are bad when you are in power, especially in mid-term when many people wish to register a protest, safe in the knowledge that the result will not bring about a change of government. But I always sent public messages of support to our candidates and spoke privately to them afterwards to congratulate or – more usually – to console.

DEFENCE AND UNILATERALISM

Inevitably, defence was the political issue on which the Falklands War had the greatest bearing. During the Falklands campaign itself the nuclear issue was almost entirely edged out of public debate, though my speech at the UN Special Session on disarmament in June 1982 was an attempt to show how the same fundamental principles underlay the whole of defence policy.* However, in the autumn of that year, I began to be more concerned about the presentation of our nuclear strategy. I was anxious that the unilateral disarmers were still making the running on nuclear issues. Although public opinion was with us on the principle of the nuclear deterrent and opposed to unilateralism, there was a good deal of opposition to Trident II, mainly on grounds of cost, and to the stationing of Cruise missiles. Underlying both was a disagreeable streak of anti-Americanism. Accordingly, on 20 October and 24 November I chaired meetings of the Liaison Committee of Ministers and Central Office officials to explore the facts and refine the arguments.

Unilateralism became the official policy of the Labour Party at the 1982 Party Conference, when the necessary two-thirds majority was secured. Michael Foot personally had long been committed to the unilateralist position. It had an appeal in the universities and among some intellectuals and received a good deal of covert support from those in the media, especially the BBC. Labour councils had adopted the gimmick of declaring their areas 'nuclear free zones'. Although the Campaign for Nuclear Disarmament (CND) had begun to lose support from the high point it had reached in 1981, it remained dangerously strong.

Of the two specific aspects of nuclear policy at the centre of debate – the independent deterrent and the stationing of medium-range nuclear missiles – it was the second which was the more controversial. Cruise

* See pp. 236–7.

missiles would have to be deployed sometime in 1983 and we could expect a major campaign to prevent this.

Ultimate control of Cruise missiles was the most tricky issue. The decision to modernize medium-range nuclear missiles in Europe, it will be recalled, had been made under pressure from the Europeans, particularly the Germans, anxious to prevent any 'decoupling' of the American and European wings of NATO. The Americans had developed and paid for the missiles, and therefore owned them, massively reducing the cost to European governments. There was a strong feeling in the US Congress that any US-owned missiles should be subject to US control. However, American ownership obviously carried implications if it ever came to decisions about use.

In Britain, distrust of the United States surfaced on the question of whether there should be a 'dual key' – that is whether there should be a technical arrangement to ensure that the US could not fire these weapons without the consent of the British Government. That would go beyond the existing agreement that the US would not use nuclear weapons based in Britain without an Anglo-American 'joint decision'.

The United States had offered us the possibility of dual key right at the start, but to exercise that option we would have had to buy the weapons ourselves, which would have been hugely expensive. John Nott, before he left his post as Defence Secretary, had been attracted by the dual key option. But neither Michael Heseltine, his successor, nor I shared his view. The UK had never exercised *physical* control over systems owned and manned by the US. It was in my view neither fair nor necessary to ask the US to break with that precedent now. Also the more the Soviets were told about how and in what conditions Cruise missiles would be fired, the less credible they would be as a deterrent. The Soviets might be persuaded – and for the purposes of deterrence it did not matter whether they were right or wrong – that at the last moment a British Government might not agree to their use. Finally, the use of a dual key in the United Kingdom would have raised the whole question of arrangements elsewhere in Europe. In West Germany both government and public opinion would, as I have noted, only agree to deploying Cruise and Pershing II missiles if there was no German finger on the trigger.

So for all these reasons I satisfied myself through discussions with Washington that the position in reality was satisfactory from the point of view of British security and defence, and on 1 May 1983 I cleared personally with President Reagan the precise formula we should use to describe it. But I knew that it would be difficult to defend our line: not only anti-nuclear protesters but a sizeable number of our own supporters in and out of Parliament had their doubts. Moreover, most of the newspapers were opposed to us on the question of dual key.

The timing of deployment was bound to be a sensitive matter, especially with an election campaign ahead. We were anxious to avoid very visible signs of deployment in the run-up to or during the 1983 general election campaign, with demonstrations stretching police resources. Until almost the last moment we had been planning an autumn election. But as events happened we had an election in June, so this was not the problem which it might have been. (The launchers and warheads duly arrived in November.)

Elsewhere in Europe the situation was still more difficult. There was already a good deal of public criticism in Germany and Italy of NATO's offer of the zero-option, which was widely felt to be unrealistic. And the Soviets were mounting a major public relations campaign.

It was crucial that NATO's policy on arms control be well presented and that the alliance should stick together. On Wednesday 9 February I had a meeting at Downing Street with George Bush to discuss these matters. The Vice-President had a special remit from President Reagan to keep in touch with European governments and he did this with great skill. He was always very well briefed and had a friendly, straightforward manner, the proof that this reflected personality rather than artifice being that his staff were well known to be devoted to him. I now urged the Vice-President that the American Administration should take a new initiative in the INF negotiations. The aim should be to seek an interim agreement whereby limited reductions on the Soviet side would be balanced by reduced deployments on the part of the United States, without abandoning the zero-option as our ultimate goal – that is the complete elimination of intermediate-range nuclear weapons.

Mr Bush reported my views back to President Reagan who replied in a message to me on Wednesday 16 February. The President was at this stage somewhat noncommittal about a new initiative but said that he would be willing to consider seriously any reasonable alternative idea for producing the same result as the zero-option. This did not seem to me to be sufficient. I replied two days later on the hot-line. I stressed the success of Vice-President Bush's visit to Europe, but pointed out that one of its effects had been to raise expectations. I hoped that the speech which President Reagan was due to make shortly on these matters would go beyond a restatement of the US position and begin to indicate how it might be developed. As things turned out, the President's statement contained nothing new. So I continued the private pressure for further movement, while remaining in public totally supportive of the American position.

Then on Monday 14 March President Reagan sent me another message. He said that he had directed that a prompt review of the US position on INF negotiations should be made as a basis for new instructions to the US arms negotiating team. In the meantime, he asked that there should be no European calls for US flexibility and specifically asked me to express confidence in the very close co-ordination of our policies. I replied warmly welcoming his decision. On Wednesday 23 March the President told me the results of his review. While sticking to the ultimate objective of the zero-option, the chief US negotiator, Paul Nitze, would tell the Soviets at Geneva before the end of the current round of negotiations that the US was indeed prepared to negotiate an interim agreement. The Americans would stop deployment of a (still to be specified) number of warheads, on condition that the USSR reduced the number of warheads on its mobile long-range INF missiles to one equal with the US on a global basis. The President said that it was his tentative judgement that they should not offer specific numbers at this time. Again, I welcomed his decision, but argued that he should consider giving specific figures. In fact the President's proposal announced on 30 March did not do so. But his modest flexibility did have a beneficial effect on public opinion and incidentally helped us in Britain fighting the general election campaign soon to be upon us.

ECONOMIC RECOVERY

In that election campaign, defence would be of great political importance. Yet I had no doubt that the result would ultimately depend on the economy. Our economic course had already been set in the 1981 budget. We now had to see the strategy through. It was a remarkable testament to the soundness of public finances by this stage that we managed to pay for the Falklands War out of the Contingency Reserve without a penny of extra taxation and with barely a tremor in the financial markets. The economy was already beginning to recover and would have done so more rapidly but for sluggish world conditions. Geoffrey Howe's 1982 budget was designed to encourage that recovery by helping business, while keeping inflation and interest rates coming down by reducing government borrowing. The principal measure of direct assistance to industry in the 1982 budget was a reduction in the National Insurance Surcharge. We were able to make further reductions at the time of the 1982 Autumn Statement and again in the 1983 budget. These made a direct contribution to cutting industry's wage-related costs and helped to increase employment.

Another means of strengthening industry without becoming involved in the futile task of 'picking winners' was to promote the application of the new 'information technology' (IT). This was something in which I took a particularly close interest. As a scientist, I was fascinated by the technology itself; as a passionate advocate of free enterprise capitalism I was convinced that, given the right framework of laws and an appropriately educated workforce, it could widen choice, generate wealth and jobs and improve the quality of people's lives. Both Keith Joseph at Education and Ken Baker at Industry felt as I did. We designated 1982 Information Technology Year and we all made special efforts to widen understanding of what IT could do for business. Of course, it was the young people who found it easiest to learn the new skills and one of our most valuable and appreciated initiatives was to put a desk-top computer in every secondary school.

By now the question we were being asked was not whether economic recovery would come but rather how fast and how sustainable it would be, and also when unemployment would begin to fall. Since the whole basis of our approach to economic policy was that politicians and civil servants do not know all the answers, I never felt tempted to pick figures out of the air. But I did my best to encourage confidence because as long as the fundamentals – the public finances, monetary policy, tax levels and so on – are sound, confidence itself leads to higher investment and higher consumer spending and so helps recovery. For example, on Tuesday 19 April 1983 I addressed the CBI annual dinner at the London Hilton. We were only weeks away from the election, though neither the audience – nor even the guest speaker – knew it. I reminded them that when I had last been their guest two years earlier there was plenty to worry about in the state of the economy:

> Indeed, we had just read an open letter which predicted doom and gloom indefinitely unless we changed our policies. It was signed by no fewer than 364 economists – enough . . . to provide me with bad advice for every day of the year except All Fools' Day.

Since then, however, cuts in the NIS had put £2 billion a year back into the hands of private companies. Personal tax had also been cut by raising thresholds faster than inflation. Interest rates were seven percentage points below their peak, saving industry about another £2 billion. The exchange rate had fallen from a high point of $2.45 in October 1980 to $1.54 now. This was providing a boost for exporters. Industrial output, housing starts, and car sales were all up. There was plenty of evidence of recovery – above all, one that was soundly based.

The money supply and government borrowing had been brought under control. Public spending was at last expected to begin falling as a share of GDP, if only slightly, now that the economy was growing again. Our overseas debts had been virtually halved. Productivity in industry was greatly improved. Most dramatically, inflation had fallen from 20 to 4 per cent – its lowest level for 13 years. Success against inflation was the single achievement to which we drew most attention as we approached the election, not least because Labour looked set to promise huge increases in spending and borrowing which could never be honestly financed and which would have sent prices soaring again. The black spot in the record was, of course, unemployment, which was still well over three million. It would be vital in the campaign to explain why this was so and what we were doing about it. Our ability to deal with this issue successfully would be a test not only of our eloquence and credibility but also of the maturity and understanding of the British electorate.

TRADE UNIONS

Unlike some of my colleagues, I never ceased to believe that, other things being equal, the level of unemployment was related to the extent of trade union power. The unions had priced many of their members out of jobs by demanding excessive wages for insufficient output, so making British goods uncompetitive. So both Norman Tebbit, my new Secretary of State for Employment, and I were impatient to press ahead with further reforms in trade union law, which we knew to be necessary and popular, not least among trade unionists.

Norman wasted no time. Towards the end of October 1981 he sought Cabinet agreement for what was to become the Employment Act, 1982. There were to be six main areas covered.

We would raise substantially the levels of compensation for those unfairly dismissed in a closed shop.

In existing closed shops there would be periodic ballots to test support among employees for their continuation.

We would make unlawful what were called 'union labour only'

requirements in contracts, which discriminated against companies not operating a closed shop.

Henceforth, employers would be able to dismiss those taking part in a strike or other industrial action without having to run the risk of claims for unfair dismissal, provided that all of those taking part in the strike were dismissed.

The definition of a lawful trade dispute was to be further restricted in a number of ways, closing loopholes in Jim Prior's legislation to limit immunities in case of secondary action.

By far the most important of Norman's proposals related to the immunity currently extended to trade union funds. By virtue of Section 14 of Labour's Trade Union and Labour Relations Act, 1974, trade unions enjoyed virtually unlimited immunity from actions for damages, even if industrial action was not taken in contemplation or furtherance of a trade dispute. They could not be sued for their unlawful acts or for unlawful acts done on their behalf by their officials. This breadth of immunity was quite indefensible. As long as unions were able to shelter behind it they had no incentive to ensure that industrial action was restricted to legitimate trade disputes and that it was lawful in other ways. Norman therefore proposed that this immunity should be reduced to that enjoyed by individuals under our 1980 legislation.* Both of these immunities would be restricted further by our proposals on 'union labour only' requirements and changes to tighten the definition of a trade dispute, which removed the immunity for disputes not mainly about pay and conditions and for disputes between trade unions.

The unions were bound to put up fierce opposition to moves which would expose them to contempt proceedings and payment of damages. Undoubtedly, they would claim that we were seeking to prevent their defending their members' interests. So it was vital for us to explain the fairness of our proposals, and to emphasize that trade unions would only be at risk if they acted in ways which were unlawful for everybody else. We believed that the general public would see this as reasonable. We proposed also to set limits on the damages which could be awarded against a trade union, though of course there would be no limit on the fines which a court could impose for contempt – a most important qualification.

There was at first some opposition in Cabinet to Norman's proposals, not all of which came from predictable quarters. But most of us were full of admiration for his boldness. He went away to consider

* See p. 107.

some of the points made in discussion, but the package agreed by Cabinet in November was more or less on the lines he wanted. Norman announced our intentions to the House of Commons later that month. The bill was introduced the following February and the act's main provisions finally came into force on 1 December 1982.

Far from being unpopular, these proposals were soon being criticized in some quarters on the grounds that they did not go far enough. The SDP were trying to out-flank us by urging greater use of mandatory secret ballots. Many of our own supporters wanted to see action to stop the abuses connected with the 'political levy', a substantial sum extracted from trade unionists largely for the benefit of the Labour Party. There was continuing pressure to do something to prevent strikes in essential services – pressure which always increased when there was a threat of public sector strikes, as happened frequently during 1982. But it would not have been practical to deal with all of these issues at once in a single bill: each raised complicated questions and we could not afford to make mistakes in this vital area. I was convinced that the giant step being taken by Norman on the immunity of trade union funds was sufficient for the moment. I was glad, however, that the atmosphere had changed and that the dangers of trade union power were now so much more widely understood. We were winning that battle too.

Norman and I had further discussions in the summer of 1982. In September he came forward with a paper containing his thoughts for new industrial relations legislation which would be formally submitted to 'E' Committee, with a view to inclusion in the manifesto. Norman had already announced that we would undertake consultations with interested parties on legislation that would require trade unions to use secret ballots for the election of their leaders. There was strong support in both Houses for mandatory secret ballots before industrial action. But we were divided on this.

Ministers now discussed what should be the priorities for the forthcoming consultative green paper. We agreed to concentrate on ballots for the election of trade union leaders, mandatory strike ballots, and the political levy. Norman had reservations about the use of compulsory ballots before strikes. We had previously concluded that these should be voluntary. Moreover, there were doubts whether or not the use of ballots would actually reduce the frequency and length of strikes. But I was very aware of the great advantages of linking trade union reform to the unassailable principle of democracy, and I was keen to see that the proposals on strike ballots were expressed in a positive way in the green paper.

ABOVE: With Helmut Schmidt at a press conference following the Anglo-German talks in May 1979 (Ian Gow behind) – my first meeting with a foreign leader as Prime Minister

RIGHT: Meeting Christopher and Mary Soames with Peter Carrington, as they returned from the newly independent Zimbabwe in April 1981

ABOVE: Arriving in Dubai for talks with Shaikh Rashid, April 1981

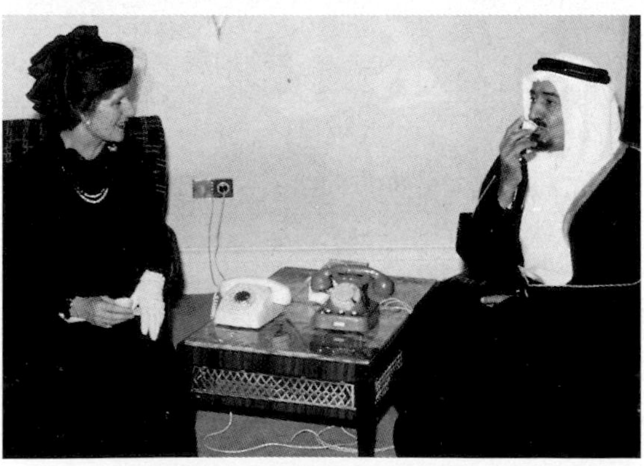

LEFT: Meeting with King Khalid during a visit to Saudi Arabia, April 1981

ABOVE: Being met by Indira Gandhi on a visit to India in April 1981

BELOW: Being met by Rajiv and Sonia Gandhi on a visit to India in April 1985

LEFT: Meeting children on my visit to China in September 1982

BELOW: With the press at a refugee camp on the Thai/Burmese border following my meeting with Prince Sihanouk in August 1988

BELOW: Inspecting troops in Malaysia during the April 1985 Far Eastern tour

RIGHT: On a trip to the Negev Desert with Shimon Peres during my visit to Israel in May 1986

BELOW: Welcoming banners at Ramat Gan in Israel, May 1986

ABOVE: With Denis during the visit to Kenya in January 1988

BELOW: Inspecting the tanks of the Jordanian Army with King Hussein during my visit to Jordan in September 1985

RIGHT: Meeting Sumo wrestlers during the visit to Japan in September 1982

BELOW: Meeting Deng Xiaoping in Peking in December 1984

LEFT: Dinner during my visit to Japan in 1982 with the late Emperor Hirohito and his daughter-in-law, now Empress of Japan

ABOVE: Photocall at Chequers with the Gorbachevs during their first visit to Britain in December 1984

RIGHT: Meeting President Gorbachev during his stop-over at Brize Norton in December 1987

We published the green paper under the title *Democracy in Trade Unions*, in January 1983. Ministers discussed in April where we should go from there. We had no difficulty deciding in favour of proposals relating to trade union elections and strike ballots. Two other issues proved much more difficult: the prevention of strikes in essential services and the political levy.

Public sector strikes and consequent disruption to the lives of the general public had been a feature of life in post-war Britain. Nineteen eighty-two was a particularly difficult year. There were two rail disputes. There was also a long and distressing strike in the National Health Service over pay, which began when ancillary workers took action in May and ended in mid-December. And industrial action in the water industry intensified interest in the whole question of how to deal with the disruption of essential services. But the practical difficulties of tackling the problem were immense. How should one define an 'essential service'? How much would it cost the taxpayer in extra pay to secure 'no strike' agreements? What should be the penalty for failure to observe a 'no strike' agreement?

The political levy was a second difficult subject. It was paid by trade unionists into political funds held by their unions, the principal use of which was, as I have noted, in fact to support the Labour Party. Payment was on the basis of 'contracting out': that is, trade unionists contributed automatically unless they specified otherwise. On the face of it, it would have been fairer to base the system on a principle of 'contracting in' and some argued for the change. But 'contracting in' would have wreaked havoc with the Labour Party's finances because of its heavy dependence on the unions. Had we introduced such a measure, there would undoubtedly have been pressure to change the system by which some companies donated to political parties, from which, of course, the Conservative Party heavily benefited. I never believed that the cases were parallel: after all, trade unionists in a closed shop could find it very difficult to avoid paying the political levy, especially when the employer had an agreement with the union to just 'check off' the levy from the employee. By contrast, shareholders who did not approve of company donations to a political party could either hold the Board to account for their decisions or simply sell their shares. But the funding of political parties was a sensitive topic. If we brought forward radical proposals on the eve of a general election, we would be accused both of attempting to crush the Labour Party financially and of unfairness on the matter of corporate donations.

On Tuesday 10 May I held a meeting of ministers at which we decided our manifesto commitment. On essential services, the introduction of strike ballots would clearly help reduce the risk of strikes in these areas. But we would also consult further about the need for industrial relations in specified essential services to be governed by adequate procedure agreements, breach of which would deprive industrial action of immunity. On the question of the political levy, we had evidence from the consultations on the green paper that there was widespread disquiet about the operation of the system and we proposed to consult with the TUC to see what action they were prepared to take, failing which we would act ourselves. These were matters to which we would have to return after the election. But we had made substantial progress in reducing the overbearing power of trade unions – much more than the fainthearted had ever believed possible. And far from proving a political incubus it was one of our strongest appeals to the voters.

POLICY WORK

For all sorts of reasons it is much easier to prepare for an election when you are in government than in Opposition. You have more information available about forthcoming events and more power to shape them. But parties in government have disadvantages as well, and you face two risks in particular. First, ministers can get out of the habit of thinking politically and become cocooned in their departments. Having to face, as I did, rigorous cross-questioning from an often hostile House of Commons twice a week, there was little danger that I, personally, would succumb to this: but others might. The second risk is that having implemented its manifesto, a government may run out of ideas. It is part of the job of ministers to see that this does not happen in their own areas of responsibility, and the job of the prime minister to prevent it happening to the government as a whole.

One of the main obstacles to the kind of forward thinking which all governments should do is the unauthorized disclosure of information by disaffected ministers or civil servants. A particularly serious problem arose in the last half of the 1979–83 Parliament. In March 1982 Geoffrey Howe asked officials to undertake an examination of long-term public expenditure up to and including 1990 and its implications for levels of taxation: their report was presented to me on 28 July. Spending ministers were inclined to think that this was just another exercise to soften them up for cuts in public expenditure. But in fact it was intended to get us all to examine how the long-term momentum for the expansion of the state and public spending might be curbed and reversed. As it turned out the paper was excessively gloomy and its most likely scenario underestimated very substantially the economic growth rate for the 1980s. To make matters worse, the CPRS prepared its own paper to accompany the Treasury paper, which contained a number of very radical options that had never been seriously considered by ministers or by me. These included, for example, sweeping changes in the financing of the National Health Service and extensions of the use of charging. I was horrified by this paper. As soon as I saw it, I pointed out that it would almost certainly be leaked and give a totally false impression. That is exactly what happened.

When the papers were discussed at Cabinet in early September, they made no great impact on our thinking. Our main conclusions could have been reached without any such exercise: that there should be no major new expenditure commitments pending further consideration, and that we should generally examine the scope for changing policies in ways which would bring public spending under proper control. My separate meetings with Keith Joseph on education and Norman Fowler on Health and Social Security confirmed that neither of them felt in any way attracted to the particular proposals which had been put forward, many of which were neither desirable nor practicable. But that failed to stop the media frenzy. A fairly full account of the CPRS paper duly appeared in the *Economist*. The *Observer* developed the story. The *Economist* later gave a blow-by-blow account of discussions at Cabinet. The *Observer* and then *The Times* revealed still more information. Of course, the Opposition had a field day. We were to be plagued by talk of secret proposals and hidden manifestos up to polling day and beyond. It was all the greatest nonsense.

There were two lessons from this incident which I never forgot. The first was that we had political opponents about us who would stop at nothing to distort and thereby prevent our forward thinking on policy. The second lesson was of equal importance: it was unacceptable for highly controversial proposals to come before Cabinet without the prior knowledge and approval of the ministers responsible. This raised acutely what role there could be for the CPRS.

In earlier days, the CPRS had been a valuable source of sound long-range analysis and practical advice. But it had become a freelance 'Ministry of Bright Ideas', some of which were sound, some not, many remote from the Government's philosophy. Moreover, as I have noted earlier, a government with a clear sense of direction does not need advice from first principles. Now, as this incident had shown, the

CPRS could become a positive embarrassment. That was why, shortly after the election, I was to dissolve the 'Think-Tank', and ask two of its members to join the in-house Policy Unit which worked more closely with me.

Ferdy Mount was now head of my Policy Unit. I had long been a great admirer of Ferdy's witty and thoughtful articles even when, as over the Falklands, I did not agree with his views; and I was delighted when in April 1982 he agreed to succeed John Hoskyns. Ferdy was particularly interested in all that goes under the heading of social policy – education, criminal justice, housing, the family and so on, to which, in the wake of the 1981 urban riots, I was increasingly turning my attention. In late May he prepared for me a paper which contained the outline of an approach to 'renewing the values of society':

> This Government came to power asserting that it is the exercise of responsibility which teaches self-discipline. But in the early stages of life it is the experience of authority, when exerted fairly and consistently by adults, which teaches young people how to exercise responsibility themselves. We have to learn to take orders before we learn how to give them. This two-way relationship between obedience and responsibility is what makes a free, self-governing society. And in the breakdown of that relationship we can trace the origins of so much that has gone wrong with Britain.
>
> If we can rebuild this relationship, we might begin to restore also respect for law and order, respect for property, and respect for teachers and parents. But the rebuilding itself has to be a two-way business. On the one hand, we need to restore effective authority to teachers and parents. On the other hand, we need to offer young people a taste of responsibility and a useful role in society.

At this stage it was the themes rather than the particular measures which needed to be worked out, and Ferdy and I discussed what these should be. In education, for example, we wanted to increase parent power, widen the variety within the state sector and see whether we could come up with workable proposals for education vouchers. We were concerned about the lack of knowledge displayed by many children about our country and society, and our history and culture. Of course, these and other topics – like all the really great issues – were never going to be amenable to instant action. But both Ferdy and I were convinced that at the heart of the Conservative mission is something more than economics – however important economics might be: there is a commitment to strengthen, or at least not undermine, the traditional virtues which enable people to live fulfilling lives without being a threat or a burden to others. This was the beginning of many of the themes and ideas which would dominate my third term of office.

Indeed, as early as June 1982 I set up an *ad hoc* group of ministers to see how this ambitious programme could be developed, comprising Keith Joseph, Willie Whitelaw, Geoffrey Howe, Norman Tebbit, Michael Heseltine, Norman Fowler and Neil Macfarlane (as Sports minister). I invited Janet Young to join us in October. The group was officially – though rather misleadingly – known as the 'Family Policy Group'; the first meeting was held in July 1982 and detailed work was now commissioned. All sorts of questions came within its remit, including the reform of the taxation of husband and wife, education vouchers, reducing crime and the widening of home ownership through increased discounts for the sale of council houses.

It is never easy to make the transition from policy-making in government to writing a party manifesto. In 1982 I used a special exercise to ease the problem. In September I wrote to Cabinet ministers requesting them to prepare a 'Five-Year Forward Look' for their departments. These papers were to summarize what had been achieved, what was under way and what still needed to be done. I received most of these papers just before Christmas and looked through them over the holiday. As someone once said of British Rail food, there was a considerable variation in quality. Relatively little new could be said on Treasury matters because the strategy was clear and the real test was to follow through the policies we already had. Similarly, as regards the Health Service the main priority at that stage was to defend our record and explain what had been achieved, rather than embark on politically difficult new initiatives.

By contrast, in both housing and local government there was more room for new thinking. The 'Right to Buy' had proved a huge success, but the wider we could extend home ownership in this way the more difficult it would be for Labour to oppose it. In employment, we were preparing for the introduction of the Youth Training Scheme and discussing the next step in trade union reform which would eventually result in the 1984 Employment Act.

In education, Keith Joseph had begun what would be a long process of reform. Falling school rolls had allowed us to increase to record levels public spending per pupil and to achieve the best ever pupil-teacher ratios. But extra resources only permit improved standards:

they do not ensure them. So Keith was pressing for changes in teacher training. He was issuing new guidelines for the school curriculum. Keith and I were also anxious to do something more to increase parents' power to choose by seriously investigating the possibilities of vouchers or at least a combination of 'open enrolment' and 'per capita funding', that is a kind of voucher applying just to the state sector.

There was a new momentum for fresh thinking at No. 10 and ministers had taken stock of their policies. By the end of 1982, although I was still not expecting an early general election, I felt that the Government was moving, as it should, into the run-up for the next campaign. There were plenty of possibilities for mishap, but our general political position was strong and the economic prospect was improving. Indeed, well before the end of the year I had authorized the setting-up of party policy groups to consider these and other proposals for the manifesto. Speculation about the date of the election soon began.

CHAPTER XI

Home and Dry

The background to and course of the 1983 general election campaign

THE MANIFESTO

The central importance of the manifesto in British general elections often strikes foreign observers as slightly odd. Party manifestos in Britain have acquired greater and greater significance over the years and have become increasingly detailed. In the United States and continental Europe, party 'platforms' have less authority and as a result they are not nearly as closely studied. Even in Britain it is only relatively recently that manifestos have been so full of detailed proposals.

The first Conservative manifesto was Sir Robert Peel's 1835 address to his electors in Tamworth. The 'Tamworth manifesto', for all the obvious differences, has one basic similarity with the Conservative manifesto today: it was then and is now very much the party leader's own statement of policies.

I was never encumbered with the ramshackle apparatus of committees and party rules which makes the drafting and approval of Labour's manifesto such a nightmare. However, the party leader cannot dictate to senior colleagues: the rest of the government and parliamentary party need to feel committed to the manifesto's proposals and consequently there has to be a good deal of consultation. I discussed the question with Cecil Parkinson and we agreed that Geoffrey Howe was the right person to oversee the manifesto-making process. There has never been a more devout believer in the virtues of consultation than Geoffrey. It had been necessary to exclude the Treasury from the Falklands War Cabinet and naturally he welcomed this chance to widen his role. As Chancellor of the Exchequer he had the seniority and experience to supervise the required policy work. Looking back, this arrangement was successful in one of its aims – that of reducing the burden on me – but, as we shall see, it turned out to have significant drawbacks. In 1987 I decided to oversee the preparation of the manifesto myself.

The whole process began almost a year before the election. On Saturday 19 June 1982 I approved the setting up of party policy groups with the remit of identifying 'tasks for Conservative administration during the rest of this decade; to make proposals for action where possible; where not possible, to identify subjects for further study'. Eleven such groups were originally envisaged, though in fact two were never set up: we dropped the idea of a group on 'constitutional reform' because I felt that there was really nothing of note to say on that subject, and the terms of reference on 'the extension of choice' turned out to be too vague. (This was a theme better dealt with in detail by the other groups.) The nine we did set up covered unemployment, enterprise, family and women's affairs, education, the cities and law and order, the poverty trap, the European Community, nationalized industries and urban transport. We decided that the chairman of each group should be a parliamentarian – an MP or peer – who would help to select members for their group from among the Conservative-minded in the worlds of business, academe, voluntary service and local government. To keep the Government informed, special advisers to the relevant Cabinet ministers would sit in on the meetings. (Special advisers are political appointees, and so free from the constraints of political neutrality which prevent the use of civil servants in such roles.) Secretarial and research work was done by members of the Conservative Research Department.

Essentially, the policy groups had two purposes. The first and more important was to involve the Party as a whole in our thinking for the future. In this I believe they were successful. The second was to come up with fresh ideas for the manifesto, and unfortunately in this purpose they failed. For one reason or another it took too long to find appropriate chairmen and the right balance of group members. It was not until October or November 1982 that the groups actually got down to work – originally, optimistically, we had thought that they might get started in July. The groups were due to report only at the end of March 1983, but by then of course we in government were all well advanced on our own policy work. Another problem is the human vanity of wanting to demonstrate that you are on the inside track. All too often their proposals trickled out through the press. Indeed, *The Times* published a detailed account of the report from the Education Policy Group.

The fact is that the really bold proposals in any manifesto can only be developed over a considerable period of time. Relying on bright ideas thought out at the last moment risks a manifesto that would be incoherent and impossible to carry out. So, in the end, the real work for the 1983 manifesto had to be done in No. 10 and by ministers in departments.

As head of my Policy Unit at No. 10, Ferdy Mount was ideally placed for manifesto drafting, and uniquely gifted for it too. He was able to see how ministers were thinking from the 'Forward Look' papers I received at the end of 1982. The next step was taken in February 1983, when Geoffrey Howe wrote to Cabinet colleagues, asking them to send him their suggestions for the manifesto not later than April. Their submissions would then be accepted, sharpened up or rejected by a smaller group of ministers and advisers directly responsible to me. The Treasury would keep a weather eye on the cost of proposals – another advantage of Geoffrey's close involvement – with the result that we were able to say during the election that all of our proposals had been taken into account in the latest Public Expenditure White Paper. Since we expected the contrast between Tory prudence and Labour profligacy to be a central issue in the campaign, this made political as well as economic sense.

Ferdy, Geoffrey Howe, and Geoffrey's special adviser, Adam Ridley, worked intensively together on Ferdy's first draft during March and early April. Subsequently, they were joined by Cecil Parkinson, Keith Joseph, Norman Tebbit, David Howell and Peter Cropper (the director of the Conservative Research Department), over the weekend of 9–10 April at which departmental submissions were fully considered. By the end of April we had a fairly complete draft, on which I worked with Geoffrey, Cecil, Ferdy and Adam at Chequers on Sunday 24 April. Shortly afterwards, the Party's Advisory Committee on Policy met under Keith Joseph's chairmanship to give it the Party's final seal of approval: interestingly, in the light of later events, the main criticism came from the two representatives of the '22 Committee who thought that we were not doing enough to reform the rates. On Wednesday 4 May chapters of the draft manifesto were sent for checking and agreement to individual ministers. A few final changes were made later still at my last pre-election strategy meeting at Chequers the following Sunday, after which it was at last ready to go to the printers. It was finally submitted in proof to an unofficial meeting of Cabinet.

The most important pledges in the manifesto fell into three groups. First, we promised to accelerate privatization, which was fundamental to our whole economic approach. If elected, we committed ourselves to sell British Telecom, British Airways, substantial parts of British

Steel, British Shipbuilders, British Leyland and as many as possible of Britain's airports. The offshore oil interests of British Gas would also be privatized and private capital would be introduced into the National Bus Company. This was an ambitious programme – far more extensive than we had thought would ever be possible when we came into office only four years before.

The second important group of pledges concerned trade union reform. Building on the consultations on our Trade Union Democracy Green Paper, we promised legislation to require ballots for the election of trade union governing bodies and ballots before strikes, failing which unions would lose their immunities. As I have noted, there was also a cautious pledge to consider legislation on the trade union political levy and on strikes in essential services. The caution was justified: we legislated on the former. At a time when Labour was promising to repeal our earlier trade union reforms, we were moving ahead with new ones: the contrast was stark, and we were sure the voters would appreciate the fact.

The third significant group of manifesto proposals related to local government. In particular, we promised to abolish the Greater London Council (GLC) and the Metropolitan County Councils, returning their functions (which we had already limited) to councils closer to the people – the boroughs in London, and the districts in the other metropolitan areas. The proposal surprised most people and was subsequently portrayed as a last-minute measure, sketchily thought out. The truth was very different. The previous year a Cabinet committee had examined the issue very thoroughly and recommended abolition, though past experience of leaks led me not to put the question to Cabinet for final decision until shortly before the election. We also promised to introduce what came to be known as 'rate-capping' – legislation enabling us to curb the extravagance of high-spending councils, in the interests of local ratepayers and the wider economy.

Though the manifesto took our programme forward, it was somehow not an exciting document. The first years of Conservative administration had been dominated by the battle against inflation and by a different kind of warfare in the South Atlantic. Great as the achievements were, neither economics nor defence is the kind of issue that generates exciting material for manifestos. Social policy is very different, but we were only really starting to turn our attention to this area, which was to become increasingly important in the next two Parliaments. And on this occasion at least, perhaps Geoffrey Howe was too safe a pair of hands. I was somewhat disappointed, though tactically I could see that it made sense for us to produce a tame manifesto and to concentrate on exposing Labour's wildness.

Perhaps the most important feature of the manifesto was what it did not contain. It did not promise a change of direction or an easing of the pace. It gave no quarter to the advocates of socialism and corporatism. In the foreword I stated my vision of Britain and the British:

> . . . a great chain of people stretching back into the past and forwards into the future. All are linked by a common belief in freedom, and in Britain's greatness. All are aware of their own responsibility to contribute to both.

Was I right in believing that this was the spirit of the time? Or was socialism what the people really wanted? The electorate would shortly give their answer.

PLANNING THE CAMPAIGN

On Wednesday 5 January 1983 I set aside a full day for discussion of our general election strategy. It was in the recess, so we held it at Chequers, always a relaxing place to think things out. The first half of the morning was spent with Cecil Parkinson, Michael Spicer (Deputy Chairman of the Party), Ian Gow and David Wolfson. We reached provisional decisions on a number of practical issues.

One of the most important things was to decide who would accompany me on my campaign tours. A coach had been hired and specially fitted out to take me around the country. We tried to keep the team as small as possible, though when the election was underway there always seemed to be a sizeable number on the bus. My PPS, Ian Gow, was a natural choice, with Michael Spicer taking his place on days when he had constituency engagements. At various times either Derek Howe or Tony Shrimsley would act as Press Officer. John Whittingdale, years later my political secretary and then only twenty-three, was chosen to do research. From Downing Street, Alison Ward and Tessa Gaisman would type the speeches, while one of the 'Garden Room girls' would keep me regularly in touch with No. 10 in case something happened which required my immediate attention. And last, but by no means least, we would be accompanied by my daughter Carol, who wrote and published a daily diary of the campaign. Harvey

Thomas would go ahead to set up arrangements for meetings and reconnoitre for the press, while his wife typed text for the Autocue, which I now used for all big speeches. Travelling in the coach was bound to be tiring but we knew it would allow us to obtain better press and television pictures. Often it would be possible for me to fly or take the train to the spot at which the tour itself began, using the travel time to work on speech notes and briefing.

At this meeting we considered the arrangements for the manning of the correspondence unit which would be set up to deal with my mail during the election period. I decided to ask Sir John Eden, a former minister who was not standing again for Parliament, to take on this task. There was also the problem of deciding who should serve on the Questions of Policy Committee at Central Office, set up at each election to give authoritative answers to difficult questions put to our candidates. I concluded that Angus Maude, who was also standing down as a Member of Parliament, was the ideal person to chair this Committee.

Later that morning at Chequers we were joined by several other senior people from Central Office. They reported on their plans. One difficulty that came around at every election was to know when to produce the Conservative Research Department's lengthy and rightly famous *Campaign Guide* – an encyclopaedia of political facts used by people of all political persuasions, including left-wing journalists too lazy to do their own research. The *Campaign Guide*'s appearance invariably triggered election speculation. We decided to aim at a publication date in July, though in the event the election came earlier and it had to be produced in a great rush to be ready for the start of the campaign in May. We discussed other literature which would be required for the constituencies. A Boundary Commission report was due and though the Party would benefit substantially from its proposals for the redistribution of seats, by the same token it was difficult to identify precisely the critical marginal seats in which the election would be won or lost. And it was vital that we focus our efforts on the marginals.

We discussed how to handle television: it was likely to be even more important than in earlier elections, though the new breakfast television would have less impact than had often been predicted. Gordon Reece had come over from the United States to help with this aspect of the campaign. Gordon was a former television producer with a unique insight into the medium. He had a much better grasp of popular taste than might have been expected from a man whose principal diet was champagne and cigars. He was always cheerful himself and he never failed to cheer others too. In fact, this was one of the few occasions when I can remember disagreeing with Gordon. He argued that we should be prepared to accept a series of televised debates between myself and Michael Foot, and (separately) with the Alliance leaders. This was an exceptional suggestion: British prime ministers have never accepted challenges to election debates of this kind. The calculation usually is that prime ministers have nothing to gain from them, and quite a lot to lose. But I stood so much better in the polls than Michael Foot that Gordon thought that on this occasion the orthodoxy was wrong and that I could only gain from such a confrontation. I rejected the idea. I disliked the way that elections were being turned into media circuses. And, as I have already said, I did not underrate Michael Foot as a debater. In any case, the arguments were too important to be reduced to a 'sound bite' or a gladiatorial sport.

One of our principal assets was the state of the Party's organization. Cecil Parkinson had done wonders for Central Office. He had brought the Party's finances into order in the year or so since he had become Chairman: this was essential, because it is only by husbanding resources in mid-term that you can afford to spend as heavily as required in a general election campaign. Cecil had also brought in some very able people. Peter Cropper had reintroduced rigorous standards in the Research Department. Tony Shrimsley, in charge of press relations, was a highly professional and talented journalist who shared my own outlook; sadly, this was to be his last campaign – he was probably already fatally ill. Cecil had placed Chris Lawson in charge of a new Marketing Department, which dealt with opinion research and publicity; Chris was that rare and useful animal, a businessman with acute political instincts.

In the afternoon Tim Bell presented a paper summarizing the strengths and weaknesses of our position, based upon opinion polls. Tim had a more sensitive set of antennae than most politicians. He could pick up quicker than anyone else a change in the national mood. And, unlike most advertising men, he understood that selling ideas is different from selling soap. Tim set out a communications strategy whose main theme was 'keep on with the change', an approach which I welcomed. Its wisdom lay in the perception that it was the Conservative Government rather than the Opposition parties which was the radical force in British society. As we ourselves had shown in 1979, there are few more potent slogans for an Opposition than that it is 'time for a change'. Tim showed that we could deprive Labour of that slogan and turn the argument against them.

We held another all-day session on general election strategy at

Chequers on Thursday 7 April. Manifesto work was in its final stages by then and I was worried that campaign planning seemed to be taking place in a separate compartment. However, that could not be helped. The key members of the Central Office team, along with Tim Bell, Ferdy Mount, David Wolfson, Ian Gow and myself ran over the style and content of the campaign and, in particular, my part in it. By now speculation about an early general election was feverish and there was little or nothing that I could do to prevent it, without firmly ruling out an early election, which of course would have been a very foolish thing to do. I had already stated in public that I would not go to the country before the end of our fourth year and at this meeting I made no secret of the fact that my own instincts were against an early election; I had in mind an election in October. Certainly, the argument was finely balanced. Were we to wait, there was a danger that if the polls started to turn in Labour's favour the prospect of their grossly irresponsible economic policies being implemented would weaken sterling and hold back investment. It is also generally true, as Jim Callaghan learnt to his cost when he postponed the election in the autumn of 1978, that in politics the 'unexpected happens'. However, on the other side of the argument, I was convinced that we were now seeing sustainable economic recovery, which would continue to strengthen the longer we waited: clearly, the more solid economic good news we could show the better.

But, of course, the overriding consideration in choosing an election date is whether or not you think you are going to win. On Sunday 8 May I had a final Chequers meeting with Cecil Parkinson, Willie Whitelaw, Geoffrey Howe, Norman Tebbit, Michael Jopling, Ferdy Mount, David Wolfson and Ian Gow. There had been local government elections on Thursday 5 May and we knew that the results would tell us a good deal about our prospects. Central Office staff had worked furiously to provide a detailed computer analysis by the weekend. We also had the evidence provided by private and public opinion polls.

Even when Cecil Parkinson took us through the information Central Office had brought together, I had some lingering doubt about whether the prospects really were good enough. I needed some convincing: calling an election is a big decision, and by constitutional convention it is a matter for the prime minister alone, however much advice is on offer. It was also, of course, a decision that I had never had to make before. Cecil and the others argued for June. It was pointed out that the main economic indicators would look slightly better then than in the autumn because inflation was due to rise slightly in the second half of the year. We would also probably face a by-election in Cardiff if we did not go soon: the Welsh Nationalists were threatening to move the writ and we had no way of stopping them. By-elections are unpredictable and there was the risk that the third-party bandwagon could be persuaded to roll if it went ahead. But the argument that told most with me was the level of election fever. The speculation was becoming impossible. Of course, I would be accused of 'cutting and running' if I went to the country in June, but the same critics would say I was 'clinging to power' if I put the election off; and probably the most damaging thing is to look as if you are afraid of testing your mandate.

By long-established custom, elections take place on a Thursday: if we were to go in June, which Thursday should it be? Again, Cecil and Central Office had done their homework, preparing a list of forthcoming events. From this it seemed that the second Thursday in June would be best, although this meant that the campaign would have to include a Bank Holiday – something electioneers prefer to avoid since it is almost impossible to campaign over that weekend. But Ascot began the following Monday and I did not like the idea of television screens during the final or penultimate week of the campaign filled with pictures of toffs and ladies in exotic hats while we stumped the country urging people to turn out and vote Conservative. Therefore, if we went in June it would have to be the 9th, rather than the 16th or 23rd.

These were persuasive arguments. But I did not make up my mind finally that day, returning to No. 10 only provisionally convinced. When I am making a big decision, I always prefer to sleep on it.

UNFINISHED BUSINESS

The following morning just before 7 o'clock I rang down to the duty clerk asking my principal private secretary, Robin Butler, to see me as soon as he came in: Robin would arrange for an audience with the Queen later that morning. I had decided to seek a dissolution and go to the country on Thursday 9 June.

There was now much to be done. I saw the Chief Whip and the Party Chairman to tell them of my decision, summoned a special Cabinet for 11.15 a.m. and went on to the Palace at 12.25 p.m. The rest of the day was spent discussing final election campaign preparations and the manifesto, and recording interviews. We had some important decisions to make about government business in Parliament. Two major bills – the Telecommunications and the Police and Criminal Evidence Bills – would have to be abandoned, though of course we would be able to reintroduce them if we formed the next government. The Finance Bill had to become law before Parliament dissolved – without it government authority to levy taxation would lapse – and to secure a quick passage for the bill we had to negotiate with the Opposition. Labour was inept: they gave us a parting gift by forcing the abandonment of a number of tax cuts proposed in the Finance Bill, including increases in the threshold at which the higher rate of income tax would begin and in the amount of tax relief for mortgages. They were quite happy to brand Labour the party of higher taxation: so were we.

I also had to make some decisions about my future engagements as Prime Minister, particularly meetings already arranged with foreign visitors: which, if any, should I see? A number of meetings were cancelled, but I carried on with as much of my diary schedule as I could. On Wednesday 11 May, I had talks and lunch with Robert Muldoon, Prime Minister of New Zealand, who had proved such a good friend to Britain in the Falklands crisis. That evening I also saw Alexander Solzhenitzyn and his wife. This courageous man sent a timely message to the British people at a press conference he gave, describing supporters of unilateral disarmament as 'naïve'.

Another question was whether I should go to the United States for the forthcoming G7 summit at Williamsburg at the end of May. I decided immediately that I had to cancel my planned visit to Washington on 26 May for pre-summit talks with President Reagan. As for the Williamsburg summit itself, I was minded to go but kept my options open for the moment. Politicians always have to be careful not to be seen spending more time with opposite numbers abroad than with their own people and that is never truer than in an election campaign. But the summit was important in its own right, not least because the President himself would be chairing it. Moreover, it would show Britain in a leading international role and lend international endorsement to the sort of policies we were pursuing.

We deliberately started our campaign later than the other parties. The electorate quickly becomes bored with incessant party politicking and it is important not to peak too soon: the ideal is to make an increasing impact in the last few days before polling day itself. Labour's manifesto, all over the newspapers shortly before the dissolution of Parliament, was an appalling document. It committed the party to a non-nuclear defence, withdrawal from the European Community, enormously increased public spending and a host of other irresponsible policies and was dubbed by one of the wittier Shadow Cabinet ministers 'the longest suicide note ever written'. We were very keen to publicize it and I understand that Conservative Central Office placed the largest single order for copies. But at my customary address to the '22 that evening, I warned the Party against overconfidence: even a short election campaign is quite long enough for things to go badly wrong.

The next day I flew to Scotland to address the Scottish Conservative Party Conference in Perth. The hall in Perth is not large, but it has excellent acoustics. It is one of the best places to speak anywhere in Britain – perhaps only Blackpool Winter Gardens is better. In spite of a sore throat from the tail-end of a heavy cold, I enjoyed myself. Not only do I always recall that this is the nation of Adam Smith: the romantic strain of Scottish Toryism appeals to the non-economist in me too. As always after visits to the Scottish Conference, I returned to London encouraged and in fighting spirit. The atmosphere had been one of buoyant enthusiasm – a good omen for the campaign.

That weekend I was also able to study the results of our first major 'state of battle' opinion poll survey. It showed that we had a 14 per cent lead over Labour and that there had been a fall in support for the Alliance. This was, of course, very satisfactory. I was glad to note that there was no evidence that people thought I had been wrong to call the election; indeed, the great majority thought it was the correct decision. But the poll also showed that if the Alliance looked in with a chance there was considerable potential for an increase in its support from weakly committed Conservative and Labour voters. Obviously this was something we would have to guard against.

THE CAMPAIGN BEGINS

In 1983, as in 1979 and 1987, we usually began the morning with a press conference on a prearranged topic. Before the press conference I was briefed in Central Office – during this election by Stephen Sherbourne, who managed to be both quick and methodical and who would shortly join my team in Downing Street as political secretary. This briefing took place at 8.30 a.m. in a cramped room at Central Office. We would begin by approving the day's press release and go on to consider questions likely to come up. Someone from the Conservative Research Department would come in part way through the briefing to report what had happened at Labour's press conference – somewhat easier then than now, for at that time Labour headquarters was at Transport House, just across the road from Central Office in Smith Square. It was convenient too that Labour's daily schedule ran ahead of ours. Our press conference would begin at 9.30 a.m. and was planned to last an hour. We had arranged my tours so that I spent very few nights away from London, and therefore I was nearly always available to chair it. I would field some of the questions myself, but try to give whichever ministers were appearing beside me that morning a chance to make their points. We were willing to change the subject of the day almost up to the last minute. In fact, during this campaign we were able to keep to the planned topics, though extra press conferences, which I did not attend, were arranged to deal with particular matters like Labour's social security spending pledges.

Our main aim both in the press conferences and speeches was to deal with the difficult question of unemployment by showing that we were prepared to take it head on and prove that our policies were the best to provide jobs in the future. So successful were we in this that by the end of the campaign the opinion polls showed that we were more trusted to deal with this problem than Labour. People knew that the real reasons for the high level of unemployment were not Conservative policies but rather past overmanning and inefficiency, strikes, technological change, changes in the pattern of world trade and the international recession. Labour lost the argument when they tried to place the whole blame for this deep-seated problem on the callous, uncaring Tories.

Then there were the speeches. During the campaign I used Sundays – almost the only time available – to work on speeches for the forthcoming week with Ferdy Mount and others at Chequers. I often saw Ferdy for final revision when I arrived back in No. 10 from campaigning during the day. He had prepared about half a dozen speech drafts on different topics before the campaign. The actual speeches I delivered consisted of extracts from these, with additional material often provided by Ronnie Millar and John Gummer, and topical comment addressing the issue of the day. I would put on the finishing touches in the campaign coach, trains, aeroplanes, cars and just about anywhere else you can imagine along the campaign trail. There were a few big speeches during this election but a large number of short speeches on 'whistle stops', often delivered off the back of a lorry on a small mobile platform, always off the cuff. I preferred the whistle stops, particularly when there were some hecklers. People tell me that

I am an old-fashioned campaigner; I enjoy verbal combat, though it has to be said that neither I nor the crowds derived much intellectual challenge from the monotonous chants of the CND and Socialist Worker protesters who followed me round the country.

Third, there were the tours themselves. The basic principle, of course, is that you should concentrate the Leader's appearances in marginal seats. One day on the campaign bus David Wolfson chided me for waving too much to people watching us pass: 'only wave in marginals, Prime Minister'. As the importance of television and the 'photo-opportunity' increases, the leader's physical location on a particular day is rather less important than it once was. In this election, moreover, our objective was to hold our vote and our seats so that (with a limited number of exceptions) my task was to concentrate on campaigning in Conservative-held seats. But one thing you must do is to visit all the main regions of the country: nothing is more devastating to candidates and party workers than to think they have been written off.

Finally, there were the interviews. These came in quite different styles. Brian Walden on *Weekend World* would ask the most probing questions. Robin Day on *Panorama* was probably the most aggressive, though in this campaign he made the mistake of plunging into detail on the problem of calculating the impact of unemployment on the public finances – a gaffe when cross-examining a former Minister of National Insurance. I made a gaffe of my own calling Sir Robin 'Mr Day' throughout. Alistair Burnet specialized in short, subtle questions which sounded innocuous but contained hidden dangers. One needed all one's nimbleness of wit to make it unscathed through the minefields. Then there were the programmes on which members of the public asked questions. My favourite was always the *Granada 500* when a large audience quizzes you about the things which really matter to them.

Our manifesto was launched at the first Conservative press conference on Wednesday 18 May. The whole Cabinet was there. I ran through the main proposals, and then Geoffrey Howe, Norman Tebbit and Tom King made short statements on their sections of the manifesto. After that I invited questions. Manifestos rarely make the headlines unless, as on this occasion, something goes wrong. The press will consign carefully thought-out proposals for government to an inside page and concentrate on the slightest evidence of a 'split'. At the press conference a journalist asked Francis Pym about negotiations with Argentina. I felt that Francis's reply risked being ambiguous, so I interrupted to make clear that while we would negotiate on commercial and diplomatic links, we would not discuss sovereignty. The press highlighted this: but there was in fact no split. That's politics.

D-21 TO D-14

In Britain the general election campaign is only about four weeks long, usually less. For planning purposes during elections we always used the so-called 'D- (minus)' system, numbering each day in a countdown to 'D-Day' – polling day itself. The most intense period of the campaign is from D-21 on, which in this case fell on Thursday 19 May. We opened our campaign on D-20, Friday 20 May, two days after the launch of the manifesto. The first of our five Party Election Broadcasts (PEBs) had been shown on D-23.

It was not Francis Pym's week. He told a questioner on BBC's *Question Time* that in his opinion 'landslides on the whole don't produce successful governments.' Naturally, people drew the inference that he did not want us to win a large majority. Of course, this was all very well for those with safe seats like Francis himself. But it was distinctly less good news for candidates in the Conservative marginals and those of our people hoping to win seats from other parties. And since complacency was likely to be our worst enemy in the campaign this remark struck a wrong note.

The first regular press conference on the campaign took place on Friday 20 May. Geoffrey Howe challenged Labour on the cost of their manifesto proposals and said that if they did not publish them we would. This was the first deployment of a very effective campaign theme. Patrick Jenkin, taking it up, drew attention to Labour's plans for nationalization and regulation of industry. There were a number of questions about the economy. But, inevitably, what the press really wanted to know was what I thought about Francis's remark. We had seen this coming and I had discussed what to say at the briefing session earlier that morning. Francis had been Chief Whip under Ted Heath and I made that the basis of my reply:

> I think I could handle a landslide majority all right. I think the comment you're referring to was natural Chief Whip's caution. Ex-Chief Whip's caution. You know there's a club of Chief Whips. They're very unusual people.

I left after the press conference for my first campaign tour, which was in the West Country. At 10.45 a.m. we drove from Central Office to Victoria Station, and from there went by train to Gatwick to catch the flight to St Mawgan in Cornwall. A group of around 40 or 50 journalists joined us, sitting together at the back of the plane. It was a pleasant rural day. I visited the fish market at Padstow Harbour and went on to Trelyll Farm, near Wadebridge. There I was caught out by the press. I was standing on a heap of cut grass and the *Daily Mirror* photographer asked me to pick some up. I saw nothing wrong with that, and so I obliged. He took his photograph – and the picture duly appeared the following day with the caption 'Let them eat grass'. It does not do to be too co-operative.

It was on Monday 23 May (D-17) that my campaign began in earnest. We started as usual with a briefing meeting for that morning's press conference where we spent some time discussing the Party's advertising. Saatchi & Saatchi had devised some brilliant advertisements and posters in 1979. Most of those they produced in 1983 were not quite as good, although there were exceptions. One compared the Communist and Labour Party manifestos by printing side by side a list of identical commitments from each. It was a long list. A second poster set out 14 rights and freedoms that the voter would be signing away if Labour was elected and carried out its programme. Another poster aimed at winning us support from ethnic minorities with the slogan 'Labour Think He's Black, Conservatives Think He's British' caused some controversy. But I thought it was perfectly fair. I did, however, veto one showing a particularly unflattering picture of Michael Foot with the slogan: 'Under The Conservatives All Pensioners Are Better Off'. Maybe that was a fair political point too: but I do not like personal attacks.

My speech that evening was at the Cardiff City Hall. It was a long speech, made a little longer but much more lively when I broke away from the text, which always seems to help the delivery. I covered all the main election issues – jobs, health, pensions, defence – but the lines I liked best related to Labour's plans for savings:

> Under a Labour government, there's virtually nowhere you can put your savings where they would be safe from the state. They want your money for state socialism, and they mean to get it. Put your savings in the bank – and they'll nationalize it. Put your savings in a pension fund or a life assurance company – and a Labour government would force them to invest the money in their own socialist schemes. If you put money in a sock they'd probably nationalize socks.

I had returned early to No. 10 from Tuesday's daily tour in order to prepare for a Question and Answer session with Sue Lawley on *Nationwide*. This unfortunately degenerated into an argument about the sinking of the *General Belgrano*.

The Left thought it was scoring points by keeping the public's attention focused on this, exploiting minor discrepancies to support its theory of a ruthless government intent on slaughter. This was not only odious; it was inept. The voters overwhelmingly accepted our view that protecting British lives came first. On the *Belgrano*, as on everything else, the Left's obsessions were at variance with their interests. But I found the whole episode distasteful.

Wednesday 25 May was a difficult day for both the major parties, though we suffered far less damage than Labour. The Labour Party was so ineffective during the campaign that the newspapers, in desperation for stories, concentrated heavily on leaked documents. The main interest on this occasion was the leaking of a draft report of the Treasury and Civil Service Select Committee, which attacked our economic policies. Cecil Parkinson contacted Edward du Cann, the Committee Chairman, who promptly issued a statement drawing attention to the fact that the report had not been approved by the committee. It was typical of the Labour Party's lack of grip that they completely missed this opportunity to embarrass us, preferring to spend their morning press conference talking about 'women's issues'. We were amazed. As we joked about it I said to my male colleagues at the briefing session: 'if they have their way, you'll soon be having the babies.'

Our press conference that day, though allegedly on defence, was in fact devoted to the revelation that our candidate at Stockton South had once been a member of the National Front. He had left the National Front some years before and now claimed to be an orthodox Conservative and regretted his past. As far as we were concerned this was a peripheral embarrassment but some left-wing journalists seemed to see themselves as Woodward and Bernstein, fighting the Establishment. Again, it served to distract the Labour Party from issues of genuine interest to the public.

The Labour Party was now in deep trouble. That same day – the very day we had chosen to devote to defence – Jim Callaghan made a speech in Wales rejecting unilateral nuclear disarmament. The newspapers were full of contradictory statements about Labour's position on nuclear weapons. Even among Labour front-benchers there was disarray: you could choose between Michael Foot, Denis Healey and John Silkin – each seemed to have his own defence policy. Michael

Heseltine at our press conference and throughout the campaign was devastating in his criticisms of Labour's policy.

I always realized that there were a few issues on which Labour was especially vulnerable – issues on which they had irresponsible policies but ones to which the public attached great importance. They were the 'gut issues'. Defence was one. Another was public spending, where the voters always have a suspicion that Labour will spend and tax too much. For that reason I was very keen that Geoffrey Howe do a more comprehensive costing of Labour's manifesto promises than usual. He produced a superb analysis that ran to twenty pages. It showed that Labour's plans implied additional spending in the life of a Parliament of between £36–43 billion – the latter figure almost equal to the total revenue of income tax at that time. Labour's economic credibility never recovered. Indeed, Labour's profligacy has been its Achilles heel in every election I have fought – all the more reason for a Conservative government to manage the nation's economic affairs prudently.

That Wednesday my election tour took me to the East of England, travelling by aeroplane and coach. It was a beautiful day. I spent part of it campaigning in East Dereham in Norfolk for Richard Ryder. As I have noted, he had been my political secretary, and I was glad to be able to help. And, of course, his wife, Caroline, had also worked for me. Almost a family occasion. I addressed a crowd in the packed market square. There were a few hecklers which made it more fun. I let rip with an old-fashioned barnstorming speech. Later someone told me that above the platform where I had stood to deliver the speech there was a large cinema sign advertising a film called *The Missionary*.

D-14 TO D-7

On Thursday 26 May (D-14) the opinion polls reported in the press gave us anything between a 13 and 19 per cent lead over Labour. The principal danger from now on would be complacency among Conservative voters rather than any desperate Labour attempts at a comeback.

Thursday was to be another pleasant day of traditional campaigning, this time in Yorkshire. One highlight was lunch in Harry Ramsden's Fish and Chip Shop – the 'biggest fish and chip shop in the Free World' – in Leeds. I thoroughly enjoyed myself but the occasion was quite chaotic, with cameramen crashing around among the startled diners.

That evening I spoke at the Royal Hall, Harrogate, dwelling on a theme which was central to my political strategy. The turbulence of politics in the 1970s and 1980s had overturned the set patterns of British politics. Labour's own drift to the left and the extremism of the trade unions had disillusioned and fractured its traditional support. The SDP and the Liberals failed to grasp the significance of what was happening. They projected their appeal to the middle-class Left, especially those who worked in the public sector, probably, I suspect, because Roy Jenkins and Shirley Williams instinctively sought out their own kind and allowed that instinct to overcome their judgement. In fact, the more numerous and dissatisfied Labour supporters were in the rising working and lower-middle class – the same group that in America Ronald Reagan was winning over and who were known as 'Reagan Democrats'. They were benefiting from the opportunities we had made available, especially the sale of council houses; more important, they shared our values, including a strong belief in family life and an intense patriotism. We now had an opportunity to bring them into the Conservative fold, and I directed my speech at Harrogate to doing just that:

> In this country the things that most of us believe in are greater than the things that divide us. There are people in all walks of life who share our vision, but who have not voted for us in the past. At this election there is so much at stake that I feel I must say to them: the Labour Party today is not the party you used to support. It no longer stands for the traditions and liberties which made this country great. It is the Conservative Party that has stayed true to those traditions and those liberties.

Politicians generally dislike elections. But one advantage is that in the course of a campaign you see a great deal of the country that would otherwise be concealed in reports and memoranda. For example, no official report could convey the excitement of the advanced electronics factories around Reading that I visited on the Friday. It was also my first encounter with the portable telephone.

By the time that I arrived back in London there had been yet another extraordinary development in Labour's campaign. Labour's General Secretary, Jim Mortimer, reported to an astonished press corps that 'the unanimous view of the campaign committee is that Michael Foot is the Leader of the Labour Party.' With statements like that one wondered how long either of them would keep his job.

My own mind that evening was very much on the forthcoming G7 economic summit at Williamsburg, for which I would leave for the United States at midday on Saturday. President Reagan was keen to have me there. He had sent me a message on 10 May to say that he would perfectly understand if I was not able to come to Washington for a pre-summit bilateral meeting, but that he very much hoped I would go to Williamsburg. The message concluded:

> I wish you every success in the election and in gaining another mandate to carry out the courageous and principled policies which you have begun.

Above all, he wanted me to win – just as I always wanted him to win. I received a report whose authenticity I had no reason to doubt that the President had said that no pressure was to be put on me one way or another about attending the summit. 'Hell,' he was reported to have said, 'the main thing is for her to get re-elected.' I shared his analysis.

Whatever its electoral implications for me, there was no doubt that the Williamsburg summit was of real international importance. President Reagan was determined to make a success of it. At previous G7 summits the scope for genuine discussion had been somewhat limited by the fact that a draft communiqué had been drawn up even before the leaders met. This time the Americans had insisted that we should discuss first and draft later, which, however inconvenient for officials, was far more sensible. But I took along a British draft just in case it was needed.

The atmosphere at Williamsburg was excellent, not just because of the President's own radiant good humour but because of the place itself. In the surroundings of this restored Virginian town each head of government stayed in a separate house. We were welcomed by friendly townspeople in old-style colonial dress. There was a complete contrast with the perhaps overluxurious feel of Versailles.

I had a long tête-à-tête discussion with the President. It ranged over a wide field: from nuclear disarmament negotiations to the state of the American economy and the protectionist leanings of the US Congress – something which was giving us increasing concern. Later I had a short but important talk with Prime Minister Nakasone of Japan. I had met him when I visited his country as Leader of the Opposition. He was perhaps the most articulate and 'western' of Japan's leaders in the period when I was Prime Minister, raising his country's international profile and fostering close links with the United States. On this occasion, my main interest was to press for Nissan to finalize its decision to invest in Britain, which I hoped would create thousands of jobs. Understandably, Mr Nakasone's line was that this was a decision for the company. I should add here that it had been reported in the British press that Nissan would not have gone ahead with their investment had Labour been elected. This was publicly denied by the company, but it was probably true.

The two main objectives which President Reagan and I shared for the summit were the reaffirmation of sound economic policies and a public demonstration of our unity behind NATO's position on arms control, especially as regards the deployment of Cruise and Pershing II missiles. I introduced the discussion on arms control at dinner on Saturday. In fact, by that morning we had what most of us considered a satisfactory draft communiqué. France's position – as a country outside the NATO command structure – required to be taken into account. But President Mitterrand said that he had no dispute with the substance of our proposal. In fact, he came up with an amendment that we were able to accept, because it strengthened it in the direction we wanted. It seems improbable that President Mitterrand realized this.

Pierre Trudeau of Canada did have a problem with a strong line on deterrence. He urged us all to 'speak more softly' to the Soviet Union. There followed some exchanges between the two of us which I later described in a letter to him as 'on the lively side'. In the end, a thoroughly satisfactory text on arms control emerged.

The text on the economy was pretty satisfactory as well, except for a little misty language on exchange rate co-ordination. President Mitterrand had been tempted at one stage by grand talk of a 'new Bretton Woods', shorthand for the system of fixed exchange rates which had operated from 1944 to 1973. But he did not press this view at Williamsburg.

I came home by the overnight British Airways flight, confident that the outcome of the summit vindicated my approach to the crucial election issues of defence and the economy. This summit also marked a change in the relationship between President Reagan and the other heads of government. They might previously have admired his eloquence and devotion to principle: but they had sometimes been dismissive of his grasp of detail. I, myself, had felt some concern about this earlier. Not so on this occasion. He had plainly done his homework. He had all the facts and figures at his fingertips. He steered the discussions with great skill and aplomb. He managed to get all he wanted from the summit, while allowing everyone to feel that they had got at least some of what *they* wanted, and he did all this with an immense geniality. What President Reagan demonstrated at Williamsburg was that in international as in domestic affairs he was a master politician.

Monday 30 May was a Bank Holiday. That day Denis Healey released what the Labour Party claimed was the 'real' Conservative manifesto, a fantastical affair, full of lies, half-truths and scares culled from reports of leaked documents, especially the CPRS long-term public expenditure document, the whole thing imaginatively embellished. I was not surprised. Labour had tried this tactic in 1979: it had not worked then either. Once again, Labour was catering not to the interests of the voter but to its own obsessions. They failed to realize that propaganda can never persuade people of the incredible. Apparently, you can persuade the press of this, however.

On Tuesday evening I was to speak at George Watson's College in Edinburgh. My idea was to use the occasion to report on Williamsburg and to defend our record on the social services. But looking at the material we already had written, I realized that we had a lot of work still to do and the whole thing was finished in a tremendous rush, as not infrequently happens with my speeches. Several of us spent the early evening before the speech crawling around the floor of my room at the Caledonian Hotel, sticking together bits of text with sellotape. After that we flew further north to Inverness, where we stayed the night. A large crowd of chanting protesters outside our hotel serenaded us to sleep.

The next day (Wednesday 1 June, D-8) I held a press conference, gave television interviews, visited two Scottish factories, flew to Manchester, visited a bakery in Bolton and a brewery in Stockport, and flew back to London to begin work on another speech. I am not usually much affected either by pressure of work or by attacks from opponents. But this day was a little different. Denis Healey made the tasteless remark that I had been 'glorying in slaughter' during the Falklands War. I was both angry and upset. We had deliberately decided not to raise the Falklands in the campaign and had done nothing whatsoever to make it an issue. The remark hurt and offended many people besides me – not all of them Conservatives – particularly the relatives of those who had fought and died in the war. Mr Healey later made a half-hearted retraction: he had meant to say 'conflict' rather than 'slaughter' – a distinction without a difference. Neil Kinnock returned to the subject a few days later, in an even more offensive form, if that were possible. These remarks were all the more revealing because they were politically stupid: indeed they did enormous harm to Labour. They were not made from political calculation, but can only have emerged from something coarse and brutal in the imagination.

D-7 TO D-DAY

Nonetheless at Thursday morning's press conference there was yet more about the *General Belgrano* and I could not conceal my irritation at the failure of some journalists to grasp the harsh reality of war. I said:

> I think it is utterly astonishing that your only allegation against me is that I in fact changed the rules of engagement with the consent of the War Cabinet to enable a ship which was a danger to our task force to be sunk.

On Friday, after the press conference, Cecil and I had now to decide whether we needed a full-scale newspaper advertising campaign over the weekend. Two opinion polls that day showed us with leads of 11 and 17 per cent over Labour. We were being told that we were home and dry. But many voters make up their minds in the last week, some indeed as they are on their way to the polling station; so I have always been a wary campaigner. Cecil was an equally battle-scarred electioneer and we had planned to run expensive three-page advertisements in the Sunday newspapers. But we decided to take a risk and save the money, cutting the advertisements to a more economical two pages. On this my political calculations coincided with my instincts as a Grantham grocer's daughter. Obvious extravagance is bad advertising.

I spent Saturday (D-5) campaigning in Westminster North, then going on to the constituencies in Ealing and Hendon close to my own. I campaigned in Finchley for most of the afternoon and then went to support our candidate in Hampstead and Highgate.

On my return to No. 10 work began almost at once on the speech I was to deliver the next day at our Youth Rally at Wembley Conference Centre. My speech writers and I worked late into the night, breaking for a hot meal which I served up in the kitchen from the capacious store of precooked frozen food I always kept there for such occasions. Shepherd's pie and a glass of wine can do a great deal to improve morale. Speech writing was for me an important political activity. As one of my speech writers said, 'no one writes speeches for Mrs Thatcher: they write speeches with Mrs Thatcher.' Every written word goes through the mincing machine of my criticism before it gets into a speech. These are occasions for thinking creatively and politically and for fashioning larger themes into which particular policies fit. I often found myself drawing on phrases and ideas from these sessions when I was speaking off the cuff, answering questions at Prime Minister's Question Time and for television interviews. This helped to preserve me from the occupational hazard of long-serving ministers: so I was never accused of thinking like a civil servant. (They had to think like me.) These occasions often continued long into the night and can perhaps be described as fraught but fun.

So was the Youth Rally. Some of the sourer critics chose to take offence at joke remarks made by the comedian who preceded my appearance on stage. What they really took offence at was the broad social appeal of the new Conservative Party demonstrated both by the unconventional people on the stage and in the audience. As one punk rocker told a journalist at the time: 'Better the iron lady than those cardboard men.'

One of the opinion polls on Sunday put the Alliance ahead of Labour for the first time. This gave the last days of the campaign a new feel and a new uncertainty. But personally I never believed that the Alliance would beat Labour into third place – even though the Labour leaders were doing their best to ensure it did.

I chaired our last press conference of the campaign on Wednesday morning (D-1), accompanied by more or less the same team as had launched the manifesto. There was an end-of-term feeling among the journalists, which we felt confident enough to share. I said that the vital issues on which the voters must decide between the parties were defence, jobs, social services, home ownership and the rule of law. I was keen to answer the charge that a large Conservative majority would lead us to ditch our manifesto policies and pursue a 'hidden agenda' of an extreme kind. I argued that a large Conservative majority would in fact do something quite different: it would be a blow against extremism in the Labour Party. And that, I think, was the real underlying theme of the 1983 general election.

Election day itself is an oddly frustrating time. I always voted early and then visited the Finchley committee rooms, each of which would be receiving information as to which of our known supporters had voted: later in the day party workers would visit those who had not done so to urge them on to the polling stations. All the opinion polls suggested a Tory landslide. But I have seen too many electoral upsets in my life to take such things for granted.

The Finchley count takes place in Hendon Town Hall. The result was late in coming through because of the number of other candidates anxious to gain publicity for their cause by fighting against me. It was made later still on this occasion because one of them successfully demanded a re-count. (My eventual majority was 9314.) It was not until well into the early hours of the morning that my result was declared and I was safely returned for the eighth time.

While waiting for my own count to finish I watched the national results coming in on television. The first three were not particularly encouraging: in both Torbay and Guildford the Alliance vote was up substantially, though we held the seats. Then there was worse news: we lost Yeovil to the Liberals. But the turning point came soon after – the first Tory gain from Labour: Nuneaton. From then on the shape and size of our victory became clearer and clearer. It really was a landslide. We had won a majority of 144: the largest of any party since 1945.

I returned to Conservative Central Office in the early hours. I was greeted by cheering party staff as I entered and gave a short speech of thanks to them for their efforts. After that I returned to No. 10. Crowds had gathered at the end of Downing Street and I went along to talk to them as I had on the evening of the Argentine surrender. Then I went up to the flat. Over the previous weeks I had spent some time clearing things out, in case we lost the election. Now the clutter could build up again.

CHAPTER XII

Back to Normalcy

Politics, the economy and foreign affairs from the election to the end of 1983

Political success is a good deal pleasanter than political failure, but it too brings its problems. Conventional wisdom, reinforced by classical mythology, has it that this is all a matter of hubris or at least of complacency. But it is not always so. Nor was it in fact during the somewhat troubled six months which followed the 1983 general election. On this occasion there were subtler problems. One was that the media, having felt obliged during the election campaign to cover real political arguments about practical choices, soon reverted to the more amusing sport of scoring points off the Government. And there was a second problem, which we encountered increasingly over the years, that the less the socialist threat seemed, the more people were inclined to jib at the inevitable difficulties and disappointments of running a free enterprise economy.

In 1983 we also had two other problems to face – one of our own making and one not. The first was that the 1983 manifesto did not inspire the Government with the sort of crusading spirit which would have got us off to a good start in the new Parliament. Some of the main pledges were popular enough, such as the abolition of the GLC and Metropolitan Counties and the introduction of rate-capping, but they ran into a difficulty with which any reforming administration must bear: that the generalized approval of the silent majority is no match for the chorus of disapproval from the organized minority. The left-wing municipal socialists and their subsidized front organizations were astute campaigners, trained and adept at exploiting every weakness of presentation of the Government's case. Much of the manifesto promised 'more of the same' – not the most inspiring of cries, although there is no doubt that a lot more was needed. We had not yet cut taxes anything like as much as we wished. There was more work to be done on trade union law and the privatization programme – which would perhaps constitute the really big advance of this Parliament – was barely under way; the bill to privatize British Telecom, which had fallen with the election, had to be reintroduced.

The second problem was one for which we could not be blamed – that there was still too much socialism in Britain. The fortunes of socialism do not depend on those of the Labour Party: in fact, in the long run it would be truer to say that Labour's fortunes depend on those of socialism. And socialism was still built into the institutions and mentality of Britain. We had sold thousands of council homes; but 29 per cent of the housing stock remained in the public sector. We had increased parents' rights in the education system; but the ethos in classrooms and teachers' training colleges remained stubbornly left wing. We had grappled with the problem of bringing more efficiency into local government; but the Left's redoubts in the great cities still went virtually unchallenged. We had cut back trade union power; but still almost 50 per cent of the workforce in employment was unionized, far more than our main competitors, and of them around 4 million were working in a union closed shop. Moreover, as the miners' strike would shortly demonstrate, the grip of the hard Left on union power was still unbroken. We had won a great victory in the Falklands War, reversing the years in which British influence seemed doomed to an inexorable retreat; but there was still a sour envy of American power and sometimes a deeper anti-Americanism, shared by too many across the political spectrum.

In all this, my problem was simple. There was a revolution still to be made, but too few revolutionaries. The appointment of the first Cabinet in the new Parliament, which took place incongruously to the background accompaniment of traditional military music and the Trooping of the Colour, seemed a chance to recruit some.

THE NEW GOVERNMENT

I began by dropping one would-be pilot, whose sense of direction had on several occasions proved faulty. In following Peter Carrington with Francis Pym as Foreign Secretary I had exchanged an amusing Whig for a gloomy one. Even the prospect of a landslide during the election made him utter dire warnings. Francis and I disagreed on the direction of policy, in our approach to government and indeed about life in general. But he was liked in the House of Commons which always warms to a minister who is believed to be out of step with the Government, something which is often mistaken for independence of mind. I hoped he would consent to become Speaker and I still believe that he would have done the job well. (In fact, I am not at all clear that we would have been able to ensure Francis got the job for it is, of course, a decision for the House itself.) But in any case he was having none of it. He preferred to go to the back-benches where he was a not very effective critic of the Government.

I also asked David Howell and Janet Young to leave the Cabinet. David Howell's shortcomings as an administrator had been exposed when he was at Energy and nothing I saw of his performance at Transport suggested to me that my judgement of him was wrong. He had the detached critical faculty which is excellent in Opposition or in the Chairman of a Select Committee, but he lacked the mixture of creative political imagination and practical drive to be a first-class Cabinet minister. I asked Janet Young to make way for Willie Whitelaw as Leader of the Lords. She was very well liked by their lordships, but had turned out not to have the presence to lead the Lords effectively and she was perhaps too consistent an advocate of caution on all occasions. She stayed on in the Government outside the Cabinet as a Minister of State at the Foreign Office. I regretted the loss of both David and Janet on personal grounds, for they had been close to me in Opposition.

Willie Whitelaw clearly fitted the bill as Janet's successor. Willie had become, quite simply, indispensable to me in Cabinet. When it really mattered I knew he would be by my side and because of his background, personality and position in the Party he could sometimes sway colleagues when I could not. Yet Willie had not had an easy time as Home Secretary. In part, this is because Home Secretaries never do have an easy time; it is sometimes said that they possess a unique combination of responsibility without power, taking the blame for matters ranging from breaches of royal security, to the misdemeanours of police officers, prison break-outs and the occasional riot, when their power to prevent them is indirect or nonexistent. But there was more to it than that. Willie and I knew that we did not share the same instincts on Home Office matters. I believe that capital punishment for the worst murders is morally right as retribution and practically necessary as a deterrent: Willie does not. My views on sentencing in general and on immigration are a good deal tougher than his. And, flatteringly but often awkwardly, the great majority of the Conservative Party and the British public agreed with me and showed it regularly at our Party Conferences.

I chose Leon Brittan to be Willie's successor at the Home Office.

I never appointed a Home Secretary who shared all my instincts on these matters, but I thought that at least Leon would bring a keen lawyer's mind and intellectual rigour to the job. He would have no time for the false sentimentality which surrounds so much discussion of the causes of crime. From the Treasury he brought with him a well-deserved reputation as a good administrator who worked hard. Leon was the best Chief Secretary to the Treasury during my premiership. His was a powerful mind and I thought he should be given his chance.

With hindsight, I think that I should have promoted him to head another department first. He needed the experience of running his own ministry before moving to one of the three great offices of state. Too rapid promotion can jeopardize politicians' long-term future. It turns press and colleagues against them; they become touchy and uncertain about their standing; and all this makes them vulnerable. Leon suffered in this way, but he also had great strengths. For example, he proved extremely capable in devising the package of measures to tighten up the sentencing of violent criminals which we introduced after the rejection of capital punishment by the House of Commons on a free vote in July. He was to prove tough and competent during the miners' strike in 1984–5. Yet there were also weaknesses, which had nothing to do with the circumstances of his appointment. Like other brilliant lawyers I have known, he was better at mastering and expounding a brief than in drawing up his own. Moreover, everybody complained about his manner on television, which seemed aloof and uncomfortable. Of course, there have been plenty of complaints over the years about my manner too, so I had a good deal of sympathy with him. But that did not change the situation, particularly since I was shortly to lose from my Cabinet a really gifted presenter of policy.

I made Nigel Lawson Chancellor of the Exchequer – an enormous and to most people unexpected promotion. Whatever quarrels we were to have later, if it comes to drawing up a list of Conservative – even Thatcherite – revolutionaries I would never deny Nigel a leading place on it. He has many qualities which I admire and some which I do not. He is imaginative, fearless and – on paper at least – eloquently persuasive. His mind is quick and, unlike Geoffrey Howe whom he succeeded as Chancellor, he makes decisions easily. His first budget speech shows what good reading economics can make. Nigel was, I knew, a genuinely creative economic thinker. Unlike creative accountancy, creative economics is a rare and valuable thing. I doubt whether any other Financial Secretary to the Treasury could have come up with the inspired clarity of the Medium Term Financial Strategy, which guided our economic policy until Nigel himself turned his back on it in later years. As Chancellor, Nigel's tax reforms had the same quality about them – a simplicity which makes everyone ask why no one thought to do this before.

Nigel was well aware of his own virtues. In January 1981 when I had appointed Leon Brittan as Chief Secretary to the Treasury over Nigel's head, at Geoffrey Howe's request, Nigel came to see me to complain: he felt slighted and was evidently cross. But I told him that his time for promotion would come and I would see that it did. Later as Secretary of State for Energy he showed that among his other qualities he was a first-class administrator. So I had by now come to share Nigel's high opinion of himself. And for most of the 1983 Parliament I had no cause to revise that judgement; on most issues I never revised it.

But what to do with Geoffrey Howe? The time had come to move Geoffrey on. Four gruelling years in the Treasury was enough and it seems a kind of psychological law that Chancellors naturally incline towards the Foreign Office. Partly this is simply because that is the next logical step. But it is also because international finance is nowadays so important that Chancellors have to take a keen interest in the IMF, the G7 and the European Community and so the longing to tread the world stage naturally takes hold of them. I wanted to promote Geoffrey as a reward for all he had done. But I had doubts about his suitability for the Foreign Office. And, in retrospect, I was right. Geoffrey was, indeed, very good at the business of negotiation of a text line by line, for which his training as a lawyer and his experience at the Treasury fitted him. He was a perfect right-hand man for the European Councils I attended. But he fell under the spell of the Foreign Office where compromise and negotiation were ends in themselves. This magnified his faults and smothered his virtues. In his new department he fell into the habits which the Foreign Office seems to cultivate – a reluctance to subordinate diplomatic tactics to the national interest and an insatiable appetite for nuances and conditions which can blur the clearest vision. In the end Geoffrey's vision became finding a form of words. To the extent that Geoffrey did have a cause to guide him in foreign affairs it was one on which the two of us were far apart, though I did not give this much thought at the time. For Geoffrey harboured an almost romantic longing for Britain to become part of some grandiose European consensus. I never heard him define this misty Europeanism, even in the last turbulent days of my Premiership, but it was for him a touchstone (along with liberal views on Home Office matters) of highmindedness and civilized values. It was to bring us all no end of trouble.

My first choice for the job of Foreign Secretary had been Cecil Parkinson. He and I agreed on economic and domestic policy. Neither of us had the slightest doubt that Britain's interests must come first in foreign policy. He had served in the Falklands War Cabinet. He had just masterminded the most technically proficient general election campaign I have known. He seemed to me right for this most senior job.

However, my hopes were disappointed. In the early evening on election day after I had returned from my own constituency Cecil visited me in Downing Street and told me that he had been having an affair with his former secretary, Sara Keays. This gave me pause. But I did not immediately decide that it was an insuperable obstacle to his becoming Foreign Secretary. I was still thinking about the election. Indeed, I marvelled that with all this on his mind he had run such a magnificent campaign. I was even relieved that he had spared me the concern and distraction that it would cause at such a time. But the following day, shortly before Cecil was due for lunch at No. 10, I received a personal letter from Sara Keays's father. It revealed that she was pregnant with Cecil's child. When Cecil arrived I showed him the letter. It must have been one of the worst moments of his life.

It was immediately obvious that I could not send Cecil to the Foreign Office with such a cloud hanging over him. I urged him to discuss the personal questions with his family. Meanwhile I decided to make him Secretary of State for the newly combined Departments of Trade and Industry. It was a job I knew he would do well – and it was a less senior and less sensitive post than Foreign Secretary would have been.

In September I appointed John Gummer to succeed Cecil as Party Chairman (I would have appointed a new Chairman sooner or later in any case). John had been a Vice-Chairman of the Party under Ted Heath and so knew Central Office well. He is also a gifted speaker and writer. Nor was there any need for a leading minister, let alone a politician of Cecil's stature, to be Chairman immediately after an election. Unfortunately, John Gummer was not a born administrator and when we ran into political trouble he did not carry the weight to help us get out of it.

An appointment that strengthened the Party, however, was that of John Wakeham who became Chief Whip. John would probably not dissent from his reputation as a 'fixer'. He was on the right of the

Party, a highly competent accountant, who had tried to make sense for me of British Leyland's elliptical accounts. He had a manner which exuded self-confidence, a good deal of which was deserved. These talents made him a highly effective party manager.

Within months I had to make further important changes. At the beginning of October Cecil Parkinson, with the agreement of Sara Keays, issued a statement to the press revealing their affair and the fact that she was pregnant. I wanted if possible to keep Cecil – a political ally, an able minister and a friend. At first, it seemed that I might succeed. There was no great pressure from within the Party for him to go: on the whole his colleagues in government and on the back-benches were supportive. The Party Conference took place the week after Cecil's statement and his ministerial speech was well received. However, very late on Thursday evening, as I was completing my own speech for the following day, the Press Office at No. 10 rang my hotel suite. They told my private secretary that Sara Keays had given an interview to *The Times* and that the story dominated Friday's front page. I called a meeting immediately, with Willie Whitelaw, John Gummer and Cecil himself. It was clear that the story was not going to die down and, though I asked Cecil to hold back from resigning that evening, we all knew that he would have to go.

Early next morning Cecil came in to see me and said that he and Ann had decided that he should resign. There was only one problem. He had a public engagement to open the new Blackpool Heliport and to unveil a commemorative plaque. Clearly, it was impossible for him to go ahead with this. Denis stepped into the breach and unveiled the plaque, which poignantly had Cecil's name on it.

Thankfully, this did not mean the end of Cecil's political career. But he had to endure four years in the political wilderness and lost whatever chance he might have had of climbing to the very top of the political ladder.

In everything but the short term, Cecil's resignation weakened the Government. He had proved an effective minister and, though he was only at the DTI a short time, had made a big impact, particularly on the City of London. It was Cecil who took the difficult but correct decision to introduce legislation to exclude the Stock Exchange from the operation of the Restrictive Trade Practices Act and so to terminate the court case which had been brought against it by the Director-General of Fair Trading. In return the Stock Exchange made a commitment to dismantle long-standing restrictions on trading and the process was begun that led to the Financial Services Act (1986) and the 'Big Bang' in October of that year. These reforms allowed the

City to adapt to the highly competitive international markets in which it now operates and have been crucial to its continued success.

I asked Norman Tebbit to move from Employment to take over the DTI and shifted Tom King from Transport as Norman's replacement. This enabled me to bring Nick Ridley into the Cabinet, as Transport Secretary. Nick's arrival in Cabinet was a silver lining to the cloud that hung over us following Cecil's departure. Like Keith Joseph, Nick was someone who wanted office in order to do what he believed was right. Although in my experience there are few politicians for whom doing the right thing is of no importance, there are fewer still for whom it is the only consideration. Nick and Keith were among them. Nick provided the Government (and me in particular) not only with a clear vision but also with technical solutions to policy problems. At Transport he pressed ahead with privatization and deregulation. And in the later years of the Government he was someone I could rely upon for complete loyalty and honest dealing. Indeed, it was an excess of honesty that ultimately brought him down. (The American journalist, Michael Kinsley, has defined a 'gaffe' as telling an inconvenient truth. I have to say that my own experience bears out the accuracy of his definition.)

Such was the team on which the success of the Government's second term depended. I hoped that they would share the zeal and enthusiasm of their captain.

THE STUTTGART EUROPEAN COUNCIL

At the end of the week in which I formed the new Government I flew to Stuttgart for the postponed European Council, which was chaired by Chancellor Kohl. We had not ourselves asked for the postponement of the Council, which had originally been planned for 6–7 June, but once the proposal was made we welcomed it since it allowed more time to campaign. Probably our European partners thought that they might extract a few more concessions from a newly re-elected government than from one under the domestic pressures that elections pose.

The main issue at Stuttgart would, as usual, be money – 'our money' in particular – though I was discreet enough on this occasion not to use the phrase. I had to ensure a satisfactory refund for Britain in 1983 and to make as much progress as possible towards a long-term solution that would continue to cut our net contributions to the

Community. This involved achieving long-term reform of the Community's finances.

Had I had to argue my case on grounds of equity alone I would have been far from sanguine about the likely outcome. But by now the Community was on the edge of bankruptcy: the exhaustion of its 'own resources' was only months away and it was possible to increase them only by agreement of all the member states to raise the 1 per cent VAT 'ceiling'. This had the effect attributed by Dr Johnson to the imminent prospect of the gallows: the minds of our European partners were beginning to concentrate wonderfully. The requirement of unanimity gave me a strong hand and they knew that I was not the person to underplay it. Of course, it would have been perfectly possible for the Community to live within the discipline imposed by the 1 per cent ceiling, if it had had the will to cut out the waste, inefficiency and plain corruption in its own programmes: after all, VAT revenues are remarkably buoyant. But I knew full well that the will was lacking and that profligacy and that particular degree of irresponsibility which is bred by unaccountable bureaucracy would continue for as long as difficult decisions could be postponed.

It was clear that West Germany's attitude would be crucial. The Germans were the Community's largest net contributors. Admittedly, West German farmers enjoyed the benefits of the extravagant Common Agricultural Policy, but at a certain point the interests of the West German taxpayer would become paramount. The Germans followed our lead in opposing an increase in 'own resources' until the Community's finances had been put on a sounder footing. But we had some suspicions that they would waver when the pressure mounted. They also resented – and I do not blame them – having to contribute towards the funding of the British rebate which I had won. But my answer to that, of course, was to urge them to exercise leadership to sort out the fundamental imbalance of the Community's finances once and for all. Chancellor Kohl was not usually the most energetic of Council participants unless some German domestic issue was directly involved, but I knew that he would want to make a success of the Stuttgart Council to crown his first European presidency. I hoped that this and the other circumstances I have described would work in favour of an outcome I could accept.

The Council decided to leave negotiations on the future financing of the Community to the Foreign and Finance ministers, initially at least; they would report to the next full Council in December. The Commission had already produced its own proposals, some of which we favoured and others we did not. A refund was agreed for Britain to cover the year 1983. But the real decisions were postponed for another six months – six months nearer the time when the Community would find itself broke.

I was not disappointed with this outcome and I subsequently took every opportunity to praise Chancellor Kohl's handling of the Council. The results were rather better for Britain than they first appeared. The 1983 refund was less than we might have hoped. But when you took the four years to 1983 together we had obtained a refund of about two-thirds of our unadjusted net contribution, which was the goal we had publicly set ourselves. Considering the strong opposition we met from France, I felt that was a useful achievement. There was some speculation in the British newspapers that I had weakened the British position as regards the increase in the VAT 'ceiling', but this was only a negotiating ploy and a close reading of the communiqué – as well as any reading of my own mind – would demonstrate that I had done no such thing. (This was, indeed, to become very publicly apparent before the end of the year.)

There was one other aspect of the Stuttgart Council. The Council issued what was called – in the grandiloquent language which had been used about this subject since before we joined – a 'Solemn Declaration on European Union'. I took the view that I could not quarrel with everything, and the document had no legal force. So I went along with it.

When I was questioned later about the declaration in the House of Commons, I replied: 'I must make it quite clear that I do not in any way believe in a federated Europe. Nor does that document.' Certainly it did not transfer powers to a centralized Europe in the way that the Maastricht Treaty was to do. But the high-flown language of the declaration has become familiar from later developments: the linguistic skeleton on which so much institutional flesh would grow was already visible.

THE ECONOMY

It sometimes happens in politics that relatively small matters, with no obvious connection between them, combine to create a political atmosphere in which the Government seems to do nothing right. I have suggested earlier some underlying reasons why such an atmosphere developed at the start of our second term. But there were other problems. There continued to be misunderstanding and resentment of the new system by which the retirement pension was uprated in line with inflation. Many of our best supporters were angry that proposals to reintroduce capital punishment were thrown out on a free vote by a Conservative-dominated House of Commons, some of whose members had undoubtedly dissembled their views (or worse) to those who had selected them. Also, shortly afterwards Members of Parliament decided to vote themselves a pay rise considerably greater than the Government had recommended, at a time when unemployment was rising and many people could expect little or no increase.

But this malaise would have had little importance had it not been for the economy. The underlying economy was sound: indeed, as we pressed ahead with further structural changes, especially privatization, it would steadily become sounder still. When I spoke in the House of Commons on 22 June 1983, introducing the Queen's Speech, I could point to the lowest rate of inflation since 1968, to higher output and to record levels of productivity. But part of the trouble was that after an election a government's past achievements are immediately discounted. As one of my advisers put it, paraphrasing La Rochefoucauld: 'the only gratitude in politics is for favours still to be received.' And we had been so lucky in choosing the date of the election (though it was not all luck) that expectations about the rate of future progress had risen too high. Inflation started to move up from the low point of 3.7 per cent in May and June to reach 5.3 per cent in December, though it would stay at that level or lower for the next twelve months. Unemployment also began to rise again, remaining above three million, and it seemed very difficult to predict when the higher economic growth which was now apparent would begin to bring the total down. Although the interest rate actually fell, mortgage rates rose to meet the extra demand for mortgages – in itself a sign of the progress we were making towards a property-owning democracy, but naturally unpopular with borrowers. All this led to accusations that the Government had 'cooked the books' on the economy before the election.

It was public spending which became the focus of this attack. Indeed, there had been tell-tale signs of trouble in the weeks before the election. In April, the first month of the new financial year, the PSBR was well above target and it soon became clear that the provisional outturn for the PSBR for 1982–3 – a figure we regularly published – would be £9.2 billion, £1.7 billion higher than the budget estimate. It was possible that lower than expected revenues were part of the problem. But there had been an earlier misjudgement about the extent to which cash limits would be underspent, and much of the problem arose from the action we took to correct this. The previous winter we had had such strong evidence that capital programmes were being underspent that we had taken positive action to encourage spending up to target. (In principle, it is right to spend up to planned levels, otherwise you pile up spending for future years, damage the construction industry and increase unemployment.)

I had discussed the problem with the then Chancellor, Geoffrey Howe, on Thursday 21 April. As so often, it seemed that the Ministry of Defence had been the main villain. The last instruction from the Treasury to the MoD before the budget had been to minimize their underspending. The MoD had complied with unwonted energy. Having been predicting a substantial underspend, they turned out to be overspending with a vengeance. Geoffrey and I were appalled and decided to give the MoD a much-needed rebuke. But the damage had been done.

After the election the new Chancellor had another look at the borrowing figures. Nigel Lawson found himself in an unenviable position. The Treasury's summer forecast had just been completed and it suggested that the PSBR for the current financial year would be overrun by £3 billion. Inevitably there was a large margin of error in these figures – as always with the PSBR which is constituted by the difference between two enormous sums of money, public sector income and expenditure. But the signs were bad. To add to the problem, the money supply figures for May were poor and we knew that sterling, though high at the time, might soon come under pressure if American interest rates kept on rising. In any case, if we were really on course for a huge overshoot in the PSBR, something had to be done.

When on Wednesday 29 June I received a note from Nigel setting out how he wished to act I too became distinctly worried and emerged no less so from the discussion I had with him the following evening. It is never an easy matter to rein back public spending part way through a fiscal year, but the argument for early action was overwhelming. The earlier you make a cut the less drastic it has to be and the more chance you have of sustaining your credibility with the markets, which is a useful bonus. The obverse of this, however, was that to announce further public expenditure cuts just weeks into a new Parliament would be extremely unpopular and politically embarrassing. The public would think that we had deceived them at the election and spending ministers would feel bounced. Nigel fully understood this and it was a mark of his courage that he recommended immediate action.

He made three proposals. The first was to raise more money for the Government by selling an extra tranche of BP shares. But while this might help fund the PSBR it did not allow escape from the need for real cuts in spending. It was not possible to take action on the non-cash-limited programmes in mid-year, so that we had to concentrate on cash-limited spending. But should the cash squeeze apply to all of this spending or just some of it? Nigel's initial view was that it should only apply to the non-pay element of central government spending because pay was extremely difficult to hold down successfully. My advisers and I queried this and after Nigel and I talked the matter through at Chequers the following Saturday we settled on a package that included the pay bill within the squeeze. Alan Walters shared Nigel's view that immediate action had to be taken and urged a 3 per cent reduction in cash limits, greater than Nigel originally proposed. In fact, we settled on a 1 per cent reduction in the pay bill and a 2 per cent reduction in other cash limits.

Nigel had one further ingenious proposal, originally suggested by Leon Brittan earlier in the year: the introduction of 'end-year flexibility'. By Treasury convention, departments which failed to spend up to their allocation during the financial year were not allowed to carry over the unspent sum into the following year; they lost the money, in effect. The result, of course, was that departments which found themselves underspending as the end of the financial year approached tended to put on a spurt to use up their allocation and public spending would surge. 'End-year flexibility' sought to diminish this effect by permitting them to carry over a proportion of that underspending into the next year.

Altogether these proposals for asset sales, public spending cuts and an improvement in the technique of public expenditure control would, we believed, reduce that year's public expenditure by more than £1 billion.

Nigel and I expected trouble at Cabinet. It would have been helpful if we could have briefed ministers in advance, but we knew that if papers were circulated the proposals would probably leak. In the end some ministers were briefed individually, as were the Permanent Secretaries of their Departments, but despite our precautions when Cabinet met on Thursday 7 July to discuss the proposals, they had already appeared in print, splashed across the front pages that morning. This did not make the meeting any easier. But Cabinet faced up to what had to be done and Nigel was able to announce the decisions to the House of Commons that afternoon. We emphasized that these were not cuts in planned public spending but rather a package of savings necessary to remain within it. It was perhaps too much to hope that this distinction would be widely grasped.

DIPLOMACY: VISITS TO THE NETHERLANDS, WEST GERMANY, CANADA AND THE UNITED STATES

I spent most of August on holiday in Switzerland, getting over an awkward and painful eye operation that I had had at the beginning of the month. On Friday 29 July I had been at the passing out parade at the RAF College at Cranwell. When the parade and the fly-past were over I turned and walked up some steps into the College for lunch. All of a sudden something happened to my right eye: black spots floated across the field of vision. I rubbed, but they wouldn't go away. Later when I was back at Chequers I bathed the eye. But it did not improve.

On Sunday I rang my doctor. I went over to his house, not far from Chequers, and he examined the eye – having heard my description of what had happened he already had an eye specialist there. He told me that he thought I had a torn and detached retina and suggested laser treatment, followed by two days lying down until we could be sure that it had worked. Lying still for very long was something I found difficult, but I filled part of the time enjoyably enough listening to novels on tape. On Wednesday I went to his surgery to receive the verdict. I had packed an overnight case, as an insurance policy, half-thinking that I would not need it. But the news was bad. He examined me again and said that there had been no improvement at all; if anything, my eye was worse. As a precaution he had already booked an operating theatre for later that day and I went straight to hospital where the operation was successfully performed.

By the time I returned to England from my Swiss holiday I felt fully recovered, which was all to the good since I had to make several important foreign visits in September.

The first of these was to the Netherlands and West Germany. The two issues which dominated my talks in both countries were the deployment of Cruise and Pershing missiles and the approaching European Council in Athens, which was due to be held in December. On Monday 19 September I arrived in the Netherlands to be met by the Dutch Prime Minister, Ruud Lubbers. I liked Mr Lubbers, a young practical businessman who now applied his talents to good effect in Dutch politics. Although his instincts were federalist, like the leaders of other small countries in the European Community, in day-to-day Community business we often found ourselves on the same side. This was very much a short working visit with no formal speeches. Over lunch, I discussed the general political scene with Mr Lubbers and his Foreign minister, Hans Van Den Broek – another Dutchman whose company and conversation I enjoyed, even when I did not agree with him. The Dutch Government, being a coalition, was in its usual somewhat fragile condition, with problems over its budget and in the background the question of nuclear arms exercising a general destabilizing influence.

The summit's plenary session in the afternoon was entirely devoted to European Community matters. There was a large measure of agreement between us on the fundamental practical questions, but the Dutch urged compromise in the run-up to Athens and I was not going to give the impression that our stance was weakening. We seemed to be getting nowhere in our campaign for a tough guideline on future CAP expenditure. Moreover, I was concerned that the Community should not drift further into protectionism. As regards the future financing of the Community, there was no question of my agreeing at Athens to an increase in the Community's 'own resources' in isolation from the other essential conditions we had laid down. I also sought to draw Dutch attention to something which is still not properly grasped: if the Community expected the Germans to go on paying an open-ended share of its costs this would store up political trouble for the future. He who paid the piper would eventually wish to call the tune.

From the Netherlands I flew on to West Germany, where I visited British forces. On Wednesday afternoon (21 September) I arrived in Bonn for talks and dinner with Chancellor Kohl. He and I discussed the approach to the Athens summit. I told him that it would be deplorable if the impetus he had given to reform at Stuttgart were now lost. So I was relieved when Herr Kohl said that sorting out the CAP and the system of financing the Community must take priority over new policies. He also told me that the European Community was 'politically essential to Germany' but it was 'no good having the Community as a roof over Germany if the roof was leaking' – an interesting metaphor, I thought; and anyone dealing with the European Community should pay careful attention to metaphors. We in Britain were inclined to minimize their significance – whether about 'roofs' or 'trains' – and to concentrate on the practicalities – mending the leaking roof, in Chancellor Kohl's phrase. We had to learn the hard way that by agreement to what were apparently empty generalizations or vague aspirations we were later held to have committed ourselves to political structures which were contrary to our interests. But this is to anticipate a little.

However, I was already beginning to feel – I did so increasingly as the years went by – that there was an imbalance in western diplomacy. European Community heads of government and ministers met regularly, drawn together initially by Community problems, but at the same time discussing wider international issues. By contrast, there was not enough contact and understanding between the European countries and our transatlantic allies in NATO – the United States and Canada. I hoped that my visit to Canada and the United States at the end of September would do something to put this right.

The Canadian visit was, in fact, made on their initiative. The sensitive question of the patriation of the Canadian Constitution from the Westminster Parliament was now behind us.* My visit was an opportunity to emphasize the value of trade and investment links and, still more important, to try to persuade Canadians to take a larger and more vigorous part in the western alliance than they had under their present Prime Minister, Pierre Trudeau. It was common knowledge that Pierre Trudeau and his Liberal Government – who sometimes seemed more interested in the politics of the Third World than in the great East-West issues – were extremely unpopular. But I would also be meeting the Conservative prime ministers of the provinces of Ontario and Alberta, as well as the new Conservative leader at federal level, Brian Mulroney, who had just been elected to the Canadian Parliament and who was firm favourite to replace Pierre Trudeau as Prime Minister at the next election.

I flew into Ottawa on the evening of Sunday 25 September and had supper at the High Commission, one of the great historic buildings in Ottawa. Two of the paragraphs of the speech I was to deliver the following day to the Canadian House of Commons were in French and a French teacher had been specially laid on when I arrived so that I could get my pronunciation just right and avoid international incidents.

The following morning I had talks with Pierre Trudeau and his Cabinet. East-West issues provided the main point of contention, as I had thought they would. Mr Trudeau's line was that technicians had taken over arms control negotiations from the politicians, and that this was why they were getting nowhere. I did not agree. After all, disarmament talks were bound to be highly technical: if we got the

* Until 1982 the Canadian Constitution was still based on British Acts of Parliament, which only Westminster could amend, though of course in every practical sense Canada has long been an independent state. In that year at Canadian request we legislated to 'patriate' the constitution and the process of amendment, passing it over to full Canadian control.

technicalities wrong we would be in trouble. However, Mr Trudeau developed his theme, arguing that the shooting down of the South Korean Airliner by the Soviets – with the loss of Canadian lives – on 1 September also demonstrated the dangers when politicians were not in command. He understood that the aircraft had been shot down on the orders of a local military commander without reference to Moscow. I replied that what this really showed was that the Soviet command structure and rules of engagement were unsound, because these should not have allowed an aircraft to be shot down without political direction. What liberal leftists like him seemed unable to grasp was that such acts of brutality as the shooting down of a civilian aircraft were by no means uncharacteristic of the communist system itself.

Later that morning I had a private meeting with Mr Trudeau. We discussed international affairs – Hong Kong, China, Belize – but most interesting for me was his impression of Mikhail Gorbachev, of whom I had heard but whom I did not yet know. Mr Gorbachev had visited Canada earlier in the year, under the pretext of examining Canada's agricultural achievements but really with a view to discussing long term security questions. Pierre Trudeau had found him sticking to the conventional line as regards the INF negotiations, but without the blinkered hostility which characterized the other Soviet leaders. Mr Gorbachev had apparently been prepared to argue and make at least verbal concessions. I did not at this time foresee the importance of Mr Gorbachev for the future. The conversation served mainly to confirm my view that we must persuade the new Soviet leader, Yuri Andropov, to visit the West. How were we to make a proper assessment of the Soviet leaders if we did not have personal contact with them? Still more important, how were we to persuade them to see further than their own propaganda if we never showed them what the West was really like?

After lunch I had my first meeting with Brian Mulroney. Mr Mulroney was undergoing that most misleading of experiences – a political honeymoon. He was charming and charismatic but he lacked any real political experience. It was to his credit that he fully realized this and at his request I spent most of our time talking about my own experience of Opposition and government. Brian Mulroney and I were to become good friends, though we were very different sorts of politician and were to have some serious disagreements. As Leader of the Progressive Conservatives I thought he put too much stress on the adjective as opposed to the noun.

The speech I delivered to the Canadian Parliament that afternoon went very well. It was a more powerful defence of values and principles than they were used to hearing from their own Government and was interrupted by frequent applause. Apart from one or two MPs, I received a standing ovation which included members of the Diplomatic Corps. This itself provided an interesting vignette of attitudes behind the Iron Curtain: the Soviet, Czech and Bulgarian Ambassadors remained rooted to their seats, while the Hungarian and the Pole rose enthusiastically to join the applause.

That evening a dinner was given for me by Mr Trudeau in Toronto. A problem I was to find throughout this visit first surfaced acutely on this occasion. The dinner was preceded by a walkabout through a large crowd of Liberal Party supporters and the guests at the dinner itself seemed similarly partisan, though very welcoming. Although it was polite and friendly, Mr Trudeau's speech emphasized the political differences between us. As he spoke, I took notes and used these as the basis of my off-the-cuff reply which took the form of a forthright defence of free enterprise. This brought cheers from the back of the hall though, as one of my party remarked, whether these came from Conservatives who had infiltrated the gathering or from Liberals who had been converted was unclear.

From Canada I flew to Washington for a meeting with President Reagan. Overall, the President's domestic political position was strong. In spite of the difficulties which the US budget deficit was causing, the American economy was in remarkably good shape. It was growing faster with markedly less inflation than when he came into office and there was widespread appreciation of this. As he himself used to say: 'now that it is working, how come they don't call it Reaganomics any more?' The President had also set his imprint on East-West relations. The Soviets were now definitely on the defensive in international relations. They were the ones who would have to decide how to react to the forthcoming deployment by NATO of intermediate-range nuclear weapons. And they were in the dock as a result of the shooting down of the Korean Airliner. In Central America the Government of El Salvador which the United States had been backing against communist insurgency was looking stronger. Perhaps only in the Middle East had the Administration's policy not proved even a qualified success. Arab-Israeli peace talks were unlikely to be resumed and there was a growing danger of the US and its allies becoming irrevocably sucked into the turbulent politics of the Lebanon. The President had yet to announce whether he would stand for a second term, but I thought and hoped that he would and it looked as if he would win.

Our discussion that morning and over the lunch which followed covered a wide canvas. The President was optimistic about events in Central America. As he put it, El Salvador had not been in the news for a long time – because the Government there was winning and so the American media were deprived of their nightly stories told from the viewpoint of the guerillas. I raised the question of the US resuming the supply of arms to Argentina, telling him that a decision to do this would simply not be understood in Britain. The President said that he was aware of that, but there would be great pressure for the resumption of arms supplies if a civilian regime were established in Buenos Aires.

I also took the opportunity to explain our opposition, which hitherto the Americans had always supported, to the inclusion of the British and French independent nuclear deterrents in the arms talks between the United States and the Soviet Union. The Soviet insistence on the inclusion of our deterrents was simply a device to divert attention from the American proposal for deep reductions in strategic nuclear weapons. From the point of view of Britain, our deterrent constituted an irreducible minimum, but it was only 2.5 per cent of the Soviet strategic arsenal. I repeated what I had told the Senate Foreign Relations Committee that morning: the inclusion of the British deterrent would logically mean that the United States could not have parity with the Soviet Union. Would that really be acceptable to the United States? Or if, say, the French decided to increase their nuclear weapons, would the United States really be prepared to cut its by an equivalent amount? The President seemed to take my point, which I found reassuring. I for my part was able to reassure him as regards the timetable for deployment of Cruise and Pershing missiles in Europe. He had been concerned to learn that the crucial debate on this matter in the Bundestag had been delayed. He had no doubt about the firmness of Chancellor Kohl but he was not so sure about some of those around him. He was convinced that the whole Soviet strategy was still aimed at preventing deployment. I said that he should be in no doubt that Britain would deploy the intermediate-range nuclear missiles as planned, and I believed that West Germany would do the same.

However, our discussion turned on the strategy we should pursue towards the Soviet Union generally over the years ahead. I had been giving a good deal of thought to this matter and had discussed it with the experts at a Chequers seminar.* I began by saying that we had to make the most accurate assessment of the Soviet system and the

* See pp. 451–3.

Soviet leadership – there was plenty of evidence available about both subjects – so as to establish a realistic relationship: whatever we thought of them, we all had to live on the same planet. I congratulated the President on his speech to the UN General Assembly after the shooting down of the Korean Airliner and said how right he was to insist that despite this outrage the arms control negotiations in Geneva should continue. The President agreed that now was not the time to isolate ourselves from the Soviet Union. When the USSR failed to prevent NATO's INF deployment they might start to negotiate seriously. Like me, he had clearly been considering the way in which we should deal with the Soviets once that happened.

The President argued that there were two points on which we had to form a judgement. First, the Russians seemed paranoid about their own security: did they really feel threatened by the West or were they merely trying to keep the offensive edge? The second question related to the control of Soviet power itself. He had always assumed that in the Soviet Union the Politburo controlled the military. But did the fact that the first public comments on the Korean Airliner incident had come from the military indicate that the Politburo was now dominated by the generals? As regards negotiation with the Soviets, we should never forget that the main reason why they were at the negotiating table in Geneva at all was the build-up of American defences. They would never be influenced by sweet reason. However, if they saw that the United States had the will and the determination to build up its defences as far as necessary, the Soviet attitude might change because they knew they could not keep up the pace. He believed that the Russians were now close to the limit in their expenditure on defence: their internal economic difficulties were such that they could not substantially increase the proportion of their resources devoted to the military. The United States, on the other hand, had the capacity to double its military output. The task was to convince Moscow that the only way it could remain equal was by negotiations because they could not afford to compete in weaponry for very much longer. The President recalled a cartoon which had Mr Brezhnev saying to a Russian general, 'I liked the arms race better when we were the only ones in it.'

Now that the Soviet system has crumbled along the lines he envisaged, his words seem prophetic. It may be that one reason why President Reagan and I made such a good team was that, although we shared the same analysis of the way the world worked, we were very different people. He had an accurate grasp of the strategic picture but left the tactical detail to others. I was conscious that we must manage our relations with the communists on a day-to-day basis in such a way that events never got out of control. This was why throughout my discussion with the President I kept on coming back to the need to consider precisely how we should deal with the Soviets when they faced up to reality and returned to the negotiating table in a more reasonable frame of mind.

That evening I made a speech at a dinner held by the Winston Churchill Foundation of the United States in which I set out my views on these questions:

> We have to deal with the Soviet Union. But we must deal with it not as we would like it to be, but as it is. We live on the same planet and we have to go on sharing it. We stand ready therefore, if and when the circumstances are right, to talk to the Soviet leadership. But we must not fall into the trap of projecting our own morality on to the Soviet leaders. They do not share our aspirations; they are not constrained by our ethics; they have always considered themselves exempt from the rules that bind other states.

I also had a slightly different message which I wanted those who did not share all of President Reagan's and my analysis to heed:

> Does it need saying that the Soviet Union has nothing to fear from us? For several years after the war the United States had a monopoly of nuclear weapons, but it was a threat to no one. Democracies are naturally peace-loving. There is so much which our people wish to do with their lives, so many uses for our resources other than military equipment. The use of force and the threat of force to advance our beliefs are no part of our philosophy.

The speech was widely reported and generally well received in the United States. But I was soon to feel, in the light of America's response to a political crisis in a small island in the Caribbean, that at least part of the message had not been understood.

PROBLEMS IN THE TRANSATLANTIC RELATIONSHIP: LEBANON AND GRENADA

Unexpectedly, the autumn of 1983 turned out to be a testing time for Anglo-US relations. This was because we adopted different attitudes towards crises in the Lebanon and in Grenada.

These events took place against the background of great strategic decisions for the West. November 1983 was the time we had agreed for the deployment of intermediate-range missiles in Britain and West Germany: I had to ensure that nothing interfered with it. Doing so depended to a large degree on demonstrating that the United States could indeed be relied upon as a trustworthy ally.

I had wider objectives as well. I needed to ensure that whatever short-term difficulties we had with the United States, the long-term relationship between our two countries, on which I knew Britain's security and the free West's interests depended, would not be damaged. I was equally determined that international law should be respected and that relations between states should not be allowed to degenerate into a game of *realpolitik* played out between contesting power blocs. Britain had fought the Falklands War in defence of a principle of international law – as well as to defend our people.

This is not the place to describe the full tragedy of the Lebanon. That formerly prosperous and democratic state has been shattered by civil war since the early 1970s and made to serve as the battleground for the competing ambitions of Syrians, Palestinians, Islamic fundamentalists, Israelis and local warlords.

Shortly before the end of the Falklands War Israel had launched a full-scale invasion of Lebanon, which led in August 1982 to the deployment of a mainly American Multi-National Force (MNF) in Beirut. The MNF was withdrawn after a brief period but returned in September following the massacres that took place in the Palestinian refugee camps in the suburbs of Beirut which shocked the world. At this point it consisted of American, French and Italian forces. The Lebanese Government asked Britain to make a contribution too. I was reluctant, and explained that in my view we were overextended as it was. But they sent a special envoy to see me who told me that Britain held a unique position and that it was vital that it be represented in the Force. So I agreed, with the support of Michael Heseltine and Geoffrey Howe, that about 100 of our men currently stationed in Cyprus with the UN should join the MNF. In practice, the British contingent had a slightly different role from the others, manning no substantial fixed positions. The mandate of the MNF was to assist the Lebanese Government and the Lebanese Armed Forces to restore their authority over the Beirut area and so help to ensure the safety of the population there.

I am always uneasy about any commitment of British forces if it is made without very clear objectives. The original limited mandate of the MNF was indeed clear, at least on paper. But later in September we came under strong pressure from the Americans and the Italians to increase our commitment and to extend the mandate. The doubt in everyone's mind was whether the current force would be sufficient to allow the Lebanese Government and Army to restore their authority. But if it was not sufficient, that fact was, of course, as much an argument for withdrawing the MNF as for expanding it. I held a meeting to discuss these matters with ministers and advisers at Chequers on Friday 9 September. I was alarmed by reports that the US seemed determined to take a much tougher line with the Syrians than seemed sensible. Although Syria was certainly an obstacle to progress, its support for any solution to the Lebanese crisis would be essential.

The military and political situation in the Lebanon was deteriorating. In the Chouf mountains south of Beirut, the forces of the Druze minority, historically friendly to Britain, were locked in a conflict with the Lebanese Army which neither side seemed able to win: it looked like a military stalemate. The Druze were under pressure from their Syrian backers to secure wider objectives than they themselves probably wanted. Certainly, they had no quarrel of their own with the British and sought to avoid firing on our position. On one occasion during a small lunch party at Downing Street I was told that a Druze shell had fallen close to our troops. Michael Heseltine was at the lunch, so I asked him to telephone the Druze leader, Walid Jumblatt, to have the shelling stopped – and it was. Our force was small, exposed and isolated, and I was becoming increasingly concerned about what might happen.

For their part, the Lebanese Government and the Christian President Amin Gemayel were unable to free themselves from their identification with the old Phalange movement and so could not draw on wider Lebanese support. As a result they had to lean increasingly on the Americans. Three-quarters of the Lebanon was now occupied by the Syrians or the Israelis and the prospects for peace and stability for the remainder seemed bleak.

Then on Sunday 23 October a suicide bomber drove a lorry laden with explosives into the basement of the US Marine headquarters in Beirut. The building was totally destroyed. A second bomb shortly afterwards did the same to the headquarters of the French Paratroopers. Altogether 242 American and 58 French troops were killed – in total more than Britain had lost in the Falklands War. Responsibility was claimed by two militant Shia Muslim groups. My immediate reaction was one of shock at the carnage and disgust at the fanatics who had caused it. But I was also conscious of the impact it would have on the position and morale of the MNF. On the one hand, it would be wrong to give the terrorists the satisfaction of seeing the international force driven out. On the other, what had happened highlighted the enormous dangers of our continued presence and the question arose about whether we were justified in continuing to risk the lives of our troops for what was increasingly no clear purpose.

At this point my attention was abruptly diverted by events on the other side of the world. The humiliation inflicted on the United States by the Beirut bombing undoubtedly influenced its reaction to the events which were taking place on the island of Grenada in the eastern Caribbean.

On Wednesday 19 October 1983 a pro-Soviet military coup had overthrown the Government of Grenada. The new regime were certainly a vicious and unstable bunch. With the exception of General Austin, who led the coup, they were all in their twenties and a number of them had a record of violence and torture. Maurice Bishop, the overthrown Prime Minister, and five of his close supporters were shot dead. There was outrage at what had happened among most of the other Caribbean countries. Jamaica and Barbados wanted military intervention in which they would have liked the Americans and us to take part. My immediate reaction was that it would be most unwise of the Americans, let alone us, to accede to this suggestion. I was afraid that it would put foreign communities in Grenada at severe risk. There were some 200 British civilians there and many more Americans. The main organization of Caribbean States, CARICOM, was not prepared to agree to military intervention in Grenada. However, the Organization of Eastern Caribbean States, the OECS, decided unanimously to put together a force and called on other governments to help in restoring peace and order in the island. Clearly, the American reaction would be crucial.

It was easy to see why the United States might be tempted to go in and deal with the thugs who had taken over in Grenada. But as I always pointed out to the Americans afterwards, though apparently to little effect, Grenada was not transformed from a democratic island paradise into a Soviet surrogate overnight in October 1983. The Marxist Maurice Bishop had already come to power there through an earlier coup in March 1979: he had suspended the Constitution and put many of his opponents in gaol. He was, indeed, a personal friend of Fidel Castro. The Americans had had hostile relations with his Government for years. Bishop was, admittedly, something of a pragmatist and had even made a visit to the United States at the end of May 1983. It seems that it was, in part, a dispute about the Grenada Government's attitude to private enterprise which brought about the clash with his colleagues in the Marxist 'New Jewel Movement' that ultimately led to his fall.

The new 'hemispheric' strategy which President Reagan's Administration was pursuing, combined with experience of living beside the Soviet satellite of Cuba, in our view led the United States to exaggerate the threat which a Marxist Grenada posed. Our intelligence suggested that the Soviets had only a peripheral interest in the island. By contrast, the Government of Cuba certainly was deeply involved. A new airfield was being constructed as an extension to the existing airport. It was due to open in March 1984, though aircraft would be able to land there from about January. The Americans saw this as having a military purpose. It did indeed seem likely that the Cubans, who were providing the workforce for the project – and an uncertain number of Cuban military personnel also – regarded it in this light. For them, it would be a way of managing more easily the traffic of their thousands of troops in Angola and Ethiopia back and forth to Cuba. It would also be useful if the Cubans wished to intervene closer to home. But our view remained that the Grenada Government's main purpose was, as they claimed, a commercial one, planning to cater for the undoubtedly exaggerated projections of their currently minimal tourist industry. So the position on the eve of the overthrow of Maurice Bishop was that Grenada had an unsavoury and undemocratic regime with close and friendly relations with Cuba. On such an analysis, the coup of 19 October 1983, morally objectionable as it was, was a change in degree rather than in kind.

On Saturday 22 October – the day before the Beirut bomb outrages – I received a report of the conclusions of the United States National Security Council meeting about Grenada. I was told that it had been decided that the Administration would proceed very cautiously. An American carrier group based on the USS *Independence*, which had been heading for the Mediterranean, had been diverted south to the Caribbean; it was now east of the southern tip of Florida and due north of Puerto Rico. An amphibious group with 1900 marines and two landing craft was 200 miles further east. The *Independence* would reach the area the following day but would remain well to the east of Dominica and well to the north of Grenada. The amphibious group would reach the same area later on the following day. The existence of this force would give the Americans the option to react if the situation warranted it. It was emphasized, however, that they had made no decision going beyond these contingency deployments. They had received a firm request from the east Caribbean heads of government to help them restore peace and order in Grenada. Jamaica and Barbados were supporting the request. If the Americans took action to evacuate US citizens they promised to evacuate British citizens as well. We were also assured that there would be consultation if they decided to take any further steps.

That evening I spent a good deal of time talking it all over on the telephone from Chequers. I spoke with Richard Luce, now back in the Foreign Office as Minister of State (Geoffrey Howe was in Athens), Willie Whitelaw and Michael Heseltine. I approved the order that HMS *Antrim* should sail from Colombia to the area of Grenada, remaining beyond the horizon. In public it should be made clear that this was a precautionary move designed to help with the evacuation of British subjects from Grenada should this be required. In fact, it did not seem necessary. The Deputy High Commissioner in Bridgetown (Barbados) reported after a day's visit to Grenada that British citizens were safe, that the new regime in Grenada was willing to allow arrangements to be made for them to leave if they wished and that Sir Paul Scoon, the Governor-General (the Queen's representative on the island) was well and in reasonably good heart. He did not request our military intervention, either directly or indirectly.

Suddenly the whole position changed. What precisely happened in Washington I still do not know, but I find it hard to believe that outrage at the Beirut bombing had nothing to do with it. I am sure that this was not a matter of calculation, but rather of frustrated anger – yet that did not make it any easier for me to defend, not least to a British House of Commons in which anti-American feeling on both right and left was increasing. The fact that Grenada was also a Commonwealth member, and that the Queen was Head of State, made it harder still.

At 7.15 in the evening of Monday 24 October I received a message from President Reagan while I was hosting a reception at Downing Street. The President wrote that he was giving serious consideration to the OECS request for military action. He asked for my thoughts and advice. I was strongly against intervention and asked that a draft reply be prepared at once on lines which I laid down. I then had to go to a farewell dinner given by Princess Alexandra and her husband, Angus Ogilvy, for the outgoing American Ambassador, J. J. Louis, Jnr. I said to him: 'Do you know what is happening about Grenada? Something is going on.' He knew nothing about it.

I received a telephone call during the dinner to return immediately to No. 10 and arrived back at 11.30 p.m. By then a second message had arrived from the President. In this he stated that he had decided to respond positively to the request for military action. I immediately called a meeting with Geoffrey Howe, Michael Heseltine and the military and we prepared my reply to the President's two messages, which was sent at 12.30 a.m. There was no difficulty in agreeing a common line. My message concluded:

> This action will be seen as intervention by a western country in the internal affairs of a small independent nation, however unattractive its regime. I ask you to consider this in the context of our wider East-West relations and of the fact that we will be having in the next few days to present to our Parliament and people the siting of Cruise missiles in this country. I must ask you to think most carefully about these points. I cannot conceal that I am deeply disturbed by your latest communication. You asked for my advice. I have set it out and hope that even at this late stage you will take it into account before events are irrevocable.

I followed this up twenty minutes later by telephoning President Reagan on the hot-line. I told him that I did not wish to speak at any length over the telephone but I did want him to consider very carefully the reply which I had just sent. He undertook to do so but said, 'we are already at zero.'

At 7.45 that morning a further message arrived, in which the President said that he had weighed very carefully the considerations that I had raised but believed them to be outweighed by other factors. In fact, the US military operation to invade Grenada began early that morning. After some fierce fighting the leaders of the regime were taken prisoner.

At the time I felt dismayed and let down by what had happened. At best, the British Government had been made to look impotent; at worst we looked deceitful. Only the previous afternoon Geoffrey had told the House of Commons that he had no knowledge of any American intention to intervene in Grenada. Now he and I would have to explain how it had happened that a member of the Commonwealth had been invaded by our closest ally, and more than that, whatever our private feelings, we would also have to defend the United States' reputation in the face of widespread condemnation.

The international reaction to American intervention was in general strongly adverse. It certainly gave a propaganda boost to the Soviet Union. In its early reports, Soviet television news apparently thought that Grenada was a province of southern Spain. But soon their propaganda machine began firing on all cylinders. The Cubans were portrayed as having played an heroic role in resisting the invasion. When I went to the Commonwealth Heads of Government Meeting in New Delhi the following month it was still Grenada which was the most controversial topic of discussion. President Mugabe claimed that American action in Grenada would provide a precedent for South Africa in dealing with her neighbours. My own public criticism of American action and refusal to become involved in it also led to temporarily bad relations with some of Britain's long-standing friends in the Caribbean. It was an unhappy time.

In Britain we had to face strong pressure, not least in the House of Commons, to renegotiate the arrangements for the deployment of Cruise missiles. The argument was that if the Americans had not consulted us about Grenada, why should they do so as regards the use of Cruise missiles. Similarly, the new leader of the SDP, David Owen, wrote in the *Daily Mail* on 28 October that 'British public opinion will simply not accept any longer the Prime Minister's refusal to insist on a dual mechanism to cover the launching procedures for any Cruise missiles that are deployed in Britain before the end of this year.'

So when President Reagan telephoned me on the evening of Wednesday 26 October during an emergency House of Commons debate on the American action I was not in the sunniest of moods. The President began by saying, in that disarming way of his, that if he was in London and dropped in to see me he would be careful to throw his hat through the door first. He said he very much regretted the embarrassment that had been caused and wanted to explain how it had all happened. It was the need to avoid leaks of what was intended which had been at the root of the problem. He had been woken at 3 o'clock in the morning with an urgent plea from the OECS. A group had then convened in Washington to study the matter and there was already fear of a leak. By the time he had received my message setting out my concerns the zero hour had passed and American forces were on their way. The military action had gone well and the aim was now to secure democracy.

There was not much I felt able to say and so I more or less held my peace, but I was glad to have received the telephone call. At that Thursday's Cabinet there was a long discussion of what had happened. I told my colleagues that our advice against US intervention had, I believed, been sound. But the US, for its part, had taken a different view on an issue which directly touched its national interests. Britain's friendship with the United States must on no account be jeopardized.

Just as events in the Lebanon had affected American action in Grenada, so what I had seen in the crisis over Grenada affected my attitude to the Lebanon. I was concerned that American lack of consultation and unpredictability might be repeated there with very damaging consequences.

Naturally, I understood that the United States wanted to strike back after the terrorist outrage against its servicemen in Beirut. But whatever military action now took place, I wanted it to be a lawful, measured and effective response. I sent a message to President Reagan on 4 November welcoming assurances which Geoffrey Howe had received from George Shultz that there would be no hasty reaction by the Americans in retaliation and urging that a more broadly based Lebanese Government be constructed. The President replied to me on 7 November, emphasizing that any action would be a matter of self-defence, not of revenge, but adding that those who committed the atrocity must not be allowed to strike again if it was possible to prevent them. A week later he sent me a further message saying that although he had not yet made a final decision he was inclined to take decisive but carefully limited military action. The US had reports of planning for other terrorist acts against the MNF and he intended to deter these. He added that, because of the need for absolute secrecy, knowledge of his current thinking was being severely limited within the US Government.

I quickly replied to the President. I said that I well understood all the pressures upon him to take action but I wanted to give him my frank views about the decision which only he could take. Any action must in my view be clearly limited to legitimate self-defence. It would be necessary to ensure the avoidance of civilian casualties and minimize the opportunities for hostile propaganda. Surprise was likely to be difficult because a range of possible targets had been publicly discussed by the media for days past. I was glad that he did not envisage involving Israel or targeting Syria or Iran, action against either of which would be very dangerous. I hoped that my message was as clear as it could be: I did not believe that retaliatory action was advisable. However, in the end France did launch air strikes – at

American urging, as President Mitterrand told me later. And in response to attacks on its aircraft, the United States struck at Syrian positions in central Lebanon in December.

These retaliations in the Lebanon failed to have any effect. The position there continued to deteriorate. The real question was no longer whether there should be a withdrawal but how to effect one. In February 1984 the Lebanese Army lost control of West Beirut and the Lebanese Government collapsed. The time had clearly come to get out and a firm joint decision with the United States and other members of the MNF was accordingly made to do so and detailed plans for this tricky operation were drawn up. I left it to the British commander on the ground to make the final decision as to what time of the day to move. He decided that it should be done by night. But I suddenly learned that President Reagan would be making a broadcast that evening to tell the American people what would be happening and why. Obviously it became necessary to alert our men to be ready to move as soon as they could. Then, at the last minute, while I was at Buckingham Palace for an audience with the Queen, I received a message that the President was reconsidering the decision and would not after all broadcast. As it turned out – not greatly to my surprise – the postponement decision promptly leaked and the President had to make his broadcast in any case. Clearly, we could not carry on like this, putting the safety of British troops at risk: so I refused to countermand the planned withdrawal of our men to British naval vessels lying offshore, which was duly effected with the British Army's usual professionalism. In fact, all the MNF forces were shortly withdrawn to ships away from the perils they would have faced on shore. Nothing could now be done to save the Lebanon; the reconstituted Lebanese Government increasingly fell under the control of a Syria whose hostility to the West was now reinforced; and in March the MNF force returned home.

The American intervention in the Lebanon – well intentioned as it was – was clearly a failure. It seemed to me that what happened there contained important lessons which we should heed. First, it is unwise to intervene in such situations unless you have a clear, agreed objective and are prepared and able to commit the means to secure it. Second, there is no point in indulging in retaliatory action which changes nothing on the ground. Third, one must avoid taking on a major regional power, like Syria, unless one is prepared to face up to the full consequences of doing so.

By contrast, American intervention in Grenada was, in fact, a success. Democracy was restored, to the advantage not only of the islanders themselves but also of their neighbours who could look forward to a more secure and prosperous future. No one would weep any tears over the fate of the Marxist thugs whom the Americans had dislodged. Yet even governments acting on the best of motives are wise to respect legal forms. Above all, democracies have to show their superiority to totalitarian governments which know no law. Admittedly, the law on these matters is by no means clear, as was confirmed for me during a seminar I held after the Grenada affair to consider the legal basis for military intervention in another country. Indeed, to my surprise, I found that the lawyers at the seminar were more inclined to argue on grounds of *realpolitik* and the politicians were more concerned with the issue of legitimacy. My own instinct was – and is – always to found military action on the right of self-defence, which ultimately no outside body has the authority to question.

THE EUROPEAN COUNCIL AT ATHENS

Grenada was still very much on my mind when I went to Bonn for one of my regular Anglo-German summits with Chancellor Kohl on Tuesday 8 November. Like me, Chancellor Kohl was worried about the impact of the American action on European public opinion in the run-up to the deployment of Cruise and Pershing missiles later that month. The West German Government had originally been very critical of the Grenada operation but had since toned this down. Helmut Kohl was showing a good deal of courage as well as political cunning in handling West German public opinion at this crucial time, and I admired him for it.

The main purpose of my visit, however, was to seek German support for the line I would take at the European Council in Athens, now just a few weeks away. So Athens was the principal topic of my discussion with him, in which we were later joined by Geoffrey Howe and the German Foreign minister, Hans-Dietrich Genscher. I began by making what I hoped would be the welcome suggestion that the next President of the European Commission should come from Germany, if the German Government wished to put forward a candidate. As I had rather expected, it appeared that they did not. Chancellor Kohl said that he agreed with me that the Commission was too big and tended to create unnecessary work. Then a little more diplomacy: I said that our aim was to build on the excellent foundation laid under the German presidency. After this we got down to business. I stressed the need for firm control of spending on the CAP if there was to be anything left of the Community's 'own resources' for other purposes, such as the development of the electronics industry, which the Germans wanted. I also warned against allowing growing protectionism to create another area of disagreement with the United States. The Germans were most interested in the future level of MCAs,* which affected German farmers' incomes, and the steel industry where they considered that they were receiving a raw deal and that the Italians were using subsidies to undercut German producers. I hoped that at the end of this discussion each side had understood the areas on which we would stand firm and those where compromise was possible. In particular, I hoped that the Germans realized how serious I was about achieving my objectives on the budget question at Athens.

As usual before European Councils I held a number of preparatory meetings with ministers and officials. This was partly to ensure that I was thoroughly briefed, but also to sort out with colleagues our precise objective on each issue. It was not enough to decide what was ideal for us: I had also to establish and fully master the least bad alternatives. All too often the ideal was not attainable.

In the meetings for Athens on the budget question both Nigel Lawson and I felt that we had to be really tough in pressing for the required package if there were to be any question of our agreeing to an increase in the Community's 'own resources'. We had to be satisfied with the way the burden on Britain was measured. The result must reflect our ability to pay. And whatever system was finally agreed must be able to be relied upon to work over time and without significant damage to the UK position. Above all, to take into account relative prosperity, we decided to press the view that if a member state's GDP per head was 90 per cent or less of the Community average it should make no net contribution at all, with states above that threshold making progressively higher contributions the richer they were. (This scheme was known as 'the safety net' or 'threshold' system.)

I wanted to ensure that at Athens I was given a proper opportunity to have the budget discussed early on, because the talks would be long and hard. So I wrote to the Council President, the Greek Prime Minister Andreas Papandreou, asking that we start the Council by dealing with the budget imbalances and linked issues. My letter, however, crossed with one from him in which he said that he wanted to deal with agriculture first. It was not a good start.

* Monetary Compensatory Amounts (MCAs) were a system of border taxes and levies on CAP products.

Yet when I left for Athens there did seem grounds for reasonable optimism. The Germans appeared to understand our position and there had even been encouraging signs from the French. It was to be a somewhat longer summit than usual and I hoped the time would be used productively.

The Community heads of government met in the magnificent Zappeion Hall, a classical Greek building adapted to the needs of a modern conference centre. At the first session of the Council that afternoon I was sitting opposite President Mitterrand and Chancellor Kohl. I noticed that whereas my own table was covered with piles of heavily annotated briefing on different complex agricultural and financial issues, no such encumbrance appeared in front of my French and German counterparts. This doubtless made for an impression of appropriately Olympian detachment, but it also suggested that they had not mastered the detail. And this turned out to be the case. Throughout the meeting Chancellor Kohl seemed unwilling or unable to make much effective contribution. Worse, President Mitterrand appeared not only badly briefed on the issues but strangely – I think genuinely – misinformed about his own Government's position, as it had previously been set out by French ministers and officials.

The Greek Presidency did not assist much either. Mr Papandreou always proved remarkably effective in gaining Community subsidies for Greece but he was less skilful in his present role as President of the European Council. As his earlier letter to me had proposed, he insisted on trying to reach agreement on agriculture before moving on to the question of finance and the British budget contribution. Obviously, it would have made better sense to face the Community countries with the financial realities first and then deal with the agricultural issues, from which so much of the financial problem derived and on which different countries had sharply opposing national interests. And we never seemed to get by without a tear-jerking homily on the predicament of Ireland from the Irish Prime Minister, Dr Garret FitzGerald, who was determined if he could to exempt his country from the disciplines on agricultural spending. I made it clear that any preferential treatment for the Republic would have to be matched by similar treatment for Northern Ireland. The first day was more or less a write-off.

I was, therefore, already pessimistic by the time I returned that night to the British Ambassador's Residence to discuss with my officials how we should conduct ourselves the following day (Monday). But it was only on the Monday that it became obvious that the summit would indeed fail. When the Council met, to my astonishment President Mitterrand made it clear that France's position on the budget had completely changed. France was no longer prepared to support us in pressing for a long-term settlement of the British budget problem. In repeated interjections, I said that I would not agree to an increase in the Community's 'own resources' unless spending on the CAP was contained and decreased as a share of the total budget and unless member states' contributions were fair and in line with the ability to pay. The argument continued, but I was clearly getting nowhere.

On Tuesday I had a working breakfast with President Mitterrand. We were so far apart that there was no point in spending much time discussing Community issues at all and we largely concentrated instead on the Lebanon. The French President seemed blissfully unaware of the damage his own turnabout had done. He said jokingly that unless we demonstrated that discussions between Britain and France were continuing, the press would soon be talking about a return to the Hundred Years' War. So in what I hoped was a suitably nonbelligerent way I told him how his attitude at the Council had taken me by surprise, given the fact that I was going along with the proposals on the budget which the French Finance minister, one M. Jacques Delors, had been advancing. The President asked me precisely what I meant and I explained. But I received no very satisfactory or clear response.

Where we did see eye to eye – at least in private – was about Germany. I said that even though the Germans were willing to be generous because they received other political benefits from the Community, a new generation of Germans might arise who would refuse to make such a large contribution. This would risk a revival of German neutralism – a temptation which, as President Mitterrand rightly said, was already present.

The meeting had been an amicable one and I tried to keep the atmosphere relatively friendly after the Council broke up, as in press interviews I avoided being too harsh about France's performance. After all, M. Mitterrand was to be the next President of the Council and so it would fall to him to chair the crucial meetings as we at last approached the time when the Community's money ran out. It did cross my mind that he might have wished to delay a settlement until he could take credit for it in his own presidency.

No communiqué was issued at the end of the Athens Council: we had had no time in plenary sessions to discuss any of the wider international issues and agree a line on them. The Council was widely and accurately described as a fiasco. But my frustration was diminished by the fact that I knew that time was on my side.

CHAPTER XIII

Mr Scargill's Insurrection

The background to and course of the year-long miners' strike of 1984–1985

PRELUDE

The 1983 general election result was the single most devastating defeat ever inflicted upon democratic socialism in Britain. After being defeated on a manifesto that was the most candid statement of socialist aims ever made in this country, the Left could never again credibly claim popular appeal for their programme of massive nationalization, hugely increased public spending, greater trade union power and unilateral nuclear disarmament. But there was also undemocratic socialism, and it too would need to be beaten. I had never had any doubt about the true aim of the hard Left: they were revolutionaries who sought to impose a Marxist system on Britain whatever the means and whatever the cost. Many of them made no effort to conceal their purpose. For them the institutions of democracy were no more than tiresome obstacles on the long march to a Marxist Utopia. While the electoral battle was still being fought their hands had been tied by the need to woo more moderate opinion, but in the aftermath of defeat they were free from constraint and thirsting for battle on their own terms.

The hard Left's power was entrenched in three institutions: the Labour Party, local government and the trade unions. From all three bases they now proceeded to challenge our renewed mandate. Predictably, it was the National Union of Mineworkers (NUM), led by its Marxist president, Arthur Scargill, who were destined to provide the shock troops for the Left's attack. The intention was plain. Within a month of the 1983 election Mr Scargill was saying openly that he did not 'accept that we are landed for the next four years with this Government'. And this would be an attack directed not only against the Government, but against anyone and anything standing in the way of the Left, including fellow miners and their families, the police, the courts, the rule of law and Parliament itself.

After the experience of the Conservative Government of 1970–74 I hardly doubted that one day we would have to face another miners' strike. From the time of Mr Scargill's election to the leadership of the NUM in 1981 I knew it. I had no desire for such a strike. There was no economic rationale for it. The National Coal Board (NCB), the Government and the great majority of miners wanted a thriving, successful, competitive coal industry. But history intertwined with myth seemed to have made coal mining in Britain a special case: it had become an industry where reason simply did not apply. Britain's industrial revolution was to a large extent based on the easy availability of coal. At the industry's height on the eve of the First World War it employed more than a million men to work over 3,000 mines. Production was 292 million tons. Thereafter decline was continuous, and relations between miners and owners frequently bitter. Conflict in the coal industry precipitated Britain's only general strike in 1926. (Prefiguring later developments, the miners' union split during the year-long coal strike that followed the general strike, and a separate union was set up in Nottinghamshire.) Successive governments between the wars found themselves dragged ever deeper into the task of rationalizing and regulating the industry, and in 1946 the post-war Labour Government finally nationalized it outright. By that time production was down to 187 million tons at 980 pits, with a workforce of just over 700,000.

Government now began setting targets for coal production and investment in a series of documents inaugurated by the 'Plan for Coal' in 1950. These consistently overestimated both the demand for coal and the prospects for improvements in productivity within the industry. The only targets that were met were those for investment. Public money was poured in, but two problems proved insoluble: overcapacity and union resistance to the closure of uneconomic pits. As the industry declined miners relied more and more on industrial muscle to keep themselves in work.

By the 1970s the coal mining industry had come to symbolize everything that was wrong with Britain. In February 1972 mass pickets led by Arthur Scargill forced the closure of the Saltley Coke Depot in Birmingham by sheer weight of numbers. It was a frightening demonstration of the impotence of the police in the face of such disorder. The fall of Ted Heath's Government after a general election precipitated by the 1973–4 miners' strike lent substance to the myth that the NUM had the power to make or break British Governments, or at the very least the power to veto any policy threatening their interests by preventing coal getting to the power stations.

I have already described the threat of a miners' strike which we faced in February 1981 and the way in which this was averted.* From then on it was really only a question of time. Would we be sufficiently prepared to win the fight when the inevitable challenge came? A milestone was reached when Mr Scargill won the union presidency at the end of 1981 and the power of the NUM and the fear it inspired came into the hands of those whose objectives were openly political.

It fell mainly to Nigel Lawson who became Secretary of State for Energy in September 1981 to build up – steadily and unprovocatively – the stocks of coal which would allow the country to endure a coal strike. We were to hear a lot of the word 'endurance' over the next few months. To maximize endurance it was vital that coal stocks be in place at the power stations and not at the pit heads, from which miners' pickets could make movement impossible. But coal stocks were not the only element determining power station endurance. Some Central Electricity Generating Board (CEGB) power stations were oil fired. Ordinarily they were used only part of the time, to meet peak demand, but if needed they could be run continuously to help meet the 'base load' – that element of electricity demand that is more or less constant. 'Oilburn' was expensive, but would add significantly to the system's ability to withstand a strike. An additional advantage was that oil supplies to the power stations were relatively secure. Nuclear-powered stations, providing about 14 per cent of supply, were mostly some distance away from the coal fields and of course their primary fuel supply was also secure. Over the next few years more Advanced Gas-cooled Reactors (AGRs) would be coming on stream and would steadily reduce our dependence on coal-fired power. We were still building a cross-Channel link which would allow us to buy power from France, though we already had a link in operation between the English and Scottish systems ('the Scottish interconnector'). We also did our best to encourage industry to hold more stocks.

Danger began to loom in the autumn of 1983. Peter Walker was now Secretary of State for Energy, a job to which I had appointed him after the general election in June. As he had shown at Agriculture in our first Parliament, he was a tough negotiator. He was also a skilled communicator, something which I knew would be important if we were to retain public support in the coal strike which the militants

* See pp. 139–43.

would some day force upon us. Peter regularly telephoned newspaper editors in person to put over our case. This was never my preferred way, but I recognized its effectiveness during the strike. Unfortunately, Peter Walker never really got on with Ian MacGregor, and this sometimes created tensions.

Ian MacGregor took over as Chairman of the NCB on 1 September. He had been an excellent Chairman of the British Steel Corporation, turning the Corporation around after the damaging three-month steel strike in 1980. If Britain's coal industry was ever to become a successful business rather than a system of outdoor relief, he had the experience and determination to make this happen. Unlike the militant miners' leaders, Ian MacGregor genuinely wanted to see a thriving coal industry making good use of investment, technology and human resources. Perhaps his greatest quality was courage. Within the NCB itself he often found himself surrounded by people who had made their careers in an atmosphere of appeasement and collaboration with the NUM and who greatly resented the changed atmosphere he brought with him. Yet it transpired that Ian MacGregor was strangely lacking in guile. He was quite used to dealing with financial difficulties and hard bargaining. But he had no experience of dealing with trade union leaders intent on using the process of negotiation to score political points. Time and again he and his colleagues were outmanoeuvred by Arthur Scargill and the NUM leadership. During the strike Peter Walker and I followed with constant anxiety every phase of the battle for public opinion. The NUM leadership used every device to distort the truth and misinform the public and their own members.

On Friday 21 October 1983 an NUM delegate conference voted for a ban on overtime in protest at the Board's 5.2 per cent pay offer and at prospective pit closures. In itself, with coal stocks as high as they were, an overtime ban was unlikely to have much effect. It probably had an ulterior purpose: to increase tension among the miners and so make them more prepared for a strike when the NUM leadership thought that one could successfully be engineered. We always knew that it was pit closures that were more likely to ignite a strike than a dispute about pay. The case for closures on economic grounds remained overwhelming. Even Labour had acknowledged it: thirty-two pits had been closed under the Labour Government between 1974 and 1979. Mr Scargill, however, denied the economic case for closure. His line was that no pit should be closed unless it was physically exhausted. Indeed, he denied the existence of 'uneconomic pits': in his view a pit that made a loss – and there were many – simply required further investment. Called to give evidence before a Select

Committee, he had been asked whether there was any level of loss that he would deem intolerable. He replied memorably: 'As far as I am concerned, the loss is without limit.'

During the autumn and winter of 1983–4 Ian MacGregor formulated his plans. At that time manpower in the industry was 202,000. The Monopolies and Mergers Commission had produced a report into the coal industry in 1983 which showed that some 75 per cent of the pits were making a loss. Faced with this, Mr MacGregor began with the aim of bringing the industry to break-even point by 1988. In September 1983 he told Government that he intended to cut the workforce by some 64,000 over three years, reducing capacity by 25 million tons. There was, though, never any secret 'hit list' of pits due for closure: decisions as to which pits were to be closed would be made on a pit-by-pit basis under the existing colliery review procedure. He came back to us in December 1983 indicating that he had decided to accelerate the programme, aiming to cut the workforce by 44,000 over the next two years; to achieve this he urged us to extend the existing redundancy scheme to include miners under the age of fifty. The terms we agreed in January 1984 were extremely generous: £1,000 for each year of service, paid as a lump sum, the scheme to operate for two years only, so that a man who had been in the pits all his working life would get over £30,000. In the coming year, 1984–5, Mr MacGregor proposed 20,000 redundancies. We were confident that this figure could be achieved without anyone being forced to leave the industry against their will. Around twenty pits would close and annual capacity would be reduced by 4 million tons a year.

As discussions continued accusations began to fly about a 'hit list' of pits. The rhetoric of the NUM leadership took ever greater leave of reality – in particular, of the economic reality that the industry was receiving £1.3 billion of subsidies from the taxpayer in 1983–4. It sounded as if Mr Scargill was preparing to lead his troops into battle. At the end of February there was an early intimation of the violence which would characterize the strike when Ian MacGregor – then 70 years old – was knocked to the ground at a Northumberland colliery by demonstrating miners. I was shocked and wrote to convey my sympathy. Far worse was to come.

Obviously we realized that a strike was always possible, but we doubted whether it would happen before the end of 1984, when winter set in and the demand for coal was at its annual peak. To begin a strike in the spring would be the worst possible tactic for the NUM. But this was a point on which Mr Scargill misled his own members: in February he was making wild claims, saying that the CEGB had only eight weeks of coal stocks. In fact stocks were far higher – something that could have been deduced from figures in the public domain. However, the union had a tradition of balloting its members before strike action took place, and there was good reason to think that Mr Scargill would not get the necessary majority (55 per cent) to call a national strike at any point in the immediate future. Since he had become President the NUM membership had voted against strike action three times already. We could not have foreseen the desperate and self-destructive tactics he chose to adopt.

THE STRIKE BEGINS

On Thursday 1 March the NCB announced the closure of the Yorkshire colliery of Cortonwood. The announcement was not particularly well handled by the local NCB: the impression was given that the colliery review procedure was being by-passed, whereas in fact the NCB had had no such intention. But the executive of the radical Yorkshire area of the NUM – Mr Scargill's home ground – announced a strike in protest at the decision, relying on a local ballot held two years previously to provide authority for their action.

Cortonwood may have triggered the strike, but it was not the cause. The truth is that once the NUM leadership had become determined to resist the closure of any pit on economic grounds the strike was inevitable, unless the NCB had been prepared to abdicate effective control of the industry. Even if Cortonwood had never happened, a meeting between the NCB and the mining unions on 6 March might have had the same result. Ian MacGregor outlined his plans for the coming year and confirmed the figure of twenty closures. The reaction from the NUM was swift. That same day the Scottish NUM called a strike from 12 March. Two days later, on Thursday 8 March, the national executive of the NUM met and gave official support to the Yorkshire and Scottish strikes.

Under rule 43 of the NUM constitution a national strike could only be called if the union held a national ballot and a majority of 55 per cent voted in favour. The militant majority on the executive doubted whether they could win such a national ballot, but they found a procedural way round the problem. Under rule 41 of the constitution, the national executive could give official sanction to strikes declared by the constituent areas that made up the union. If all the areas could be pushed into action individually, this would have the effect of a national strike without the need for a national ballot. If any proved difficult, pickets could be sent from striking areas to intimidate them into joining the dispute. This ruthless strategy very nearly worked. But in the end it proved to be a disaster for its authors.

The strike began on Monday 12 March. Over the following two weeks the brutal weight of the militants' shock troops descended on the coal fields and for a moment it seemed as if rationality and decency would go under. At the beginning of the first day of the strike 83 pits were working and 81 were out. Ten of these, I was told, were not working due to heavy picketing rather than any positive desire to join the strike. By the end of the day the number of pits not working had risen to about 100. The police were fighting a losing battle to ensure that those who wished to work could do so. The Home Office – both ministers and officials – gave them the fullest support, but the situation worsened. On Tuesday morning the flying pickets again descended. On that day it so happened that I was due to see Ian MacGregor about the Channel Tunnel – a quite separate matter in which he had an interest. Peter Walker joined us afterwards and we discussed the situation in the coal fields. Mr MacGregor told me that he had applied for and obtained a civil injunction in the High Court against the NUM executive to restrain the use of flying pickets, using our new trade union law. However, his impression was that the police were failing to uphold the criminal law and that pickets had been able to prevent people going to work. The threat of violence had already resulted in the postponement of plans to hold a strike ballot in the Lancashire area. The Nottinghamshire and Derbyshire areas were due to vote on Thursday but there was a real danger that the vote would be frustrated or that intimidation would force miners to stay at home. I told him that I was dismayed at this news. It was a repetition of what had happened in Saltley in 1972. The criminal law had to be upheld. I said that helping those who wished to work was not enough: intimidation must be stopped.

I went straight out of this meeting and asked to speak to Leon Brittan. As luck would have it the next meeting that day had originally been called to discuss the issue of strikes in essential services, on which we had a manifesto commitment, and Leon and other relevant ministers were already on their way. At the meeting I repeated that we must uphold the criminal law as it related to picketing. Leon shared my unease at what was happening. His view was that the police already had all the powers they needed to deal with the problem, including the power to turn pickets back and to disperse them if they assembled in excessive numbers. He told us that he had made this position clear in public and would repeat the message. But, of course, there were tight constitutional limits on what he, as Home Secretary, could do to instruct the police on their duties. We agreed that Michael Havers would set out the legal position to the House. I was determined that the message should go out from government loud and clear: there would be no surrender to the mob and the right to go to work would be upheld.

Mass picketing continued. By Wednesday morning only twenty-nine pits were working normally. The police were by now drafting in officers from around the country to protect the miners who wanted to work: 3000 police officers from seventeen forces were involved. At this point in the dispute the violence centred on Nottinghamshire, where the flying pickets from Yorkshire were determined to secure a quick victory. However, the Nottinghamshire men went ahead with their ballot and the result that Friday showed 73 per cent against the strike. Area ballots the following day in the Midlands, the North-West and the North-East coalfields also gave heavy majorities against strike action. Altogether, of the 70,000 miners balloted, over 50,000 voted to work.

Early though it was, this was one of the turning points of the strike. The huge police operation was highly effective and together with the moral force of the ballot results it reversed the trend towards a shut down of the pits. The first, crucial battle had been won. On Monday morning the latest information was telephoned through to me in Brussels, where I was attending a European Council. Forty-four pits were now working, compared with just eleven on Friday. In the areas which had voted for a return to work the great majority of pits had gone back. The militants knew that if it had not been for the courage and competence of the police the result would have been very different and from now on they and their mouthpieces in the Labour Party began a campaign of vilification against them.

On the day the NUM executive met, I told Cabinet that I would set up a committee of ministers under my chairmanship to monitor the strike and to decide what action should be taken. Willie Whitelaw was a member, of course, and deputized for me when I could not be present, though this was rarely necessary. Peter Walker, as Energy Secretary, and Leon Brittan, as Home Secretary, were crucial figures. The Chancellor, Nigel Lawson, was directly concerned as the issue was of vital importance to the economy; he also brought to bear his experience as former Energy Secretary. Norman Tebbit (Trade and Industry), Tom King (Employment) and Nick Ridley (Transport), all had obvious contributions to make. We sought to minimize the impact of the strike on industry to prevent the strike spreading by sympathy action and to keep coal stocks moving by road and rail. In Scotland, George Younger had responsibility both for Scottish mining and for Scotland's police. All these ministers or their deputies regularly attended. When issues of law arose the Attorney-General, Michael Havers, also joined us. The group met about once a week, though more frequently when conditions required it. In practice the large membership sometimes proved unwieldy and so Peter Walker and I made some important decisions in smaller meetings, called *ad hoc* to deal with developments as they arose, particularly when notice was short.

There was a wider question relating to the work of this committee, however: to determine the proper role of government in the strike. I repeatedly made it clear that prime responsibility for dealing with the strike lay with the managements of the NCB and those other nationalized industries involved (the CEGB, BSC and British Rail (BR)). They operated within financial and other constraints set by government and by statute. But so much was at stake that no responsible government could take a 'hands-off' attitude: the dispute threatened the country's economic survival. Consequently, I tried to combine respect for their freedom of action with clear signals as to what would or would not be financially and politically acceptable. The Opposition never seemed to be able to make up their mind whether we were intervening too much or too little. Their uncertainty, combined with the successful outcome, suggests to me that perhaps we got the delicate balance about right.

The Government's relationship with the police and the courts was an even more sensitive issue during the strike. Britain had no national police force: the police were organized into fifty-two local forces, each headed by a Chief Constable who had operational control. Authority was divided between the Home Secretary, local police authorities (made up of local councillors and magistrates) and Chief Constables. Inevitably during the miners' strike this tripartite system of policing was put under considerable strain: challenges to the rule of law posed by violence on the scale that took place during this strike clearly needed to be dealt with, swiftly and efficiently, at national level. Accordingly, the National Reporting Centre (NRC) – originally set up in 1972 – was activated in Scotland Yard, allowing the police to pool intelligence and to co-ordinate assistance from one force to another under the 'mutual aid' provisions of the 1964 Police Act. However, the tripartite system survived a good deal better than the Labour Party's hysterical denunciations might have suggested. Problems did arise in financing the extra police costs under this system, but these were resolved by steadily taking more and more of the burden on to the Exchequer.

Mob violence can only be defeated if the police have the complete moral and practical support of government. We made it clear that the politicians would not let them down. We had already given them the equipment and the training they would need, learning the lessons of the 1981 inner-city riots. More recently the police had shown themselves skilled in tackling violence masquerading as picketing when pickets from the National Graphical Association (NGA) had tried to close down Eddie Shah's newspaper in Warrington in November 1983. On that occasion the police had made it clear that force of numbers would not be allowed to prevent people from going to work if they wished to do so. They had also for the first time made effective use of powers to prevent a breach of the peace by turning back pickets before they arrived at their destination.

Another prerequisite of effective policing is that the law should be clear. Early in the strike Michael Havers made a lucid statement in a written answer to the Commons, setting out the scope of police powers to deal with mass picketing, including the power (mentioned above) to turn back pickets on their way to the picket line when there are reasonable grounds to expect a breach of the peace. These common law powers long predated our trade union legislation, and were matters of criminal rather than civil law. In the second week of the strike the Kent NUM challenged those powers in court, but they lost the case. The prevention of large numbers of pickets assembling to intimidate those who wished to work would be vital to the outcome of the dispute.

The relationship between government and the courts was, if anything, more sensitive still. It is right that people should have been vigilant on this question. The independence of the judiciary is a matter of constitutional principle, though the administration of the courts falls properly within the sphere of government responsibilities. As the incidents of violence accumulated it became a real concern to us that so few of those charged had been brought to court and convicted. It is vital if the rule of law is to prevail that criminal actions as visible as those during the strike be punished quickly: people need to see that the law is working. A backlog of cases built up, stemming partly from the delaying tactics of offenders and their solicitors, partly from the obstruction of some magistrates in areas where there was sympathy with the strikers' cause. The sheer number of cases also imposed a sudden strain on the system. In time we made available more buildings and professional stipendiary magistrates and the backlog began to be cleared. Stipendiary magistrates get through many more cases than their lay counterparts, but the Lord Chancellor could only respond to requests for help and had no power to make appointments unasked. Another problem was that policemen trying to defend themselves against hails of missiles and other assaults have little time to assemble detailed evidence. Cases were difficult to sustain. In the end all too many of the men of violence went unpunished.

By the last week of March the situation was fairly clear. The strike was unlikely to be over quickly. At the majority of pits Mr Scargill and his colleagues had a tight grip, which it would not be easy to break. But in our planning over the previous two years we had not allowed ourselves to assume that any coal would be mined during a strike, whereas in fact a substantial section of the industry was still working. If we could move this coal to the power stations then the prospects for endurance would be transformed. This calculation had an enormous impact on our strategy. We had to act so that at any one time we did not unite against us all the unions involved in the use and distribution of coal. This consideration meant that we all had to be very careful when and where the civil law was used and the NCB suspended – though it did not withdraw – its civil action.

Although Mr Scargill had been very anxious to avoid a ballot before the strike began, it was clear to us that he wanted to keep the possibility open. Indeed the following month an NUM Special Delegate Conference voted to reduce the majority required for a strike from 55 per cent to 50 per cent. Also at the beginning of the strike we had hopes that moderates on the NUM executive might succeed in forcing a ballot. This made it even more important to keep the balance of opinion among miners favourable to our cause because it seemed that much of the opposition to the strike came from miners angry not to have been allowed to vote. Would a ballot held during a strike, with emotions raised, produce a majority for or against Mr Scargill? I was not entirely sure.

The NUM leadership was desperate to prevent the movement of coal by rail, by road or by sea. Although at times during the dispute there were problems in the docks and they had some limited success in slowing rail traffic, the lorry drivers refused to be intimidated by the dockers or anyone else. Increasingly, and to a degree that we had not anticipated, road haulage firms were able to keep coal moving to the power stations and other main industrial customers. The steel workers had endured their own long and damaging strike and they were not keen to see plant destroyed and jobs lost in their own industry simply in order to demonstrate sympathy with the NUM – a union which had earlier shown remarkably little sympathy towards them. However, it was the power workers whose attitude was most crucial. If they struck, or acted in sympathy with the miners to prevent us moving to maximum oilburn, we would have had great difficulties. But their attitude was simply that they were not a party to the strike and that their job was to see that the people of Britain had light and power. Nor were their leaders prepared to be browbeaten by other trade union bosses into doing what they regarded as fundamentally wrong.

Everything turned on maximizing endurance. I received weekly reports from the Department of Energy setting out the position and I read them very carefully indeed. Early in the strike the power stations were consuming coal at the rate of about 1.7 million tons a week, though the net reduction in stocks was smaller because some deliveries were getting through. The CEGB estimated endurance at about six months but this assumed a build-up to maximum oilburn – that is, using oil-fired stations at full capacity – which had not yet begun. We had to judge when this should be set in train because it would certainly be described as provocative by the NUM leadership. We held off while there seemed a prospect that NUM moderates might force a ballot. However, I decided on Monday 26 March that this nettle must now be grasped.

Industrial stocks were, of course, much lower than those at the power stations: the cement industry was particularly vulnerable and important. But it was BSC whose problems were most immediate. Their integrated steel plants at Redcar and Scunthorpe would have to close in the next fortnight if supplies of coke and coal were not delivered and unloaded. Port Talbot, Ravenscraig and Llanwern had stocks sufficient for no more than three to five weeks. Not surprisingly, BSC was extremely concerned as the position changed from day to day.

This was the state of uncertainty as we ended the first month of the strike. Perhaps the only thing one could be sure of was Mr Scargill's intentions. He wrote in the *Morning Star* on 28 March that 'the NUM is engaged in a social and industrial Battle of Britain . . . what is urgently needed is the rapid and total mobilization of the Trade Union and Labour movement.' It was still unclear whether he would get it.

The stalemate continued during April. There still seemed the possibility of a ballot for a national strike whose result no one could guess. In spite of continuing heavy picketing, there were some signs of a drift back to work, particularly in Lancashire – though it was only a drift. The leaders of the rail unions and the seamen promised to support the miners in their struggle: there were many declarations of this kind during the strike, but their members were less enthusiastic. The first court cases against the NUM began: two coke hauliers began legal action against the South Wales NUM picketing of Port Talbot steelworks.

From early in the dispute we were worried that the NCB was failing to put across its case, both to its own employees and to the general public. This was not something that government could do for them, though later (as will be seen) we pressed them to improve their presentation. But on the question of upholding the law it was our role to speak, and we did so vigorously. When I was interviewed on *Panorama* by Sir Robin Day on Monday 9 April I strongly defended the police handling of the dispute:

> The police are upholding the law. They are not upholding the Government. This is not a dispute between miners and government. This is a dispute between miners and miners . . . it is the police who are in charge of upholding the law . . . [they] have been wonderful.

A few days later, the police were on a different front line. On 17 April WPC Yvonne Fletcher was killed by machine-gun fire from the Libyan Embassy in St James's Square while policing a peaceful demonstration. The whole country was shocked. In spite of which, Mr Scargill was to open contacts with Libyan officials, and an NUM official even met Colonel Gaddafi in the hope of raising money to continue the strike. It was as if there was a preternatural alliance between these different forces of disorder.

A LONG SLOG

In May there were brief but revealing contacts between the NCB and the NUM leadership – the first since the strike began. The talks took place on Wednesday 23 May; I had a full report the next day. Mr Scargill would allow no one to speak for the NUM side but himself: the other members of his executive had clearly been told to keep quiet. The NCB had given two presentations, one on the marketing prospects of the coal industry and another on the physical condition of the pits, some of which were now in danger of becoming unworkable because of the strike. At the end of each presentation the NUM representatives declined to comment or to ask questions. Mr Scargill then made a prepared statement. He insisted that there could be no discussion of pit closures on grounds other than exhaustion – certainly no question of closing pits on economic grounds. Ian MacGregor made some brief remarks to the effect that he saw no purpose in continuing the meeting in the light of this, but nevertheless he suggested further talks between two senior members of the NCB and two senior representatives of the NUM. Mr Scargill again insisted that the withdrawal of all closure plans was a precondition for any talks. There the meeting ended. But at that point the NUM sprung a trap. They asked to be allowed to stay in the room in which the meeting had just taken place for a discussion among themselves. Ian MacGregor saw this as a perfectly innocent request and readily agreed. The NCB representatives left the room. But later we discovered that the NUM had managed to persuade the press that this was a 'walkout' by the NCB. Many people seized on the episode as evidence that Ian MacGregor was unwilling to talk. It was a classic example of the dangers of negotiating with people like Mr Scargill.

Week by week the strike grew more bitter. There was evidence that many miners were losing their early enthusiasm for it and questioning Mr Scargill's forecasts of limited power station endurance. The NUM leadership responded by increasing the allowances they paid to pickets – they paid nothing at all to strikers who did not turn out to picket – recruiting non-miners to the task. There was a general escalation of the level of violence. Their tactic evidently was to achieve maximum surprise by concentrating large numbers of pickets at a particular pit at the shortest possible notice. Perhaps the most shocking scenes of violence were those which took place outside Orgreave Coke Works in an attempt to prevent coke convoys reaching the Scunthorpe steelworks. On Tuesday 29 May over 5,000 pickets engaged in violent clashes with the police. The police were pelted with all kinds of missiles, including bricks and darts, and sixty-nine people were injured. Thank goodness they at least had proper protective riot gear, I thought, as, like so many millions of others, I watched the terrible scenes on television.

Speaking in Banbury the next day I said:

> You saw the scenes . . . on television last night. I must tell you that what we have got is an attempt to substitute the rule of the mob for the rule of the law, and it must not succeed. There are those who are using violence and intimidation to impose their will on others who do not want it. They are failing because of two

> things. First, because of the magnificent police force, well trained for carrying out their duties bravely and impartially. And secondly, because the overwhelming majority of people in this country are honourable, decent and law-abiding and want the law to be upheld and will not be intimidated. I pay tribute to the courage of those who have gone into work through these picket lines . . . the rule of law must prevail over the rule of the mob.

Over the next three weeks there were further violent clashes at Orgreave, but the pickets never succeeded in halting the road convoys. The battles at Orgreave had an enormous impact and did a great deal to turn public opinion against the miners.

It was at about this time that we had the first clear evidence of large-scale intimidation in the mining villages. This problem grew steadily worse as the strike went on. Working miners were not the only targets: their wives and children were also at risk. The sheer viciousness of what was done provides a useful antidote to some of the more romantic talk about the spirit of the mining communities. In its very nature intimidation is extremely difficult for the police to combat, though as time went on officers in uniform and teams in plain clothes were specially deployed to tackle it.

There was a good deal of public criticism of the failure of the nationalized industries to use the civil remedies which our trade union laws had provided. As the violence continued and the problems of BSC in particular increased, the ministerial group frequently discussed whether to encourage the use of the civil law against the NUM and other unions involved in secondary action. Failure to take civil action against the unions and their funds put all the pressure on to the criminal law and onto the police whose duty it was to uphold it. It was also pointed out that, if successful, legal action against union funds would restrict their ability to finance mass pickets and to engage in unlawful action. People were saying openly that our trade union reforms were being discredited by the failure of the nationalized industries involved to use the legal remedies. Instinctively, I had a good deal of sympathy with this view, as did my advisers.

However, Peter Walker persuaded us that use of the civil law might alienate the support we had among working miners or moderate trade unionists. The chairmen of the BSC, NCB, BR and CEGB agreed with him, at least for the present: they met towards the end of June and decided that in all the circumstances this was not the time to apply for an injunction. Nor were the police convinced that civil action would make their job on the picket lines any easier. Of course, that did not prevent others – whether businessmen or working miners – making use of the new laws. The fact was that throughout this dispute there was much to be said for emphasizing the point that it was the basic criminal law of the country which was being flouted by the pickets and their leaders, rather than 'Thatcher's laws'.

Peter Walker's argument won the day, and the NCB went on to win the strike. In a sense, therefore, the outcome justified the tactic. But could the same result have been achieved earlier through civil action leading, by way of the NUM's defiance, to sequestration of union funds? Such 'might-have-beens' are always impossible to resolve. Looking back, however, we might reasonably have urged the nationalized industries to take action against the NUM and at an earlier stage. When the working miners actually did so on their own initiative – the best possible outcome but not something on which we should have relied – this put enormous pressure on Mr Scargill and severely circumscribed the ability of the NUM to keep the strike going. Since then, however, the use of 'Thatcher's laws' has become standard in Britain's industrial relations and the number of strikes and industrial disputes has plummeted.

Meanwhile, we kept a very close watch on the number of pits reopening and men working. In July and August many pits close to take their annual holidays and we had some hopes that there would be a large-scale return to work when the holiday period ended, though there were fears too that pits that had been working before the holidays would fail to reopen due to renewed efforts by the pickets. The cost of being on strike to miners and their families was one consideration in estimating what would happen. But perhaps psychology was more important. A really large return to work after the holiday might create its own momentum. For his part, Mr Scargill would try to persuade his troops that with autumn approaching there was hope of the NCB being forced to back down by a government unwilling to impose winter power cuts.

It was clearly very important that the NCB should do everything possible to get its case over to those tempted to give up the strike and return to work. On my recommendation, Tim Bell, who had given me so much good advice on presentation in the past, had begun to advise Ian MacGregor. There was certainly a powerful positive case to deploy: massive new investment was available for the pits under existing plans, though this was now being held up, and if work resumed there was the promised pay rise for miners to look forward to. There was also the negative side: pits might never reopen because of deterioration which occurred while the strike continued. Customers were being lost, probably permanently: no one in industry tempted by our subsidies to change from other fuels to coal was likely to have much faith in the reliability of coal supplies from now on. It would also have been possible to go ahead with pit closures on economic grounds while the strike was still on, and we debated this. But on balance the risk of alienating moderate miners was too great. We also had to consider whether to encourage more miners to take the uniquely generous redundancy terms on offer. There were two problems with respect to redundancy: first, even if large numbers of miners took up the offer, there was no guarantee that they would be from the pits we needed to close. And the savings lay in closing uneconomic pits. Second, there was a real risk that it was the moderate miners, sickened by the violence and intimidation, who would find redundancy most attractive, leaving the hardliners in a majority in particular areas or even nationally. So again we held fire.

July proved to be one of the most difficult months of the strike. On Monday 9 July almost out of the blue the TGWU called a national dock strike over a supposed breach of the National Dock Labour Scheme (NDLS). The NDLS had been established by the Attlee Government with the aim of eliminating casual labour in the docks. Based on statute, it operated in the majority of British ports, establishing a closed shop and giving the union extraordinary powers. The occasion for the strike was BSC's use of contract labour to move iron ore by road from stockpiles in the docks at Immingham to the Scunthorpe steelworks. In fact, BSC were satisfied that neither the scheme nor local agreements had been breached. Under the scheme's absurd provisions 'shadow' labour consisting of registered dock workers was required to stand and watch the work as it was being done by contractors. This had been complied with in the 'normal way'. We hoped that the National Dock Labour Board, which included union representatives, would give an early ruling to this effect. But the TGWU leadership was strongly committed to supporting Mr Scargill and plainly welcomed the opportunity to call a strike.

We had already made an extensive study of the implications of a national dock strike in 1982. It seemed likely that the strike – which would probably only seriously affect those ports which were part of the NDLS – would have little direct impact on the outcome of the coal strike. We were not importing coal for the power stations, because it would have risked losing us the support of working miners. But a dock strike would have serious implications for BSC by disrupting its imports of coal and iron ore. Indeed, it looked as if a major motive for the strike had been the desire of the left-wing TGWU leadership to assist the miners by tightening their grip on the major steel plants, counteracting BSC's success in by-passing secondary action on the railways by organizing road deliveries. The general effect on trade would be very serious – particularly on imports of food – though about a third of non-bulk cargo was carried by roll-on – roll-off ships (known as 'RO-RO'), much of which was driver-accompanied and passed through 'non-scheme' ports such as Dover and Felixstowe. Everything would depend on how well the strike was supported and whether it was confined to the NDLS ports.

Our regular meetings of the ministerial group on coal now had to deal with two strikes rather than one. I told the group on the day after the dock strike began that it was vital to make a major effort to mobilize opinion over the next forty-eight hours. We should urge the port employers to adopt a resolute approach and use all available means to strengthen opposition to the strike among workers in industries likely to be damaged by it, and indeed among the public. It must be clearly demonstrated that the pretext for the strike was false and that those taking this action already enjoyed extraordinary privileges. We should make the point that it was estimated that 4,000 out of the 13,000 dockers registered under the NDLS were surplus to the requirements of the industry. Of course, this was not the right time to abolish the NDLS – in the middle of a coal strike – but we should aim for the present to solve the dispute without ruling out future change. We mobilized the Civil Contingencies Unit to prepare to meet the crisis but avoided proclaiming a state of emergency, which might have meant the use of troops. Any sign of overreaction to the dock strike would have given the miners and other union militants new heart. Our strategy had to be to end the dock strike as quickly as possible, so that the coal dispute could be played as long as was necessary.

The earliest indications were that the dock strike would prove extremely difficult. On Monday 16 July I met the General Council of British Shipping for lunch and I found them in defeatist mood. This was an instance of something I came to know well: employers were always advising me to be tough except in their own industry. They told me that the strike was of greater extent than anything they had seen before in the docks.

I had called an *ad hoc* ministerial meeting that evening to review the overall position and we ran though the options. We recognized that if picketing spread to 'non-scheme' ports there was a high probability that civil action would be taken against the TGWU, and that there would be a strong case for activating the NCB's suspended injunction against the NUM. The conflict seemed to be on the verge of a significant escalation.

My recognition of the importance of presentation, however, did lead me to take a specific initiative, which was to set up a group of junior ministers from the departments concerned to co-ordinate government statements during the crisis, under the chairmanship of Tom King, then Employment Secretary. Peter Walker was not particularly pleased. He always liked to play his cards very close to his chest and although he did so with consummate skill there was a risk that one branch of government would lose confidence or lack proper information about what we were trying to do. In the end it was a great success: for once all of us in government contrived to sing the same song day after day.

In the event the dock strike proved far less of a problem than we had feared. Whatever the views of their leaders, the ordinary dockers were simply not prepared to support action which threatened their jobs: even those at the NDLS ports were less than enthusiastic, fearing that a strike would hasten the demise of the scheme itself. But the decisive role was played by the lorry drivers who had an even greater direct interest in getting goods through and were not prepared to be bullied and threatened. By 20 July the TGWU had no alternative but to call off the strike. It had lasted only ten days.

The end of the dock strike was only one of a number of important developments at this time. Following the fruitless meeting between the NCB and NUM on 23 May, talks had resumed at the beginning of July. Our hope was that they would end quickly and that the NCB would succeed this time in exposing the unreasonableness of Mr Scargill's position. There would then be a chance that striking miners would realize that they had no hope of winning and a return to work would begin.

However, the talks had drifted on, and there were indications that the NCB was softening its negotiating position. One problem was that each new round of negotiations naturally discouraged a return to work: few would risk going back if a settlement seemed to be in the offing. More troubling still, there was a real danger that the talks would end by fudging the issue on the closure of uneconomic pits: a formula was being developed based upon the proposition that no pit should be closed if it was capable of being 'beneficially developed'. The NCB was also prepared to give a commitment to keep open five named pits that the NUM had claimed were due for closure. We were very alarmed. Not only were there ambiguities in the detailed wording of the proposals, but (far worse) a settlement on these lines would have given Mr Scargill the chance to claim victory.

But on 18 July, two days before the end of the dock strike, negotiations collapsed. I have to say I was enormously relieved.

A week later we reached what was for me a very important moment in the history of the strike, though this was something very few people knew about at the time. On Wednesday 25 July I held a meeting in conditions of strict security to discuss power station endurance with Peter Walker and Sir Walter Marshall, Chairman of the CEGB. That very day Norman Tebbit had written to me expressing anxiety that time was not on our side in the coal strike. He had seen estimates of power station endurance that suggested stocks would be exhausted by mid-January: if this were so, he argued that we needed as soon as possible to consider measures to win the strike by the autumn, since he thought we could not afford to go on to the very brink of endurance.

I perfectly understood Norman's concern and it was partly because I shared his instinctive distrust of the figures – and could not quite believe Peter Walker's laid-back optimism – that I had asked for the meeting with Peter and Walter Marshall. The message I received at the meeting was extremely encouraging. Walter Marshall confirmed the position as Peter had previously described it. If supplies of coal from Nottinghamshire and other working areas to the power stations were maintained at the present level the safe date for endurance would be June 1985. In fact, the CEGB believed they could keep the power stations running until November 1985. He showed me a chart which demonstrated that coal, nuclear and oil generation taken together almost exactly matched the (lower) summertime demand. Indeed, if endurance could be extended into the spring of 1986 – which we might manage by getting more miners back to work for example – it would then be possible to go on into the following winter.

However, all these predictions were extremely sensitive to variations in the supply of coal from the Nottinghamshire pits. Walter Marshall stressed how important it was to maintain their output. Small improvements in supplies from these pits increased endurance dramatically: small shortfalls curtailed it equally dramatically. It would be essential to maintain transport from the Nottinghamshire pits and although road transport had made a great contribution, deliveries by rail could not be dispensed with. Enormous quantities of coal had to be moved, and pithead stockyards in many of the working pits were comparatively small – they had been built on the 'merry-go-round' system, by which trains ran directly to the power stations and back again on a daily basis. Accordingly, it was vital that we keep the rail unions working, if necessary at the price of concessions in pay talks.

Walter Marshall confirmed that importing coal for the power stations would be a mistake. This would annoy even the Nottinghamshire miners. It would be better to dedicate imports to industry and avoid getting the CEGB embroiled in the argument. Looking to the longer term, he also set out his programme for increasing endurance to at least twelve months rather than the six months provided for in the current plans. We never forgot the possibility of a second strike after the present one was finished.

The combination of Walter Marshall's natural ebullience, his mastery of detail and the determination he showed to avoid power cuts raised my spirits enormously. Over the next couple of days I spoke individually to Norman Tebbit and several other colleagues to give them the message. We were all able to take our holidays in a better frame of mind than we would otherwise have done.

On Tuesday 31 July I spoke in a debate in the House of Commons on a Censure Motion which the Labour Party had been ill-advised enough to put down. The debate went far wider than the coal strike. But the strike was on everyone's minds and inevitably it was the exchanges on this matter which caught the public attention. I did not mince my words:

> The Labour Party is the party which supports every strike, no matter what its pretext, no matter how damaging. But, above all, it is the Labour Party's support for the striking miners against the working miners which totally destroys all credibility for its claim to represent the true interests of working people in this country.

I went on to deal with Neil Kinnock:

> The Leader of the Opposition went silent on the question of a ballot until the NUM changed its rules to reduce the required majority. Then he told the House that a national ballot of the NUM was a clearer and closer prospect. That was on 12 April – the last time that we heard from him on the subject of a ballot. But on 14 July he appeared at an NUM rally and said, 'there is no alternative but to fight: all other roads are shut off.' What happened to the ballot?

Answer came there none.

Neil Kinnock had succeeded Michael Foot as Leader of the Labour Party in October 1983. I faced him across the despatch box of the House of Commons for seven years. Like Michael Foot, Neil Kinnock was a gifted orator; but unlike Mr Foot he was no parliamentarian. His Commons performances were marred by verbosity, a failure to master facts and technical arguments and, above all, a lack of intellectual clarity. This last drawback reflected something deeper. Mr Kinnock was entirely a product of the modern Labour Party – left-wing, close to the unions, skilful at party management and political manipulation, basically convinced that Labour's past defeats resulted from weaknesses of presentation rather than errors of policy. He regarded words – whether speeches or the texts of manifestos and policy documents – as a means of concealing his and the Labour Party's socialism rather than of converting others to it. So he forcefully – and on occasion courageously – denounced Trotskyists and other left-wing troublemakers, not for their brutal tactics or their extreme revolutionary objectives but because they were an embarrassment to his and Labour's ambitions. Being Leader of the Opposition, as I well remembered, is not an easy assignment. Leading the Labour Party in Opposition must be a nightmare. But I found it difficult to sympathize with Mr Kinnock. He was involved in what seemed to me a fundamentally discreditable enterprise, that of making himself and his party appear what they were not. The House of Commons and the electorate found him out. As Opposition Leader he was out of his depth. As Prime Minister he would have been sunk.

As we entered August we had some reason to hope that the worst of the strike was behind us. Arthur Scargill and the militants were becoming increasingly isolated and frustrated. The dock strike had collapsed. The Government's attitude and the NCB's stance were now generally perceived in a more sympathetic light. The Labour Party was in disarray. Although the return to work remained a trickle – about 500 during July – there was no sign of any weakening of determination at the working pits. Finally, on Tuesday 7 August two Yorkshire miners began a High Court action against the Yorkshire NUM for striking without a ballot. This proved to be a vital case and led eventually to the sequestration of the whole of the NUM's assets.

One sign of the militants' frustration was an increase in violence against working miners and their families. The situation appeared to be under control in Nottinghamshire, but things were getting worse in Derbyshire, partly because it was more deeply divided and also because it was closer to the Yorkshire coal fields from which the flying pickets largely came. Ian MacGregor was in touch with us in No. 10

and with the Home Office. He feared that such intimidation, appalling in itself, might also slow the return to work and could frighten miners currently working into staying away. The police thought that there might have been a change of tactics on the part of the NUM: frustrated by the failure of mass picketing, perhaps they were taking to guerilla warfare based on the intimidation of individuals and companies. The police stepped up their measures to protect the Derbyshire miners: 'freephone' lines to police stations were installed; detective squads set out to counter intimidation; and uniformed policemen patrolled the villages.

There was also the threat of another dock strike. A tense situation had developed at Hunterston, the deep-water port in Scotland which supplied BSC's Ravenscraig plant. An important cargo of coal, of the kind necessary for Ravenscraig's coke ovens, was aboard the bulk carrier *Ostia*, presently moored in Belfast Lough. BSC told us that if it were not landed quickly they would have to start to run down Ravenscraig. Steel furnaces cannot be shut down fully without irreversible damage and there was every likelihood that the whole plant would have to close for good if coal supplies were halted. As with the earlier dock strike, absurd restrictive practices were the pretext for the strike threat. The normal operation at Hunterston for BSC-destined cargo was divided between work done aboard ship by TGWU registered dockers and work done on-shore by members of the steel union, the ISTC. But 90 per cent of the cargo could be unloaded even without 'trimming'. BSC wanted to use its employees to unload this coal, but the TGWU was likely to claim that such action was contrary to the National Dock Labour Board agreement in order to provoke a new docks dispute. BSC told us that they were prepared to go to court if the cargo could not be unloaded.

This was a very delicate question and Norman Tebbit stayed in close contact with BSC. The National Dock Labour Board was asked to offer a ruling but delayed and, finally, funked the issue altogether. BSC began the rundown of Ravenscraig on 17 August; they told us that unless the coal was landed by 23–4 August, their furnaces would have to be 'banked' on 28–9 August – that is, kept running at a minimum level, without production. Total closure would follow if coal supplies did not resume.

In the end, after putting off the decision as long as possible, BSC had its employees start unloading the *Ostia* on the morning of Thursday 23 August. Although BSC acted in conformity with a local port agreement of 1984, TGWU dockers immediately walked out and the union called a second national dock strike.

But in Scotland public opinion was strongly opposed to any action that threatened the future of Ravenscraig. So we had doubts whether the union could sustain a strike across the whole of Scotland, let alone in the United Kingdom as a whole. And we were right. This strike was to cause us much less worry than the first. Though to begin with the strike received considerable support from registered dockers, a majority of ports remained open. Finally, the TGWU called it off on 18 September.

On holiday in Switzerland and Austria between 9 and 27 August I followed the story of the *Ostia* by telex. In my absence, Peter Walker took effective charge of day-to-day policy in the coal strike. But a prime minister is never really on holiday. I found myself accompanied by the local ambassador, who had previously been one of my private secretaries, five 'Garden Room girls' on duty round the clock, a technician to superintend communications with Downing Street and the usual roster of detectives. Red boxes came through the 'diplomatic bag'. The telex chattered constantly. At least one important decision was demanded of me by Willie Whitelaw over the telephone. Clarissa Eden once said that she sometimes felt that the Suez Canal flowed through her dining-room at No. 10. I sometimes thought at the end of the day that I would look out of the window and see a couple of Yorkshire miners striding down the Swiss slopes. And somehow neither the beautiful mountain scenery nor even my favourite reading – thrillers by Frederick Forsyth and John Le Carré – provided a distraction.

On my return I found the situation much as I had left it, though with one – as it was to turn out – fateful exception. There was a good deal of violence and intimidation still going on. By now 5,897 arrests had been made in the course of the dispute; there had been 1,039 convictions, the most severe sentence being nine months' imprisonment. Stipendiary magistrates would sit for the first time in early September at Rotherham and Doncaster. Others were ready elsewhere. Labour's Energy spokesman, Stan Orme, was trying to mediate in the coal strike, which served perhaps more to minimize Labour embarrassment than to bring the end of the dispute any closer. Robert Maxwell was also trying to muscle in. He announced in early September that he was holding himself ready to mediate, but the whole thing collapsed in recrimination before the two sides had even met. The NUM blamed the Government.

FROM THE JAWS OF VICTORY?

The most serious development, however, had been a circular issued on 15 August by the NCB to members of the National Association of Colliery Overmen, Deputies and Shotfirers (NACODS). By law coal could only be mined in the presence of suitably qualified safety personnel – the great majority of whom were members of NACODS. In April, NACODS members voted to strike, but the margin was less than the two-thirds required by union rules. Up to mid-August the NCB had varied in its policy towards NACODS: in some areas members were being allowed to stay away from striking pits where no work was being done, in others they were being required to cross picket lines. The NCB circular now generalized the latter policy, threatening to withhold pay from NACODS members who refused to comply.

The NCB circular played into the hands of those leaders of NACODS, particularly its president, who were strongly sympathetic to the NUM. Here at last was an issue on which they could persuade their members to strike. It was easy to understand why the NCB acted as they did. But it was a major error, subsequently compounded by their failure to perceive the swing in favour of a strike among NACODS members, and it almost precipitated disaster.

September and October were always likely to be difficult months. The miners would be looking forward to the winter when demand for electricity was at its highest and power cuts most likely. At the TUC Conference in early September a majority of trade unions – strongly opposed by the electricity and power workers – pledged support for the miners, though in most cases they had no intention of giving it. When the forthright electricians' leader Eric Hammond made a powerful speech pointing this out, he was heavily barracked for his pains. Neil Kinnock also spoke at the conference, coming as near as he ever did to outright condemnation of picket line violence, but without taking any action to expel from his party those who supported it. Meanwhile, Mr Scargill reaffirmed his view that there was no such thing as an uneconomic pit, only pits which had been starved of the necessary investment.

Negotiations between the NCB and the NUM were resumed on 9 September. As arguments continued about forms of words, it was difficult for the general public to work out precisely what separated the two parties. I was always concerned that Ian MacGregor and the

NCB team would unwittingly give away basic principles for which the strike was being fought. In the July talks he had already moved from the principle of closing 'uneconomic' pits to the much more dubious concept of closing pits which could not be 'beneficially developed'. Thankfully, Mr Scargill had not been prepared to adopt this ambiguous objective. Peter Walker and I felt throughout that Ian MacGregor did not fully comprehend the devious ruthlessness of the NUM leaders he was arguing with. He was a businessman, not a politician, and thought in terms of reasonableness and reaching a deal. I suspect that Mr MacGregor's view was that once he got the miners back to work he would be able to restructure the industry as he wished, whatever the precise terms on which a settlement had been reached. The rest of us, from long experience, understood that Arthur Scargill and his friends would exploit a fudged formula and that we should be back where we started. It was crucial for the future of the industry and for the future of the country itself that the NUM's claim that uneconomic pits should never be closed should be defeated, and be seen to be defeated, and the use of strikes for political purposes discredited once and for all.

It was also in September that I first met in person members of the 'Miners' Wives Back to Work Campaign', whose representatives came to see me at 10 Downing Street. I was moved by the courage of these women, whose families were subject to the abuse and intimidation. They told me a great deal and confirmed some of my suspicions about the NCB's handling of the strike. They said that the majority of miners still did not understand the full extent of the NCB's pay offer and plans for investment: more needed to be done to put across the NCB's case to striking miners, many of whom relied on the NUM for their information. They confirmed that while talks between the NCB and the NUM were going on, or were in prospect, it was extremely difficult to persuade men to return to work. They explained to me how small shops in the coalfields were being blackmailed into supplying food and goods for striking miners and withholding them from working miners. But perhaps the most shocking thing they had to say was that local NCB management in some areas were not anxious to promote a return to work and in one particular area were actively siding with the NUM to discourage it. In this overunionized industry I found that all too likely.

Of course, the vital thing for these women was that the NCB should do everything it could to protect miners who had led the return to work, if necessary transferring them to pits where there were fewer militants and giving them priority in applications for redundancies. I said that we would not let them down, and I think I kept my word. The whole country was in their debt.

One working miner's wife, Mrs McGibbon from Kent, spoke at the Conservative Party Conference, describing the harrowing experiences which she and her family had undergone. The vile tactics of the strikers knew no limit. Even her small children were targets: they were told that their parents were going to be killed. Shortly after she had spoken the *Morning Star* published her address. A week later her home was attacked.

On 11 September the National Working Miners' Committee was formed. This was an important development in the history of the working miners' movement. I heard a good deal informally about what was happening on the ground through David Hart, a friend who was making great efforts to help the working miners. I was eager to learn everything I could.

On Wednesday 26 September I went to York. I visited the Minster, which had recently been struck by lightning and badly damaged in the fire which followed – divine punishment, some suggested, for the wayward theology of leading Anglican clerics. I also discussed with the Yorkshire police and local people the damage the strike was doing to the local community. At lunch with Conservative Party activists, some of those from Barnsley confirmed the impression that we had received throughout the strike: that the NCB's publicity of its case was truly dreadful. There were, too, the accounts of intimidation with which I had become all too familiar. Nor could one doubt the economic hardship which Mr Scargill's obduracy was imposing on his own supporters. I was told that miners were digging up rootcrops from the fields to feed themselves and their families.

One positive result of the visit was my meeting with Michael Eaton, Director of the NCB's North Yorkshire area and the man who had developed the new pit at Selby.

I heard again in York, as I had from advisers previously, how effective he was. He has a wonderful soft Yorkshire voice and a good way of explaining things, so I suggested his appointment as a national spokesman to help improve NCB's presentation. Mr Eaton did a fine job, though unfortunately his position was made difficult as a result of jealousy and obstruction elsewhere in the NCB's ranks.

Meanwhile the threat from NACODS crept up on us. The leadership of NACODS was now clearly intent on a strike and announced that a strike ballot was to be held on 28 September. An agreement on the outstanding issues seemed within reach at one point but was repudiated by the union president on his return from holiday. At first the NCB was optimistic about the result of the ballot, but ominously as the days went by their assessments grew less and less hopeful. I had a meeting with Ian MacGregor and Peter Walker at Chequers on Sunday 23 September and we discussed what would happen if the two-thirds majority required for a strike was obtained. It was possible that NACODS might just use the result to put pressure on the NCB management to resolve their grievances. Alternatively, they might call a strike. We thought that in that event NACODS men in areas where the mines were working would themselves remain at work. But there was little chance of this happening in borderline areas like Derbyshire and it was clear that a NACODS strike would make it even more difficult to bring about a return to work by miners in the more militant areas. NACODS men were not the only NCB employees with the necessary safety qualifications. Many members of the British Association of Colliery Managers (BACM) were also qualified, but it would be difficult to persuade them to go underground and perform these tasks in the face of NACODS hostility. And while there were some NUM members who had passed the requisite examinations and were awaiting promotion to safety work grades, they too could provide only limited cover.

On Tuesday 25 September Peter Walker told the ministerial group on coal that it now looked likely that NACODS would vote for a strike. He was right: when the result came through on Friday we discovered that 82.5 per cent had voted in favour.

This was very bad news. Throughout the coal strike events swung unpredictably in one direction then another – suddenly things would move our way, then equally suddenly move against us – and I could never let myself feel confident about the final outcome.

Apart from the initial few days of the strike in March, this was the time when we felt most concern. Some in Whitehall feared that a bandwagon might begin to roll in Mr Scargill's favour. We could not know what effect the TUC resolution of support for the NUM would have. We were now approaching the autumn and the militants might gain new heart. And there was the threatened NACODS strike.

It was suggested to us that most members of NACODS had voted for a strike in order to strengthen their leadership's negotiating hand and that the vote did not mean that a strike would inevitably take place. After the ballot the NACODS executive had announced a nine-day delay before industrial action would actually begin, lending some plausibility to this interpretation. But for most of the leadership itself the original dispute about crossing picket lines was a secondary matter; their real aim was to secure an end to the miners' strike on the NUM's terms. Our best chance of avoiding a strike by NACODS – or of minimizing its effects if one could not be avoided – would be to drive a wedge between the union leaders and their members. It was therefore vital that the NCB should be as conciliatory as possible on the points of substance.

The NCB and NACODS held talks on Monday 1 October. Agreement was reached on pay and on guidelines as regards crossing picket lines, the NCB withdrawing its circular of 15 August. The following day there were discussions on machinery for the review of pit closures and the possibility of some form of arbitration in cases of disagreement. This was to remain the most difficult question. No matter how elaborate the process of consultation, the NCB could not concede to a third party the right of ultimate decision over pit closures. This, although generally understood, was best not set out too starkly.

All this time we were faced with hostile outside comment and pressure. The Labour Party Conference wholeheartedly backed the NUM and condemned the police. Worst of all, perhaps, was Neil Kinnock's speech in which, under pressure from the left wing and trade unions, he retreated from the tougher line he had taken at the TUC Conference. He took refuge in a general condemnation of violence which made no distinction between the use of violence with the aim of breaking the law and the use of force to uphold it. He even contrived to equate violence and intimidation with the social ills from which he claimed Britain was suffering: 'the violence of despair . . . of long-term unemployment . . . loneliness, decay and ugliness'. No wonder that the Labour Party lost so much support in Nottinghamshire, where miners and their families knew what violence really was, even if the Leader of the Labour Party did not.

As always, the Conservative Party Conference followed straight on from Labour's. Much of my time at Brighton was spent following as best I could the course of negotiations between the NUM and the NCB at the Advisory, Conciliation and Arbitration Service (ACAS). A delegation from NACODS was also present at ACAS, though not directly involved in the negotiations. It was clear that NACODS was trying to win terms for the NUM which would have allowed Mr Scargill to claim victory. NACODS leaders were making threats with this in mind, claiming that their members could not be restrained much longer from beginning their strike and so on. Tactics became at this stage of the greatest importance. The NCB tabled a paper which accepted an independent review body on pit closures and they committed themselves to give proper consideration to its views, though obviously they would retain the right to take management decisions.

ACAS then put forward a variation on this which the NCB immediately accepted and the NUM promptly rejected. We were still not to know how NACODS would react. But for once the NCB had obtained an important tactical advantage in negotiations.

These discussions spanned our Party Conference. Leon Brittan and Peter Walker both delivered powerful defences of our position during it. But the event which dominated our thoughts at that time was the IRA bomb at the Grand Hotel which killed five of our friends and came near to killing me, members of the Cabinet and many others.*

Among the messages I received afterwards was one from Mrs Gandhi, whom I knew well and admired. Within three weeks she was the victim of a brutal assassination by two of her own bodyguards.

THE TIDE TURNS

Towards the end of October the situation changed sharply once again. Three events within a week were particularly hopeful for us and must have come as hammerblows to Mr Scargill. First, on Tuesday 24 October the NACODS executive agreed not to strike after all. Precisely what happened is unclear. In all probability the moderates on the executive convinced the hardliners that their members simply would not act as stooges for Mr Scargill.

Second, it was at this point that the civil law at last began to bite. I have already mentioned a case which had been brought against the NUM by two Yorkshire miners: the High Court had ruled in the two miners' favour that the strike in Yorkshire could not be described as 'official'. The NUM had ignored the ruling and as a result a writ had been served on an astonished Mr Scargill actually on the floor of the Labour Party Conference. On 10 October both he and the union had been found in contempt of court and fined £1,000 and £200,000 respectively. Mr Scargill's fine was paid anonymously, but the NUM refused to pay and the High Court ordered its assets to be sequestrated. It soon became evident that the NUM had prepared for this event, but the financial pressure on the union was now intense and its ability to organize was greatly hampered.

Finally, on Sunday 28 October – only three days after the sequestration order – the *Sunday Times* revealed that an official of the NUM had visited Libya and made a personal appeal to Colonel Gaddafi for

* See pp. 379–83.

his support. This was astonishing news and even Mr Scargill's friends were dismayed. At the beginning of October, Mr Scargill (travelling under an alias as 'Mr Smith') had visited Paris with his colleague Mr Roger Windsor to meet representatives of the French communist trade union, the CGT. Present at the meeting was a Libyan whom Mr Scargill later claimed to be a representative of Libyan trade unionists – a rare breed, in fact, since Colonel Gaddafi had dissolved all trade unions when he came to power in 1969. It seems likely that Colonel Gaddafi made a donation to the NUM, though the amount is uncertain. The sum of £150,000 has been suggested. Mr Windsor's visit to Libya was a follow-up to the Paris meeting.

A further sum was certainly received from an equally unlikely source: the nonexistent 'trade unions' of Soviet-controlled Afghanistan. And in September reports had begun to surface that the NUM was receiving assistance from Soviet miners – a group whose members would have looked with envy on the freedoms, incomes and working conditions of their British equivalents. There was further confirmation in November. It was quite clear that these initiatives had the support of the Soviet Government. Otherwise the Soviet miners would not have had access to convertible currency. Our displeasure at this was made very clear to the Soviet Ambassador and I raised the matter with Mr Gorbachev when he visited Britain for the first time in December, who claimed to be unaware of it.*

All this did the NUM's cause great harm, not least with other trade unionists. The British people have plenty of sympathy for someone fighting for his job, but very little for anyone who seeks help from foreign powers out to destroy his country's freedom.

In November the ground continued to slip from under the NUM leadership. The NCB seized the moment to launch a drive to encourage the return to work. It was announced that miners who were back at work on Monday 19 November would qualify for a substantial Christmas bonus. The NCB mounted a direct mail campaign to draw the attention of striking miners to the offer. Combined with the growing disillusionment with Mr Scargill, this had an immediate effect. In the first week after the offer 2,203 miners returned to work, six times more than in the previous week. The most significant return to work was in North Derbyshire. Our strategy was to let this trend continue without trying to take any explicit political credit for it, which could have been counter-productive. I told ministers that the figures should

* In fact, I have since seen documentary evidence suggesting that he knew full well and was among those who authorized payment.

be allowed to speak for themselves, but that we should continue to emphasize just how much was on offer. I was keen to bring it home to the public that, in spite of all Mr Scargill's efforts, the trend was now firmly in the right direction.

Speaking at the Lord Mayor's Banquet on Monday 12 November I said:

> The Government will hold firm. The Coal Board can go no further. Day by day, responsible men and women are distancing themselves from this strike. Miners are asserting their right to go to their place of work. Those in other unions now see clearly the true nature and purpose of those who are leading this strike.
>
> This has been a tragic strike but good will emerge from it. The courage and loyalty of working miners and their families will never be forgotten. Their example will advance the cause of moderate and reasonable trade unionism everywhere. When the strike ends it will be their victory.

In fact, I remained in touch with representatives of the working miners. I was keen to see them but there appeared to be some rivalry between two groups: to have seen one without the other would have caused resentment and to have seen both together would have been undiplomatic. I accepted Peter Walker's advice to this effect, but I told my Private Office that when the strike was over I would have representatives of all the working miners and their wives to No. 10 for a reception – which indeed I did. (I met some also at a private buffet hosted by Woodrow Wyatt at the end of March the following year.)

Like many others, I suspect, I had been impelled to reflect a great deal in the course of the strike on the threats to democracy. Back in July I had addressed an eve of recess meeting of the '22 Committee on the subject of the 'enemy within'. The speech had attracted a good deal of hostile comment: critics had tried to distort my meaning by suggesting that the phrase was a reference to the miners at large rather than the minority of Marxist militants, as I had intended. I returned to the theme in the Carlton Lecture, which I delivered in the traditional home of Conservatism – the Carlton Club – on the evening of Monday 26 November. I was the second Carlton lecturer: the first had been Harold Macmillan, who had recently attacked our handling of the miners' strike in a characteristically elegant maiden speech in the Lords. Of course, in contemplating the threat of anti-democratic extremism I had in mind not only the NUM leadership but also the terrorists, who had demonstrated their murderous intent at the Brighton Grand Hotel just weeks before. I reflected:

> There has come into existence a fashionable view, convenient to many special interest groups, that there is no need to accept the verdict of the majority: that the minority should be quite free to bully, even coerce, to get the verdict reversed. Marxists, of course, always had an excuse when they were outvoted: their opponents must have 'false consciousness': their views didn't really count. But the Marxists, as usual, only provide a bogus intellectual top-dressing for groups who seek only their own self-interest.
>
> . . . Now that democracy has been won, it is not heroic to flout the law of the land as if we still struggled in a quagmire where civilization had yet to be built. The concept of fair play – a British way of saying 'respect for the rules' – must not be used to allow the minority to overbear the tolerant majority. Yet these are the very dangers which we face in Britain today. At one end of the spectrum are the terrorist gangs within our borders, and the terrorist states which finance and arm them. At the other are the hard Left operating inside our system, conspiring to use union power and the apparatus of local government to break, defy and subvert the laws.

The return to work continued. But so did the violence. Violence and intimidation well away from the pitheads were more difficult for the police to prevent and required fewer people to perpetrate: consequently it was on such tactics that the militant miners now concentrated. There were many incidents. One that particularly struck me took place on Friday 23 November when Michael Fletcher, a working miner from Pontefract in Yorkshire, was attacked and beaten by a gang of miners in his own home. No fewer than nineteen men were arrested for the crime. Then a week later came one of the most appalling events of the strike: a three-foot concrete post was thrown from a motorway bridge onto a taxi carrying a South Wales miner to work. The driver, David Wilkie, was killed. I wondered whether there was any limit to the savagery of which these people were capable.

With the passing of the 19 November deadline for the Christmas bonus the return to work slowed somewhat. One of the wives of the working miners sent me a message explaining that there were two additional reasons. First, some striking miners who intended to go back to work would only return after Christmas, to avoid intimidation of their families over the holiday. Second, there was news of fresh talks being planned between the NUM and the NCB, and talks always had a negative effect on the movement back to work.

But further talks were difficult to avoid, although Mr Scargill's intransigence would probably ensure that they went nowhere. Using Robert Maxwell as an intermediary, key figures in the TUC were anxious to find some way of concluding the strike which would allow Mr Scargill and the militants to save face. In fact, of course, it was only by ensuring that they lost face and were seen to be defeated and rejected by their own people that we could tame the militants. I suspect that some of the union leaders knew this. Certainly, some of them had reason to know it. Norman Willis, General Secretary of the TUC, had pursued a thoroughly honourable line throughout, unlike the leaders of the Labour Party. Earlier that month he had spoken at an NUM rally in South Wales. Attempts were made to shout him down when he condemned violence on the picket line and in a chilling moment, which I and millions of others watched on television, a noose was lowered from the ceiling and suspended just above his head.

David Basnett, General Secretary of the GMWU, and Ray Buckton, General Secretary of ASLEF, had a private meeting with Peter Walker in which they revealed their desire for the TUC to play a role. I considered how we should respond. On the one hand, the last thing I wanted was to bring the TUC into No. 10 in their old capacity as power brokers. On the other hand, a clumsy rebuff could alienate moderate opinion among the unions.

So Peter Walker and Tom King had a lengthy meeting with seven of the main union leaders on the evening of Wednesday 5 December. It was clear that none of the seven really had any idea how to end the strike. I discussed how to deal with the TUC initiative with Peter Walker and officials on the morning of Thursday 13 December at Downing Street. Apparently the TUC were proposing to put to the NUM and the NCB the idea of a return to work followed by discussion of a new Plan for Coal, the talks to have a time limit of perhaps eight to twelve weeks. The TUC wanted to know whether we would endorse this approach. Peter Walker saw some advantages in it. I was more conscious of the difficulties. There were three principles, I said, to which we must adhere. First, any talks on the future of the industry must take place after the return to work. Second, nothing should be agreed which would undercut the position of the working miners. Third, it was essential to prevent the NUM claiming that the programme of pit closures had been withdrawn or even that there would be no pit closures while talks continued. It should be clearly seen that the NCB was free to operate the existing colliery review procedure, as modified by the provisions of the agreement with NACODS. However, I agreed that Peter should meet the TUC on Friday morning to tell them that the Government would go along with their efforts to bring the strike to an end on the basis of a return to work followed by talks on the future of the industry. The colliery review procedure, modified by the NACODS agreement, would remain in place.

Peter and Tom met the TUC delegation the following day. Nothing came of the meeting. The TUC had no authority from Mr Scargill to negotiate and they concluded that no initiative to end the strike was now possible before Christmas.

As the year ended, our main objective was to encourage a further return to work from 7 January, the first working Monday in the New Year. Though the NCB's bonus offer had expired, there was still a strong financial incentive for strikers to return to work in the near future because they would pay little, if any, income tax on their wages if they went back before the end of the tax year on 31 March. The great strategic prize would be to get more than 50 per cent of NUM members back to work: if we could secure that, it would be equivalent in practical and presentational terms to a vote in a national ballot to end the strike. This would require the return of a further 15,000 to work, which the NCB were busily preparing a new campaign of letters and press advertising to achieve.

It was also vital that the miners and the public at large should be told that there would be no power cuts that winter, contrary to Mr Scargill's ever more desperate and incredible predictions. We held off making such an announcement until we could be absolutely certain, but finally on 29 December Peter Walker was able to issue a statement saying that he had been informed by the Chairman of the CEGB that at the level of coal production that had now been achieved there would be no power cuts during the whole of 1985.

THE STRIKE BEGINS TO CRUMBLE

The question now was what the effect of all this would be on the return to work in January. The rate of return was initially affected in some areas by bad weather, which also had some negative effects on the movement of coal. (I had been worried earlier that we would have a cold winter, but fortunately the weather was generally good.) But as January continued the rate of return increased. By the middle of the month there were almost 75,000 NUM members not on strike and the rate of return was running at about 2,500 a week. Plainly the end was near.

The pattern which seemed to be emerging was for working miners to establish a 'bridgehead' at a strike-bound pit: fifty or more of those most anxious to return would go in together, often on a Thursday or Friday when their action attracted least attention. After that things could move quite fast. The increase in production was bound to be slower than the rate of return to work, but the trend there was also clearly in the right direction.

The one thing which could be relied upon to slow down the progress was further negotiations: and so it proved. When news broke of 'talks about talks', which were arranged between the NCB and the NUM on Monday 21 January, the effect was to cut the rate of return to rather less than half that of the previous week.

Meanwhile, public attention increasingly focused on the attempts of the sequestrators to trace and recover NUM funds which had been transferred abroad. In early December further legal action by working miners had led to the removal of the NUM's trustees and the appointment of an official receiver. These were, of course, principally questions for the courts. However, even with the full armoury of the law, there were such difficulties in tracing the funds that the sequestrators might not even have been able to cover their costs. Accordingly, Michael Havers told the Commons on Tuesday 11 December that the Government would indemnify them against the loss. We could not stand by and see the intention of the court frustrated. We were also involved in trying to ensure maximum co-operation from foreign governments – Ireland and Luxemburg – in whose jurisdictions the NUM had lodged its money. Towards the end of January some £5 million was recovered.

If the position of Mr Scargill looked hopeless, that of the Labour Party looked ridiculous. There was another Censure Debate in the House of Commons at this time in which I spoke for the Government. As on the previous occasion I challenged Mr Kinnock to tell us where he stood, even if belatedly:

> Throughout the strike the Rt. Hon. Gentleman has had the choice between standing up to the NUM leadership and keeping silent. He has kept silent. When the leadership of the NUM called a strike without a ballot, in defiance of union rules, the Rt. Hon. Gentleman stayed silent. When pickets tried by violence to close down pits in Nottinghamshire and elsewhere, against the democratically expressed wishes of the local miners, the Rt.

Hon. Gentleman stayed silent. When the NUM tried to impose mob rule at Orgreave, the Rt. Hon. Gentleman stayed silent. Only when the General Secretary of the TUC had the courage to tell the leadership of the NUM that its tactics were unacceptable did the Rt. Hon. Gentleman take on the role of Little Sir Echo . . . I challenge the Leader of the Opposition. Will he urge the NUM to accept that agreement or will he not? [Hon. Members: 'Answer!'] He will not answer, because he dare not answer.

The real question now was how and when would the strike end. In early February the numbers returning to work were again down because of the prospect of a resumption of talks. The TUC continued to seek to act as an intermediary between the NCB and the NUM. By this time, the NCB had rightly deduced that in negotiations they should put everything on paper so that there was less chance of the NUM leadership distorting it for their own tactical advantage. For his part, Mr Scargill continued to confirm in public that he would not agree to the closure of pits on economic grounds. Not surprisingly, working miners and their families were worried and perplexed by the continuing talk of negotiations. On Monday 4 February I wrote to the wife of a working miner to reassure her:

> I do understand your fear that the NUM leadership may yet evade responsibility for the misery they have caused – but I believe that the Coal Board have been, and are being, resolute about their position. For my part, I have made clear that there can be no fudging of the central issue, and no betrayal of the working miners to whom we owe so much . . .

By this time, the NUM leadership could have no doubt about how far events had swung against them since the NACODS dispute the previous autumn. The NACODS leaders now began to press the NCB to resume negotiations and so assist the NUM. But, learning from past mistakes, the NCB avoided giving NACODS any excuse for a renewed threat of industrial action.

The TUC leaders also remained anxious to save the militants from humiliating defeat. But Mr Scargill clearly had no intention of budging: indeed he had already stated publicly that he would prefer a return to work without an agreement to acceptance of the NCB's proposals. For its part, the NCB had told the TUC that there was no basis for negotiation on the terms still demanded by the NUM. I recognized that, although their motives were decidedly mixed, the TUC leaders and particularly the General Secretary had been acting in good faith. They must have realized by now that there was no possibility of doing business with Mr Scargill. Consequently, when a delegation from the TUC asked to see me, I agreed.

I met Norman Willis and other union leaders at No. 10 on the morning of Tuesday 19 February. Willie Whitelaw, Peter Walker and Tom King joined me on the Government side. The meeting was good natured. Norman Willis put as fair a construction on the NUM's negotiating stance as anyone could. In reply I said that I appreciated the TUC's efforts. I too wanted to see the strike settled as soon as possible. But this required a clear resolution of the central issues of the dispute. It was in no one's interest to end the strike with an unclear formula: arguments about interpretation and accusations of bad faith could provide the basis for another dispute. I could not agree with Mr Willis that there was evidence of a significant shift in the NUM executive's position. I gave an assurance that the NACODS agreement would be fully honoured and that I saw no difficulties about implementing it. An effective settlement of the dispute required clear understandings about procedures for closure, acknowledgement of the NCB's right to manage and to make the final decisions, and an acknowledgement that the Board would take the economic performance of pits into account when those decisions were made.

THE END OF THE STRIKE

It was now evident to the miners and to the public that the TUC were neither willing nor able to stop events taking their course. Large numbers of miners were going back to work and the rate of return was increasing. On Wednesday 27 February the magic figure was reached: more than half the members of the NUM were now not on strike. On Sunday 3 March an NUM Delegates' Conference voted for a return to work, against Mr Scargill's advice, and over the next few days even the most militant areas returned. That Sunday I gave an interview to reporters outside No. 10. I was asked who if anyone had won. I replied:

> If anyone has won, it has been the miners who stayed at work, the dockers who stayed at work, the power workers who stayed at work, the lorry drivers who stayed at work, the railwaymen

> who stayed at work, the managers who stayed at work. In other words, all of those people who kept the wheels of Britain turning and who, in spite of a strike, actually produced a record output in Britain last year. It is the whole working people of Britain who kept Britain going.

And so the strike ended. It had lasted almost exactly a year. Even now we could not be sure that the militants would not find some new excuse to call a strike the following winter. So we took steps to rebuild coal and oil stocks and continued to watch events in the coal industry with the closest attention. I was particularly concerned about the dangers faced by the working miners and their families now that the spotlight had moved away from the pithead villages. In May I met Ian MacGregor to emphasize how vital it was that they should receive the necessary consideration and support.

As an industrial dispute the coal strike had been wholly unnecessary. The NUM's position throughout the strike – that uneconomic pits could not be closed – was totally unreasonable. Never while I was Prime Minister did any other group make a similar demand, let alone strike for it. Only in a totalitarian state with a siege economy – with nationalization, the direction of labour and import barriers – could the coal industry have functioned, even for a time, irrespective of financial realities and the forces of competition. But for people like Mr Scargill these were desirable things. The impossibility of the NUM's policy on pit closures is a further clue – as if public statements were not enough – to the real nature of the strike itself.

The strike certainly established the truth that the British coal industry could not remain immune to the economic forces which applied elsewhere in both the public and private sectors. In spite of heavy investment, British coal has proved unable to compete on world markets and as a result the British coal industry has now shrunk far more than any of us thought it would at the time of the strike.*

Yet the coal strike was always about far more than uneconomic pits. It was a political strike. And so its outcome had a significance far beyond the economic sphere. From 1972 to 1985 the conventional wisdom was that Britain could only be governed with the consent of the trade unions. No government could really resist, still less defeat, a major strike; in particular a strike by the miners' union. Even as we were reforming trade union law and overcoming lesser disputes, such as the steel strike, many on the left and outside it continued to believe

* See pp. 685–6.

that the miners had the ultimate veto and would one day use it. That day had now come and gone. Our determination to resist a strike emboldened the ordinary trade unionist to defy the militants. What the strike's defeat established was that Britain could not be made ungovernable by the Fascist Left. Marxists wanted to defy the law of the land in order to defy the laws of economics. They failed, and in doing so demonstrated just how mutually dependent the free economy and a free society really are. It is a lesson no one should forget.

CHAPTER XIV

Shadows of Gunmen

The political and security response to IRA terrorism – 1979–1990

THE BRIGHTON BOMB

As usual, by the end of the week of our 1984 Party Conference in Brighton I was becoming frantic about my speech. A good conference speech cannot just be written in advance: you need to get the feel of the conference in order to achieve the right tone. I spent as much time as I could working on the text with my speech writers on Thursday afternoon and evening, rushed away to look in at the Conservative Agents' Ball and returned to my suite at the Grand Hotel just after 11 o'clock.

By about 2.40 a.m. the speech – at least from my point of view – was finished. So while the speech writers themselves, who had been joined for a time by Norman Tebbit, went to bed, my long-suffering staff typed in what I was (fairly) confident would be the final changes to the text and prepared the Autocue tape. Meanwhile, I got on with some government business.

At 2.50 a.m. Robin Butler asked me to look at one last official paper – it was about the Liverpool Garden Festival. I gave Robin my view and he began to put away the papers. At 2.54 a.m. a loud thud shook the room. There was a few seconds' silence and then there was a second slightly different noise, in fact created by falling masonry. I knew immediately that it was a bomb – perhaps two bombs, a large followed by a smaller device – but at this stage I did not know that the explosion had taken place inside the hotel. Glass from the windows of my sitting-room was strewn across the carpet. But I thought that it might be a car bomb outside. (I only realized that the bomb had exploded above us when Penny, John Gummer's wife, appeared a little later from upstairs, still in her night clothes.) The adjoining bathroom was more severely damaged, though the worst I would have suffered had I been in there were minor cuts. Those who had sought to kill me had placed the bomb in the wrong place.

Apart from the broken glass and a ringing fire alarm, set off by the explosion, there was a strange and, as it turned out, deceptive normality. The lights, thankfully, remained on: the importance of this played on my mind for some time and for months afterwards I always kept a torch by my bed when I was staying the night in a strange house. Denis put his head round the bedroom door, saw that I was all right and went back inside to dress. For some reason neither of us quite understands he took a spare pair of shoes with him, subsequently worn by Charles Price, the American Ambassador, who had lost his in the confusion of leaving the hotel. While Crawfie gathered together my vanity case, blouses and two suits – one for the next day – Robin Butler came in to take charge of the government papers. I went across the landing to the secretaries' room to see if my staff were all right. One of the girls had received a nasty electric shock from the photocopier. But otherwise all was well. They were as concerned about my still only partly typed-up speech as they were for themselves. 'It's all right,' they assured me, 'we've got the speech.' A copy went straight into my briefcase.

By now more and more people were appearing in the secretaries' room with me – the Gummers, the Howes, David Wolfson, Michael Alison and others, unkempt, anxious but quite calm. At this stage none of us had any clear idea about the extent of the damage, let alone injuries. While we talked, my detectives had been checking out as best they could our immediate security. There is always a fear of a second device, carefully timed to catch and kill those fleeing from the first explosion. It was also necessary for them to find a way out of the hotel which was both unblocked and safe.

At 3.10 a.m., in groups, we began to leave. It turned out that the first route suggested was impassable and we were turned back by a fireman. So we went back and waited in the office. Later we were told that it was safe to leave and we went down by the main staircase. It was now that I first saw from the rubble in the entrance and foyer something of the seriousness of the blast. I hoped that the porter had not been injured. The air was full of thick cement dust: it was in my mouth and covered my clothes as I clambered over discarded belongings and broken furniture towards the back entrance of the hotel. It still never occurred to me that anyone would have died.

Ten minutes later Denis, Crawfie and I arrived in a police car at Brighton Police Station. We were given tea in the Chief Constable's room. Soon friends and colleagues started to arrive to see me. Willie Whitelaw came in. So did the Howes, accompanied by their little dog 'Budget'. But it was Leon Brittan, as Home Secretary, and John Gummer, as Party Chairman, with whom I had most to discuss. At this stage none of us knew whether the conference could continue: had the conference hall itself been attacked? But I was already determined that if it was physically possible to do so I would deliver my speech. There was discussion about whether I should return to No. 10; but I said, 'No: I am staying.' It was eventually decided that I would spend the rest of the night at Lewes Police College. I changed out of evening dress into a navy suit and, as I left the Police Station with Denis and Crawfie, I made a brief statement to the press. Then we were driven at great speed to Lewes.

Nobody spoke during the journey. Our thoughts were back at the Grand Hotel. Whether by chance or arrangement, there was no one staying at the College. I was given a small sitting-room with a television and a twin-bedded room with its own bathroom. Denis and the detectives shared rooms further down the corridor. Crawfie and I shared too. We sat on our beds and speculated about what had happened. By now I was convinced that there must have been casualties. But we could get no news.

I could only think of one thing to do. Crawfie and I knelt by the side of our beds and prayed for some time in silence.

I had brought no night clothes with me and so I lay down fully clothed and slept fitfully for perhaps an hour and a half. I awoke to the sound of the breakfast television news at 6.30 a.m. The news was bad, much worse than I had feared. I saw pictures of Norman Tebbit being pulled out of the rubble. Then came the news that Roberta Wakeham and Anthony Berry MP were dead. I knew that I could not afford to let my emotions get control of me. I had to be mentally and physically fit for the day ahead. I tried not to watch the harrowing pictures. But it did not seem to do much good. I had to know each detail of what had happened – and every detail seemed worse than the last.

I bathed quickly, changed and had a light breakfast with plenty of black coffee. It was soon clear that the conference could go ahead. I said to the police officer in charge that I must get back to Brighton to open the conference on time.

It was a perfect autumn day and as we drove back into Brighton the sky was clear and the sea completely calm. I now had my first sight of the front of the Grand Hotel, a whole vertical section of which had collapsed.

Then we went on to the Conference Centre itself, where at 9.20 a.m. the conference opened; and at 9.30 a.m. precisely I and the officers of the National Union* walked on to the platform. (Many of them had had to leave clothes in the hotel, but Alistair McAlpine had persuaded the local Marks & Spencer to open early and by now they were smartly dressed.) The body of the hall was only about half full, because the rigorous security checks held up the crowds trying to get in. But the ovation was colossal. All of us were relieved to be alive, saddened by the tragedy and determined to show the terrorists that they could not break our spirit.

By chance, but how appropriately, the first debate was on Northern Ireland. I stayed to listen to this but then left to work on my speech which had to be completely revised. Michael Alison (my Parliamentary Private Secretary) and I retired to an office in the Centre where we removed most of the partisan sections of the speech: this was not a time for Labour-bashing but for unity in defence of democracy. Whole new pages had to be written, though there were tough sections on law and order which could be used as they stood. Ronnie Millar then polished the text as he and I went through it. All the while, and in spite of attempts by my staff to minimize the interruptions, I was receiving messages and fleeting visits from colleagues and friends. I knew that John Wakeham had not yet been freed from the rubble and several people were still missing. A steady stream of flowers arrived which later were sent on to the hospital where the injured had been taken.

As in earlier days, I delivered the speech from a text rather than Autocue and ad libbed a good deal as well. But I knew that far more important than what I said was the fact that I, as Prime Minister, was still able to say it. I did not dwell long in the speech on what had happened. But I tried to sum up the feelings of all of us.

> The bomb attack . . . was an attempt not only to disrupt and terminate our conference. It was an attempt to cripple Her Majesty's democratically elected government. That is the scale of the outrage in which we have all shared. And the fact that we are gathered here now, shocked but composed and determined, is a sign not only that this attack has failed, but that all attempts to destroy democracy by terrorism will fail.

* The National Union of Conservative and Unionist Associations – the voluntary wing of the Party.

I did not linger after my speech but went immediately to the Royal Sussex County Hospital to visit the injured. Four people had already died. Muriel McLean was on a drip feed: she would die later. John Wakeham was still unconscious and remained so for several days. He had to be operated on daily for some time to save his legs which had been terribly crushed. By chance we all knew the consultant in charge, Tony Trafford, who had been a Conservative MP. I spent hours on the telephone trying to get the best advice possible from experts in dealing with crush injuries. In the end it turned out that there was a doctor in the hospital from El Salvador who had the expertise required. Between them they managed to save John's legs. Norman Tebbit regained consciousness while I was at the hospital and we managed a few words. His face was bloated as a result of being trapped for so long under the rubble: I scarcely recognized him. I also talked to Margaret Tebbit who was in the intensive care unit. She told me she had no feeling below the neck. As a former nurse, she knew well enough what that meant.

I left the hospital overcome by such bravery and suffering. I was driven back to Chequers that afternoon faster than I have ever been driven before, with a full motorcycle escort. As I spent that night in what had become my home I could not stop thinking about those unable to return to theirs.

THE IRISH DILEMMA

What happened in Brighton shocked the world. But the people of Northern Ireland and the security forces face the ruthless reality of terrorism day after day. There is no excuse for the IRA's reign of terror. If their violence were, as the misleading phrase often has it, 'mindless' it would be easier to grasp as the manifestation of a disordered psyche. But that is not what terrorism is, however many psychopaths may be attracted to it. Terrorism is the calculated use of violence – and the threat of it – to achieve political ends. In the case of the IRA those ends are the coercion of the majority of the people of Northern Ireland, who have demonstrated their wish to remain within the United Kingdom, into an all-Ireland state. Along with the political objective go crimes of other kinds – robbery, protection, fraud to name but a few.

There are terrorists in both the Catholic and Protestant communities, and all too many people prepared to give them support or at least to acquiesce in their activities. Indeed, for a person to stand out against the terrorists carries great personal risk. The result is that it is impossible to separate entirely the security policy, required to prevent terrorist outrages and bring the perpetrators to book, from the wider political approach to the long-standing 'Northern Ireland problem'. For some people that connection implies that you should make concessions to the terrorist, in particular by weakening the Union between Ulster and Britain. But it never did so for me. My policy towards Northern Ireland was always one aimed above all at upholding democracy and the law: it was always therefore determined by whatever I considered at a particular time would help bring better security.

The IRA are the core of the terrorist problem; their counterparts on the Protestant side would probably disappear if the IRA could be beaten. But the best chance of beating them is if three conditions are met. First, the IRA have to be rejected by the nationalist minority on whom they depend for shelter and support.* This requires that the minority should be led to support or at least acquiesce in the constitutional framework of the state in which they live. Second, the IRA have to be deprived of international support, whether from well-meaning but naïve Irish Americans, or from Arab revolutionary regimes like that of Colonel Gaddafi. This requires constant attention to foreign policy aimed at explaining the facts to the misinformed and cutting off the weapons from the mischievous. Third, and linked to the other two, relations between Britain and the Republic of Ireland have to be carefully managed. Although the IRA have plenty of support in areas like West Belfast within Northern Ireland, very often it is to the South that they go to be trained, to receive money and arms and to escape capture after crimes committed within the United Kingdom. The border, long and difficult to patrol, is of crucial significance to the security problem. Much depends on the willingness and ability of the political leaders of the Republic to co-operate effectively with our intelligence, security forces and courts. So it was that through-

* In this chapter and elsewhere nationalist is generally used as an alternative to 'Catholic' and Unionist to 'Protestant'. While it is true that the political and ethnic division in Northern Ireland is largely (though not always) consistent with and sometimes worsened by religious division, it is misleading to describe it in essentially religious terms. The IRA gunmen who murder and the hunger strikers who committed suicide are not in any proper sense 'Catholic' nor are 'loyalist' sectarian killers 'Protestant'. They are not even in any meaningful sense Christians.

out my time in office security issues and political initiatives were intertwined.

My own instincts are profoundly Unionist. There is therefore something of a paradox in that my relations with the Unionist politicians were so uncomfortable most of the time. Airey Neave and I felt the greatest sympathy with the Unionists while we were in Opposition. I knew that these people shared many of my own attitudes, derived from my staunchly Methodist background. Their warmth was as genuine as it was usually undemonstrative. Their patriotism was real and fervent, even if too narrow. They had often been taken too much for granted. From my visits to Northern Ireland, often after terrible tragedies, I came to have the greatest admiration in particular for the way in which the little rural Protestant communities would come together, looking after one another, after some terrible loss. But, then, any Conservative should in his bones be a Unionist too. Our Party has always, throughout its history, been committed to the defence of the Union: indeed on the eve of the First World War the Conservatives were not far short of provoking civil disorder to support it. That is why I could never understand why leading Unionists – apparently sincerely – suggested that in my dealings with the South and above all in the Anglo-Irish Agreement, which I shall discuss shortly, I was contemplating selling them out to the Republic.

But what British politician will ever fully understand Northern Ireland? I suspect that even the most passionate English supporters of Ulster do so less than they imagine. Certainly, time and again I found that apparently innocuous words and phrases had a special significance in the overheated political world of Ulster – indeed the mere use of that term to describe the province is an example, allegedly denoting a 'Protestant' bias. In the history of Ireland – both North and South – which I tried to read up when I could, especially in my early years of office, reality and myth from the seventeenth century to the 1920s take on an almost Balkan immediacy. Distrust mounting to hatred and revenge is never far beneath the political surface. And those who step onto it must do so gingerly.

I started from the need for greater security, which was imperative. If this meant making limited political concessions to the South, much as I disliked this kind of bargaining I had to contemplate it. But the results in terms of security must come through. In Northern Ireland itself my first choice would have been a system of majority rule – devolved government on the same lines as Westminster, and subject to its supremacy – with strong guarantees for the human rights of the minority, and indeed everyone else. That is broadly the approach which Airey and I had in mind when the 1979 manifesto was drafted. But it was not long before it became clear to me that this model was not going to work, at least for the present. The nationalist minority were not prepared to believe that majority rule would secure their rights – whether it took the form of an assembly in Belfast, or more powerful local government. They insisted on some kind of 'power sharing' – that in some way both sides should participate in the executive function – as well as demanding a role for the Republic in Northern Ireland, both of which proposals were anathema to the Unionists.

I had always had a good deal of respect for the old Stormont system.* When I was Education Secretary I was impressed by the efficiency of the Northern Ireland education service. The province has kept its grammar schools and so has consistently achieved some of the best academic results in the United Kingdom. But majority rule meant permanent power for the Protestants, and there was no getting away from the fact that, with some justice, the long years of Unionist rule were associated with discrimination against the Catholics. I believe the defects were exaggerated, but Catholic resentment gave rise to the civil rights movement at the end of the 1960s, which the IRA was able to exploit. By early 1972 civil disorder existed on such a scale that Stormont was suspended and replaced by direct rule from London. At the same time the British Government gave a guarantee that Northern Ireland would remain a part of the United Kingdom so long as the majority of its people wished, and this has remained the cornerstone of policy under governments of both parties.

The political realities of Northern Ireland prevented a return to majority rule. This was something that many Unionists refused to accept, but since 1974 they had been joined in the House of Commons by Enoch Powell, who helped to convert some of them to an altogether different approach. His aim was that of 'integration'. Essentially, this would have meant eliminating any difference between the government of Northern Ireland and that of the rest of the UK, ruling out a return to devolution (whether majority rule or power sharing) and any special role for the Republic. Enoch's view was that the terrorists thrived on uncertainty about Ulster's constitutional position: that uncertainty would, he argued, be ended by full integration combined with a tough security policy. I disagreed with this for two reasons. First, as I have

* A system of majority rule had existed in the province from the creation of Northern Ireland in the partition of 1920 until 1972, known as 'Stormont' (from the location of government buildings on the edge of Belfast).

said, I did not believe that security could be disentangled from other wider political isssues. Second, I never saw devolved government and an assembly for Northern Ireland as weakening, but rather strengthening the Union. Like Stormont before it, it would provide a clear alternative focus to Dublin – without undermining the sovereignty of the Westminster Parliament.

FIRST ATTEMPTS AT DEVOLUTION

Such were my views about Northern Ireland's future on entering office. My conviction that further efforts must be made on both the political and security fronts had been strengthened by the events of the second half of 1979.* In the course of that October we discussed in government the need for an initiative designed to achieve devolution in Northern Ireland. I was not very optimistic about the prospects but I agreed to the issue of a discussion document setting out the options. A conference would be called of the main political parties in Northern Ireland to see what agreement could be reached.

On Monday 7 January 1980 the conference opened in Belfast. Since the traumas of the late 1960s and early 1970s the forces of Unionism in Northern Ireland have been divided, adding factional rivalry to all the other problems faced by Ulster. On this occasion the largest Unionist group, the Official Unionist Party (OUP), refused to attend. Dr Paisley's more militant Democratic Unionist Party (DUP), the mainly Catholic nationalist Social Democratic and Labour Party (SDLP) and the moderate middle-class Alliance Party did attend but, not altogether surprisingly, there was no real common ground.

We adjourned the conference later in March and began to consider putting forward more specific proposals ourselves in the form of a white paper. Ministers discussed a draft paper from Northern Ireland Secretary Humphrey Atkins in June. I had various changes made in the text in order to take account of Unionist sensitivities. I was no more optimistic than earlier that the initiative would succeed, but I felt that it was worth the effort and agreed that the white paper should be published in early July. It described areas – not including security – in which powers might be transferred to an executive chosen by an assembly in the province. It also spelt out two ways of choosing that

* See pp. 56–9.

executive, one inclining towards majority rule and the other towards power sharing. Discussions with the Northern Irish parties went on during the summer and autumn. But by November it was clear that there would not be sufficient agreement among them to go ahead with the assembly.

In any case, by now Republican prisoners inside the Maze Prison had begun the first of their two hunger strikes. I decided that no major political initiative should be made while the hunger strike was continuing: we must not appear to be bowing to terrorist demands. I was also cautious about any high-profile contacts with the Irish Government at such a time for the same reason.

Charles Haughey had been elected leader of his Fianna Fáil Party and Taoiseach in mid-December 1979. Mr Haughey had throughout his career been associated with the most Republican strand in respectable Irish politics. How 'respectable' was a subject of some controversy: in a famous case in 1970 he had been acquitted of involvement while an Irish minister in the importing of arms for the IRA. That very fact, however, might inhibit his Republicanism. I found him easy to get on with, less talkative and more realistic than Garret FitzGerald, the leader of Fine Gael. Charles Haughey was tough, able and politically astute with few illusions and, I am sure, not much affection for the British. He had come to see me in May at No. 10 and we had had a general and friendly discussion of the scene in Northern Ireland. He kept on drawing the parallel, which seemed to me an unconvincing one, between the solution I had found to the Rhodesian problem and the approach to be pursued in Northern Ireland. Whether this was Irish blarney or calculated flattery I was not sure. He left me a gift of a beautiful Georgian silver teapot, which was kind of him. (It was worth more than the limit allowed for official gifts and I had to leave it behind at No. 10 when I left office.) By the time that I had my next talk with Mr Haughey when we were attending the European Council in Luxemburg on Monday 1 December 1980 it was the hunger strike which was the Irish main concern.

THE HUNGER STRIKES

To understand the background to the hunger strikes it is necessary to refer back to the 'special category' status for convicted terrorist prisoners in Northern Ireland which had been introduced, as a concession to the IRA, in 1972.* This was, and quickly appeared, a bad mistake. It was ended in 1976. Prisoners convicted of such offences after that date were treated as ordinary prisoners – with no greater privileges as regards clothing and association than anyone else. But the policy was not retrospective. So some 'special category' prisoners continued, being held apart and under a different regime from other terrorists. Within the so-called 'H blocks' of the Maze Prison where the terrorist prisoners were housed, protests had been more or less constant, including the revolting 'dirty protest', consisting of fouling cells and smashing up furniture. On 10 October a number of prisoners announced their intention of beginning a hunger strike on Monday 27 October unless certain demands were met. Of these, the most significant were that they should be able to wear their own clothes, associate freely with other 'political' prisoners and refrain from prison work.

There were several discussions among ministers in the interim to see what concessions might be made to avert the strike. All my instincts were against bending to such pressure, and certainly there could be no changes in the prison regime once the strike had begun. There was never any question of conceding political status. But the RUC Chief Constable believed that some concessions before the strike would be helpful in dealing with the threatened public disorder which such a strike might lead to and though we did not believe that they could prevent the hunger strike, we were anxious to win the battle for public opinion. Accordingly, we agreed that all prisoners – not just those who had committed terrorist crimes – might be permitted to wear 'civilian type' clothing – but not their own clothes – as long as they obeyed the prison rules. As I had foreseen, these concessions did not in fact prevent the hunger strike.

To the outside world the issue at stake must have seemed trivial. But both the IRA and the Government understood that it was not. The IRA and the prisoners were determined to gain control of the prison and had a well-thought-out strategy of doing this by whittling away at the prison regime. The purpose of the privileges they claimed was not to improve prisoners' conditions but to take power away from the prison authorities. They were also keen to establish once again, as they felt they had in 1972, that their crimes were 'political', thus

* Convicted criminals sentenced to more than nine months' imprisonment who claimed political motivation and were acceptable to the paramilitary leaders in the gaols were accorded special category status – allowed to wear their own clothes, exempted from work, and segregated in compounds.

giving the perpetrators a kind of respectability, even nobility. This we could not allow. Above all, I would hold fast to the principle that we would not make concessions of any kind while the hunger strike was continuing. The IRA were pursuing with calculated ruthlessness a psychological war alongside their campaign of violence: they had to be resisted at both levels.

As the hunger strike continued and the prospect approached of one or more of the prisoners dying we came under a good deal of pressure. When I met Mr Haughey in the margins of the Luxemburg European Council on Monday 1 December 1980 he urged me to find some face-saving device which would allow the strikers to end their fast, though he said that he fully accepted that political status was out of the question. I replied that the Government could not go on making offers. There was nothing left to give. Nor was I convinced, then or later, that the hunger strikers were able to abandon the strike, even if they had wanted to, against the wishes of the IRA leadership. I had no objection to restating what we had already said, but there would be no more concessions under duress.

We met again exactly a week later for our second Anglo-Irish summit in Dublin. This meeting did more harm than good because, unusually, I did not involve myself closely enough in the drafting of the communiqué and, as a result, allowed through the statement that Mr Haughey and I would devote our next meeting in London 'to special consideration of the totality of relationships within these islands'. Mr Haughey then gave a press briefing which led journalists to write of a breakthrough on the constitutional question. There had of course been no such thing. But the damage had been done and it was a red rag to the Unionist bull.

The Catholic Church was also a factor in dealing with the hunger strike. I explained the circumstances personally to the Pope on a visit to Rome on 24 November. He had as little sympathy for terrorists as I did, as he had made very clear on his visit to the Republic the previous year. After the Vatican brought pressure on the Irish Catholic hierarchy, they issued a statement calling on the prisoners to end their fast, though urging the Government to show 'flexibility'.

Talk of concessions and compromises continued and intensified as we approached the point where one or more of the prisoners was likely to die. It was impossible to predict exactly when this would happen. But then on Thursday 18 December one of the prisoners began to lose consciousness and the strike was abruptly called off. The IRA claimed later that they had done this because we had made concessions, but this was wholly false. By making the claim they sought to excuse their defeat, to discredit us, and to prepare the ground for further protests when the nonexistent concessions failed to materialize.

I had hoped that this would see the end of the hunger strike tactic, and indeed of all the prison protests. But it was not to be so. In January 1981 we tried to bring an end to the 'dirty protest', but within days prisoners who had been moved to clean cells had begun to foul them. Then we received information in February that there might be another hunger strike. It was begun on 1 March 1981 by the IRA leader in the Maze, Bobby Sands, and he was joined at intervals by others. Simultaneously the 'dirty protest' was finally ended, ostensibly to concentrate attention on the hunger strike.

This was the beginning of a time of troubles. The IRA were on the advance politically: Sands himself *in absentia* won the parliamentary seat of Fermanagh and South Tyrone, at a by-election caused by the death of an Independent Republican MP. More generally, the SDLP was losing ground to the Republicans. This was a reflection not just of the increasing polarization of opinion in both communities, which it was the IRA's objective to achieve, but also of the general ineffectiveness of the SDLP MPs. There was some suggestion, to which even some of my advisers gave credence, that the IRA were contemplating ending their terrorist campaign and seeking power through the ballot box. I never believed this. But it indicated how successful their propaganda could be.

Michael Foot, then Leader of the Opposition, came to see me, asking for concessions to the strikers. I was amazed that this thoroughly decent man could take this line and told him so. I reminded him that the conditions in the Maze Prison were among the best in any prison anywhere, well above the general standards prevailing in Britain's overcrowded gaols. We had since gone even further in making improvements than the European Commission on Human Rights had recommended the previous year. I told Michael Foot that he had shown himself to be a 'push-over'. What the terrorist prisoners wanted was political status, and they were not going to get it.

Bobby Sands died on Tuesday 5 May. The date was of some significance for me personally, though I did not know it at the time. From this time forward I became the IRA's top target for assassination.

Sands's death provoked rioting and violence, mainly in Londonderry and Belfast, and the security forces came under increasing strain. It was possible to admire the courage of Sands and the other hunger strikers who died, but not to sympathize with their murderous cause. We had done everything in our power to persuade them to give up their fast.

So had the Catholic Church. I realized that the Church might be able to bring pressure to bear on the hunger strikers, which I could not. So I went as far as I could to involve an organization connected with the Catholic hierarchy (the Irish Commission for Justice and Peace (ICJP)), hoping that the strikers would listen to them – though our reward was to be denounced by the ICJP for going back on undertakings we had allegedly made in the talks we had had with them. This false allegation was supported by Garret FitzGerald who became Taoiseach in place of Mr Haughey at the beginning of July 1981. I wrote to the new Taoiseach to say that he should not be misled into thinking that the problem of the hunger strike was susceptible to an easy solution, wanting only a little flexibility on our part. The protesters were trying to secure a prison regime in which the prisoners – and not the prison officers – determined what went on.

I also saw the Catholic Primate of All-Ireland, Cardinal O'Fiaich, in No. 10 on the evening of Thursday 2 July in the forlorn hope that he might use his influence wisely. Cardinal O'Fiaich was not a bad man; but he was a romantic Republican, whose nationalism seemed to prevail over his Christian duty of offering unqualifed resistance to terrorism and murder. He believed that the hunger strikers were not acting under IRA orders: I was not convinced. He made light of the demands of the prisoners for special category status, and it soon became clear why. He told me that the whole of Northern Ireland was a lie from start to finish. At the root of what the hunger strikers believed they were striking for was a united Ireland. He asked when the time would come that the British Government would admit that its presence was divisive. The only solution was to bring together all the Irish people under a government of Irishmen, whether in a federal or a unitary state. I replied that the course he advocated could not become the policy of the British Government because it was not acceptable to the majority of the population of Northern Ireland. The border was a fact. Those who sought a united Ireland must learn that what could not be won by persuasion would not be won by violence. We spoke bluntly, but it was an instructive meeting.

In striving to end the crisis, I had stopped short of force-feeding, a degrading and itself dangerous practice which I could not support. At all times hunger strikers were offered three meals a day, had constant medical attention and, of course, took water. When the hunger strikers fell into unconsciousness it became possible for their next of kin to instruct the doctors to feed them through a drip. My hope was that the families would use this power to bring an end to the strike. Eventually, after ten prisoners had died, a group of families announced that they would intervene to prevent the deaths of their relatives and the IRA called off the strike on Saturday 3 October. With the strike now over, I authorized some further concessions on clothing, association and loss of remission. But the outcome was a significant defeat for the IRA.

However, the IRA had regrouped during the strikes, making headway in the nationalist community. They now turned to violence on a larger scale, especially on the mainland. The worst incident was caused by an IRA bomb outside Chelsea Barracks on Monday 10 October. A coach carrying Irish Guardsmen was blown up, killing one bystander and injuring many soldiers. The bomb was filled with six-inch nails, intended to inflict as much pain and suffering as possible. I went quickly to the scene and with horrified fascination pulled a nail out of the side of the coach. To say that the people capable of this were animals would be wrong: no animal would do such a thing. I went on to visit the casualties at the three London hospitals to which they had been taken. I came away more determined than ever that the terrorists should be isolated, deprived of their support and defeated.

DEALINGS WITH THE IRISH REPUBLIC

After Garret FitzGerald had overcome his initial inclination to play up to Irish opinion at the British Government's expense I had quite friendly dealings with him – all too friendly, to judge by Unionist reaction to our agreement after a summit in November 1981 to set up the rather grand sounding 'Anglo-Irish Inter-Governmental Council', which really continued the existing ministerial and official contacts under a new name. Garret FitzGerald prided himself on being a cosmopolitan intellectual. He had little time for the myths of Irish Republicanism and would have liked to secularize the Irish Constitution and state, not least – but not just – as a way of drawing the North into a united Ireland. Unfortunately, like many modern liberals, he overestimated his own powers of persuasion over his colleagues and countrymen. He was a man of as many words as Charles Haughey was few. He was also, beneath the skin of sophistication, even more sensitive to imagined snubs and more inclined to exaggerate the importance of essentially trivial issues than Mr Haughey.

How Garret FitzGerald would have reacted to the new proposals we made in the spring of 1982 for 'rolling devolution' of powers to a Northern Ireland Assembly it is difficult to know. But in fact by now the whirligig of Irish politics had brought Charles Haughey back as Taoiseach and Anglo-Irish relations cooled to freezing. The new Taoiseach denounced our proposals for devolution as an 'unworkable mistake' in which he was also joined by the SDLP. But what angered me most was the thoroughly unhelpful stance taken by the Irish Government during the Falklands War, which I have mentioned earlier.*

Jim Prior, who succeeded Humphrey Atkins as Secretary of State for Northern Ireland shortly before the end of the second hunger strike, was a good deal more enthusiastic and optimistic about the proposals in our white paper than I was. Ian Gow, my PPS, was against the whole idea and I shared a number of his reservations. Before publication, I had the text of the white paper substantially changed in order to cut out a chapter dealing with relations with the Irish Republic and, I hoped, minimize Unionist objections: although Ian Paisley's DUP went along with the proposals, many integrationists in the Official Unionist Party were critical. Twenty Conservative MPs voted against the bill when it came forward in May and three junior members of the Government resigned.

If the aim of the white paper initiative was to strengthen the moderates in the nationalist community it certainly did not have this effect. In the elections that October to the Northern Ireland Assembly Sinn Fein won 10 per cent of the total, over half of the vote won by the SDLP. For this, of course, the SDLP's own tactics and negative attitudes were heavily to blame: but they continued them by refusing to take their seats in the assembly when it opened the following month. The campaign itself had been marked by a sharp increase in sectarian murders.

The IRA were still at work on the mainland too. I was chairing a meeting of 'E' Committee in the Cabinet Room on the morning of Tuesday 20 July 1982 when I heard (and felt) the unmistakeable sound of a bomb exploding in the middle distance. I immediately asked that enquiries be made, but continued the meeting. As the morning wore on I noticed, looking out of the window, that the soldiers had not arrived on Horse Guards for their parade. When the news finally came through it was even worse than I feared. Two bombs had exploded, one two hours after the other, in Hyde Park and Regent's Park, the intended victims being in the first case the Household Cavalry and in the second the band of the Royal Green Jackets. Eight people were killed and 53 injured. The carnage was truly terrible. I

* See pp. 191, 216, 223, 225.

heard about it first hand from some of the victims when I went to the hospital the next day.

The return of Garret FitzGerald as Taoiseach in December 1982 provided us with an opportunity to improve the climate of Anglo-Irish relations with a view to pressing the South for more action on security. But I was wary about allowing the Irish to set the pace: Dr FitzGerald's understanding of Unionist sensibilities was no greater than Mr Haughey's and I had plenty of experience already of the exaggerated construction which both nationalists and Unionists placed on even bland pledges of Anglo-Irish co-operation.

I had a meeting with Dr FitzGerald at the European Council at Stuttgart in June 1983. I shared the worry he expressed about the erosion of SDLP support by Sinn Fein. However uninspiring SDLP politicians might be – at least since the departure of the courageous Gerry Fitt – they were the minority's main representatives and an alternative to the IRA. They had to be wooed. But Dr FitzGerald had no suggestions to make about how to get the SDLP to take part in the Northern Ireland Assembly, which was pointless without their participation. He pressed me to agree talks between officials on future co-operation.

I did not think there was much to talk about, but I accepted the proposal. Robert Armstrong, head of the civil service and Cabinet Secretary, and his opposite number in the Republic, Dermot Nally, became the main channels of communication. Over the summer and autumn of 1983 we received a number of informal approaches from the Irish, by no means consistent or clear in content. It became apparent that Dr FitzGerald's Government did not speak with a single voice. At various times and with various degrees of specificity they seemed to be offering to amend Articles 2 and 3 of the Irish Constitution, by which the Republic claims sovereignty over Northern Ireland. We became increasingly sceptical of their ability to deliver this, since it would involve a referendum and divide the Irish Government. We also had well-justified doubts about talk of a more helpful line from the SDLP. On the security side the Irish were offering better co-operation, but proposing also a direct role for the Irish police (the Garda), and possibly the Irish Army, in Northern Ireland itself, as well as a Southern involvement in the Northern courts. They urged another attempt at devolution and, surprisingly, appeared ready to contemplate a return to majority rule.

Most of these ideas were impossible, implying some kind of joint sovereignty over Northern Ireland. Moreover, I disliked intensely this kind of bargaining about security. It seemed to me that to withhold full co-operation to catch criminals and save lives because one wanted some political gain was fundamentally wrong. But the Irish side did not see it like that.

I allowed the talks between the two sides to continue. I also had in mind the political danger of seeming to adopt a negative reaction to new proposals. This in turn meant that I had, within limits, to treat seriously the Republic's so-called 'New Ireland Forum'. This had originally been set up mainly as a way of helping the SDLP at the 1983 general election but Garret FitzGerald was now using it as a sounding board for 'ideas' about the future of Northern Ireland. Since the Unionist parties would take no part in it the outcome was bound to be skewed towards a united Ireland. For my part I was anxious that this collection of nationalists, North and South, might attract international respectability for moves to weaken the Union, so I was intensely wary of them.

BACKGROUND TO THE ANGLO-IRISH AGREEMENT, 1983–1985

I saw Garret FitzGerald at Chequers on the morning of Monday 7 November 1983 for our second bilateral summit. It was a modestly useful discussion, but the Irish always had difficulty understanding that joint sovereignty was a nonstarter. Immediately after the Irish team left I held a further meeting with ministers and officials. I felt that we must now come up with our own proposals and I asked Robert Armstrong to draw up an initial paper setting out the options. I laid special stress on the need for secrecy; a leak would destroy the prospects for a new initiative. This meeting, from our side, was the origin of the later Anglo-Irish Agreement.

The need for Irish help on security was again evident after the appalling murder by the Irish National Liberation Army (INLA) of worshippers at the Pentecostal Gospel Hall at Darkley in County Armagh on Sunday 20 November. In spite of all the fine words about the need to defeat terrorism which I had been hearing from the Taoiseach, the Irish Justice minister refused to meet Jim Prior to review security co-operation and the Garda Commissioner similarly refused to meet the Chief Constable of the RUC.

Then the IRA struck again on the mainland. After lunch on Saturday 17 December I left Chequers to attend a carol concert in the Royal Festival Hall. While I was there I received news that a car bomb had exploded just outside Harrods. I left at the first opportunity and went to the scene. By the time I arrived most of the dead and injured had been removed but I shall never forget the sight of the charred body of a teenage girl lying where she had been blown against the store window. Even by the IRA's own standards this was a particularly callous attack. Five people including two police officers died. The fact that one of the dead was an American should have brought home to US sympathizers with the IRA the real nature of Irish terrorism.

The Harrods bomb was designed to intimidate not just the Government but the British people as a whole. The IRA had chosen the country's most prestigious store at a time when the streets of London were full of shoppers in festive mood looking forward to Christmas. There was an instinctive feeling – in reaction to the outrage – that everyone must go about their business normally. Denis was among those who went to shop in Harrods the following Monday to do just that.

Two days after the bomb we received word that the Irish Cabinet was to meet the following day to consider proscribing Sinn Fein south of the border. I summoned a meeting of ministers straight away to consider our response. Clearly if the Irish proscribed, we would take similar action. But our tentative conclusion was that proscription would not directly affect the fight against Irish terrorism in Great Britain, and would probably lead to disorder and violence in Northern Ireland. In the event the Irish Cabinet decided not to go ahead.

On Christmas Eve I visited the province myself, meeting members of the security forces and the general public. I was all but mobbed by cheering well-wishers in the main street of Bangor, a seaside town in County Down, and added to my rapidly growing collection of Tyrone crystal, purchased on Ulster visits, while Denis acquired another tie.

By the end of the year the prospects for some kind of negotiation seemed reasonable, but the acid test for me would be the question of security. Not that the picture on security was wholly bad. The Irish Government devoted significant resources to security – more on a per capita basis than the United Kingdom. Also co-operation between Dublin and London was good. The real area of difficulty lay in cross-border co-operation between the Garda and the RUC. In spite of our efforts to help, Garda training and use of information were unsatisfactory. These shortcomings were worsened by personal mistrust between Garda and RUC personnel. We wanted to find solutions to these problems, some of which required the Irish to deploy more resources to the border, others of which were really a matter of political will. The best hope on both accounts seemed to lie with an Anglo-Irish

Agreement which would acknowledge in a public way the Republic's interest in the affairs of the North, while keeping decision-making out of its hands and firmly in ours. This was what I now set out to achieve.

In January and February 1984 I held meetings to run through the options. The Irish were keen to pursue possibilities of joint policing and even mixed courts (with British and Irish judges sitting on the same bench), about both of which I had the gravest reservations – reservations which grew stronger still as time went on. The idea, favoured by Dr FitzGerald, of the Garda policing nationalist areas like West Belfast seemed quite impractical: not only would the Unionists have been outraged, the Garda officers would probably have been shot on sight by the IRA. As for joint Anglo-Irish courts, this would have cast doubt on the whole administration of justice which had taken place in the province. Majority decisions in terrorist cases by a mixed court would have been disastrous. The same arguments, with slightly less though sufficient force, applied to the proposal for three-judge courts in Ulster, which was another option favoured by the Irish.

We decided to put forward our own proposals at the beginning of March. Robert Armstrong travelled to Dublin and presented our ideas orally – no papers were exchanged until much later in the talks. Our main idea was to establish a Joint Security Commission, to work up proposals that might include a measure of joint policing along a zone on both sides of the border – the element of reciprocity was crucial to us. We were prepared also to consider other measures with respect to the criminal law and local government in Northern Ireland.

The Irish responded immediately by ruling out the idea of a security zone, though encouraging further talks. They made a counter-approach in May, still based on the idea of 'joint sovereignty', though they sought to get around our fundamental objections by using the term 'joint authority'. I was not at any point prepared to concede this, but at the end of May I authorized Robert Armstrong to develop the idea of a consultative role for the Republic in Northern Ireland. I also requested a study of a quite different approach to the problem: redrawing the existing border with the Republic, which followed the old Irish county lines. My instinct was that there might be political and security gains from getting rid of the anomalies, in the event that our talks with the Irish came to nothing.

There was an important development over the summer: the Irish for the first time explicitly put forward the idea of amending Articles 2 and 3 of their Constitution to make Irish unity an aspiration rather than a legal claim. This was attractive to me, in that I thought it should reassure the Unionists. But it was clear that the Irish would expect a good deal in return, and I still doubted their capacity to deliver the referendum vote. So the net effect of their proposal was actually to make me more pessimistic and suspicious. Also they were trying to go too far too fast. The Irish still hankered after joint authority (indeed this lay behind the subsequent contrary interpretations we and they placed on the provisions of the Anglo-Irish Agreement). I made these points forcefully to Dr FitzGerald when he came to see me at No. 10 on Monday 3 September.

Jim Prior resigned as Northern Ireland Secretary in September 1984 to become chairman of GEC. I brought Douglas Hurd, a former Foreign Office mandarin and a talented political novelist, who had been Ted Heath's political secretary at No. 10 but who had shown a willingness to work in the new ideological climate, into the Cabinet as his replacement. Shortly afterwards I widened the circle of those involved on our side of the talks to include senior officials in the Northern Ireland Office (NIO). We held a meeting of ministers and officials in early October which brought out the likely extent of Unionist objections, and in particular the fact that amendment of Articles 2 and 3 might cut little ice with them; indeed, I was told that 'an aspiration to unity' was scarcely less offensive to the Unionists than an outright claim.

It was at this point that the IRA bombed the Grand Hotel in Brighton. I was not going to appear to be bombed to the negotiating table; the incident confirmed my feeling that we should go slowly, and I feared too that it might be the first of a series which might poison the atmosphere so much that an agreement would prove impossible.

In what remained of October and in early November we toughened our negotiating position. On a visit to Dublin Douglas Hurd and Robert Andrew (the Permanent Secretary of the NIO) made it clear to the Irish that we did not believe that an ambitious package involving amendment of Articles 2 and 3 was possible. It seemed to me that a breakdown might not be far off.

On Wednesday 14 November 1984 I held a meeting of ministers and officials to review the position. I was to meet Garret FitzGerald at our regular Anglo-Irish summit the following week and I was alarmed by the lack of realism which still seemed evident in the Irish proposals. I decided that while I would go to the summit willing to make progress on co-operation I would disabuse him in no uncertain terms of the possibility of joint authority.

When Dr FitzGerald and I met at Chequers on Sunday 18 and Monday 19 November I tried to do just this. I was prepared to offer a Joint Security Commission (though operational security matters in Northern Ireland would remain in our hands) but Dr FitzGerald was still talking of the minority needing to be 'policed by people from their own community'. He was still arguing for power sharing in the Northern Ireland Assembly as a precondition for the SDLP taking part in it, which was almost equally unrealistic given Unionist attitudes. As foreseen, we disagreed sharply over the Irish desire for joint authority. But I agreed that talks at an official level should continue.

At my press conference afterwards I was asked about the conclusions of the New Ireland Forum which had issued a report earlier in the year setting out three 'options' for the future government of Ireland: unification, confederation and joint authority. I listed them and said that each of them was 'out'. There seemed no point in pretending that these were acceptable approaches when they were not. Almost immediately a wave of Irish indignation broke against the defences of Downing Street. Dr FitzGerald attacked me in a 'private' address to his own Parliamentary Party, and was reported to have described my remarks as 'gratuitously offensive'. The Irish Minister of Justice warned our Ambassador that the current crisis in relations was such that the Irish public's tolerance of the IRA would grow and that the Irish Government's ability to deal with terrorism had been weakened.

I was therefore somewhat surprised to hear that the Taoiseach wanted a private meeting with me when I was at Dublin Castle for the European Council in early December. I agreed and we had a short discussion in which he pleaded that extra sensitivity was needed in what was said after eight hundred years of misunderstandings. I felt at the end that I had gained an insight into every one of those eight hundred years.

Nevertheless, discussions with the Irish continued through the first half of 1985. In January they agreed to begin detailed consideration of an agreement on the basis of a British draft, based on the idea of consultation rather than joint authority. But more and more leaks appeared about proposals on joint courts and joint policing from the Irish side. This worsened Unionist distrust still further.

In our discussions with the Irish of a joint Anglo-Irish body as a framework for consultation there was a succession of misunderstandings and disagreements. Although the idea of amending Articles 2 and 3 was clearly now off the agenda, we pressed the Irish for some kind of firm declaration committing them to the principle that unification could only come about with the consent of the majority in Northern Ireland. We hoped that such a declaration would reassure the Unionists, to the extent that such a thing was possible. The Irish wanted the proposed joint body to have a much bigger say over economic and social matters in the North than we were prepared to concede. Nor did the gains we could hope for on security become any clearer. I found myself constantly toning down the commitments which were put before me in our own draft proposals, let alone being prepared to accept those emanating from Dublin. If the arrangements worked badly we must leave ourselves a retreat. In early June I insisted that there should be a review mechanism built into the Anglo-Irish Agreement. I also continued to resist Irish pressure for joint courts and SDLP demands for radical changes in the Ulster Defence Regiment (UDR) and the RUC.

When I met Dr FitzGerald at the Milan European Council on the morning of Saturday 29 June 1985 he said that he was prepared to have the Irish Government state publicly that there could be no change in the status of Northern Ireland without the consent of the majority of the people and acknowledge the fact that this consent did not exist. He was prepared to have a special Irish task force sent to the south side of the border to strengthen security. He was also prepared to have Ireland ratify the European Convention on the Suppression of Terrorism (ECST). But he was still pressing for joint courts, changes in the RUC and the UDR – to be announced as 'confidence-building measures', rather than as part of the agreement itself – and now added the proposal for a major review of sentences for terrorist prisoners if the violence was brought to an end. It remained to be seen whether he could deliver on his promises. But in any case the demands were still unrealistic, as I told him. I could go no further than considering the possibility of joint courts: I was certainly not going to give an assurance in advance that they would be established. I considered a review of sentences quite out of the question and he did not press the point. I warned him that announcing measures on policing at the same time as the Anglo-Irish Agreement would cause a sharp Unionist reaction and jeopardize the whole position.

At this point Dr FitzGerald became very agitated. He declared that unless the minority in Northern Ireland could be turned against the IRA, Sinn Fein would gain the upper hand in the North and provoke a civil war which would drag the Republic down as well, with Colonel Gaddafi providing millions to help this happen. A sensible point was being exaggerated to the level of absurdity. I said that of course I shared his aim of preventing Ireland falling under hostile and tyrannical forces. But that was not an argument for taking measures which would simply provoke the Unionists and cause unnecessary trouble.

By the time our meeting ended, however, I felt that we were some way towards an agreement, though there were still points to resolve. I also knew that a lot of progress had been made in the official talks, so I had good reason to believe that a successful conclusion was possible. Dr FitzGerald and I even discussed the timing and place of the signing ceremony.

THE ANGLO-IRISH AGREEMENT – AND REACTIONS: 1985–1987

At two o'clock on the afternoon of Friday 15 November Garret FitzGerald and I signed the Anglo-Irish Agreement at Hillsborough Castle in Northern Ireland. It was not perfect from either side's point of view. Article 1 of the agreement affirmed that any change in the status of Northern Ireland would only come about with the consent of a majority of the people of Northern Ireland and recognized that the present wish of that majority was for no change in the status of the province. I believed that this major concession by the Irish would reassure the Unionists that the Union itself was not in doubt. I thought that given my own well-known attitude towards Irish terrorism they would have confidence in my intentions. I was wrong about that. But the Unionists miscalculated too. The tactics which they used to oppose the agreement – a general strike, intimidation, flirting with civil disobedience – worsened the security situation and weakened their standing in the eyes of the rest of the United Kingdom.

The agreement allowed the Irish Government to put forward views and proposals on matters relating to Northern Ireland in a wide range of areas, including security. But it was made clear that there was no derogation from the sovereignty of the United Kingdom. It was for us, not the Irish, to make the decisions. There was no commitment to do anything more than consider the possibility of mixed courts. If there was devolution in Northern Ireland, which the agreement committed us to work for, those areas of policy devolved would be taken out of the hands of the Anglo-Irish Inter-Governmental Conference. (Garret FitzGerald, showing some courage, publicly accepted this implication of the agreement at the press conference which followed the signing.) The agreement itself would be subject to review at the end of three years or earlier if either Government requested. The Taoiseach also said that it was the intention of his Government to accede as soon as possible to the ECST.

The real question now was whether the agreement would result in better security. The strong opposition of the Unionists would be a major obstacle. By contrast, international – most importantly American – reaction was very favourable. Above all, however, we hoped for a more co-operative attitude from the Irish Government, security forces and courts. If we got this the agreement would be successful. We would have to wait and see.

One person who was not going to wait was Ian Gow. I spent some time trying to persuade him not to go but he insisted on resigning as a Treasury minister. This was a personal blow to me, though I am glad to say that the friendship between the two of us and our families was barely affected. Ian was one of the very few who resigned from my Government on a point of principle. I respected him as much as I disagreed with him.

By the end of the year, however, I had become very worried about the Unionist reaction. It was worse than anyone had predicted to me. Of the legitimate political leaders, Ian Paisley was in the forefront of the mass campaign against the agreement. But far more worrying was the fact that behind him and other leaders stood harder and more sinister figures who might all too easily cross the line from civil disobedience to violence. As I told Dr FitzGerald when I saw him on the morning of Tuesday 3 December in Luxemburg, it was now vital to show immediate practical results from the agreement, particularly as regards security co-operation, Irish accession to the ECST and a co-operative attitude by the SDLP to devolution. But now, as later, it seemed to me that he could not grasp how important it was to achieve the support or at least the acquiescence of the Unionist majority.

Shortly before the agreement, Tom King had taken over as Secretary of State for Northern Ireland. Tom was initially highly sceptical about the value of the agreement – indeed within weeks of taking office he had sent me a minute arguing that the balance of the agreement as drafted was heavily in favour of the Irish – though he later became more enthusiastic. Both of us agreed that the political priority was to win over the support of at least some Unionist leaders and that wider Unionist opinion which I felt was probably more understanding of what we were trying to achieve. I was convinced that the people who met me on my visits to Northern Ireland could harbour no doubts about my commitment to their safety and freedom. Indeed, this was confirmed for me when I invited nonpolitical representatives of the majority community from business and the professions to lunch at No. 10 on Wednesday 5 February 1986. Their view was that for many people the real concerns in Northern Ireland were with jobs, housing, education – in short the sort of issues which are at the centre of politics on the mainland. I was also confirmed in my impression that one of the problems of Northern Irish politics was that it no longer attracted enough people of high calibre.

I invited Jim Molyneaux and Ian Paisley to Downing Street on the morning of Tuesday 25 February. I told them that I believed that they underestimated the advantages which the agreement offered, both in the reaffirmation of Northern Ireland's status within the United Kingdom and in terms of cross-border security co-operation. I recognized that they were bitter at not having been consulted during the negotiation of the agreement. I offered to devise a system which would allow full consultation with them in future and which would not just be confined to matters discussed in the Anglo-Irish Inter-Governmental Conference. Security, for example, could be included. I also said that we were prepared in principle to sit down at a round-table conference with the parties in Northern Ireland to consider, without any preconditions, the scope for devolution. Third, we were ready for consultations with the Unionist parties on the future of the existing Northern Ireland Assembly and on the handling of Northern Ireland business at Westminster. I made it plain that I would not agree to even temporary suspension of the Anglo-Irish Agreement, but the agreement would be operated 'sensitively'. At the time this seemed to go down well. I went on to warn of the damage which would be done if the proposed general strike in Northern Ireland on 3 March took place. Ian Paisley said that he and Jim Molyneaux knew nothing of the plans. They would reach their decisions when they had considered the outcome of the present meeting. It was a reasonably successful meeting. But the following day after they had consulted their supporters in Northern Ireland they came out in support of the strike.

Nor did I find the SDLP any more co-operative. I saw John Hume in my room in the House of Commons on the afternoon of Thursday 27 February. I urged that the SDLP should give more open support to the security forces, but to no avail. He seemed more interested to score points at the expense of the Unionists. A few days later I wrote to Garret FitzGerald urging him to get the SDLP to adopt a more sensible and statesman-like approach.

But by now Dr FitzGerald and his colleagues in Dublin were adding their own fuel to the flames, publicly exaggerating the powers which the Irish had obtained through the agreement, a tactic which was of course entirely self-defeating. Nor, in spite of detailed criticisms and suggestions, could we get the Irish to make the required improvements in their own security. The Irish judicial authorities were proving no more co-operative either, having sent back warrants for the arrest and extradition of Evelyn Glenholmes from the Irish Republic on suspicion of involvement in terrorism because, among other things, they claimed that a full stop was missing.

In any case, Garret FitzGerald's Government's own position was weakening. In spite of our representations, he was back-tracking on his commitment to get the European Convention on the Suppression of Terrorism though the Dáil. His Government was now in a minority and he told us that he was under pressure to accept the requirement that we should make a *prima facie* case before extradition to the United Kingdom was granted. This would actually have worsened the situation on extradition, reviving past difficulties which recent Irish judge-made law had overcome. Dr FitzGerald told us that he was resisting the pressure, but it soon became clear that he was seeking a *quid pro quo*. He wanted us to introduce three-judge courts for terrorist trials in Northern Ireland. Following a meeting with the Taoiseach in Dublin, Tom King brought forward a paper supporting the idea, which Geoffrey Howe and Douglas Hurd also backed. But the lawyers were outraged and my sympathies lay with them. I did not believe that there was a case for three-judge courts, nor did I see why we should make concessions to get the Irish Government to carry out its commitments. The proposal was turned down at a ministerial meeting at the beginning of October 1986.

In the end Dr FitzGerald managed to pass his legislation, but with the proviso that it would not come into effect unless the Dáil passed a further resolution a year later, which stored up trouble for the future. Shortly afterwards, in January 1987, his Coalition Government collapsed and the subsequent election brought Charles Haughey back to the office of Taoiseach. This heralded more difficulties. Mr Haughey and his Party had opposed the agreement, though his formal position was now that he would be prepared to make it work. I knew, though, that he felt much less commitment to it and I suspected that he would be prepared to play up to Republican opinion in the South more than had his predecessor.

The security position in the province had also worsened. I received a report from George Younger on the strength of the IRA north and south of the border which convinced me that a new drive against them was necessary. There was a rising trend of violence, particularly against personnel in the security forces, and cross-border co-operation was still not effective. The scale of the supplies of arms being received by the IRA, on which we already had a good deal of intelligence, was confirmed by the interception of the *Eksund* – with its hoard of Libyan arms – by French customs in October.

IRA ATTACKS AND EXTRA SECURITY MEASURES, 1987–1990

I was at the reception which follows the Remembrance Day Service at the Cenotaph when I received news that a bomb had exploded at Enniskillen in County Fermanagh. It had been planted yards away from the town War Memorial in an old school building, part of which collapsed on the crowd which had assembled for the service. Eleven people were killed, and more than sixty injured. No warning was given.

The next day (Monday 9 November) I met a delegation of Jim Molyneaux, Ken Maginnis, the local MP, and people from Enniskillen. They wanted me to go much further in tightening security, by ending the present 50 per cent remission available to sentenced terrorist prisoners,* by proscribing Sinn Fein, by tightening control of the border, by ending the so-called 'right to silence' (the provision whereby the refusal to answer questions cannot be adduced as evidence of guilt in court) and by bringing back internment.** I too believed that there must be a new review of security: indeed, I had already initiated one. I would see which if any of these was practicable.

At least I felt that I could make one personal gesture which would be appreciated. On Sunday 22 November I flew to Northern Ireland to attend a Remembrance Service at St Martin's Cathedral, Enniskillen. It was a cold, wet day. After the service I talked briefly to the bereaved, including Mr Gordon Wilson whose daughter Marie had died beside him in the explosion and who had publicly forgiven the murderers in terms which inspired – perhaps shamed – those who heard him.

From now on the requirements for practical improvements in security, reviewed after each new tragedy, increasingly dominated my policy towards both Northern Ireland and the Republic. It slowly became clear that the wider gains for which I had hoped from greater support

* Prisoners on the mainland received 33 per cent remission: we acted to remove this extraordinary anomaly by reducing remission in Northern Ireland to the same level the following year.

** Internment – detention without trial – had been introduced at the height of the troubles in 1971, and phased out by 1975.

by the nationalist minority in Northern Ireland or the Irish Government and people for the fight against terrorism were not going to be forthcoming. Only the international dimension became noticeably easier to deal with as a result of the agreement. My reluctant conclusion was that terrorism would have to be met with more and more effective counter-terrorist activity; and that in fighting terror we would have to stand almost alone, while the Irish indulged in gesture politics.

Nonetheless, I kept up the pressure on the Irish for effective extradition arrangements of terrorists suspected of offences committed within the United Kingdom. Predictably, the Haughey Government was unwilling to confirm the Extradition Act that Dr FitzGerald had passed at the end of his administration without trying to exact a price. We heard the familiar plea for three-judge courts, followed by a new demand for our Attorney-General to provide his Irish counterpart with a note confirming his intention to prosecute founded on a sufficiency of evidence – a note that could be scrutinized by the Irish courts. This was an impossible scheme and we rejected it. The upshot was new Irish legislation that for a time brought extradition to a halt altogether.

In the meantime our own review of security had come to a number of conclusions, principally the redeployment of the army to strengthen anti-terrorist operations and to patrol in areas close to the border. As a matter of courtesy I wrote to Mr Haughey in January 1988 informing him of what we were doing. But it soon appeared that a more far-reaching review of security was required – and that we could rely only on a thoroughly unhelpful attitude from the Irish in the course of it.

On Sunday 6 March three Irish terrorists were shot dead by our security forces in Gibraltar. There was not the slightest doubt about the terrorists' identity or intentions. Contrary to later reports, the Spanish authorities had been extremely co-operative. The funeral of the terrorists was held in Milltown Cemetery, Belfast. From the thousands attending you would imagine that these people were martyrs not would-be murderers. The spiral of violence now accelerated. A gunman attacked the mourners, three of whom were killed and 68 injured. It was at the funeral of two of these mourners that what was to remain in my mind as the single most horrifying event in Northern Ireland during my term of office occurred.

No one who saw the film of the lynching of the two young soldiers trapped by that frenzied Republican mob, pulled from their car, stripped and murdered, will believe that reason or goodwill can ever be a substitute for force when dealing with Irish Republican terrorism. I went to be with the relatives of our murdered soldiers when the bodies were brought back to Northolt; I shall not forget the remark of Gerry Adams, the Sinn Fein leader, that I would have many more bodies to meet in that way. I could hardly believe it when the BBC initially refused to supply to the RUC film which might have been useful in bringing to justice the perpetrators of this crime, though they later complied. But I knew that the most important task was for us to use every means available to beat the IRA. On the same day as the news came in of what had happened I told Tom King that there must be a paper brought forward setting out all the options. I was determined that nothing should be ruled out.

On the afternoon of Tuesday 22 March I held an initial meeting. The policing of funerals was already under review. I said that the security forces must take all necessary steps, including extensive searches in nationalist areas, to apprehend those responsible for the murder of the British Army corporals. Measures to improve the chances of securing convictions in Northern Ireland courts – such as the use of DNA finger-printing, and the ending of the 'right to silence' and measures to seize the finances of groups which practised or supported violence – should be investigated. Cross-border security co-operation must be strengthened and security on the border itself must be improved. We must examine whether the instructions about the circumstances in which the security forces could use their weapons (the 'yellow card') should be reviewed in case they were too restrictive. In addition, I said that more far-reaching measures must now be considered. Perhaps Sinn Fein should be banned. We should consider the introduction of selective internment, which would be much more effective if it were introduced simultaneously in the Republic. I wondered whether the introduction of identity cards in Northern Ireland might enable us to control more easily the movements of suspects. Should the numbers of soldiers in Northern Ireland be increased? Should the present doctrine of so-called 'police primacy' be reversed to give the army control in security matters? Could we do more to deprive the terrorists of the 'oxygen of publicity' (a phrase I borrowed with permission but without attribution from the Chief Rabbi)? In fact, many of these possibilities would have to be jettisoned on one ground or another. But I felt that I owed it to those two soldiers and their families to ensure that nothing which could save other young lives was overlooked.

This far-reaching security review continued during the spring. Mr Haughey added to the problem of restoring confidence and stability in Northern Ireland by an astonishing speech which he made in the United States in April. This listed all of his objections to British policy, lumping together the Attorney-General's decision not to initiate prosecutions following the Stalker-Sampson Report into the RUC,* the Court of Appeal's rejection of the appeal of the so-called 'Birmingham Six'** (as if it was for the British Government to tell British courts how to administer justice), the killing of the terrorists in Gibraltar and other matters. There was no mention in his speech of IRA violence, no acknowledgement of the need for cross-border co-operation and no commitment to the Anglo-Irish Agreement. It was a shabby case of playing to the American Irish gallery.

I wrote to Mr Haughey on Wednesday 27 April to protest in the most vigorous terms. I took him to task not only for what he had said but for what he had failed to deliver on cross-border security co-operation. In spite of an ill-judged speech by Geoffrey Howe in which he said that he did not 'underestimate the hurt felt by the Irish in recent months', I let it be known that there was no possibility of ordinary relations with Dublin resuming until I received a reply to my letter – a reply which was not forthcoming until Wednesday 15 June. The reply, when it came, was short and noncommittal. But I felt that my sharp letter had done some good when I received a long message from Mr Haughey prior to my meeting with him at the end of the European Council in Hanover on Tuesday 28 June. In this he reaffirmed in the strongest terms his opposition to terrorism, repeated his commitment to the Anglo-Irish Agreement and conveyed his personal support for security co-operation. But the statement also showed what we were up against; for he made clear that his whole approach was based on the objective of a united Ireland and that he saw the Anglo-Irish Agreement as a staging post to that. That was utterly unacceptable to us.

At the next European Council in Hanover I took up the question of security co-operation, which was of far more importance to me than any personal differences. I said that though Mr Haughey had affirmed that he had difficulties with Irish public opinion about this, I had difficulty myself about bombs, guns, explosions, people being beaten to death and naked hatred. I had had to see ever more young men in the security forces killed. We knew that the terrorists went over the

* The Stalker-Sampson Report was the outcome of a police enquiry into a series of fatal incidents in 1982 in which the RUC was alleged to have operated a 'shoot-to-kill' policy in dealing with terrorist suspects.

** The 'Birmingham Six' were six Irishmen convicted of multiple murders resulting from the IRA bombing of two pubs in Birmingham in 1974. A long campaign was undertaken to prove the convictions unsafe, eventually resulting in their release. At this time, however, their latest appeal had just been rejected by the Court of Appeal.

border to the Republic to plan their operations and to store their weapons. We got no satisfactory intelligence of their movements. Once they crossed the border they were lost. Indeed, we received far better intelligence co-operation from virtually all other European countries than with the Republic. If it was a question of resources, then we were ready to offer equipment and training. Or if this were politically difficult, there were other countries who could offer such help. There was no room for amateurism.

Mr Haughey defended the Irish Government's and security forces' record. But I was not convinced. I said that I wondered whether Mr Haughey realized that the biggest concentration of terrorists anywhere in the world save Lebanon was to be found in Ireland. The border was virtually open so far as terrorists were concerned. I accepted that the Republic's resources were limited, but I was not satisfied that they were using them to best effect. I said that the results of the Anglo-Irish Agreement so far had been disappointing. Nor was I any less disappointed by the attitude of the SDLP. As for the suggestion that all would be peace and light if there were a united Ireland, as Mr Haughey's recent message had suggested, the reality was that there would be the worst civil war ever. In any case, most nationalists in the North would prefer to continue to live there because they were much better provided for than in the Republic. Indeed, there continued to be a substantial flow of Irish immigrants to the UK, who were a significant burden on the welfare system.

Surprisingly, perhaps, though we were both pretty outspoken, neither of us, I believe, left our meeting with any ill will or rancour. Mr Haughey knew where I stood. He had, as it turned out, taken seriously at least some of what I had said about the shortcomings of Irish security co-operation. I, for my part, felt that I understood him better than I had before – and better perhaps than I ever did Garret FitzGerald.

There was a surge in IRA violence from early August. It began with an IRA bomb at an Army Communications Centre in Mill Hill in North London. One soldier was killed. This was the first mainland bomb since 1984. I was at Alice Springs on a visit to Australia when I learnt the news. Irish Republican sympathizers – on the streets and in the media – did their best to disrupt my tour. There were some particularly awkward moments in Melbourne where crowds of both opponents and well-wishers were funnelled into an overcrowded shopping precinct by Australian police, inexperienced in dealing with such situations. But I took every opportunity to express my contempt for the IRA. In a television interview I said that 'they should be wiped off the civilized world.'

The bombing campaign continued. I was on holiday in Cornwall when I was woken very early on Saturday 20 August to be told of an attack at Ballygawley in County Tyrone on a bus carrying British soldiers travelling from Belfast back from a fortnight's leave. Seven were dead and twenty-eight injured. I immediately decided to return to London and helicoptered into the Wellington Barracks at 9.20 a.m. Archie Hamilton (my former PPS, who was now Armed Forces minister) came straight in to No. 10 to brief me. He told me that the bus had not been on its designated route at the time of the explosion but on a parallel road some three miles away. A very large bomb, wire-controlled, had been laid in wait for the bus and then detonated. I questioned whether this could be a safe way of moving our troops around the province. But I accepted that perhaps there was no such thing as a 'safe way'.

Ken Maginnis MP, whose constituency was yet again the scene of this tragedy, came in to see me over lunch, accompanied by a local farmer who had been first on the scene and a surgeon at the local hospital who had operated on some of the wounded. Then that evening I held a long meeting with Tom King, Archie and the security forces chiefs for the province.

Although the bus had been travelling on a forbidden route this did not seem to be material to what had happened. The IRA had from 1986 acquired access to Semtex explosive material, produced in Czechoslovakia and probably supplied through Libya. This substance was extremely powerful, light and relatively safe to use and as a result had given the terrorists a new technical advantage. The device could, therefore, have been planted very quickly and so the attack could have occurred on either route. It was also clear that the IRA had been planning their campaign for some time. The RUC reported that the terrorists were well prepared and had been successful in bringing large quantities of arms and explosives from the South. We then went on to discuss the co-ordination of intelligence, security co-operation with the Republic, the need to control the availability of fertilizers (which could be used as a basis for making bombs), the position on sentencing and remission and other matters. I called for more papers on all these subjects and for a vigorous follow-through on all the issues of security which I had raised after the murder of our soldiers in West Belfast earlier in the year.

Later that month I held several meetings to go through in detail what further action we should take. On the evening of Tuesday

6 September I chaired a meeting of the ministers and officials concerned. I noted that the expected IRA offensive had materialized. We had a number of possible proposals for action. But we would not be announcing a package of measures. Some would become public knowledge as they were implemented or introduced in Parliament. But in other areas I wanted to keep the terrorists guessing. Consequently it would not be possible to brief the Irish Government on our intentions, although we would inform them of individual measures shortly before their introduction.

Then we went through the possibilities one by one. Some measures – like the proscription of Sinn Fein or the removal of British citizenship from undesirables with British/Irish dual citizenship,* or the introduction of minimum sentences for terrorist offences – looked less promising the more they were discussed. But others – cutting back on the 50 per cent remission for all prisoners in Northern Ireland, ensuring that those convicted of certain terrorist offences would serve consecutively with a new sentence the unexpired portion of an earlier remitted sentence, measures to deal with terrorist finance, improvement of intelligence co-ordination – all these required further work.

I continued to go through the possibilities with ministers at a second meeting on the afternoon of Thursday 29 September. At this meeting I particularly concentrated on the army's role. It was important to reduce the number of unnecessary commitments of army manpower in Northern Ireland in order to allow them to concentrate their efforts where they were most required.

One measure which we announced publicly in October was the prohibition of broadcast statements by Sinn Fein and other Northern Irish supporters of terrorism. This immediately provoked cries of censorship: but I have no doubt that not only was it justified but that it has worked, and there is some reason to believe that the terrorists think so too. Measures to cut Northern Ireland remission and to change the 'right to silence' in Northern Irish courts were also introduced, as was action against terrorist finance.

More and more in the struggle to bring peace and order to Northern Ireland, we were being forced back on our own resources. Because of the professionalism and experience of our security forces, those resources were adequate to contain, but not as yet to defeat the IRA. Terrible tragedies continued to occur. Yet the terrorists did not man-

* In Irish law every person born in Ireland is an Irish citizen from birth, but those born in Northern Ireland do not become Irish citizens unless they declare themselves so to be.

age to make even parts of the province ungovernable, nor were they successful in undermining the self-confidence of Ulster's majority community or the will of the Government to maintain the Union.

The fact remained that the contribution which the Anglo-Irish Agreement was making to all this was very limited. The Unionists continued to oppose it – though with less bitterness as it became clear that their worst fears had proved unfounded. It never seemed worth pulling out of the agreement altogether because this would have created problems not only with the Republic but, more importantly, with broader international opinion as well.

Still, I was disappointed by the results. The Patrick Ryan case demonstrated just how little we could seriously hope for from the Irish. Ryan, a nonpractising Catholic priest, was well known in security service circles as a terrorist; for some time he had played a significant role in the Provisional IRA's links with Libya. The charges against Ryan were of the utmost seriousness, including conspiracy to murder and explosives offences. In June 1988 we had asked the Belgians to place him under surveillance. They, in turn, pressed us strongly to apply for extradition. So the application was made in close co-operation with the Belgian authorities. The Belgian court which considered the extradition request gave an advisory opinion, which we knew to have been favourable – something which the Belgian Government never denied – to the Minister of Justice. The latter then took the decision to the Belgian Cabinet. The Cabinet decided to ignore the court's opinion and to fly Ryan to Ireland, only telling us afterwards. Presumably this political decision was prompted by fear of terrorist retaliation if the Belgians co-operated with us.

We now sought the extradition of Ryan from the Republic; but this was refused, initially on what seemed a technicality, though the Irish Attorney-General later suggested that Ryan would not receive a fair trial before a British jury. I wrote a vigorous protest to Mr Haughey. I had already taken up the matter personally with him and with the Belgian Prime Minister, M. Martens, at the European Council in Rhodes on Friday 2 and Saturday 3 December 1988. I told both of them how appalled I was. I was particularly angry with M. Martens. I reminded him how his Government's attitude contrasted with all the co-operation we had given Belgium over those British people charged in relation to the Heysel Football Stadium riot.* I was

* British football fans had attacked Italian fans at the Heysel Stadium in Brussels in 1985, crushing thirty-eight of them to death when a wall collapsed. Twenty-six were later extradited from Britain to face charges in Belgium.

unconvinced and unmoved by M. Martens's explanations. His Government had clearly taken its decision in contradiction to and in defiance of legal advice. As I warned him I would, I then told the press of my views in very similar terms. But as a Belgian government under the same M. Martens later showed at the time of the Gulf War, it would take more than this to provide them with a spine. And Patrick Ryan is still at large.

I had moved Peter Brooke to become Northern Ireland Secretary in the reshuffle of July 1989. Peter's family connections with the province and his deep interest in Ulster affairs made him seem an ideal choice. His unflappable good humour also meant that no one would be better suited for trying to bring the parties of Northern Ireland together for talks. Soon after his appointment I authorized him to do so: these talks were still continuing at the time I left office.

Meanwhile, the struggle to maintain security continued. So did the IRA's murderous campaign. On Friday 22 September ten bandsmen were killed in a blast at the Royal Marines School of Music at Deal. The following summer the IRA's mainland campaign resumed. June 1990 saw bombs explode outside Alistair McAlpine's former home and then at the Conservative Party's Carlton Club. But it was the following month that I experienced again something of that deep personal grief I had felt when Airey was killed and when I learned, early on that Friday morning at Brighton in 1984, of the losses in the Grand Hotel bomb attack.

Ian Gow was singled out to be murdered by the IRA because they knew that he was their unflinching enemy. Even though he held no government office, Ian was a danger to them because of his total commitment to the Union. No amount of terror can succeed in its aim if even a few outspoken men and women of integrity and courage dare to call terrorism murder and any compromise with it treachery. Nor, tragically, was Ian someone who took his own security precautions seriously. And so the IRA's bomb killed him that Monday morning, 30 July, as he started up his car in the drive of his house. I could not help thinking, when I heard what had happened, that my daughter Carol had travelled with Ian in his car the previous weekend to take the Gows' dog out for a walk: it might have been her too. I went down to Eastbourne to see Jane Gow in the early afternoon and we spoke for an hour or so. That evening I went to a service in the Anglo-Catholic church where Ian and Jane always worshipped and I was moved to see it full of people who had come in from work at the end of the day to mourn Ian's loss. Whenever Jane came to Chequers to see me she used to play the piano there – she is a fine pianist. She once remarked to me, speaking of the loss of Ian, 'people say it gets better, but it doesn't.' That must always be true of someone you love, whatever the manner of their death. But for some reason the loss of a friend or family member by violence leaves an even deeper scar.

The IRA will not give up their campaign unless they are convinced that there is no possibility of forcing the majority of the people of Northern Ireland against their will into the Republic. That is why our policy must never give the impression that we are trying to lead the Unionists into a united Ireland either against their will or without their knowledge. Moreover, it is not enough to decry individual acts of terrorism but then refuse to endorse the measures required to defeat it. That applies to American Irish who supply Noraid with money to kill British citizens; to Irish politicians who withhold co-operation in clamping down on border security; and to the Labour Party that for years has withheld its support from the Prevention of Terrorism Act which has saved countless lives.

Ian Gow and I had our disagreements, above all about the Anglo-Irish Agreement: but for the right of those whose loyalties are to the United Kingdom to remain its citizens and enjoy its protection I believe, as did Ian, that no price is too high to pay.

In dealing with Northern Ireland, successive governments have studiously refrained from security policies that might alienate the Irish Government and Irish nationalist opinion in Ulster, in the hope of winning their support against the IRA. The Anglo-Irish Agreement was squarely in this tradition. But I discovered the results of this approach to be disappointing. Our concessions alienated the Unionists without gaining the level of security co-operation we had a right to expect. In the light of this experience it is surely time to consider an alternative approach.

CHAPTER XV

Keeps Raining all the Time

The mid-term political difficulties of 1985–1986

A POLITICAL MALAISE

Whatever long-term political gains might accrue from the successful outcome of the miners' strike, from the spring of 1985 onwards we faced accumulating political difficulties. Matters of no great importance in themselves, and often of limited interest to the general public, were invested within the hyperactive and incestuous world of Westminster with huge significance. The phenomenon is by no means uniquely British: my American friends tell me frequently of the gulf which separates the priorities of the 'beltway' from those outside it. So any democratic politician must be able to distinguish between the two – and recognize the pre-eminence of the second.

That spring the Labour Party started to move ahead of us in the opinion polls. In the local elections in May we lost control of a number of shire counties, mainly to the benefit of the SDP/Liberal Alliance. Francis Pym took the opportunity to launch a new grouping of Conservative MPs critical of my policies. The group was officially known as 'Centre Forward'. Its failure to come up with any coherent alternative, however, caused it to be dubbed in a *Times* editorial as 'Centre Backward'. A number of Francis's supporters hurried to disclaim any connection with the group and after the initial flurry of publicity it sank into oblivion. But that did not alter the fact that, as the columns of the press showed daily, there were rumblings of dissent within the Parliamentary Party. I could not ignore them.

Opinions frayed further in July – always a bad-tempered time in British politics as MPs become restless to return to their constituencies, or in some cases to their villas in Chianti-shire. On Thursday 4 July we had a spectacularly bad by-election result at Brecon and Radnor, which was won by the Alliance on a swing of almost 16 per cent from the Conservatives: our candidate came in third. It was described –

not quite accurately – as the worst Tory defeat since 1962. By-election results always have to be taken seriously, even though they are a poor indication of what would happen at a general election when people know they are voting for a government rather than registering a protest. But the press was full of unattributable criticism of the Government and of me personally which, having about it an unmistakeable whiff of panic, confirmed that the Parliamentary Party had a bad case of the wobbles.

Then a fortnight later the publication of our acceptance of the Top Salary Review Board (TSRB) recommendations provided the occasion for a large back-bench revolt in the House of Commons. What caused the outrage was the large increases for top civil servants. There was no doubt in my mind that we could not retain the right people in vitally important posts in government administration unless their salaries bore at least some comparison with their counterparts in the private sector. The cost of doing this to the public purse was, of course, only a tiny fraction of even a modest increase to large groups of public sector workers. I came to the conclusion that it was best to put the anomaly right at one go. When the Labour Party erupted I reminded them that Jim Callaghan had done the same thing in 1978. That said, we did not handle the issue well. Fear of leaks meant that those entrusted with explaining the rationale of our policy simply did not know about it in time. Even Bernard Ingham had been kept in the dark which, when he raised the matter with me afterwards, I conceded was absurd. In future we handled the TSRB announcements much more carefully. But for this occasion the damage had been done.

Generally, a political malaise spreads because underlying economic conditions are bad or worsening. But this was not the case on this occasion. True, inflation had moved upwards from the low point it had reached after the election and unemployment, always a lagging indicator, remained stubbornly high; but the economy was growing quite fast. It became clear to me that the root of our problems was presentation and therefore personnel. Of course, there is a tendency for all governments – particularly Conservative governments – to blame presentation and not policy for their woes: but in 1985 it really was the case that some ministers were not in the right jobs and could not explain our policies to the people. So there was only one way of changing the image of the Government and that was by changing its members. A reshuffle was required.

THE 1985 RESHUFFLE

My first discussion about the 1985 reshuffle was with Willie Whitelaw and John Wakeham, now Chief Whip, over supper in the flat at No. 10 in late May. Willie and John were both shrewd and party to the gossip which constitutes parliamentary opinion. Each had his own personal likes and dislikes, which I would privately try to discount, but I listened to their advice very carefully. They urged on me a July reshuffle. I could not agree with them. I hated sacking ministers and I could not prevent myself thinking what it meant to them and their families, suddenly losing salary, car and prestige.* I used to like to feel that they would have the long summer recess in office before coming back in September to learn the bad news. The trouble was that the press would then spend the whole of that period speculating on who was to stay and who would go. So I eventually agreed to reshuffles at the end of July; but not yet.

Planning a reshuffle is immensely complex. There is never a perfect outcome. It is necessary to get the main decisions about the big offices of state right and then work outward and downward from these. Nor is it possible always to give the best positions to one's closest supporters. Not only must the Cabinet to some extent reflect the varying views in the Parliamentary Party at a particular time: there are some people that it is better to bring in because they would cause more trouble outside. Peter Walker and, to a lesser extent, Kenneth Clarke are examples, precisely because they fought their corner hard. There is another problem: I generally found that the Left seemed to be best at presentation, the Right at getting the job done – although Norman Tebbit and Cecil Parkinson managed to do both.

I wanted to ensure that the Government's policies were presented properly between now and the general election. This meant some movement in the most senior three posts – Chancellor, Foreign Secretary and Home Secretary. Nigel Lawson was turning out to be an effective tax-reforming Chancellor. Geoffrey Howe seemed a competent Foreign Secretary; I had not yet taken the full measure of our disagreements. Leon Brittan was the obvious candidate to be moved:

* Three months' redundancy pay had been available to ministers in the Lords since 1984, and we introduced legislation to extend the scheme to the Commons in July 1990. Due to lack of time the scheme was only enacted in February 1991.

however unfairly, he just did not carry conviction with the public. I knew that he would be devastated, but it had to be done.

I asked Leon to come to Chequers on Sunday afternoon 1 September where Willie, John and I were putting the final touches to the decisions. Willie is a good judge of character. He told me that the first thing Leon would ask when I broke the news to him was whether he would keep his order of precedence in the Cabinet list. To my surprise, this was indeed what he asked. Forewarned, I was able to reassure him. I was also able to say – and mean it – that with complex Financial Services legislation coming up to provide a framework of regulation for the City Leon's talents would be well employed at the Department of Trade and Industry to which I was moving him.

I replaced Leon at the Home Office with Douglas Hurd, who looked more the part, was immensely reassuring to the police, and, though no one could call him a natural media performer, inspired a good deal of confidence in the Parliamentary Party. He had become a harder and wiser man through serving as Secretary of State for Northern Ireland. He also knew the department, having earlier been Leon's number two there. By and large, it was a successful appointment.

I had to move Leon; but was I right to move him to the DTI? Although the main fault in what lay ahead certainly resided elsewhere, Leon's attitude on going to his new department carried its own dangers. He was obviously shaken – friends later described him as somewhat demoralized – and determined to make his political mark. As a result he proved oversensitive about his position when the Westland affair blew up. All this made for errors of judgement when facing a ruthless opponent like Michael Heseltine. It turned out that the DTI had even more pitfalls for this civilized but not very streetwise politician than did the Home Office. At the time, however, it seemed that this was a job which would put Leon less in the limelight, while making the most of his formidable intellect and phenomenal industry, which was what I wanted. But even had Leon weathered Westland he would have found himself in difficulties over the question of privatizing BL.

Leon's position turned out therefore to be the key to the plan for the reshuffle. It might have worked out differently. For I thought long and hard about bringing Cecil Parkinson back to the Cabinet. I missed his dry views and great presentational skills. But my advisers were divided on the merits of doing so and in the end I reluctantly concluded that it was too soon.

There were three departures from the Cabinet. Nigel Lawson had become almost as irritated with Peter Rees as Chief Secretary as

Geoffrey Howe had been with John Biffen. Peter was an able tax lawyer and an amiable colleague. I always got on well with him. But I took the view that a Chancellor has the right to select his own subordinates. At Nigel's request, I replaced Peter with John MacGregor. John had a good financial brain as he had shown as part of the Shadow Treasury team. Although I considered him very much a Ted Heath man, I had been impressed by his acumen and diligence and felt he would do this demanding job well – which he did.

Grey Gowrie – after only a year in Cabinet, as Leader of the House of Lords – to my great regret decided that he wanted to earn more than a Cabinet member who was a peer – and therefore had no MP's salary – was able to do. He decided to go back into business. He had a fine, highly cultivated mind and great style. I had offered him the job of Secretary of State for Education, planning to keep Keith Joseph, who I knew was thinking of retirement, as minister without portfolio. But that was not to be. Keith agreed to stay at Education a little longer.

I regretted in a different way the loss of Patrick Jenkin. No one could have been more conscientious than Patrick – loyal, kind, selfless. But I could not have the constant haemorrhage of political support which his inability to put over a case in the Department of the Environment caused. I was becoming increasingly worried about what to do with the rating system which would be an even more difficult issue than GLC abolition. So I appointed Ken Baker to succeed Patrick. It was a good decision. Ken turned the tables on the Left, proved a superb communicator of our policies and was the foster-father of the community charge.

I had brought David Young into the Cabinet as minister without portfolio the previous year and I now had him succeed Tom King, who went to be Secretary of State for Northern Ireland. It is difficult to conceive of a greater contrast than David and Tom. I had started off with a wrong view of Tom King, inherited from Opposition. I had thought that he was a man with a taste for detail who, when I made Michael Heseltine Secretary of State for the Environment in 1979, would complement Michael's very broad-brush approach. I then made the uncomfortable discovery that detail was not at all Tom's forte, as the way in which we became steadily more enmeshed in almost incomprehensible formulae for rate support grant amply demonstrated. At Employment – in particular on the whole question of trade union political funds where he adopted a half-hearted compromise – he had not shown himself to best effect. Norman Tebbit, his predecessor, was unimpressed; and I felt rightly so. At Northern Ireland,

Tom subsequently demonstrated the other side of his character, which was a robust, manly good sense that won even hardened opponents to his point of view, at least as far as is possible in Northern Ireland. Even though from the standpoint of Ulster affairs it was a slightly difficult time to put in a new Secretary of State, with negotiation of the Anglo-Irish Agreement in its final stages, Tom went with good grace and to good effect.

David Young did not claim to understand politics: but he understood how to make things happen. He had revolutionized the working of the Manpower Services Commission (MSC) and at the Department of Employment his schemes for getting the unemployed back into work made a major contribution to our winning the 1987 general election. He shared Keith Joseph's and my view about how the economy worked and how jobs were created – not by government but by enterprise. He understood the relationship between the price of labour and the number of jobs. And he had that sureness of touch in devising practical projects which make sense in the marketplace that few but successful businessmen ever acquire. The 'Action for Jobs' programme was the single most effective economic programme we launched in my term in office. As a general rule I did not bring outsiders directly into Cabinet, feeling that previous experience of this – as with John Davies in Ted Heath's Government – had not been altogether happy. David Young was an exception and proved eminently worthy of being so.

If the Government's presentation was to be improved something had to be done about Conservative Central Office. Central Office rightly claims that it is a universal scapegoat for whatever goes wrong. It is blamed by the Government when the Party is restive or lethargic. It is blamed by the Party when the Government seems insensitive or out of touch. But equally there is no doubt that the performance of Central Office is variable and by this point it was causing alarm. John Gummer just did not have the political clout or credibility to rally the troops. I had appointed him as a sort of nightwatchman: but he seemed to have gone to sleep on the job. It was time for a figure of weight and authority to succeed him and provide the required leadership. In many ways, the ideal man seemed to be Norman Tebbit. Norman is one of the bravest men I have ever met. He will never deviate on a point of principle – and those principles are ones which even the least articulate Tory knows he shares.

There were, though, arguments against Norman's appointment. He was still not well and would indeed have to undergo more painful surgery at a very difficult political time for us. He was not a first-class administrator. I later came to have some vigorous arguments with him. There were also those who said that he and I were too close politically. They argued that what was needed, in John Biffen's foolish phrase, was a more 'balanced ticket', which seemed to me a recipe for paralysis.

But there was no doubt in my mind that Norman was the man for the job, and so it proved. I knew he wanted it, though he never asked me for it. I thought that one day he might succeed me if we won the election, though Party Chairmanships have generally been something of a poisoned chalice. Above all, I knew that the rank and file of the Party would give their all for Norman Tebbit, whom everyone admired for bearing his sufferings with such heroism, never complaining but never concealing either that, whatever politics might bring, it was his own family and Margaret Tebbit's needs which came first. Norman was better than an inspiration: he was an example. So I appointed him Chairman of the Party; he remained a member of the Cabinet as Chancellor of the Duchy of Lancaster. At least for the moment, party morale soared.

Norman needed a Deputy Chairman who would be able to make those visits to the Party around the country which Norman's health precluded him from doing. Only someone with a high profile already could do this successfully and I decided that Jeffrey Archer was the right choice. He was the extrovert's extrovert. He had prodigious energy; he was and remains the most popular speaker the Party has ever had. Unfortunately, as it turned out, Jeffrey's political judgement did not always match his enormous energy and fund-raising ability: ill-considered remarks got him and the Party into some awkward scrapes, but he always got himself out of them.

I also made quite a large number of changes in the ranks of junior ministers. Two future Cabinet ministers came into the Government – Michael Howard at the DTI and John Major who moved from the Whips' Office to the DHSS. John Major was certainly not known to be on the right of the Party during his first days as an MP. When as a whip he came to the annual whips' lunch at Downing Street with the other whips he disagreed with me about the importance of getting taxation down. He argued that there was no evidence that people would rather pay lower taxes than have better social services. I did not treat him or his argument kindly and some people, I later heard, thought that he had ruined his chances of promotion. But in fact I enjoy an argument and when the whips' office suggested he become a junior minister I gave him the job which I myself had done first, dealing with the complex area of pensions and national insurance. If that did not alert him to the realities of social security and the dependency culture, nothing would.

I felt that the reshuffle had given the Party and the Government a lift. I believed that we had created a stronger administration, good at both policy and presentation, that could weather any storm and see us through to the next election. But it was not to be. 'The best laid schemes o' mice an' men [and women], Gang aft a-gley.'

THE WESTLAND AFFAIR

There are differing views even now of what the Westland affair was really about. At various times Michael Heseltine claimed that it was about Britain's future as a technologically advanced country, the role of government in industry, Britain's relationship with Europe and the United States and the proprieties of constitutional government. Of course, these are all interesting points for discussion. But Westland was really about none of these things. Michael Heseltine's own personality – not mine or any other member of the Government's – alone provides a kind of explanation for what arose. Michael is one of the most talented people in politics. His talents are selective and cultivated to what always seemed to me the point of exaggeration. But anyone who has seen him on television or on a public platform will quickly accept that they are real enough.

Michael and I are similar in some ways, very different in others. We are ambitious, single-minded and believe in efficiency and results. But whereas with me it is certain political principles that provide a reference point and inner strength, for Michael such things are unnecessary. His own overwhelming belief in himself is sufficient. Shortly before Christmas 1985 when the Westland affair was rapidly getting out of hand he sent me a handwritten letter in which he wrote that he knew I would 'understand the depth of [his] convictions in this matter'. He was all too correct.

My relations with Michael Heseltine had never been easy. When I became Leader of the Party in 1975 I wanted to move him out of his post as Shadow Industry spokesman where his interventionist instincts were out of place. He agreed to take the Environment portfolio on condition that he did not have to do so in Government. Working with Hugh Rossi – a great expert on housing – Michael presented our policy on the sale of council houses very effectively. After our election victory I offered him the Department of Energy – an important job at the time, since the fall of the Shah was sending oil prices sharply upwards. Hearing this, he said that if that was all, he would prefer to become Secretary of State for the Environment. I bowed to this. There Michael – assisted by Tom King – did not prove particularly successful in curbing local authority spending. He came up with no feasible alternative to the rating system, which was at the root of much of the problem since many voters did not pay local authority rates. But Michael was far less interested in local authority finance than in being 'Minister for Merseyside'. In that capacity he made a great impression, which was undoubtedly politically helpful to us. Though for the most part his efforts had only ephemeral results, I would not blame him for that: Liverpool has defeated better men than Michael Heseltine. Apart from the sale of council houses and Merseyside, what came to obsess Michael was introducing new management systems into government. This seemed to me a most commendable interest and I encouraged him, arranging at one point a seminar with other ministers to discuss it.

But Michael was clearly restless and when John Nott told me that he did not intend to stand again for the next Parliament, I decided to give Michael his big chance and put him into Defence. There Michael's strengths and weaknesses were both apparent. He defended our approach to nuclear arms with great panache and inflicted a series of defeats on CND and the Labour Left. He reorganized the MoD, rationalizing its traditional federal structure. Supported by me in the face of departmental obstruction, he brought in Peter Levene to run defence procurement on sound business lines.

These were real achievements. But Michael's sense of priorities was gravely distorted by his personal ambitions and political obsessions. For while Michael Heseltine was becoming increasingly obsessed with a small West Country helicopter company with a turnover of something over £300 million, far more important issues escaped his interest. In particular, the Nimrod Airborne Early Warning System project which would have to be cancelled by George Younger in December 1986 after £660 million had been spent was running into grave difficulties while Michael Heseltine was at Defence. It would have been inconceivable for Leon Brittan, who was to fare so badly at Michael's hands, to have let such a situation continue. The Nimrod affair constituted a unique – and uniquely costly – lesson in how not to monitor and manage defence procurement. A minister has to be prepared to work through the details if he is going to come to the right decisions and this Michael was always unwilling to do.

However complex the psychological drives of Michael Heseltine, the basic issue at stake in Westland was clear enough. It was whether the directors and shareholders of a private sector firm, heavily but not exclusively dependent on government orders, should be free to decide its future, or whether government should do so. In this sense an important issue was indeed at stake in Westland. If government manipulates its purchasing power, if it arbitrarily changes the rules under which a particular company's financial decisions have to be made, and if it then goes on to lobby directly for a particular commercial option – these things are abuses of power. All my reading, thinking and experience has taught me that once the state plays fast and loose with economic freedom, political freedom risks being the next casualty.

The Westland helicopter company was small by international aerospace standards but it was Britain's only helicopter manufacturer. Unlike the bulk of the aerospace industry it was never nationalized by the Labour Government and was reasonably profitable into the early 1980s. It then began to run into financial trouble. Mr Alan Bristow bid for the company in April 1985 and it was in the light of this that on 30 April Michael Heseltine informed me and other members of the Cabinet's Overseas and Defence Committee of the Ministry of Defence's view of Westland. Westland hoped to obtain an order from the Indian Government for helicopters partly financed from our Overseas Aid budget. But they were also looking to the MoD for crucial new orders: from Michael's minute it was clear that they would look in vain. He made no suggestion at this stage that Westland was of strategic significance to Britain. Indeed, he emphasized that he would not wish to give the company extra orders for which there was no defence need. He added that even with the best will in the world it was difficult to see a single British specialist helicopter company competing in worldwide markets in the longer term.

In mid-June we learned that Mr Bristow was threatening to withdraw his bid unless the Government provided assurances of future MoD orders and agreed to waive its right to repayment of over £40 million of launch aid provided by the DTI for Westland's latest helicopter. I held a series of meetings with Michael Heseltine, Norman Tebbit, Nigel Lawson and others. At the meeting on Wednesday 19 June Michael suggested a scheme by which we could provide £30 million in aid to the company, but explained that what was important to the defence programme was not the existing Westland company but rather Britain's capability to service existing helicopters and to develop the EH101 project (see below). In spite of that, we all agreed that it was desirable to avoid Westland going into receivership, which appeared likely if the Bristow bid was withdrawn. In the end we decided that rather than provide aid to the company in the midst of a takeover bid (which in any case might have breached company law), Norman Tebbit should encourage the Bank of England to bring together the main creditors with the object of putting in new management and developing a recovery strategy as an alternative to receivership.

As a result Mr Bristow withdrew his bid and in due course Sir John Cuckney took over as Chairman, bringing his extraordinary talents to the task of securing Westland's future. Shortly afterwards it emerged that a large privately owned American company was considering making a bid for Westland. The new Westland management opposed this particular bid. Norman Tebbit and Michael Heseltine were also against it. But while noting the general arguments against an American takeover I made it clear even at this stage that a different American offer would have to be judged on its merits.

The situation of Westland was one of the first difficult issues which Leon Brittan had to face when he took over at the DTI in September. On Friday 4 October Leon sent me a thorough assessment of the position. The matter was urgent. It seemed likely that the company would have to go into receivership if a solution could not be found before the end of November. Leon urged me to take up the issue of India's proposed helicopter order with Rajiv Gandhi when he visited Britain in October. As part of the proposed financial reconstruction of the company the Government was asked to underwrite some helicopter sales. We would also have to decide what to do about the launch aid, which seemed unlikely to be recovered. What would be the most controversial aspect of the package put forward by Sir John Cuckney, however, was the introduction of a new large minority shareholder to raise new capital. No British company was prepared to take such a shareholding. The most likely candidate was the large American company, Sikorsky. Westland were in contact with their European counterparts, but the prospects of a European solution within the timetable did not look good.

It was from a note of a meeting on Wednesday 16 October between Leon Brittan and Michael Heseltine that I first read about Michael Heseltine's concern that Sikorsky would turn Westland into 'merely a metal bashing operation'. Michael did not wish to go so far as to oppose Sikorsky's taking the 29.9 per cent in any circumstances, but he did think it important to make every effort to find an acceptable European shareholder instead. More ominously, he apparently did not think that Sir John Cuckney was the right person to deal with negotiations with the European companies, since the latter looked to their governments for guidance in such matters. Michael argued that the approaches needed to be made at a political level by the Ministry of Defence.

It was now becoming clear that the preference of the Westland board was likely to be for Sikorsky, while Michael Heseltine's preference was very different. Other things being equal, we would all have preferred a European solution. Since 1978, European governments had agreed to make every effort to meet their needs with helicopters made in Europe. This did not, of course, mean that we were bound to rule out purchases of non-European helicopters, but it did obviously incline us in the European direction.

I still do not understand why anyone later imagined that the Westland board, Leon Brittan and I were all biased against a European option. In fact, the Government bent over backwards to give that option and Michael Heseltine every opportunity to advance their arguments and interests. Yet in the frenzy which followed there was almost no limit to the deviousness and manipulation we were accused of employing to secure Sikorsky its minority holding.

At the end of November the opposition between the Westland board's views and Michael Heseltine came out into the open. Sikorsky made an offer for a substantial stake in Westland which the Westland board was inclined to accept. But entirely off his own bat Michael now called together a meeting of the National Armaments Directors (NADs) of France, Italy and Germany as well as the United Kingdom to agree a document under which the respective governments would refrain from buying helicopters other than those designed and built in Europe. This was more than a blatant departure from the Government's policy of maximizing competition to get the best value for money: it also placed Westland in an almost impossible position. There was now an obvious risk that if Westland concluded its deal with Sikorsky it would not be deemed to meet the NADs criterion and would be excluded from all further orders from the four governments, including the UK. It was my view – and Leon Brittan's – that the Government must not seek to prevent any particular solution to Westland's problems: it must be for the company to decide what to do. Yet by a stroke of a pen Michael Heseltine was effectively ruling out the company's preferred option for its future. If Westland were to be able to make a free decision it would be necessary for the Government to overrule the NADs decision. This, of course, meant overruling Michael.

I realized that we might have to do this. Although these were essentially matters for the company, the closer that we looked at the

European option the less substantial did it seem. The three European companies concerned – Aérospatiale (France), MBB (West Germany) and Agusta (Italy) – were, as Michael certainly knew, subject to pressure from their own governments. Aérospatiale and Agusta were state-owned and MBB was substantially financed by the West German Government. All the European companies were short of work and promises of more work for Westland from Europe seemed likely to remain just promises. By contrast, Westland had been collaborating with Sikorsky for several decades and had produced a number of models under licence from them. Indeed, most of not just Westland's but Agusta's existing helicopter designs were of American origin. Michael Heseltine argued that if Sikorsky took even a minority stake in Westland they would use their position to put pressure on the Ministry of Defence to order American-designed Blackhawk helicopters. In fact, it was widely rumoured that the armed services would have liked the MoD to do just that rather than wait for the European equivalent which was now still only at the stage of feasibility study. My own personal view of all this was of little importance, but I could well understand, as would anyone else conversant with the facts, why Westland had their preference for the American option and how angry they and Sikorsky were with Michael Heseltine's manoeuvrings.

Nor, by now, was the 'American' option American only. Sikorsky had been joined by Fiat in their bid. Not to be outdone, however, Michael Heseltine suddenly revealed that British Aerospace would be ready to join the European consortium, thus making it less 'foreign'. There were several accounts of how precisely this had occurred: I had my own opinions.

I held two meetings with Michael Heseltine, Leon Brittan, Willie Whitelaw, Geoffrey Howe, Norman Tebbit and Nigel Lawson to discuss Westland on Thursday 5 December and the following day. (British Aerospace entered the field between the first and second meetings.) By the time of the second meeting Michael had totally changed his line from the one he had pursued in April. Suddenly the issue had become whether it was right to allow a significant British defence contractor to come under foreign control. But the real issue was whether the Government should reject the recommendation from the NADs, thus leaving Westland to reach their decision whether to accept the Sikorsky offer or that from the European consortium on straightforward commercial grounds. By the end of the second meeting it was clear that for most of us the argument had been won by Leon Brittan: the NADs decision should be set aside. But Geoffrey, Norman and, of course, Michael strongly dissented and so I decided that a decision should be reached in a formal Cabinet Committee. 'E'(A)* enlarged as appropriate would meet on Monday 9 December.

Over the weekend the pace quickened and tempers frayed. Michael Heseltine blocked a joint MoD and DTI paper on Westland and had it redrafted to emphasize the risks of a Sikorsky bid. Leon Brittan was furious, but allowed it to go forward to 'E'(A). This was a mistake. Michael said that the French Defence minister also telephoned over the weekend to place unspecified sub-contract work on the 'Super Puma' helicopter with Westland provided it was not sold to Sikorsky. Monday morning's newspapers covered the row between Michael and Leon.

The main argument of substance which Michael Heseltine advanced was that the attitude of the Europeans to a Sikorsky deal would jeopardize future collaboration between Westland and the European defence companies. Some of this work was certainly important. Westland's collaboration with Agusta on a large helicopter known as the EH101 was due to become the main basis of its business in later years. By contrast, the projected troop-carrying helicopter known as the NH90 was at a very early stage. In fact these fears were exaggerated. Though the NH90 was abandoned in April 1987, the EH101 subsequently went ahead successfully. Neither decision had anything to do with the ownership of Westland.

But the real sleight of hand was Michael's suggestion that as a result of the recommendations of NADs two projected European battlefield helicopters – an Anglo-Italian model and a Franco-German one – could be rationalized and that the savings in development costs which for the UK might amount to £25 million over the next five years would become available for extra work for Westland. This would enable additional helicopter orders to be placed by the MoD to help fill the gap in production work. Whether or not one thought that this £25 million was in fact likely to be saved or whether this was the best way to spend it seemed almost beside the point. It appeared that for Michael Heseltine the procurement budget of the MoD and arrangements with other governments were to be manipulated in whatever way necessary to secure his own preferred future for this modest helicopter company. What small sense of proportion Michael possessed had vanished entirely.

At the 'E'(A) meeting on 9 December Sir John Cuckney, who had been invited to attend and speak, brought matters down to earth. Westland needed fundamental reconstruction and an improved

* The principal sub-committee of 'E', the economic committee of the Cabinet.

product range and it was the view of his board that this was best met by Sikorsky. The longer it took to make the decision the greater would be the pressure on the share price. Westland's accounts were due to be published on 11 December and the company could not maintain market confidence if publication was delayed much beyond that.

There was a majority at the meeting in favour of overturning the NADs' recommendation, but instead of terminating the discussion and summing up the feeling of the meeting in favour of that, I gave Michael Heseltine (and Leon Brittan) permission to explore urgently the possibility of developing a European package which the Westland board could finally accept. But if this had not been done and a package which the Westland board could recommend had not been produced by 4 p.m. on Friday 13 December, we would be obliged to reject the NADs recommendation.

In fact, the Westland board did not accept the European bid and chose to recommend that from Sikorsky-Fiat. But Michael had now developed another fixation or perhaps tactic. At the 'E'(A) meeting it was recognized in discussion that the timetable would allow for another meeting of ministers before the Friday deadline. But there was no decision to call a meeting; and indeed none was necessary. What was the point? Westland's board knew precisely where they stood: it was up to them and the shareholders. Michael had already started muttering. He urged John Wakeham to get me to call another meeting, saying it was a constitutional necessity under Cabinet government. It so happened that officials had rung round to see whether people would be available if a further meeting was called: but that was very definitely not a summons to a meeting, because no meeting had been arranged. This was of little consequence, however, because from this point on Michael became convinced that he was the victim of a plot in which more and more people seemed to be involved. Obviously, it now involved Cabinet Office civil servants. Who might be revealed as a conspirator next?

The next twist came soon. Without any warning Michael raised the issue of Westland in Cabinet on Thursday 12 December. This provoked a short, ill-tempered discussion, which I cut short on the grounds that we could not discuss the issue without papers. Nor was it on the agenda. The full account of what was said was not circulated, though a summary record should have been sent round in the minutes. Unfortunately, by an oversight this was not done. The Cabinet Secretary noticed the omission himself and rectified it without prompting. However, Michael Heseltine was not satisfied with the brief record, complaining that it did not record his 'protest'. For Michael the plot was thickening fast.

Michael continued his campaign up to and over Christmas. He lobbied back-benchers. He lobbied the press. He lobbied bankers. He lobbied industrialists. GEC, of which Jim Prior was chairman, mysteriously developed an interest in joining the European consortium. The consortium itself came forward with a new firm bid. Each new development was adduced as a reason to review the Government's policy. The battle was fought out in the press. There was an increasingly farcical air about the affair, which was making the Government look ridiculous. There was even a completely contrived 'Libyan scare'. Michael Heseltine suggested that the long-standing involvement of the Libyan Government in Fiat raised security questions about the Sikorsky bid. In fact, Fiat would have owned 14.9 per cent of Westland and Libya owned 14 per cent of Fiat. Fiat already supplied many important components for European defence equipment. The Americans, who were even more sensitive than we were about both security and Libya, seemed quite content for Fiat to be involved with Sikorsky.

I rejected Michael's argument that we needed now to come down in favour of the European bid. But the public row between Michael and Leon continued over Christmas.

Westland's board were still extremely anxious about whether they could look forward to British and European government business. In answer to John Cuckney, I wrote to say that 'as long as Westland continues to carry on business in the UK, the Government will of course continue to regard it as a British and therefore European company and will support it in pursuing British interests in Europe.' Michael had wanted to include a good deal of other less reassuring material in my reply but I rejected this. Imagine, therefore, my admiration when I found early in the New Year that Lloyds Merchant Bank had sent him a letter which enabled him to make all the points in his published reply about what – in Michael's view – would happen if Westland chose Sikorsky rather than the bid of the European consortium. It was in response to Michael's letter that the Solicitor-General wrote to him of 'material inaccuracies'. The leaking of the Solicitor-General's letter to the press magnified the Westland crisis and eventually led to Leon Brittan's resignation; but all that lay in the future.

I now knew from Michael's behaviour that unless he were checked there were no limits to what he would do to secure his objectives at Westland. Cabinet collective responsibility was being ignored and my own authority as Prime Minister was being publicly flouted. This had to stop.

Westland was placed on the agenda for the Cabinet of Thursday 9 January. At that meeting I began by rehearsing the decisions which had been made by the Government. I then ran over the damaging press comment which there had been in the New Year. I said that if the situation continued, the Government would have no credibility left. I had never seen a clearer demonstration of the damage done to the coherence and standing of a Government when the principle of collective responsibility was ignored. Leon Brittan then Michael Heseltine put their respective cases. After some discussion, I began to sum up by pointing out that the time was approaching when the company and its bankers at a shareholders' meeting had to decide between the two consortia. It was legally as well as politically important that they should come to their decision without further intervention directly or indirectly by ministers or by other people acting on their behalf. That must be accepted and observed by everyone and there must be no lobbying or briefing directly or indirectly. Because of the risks of misinterpretation during this period of sensitive commercial negotiations and decisions, answers to questions should be cleared inter-departmentally through the Cabinet Office so as to ensure that all answers given were fully consistent with the policy of the Government.

Everyone else accepted this. But Michael Heseltine said that it would be impossible to clear every answer through the Cabinet Office and that although he did not envisage making any new statements he must be able to confirm statements already made and answer questions of fact about procurement requirements without any delay. I suspect that no one present saw this as anything other than a ruse. No one sided with Michael. He was quite isolated. I again summed up, repeating my earlier remarks and adding that consideration should also be given to the preparation under Cabinet Office auspices of an inter-departmentally agreed fact sheet which could be drawn upon as a source of answers to questions. I then emphasized the importance of observing collective responsibility in this and in all matters. At this Michael Heseltine erupted. He claimed that there had been no collective responsibility in the discussion of Westland. He alleged a breakdown in the propriety of Cabinet discussions. He could not accept the decision recorded in my summing up. He must therefore leave the Cabinet. He gathered his papers together and left a Cabinet united against him.

I have learnt that other colleagues at the meeting were stunned by what had happened. I was not. Michael had made his decision and that was that. I already knew whom I wanted to succeed him at

Defence: George Younger was precisely the right man for the job, which I knew he wanted.

I called a short break and walked through to the Private Office. Nigel Wicks, my principal private secretary, brought George Younger out; I offered him, and he accepted, the Defence post. I asked my office to telephone Malcolm Rifkind to offer him George's former post of Scottish Secretary, which he too subsequently accepted. We contacted the Queen to ask her approval of these appointments. Then I returned to Cabinet, continued the business and by the end of the meeting I was able to announce George Younger's appointment. Within the Cabinet at least all had been settled.

I had no illusion about the storm which would now break. And yet it remained a storm in a teacup, a crisis created from a small issue by a giant ego. Whether Michael Heseltine had come to the Cabinet having decided to resign I do not know. But the speed with which he was able to prepare the twenty-two-minute statement he delivered that afternoon, detailing my alleged misdemeanours, at least suggests that he was well prepared. I knew that, whatever disagreements there might be between me and other members of the Cabinet, they had witnessed for themselves that Michael was in the wrong.

As it happened, the main task of replying to Michael Heseltine fell to Leon Brittan. When the House reassembled on Monday 13 January, at a meeting that morning Willie, Leon, George, the Chief Whip and others discussed with me what should be done. It was decided that Leon, rather than I, would make a statement on Westland in the House that afternoon. It went disastrously wrong. Michael Heseltine trapped Leon with a question about whether any letters from British Aerospace had been received bearing on a meeting which Leon had had with Sir Raymond Lygo, the Chief Executive of British Aerospace. It was suggested (as it transpired quite falsely) that at his meeting with Sir Raymond Lygo Leon had said that British Aerospace's involvement in the European consortium was against the national interest and that they should withdraw. The letter in question which had arrived at No. 10 and which I saw just before coming over to the House to listen to Leon's statement had been marked 'Private and Strictly Confidential'. Leon felt that he had to respect that confidence, but in doing so he used a lawyer's formulation which opened him to the charge of misleading the House of Commons. He had to return to the House later that night to make an apology. In itself it was a small matter; but in the atmosphere of suspicion and conspiracy fostered by Michael Heseltine – who mysteriously knew all about this confidential missive – it did great harm to Leon's credibility. I defended his action on the grounds that he had a duty to respect the confidentiality of the letter. The letter itself was subsequently published with the permission of its author, Sir Austin Pearce, but it contributed little to the debate since the day after that Sir Raymond withdrew his allegations as having been based on a misunderstanding. By then, however, Leon's political position was all but irrecoverable.

But none of this made my life any easier when I had to reply to Neil Kinnock in the debate on Westland on Wednesday 15 January.

My speech was low-key and strictly factual. It demonstrated that we had reached our decisions on Westland in a proper and responsible way. Indeed, as I listed all the meetings of ministers, including Cabinet Committees and Cabinets which had discussed Westland, I half felt that I had been guilty of wasting too much of ministers' time on an issue of relative unimportance. Although it set out all the facts, my speech was not well received. The press were expecting something more fiery.

Michael Heseltine spoke, criticizing the way in which collective responsibility had been discharged over Westland and quite ignoring the fact that he had walked out of a Cabinet meeting on Westland because he was the only minister unwilling to abide by a Cabinet decision.

Leon summed up for the Government in a speech which I hoped would restore his standing in the House and which seemed a modest success. The press, however, still kept up the pressure on him and there was plenty of criticism of me as well. It seemed, though, that given time we were over the worst. It was not to be. On Thursday 23 January I had to make a difficult statement to the House. It outlined the results of the leak enquiry into the disclosure of the Solicitor-General's letter of 6 January. The tension was great, speculation at fever pitch. The enquiry concluded that civil servants at the Department of Trade and Industry had acted in good faith in the knowledge that they had the authority of Leon Brittan, their Secretary of State, and cover from my office at No. 10 for proceeding to reveal the contents of Patrick Mayhew's letter. For their part, Leon Brittan and the DTI believed that they had the agreement of No. 10 to do this. In fact I was not consulted. It is true that, like Leon, I would have liked the fact that Michael Heseltine's letter was thought by Patrick Mayhew to contain material inaccuracies needing correction to become public knowledge as soon as possible. Sir John Cuckney was to hold a press conference to announce the Westland board's recommendation to its shareholders that afternoon. But I would not have approved of the leaking of a law officer's letter as a way of achieving this.

In my statement I had to defend my own integrity, the professional conduct of civil servants who could not answer for themselves and, as far as I could, my embattled Trade and Industry Secretary. I never doubted that as long as the truth was known and believed all would ultimately be well. Yet it is never easy to persuade those who think that they know how government works, but in fact do not, that misunderstandings and errors of judgement do happen, particularly when ministers and civil servants are placed under almost impossible pressure day after day after day, as they were by Michael Heseltine's antics.

Alas, Leon's days were numbered. It was a meeting of the '22 Committee, not any decision of mine, which sealed his fate. He came to see me on the afternoon of Friday 24 January and told me that he was going to resign. I tried to persuade him not to; I hated to see the better man lose. His departure from the Cabinet meant the loss of one of our best brains and cut short what would have been, in other circumstances, a successful career in British politics. I hoped that he would return to the Government in due course. But I was by now thinking hard about my own position. I had lost two Cabinet ministers and I had no illusions that, as always when the critics sense weakness, there were those in my own Party and Government who would like to take the opportunity of getting rid of me as well.

But I also had staunch friends who rallied round. Not the least of these was President Reagan who telephoned me on Saturday evening at No. 10. He said that he was furious that anyone had the gall to challenge my integrity. He wanted me to know that 'out here in the colonies' I had a friend. He urged me to go out 'and do my darndest'. I appreciated his call. I told him that this was indeed a difficult moment but I intended to put my head down and battle through.

I knew that the big test would come in the House of Commons the following Monday when I was to answer Neil Kinnock once more in an emergency debate on Westland. I spent the whole of Sunday with officials and speech writers. I went through all of the papers relating to the Westland affair from the beginning, clarifying in my own mind what had been said and done, by whom and when. It was time well spent.

Neil Kinnock opened the debate that Monday afternoon with a long-winded and ill-considered speech which certainly did him more harm than it did me. But I knew as I rose to speak that it was my performance which the House was waiting for. Once again, I went over all the details of the leaked letter. It was a noisy occasion and there were plenty of interruptions. But the adrenalin flowed and I gave as good as I got. The speech does not now read as anything exceptional. But it undoubtedly turned the tide. I suspect that Conservative MPs had by now woken up to the terrible damage which had been done to the Party. They would have found in their constituencies that weekend that people were incredulous that something of such little importance could be magnified into an issue which threatened the Government itself. So by the time I spoke what Tory MPs really wanted was leadership, frankness and a touch of humility, all of which I tried to provide. Even Michael Heseltine deemed it expedient to protest his loyalty.

Some of the details raised in Westland continued to fascinate the *cognoscenti*, but they were a small and shrinking band. Westland shareholders accepted the Sikorsky bid and though there were to be some difficult times for the company the doom-laden consequences for it and Britain's industrial base about which Michael Heseltine had warned so eloquently never materialized.

Some said I should have sacked Michael weeks before his resignation. Certainly, there is weight in the criticism that I allowed Michael too much leeway, not too little. At a meeting in No. 10 on 18 December, Leon Brittan urged me to sack him and was brutally dismissive of those who on tactical grounds urged the opposite. But it is necessary to remember two things. First, to begin with the issues were not as clear-cut as they became. Although, as I was later to stress to the House of Commons, decisions on defence procurement are for the Cabinet as a whole not just for the Defence Secretary, Michael certainly did have a legitimate role to play in deciding Westland's future. The problem was that he did not stick to the limits of that role and not only sought to impose his own views on a private company but did so without respect for collective responsibility in the Government. Second, Michael was at that time a popular and powerful figure in the Party. No one survives for long as Prime Minister without a shrewd recognition of political realities and risks. It seemed to me that I should weather the storm best by reacting to events as they occurred, not trying to bring about a crisis, but sticking to the essential issues. In retrospect, I think that this paid off. Michael gained plenty of publicity but did himself great damage by storming out as he did: if he had not gone voluntarily he might have been still more troublesome on the back-benches.

But the most damaging effect of the Westland affair was the fuel which had been poured on the flames of anti-Americanism. And that fire, once lit, proved difficult to extinguish.

The kind of rhetoric which had been used by Michael Heseltine and his supporters about the American industrial 'threat' in the helicopter industry certainly touched a raw nerve. The Left always thought the worst of American motives because they saw the United States as the most vigorous, powerful and self-confident force for capitalism. Some on the far right – Enoch Powell with whom I so often agreed on other matters was the most obvious example – distrusted America on narrow nationalistic grounds: and for some in the Tory Party the memories of America's actions at the time of Suez remained for ever fresh. The more fanatical European federalists were anti-American for other reasons: they saw the strong cultural and sentimental links between Britain and the United States as detracting from our commitment to Europe. This was essentially an anti-Americanism of the political élites. But there was also a popular variety, which was more worrying. The British people by and large did not understand or properly appreciate President Reagan. And by now the emergence of Mr Gorbachev in the Soviet Union, someone with an unusual understanding of how to play on western public opinion and who as a communist would always receive the benefit of the doubt from the left-wing media, provided an apparently favourable contrast with President Reagan. There was a feeling that the Soviets were the model of sweet reason, the United States of recklessness. These were the rich seams which Michael Heseltine opened up in the Westland affair and which others were now to exploit.

BRITISH LEYLAND

On the heels of Westland came the question of privatizing British Leyland (BL).* Paul Channon, who had been Trade minister at the DTI and whom I appointed to succeed Leon, was faced within days of taking office with a fresh crisis and one which unlike Westland affected the jobs of many thousands of people and concerned a significant number of Conservative MPs, including ministers.

I had not always seen eye to eye with Norman Tebbit over BL. I felt that the company was continuing to perform badly and wanted to take a tougher line with it. There had certainly been improvements. Productivity was up, days lost by strikes were down, losses were smaller. But the management was still poor. Moreover, the same old bromides were used to justify failure. Next year or the year after was

* See Chapters 4 and 23.

always the time when losses would be turned to profit as long as new investment was provided by the taxpayer today. The only alternative to going along with what BL management wanted was its complete collapse which they rightly thought we could not allow. Forecasts were always being revised downwards – and then not met. UK market share hovered around 17 or 18 per cent in spite of expectations that with its new models BL would have taken 25 per cent. The company's 1984 results were unsurprisingly much worse than predicted. The Government had to stand behind BL's large and increasing borrowings under the so-called 'Varley-Marshall' assurances.

I wanted to cut back BL's investment programme and believed that one way of doing this was to buy in engines from Honda – with which BL planned to develop its existing collaboration – rather than for Austin Rover to develop its own new engines. In spite of several attempts during the spring and summer of 1985, I did not get very far. I did not feel that the DTI was sufficiently serious and I knew that BL itself was positively hostile. In such circumstances there is little a prime minister can do – even one so well advised as I was on these matters by my Policy Unit* and outside experts.

There must, I felt, be a new management and new Chairman at BL, tighter financial discipline and, above all, a renewed drive for privatization. From October 1985 on Leon Brittan concentrated closely on all these aspects but it was privatization which increasingly took centre stage. Jaguar had already been successfully sold off. Unipart, which handled BL's spare parts, should have been privatized too, though BL seemed to be reluctant to move ahead with this. But, most important, we had secretly been in contact with General Motors (GM) which was interested in acquiring Land Rover, including Range Rover, Freight Rover (vans) and Leyland Trucks (heavy vehicles). These negotiations too seemed to drag on and on; so I was pleased when Leon sent me on 25 November his proposals for moving ahead with the deal.

Apart from (though having a bearing upon) the price, there were three tricky questions which required attention.

- First, we had to consider the consequences for jobs of the rationalization of the GM (Bedford) and BL (Leyland) truck businesses, which was undoubtedly one of the attractions for

* John Redwood had arrived in 1983 to be the extremely effective head of the Policy Unit. He and Peter Warry kept a shrewd and sceptical eye on BL's finances, briefing me regularly.

GM of their proposal. We thought that up to 3000 jobs might go: but the choice in an industry where there was great overcapacity was not between job losses and no job losses but between some jobs going and a possible collapse of one or other – or conceivably both – truck producers.

- Second, we had to consider the position of the rest of BL's operations: the volume car business of Austin Rover, which would be left to pay off the accumulated debt, and which GM had no intention themselves of taking on.
- Third, the thorniest issue would be the future control of Land Rover, which GM were determined to acquire but on which public opinion would require safeguards that it should in some sense 'stay British'.

Suddenly, however, we were facing an *embarras de richesses*. Before we had fully come to grips with the GM offer, code-named 'Salton', the still more intriguingly code-named 'Maverick' put in an appearance. At the end of November the Chairman of Ford of Europe came to see Leon Brittan to say that Ford were considering making an offer for Austin Rover and Unipart. The company fully recognized the political sensitivity of this and it probably also understood how much opposition to expect from BL, which would much prefer to stick with its cosier relationship with Honda. So Ford wanted the green light from the Government first. Leon Brittan, Nigel Lawson and I discussed what should be done at a meeting on the afternoon of Wednesday 4 December. There was no doubt in our minds of the political difficulties involved. Although Ford said that they intended to keep the main BL and Ford plants open there would be opposition from MPs fearful of job losses in the areas affected. Ford's productivity was worse than BL's, their newest models were not selling well and they were worried about Japanese penetration of their European markets. There might be problems about collaboration with Honda on which BL had come to depend. There were possible criticisms as regards the effect on competition in car manufacture. But for all that the Ford offer was certainly worth pursuing. Some people would say that once successful negotiations had taken place with Ford and GM we would have disposed of Britain's own car-making capacity at a stroke. But others would welcome the privatization, which would end the drain on the public purse and secure a viable future for the car industry in Britain. So contacts with Ford went ahead.

Whether we could have succeeded in pushing through this ambitious privatization programme in a more favourable political climate must be a matter of speculation. But it could not have come at a worse time. To Paul Channon's horror – and mine – at the start of February the weekend press was full of details of what was planned. BL had almost certainly leaked it when we were at our most vulnerable as a result of the Westland affair. On Monday 3 February Paul Channon had to confirm these contacts in an emergency statement to the House. All hope of confidential commercial discussion had been destroyed. Irrationality swept through the debate.

Paul had an almost impossible task, which, however, he undertook with great courage and skill. A kind of pseudo-patriotic hysteria swept politics and the media. Ted Heath talked of our responding to the efforts of workers and management at BL by saying, 'now we will sell you out to the Americans.' Not even the Cabinet was immune. Norman Fowler, whose constituency was affected by BL, let it be known that he was fighting the deal. When the Norman Fowlers of this world believe that they can afford to rebel, you know that things are bad.

I chaired an extremely difficult meeting of the Cabinet on Thursday 6 February in the course of which it became clear to me that there was no way in which the Ford deal could be put through. In these circumstances it was essential to limit the damage and try to press ahead with the negotiations with GM. Paul Channon told the House that afternoon that in order to end the uncertainty we would not pursue the possibility of the sale of Austin Rover to Ford. It was humiliating and did less than justice to Ford, which had provided so many jobs in Britain. But in politics you have to know when to cut your losses.

The question now was whether, having relieved the immediate pressure, we could still strike a satisfactory deal with GM. I saw Paul after his statement and said that we must push ahead as fast as possible with this and the sale of Unipart. Now the news was out, however, we were faced with a rash of alternative bids. Few of them were serious and all of them were an embarrassment rather than a help at this late stage. Most politically sensitive was the proposal for a management buy-out of Land Rover. GM remained – in our and BL's view – by far the best option because that company was interested in all, not just some, divisions; because of its financial strength; and because of the access to its distribution network.

On Wednesday 19 February I set up a small ministerial group – what John Biffen would have called a 'balanced ticket' – to consider this increasingly complex and difficult matter. The main members were Willie Whitelaw, Nigel Lawson, Norman Tebbit, Peter Walker, John Biffen, Norman Fowler and of course Paul Channon. Paul remained in charge of the detailed negotiations with GM. These carried on well into March. Sometimes it looked as if we could gain a sufficient undertaking from GM as regards control of Land Rover. We had had to harden our position considerably, insisting that GM could have no more than 49 per cent voting strength and that GM's right to manage the business would be subject to the overriding control of the (British) board.

GM in the end were not prepared to wear this and I do not blame them. They were not willing to proceed with a deal for Leyland Trucks and Freight Rover which excluded Land Rover and so the talks ended. When this was announced by Paul to the House of Commons on Tuesday 25 March, one after another of our back-benchers stood up to say that a great opportunity had been lost and that the GM deal should have gone through. I did not disguise my irritation with them and told several later that they should have spoken up when the going was rough.

This whole sorry episode had harmed not just the Government but Britain. Time and again I had drawn attention to the benefits Britain received as a result of American investment. The idea that Ford was foreign and therefore bad was plainly absurd. Their European headquarters was located in Britain, as was their largest European Research and Development Centre. All of the trucks and most of the tractors that Ford sold in Europe were made in Britain. Ford's exports from the UK were 40 per cent more by value than those of BL. Would Britain have really been better off if BL had taken over Ford? The notion is ridiculous. But it was not just a matter of Ford. Over half the investment coming into Britain from abroad was from the United States. Both Ford and GM were offended and annoyed by the campaign waged against them. Britain just could not afford to indulge in self-destructive anti-Americanism of this sort. Yet it would continue and was shortly to be raised to fever pitch – not just in the area of industrial policy but that of defence and foreign affairs, where passions ignite more easily.

THE US RAID ON LIBYA

I was at Chequers on Friday 27 December 1985 when I learnt that terrorists had opened fire on passengers waiting on the concourse at the Rome and Vienna Airports, killing seventeen people. It soon became clear that the gunmen were Palestinian terrorists from the

Abu Nidal group. They had apparently been trained in the Lebanon, but evidence soon emerged of a Libyan connection. Certainly, the Libyan Government did not stint in its praise for the attacks, describing them as 'heroic actions'. We and the Americans already had a large amount of shared intelligence about Libya's support for terrorism. The question was not whether Colonel Gaddafi headed a terrorist state but rather what to do about it. Britain had adopted a much tougher attitude towards Libya than other European countries ever since the murder of WPC Yvonne Fletcher in 1984. But the Americans wanted us and the rest of Europe to go further still by imposing economic sanctions, in particular ending purchases of Libyan oil, 75 per cent of which was bought by the Europeans.

On Tuesday 7 January the United States unilaterally imposed sanctions on Libya with little or no consultation and expected the rest of us to follow. I was not prepared to go along with this. I made it clear in public that I did not believe that economic sanctions against Libya would work. The US State Department was highly displeased and even suggested that Britain was the least helpful of their European allies – something which was quite unjust since we were already applying stiff measures against Libya as regards arms, credits and immigration and had closed down the Libyan 'People's Bureau'. One reason why the United States considered Britain particularly difficult was because of my un-European habit of straight talking when I disagreed. When I discussed how to deal with Libya with President Mitterrand in Lille in mid-January he sounded a good deal more hawkish than I was. No doubt the Americans were receiving a similar impression.

In late January, February and March tension between the United States and Libya rose as US naval forces started manoeuvres in an area of the Gulf of Sirte which Libya, in violation of international law and opinion, claimed as its own territorial waters. On Monday 24 March US aircraft were attacked by Libyan missiles fired from the shore. US forces struck back at the Libyan missile sites and sank a Libyan fast patrol boat.

I had to consider what our reaction would be. I was conscious that we had 5,000 British subjects in Libya, while the United States had only 1,000. I was also aware of the possibility of Libyan action against our base in Cyprus. But I told Cabinet that in spite of this we must endorse the right of the United States to maintain freedom of movement in international waters and air space and its right to self-defence under the UN Charter.

Meanwhile, the Americans may have started to see who their true friends were. I learned that the French were expressing reservations about any policy of confrontation with Colonel Gaddafi, arguing that any US military action would win Libya Arab support and urging the need to avoid 'provocation'.

Then in the early hours of Saturday 5 April a bomb exploded in a discothèque frequented by US servicemen in West Berlin. Two people – one a US soldier – were killed and some 200 others – including 60 Americans – were injured. US intelligence, confirmed by ours, pointed to a Libyan involvement. For the Americans this was the final straw.

Just before 11 p.m. on the night of Tuesday 8 April I received a message from President Reagan. He requested our support for the use of the American F1–11s and support aircraft based in Britain in strikes against Libya, and he asked for an answer by noon the following day. At this stage there was nothing to indicate the precise nature of US objectives and targets. I immediately called in Geoffrey Howe and George Younger to discuss what should be done. At 1 a.m. I sent an interim reply to the President. Its main purpose was to ask him to think further. I emphasized that my basic instinct was to support the United States but I also expressed very considerable anxiety about what was proposed. I wanted more information on the targets in Libya. I was worried that US action might begin a cycle of revenge. I was concerned that there must be the right public justification for the action which was taken, otherwise we might just strengthen Gaddafi's standing. I was also worried about the implications for British hostages in the Lebanon – and, as events were to turn out, rightly so.

Looking back, I think that this initial response was probably too negative. Certainly the Americans thought so. But it had the practical benefit of making them think through precisely what their objectives were and how they were to justify them, which is certainly one service to be expected of a friend. Two other considerations influenced me. First, I felt that there was an inclination to precipitate action in the United States, which was doubtless mirrored there by a perception of lethargy in Europe. Second, even at this stage I knew that the political cost to me of giving permission for the use of US bases by the United States in their strikes against Libya would be high. The Government's fortunes were just recovering from the low point of Westland and BL: but that recovery was fragile. I could not take this decision lightly.

Geoffrey, George, officials and I met the following morning at 7.45 at No. 10. A message had been received from the White House saying that the final reply to the original request was not now required by noon. I decided to use the time available by having lists of possible Libyan targets drawn up which would be as narrow as possible. More in hope than anticipation, a list of non-military actions which the US might take was also drawn up. I held a further meeting in the early afternoon, but there was little we could usefully do until I received the President's reply to my message. I waited with some anxiety throughout the afternoon and evening.

Some time after midnight President Reagan's response came through on the hot-line. It was a powerful, detailed and not uncritical answer to the points I had raised. President Reagan stressed that the action he planned would not set off a new cycle of revenge: for the cycle of violence began a long time ago, as the story of Gaddafi's terrorist actions demonstrated. He drew attention to what we knew from intelligence about Libyan direction of terrorist violence. He argued that it was the lack of a firm western response which had encouraged this. He felt that the legal justification for such action was clear. The President emphasized that the US action would be aimed at Gaddafi's primary headquarters and immediate security forces, rather than the Libyan people or even troop concentrations of the regular armed forces. The strikes would be at limited targets. I was particularly impressed by the President's sober assessment of the likely effect of what was planned. He wrote:

> I have no illusion that these actions will eliminate entirely the terrorist threat. But it will show that officially sponsored terrorist actions by a government – such as Libya has repeatedly perpetrated – will not be without cost. The loss of such state sponsorship will inevitably weaken the ability of terrorist organizations to carry out their criminal attacks even as we work through diplomatic, political, and economic channels to alleviate the more fundamental causes of such terrorism.

I read and reread the President's message. He was clearly determined to go ahead.

The more I considered the matter the clearer the justification for America's approach to Libya seemed. The phenomenon of the terrorist state which projects violence against its enemies across the globe, using surrogates wherever possible, is one which earlier generations never confronted. The means required to crush this kind of threat to world order and peace are bound to be different too. There was no doubt of Gaddafi's culpability. Nor when the most powerful country in the free world decided to act against him must there be any doubt where Britain stood. Whatever the cost to me, I knew that the cost to Britain of not backing American action was unthinkable. If the United States was abandoned by its closest ally the American people and their Government would feel bitterly betrayed – and reasonably so. From this point on, my efforts were directed not at trying to hold America back but to giving her Britain's full support, both as regards use of bases and in justifying its action against what I knew would be a storm of opposition in Britain and Europe. This did not mean, however, that I would go along with every American suggestion. It remained vital that the air strikes be limited to clearly defined targets and that the action as a whole could be justified on grounds of self-defence.

The first task next day was to convince my colleagues of what needed to be done. Geoffrey Howe was against the American action, but once the decision had been made to support it he defended the line staunchly in public. George Younger supported it from the first.

That afternoon I sent a further message to President Reagan. I pledged 'our unqualified support for action directed against specific Libyan targets demonstrably involved in the conduct and support of terrorist activities'. I pledged support for the use of US aircraft from their bases in the UK, as long as that criterion was met. But I questioned some of the proposed targets and warned that if there ensued more wide-ranging action the Americans should recognize that even those most keen to give them all possible support would then find themselves in a difficult position.

It is all but impossible to keep anything secret in Washington, which was now awash with rumours of US preparations for military action against Libya. This did not make it any easier to maintain a discreet silence about our own attitude. At one point on Friday it seemed that the US was not intending to use the F1–11s based in Britain, which would of course have substantially eased our predicament. But later in the evening it appeared that they would indeed wish to do so. Later still I received a message from President Reagan thanking me for our offer of co-operation and confirming that the targets would be closely defined under three categories: those which were directly terrorist related; those having to do with command, control and logistics which were indirectly related; and those relating to defence suppression – that is radar and other equipment which would endanger the incoming American aircraft.

On Saturday morning General Vernon Walters came to see me to explain American intentions in more detail. I began by saying how appalled I was that the gist of my exchanges with President Reagan was by now openly reported in the US press. This meant, of course, that the propaganda battle was even more important. I eagerly welcomed General Walters's offer to show us in advance the statement from the President which would announce and explain the Libyan raid. He and I also discussed how much intelligence information could be used in public to justify the action. I was always more reluctant to reveal intelligence than were the Americans. But on this occasion it was obviously vital to do so if the general public were to be convinced of the truth of the allegations we were making against Gaddafi. In fact, although I do not believe that anyone's life was endangered as a result of these revelations, it is certainly true that a fair amount of intelligence dried up. I also discussed with General Walters the President's latest list of targets which I found reasonably reassuring. I suspect that the General knew precisely which targets the US would hit by the time he came to see me. If so, it was very wise of him not to say what they were. I hoped that he would be even more discreet in the rest of his trip to Paris, Rome, Bonn and Madrid where he was to explain the intelligence on which the US was acting and ask for European support.

Now that America was actually asking the Europeans for assistance which involved a political price they showed themselves in a less than glorious light. Chancellor Kohl apparently told the Americans that the US should not expect the wholehearted support of its European allies and said that everything would turn on whether the action succeeded. The French who just recently had indulged in at least private sabre rattling refused to allow the F1–11s to cross French airspace. The Spanish said that the American aircraft could fly over Spain, but only if it was done in a way which would not be noticed. Since this condition could not be met, they had to fly through the Straits of Gibraltar.

Speculation was now rife. We could not confirm or deny our exchanges with the Americans. The Labour and Liberal Parties insisted that we should rule out the use of American bases in the UK for the action which everyone now seemed to expect. It was important to ensure that senior members of the Cabinet backed my decision. At midday on Monday (14 April) I told the Cabinet's Overseas and Defence Committee what had been happening in recent days. I said that it was clear that the US was justified in acting in self-defence under Article 51 of the UN Treaty. Finally, I stressed that we had to stand by the Americans as they had stood by us over the Falklands.

That afternoon it was confirmed by telephone from Washington that American aircraft would soon take off from their British bases. I received the news shortly before attending a long-standing engagement at the *Economist*: this was a reception to celebrate either the great Victorian constitutionalist Walter Bagehot or Norman St John Stevas, his contemporary editor, depending on your point of view. As I entered the *Economist* building off St James's, Andrew Knight, the magazine's editor, remarked with some concern how pale I looked. Since my complexion is never ruddy, I must have appeared like Banquo's ghost. But I wondered how Andrew Knight would have looked if he knew about those American F1–11s heading secretly and circuitously towards Tripoli. Nevertheless I praised Bagehot, kissed Norman and returned to No. 10.

Late that night I received a message from President Reagan saying that the US aircraft would shortly strike at five named terrorist-associated targets in Libya. The President confirmed that the text of his televised statement to the American people took into account our advice to stress the element of self-defence to get the legal position right. My own statement to the House of Commons on the raid for the following day was already being drafted.

The American attack was, as we had foreseen, carried out principally by sixteen F1–11s based in the UK, though a number of other aircraft were also used. The attack lasted forty minutes. Libyan missiles and guns were fired but their air defence radars were successfully jammed. The raid was undoubtedly a success, though sadly there were civilian casualties and one aircraft was lost. Television reports, however, concentrated all but exclusively not on the strategic importance of the targets but on weeping mothers and children.

The initial impact on public opinion in Britain, as elsewhere, was even worse than I had feared. Public sympathy for Libyan civilians was mixed with fear of terrorist retaliation by Libya. Conservative Central Office received large numbers of telephoned protests, as did the No. 10 switchboard. Worries were expressed about the fate of British nationals there and the potential for hostage taking. Opposition critics, Conservative back-benchers and Tory newspapers alike were bitterly critical of the fact that I had given permission for the use of the bases. I was depicted as cringing towards the US but callous towards their victims. I reported fully on what had happened to the Cabinet, some of whose members I subsequently learnt thought that they ought to have known about the raid beforehand. Later that afternoon I made my statement to a largely sceptical or hostile House of Commons. President Reagan telephoned me afterwards to fill me in on what had been happening and to wish me well in fighting off the criticism he knew I faced. He said that when in his speech on television the previous night he had referred to the co-operation of European allies, he had had only one country in mind – the United Kingdom.

I was to speak in the emergency debate on the Libyan raid in the

House on Wednesday afternoon. It was intellectually and technically the most difficult speech to prepare because it depended heavily on describing the intelligence on Libya's terrorist activities and we had to marshal the arguments for self-defence in such circumstances. Every word of the speech had to be checked by the relevant intelligence services to see that it was accurate and that it did not place sources at risk. The debate was rank with anti-American prejudice. Neil Kinnock misquoted President Reagan's televised broadcast; but he did so once too often. I had heard him do this earlier in the day and I had the full text of what the President had actually said given to Cranley Onslow, the Chairman of the '22 Committee Executive. Mr Kinnock said:

> The purpose of the bombing raid on Tripoli and Benghazi on Monday night was said by President Reagan to be to 'bring down the curtain on Gaddafi's reign of terror'. I do not believe that anyone can seriously believe that that objective has been or will be achieved by bombing.

Cranley Onslow interrupted to point out that the President had said precisely the opposite:

> *I have no illusion* [my italics] that tonight's action will bring down the curtain on Gaddafi's regime, but this mission, violent as it was, can bring closer a safer and more secure world for decent men and women.

As the Victorians used to say: 'collapse of stout party'.

My speech steadied the Party and the debate was a success. But there was still a large measure of incomprehension even among our supporters. I went that Friday to Cranley Onslow's constituency. I felt that people were looking at me strangely, as if I had done something terrible, which given the sensational and biased media coverage you could understand. When I explained to party workers at a reception that our action had been taken to protect the victims of future terrorism, they understood: but the accusation of heartlessness stuck – and it hurt. Yet the Libyan raid was also a turning point; and three direct benefits flowed from it.

First, it turned out to be a more decisive blow against Libyan-sponsored terrorism than I could ever have imagined. We are all too inclined to forget that tyrants rule by force and fear and are kept in check in the same way. There were revenge killings of British hostages organized by Libya, which I bitterly regretted. But the much vaunted Libyan counter-attack did not and could not take place. Gaddafi had not been destroyed but he had been humbled. There was a marked decline in Libyan-sponsored terrorism in succeeding years.

Second, there was a wave of gratitude from the United States for what we had done which is still serving this country well. The *Wall Street Journal* flatteringly described me as 'magnificent'. Senators wrote to thank me. In marked contrast to feelings in Britain, our Washington embassy's switchboard was jammed with congratulatory telephone calls. It was made quite clear by the Administration that Britain's voice would be accorded special weight in arms control negotiations. The Extradition Treaty, which we regarded as vital in bringing IRA terrorists back from America, was to receive stronger Administration support against filibustering opposition. The fact that so few had stuck by America in her time of trial strengthened the 'special relationship', which will always be special because of the cultural and historical links between our two countries, but which had a particular closeness for as long as President Reagan was in the White House.

The third benefit, oddly enough, was domestic, though it was by no means immediate. However unpopular, no one could doubt that our action had been strong and decisive. I had set my course and stuck to it. Ministers and disaffected MPs might mutter; but they were muttering now about leadership they did not like, rather than a failure of leadership. I had faced down the anti-Americanism which threatened to poison our relations with our closest and most powerful ally, and not only survived but emerged with greater authority and influence on the world stage: this the critics could not ignore. And such are the paradoxes of politics that within the year this wave of anti-Americanism had come to the Government's aid. Labour was emboldened foolishly to stress an anti-American defence policy – which provoked strong reactions from Cap Weinberger and Richard Perle. When the British people were told that 'if you want us to go, we will go' they woke up to reality. Labour's anti-Americanism, in vogue the year before, steadily became more of an albatross and when the election came it helped to sink them.

As the spring of 1986 moved into summer the political climate began slowly, but unmistakeably, to improve.

CHAPTER XVI

Men to Do Business With

East-West relations during the second term – 1983–1987

REASSESSING THE SOVIET UNION

As 1983 drew on, the Soviets must have begun to realize that their game of manipulation and intimidation would soon be up. European governments were not prepared to fall into the trap opened by the Soviet proposal of a 'nuclear-free zone' for Europe. Preparations for the deployment of Cruise and Pershing missiles went ahead. In March President Reagan announced American plans for a Strategic Defence Initiative (SDI) whose technological and financial implications for the USSR were devastating. Then, at the beginning of September the Soviets shot down a South Korean civilian airliner, killing 269 passengers. Not just the callousness but the incompetence of the Soviet regime, which could not even bring itself to apologize, was exposed. The foolish talk, based on a combination of western wishful thinking and Soviet disinformation, about the cosmopolitan, open-minded, cultured Mr Andropov as a Soviet leader who would make the world a safer place was silenced. Perhaps for the first time since the Second World War, the Soviet Union started to be described, even in liberal western circles, as sick and on the defensive.

There was a new chill in East-West relations. We had entered a dangerous phase. Both Ronald Reagan and I were aware of it. We knew that the strategy of matching the Soviets in military strength and beating them on the battlefield of ideas was succeeding and that it must go on. But we had to win the Cold War without running unnecessary risks in the meantime.

The Cold War itself had never really ended, at least from the Soviet side: there were merely variations of chill. At times, as in Korea and Vietnam, it had been far from cold. But it was always, as I never forgot, a conflict of one system against another. In this sense, the analysis of the communist ideologues was right: ultimately, our two

Addressing the United Nations General Assembly in November 1989

ABOVE: Being met by Crown Prince Fahd of Saudi Arabia on my arrival in Riyadh in April 1981

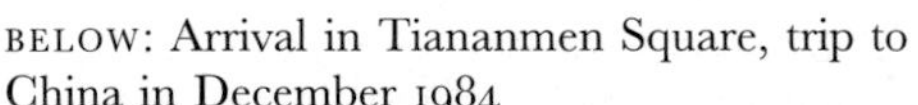

BELOW: Arrival in Tiananmen Square, trip to China in December 1984

RIGHT: Visit to Tokhai Power Station, Japan, in September 1982

BELOW: Test driving the new Challenger tank during a visit to Germany in September 1988

ABOVE: On holiday in Cornwall in August 1986 – walking at Constantine Bay with Denis – following an operation on my hand. After seeing the pictures on television my doctor telephoned to reprimand me for not resting up after the operation

BELOW: On holiday in Austria in August 1985

ABOVE: Speaking to the press outside the White House in July 1987

RIGHT: With Denis and the Reagans on the balcony of the White House, July 1987

ABOVE: Some of the Commonwealth leaders who attended the Special Commonwealth Conference in London, August 1986
From l-r: *back row* Rajiv Gandhi, Brian Mulroney, Sonny Ramphal, Bob Hawke, Robert Mugabe
front row self, Sir Lynden Pindling, Kenneth Kaunda

BELOW: Participants at the London G7 Summit in June 1984 meeting with Her Majesty the Queen at the Buckingham Palace Picture Gallery
From l-r: Helmut Kohl, HMQ, Ronald Reagan, self, Yasuhiro Nakasone, François Mitterrand

RIGHT: Signing and exchanging of the Channel Tunnel Agreement with President Mitterrand, in Canterbury, 12 February 1986

BELOW: Line up of G7 participants in front of the Pyramid at the Louvre, in July 1989
From l-r: Jacques Delors, Ciriaco de Mita, Helmut Kohl, George Bush, François Mitterrand, self, Brian Mulroney, Sosuke Uno

Dear Margaret – As you can see, I agree with every word you are saying. I always do. Warmest Friendship.
Sincerely Ron

ABOVE: At the dinner at Number Ten held in honour of President Reagan when he visited Britain in July 1988; on the right is George Shultz

LEFT: Arriving at Camp David by helicopter in November 1989 for talks with George Bush accompanied by Sir Antony Acland, the British Ambassador to the United States

opposing systems were incompatible – though, because both sides possessed the means of nuclear destruction, we had to make the adjustments and compromises required to live together. What we in the West had to do now was to learn as much as we could about the people and the system which confronted us and then to have as much contact with those living under that system as was compatible with our continued security. In a cold as in a hot war it pays to know the enemy – not least because at some time in the future you may have the opportunity to turn him into a friend.

Such was the thinking which lay behind my decision to arrange a seminar at Chequers on Thursday 8 September 1983 to pick the brains of experts on the Soviet Union. The difficulty of tapping into outside thinking even in our own open democratic system of government shows just why closed totalitarian systems are so sluggish and mediocre. I had been used to wide-ranging seminars from our days in Opposition and had always found them stimulating and educative. But instead of the best minds on the Soviet system I now found myself presented with a list of the best minds in the Foreign Office, which was not quite the same thing. I minuted on the original list of suggested participants:

> This is NOT the way I want it. I am not interested in gathering in every junior minister, nor everyone who has ever dealt with the subject at the FO. The FO must do their preparation before. I want also some people who have really studied Russia – the Russian mind – and who have had some experience of living there. More than half the people on the list know less than I do.

Back to the drawing board.

In fact, by the time the seminar went ahead I felt that we did have the right people and some first-class papers. The latter covered almost all of the factors we would have to take into account in the years ahead in dealing with the Soviets and their system. We discussed the Soviet economy, its technological inertia and the consequences of that, the impact of religious issues, Soviet military doctrine and expenditure on defence, and the benefits and costs to the Soviet Union of their control over eastern Europe. The one issue which, in retrospect, we underestimated – though it figured briefly – was the nationality question, failure to solve which would ultimately lead to the break-up of the Soviet Union itself. Perhaps for me the most useful paper was one which described and analysed the power structure of the Soviet state, and which put flesh on the bones of what I had already learnt in Opposition from Robert Conquest.

Of course, the purpose of this seminar was not ultimately academic: it was to provide me with the information on which to shape policy towards the Soviet Union and the eastern bloc in the months and years ahead. There were always – right up to the last days of the Soviet Union – two opposite outlooks among the Sovietologists.

At the risk of over-simplification, these were as follows. On the one hand, there were those who played down the differences between the western and Soviet systems and who were generally drawn from political analysis and systems analysis. They were the people who appeared night after night on our television screens analysing the Soviet Union in terms borrowed from liberal democracies. These were the optimists, in search of light at the end of even the longest tunnel, confident that somehow, somewhere, within the Soviet totalitarian system rationality and compromise were about to break out. I remember a remark of Bob Conquest's that the trouble with systems analysis is that if you analyse the systems of a horse and a tiger, you find them pretty much the same: but it would be a great mistake to treat a tiger like a horse. On the other hand, there were those – mainly the historians – who grasped that totalitarian systems are different in kind, not just degree, from liberal democracies and that approaches relevant to the one are irrelevant to the other. These analysts argued that a totalitarian system generates a different kind of political leader from a democratic one and that the ability of any one individual to change that system is almost negligible.

My own view was much closer to the second than to the first of these analyses, but with one very important difference. I always believed that our western system would ultimately triumph, if we did not throw our advantages away, because it rested on the unique, almost limitless, creativity and vitality of individuals. Even a system like that of the Soviets, which set out to crush the individual, could never totally succeed in doing so, as was shown by the Solzhenitsyns, Sakharovs, Bukovskys, Ratushinskayas and thousands of other dissidents and *refuseniks*. This also implied that at some time the right individual could challenge even the system which he had used to attain power. For this reason, unlike many who otherwise shared my approach to the Soviet Union, I was convinced that we must seek out the most likely person in the rising generation of Soviet leaders and then cultivate and sustain him, while recognizing the clear limits of our power to do so. That is why those who subsequently considered that I was led astray from my original approach to the Soviet Union because I was dazzled by Mr Gorbachev were wrong. I spotted him because I was searching for someone like him. And I was confident that such a person could exist, even within that totalitarian structure, because I believed that the spirit of the individual could never ultimately be crushed in the Kremlin any more than in the Gulag.

At the time of my Chequers seminar, although as I have explained East-West relations were worsening – and would become worse still when the Soviets pulled out of arms control talks in Geneva in response to the stationing of Cruise and Pershing missiles – it did seem that there would soon be important changes in the Soviet leadership. Mr Andropov, though he was no liberal, did undoubtedly want to revive the Soviet economy, which was in fact in a far worse state than any of us realized at the time. In order to do this he wanted to cut back bureaucracy and improve efficiency. Although he had inherited a top leadership which he could not instantly change, the high average age of the Politburo would present him with the opportunity of filling vacancies with those amenable to his objectives. There were already doubts about Andropov's health. If he lived for just a few more years, however, it seemed likely that the leadership would pass to a new generation. The two main contenders appeared to be Grigory Romanov and Mikhail Gorbachev. I asked for all the information we had about these two. It was not very much and a good deal was vague and anecdotal. It was soon obvious to me, however, that – attractive as was the idea of seeing a Romanov back in the Kremlin – there would probably be other unpleasant consequences. Romanov as First Secretary of the Communist Party in Leningrad had won a reputation for efficiency but also as a hardline Marxist which, like many of the sort, he combined with an extravagant lifestyle. And I confess that when I read about those priceless crystal glasses from the Hermitage being smashed at the celebration of his daughter's wedding some of the attraction of the name was lost as well.

Of Mr Gorbachev what little we knew seemed modestly encouraging. He was clearly the best educated member of the Politburo, not that anybody would have described this group of elderly soldiers and bureaucrats as intellectuals. He had acquired a reputation for being open-minded; but of course this might be just a matter of style. He had risen steadily through the Party under Khrushchev, Brezhnev and now Andropov, of whom he was clearly a special protégé; but that might well be a sign of conformity rather than talent. Nevertheless, I heard favourable reports of him from Pierre Trudeau in Canada later that month. I began to take special notice when his name was mentioned in reports on the Soviet Union.

VISIT TO HUNGARY

For the moment, however, relations with the Soviets were so bad that direct contact with them was almost impossible. It seemed to me that it was through eastern Europe that we would have to work. The Deputy Prime Minister of Hungary, Mr Marjai, had come to see me in March, before the general election, and had renewed an invitation from his Government for me to visit Hungary. I had been fascinated by what he told me about the Hungarian 'economic experiment'. At one point Mr Marjai, having noted the importance of profits and incentives, declared that it was not for the government to hand out money because the government did not have money. I commented that these remarks could have been made in one of my own speeches.

Hungary was the choice for my first visit as Prime Minister to a Warsaw Pact country for several reasons. The Hungarians had gone furthest along the path of economic reform, although they were anxious to describe it as anything but capitalism. A certain amount of liberalization had occurred, though outright dissent was punished. The strategy of János Kádár, officially First Secretary of the Hungarian Communist Party but in fact unchallenged leader, was summed up in the telling if hardly original slogan, 'he who is not against us is with us.' He used economic links with the West to provide his people with a tolerable standard of living while constantly asserting Hungary's loyalty to the Warsaw Pact, socialism and the Soviet Union: a necessary consideration, given that some 60,000 Soviet troops had been 'temporarily' stationed in Hungary since 1948. By this time Mr Kádár seemed to be regarded with some respect, perhaps even affection, by many Hungarians because he was credited with avoiding a repetition of the events of 1956, while allowing a gradual process of reform to continue. Although he himself had been tortured by his comrades, his own past included the incidents of villainy which marked the careers of all that generation of old communist leaders: he had been responsible for the torture and trial of Cardinal Mindszenty, the execution of his friend, Foreign minister Rajk, and the betrayal of the Revolution of 1956. However, he denied to me personally that he had had any responsibility for the execution of Imre Nagy, the reformist communist leader; indeed he said he had obtained an undertaking from the Soviets that Nagy would be allowed to live. In any case, the fact that Kádár had been in power for so long meant that he had come to know the Soviets and their thinking better than any other eastern European leader. In particular, he knew Mr Andropov, who had been the Soviet Ambassador in Budapest at the time of the 1956 uprising, and, we believed, remained close to him. I hoped that he would report back to the Soviet leader what I had to say.

I stepped off the plane at 10 o'clock on the night of Thursday 2 February 1984 to be met by the Hungarian Prime Minister, Mr Lázár, and then walked across the thick snow to inspect a flood-lit Guard of Honour. My first official engagement the next morning was a private discussion with Mr Lázár, a self-effacing functionary who gave every sign of loyalty to the communist system. But what he had to say showed the roots of that loyalty. He warned me that the worst possible thing I could do on my visit was to cast doubt on Hungary's remaining part of the socialist bloc. The Hungarians had been concerned at what Vice-President George Bush had said to this effect in Vienna after making a successful visit to the country. I realized that formal adherence to the Soviet system was the price of the limited reforms they had been able to make. I immediately said that I understood and I was careful then and later to keep my word.

Later that morning I saw Mr Kádár. He had only four more years left in power. But he was still vigorous and very much in charge. He was a square-faced, large-boned, healthy complexioned man with an air of easy authority and an apparently reasonable frame of mind in discussion. He did not rely, as so many other communist leaders did, on serried ranks of advisers and we were accompanied only by interpreters.

The main message I tried to get across was that the West and President Reagan personally were genuinely seeking disarmament. What we wanted was to preserve our own security, but at a lower level of weaponry, particularly nuclear weaponry. I told Mr Kádár that I knew from President Reagan, who was a close friend, just how personally hurt he had been by an earlier response to an attempt to get a better understanding with the Soviet Union. I recalled the tone in which President Reagan had spoken, when the two of us were walking in the garden of the United States Embassy in Paris, about a personal letter he had written in his own hand to President Brezhnev telling him of America's desire for peace. He awaited the reply eagerly. It took a long time to come. And when it did, it consisted of just the standard, official typed letter, short and dismissive. Since then, I added, President Reagan had indeed been increasing the military strength of the United States but he wanted relations between NATO and the Warsaw Pact improved.

I went on to try to gain a clearer picture from Mr Kádár of the situation in the USSR. He told me about the personalities of the Soviet leaders he had known: as he put it 'the Russians are individuals too'. Khrushchev was impulsive. Mr Kádár had told him that he was like an old Bolshevik – instead of saying 'Good Morning', he tended to punch you in the stomach. Brezhnev he described as very emotional. Andropov was different again. He described him as very tough and calculating, but someone who was capable of listening. He confirmed that Andropov was ill, but said that he was mentally intact and never stopped working. He also told me that his condition was improving but that the Hungarians were crossing their fingers for him. He added that the Soviet leadership was becoming stronger and younger people were entering it, that they wanted peace and were prepared to have talks about it. Of course, this picture of life in the Kremlin could hardly be taken at face value, given Mr Kádár's long association with Mr Andropov. And given that Andropov died six days later, what he told me about the latter's health was either wildly optimistic or a diplomatic lie. But his insights were interesting nonetheless.

So too was my first experience of what life in a communist country was like for ordinary people. On Saturday morning I visited Budapest's large central covered market, talked to stall holders and shoppers and bought honey, pimentos and spices. Huge friendly crowds gathered, in spite of the intense cold. The market was better stocked than I imagined it would be. But what remains in my mind even to this day was the warm, even passionate, welcome from the crowd of shoppers. It was not just that I was a western head of government that evoked this, but my reputation as a strong anti-communist political leader – a reputation further burnished internationally by the Falklands War two years before and even by the Soviet attacks on me as the Iron Lady. I responded warmly to the crowd and, on my return to London, found that several journalists were reporting my discovery that 'communists were human beings too.' What I had in fact discovered – or rather had confirmed – was that human beings in communist countries were not in fact communists at all but retained a thirst for liberty.

I was also struck by the people's pride in the old Hungary – which has since become the basis for the new post-communist one. At Szentendre I visited the local museum and art gallery which had a valuable collection of porcelain. I was shown round by a distinguished elderly curator, wearing well-cut but worn clothes, and immaculately polished but creased shoes. He had that indefinable air of someone who has known better days, as indeed he had. He was an aristocrat who had lost his property, but at the time of the communist revolution, rather than go into exile, he had remained to pass on his extraordinary knowledge of Hungarian history and culture to a new generation, who might otherwise forget it. Both from what he told me then of his country's past and what I had noticed earlier in my discussions with Mr Kádár, all Hungarians – even the communist rulers – had a strong sense of their country's identity.

The one surprise – and disappointment – of my visit was how far even Hungary was from a free economy. There were some small businesses, but they were not allowed to grow beyond a certain size. The main emphasis of Hungary's economic reforms was not on increasing private ownership of land or investment but rather on private or co-operative use of state-owned facilities. I visited a housing project at Szentendre in which the British firm, Wimpey, was involved. I found, on asking the people that I met there, that though they could buy their own flats they could not sell them freely on the market but only back to the state – more or less the same policy, it must be said, that the Labour Party in Britain had adopted towards the sale of council houses.

I reported my impressions in a message to President Reagan:

> [The Hungarian] economic experiment is conducted within very strict limits: the single political party, the controlled press, the sham Parliament, the state ownership of all but the smallest economic units, but above all the close alliance with Moscow. Kádár and Lázár made it perfectly plain that these things cannot change. . . . I am becoming convinced that we are more likely to make progress on the detailed arms control negotiations if we can first establish a broader basis of understanding between East and West. But I am under no illusions that it will be very hard to achieve that. It will be a slow and gradual process, during which we must never lower our guard. However, I believe that the effort has to be made.

In retrospect, my Hungarian visit was the first foray in what became a distinctive British diplomacy towards the captive nations of eastern Europe. The first step was to open greater economic and commercial links with the existing regimes, making them less dependent upon the closed COMECON system. Later we were to put more stress on human rights. And, finally, as the Soviet control of eastern Europe began to decay, we made internal political reforms the condition of western help. My visit to Hungary which began this successful diplomatic strategy had turned out to be altogether more significant than I could have imagined.

MOSCOW: ANDROPOV'S FUNERAL

Just a few days after my return from Hungary Mr Andropov was dead. Nevertheless the funeral, to which I decided to go, would give me the opportunity to meet the man who to our surprise emerged as the new Soviet leader, Mr Konstantin Chernenko. We had thought that Mr Chernenko was too old, too ill and too closely connected with Mr Brezhnev and his era to succeed to the leadership – and as events turned out we were more astute than his colleagues in the Politburo. But at least western commentators were unlikely to portray this ageing time-server as heralding an overnight transformation of totalitarianism into liberal democracy.

My party landed at Moscow Airport at 9.30 p.m. on Monday 13 February. It was bitterly cold and as I trod gingerly around the ice patches I wished that I was wearing a thick Russian fur coat. I spent the night at our embassy – a magnificent house, facing the Kremlin across the Moskva river, which was constructed at the end of the last century for a Ukrainian sugar magnate. (Later, when we would otherwise have had to give it up at the end of the lease, I did a deal with Mr Gorbachev for us to keep our splendid building in exchange for the Soviets keeping their current embassy in Britain when that lease expired. One of the few points on which the Foreign Office and I agreed was the need for British embassies to be architecturally imposing and provided with fine pictures and furniture.)

The day of the funeral was bright, clear and if anything even colder than when I arrived. At these occasions visiting dignitaries did not have seats: we had to stand for several hours in a specially reserved enclosure. Later I met the new Soviet leader for a short private meeting at which he read rapidly, stumbling over his words from time to time, from a prepared text. He was accompanied by the Soviet Foreign minister, Mr Gromyko. It was a formal affair, covering all the old ground of disarmament issues. I was unimpressed.

With long hours of standing I was glad that Robin Butler had persuaded me that I should wear fur-lined boots, rather than my usual high heels. They had been expensive. But when I met Mr Chernenko the thought crossed my mind that they would probably come in useful again soon.

VISIT OF THE GORBACHEVS TO BRITAIN

I now had to consider the next step in my strategy of gaining closer relations – on the right terms – with the Soviet Union. Clearly, there must be more personal contact with the Soviet leaders. Geoffrey Howe wanted us to extend an invitation to Mr Chernenko to come to Britain but I said that it was too early to do this. We needed to see more about where the new Soviet leader was heading first. But I was keen to invite others and accordingly invitations went to several senior Soviet figures, including Mr Gorbachev. It quickly appeared that Mr Gorbachev was indeed keen to come on what would be his first visit to a European capitalist country and wanted to do so soon. By now we had learned more about his background and that of his wife, Raisa, who, unlike the wives of other leading Soviet politicians, was often seen in public and was an articulate, highly educated and attractive woman. I decided that the Gorbachevs should both come to Chequers, which has just the right country house atmosphere conducive to good conversation. I regarded the meeting as potentially of great significance. Indeed, before their arrival I held a further seminar with Soviet experts to cover the issues and work out the approach I would take.

The Gorbachevs drove down from London on the morning of Sunday 16 December, arriving in time for lunch. Over drinks in the Great Hall Mr Gorbachev told me how interested he had been to see the farm land on the way to Chequers and we compared notes about our countries' different agricultural systems. This had been his responsibility for a number of years and he had apparently achieved some modest progress in reforming the collective farms, but up to 30 per cent of the crops were lost because of failures of distribution.

Raisa Gorbachev too was making her first visit to western Europe and she knew only a little English – as far as I could tell her husband knew none; but she was dressed in a smart western style outfit, a well-tailored grey suit with a white stripe – just the sort I could have worn myself, I thought. She had a philosophy degree and had indeed been an academic. Our advice at this time was that Mrs Gorbachev was a committed, hardline Marxist; her obvious interest in Hobbes's *Leviathan*, which she took down from the shelf in the library, might possibly have confirmed that. But I later learned from her – after I had left office – that her grandfather had been one of those millions of kulaks killed during the forced collectivization of agriculture under Stalin. Her family had no good reason for illusions about communism.

We went into lunch – I was accompanied by a rather large team of Willie Whitelaw, Geoffrey Howe, Michael Heseltine, Michael Jopling, Malcolm Rifkind (Minister of State at the Foreign Office), Paul Channon and advisers; he and Raisa by Mr Zamyatin, the Soviet Ambassador, and the quietly impressive Mr Alexander Yakovlev, the adviser who was to play a large part in the reforms of the 'Gorbachev years'. It was not long before the conversation turned from trivialities – for which neither Mr Gorbachev nor I had any taste – to a vigorous two-way debate. In a sense, the argument has continued ever since and is taken up whenever we meet; and as it goes to the heart of what politics is really about, I never tire of it.

He told me about the economic programmes of the Soviet system, the switch from big industrial plant to smaller projects and 'businesses', the ambitious irrigation schemes and the way in which the industrial planners adapted industrial capacity to the labour force to avoid unemployment. I asked whether this might not all be easier if reform were attempted on a free enterprise basis, with the provision of incentives and a free hand for local enterprises to run their own show, rather than everything being directed from the centre. Mr Gorbachev denied indignantly that everything in the USSR was run from the centre. I took another tack. I explained that in the western system everyone – including the poorest – ultimately received more than they would from a system which depended simply on redistribution. Indeed, in Britain we were attempting to cut taxes in order to increase incentives so that we could create wealth, competing in world markets. I said I had no wish to have the power to direct everyone where he should work and what he or she should receive.

Mr Gorbachev, however, insisted on the superiority of the Soviet system. Not only did it produce higher growth rates, but if I came to the USSR I would see how the Soviet people lived – 'joyfully'. If this were so, I countered, why did the Soviet authorities not allow people to leave the country as easily as they could leave Britain?

In particular, I criticized the constraints placed on Jewish emigration to Israel. He claimed that 80 per cent of those who had expressed the wish to leave the Soviet Union had been able to do so. I said that this was not my information. But he repeated the Soviet line, which I did not believe either, that those forbidden to leave had been working in areas relating to national security. I knew there was no purpose in persisting now; but the point had been registered. The Soviets had to know that every time we met their treatment of the *refuseniks* would be thrown back at them.

We now left the dining-room and had coffee in the main sitting-room. All of my team except Geoffrey Howe, my private secretary Charles Powell, and the interpreter left. Denis showed Mrs Gorbachev around the house.

If at this stage I had paid attention only to the content of Mr Gorbachev's remarks – largely the standard Marxist line – I would have to conclude that he was cast in the usual communist mould. But his personality could not have been more different from the wooden ventriloquism of the average Soviet *apparatchik*. He smiled, laughed, used his hands for emphasis, modulated his voice, followed an argument through and was a sharp debater. He was self-confident and though he larded his remarks with respectful references to Mr Chernenko, from whom he brought a not very illuminating written message, he did not seem in the least uneasy about entering into controversial areas of high politics. This was even more so in the hours of discussion which followed. He never read from a prepared brief, but referred to a small notebook of manuscript jottings. Only on matters of pronunciation of foreign names did he refer to his colleagues for advice. His line was no different from what I would have expected. His style was. As the day wore on I came to understand that it was the style far more than the Marxist rhetoric which expressed the substance of the personality beneath. I found myself liking him.

The most practical piece of business I had to discuss on this occasion was arms control. It was an important moment. Secretary of State Schultz and Foreign minister Gromyko were due to meet early in the New Year in Geneva to see whether the stalled arms talks could be revived. I had found in talking to the Hungarians that the best basis on which to discuss arms control in a relatively serene atmosphere was to state that our two opposing systems must live side by side, with less hostility and lower levels of armaments. I did the same again now.

I added that as perhaps the last generation of politicians that remembered the Second World War, we had a bounden duty to ensure that no such conflict would occur again. On this basis our detailed discussions began: two things quickly became clear. The first was just how well briefed Mr Gorbachev was about the West. He commented on my speeches, which he had clearly read. He quoted Lord Palmerston's dictum that Britain had no eternal friends or enemies but only eternal interests. He had been closely following leaked conversations from the American National Security Council, which had appeared in the American press, to the effect that the US had an interest in not allowing the Soviet economy to emerge from stagnation.

At one point, with a touch of theatre, he pulled out a full-page diagram from the *New York Times*, illustrating the explosive power of the weapons of the two superpowers compared with the explosive power available in the Second World War. He was well versed in the fashionable arguments then raging about the prospect of a 'nuclear winter' resulting from a nuclear exchange. I was not much moved by all this. I said that what interested me more than the concept of the nuclear winter was avoiding the incineration, death and destruction which would precede it. But the purpose of nuclear weapons was, in any case, to deter war not to wage it. They had given us a greater degree of protection from war than we had ever known before. Yet this could – and must – now be achieved at a lower level of weaponry. Mr Gorbachev argued that if both sides continued to pile up weapons this could lead to accidents or unforeseen circumstances and with the present generation of weapons the time for decision-making could be counted in minutes. As he put it, in one of the more obscure Russian proverbs, 'once a year even an unloaded gun can go off.'

The other point which emerged was the Soviets' distrust of the Reagan Administration's intentions in general and of their plans for a Strategic Defence Initiative (SDI) in particular. I emphasized on more than one occasion that President Reagan could be trusted and that the last thing he would ever want was war. I spoke, as I had in Hungary, about the desire for peace which lay behind his earlier letter to President Brezhnev. In this he was continuing something which was characteristic of America. The United States had never shown any desire for world domination. When, just after the war, they had enjoyed a monopoly of nuclear weapons, they had never used that monopoly to threaten others. The Americans had always used their power sparingly and shown outstanding generosity to other countries. I made it clear that, while I was strongly in favour of the Americans going ahead with SDI, I did not share President Reagan's view that it was a means of ridding the world entirely of nuclear weapons. This seemed to me an unattainable dream – you could not disinvent the knowledge of how to make such weapons. But I also reminded Mr Gorbachev that the Soviet Union had been the first country to develop an anti-satellite (ASAT) capability. It was clearly not feasible to think in terms of stopping research into space-based systems. The critical stage came when the results of that research were translated into the production of weapons on a large scale.

As the discussion wore on it was clear that the Soviets were indeed very concerned about SDI. They wanted it stopped at almost any price. I knew that to some degree I was being used as a stalking horse for President Reagan. I was also aware that I was dealing with a wily opponent who would ruthlessly exploit any divisions between me and the Americans. So I bluntly stated – and then repeated at the end of the meeting – that he should understand that there was no question of dividing us: we would remain staunch allies of the United States. My frankness on this was particularly important because of my equal frankness about what I saw as the President's unrealistic dream of a nuclear-free world.

The talks were due to end at 4.30 p.m. to allow Mr Gorbachev to be back for an early evening reception at the Soviet Embassy, but he said that he wanted to continue. It was 5.50 p.m. when he left, having introduced me to another pearl of Russian popular wisdom to the effect that, 'Mountain folk cannot live without guests any more than they can live without air. But if the guests stay longer than necessary, they choke.' As he took his leave, I hoped that I had been talking to the next Soviet leader. For, as I subsequently told the press, this was a man with whom I could do business.

SDI

President Reagan's Strategic Defence Initiative, about which the Soviets and Mr Gorbachev were already so alarmed, was to prove central to the West's victory in the Cold War. Although, as I have noted, I differed sharply from the President's view that SDI was a major step towards a nuclear weapon-free world – something which I believed was neither attainable nor even desirable – I had no doubt about the rightness of his commitment to press ahead with the programme. Looking back, it is now clear to me that Ronald Reagan's original decision on SDI was the single most important of his presidency.

In Britain, I kept tight personal control over decisions relating to SDI and our reactions to it. I knew that irreparable harm could have been done to our relations with the United States had the wrong line or even tone been adopted. I was also passionately interested in the technical developments and strategic implications. This was one of those areas in which only a firm grasp of the scientific concepts involved allows the right policy decisions to be made. Laid back generalists from the Foreign Office – let alone the ministerial muddlers in charge of them – could not be relied upon. By contrast, I was in my element.

When I was Leader of the Opposition I had had several briefings from military experts about the technical possibilities of SDI and indeed about the advances already made by the Soviet Union in laser and anti-satellite technology. These left me fearful that they were already moving ahead of us. I collected and read articles from *Aviation Week & Space Technology* and the scientific press. Consequently, when I began to read reports of the new Reagan Administration's thinking in this area I immediately understood that we too needed access to the best expert advice in order to assess the potentially revolutionary implications. Neither the Foreign Office nor the Ministry of Defence took SDI sufficiently seriously. Time and again I had to press for papers which had been promised and these, when they came, consistently underrated the technical possibilities opened up by the research and the American Administration's determination to press ahead with it. In fact, the only time I found much enthusiasm was when there appeared to be possibilities – which, by contrast, the MoD significantly exaggerated – for British firms to win large contracts for the research.

In formulating our approach to SDI, there were four distinct elements which I bore in mind. The first was the science itself. The American aim in SDI was to develop a new and much more effective defence against ballistic missiles. This would be what was called a 'multi-layered' Ballistic Missile Defence (BMD), using both ground and space-based weapons. This concept of defence rested on the ability to attack incoming ballistic missiles at all stages of their flight, from the boost phase when the missile and all its warheads and decoys were together – the best moment – right up to the point of re-entry of the earth's atmosphere on its way to the target. Scientific advances opened up new possibilities to make such defence far more effective than the existing Anti-Ballistic Missile (ABM) defences. The main advances which appeared likely were in the use of kinetic energy weapons (which were non-nuclear and which, when launched at high speed against the nuclear missile, would smash it) and in the use of laser weapons. Even more challenging than the development of these different elements of SDI, however, was the requirement for an enormously powerful and sophisticated computer capability to direct and co-ordinate the system as a whole. Such an undertaking would not only require huge sums of money but also test the ultimate creative abilities of the western and communist systems competing for it.

The second element to be considered was the existing international agreements limiting the deployment of weapons in space and ABM systems. The 1972 ABM Treaty, as amended by a 1974 Protocol, allowed the United States and the Soviet Union to deploy one static

ABM system with up to one hundred launchers in defence of either an Inter-Continental Ballistic Missile (ICBM) silo field or the national capital. The precise implications of the treaty for the research, testing, development and deployment of new kinds of ABM system were subject to heated legalistic dispute. The Soviets had started out with a 'broad interpretation' of the treaty which they narrowed when it later suited them. Within the American Administration there were those who pressed for a 'broader than broad' interpretation which would have placed almost no effective constraint on the development and deployment of SDI. The Foreign Office and the Ministry of Defence always sought to urge the narrowest possible interpretation, which the Americans – rightly in my view – believed would have meant that SDI was stillborn. I always tried to steer away from this phraseology and made it clear in private and public that research on whether a system was viable could not be said to have been completed until it had been successfully tested. Underneath the jargon, this apparently technical point was really a matter of straight common sense. But it was to become the issue dividing the United States and the USSR at the Reykjavik summit and so assumed great importance.

The third element in the calculation was the relative strength of the two sides in Ballistic Missile Defence. Only the Soviet Union possessed a working ABM system (known as GALOSH) around Moscow, which they were currently up-grading. The Americans had never deployed an equivalent system. The United States assessed that the Soviets were spending in the order of $1 billion a year on their research programme of defence against ballistic missiles. Also the Soviets were further advanced in anti-satellite weapons. There was, therefore, a strong argument that the Soviets had already acquired an unacceptable advantage in this whole area.

The fourth element was the implications of SDI for deterrence. I started off with a good deal of sympathy for the thinking behind the ABM Treaty. This was that the more sophisticated and effective the defence against nuclear missiles, the greater the pressure to seek hugely expensive advances in nuclear weapons technology. I was always a believer in a slightly qualified version of the doctrine known as MAD – 'mutually assured destruction'. The threat of (what I preferred to call) 'unacceptable destruction' which would follow from a nuclear exchange was such that nuclear weapons were an effective deterrent against not just nuclear but also conventional war. I had to consider whether SDI was likely to undermine that. On one argument, of course, it would. If any power believed that it had a completely effective shield against nuclear weapons it had, in theory, a greater temptation to use them. I knew – and post-war experience demonstrated beyond doubt – that the United States would never start a war by launching a first strike against the Soviet Union, whether it believed that it was secure from retaliation or not. The Soviets, by contrast, claimed to have no such confidence.

But I soon began to see that SDI would strengthen not weaken the nuclear deterrent. Unlike President Reagan and some other members of his Administration I never believed that SDI could offer one hundred per cent protection, but it would allow sufficient United States missiles to survive a first strike by the Soviets. Theoretically, the US would then be in a position to launch its own nuclear weapons against the Soviet Union. It follows that the Soviets would be far less likely to yield to the temptation to use nuclear weapons in the first place.

The decisive argument for me, however, was precisely the one which made me reject President Reagan's vision of a nuclear weapon-free world. It was that you could not ultimately hold back research on SDI any more than you could prevent research into new kinds of offensive weapons. We had to be the first to get it. Science is unstoppable: it will not be stopped for being ignored. The deployment of SDI, just like the deployment of nuclear weapons, must be carefully controlled and negotiated. But research, which necessarily involved testing, must go ahead.

DISCUSSION OF SDI AT CAMP DAVID

It was the subject of SDI which dominated my talks with President Reagan and members of his Administration when I went to Camp David on Saturday 22 December 1984 to brief the Americans on my earlier talks with Mr Gorbachev. This was the first occasion on which I had heard President Reagan speaking about SDI. He did so with passion. He was at his most idealistic. He stressed that SDI would be a defensive system and that it was not his intention to obtain for the United States a unilateral advantage. Indeed, he said that if SDI succeeded he would be ready to internationalize it so that it was at the service of all countries, and he had told Mr Gromyko as much. He reaffirmed his long-term goal of getting rid of nuclear weapons entirely.

These remarks made me nervous. I was horrified to think that the

United States would be prepared to throw away a hard-won lead in technology by making it internationally available. (Fortunately the Soviets never believed that he would.) But I did not raise this directly. Instead, I concentrated on my areas of agreement with the President. I said that it was essential to pursue the research, but that if this reached the point where a decision had to be made to produce and deploy weapons in space a very different situation would arise. Deployment would not be consistent either with the 1972 ABM Treaty or the 1967 Outer Space Treaty. Both of these would have to be renegotiated. I also explained my concern about the possible intermediate effect of SDI on the doctrine of deterrence. I was worried that deployment of a Ballistic Missile Defence (BMD) system would be destabilizing and that while it was being constructed a pre-emptive first strike against it would become an attractive option. But I acknowledged that I might well not be fully informed of all the technical aspects and wanted to hear more. In all this I was keen to probe the Americans, not just in order to learn more of their intentions but to ensure that they had clearly thought through the implications of the steps they were now taking.

What I heard, now that we got down to discussion of the likely reality rather than the grand vision, was reassuring. President Reagan did not pretend that they yet knew where the research could finally lead. But he emphasized that – in addition to his earlier arguments in favour of SDI – keeping up with the United States would impose an economic strain on the Soviet Union. He argued that there had to be a practical limit as to how far the Soviet Government could push their people down the road of austerity. As so often, he had instinctively grasped the key to the whole question. What would the effects be of SDI on the Soviet Union? In fact, as he foresaw, the Soviets did recoil in the face of the challenge of SDI, finally renouncing the goal of military superiority which alone had given them the confidence to resist the demands for reform in their own system. But of course this still lay in the future.

What I wanted now was an agreed position on SDI to which both the President and I could lend our support, even though our long-term view of its potential was different. I had been thinking about this over the last few days and particularly on the long flight from Peking where I had been for the signing of the Joint Declaration on Hong Kong. I now jotted down, while talking to National Security Adviser Bud McFarlane, the four points which seemed to me to be crucial.

My officials then filled in the details. The President and I agreed a text which set out the policy.

The main section of my statement reads:

> I told the President of my firm conviction that the SDI research programme should go ahead. Research is, of course, permitted under existing US/Soviet treaties; and we, of course, know that the Russians already have their research programme and, in the US view, have already gone beyond research. We agreed on four points: (1) the US, and western, aim was not to achieve superiority, but to maintain balance, taking account of Soviet developments; (2) SDI-related deployment would, in view of treaty obligations, have to be a matter for negotiation; (3) the overall aim is to enhance, not undercut, deterrence; (4) East-West negotiation should aim to achieve security with reduced levels of offensive systems on both sides. This will be the purpose of the resumed US-Soviet negotiations on arms control, which I warmly welcome.

I subsequently learnt that George Schultz thought that I had secured too great a concession on the Americans' part in the wording; but in fact it gave them and us a clear and defensible line and helped reassure the European members of NATO. A good day's work.

VISIT TO WASHINGTON: FEBRUARY 1985

I again visited Washington in February 1985. Arms talks between the Americans and the Soviet Union had now resumed, but SDI remained a source of contention. I was to address a joint meeting of Congress on the morning of Wednesday 20 February and I brought with me from London as a gift a bronze statue of Winston Churchill, who had also many years before been honoured with such an invitation. I worked specially hard on this speech. I would use the Autocue for its delivery. I knew that Congress would have seen the 'Great Communicator' himself delivering faultless speeches and I would have a discriminating audience. So I resolved to practise speaking the text until I had got every intonation and emphasis right. (Speaking to Autocue, I should add, is a totally different technique to speaking from notes.) In fact, I borrowed President Reagan's own Autocue and had it brought back to the British Embassy where I was staying. Harvey Thomas, who accompanied me, fixed it up and, ignoring any jetlag, I practised until 4 a.m. I did not go to bed, beginning the new working day with my usual black coffee and vitamin pills, then gave television interviews from 6.45 a.m., had my hair done and was ready at 10.30 to leave for the Capitol. I used my speech, which ranged widely over international issues, to give strong support for SDI. I had a terrific reception.

I regarded the *quid pro quo* for my strong public support of the President as being the right to be direct with him and members of his Administration in private. It was a little more awkward on this occasion for I had brought Geoffrey Howe and Michael Heseltine with me for my meeting and working lunch with the President, which made for a more stilted and less satisfactory conversation than on other occasions. (I did not bring them again.) But I went to the heart of what was worrying me. I told President Reagan that I thought it was important to avoid exaggerated rhetoric about SDI. We must not get into a situation where people were told that nuclear weapons were wicked, immoral and might soon be rendered unnecessary by the development of defensive systems. Otherwise the British public's support for them would be eroded. I think that the President took this point. He, for his part, emphasized that SDI was not going to be a bargaining chip. The United States would not go to Geneva and offer to give up SDI research if the Russians reduced nuclear weapons by a certain amount. He was to prove as good as his word.

REYKJAVIK

The following month (March 1985) saw the death of Mr Chernenko and, with remarkably little delay, the succession of Mr Gorbachev to the Soviet leadership. Once again I attended a Moscow funeral: the weather was, if anything, even colder than at Yuri Andropov's. Mr Gorbachev had a large number of foreign dignitaries to see. But I had almost an hour's talk with him that evening in St Katherine's Hall in the Kremlin. The atmosphere was more formal than at Chequers and the silent, sardonic presence of Mr Gromyko did not help. But I was able to explain to them the implications of the policy I had agreed with President Reagan the previous December at Camp David. It was clear that SDI was now the main preoccupation of the Soviets in arms control.

Mr Gorbachev brought, as we had expected, a new style to the Soviet Government. He spoke openly of the terrible state of the Soviet economy, though at this stage he was still relying on the methods associated with Mr Andropov's drive for greater efficiency rather than radical reform. An example of this was the draconian measures he took against alcoholism. As the year wore on, however, there was no evidence of improvement in conditions in the Soviet Union. Indeed, as our new – and first-class – ambassador to Moscow, Brian Cartledge, who had been my foreign affairs private secretary when I first became Prime Minister, pointed out in one of his first despatches, it was a matter of, 'jam tomorrow and, meanwhile, no vodka today'.

A distinct chill entered into Britain's relations with the Soviet Union as a result of expulsions which I authorized of Soviet officials who had been spying. The defection of Oleg Gordievsky, a former top KGB officer, meant that the Soviets knew how well informed we were about their activities. I had several meetings with Mr Gordievsky and had the highest regard for his judgement about events in the USSR. I repeatedly tried – without success – to have the Soviets release his family to join him in the West. (They eventually came after the failed coup in August 1991.)

In November President Reagan and Mr Gorbachev had their first meeting in Geneva. Not much of substance came out of it – the Soviets insisted on linking cuts in strategic nuclear weapons to an end to SDI research – but a good personal rapport quickly developed between the two leaders (though not, sadly, between their wives). There had been some concern expressed that President Reagan might be outmanoeuvred by his sharp-witted and younger Soviet counterpart. But he was not, which I found not at all surprising. For Ronald Reagan had had plenty of practice in his early years as President of the Screen Actors Guild in dealing with hard-headed trade union negotiations – and no one was more hard-headed than Mr Gorbachev.

During 1986 Mr Gorbachev showed great subtlety in playing on western public opinion by bringing forward tempting, but unacceptable, proposals on arms control. Relatively little was said by the Soviets on the link between SDI and cuts in nuclear weapons. But they were given no reason to believe that the Americans were prepared to suspend or stop SDI research. Late in the year it was agreed that President Reagan and Mr Gorbachev – with their Foreign ministers – should meet in Reykjavik, Iceland, to discuss substantive proposals.

In retrospect, the Reykjavik summit on that weekend of 11 and 12 October can be seen to have a quite different significance than most of the commentators at the time realized. A trap had been prepared for the Americans. Ever greater Soviet concessions were made during the summit: they agreed for the first time that the British and French deterrents should be excluded from the INF negotiations; and that cuts in strategic nuclear weapons should leave each side with equal numbers – rather than a straight percentage cut, which would have left the Soviets well ahead. They also made significant concessions on INF numbers. As the summit drew to an end President Reagan was proposing an agreement by which the whole arsenal of strategic nuclear weapons – bombers, long-range Cruise and ballistic missiles – would be halved within five years and the most powerful of these weapons, strategic ballistic missiles, eliminated altogether within ten. Mr Gorbachev was even more ambitious: he wanted the elimination of all strategic nuclear weapons by the end of the ten-year period.

But then suddenly, at the very end, the trap was sprung. President Reagan had conceded that during the ten-year period both sides would agree not to withdraw from the ABM Treaty, though development and testing compatible with the Treaty would be allowed. Mr Gorbachev said that the whole thing depended on confining SDI to the laboratory – a much tighter restriction that was likely to kill the prospect of an effective SDI. The President rejected the deal and the summit broke up. Its failure was widely portrayed as the result of the foolish intransigence of an elderly American President, obsessed with an unrealizable dream. In fact, President Reagan's refusal to trade away SDI for the apparent near fulfilment of his dream of a nuclear-free world was crucial to the victory over communism. He called the Soviets' bluff. The Russians may have scored an immediate propaganda victory when the talks broke down. But they had lost the game and I have no doubt that they knew it.* For they must have realized by now that they could not hope to match the United States in the competition for military technological supremacy and many of the concessions they made at Reykjavik proved impossible for them to retrieve.

My own reaction when I heard how far the Americans had been prepared to go was as if there had been an earthquake beneath my feet. I supported the idea of a 50 per cent reduction in strategic ballistic missiles over five years, but the President's proposal to eliminate them altogether after ten years was a different matter. The whole system of nuclear deterrence which had kept the peace for forty years was close to being abandoned. Had the President's proposals gone through, they would also have effectively killed off the Trident missile, forcing us to acquire a different system if we were to keep an independent nuclear deterrent. My intense relief that Soviet duplicity had finally caused these proposals to be withdrawn was balanced by a gnawing anxiety

* In February 1993 former senior Soviet officials confirmed precisely this point at a conference at Princeton University on the end of the Cold War.

that they might well be put forward on some new occasion. I had always disliked the original INF 'zero option', because I felt that these weapons made up for western Europe's unpreparedness to face a sudden, massive attack by the Warsaw Pact; I had gone along with it in the hope that the Soviets would never accept. But extending this approach more generally to all strategic ballistic missiles would have left the Soviets confronting western Europe with a huge superiority of conventional forces, chemical weapons and short-range missiles. It also undermined the credibility of deterrence: talk about eliminating strategic ballistic missiles (and possibly nuclear weapons altogether) at some point in the future raised doubts in people's minds about whether the United States was prepared to use nuclear weapons in the present. Somehow I had to get the Americans back onto the firm ground of a credible policy of nuclear deterrence. I arranged to fly to the United States to see President Reagan.

FURTHER DISCUSSIONS OF NUCLEAR STRATEGY AT CAMP DAVID

I have never felt more conscious than in the preparation for this visit of how much hung on my relationship with the President. It seemed to me that we were poised between a remarkable success and a possible catastrophe. I received the fullest briefing from the military about the implications of a defence strategy involving the elimination of all ballistic missiles. It was argued in some quarters in the US Administration that NATO strategy would not be undermined by the elimination of strategic ballistic missiles, and that aircraft, Cruise missiles and nuclear artillery, in all of which it was thought the West had a superiority, would provide an even better deterrent. In fact, NATO's whole strategy of flexible response – dependent as it was on a full range of possible military, including nuclear, responses to a Soviet attack – would have ceased to be viable. The so-called 'Air Breathing Systems' (Cruise missiles and bombers) were less certain to penetrate Soviet defences and generally more vulnerable to a pre-emptive strike. That would weaken their deterrent value. Europe would be dangerously exposed.

Just as important were the political considerations. To provide a credible British deterrent using Cruise missiles rather than Trident might be twice as expensive. Was it really likely that in an atmosphere full of talk of a world free of nuclear weapons we would ever obtain public support for such a programme? The more closely I examined the implications, the worse they were.

Percy Cradock (my Special Adviser on security matters), Charles Powell and I drafted and redrafted the arguments I would use with President Reagan. These must be logically coherent, persuasive, crisp and not too technical.

I flew into Washington on the afternoon of Friday 14 November. That evening I practised my arguments in meetings with George Schultz and Cap Weinberger. I saw George Bush for breakfast the following morning and then left for Camp David where I was met by President Reagan.

To my great relief I found that the President quickly understood why I was so deeply concerned about what had happened in Reykjavik. He agreed the draft statement which we had finalized after talking to George Schultz the previous day and which I subsequently issued at my press conference. This stated our policy on arms control after Reykjavik. It ran as follows:

> We agreed that priority should be given to: an INF agreement, with restraints on shorter range systems; a 50 per cent cut over 5 years in the US and Soviet strategic offensive weapons; and a ban on chemical weapons. In all three cases, effective verification would be an essential element. We also agreed on the need to press ahead with the SDI research programme which is permitted by the ABM Treaty. We confirmed that NATO's strategy of forward defence and flexible response would continue to require effective nuclear deterrence, based on a mix of systems. At the same time, reductions in nuclear weapons would increase the importance of eliminating conventional disparities. Nuclear weapons cannot be dealt with in isolation, given the need for stable overall balance at all times. We were also in agreement that these matters should continue to be the subject of close consultation within the alliance. The President reaffirmed the United States' intention to proceed with its strategic modernization programme, including Trident. He also confirmed his full support for the arrangements made to modernize Britain's independent nuclear deterrent, with Trident.

I had reason to be well pleased.

PREPARATION FOR MOSCOW VISIT

It is easy to imagine what the effect of the Camp David statement must have been in Moscow. It meant the end of the Soviets' hope of using SDI and President Reagan's dream of a nuclear weapons-free world to advance their strategy of denuclearizing Europe, leaving us vulnerable to military blackmail and weakening the link between the American and European pillars of NATO. It also demonstrated that, whether they liked it or not, I was able to have some influence on President Reagan on fundamental issues of alliance policy. Mr Gorbachev, therefore, had as much reason to do business with me as I with him. Add to this the fact that the Soviets often preferred to deal with right-wing western governments, because they regarded them as hard-headed negotiators who would nonetheless keep a bargain when it has been reached, and that I had struck up such a good personal relationship with Mr Gorbachev at Chequers before he became leader, and it is no surprise that I was soon invited to Moscow.

I prepared myself very thoroughly. On Friday 27 February 1987 I held an all-day seminar on the Soviet Union at Chequers. The two opposing tendencies among Sovietologists, which I have mentioned earlier, were apparent on this occasion. The enthusiasts stressed the scope and energy of Mr Gorbachev's reforms. The sceptics emphasized the orthodox communist objectives which Mr Gorbachev was pursuing and the limited effect even these modest measures of reform were having. On balance, the sceptics probably had the better of the argument. The view was that fundamental change was not on the agenda, only limited change which fully preserved the powers and guiding role of the Communist Party. Although Mr Gorbachev might want to enjoy the fruits of the incentive system, he could not take the risk of adopting it. Reform would, therefore, be conducted firmly within the bounds of the socialist system. In retrospect, it is possible to see that this analysis was flawed by a confusion between the *intentions* of Mr Gorbachev, which at any particular time were limited both by his communist way of thinking and by the circumstances of the moment, and the *effects* of his reforms, which unleashed forces that would sweep away the Soviet system and the Soviet state.

The seminar was only one aspect of my preparations. I also read through in detail the – usually long and indigestible – speeches which Mr Gorbachev had been making. Even though the political language was so different from that which I would have used, I felt that something new was emerging from them. Of these, by far the most important to date was that which he delivered to the Central Committee of the Communist Party towards the end of January 1987. In this he placed a new emphasis on democratizing the Party and, at the local level, the Soviet body politic itself: the forthcoming Soviet local elections would allow the nomination of more candidates than seats available in a small number of multi-member constituencies. This would prove to be the beginning – though only the beginning – of the replacement of democratic centralism by real democracy in the Soviet Union.

Soviet politics worked on the basis of slogans. These could not be taken at face value nor given a western interpretation. But, equally, they had to be taken seriously. The slogans under Mr Gorbachev were definitely changing. *Perestroika* (restructuring) had taken over from *uskorenie* (acceleration), reflecting his understanding that the fundamental problems of the Soviet economy required not just more of the same – central controls, discipline, efficiency drives – but real radical change. Similarly, the new talk of *glasnost* (openness) was based on an understanding that, unless the facts were known and at least some of the truth told about what was going on, conditions could never improve.

In the two years since Mr Gorbachev had become Soviet leader, the political reforms were already more evident than the economic benefits. Although there was precious little evidence of the Soviet economy working better, there was far more discussion of the need for political freedom and democracy. Mr Gorbachev had gone to great lengths to win over some of the leading dissidents, particularly Professor Sakharov, to support his programme. The truth about the horrors of Stalin – though not yet of Lenin – began to be published. The Soviets started to show greater sensitivity on matters of human rights, allowing more – though by no means all – Soviet Jews who wished to emigrate to do so. Whatever Mr Gorbachev's long-term goals, there was no doubt in my mind that he was making the Soviet Union something better than a 'prison house of nations' and we ought to support him in his efforts.

Such support was certainly needed. Although there was a freer political atmosphere and the improvements in political conditions endeared him to some of the intellectuals, ordinary Soviet citizens saw no real material progress. And though many members of the Politburo and the Central Committee had been replaced, it did not follow that all these replacements necessarily supported Mr Gorbachev and reform. There were worries too about the attitude of the army and the KGB.

All this posed the Soviet leader with a dilemma – and created a dilemma for us too.

Above all, the West had to ensure that Mr Gorbachev's reforms led to practical improvements in our own security. Were the Soviets prepared to reduce their military threat? Were they prepared to withdraw from Afghanistan? Would they end their policy of international subversion? We must press them on all these matters, but not in such a way that Mr Gorbachev's reform programme was discredited and so reversed, either by him or a hardline successor.

In the course of March I welcomed a stream of visitors to No. 10 and Chequers to brief me before my visit. The Chief Rabbi came to see me about the plight of the *refuseniks*. Peter Walker gave me his own impressions of the Soviet Union, gained on a recent visit. I discussed arrangements for the trip with the Soviet Ambassador. General Abrahamson, the Pentagon's Director of the SDI programme, came to Chequers to give me an up-to-date account of the state of research and the strategic issues. Oleg Gordievsky gave me the benefit of his analysis. So did the human rights activist, Yuri Orlov.

I was not going to Moscow as the representative of the West, let alone as a 'broker' between the USSR and the United States, but it was clearly very important that other western leaders should know the line I intended to take and that I should gauge their sentiments beforehand. I knew President Reagan's mind and had, I knew, his confidence. I therefore limited myself to sending him a lengthy message. There was only one specific policy point at issue which I felt it necessary to raise. This was a proposal, which I had made to the Americans and which they were studying but were not so far prepared to accept, that the United States should give the Soviets an assurance about the shape and time-scale of SDI – what was known in the jargon as 'predictability'. My argument was that since it would take a number of years before the decision about the deployment of SDI need be reached there was no point in alarming the Soviets unnecessarily now.

I also arranged to meet President Mitterrand and then Chancellor Kohl on Monday 23 March. The French President – socialist or not – has the use of a number of delightful châteaux. He also seems to have access to the best chefs in the French Republic. Lunch with him at the Château de Benouville in Normandy was no exception. And of course each dish had to have a traditional Norman flavour, with sauces of cider or calvados and some of that aromatic Camembert against which the health-conscious bureaucrats of the European Community were to labour in vain. President Mitterrand's attitude to the Soviets was very like my own. He believed, as I did, that Mr Gorbachev was prepared to go a long way to change the system. One of his shrewdest and most perceptive observations was that the Soviet leader would find that 'when you change the form, you are on the way to changing the substance.' But the French President knew too that the Soviets respected toughness. He said that we must resist the attempt to denuclearize Europe. I warmly agreed.

Nor did I find any disagreement with Chancellor Kohl. The division of Germany, past history and the existence of large numbers of Germans living as minorities throughout the Soviet bloc gave this very German leader a clear insight into the USSR. Moreover, as he reminded me, West Germany had for many years been the main target of Soviet propaganda. He had doubts about whether Mr Gorbachev would survive: he was running a high-risk policy. Nor should we assume that his reforms – which Chancellor Kohl saw as intended to modernize a communist system, not create a democratic system – could be carried through without suffering. Helmut Kohl always had a strong sense of history and he reminded me that from the time of Peter the Great the reforms of Russian leaders had not been without their victims.

My last public pronouncement about the Soviet Union before I left had been my speech to the Conservative Central Council in Torquay on Saturday 21 March. It would have been easy to tone down my criticism of the Soviet regime. But I was not prepared to do so. Too often in the past western leaders had placed the search for trouble-free relations with foreign autocrats above plain speaking of the truth. I said:

> We have seen in Mr Gorbachev's speeches a clear admission that the communist system is not working. Far from enabling the Soviet Union to catch up with the West, it is falling further behind. We hear new language being used by their leaders. Words which we recognize, like 'openness' and 'democratization'. But do they have the same meaning for them as they do for us? Some of those who have been imprisoned for their political and religious beliefs have been released. We welcome that. But many more remain in prison or are refused permission to emigrate. We want to see them free, or reunited with their families abroad, if that is what they choose . . . When I go to Moscow to meet Mr Gorbachev next week, my goal will be a peace based not on illusion or surrender, but on realism and strength . . . Peace needs confidence and trust between countries and peoples. Peace means an end to the killing in Cambodia, an end to the

> slaughter in Afghanistan. It means honouring the obligations which the Soviet Union freely accepted in the Helsinki Final Act in 1975 to allow free movement of people and ideas and other basic human rights . . . We shall reach our judgements not on words, not on intentions, not on promises, but on actions and results.

VISIT TO THE SOVIET UNION: MARCH–APRIL 1987

I left Heathrow for Moscow just after midday on Saturday 28 March. I always used a special VC10 for these flights. A dozen of these aircraft were permanently based at Brize Norton and two or three of them had been adapted for ministerial overseas visits. The VC10 was not a modern aircraft and was rather noisy. But it was pleasant to fly in and had two big advantages. One was that there was plenty of space for me and my staff. There were tables to work at. There was a separate compartment for me to get an hour or two's sleep when allowed respite from writing speeches and reading papers. There was even room for journalists towards the rear of the aircraft. The other advantage was the RAF staff who provided us with delicious food, drink and friendly service.

When I landed, there was an official welcoming ceremony which began at Moscow Airport, where I was presented with a large bouquet of red roses which proved remarkably photogenic against my plain black coat and fox-fur hat. We then sped down the centre of the road, reserved for high officials and their guests, to the Kremlin. There I had to make my way down the length of St George's Hall, under its glittering crystal chandeliers, to meet Mr and Mrs Gorbachev and to exchange formal pleasantries. I cannot deny that I enjoyed the splendour of these occasions, but I sometimes reflected that the traditional formalities were intended to clothe in the trappings of legitimacy regimes that had neither historic nor democratic credentials.

On Sunday morning I was driven fifty miles out from Moscow to the Russian Orthodox Monastery at Zagorsk. I knew that this was a very important time for Orthodox Christians in Russia who, the following year, would be celebrating the millennium of their Church. The Soviet authorities had allowed some churches to reopen and the numbers of seminarians to increase a little. There was also a slight increase in the amount of religious literature allowed. As the

Khrushchev years showed – when religious persecution sharply increased, even though in other areas liberalization occurred – there was no guarantee that the pressure on Christians would be removed just because of *glasnost* and *perestroika*. I felt it important that I should show solidarity.

Crowds were waiting outside the gates of the monastery when I arrived. Against the wishes of the communist Minister for Religious Affairs (sic) who accompanied me, I insisted on getting out of the car to speak to them. Then I got back in and we were taken into the grounds of the monastery itself. I had never attended an Orthodox liturgy. I was struck by the richness of the singing, the clouds of incense, the gorgeous vestments, the sensuousness of the total experience. It was a far cry from the Sunday service at Finkin Street Methodist Church in Grantham. I was also moved by the devotion of the worshippers – it would be too much to say 'the congregation', for so much of what was going on was evidently a matter of private prayer, with people coming in and out to attend a part of the apparently endless ritual. I stayed for forty minutes or so and then lit one of the long, thin unbleached Orthodox candles, placing it in the sandbox which contained so many others. I reflected that it would take more than limited reforms of the communist system to contain the power of this Christian revival.

The best that can be said of most of the Russian Orthodox leaders was that they probably had little choice other than to collaborate so closely with the communists. The worst that can be said was that they were active KGB agents. Certainly, the speech which was given by the Deputy Patriarch over lunch could have been drafted by Agitprop: it concentrated heavily on the need to get rid of all nuclear weapons. Discarding my own prepared text, I answered by stressing instead the need to release prisoners of conscience. In the car, on the way back to Moscow, I asked the Minister for Religious Affairs whether there were still people in gaol for their religious beliefs. He said, 'No, unless they are in for something else.' Such as possessing a Bible, I thought.

That afternoon it had been arranged, at my suggestion, that I should do a 'walkabout' of the sort which comes so easily to western politicians but which the Soviets typically – and perhaps for good reason – avoided. (Mr Gorbachev, though, was in this, as in other matters, a western-style politician.) As I walked around a large housing estate in a bleak suburb of Moscow in the slushy snow and bitter wind, more and more people gathered to meet me. Soon they poured in from everywhere, a huge crowd cheering, smiling, wanting to shake hands. As in Hungary I was being received rapturously as an anti-communist by those who knew the system even better than I did.

That evening I attended a performance of *Swan Lake* at the Bolshoi Theatre with the Gorbachevs. We shared a box. Like all good Russians, they were both clearly enthusiasts for the ballet. I too enjoy the ballet, almost as much as the opera, so we found this in common. During the interval the Gorbachevs held a small supper party for me in a private room. It was a relaxed occasion. For some reason the conversation turned from the story of *Swan Lake* to the subject of bread-making in the Soviet Union. Mr Gorbachev said that, partly as a result of help which the Soviet Union had received from ICI, the quality of Soviet bread was now much better than it had been. But it was difficult to please people. When the quality had been lower, it had been necessary to add salt. Now that the quality had improved, so that salt was no longer necessary for the bread, the people still preferred salty bread. He had told the Soviet minister responsible for bread-making to go on television to explain to the people that they were now getting better bread, even though it was not what they were familiar with. Ironically, a similar point had recently been made by the great dissident Vladimir Bukovsky. He remarked that whenever the Soviet media reported that scientists had found that some food – sausage, say – was bad for your health, the ordinary Russians reacted immediately by telling each other: 'So they're running out of sausage.' Such are the unanticipated consequences of collectivism.

We drank some excellent Georgian wine. I was encouraged to have another glass when Mr Gorbachev assured me that it helped some Georgians to live to be a hundred. He was very conscious of the unpopularity of the action he had taken against alcoholism. This had already resulted in a decline in deaths at work and road accidents. But it was an uphill struggle. He had read that people in the West thought that *perestroika* was doomed because he had taken away alcohol from the people and privileges from party officials. We lingered rather too long over supper and the audience had been sitting in semi-darkness for some time when we returned. When we bade farewell Mr Gorbachev was still in a jovial mood and said that he looked forward to our meeting tomorrow.

Monday began for me with a meeting of what it would be perhaps impolite but only accurate to describe as impeccably distinguished Soviet stooges. This group of tame artists, academics and scientists took up again the themes which had been prominent in the Deputy Patriarch's speech. They knew, presumably, that I was to have lunch with Dr Sakharov and other dissidents and wanted to extol the merits of communism first. Then I left for my discussions with Mr Gorbachev in the Kremlin.

I sat across the table from him, a long flower vase between us. I was accompanied by just one member of my staff and an interpreter. It was soon clear that he, glancing from time to time at the notes in front of him, intended to take me to task for my Central Council speech. He said that when the Soviet leaders had studied it they had felt the breeze of the 1940s and '50s. It reminded them of Winston Churchill's speech at Fulton, Missouri (about the 'Iron Curtain') and the Truman doctrine. They had even considered whether they might have to cancel the visit.

I did not apologize. I said that there was one point which I did not make in my Central Council speech but which I would make now. This was that I knew of no evidence that the Soviet Union had given up the Brezhnev doctrine or the goal of securing world domination for communism. We were ready to fight the battle of ideas: indeed this was the right way to fight. But instead we in the West saw Soviet subversion in South Yemen, in Ethiopia, in Mozambique, in Angola and in Nicaragua. We saw Vietnam being supported by the Soviet Union in its conquest of Cambodia. We saw Afghanistan occupied by Soviet troops. We naturally drew the conclusion that the goal of worldwide communism was still being pursued. This was a crucial consideration for the West. We recognized that Mr Gorbachev was committed to internal reforms in the Soviet Union. But we had to ask ourselves whether this would lead to changes in external policies.

I went on to show that I had read Mr Gorbachev's speeches with as much care as he seemed to have read mine. I told him that I had found his January Central Committee speech fascinating. But I wanted to know whether the internal changes he was making would lead to changes in the Soviet Union's foreign policies as well. I added that I had not expected that we would have generated quite so much heat so early in the discussion. Mr Gorbachev replied with a roar of laughter that he welcomed 'acceleration' and was pleased we were speaking frankly.

The conversation went back and forth, not just covering regional conflicts (with me placing much of the blame on the Soviet Union and Mr Gorbachev blaming the West), but going right to the heart of what differentiated the western and communist systems. This I described as being a distinction between societies in which power was dispersed and societies based on central control and coercion.

Mr Gorbachev was as critical of Conservatism as I was of communism. But he was a good deal less well informed about it. His view was that the British Conservative Party was the party of the 'haves' in Britain and that our system of what he called 'bourgeois democracy' was designed to fool people about who really controlled the levers of power. I explained that what I was trying to do was to create a society of 'haves', not a class of them.

We then turned to arms control. As at our meeting at Chequers, he showed that he was well versed in all that was being written about the Soviet Union in the West. He knew that it was being openly said that the Soviet Union would need to reduce its military budget to finance the development of the civil economy and that the Soviets were desperate for arms agreements. He was clearly extremely sensitive and worried about being humiliated by the West. In particular, he blamed me for frustrating the moves towards the elimination of nuclear weapons which had been discussed at Reykjavik. (So the Camp David statement had indeed been noticed.) I found myself arguing, yet again, the case for the retention of the nuclear deterrent. I also said that it was quite clear to me that the Soviet Union's objective was to bring about the denuclearization of Europe, leaving the USSR with a preponderance of conventional and chemical weapons. But I welcomed the fact that Mr Gorbachev had now broken the link, to which the Soviets had previously held, between an INF Agreement and other arms control issues, such as SDI. At this point I returned – rather late because our animated argument had overrun the scheduled time limit – to lunch with the Sakharovs and other former dissidents who were now supporting the Gorbachev reforms. I was impressed by what they told me of the changes being made. But I told them that it was not enough to support Mr Gorbachev now; they should be prepared to support him in five to ten years' time when the going got really tough. I said that the costs of reform would be apparent long before the benefits.

I then returned to the Kremlin to continue my talks with Mr Gorbachev. St Katherine's Hall, where we had met that morning, was now being rearranged for the plenary session which was due to follow. So we were moved to the 'Red Room' of the Kremlin, which Mr Gorbachev said he hoped might improve my views. The afternoon discussion was less contentious and more informative. He explained to me the economic reforms he was making and the problems still to be faced. This led on to technology. He claimed to be confident about the Soviet Union's capacity for developing computers in competition with the United States. But I was not convinced. And that led back to SDI which Mr Gorbachev promised the Soviets would match – in some way that he would not disclose. I tried to interest him in my proposal for greater 'predictability' as regards the progress of the American SDI programme, but apparently to no avail.

Then I pressed Mr Gorbachev on human rights in general and the treatment of the Jews in particular. I also raised the question of Afghanistan, where I had the impression that he was searching for some way out. Finally, I listed the points which I thought we could agree on for a public account of our discussion which, he agreed, had contributed to better relations and greater confidence between us. But it was now very late. Guests were already assembling for the formal banquet at which I was to speak. The plenary session was abandoned. Putting diplomacy ahead of fashion, I abandoned my plans to return to the embassy and change: I attended the banquet in the short wool dress I had been wearing all day. I felt rather like Ninotchka in reverse.

Tuesday began with a rather dull meeting with Prime Minister Ryzhkov – apparently a pleasant, competent man, who, alas, could never quite escape from the armour of his communist training – and other Soviet ministers. I had hoped to learn more about the Soviet economic reforms, but we got bogged down once again in arms control and then in bilateral trade issues.

Far more exciting and worthwhile for all concerned was the interview which I gave to three journalists from Soviet Television. I learnt afterwards that this had an enormous impact on Soviet opinion. Most of the questions related to nuclear weapons. I defended the West's line and indeed the retention of the nuclear deterrent. I went on to point out that there were more nuclear weapons in the Soviet Union than in any other country and that the Soviets had led the way on deploying short- and intermediate-range weapons as well. I reminded them of their huge superiority in conventional and chemical weapons. I pointed out that the Soviet Union was ahead of the United States in ABM defences. Nobody had ever told ordinary Russians these facts. They learned them from my interview for the first time. The interview was allowed to go out uncut from Soviet television, which I afterwards regarded as proof that my confidence in Mr Gorbachev's basic integrity was not misplaced.

That evening the Gorbachevs gave me dinner in an old mansion, converted many years before for entertaining foreign guests. The atmosphere was, perhaps deliberately, as close to that of Chequers as I ever found in the Soviet Union. In the rooms around which Mr Gorbachev showed us, Churchill, Eden, Stalin and Molotov had smoked, drunk, and argued. We were a small group, the Gorbachevs being joined by just the Ryzhkovs, who did not take a very active part in the conversation. A brightly burning log fire – again like Chequers

– illumined the room to which we later withdrew to put right the world's problems over coffee and liqueurs. I saw two interesting examples of the way in which old Marxist certainties were being challenged. There was a lively argument between the Gorbachevs, which I provoked, about the definition of the 'working class' about which we heard so much in Soviet propaganda. I wanted to know how they defined this in the Soviet Union – a point of some substance in a system in which, as the old Polish saying goes, 'we pretend to work and they pretend to pay us.' Mrs Gorbachev thought that anyone who worked, whatever his job or profession, was a worker. Her husband argued initially that only the blue-collar workers counted. But he then reconsidered and said that this was largely an historical or 'scientific' (that is Marxist) term which did not do justice to the diversity of today's society.

The second indication of a break with old socialist certainties was when he told me – with tantalizingly little detail – of plans which were being discussed for increasing people's incomes and then having them make some payment for public services like health and education. Not surprisingly, such plans, whatever they were, came to nothing.

The following morning I had breakfast with *refuseniks* at the British Embassy. Theirs was a disturbing tale of heroism under mainly petty but continual persecution. Every obstacle, short of total prohibition, was put in the way of their worship and expression of cultural identity. They were discriminated against at work – if they found work. They told me that giving private tuition was the easiest way to earn a living: for these were educated people whose talents the Soviet state should have been able to draw upon. One of their leaders, Iosif Begun, brought me a tiny Star of David, which he had carved out of horn while he was in prison and which I have always kept.

Later that morning I left Moscow for Tbilisi in Georgia. I had wanted to see a Soviet republic other than Russia and I knew that Georgia would present a great cultural and geographical contrast. This certainly proved to be the case. From all that I saw – and from the excellent and exotic food and Georgian wine – it was clear to me that given the right political and economic conditions this was an area where the tourist industry could flourish. But, as in the detective story, perhaps the most important feature of my admittedly brief visit was the 'dog which did not bark'. Although I was presented with all the evidence of a vigorous folklore and although I knew how ancient and distinctive Georgia was – only coming under the control of Russia at the beginning of the nineteenth century – there was still no evidence of that desire for national self-assertion and independence which was to come.

That night I left Tbilisi Airport for London. It had been, quite simply, the most fascinating and most important foreign visit I had made. I could sense in the four days I spent in the Soviet Union that the ground was shifting underneath the communist system. De Tocqueville's insight that 'experience shows that the most dangerous moment for a bad government is generally that in which it sets about reform' sprang to my mind. The welcome I had received – both the warm affection from the Russian crowds, and the respect of the Soviet authorities in long hours of negotiations – suggested that something fundamental was happening under the surface. The West's system of liberty which Ronald Reagan and I personified in the eastern bloc (thanks, ironically, to the effects of communist propaganda) was increasingly in the ascendant: the Soviet system was showing its cracks. I sensed that great changes were at hand – but I could never have guessed how quickly they would come.

CHAPTER XVII

Putting the World to Rights

Diplomacy towards and visits to the Far East, the Middle East and Africa – 1984–1990

When I was in Opposition I was very doubtful of the value of high-profile public diplomacy. To some extent I remain so. My political philosophy in domestic affairs is founded on a deep scepticism about the ability of politicians to change the fundamentals of the economy or society: the best they can do is to create a framework in which people's talents and virtues are mobilized not crushed. Similarly, in foreign affairs, the underlying realities of power are not transformed by meetings and understandings between heads of government. A country with a weak economy, an unstable social base or an ineffective administration cannot compensate for these – at least for long – with an ambitious diplomatic programme. That said, my experience as Prime Minister did convince me that a skilfully conducted foreign policy based on strength can magnify a country's influence and allow progress to be made in dealing with thorny problems around the world. As the years went by, I put increasing effort into international diplomacy.

But it is still necessary to have a clear idea of the potential and the limits of statesmanship. The twin, opposing, temptations of the statesman are hubris and timidity. It is easy to subscribe to ringing declarations and ambitious global plans. It is a great deal harder to balance vision with practical measures and persistence. Under some circumstances, to try definitively to 'solve' a long-standing problem will be to make it worse. Under others, even a brief delay will mean an opportunity lost. The statesman has to be able to distinguish between the two, always knowing the destination; never presuming that the path is open; then, when it is, pressing ahead with every means available.

And in all this one should never lose sight of the importance of the personal chemistry which exists between those who conduct their nation's affairs. I found myself liking and respecting – and sometimes heartily disliking and distrusting – heads of government not just as politicians but as people. I did so irrespective of colour, creed or political opinion. Personal relations must never become a substitute for hard-headed pursuit of national interests. But nor should any statesman ignore their importance. Foreign visits allowed me to meet, talk to and seek to influence heads of government on their own ground. These visits gave me insights into the way those I dealt with in the clinical atmosphere of great international conferences actually lived and felt. Moreover, it gave others a chance to know me. Longevity has its drawbacks and difficulties in domestic politics, where the media are always longing for a new face. But in foreign affairs there is a huge and cumulative advantage in simply being known both by politicians and by ordinary people around the world.

All of these elements were present in my dealings with and visits to the Far East, the Middle East and Africa. In these regions – in the last case a whole continent – the struggle between East and West was being waged by influence and by arms. But in each that contest also worked upon other issues particular to the region.

In the Far East, the dominant long-term questions concerned the future role and development of a political and military super-power, the People's Republic of China, and an economic super-power, Japan; though for Britain, it was the future of Hong Kong which had to take precedence over everything else.

In the Middle East, it was the Iran-Iraq War, with its undercurrent of destabilizing Muslim fundamentalism, which cost most lives and threatened most economic harm. But I always felt that the Arab-Israeli dispute was of even more abiding importance. For it was this which time and again prevented the emergence – at least until the Gulf War – of a solid bloc of more or less self-confident pro-western Arab states, no longer having to look over their shoulders at what their critics would make of the plight of the landless Palestinians.

Finally, in Africa – where, as in the Middle East, Britain was not just another player in the great game, but a country with historic links and a distinct, if not always favourable, image – it was the future of South Africa which dominated all discussion. For reasons which will become clear, no one had a better opportunity – or a more thankless task – than I did in resolving an issue which had poisoned the West's relations with black Africa, left isolated the most advanced economic power in that continent and been used, incidentally, to justify more hypocrisy and hyperbole than I heard on any other subject.

THE FAR EAST

Hong Kong

My visit to China in September 1982 and my talks with Zhao Ziyang and Deng Xiaoping had had three beneficial effects.* First, confidence in Hong Kong about the future had been restored. Second, I now had a very clear idea of what the Chinese would and would not accept. Third, we had a form of words which both we and the Chinese could use about the future of Hong Kong which would provide a basis for continuing discussion between us. But there was a real risk that each of these gains would be transitory. Confidence in the colony was fragile. It was by no means clear how we could persuade the Chinese to be more forthcoming with their assurances. And – what I found most worrying – the Chinese proved very reluctant to get on with the talks which I had envisaged when I left Peking. For months nothing happened. I asked the advice of that old China hand, Henry Kissinger: his response was 'don't worry – that's just their way.' But I was worried and became more so as time passed.

On the morning of Friday 28 January 1983 I held a meeting with ministers, officials and the Governor of Hong Kong to review the position. We had learnt that in June the Chinese were proposing unilaterally to announce their own plan for Hong Kong's future. We were all agreed that we must try to prevent this happening. I myself had been doing some fundamental rethinking about our objectives. I proposed that in the absence of progress in the talks we should now develop the democratic structure in Hong Kong as though it were our aim to achieve independence or self-government within a short period, as we had done with Singapore. This would involve building up a more Chinese government and administration in Hong Kong, with the Chinese members increasingly taking their own decisions and with Britain in an increasingly subordinate position. We might also consider using referenda as an accepted institution there. Since then legislative elections have demonstrated a strong appetite for democracy among the Hong Kong Chinese, to which the Government has had to respond. At that time, however, nobody else seemed much attracted by my ideas: and in the end I had reluctantly to concede that since the Chinese would not accept such an approach it was not then worth

* See pp. 259–62.

studying further. But I could not just leave things as they were, so in March 1983 I sent a private letter to Zhao Ziyang which broke the deadlock and got Anglo-Chinese talks off the ground again. This went marginally further than I had in Peking. There I had told Mr Deng that I would be prepared to consider making recommendations to Parliament about Hong Kong's sovereignty if suitable arrangements could be made to preserve its stability and prosperity. I now subtly strengthened the formulation:

> Provided that agreement could be reached between the British and Chinese Government on administrative arrangements for Hong Kong which would guarantee the future prosperity and stability of Hong Kong, and would be acceptable to the British Parliament and to the people of Hong Kong as well as to the Chinese Government, I *would be prepared to recommend* to Parliament that sovereignty over the whole of Hong Kong should revert to China. [my italics]

Geoffrey Howe and the Foreign Office wanted to go further: they argued strongly that I should concede early in the talks that British administration would not continue. I saw no reason to make such a concession. I wanted to use every bargaining card we had to maximum effect. Just how few such cards there were, however, quickly became apparent.

There were three rounds of talks over the summer in which no progress was made. When we took stock of the situation at a meeting on Monday 5 September it was clear that the talks would break down when they resumed on 22 September unless we conceded administration as well as sovereignty to the Chinese. One particular problem was that the timing of the talks was publicly known and it had become the practice at the end of each session to announce the date of the next. If the Chinese decided to hold up progress or break off altogether it would immediately become apparent and damage would be done to confidence in Hong Kong.

This is indeed what happened after the 22–23 September talks. Intensified Chinese propaganda and anxiety at the absence of any reassuring element in the official communiqué caused a massive capital flight out of the Hong Kong dollar and a sharp fall in its value on the foreign exchanges.

Early on Sunday morning, 25 September, I received a telephone call from Alan Walters, who was then in Washington and had been unable to track down either Nigel Lawson or the Governor of the

Bank of England. Alan was convinced that the only way to prevent a complete collapse of the currency and all the serious political consequences that entailed was to restore the currency board system – backing the Hong Kong dollar at a par value with the United States dollar. (The Hong Kong Government's reserves were big enough to make this possible.) Although I was largely convinced by Alan's arguments and accepted the urgent need for action, I still had some concerns – mainly whether our exchange reserves would be put at risk. But I informed the Treasury of what I considered was a dangerous crisis that needed immediate defusing, and they got in touch with Nigel and the Governor of the Bank. The following Tuesday I met Nigel, the Governor and Alan at the Washington embassy. Although Nigel was at first reluctant and the Governor had reservations, they eventually agreed with me that a restoration of the currency board was the only solution. As always this news soon leaked out to financial markets, confidence was restored and the crisis of the Hong Kong dollar was over. We sealed it later on 16 October 1983 by fixing the Hong Kong dollar at an exchange rate of 7.80 Hong Kong dollars for a US dollar. The financial press thought it was 'an unalloyed success'. And so time has proved it to be.

But it was also necessary to see that Anglo-Chinese talks began again. On 14 October I sent a further message to Zhao Ziyang expressing our willingness to explore Chinese ideas for the future of Hong Kong and holding out the possibility of a settlement on those lines. I had by now reluctantly decided that we would have to concede not just sovereignty but administration to the Chinese. On 19 October the talks were accordingly resumed.

I hoped that by pointing out in my message those aspects of the Chinese negotiating position which might conceivably lead to as much autonomy for and as little change in the way of life of the people of Hong Kong as possible, we might make some progress. In November I authorized that working papers on the legal system, financial system and external economic relations of Hong Kong be handed over to the Chinese. But their position hardened. They now made it clear that they were not prepared to sign a treaty with us at all but rather to declare 'policy objectives' for Hong Kong themselves. By now I had abandoned any hope of turning Hong Kong into a self-governing territory. The overriding objective had to be to avoid a breakdown in the negotiations, so I authorized our ambassador in Peking to spell out more clearly the implications of my 14 October letter: that we envisaged no link of authority or accountability between Britain and Hong Kong after 1997. But I felt depressed.

At this time I received further advice from someone whose experience in dealing with the Chinese I knew to be unequalled. At the Commonwealth Heads of Government Meeting (CHOGM) in New Delhi I discussed our problems in dealing with the Chinese with Lee Kuan Yew, the Prime Minister of Singapore. Unfortunately, the discussion was interrupted on several occasions and Mr Lee telephoned through to me his full advice later. This was that we should send a very senior minister or emissary to convey our proposals at the highest possible level of the Chinese Government. It was crucial, he said, that we should adopt the right attitude – neither defiant nor submissive, but calm and friendly. We should say clearly that the fact was that if China did not wish Hong Kong to survive, nothing would allow it to do so. This, of course, was precisely the point that Deng Xiaoping had put to me in September 1982. I had managed then to persuade him that there was an international price to be paid if he simply took over without any regard for the prosperity and system of Hong Kong. But I now had to accept that China's concern for its international good name would allow us only so much latitude. Mr Lee's advice therefore confirmed me in the course upon which I had decided the previous month. The question remained: what would be the basis of the Chinese administration? From now on we must concentrate on the questions of autonomy and preservation of the existing legal, economic and social system after 1997.

Whatever concessions we had to make, I was determined that the representatives of the people of Hong Kong – the 'unofficial' members of the Hong Kong Executive Council (EXCO) – should be consulted at each crucial stage. Geoffrey Howe and I met them on the morning of Monday 16 January 1984 at Downing Street. As always, I was struck by their common sense and realism about the highly unpalatable options they knew we had to consider. They basically shared our objective, which was the highest degree of autonomy for Hong Kong we could get backed by the best possible Chinese assurances. After this meeting I began to think hard about how best we could give undertakings of a right of entry to the United Kingdom to those in Hong Kong who would be putting themselves and their families at risk through sensitive work for the Hong Kong Government in the period up to 1997. When I discussed the matter with ministers and officials in July I said that we should err on the side of generosity. It must never be said that the United Kingdom repaid loyalty with disloyalty.

The single most difficult issue which we now faced in negotiations with the Chinese was the location of the 'Joint Liaison Group' which would be established after the planned Anglo-Chinese Agreement had been signed to make provision for the transition. I was worried that during the transition this body would become an alternative power centre to the Governor or, worse, that it would create the impression of some kind of Anglo-Chinese 'Condominium' which would have destroyed confidence. But I also insisted that it should continue for three years after 1997 so as to maintain confidence after the handover of administration had taken place. I wrote to Mr Zhao to this effect.

Geoffrey Howe had visited Peking in April and now returned in July, accompanied by Sir Percy Cradock, and successfully reached a compromise on the Joint Liaison Group, which would not operate in Hong Kong before 1988. Geoffrey's patient negotiations eventually secured agreement. It was no triumph: but nor could it be, considering the fact that we were dealing with an intransigent and overwhelmingly superior power.

The terms had three main advantages. First, they constituted what would be an unequivocally binding international agreement. Second, they were sufficiently clear and detailed about what would happen in Hong Kong after 1997 to command the confidence of the people of Hong Kong. Third, there was a provision that the terms of the proposed Anglo-Chinese Agreement would be stipulated in the Basic Law to be passed by Chinese People's Congress: this would in effect be the constitution of Hong Kong after 1997.

Geoffrey was always good at the actual process of negotiation, though we sometimes fell out as to what was possible as a result of negotiations. In this case, though, he had shown an impressive grasp of the issues throughout; moreover, his meeting with Mr Deng was highly effective in reassuring the Chinese that we were to be trusted and so paving the way for me to return to Peking to sign the Joint Agreement. I congratulated Geoffrey in Cabinet on his return – and I meant every word.

My visit to China in December to sign the Joint Agreement on Hong Kong was a much less tense occasion than my visit two years earlier. The difficult negotiations were already concluded. We had won the support, with some reservations, of the Unofficial Members of EXCO for the agreement. I had explained its contents to President Reagan and won American support as well. The main purpose, therefore, of my talks in Peking must be to strengthen the trust which the Chinese had in our good faith as regards the management of the transition till 1997 and to reinforce in every way possible their sense of obligation to carry through the agreement.

I arrived in Peking on the evening of Tuesday 18 December. The official welcoming ceremony was at 9 o'clock the following morning: at it I reviewed a Guard of Honour in Tiananmen Square, where less than five years later the massacre of protesters took place which would suddenly throw doubt on the carefully negotiated agreement I was here to conclude.

The rest of the morning was spent in some two and a half hours of talks with Prime Minister Zhao Ziyang. The mood was friendly and relaxed: but it was clear to me that the Chinese were as concerned about the transitional period as I was. They wanted to maintain stability and prosperity: but they had their own ideas about how this should be done. I emphasized that it all came down to the drafting of the Basic Law. It must be suited to the capitalist system and consistent with the Hong Kong legal system. I stressed how important it was that China had expressed willingness to solicit opinions from a wide range of people within Hong Kong. I then broached what I knew would be an even more sensitive topic. I said that the Chinese would be aware of our proposals for the constitutional development of Hong Kong – essentially strengthening in a modest way democracy and autonomy, though I was careful not to use these words. Mr Zhao answered that the Chinese Government was not prepared to make any comment on constitutional development in the transitional period. In principle, the Chinese too wanted more Hong Kong people involved in the administration. But that process must not adversely affect stability and prosperity or the smooth transfer of government in 1997. I left it at that; it was as far as I felt it was prudent to go at this meeting.

In the afternoon I talked to the Chinese Communist Party General Secretary, Hu Yaobang, whose influence I had been told was greater than some outside observers thought. I had earlier met the diminutive Mr Hu when he visited London. He was widely considered – perhaps too widely for his own interests as it turned out – to be Deng Xiaoping's preferred successor and was known as a reformist. I had said quite openly to him in London that many of us hoped that those like him who had lived through the Cultural Revolution would bring a new approach to China's affairs. He went on to tell me, with tears in his eyes, about the suffering he personally had endured at this time. It would be nice to believe that he could understand at least some of my worries about Hong Kong's future: but perhaps human nature is not quite that simple.

I then went on to the crucial meeting with Deng Xiaoping. The most important immediate guarantee of Hong Kong's future was Mr Deng's goodwill. I told him that the 'stroke of genius' in the negotiations had been his concept of 'one country, two systems'. He, with becoming modesty, attributed the credit for this to Marxist historical dialectics, or to use what appeared to be the appropriate slogan, 'seeking truth from the facts'. Apparently, the concept of 'one country, two systems' had been devised originally from Chinese proposals of 1980 for dealing with Taiwan. (In fact, it proved a good deal more appropriate for Hong Kong: the Taiwanese attitude was clearly 'one country, one system – ours' – and given their economic success and their move to democracy, I can see their point.)

The Chinese had set out in the agreement a fifty-year period after 1997 for its duration. I was intrigued by this and asked why fifty years. Mr Deng said that China hoped to approach the economic level of advanced countries by the end of that time. If China wanted to develop herself, she had to be open to the outside world for the whole of that period. The maintenance of Hong Kong's stability and prosperity accorded with China's interest in modernizing its economy. This did not mean that in fifty years China would be a capitalist country. Far from it. He said that the one billion Chinese on the mainland would pursue socialism firmly. If Taiwan and Hong Kong practised capitalism that would not affect the socialist orientation of the bulk of the country. Indeed the practice of capitalism in some small areas would benefit socialism. (Since then, it has become clear that Chinese socialism is whatever the Chinese Government does; and what it has been doing amounts to a thorough-going embrace of capitalism. In economic policy, at least, Mr Deng has indeed sought truth from facts.)

I found his analysis basically reassuring, if not persuasive. It was reassuring because it suggested that the Chinese would for their own self-interest seek to keep Hong Kong prosperous. It was unpersuasive for quite different reasons. The Chinese belief that the benefits of a liberal economic system can be had without a liberal political system seems to me false in the long term. Of course, culture and character affect the way in which economic and political systems work in particular countries. The crackdown after the Tiananmen Square massacre in June 1989 convinced many outside observers that in China political and economic liberty were not interdependent. Certainly, after those terrible events we reassessed what needed to be done to secure Hong Kong's future. I was reinforced in my determination to honour Britain's obligations to those on whom British administration and Hong Kong's prosperity depended up to 1997. In any case, I always felt Britain would benefit economically from talented, entrepreneurial Hong Kong people coming here.

So in 1990 we legislated to give British citizenship to 50,000 key people in the Colony and their dependants – though the essential purpose of the scheme was to provide sufficient reassurance to persuade them to stay at their posts in Hong Kong where they were vitally needed. We were also brought under strong pressure immediately to accelerate the process of democratization in Hong Kong. There were, in any case, strong moral arguments for doing so. But all my instincts told me that this was the wrong time. The Chinese leadership was feeling acutely apprehensive. Such a step at that moment could have provoked a strong defensive reaction that might have undermined the Hong Kong Agreement. We needed to wait for calmer times before considering moves towards democratization within the scope of the agreement.

If it was China's recognition that she could benefit from extending the notion of 'one country, two systems' to Hong Kong which allowed the Hong Kong Agreement to be reached, something more would be needed in the long term. At some point the increasing momentum of economic change in China itself will lead to political change. Keeping open the channels of trade and communication, while firmly pressing for human rights in China to be upheld, are the best means of ensuring that this great military power, on the verge of becoming a great economic power, becomes also a reliable and predictable member of the international community.

Japan

Japan is not only a great economic power and a leading democratic nation in the region, but of great importance to Hong Kong. The confidence of Hong Kong is much affected by the confidence of Japanese investors there, who also regard it as the gateway to mainland China. For reasons of wartime history, the Japanese were shy of making public statements about China. But they had close contacts with and a deep insight into what was happening there. So I always sounded out Japanese politicians on their impressions of thinking in Peking.

However, the main subject of (often difficult) negotiations with the Japanese during my time as Prime Minister was trade. We pressed the Japanese to open up their markets to our goods, to liberalize their financial and retail distribution systems and to work towards the reduction of their huge and destabilizing balance of trade surpluses with the West.

Much of the criticism of the Japanese was unfair. They were everybody's scapegoat. The Japanese should not have been blamed for prudently saving more – and so having more to invest at home, overseas or, indeed, financing the US budget deficit. Nor should the Japanese have been blamed for producing first-class cars, cheaper video recorders and advanced cameras, bought eagerly by western consumers. Yet in both cases they were.

Far more important was to ensure that their markets should be as open to our goods as ours were to theirs. In fact, in addition to tariffs, which of course were subject to GATT regulations, there were two big obstacles. The first was that their distribution system was inefficient, fragmented and overmanned and their administrative system was difficult to get around. The second was a cultural difference. For example, Japanese consumers automatically prefer to buy home-produced goods: government action can do little to change that. More potentially amenable to international pressure was that the Japanese offered terms of aid which we could not match and so secured foreign contracts.

The Japanese have also regularly been pilloried by western governments for not taking a more active international role in upholding security when we – and even more so Japan's immediate East Asian neighbours – would not wish Japan to rearm and act as a great or even a regional power. As was shown in the Gulf War, Japan is increasingly willing to pay for others, particularly the United States, to uphold international order and security. The fact that, in both the economic and security fields, much western criticism of Japan is unfair does not, however, mean that we should be anything other than tough-minded and realistic in dealing with Japan. But the Japanese must also be treated with genuine (and deserved) respect and their own sensitivities understood.

My second visit to Japan was in the autumn of 1982 on my way to China and Hong Kong. It set something of a pattern. I stressed to my hosts – both politicians and businessmen – my concern at the difficulty which British companies faced in penetrating Japanese markets. The Japanese themselves had promised action to deal with this, but it was a long time in taking effect. There were, though, more positive elements to the visit. I met members of the Keidanren – the Japanese CBI – and was struck by the fact that the top Japanese industrialists I encountered seemed often to be engineers, people with a practical understanding of the manufacturing processes of their firms and able to contribute to innovation. This was in marked contrast to Britain where, all too often, 'management' seemed to be qualified in administration and accountancy. It was, I thought, a clue to Japanese industrial success.

While in Japan I met the President of Nissan, whose company was considering at that time whether to go ahead with the construction of the plant it eventually built in Sunderland. We had a useful talk, though I could not at this stage draw from him any explicit commitment. Negotiations were at first known only to a small group. But agreement was finally reached in January 1984. I was convinced that the Nissan project made as much sense for Japan as it did for us. By exporting investment to Britain they would undercut protectionist pressures against them, bring in income for years ahead as well, of course, as providing incomes and jobs in the recipient country.

During my visit I also went to the Tsukuba Science City. This was fascinating. But I thought the decision to concentrate scientists in one particular location away from the great industrial centres was questionable. Interestingly, I found a number of Japanese who shared that view. This is all the more important because Japan's research is often on the technological side, whereas, by contrast, Britain's emphasis is on basic science. (Most of Japan's advances in industry have come from the application of well-established scientific principles.)

At this time the export of Japanese machine tools to the West was one of the most vexed issues of dispute. At Tsukuba I saw just how advanced the Japanese were. I was photographed shaking hands with a robot and, to my astonishment, found that it even had smooth, delicately jointed fingers. It was a demonstration that the Japanese not only had advanced electronics: they had managed to develop and apply that technology far more successfully than we had.

Under Prime Minister Nakasone, Japan began to play a more active role in international affairs. So, when he made a visit to Britain in June 1984, I felt that I was dealing with a Japanese leader who understood and sympathized with western values and had shown that he was prepared to make steps in the right direction on economic policy. The talks I had with him in the morning and over lunch on Monday 11 June 1984 could, therefore, concentrate as much on wider international issues as on Anglo-Japanese bilateral trade disputes. Mr Nakasone gave me an account of his dealings with the Chinese. I told him about the state of our negotiations on Hong Kong. This was, of course, nearing the end of that period of freeze in the Cold War which preceded the advent of Mr Gorbachev. Mr Nakasone showed a shrewd understanding of what Japan's role in these circumstances should be. He said that the Soviets would come out of their hibernation only when they decided to do so and that the West should wait for this. But he had continued to urge on the USSR the need for dialogue. He believed that the Soviets would need Japanese expertise and capital to develop Siberia and that this would in the long run be a powerful influence. In fact, this accurate and imaginative approach, which could yield enormous benefits, has still not been applied, mainly because of the dispute between (now) Russia and Japan over the Kurile Islands. I also discussed with Mr Nakasone Japanese investment in Britain. He said that half of the Japanese companies now established within the European Community were in the United Kingdom. 'Not enough,' I replied. 'I would like two dozen more.' He went away in no doubt about the welcome Britain would accord to Japanese investment.

My next visit to Tokyo was for the G7 economic summit in May 1986. The main issues at the summit were not economic at all but rather political. In the wake of the US-Libyan raid, international terrorism was the principal item on the agenda. The appalling consequences of the nuclear disaster at Chernobyl were also still being assessed and discussed. On terrorism I was determined to support the Americans with a strong statement in the communiqué. I was glad to learn from President Reagan when I saw him in Tokyo on the afternoon of Sunday 4 May, on the eve of the summit, that he could go along with what I proposed.

Both President Reagan and I were keen that the summit should be a success for the Japanese. The President was a strong supporter of Prime Minister Nakasone and was rather more inclined to be optimistic about the changes which had been promised in Japan's economic practices than I was. But I had to agree with him that Mr Nakasone had the right instincts in international affairs and it was important not to endanger his position.

In fact, there was not much practically to show for the vigorous efforts we had made to have the Japanese open up their markets. There was, for example, still heavy discriminatory tax on imported liquor. Whisky was the fourth largest single UK export to Japan. This being my own favourite nightcap, I felt a truly proselytizing zeal to encourage the taste for it. The former Governor of the Bank of Japan, Mr Maekawa, had also produced a report on ways to reform the Japanese financial and commercial system so as to allow the reduction of Japan's huge trade surplus. But it was better on generalities than specifics.

Japan's trade surplus was sharply up again in 1986. But the Japanese had allowed the yen to rise in value, something which was far from popular among Japanese industrialists, and this would probably be the most important factor towards achieving a better balance of international trade relations in the future. The other good news from our point of view was that by now forty Japanese manufacturing companies were operating in the UK, creating over 10,000 jobs; and the

Nissan plant was expected to start full-scale production that summer with total employment of around 3,000 people. On the cultural level, contacts between our two countries were good. The Japanese had begun a policy of endowing teaching posts at British universities. The eldest son of the Crown Prince of Japan had recently completed two years at Oxford University. Our own Prince and Princess of Wales were due, in turn, to visit Japan.

I talked to Mr Nakasone shortly after the end of the summit. After congratulating him on the organization – which was far better than the previous Tokyo summit I had attended – and discussing the inevitable subject of Scotch whisky, I said that I wanted to try to ensure that in future relations between Britain and Japan were not dominated by the trade imbalance. That was still not possible at the moment. Some sizeable purchases by the Japanese of aircraft would help. But I was clear in my own mind that we must get beyond these issues to those of wider international importance if Japan was to play her proper role in world affairs.

Japanese politics are *sui generis*. Leaders 'emerge' from negotiations between factions. Decisions are taken through gradually developed consensus rather than debate. And in spite of his achievements in establishing Japan as a major player on the international stage, Mr Nakasone was unable to buck the convention by which the nominees of other factions in the governing Japanese Liberal Democratic Party (LDP) must have their turn in office.

It was his successor, Mr Takeshita, as head of the largest faction in the LDP, who took the most important decisions to make structural changes in the Japanese economy. Of most importance from our point of view, it was he who removed the discrimination against Scotch whisky and opened up the Japanese Stock Exchange to two of the best-known British stockbrokers who had been excluded. I said to Mr Takeshita when he came to London to see me that he was the fourth Prime Minister with whom I had raised the issue of the Stock Exchange. He promised action but asked for time. And he proved as good as his word. I did not have to raise it with a fifth. Partly as a result, however, of public resentment at the introduction of a new, though modest consumption tax and partly as a result of political scandal, Mr Takeshita resigned in May 1989. His successor, Mr Uno, after just a few months in office, soon resigned too. So it was the comparatively young and relatively unknown Prime Minister Toshiki Kaifu who was in office when I made what turned out to be my last visit to Japan as Prime Minister in September 1989.

Mr Kaifu was to host a meeting of the International Democratic

Union (IDU) – the international organization of Conservative Parties which Ronald Reagan and I had founded. Inevitably, the IDU comprised a variety of right-of-centre parties: but it had the advantage over its junior partner, the European Democratic Union (EDU), that it was not dominated by the Christian Democrats and included the American Republican Party. (The star of that year's conference was undoubtedly the Swedish Conservative leader – since Prime Minister – who delivered a speech of such startling Thatcherite soundness that in applauding I felt as if I was giving myself a standing ovation.)

Mr Kaifu had his own domestic reasons for wanting the occasion to be a success. He had no strong power base of his own within the LDP and needed to cut something of an international figure in order to win back alienated LDP voters before the forthcoming general election. For my part I wanted to help him as much as I could. He was strongly pro-western, a man of integrity, and not at all in the somewhat reticent, introverted mould of some Japanese politicians that I met. I had not really got to know Mr Kaifu before I came to Japan – though he had been to see me at No. 10 as part of a group on previous occasions. I was told that his favourite sayings were: 'politics begins with sincerity' and 'perseverance leads to success.' It seemed an uncontroversial philosophy.

I had a long talk with Prime Minister Kaifu on the afternoon of Wednesday 20 September. Some of the worst causes of disagreement between Japan and the West, including Britain, were by now being overcome. Japan's external surplus had begun to fall somewhat – though the fact that the yen had depreciated against the dollar threatened problems with the Americans in the future. Japanese investment in Britain was now greater than ever: in fact we were attracting more Japanese manufacturing investment than anywhere else in the European Community. Japan had become one of Britain's fastest growing major markets. My discussions with the Prime Minister covered that perennial topic, Scotch whisky – where the ever ingenious Japanese had devised whisky 'lookalikes' to circumvent the tax changes which had been introduced.

But we were also able to range much more widely over international and indeed Japanese domestic affairs. Mr Kaifu had twice been Education minister and so we had something special in common. He spoke eloquently about social issues, in particular the decline of the family and the need to come to terms with the demographic factor of a rapidly ageing population. These were matters which were also increasingly preoccupying me. But I felt that Japan's highly developed sense of community and ability to combine material progress with an attachment to traditional values in some ways equipped them better to face these challenges than did our western culture. I have always connected this with the fact that Japan has the lowest level of violent crime in the developed world.

At the end of our talk I gave a television interview jointly with Mr Kaifu about global environmental issues, an area in which the Japanese were beginning to play a large role. I hoped that it would boost his standing, and was told that it had done so. But after the customary two years, Mr Kaifu was soon in his turn to join the ranks of former Japanese prime ministers whose international achievements were an insufficient antidote for factional weakness.

By the time I left office, the West and Japan were beginning seriously to come to terms with the question of where Japan's future lay. Only with the end of the Cold War has the full importance of this become apparent. Japan can have a huge role in bringing Russia to prosperity and stability by providing the capital and technology for the development of Siberia. At the same time, Japan has very close links with China. Japan's attitude to East Asia, where newly industrialized countries' economies are racing ahead, is also of great importance in determining whether the dominant approach will be one of free trade or protection. Above all, relations between the United States and Japan are vital to the security of the region, and indeed on a global scale too, where Japan has the resources and America the technology – and enjoys the trust – to support any kind of 'new world order'.

East Asia and Australia

British policy 'East of Suez' still matters. Indeed, there is a strong argument that it will matter more and more. East Asia contains some of the fastest growing economies in the world. The newly industrialized countries of the Asian Pacific region, like South Korea, Taiwan, Indonesia and Singapore – which, together with Hong Kong, make up the five 'little tigers' – have to be fully integrated into a global free-trading economy if our industries are to compete effectively. They will increasingly provide us not just with competition but markets. They would all welcome more European – particularly British – contact as a counterweight to the other dominant influences in the region – the United States, China and Japan. In the longer term it is still unclear if and when countries like (an eventually reunited) Korea and Indonesia (with the world's fourth largest population – and the largest Muslim country) will develop wider political ambitions.

Britain has a traditional presence in the region. Australia should also now be considered at least as much a power in its own right as a partner in the Anglo-Saxon world. Individually and through the Commonwealth, Britain and Australia have an interest in nudging political development in the direction of democracy. So for all these reasons I was keen to visit the region so as to exert influence and drum up business for British companies.

I had had to postpone my visit to South-East Asia because of the miners' strike. This put out some of the initial arrangements. So when I eventually departed on the morning of Thursday 4 April 1985 it was with a schedule originally devised for a fortnight but telescoped into ten days.

The first leg of the tour was Malaysia. We ought to have had better relations with Malaysia than we actually did. This was in part because the Prime Minister of Malaysia, Dr Mahathir, felt that in the past we had not treated his country with sufficient respect as an independent nation. It may not have been just chance that Britain always seemed to be at the bottom of the list when bids for contracts in Malaysia were considered. In fact, I got on rather well with Dr Mahathir and developed an increasing respect for him. He was tough, shrewd and practical. He had a refreshingly matter-of-fact outlook on everything that related to his country. Several years later, when, almost overnight, environmental issues had become all the rage in international gatherings, he put down some of the more extreme conservationists by saying that he was not prepared to keep tribesmen in his country living under conditions which promised a life expectancy of about forty-five simply in order to allow them to be studied by academics.

When I left Malaysia I felt that Dr Mahathir and I had established a good understanding, and so indeed it proved. When I first arrived he had been highly critical of the Commonwealth, seeing it as a kind of post-colonial institution. But I persuaded him to come to the next CHOGM. I had made a convert. Indeed in 1989, he himself hosted the CHOGM in Kuala Lumpur. It turned out to be the best organized I ever attended. Slightly less diplomatically beneficial were my talks with the very cultured, sophisticated earlier Prime Minister of Malaysia, Tunku Abdul Rahman. We found ourselves, as so often seemed the case in Commonwealth countries, discussing South Africa. I remarked that it would have been better if we had kept South Africa inside the Commonwealth, where we could have influenced her more effectively. Tunku Abdul Rahman looked surprisingly displeased. I soon learnt why. He told me that he had been principally responsible for throwing South Africa out in the first place. Clang.

From Malaysia I went, via Singapore and Brunei, to Indonesia. Everything about Indonesia is remarkable. A state created out of some 17,000 islands, a mix of races and religions, based on an artificially created philosophy – the five principles of 'Pancasila' – it is a marvel that Indonesia has been kept together at all. Yet it has an economy which is growing fast, more or less sound public finances, and though there have been serious human rights abuses, particularly in East Timor, this is a society which by most criteria 'works'. At the top, President Soeharto is an immensely hard-working and effective ruler. I was struck by the detailed interest he took in agriculture – something which is all too rare in oil-rich countries like Indonesia. He spent hours on his own farm where experiments in cross-breeding livestock to maximize nutrition were the order of the day. The architect of the technological and industrial base of Indonesia was Dr Habibie, a German-trained scientist of immense energy and imagination.

It was on the final day of my stay in Indonesia that I first realized that I had become an internationally known figure – and not just in Europe, the scene of so many bitter arguments, or in the United States, where I always received a warm reception, but in parts of the world entirely foreign to me. I flew up to Bandung to inspect Dr Habibie's excellent Institute of Technology. As I got off the aeroplane I was met by girls throwing rose petals on the ground in front of me and then all the way from the airport by crowds five to six deep along the roadside crying 'Tacher, Tacher'.

Later that day I arrived in Colombo, Sri Lanka. President Jayewardene I already knew and had liked at once. He was an elderly, distinguished lawyer of great integrity and someone who peppered his speech, as I am inclined to do, with talk of 'the rule of law', not a bad refrain for any politician. At this time he was beginning to be faced by Tamil terrorism, which ultimately Sri Lanka alone was not able to suppress. He explained to me in the car the various concessions he had made for regional autonomy – Sri Lanka is a relatively modern construct and real unification of Ceylon came only in the 1830s. I judged that if anyone could restore peace and order without large-scale violence it was such a man as this.

Early the following morning I set off for the opening ceremony of the Victoria Dam Power Station, which as I have explained earlier,* was largely paid for out of British Overseas Aid. Although it was still before 10 o'clock in the morning and we were well up in the hills, the

* See p. 75.

heat was almost unbearable. First, I visited the power station and dam. Then there was a long march past of children in different costumes; dances were performed; flowers were thrown. The Sri Lankan minister with me made his speech. By now we were under a large awning and it was with relief that I saw that someone had brought him a glass of water. Then it was my turn to speak. But no water. By now the atmosphere was even more stifling. I was glad to get back in the car to be driven on to Kandy. The President came with me. But for some reason I still couldn't get any water. Nearly five hours after leaving Colombo I reached the government guesthouse and I at last got my glass of water. I gulped it gratefully.

Next day I was due to address the Sri Lankan Parliament. It is easy to imagine my horror when, having been introduced by the Speaker, I looked around and found . . . no water. The Parliament building is magnificent inside and out: but it is also excessively air-conditioned and the atmosphere is dry as dust. Part of the way through my speech I had such a fit of coughing that I had to stop and wait until a glass of water was found for me. I had learnt my lesson. From now on a crate of fizzy Ashbourne water would accompany me on my travels.

I returned to Britain by way of India where I met Rajiv Gandhi for the first time since he had become Prime Minister after his mother's assassination. (At this stage I was on good terms with him: it was only later that year at the CHOGM in Nassau that we fell out over South Africa.) My abiding impression was of the tight security which surrounded him and his wife Sonia. They were living in a small, rather cramped house, unwilling or unable to return to the house where Mrs Gandhi had met her death. I laid a wreath at the site of my old friend's funeral pyre.

I was due to attend the Bicentennial celebration in Australia in the late summer of 1988. I had really rather doubted whether my presence was necessary at all. I had earlier suggested to the Australian Prime Minister, Bob Hawke, that, with the Queen, other members of the Royal Family and numerous foreign dignitaries, perhaps I would be one Englishwoman too many. But he insisted that I should come, and so I did. Although I had some famous rows with Bob Hawke, I found him easy to deal with: like me, he was blunt and direct. But on this occasion, he was to prove consideration itself.

I had decided to combine this Australian visit with another foray into South-East Asia. On this occasion I was able to spend rather longer than previously in Singapore. That little island's economy continued to astonish. Its GDP was rising at over 9 per cent a year and its total trade was up over the same period by a third. It was therefore pleasant to receive congratulations from Prime Minister Lee Kuan Yew about the state of the British economy, though I said that in my view we were growing somewhat too fast. His only criticism was of me personally – for undertaking a programme of foreign visits which he described as 'absolute madness', adding that he did not know anyone else who would even contemplate it. He was full of his usual shrewd observations about world trouble spots like Cambodia, North Korea and the Middle East. I always found him most perceptive about China. He maintained that although entrenched habits in China were deeply authoritarian, communism itself went against the grain of the Chinese character and could not in the very long term succeed. Lee Kuan Yew is of course by origin Chinese himself: I used to tell him that in many ways I wished he had stayed at home – that way China might have found its way to capitalism twenty years earlier.

Then it was on to Australia. I arrived in Perth, went on to Alice Springs, and arrived at Canberra. Here I visited the new Parliament building, erected to celebrate the Bicentennial, and was met by Bob Hawke, who introduced me to his Cabinet, in which Paul Keating was then Finance minister. Whatever differences of outlook we had on other matters, I found Mr Keating refreshingly orthodox on finance – a far cry from the British Labour Party. In my speech at the lunch which followed I stressed the importance of Australia's role as a regional power. The fact was that the economic growth of many countries in the area was going ahead far faster than political progress. I believed that Australia, as one of the world's oldest and most developed democracies, could make a vital contribution to regional stability.

My tour finished up in Brisbane. I visited the British Pavilion at the EXPO '88 World Trade Fair. I was disappointed by what I saw and said so with some vigour on my return to England. It was not the fault of those directly concerned, but rather of cheese-paring by the British Government, that our pavilion just did not match those of other major countries. As with embassy buildings, I always insisted that cutting back on expenditure on generating the right image of Britain abroad is sheer foolishness. From now on I took a direct interest in the matter: for example, I told David Young, as Trade and Industry Secretary, that we must have the best national exhibition at the Seville EXPO in 1992, and I believe we did.

My day ended in Brisbane with attendance at a splendid production of the 'Last Night of the Proms' – which the Australians immediately christened the 'Last Night of the Poms'. Whatever the shortcomings of the pavilion, British popular culture was on vigorous form.

From Australia I flew via Malaysia to Thailand. It was my first visit. But I soon found myself in much the same frame of mind as at Brisbane, for it was clear that our large and impressive embassy building in Bangkok was not being properly maintained. Next morning I visited the United Nations Refugee Camp on the Thai border with Cambodia. It was quite a trip to get there – aeroplane, then helicopter, then Land Rover. It was huge, more like a large town than a temporary camp. Prince Sihanouk, his wife and daughter were in charge. I quickly noticed that there were very few men: it turned out that the great majority were away fighting the Vietnamese Army inside Cambodia. I also noticed immediately how the refugees venerated Prince Sihanouk, approaching him, as is the – for a westerner – rather disturbing habit, on their knees. He delivered a rousing and justified philippic against Pol Pot and the Khmer Rouge while I was there. Later I detected in conversation with him that wiliness and toughness which accounted, against all odds and predictions, for his political survival in a very dangerous game.

I had worn a simple cotton dress and flat shoes to visit the refugee camp. But I was struck by the fact that many of the women there were wearing attractive new dresses, looking remarkably elegant. My hair had also suffered from the wind, heat and humidity. So when I returned to Bangkok I asked the embassy to find someone who would set it for me and was pleasantly surprised to find myself in the hands of a lady whom I still consider to be one of the best hairdressers I have ever had.

It is easy to fall in love with Thailand, in spite of its seamy side which was kept well hidden from me. As a staunch monarchist myself, I was particularly moved by my discussions with the King and Queen of Thailand. Perhaps every national monarchy has to find its own particular style. Certainly, King Bhumibol had done so. Hearing him speak with equal passion about problems of peasant agriculture and matters of high politics I could well understand the unique regard in which the Thai monarchy was held and how, though generals and civilian governments might come and go, the monarchy itself had remained the enduring source of legitimacy.

I returned to Britain by way of Dubai and took the opportunity of visiting HMS *Manchester*, acting as part of the Armilla Patrol protecting shipping in the Gulf. I do not really enjoy the heat: but at least I thought I would never experience anything worse than the temperature overlooking Sri Lanka's Victoria Dam Power Project three years earlier. I was wrong. It was over 120 degrees as Denis and I stood waiting on the tarmac for the helicopter to take us from Dubai Airport aboard HMS *Manchester*. I was fascinated to explore the ship, climbing up and down ladders and along the narrow gangways from the galley to the Sea Dart missile loading bay. I stayed longest in the Operations Room. It did not take much imagination to envisage how easily mistakes can be made, in spite of all the checks and double checks, under great tension, in that darkened enclosed space. Below decks it was slightly cooler, though not much. The Chief Cook who was baking an apple and blackcurrant pie told me that the temperature in the galley was 105 degrees. I decided that it was time for this particular politician to 'get out of the kitchen' and left. I had enjoyed myself. But that iced whisky and soda back aboard the VC10 never tasted better.

THE MIDDLE EAST

Egypt and Jordan

Little progress was made during my time as Prime Minister in solving the Arab-Israeli dispute. It is important, though, to be clear about what such a 'solution' can and cannot be. The likelihood of a total change of heart among those concerned is minimal. Nor will outside influences ever be entirely removed from the region. Certainly, the end of Soviet communist manipulation of disputed issues makes it potentially easier to reach agreement with moderate Arabs and allows the United States to place clearer limits on its support for particular Israeli policies. But ultimately the United States, which was the power most responsible for the establishment of the state of Israel, will and must always stand behind Israel's security. It is equally, though, right that the Palestinians should be restored in their land and dignity: and, as often happens in my experience, what is morally right eventually turns out to be politically expedient. Removing, even in limited measure, the Palestinian grievance is a necessary if not sufficient condition for cutting the cancer of Middle East terrorism out by the roots. The only way this can happen, as has long been clear, is for Israel to exchange 'land for peace', returning occupied territories to the Palestinians in exchange for credible undertakings to respect Israel's security. It may be that the (thankfully ineffective) scud missile attacks of the Gulf War, demonstrating that Israel cannot preserve her security just by enlarging her borders, will eventually pave the way for such a compromise. That is to anticipate: for during my time as Prime Minister all initiatives eventually foundered on the fact that the two sides ultimately saw no need to adjust their stance. But that did not mean that we could simply sit back and let events take their course. Initiatives at least offered hope: stagnation in the Middle East peace process only ever promised disaster.

In September 1985 I visited the two key moderate Arab states, Egypt and Jordan. President Mubarak of Egypt had continued to pursue, though with greater circumspection, the policies of his assassinated predecessor, Anwar Sadat. King Hussein of Jordan had put forward a proposal for an international peace conference, as a prelude to which US Ambassador Murphy was to meet a joint Jordanian-Palestinian delegation. The Egyptians were keen to see the Jordanian initiative succeed. But the sticking point was which Palestinian representatives would be acceptable to the Americans, who would have nothing directly to do with the PLO. President Mubarak felt that the Americans were not being sufficiently positive. I had some sympathy for this point of view, though I restated what I said was a cardinal principle for the US, as for Britain, that we would not agree to talks with those who practised terrorism. I felt that President Mubarak and I understood one another. He was a large personality, persuasive and direct – the sort of man who could be one of the key players in a settlement.

My main public gesture in Egypt on behalf of British business was the unromantic one of opening the British-built Cairo Waste Water Project, in effect the city's sewer. But before leaving Egypt I made the statutory – though no less fascinating – tour of Karnak and Luxor. It was very hot. By this time I had learned my lesson: I had my own bottled mineral water with me in the car. But a minor disaster ensued when my staff, credulously believing that a bottle labelled mineral water at the museum actually contained such a thing, promptly all went down with severe stomach upsets. I suspect that they were even more pleased than I was when we arrived that evening (Wednesday 18 September) at Amman.

I already knew King Hussein well and liked him. He had come to see me in Downing Street on a number of occasions. Like President Mubarak, but more so, King Hussein was vexed with the Americans, believing that, having encouraged him to take a peace initiative, they were now drawing back under domestic Jewish pressure. I understood what he felt. He had been taking a real risk in trying to promote his initiative and I thought he deserved more support. I wanted to do what I could to help. So when the King told me that two leading

PLO supporters would be prepared publicly to renounce terrorism and accept UNSCR 242 I said that if they would do this, I would meet them in London. I announced this at my press conference. It would have been the first meeting between a British minister and representatives of the PLO. Later, when they arrived in London, I checked to see if they were still prepared to adhere to these conditions. One did. But the other could not: he was afraid for his life. So I could not see them. I am glad to say that King Hussein supported me in that decision. But it demonstrated – if that was necessary – how treacherous these waters were.

Before leaving Jordan I was taken out to see a Palestinian refugee camp. Denis used to say to me that these camps always tore his heart out. This was no exception. It was clean, well organized, orderly – and utterly hopeless. It was in effect run by the PLO who had, of course, a vested interest in making such camps a permanent recruiting ground for their revolutionary struggle. The most talented and educated Palestinians would not remain long there, preferring to join the Palestinian diaspora all over the Arab world. I talked to one old lady, half blind, lying in the shade of a tree outside her family's hut. She was said to be about 100. But she had one thing above all on her mind, and spoke about it: the restoration of the Palestinians' rights.

Israel

I had been to Israel several times before I became Prime Minister; and each time I visited what for the world's three great religions is 'the Holy Land' it made an indelible impression. Anyone who has been to Jerusalem will understand why General Allenby, on taking the city from the Turks, dismounted to enter it on foot, as a mark of respect.

I have enormous admiration for the Jewish people, inside or outside Israel. There have always been Jewish members of my staff and indeed my Cabinet. In fact I just wanted a Cabinet of clever, energetic people – and frequently that turned out to be the same thing. My old constituency of Finchley has a large Jewish population. In the thirty-three years I represented it I never had a Jew come in poverty and desperation to one of my constituency surgeries. They had always been looked after by their own community.

I believe in what are often referred to as 'Judaeo-Christian' values: indeed my whole political philosophy is based on them. But I have always been wary of falling into the trap of equating in some way the

Jewish and Christian faiths. I do not, as a Christian, believe that the Old Testament – the history of the Law – can be fully understood without the New Testament – the history of Mercy. But I often wished that Christian leaders would take a leaf out of the teaching of Britain's wonderful former Chief Rabbi, Immanuel Jakobovits, and indeed that Christians themselves would take closer note of the Jewish emphasis on self-help and acceptance of personal responsibility. On top of all that, the political and economic construction of Israel against huge odds and bitter adversaries is one of the heroic sagas of our age. They really made 'the desert bloom'. I only wished that Israeli emphasis on the human rights of the Russian *refuseniks* was matched by proper appreciation of the plight of landless and stateless Palestinians.

The Israelis knew when I arrived in their country in May 1986 that they were dealing with someone who harboured no lurking hostility towards them, who understood their anxieties, but who was not going to pursue an unqualified Zionist approach. Above all, I could be assured of respect for having stood up to terrorism at home and abroad. (It was only a matter of weeks since I had been one of the very few to support the American raid on Libya.) The Israelis were also aware of the tough line we were taking with the Syrians about the attempt of Nezar Hindawi, who had clear links to the Syrian Embassy and Government, to place a bomb on an El Al aircraft at Heathrow. So if anyone was in a good position to speak some home truths without too much fear of being misunderstood it was I.

I was looking forward to seeing Prime Minister Shimon Peres again. I knew him to be sincere, intelligent and reasonable. I had met him many times. It was a great pity that he would shortly, under the arrangement reached with the Likud Party in the national coalition, hand over the premiership to the hardline Yitzhak Shamir. Both Mr Peres and I wondered in the light of past history how people would react to seeing the Union Jack and the Star of David flying side by side. But we need not have worried. I arrived to be greeted by welcoming crowds at Tel Aviv, and was driven up to Jerusalem to stay at the King David Hotel – so full of associations for me and for all British people.* Outside the hotel even larger crowds were cheering in the darkness. I insisted on getting out of the car to see them, which threw the security men into a fit of agitation. But it was worth it: the people were delighted.

I breakfasted the following morning with Teddy Kollek, the Mayor

* On 22 July 1946 91 people were killed when the hotel was bombed by Jewish terrorists from a group led by Menachem Begin.

of Jerusalem. I knew him well: he combined a warm humanity with formidable administrative zeal and – a still more valuable combination – loyalty to his own people with a sympathetic understanding of the problems of the Arabs. The whole day – Sunday 25 May – was full of evocative demonstrations of Israel's history and identity. Naturally, I attended the Yad Vashem Memorial to the Holocaust: as on every occasion, I came out numb with shock that human beings could sink to such depravity.

I went on to a meeting with Mr Shamir. It was impossible to imagine anyone more different from Shimon Peres. This was a hard man, though undoubtedly a man of principle, whose past had left scars on his personality. There was no hostility between us: but nor could there ultimately be any meeting of minds about the way forward. It was clear that there was no possibility of Mr Shamir himself giving up 'land for peace' and the Jewish settlements on the West Bank would continue to go ahead.

I believed that the real challenge was to strengthen moderate Palestinians, probably in association with Jordan, who would eventually push aside the PLO extremists. But this would never happen if Israel did not encourage it; and the miserable conditions under which Arabs on the West Bank and in Gaza were having to live only made things worse. I also believed that there should be local elections on the West Bank. But at that time one of the strongest opponents of concessions on this – or anything else it seemed – was the then Defence minister, Mr Rabin, with whom I had breakfast on Monday. He proceeded to read out his views to me for forty minutes with barely time for a bite of toast.

But I was not to be put off. I repeated my proposals for local elections in a speech that afternoon to a group of Israeli MPs at the Knesset – the Israeli Parliament – chaired by the eloquent and respected Abba Eban.

Later I went to a dinner with carefully selected moderate Palestinians – mostly businessmen and academics – of precisely the sort I felt the Israelis should be prepared to deal with. They poured out their complaints, particularly about their treatment on the West Bank and especially in Gaza, where conditions were worst, partly because of insensitive security policing and partly, it seemed, because of economic discrimination in favour of Jewish business. I promised to take these matters up with Mr Peres – and did so in detail the following day – but I also made clear to them the need to reject terrorism and those who practised it. Although the general view was that only the PLO were able to represent the Palestinians, I also detected in conversations with smaller groups that this did not mean that there was any great love for that organization.

During my visit I had two long discussions with Mr Peres. He was conscious of the need to keep King Hussein's now faltering peace initiative in play, not least so as to avoid destabilizing Jordan itself. But he was obviously highly sceptical about the proposal for an international peace conference. For all his understanding of the need for some kind of compromise, I did not come away with any real optimism. In fact, the succession of Mr Shamir as Prime Minister would soon seal off even these few shafts of light.

However intractable the diplomatic issues were, there was no doubt about the warmth of my reception in Israel, which indeed continued to grow as the visit went on. On Tuesday on my way to the airport for my return flight I stopped at Ramat Gan, a suburb of Tel Aviv that was twinned with Finchley. I had expected that I would be meeting the mayor and a few other dignitaries, perhaps some old acquaintances. Instead, 25,000 people were awaiting me. I was plunged into – at times, to the horror of my detectives and staff, almost sank into – a huge crowd of cheering residents, before being squeezed through and onto a large platform from which I had to give an unscripted speech – always the best. Later, during the Gulf War scud missiles from Iraq fell on Ramat Gan. The people of Finchley raised money to rebuild the houses that had been destroyed. This, I thought, was what 'twinning' should be all about.

AFRICA

The Problem of South Africa

I no more shared the established Foreign Office view of Africa than I did of the Middle East. Whereas Israel was considered the pariah of the Middle East with which we would be ill-advised too closely to associate, this role was allotted within Africa to South Africa. The basic, if usually unstated, assumption seemed to be that Britain's national interests required that we should ultimately be prepared to go along with the opinions of the radical black African states in the Commonwealth. In fact, a clear-sighted analysis suggested something rather different.

Admitted that fundamental changes must be made in South Africa's system, the question was of how best to achieve them. It seemed to me that the worst approach was to isolate South Africa further. Indeed, the isolation had already gone too far, contributing to an inflexible, siege mentality among the governing Afrikaner class. It was absurd to believe that they would be prepared to relinquish power suddenly or without acceptable safeguards. Indeed, had that occurred the result would have been anarchy in which black South Africans would have suffered most.

Nor, I knew, could the latter be considered a homogeneous group. Tribal loyalties were of great importance. For example, the Zulus are a proud and self-conscious nation with a distinct sense of identity. Any new political framework for South Africa had to take account of such differences. Not least because of these complexities, I did not believe that it was for outsiders to impose a particular solution. What I wanted to achieve was step-by-step reform – with more democracy, secure human rights, and a flourishing free enterprise economy able to generate the wealth to improve black living standards. I wanted to see a South Africa which was fully reintegrated into the international community. Nor did I ever feel, for all the sound and fury of the Left, that this was anything other than a high ideal of which no one need be ashamed.

It was also true that Britain had important trading interests in the continent and that these were more or less equal in black Africa on the one hand and South Africa on the other. South Africa had by far the richest and most varied range of natural resources of any African country. It was the world's largest supplier of gold, platinum, gem diamonds, chrome, vanadium, manganese and other vital materials. Moreover, in a number of these cases South Africa's only real rival was the Soviet Union. Even if it had been morally acceptable to pursue a policy which would have led to the collapse of South Africa, it would not therefore have made strategic sense.

South Africa was rich not just because of natural resources but because its economy was at least mainly run on free enterprise lines. Other African countries, well endowed with natural resources, were still poor because their economies were socialist and centrally controlled. Consequently, the blacks in South Africa had higher incomes and were generally better educated than elsewhere in Africa: that was why the South Africans erected security fences to keep intended immigrants out, unlike the Berlin Wall which kept those blessed with a socialist system in. The critics of South Africa never mentioned these inconvenient facts. But simply because I recognized them did not mean that I held any brief for apartheid. The colour of someone's skin should not determine his or her political rights.

President P. W. Botha was to visit Europe on the occasion of the fortieth anniversary of the Normandy Landings and I sent him an invitation to come to see me at Chequers. He had a whole programme of visits in Europe, made possible by an agreement that he had reached earlier in the year with President Machel of Mozambique which seemed a promising development to many European states. Nevertheless, my invitation provoked accusations that I was 'soft' on apartheid. On Wednesday 30 May Bishop Trevor Huddleston, the veteran anti-apartheid campaigner, came to Downing Street to put the case against my seeing Mr Botha. His argument was that the South African President should not be accorded credibility as a man of peace and that South Africa should not be allowed to re-enter the international community until it changed its internal policies. This seemed to me to miss the point. It was South Africa's isolation which was an obstacle to reform. Before his European trip, the only country that Mr Botha had visited in recent years was Taiwan.

One thing which the opponents of apartheid – perhaps because so many of them were socialists – never seemed fully to grasp was that capitalism itself was probably the greatest force for reform and political liberalization in South Africa, as it was in the communist countries. South Africa could not fulfil its economic potential unless black labour was brought in to the cities and trained. Capitalism in South Africa was already creating a black middle class which would ultimately insist on a share of power.

President Botha came to Chequers on the morning of Saturday 2 June. I had a private conversation with him which lasted some forty minutes and then I was joined over lunch by Geoffrey Howe, Malcolm Rifkind and officials – the South African President by his Foreign minister R. F. ('Pik') Botha. President Botha told me that South Africa never received any credit for the improvements which had been made in the conditions of the blacks. Although there was some truth in this, I had to tell him also how appalled we were by the forced removal of blacks from areas which had been designated for white residents only. I went on to raise the case of the imprisoned Nelson Mandela whose freedom we had persistently sought. It was my view, moreover, that no long-term solution to South Africa's problems could be achieved without his co-operation. But the main discussion concentrated on Namibia, the former South African colony, where South Africa had reimposed direct rule the previous year. Our policy was to support Namibian independence. There was little progress here: South Africa had no intention of allowing Namibia to become independent while Cuban troops remained in Angola, but there was no prospect of Cuban withdrawal until civil war ended in Angola – which at the time seemed a forlorn hope. The South Africans clearly wanted to have more secure relations with their neighbours and hoped that the carrot of economic aid from South Africa might enable better relations to be built. In fact, for the reasons outlined above, this was to be a vain hope because the South African social and political system had begun to hamper economic growth.

I did not particularly warm to President Botha, whom I had met previously, but to do him justice he listened carefully to what I said. I found that when I raised specific circumstances he was willing to look into them personally and where he undertook to take action he proved as good as his word. The most important result of this meeting, however, was that from now on I was able to send him private messages on delicate matters which probably constituted almost the only helpful contact he had with western governments. As I told the Cabinet afterwards, it must be right to expose him as much as possible to our views. The arguments in favour of dialogue with the Soviet Union applied with at least as much force to the need to maintain contacts of this kind with South Africa.

The year 1985 was one of mounting crisis for South Africa. There was widespread rioting. A state of emergency was declared in many parts of the country. Foreign banks refused to renew South African credit and the South African Government declared a four-month freeze on the repayment of the principal of foreign debt. My old friend Fritz Leutwiler, former head of the Swiss Central Bank, was appointed as a mediator between the banks and the South African Government. We kept in contact so I knew what was happening. The international pressure on South Africa continued to mount. President Reagan, who was as opposed to economic sanctions as I was, introduced a limited package of sanctions to forestall pressure from Congress. It was clear that the Commonwealth Heads of Government Meeting in the Bahamas at Nassau that October would be a difficult one for me.

So in September I held a seminar at Chequers to clarify our thinking on tactics towards South Africa. Apart from Geoffrey Howe, Malcolm Rifkind, Paul Channon and Ian Stewart (from the Treasury), there were present a range of businessmen, academics and one or two interested and well informed MPs. None of us would have 'started from here' had we the choice. On the one hand the reform process in South Africa had ground to a halt: the constitutional reforms had proved a dead end because they did not involve even moderate middle-class blacks. On the other, the European Community was moving towards imposing sanctions. We had placed a reserve on the measures agreed by the Community earlier that month, though in fact, on closer inspection, most of these turned out to accord with our existing practice and I agreed to lift it before the CHOGM. One idea which was raised at the meeting was sending a 'contact group' of 'eminent persons' to try to get talks off the ground between the South African Government and representatives of the black community.

In the run up to the conference I did what I could to try to slow down the Gadarene rush towards imposing sanctions. I wrote to Commonwealth heads of government urging that instead we try to bring about negotiations between the South African Government and representatives of the black population. But it was already clear that we would be in for plenty of posturing from those intent on cutting a figure on the international stage.

The CHOGM at Nassau

I saw Brian Mulroney in Nassau on the first evening of the conference. He urged me to take the initiative by proposing a package of measures representing the lowest common denominator of Commonwealth agreement. All would be committed to it as the minimum, but it would be open to individual governments to do more if they chose. I told him that experience had taught me never to put forward ideas at too early a stage and I ended by saying: 'I have made my final – and I mean final – step in accepting the European position on sanctions. I don't relish being isolated within the Commonwealth, but if necessary so be it.' I took the same line in similar meetings with Robert Mugabe, Kenneth Kaunda and Bob Hawke.

Bob Hawke opened the conference debate on South Africa, obviously seeking a compromise. Kenneth Kaunda followed with an emotional call for sanctions. I tried to meet both points of view in my reply. I began by detailing the evidence of social and economic change in South Africa. I carefully cited the number of black South Africans who had professional qualifications, who had cars, who were in business. Of course, there was a long way to go. But we were not faced with a static situation. The speech had an effect, as I saw from the reactions of those around the table. But natural caution had led me to have a fall-back position prepared: after my meeting with Brian Mulroney my officials had worked up a note of options for further measures, which I would take with me to the heads of government retreat over the weekend at Lyford Cay, where I knew that the real business would be done.

Lyford Cay is a beautiful spot with interesting historical associations. Private houses in the estate had been made available for the delegations. The central club there was effectively the Conference Centre. In a rather nice touch the Prime Minister of the Bahamas had seen that the house allocated to me and my delegation was the one where the Polaris agreement had been signed by Harold Macmillan and John Kennedy in 1962. At Lyford Cay a drafting committee of heads of government was somehow formed and in the course of Saturday morning drew up a draft communiqué on South Africa. Meanwhile I got on with other work. At 2 o'clock Brian Mulroney and Rajiv Gandhi arrived at the house to show me their best efforts. Alas, I could not give them high marks and spent the best part of two hours explaining why their proposals were unacceptable to me. I suggested that the text should include a firm call for an end to violence in South Africa as a condition for further dialogue: but this they considered far too controversial.

After dinner I was invited to join a wider group and put under great pressure to agree to the line they wanted. Bob Hawke bitterly attacked me. I replied with vigour. In a steadily worsening atmosphere, the argument went on for some three hours. Fortunately, I can never be defeated by attrition.

Overnight, I had officials prepare an alternative text to be presented at the plenary session due to begin at 10.30 next morning, before which a dejected Sonny Ramphal, the Commonwealth Secretary-General, begged me to compromise and show goodwill. There was certainly not much goodwill evident when the meeting began. The British text was not even considered. I was lectured on my political morality, on my preferring British jobs to black lives, on my lack of concern for human rights. One after the other, their accusations became more vitriolic and personal until I could stand it no longer.

To their palpable alarm I began to tell my African critics a few home truths. I noted that they were busily trading with South Africa at the same time as they were attacking me for refusing to apply sanctions. I wondered when they intended to show similar concern about abuses in the Soviet Union, with which of course they often had not just trade but close political links. I wondered when I was going to hear them attack terrorism. I reminded them of their own less than impressive record on human rights. And when the representative from Uganda took me to task for racial discrimination, I turned on him and reminded him of the Asians which Uganda had thrown out on racial grounds, many of whom had come to settle in my constituency in North London, where they were model citizens and doing very well. No one spoke for my position, though President Jayewardene of Sri

Lanka caused something of a ripple when he said that in any case he had no intention of ending trade links with South Africa because it would throw the Sri Lankan tea planters out of work. The heads of government of some of the smaller states also told me privately that they agreed with me.

Over the lunch break I made a tactical decision as to which of the prepared options I would concede. My modest choice was to take unilateral action against the import of krugerrands and withdraw official support for trade promotion with South Africa. I would only do this, however, if there was a clear reference in the communiqué to the need to stop the violence. Then at 3.30 p.m. I went to join the 'drafting committee' in the library.

As I entered the room they all glared at me. It was extraordinary how the pack instinct of politicians could change a group of normally courteous, in some cases even charming, people into a gang of bullies. I had never been treated like this and I was not going to stand for it. So I began by saying that I had never been so insulted as I had by the people in that room and that it was an entirely unacceptable way of conducting international business. At once the murmurs of surprise and regret rose: one by one they protested that it was not 'personal'. I answered that it clearly was personal and I wasn't having it. The atmosphere immediately became more subdued. They asked me what I would accept. I announced the concessions I was prepared to make. I said that this was as far as I was going: if my proposals were not accepted I would withdraw and the United Kingdom would issue its own statement. The erstwhile 'draftsmen' went into a huddle. Ten minutes later it was all over. I suddenly became a stateswoman for having accepted a 'compromise'. A text was agreed and at a plenary session later that evening was accepted without amendment.

Though I was genuinely hurt and dismayed by the behaviour I had witnessed, I was not displeased with the outcome. In particular, I was glad that the Commonwealth heads of government endorsed an idea with which several of us had been toying – the sending of a group of 'eminent persons' to South Africa to report back on the situation to a future conference. This had the great merit of giving us time – both to press the South Africans for further reform and to fight the diplomatic battle. I sought to persuade Geoffrey Howe to be an 'eminent person' but he was most reluctant to do so. He probably rated its chances of success as poor, and events proved him right. I may, myself, have been less than tactful. For when he protested that he was Foreign Secretary and could not do both jobs, I said that I could just about cope with his as well while he was away. Since by now I was firmly in charge of our approach to South Africa, making the main decisions directly from No. 10, that may have been close to the bone. One advantage of those eventually chosen as members of the 'Eminent Persons Group' was that a distinguished black African, the Nigerian General Obasanjo, would act as chairman of the group and would see for himself what the reality of life in South Africa was. But this advantage was more than cancelled out by the problems created by Malcolm Fraser, still full of rancour at his election defeat by Bob Hawke, longing to achieve a high international profile once more and consequently making a thoroughly 'eminent person' of himself.

At the press conference after the summit I described, with complete accuracy, the concessions I had made on sanctions as 'tiny', which enraged the Left and undoubtedly irritated the Foreign Office. But I did not believe in sanctions and I was not prepared to justify them. I was able to leave the shores of Nassau with my policy intact, albeit with my personal relations with Commonwealth leaders somewhat bruised: but that, after all, was not entirely my fault. And there were thousands of black Africans who would keep their jobs because of the battle I had fought.

More arguments about sanctions in the EC and the Commonwealth

I had no illusions that I had succeeded in doing anything more at Nassau than stave off for the present the pressure for sanctions against South Africa. It remained to be seen what would come of the 'eminent persons' visit to southern Africa. In fact it was an unmitigated disaster. Whether to scupper the initiative or for quite unconnected reasons, the South African armed forces launched raids against African National Congress (ANC) bases in Botswana, Zambia and Zimbabwe and the EPG cut short their visit.

This gave me a very difficult hand to play at the European Council meeting at the Hague in June 1986 – and because the actions of European Community countries, unlike most Commonwealth members, could have a real impact on the South African economy this was at least as important a forum for the sanctions issue as was CHOGM. The Dutch themselves – the Netherlands having been the original home of the Afrikaners – suffered from a pervasive guilt complex about South Africa, which did not make them ideal chairmen. But Chancellor Kohl – who, at least at this stage, was as strongly opposed to sanctions as I was – led the debate. I supported him, followed by the Prime Minister of Portugal. In the end we agreed to consider introducing later in the year a ban on new investment and sanctions on imports of South African coal, iron, steel and krugerrands. But it was also agreed that Geoffrey Howe should, as a sort of lone 'eminent person' and in view of the fact that Britain would shortly be taking on the presidency of the Community, visit South Africa to press for reform and the release of Nelson Mandela.

Geoffrey was extremely reluctant to go and it must be said that his reluctance proved justified since he was insulted by President Kaunda and brushed off by President Botha. I later learned that he thought I had set him up for an impossible mission and was deeply angry about it. I can only say that I had no such intention. I had a real admiration for Geoffrey's talent for quiet diplomacy. If anyone could have made a breakthrough he would have done it.

Shortly after Geoffrey's return I had to face the Special Commonwealth Conference on South Africa which we had agreed at Lyford Cay to review progress. It had been decided that seven Commonwealth heads of governments would meet in London in August. The worst aspect was that because of President P.W. Botha's obstinacy we did not have enough to show by way of progress since the Nassau CHOGM. There had been some significant reforms and the partial state of emergency had been lifted in March. But a nationwide state of emergency had been imposed in June, Mr Mandela was still in prison, and the ANC and other similar organizations were still banned. With the fiasco of the 'Eminent Persons Group' in addition, there was no prospect of peaceful political dialogue between the South African Government and representatives of the black population. The US Congress was exerting increasing pressure for tough sanctions and later in the year forced a change in the Administration's policy by overruling President Reagan's veto on a new sanctions bill. It was clear that I would have to come up with some modest package of measures, though whether this would arrest the march towards full-scale economic sanctions was doubtful. In any case, I had a little list. For use as a diplomatic weapon of a rather different kind I had another little list of Commonwealth countries which applied detention without trial and similar illiberal practices – just in case.

The media and the Opposition were by now quite obsessive about South Africa. There was talk of the Commonwealth breaking up if Britain did not change its position on sanctions, though there was never any likelihood of either event. I was always convinced – and my postbag showed – that the views and priorities of these commentators were quite unrepresentative of what the general public felt. But that did not make it any more pleasant. On the eve of the conference Denis and I visited Edinburgh where the Commonwealth Games were to be held. We went to see the competitors – those at least whose countries had not boycotted the event – in the Games 'village', to be met by a few catcalls and some sour criticism. I did not disagree with Denis when he remarked that this was 'one of the most poisonous visits' we had ever made. It was a relief to dine that evening with my good friend Laurens van der Post who talks good sense about South Africa and who had been very helpful when we were negotiating independence for Zimbabwe.

Then it was back to more irrationality as the Special Conference opened in London. My meetings with heads of government before the official opening filled me with gloom. Brian Mulroney urged me to have Britain 'give a lead' and seemed to want me to reveal my negotiating hand to him in advance: but this I had no intention of doing, having on many an occasion seen such 'concessions' pocketed and then immediately forgotten. Kenneth Kaunda was in a thoroughly self-righteous and unco-operative frame of mind when I dropped in to see him at his hotel. He predicted that if sanctions were not applied, South Africa would go up in flames. I wound up the meeting smartly and said that it would be better if we postponed our discussion. Later I told Rajiv Gandhi that I would be prepared to move 'a little' at the conference. He seemed rather more amenable than he had been at Nassau, as indeed he usually was in private.

In fact, the formal discussions were every bit as unpleasant as at Lyford Cay, though at least they were shorter. My refusal to go along with the sanctions they wanted was attacked by Messrs Kaunda, Mugabe, Mulroney and Hawke. I found no support. Their proposals went well beyond what had been proposed the previous year. At Nassau they had wanted to cut off air links with South Africa, to introduce a ban on investment, agricultural imports, the promotion of tourism and other measures. Now they were demanding not only that these sanctions go ahead, but a whole raft of additional measures: a ban on new bank loans, imports of uranium, coal, iron and steel and the withdrawal of consular facilities. Such a package sacrificed the living standards of South Africa's black population to the posturing of South Africa's critics and the interests of their domestic industries. I was simply not prepared to endorse it. Instead, I had a separate paragraph inserted into the communiqué detailing our own approach which noted our willingness to go along with a ban on South African coal, iron and steel imports, if the European Community decided on it, and to introduce straight away voluntary bans on new investment and the promotion of tourism in South Africa. In the event we in the Community decided against the sanctions on coal, to which the

Germans were particularly strongly opposed, though the other sanctions proposed at the Hague were introduced in September 1986.

Perhaps the most extraordinary feature of these discussions was that they seemed to be carried on without regard to what was happening in South Africa itself. P. W. Botha's Government was unimaginative and inflexible and the nationwide state of emergency had been imposed. But, as I was informed by our excellent new ambassador, Robin Renwick, and by others who had dealings with the real rather than the bogus South Africa, fundamental changes were taking place. Black trade unions had been legalized, the Mixed Marriages Act had been repealed, influx controls had been abolished and the general policy (though not without exceptions) of forced removals of blacks had ended. So had job reservation for whites and the very unpopular pass laws. Still more important, there was a practical breakdown of apartheid at the work place, in hotels, in offices and in city centres. The repeal of the Separate Amenities Act had been proposed and seemed likely to be implemented. In all these ways 'apartheid', as the Left continued to describe it, was if not dead at least rapidly dying. Yet South Africa received no credit for this, only unthinking hostility.

I was less prepared than ever to go along with measures which would weaken the South African economy and thus slow down reform. So as the 1987 CHOGM at Vancouver approached I was still in no mood for compromise. In some respects the position was easier for me than it had been at Nassau and in London. Events in Fiji and in Sri Lanka were likely to occupy a good deal of attention at the conference. My line on sanctions was well known and the domestic pressure on me had decreased: I had made headway in winning the sanctions argument at home during the London conference. But it would not all be plain sailing. It seemed to me that the Canadians, our hosts, wanted to be more African than the Africans – particularly since countries like Zimbabwe knew that they could not possibly afford to implement full-scale sanctions themselves and hoped that we would do it for them. Brian Mulroney was keen to gain agreement for setting up a committee of Commonwealth Foreign ministers to monitor events in South Africa, which seemed to me not just a waste of time but counter-productive – as I told Mr Mulroney at a meeting with him on the eve of the conference. I said that its only purpose would be to satisfy the ego of the Commonwealth heads of government and I would criticize it publicly and strongly.

I also had a talk with President Kaunda who was under some pressure to set his own country's economic affairs in order to meet the requirements of the IMF. Our views were no more similar on South

Africa than they had been. At one point I said that I regretted that I had not yet been able to visit Africa, apart from my attendance at the Lusaka CHOGM in 1979. Mr Kaunda said that Africa was not at all my area, which I found intensely irritating. I retorted that he himself had charged me with the duty of bringing Rhodesia to full independence as Zimbabwe at the Lusaka Conference and that I had accomplished it. But his off-hand remark did confirm me in my intention of making a visit soon to black African countries.

In my speech to the conference I pointed out just how damaging sanctions and disinvestment were to those we were allegedly trying to help. I gave the example of an Australian firm which had just closed a fish-canning factory near Cape Town putting 120 non-whites out of jobs. I noted that a general ban on fruit and vegetable exports would destroy between 100,000 and 200,000 non-white jobs – and all those affected would have no social security benefits to fall back on. Nearer the knuckle, I said that I well understood why neighbouring countries had not imposed the whole range of sanctions. Eighty per cent of Zimbabwe's external trade passed through South Africa. A million migrant workers earned their living there. Over half of Lesotho's GNP came from their remittances. So I was more firmly convinced than ever that sanctions were not the answer. Of course, such arguments cut little ice with those determined on gestures.

As usual, the main decisions were deferred for the – this time mercifully quite brief – retreat at the Lake Okanagan resort up in the mountains. The discussions took place and meals were provided at a central hotel with individual chalets dotted around it. It was bitterly cold at Lake Okanagan. But the Africans, of course, felt it more than I did. They turned up at the central hotel with blankets over their shoulders. Rajiv Gandhi obviously considered that exercise was the best way to keep warm and always seemed to appear in a tracksuit having jogged between meetings.

The atmosphere at our discussions was not much warmer. I was not prepared to go along with the draft communiqué which they wanted. At a dinner given by Rajiv Gandhi back in Vancouver I was left to kick my heels for forty-five minutes on my own waiting for other heads of government to turn up. They had in fact been holding a press conference on South Africa to which I had not been invited and of whose existence I was unaware.

But we had given as good as we got. In reply to the sanctimonious criticism of our Canadian hosts, I had figures released which showed that Canada's imports from South Africa had risen. It was a useful comment on the Commonwealth heads' sincerity. Not just Mr Mulroney, but almost everyone else it seemed, exploded with indignation at this intrusion of fact upon rhetoric. My suspicion that in this the political leaders were out of step with the people was confirmed when I received a rapturous reception from the crowds in Vancouver: one man kept on shouting 'Hang in there girl, hang in there.' I did.

Visits to Black Africa

Whatever Kenneth Kaunda thought of it, I was now determined to pay a visit to black Africa. It seemed absurd to allow the public arguments about South Africa to get in the way of that. I knew perfectly well from private discussions with African leaders that many of them wanted closer links with Britain. They also generally respect strength in leaders. No one gets very far in African politics without being tough. I also intended to use my visit for a purpose which was to become still more important during the rest of my premiership: I wanted to spread the message that a combination of limited government, financial orthodoxy and free enterprise would work for prosperity in underdeveloped countries as well as it did in the prosperous West. I chose Kenya and Nigeria for my first African political safari. In both cases this was with good reason.

Kenya was the most pro-western, most free enterprise of the important black African states. Nigeria was the most populous African state – one in four Africans is a Nigerian – and a country of huge potential, if only it could achieve sound public finances and public administration. Both President Moi of Kenya and General Babangida of Nigeria were pro-British, though Nigerian feeling towards us was more volatile and on the South African question extremely hostile. Britain was the largest foreign investor in both countries – and in the case of Kenya the largest aid donor too.

I arrived in Nairobi on the evening of Monday 4 January 1988, to be met by President Moi. He had a dignified, rather grave manner, with something of the tribal chief about him: we always got on well. But his human rights record was no better than that of many Commonwealth heads of government. Although we disagreed about South Africa, he was a moderate and one of the forces for common sense at CHOGMs.

Denis and I and our party stayed at the government guesthouse, which left something to be desired. Denis tried to run a bath but found that there was no water and it had to be brought up in dustbins from the cellar: we heated it up on gas rings in the kitchen. Then no sooner did we have hot water than the lights went out.

But whatever difficulties there were with the facilities, there was none with the welcome. President Moi, who loved nothing better than to get out of Nairobi into the countryside, accompanied me on a fascinating itinerary. Kenya, unlike some other African countries, has never lost sight of the importance of agriculture. Great efforts were clearly being put into improving it. I visited a Masai rural training centre and inspected their lugubrious cattle, toured a tea plantation, met a polygamous sugar farmer with twenty-three immaculately turned-out young children and then went on to what was described as a 'Women's Poultry Project'. This visit had been suggested by the British Overseas Development Administration (ODA) as a model small agricultural project. Unfortunately, the Kenyan Government, on learning that I was to go there, upgraded the whole project and moved the chickens into conditions of great luxury, which of course largely destroyed the point of the visit. Everywhere I went I was struck by the good-humoured reception I received. The bitternesses of the 1950s had clearly been forgotten. It was an encouraging start.

I then went on to make a fleeting visit to Nigeria. I arrived at Lagos on the morning of Thursday 7 January and had talks with General Babangida. He was a forceful, intelligent man, trying to put Nigeria's economy on to a sounder footing and in due course, we hoped, to create the conditions for a restoration of democracy. We had helped Nigeria in its dealings with the IMF and this was appreciated. General Babangida seemed to be open to my suggestions about the need to curb Nigeria's budget deficit, cut inflation and provide reassurances for foreign investors. We also saw eye to eye about the dangers of Soviet and Cuban involvement in Africa.

The next day I flew to the very north of the country to attend a Durbar as the guest of the Emir of Kano. It was a difficult landing because of the cloud of fine Sahara sand suspended in the air. Denis was sitting in the aeroplane cockpit and he told me afterwards that there had only been a relatively brief period of visibility before landing. This real danger was, however, entirely subordinated to one manufactured by the British press. On the way up to the Emir's box, from where I was to view the horses and camels parading below, I lost contact with the rest of my staff who were jostled by an overenthusiastic crowd and then treated with some vigour by anxious security guards confused about their identity. Bernard Ingham received a none too gentle rifle butt in the stomach. Later in the day an anxious Nigel Wicks, my principal private secretary at No. 10, rang up to see whether we were still in one piece. In fact – unaware of the confusion – I had been enjoying myself hugely, holding on to a rather fabulous hat I was wearing with the Nigerian national colours on it as horsemen charged in a cloud of dust up to where the Emir, Denis and I were seated. At the end I was presented with a horse myself as a gift; but, arguing that it would be happier with its own horse acquaintances than in a British stable, I prevailed on my hosts to keep it for me.

The success of this visit convinced me that I should make a more ambitious foray into Africa the following year and this was now arranged. I would go first to Morocco – which is essentially part of the Arab world – and then on to Zimbabwe, Malawi, possibly Namibia, and Nigeria once more.

I already had the greatest regard for King Hassan of Morocco, who was always underrated as a player in Middle Eastern politics. I had met him in London two years earlier when he was on a state visit. On this occasion our talk was mainly of the Arab-Israeli dispute and military co-operation between Britain and Morocco. As well as being enormously cultivated – he speaks half a dozen languages and can make an impromptu speech in any of them – the King has an icy nerve. When I heard from him about the measures he took to protect himself from further assassination attempts I understood that he, like me, understood what it meant to live as a terrorist target.

Then I flew to Lagos. This was just a stop-over visit and General Babangida came to the airport to have lunch with me. I was glad to learn that he was not just pressing ahead with, but actually toughening, the economic reform programme on which Nigeria had embarked. With our support, Nigeria now had the approval of the IMF and its main western creditors and had secured a rescheduling of debt to its public sector creditors. It is never an easy task to govern a country like Nigeria – it is a somewhat artificial creation divided between the Muslim North and the Christian and pagan South – let alone to do so under conditions of economic austerity.

I arrived at Harare, Zimbabwe, at 10 o'clock that night, to be met by Robert Mugabe and a floodlit, noisy tribal welcome. It was nearly ten years since I had convened the Lancaster House Conference which led to Mr Mugabe peacefully taking power in Zimbabwe. Since then Britain had provided more than £200 million in aid and military training. Britain was also the largest investor. Zimbabwe could still boast of one of the strongest African economies outside South Africa. But Mr Mugabe's doctrinaire socialism, suspicion of foreign investment and reluctance to accept the prescriptions of the IMF and the World Bank were taking their toll. I had little reason to expect that I could persuade him to my point of view on the South African sanctions question, but I hoped that I might succeed in bringing him to accept the need for changes in economic policy. At my talks with him the following morning I sought to do this by describing my own economic policies in the United Kingdom where we were reducing the role of the state in the economy and encouraging free enterprise: this, I said, was why our economy was growing and enabling us to provide aid for Zimbabwe. I also drew attention to a recent World Bank study which showed that those African countries which followed programmes recommended by the IMF did better than those which did not. Mr Mugabe recognized, at least in principle, the need to devise an investment code so as to give assurance to foreign investors. But I was not convinced that the rest of my message really went home. Much of our discussion, however, was about the situation in neighbouring African states, not least Mozambique. I was shortly to learn more about this.

Later that morning I flew out with President Mugabe to the training camp at Nyanga on the border with Mozambique. There I was met by President Chissano of Mozambique and the three of us had lunch in a tent on a bluff overlooking a deep valley. Then I watched the British troops training Mozambique soldiers to fight the RENAMO guerillas. I could not help reflecting how impossible this prospect would have seemed back in 1979 when I was trying to bring Rhodesia back to peace and legality. It would probably have seemed hardly less improbable to those of my left-wing critics who considered my stand against sanctions as a kind of racist impulse.

The following evening (Thursday 30 March) I flew from Harare to Blantyre, Malawi. The journey was short and so my VC10 was flying lower than usual – too low for comfort, since at one point we were fired on with missiles by RENAMO. Fortunately they missed. I was met at the airport – with another floodlit tribal greeting – by President Banda. It was an unforgettable occasion. He was an extraordinary man. Although probably in his early nineties, I found him, in my talks, bright, alert and humorous. Almost alone, he had built up Malawi, a poor country, into one with sound finances and sensibly developed agriculture. I stayed with him in his official residence, the Sanjika Palace, where I would come across him wearing dark formal dress and a black hat which he would doff when I met him in the corridor. There was another, less agreeable, side to his regime. Opponents quickly found themselves in jail and traders who, like several of my own Asian constituents, tried to get their money out of the country had their property confiscated.

Early next morning I helicoptered out to the Mankhokwe Refugee

Camp on the border with Mozambique. Most of the flight was over mountains which then dropped away to a plain on which a vast refugee camp housing over 600,000 people had been built. These refugees had fled from the civil war in Mozambique. What they told me about the atrocities committed and the reign of fear created in their villages by RENAMO was truly horrifying. I saw some of those who had just recently fled: they had not eaten for several days and had travelled by night. Their eyes had that deadness which total exhaustion brings. After this, I could never be tempted to regard RENAMO as anti-communist freedom fighters in the way that some right-wing Americans continued to. They were terrorists.

That night President Banda hosted a state banquet for me. It was a memorable occasion, not least because it lasted over five hours. Each new dish which was brought in was presented first to the President before being served to his guests. My own gaze fell on a giant chocolate cockerel: I can never resist chocolate. Zulus sang and danced throughout the banquet. Then Dr Banda rose to speak. An hour later his account of his life and experiences had only reached 1945. Some of his guests had actually fallen asleep. At this point the lady who acted as his hostess gave him a hard nudge and reminded him of the time. We got through the next forty-three years in five minutes flat. In consideration of those present I cut down my own speech accordingly.

Hardly anyone knew that from Blantyre I intended to fly to Windhoek, Namibia: the press who were with us were only told after we had taken off. The UN plan to bring Namibia (formerly South-West Africa) to democratic independence had been drawn up in the late 1970s but only now, as a result of American efforts to broker a settlement of the Angolan civil war – to which we had given strong support – was it possible to put it into effect. Security Council Resolution 632 of 16 February 1989 was to be implemented from Saturday 1 April – the day on which I arrived in Windhoek – with a view to elections later in the year.

On my arrival I was met by the three key figures – the UN Special Representative (Mr Ahtisaari), the UN Force Commander (General Prem Chand) and the South African Administrator-General (Mr Pienaar). Denis and I then visited and had lunch with the small British Signals contingent in their base camp, visited the Rossing Uranium Mine – where I was much impressed by the housing and welfare services provided for the employees – and then returned to Windhoek. By now it was clear that the whole UN solution to the Namibian problem was at mortal risk. In flagrant disregard of previous undertakings that no armed personnel would come south of the 16th Parallel (well within Angola) hundreds of SWAPO (South-West Africa People's Organization) troops had crossed the border into Namibia with military equipment. I was not in the least convinced by the reaction of the SWAPO leader – Sam Nujoma – who claimed that his organization was faithfully abiding by the cease-fire and that the so-called invaders must be South Africans in disguise.

But nor did I believe that it would do anything but harm – not least to South Africa – if the South Africans now responded by unilaterally moving their own forces out of barracks to drive SWAPO back. I met Pik Botha, the South African Foreign minister, at Windhoek Airport. I said that SWAPO had done wrong and therefore South Africa must act with scrupulous correctness. 'Never put yourself in the wrong', I said, 'particularly when your opponents have just done so.' I told him that he must get in touch with the UN representative and General Prem, present his evidence before them and ask for their authority to get his troops and helicopters out of barracks. I rang Mr Ahtisaari myself to alert him to what was happening.

In fact, the UN did authorize the South Africans to use their forces. But it was all legal. Though there were many casualties, a full-scale confrontation was avoided, assembly points were designated to which SWAPO units reported to be escorted back across the border with their arms by UN forces, a new cease-fire was agreed – and this now held. That autumn SWAPO won the elections for the Namibian Constituent Assembly and Mr Nujoma became President – in which capacity he thanked me when I was at the United Nations in September 1990 for my intervention. In fact, I had held no brief for SWAPO. But I did believe that only with the issue of Namibia sorted out could there be peaceful change in South Africa. I had been the right person in the right place at the right time.

But my activities in black Africa had little impact on 'Commonwealth opinion'. Nor, it seemed, did changes in South Africa itself.

Rhetoric and Reality in South Africa, 1989–1990

I had always felt that fundamental reform would never take place while P. W. Botha was President. But in January 1989 Mr Botha suffered a stroke and the following month was succeeded as National Party Leader by F. W. de Klerk, who became President in August. It was surely right to give the new South African leader the opportunity to make his mark without ham-fisted outside intervention.

The 1989 CHOGM was due to take place in October in Kuala Lumpur, hosted by Dr Mahathir. I went there with a new Foreign Secretary, John Major, and a renewed determination not to go further down the path of sanctions. I also tried to raise the sights of those present to the great changes which were taking place in the world around them. Introducing the session on the 'World Political Scene' I drew attention to the momentous changes occurring in the Soviet Union and their implications for all of us. I said that there was now the prospect of settling regional conflicts – not least those in Africa – which had been aggravated by the international subversion of communism. Throughout the world we must now ardently advocate democracy and a much freer economic system. I secretly hoped that the message would not be lost on the many illiberal, collectivist Commonwealth countries whose representatives were present.

But the debate on South Africa brought out all the old venom. Bob Hawke and Kenneth Kaunda argued the case for sanctions. I intervened to read out a letter I had recently received from a British company which had invested in pineapple-canning in South Africa, but found its export markets in the USA and Canada cut off by sanctions and had therefore been forced to close, putting 1,100 black and 40 white South Africans out of work. That was the only sense in which sanctions 'worked'. I also quoted figures to show that Britain's share of South African imports and exports had fallen further over the last eight years than that of the rest of the Commonwealth, adding that our share had largely been picked up by Japan and Germany. I pointed out that Britain was providing substantial help for black South Africans, their education, their housing, rural projects, refugees from Mozambique and aid to the 'front line' states. We were assisting 'Operation Hunger' which provides meals for millions of poor South Africans. By contrast, the aim of many others at the CHOGM seemed to be to multiply the number of those who were hungry.

By now I was quite used to the vicious, personal attacks in which my Commonwealth colleagues liked to indulge. John Major was not: he found their behaviour quite shocking. I left him back in Kuala Lumpur with the other Foreign ministers to draft the communiqué while I and the other heads of government went off to our retreat in Langkawi. While I was there my officials faxed through a text which the Foreign ministers apparently thought we could all 'live with'. But I could only live with it if I also put out a separate unambiguous statement of our own views. I had it drafted and sent back to John Major in Kuala Lumpur. Contrary to what the press – almost as eager for 'splits' as they were for describing Britain's 'isolation' – subsequently alleged, John was quite happy to go along with issuing a separate British document and made some changes to it, which I agreed. I suspect that he had had his fill of Commonwealth diplomacy already. The issue, however, of our separate document prompted howls of anger from the other heads of government. At the session of CHOGM at which Dr Mahathir reported on the retreat at Langkawi Bob Hawke intervened to protest about what Britain had done. Brian Mulroney followed this up. It was, in fact, clearly planned. They arrived at the meeting together and signalled to each other before Bob Hawke spoke. I replied by saying that I owed nobody an explanation and was astounded that anyone should object to a nation putting forward its own viewpoint. They had put forward their views in speeches and press conferences and Britain had as much right to free speech as they did. That ended the discussion.

In South Africa as 1990 opened the movement which I had hoped and worked for began. There were indications that Nelson Mandela would, after all the years of pressure, not least from me, shortly be released. I told our ambassador, Robin Renwick, that I would welcome the chance to see President de Klerk at Chequers if he visited Europe in the spring. I told the Foreign Office – who did not like it one bit – that as soon as Mr Mandela was freed I wanted us to respond rapidly by rescinding or relaxing the measures we had taken against South Africa, starting with the relatively minor ones which rested with us alone and did not have to be discussed with the European Community.

On 2 February 1990 President de Klerk made a speech which announced Mr Mandela's and other black leaders' imminent release, the unbanning of the ANC and other black political organizations and promised an end to the state of emergency as soon as possible. I immediately went back to the Foreign Office and said that once the promises were fulfilled we should end the 'voluntary' ban on investment and encourage the other European Community countries to do likewise. I asked Douglas Hurd – now Foreign Secretary – to propose to other Community Foreign ministers at his forthcoming meeting with them an end to the restrictions on purchase of krugerrands and iron and steel. I also decided to send messages to other heads of government urging practical recognition of what was happening in South Africa.

In April I was briefed by Dr Gerrit Viljoen, the South African Minister for Constitutional Development, on the contacts between the South African Government and the ANC, now effectively led once more by Mr Mandela. I was disappointed by the fact that Mr Mandela kept repeating the old ritual phrases, arguably suitable for a movement refused recognition, but not for one aspiring to a leading and perhaps dominant role in government. The South African Government was formulating its own ideas for the constitution and was moving towards a combination of a lower house elected by one-man one-vote with an upper chamber with special minority representation. This would help to accommodate the great ethnic diversity which characterizes South Africa, although in the long run some sort of cantonal system may be needed to do this efficiently.

By the time that President de Klerk set off for his talks with European leaders in May, discussions with the ANC had begun in earnest. I was also glad that the South African Government was paying due regard to Chief Buthelezi, who had been such a stalwart opponent of violent uprising in South Africa while the ANC had been endorsing the Marxist revolution, to which some of its members are still attached.

Talks with President de Klerk and Mr Mandela

President de Klerk, Pik Botha and their wives came to talks and lunch at Chequers on Saturday 19 May. I felt that Mr de Klerk had grown in stature since my last meeting with him a year ago. It struck me that there were parallels with Mr Gorbachev – though perhaps neither would have welcomed the comparison: in each case one man brought to power through an unjust and oppressive system had the combination of vision and prudence to set about changing that system. My talks with Mr de Klerk focused on his plans for the next steps in bringing the ANC to accept a political and economic system which would secure South Africa's future as a liberal, free enterprise country. The violence between blacks, which was to get worse, was already the single biggest obstacle to progress. But he was optimistic about the prospects for agreement with the ANC on a new constitution; and he thought that the ANC wanted this too.

We discussed what should be done about sanctions. He said that he was not like a dog begging for a biscuit, seeking specific rewards for actions he took. What he wanted was the widest possible international recognition of and support for what he was doing, leading to a fundamental revision of attitudes towards South Africa. This seemed to me very sensible. Mr de Klerk also invited me to South Africa. I said that I would love to come but I did not want to make things more difficult for him at this particular moment. There was, I knew, nothing more likely to sour his dealings with other governments who had been proved wrong about South Africa than for me to arrive in his country as a kind of proclamation that I had been right. (In fact, it is a disappointment to me that I was never to go to South Africa as Prime Minister and I only finally accepted his invitation after I left office.)

On Wednesday 4 July I held talks and had lunch at Downing Street with the other main player in South African politics, Nelson Mandela. I had seen him briefly in the spring when he had been feted by the media Left, attending a concert in Wembley in his honour, but this was the first time I really got to know him. The Left were rather offended that he was prepared to see me at all. But then he, unlike them, had a shrewd view as to what kind of pressure for his release had been more successful. I found Mr Mandela supremely courteous, with a genuine nobility of bearing and – most remarkable after all he had suffered – without any bitterness. I warmed to him. But I also found him very outdated in his attitudes, stuck in a kind of socialist timewarp in which nothing had moved on, not least in economic thinking, since the 1940s. Perhaps this was not surprising in view of his long years of imprisonment: but it was a disadvantage in the first few months of his freedom because he tended to repeat these outdated platitudes which in turn confirmed his followers in their exaggerated expectations.

I made four main points in our discussion. First, I urged him to suspend the 'armed struggle'. Whatever justification there might have been for this was now gone. Second, I supported the South African Government's arguments against having an elected Constituent Assembly to draw up a constitution. It seemed to me that in order to maintain both the confidence of the white population and law and order it should be for the Government, the ANC and Inkatha (Chief Buthelezi's movement) and others to agree on a constitution now. Third, I pointed out the harm which all his talk of nationalization could do to foreign investment and the economy in general. Finally, I said that I thought he should meet Chief Buthelezi personally – which he was refusing to do. This was the only hope for ending the violence between their supporters. Our relationship was unharmed by my straight talking. In spite of his socialist outlook, I believed that South Africa was lucky to have a man of Mr Mandela's stature at such a time. Indeed, I hoped he would assert himself more at the expense of some of his ANC colleagues.

It was only shortly before I left office that President de Klerk again came to see me at Chequers – on Sunday 14 October. There had been some progress since I had seen Mr Mandela in June. The ANC had agreed to suspend the 'armed struggle' and the two sides had agreed in principle on the arrangements for the return of South African exiles and the release of the rest of the political prisoners. The remaining features of the old apartheid system were being dismantled. The Land Acts were due to be repealed and the Population Registration Act – the last remaining legislative pillar of apartheid – would go when a new constitution was agreed. Only state education remained segregated but movement on this – for the whites – very sensitive matter had also begun. However, violence between blacks had sharply worsened and this was poisoning the atmosphere for negotiations.

The South Africans were being careful about pressing for the lifting of the remaining sanctions. The most important contribution to this would have been that of the ANC: but they stubbornly refused to recognize that the case for sanctions – to the extent it had ever existed – was dead. Within the European Community, the key to a formal change of policy now was Germany, but for domestic political reasons Chancellor Kohl was still unwilling to act. The Americans held back for similar reasons. However, as President de Klerk told me, in practice most of the economic sanctions were being steadily eroded and what really mattered to the South Africans now was access to foreign loans and investment. (In fact, sanctions were gradually dismantled over the next few years: indeed the international community began to prepare financial aid for South Africa to undo the damage that sanctions had wrought.)

President de Klerk was clearly frustrated that the further round of informal talks with the ANC on the constitution for which he had been pressing had still not occurred. The longer the process continued the more opportunity there was for hardliners – on either side – to derail the negotiations. The main principle to which he held was that there must be power sharing in the Executive. In the new South Africa no one must have as much power as he himself had now. In some respects he thought that the Swiss Federal Cabinet was a guide to what was needed. This seemed to me to be very much on the right lines – not that either hybrid constitutions or federal systems have much inherent appeal, but in states where allegiances are at least as much to subordinate groups as to the overarching institutions of the state itself these things may constitute the least bad approach. It remains to be seen whether the ANC leadership is prepared to recognize this. With all the risks of violence and all the shortcomings of the various political factions, South Africa remains the strongest economy on the continent and has the most skilled and educated population.

It would be a tragedy if it cannot exploit these advantages to build a genuine democracy, which respects minority rights, on the foundation of a free economy.

CHAPTER XVIII

Jeux Sans Frontières

Relations with the European Community – 1984–1987

TWO VISIONS OF EUROPE

The wisdom of hindsight, so useful to historians and indeed to authors of memoirs, is sadly denied to practising politicians. Looking back, it is now possible to see the period of my second term as Prime Minister as that in which the European Community subtly but surely shifted its direction away from being a Community of open trade, light regulation and freely co-operating sovereign nation-states towards statism and centralism. I can only say that it did not seem like that at the time. For it was during this period that I not only managed to secure a durable financial settlement of Britain's Community budget imbalance and began to get Europe to take financial discipline more seriously, but also launched the drive for a real Common Market free of hidden protectionism. It was clear to me from the start that there were two competing visions of Europe: but I felt that our vision of a free enterprise *Europe des patries* was predominant.

Now I see the period somewhat differently. For the underlying forces of federalism and bureaucracy were gaining in strength as a coalition of Socialist and Christian Democrat governments in France, Spain, Italy and Germany forced the pace of integration and a commission, equipped with extra powers, began to manipulate them to advance its own agenda. It was only in my last days in office and under my successor that the true scale of the challenge has become clear.

At this time I genuinely believed that once our budget contribution had been sorted out and we had set in place a framework of financial order, Britain would be able to play a strong positive role in the Community. I considered myself a European idealist, even if my ideals differed somewhat from those expressed with varying degrees of sincerity by other European heads of government. I told a dinner of Conservative MEPs on Thursday 8 March 1984:

> I don't want to paper over the cracks. I want to get rid of the cracks. I want to rebuild the foundations.
>
> . . . I want to solve [the current problems] so that we can set about building the Community of the future. A Community striving for freer trade, breaking down the barriers in Europe and the world to the free flow of goods, capital and services; working together to make Europe the home of the industries of tomorrow; seizing the initiative on world problems, not reacting wearily to them; forging political links across the European divide and so creating a more hopeful relationship between East and West; using its influence as a vital area of stability and democracy to strengthen democracy across the world.
>
> That is my vision.

It was also, incidentally, the vision on which we were to fight the European Assembly elections later that year and do remarkably well, winning 45 out of the 81 United Kingdom seats.

REFORMING COMMUNITY FINANCES: BRITAIN'S BUDGET CONTRIBUTION

Before there was any hope of moving far towards those wider objectives I had to get more understanding and support from other Community heads of government for our position. The French presidency of the first half of 1984 seemed to offer an opportunity which must be grasped. The events in Athens the previous December – where the only thing to record was disagreement – were widely considered to have reduced Community negotiations to the level of farce.* President Mitterrand was, I knew, someone who relished a diplomatic success and would probably be prepared to sacrifice French national interests – at least marginally – in order to secure one. In January (in Paris) and in early March (at Chequers) I had talks with him. In January Geoffrey Howe and I also discussed the Community budget and other matters with the Italian Government in Rome. The following month Chancellor Kohl and I held talks at No. 10. These meetings were pleasant enough,

* For discussion of the Athens European Council, see Chapter 12, pp. 335–8.

but no clear undertakings were given. The Foreign Affairs Councils – that is the meetings of Community Foreign ministers – in February and March advanced matters no further. But I was reasonably optimistic that the European Council in Brussels, which I was to attend on Monday 19 and Tuesday 20 March, might give us the lasting, satisfactory solution on the British budget contribution which I wanted.

By the time I reached Brussels three possible 'solutions' to the budget question had been advanced – one by the Commission President, Gaston Thorn, one by the Germans, and one by the French presidency. None was satisfactory to us, but all of them acknowledged the principle behind our 'threshold' proposal at Athens – that a country's prosperity should be taken into account in determining its net contribution. We were getting down to brass tacks. I was also glad that President Mitterrand, unlike his Greek predecessor, had chosen a more sensible order of discussion at the Council, beginning with the issues of budget discipline and budget imbalances. After initial discussion, officials went away to work on the text relating to the budget while we moved on to the issue of increasing the Community's 'own resources'. On this, the line-up was predictable. The President of the Commission wanted an increase in the current VAT ceiling, not just to 1.4 per cent but to a minimum of 1.6 per cent. Garret FitzGerald wanted a minimum of 1.8 per cent. President Mitterrand suggested 1.6 per cent. Chancellor Kohl and I would have none of this: 1.4 per cent was as far as we could possibly go – and that was only after other matters relating to the budget and agricultural spending had been satisfactorily resolved.

The Council was due to meet again at about 11 o'clock the next morning. President Mitterrand and Chancellor Kohl had a working breakfast – something which was to become a feature of European Councils because it was widely and probably accurately believed that these were the occasion of the Franco-German deals which heavily influenced or in some cases virtually determined the outcome of the Council. I met President Mitterrand after his meeting with Chancellor Kohl and gained the impression that we were heading for a successful outcome.

When the heads of government reconvened later that morning the session began with a gush of Euro-idealism. Chancellor Kohl and President Mitterrand became quite lyrical on the subject of getting rid of frontier controls, which they seemed to invest with a high symbolic significance. Then President Mitterrand urged that Europe should not be left behind by the USA in the space race. The Italian Foreign minister became still more enthusiastic, urging that Europe should be in the vanguard of moves against the 'militarization of space'. It seemed to me that it would be more sensible to concentrate on sorting out the Community budget first and at last we got down to business.

Now the high-mindedness quickly disappeared. The Irish Prime Minister tried and failed to gain a special exemption from the measures to limit milk production that the rest of us wanted. He promptly invoked the Luxemburg compromise and walked out. At 4 p.m. there was a long adjournment in order to study a new text of the draft communiqué. On resuming, we discussed once again the budgetary problems. The Italians and the Greeks stood out against giving Britain any permanent agreement to reduce our net budget contributions; more serious for us, President Mitterrand seemed to side with them. I intervened to say that I had fought this battle for five years and that I intended to have a system which was fair and which would last. At this point – whether spontaneously or by previous agreement with President Mitterrand I do not know – Chancellor Kohl upped and offered Britain a 1,000 million ecus rebate for five years – much less than I wanted and still only a temporary arrangement. Almost immediately France and the others agreed with Germany. I found myself isolated. I refused to accept his proposal. Nothing more could be done. No agreed communiqué was issued. To rub salt into the wound, France and Italy at a Foreign Affairs Council immediately after the heads of government summit broke up blocked payment of our 1983 refund.

I had not expected such a totally negative outcome. So the question immediately arose as to whether we should withhold payments to the Community budget. This was partly a legal and partly a political question. We had always been advised that if we withheld contributions we would almost certainly lose any subsequent case before the European Court. In this instance, however, we were on somewhat stronger legal ground because the Community was withholding rebate payments to which we were entitled by previous agreement. Probably, we would have lost the case anyway. But it might have been politically worth fighting – that is we might have thus secured a favourable compromise – if we had enjoyed the united backing of the Parliamentary Party. Unfortunately, there was a hard core of Euro-enthusiasts on the Tory back-benches who instinctively supported the Community in any dispute with Britain. Though a clear minority, they robbed us of the advantages of unity. So as on previous occasions, I decided not to go down the path of withholding contributions. And we had other cards to play.

On the basic question of whether I had been right to refuse what was on offer there was little dispute. A letter I received from one parliamentary colleague began:

> Glory Glory Halleluia and many congratulations on your courageous and absolutely correct stand at the EEC summit tonight.

Apart from my own summits with the other European heads of government in the run up to important Councils, I always received up-to-the-minute reports from our embassies and officials on what could be deduced of the private intentions of other governments and the state of public and press opinion in their countries. The two crucial players would be France – which still held the presidency – and Germany. Before the European Assembly election campaign got under way I tried to persuade President Mitterrand and Chancellor Kohl to agree to sort out the budget. In this I was certainly being a 'better' European than they were: for public opinion in Britain was all for intransigence. But I suspect that the French President, at least, was not minded to reach a deal until the elections had come and gone. My attempts failed.

As the Council approached it still seemed to us that President Mitterrand had not yet finally decided between two possible courses of action – a solution which would be a diplomatic triumph for France (in the chair) or a failure which would all be down to 'Perfidious Albion'. Whatever his private political calculations, the French President was also now publicly calling for yet another 'relaunch' of the Community, something which was music to Chancellor Kohl's ears. So when we prepared our own paper on the Community's future for the forthcoming summit, I accepted that it should be liberally sprinkled with *communautaire* phrases.

The French President's intentions continued to be unclear. Whether the French themselves were confused or whether these were tactics designed to confuse us in the best tradition of Gallic gamesmanship we could not yet tell. A number of apparently unco-ordinated French ideas to settle the budget were in circulation; which, if any, had the President's own support was unknown. Then on the eve of the Council, President Mitterrand departed for Moscow with an air of nonchalance, which may itself have been an aspect of psychological warfare.

What would the German position be? There were some reasons for optimism. It seemed that Chancellor Kohl was now definitely anxious for a successful summit. At Brussels, where he had been blamed for the failure of the budget negotiations, he had learnt the danger of taking ill-thought-out initiatives. We thought that he would support the French presidency and that he would probably be willing to agree to a better deal for Britain than he had proposed at Brussels. The most encouraging consideration was that he needed the Community's agreement to enable him to provide a politically necessary subsidy for his farmers – and for Chancellor Kohl domestic political considerations always came first. As by far the largest net contributors to the Community, the Germans wanted both to set a limit to their contributions – as we did – and to ensure that they did not finish up paying for the whole of our own rebate. But they were surprisingly vague on how precisely to achieve this.

THE FONTAINEBLEAU EUROPEAN COUNCIL

The European Council was held at Fontainebleau, just outside Paris, on Monday 25 and Tuesday 26 June. On the short flight in the Andover from Northolt to Orly I finalized our tactics. Geoffrey Howe and I shared the same analysis. We wanted an agreement at this meeting but only if it was close enough to our terms. We had our reasons. After France the presidency would go to Ireland which would be no improvement – indeed worse because the French themselves, for the reasons I have outlined, were likely to be more difficult when they were not in the chair. Moreover, we had no agreement on rebates for the current year, nor for the future; and our 1983 refund of 750 million ecus (£400 million) was still being held up. I was prepared to accept, if necessary, a different formula from that which we had advanced, but the money rebated must be enough and the arrangement had to be lasting.

I arrived at lunchtime at the Château of Fontainebleau to be met by President Mitterrand and a full guard of honour. The French know how to do these things properly. Whereas Versailles provided the heads of government with an experience of the splendour of France in the *Grand Siècle*, Fontainebleau – the creation of Francis I who vied with our own Henry VIII on the famous Field of Cloth of Gold – represents the height of French Renaissance culture. Lunch took place in the Château's Hall of Columns and then we went through into the Ballroom, which was heavily disguised by interpreters' booths, for the first session of the Council. Without any warning, President Mitterrand asked me to open the proceedings by summing up the results of the recent economic summit in London. Others then joined in to give their own views and two hours elapsed. I started to fidget. Were these just delaying tactics? At last we got on to the budget. Again I opened, demonstrating what I thought unsatisfactory about the other schemes which had been put forward to provide a solution and argued for our own ideas of a formula. There was further discussion. Then President Mitterrand remitted the matter to the Foreign ministers to discuss later in the evening. Our meeting now returned to generalities, in particular President Mitterrand's lively account of his recent visit to Moscow.

That evening we drove back along the road through the forest to our hotel at Barbizon. This little village attracts artists and gastronomes. Anyone who has eaten at the local Hôtellerie du Bas-Bréau will know why: the food was simply delicious.* Over dinner I was wondering what the Foreign ministers were going to come up with. As we drank our coffee, we saw that the Foreign ministers were taking theirs outside on to the terrace and naturally concluded that they had done their work. Far from it. It appeared that over dinner the French Foreign minister, M. Cheysson, had been regaling his colleagues with his own recollections of Moscow. President Mitterrand did not conceal his displeasure and the Foreign ministers quickly went inside again to get down to discussing the budget.

For our part, the heads of government spent some time discussing the future of the Community. We got on to the question of the number of commissioners once enlargement to take in Spain and Portugal had occurred. I was alone in being prepared to settle for one commissioner per country so as to reduce the number from sixteen to twelve. I asked M. Thorn (with whom I often saw eye to eye – he did not have the grandiose ambitions and bureaucratic leanings of his successor) whether there was really enough work for seventeen commissioners. He said no. But my colleagues from France, Germany and Italy were not prepared to reduce their representation. So the Commission ended up with the full complement – and the devil makes work for idle hands.

At about 11.30 p.m. M. Cheysson emerged once more to tell us that the Foreign ministers had 'clarified the points of difference'. In fact, the French had apparently managed to persuade the Foreign ministers to favour a rebate system giving us back a simple percentage of our net contribution. On such a percentage system there would be

* I am a great collector of menus. For the connoisseur I reproduce the menu for dinner on 25 June: *Assortiment de foie gras d'oie; Homard breton rôti, beurre Cancalais; Carré d'agneau aux petites girolles; Asperges tièdes; Fromages de la Brie et de Fontainebleau; Soufflé chaud aux framboises; Mignardises et fours frais.* All washed down with the finest wines.

no link between net contributions and relative prosperity – unlike the 'threshold' system we had been arguing for. We had privately envisaged that this is how matters might eventually turn out.

But a percentage of what? Everyone could agree that it would be a percentage of the gap between the sums we paid into the Community and the sums we received from it. The French proposed in calculating our contributions to take into account only those payments to the Community that Britain made under VAT. That formula, however, ignored the considerable sums we also contributed through tariffs and levies. All our previous proposals had been based on this larger sum, but in the end we had to accept the calculation based on VAT.

And, finally, how big a percentage would the rebate be? If we were to drop the threshold idea – and therefore any link between net contribution and prosperity – it would need to be pretty big. Indeed, I had in mind a figure of well over 70 per cent. But it seemed from the Foreign ministers' meeting that we were now likely to be offered at most something between 50 and 60 per cent with a temporary two-year sweetener that would bring the refund up to 1000 million ecus a year for the first two years. How Geoffrey, who had been splendidly staunch in the negotiations so far, had allowed the Foreign ministers to reach such a conclusion I could not understand.

I was in despair. I told the heads of government that Britain had never been treated fairly from the beginning: I was not prepared to go back to talking about a temporary sum: if this was the best they had to offer the Fontainebleau Council would be a disaster.

Geoffrey, civil servants and I then met to discuss what should be done. Our officials – who, I knew, had the brains, experience and determination required to retrieve something from this débâcle – set to work with their opposite numbers all through the night and into the early morning. As a result of their efforts, the next day began a great deal better than the previous one had ended.

President Mitterrand's and Chancellor Kohl's breakfast the following morning probably cleared the way for a settlement. President Mitterrand opened the formal session by saying that we must try for an agreement on the budget, but if we had not succeeded by lunchtime we should go on to other things. I made it clear that I was now ready to negotiate on the basis of a percentage agreement, but I held my ground for a figure of over 70 per cent. Quite soon, and sensibly, President Mitterrand adjourned the main session so that bilateral meetings could take place.

How hard should I hold out on the figure? As I have said, there were good reasons for my wanting a settlement now. And with the Community running right up against the financial buffers of the 1 per cent VAT ceiling (on raising which they knew we had a veto) there were equally good reasons for other Community members to be co-operative. I saw President Mitterrand and Chancellor Kohl separately. At this stage the French President would not move above 60 per cent. Chancellor Kohl would go as far as 65 per cent. I carefully appraised the situation and came to the conclusion that I could obtain a deal on the basis of a two-thirds refund. But I was determined to get the full 66 per cent. It was only when the full session resumed that I managed to do so. I said that it would be absurd to deny me my 1 percentage point. The French President smiled and said: 'Of course, Madame Prime Minister, you must have it.' And so the agreement was reached.

Or almost. When the agreement was being drafted an attempt was made to exclude the costs of enlargement from this refund arrangement. I resisted this fiercely and won. The heads of government also agreed to release our 1983 refund.

Immediately, Chancellor Kohl raised his point about a special subsidy for his farmers. He said that as Germany had facilitated the budget settlement by providing the greater part of the money, he felt he was entitled to subsidize his own farmers, in effective contravention of the CAP. This did not please the Dutch because they would in practice have to subsidize their farmers to the same extent; but the Netherlands had neither the stomach nor the strength to oppose Germany. So Chancellor Kohl got his way.

After more argument, principally between me and Garret FitzGerald, about how to deal with the already overspent 1984 Community budget, President Mitterrand wound up the conference and we retired to a late lunch in high spirits because the deadlock on the budget had been broken.

At my press conference and at the time of my later statement to the House of Commons on the outcome of Fontainebleau there was some criticism that I had not got more. But the crucial achievement was to have gained a settlement which would last as long as the increased 'own resources' from the new 1.4 per cent VAT ceiling itself lasted. Of course, in a sense that was not 'permanent': but it meant that I would not have to go back every year to renegotiate the rebate until the new VAT limit ran out, and that when it did so I would be in just as strong a position as I had been at Fontainebleau to veto any extra 'own resources' unless I had a satisfactory deal on Britain's budget contribution. More generally, the resolution of this dispute meant that the Community could now press ahead both with the enlargement and with the Single Market measures which I wanted to see. In every negotiation there comes the best possible time to settle: this was it.

ENLARGEMENT OF THE COMMUNITY

It had generally been expected that once we and the Germans had agreed to increase the Community's 'own resources' the admission of Spain and Portugal would run fairly smoothly. In fact it took two European Councils at Dublin and at Brussels to sort it out. The Irish having assumed the Community presidency, the Dublin Council was set for Monday 3 and Tuesday 4 December. I was always the odd 'man' out on such occasions simply because as the IRA's prime political target I had to be surrounded by especially tight security. The Irish Government and Army went to great lengths to achieve this and I always expressed my gratitude to them for it. But I could barely venture out of Dublin Castle, where I would stay, helicoptering back and forth only as strictly necessary.

At least on this occasion it was not Britain but Greece which was marked out as the villain of the piece – and with some justice. The two outstanding issues as regards the terms for Spain's and Portugal's entry had turned out to be wine and fish, on both of which the Iberian countries were heavily dependent. The negotiations seemed to be nearing a mutually satisfactory conclusion. It was at this point that Mr Papandreou, the left-wing Greek Prime Minister, suddenly treated us to some classical theatre. A charming and agreeable man in private, his whole persona changed when it was a question of getting more money for Greece. He now intervened, effectively vetoing enlargement unless he received an undertaking that Greece should be given huge sums over the next six years. The occasion for this arose as a result of discussions which had been going on for some time about an 'Integrated Mediterranean Programme' of assistance, from which Greece would be the main beneficiary. It seems that the Greeks' appetite had been further whetted by unauthorized discussion of large sums within the Commission. Mr Papandreou's statement threw the Council into disarray. Everyone resented not just the fact that Greece was holding us to ransom, nor even the particular tactics used, but still more the fact that, though Greece had been accepted into the Community precisely to entrench its restored democracy, the Greeks would not now allow the Community to do exactly the same for the former dictatorships of Spain and Portugal.

As it happened I talked to Sr. Felipe González, the Spanish Prime Minister, when we were both in Moscow for Mr Chernenko's funeral the following March. Sr. González, whom I liked personally however much I disagreed with his socialism, was indignant about the terms being offered Spain for entry into the Community. I had a good deal of sympathy with him. I had earlier stressed to President Mitterrand just how vital it was to get Spain and Portugal in quickly and not let short-term selfish considerations stand in the way of what must be done to strengthen democracy in Europe. But I now cautioned Sr. González against holding out for better terms, which I doubted he would get. I said it was better to argue the case from within. For whatever reason, he accepted the advice and at the otherwise fairly uneventful Brussels Council the following month, chaired by Italy, negotiations for the entry of Spain and Portugal were effectively completed. There would be a special bonus to Britain in having Spain in because she would over time have to dismantle discriminatory tariffs against our car imports, which had long been a source of irritation in the motor industry.

But the Greek Danegeld had to be paid. I was alone in Brussels in arguing vigorously against the size of the bill we were presented for the 'Integrated Mediterranean Programmes'. The Germans seemed strangely reluctant to defend their own financial interests and refused our attempts made at ministerial and official level to set up a working partnership with them. Even France and Italy turned out to be net contributors. Greece could expect a bonanza.

At Brussels I also launched an initiative on deregulation designed to provide impetus to the Community's development as a free trade and free enterprise area. It was intended to fit in with our own economic policy: I have never understood why some Conservatives seem to accept that free markets are right for Britain but are prepared to accept *dirigisme* when it comes wrapped in the European flag. In my statement to the Council, I employed a little ridicule to make my point about the way in which directives spewed forth from Brussels. I noted that the Treaty of Rome was a charter for economic liberty and we must not allow ourselves to change it into a charter for thousands of minor regulations. We should seek to cut the bureaucracy on business and see that labour markets worked properly so as to create jobs. Some Community legislation had been amended up to forty times:

we should think what this meant for the small trader. I pointed to a large pile of directives in front of me on VAT and company law. There had been fifty-nine new regulations in 1984. Of these my three favourites were: a draft directive on sludge in agriculture; a draft directive on trade in mincemeat; and a draft directive amending the main regulation on the common organization of the market in goat meat.

I received a good deal of support for the initiative; but of course it was for the Commission – the source of the problem – to follow it through. It would take more than this modestly useful gesture to change the way the Commission worked: and soon we would entrust still further powers to it.

It was at Brussels that the new Commission was approved with M. Delors as its President. At the time, all that I knew was that M. Delors was extremely intelligent and energetic and had, as French Finance minister, been credited with reining back the initial left-wing socialist policies of President Mitterrand's Government and with putting French finances on a sounder footing. The French socialist is an extremely formidable animal. He is likely to be highly educated, entirely self-assured, a *dirigiste* by conviction from a political culture which is *dirigiste* by tradition. Such was M. Delors.

I nominated Lord Cockfield as the new British European Commissioner. I was no longer able to find a place for him in the Cabinet and I thought that he would be effective in Brussels. He was. I always paid tribute to the contribution he made to the Single Market programme. Arthur Cockfield was a natural technocrat of great ability and problem-solving outlook. Unfortunately, he tended to disregard the larger questions of politics – constitutional sovereignty, national sentiment and the promptings of liberty. He was the prisoner as well as the master of his subject. It was all too easy for him, therefore, to go native and to move from deregulating the market to reregulating it under the rubric of harmonization. Alas, it was not long before my old friend and I were at odds.

In retrospect, the Dublin and Brussels summits had been an interlude – even if a lively one – between the two great issues which dominated Community politics in these years – the budget and the Single Market. The Single Market – which Britain pioneered – was intended to give real substance to the Treaty of Rome and to revive its liberal, free trade, deregulatory purpose. I realized how important it was to lay the groundwork in advance for this new stage in the Community's development.

The pressure from most other Community countries, from the European Commission, from the European Assembly and from influential figures in the media for closer European co-operation and integration was so strong as to be almost irresistible. But what kind of integration? My aim had to be to ensure that we were not driven helter-skelter towards European federalism. The thrust of the Community should be towards achieving the genuine Common Market envisaged in the original treaty, a force for free trade not protectionism. To do this I would have to seek alliances with other governments, accept compromises and use language which I did not find attractive. I had to assert persuasively Britain's European credentials while being prepared to stand out against the majority on issues of real significance to Britain. Such an approach was never going to be easy.

THE MILAN EUROPEAN COUNCIL

I hoped that a significant first step would be the paper which Geoffrey Howe and I worked up for the Milan Council, hosted and chaired by Italy, on Friday 28 and Saturday 29 June. The language and direction of this paper were ostentatiously *communautaire*. It covered four areas: the completion of the Common Market, strengthened political co-operation, improvements in decision-making and better exploitation of high technology. The most significant element was that dealing with 'political co-operation', which in normal English means foreign policy. The aim was closer co-operation between Community member states, which would nonetheless reserve the right of states to go their own way.

At that time there seemed a number of good reasons for this approach. The Falklands War had demonstrated to me how valuable it would be if all Community members were prepared to commit themselves to supporting a single member in difficulties. President Mitterrand had been a staunch ally: but some of the other members of the Community had wavered and the instincts of one or two were downright hostile. Even more important perhaps was the need for western solidarity in dealing with the eastern bloc. Foreign policy co-operation within the European Community would help strengthen the West, as long as good relations with the United States remained paramount. What I did not want to do, however, was to have a new treaty grafted on to the Treaty of Rome. I believed that we could achieve both closer political co-operation – as well as make progress towards a Single Market – without such a treaty; and all my instincts warned me of what federalist fantasies might appear if we opened this Pandora's box.

I was keen to secure agreement for our approach well before the Milan Council. So when Chancellor Kohl came to see me for an afternoon's talks at Chequers on Saturday 18 May I showed him the paper on political co-operation and said that we were thinking of tabling it for Milan. I said that what I wanted was something quite separate from the Treaty of Rome, basing co-operation on an inter-governmental agreement. Chancellor Kohl seemed pleased with our approach and in due course I also sent a copy to France. Imagine my surprise, then, when just before I was to go to Milan I learnt that Germany and France had tabled their own paper, almost identical to ours. Such were the consequences of prior consultation.

The ill-feeling this created was, in its way, an extraordinary achievement, given the fact that nearly all of us had come there with a view to proceeding in roughly the same direction. Matters were not helped by the chairmanship of the Italian Prime Minister, Bettino Craxi. Sig. Craxi, a socialist, and his Foreign minister, the Christian Democrat Sig. Andreotti, were political rivals but they shared a joint determination to call an Inter-Governmental Conference (IGC). Such a conference, which could be called by a simple majority vote, would be necessary if there were to be changes in the Treaty of Rome, which themselves, however, would have to be agreed by unanimity. An IGC seemed to me unnecessary (as I said) and dangerous (as I thought). Quite what the French and Germans wanted was unclear – beyond their desire for a separate treaty on political co-operation. They certainly wanted more moves towards European 'integration' in general and it had to be likely that they would want an IGC if one were attainable as – for reasons I shall explain shortly – it was. It is also possible that some kind of secret agreement had been reached on this before the Council began. Certainly when I had a bilateral meeting with Sig. Craxi early on Friday morning he could not have been more sweetly reasonable; an IGC was indeed mentioned as a possibility, but I made it very clear that I thought that the relevant decisions could largely be taken at the present Council without the postponement inevitable if a full IGC were to be called. I came away thinking how easy it had been to get my points across.

It is worth recalling just how the pressure for an IGC had built up in the first place. A year earlier, in one of those gestures which seem to be of minor significance at the time but adopt a far greater one in the light of events, we had agreed (at Fontainebleau) to set up an *ad hoc* committee under the chairmanship of the Irish Senator James Dooge to suggest improvements in European co-operation. Some of the committee's proposals were sensible, such as its stress on more effective political co-operation and a Single Market; some were objectionable like the 'achievement of a European social area', which prefigured the approach of the later Social Charter; and some were plainly dotty, such as the promotion of 'common cultural values'. But above all the Dooge Committee proposed an IGC to ratify all its proposed treaty amendments with a view to the creation of a 'European Union'. So such a proposal was inevitably on the table at Milan. And once this happened the proposed IGC seemed the perfect vehicle for almost everyone else's particular ideas about European development. This made it difficult to resist.

It was, in fact, Sig. Craxi himself as President who suggested at the Council that we should have an IGC. Battle lines were quickly drawn. I argued that the Community had demonstrated that it did have the capacity to take decisions under the present arrangements and that we should now at the Milan Council agree upon the measures needed to make progress on the completion of the Common Market internally and political co-operation externally. There would, I granted, be a need for improved methods of decision-taking if these ends were to be met. I proposed that we agree now to greater use of the existing majority voting articles of the Rome Treaty, while requiring any member state which asked for a vote to be deferred to justify its decision publicly. I called for a reduction in the size of the Commission to twelve members. I also circulated a paper suggesting some modest ways in which the European Assembly might be made more effective. I suggested that the Luxemburg European Council, due to meet in December, should as necessary constitute itself as an IGC. There agreements could be signed and conclusions endorsed. But I did not see any case for a special IGC working away at treaty changes in the meantime.

But it was to no avail. Having come to Milan in order to argue for closer co-operation I found myself being bulldozed by a majority which included a highly partisan chairman. I was not alone: Greece and Denmark joined me in opposing an IGC. Geoffrey Howe would have agreed to it. His willingness to compromise reflected partly his temperament, partly the Foreign Office's *déformation professionnelle*. But it may also have reflected the fact that Britain's membership of the European Community gave the Foreign Office a voice in every aspect of policy that came under the Community. And the more the Community moved in a centralized direction the more influential the

Foreign Office became in Whitehall. Inevitably, perhaps, Geoffrey had a slightly more accommodating view of federalism than I did.

In any case, to my astonishment and anger Sig. Craxi suddenly now called a vote and by a majority the Council resolved to establish an IGC. My time – not just at the Council but all of those days of work which preceded it – had been wasted. I would have to return to the House of Commons and explain why all of the high hopes which had been held of Milan had been dashed. And I had not even had an opportunity while there to go to the opera.

SINGLE MARKET-MINDEDNESS

Annoyed as I was with what had happened, I realized that we must make the best of it. I made it clear that we would take part in the IGC: I saw no merit in the alternative policy – practised for a time in earlier years by France – of the so-called 'empty chair'. There has to be a major matter of principle at stake to justify any nation's refusing to take part in Community discussions. That was not the case here: we agreed with the aims of enhanced political co-operation and the Single Market; we disagreed only with the means (i.e., the IGC) to effect them. In general, too, I believed that it was better to argue our case at the earlier stage, either in the Council or in the IGC, rather than in the last ditch, when the proposal had become an amendment to the Treaty of Rome. My calculations here, however, depended upon fair dealing and good faith in discussions between heads of government and with the Commission. As time went on, I had reason to question both.

There now followed an apparently endless stream of meetings and texts in preparation for the European Council which would meet at Luxemburg in December. The reports of some of these discussions, which I read, illustrated how widely differing were the objectives of different participants. M. Delors urged fulfilment of what he had described as the 'two great dreams' for Europe – an area without frontiers and monetary union. Every exemption or derogation which other countries, like Britain, sought seemed to be regarded as a kind of betrayal. I was told that at one time or another he had denounced almost every member state except Italy, Belgium and the Netherlands.

The second prize for overambition had to go to the Italians. Sig. Craxi and Sig. Andreotti had come to regard the expansion of the powers of the European Assembly as the touchstone of their federalist principles. They wanted to give the assembly a power of 'co-decision' with the Council, something which would have effectively paralysed the Community by subjecting heads of government to perpetual interference by this inchoate, inexperienced and frequently irresponsible body.

The smallest European countries were really aiming at the fastest and – for them – cheapest route to European economic and political union and so were likely to go along with any moves in that direction which did not alienate the Germans and the French. It was all summed up in a letter to me from M. Jacques Santer, the Prime Minister of tiny Luxemburg, which would host the Council. He urged that we should 'recall our great objective of monetary and economic union', and added: 'a resolutely ambitious attitude will without doubt allow us to achieve stimulating results and provide a starting point for the economic and psychological changes which are essential as Europe assumes its new role.' We in the British delegation were inclined to dismiss such rhetoric as cloudy and unrealistic aspirations which had no prospect of being implemented. We were correct in believing them to be lacking in realism; where we were mistaken was in underestimating the determination of some European politicians to put them into effect.

More important to British calculations at the time was what the French and Germans wanted out of it all. By now, the Franco-German axis was again as strong as it had been under President Giscard and Chancellor Schmidt. President Mitterrand and Chancellor Kohl, in contrast to their predecessors, had little in common personally. Chancellor Kohl has the sure touch of a German provincial politician, which has always stood him well politically. Only recently – since German reunification in fact – has he struck out with a distinctive German foreign policy. For most of the 1980s, he seemed willing to subordinate German interests to French guidance, since this reassured Germany's neighbours. Furthermore as a Christian Democrat, he is more of the social than of the economic Right and so sees the world from a perspective far closer to that of the Socialist President of France than would any British Conservative. President Mitterrand is cultivated and cosmopolitan, but somewhat aloof in French domestic politics. Like so many Frenchmen of his generation, he is driven by a fear of the consequences of German domination. But, whatever he said to me in private, his public line and his actions would for this very reason always be directed towards keeping the Germans bound into the European Community, where the French might be able to exercise greater influence over them. Consequently, I knew that the French attitude at the forthcoming Council would be to press hard for closer 'European Union', since this is the phrase which allows both nations to pursue their own national interests with respectability. These trends were, as I shall describe, to become still more important as time went by.

I had one overriding positive goal. This was to create a single Common Market. The Community's internal tariffs on goods had been abolished by July 1968. At the same time it had become a customs union, which Britain had fully accepted in July 1977. What remained were the so-called 'non-tariff' barriers. These came in a great variety of more or less subtle forms. Different national standards on matters ranging from safety to health, regulations discriminating against foreign products, public procurement policies, delays and overelaborate procedures at customs posts – all these and many others served to frustrate the existence of a real Common Market. British businesses would be among those most likely to benefit from an opening-up of other countries' markets. For example, we were more or less effectively excluded from the important German insurance and financial services markets where I knew – as I suspect did the Germans – that our people would excel. Transport was another important area where we were stopped from making the inroads we wanted. The price which we would have to pay to achieve a Single Market with all its economic benefits, though, was more majority voting in the Community. There was no escape from that, because otherwise particular countries would succumb to domestic pressures and prevent the opening-up of their markets. It also required more power for the European Commission: but that power must be used in order to create and maintain a Single Market, rather than to advance other objectives.

I knew that I would have to fight a strong rear-guard action against attempts to weaken Britain's own control over areas of vital national interest to us. I was not going to have majority voting applying, for example, to taxation which the Commission would have liked us to 'harmonize'. Competition between tax regimes is far more healthy than the imposition of a single system. It forces governments to hold down government spending and taxation, and to limit the burden of regulations; and when they fail to do these things, it allows companies and taxpayers to move elsewhere. In any event, the ability to set one's own levels of taxation is a crucial element of national sovereignty. I was not prepared to give up our powers to control immigration (from non-EC countries), to combat terrorism, crime, and drug trafficking and to take measures on human, animal and plant health, keeping out carriers of dangerous diseases – all of which required proper frontier controls. There was, I felt, a perfectly practical argument for this: as an island – and one quite unused to the more authoritarian continental systems of identity cards and policing – it was natural that we should apply the necessary controls at our ports and airports rather than internally. Again, this was an essential matter of national sovereignty, for which a government must answer to its own Parliament and people. I was prepared to go along with some modest increase in the powers of the European Assembly, which would shortly and somewhat inaccurately be described as a Parliament: but the Council of Ministers, representing governments answerable to national Parliaments, must always have the final say. Finally, I was going to resist any attempt to make treaty changes which would allow the Commission – and by majority vote the Council – to pile extra burdens on British businesses.

Right up to the beginning of the Luxemburg Council I thought that we could rely on the Germans to support us in opposing any mention of the EMS and economic and monetary union in the revisions of the treaty. Then, as now, however, there was an inherent tension between, on the one hand, the German desire to retain control over their own monetary policy to keep down inflation and, on the other, to demonstrate their European credentials by pressing further towards economic and monetary union.

I had discussed this with the Chancellor of the Exchequer and he and I were at one. A few days before the Council began Nigel Lawson set out his views with admirable clarity in a note urging me to stand firm. He recalled that Chancellor Kohl had told me the previous day that the Germans, like us, were totally opposed to any amendment to the monetary provisions of the Treaty of Rome. But he added that if the position deteriorated I would have to have some possible form of words up my sleeve. Nigel stressed that it would be essential that the language used should contain no obligation on us to join the ERM, make it clear that exchange rate policy is the responsibility of national authorities, minimize any extension of Community competence and avoid any treaty reference to EMU. He concluded that having reviewed the options he was bound to say that the better course by far looked to be not to get caught up in this whole exercise. I agreed.

THE LUXEMBURG EUROPEAN COUNCIL

I arrived in Luxemburg at 10 o'clock on Monday morning, 2 December 1985. The first session of the Council began soon afterwards. The heads of government went through the draft treaty – what would become the Single European Act – which the presidency and the Commission had drawn up. At first the discussion dragged on, with several hours being spent on a single clause. The ability of those present to argue at great length and with much repetition about matters of little interest was, as ever, astonishing. It would have been far better to have agreed on the principles and then let others deal with the details, referring back to us. But of course it would have been better if, as I had wanted originally, there had been no IGC, no new treaty and just some limited practical agreements.

I was also dismayed that the Germans shifted their ground and said that they were now prepared to include monetary matters in the treaty. I was, however, able in a side discussion with Chancellor Kohl to reduce the formula to what I considered insignificant proportions which merely described the *status quo*, rather than set out new goals. This added to the phrase 'Economic and Monetary Union' the important gloss 'co-operation in economic and monetary policy'. The former had been the official objective, unfortunately, since October 1972: the latter, I hoped, would signal the limits the act placed on it. But this formulation delayed M. Delors's drive to monetary union only briefly.

Perhaps even those heads of government with the most insatiable thirst for Euro-jargon had become a little bored after the first day. Certainly, Tuesday's discussions, though long and intense, were far more productive. It was midnight when I gave my press conference on the conclusions of the Council. I was pleased with what had been achieved. We were on course for the Single Market by 1992. I had had to make relatively few compromises as regards wording; I had surrendered no important British interest; I had had to place a reservation on just one aspect of social policy in the treaty.* Italy, which had insisted on the IGC in the first place, had not only applied the most reservations on it but also demanded that it must be agreed by the European Assembly.

Perhaps I derived most satisfaction from the inclusion in the official record of the conference of a 'general statement' recording that:

> Nothing in these provisions shall affect the right of member states to take such measures as they consider necessary for the purpose of controlling immigration from third countries, and to combat terrorism, crime, the traffic in drugs and illicit trading in works of art and antiques.

* Britain and Ireland – as island countries – were permitted to retain or take new measures on grounds of health, safety, environment and consumer protection.

I had insisted on the insertion of this statement. I said that otherwise terrorists, drug dealers and criminals would exploit the provisions of the act to their own advantage and to the danger of the public. Without it I would not have agreed the Single European Act. In fact, neither the Commission, nor the Council nor the European Court would in the long run be prepared to uphold what had been agreed in this statement any more than they would honour the limits on majority voting set out in the treaty itself. But this is to anticipate.

The first fruits of what would be called the Single European Act were good for Britain. At last, I felt, we were going to get the Community back on course, concentrating on its role as a huge market, with all the opportunities that would bring to our industries. Advantages will indeed flow from that achievement well into the future, even though harmonization and standardization regularly threaten to become ends in themselves. The trouble was – and I must give full credit to those Tories who warned of this at the time – that the new powers the Commission received only seemed to whet its appetite.

Even at the time different people had very different ideas of the significance of what had been agreed at Luxemburg. M. Delors described it as a 'compromise of progress', regretted that his proposal for extra power for the European Assembly did not find favour, but welcomed what had been said about monetary matters since he regarded the ecu as 'part of the European dream'. The Dutch, natural federalists, were also disappointed. But some of them lived in hope. A comment in one of the Dutch papers said that 'the ideal of European unity would have to wait until there was a new incumbent in No. 10.' The Germans, rightly, saw that the momentum towards their objective of European Union had been resumed. Welcoming the outcome, Chancellor Kohl told the Bundestag that the Council had 'taken the political and institutional development of the Community a decisive step forward'.

At the time I had a different view. Answering questions in the House of Commons on the outcome of Luxemburg I said at one point:

> I am constantly saying that I wish that they would talk less about European and political union. The terms are not understood in this country. In so far as they are understood over there, they mean a good deal less than some people over here think they mean.

Looking back, I was wrong to think that. But I still believe it was right to sign the Single European Act, because we wanted a Single European Market.

European affairs took second place for me during the rest of this Parliament, with just a few exceptions. The main decisions had been made and even the Commission's search for new 'initiatives' had been slowed for the moment by the need to work out and implement the Single Market programme. The Community was overspending its resources, but had not yet reached the new limits of VAT revenue which had been set. Enlargement had to be carried out. There was plenty to be getting on with.

THE LONDON EUROPEAN COUNCIL

Britain took up the presidency and the European Council met in London on Friday 5 and Saturday 6 December 1986. We were to meet in the Queen Elizabeth II Conference Centre. The great expense and unpleasing design of this building can only be justified by the unsightliness of the original gaping hole – an overflow car park – which it filled. I took a close interest in the physical as well as the diplomatic preparations for our big summits. For example, I had earlier had the swivel chairs around the big conference table at the 'QE II' replaced by light wooden ones: I always thought there was something to be said for looking at your opposite number in the eye without his being able to swivel sideways to escape. On this occasion I took care to have the battleship-grey walls covered up with beige hangings and pictures, deliberately having some drawings by Henry Moore, borrowed from the Moore Foundation, placed opposite President Mitterrand, who I knew loved Moore as much as I did.

Undoubtedly, the main achievement of the British presidency was adoption of or agreement to a record number of measures to implement the Single Market. This was the sort of solid progess the Community needed, rather than flashy publicity-seeking initiatives which came to nothing or just caused bad feeling.

But the London Council itself could only be a modest success. On the way into dinner Chancellor Kohl had made it clear to my private secretary, Charles Powell, that there was no question of Germany being able to take major decisions on agriculture – the most vexed question at this time – before their forthcoming elections. If nothing dramatic could be accomplished on agriculture or the budget, however, the Council was notable for the emergence of M. Delors as a new kind of European Commission President – a major player in the game. I had a brief foretaste of this at the first evening's dinner, when, to my surprise and unconcealed irritation, he used the discussion period before dinner to launch into a long speech about the parlous financial state in which the Community found itself as a result of the CAP and to put forward a range of quite detailed suggestions. I replied that we should have all been told this before: it was plain from what he said that the Community was broke. I agreed that M. Delors should visit European capitals, as he proposed, to try to find a solution. But this sort of thing ought not to be repeated. I reflected to myself that no one could have imagined a top British civil servant springing surprises on ministers in this way: it illustrated all too well what was wrong with the Commission – that it was composed of a new breed of unaccountable politicians.

As President of the Community I had to give a press conference reporting on the outcome, at which I was accompanied by M. Delors. This time – again to my surprise – he refused to say anything, even when I asked him to comment on one of my answers. I continued to urge him, but to no avail. 'I had no idea you were the strong silent type,' I remarked.

M. Delors soon broke his silence. Three days later I gave a speech reporting on the presidency to the European Assembly in Strasbourg on Tuesday 9 December. It could not have been more *communautaire*. But when I sat down, M. Delors – a quite new M. Delors whom I had never seen or heard before – began to speak. It was Euro-demagogy, designed to play to the prejudices of his audience, to belittle the British presidency and to ask for more money. I was not having this. When he finished I stood up and demanded a right of reply – something quite unknown, apparently, in this 'Parliament'. Speaking off the cuff, I answered the points which had been raised, as I would in a wind-up speech in the House of Commons. And I did not fail to observe how he had said none of this when he had had the chance at the press conference we had held together. He came in late to the lunch afterwards and took his place beside me. I told him then that time after time I had stood up for his position in the House of Commons, refusing to rule out extra money, even though under the most intense pressure. Of one thing he could be sure, I said: that would never happen again.

In the two years of European politicking that led up to the Single European Act, I had witnessed a profound shift in how European policy was conducted – and therefore in the kind of Europe that was taking shape. A Franco-German bloc with its own agenda had re-emerged to set the direction of the Community. The European Commission, which had always had a yen for centralized power, was now led by a tough, talented European federalist, whose philosophy justified centralism. And the Foreign Office was almost imperceptibly moving to compromise with these new European friends. We could, of course, look to the veto, to legal safeguards, and to declared exemptions. In the future, however, these would increasingly be circumvented where they were not overthrown entirely.

CHAPTER XIX

Hat Trick

The preparations for and course of the 1987 general election campaign

All election victories look inevitable in retrospect; none in prospect. The wounds which Westland, BL and reaction to the US raid on Libya inflicted on the Government and the Conservative Party would take some time to heal. Economic recovery would in time provide an effective salve, as it became clear that our policies were delivering growth with low inflation, higher living standards and – from the summer of 1986 – steadily falling unemployment. But in the meantime, Labour had developed a thirst for power, moderated their image and gained a lead in the opinion polls. It was important that I should unify the Party around my authority and vision of Conservatism. This would not be easy.

STYLE AND TONE

Perhaps the most damaging accusation made against me during the Westland affair was that I did not listen. Like most allegations which stick, this contained a grain of truth. Once I begin to follow a train of thought I am not easily stopped. This has its advantages. It means that I can concentrate on a tricky point almost no matter what is going on in the background, a useful ability, for example, at Prime Minister's Question Time. But it does, of course, also mean that I am inclined to talk over people and ignore timid or inarticulate objections and arguments. People who do not know me and how I work conclude that I have not taken in what has been said to me. Those who know me better will confirm, however, that this is generally not the case. I will often go away afterwards to revise my views in the light of what

I have heard. Indeed, I have even been accused by some supporters of taking too much notice of those who do not agree with me.

The suggestion that I do not listen, particularly when it comes from ex-ministers, can, however, simply mean that I do not agree with their views. You might say I 'chair from the front'. I like to say what I think quite early on and then see whether arguments are adduced which show me to be wrong, in which case I have no difficulty in changing my line. This is, of course, not the traditional formal way of chairing meetings. My experience is that a group of men sitting round a table like little better than their own voices and that nothing is more distasteful than the possibility that a conclusion can be reached without all of them having the chance to read from their briefs. My style of chairmanship certainly nonplussed some colleagues, who knew their brief a good deal less well than I did. But I adopt this technique because I believe in argument as the best way of getting to the truth – not because I want to suppress argument. In fact, I would go further: nothing is more important to successful democratic government than the willingness to argue frankly and forcefully – unless, perhaps, it is the willingness to recognize collective responsibility when the decision is made.

So I set in train a series of steps to make plain that the Government encompassed – and was receptive to – a wide range of views. My first concern was to deal with the impression – that was apparently very widespread – that the Government was unaware of people's worries. I could do this without diluting the Thatcherite philosophy because, whatever commentators imagined, the hopes and aspirations of the great majority were in tune with my beliefs. It was because I did listen to people that I knew this. But I never confused the leader page of the *Guardian* with *vox populi*.

I used my speech to the Scottish Party Conference in Perth on Friday 16 May (1986) to stress that we were indeed listening to what people were concerned about. And in some cases we had already acted to put matters right. The Scots had been up in arms because of the effects of the domestic rate revaluation, which had sent some people's rates bills soaring while others had apparently inexplicably dropped. So I reminded the 1986 Scottish Conference:

> A year ago, when I came to this same conference, you made clear your deep worries about rates. We listened. We understood. We're dealing with it. And because of the urgency, domestic rates will be abolished in Scotland ahead of England and Wales.

I went on to promise the same radical but sensitive approach to people's concerns in education, where there was much discontent, and health where there was still more. I acknowledged:

> There are genuine concerns. How long will your elderly relative have to wait for the hip operation which will relieve so much pain? Will the expectant mother be cared for by the same medical team throughout her pregnancy? . . . I know your worries, and we are determined to deal with them . . .

What was important in this speech, and was remarked upon, was the tone. Of course, it is never enough just to listen: you have to come up with answers. But this was a time to demonstrate sensitivity and the speech went down well.

RESHUFFLE

A second step towards getting the Government and Party off to a new start was provided by the reshuffle a little later that month. Keith Joseph had decided that he now wished to leave the Cabinet. The departure of my oldest political friend and ally, indeed mentor, saddened me. He was irreplaceable; somehow, politics would never be the same again. But Keith's departure gave rise to important changes. What I needed was ministers who could fight battles in the media as well as in Whitehall.

Any analysis of the opinion polls revealed that where we were strong was on economic management; where we were weak was on the so-called 'caring issues'. There is nothing new about this. No matter how unjust – and I personally resented the injustice because I have always found no one more willing to give time and money without reward than the typical Conservative – this is what was to be expected. In Health I felt that the best answer was to set out the record: but there was no evidence that it made much impact; indeed, it was widely disbelieved. In Education, however, the Conservatives were trusted because although people thought we would spend less than Labour on schools they rightly understood that we were interested in standards – academic and nonacademic – parental choice and value for money; and they knew that Labour's 'loony Left' had a hidden agenda of social engineering and sexual liberation. Ken Baker had won hands-down the propaganda battle against the Left in the local authorities and he and

William Waldegrave, stimulated by the advice of Lord Rothschild, had set out what I had long been looking for – an alternative to the rates. But I felt that a first-class communicator like Ken Baker was now needed at Education.

John Moore, who had done an excellent job pressing ahead the privatization programme from the Treasury and was highly regarded by Nigel Lawson, now entered the Cabinet as Transport Secretary. I had high hopes of John. He was of my way of thinking. He was conscientious, charming, soft spoken and in some ways he had the strengths of Cecil Parkinson – that is, he was right-wing but not hard or aggressive. He came across very well on television, where in the subsequent election campaign he managed to be tough and sweetly reasonable at the same time. I had no doubt that John Moore would be an asset to the Government and a loyal supporter to me.

I moved Nick Ridley to the sprawling Department of the Environment. Nick could not match Ken or John in presentation. But we still needed to come up with some radical policies for our manifesto and the third term. No one, I knew, was better suited to find the right answers to the complicated issues which faced us in Nick's new field of responsibility. Housing was certainly one area which required the application of a penetrating intellect. The sale of council houses had led to a real revolution in ownership. But the vast, soulless high rise council estates remained ghettoes of deprivation, poor education and unemployment. The private rented sector too, in spite of some liberalization through the shorthold, had continued to shrink, holding back labour mobility. Housing benefit and housing finance generally was a jungle, always threatening to swallow up the best laid schemes. The community charge had to be thought through in detail and implemented in England and Wales.* And further ahead lay the vexed question of pollution of the environment.

Nick flourished at Environment. He was never popular with the general public who saw what appeared to be a chain-smoking, dishevelled, languid aristocrat; by contrast, he was the object of universal respect and great affection from those who worked with him, above all his officials. Nick had those virtues which seem only to be cultivated in private: he was completely unaffected; he treated people and arguments on their merits; he was incapable of guile; and he was always seeking to take on the unrewarding and unpopular tasks.

On the evening of Thursday 24 July I spoke to the '22 Committee to give the traditional 'end of term' address. This was always an

* See Chapter 22.

important occasion, but particularly so on this occasion. My task was to ensure that the Parliamentary Party left in the past all the agonized debates about Westland, BL and Libya and came back in the autumn determined to demonstrate the unity and self-confidence required to fight and win the arguments – and then a general election. There is no point in telling back-bench politicians, who are in regular touch with their constituents, that things are good when they are not. All that achieves is to undermine confidence in you. So in an unvarnished speech I told them that they had had to take a lot of difficulties on the chin in the last year, but those difficulties had nothing to do with our fundamental approach, which was correct. They had resulted from throwing away the precious virtue of unity and also because, as over Libya, we had had to do genuinely difficult things which were right. I was glad to get warm and noisy applause for this, not simply because I prefer applause to execration, but because such a warm response to such a strong speech meant that the Party was recovering its nerve.

The summer of 1986 was important too in another regard. At Conservative Central Office Norman Tebbit, the Chairman of the Party, had been having a very hard time. As Norman used to say, he was the 'lightning conductor' for me. A good deal of criticism of Norman found its way into the press and at one point he believed that it was coming from me or my staff. Norman arrived one day at Downing Street armed with a sheaf of critical press cuttings, asking where these rumours came from. I was surprised to read these cuttings – my press summary did not convey the flavour of these vicious attacks – but I reassured Norman that they certainly did not come from me, or my staff, nor – I emphasized strongly – did they reflect my views. These tensions build up when people do not see one another frequently enough to give vent to tensions and clear up misunderstandings: and the civil service machine never likes to give enough time in diaries to party political matters. Relations improved, I am glad to say, when Stephen Sherbourne, my political secretary who understood politics as well as any Cabinet minister and whose shrewdness never failed me, ensured that Norman and I had regular weekly meetings.

THE STRATEGY GROUP AND POLICY GROUPS

My third step was to involve senior Cabinet ministers in the strategy for the next election. In June Willie Whitelaw and John Wakeham, the Chief Whip, sent me a memorandum urging me to set up the group of ministers which was to be officially known as the Strategy Group and, no doubt to the great pleasure of its male members, was soon known by the press as the 'A-Team'. Its purpose would be to plan for the next election, discussing policy, presentation and tactics. I agreed that, apart from Willie and John, the group should consist of Geoffrey Howe, Nigel Lawson, Douglas Hurd and Norman Tebbit. I vetoed the suggested inclusion of Peter Walker, and although I would have liked to have Nick Ridley as a permanent member of the group, I decided that it should be confined to the Deputy Prime Minister, the three great offices of state, the Chairman of the Party and the Chief Whip. Plainly, these had to be members. To have included other ministers would have provoked the usual political jealousies and back biting. Other colleagues, though, were invited when their departmental responsibilities were under discussion. Since it was a political rather than a government group it was serviced by Stephen Sherbourne and Robin Harris, the Director of the Conservative Research Department. As head of my Policy Unit, Brian Griffiths regularly attended too. The group met on Monday mornings.

We began by looking through the programme of main events for the week and the response they required. As we got nearer to the election Norman Tebbit would often give us a brief report on the state of party preparations. But the main item was usually a paper from a Cabinet minister – either a permanent member of the group or another colleague – on his departmental plans for the future. Several ministers who today enjoy a reputation for radicalism had originally arrived at our meetings with proposals that would not, as I would privately put it, pull the skin off a rice pudding – and left with the distinct feeling that much, much more was required of them.

At about the same time as the Strategy Group was established I set up eleven party policy groups. On this occasion I made the chairman of each group the Cabinet minister whose responsibilities covered its area of interest. Apart from the obvious areas – the economy, jobs, foreign affairs and defence, agriculture, the NHS – there were separate groups on the family (under Nicholas Edwards, Welsh Secretary) and young people (under John Moore – the nearest we had in Cabinet to a young person). At least on this occasion, unlike 1983, the groups were set up promptly and for the most part managed to send in their reports on time. The fact that Cabinet ministers chaired groups on their own areas meant, naturally, that even though outside experts and back-benchers were members, the groups' conclusions bore an unremarkable similarity to the suggestions for policy initiatives advanced by departments. As in 1983, however, their real value was to make the Party feel fully involved in what was happening. In this sense they were a counterpart to the Strategy Group which served the same purpose as regards the Cabinet and Government.

In general, the contents of the reports were not particularly exciting. It is, though, worth noting that Nigel Lawson's policy group, bearing the unmistakable imprint of its chairman, advocated early entry into the ERM (possibly even before the election which would have been potentially disastrous), made no reference to the need to control public borrowing and did not even mention his own invention, the MTFS, which I regarded as the anchor for the whole of our economic strategy. This approach never made its way into the manifesto, but somehow it made its way into policy.

THE 1986 CONSERVATIVE PARTY CONFERENCE

None of us had any doubts about the importance of the 1986 Party Conference in Bournemouth. This was likely, though not certain, to be our last Party Conference before the general election. Labour's Conference the week before had been marked by highly professional presentation which, though it deliberately subordinated substance to public relations, was undoubtedly effective. Their device of substituting a red rose for the red flag as their Party's symbol, impudent as it was, marked a shrewd understanding that whatever else the electorate might vote for, it would not be socialism. Still, their overconfidence persuaded the Labour leadership to offer a number of hostages to fortune – notably a neutralist and anti-American defence policy that was to leave them immensely vulnerable to our attacks in the election campaign.

A temptation which Norman Tebbit and I found easy to resist was that of trying to copy Labour tactics. One of the first rules of campaigning is to play to your own strengths: only if these are insufficient should you think about aping other people's. This meant that we must stress our record of achievement, not just by reeling off figures but by portraying it as the basis for further progress – or, as the slogan Norman picked for the conference had it, for 'Our Next Move Forward'. When Norman told me what he intended I was impressed. In the late summer and early autumn he had pressed ministers to come up with crisp statements of what had been achieved and targets which should be met, preferably within a given time-span. All of this material was cleared with the Treasury to see that there were no hidden public expenditure implications. By the time that we arrived at Bournemouth the material was ready and each day of the conference was marked by practical policy announcements which the media could not help but compare favourably with the glitzy Labour Conference which preceded ours. Happily, the Bournemouth Conference coincided with increasing evidence of prosperity, not least the fall in unemployment. As a result it gave us a lift of morale and in the polls which, in retrospect, set us on course for winning the next election.

I took even more trouble with my speech at Bournemouth than on other occasions. The very success of the speeches which the conference had already heard made this a more difficult occasion. I had to sum up but not to repeat: above all, I had to provide a theme which would fire our people over the next few months.

Throughout the year I had collected in a file called 'ideas for speeches' articles, speeches and different briefing and policy items which came across my desk. Stephen Sherbourne and the Research Department always provided me with a collection of the most stimulating articles of the week. Stephen also put in for me copies of speeches by those whose ideas he knew I particularly valued, such as Nick Ridley, David Young and Nigel Lawson.

During the summer recess I would have a meeting to discuss the general themes I should put across in my conference speech. Speech contributions were commissioned from ministers, advisers, friendly journalists, and academics. On this occasion we began speech writing with no fewer than twelve separate contributions and two and a half hefty files of background material. The weekend before the conference different draft speech sections would be laid out and put together – literally – along the table in the Great Parlour at Chequers. Linking passages would be written and then the still disjointed and often repetitive first draft would be typed up. Everyone breathed a sigh of relief when they knew that we at least had a speech of some sort; even though past experience suggested that this might bear little relationship to the final text. Then would come the long hours of refining and polishing until midnight (if we were lucky).

On the Friday morning I used to mark up the text with my own special code, noting pauses, stress and where to have my voice rise or fall. (I would familiarize myself with the speech using this text and always have it with me, even though when I spoke it would be from the Autocue tape.)

My task in this year's speech was to provide a trailer to the arguments on which we would fight the election and to give a thematic unity to the various reforms of the 'Next Move Forward'. What would prove to be the single most important element in our victory – namely the rising prosperity achieved by our economic policies – was more a back-drop than a theme in the conference and my speech. Our second campaign theme was foreshadowed in my fierce attack on the Labour Party's defence policy.

The Labour Conference had voted for a non-nuclear defence policy, including the closure of American nuclear bases in the UK. Mr Kinnock had also made it clear that there were no circumstances in which he would ask the United States to use nuclear weapons in the defence of Britain. This, of course, went further than Labour had ever done before, because it meant that from the first day on which a Labour government took power Britain would be regarded by the Soviets as no longer under the American and NATO 'nuclear umbrella'. I said:

> Labour's defence policy – though 'defence' is scarcely the word – is an absolute break with the defence policy of every British Government since the Second World War. Let there be no doubt about the gravity of that decision. You cannot be a loyal member of NATO while disavowing its fundamental strategy. A Labour Britain would be a neutralist Britain. It would be the greatest gain for the Soviet Union in forty years. And they would have got it without firing a shot.

But my main positive theme which was to be at the centre of our manifesto too was contained in the section of my speech entitled 'power to the people'. This drew attention to the wider home and share ownership attendant on privatization and looked ahead to the manifesto reforms of education and housing designed to give ordinary people more choice in public services. I said:

> The great political reform of the last century was to enable more and more people to have a vote. Now the great Tory reform of

> this century is to enable more and more people to own property. Popular capitalism is nothing less than a crusade to enfranchise the many in the economic life of the nation. We Conservatives are returning power to the people.

When all is said and done, however, a speech is a theatrical as well as a political event. Just before 2.30 p.m. on Friday 10 October I walked onto the platform amid the usual uproar, which increased when people saw that I was wearing a rose on my lapel. I began by saying:

> There is just one thing I would like to make clear. The rose I am wearing is the rose of England.

ELECTION PREPARATIONS AND THE MANIFESTO

When Parliament reassembled the Party was in a quite different frame of mind than it had been just a few months earlier. We had a brief legislative programme on the advice of David Young, so crucial legislation would not be abandoned if we went for an early election the following summer. Our position in the opinion polls had begun to improve. The Strategy Group and the policy groups were meeting regularly. Norman kept me informed of the work which was going on in Central Office to prepare for the election when it came. Already, on 2 July, he had given me a paper setting out his view of possible election dates.

The compilation of documents which constitute the Party's plans for an election campaign is traditionally called the 'War Book'. On 23 December Norman sent me the first draft 'as a Christmas present'. I was not unhappy to see the end of 1986 but I felt a new enthusiasm as I considered the fresh policies and the battle for them which would be required in 1987.

On Thursday 8 January I discussed with Norman and others the papers he had sent me about the election campaign. We met at Alistair McAlpine's house in order to escape detection by the press, which had already started to speculate about election dates. Many details of the campaign had not been worked out as yet, but I found myself largely in agreement with the suggestions. I did, however, have one continuing worry; this was about the advertising. Several months earlier I had asked whether Tim Bell, who had worked with me on previous elections, could do so again now. I understood that he was a consultant to Saatchis. But in fact the rift between them was greater than I had imagined and the suggestion was never taken up. I might have been prepared to insist, but this would have caused more important problems with Norman and Central Office. In any case I continued to see Tim socially. At this stage in January, though, I still hoped that Saatchis would exhibit the political nous and creativity we had had from them in the past.

I regarded the manifesto as my main responsibility. Brian Griffiths and Robin Harris brought together in a single paper the proposals which had come in from ministers and policy groups. We discussed this at Chequers on Sunday 1 February. Nigel Lawson, Norman Tebbit and Nick Ridley – in their different ways the three best brains of the Cabinet – were there. It was as important at this stage to rule out as to rule in different proposals: I like a manifesto which contains a limited number of radical and striking measures, rather than irritating little clutches of minor ones. It was at this meeting that the main shape of the manifesto proposals became clear.

We agreed to include the aim of a 25 per cent basic rate of income tax. We would not include a figure for the reduction of the top rate, though we were thinking about a top rate of 50 per cent. I kept out of the manifesto any commitment to transferable tax allowances between husband and wife which, if they had been implemented along the lines of the earlier green paper, would have been extremely expensive. I commissioned further work on candidates for privatization which I wanted to be spelt out clearly in the manifesto itself. Education would, we all agreed, be one of the crucial areas for new proposals in the manifesto. Largely as a result of work done by Brian Griffiths, I was already clear what these should be. There must be a core curriculum to ensure that the basic subjects were taught to all children. There must be graded tests or benchmarks against which children's knowledge should be judged. All schools should have greater financial autonomy. There must be a new per capita funding system which, along with 'open enrolment',* would mean that successful, popular schools were financially rewarded and enabled to expand. There must be more powers for head teachers. Finally, and most controversially, schools must be given the power to apply for what at this stage we were describing as 'direct grant' status, by which we meant that they could become in effect 'independent state schools' – a phrase that the DES

* See p. 591.

hated and kept trying to remove from my speeches in favour of the bureaucratically flavoured 'Grant-Maintained Schools' – outside the control of Local Education Authorities.

Housing was another area in which radical proposals were being considered: Nick Ridley had already drawn up papers which were yet to be properly discussed. But his main ideas – all of which eventually found their way into the manifesto – were to give groups of tenants the right to form tenants' co-operatives and individual tenants the right to transfer ownership of their house (or flat) to a housing association or other approved institution – in other words to swap landlords. Housing Action Trusts (HATs), modelled on the highly successful Urban Development Corporations, were to be set up to take over bad estates, renovate them and then pass them on to different tenures and ownerships. We would also reform local authority housing accounts to stop housing rents being used to subsidize the rate fund when they should have gone towards repairs and renovation.

We were by now under a good deal of political pressure on the Health Service and discussed at our meeting how to respond. However good the record of the service as a whole, there was plenty of evidence that it was not sufficiently sensitive to patients' wishes, that there was much inefficiency and that some areas and hospitals were performing inexplicably worse than others, treating fewer patients etc. Norman Fowler at the 1986 Party Conference had set out a number of targets, backed up by special allocations of public spending, for increases in the number of particular sorts of operation. This announcement had gone well. I was reluctant to add the Health Service to the list of areas in which we were proposing fundamental reform – not least because not enough work had yet been done on it. The NHS was seen by many as a touchstone for our commitment to the welfare state and there were obvious dangers of coming forward with new proposals out of the blue. The direction of reform which I wanted to see was one towards bringing down waiting lists by ensuring that money moved with the patient, rather than got lost within the bureaucratic maze of the NHS. But that left so many questions still unanswered that I eventually ruled out any substantial new proposals on Health for the manifesto.

After the meeting I wrote to Cabinet ministers asking them to bring forward any proposals which required policy approval for implementation in the next Parliament. Once this had been received, legislation could then be drafted for introduction in the new Parliament. To knock all these submissions into a coherent whole I established a small Manifesto Committee that reported directly to me. Chaired by John

MacGregor, Chief Secretary to the Treasury, its other members were Brian Griffiths, Stephen Sherbourne, Robin Harris and John O'Sullivan, a former Associate Editor of *The Times*, who had joined my Policy Unit as a special adviser and who drafted the manifesto.

The manifesto was designed to solve a serious political problem for us. As a party which had been in government for eight years, we had to dispel any idea that we were stale and running out of ideas. We therefore had to advance a number of clear, specific, new and well-worked-out reforms. At the same time we had to protect ourselves against the jibe: if these ideas are so good, why haven't you introduced them before? We did so by presenting our reforms as the third stage of a rolling Thatcherite programme. In our first term, we revived the economy and reformed trade union law. In our second, we extended wealth and capital ownership more widely than ever before. In our third, we would give ordinary people the kind of choice and quality in public services that the rich already enjoyed. Looking back, once the manifesto was published, we heard no more about the Government running out of steam.

The manifesto was the best ever produced by the Conservative Party. This was not just because it contained far-reaching proposals to reform education, housing, local government finance, trade unions and for more privatization and lower taxes. It was also because the manifesto projected a vision and then arranged the policies in a clear and logical away around it. So, for example, the proposals on education, housing and trade unions (requiring more use of secret ballots and protecting individual unionists' rights not to join a strike) came almost at the very front of the document, highlighting the fact that we were embarked upon a great programme of ambitious social reform to give power to the people. Those we wanted to empower were not just (or even mainly) those who could afford their own homes or private schools for their children or who had large investments, but those who lacked these advantages.

The manifesto went to the heart of my convictions. I believe that Conservative policies must liberate and empower those whom socialism traps, demoralizes and then contemptuously ignores. This, of course, is precisely what socialists most fear; it makes a number of paternalist Tories uneasy too.

I held a meeting at Chequers on Tuesday 21 April with Willie Whitelaw, Norman Tebbit, David Young, Peter Morrison (Norman's Deputy at Central Office) and the draftsmen and advisers to go through the whole text. Then the redrafting and checking began. Brian and John reported back to me. Stephen Sherbourne, with his special kind of tactful ruthlessness, kept all involved to the increasingly tight deadlines which had to be met. The main new development – and a substantial improvement – was suggested by David Young. This was to bring together the record of government achievements, entitled 'Our First Eight Years', in a separate document, to go in a wallet alongside the manifesto. David had great flair and energy, essential for this kind of work, and I left him in charge of overseeing the manifesto's visual presentation and indeed involved him as much as possible in the wider election preparations.

Because a good deal of misleading comment has been made about the background to and course of the 1987 general election campaign it is worth setting some matters straight at the outset. According to some versions of events this was all about a battle between rival Tory advertising agencies; according to other accounts the main participants – particularly myself – behaved in such an unbalanced way that it is difficult to see why we were all not carried off to one of our new NHS hospitals by the men in white coats, let alone re-elected. This was not to be a happy campaign; but it was a successful one and that is what counts. There were disagreements – but good old-fashioned stand-up rows, in which most of us regret what we have said and try to forget about it without bearing grudges, feature in all election campaigns. (As far as I can gather there were no rows in what was generally seen as a smooth running and happy Labour campaign.) As it turned out, the talents and character of all the main participants in the Conservative campaign contributed to the victory, though perhaps the creative tension was more tense than creative on occasion.

Apart from the manifesto and the practical preparations for the campaign, there was one other task which concerned us in the early months of 1987. This was the need to deal with the SDP-Liberal Alliance. The Alliance was by now led by the at first attractive but later increasingly ridiculous duo of the two Davids, Steel and Owen: it sought to represent itself as a credible, radical third force and if it did so might attract what (in the psephological jargon we all found it impossible to avoid) is called 'soft' Tory support. Within the Conservative Party there was a rumbling debate about how to deal with the Alliance. Some Conservatives on the left of the Party, who doubtless had more than a sneaking sympathy with the Alliance criticisms of my policies, were all for treating them lightly – or just ignoring them.

Neither Norman Tebbit nor I saw things like this. The fact was that, for all the posturing, the SDP were retread socialists who had gone along with nationalization and increased trade union power when in office, and had only developed second thoughts about socialism when their ministerial salaries stopped in 1979. The Liberals have always, for their part, been the least scrupulous force in British politics, specializing in dubious tactics – fake opinion polls released on the eve of by-elections to suggest a nonexistent Liberal surge were a well-loved classic. Another tactic, which the SDP quickly borrowed, was to support one policy when talking to one group and a quite different one when talking to another. The analysis which Norman had done at Central Office showed quite clearly that there were splits and inconsistencies which we must exploit – and do so as far as possible before the election campaign itself began, when such matters risked becoming submerged.

So Norman and I agreed that at the Central Council in Torquay on Saturday 21 March 1987 we would both use the occasion to launch an assault on the Alliance. I called the Alliance 'the Labour Party in exile', recalled the SDP leaders' leading role in the last Labour Government and ended with a quotation from an old music hall song:

> I gather at the next election they are hoping to be asked to give us an encore – the two Davids in that ever-popular musical delight: 'Don't tell my mother I'm half of a horse in a panto.'

While the manifesto was being drafted, I was discussing with Norman Tebbit what I hoped would be the final shape of the campaign and my own role in it. At our meeting on Thursday 16 April we went over press conference themes, advertising and party election broadcasts. By now I was in a mood for an early – June – election. We would have served the four years I always felt a government should. I felt in my bones that the popular mood was with us and that Labour's public relations gimmicks were starting to look just a little tired.

As is the way of these things, the most appropriate date eventually wrote itself into our programme – Thursday 11 June. By then we would have seen the results of the local elections which, as in 1983, would be run through the number-crunchers of Central Office to make it into a useful guide for a general election. It would be supplemented by other private polls Norman had commissioned: this was particularly necessary for Scotland and London where there were no local elections that year. Some polling in individual key constituencies would also be done: though such are the problems of sampling in constituency polls that no one would attach too much weight to these. I saw this analysis and heard senior colleagues' views at Chequers on Sunday: I knew by then that the manifesto was in almost final form. I had been through the final text with the draftsmen and with Nigel and Norman on that Saturday.

We had one last disagreement. Nigel wished to include a commitment to zero inflation in the next Parliament. I thought this was a hostage to fortune. Events unfortunately proved my caution right.

As always, I slept on the decision about whether to go to the country, and then on Monday 11 May I arranged to see the Queen at 12.25 p.m. to seek a dissolution of Parliament for an election on 11 June.

CLOTHES

In my case, preparation for the election involved more than politics. I also had to be dressed for the occasion. I had already commissioned from Aquascutum suits, jackets and skirts – 'working clothes' for the campaign.

I took a close interest in clothes, as most women do: but it was also extremely important that the impression I gave was right for the political occasion. In Opposition I had worn clothes from various suppliers. And if I had had any doubts about the importance of getting these matters very carefully organized, they were dissipated by the arrival of an outfit ordered for the Opening of Parliament in 1979. It was a beautiful sapphire blue suit with a matching hat. I had no time for a fitting and as I put it on with just a few minutes in hand I found to my horror that it neither fitted nor suited me and had to rush away to change into something else. It was a lesson not to order from a sketch, which can disguise unwanted bulges that are too painfully obvious to the real customer.

From the time of my arrival in Downing Street, Crawfie helped me choose my wardrobe. Together we would discuss style, colour and cloth. Everything had to do duty on many occasions so tailored suits seemed right. (They also have the advantage of gently passing by the waist.) The most exciting outfits were perhaps those suits I had made – in black or dark blue – for the Lord Mayor's Banquet. On foreign visits, it was, of course, particularly important to be appropriately dressed. We always paid attention to the colours of the national flag when deciding on what I should wear. The biggest change, however, was the new style I adopted when I visited the Soviet Union in the spring of 1987, for which I wore a black coat with shoulder pads, that Crawfie had seen in the Aquascutum window, and a marvellous fox fur hat. (Aquascutum have provided me with most of my suits ever since.)

With the televising of the House of Commons after November 1989 new considerations arose. Stripes and checks looked attractive and cheerful in the flesh but they could dazzle the television viewer. One day when I had just not had enough time to change before going to the House, I continued to wear a black and white check suit. Afterwards a parliamentary colleague who had seen me on television told me, 'what you said was all right, but you looked awful.' I learned my lesson. People watching television would also notice whether I had worn the same suit on successive occasions and even wrote in about it. So from now on Crawfie always kept a note of what I wore each week for Prime Minister's Questions. Out of these notes a diary emerged and each outfit received its own name, usually denoting the occasion it was first worn. The pages read something like a travel diary: Paris Opera, Washington Pink, Reagan Navy, Toronto Turquoise, Tokyo Blue, Kremlin Silver, Peking Black and last but not least English Garden. But now my mind was on the forthcoming campaign: it was time to lay out my navy and white check suit, to be known as 'Election '87'.

THE ELECTION CAMPAIGN

The Conservative Party, as I pointed out earlier, deliberately makes a slow start in elections. A slow start, however, is one thing: no start at all is quite another. As the days went by, it seemed to me that the Opposition parties were making most of the running – though at one moment they fell over their own feet when Denis Healey told an astonished world direct from the Soviet capital, where he had been seeking to establish Labour's international credentials, that Moscow was 'praying for a Labour victory'.

On Friday, I spoke at the Scottish Party Conference in Perth. But of course at that stage our manifesto had not been published, so my main message was a warning of what to expect from Labour, which would try to conceal its true nature and purpose: I told people to expect an 'iceberg manifesto' from Labour with 'one-tenth of its socialism visible, nine-tenths beneath the surface'.

On Tuesday 19 May, I chaired the first press conference of the campaign to launch our manifesto: the Alliance's had already appeared, and disappeared, and Labour's, which would be more notable for omissions than contents, would be launched the same day. Our manifesto launch was not quite all that I had wished. The press conference room at Central Office was far too crowded, hot and noisy. Cabinet ministers – all of whom were present in order to demonstrate the strength of the 'team' – were crowded in too, so much so that the television shots of the conference looked truly awful. Nick Ridley explained our housing policy and I hoped that the journalists might be tempted actually to read the detailed policies of the manifesto. I was certainly determined that our candidates should do so and I took them through it in my speech to their conference in Central Hall, Westminster, the following morning.

But I also used the speech for another purpose. Our political weak point was the social services, especially Health, so I went out of my way to tell the candidates, and through them the voters, that the Government was committed to the principle of a National Health Service which I said was 'safe only in our hands'. We had a notably cautious section on Health in the manifesto. That done, I devoted most of the campaign to stressing our strong points on the economy and defence. This did not prevent Health emerging later in the campaign as an issue; but it meant that we had armed ourselves against Labour's attack and done our best to soothe the voters' anxieties.

D-21 TO D-14

Thursday was my first day out in the campaign Battle Bus. This was a new high-tech version of the coach I had used in 1983. It was packed with every kind of up-to-date technology – a computer, different kinds of radio telephones, a fax, a photocopier and an on-board technician to look after it all. Painted blue, the Battle Bus bore the slogan 'Moving Forward with Maggie'. My first photo-opportunity beside the bus was at Docklands, chosen as an example of our Conservative theme of 'regeneration'. I left Docklands to return to No. 10 at lunchtime. In the meantime, the Battle Bus had to undergo some regeneration having collided with a BMW. But the bus's dents were hammered out overnight and it appeared almost spick and span for the following day.

I always held my adoption meeting in Finchley on a Thursday rather than a Friday because the large Jewish population would otherwise be preparing for the Sabbath. In my speech that Thursday evening I concentrated heavily on defence, targeting not just the Labour Party but the Alliance, to the latter's great irritation.

Our first regular press conference of the campaign was on Friday (22 May). The subject was officially defence and George Younger made the opening statement. We had suddenly been given a great opportunity to sink the Alliance parties which some Tory strategists – but not I – thought were the principal electoral threat to us. Instead, the two Davids sank themselves. The passage in our manifesto claimed that their joint defence policy, because it amounted to unilateral nuclear disarmament by degrees, would just as surely as Labour's eventually produce a 'frightened and fellow-travelling Britain' vulnerable to Soviet blackmail. This was not, of course, an allegation of a lack of patriotism, but a forecast of what weakness would inevitably lead to. David Owen, however, failed to make this distinction and took enormous offence. We could hardly believe our luck when for several days he concentrated the public's attention on our strongest card, defence, and his weakest one, his connection with the Liberal Party's sandal-wearing unilateralists. The Alliance never recovered from this misjudgement.

But we were not without our difficulties. I was questioned on education, on which it was suggested that there were contradictions between my and Ken Baker's line on 'opted-out', grant-maintained schools. In fact, we were not suggesting that the new schools would be fee paying in the sense of being private schools: they would remain in the public sector. Moreover, the Secretary of State for Education has to give his approval if a school – whether grant-maintained or not – wishes to change from being a comprehensive school to becoming a grammar school.

That said, however – and over the next few days it all had to be said repeatedly by Ken Baker – I was saddened that we had had to give all these assurances. It is my passionate belief that what above all has gone wrong with British education is that since the war we have, as I put it at this time, 'strangled the middle way'. Direct grant schools and grammar schools provided the means for people like me to get on equal terms with those who came from well-off backgrounds. I would have liked grant-maintained schools – combined with the other changes we were making, and perhaps supplemented by a voucher applying in public and private sectors alike – to move us back to that 'middle way'. I also wanted a return to selection – not of the old eleven-plus kind but a development of specialization and competition so that some schools would become centres of excellence in music, others in technology, others in science, others in the arts etc. This would have given specially gifted children the chance to develop their talents, regardless of their background.

If you are to have specialization of the sort I would like to see you ought to allow the school, which has become a centre of excellence in some field, to control its admission procedures. Competition between schools and individuals will also be more effective if there is some ability to 'top up' grants received from the state. I hope that we can go further along these lines. We ought to if the full Conservative vision for education is to be fulfilled. But at this stage it was clearly not going to be possible.

Some critics argued that this early row resulted from the fact that our reforms had not been fully thought through. That is certainly true of some of the details, even though the main lines were clear. But what was really behind the dispute was that, as I often did in government, I was using public statements to advance the argument and to push reluctant colleagues further than they would otherwise have gone. In an election campaign this was certainly a high-risk strategy. But without such tactics Thatcherism would be a merely theoretical viewpoint.

At the end of the first week we had established ourselves as the only party which had new, fresh ideas. But I felt that we had not gained the momentum from our manifesto which we might have expected and I was starting to be concerned about the tactics of the campaign.

My tour that day took me to the North-West. I made a speech to a large crowd of supporters from the Bury North constituency in the middle of a field. It was just the sort of lively, old-fashioned campaigning which I enjoyed.

Sunday was spent with interviews and working on speeches. Unlike 1983, each of my speeches in this campaign was for the particular occasion rather than drawn from previously prepared material. John O'Sullivan, Ronnie Millar and Stephen Sherbourne were the 'home team' of speech writers. The general rule was that I would look at the speech draft overnight, make the changes required and work on the detail through the following day right up to the delivery of the speech itself. This made for fresh and interesting speeches which were probably better than in the 1983 campaign; but it was also much more difficult to link the theme of the speech with other themes of the day from the morning press conference, my tour, other ministerial speeches or external events.

At Monday's press conference we took the economy as the subject of the day and Nigel Lawson made the opening statement. This was a good campaign for Nigel. Not only did he demonstrate complete command of the issues, he also spotted the implications of Labour's tax and national insurance proposals – especially their planned abolition of the married man's tax allowance and of the upper limit on employees' national insurance contributions – for people on quite modest incomes. This threw Labour into total disarray in the last week of the campaign and revealed that they did not understand their own policies. Nigel had earlier published costings of the Labour Party's manifesto at some £35 billion over and above the Government's spending plans. As I was to say later in a speech: 'Nigel's favourite bedside reading is Labour policy documents: he likes a good mystery.'

At this stage, however, defence continued to dominate the headlines, partly because we had deliberately concentrated our early fire on it, but mainly because of Neil Kinnock's extraordinary gaffe in a television interview in which he suggested that Labour's response to armed aggression would be to take to the hills for guerilla warfare. We gleefully leapt upon this and it provided the inspiration for the only good advertisement of our campaign, depicting 'Labour's Policy on Arms' with a British soldier, his hands held up in surrender. On Tuesday evening, after a day's campaigning in Wales, I told a big rally in Cardiff:

> Labour's non-nuclear defence policy is in fact a policy for defeat, surrender, occupation, and finally, prolonged guerilla fighting . . . I do not understand how anyone who aspires to government can treat the defence of our country so lightly.

The speech went very well. Under Harvey Thomas's supervision our rallies had by now moved into the twentieth century with a vengeance. Dry ice shot out over the first six rows, enveloping the press in a dense fog; lasers flashed madly across the auditorium; our campaign tune, composed by Andrew Lloyd Webber for the occasion, blared out; a video of me on international visits was shown; and then on I walked to deliver my speech, feeling something of an anti-climax.

Wednesday's press conference was of particular importance to the campaign because we took education as the theme, with Ken Baker and me together, in order to allay the doubts our early confusion had generated and to regain the initiative on the subject, which I regarded as central to our manifesto. It went well.

But my tours, by general agreement, did not. Neil Kinnock was gaining more and better television coverage. He was portrayed – as I had specifically requested at the beginning of the campaign that I should be – against the background of cheering crowds, or doing something which fitted in with the theme of the day. The media – far more I suspect than the general public – were entranced by the highly polished party election broadcast showing Neil and Glenys walking hand in hand, bathed in a warm glow of summer sunlight, to strains of patriotic music, looking rather like an advertisement for early retirement. This probably encouraged them to give favourable coverage to the Kinnock tours. And what was I doing on Wednesday? I was visiting a training centre for guide dogs for the blind. The symbolism and significance were lost not just on the media but on me too – and much as I enjoyed looking at the dogs, they did not have a vote. I felt that I was not meeting enough real people. I was going to too many factories and firms. This was partly because of the very tight constraints on security which dictated the tour programme. But the basic strategy was wrong because the tour was organized around photo-opportunities – and no one was seeing the photos.

I began to improvise a little on my own account. That afternoon on our way back from the West Country I had the coach stop at a farm shop, plentifully stocked with bacon, chutney and cream. The following press coaches stopped too and we all piled into the shop. I bought cream and everyone seemed to follow suit. This, I felt, had been my personal contribution to the rural economy; perhaps we might even get some reasonable television film footage at last.

D-14 TO D-7

One week into the campaign and in spite of our own difficulties the political situation was still favourable. Our lead in the polls was holding up. Indeed, the polls recorded little net change in party strength during the campaign, though as will be seen there were a few rogue polls which caused some alarm. There had been a big erosion of support for the Alliance, whose campaign was marred by splits and that basic incoherence which is the nemesis of people who eschew principle in politics. Neil Kinnock kept away from the main London-based journalists and Bryan Gould took most of the press conferences. By the second week, however, this tactic was beginning to rebound and the Fleet Street press were becoming frustrated and critical: they were able to cross-question me day after day and they expected to enjoy a similar sport with the Leader of the Opposition. In this they were enthusiastically encouraged by Norman Tebbit, who by temperament and talent was perfectly suited to maul Neil Kinnock and did so effectively in successive speeches as the campaign wore on.

Thursday's press conference was on the NHS. Norman Fowler had devised a splendid illustration of new hospitals built throughout

Britain, marked by lights on a map which were lit up when he pressed a switch. Like the Kinnocks' election broadcast, I had him repeat the performance by popular demand. Sadly, like so much of the campaign, it did not come over properly on television. The press conference went smoothly. But what was worrying me, as usual, was my speech that evening in Solihull.

We had worked on the draft late until 3.30 a.m. but I was still not happy with it. I continued to break away to work on it whenever I could during the day – that is when I was not meeting candidates, talking to regional editors, admiring Jaguars at the factory and then meeting crowds at the Home and Garden exhibition at the Birmingham NEC. As soon as we arrived at Dame Joan Seccombe's house – she is one of the Party's most committed volunteers – I left the others to enjoy her hospitality and closeted myself away with my speech writers, working frantically on the text right up to the last moment. For some mysterious reason the more you all suffer in preparing a speech, the better it turns out to be and this speech was very good indeed. It contained one wounding passage which drew a roar of approval from the audience:

> Never before has the Labour Party offered the country a defence policy of such recklessness. It has talked of occupation – a defence policy of the white flag. During my time in government white flags have only once entered into our vocabulary. That was the night, when at the end of the Falklands War, I went to the House of Commons to report: 'The white flags are flying over Port Stanley.'

But I was to broaden the attack on Labour in this speech. I levelled my sights at the 'loony Left's' policy of municipal socialism and sexual propaganda on the rates. This drew applause which surprised even me. It became clear that there was real public anxiety about the extremism cloaked by Labour's moderate image. I set out with renewed energy in every speech to win over traditional Labour supporters. Indeed, this became one of my principal themes.

Nick Ridley explained our housing policy at the Friday morning press conference. Then I set off on my tour. This was one of our more successful days, including good photo-opportunities, the chance to meet real people and even a spot of heckling from a Labour councillor when I was making a speech through a loudspeaker to a large crowd on a sports field. The television cameras covered what was thought to be my receiving from No. 10 the news that a British diplomat kidnapped in Tehran had been released: in fact I knew this anyway and the person I was speaking to over the telephone was a secretary at Conservative Central Office. The best picture of the campaign was in Tiptree, in John Wakeham's constituency. Followed by three tractors pulling trailers full of perspiring press-men and photographers, I was driven out into a blackcurrant field to be photographed looking through binoculars at a bird sanctuary. It was a surreal picture of splendid isolation.

With ten days to go, David Young gave the press conference on Monday 1 June, arguing that voting Conservative was the only way to keep unemployment coming down. Using striking graphics, he summarized the elements of what we called 'Labour's job destruction package', showing how thousands of jobs would go as a result of their policies for defence cuts, sanctions on South Africa and extra powers for trade unions. It was a good performance and I was glad that we were at last beginning to get across our strong card of economic prosperity.

The next day, after chairing our press conference, which again was on the economy, I flew to Scotland. By now the Labour Party had decided that they had better keep off policy altogether and they leaked that instead they would concentrate on personal attacks on me. Neil Kinnock did not do this with great subtlety: he described me as 'a would-be empress' and the Cabinet as 'sycophants and doormats'. I was determined to make this tactic rebound on them. I spoke at a rally that night in Edinburgh:

> This week [Labour] are resorting to personal abuse. This is an excellent sign. Personal abuse is no substitute for policy. It signals panic. In any case, let me assure you it will not affect me in the slightest. As that great American Harry Truman observed: 'if you can't stand the heat, get out of the kitchen.' Well, Mr Chairman, after eight years over the hot stove I think I can say, with all due modesty, that the heat is entirely tolerable.

In spite of the bad weather it had been a pleasant, old-fashioned day of campaigning. Denis enjoyed it too. We visited the Scottish & Newcastle Brewery in Edinburgh and Denis with somewhat feigned reluctance downed the obligatory pint on my behalf. Next morning after giving press and television interviews I flew to Newcastle and went on to the Gateshead Metro shopping centre where, amid the large crowds which gathered as I went into different shops, I felt that I was at last making proper contact with the electorate.

My satisfaction, however, was marred by the onset of extremely painful toothache. I had been to the dentist before the campaign began and nothing seemed amiss. But the pain grew worse as the afternoon wore on and later that evening after I returned to London I went to the dentist once more. There was apparently an abscess under my tooth which would need proper treatment later. For the moment I had to rely on pain killers. By the time I got back to London I had something else unpleasant to think about. I was told in the course of the afternoon that the next day's Gallup poll would show a definite shift from us to Labour for the first time, cutting our lead to 4 per cent.

D-7 TO D-DAY

I could not get to sleep that night because of my tooth. At about 4.00 a.m. Crawfie gave me some pain killers. They did the trick for the toothache and allowed me to get some rest. But they made me feel and – as I have later learned – look catatonic when, first thing the following morning, I went across to Central Office. This has gone down in political mythology as 'wobbly Thursday' or 'black Thursday': since we did not wobble but the news looked black I prefer the second description.

The subject of the day was pensions and social security. I had expressly told Central Office that I wanted Health to be covered as well but this had not been done, which angered me. At the press conference briefing my toothache had come on again and I tore into Norman Fowler's draft press release, rather unfairly, until David Wolfson, who is one of the few people who gets away with this sort of thing, told me to 'shut up' and read it through first before making any more changes. I did so, agreed it and then faced the news about the poll. The worst was that there would be another poll by Marplan for the next day which was the subject of wild speculation. It would show whether the Gallup result was just a rogue poll, or whether our position really was slipping away.

I had talked to David Young the previous night about my worries about the campaign, which seemed to me to be unfocused and not to stress sufficiently our strongest themes, in particular the record of economic prosperity. The following day, Norman Tebbit and I had a ding-dong row. This cleared the air. We agreed that some of our younger ministers, like John Moore and Kenneth Clarke, should be given a higher billing. I arranged to appear upon the David Frost programme from which I had been withdrawn. But at this stage we had still not agreed on the advertising for the following week.

The press conference that day was widely considered to be a disaster for us and I was held to blame. The issue arose of private health care. I refused to be apologetic for the fact that I used private health insurance to have minor operations done speedily, without adding to the queue for NHS treatment and using my own money. What I said was immediately exploited as being insensitive, callous and uncaring. I was aware that the press conference had not been a success in public relations terms. But I was not going to back down, however much others around me hoped that I would stay silent on the matter in the interviews when it was bound to be raised. Moreover, my instincts were right and that of the professionals wrong. The press set out on what turned out to be a fruitful hunt for examples of Labour politicians and their families who used private health care. By the end of the campaign I had won this argument – and it was definitely worth winning.

After the press conference I set out my ideas for a major advertising campaign, which I had previously privately discussed with Tim Bell, who had of course been effectively excluded from the campaign by Central Office and Saatchis. I wanted this to be based heavily on our record of achievements, which may have seemed dull to the creative and unpolitical minds of communications specialists but which – as was subsequently demonstrated again at the 1992 general election – are what the electorate is really likely to vote on. Saatchis were to devise one set of advertising for me to see and approve: meanwhile Tim Bell and David Young were working on another which I believed would be better. I went to the Alton Towers theme park in Staffordshire, without being quite in the mood for jollity, still worried about what would come of the advertising, even more concerned about the mysterious opinion poll we were waiting for. There was media speculation that it would show our lead down to 1 per cent. While at Alton Towers I overheard a BBC newscaster remark, 'that's it: she's downhill all the way now.'

I had little time to deal with the advertising when I arrived back at No. 10. I liked the material Tim Bell had prepared. Norman Tebbit, who is always a big man in such situations, frankly acknowledged that the new ideas for the advertising were better. I left him and David Young to deal with it all while I went on with the briefing for my interview with Jonathan Dimbleby. There is only one complaint I still allow myself to nurture against my staff in No. 10: that is that I was not told before I went on television about the results of the poll, which put us back in a healthy lead and showed that the earlier one was not to be taken seriously. Perhaps it was as well, for it was a tough interview and I really fought back. At least one good – if extremely expensive – thing came out of that rogue poll: for it prompted me to insist on that newspaper advertising blitz on the lines I wanted, which consolidated our support.

I was due to speak in Chester on Friday. I did not really concentrate on my draft speech until I was in the train that morning to Gatwick. I found it far too theatrical. I was expected to use 'props' – to ensure that television news concentrated on certain passages – a large key to illustrate the advances in home ownership was just one of several. Stephen Sherbourne and John Whittingdale were promptly asked to bring this flight of fancy down to earth. As is often the case with speeches, panic proved productive. The revised text was first class: the audience approved as well.

Over the weekend I had several more big interviews. The *Today Programme* on Saturday morning was characteristically hostile. However, I enjoyed Channel 4's *Face the People* later that morning, in which voters from marginal constituencies questioned me on our policies. I loved these occasions: the questions are real and have a life and a depth that one-to-one interviews never evoke. On Sunday I was interviewed by David Frost. The questioning was tough but fair, concentrating heavily once more on the private health issue. We all felt that it had gone quite well.

This was also the day of our final 'family rally' at Wembley where, as in 1983, television personalities, actors, comedians and musicians gave us their public support. Ronnie Millar had written a version of the *Dad's Army* theme song, 'Who do you think you are kidding, Mr Kinnock?', to which the audience sang along as at a pantomime. This went down very well and when my turn came to speak I picked up the theme predicting that millions of traditional Labour voters, disgusted with their Party's swing to the left and neutralism, would soon be joining 'Mum's Army'. To my surprise it was the lead item on that evening's TV news. I felt that this important message, at least, was getting across.

On Monday, after chairing our press conference and then recording an interview with Sir Robin Day, I left for the G7 economic summit in Venice. I had decided before the campaign began that I would almost certainly go to the G7, just as I had gone to Williamsburg in 1983. My role as 'international statesman' was a more important element in our election campaign this time; so there were even stronger political arguments for making the visit. In any case, I never missed the opportunity of talking with President Reagan as I would both at the dinner that evening which concentrated on arms control and at my tête-à-tête meeting with him the following morning before the first formal session on the economy. There was a real point at issue on arms control, on which I wanted to make my position clear. Chancellor Kohl wanted to press ahead with negotiation with the Soviets for the removal of shorter-range nuclear weapons. I was not prepared to see British forces in Germany left without their protection and said so forcefully over dinner. I would not subscribe to any communiqué which established the goal of further reductions, at least until agreement to eliminate chemical weapons and redress the imbalance in conventional forces. In this, I received the crucial backing of President Reagan.

I was back in Britain by 2.30 on Tuesday afternoon. A draft of my speech for Harrogate that evening was waiting for me with Stephen Sherbourne and the speech writers when I landed at Gatwick. To my relief and their amazement I liked it. It was essentially a summary of what I, at least, thought were the three main themes of the election: Conservative prosperity, Labour extremism, especially on defence, and the new reforms of education and housing to give more power to the people. On the way to the hall at Harrogate I had been given the results of the specially large – and therefore significant – Gallup 2000 poll. They showed us with a 7-point lead. 'Not enough,' I said. But it was good news all the same. It seemed that our opinion poll rating had been practically level throughout the entire campaign.

I returned to London, but I did not ease up. On Wednesday morning I answered questions on the *Election Call* 'phone-in programme. I spent most of the afternoon campaigning in Portsmouth and Southampton.

After voting myself, I spent Thursday morning and early afternoon in Finchley visiting our Committee Rooms and then, as the time for getting late voters out to the poll approached, I returned to No. 10. Norman Tebbit came over and we had a long talk over drinks in my study, not just about the campaign and the likely result, but also about Norman's own plans. He had already told me that he intended to leave the Government after the election because he felt that he should spend more time with Margaret. There was not much I could say to try to persuade him otherwise, because his reasons were as personal as they were admirable. But I did bitterly regret his decision. I had too few like-minded supporters in the Government, and of these none had Norman's strength and acumen.

I had supper in the flat and listened to the television comment and speculation about the result. Before I left for Finchley at 10.30 p.m. I heard Vincent Hanna on the BBC forecasting a hung Parliament. ITV was talking about a Conservative majority of about 40. I felt reasonably confident that with the Alliance vote having clearly collapsed we would have a majority, but I was not at all confident how large it would be. My own result would be one of the later ones; but the first results began to come in just after 11 p.m. We held Torbay with a larger than predicted majority. Then we held Hyndburn, the second most marginal seat, then Cheltenham, a seat targeted by the Liberals, and then Basildon. At about 2.15 a.m. we had passed the winning post. My own majority was down by 400, though I secured a slightly higher percentage of the vote (53.9 per cent).

I was driven back into town, arriving at 2.45 a.m. at Conservative Central Office to celebrate the victory and thank those who had helped achieve it. Then I returned to Downing Street where I was met by my personal staff. I felt grateful to them because, whatever the deficiencies of the national campaign, they had done a superb job. I remember Denis saying to Stephen Sherbourne, as we went down the line: 'You have done as much as anyone else to win the election. We could not have done it without you.' Stephen may have been less pleased by my next remark. It was to ask him to come up to the study to begin work on making the next Cabinet. A new day had begun.

CHAPTER XX

An Improving Disposition

Reforms in education, housing and the Health Service; the situation in Scotland

THE NEW GOVERNMENT

The first priority after the 1987 election victory was to see that I had the right team of ministers to implement the reforms set out in our manifesto. The reshuffle was a limited one: five Cabinet ministers left the Government, two at their own request. The general balance of the new Cabinet made it clear that 'consolidation' was no more my preferred option after the election than before it. John Biffen, whose less than inspiring slogan this had been, left the Cabinet: this was a loss in some ways, for he agreed with me about Europe and had sound instincts on economic matters too, but he had come to prefer commentary to collective responsibility. I lost Norman Tebbit for reasons I have explained. But Cecil Parkinson, a radical of my way of thinking, rejoined the Cabinet as Energy Secretary. I made no change at Education where Ken Baker would make up in presentational flair whatever he lacked in attention to detail, nor Environment where Nick Ridley was obviously the right man to implement the housing reforms which he had conceived. These two areas – schools and housing – were those in which we were proposing the most far-reaching changes. But it was not long before I decided that there must be a major reform of the National Health Service too. In John Moore, whom I had promoted to be Secretary of State for Health and Social Services, I had another radical, anxious to reform the ossified system he had inherited. So the Government soon found itself embarked on even more far-reaching social reforms than we had originally intended.

APPROACHES TO EDUCATION REFORM

The starting point for the education reforms outlined in our general election manifesto was a deep dissatisfaction (which I fully shared) with Britain's standard of education. There had been improvements in the pupil-teacher ratio and real increases in education spending per child. But increases in public spending had not by and large led to higher standards. The classic case was the left-wing dominated Inner London Education Authority (ILEA) which spent more per pupil than any other education authority and achieved some of the worst examination results. Precisely what conditions and qualities made for good schools was a matter of vigorous debate. I had always been an advocate of relatively small schools as against the giant, characterless comprehensives. I also believed that too many teachers were less competent and more ideological than their predecessors. I distrusted the new 'child-centred' teaching techniques, the emphasis on imaginative engagement rather than learning facts, and the modern tendency to blur the lines of discrete subjects and incorporate them in wider, less definable entities like 'humanities'. And I knew from parents, employers and pupils themselves that too many people left school without a basic knowledge of reading, writing and arithmetic. But it would be no easy matter to change for the better what happened in schools.

One option would in theory have been to advance much further along the path of centralization. In fact, I did come to the conclusion that there had to be some consistency in the curriculum, at least in the core subjects. The state could not just ignore what children learned: they were, after all, its future citizens and we had a duty to them. Moreover, it was disruptive if children who moved from a school in one area to a school elsewhere found themselves confronted with a course of work different in almost all respects from that to which they had become accustomed. Alongside the national curriculum should be a nationally recognized and reliably monitored system of testing at various stages of the child's school career, which would allow parents, teachers, local authorities and central government to know what was going right and wrong and take remedial action if necessary. The fact that since 1944 the only compulsory subject in the curriculum in Britain had been religious education reflected a healthy distrust of the state using central control of the syllabus as a means of propaganda. But that was hardly the risk now: the propaganda was coming from left-wing local authorities, teachers and pressure groups, not us. What I never believed, though, was that the state should try to regiment every detail of what happened in schools. Some people argued that the French centralized system worked: but, whether it worked for France or not, such arrangements would not be acceptable in Britain. Here even the strictly limited objectives I set for the national curriculum were immediately seen by the vested interests in education as an opportunity to impose their own agenda.

The other possibility was to go much further in the direction of decentralization by giving power and choice to parents. Keith Joseph and I had always been attracted by the education voucher, which would give parents a fixed – perhaps means-tested – sum, so that they could shop around in the public and private sectors of education for the school which was best for their children. The arguments against this were more political than practical. By means testing a voucher one could even reduce the 'dead weight' cost – that is the amount lost to the Exchequer in the form of subsidy for parents who would otherwise have sent their children to private schools anyway.

However, Keith Joseph recommended and I accepted that we could not bring in a straightforward education voucher scheme. In the event, we were, through our education reforms, able to realize the objectives of parental choice and educational variety in other ways. Through the assisted places scheme* and the rights of parental choice of school under our 1980 Parents' Charter we were moving some way towards this objective without mentioning the word 'voucher'.

In the 1988 Education Reform Act we now made further strides in that direction. We introduced open enrolment – that is allowing popular schools to expand to their physical capacity (broadly judged by the numbers of children accommodated in 1979). This significantly widened choice further and prevented local authorities setting arbitrary limits on good schools just to keep unsuccessful schools full. An essential element in the same reforms was per capita funding, which meant that state money followed the child to whatever school he attended. Parents would vote with their children's feet and schools actually gained resources when they gained pupils. The worse schools in these circumstances would either have to improve or close. In effect we had gone as far as we could towards a 'public sector voucher'. I would have liked to go further still and decided that we must work up a possible full-scale voucher scheme – I hinted at this in my final

* See p. 39.

Party Conference speech – but did not have the time to take the idea further.

GRANT-MAINTAINED SCHOOLS

But we needed to do one more thing to make parental choice a reality. This was to give more powers and responsibility to individual schools – something very much in line with my instinctive preference for smaller schools rooted in real local communities and, insofar as this was possible in the state sector, reliant on their own efforts and energies. But it was Brian Griffiths who devised the extremely successful model of the 'grant-maintained (GM) schools', which are free from local education authority (LEA) control entirely and are directly funded from the DES.* With a healthy range of GM schools, City Technology Colleges, denominational schools and private schools (known as 'public' schools, much to the confusion of American visitors to Britain) parents would have a much wider choice. But, even more vital, the very fact of having all the important decisions taken at the level closest to parents and teachers, not by a distant and insensitive bureaucracy, would make for better education. This would be true of all schools, which was why we had introduced the Local Management of Schools Initiative (LMS) to give schools more control of their own budgets. But GM schools took it a giant step further.

The governors of a GM school were empowered to manage its budget (receiving their money directly without a service charge deducted by the LEA). They appointed the staff including the head teacher, agreed policy as regards admissions with the Secretary of State, decided the curriculum (subject to the core requirements) and owned the school and its assets. The schools most likely to opt out of LEA control and become GM schools were those which had a distinctive identity, which wished to specialize in some particular subject or which wanted to escape from the clutches of some left-wing local authority keen to impose its own ideological priorities.

The vested interests working against the success of GM schools were strong. The DES, reluctant to endorse a reform that did not extend central control, would have liked to impose all manner of checks and controls on their operation. Local authority officials sometimes campaigned fiercely to prevent opting out by particular schools. And,

* For the arguments about the terminology see pp. 570–1.

unexpectedly, the churches also mounted an opposition. In the face of so much hostility I had the Grant-Maintained Schools Trust set up to publicize the GM scheme and advise those interested in making use of it. In fact, GM schools proved increasingly popular, not least with head teachers who were now, in consultation with the governors, able to set their own priorities.

THE NATIONAL CURRICULUM

The decentralizing features of our policy – open enrolment, per capita funding, City Technology Colleges, Local Management of Schools and above all grant-maintained schools – were extraordinarily successful. By contrast, the national curriculum – the most important centralizing measure – soon ran into difficulties. I never envisaged that we would end up with the bureaucracy and the thicket of prescriptive measures which eventually emerged. I wanted the DES to concentrate on establishing a basic syllabus for English, Mathematics and Science with simple tests to show what pupils knew. It always seemed to me that a small committee of good teachers ought to be able to pool their experience and write down a list of the topics and sources to be covered without too much difficulty. There ought then to be plenty of scope left for the individual teacher to concentrate with children on the particular aspects of the subject in which he or she felt a special enthusiasm or interest. I had no wish to put good teachers in a strait jacket. As for testing, I always recognized that no snapshot of a child's, a class's or a school's performance on a particular day was going to tell the whole truth. But tests did provide an independent outside check on what was happening. Nor did it seem to me that the fact that some children would know more than others was something to be shied away from. Of course, not every child had the same potential and certainly not in every subject. But the purpose of testing was not to measure merit but knowledge and the capacity to apply it. Unfortunately, my philosophy turned out to be different from that of those to whom Ken Baker entrusted the drawing-up of the national curriculum and the formulation of the tests alongside it.

There was a basic dilemma. As Ken emphasized in our meetings, it was necessary to take as many as possible of the teachers and Her Majesty's Inspectorate (HMI) with us in the reforms we were making. After all, it was teachers not politicians who would be implementing them. On the other hand, the educational establishment's terms for accepting the national curriculum and testing could well prove unacceptable. For them, the new national curriculum would be expected to give legitimacy and universal application to the changes which had been made over the last twenty years or so in the content and methods of teaching. Similarly, testing should in their eyes be 'diagnostic' rather than 'summative' – and this was only the tip of the jargon iceberg – and should be heavily weighted towards assessment by teachers themselves, rather than by objective outsiders. So by mid-July the papers I was receiving from the DES were proposing a national curriculum of ten subjects which would account for 80–90 per cent of school time. They wanted different 'attainment targets', stressing that assessments should not denote 'passing' or 'failing': much of this assessment would be internal to the school. Two new bodies – the National Curriculum Council and the Schools Examination and Assessment Council – were to be set up. In fact, the original simplicity of the scheme had been lost and the influence of HMI and the teachers' unions was manifest.

All this was bad enough. But then in September I received a further proposal from Ken Baker for comprehensive monitoring of the national curriculum by the recruitment of 800 extra LEA Inspectors, who themselves would be monitored and controlled by the HMI, which would doubtless have to be expanded as well. I noted: 'it is utterly ridiculous. The results will come through in the tests and exams.' I stressed to the DES that all of these proposals would alienate teachers, hold back individual initiative at school level and centralize education to an unacceptable degree. The Cabinet sub-committee which I chaired to oversee the education reforms decided that all of the core and foundation subjects taken together should absorb no more than 70 per cent of the curriculum. But, at Ken Baker's insistence, I agreed that this figure should not be publicly released – presumably it would have caused offence with the education bureaucrats who were by now ambitiously planning how each hour of school time should properly be spent.

The next problem arose from the report by the 'Task Group on Assessment and Testing' which we had established in July 1987 to advise on the practical considerations which would govern assessment, including testing, within the national curriculum. Ken Baker warmly welcomed the report. Whether he had read it properly I do not know: if he had it says much for his stamina. Certainly I had no opportunity to do so before agreeing to its publication, having simply been presented with this weighty, jargon-filled document in my overnight box with a deadline for publication the following day. The fact that it was then welcomed by the Labour Party, the National Union of Teachers and the *Times Educational Supplement* was enough to confirm for me that its approach was suspect. It proposed an elaborate and complex system of assessment – teacher-dominated and uncosted. It adopted the 'diagnostic' view of tests, placed the emphasis on teachers doing their own assessment and was written in an impenetrable educationalist jargon. I minuted out my concerns to Ken Baker but by now, of course, it had been published and was already the subject of consultation.

In July 1988 I received the Mathematics National Curriculum papers. It was a small mountain. A complicated array of 'levels', 'attainment targets' and 'profile components' based on 'tasks' which pupils were expected to perform was surely not what teachers required. In commenting, I stressed the need for greater clarity, simplicity and a more practical approach.

Then in October I read the first report of the National Curriculum English Working Group. This too I found disappointing, as I had the earlier Kingman Committee Report on the teaching of English language – and for the same reasons. Although there was acceptance of a place for Standard English, the traditional learning of grammar and learning by heart, which I considered vital for memory training, seemed to find no favour. Unsatisfactory as all this seemed to me, the fact that many critics considered the direction of these recommendations to be controversial demonstrated just how far things had deteriorated in many classrooms. Moreover, the final report of the English Working Group responded to the criticism made of its first report and gave at least some more emphasis to grammar and spelling.

Perhaps the hardest battle I fought on the national curriculum was about history. Though not an historian myself, I had a very clear – and I had naïvely imagined uncontroversial – idea of what history was. History is an account of what happened in the past. Learning history, therefore, requires knowledge of events. It is impossible to make sense of such events without absorbing sufficient factual information and without being able to place matters in a clear chronological framework – which means knowing dates. No amount of imaginative sympathy for historical characters or situations can be a substitute for the initially tedious but ultimately rewarding business of memorizing what actually happened. I was, therefore, very concerned when in December 1988 I received Ken Baker's written proposals for the teaching of history and the composition of the History Working Group on the curriculum. The guidance offered was not rigorous enough. There was also too much emphasis given to 'cross-curricular' learning: I felt that history must be taught as a separate subject. Nor was I happy at the list of people Ken Baker was suggesting. His initial names contained no major historian of repute but included the author of the definitive work on the 'New History' which, with its emphasis on concepts rather than chronology and empathy rather than facts, was at the root of so much that was going wrong. Ken saw my point and made some changes. But this was only the beginning of the argument.

In July 1989 the History Working Group produced its interim report. I was appalled. It put the emphasis on interpretation and enquiry as against content and knowledge. There was insufficient weight given to British history. There was not enough emphasis on history as chronological study. Ken Baker wanted to give the report a general welcome while urging its chairman to make the attainment targets specify more clearly factual knowledge and increasing the British history content. But this did not in my view go far enough. I considered the document comprehensively flawed and told Ken that there must be major, not just minor, changes. In particular, I wanted to see a clearly set out chronological framework for the whole history curriculum. But the test would of course be the final report.

By the time this arrived in March 1990 John MacGregor had gone to Education. I thought that he would prove more effective than Ken Baker in keeping a grip on how our education reform proposals were implemented, though I knew that he did not have Ken's special talent for putting our case in public. On this occasion, however, John MacGregor was far more inclined to welcome the report than I had expected. It did now put greater emphasis on British history. But the attainment targets it set out did not specifically include knowledge of historical facts, which seemed to me extraordinary. However, the coverage of some subjects – for example twentieth-century British history – was too skewed to social, religious, cultural and aesthetic matters rather than political events. The detail of the history curriculum would impose too inflexible a framework on teachers. I raised these points at a meeting with John on the afternoon of Monday 19 March. He defended the report's proposals. But I insisted that it would not be right to impose the sort of approach which it contained. It should go out to consultation but no guidance should at present be issued.

By now I had become thoroughly exasperated with the way in which the national curriculum proposals were being diverted from their original purpose. I made my reservations known in an interview I gave to the *Sunday Telegraph* in early April. In this I defended the principles of the national curriculum but criticized the detailed prescription in other than core subjects which had now become its least agreeable feature. My comments were greeted with consternation by the DES.

There was no need for the national curriculum proposals and the testing which accompanied them to have developed as they did. Ken Baker paid too much attention to the DES, the HMI and progressive educational theorists in his appointments and early decisions; and once the bureaucratic momentum had begun it was difficult to stop. John MacGregor, under constant pressure from me, did what he could. He made changes to the history curriculum which reinforced the position of British history and reduced some of the unnecessary interference. He insisted that the sciences could be taught separately, not just as one integrated subject. He stipulated that at least 30 per cent of GCSE English should be tested by written examination. Yet the whole system was very different from that which I originally envisaged. By the time I left office I was convinced that there would have to be a new drive to simplify the national curriculum and testing.

THE NEXT WAVE OF EDUCATION REFORM

Education policy was one of the areas in which my Policy Unit and I had begun radical thinking about proposals for the next election manifesto – some of which we envisaged announcing in advance, perhaps at the March 1991 Central Council meeting. Brian Griffiths and I were concentrating on three questions at the time I left office.

First, there was the need to go much further with 'opting out' of LEA control. I authorized John MacGregor to announce to the October 1990 Party Conference the extension of the GM schools scheme to cover smaller primary schools as well. But I had much more radical options in mind. Brian Griffiths had written me a paper which envisaged the transfer of many more schools to GM status and the transfer of other schools – which were not yet ready to assume the full responsibility – to the management of special trusts, set up for the purpose. Essentially, this would have meant the unbundling of many of the LEAs' powers, leaving them with a monitoring and advisory role – perhaps in the long term not even that. It would have been a way to ease the state still further out of education, thus reversing the worst aspects of post-war education policy.

Second, there was the need radically to improve teacher training. Unusually, I had sent a personal minute to Ken Baker in November 1988 expressing my concerns. I said we must go much further in this area and asked him to bring forward proposals. The background to this was that Keith Joseph had set up the Council for the Accreditation of Teacher Education (CATE) in 1984 to approve teacher-training courses. But the position had barely improved. There was still too little emphasis on factual knowledge of the subjects teachers needed to teach, too little practical classroom experience acquired and too much stress on the sociological and psychological aspects. For example, I could barely believe the contents of one of the B.Ed. courses – duly approved by CATE – at Brighton Polytechnic about which one concerned Tory supporter sent in details. Entitled 'Contexts for learning', this course claimed to be enabling teachers to come to terms with such challenging questions as 'To what extent do schools reinforce gender stereotypes?' It continued: 'students are then introduced to the debate between protagonists [sic] of education and those who advocate anti-racist education.' I felt that the 'protagonists' of education had a better case.

The effective monopoly exercised by the existing teacher-training routes had to be broken. Ken Baker devised two schemes – that of 'licensed teachers' to attract those who wished to enter teaching as a second career and that of 'articled teachers' which was essentially an apprenticeship scheme of 'on the job' training for younger graduates. These were good proposals. But there was no evidence that there would be a large enough inflow of teachers from these sources significantly to change the ethos and raise the standards of the profession. So I had Brian Griffiths begin work on how to increase the numbers: we wanted to see at least half of the new teachers come through these or similar schemes, as opposed to teacher-training institutions.

The third educational policy issue on which work was being done was the universities. By exerting financial pressure we had increased administrative efficiency and provoked overdue rationalization. Universities were developing closer links with business and becoming more entrepreneurial. Student loans (which topped up grants) had also been introduced: these would make students more discriminating about the courses they chose. A shift of support from university grants to the payment of tuition fees would lead in the same direction of greater sensitivity to the market. Limits placed on the security of tenure enjoyed by university staff also encouraged dons to pay closer attention to satisfying the teaching requirements made of them. All this encountered strong political opposition from within the universities. Some of it was predictable. But undoubtedly other critics were genuinely concerned about the future autonomy and academic integrity of universities.

I had to concede that these critics had a stronger case than I would have liked. It made me concerned that many distinguished academics thought that Thatcherism in education meant a philistine subordination of scholarship to the immediate requirements of vocational training. That was certainly no part of my kind of Thatcherism.* That was why before I left office Brian Griffiths, with my encouragement, had started working on a scheme to give the leading universities much more independence. The idea was to allow them to opt out of Treasury financial rules and raise and keep capital, owning their assets as a trust. It would have represented a radical decentralization of the whole system.

IMPLEMENTING THE HOUSING REFORMS

Of the three major social services – Education, the Health Service and Housing – it was, in my view, over the last of these that the most significant question mark hung. By the mid-1980s everything in housing pointed to the need to roll back the existing activities of government. Although the country's housing stock needed refurbishment and adaptation, there was no pressing need now – as arguably there had been after the war – for massive new house building by the state. Furthermore, rising incomes and capital ownership were placing more and more people in the position to buy their homes with a mortgage.

State intervention to control rents and give tenants security of tenure in the private rented sector had been disastrous in reducing the supply of rented properties. The state in the form of local authorities had frequently proved an insensitive, incompetent and corrupt landlord. And insofar as there were shortages in specific categories of housing, these were in the private rented sector where rent control and security of tenure had reduced the supply. Moreover, new forms of housing had emerged. Housing Associations and the Housing Corporation which financed them – though they could be all too wasteful and bureaucratic on occasion – offered alternative ways of providing 'social housing' without the state as landlord. Similarly, tenant involvement in the form of co-operatives and the different kinds of trusts being pioneered in the United States offered new ways of pulling government out of housing management. I believed that the state must

* See my speech to Rand Afrikans University in May 1991.

continue to provide mortgage tax relief in order to encourage home ownership, which was socially desirable. (Far better and cheaper to help people to help themselves than to provide housing for them.) The state also had to provide assistance for poorer people with housing costs through housing benefit. But as regards the traditional post-war role of government in housing – that is building, ownership, management, and regulation – the state should be withdrawn from these areas just as far and as fast as possible.

This was the philosophical starting point for the housing reforms on which Nick Ridley was working from the autumn of 1986, which he submitted for collective discussion at the end of January 1987, and which after several meetings under my chairmanship were included in the 1987 general election manifesto.* The beauty of the package which Nick devised was that it combined a judicious mixture of central government intervention, local authority financial discipline, deregulation and wider choice for tenants. In so doing it achieved a major shift away from the ossified system which had grown up under socialism.

Central government would play a role through Housing Action Trusts (HATs) in redeveloping badly run down council estates and passing them on to other forms of ownership and management – including home ownership, ownership by housing associations and transfer to a private landlord – with no loss of tenant rights. Second, the new 'ring-fenced' framework for local authority housing accounts would force councils to raise rents to levels which provided money for repairs. It would also increase the pressure on councils for the disposal of part or all of their housing stock to housing associations, other landlords or indeed home ownership. Third, deregulation of new lets – through development of shorthold and assured tenancies – should at least arrest the decline of the private rented sector: Nick rightly insisted that there should be stronger legal provisions enacted against harassment to balance this deregulation. Finally, opening up the possibility of council tenants changing their landlords, or groups of tenants running their estates through co-operatives under our 'tenants' choice' proposals, could reduce the role of local authority landlords still further.

The most difficult aspect of the package seemed likely to be the higher council rents, which would also mean much higher state spending on housing benefit. More people on housing benefit means more welfare dependency; on the other hand, it seemed better to provide

* See p. 571.

help with housing costs through benefit than through subsidizing the rents of local authority tenants indiscriminately. Moreover, the higher rents paid by those not on benefit would provide an added incentive for them to buy their homes and escape from the net altogether.

These reforms will need time to produce results. But the new arrangements for housing revenue accounts are applying a beneficial new discipline to local authorities. And deregulation of the private rented sector will increase the supply of rented housing gradually, as ideological hostility to private landlordism recedes.* But I have to say that I had expected more from 'tenants' choice' and from HATs. The obstacle to both was the same: the deep-rooted hostility of the Left to the improvement and enfranchisement of those who lived in the ghettoes of dependency which they controlled. The propaganda against 'tenants' choice', however, was as nothing compared with that directed against HATs and, sadly, the House of Lords gave the Left the opportunity they needed.

Their lordships amended our legislation to require that a HAT could only go ahead if a majority of eligible tenants voted for it. This would have been an impossibly high hurdle, given the apathy of many tenants and the intimidation of the Left. We finished up by accepting the principle of a ballot, limiting it to the requirement of a majority of those voting. In the summer of 1988 Nick Ridley announced proposals to set up six HATs, of which – after receiving consultants' reports – he decided to go ahead with four in Lambeth, Southwark, Sunderland and Leeds. I later saw some of the propaganda by left-wing tenants' groups – strongly backed by the trade unions – which showed how effective their campaigns had been to spread alarm among tenants who were now worried about what would happen when they moved out as their flats were refurbished and about levels of rents and security of tenure. One would never have guessed that we were offering huge sums of taxpayers' money – it would probably have worked out at £100 million a HAT – to improve the conditions of people living in some of the worst housing in the country. Accordingly, the proposals for HATs in Sunderland, Sandwell, Lambeth, Leeds and finally Southwark had to be dropped, though we knew that a number of local authorities – even Labour-controlled ones – would have liked to obtain access to the HATs money if they could have overcome the opposition of the militants. As a result, no HATs were set up while I was Prime Minister, though three have been since I left office.

* See pp. 670–1.

FURTHER STEPS IN HOUSING POLICY

By the time of the July 1989 reshuffle the problems with the implementation of our 1987 manifesto housing reforms were all too apparent and it was clear that we should take stock and seek new ways of achieving our objectives. Unfortunately, in Chris Patten as the new Environment Secretary I had someone whose energies were principally (and rightly) directed at trying to smooth out the introduction of the community charge and who in any case was less interested in housing policy than in his other departmental responsibilities. This is not, though, to say that innovative thinking had come to a halt.

Since the spring of 1988 Peter Walker in Wales had been pressing a scheme which he christened 'flexi-ownership' under which public sector tenants unable to exercise the 'Right to Buy' – even with the large discounts available – would be able to acquire equity stakes in their homes that would increase as the years went by and whose value would be updated in line with local house prices. Initially, I had doubts about the idea – on financial grounds, in that people might choose to use this route rather than the 'Right to Buy' and sales and receipts would fall; on political grounds, in that those who had already exercised the 'Right to Buy' and made the sacrifices required to do so would be resentful. Both the DoE and the Treasury were strongly against. In Scotland, another variant on the same idea – called 'Rents to Mortgages' – had been devised. Under this, rent payments – less a sum for repair and maintenance – would be converted into mortgage repayments.

We discussed the possibilities of both schemes in the summer and autumn of 1988. Scotland was a different case from Wales, for – as I shall explain – home ownership was much lower. Another difference was that in Scotland the Government through 'Scottish Homes' was itself a substantial landlord: so no new legislation was needed. I therefore agreed to a Scottish experiment on these lines, while holding fire on Wales.

The ever ingenious Peter Walker now put his ingenuity to good use. He devised a similar Welsh scheme which would operate through the Development Board for Rural Wales at Newtown Powys. The DoE and the Treasury still objected on the ground that the idea could not in the end be limited to Wales and that if it were applied in England substantial 'Right to Buy' sales revenues would be lost. But I could see its political attractions; it was fairly modest, and, in any case, it was Peter Walker's brainchild and I thought he should be allowed to go ahead. I agreed to this at the end of June 1989.

The most disturbing political issue in housing at this time, however, was homelessness. It should immediately be said that the alarmingly large figures for the 'homeless' did not by definition reflect the number of people without roofs over their heads. Rather, the published 'homelessness' figures described the number of people in certain statutorily determined 'priority groups' who were accepted for housing. In other words, far from being homeless they had homes provided by local councils. Sad as the cases of some of these people might be, the problem which worried the general public – and me too – was the growing number of people (especially young people) sleeping rough on the streets of London and other big cities, who were better described as 'roofless'.

While it was certainly true that there was an insufficiency of short-term 'direct access' hostel accommodation – as opposed to the larger, more traditional hostels – and while it was true that the shortage of private rented accommodation had worsened because of rent control, this was essentially a problem of wider social, not housing, policy. Nor are behavioural problems solved by bricks and mortar. I was not prepared to endorse changes in social security benefits relating to the under-25s which were suggested by Tony Newton and the Social Security Department: I thought it vital that we should not add to the already too evident lure of the big city for young people. We wanted them back with their families, not in London living on benefits. I urged the Department of the Environment to bring in the voluntary organizations to see what they rather than the state could do. I was also convinced that far too many disturbed people, who should have been in institutions, had fallen through the central and local government safety net and found themselves with nowhere to go.

In November 1989 Chris Patten announced a package which provided £250 million over two years to London and the South-East, the areas with the worst problems, with help also to improve the management of empty properties by councils and housing associations. But I insisted that whatever Government did to help, there must be a stick as well as a carrot. Crowds of drunken, dirty, often abusive and sometimes violent men must not be allowed to turn central areas of the capital into no-go zones for ordinary citizens. The police must disperse them and prevent their coming back once it was clear that accommodation was available. Unfortunately, there was a persistent tendency in polite circles to consider all the 'roofless' as victims of middle-class society, rather than middle-class society as victim of the 'roofless'.

At the end of July 1990 I asked Chris Patten and Michael Spicer, the Housing minister, to come in and discuss with me the whole of our housing policy – both about where we stood on existing initiatives and where we should go from here. I pinpointed three specific areas – what to do about improving the condition of council estates, whether to extend 'flexi-ownership' (or 'Rents to Mortgages') in England, and the timetable for getting 'roofless' people off the streets and into decent accommodation. In September Chris Patten duly submitted a paper containing his latest thinking. It was immediately clear to me that there were some important differences between his – or more accurately the DoE's – approach and mine; this was confirmed when he and Michael Spicer came in to see me later that month.

The extension of home ownership over the last decade had been one of the Government's greatest successes. It had (in England) risen from 57 to 68 per cent of the housing stock. 'Right to Buy' sales were still running at about 80,000 a year. Councils had almost completely stopped building new houses and were now concentrating on renovation, a trend which would be accelerated by the new housing finance system. Nine councils had transferred all or part of their housing stock to housing associations – though not in the major urban areas. What was clear, however, was that the DoE saw all this as raising more problems than it solved. In their view – something, indeed, which never seemed to alter – there was a 'housing shortage' which required the public sector to provide more new low-cost homes to meet the 'demand' from a growing number of households. Consequently, measures to increase home ownership – such as the 'flexi-ownership' proposal which would be particularly attractive to poorer families – were considered undesirable because they would reduce the supply of cheap local authority housing to rent. This analysis failed to grasp that selling a house to a tenant reduced the demand for as well as the supply of rented housing and that more home ownership – even partial ownership with a small equity stake – would make even quite bad estates that much more tolerable, as the pride of ownership improved the neighbourhood. More seriously, it also assumed that the 'demand' for housing was finite, which was not true if housing was subsidized. Indeed, perverse incentives were operating to encourage the break up of large households and the formation of new smaller ones, for instance in the treatment of the housing needs of unmarried pregnant mothers. To analyse demand and supply without considering the effect of price was a perfect prescription for policy failure.

The other difference of analysis lay in our opposing views of the role of local authorities. The DoE envisaged the main thrust of renovation coming from the extension of the Estate Action programme – which worked through local authorities – under which money was provided to improve the worst estates. Many of these individual schemes were good and imaginative. Indeed, I went further than the DoE in believing that the design of estates was crucial to their success and to reducing the amount of crime. I was a great admirer of the work of Professor Alice Coleman in this area and I had her made an adviser to the DoE, to their dismay. But what I did not believe was that local authorities should be the main agents for improvement. My Policy Unit was working on an interesting alternative route which would have combined a new QUANGO – at arm's length from the DoE and not in collusion with the local authorities – which would have backed 'Community Housing Trusts'. The latter were schemes which we envisaged would combine public and private investment to upgrade the infrastructure of the estate, give residents an equity stake in their homes and under which the estates would be managed by a commercial company. It would thus be a different route to the objective for which HATs had been created, but this time bringing in private enterprise from the start and giving residents a direct financial stake in its success.

The September 1990 discussion with Chris Patten and Michael Spicer was not an inspiring one. Michael was keen to concentrate on new measures to revive the private rented sector. I agreed with him on this, but I thought that in the short term it was more important to tackle the problems of public sector housing. Chris, I suspect, thought that the best way of doing this was simply to build more public sector houses. In any case, he seemed content to work within the present local authority dominated framework. After the meeting I had a discussion with my advisers and penned a personal minute to Chris Patten in which I noted my disappointment. I added:

> I am not persuaded that we are yet being sufficiently bold in carrying forward promising and practical policy initiatives in the short term; nor have we yet explored with the necessary thoroughness and vision the full range of policy options for the longer term.

I drew particular attention to the importance of extending home ownership through the 'Right to Buy', 'Rents to Mortgages' and homesteading – providing people with the money to renovate and then become the owners of derelict properties. I reaffirmed that I wanted to get local authorities out of managing and owning housing. It was clear to me that we must now get back to the kind of fundamental policy thinking which Nick Ridley – now no longer a member of the Government – had once supplied. I said that I was going to call in outside experts and businessmen to talk through all these issues at a dinner which Chris would, of course, attend; but I had left No. 10 before the planned dinner could take place. The inertia of the DoE had won out in the end.

REFORMING THE NATIONAL HEALTH SERVICE (NHS)

Housing, like Education, had been at the top of the list for reform in 1987. But I had reserved Health for detailed consideration later. I believed that the NHS was a service of which we could genuinely be proud. It delivered a high quality of care – especially when it came to acute illnesses – and at a reasonably modest unit cost, at least compared with some insurance-based systems. Yet there were large and on the face of it unjustifiable differences between performance in one area and another. Consequently, I was much more reluctant to envisage *fundamental* changes than I was in the nation's schools. Although I wanted to see a flourishing private sector of health alongside the National Health Service, I always regarded the NHS and its basic principles as a fixed point in our policies. And so, whereas I felt under no obligation to defend the performance of our schools when criticism was made, I peppered my speeches and interviews with the figures for extra doctors, dentists and midwives, patients treated, operations performed and new hospitals built. I felt that on this record we ought to be able to stand our ground.

Some of the political difficulties we faced on the Health Service could be put down to exploitation of hard cases by Opposition politicians and the press. But there was, of course, more to it than that. There was bound to be a potentially limitless demand for health care (in the broadest sense) for as long as it was provided free at the point of delivery. The number of elderly people – the group who made greatest call on the NHS – was increasing and this added to the pressure. Advances in medicine opened up the possibility of – and demand for – new and often expensive forms of treatment.

In significant ways, the NHS lacked the right economic signals to respond to these pressures. Dedicated its staff generally were; cost conscious they were not. Indeed, there was no reason why doctors, nurses or patients should be in a monolithic state-provided system. Moreover, although people who were seriously ill could usually rely on first-class treatment, in other ways there was too little sensitivity to the preferences and convenience of patients.

If one were to recreate the National Health Service, starting from fundamentals, one would have allowed for a bigger private sector – both at the level of general practitioners (GPs) and in the provision of hospitals; and one would have given much closer consideration to additional sources of finance for health, apart from general taxation. But we were not faced by an empty slate. The NHS was a huge organization which inspired at least as much affection as exasperation, whose emergency services reassured even those who hoped they would not have to use them, and whose basic structure was felt by most people to be sound. Any reforms must not undermine public confidence.

I had had several long-range discussions with Norman Fowler, then Secretary of State at the DHSS, in the summer and autumn of 1986 about the future of the National Health Service. It was a time of renewed interest in the economics of health care. Professor Alain Enthoven of Stanford University had been advancing ideas about creating an internal market in the NHS, whereby market disciplines would be applied even though a full-scale free market would not. Some of the think-tanks were refining these concepts. So there was much to talk about. Norman provided a paper which I discussed with him and others at the end of January 1987. The objective of reform, which we even now distinguished as central, was that we should work towards a new way of allocating money within the NHS, so that hospitals treating more patients received more income. There also needed to be a closer, clearer connection between the demand for health care, its cost and the method for paying for it. We discussed whether the NHS might be funded by a 'health stamp' rather than through general taxation. Yet these were very theoretical debates. I did not believe that we were yet in a position to advance significant proposals for the manifesto. I was not even sure that we would be able to do so at an early stage in the next Parliament. Even the possibility of a Royal Commission – not a device which I would generally have preferred but one which had been used by the previous Labour Government in considering the Health Service – held some attractions for me.

Norman Fowler was much better at publicly defending the NHS than he would have been at reforming it. But his successor, John

Moore, was very keen to have a fundamental review. John and I had our first general discussion on the subject at the end of July 1987. At this stage I still wanted him to concentrate on trying to ensure better value for money from the existing system. But as the year went on it became clear to me also that we needed to have a proper long-term review. During the winter of 1987–8 the press began serving up horror stories about the NHS on a daily basis. I asked for a note from the DHSS on where the extra money the Government had provided was actually going. Instead, I received a report on all of the extra pressures which the NHS was facing – not at all the same thing. I said that the DHSS must make a real effort to respond quickly to the attacks on our record and the performance of the NHS. After all, we had increased real spending on the NHS by 40 per cent in less than a decade.

But the pressure to provide more money for the Health Service was proving all but irresistible. Many of the District Health Authorities (DHAs)* which ran the hospitals overspent in the first half of the year and then cut back by closing wards and postponing operations. They promptly blamed us, publicizing the sad cases of patients whose operations had been postponed, or, in the ghoulish phrase used among doctors, 'shroud waving'. It seemed that the NHS had become a bottomless financial pit. If more money had to be provided, I was determined that there must at least be strings attached – and the best way those strings could be woven together was in the form of a full scale NHS review.

There was another strong reason for favouring a review at this time. There was good evidence that public opinion accepted that the NHS's problems went far deeper than a need for more cash. Many of our critics in the press admitted as much. If we acted quickly we could take the initiative, put reforms in place and see benefits flowing from them before the next election.

There was a setback, however, before the review had even been decided on. John Moore fell seriously ill with pneumonia in November, almost collapsing during a meeting at No. 10. With characteristic gallantry, John insisted on returning to work as soon as he could – in

* The Department of Health and Social Security (later Health alone) was responsible for strategic planning of health care in England and Wales. Below it are the Regional Health Authorities (RHAs) responsible for a number of special services, major capital projects and regional planning, and below them are District Health Authorities, whose functions are discussed below. General practitioners, dentists, pharmacists, and opticians are the responsibility of separate bodies, now known as Family Health Service Authorities. In Scotland there is a single tier of Health Boards under the Scottish Office.

my view too soon. Not fully recovered, he could never bring enough energy to bear on the complex and arduous process of reform and produced several below par performances in the Commons. The tragedy of this was that his ideas for reform were in general the right ones, and indeed he deserves much more of the credit for the final package than he has ever been given.

I made the final decision to go ahead with a Health review at the end of January 1988: we would set up a ministerial group, which I would chair. I made it clear from the start that medical care should continue to be readily available to all who needed it and free at the point of consumption. The review would seek to reform the administrative structure of the NHS so that the best of intentions could become the best of practice. With this in mind I set out four principles which should inform its work. First, there must be a high standard of medical care available to all, regardless of income. Second, the arrangements agreed must be such as to give the users of health services, whether in the private or the public sectors, the greatest possible choice. Third, any changes must be made in such a way that they led to genuine improvements in health care, not just to higher incomes for those working in the Health Service. Fourth, responsibility, whether for medical decisions or for budgets, should be exercised at the lowest appropriate level closest to the patient.

The ministerial group met first in February. John Moore and Tony Newton represented the DHSS with Nigel Lawson and John Major for the Treasury, working with officials and advisers. Twelve background papers were commissioned covering consultants' contracts, financial information, efficiency audit, waiting times and the scope for increased charging. The Treasury representatives were especially keen on increasing and extending charges throughout the NHS. This would have discredited any other proposals for reform and ditched the review. I stamped firmly on it. Otherwise, the danger quickly appeared that we had too much information before us on secondary matters and too little about the principles of reform. Accordingly, I asked John Moore for a paper on the long-term options for the NHS for my next meeting. This duly arrived in mid-March and set out the very differing routes along which we might go.

For intellectual completeness all such reviews list virtually every conceivable bright idea for reform. This contained, if I recall aright, about eighteen. But the serious possibilities boiled down to two broad approaches in John Moore's paper. On the one hand we could attempt to reform the way the NHS was financed, perhaps by wholly replacing the existing tax-based system with insurance or, less radically, by providing tax incentives to individuals who wished to take out cover privately. There were several possible models. On the other hand, we could concentrate on reforming the structure of the NHS, leaving the existing system of finance more or less unchanged. Or we could seek to combine changes of both kinds.

I decided early in the review that the emphasis should be on changing the structure of the NHS rather than its finance. There was, admittedly, some attraction in the idea of funding the NHS by national insurance or an hypothecated tax, which would have brought home to people the true cost of health care and, under some models, allowed them to contract out of certain state services if they chose. In the early stages John Moore and the DHSS strongly favoured such a contracted out, hypothecated tax model for the not very mysterious reason that it would have guaranteed them a large, stable and increasing income for the DHSS. In effect, the DHSS would have contracted out of the annual public spending round. It was a real mystery, however, why the Treasury seemed to smile on such an approach in the early stages. If we rule out genuine disinterested intellectual curiosity, perhaps unfairly, the Treasury's motive may have been to strike an alliance with the DHSS in order to get control of the review and curb any radicalism of which it disapproved. It could then abandon its apparent support for the hypothecated tax – which indeed is exactly what it did a month or two into the review. We decided during the summer that further work on the finance side should concentrate on the possibility of tax reliefs for private health insurance premiums paid by the elderly and incentives to boost company health insurance schemes.*

On the other side of the equation – reforming the structure of the NHS – two possibilities seemed to have most appeal. The first was the possible setting-up of 'Local Health Funds' (LHFs). These were essentially a variant on the American idea of Health Maintenance Organizations (HMOs). People would be free to decide to which LHF they subscribed. LHFs would offer comprehensive health care services for their subscribers – whether provided by the LHF itself, purchased from other LHFs, or purchased from independent suppliers. The advantage of this system – which was also claimed for the American HMOs – was that it had built-in incentives for efficiency and so for keeping down the costs which would otherwise escalate as they had

* We also looked briefly at the idea of a national lottery to help fund the NHS. But while I saw some value in local lotteries to help the voluntary sector raise small amounts for particular projects, I did not like a National Health lottery because I did not think that the Government should encourage more gambling, let alone link it to people's health.

in some health insurance systems. What was not so clear was whether if they were public sector bodies there would be any obvious advantage over a reformed structure of the DHAs.

So I was impressed by a suggestion in John's paper that we should make NHS hospitals self-governing and independent of DHA control. This was a proposal – somewhat more ambitious than that which we finally adopted – by which all hospitals would (perhaps with limited exceptions) be contracted out individually or in groups through charities, privatization or management buy-outs, or perhaps leased to operating companies formed by the staff. This would loosen the excessively rigid control of the hospital service from the centre and introduce greater diversity in the provision of health care. But, most important, it would create a clear distinction between buyers and providers. The DHAs would cease to be involved in the provision of health care and would become buyers, placing contracts with the most efficient hospitals to provide care for their patients.

This buyer/provider distinction was designed to eliminate the worst features of the existing system: the absence of incentives to improve performance and indeed of simple information. The crudity of this system becomes clear when one realizes that there was at that time virtually no information about costs within the NHS. We had already begun to remedy this. But when I asked the DHSS at one review meeting how long it would be before we had a fully working information flow and was told six years, I exploded involuntarily: 'Good heavens! We won the Second World War in six years!'

Within the NHS money was allocated from regions to districts and then to hospitals by complicated formulas based on theoretical measures of need. A hospital which treated more patients received no extra money for doing so; in fact it would be likely to spend over budget and be forced to cut services. The financial mechanism for reimbursing DHAs when they treated patients from other areas was to adjust their future spending allocations several years after the event – a hopelessly unresponsive system. But with DHAs acting as buyers money could follow the patient and patients from one area treated in another would be paid for straight away. Hospitals treating more patients would generate a higher income and thus improve their services rather than having to cut back. The resulting competition between hospitals – both within the NHS and between the public and private sectors – would increase efficiency and benefit patients.

I held two seminars on the NHS at Chequers – one in March with doctors and the other in April with administrators – to brief myself more fully. Then in May we began our next round of discussions with papers from John Moore and Nigel Lawson.

Nigel took a critical view of John Moore's ideas. By now, the Treasury had become thoroughly alarmed that opening up the existing NHS structure might lead to much higher public expenditure. Despite apparent Treasury interest earlier in the idea of an 'internal market', at the end of May Nigel sent me a paper questioning the whole direction of our thinking. John Major followed up the attack with a proposal for a system of 'top-slicing' by which the existing system of allocating funds to health authorities would continue, but the extra element provided for growth in the health budget each year would be held back ('top-sliced') and allocated separately to hospitals which fulfilled performance targets set down from the centre. This was presented as a more practical and immediate way of realizing the objective of 'money following the patient'. It was, of course, nothing of the sort. Relative to the overall hospital budget the amount of money paid in relation to performance would have been small. Central control of the hospital service would if anything have been increased. And there would have been no attempt to separate buyers from providers – in the short term at any rate – and thus no real provision to make money follow the patient. In short, a characteristic Treasury device to assert its central control of spending and disguise it as extending consumer choice.

In the face of these challenges John Moore did not defend his approach very robustly and I too began to doubt whether it had been properly thought through. We had a particularly difficult meeting on Wednesday 25 May which ended with a decision to commission further work on 'top-slicing'. Meanwhile, the Treasury did not have it all their own way. I asked them for a paper on possible new tax incentives for the private sector – an idea which Nigel fiercely opposed.

Nigel's objection to tax relief for private medical insurance was essentially twofold. First, he was – as I have said earlier – a convinced fiscal purist. Tax reliefs in his view distorted the system and should be eroded and if possible removed. Second, he argued that tax relief for private health insurance would in many cases help those who could already afford private cover and so fail to deliver a net increase in private sector provision. In those cases where it did provide an incentive, it would increase the demand for health care, but without corresponding efforts to improve supply the result would just be higher prices. Neither of these objections was trivial – though taken to its logical conclusion the Treasury position implied that we should have been trying to discourage the growth in private sector provision that was already taking place. In any case, both objections missed the point that unless we achieved a growth in private sector health care, which had been slow over the past few years, all the extra demands would fail to be met by the NHS. In the long term it would be impossible to resist that pressure and public expenditure would have to rise much further than it otherwise would. I was not arguing for across the board tax relief for private health insurance premiums – though in principle that would be justified – but rather for a targetted measure. If we could encourage people over sixty to maintain the health insurance which they had subscribed to before their retirement, that would reduce the demand on the NHS from the limited group which put most pressure on its services.

Nor, of course, were we neglecting the 'supply side'. The whole approach we were taking in the review was designed to remove obstacles to supply. And in addition the review was considering a significant increase in the number of consultants' posts, which would have an impact on the private sector as well as the NHS. We had further plans to tackle restrictive practices and other inefficiencies in the medical profession, directing the system of merit awards more to merit and less to retirement bonuses, and we planned the general introduction of 'medical audit'.*

Nigel fought hard even against these limited tax reliefs but I got it through with John Moore's help in the first part of July. In other areas I was less happy. The DHSS had been shaken by the Treasury's criticisms and responded by seeking to obtain Treasury support for their proposals at a formative stage before they presented the review. This gave the Treasury an effective power of veto. Accordingly, the DHSS put forward, with Treasury agreement, a much more evolutionary approach. Though money following the patient and self-governing hospitals remained goals of policy, they were relegated to the indefinite future and 'top-slicing' took centre stage in the short term. (Indeed, this idea staggered on, ever more feebly, through almost the entire length of the review. But it failed in its purpose of diverting us from a genuine system of money following the patient, and never made its way into the white paper.)

I had no objection, in principle, to an evolutionary approach to the introduction of self-governing hospitals. We already had a model from our education reforms: hospitals could opt out of DHA control while remaining within the NHS, just as grant-maintained schools opted out of local authority control while remaining in the state sector. But

* 'Medical audit' is a process by which the quality of medical care provided by individual doctors is assessed by their peers.

I was suspicious of the distinction that was emerging between short- and long-term changes, generally worried about the slow pace of the review and thought we were losing our way.

What made me uneasy was that my Policy Unit – which had from the first championed the three reforms of the buyer/provider distinction, money following the patient and independent hospital trusts – presented me with two worrying criticisms. First, we were in danger of letting these ideas be overwhelmed by Treasury considerations of short-term cost control. Second, the reforms under discussion, while vital, extended choice to the doctor and to health service managers but not to the patient who would continue to be the dependant of a locally monopolistic DHA. What was needed to remedy this was some variant of the old idea of the GP as budget holder. In the Policy Unit's version, the GP would, like the hospital, be able to opt out of DHA control and make his own arrangements with hospitals for the treatment of his patients. The patient would therefore be able to choose between a GP who held his own budget or one who worked under the DHA. At first, this idea struck me as too radical, but it worried me that we seemed, under Treasury pressure, to be moving away from, rather than towards, radical reforms.

At the end of July 1988 I made the difficult decision to replace John Moore on the review. I took this opportunity to split the unwieldy DHSS into separate Health and Social Security departments, leaving John in charge of the latter and bringing in Ken Clarke as Health Secretary. There can be no question that John had made a very important contribution to the review. The idea of money following the patient, the distinction between buyers and providers and the concept of self-governing hospitals all emerged in the review during his period as Secretary of State. Also he had pushed hard for tax reliefs, which Ken Clarke would not have done. As he was to demonstrate during the short period in which he was my Secretary of State for Education (when he publicly discounted my advocacy of education vouchers), Ken Clarke was a firm believer in state provision. But whatever the philosophical differences between us, Ken's appointment was a useful one. His arrival at the Department of Health undoubtedly helped our deliberations. He was an extremely effective Health minister – tough in dealing with vested interests and trade unions, direct and persuasive in his exposition of government policy.

Ken Clarke now revived the idea which the Policy Unit had been urging: that GPs should be given budgets. In Ken's version GPs would hold budgets to buy from hospitals 'elective acute services' – surgery for non-life-threatening conditions such as hip replacements and cataract operations. These were the services for which the patient had (in theory at least) some choice as to timing, location and consultant and for which GPs could advise between competing providers in the public and private sector. This approach had a number of advantages. It would bring the choice of services nearer to patients and make GPs more responsive to their wishes. It would maintain the traditional freedom of GPs to decide to which hospitals and consultants they wanted to refer their patients. It also improved the prospects for hospitals which had opted to leave DHA control and become self-governing: otherwise it was all too likely that if District Health Authorities were the only buyers they would discriminate against any of their own hospitals which opted out.

Giving GPs budgets of their own also promised to make it possible for the first time to put reasonable limits on their spending – provided we could find ways of having some limit to the number of GPs within the NHS and to how much they spent on drugs, although there was always provision for emergencies. Nevertheless, the Treasury objected to practice budgets, foreseeing the creation of a powerful new lobby for extra health spending, and argued for a more direct way of cash limiting GPs. They also doubted whether all GPs would be able to manage their affairs with sufficient competence and whether many practices would be big enough to cope financially with the unpredictabilities of patient needs. If there were such problems, the patient would suffer.

I myself had initially been cautious and wanted more detail. However, the more closely we examined the concept of having GPs shop around for the best quality and value treatment for their patients, the more fruitful the idea seemed. We decided in the end to proceed again by an 'opting out' mechanism, limiting the option to the larger GP practices but extending the services covered by budgets beyond what Ken had originally proposed to include 'out-patient' services. We also gave opted-out practices an additional budget to cover the cost of prescriptions.

By the autumn of 1988 it was clear to me that the moves to self-governing hospitals and GPs' budgets, the buyer/provider distinction with the DHA as buyer, and money following the patient were the pillars on which the NHS could be transformed in the future. They were the means to provide better and more cost-effective treatment.

A good deal of work had by now been done on the self-governing hospitals. As with our education reforms, we wanted all hospitals to have greater responsibility for their affairs but the self-governing hospitals to be virtually independent within the NHS. I wanted to see the simplest possible procedure for hospitals to change their status and become independent – what I preferred to call 'trust' – hospitals. They should also own their assets, though I agreed with the Treasury that there should be some overall limits on borrowing. It was also important that the system should be got under way soon and that we had a significant number of trust hospitals by the time of the next election. By December we were in the position to start commenting on the first draft of the white paper which would set out our proposals. In January 1989 we discussed proposals for giving a proper management structure to the NHS. Then at the end of the month – after the twenty-fourth ministerial meeting I had chaired on the subject – the white paper was finally published.

Henceforth the provision and financing of health care were to be separated, with money following the patient. The old, overelaborate and distorting RAWP (Resource Allocation Working Party) funding system would be ended and replaced by a new system based on population, weighted for age and health, with some special provision for London which had its own problems. Hospitals would be free to opt out of District Health Authority control to become self-governing trusts, funded from general taxation, free to settle the pay and conditions of staff and able to sell their services in the public and private sectors. GPs in large practices would have the opportunity to hold their own NHS budgets. The remit of the independent Audit Commission would now be extended to include the NHS. There would be tax relief for the over-60s on private health insurance premiums. Throughout the system, more powers would be devolved to local hospital management.

The white paper proposals essentially simulated within the NHS as many as possible of the advantages which the private sector and market choice offered but without privatization, without large-scale extra charging and without going against those basic principles which I had set down just before Christmas 1987 as essential to a satisfactory result. But there was an outcry from the British Medical Association, health trade unions and the Opposition, based squarely on a deliberate and self-interested distortion of what we were doing. In the face of this campaign of misinformation Ken Clarke was the best possible advocate we would have. Not being a right-winger himself, he was unlikely to talk the kind of free-market language which might alarm the general public and play into the hands of the trade unions. But he had the energy and enthusiasm to argue, explain and defend what we were doing night after night on television.

What I was less convinced about, however, was whether Ken Clarke and the Department of Health had really thought through the detailed implementation of what we were doing and foreseen the transitional difficulties which might arise as we moved from one system of finance and organization to another. David Wolfson and others doubted whether District Health Authorities and hospitals had the information technology, accounting systems and general administrative expertise required to cope with the changes. Clearly, if the information on the flows of patients between districts and the costs of their treatment were inaccurate the consequences for budgets could be horrendous. I had papers prepared for me on this and arranged for a presentation from the Department of Health in June 1990, which I did not find very reassuring. With all the political problems which the community charge was causing, we could not afford to run the risk of disruption in London and the possible closure of hospital wards because the service was not capable of managing in the new more competitive environment. In the end, I decided against slowing down the reforms, while urging that the closest attention should be paid to what was happening in London.

In their different ways, the white paper reforms will lead to a fundamental change in the culture of the NHS to the benefit of patients, taxpayers and those who work in the service. By the time I left office the results were starting to come through. Fifty-seven hospitals were in the process of becoming trusts. Moreover, the political climate was changing. The stridency of the BMA's campaigns against our reforms was leading to a backlash among moderate doctors. The Labour Party had been put on the defensive and had begun themselves to talk about the need for reforms, though not of course ours.

I was determined to build on what had been achieved. I had my Policy Unit working on further proposals. We were considering the possible further encouragement of private health insurance through tax reliefs, structural reforms of the NHS to cut bureaucracy, more contracting-out of NHS ancillary services and – most far reaching – the introduction of a measure whereby anyone who waited more than a specified time for certain sorts of operation would be given a credit from their District Health Authority to be used for treatment either elsewhere within the NHS or in the private sector. The health debate was moving on and – for the first time in my lifetime – it was the Right which was winning it.

THATCHERISM REBUFFED – THE CASE OF SCOTLAND

In Education, Housing and Health the common themes of my policies were the extension of choice, the dispersal of power and the encouragement of responsibility. This was the application of a philosophy not just an administrative programme. Though there were teething troubles and mistakes along the way, this approach was successful: it was also popular. Indeed, if it had not been the Conservative Party would have lost the three general elections it fought under my leadership, not won them. But there were regional exceptions, most notably Scotland. There was no Tartan Thatcherite revolution.

That might seem strange. For Scotland in the eighteenth century was the home of the very same Scottish Enlightenment which produced Adam Smith, the greatest exponent of free enterprise economics till Hayek and Friedman. It had been a country humming with science, invention and enterprise – a theme to which I used time and again to return in my Scottish speeches. But on top of decline in Scotland's heavy industry came socialism – intended as cure, but itself developing quite new strains of social and economic disease, not least militant trade unionism. Only in the 1980s did things really begin to change for the better as Britain's transformed reputation started to attract foreign – often high technology – companies to Scotland and Edinburgh became a prosperous financial centre. Earlier, private enterprise had developed a prosperous and thriving oil industry. Even then, jobs in uncompetitive industry continued to be shed and unemployment remained higher than in England.

The fortunes of Scottish Toryism had declined in line with these long-term economic difficulties. So whereas in 1955 Conservative candidates took just over 50 per cent of the vote, in 1987 we were down to 24 per cent. And this reflected short-term as well as long-term economic conditions. Unemployment in Scotland had only started to fall four months before the 1987 general election – there was still too little economic confidence to start a recovery for the Scottish Tories.

There were now only ten Conservative MPs north of the border and this presented real difficulties in finding enough Tory back-benchers to take part in the House of Commons Select Committee monitoring the Scottish Office, which consequently could not be set up at all during the 1987 Parliament given that there were the ministries of the Scottish Office to fill. The real question now was whether the falling unemployment and economic recovery taking place would of themselves be sufficient to revive the Conservative Party's fortunes in Scotland. I never believed that they would and this indeed proved to be the case. So if it was not all a matter of economics, what was wrong?

It was certainly possible – even plausible – to point to changes in social and religious attitudes to explain this decline. The old Glaswegian Orange foundations of Unionist support which had in earlier decades been so important had irreparably crumbled. Moreover, whereas in the past it might have been possible for the Conservatives in Scotland to rely on a mixture of deference, tradition and paternalism to see them through, this was just no longer an option – and none the worse for that. But that did not explain why Scotland was so different from England now, that is after eight years of Tory government.

Although there was a much better economic record in Scotland than was usually admitted, the statistics which were most revealing were those which showed that about half Scotland's population were living in highly subsidized local authority housing compared with about a quarter in England. In short the conditions of dependency were strongly present. And the conditions of dependency are conditions for socialism. In Scotland the Left still formed its own establishment which intruders challenged at their peril. The Labour Party and the trade unions had a powerful grip on office and influence at every level – from the local authorities, through QUANGOs, right into the Scottish Office. In practice, the Left, not the Right, had held on to the levers of patronage. It had its arguments voiced by both Catholic and Protestant churches in Scotland and parrotted in the media – hardly any Scottish newspapers supported us and the electronic media were largely hostile.

The reaction of Scottish Office ministers to these difficulties had cumulatively worsened the problem. Feeling isolated and vulnerable in the face of so much left-wing hostility, they regularly portrayed themselves as standing up for Scotland against me and the parsimony of Whitehall. Yielding to this temptation brought instant gratification but long-term grief. For in adopting this tactic they increased the underlying Scottish antipathy to the Conservative Party and indeed the Union. The pride of the Scottish Office – whose very structure added a layer of bureaucracy, standing in the way of the reforms which were paying such dividends in England – was that public expenditure per head in Scotland was far higher than in England. But they never seemed to grasp – as their opponents certainly did – that if public spending was a 'good thing' there should be lots more of it. That effectively conceded the fundamental argument to the socialists. But the truth was that more public spending in a dependency culture had not solved Scotland's problems, but added to them.

There was only one answer. If a small state, low taxes, less intervention and more choice were right then we should argue for them and do so without apology. There must also be the same drive to implement this programme north as south of the border.

George Younger (who for all his decency and common sense was very much of the paternalist school of Scottish Tory politician) left the Scottish Office in 1986 to become Secretary of State for Defence. Malcolm Rifkind was the heir apparent. But I appointed him with mixed feelings. He had been a passionate supporter of Scottish devolution when we were in Opposition. He was one of the Party's most brilliant and persuasive debaters. No one could doubt his intellect or his grasp of ideas. Unfortunately he was as sensitive and highly strung as he was eloquent. His judgement was erratic and his behaviour unpredictable. Nor did he implement the radical Thatcherite approach he publicly espoused; for espouse it he certainly did. After the 1987 election Malcolm made speeches up and down Scotland attacking dependency and extolling enterprise. But as political pressures mounted he changed his tune.

The real powerhouse for Thatcherism at the Scottish Office was Michael Forsyth, whom I appointed a Parliamentary Under-Secretary in 1987, with responsibility for Scottish Education and Health. It was Michael, Brian Griffiths and I who were convinced of the need to intervene to protect Paisley Grammar School – a popular school of high academic standards and traditional ethos – which (doubtless for these very reasons) the socialist Strathclyde Council wanted to close. I was moved by the appeals I received from the staff and parents. I also saw this as a test case. We must show that we were not prepared to see the Scottish left-wing establishment lord it over people it was our duty to protect. I sent a personal minute to Malcolm Rifkind on Friday 22 January 1988 registering the strength of my views. As a result of my intervention regulations were laid so that where a Scottish education authority proposed to close, change the site or vary the catchment area of any school where the number of pupils at the school was greater than 80 per cent of its capacity, the proposal should be referred to the Secretary of State for Scotland.

I also had to take a very firm line on the issue of whether Scottish schools should be allowed to opt out of local authority control, like their English counterparts. Before this could happen in Scotland, school boards in which parents had a powerful role had to be substituted for the direct local authority control which had previously existed. But once this had been done and schools had effective governing bodies there was no reason to prevent their seeking grant-maintained status. Yet Malcolm resisted this. After receiving advice from the parliamentary business managers about the pressure on the legislative timetable, I reluctantly agreed that opting out provisions should not be included in his first Education Bill. But I pressed that such a provision should be included in the next session's Scottish Education Bill. Malcolm claimed that there was not sufficient demand for opting out in Scotland. However, from my postbag and Brian Griffiths's enquiries I knew otherwise. I insisted and had my way. In 1989 legislation was accordingly introduced to bring the opportunity of grant-maintained schools to Scotland.

Whatever the obstruction from Malcolm Rifkind, Michael Forsyth and I were not alone in believing that real changes to reduce the role of the state in Scotland were both necessary and possible. In housing, for example, 'Scottish Homes' – established in May 1989 – developed attractive and imaginative schemes to provide more choice for public sector tenants and to renovate run-down houses, selling some and letting others. Indeed, the organization generally proved more innovative than DoE efforts through Estate Action programmes in England. As regards the Government's role in industry, Bill Hughes – Chairman of the Scottish CBI whom I later appointed Deputy Chairman of the Scottish Conservative Party – devised 'Scottish Enterprise', which mobilized private sector business to take over the functions of the old, more interventionist, Scottish Development Agency and other bodies.

I became convinced, however, that it was only by having someone who shared my commitment to fundamental change in Scotland spearheading the Party's efforts there that real progress would be made. I did not want to move Malcolm Rifkind who, for better or worse, had established himself as a major political force. But the Chairman of the Scottish Conservative Party, Sir James (now Lord) Goold, for whose loyalty and dependability I always had the highest regard, had told me that he wished to stand down when I had found a suitable successor. Both he and I believed that that successor was now available in the form of Michael Forsyth.

Malcolm, however, was strongly opposed to this. I discussed the matter with him in January 1989. He went away to think of his own preferred candidates and decided to press for the appointment of Professor Ross Harper, shortly to be chosen as President of the Scottish Conservative and Unionist Association, the top post of the voluntary party in Scotland. Malcolm repeatedly argued that Michael Forsyth could not be spared from his ministerial duties in the Scottish Office.

I was not satisfied by this and insisted that Michael should become Chairman. He could run his ministerial duties in parallel, as others had done before him. So in July I overrode Malcolm Rifkind's objections and appointed Michael Chairman and Bill Hughes his Deputy.

Michael was the only Conservative politician in Scotland whom the Labour Party really feared. He was, therefore, bound to be the object of unrelenting attack in the left-wing media. But it was the opposition he faced from Conservatives which was to prove his undoing. The personal friction between him and Malcolm became steadily worse. A full-scale campaign of vilification was launched by Michael's enemies and the Scottish press was full of talk of splits and factions.

Malcolm Rifkind now also fell back with a vengeance on the old counter-productive tactic of proving his Scottish virility by posturing as Scotland's defender against Thatcherism. In March 1990, John Major delivered his first budget. Coming on the eve of the introduction of the community charge in England and Wales, it doubled from £8,000 to £16,000 the amount of savings a person could have and still not lose entitlement to community charge benefit. This reflected the argument – with which I had much sympathy – that too great a squeeze was being exerted on those who had been prudent enough to put aside some savings. Malcolm Rifkind raised no objection when this was announced to Cabinet before the budget. Nor did he make any special demands for Scotland. But the announcement provoked an outcry in Scotland where the community charge had been introduced one year earlier and where the critics accordingly wanted the community charge benefit change backdated. Under fire, Malcolm did not stand by John Major's decision. He now entered into heavily leaked discussions with me and John to have the change made retrospective for Scotland. Very reluctantly, I agreed that a special payment should be made to those concerned in Scotland from *within* the Scottish Office budget. Having damaged the reception of John's skilfully conceived budget, Malcolm then went on to revel publicly in Scotland in his 'victory'. It was suggested that he had only secured these changes by threatening resignation. He also told the press that I had fallen into line with his better judgement. This childish behaviour did the Conservative cause in Scotland great harm and prompted letters of protest from outraged Scottish Tories.

In May he entered into a public row with the British Steel Corporation over the future of the Ravenscraig steel plant, which should have been a matter for BSC to decide on commercial grounds, and even went so far – I was told – as to ask Scottish Conservative back-benchers to vote for a Labour Early Day Motion in the House of Commons on the subject. At the Scottish Party Conference the week before Malcolm also made some delphic remarks which were interpreted as suggesting that devolution was back on the agenda in Scotland. He was reverting to type.

The pressure on me to get rid of Michael Forsyth mounted during the summer of 1990. He himself was becoming depressed at the constant difficulties with Malcolm Rifkind and the unrelenting campaign pursued against him and his supporters. In August my office was flooded with letters from friends and opponents of Michael, obviously being geared up by their respective factions. By now it was clear that the opposition to him had enlisted the Scottish Tory Party establishment including Willie Whitelaw, George Younger and the senior members of the voluntary party. I had my own troubles. It had been a brave attempt to bring the Scottish Tory Party into the latter half of the twentieth century and offer leadership and vision to people who had become all too used to losing or – even worse – winning on their opponents' terms. In October 1990 I promoted Michael Forsyth to be a Minister of State at the Scottish Office with extended duties and replaced him as Chairman with (Lord) Russell Sanderson who relinquished his ministerial job at the Scottish Office. His appointment was taken as a sign that the attempt to extend Thatcherism to Scotland had come to an end. This combination of the Left and the traditional establishment of the Party to rebuff Thatcherism in Scotland was a prelude to the formation of the same alliance to oust me as leader of the Conservative Party a few weeks later – although I did not know it at the time.

The balance sheet of Thatcherism in Scotland is a lopsided one: economically positive but politically negative. After a decade of Thatcherism, Scotland had been economically transformed for the better. People moved in large numbers from the older declining industries such as steel and shipbuilding to new industries with a future such as electronics and finance. Almost all the economic statistics – productivity, inward investment, self-employment – showed a marked improvement. As a result, Scottish living standards reached an all-time high, rising by 30 per cent from 1981 to 1989, outperforming most of the English regions.

A slower start was made on reducing dependency and encouraging ownership. As late as 1979 only a third of Scots owned their own home. By the time I had left office this had risen to over half – thanks in part to the 'Right to Buy' scheme. And we had begun to enable still more local authority tenants to become home owners through 'Rents to Mortgages'.

Yet however valuable socially those initiatives were, they had little political impact. The 1992 election showed that the fall in Tory support had been halted; it had yet to be reversed. Some part of this unpopularity must be attributed to the national question on which the Tories are seen as an English party and on which I myself was apparently seen as a quintessential English figure.

About the second point I could – and I can – do nothing. I am what I am and I have no intention of wearing tartan camouflage. Nor do I think that most Scots would like me, or any English politician, the better for doing so. The Tory Party is not, of course, an English party but a Unionist one. If it sometimes seems English to some Scots that is because the Union is inevitably dominated by England by reason of its greater population. The Scots, being an historic nation with a proud past, will inevitably resent some expressions of this fact from time to time. As a nation, they have an undoubted right to national self-determination; thus far they have exercised that right by joining and remaining in the Union. Should they determine on independence no English party or politician would stand in their way, however much we might regret their departure. What the Scots (nor indeed the English) cannot do, however, is to insist upon their own terms for remaining in the Union, regardless of the views of the others. If the rest of the United Kingdom does not favour devolved government, then the Scottish nation may seek to persuade the rest of us of its virtues; it may even succeed in doing so; but it cannot claim devolution as a right of nationhood inside the Union.

It is understandable that when I come out with these kind of hard truths many Scots should resent it. But it has nothing whatever to do with my being English. A lot of Englishmen resent it too.

CHAPTER XXI

Not So Much a Programme, More a Way of Life

Family policy, the Arts, Broadcasting, Science and the Environment

INDIVIDUALS AND COMMUNITIES

The surge of prosperity – most of it soundly based but some of it unsustainable – which occurred from 1986 to 1989 had one paradoxical effect. Deprived for the moment at least of the opportunity to chastise the Government and blame free enterprise capitalism for failing to create jobs and raise living standards, the Left turned their attention to non-economic issues. The idea that the state was the engine of economic progress was discredited – and ever more so as the failures of communism became more widely known. But was the price of capitalist prosperity too high? Was it not resulting in a gross and offensive materialism, traffic congestion and pollution? Were not the attitudes required to get on in Thatcher's Britain causing the weak to be marginalized, homelessness to grow, communities to break down? In short, was not the 'quality of life' being threatened?

I found all this misguided and hypocritical. If socialism had produced economic success those same critics would have been celebrating in the streets. But socialism had failed. And it was the poorer, weaker members of society who had suffered worst as a result of that failure. More than that, however, socialism, in spite of the high-minded rhetoric in which its arguments were framed, had played on the worst aspects of human nature. It had literally demoralized communities and families, offering dependency in place of independence as well as subjecting traditional values to sustained derision. It was a cynical ploy for the Left to start talking as if they were old-fashioned Tories, fighting to preserve decency amid social disintegration.

But nor could the arguments be ignored. Some Conservatives were always tempted to appease the Left's social arguments – just as before

I became leader they had appeased their economic arguments – on the grounds that we ourselves were very nearly as socialist in practice. These were the people who thought that the answer to every criticism was for the state to spend and intervene more. I could not accept this. There was a case for the state to intervene in specific instances – for example to protect children in real danger from malign parents. The state must uphold the law and ensure that criminals were punished – an area in which I was deeply uneasy, for our streets were becoming more not less violent, in spite of large increases in police numbers and prison places. But the root cause of our contemporary social problems – to the extent that these did not reflect the timeless influence and bottomless resources of old-fashioned human wickedness – was that the state had been doing too much. A Conservative social policy had to recognize this. Society was made up of individuals and communities. If individuals were discouraged and communities disorientated by the state stepping in to take decisions which should properly be made by people, families and neighbourhoods then society's problems would grow not diminish.

This belief was what lay behind my remarks in an interview with a woman's magazine – which caused a storm of abuse at the time – about there being 'no such thing as society'. But they never quoted the rest. I went on to say:

> There are individual men and women, and there are families. And no government can do anything except through people, and people must look to themselves first. It's our duty to look after ourselves and then to look after our neighbour.

My meaning, clear at the time but subsequently distorted beyond recognition, was that society was not an abstraction, separate from the men and women who composed it, but a living structure of individuals, families, neighbours and voluntary associations. I expected great things from society in this sense because I believed that as economic wealth grew, individuals and voluntary groups should assume more responsibility for their neighbours' misfortunes. The error to which I was objecting was the confusion of society with the state as the helper of first resort. Whenever I heard people complain that 'society' should not permit some particular misfortune, I would retort, 'And what are you doing about it, then?' Society for me was not an excuse, it was a source of obligation.

I was an individualist in the sense that I believed that individuals are ultimately accountable for their actions and must behave like it.

ABOVE: Visit to the church at Zagorsk during my trip to Russia, 29 March 1987

RIGHT: Meeting the Sakharovs in Moscow, 30 March 1987

LEFT: Inspecting troops in Australia during my visit for the Bicentennial in August 1988

LEFT: Participants at the Tokyo G7 summit in May 1986 – from l-r: Ronald Reagan, self, Brian Mulroney, Yasuhiro Nakasone, François Mitterrand, Helmut Kohl

BELOW: Meeting the late President Ozal of Turkey during my Turkish visit in April 1988

RIGHT: With Prime Minister González in September 1988 during my visit to Spain immediately after the Bruges speech

LEFT: Visiting a market in Poland in November 1988

BELOW: Talking to war veterans at Gallipoli on the 75th Anniversary of the 1915 landings, April 1990

ABOVE: President Gorbachev arriving at Number Ten during his visit to Britain in September 1989

RIGHT: Walking through Gdansk with Lech Walesa during my visit to Poland in 1988

LEFT: With the Emir of Kuwait at Number Ten in October 1990

RIGHT: With Nelson Mandela during his visit to Britain in July 1990

BELOW: With Helmut Kohl during the NATO summit in London in July 1990

RIGHT: With Václav Havel at Number Ten in March 1990

ABOVE: With Boris Yeltsin at Number Ten in April 1990

RIGHT: With President Cossiga of Italy at Number Ten in October 1990, during his state visit to Britain

At the Paris CSCE summit, 20 November 1990

ABOVE: Leaving the ballet at Versailles with George and Barbara Bush

LEFT: The morning of the first ballot

But I always refused to accept that there was some kind of conflict between this kind of individualism and social responsibility. I was reinforced in this view by the writings of conservative thinkers in the United States on the growth of an 'underclass' and the development of a dependency culture. If irresponsible behaviour does not involve penalty of some kind, irresponsibility will for a large number of people become the norm. More important still, the attitudes may be passed on to their children, setting them off in the wrong direction.

I had great regard for the Victorians for many reasons – not least their civic spirit to which the increase in voluntary and charitable societies and the great buildings and endowments of our cities pay eloquent tribute. I never felt uneasy about praising 'Victorian values' or – the phrase I originally used – 'Victorian virtues', not least because they were by no means just Victorian. But the Victorians also had a way of talking which summed up what we were now rediscovering – they distinguished between the 'deserving' and the 'undeserving poor'. Both groups should be given help: but it must be help of very different kinds if public spending is not just going to reinforce the dependency culture. The problem with our welfare state was that – perhaps to some degree inevitably – we had failed to remember that distinction and so we provided the same 'help' to those who had genuinely fallen into difficulties and needed some support till they could get out of them, as to those who had simply lost the will or habit of work and self-improvement. The purpose of help must not be to allow people merely to live a half-life, but to restore their self-discipline and through that their self-esteem.

I was also impressed by the writing of the American theologian and social scientist Michael Novak who put into new and striking language what I had always believed about individuals and communities. Mr Novak stressed the fact that what he called 'democratic capitalism' was a moral and social, not just an economic system, that it encouraged a range of virtues and that it depended upon co-operation not just 'going it alone'. These were important insights which, along with our thinking about the effects of the dependency culture, provided the intellectual basis for my approach to those great questions brought together in political parlance as 'the quality of life'.

THE FAMILY

The fact that the arguments deployed against the kind of economy and society which my policies were designed to foster were muddled and half-baked did not, of course, detract from the fact that there *were* social ills and that in some respects these were becoming more serious. I have mentioned the rise in crime. The Home Office and liberal opinion more generally were inclined to cast doubt on this. Certainly, it was possible to point to similar trends throughout the West and to worse criminality in American cities. It was also arguable that the rise in the number of recorded crimes reflected a greater willingness to report crimes – rape for example – which would previously have not come to the attention of the police. But I was never greatly impressed by arguments which minimized the extent and significance of crime. I shared the view of the general public that more must be done to apprehend and punish those who committed it. I believed that while it was right that those who did not really need to go to prison should be punished in other ways, violent criminals must be given exemplary sentences. In this regard the measure we introduced in which I took greatest satisfaction was the provision in the 1988 Criminal Justice Act which empowered the Attorney-General to appeal against overlenient sentences passed by the Crown Court.

The fact that the level of crime rose in times of recession and of prosperity alike gave the lie to the notion that poverty explained – or even justified – criminal behaviour. Arguably, the opposite might have been true: greater prosperity led to more opportunities to steal. In any case, the rise in violent crime could not in any sense be regarded as an economic phenomenon. Nor could the alarming levels of juvenile delinquency. These had their origins deeper in society.

I became increasingly convinced during the last two or three years of my time in office that, though there were crucially important limits to what politicians could do in this area, we could only get to the roots of crime and much else besides by concentrating on strengthening the traditional family. The statistics told their own story. One in four children were born to unmarried parents. No fewer than one in five children experienced a parental divorce before they were sixteen. Of course, family breakdown and single parenthood did not mean that juvenile delinquency would inevitably follow: grandparents, friends and neighbours can in some circumstances help lone mothers to cope quite well. But all the evidence – statistical and anecdotal – pointed to the breakdown of families as the starting point for a range of social ills of which getting into trouble with the police was only one. Boys who lack the guidance of a father are more likely to suffer social problems of all kinds. Single parents are more likely to live in relative poverty and poorer housing. Children can be traumatized by divorce far more than their parents realize. Children from unstable family backgrounds are more likely to have learning difficulties. They are at greater risk of abuse in the home from men who are not the real father. They are also more likely to run away to our cities and join the ranks of the young homeless where, in turn, they fall prey to all kinds of evil.

The most important – and most difficult – aspect of what needed to be done was to reduce the positive incentives to irresponsible conduct. Young girls were tempted to become pregnant because that brought them a council flat and an income from the state. My advisers and I were considering whether there was some way of providing less attractive – but correspondingly more secure and supervised – housing for these young people. I had seen some excellent hostels of this sort run by the churches. Similarly, young people who ran away from home to sleep on the streets needed help. But I firmly resisted the argument that poverty was the basic cause – rather than the result – of their plight and felt that it was the voluntary bodies which could provide not just hostel places (which were often in surplus) but guidance and friendship of the sort the state never could.*

We were feeling our way towards a new ethos for welfare policy: one comprising the discouragement of state dependency and the encouragement of self-reliance; greater use of voluntary bodies including religious and charitable organizations like the Salvation Army; and, most controversially, built-in incentives towards decent and responsible behaviour. We might then reduce the problem over the next generation rather than increase it, as the last generation had done. But our attempts to rethink welfare along these lines met a number of objections. Some were strictly practical and we had to respect them. Others, though, were rooted in the attitude that it was not for the state to make moral distinctions in its social policy. Indeed, when I raised such points I was sometimes amused to detect ill-concealed expressions of disapproval on the faces of civil servants under the veneer of official politeness.

In spite of all the difficulties, by the time I left office my advisers and I were assembling a package of measures to strengthen the

* For more discussion of 'homelessness' see pp. 603–4.

traditional family whose disintegration was the common source of so much suffering. We had not the slightest illusion that the effects of what could be done would be more than marginal. Nor, in a sense, would I have wanted them to be. For while the stability of the family is a condition for social order and economic progress the independence of the family is also a powerful check on the authority of the state. There are limits beyond which 'family policy' should not seek to go.

That is why I considered it important to encourage voluntary bodies which had the right values and vision, like Mrs Margaret Harrison's 'Homestart', whose six thousand voluntary workers were themselves parents and offered friendship, common sense advice and support in the family home. I preferred if at all possible that direct help should come from someone other than professional social workers. Of course, professionals have a vital role in the most difficult cases – for example, where access to the home has to be gained to prevent tragedy. In recent years, however, some social workers have exaggerated their expertise and magnified their role, in effect substituting themselves for the parents with insufficient cause.

I was also appalled by the way in which men fathered a child and then absconded, leaving the single mother – and the taxpayer – to foot the bill for their irresponsibility and condemning the child to a lower standard of living. I thought it scandalous that only one in three children entitled to receive maintenance actually benefited from regular payments. So – against considerable opposition from Tony Newton, the Social Security Secretary, and from the Lord Chancellor's department – I insisted that a new Child Support Agency be set up, and that maintenance be based not just on the cost of bringing up a child but on that child's right to share in its parents' rising living standards. This was the background to the Child Support Act, 1991.

As for divorce itself, I did not accept that we should follow the Law Commission's recommendation in November 1990 that this should just become a 'process' in which 'fault' was not at issue. In some cases – for example where there is violence – I considered that divorce was not just permissible but unavoidable. Yet I also felt strongly that if all the remaining culpability was removed from marital desertion, divorce would be that much more common.

The question of how best – through the tax and social security system – to support families with children was a vexed one to which I and my advisers were giving much thought when I left office. There was great pressure, which I had to fight hard to resist, to provide tax reliefs or subsidies for child care. This would, of course, have swung the emphasis further towards discouraging mothers from staying at home. I believed that it was possible – as I had – to bring up a family while working, as long as one was willing to make a great effort to organize one's time properly and with some extra help. But I did not believe that it was fair to those mothers who chose to stay at home and bring up their families on the one income to give tax reliefs to those who went out to work and had two incomes.* It always seemed odd to me that the feminists – so keenly sensitive to being patronized by men but without any such sensitivity to the patronage of the state – could not grasp that.

More generally, there was the question of how to treat children within the tax and benefit system. At one extreme were those 'libertarians' who believed that children no more merited recognition within the tax and benefit systems than a consumer durable. At the other were those who would have liked a fully fledged 'natalist policy' to increase the birth rate. I rejected both views. But I accepted the long-standing idea that the tax someone paid on his income should take into account his family responsibilities. This starting point was important in deciding what to do about child benefit. This sum was paid – tax free – to many families whose incomes were such that they did not really need it and was very expensive. But, as I reminded the Treasury on a number of occasions, it had been introduced partly as an equivalent of the (now abolished) child tax allowances, so there was an argument on grounds of fairness that its real value should be sustained. As a compromise we eventually decided in the autumn of 1990 that it should be uprated for the first child but not the others: but this did not settle the larger question of what the future of child support should be. I would have liked to return to a system including child tax allowances, which I believed would have been fairer, clearer and – incidentally – extremely popular. But the fiscal purists in the Treasury were still fighting a strong action against me on this at the time I left Downing Street.

All that family policy can do is to create a framework in which families are encouraged to stay together and provide properly for their children. The wider influences of the media, schools and above all the churches are more powerful than anything government can do. But so much hung on what happened to the structure of the nation's families that only the most myopic libertarian would regard it as outside the purview of the state: for my part, I felt that over the years

* I was, though, content to make one minor adjustment. This was to provide tax relief for workplace nurseries.

the state had done so much harm that the opportunity to do some remedial work was not to be missed.

THE ARTS

Perhaps nowhere were the proper limits of what the state should do more hotly disputed than in the world of the arts. The proponents of subsidies would stress that the state today was only performing the role of generous private patrons of the past, that access to artistic treasures must not depend on personal wealth and – more practically – that every other country subsidized the arts and therefore we must too. Against that – and this was significantly the view of Nick Ridley, the only member of the Government who could really *paint* – it could be argued that no artist had a right to a living from his work and that the market should be left to operate as with any other activity. My own attitude was somewhat different from either of these. I was not convinced that the state should play Maecenas. Artistic talent – let alone artistic genius – is unplanned, unpredictable, eccentrically individual. Regimented, subsidized, owned and determined by the state, it withers. Moreover the 'state' in these cases comes to mean the vested interests of the arts lobby. I wanted to see the private sector raising more money and bringing business acumen and efficiency to bear on the administration of cultural institutions. I wanted to encourage private individuals to give by covenant, not the state to take through taxes. But I was profoundly conscious of how a country's art collections, museums, libraries, operas and orchestras combine with its architecture and monuments to magnify its international standing. It is not just or even mainly a question of revenues from tourism: the public manifestation of a nation's culture is as much a demonstration of its qualities as the size of its GDP is of its energies. Consequently, it mattered to me that culturally as well as economically Britain should be able to hold its head up in comparison with the United States and Europe. And indeed we did. London is one of the world's great centres of culture. We have, in the West End, the most vibrant commercial theatre in the world. We have probably the widest variety of museums of any city, ranging from the intimate and yet magnificent Wallace Collection to the glories of the British Museum. The performing arts, whether theatre, music or opera are represented in astonishing diversity.

But there is always more to be done – if it can be afforded. I certainly did not regret – though from the chorus of complaints about 'cuts' you would not have known it – that central government spending on the arts rose sharply in real terms while I was in Downing Street. Greater stability was provided too: from 1988 the Arts Council budget was set for a three-year period. Government funds were, wherever possible, used to attract private sponsorship for developing existing museums and galleries. For example, in March 1990 we announced the establishment of a new Museums and Galleries Improvement Fund – a joint initiative with the Wolfson Foundation. A succession of budgets included provisions to encourage covenanted giving. The most potentially significant of these was the introduction in October 1990 of a new tax relief for one-off gifts to charities from individuals and companies.

My greatest disappointment was my inability to secure for Britain the magnificent Thyssen Collection. In February 1988 my old friend Sir Peter Smithers wrote to me from Switzerland to tell me that his neighbour, Baron 'Heinie' Thyssen-Bornemisza, was keen to have his collection of Old and Modern Masters come permanently to Britain. Fifty of the Thyssen Collection pictures were on show at the Royal Academy and I had been to see them like so many others – and they were just fabulous. I asked for a report on the full Thyssen Collection and learned that it contained some supreme masterpieces including a Van Eyck *Annunciation*, Dürer's *Christ Among the Doctors* and Holbein's *Henry VIII*, as well as paintings by Carpaccio, Caravaggio, Cézanne, Degas and Van Gogh. I was determined to do all that we could to secure it for Britain. I had been to Portugal in 1984 where I had seen the Gulbenkian Collection which had been offered to Britain in the 1930s but, sadly, was let slip.

The project would have been very costly. We thought that it would require at least £200 million to satisfy the Baron's requirements: but for this we would receive a collection valued at Sotheby's at $1.2 billion. The cost would have had to be met by a combination of public and private funding to go towards the building in which the collection would be housed. It would have caused an outcry from some of the British arts lobby, who understandably thought that such sums would be better spent on them and their favoured projects. But it was worth it.

Nick Ridley and I took charge of the negotiations. Cabinet agreed the allocation of money. The international legal problems were all ironed out. Within a matter of six weeks the formal offer was taken personally by Robin Butler (the Cabinet Secretary) to Baron Thyssen in Switzerland. Alas, the real problem – insuperable as it turned out

– was that it was not clear who precisely had the final say about the disposition of the collection. Nor was it clear what the status was of a loan agreement reached with the Spanish Government to the effect that the collection would go there for a period of years. In the end, it did indeed go to Spain on loan. But I had no regrets about having made the attempt to win it for Britain. It was not only a great treasure but a good investment – in every sense.

BROADCASTING

The world of the media had in common with that of the arts a highly developed sense of its own importance to the life of the nation. But whereas the arts lobby was constantly urging government to do more, the broadcasters were pressing us to do less. Broadcasting was one of a number of areas – the professions such as teaching, medicine and the law were others – in which special pleading by powerful interest groups was disguised as high-minded commitment to some greater good. So anyone who queried, as I did, whether a licence fee – with non-payment subject to criminal sanctions – was the best way to pay for the BBC, was likely to be pilloried as at best philistine and at worst undermining its 'constitutional independence'. Criticism of the broadcasters' decisions to show material which outraged the sense of public decency or played into the hands of terrorists and criminals was always likely to be met with accusations of censorship. Attempts to break the powerful duopoly which the BBC and ITV had achieved – which encouraged restrictive practices, increased costs and kept out talent – were decried as threatening the 'quality of broadcasting'. Some of Britain's television and radio was of very high quality indeed, particularly drama and news. Internationally, it was in a class of its own. But the idea that a small clique of broadcasting professionals always knew what was best and that they should be more or less immune from criticism or competition was not one I could accept. Unfortunately, in the Home Office the broadcasters often found a ready advocate. The irony that a Reithian rhetoric should be used to defend a moral neutrality between terrorism and the forces of law and order, as well as programmes that seemed to many to be scurrilous and offensive, was quite lost.

The notion of 'public service broadcasting' was the kernel of what the broadcasting oligopolists claimed to be defending. Unfortunately, when subject to closer inspection that kernel began rapidly to disintegrate. 'Public service broadcasting' was extremely difficult to define. One element was supposed to be that viewers or listeners in all parts of the country who paid the same licence fee should be able to receive all public service channels – what was described as the concept of 'universality'. More important, though, was the idea that there should be a proper balance of information, education and entertainment offered through a wide range of high quality programmes. More recently, the public service obligation had been extended to cover particular 'minority' programmes. The BBC and the IBA – which regulated the independent television companies – mainly gave effect to this public service obligation by their influence over scheduling.

So much for the – somewhat nebulous and increasingly outdated – theory. The practice was very different. BBC1 and ITV ran programmes that were increasingly indistinguishable from commercial programming in market systems – soap operas, sport, game shows and made-for-TV films. To use Benthamite language, the public broadcasters were claiming the rights of poetry but providing us with pushpin. Good fun perhaps. But did our civilization really depend on it?

Furthermore the duopoly was being undermined by technological developments. Scarcity of available spectrum had previously determined that only a very few channels could be broadcast. But this was changing. It seemed likely that ever higher-frequency parts of the spectrum would be able to be brought into use. Cable television and direct broadcasting by satellite (DBS) also looked likely to transform the possibilities. There was more opportunity for payment – per channel or per programme – by subscription. An entire new world was opening up.

I believed we should take advantage of these technical possibilities to give viewers a far wider choice. This was already happening in countries as diverse as the United States and Luxemburg. Why not in Britain? But this vastly increased potential demand for programmes should not be met from within the existing duopoly. I wanted to see the widest competition among and opportunities for the independent producers – who were themselves virtually a creation of our earlier decision to set up Channel 4 in 1982. I also believed that it would be possible to combine more choice for viewers and more opportunity for producers with standards – both of production and of taste – that were as high as, if not higher than, those under the existing duopoly. To make assurance doubly sure, however, I wanted to establish independent watchdogs to keep standards high by exposing broadcasters to public criticism, complaint and debate.

The Peacock Committee on Broadcasting, which had been set up by Leon Brittan as Home Secretary in March 1985 and reported the following year, provided a good opportunity to look at all these matters once again. I would have liked to find an alternative to the BBC licence fee. One possibility was advertising: Peacock rejected the idea. Willie Whitelaw too was fiercely opposed to it and indeed threatened to resign from the Government if it were introduced. I felt that index-linking the licence fee achieved something of the same purpose – to make the BBC more cost-conscious and business-like. In October 1986 the ministerial committee on broadcasting which I chaired agreed that the BBC licence fee should remain at £58 until April 1988 and then be linked to the RPI until 1991. But I did not drop my long-term reservations about the licence fee as the source of its funding. It was agreed to study whether the licence fee could be replaced by subscription.

At least as important for the future was the need to break the BBC and ITV duopoly over the production of the programmes they showed. My ministerial group agreed that the Government should set a target of 25 per cent of BBC and ITV programmes to be provided by independent producers. But there was a sharp division between those of us like Nigel Lawson and David Young who believed that the BBC and ITV would use every opportunity to resist this and Douglas Hurd and Willie Whitelaw who thought that they could be persuaded without legislation. Douglas was to enter into discussions with the broadcasters and report back. In the end we had to legislate to secure it.

I also insisted, against Home Office resistance, that our 1987 general election manifesto should contain a firm commitment to 'bring forward proposals for stronger and more effective arrangements to reflect [public] concern [about] the display of sex and violence on television'. This produced the Broadcasting Standards Council of which William Rees-Mogg became the very effective chairman and which was put on a statutory basis in the 1989 Broadcasting Act.

After the election there was more time to think about the long-term future of broadcasting. Apart from the opportunities for more channels which technology offered and the continuing discussion about how to achieve the 25 per cent target for independent producers, we needed to consider the future of Channel 4 – which I would have liked to privatize altogether, though Douglas Hurd disagreed – and the still more important matter of how the existing system of allocating ITV franchises should be changed. The Peacock Committee recommended that the system be changed to become more 'transparent' and I strongly agreed with this objective. Under the Peacock proposals, if the IBA decided to award a franchise to a contractor other than the highest bidder it should be required to make a full, public and detailed statement of its reasons. This had the merit of openness and simplicity as well as maximizing revenues for the Treasury. But we immediately ran into the morass of arguments about 'quality'.

In September 1987 I held a seminar to which the main figures in broadcasting were invited to discuss the future. There was more agreement than I might have thought possible on the technical opportunities and the need for greater choice and competition. But some of those present took a dim view of our decision to set up a Broadcasting Standards Council and to remove the exemption enjoyed by the broadcasters from the provisions of the Obscene Publications Act. I was entirely unrepentant. I said that they must remember that television was special because it was watched in the family's sitting-room. Standards on television had an effect on society as a whole and were therefore a matter of proper public interest for the Government.

We had a number of discussions during 1988 about the contents of the planned white paper on broadcasting. (It was eventually published in November.) I was pressing for the phasing out of the BBC licence fee altogether to be announced in that document. But Douglas was against this and a powerful lobby on behalf of the BBC built up. In the end I agreed to drop my insistence on it and on the privatization of Channel 4. But I made more progress in ensuring that Channel 3 should be subject to much less heavy regulation under the new ITC (Independent Television Commission) than under the IBA.

Of course, one could only do so much by changing the framework of the system: as always, it was the people who operated within it who were the key. The appointment of Duke Hussey as Chairman of the BBC in 1986 and later of John Birt as Deputy Director-General represented an improvement in every respect. When I met Duke Hussey and Joel Barnett – his deputy – in September 1988 I told them how much I supported the new approach being taken. But I also did not disguise my anger at the BBC's continued ambivalence as regards the reporting of terrorism and violence. I said that the BBC had a duty to uphold the great institutions and liberties of the country from which we all benefited.

The broadcasters continued to lobby fiercely against the proposals in the Broadcasting White Paper on the process of auctioning the ITV franchises. My preferred approach was that every applicant would have to pass a 'quality threshold' and then go on to offer a financial bid, with the ITC being obliged to select the highest. Otherwise a gathering of the great and the good could make an essentially arbitrary choice with clear possibilities of favouritism, injustice and propping up the *status quo*. But the Home Office team argued that we had to make concessions – first in June 1989 in response to consultation on the white paper and then at report stage of the broadcasting bill in the spring of 1990, when they said there would be great parliamentary difficulties otherwise. These unfortunately muddied the transparency which I had hoped to achieve and produced a compromise which turned out to be less than satisfactory when the ITC bestowed the franchises the following year 'in the old-fashioned way'. Still, the new auctioning system – combined with the 25 per cent target for independent producers, the arrival of new satellite channels, and a successful assault on union restrictive practices – went some way towards weakening the monopolistic grip of the broadcasting establishment. They did not break it.

SCIENCE AND THE ENVIRONMENT

In 1988 and 1989 there was a great burst of public interest in the environment. Unfortunately, under the green environmental umbrella sheltered a number of only slightly connected issues. At the lowest but not by any means least important level, there was concern for the local environment, which I too always felt strongly about. Indeed, every time I came back from some spotlessly maintained foreign city my staff and the then Secretary of State for the Environment knew that they could expect a stiff lecture on the litter-strewn streets of parts of London. But this was essentially and necessarily a matter for the local community, though the privatizing of badly run municipal cleaning services often helped.

Then there was the concern about planning – or rather the alleged lack of it – and overdevelopment of the countryside. Here there was, as Nick Ridley became somewhat unpopular for robustly pointing out, a straightforward choice. If people were to be able to afford houses there must be sufficient amounts of building land available. Tighter planning meant less development land and fewer opportunities for home ownership.

There was also widespread public concern – some merited but much not – about the standard of Britain's drinking water, rivers and sea. The European Commission found this a fruitful area into which to extend its 'competence' whenever possible. In fact, a hugely expensive and highly successful programme was under way to clean up our rivers and the results were already evident – for example the return of healthy and abundant fish to the Thames, Tyne, Wear and Tees.

I always drew a clear distinction between *these* 'environmental' concerns and the quite separate question of atmospheric pollution. For me, the proper starting point in formulating policy towards this latter problem was science. There had always to be a sound scientific base on which to build – and of course a clear estimation of the cost in terms of public expenditure and economic growth foregone – if one was not going to be thrust into the kind of 'green socialism' which the Left were eager to promote. But the closer I examined what was happening to Britain's scientific effort, the less happy I was about it.

There were two problems. First, too high a proportion of government funding for science was directed towards the Defence budget. Second – and reflecting the same approach – too much emphasis was being given to the development of products for the market rather than to pure science. Government was funding research which could and should have been left to industry and, as a result, there was a tendency for the research effort in the universities and in scientific institutes to lose out. I was convinced that this was wrong. As someone with a scientific background, I knew that the greatest economic benefits of scientific research had always resulted from advances in fundamental knowledge rather than the search for specific applications. For example, transistors were not discovered by the entertainment industry seeking new ways of marketing pop music but rather by people working on wave mechanics and solid-state physics.

In the summer of 1987 I instituted a new approach to government funding of science. I set up 'E'(ST) as a new sub-committee of the Economic Committee of the Cabinet which I now chaired. This replaced 'E'(RD) that had been chaired by Paul Channon as Industry Secretary. I also set up a Cabinet committee of officials and experts – ACOST – to replace ACARD which had been shadowing Paul Channon's committee. 'E'(ST) and ACOST examined departmental science budgets, breaking them down between basic science and support for innovation, giving greater emphasis to the first. My ideal was to search out the brightest and best scientists and back them rather than try to provide support for work in particular sectors. What those who have no real understanding of science are inclined to overlook is that in science – just as in the arts – the greatest achievements cannot be planned and predicted: they result from the unique creativity of a particular mind.

At every stage scientific discovery and knowledge set the requirements and the limits for the approach we should pursue towards the problems of the global environment. It was, for example, the British Antarctic Survey which discovered a large hole in the ozone layer which protects life from ultra-violet radiation. Similarly, it was scientific research which proved that chlorofluorocarbons (CFCs) were responsible for ozone depletion. Convinced by this evidence, governments agreed first to cut and then to phase out the use of CFCs – for example in refrigerators, aerosols and air conditioning systems. From the time of the first international meeting and agreement in Montreal in 1987 until my last days in office when I was addressing the Second World Climate Conference in Geneva on the subject, I took the closest personal interest as the scientific evidence was amassed and analysed.

'Global warming' was another atmospheric threat which required the application of hard-headed scientific principles. The relationship between the industrial emission of carbon dioxide – the most significant though not the only 'greenhouse gas' – and climatic change was a good deal less certain than the relationship between CFCs and ozone depletion. Nuclear power production did not produce carbon dioxide – nor did it produce the gases which led to acid rain. It was a far cleaner source of power than coal. However, this did not attract the environmental lobby towards it: instead, they used the concern about global warming to attack capitalism, growth and industry. I sought to employ the authority which I had gained in the whole environmental debate, mainly as a result of my speech to the Royal Society in September 1988, to ensure a sense of proportion.

That speech was the fruit of much thought and a great deal of work. It was our outgoing ambassador at the UN, Sir Crispin Tickell, who first suggested that I should make a major speech on the subject. I decided that the Royal Society was the perfect forum. George Guise, who advised me on science in the Policy Unit, and I spent two weekends working on the draft. It broke quite new political ground. But it is an extraordinary commentary on the lack of media interest in the subject that, contrary to my expectations, the television did not even bother to send film crews to cover the occasion. In fact, I had been relying on the television lights to enable me to read my script in the gloom of the Fishmongers' Hall, where it was to be delivered; in the event, candelabra had to be passed up along the table to allow me to do so. The speech itself triggered much debate and discussion, particularly one passage:

> For generations, we have assumed that the efforts of mankind would leave the fundamental equilibrium of the world's systems and atmosphere stable. But it is possible that with all these enor-

> mous changes (population, agricultural, use of fossil fuels) concentrated into such a short period of time, we have unwittingly begun a massive experiment with the system of this planet itself . . . In studying the system of the earth and its atmosphere we have no laboratory in which to carry out controlled experiments. We have to rely on observations of natural systems. We need to identify particular areas of research which will help to establish cause and effect. We need to consider in more detail the likely effects of change within precise timescales. And to consider the wider implications for policy – for energy production, for fuel efficiency, for reforestation . . . We must ensure that what we do is founded on good science to establish cause and effect.

The relationship between scientific research and policy towards the global environment was not just a technical matter. It went to the heart of what differentiated my approach from that of the socialists. For me, the economic progress, scientific advance and public debate which occur in free societies *themselves* offered the means to overcome threats to individual and collective wellbeing. For the socialist, each new discovery revealed a 'problem' for which the repression of human activity by the state was the only 'solution' and state-planned production targets must always take precedence. The scarred landscape, dying forests, poisoned rivers and sick children of the former communist states bear tragic testimony to which system worked better, both for people and the environment.

CHAPTER XXII

A Little Local Difficulty

The replacement of the rating system with the community charge

The introduction of the community charge to replace the domestic rates turned out to be by far the most controversial of the changes promised in our 1987 general election manifesto. Whereas the other elements of those reforms – in education, housing and trade union law – took root, the community charge has since been abolished by a government consisting largely of those who framed and implemented it.

The charge became a rallying point for those who opposed me, both within the Conservative Party and on the far left. Had I not been facing problems on other fronts – above all, had the Cabinet and Party held their nerve – I could have ridden through the difficulties. Indeed, the community charge, having been modified in several ways, was beginning to work at the very time it was abandoned. Given time, it would have been seen as one of the most far-reaching and beneficial reforms ever made in the working of local government. Above all, the community charge offered a last chance of responsible, efficient, local democracy in Britain. Its abandonment will mean that more and more powers will pass to central government, that upward pressures on public spending and taxation will increase accordingly, and that still fewer people of ability will become local councillors.

PROBLEMS WITH THE OLD SYSTEM

We did not enter lightly upon the path of radical reform of local government finance. I shared much of the traditional Tory caution about turning existing financial or administrative systems upside down. If it had been possible to carry on as before I would have been quite prepared to do so. But by almost universal agreement it was not. The person who knew this best was Michael Heseltine – in fact, as it turned out, the most vocal Conservative opponent of the community charge. Michael, as Environment Secretary in the early 1980s, had tried to make the old system work by resorting to more and more complicated devices. He took a whole battery of new powers in an attempt to deal with the problem: that we lacked the means to control local government spending, though it made up a large fraction of overall public expenditure. He brought in the block grant system and 'grant-related expenditure assessments' (GREAs), 'targets' and 'hold-back', limits on local authority capital expenditure, and the Audit Commission, as well as beginning a general squeeze on the central government grant – all designed to hold down local spending and to give ratepayers an incentive to think twice before re-electing high-spending councils.*

The system became so complicated that scarcely anyone understood it. It was like the 'Schleswig-Holstein question' of the last century: Palmerston joked once that only three people ever had a real grasp of it – one of them was dead, one was mad and he himself had forgotten it. The system was also highly unpopular, wayward in its application and inexplicably unfair to historically low-spending authorities, many of whom were set targets below their GREAs. Worse still, it did not work. Ministers might exhort, bewail and threaten but local government spending grew inexorably in real terms, year after year.

So in 1981 Michael came up with new ideas. He proposed that if local authorities spent more than a certain amount over and above their GREAs all the extra would have to be paid for by domestic ratepayers. The Government also agreed that a local referendum should be held before a council could go ahead with the extra spending. This proposal had something new and important to be said for it because

* Central government grant contributes a large proportion of local authority spending. GREAs were an attempt to allocate grants to authorities on the basis of their 'need to spend', as defined by central government on the basis of dozens of indicators covering everything from an authority's population to the state of its roads. The block grant system altered the distribution of central government grant so that it provided a lower proportion of local authorities' expenditure if they spent significantly more than their GREAs – in other words, the more a council overspent, the higher the proportion of its spending ratepayers would have to meet. 'Targets' for individual local authorities (based on past spending) were introduced later in an attempt to secure year-on-year reductions in local authority spending: local authorities exceeding their targets actually lost grant ('holdback'). The Audit Commission was established in 1982 with responsibility for auditing the accounts of local authorities in England and Wales and with powers to undertake or promote work on value for money and efficiency.

it at least marginally reinforced local accountability which – as I shall explain – was at the root of the problem. But, in spite or even because of that, it drew howls of protest from local authorities and the Tory back-benchers whom they so easily influenced. The proposal had to be withdrawn.

So Michael's successors at the Department of the Environment – Tom King and then Patrick Jenkin – were left with no alternative but to apply more and more complex central controls, while the local authorities went on spending. In 1984 we took powers to limit directly the rates of selected local authorities, with powers in reserve to limit them all. This procedure – known as 'rate-capping' – was one of the most effective weapons at our disposal. Much of the overspending was concentrated in a small number of authorities, so that capping fewer than twenty could make a considerable difference. It allowed us to offer some protection from very high rates to businesses and families who were trying to make their own way in profligate Labour authorities – particularly those families on incomes just above the benefit levels, who could not rely on the state to pay their rising rates bills. But rate-capping was a complicated business: it stretched the capacity of the Department of the Environment and could be challenged in the courts. The fundamental problem remained.

I had always disliked the rates intensely. Any property tax is essentially a tax on improving one's own home. It was manifestly unfair and un-Conservative. In my constituency and in letters received from people all over the country I witnessed a chorus of complaints from people living alone – widows for example – who consumed far less of local authority services than the large family next door with several working sons, but who were expected to pay the same rates bills, regardless of their income. I had, of course, been Shadow Environment spokesman at the time of the October 1974 election when we promised to abolish the rates altogether. In fact, this was a last-minute pledge insisted upon by Ted Heath about which I had considerable doubts for we had not properly thought through what to put in their place: but I had witnessed the anger and distress caused by the 1973 rate revaluation and believed strongly that something new must replace the existing discredited system.* When I became Prime Minister I

* Rates were levied at so many pence in the pound (the 'poundage') on the basis of the rental value of the property, which was assessed by a general valuation carried out by the Inland Revenue. Since the rental market in domestic property was small and shrinking the valuations were often very artificial. In addition, obviously, their accuracy deteriorated over time; hence the need for periodic revaluations.

stopped any further rate revaluations in England. (In Scotland the system was different and a domestic rate revaluation was required by law every five years, though extensions were possible and we took powers to put off for two years a revaluation due in 1983.) But the counterpart of this decision was that the potential disruption which a rate revaluation would have caused in England grew by the year. And we could not put it off for ever.

The reliance on property taxes as a principal source of income for local government went back centuries. Rates made sense, perhaps, when the bulk of local authority services were supplied to property – roads, water and drains, and so on – but in the course of the present century local authorities have increasingly become providers of services for people, such as education, libraries and personal social services.

Moreover, the franchise for local elections has been widened dramatically. Originally, it was limited to property holders: now it is almost identical to that for parliamentary elections. The old business vote has gone too. The only serious argument for the rates – business and domestic – was that they were relatively easy to collect: people can abscond, houses and factories cannot. The rates became a painless tax for the large number of local electors who were not liable to pay them. But this was what made the old system so defective, ultimately even dangerous. Of the 35 million local electors in England, 17 million were not themselves liable for rates, and of the 18 million liable, 3 million paid less than full rates and 3 million paid nothing at all. Though some of those not liable contributed to the rates paid by others (for example, spouses and working children living at home), many people had no direct reason to be concerned about their council's overspending, because somebody else picked up all or most of the bill. Worse still, people lacked the information they needed to hold their local authority to account: the whole system of local government finance worked to obscure the performance of individual authorities. It is not surprising that many councillors felt free to pursue policies which no properly operating democratic discipline would have permitted.

This lack of accountability lay behind the continued overspending. Although central government steadily reduced the share of local government spending met from the Exchequer, the result was more likely to be higher rates than lower total public spending. That was unsatisfactory for the overall economy. But it was ruinous for local businesses and – ultimately – for local communities. In the summer of 1985 when we began seriously to look at the alternatives to the rating system, some 60 per cent of the rate income of local authorities in England was coming from business rates. In some areas, though, it was a far higher percentage. For example, in the Labour-controlled London borough of Camden it reached 75 per cent. Socialist councils were thus able to squeeze local businesses dry and the latter had no recourse except to press central government to cap the council concerned or to move out of the area. It might be imagined that the devastating effect of such policies of overspending on employment would discourage Labour authorities from such action. But I never forgot that the unspoken objective of socialism – municipal or national – was to increase dependency. Poverty was not just the breeding ground of socialism: it was the deliberately engineered effect of it.

Popular discontent with the rates surfaced strongly in the motions submitted by constituencies for our 1984 Party Conference. Conservatives in local government were unhappy at the apparatus of central controls – particularly on capital spending – and within the Department of the Environment there was concern that these controls gave rise to so many anomalies and political difficulties that they could not be sustained for many more years. Nor was it yet clear how effective rate-capping would prove. Accordingly, in September 1984 Patrick Jenkin sought my agreement to announce to the Party Conference a major review of local government finance. The Party Chairman, John Gummer, gave him strong support. But I was cautious. There was a danger of raising expectations that we could not meet. After all, there had been two previous reviews – under Michael Heseltine and Tom King – and only the most modest of mice had emerged. Unlike October 1974, we must be absolutely clear that we had a workable alternative to put in place of the present system. I authorized Patrick to say no more than that we would undertake studies of the most serious inequities and deficiencies of the present system. There would be no publicly announced 'review' and no hint that we might go as far as abolishing the rates.

Later that October I held a small meeting at Chequers to listen to a presentation of the intricacies of the Rate Support Grant system. When it ended I was more convinced than ever of the fundamental absurdities of the present system. Afterwards I discussed the proposed studies with the Junior Local Government minister, William Waldegrave, and suggested that Lord Rothschild – the former head of the CPRS in Ted Heath's time and someone for whom I had the highest regard, having worked with him on science policy when I was Education Secretary – should be brought into it. William had also worked with him at the CPRS and jumped at the idea. Much of the radical thinking which resulted was Victor Rothschild's.

By the time that the studies were complete, the political imperative for change had been dramatically demonstrated by a disastrous rate revaluation in Scotland. In Scotland there was a legislative requirement for rate revaluation every five years, though if George Younger and Michael Ancram at the Scottish Office had alerted us to the full consequences in time we could have introduced an order to stop it or mitigated its effects by making changes to the distribution of central government grant. The Scottish Conservative Party Chairman, Jim Goold, came to see me in the middle of February 1985 to describe the fury which had broken out north of the border when the new rateable values became known. The revaluation had led to a large shift in the burden from industry to domestic ratepayers and – with the high level of spending of Scottish local authorities – this was combined with large overall increases in the poundage. By the time that I chaired a proper ministerial discussion on the evening of Thursday 28 February to see what could be done about the problem it was really too late. Scottish ministers, businessmen and Tory supporters began with one voice to call for an immediate end to the rating system.

For us, south of the border, it was powerful evidence of what would happen if we ever had a rate revaluation in England. There was no legal obligation to undertake a revaluation in England by a particular year, but it could fairly be argued that without any revaluation the rates would contain more and more anomalies. As noted above, the whole basis of rating valuation by reference to rental values was dubious anyway. Of course, we could have used capital values for revaluation. But capital values can go down as well as up, so a system based on them would have been highly disruptive, unpopular and a very uncertain basis for local government finance. This was the option which Nigel Lawson and – from time to time depending on which spokesman was asked – the Labour Party favoured. But I was firmly against it, because it was still a tax on the value of someone's home and the improvements made to it.

ORIGINS OF THE COMMUNITY CHARGE

So it was that when Ken Baker, then DoE minister responsible for local government, his junior, William Waldegrave, and Lord Rothschild made their presentation to a seminar I held at Chequers at the end of March 1985 I was very open to new ideas. It was at the Chequers meeting that the community charge was born. They convinced me that we should abolish domestic rates and replace them with a community charge levied at a flat rate on all resident adults. There would be rebates for those on low incomes – though rebates should be less than 100 per cent so that everyone should contribute something, and therefore have something to lose from electing a spendthrift council. This principle of accountability underlay the whole reform.

The second element of the approach was that business rates would be charged at a single nationally set level and the revenue redistributed to all authorities on a per capita basis. The reform of business rates would also make it possible to end one of the most unsatisfactory features of the old system: 'resource equalization'. One problem with the rating system was that taxable capacity varied enormously from one authority to another, since the value and amount of property itself varied – particularly commercial and business property. 'Resource equalization' was the name given to the process by which central government redistributed income between authorities to even out the effect. As a result there were major variations across the country in the amount of rates paid on similar properties for a given standard of service, generally to the disadvantage of the South, where properties were usually valued much more highly. A great deal of money was involved, though like much else in local government finance the average voter had never heard of it. Such a system, of course, made it still harder for voters to judge whether they were getting value for money from their authority. But with the abolition of domestic rates and the distribution of the national business rate on a per capita basis, taxable capacity would no longer vary between authorities and so the need for 'resource equalization' disappeared. Obviously some authorities had greater needs than others, but this would be compensated for by giving them more in central grant. For the first time it would be possible for every council to provide the same level of service at the same level of local taxation anywhere in the country, so that much more transparent comparisons between councils could be made.

In the discussion which followed there was a lot of tough questioning but general support for the DoE approach and in particular a commitment to the strengthening of local accountability. The only alternative was to go further in the direction of centralization, for example by having central government take over specific local authority functions like education or teachers' pay, and yet tighter controls on spending. We wanted to avoid this if we could.

Nor was there any enthusiasm for the two other options which had long been canvassed – local income tax (LIT) or a local sales tax. The former would have undermined our efforts to lower income tax at the national level and would have put in the hands of Labour authorities a powerful weapon to drive out even more people of talent and energy from their areas. A sales tax would have been a recipe for absurd distortions in a country as small as Britain: prices would have varied from authority to authority, with high spending authorities driving shoppers to lower-spending neighbours only minutes away. And there would have had to be massive redistribution of revenue from one area to another to compensate for variations in the distribution of shops. Finally, both taxes would have been highly bureaucratic.

Of the ideas now put forward by the DoE team, the only proposal which I rejected was that we should consider changing the whole of local government to single-tier authorities. Then and later I was to be attracted by this on the grounds of the transparency it would have brought to the community charge figures. But we could not do everything at once.

After the Chequers seminar William Waldegrave and DoE officials went away to prepare more detailed proposals. Nigel Lawson had already expressed reservations through his Chief Secretary Peter Rees at the seminar. But it was only afterwards that it became clear just how deeply opposed he was. The DoE proposals were to come before a Cabinet committee at the end of May. A few days before the meeting Nigel sent in a Cabinet memorandum strongly challenging the community charge and urging the consideration of alternatives.

Nigel's dissenting Cabinet memorandum showed prescience in one crucial respect: he foresaw that local authorities would use the introduction of the new tax as an excuse to increase spending, knowing that they stood a good chance of persuading the voters that the Government was to blame for higher bills. I too had worries on this score, and the main aspect of the DoE's early thinking of which I was doubtful was their optimistic suggestion that enhanced accountability would make it possible to abandon 'capping' altogether. In an ideal world perhaps this would have been true. But the world which years of socialism in our inner cities had created was far from ideal. I was determined that capping powers would remain and, indeed, before the end I would find myself pressing for much more extensive community charge capping than was ever envisaged for the rates.

When the committee met I asked Nigel to work up his alternative proposals. If this was to be done it would have to be done quickly: I had it in mind – if we went ahead – to get a green paper published by the autumn of 1985, with a view to legislating in the 1986–7 session, which was a tight timetable. But his idea for a 'Modified Property Tax' was not to win any support from colleagues outside the Treasury when it was circulated in August 1985. It had most of the defects of the existing system and some more as well.

In September 1985 I promoted Ken Baker from Minister for Local Government to Secretary of State for the Environment, with responsibility for refining and then presenting the proposals. During autumn and winter that year we slogged away in Cabinet committee. Figures from the DoE made it clear that moving in a single step to a community charge would create many losers from the change, particularly (but not only) in the profligate inner London boroughs. How sharp these changes would be would depend very much on the level of the charge itself: at this stage – 1985–6 – we were advised that the average level would be under £200. But I fully realized that even with these figures there would be real difficulties in transition for which solutions had to be found.

With the abolition of 'resource equalization' and the pooling of business rates there would be large shifts in the domestic local tax burden between areas. Areas with high rateable values and low spending levels would tend to gain. Those with low rateable values and high spending would tend to lose. London had its own special problems. Inner London had received specially generous subsidies; a number of London authorities were very high spenders; there was – until we eventually abolished it – the burden of high spending by the Inner London Education Authority; there was also the fact that business rates, which socialist authorities had in the past been able to increase more or less at will, would now be limited and pooled, with the result that extra burdens would fall on domestic ratepayers. In order to deal with these changes between areas a system called the 'safety net' was devised to smooth the transition. The safety net was designed to be self-financing: it slowed down one area's losses by delaying another area's gains. This was unpopular with the gainers, but unavoidable unless the Exchequer stepped in to meet the difference. Nor could the safety net deal directly with the most politically sensitive question which was the changes in the burden between individuals and between households.

The problem of limiting individual losses raised the question of whether the community charge itself should be phased in, and if so, how. Ken Baker – always canny and cautious – wanted a very long transition period during which the rates and community charge would run alongside each other (known in the jargon as 'dual running'). Indeed in an early draft of the green paper we were to publish in

January 1986 he wanted to leave open whether the rates would ever be abolished. I intervened: it had to be clear that the community charge would replace the rates entirely and not in the very distant future. The final position which Ken Baker announced to the House of Commons on Tuesday 28 January 1986 was that the community charge would start at a low level, with a corresponding cut in the rates. But the whole burden of any increased spending would fall on the community charge from the start so that there was a clear link between higher spending and higher community charges. In subsequent years there would be further shifts from the rates to the charge. In some areas the rates would disappear within three years: they would be eliminated in all areas within ten. The green paper made it clear that we were retaining capping. On the strong advice of Scottish ministers, who reminded us continually and forcefully how much the Scottish people loathed the rates, we also accepted that we should legislate to bring in the community charge in Scotland in advance of England and Wales.

THE ABANDONMENT OF DUAL RUNNING

In May 1986 I moved Ken Baker to Education and brought in Nick Ridley to replace him at the Department of the Environment. Nick brought a combination of clarity of thought, political courage and imagination to the questions surrounding the implementation of the new system. His vision was that local authorities should enable services to be provided but, unless it was truly necessary, local authorities should not provide those services themselves. The main business of modern local government should therefore be regulation – and not too much of that – rather than owning assets and competing with private sector businesses. One way of ensuring this was through the community charge which, by bringing home to people the true cost of local government, would maximize the pressure for efficiency and low spending. Complementary to this was the expansion of competitive tendering of local government services which would result in more contracting out to the private sector. Nick's 1988 Local Government Act required that refuse collection, street cleaning, the cleaning of buildings, ground maintenance, vehicle maintenance and repair and catering services (including school meals) be put out to tender.

It was entirely consistent with this rigorous approach that Nick considered it illogical to retain capping powers, except perhaps during the transition to the new system. But I felt we needed this safeguard. He also wanted to introduce the community charge more quickly than Ken Baker had envisaged, believing that the sooner local authorities could be made truly accountable the faster we could go in bringing local government back onto the right lines. Nick had always opposed dual running and in the end he persuaded the rest of us to abandon it – though, as I shall explain, not without a little help from the Party in the country. The political arguments against dual running were powerful. Having two local taxes instead of one, even if only for a time, would have been a gift to our opponents; it would have been expensive and difficult to administer; and it would have postponed the very accountability our reforms were about.

During the winter of 1986–7 Parliament legislated to introduce the community charge in Scotland from April 1989. In February 1987 Malcolm Rifkind won our agreement to drop dual running in Scotland, though a safety net was retained, and it was on this basis that the Party north of the border fought the 1987 election. The community charge was an important issue during the campaign there. Our results were disappointing but Malcolm Rifkind wrote to me afterwards that the community charge had been 'neutral' in its effect and that it had at least defused the rates problem. In England and Wales the community charge was hardly an election issue at all.

Nevertheless, immediately the new Parliament met it became clear that many of our back-benchers had got the jitters. On 1 July the whips estimated that while over 150 were clear supporters, there were nearly 100 'doubters', with 24 outright opponents. There was a real danger that over the summer recess many of the doubters would commit themselves against the charge altogether. Nick's response was characteristically robust: to propose that we drop dual running, drastically cut down the safety net and attack the London problem by direct action to reduce ILEA's costs. But he met strong opposition from colleagues, particularly Nigel, and in the end we compromised on dual running for four years with a full safety net phased out over the same period.*

It quickly became clear that this had not done the trick. At the Party Conference in October speaker after speaker attacked dual running and back-bench opinion was also very strongly opposed to it. All this made a strong impression on us. We argued it out at a ministerial meeting on 17 November, and decided that dual running should be

* A 'full' safety net was one that ensured there would be no losses or gains from the abolition of 'resource equalization' during the first year of the charge.

abandoned except for a very few councils, all but one of them in inner London. We also ended the full safety net, setting a maximum contribution of £75 per person from the gaining authorities, so that their gains came through more quickly. (In June 1988 we abandoned dual running altogether: by that time we had made the decision to abolish ILEA, which seemed likely to reduce community charge bills in London significantly in the long term. There were serious doubts too whether the authorities scheduled for dual running were administratively competent to do the job).

It is worth noting that the changes we made in local government finance originated in and continued to reflect opinion in the Conservative Party, notwithstanding these arguments about transitional arrangements. Both the English and the Scottish Party demanded fundamental changes in the rates. It was the Scottish Party which insisted upon the early introduction of the community charge in Scotland: and if, as the Scots subsequently claimed, they were guinea pigs for a great experiment in local government finance they were the most vociferous and influential guinea pigs which the world has ever seen.

It is true that in April 1988 we had to fight off an amendment put forward by Michael Mates MP, a lieutenant of Michael Heseltine, which would have introduced a 'banding' of the community charge – that is, income would be taken into account in setting the charge. This would have defeated the whole purpose of the flat-rate charge, as well as creating damagingly high marginal rates of tax at the level of each 'band'. The proper way to help the less well off was through community charge rebates, and Nick Ridley won round many of the rebels by announcing improvements in these, making them a good deal more generous than rate rebates had been. But the most consistent pressure was from Tory MPs anxious to see that the benefits of the new system came through faster to their constituents.

The bill received its Royal Assent in July 1988. The new system would come into operation in England and Wales on 1 April 1990.

The discussions about dual running, the safety net and transitional relief which so preoccupied us in the period before the new system's introduction all reflected one fundamental point. The new system of local authority finance would be 'transparent'. That is, its clarity and directness would bring financial realities home to everyone. This, in my view, was one of its inestimable benefits. As I used to put it in my speeches explaining the community charge, it provided everyone with a 'ready reckoner'. The differing needs of any particular area would be taken into account in the central government grant. Then a standard level of community charge would be set and published. If local authorities chose to spend more than the standard level of service required then the community charge would go up. The effect would not be concealed either by complex formulae or by draining more money from business. Every elector therefore would have the information and the incentive to insist on efficiency and low levels of spending.

But the other side of this was that because the total contribution from businesses was to be held to the rise in the RPI any increase in local authority spending above the level allowed for in central government grant would be concentrated on the individual community charge payer. Each 1 per cent of extra spending would add 4 per cent to the community charge – the charge covering about a quarter of total local authority spending. Such high 'gearing' meant that if local authorities pushed up spending – using the opportunity of the introduction of a new system to do so and then blaming central government – the increase in the bills to the individual charge payer would frequently be dramatic. In many badly run (usually Labour-controlled) authorities families were stunned by the size of the estimated bills and blamed the Government. In these cases, the deep unpopularity of the community charge was in a sense proof that it was likely to work, but the political opposition rapidly began to get out of hand.

Looking back, it may have been a mistake to do away with the dual running of rates and community charge. And perhaps we were relatively too sensitive to the needs of business – as well as too willing to accept the large transfer of resources from the South to the North which was entailed by the replacement of the old business rating system with the new nationally set business rate. Business might have been expected to pay for at least some of the overspending.

Two other changes would also have helped. First, wasteful as it might have seemed, there would have been something to be said for allowing a rating revaluation under the old system to occur in England before the community charge was introduced. This would have reminded people how painful it would be to carry on with the rates and how unfair the rating system was. The gainers under the new system might have been more appreciative and the losers less vociferous if they had seen the alternative. Second, I believe that we should have legislated before the introduction of the charge for much wider and stronger powers to cap local authority spending. Of course, there is an apparent contradiction between bringing in a new system of local authority finance in order to strengthen local accountability and then taking more powers to the centre. But the contradiction is apparent rather than real. The beneficial effects of the new system could not be expected to come through immediately. We should have been more alert to the cynical abuse of their power which left-wing authorities would practise, going to any lengths to blame us and the community charge for their own overspending.

In considering all this we were assisted less than might have been predicted by what was happening in Scotland. In the first year of the new system Scottish local authorities pushed up their spending, increasing their budgets by 14 per cent in 1989–90. But Malcolm Rifkind, the new Scottish Secretary, argued strongly against capping these authorities. Because the timetable was very tight and the legal advice we received was against, I agreed somewhat reluctantly with this. In the second year of the operation of the community charge in Scotland, though, there was evidence that the benefits of increased accountability had begun to restrain local authority spending. So the indications were mixed.

PREPARING FOR THE INTRODUCTION OF THE CHARGE

It was very important that the first year's community charge in England (1990–91) was not so high as to discredit the whole system. In particular it was crucial that good authorities be able to announce community charges at or below the level we deemed necessary to achieve the standard level of service (known as the Community Charge for Standard Spending, or CCSS). But ensuring this was easier said than done.

In May 1989 Nick Ridley, Nigel Lawson and John Major (as Chief Secretary) began discussions on the level of the local authority grant settlement for 1990–91. There was a wide gap between the DoE and the Treasury. Each side had good arguments. The figures suggested by Nick Ridley were, he argued, the only ones which would lead to actual community charges below £300 (significantly, a far higher figure than we had envisaged a year before when the community charge legislation was passed). The Treasury view, with which I agreed, was that the 1989–90 settlement had been very generous – deliberately so to pave the way for the community charge. But the only result had been to lead to greatly increased local authority spending, which was up 9 per cent in cash terms. Local authorities had kept down the rates themselves in 1989–90 through the use of reserves, merely deferring increases. The lesson, the Treasury argued, was that providing more money from the Exchequer did not mean lower rates (or a lower community charge). On 25 May I summed up the discussion at a ministerial meeting by rejecting both Nick Ridley's and John Major's preferred options and going for something in the middle, which I thought would still give us a tolerable community charge while not validating the large increase in local authority spending in 1989–90. But I said that I wanted to see exemplifications of the likely community charge in each local authority area.

We were not to know it at the time, but these decisions contributed to the undoing of the community charge. At this time the Treasury was still using an inflation measure (the GDP deflator) of just 4 per cent. In fact, inflation and – most important – wage settlements were turning sharply upwards. Combined with a pretty tight grant settlement and with the determination of many local authorities to push up spending for political reasons, we were now on course for much higher levels of community charge in 1990–91 than any of us foresaw. If we had had better control over local spending we could have been sure that extra money from the centre would be used to reduce community charge bills rather than increase spending.

I moved Chris Patten to become Secretary of State for the Environment later that summer. By now Conservative back-benchers were becoming extremely restive. In July they had given Nick Ridley's last major statement as Environment Secretary – announcing the grant settlement – a rough reception. Many of them did not really understand the new system and the changes that they wanted were often mutually contradictory. Nick had at least been able to meet one of their most pressing concerns by announcing a £100 million scheme to ease the transition in areas with low rateable values, which faced large increases under the new system. But there was no doubt that the back-benchers wanted more, and their worries grew during the autumn. I received regular and depressing reports from the whips.

In early September Chris Patten, with my approval, began a review of the operation of the charge. A couple of days before, as I was about to leave for the Prime Minister's traditional autumn visit to Balmoral, Ken Baker (now the Party Chairman) had sent me in great secrecy research conducted by Central Office in ten Conservative marginal seats. This confirmed the scale of the political problem we faced. On the assumption of a 7 per cent increase in local spending the following year, 73 per cent of households and 82 per cent of individuals would lose from the introduction of the charge in 1990 compared with the rates in the previous year. If spending increased by 11 per cent the figures would rise to 79 per cent and 89 per cent respectively. Though these figures did not take account of extensive rebates, on any calculation they were pretty bad.

Now that dual running had been dropped, the only way in which we could limit the losses of individuals or households generally – as opposed to the losses of areas, which it was the function of the by now extremely unpopular 'safety net' to iron out – was by a new scheme altogether. Chris Patten and the Treasury accordingly worked up a proposal for 'transitional relief'.

Chris favoured a massive programme of transitional relief for households to limit losses to £2 a week – that is £2 a week on the basis of what we thought local authorities should spend (the CCSS), which many of them of course would exceed. Even in this limited form the scheme might cost as much as £1,500 million. Ken Baker – never backward when it came to public spending – wanted a very costly scheme too. The Treasury argued for something much more modest, targetted on the worst losers. All of this was against a difficult public expenditure round and a worsening economic situation with rising inflation. I told Chris Patten that transitional relief on the scale he was proposing was out of the question, but I also pressed the Treasury hard to take a positive and co-operative attitude. I held a meeting at the end of September to try to get agreement. I brought the two sides closer together and concluded by saying that it was essential that the scheme should be sufficiently generous to defuse genuine criticism but that it must be clear that this was indeed the last word and that the Government would not make further money available for 1990–91.

Discussions continued up to the eve of the Party Conference where David Hunt, the Local Government minister, announced a scheme costing £1.2 billion over three years. The scheme would ensure that former ratepayers (and ratepayer couples) need pay in community charges no more than £3 a week extra over and above their 1989–90 rate bills, provided that their local authority spent in line with the Government's assumptions. Pensioners and disabled people would be entitled to the same level of help even if they had not previously paid the rates (and of course many of them were entitled to rebates as well). At the same time David Hunt announced that the taxpayer would finance the safety net in England and Wales after the first year and that all gains would therefore come through in full from 1 April 1991. In spite of this, back-bench pressure increased. There was even doubt as to whether we could win the crucial Commons votes in January 1990 to authorize payment of the 1990–91 Revenue Support Grant. We met to discuss whether concessions needed to be made. Even if we had wanted to make concessions, it would not have been easy to do so because there was really no common thread to the rebels' concerns. In fact, I decided that we should hold our ground, and through the efforts of the whips and with the help of a superb speech from Chris Patten – always an able debater – we won the votes by a good margin. But I was under no illusion that victory in the House of Commons would be sufficient to convince public opinion, which had now turned strongly against the community charge.

THE POLITICAL CRISIS MOUNTS

By now the bad news about likely future levels of the charge was coming through thick and fast. By January 1990 the DoE had yet again raised its estimate of the average community charge to £340. We were heading for double the original estimate. That had been bad enough. Now in February, with local authorities likely to increase their spending by some 15–16 per cent, the latest indications were that it could be £20 or more higher.

Another piece of bad news was that the Retail Price Index Advisory Committee had in its wisdom decided that the community charge should be included in the RPI – treating it like the rates, but unlike other direct taxes. But the massive reliefs to individual charge payers should not be taken into account. This administrative fiction gave another expensive upward twist to the RPI and greatly increased the political damage which we were sustaining.

The political atmosphere was becoming grim. All my instincts told me that we could not continue as we were. On Thursday 22 March we sustained a very bad by-election defeat in Mid-Staffordshire, losing a seat in which we had had a majority of over 19,000. The press was full of outraged criticism of the community charge from Conservative supporters. I was deeply worried. What hurt me was that the very people who had always looked to me for protection from exploitation by the socialist state were those who were suffering most. These were the people who were just above the level at which community charge benefit stopped but who were by no means well off and who had scrimped and saved to buy their homes. Our new scheme of transitional relief did not protect them against overspending councils. Something more must be done.

My thoughts were crystallized by the discussion I had with Ken Baker, Tim Bell and Gordon Reece over supper at Chequers on Saturday 24 March. Their message was clear. It was vital to achieve lower levels of community charge. If this were not done the political consequences would be grave. This matched my analysis entirely.

There was widespread support for the principle that everyone should pay something towards the cost of local government, which only the community charge could ensure. When people complained about its fairness they were not usually rehearsing the hackneyed – and spurious – point about the hypothetical duke and dustman paying the same. Unless the duke were very poor or the dustman very wealthy this could not be so, because about half of local authority expenditure was met out of general taxation which did reflect 'ability to pay'. The problem was the levels at which the charge was now being levied and the fact that it was sudden and unexpected in its impact, frequently bearing down on our own people. That was what the authors of all those letters of complaint which I received were really driving at. But what could now be done?

The essential point, I felt, was to ensure that central government stepped in to protect the victims of what was essentially an arbitrary abuse of power by irresponsible local authorities. Arguments about accountability and the prospects for long-term improvement simply had to take second place.

So on Sunday morning, before I began work with my advisers at Chequers on drafting my speech to the Central Council, I rang the Chancellor, John Major. I told him that I had been reading the papers relating to community charge capping for 1990–91. I had a number of fundamental concerns. The first was political. When the community charge system had been developed we had assumed that if authorities persisted with high levels of spending, the blame for the resultant high community charges would fall on them rather than the Government. But that was not in fact happening. The public were blaming us and indeed the spending levels of a number of Conservative-controlled councils as well. Second, the impact of high community charges was falling on those in the middle income groups – what might be called the 'conscientious middle'. Those on low incomes were well protected by the various rebate arrangements. Indeed, we were having to meet a much higher public spending bill than expected for community charge rebates because the charges themselves were so high. This would be given a further twist because, since the levels of community charge were pushing up the RPI, that would carry through into a higher than expected uprating for all social security benefits next autumn. The new system was not yet bringing about increased accountability. Nor did it seem to me that this was likely to materialize in the second year either. We could give some modest protection to charge payers in

1990–91 if we went ahead with the current proposals for charge capping, and indeed we must do so. But the effect on average bills would be marginal, at best. We therefore needed to consider radical further measures in relation to 1991–2.

The main option seemed to be the introduction of a direct central control over levels of local authority spending; for example, laying down that expenditure by each authority could be no more than a certain percentage above a Standard Spending Assessment (SSA) – that is the level at which the authority needed to spend to deliver a certain nationally uniform standard of service. That, however, would need to be matched by a substantial increase in the level of government grant to local authorities, perhaps with a larger proportion of the total in the form of specific grants for particular services. I saw no reason why it should not be possible for this dual approach to reduce total public spending by local authorities. We would then have to consider whether to continue with the community charge as the sole means of financing expenditure above the level allowed for, given that at present all the extra expenditure fell on the charge. An alternative would be to place some of the burden of higher spending on the business rate. All this pointed to the need for a major internal review which would have to be carried out very speedily. It would be necessary to indicate publicly that some kind of review was under way, although the terms and manner of such an announcement needed careful thought.

John Major did not dissent from my judgement that a radical review was necessary. He also agreed that the changes we came up with must control total public expenditure. I finished by saying that I would speak very soon to Environment ministers to tell them what I wanted done.

In one form or another I was to pursue this approach over the months ahead – until, as I shall describe, unexpected legal advice caused me to revise my views about the best practical way forward. I did not, though, even then alter the view which I had now come to about the future of local government finance. I still believed that the local accountability which the community charge did so much to strengthen would have a salutary effect. It would, not so incidentally, help ensure that low-spending councils – generally Conservative – were elected. But I had also seen – and did not intend to forget – the perversity, incompetence and often straightforward malice of many local councils. High-minded talk of local democracy must not be allowed to obscure the low-level politics of the people we were up against. That meant that central government must have adequate powers – and be prepared to use them – to protect the individual citizen against rogue authorities.

But the most public opposition to the community charge came not from the respectable Tory lower-middle classes for whom I felt so deeply, but rather from the Left. From 1988 a number of Labour MPs, mostly in Scotland, had proclaimed their determination to break the law and refuse to pay the community charge and the far Left were agitating effectively in England too. They found little sympathy from the law-abiding mass of Labour supporters. But there were enough people ready to take the lead in organizing violent resistance. On Saturday 31 March, the day before the introduction of the community charge in England and Wales, a demonstration against the charge degenerated into rioting in and around Trafalgar Square. There was good evidence that a group of troublemakers had deliberately fomented the violence. Scaffolding on a building site in the square was dismantled and used as missiles; fires were started and cars destroyed. Almost 400 policemen were injured and 339 people were arrested. It was a mercy that no one was killed. I was appalled at such wickedness.

For the first time a government had declared that anyone who could reasonably afford to do so should at least pay something towards the upkeep of the facilities and the provision of the services from which they benefited. A whole class of people – an 'underclass' if you will – had been dragged back into the ranks of responsible society and asked to become not just dependants but citizens. The violent riots of 31 March in and around Trafalgar Square was their and the Left's response. And the eventual abandonment of the charge represented one of the greatest victories for these people ever conceded by a Conservative Government.

The trouble was that, because of the size of the bills now being sent out, the new system had the very same law-abiding, decent people – on whom we depended for support in defeating the mob – protesting themselves. The riot did not, therefore, shift me from my determination to continue with the community charge itself or to see the criminals of that day brought to justice. But it did reinforce the conclusions I had reached about the need to take effective action to limit the burden it was placing on what I had described to John Major as the 'conscientious middle'.

In fact, unbeknown to me, the rioters were on their way up to Whitehall as I was addressing the Central Council in Cheltenham.

I began my speech with what was to be the first of a number of increasingly risky jokes about the political threat to my leadership.

Cheltenham's reputation as the traditional retirement centre for those who governed our former empire provided the peg. I began:

> It's a very great pleasure to be in Cheltenham once again. To avoid any possible misunderstanding, and at the risk of disappointing a few gallant colonels, let me make one thing absolutely clear: I haven't come to Cheltenham to retire.

I then went almost immediately to the heart of the issue about which the Party was agonizing.:

> Many of the bills for the community charge which people are now receiving are far too high. I share the outrage they feel. But let's be clear: it's not the way the money is raised, it's the amount of money that local government is spending. That's the real problem. No scheme, no matter how ingenious, could pay for high spending with low charges.

But I did go on to announce a number of limited special reliefs. Even this modest package had necessitated my tearing up a feeble draft from the Treasury and writing it myself. Given the weak draft, the absence of colleagues and the late hour, however, I was not able to write into my speech assurances of the weight and substance I would have liked. So I had to content myself with hinting at my ideas about further capping powers to deal with overspenders.

My main message, therefore, had to be that the way to have low community charge bills was to vote Conservative in the forthcoming local elections. I pointed to some of the figures for the charge to illustrate my point.

> It costs £96 more for the privilege of living in Labour Warrington than in neighbouring Tory Trafford; £108 more in Labour Liverpool than in next-door Tory Wirral; and an appalling £339 more in Labour Camden than in adjoining Tory Westminster.

But I also drew a wider lesson, and in doing so I deliberately sought to move the political argument back to the greater questions of politics which distinguished the Conservative from the socialist approach – and back to the values for which I personally stood:

> Our struggle with the Labour Party has never been a matter just of economics. It concerns the way of life we believe is right for

> Britain now and in the future. It concerns the values by which we live. Socialism is a creed of the state. It regards ordinary human beings as the raw material for its schemes of social change. But we put our faith in people – in the millions of people who spend what they earn, not what other people earn. Who make sacrifices for their young family or their elderly parents. Who help their neighbours and take care of their neighbourhoods. The sort of people I grew up with. These are the people whom I became leader of this party to defend. The people who gave us their trust. To them I say, of course I understand your worries. They are part of the fabric of my life too, and I share the aspirations which you hold. You don't expect the moon. But you do want the opportunity to succeed for yourselves and your children.

The reception was good. But for them and for me the worries remained.

TO CAP OR NOT TO CAP?

Now I had to ensure that my colleagues threw themselves as wholeheartedly as I would into the job of protecting our people from the kind of problems we were experiencing in 1990–91. There was not much we could do as regards this year's bills. The lawyers advised that anything like the scale of capping I wanted to see was unlikely to be sustainable in the courts. Consequently, Chris Patten could only announce the capping of twenty councils. This was very disappointing. But a defeat in the courts could have put the whole system in disarray if, for example, the judges had found not just against a decision about a particular council but against the fairness of the system of SSAs which were crucial to the community charge.

All this reinforced the case for seeking new ways of holding down local government spending – and so community charges – the following year. I pressed with the Treasury and the Department of the Environment my ideas for wide-ranging direct controls over local authority spending combined with more extensive use of specific grants. I had also come round to the idea of single-tier authorities which – though the abolition of county councils would create a furore with Tory councillors – would mean that the identities of the culprits of overspending and high community charges were much clearer in the eyes of local electors.

Chris Patten was strongly opposed to any kind of comprehensive capping of local authorities. He argued against it both on the ground that it would undermine the principle of local accountability and because he thought such a system could not be got up and running in time for 1991–2. But I insisted that the DoE should work up the options. I wanted to see cuts in expenditure in some local authorities.

The local election results on Thursday 3 May 1990 strongly suggested that where Conservative councillors and candidates used the community charge in order to point up the differences between them and the Labour Party and then worked to get out the Conservative vote – rather than indulge in recrimination against the Government – they could do very well. (Indeed, some of our councillors opposed wider capping in 1990–91 on the ground that it would protect profligate Labour councils from the electoral *coup de grâce*.) Conservative successes in Wandsworth and Westminster were the results of that approach. Where the Conservatives were in control of an authority, the lower the charge it set, the better we did. The reverse was true where Labour was in office. In this respect the community charge was already transforming local government. There was the prospect that, even in a bad year for the Conservative Party nationally, local government elections could now be fought and won on genuinely local issues and the local record, rather than the political control of councils swinging according to national trends – something which had always demoralized conscientious councillors of either party.

These successes, however, did not diminish the urgency of ensuring that next year's charge levels throughout the country were kept down. Throughout May and early June papers were produced and discussions between ministers and officials held. Chris Patten and I were still at odds over the question of a general capping power. He was demanding a substantial increase in central grant, sufficient to allow us to say with credibility that responsible authorities would be able to set charges in 1991–2 no higher than in 1990–91. I put some pressure on him by refusing to allow any discussion about the level of next year's central grant until we had reached a decision on spending controls. John Major was in two minds. On the one hand, as Chancellor, he wanted to see effective controls on public spending. On the other, perhaps as a former whip, he was worried about getting the Parliamentary Party to pass the necessary new legislation for stronger capping powers. And this was a fair point. A number of our backbenchers were now in a mood not far short of outright panic and it was difficult to know how they would react to any new legislation which appeared to give them a chance – through amendments – to overturn key aspects of the community charge on which they thought their own electoral fortunes would founder. Quite how the argument would have ended up in government I do not know.

But suddenly the whole basis of our discussions was changed by new legal advice. When we had met on the morning of Thursday 17 May the lawyers advised that even new legislation on capping could be undermined by judicial review. This seemed to me to be extraordinary. It suggested that Parliament would not be allowed by the courts to fulfil its duty to protect the citizen from unreasonable levels of taxation: it cast doubt on our ability to control public expenditure and manage the economy. At that point I asked for urgent advice about how these difficulties could be overcome.

It is easy to imagine my surprise – and initial scepticism – when as I worked through my boxes overnight on Wednesday 13 June I came across a note from my private secretary reporting a telephone conversation with government lawyers earlier that evening. Their view now was that the present legislation – let alone any future legislation – might be more robust than their earlier advice had indicated.* They told us that we would be in a position to cap large numbers of authorities as long as we made clear at an early stage in the budgetary cycle what we would regard as an excessive increase in spending – and we could achieve this without the difficulties which new legislation would have brought. This legal advice was strengthened as a result of the Government's victory in a court case several days later against a number of local authorities appealing against capping.

On the evening of Tuesday 26 June I held a meeting of ministers to sort out exactly where we stood. The lawyers confirmed their advice that it was unlikely that we could have any greater certainty about capping under new legislation than under the present. I was reluctant to drop the idea of introducing a general capping power. I would have liked to combine this with the use of local referenda, so that an authority which wanted to spend more than the limit set by central government would have first to win the agreement of its electorate. This would have done a good deal to defuse the accusation that new spending controls would undermine local democracy. In the light of the

* The capping legislation allowed us to act on a number of different criteria. The lawyers now advised that we could be much more rigorous than we had thought in capping authorities which had made excessive increases of the charge year-on-year (as opposed to capping those which had an excessive level of spending in a particular year).

revised legal advice, though, I accepted that unless the courts came up with some new judgement which changed the position it would be best to cap in 1991–2 under the existing law. It was crucial, however, to achieve the greatest possible deterrent effect and so Chris Patten had to announce in July – well before local authorities set their budgets – how he intended to use his powers. The other aspect we had to discuss was the extra money which was needed to be put in in order to limit the burden on individuals. Chris was authorized to announce to the House certain extensions to the transitional relief scheme and other changes.

The relevant Cabinet committee met the following week under my chairmanship to finalize the community charge review and agree the details of the 1991–2 settlement – the amount that we were going to provide for local authorities in the form of grant and business rates, and the amount that we thought they ought to spend. Chris Patten and John MacGregor (the Chief Secretary) had already reached agreement on a package. Our purpose was to endorse this: I also wanted to ensure that it was understood that the extra money for the community charge was not a sign that the brakes had been taken off public expenditure control – far from it. We agreed that the local authorities ought to spend £39 billion, an increase of 19 per cent over the same estimate the previous year and an increase of 7 per cent over what they had actually spent. This would produce a community charge at 'standard spending' of £379. The actual community charge in a particular area would of course depend on whether the local authority spent more or less than this figure. It should be possible to keep the community charge down below an average of £400 by vigorous use of charge capping. Yet even so this sum was well over twice the original estimate of the community charge which had been given to ministers. I stressed that the extra money – almost £3 billion – going to reduce the burden of the community charge would mean less for other purposes. That was the priority we had chosen and all ministers must abide by the consequences. Otherwise we would lose control of public spending. Chris Patten announced these measures to the House of Commons shortly afterwards. Some further details and modifications were announced at the end of October.

The system of local authority finance which I bequeathed to my successor remained unpopular. During the leadership contest in November 1990 Michael Heseltine made great play with his pledge to review the community charge and this prompted John Major and Douglas Hurd to promise their own reviews as well. At the end of March 1991 Michael Heseltine, once again Environment Secretary, announced the outcome: the Government had decided to abandon the community charge and to return to a property tax, supplemented by a sharp rise in VAT from 15 to 17 per cent.

Few episodes of my period in government have generated more myths than the community charge. It is generally presented as a doctrinaire scheme forced on reluctant ministers by an authoritarian Prime Minister and eventually rejected by popular opinion as unworkable. Mistakes were certainly made in implementing the charge, but this picture is a tissue of nonsenses. As Nigel Lawson has generously conceded, few pieces of legislation have ever received such a thorough and scrupulous examination by ministers and officials in the relevant Cabinet committees as did the charge. Its difficulties arose from a number of factors: the worsening economic and inflationary situation; the fact that the estimates of the charge's level proved consistently misleading; and the certainty that any reform of local government finance, after seventeen years of nonrevaluation, would have produced many losers and therefore great unpopularity. The conclusion I draw is that whatever reform was chosen, we should have accompanied it with draconian restraints on local government spending from the centre in order to prevent local authorities – alas Conservative as well as Labour – from using the transition to jack up spending and blame it on the Government.

The fact remains that the defects in our system of local government finance were largely remedied by the charge, and its benefits had just started to become apparent when it was abandoned. Those advantages would have become steadily more evident as contracting out of local authority services and improved local authority efficiency took effect. But one further thing would have been necessary. Although the 1990–91 community charge capping proved relatively successful in holding down local authority spending, it would probably also have been necessary to introduce the much more far-reaching direct controls over council spending to which my mind had anyway been turning until our legal advice changed. It would have taken time before the disciplines of the new system began to affect the behaviour of the worst overspenders. But eventually they would have done so. However, the community charge was abandoned. The fundamental problems of local government – badly administered services, an obscure relationship with central government, lack of effective local accountability – not only remain: they will get worse.

CHAPTER XXIII

To Cut and to Please

Tax cuts, tax reform and privatization

The 1980s saw the rebirth in Britain of an enterprise economy. This was by and large a decade of great prosperity, when our economic performance astonished the world. Whereas Britain lagged behind other European Community countries in the 1960s and 1970s, our economy grew faster in the 1980s than all of them except Spain. Whereas most European economies in the 1980s grew more slowly than they had the previous decade, the British economy grew faster. From 1987 there were classic signs of 'overheating' and initial confusion about what monetary indicators were showing. Nigel Lawson's shadowing the deutschmark meant that we did not take action early enough to tighten monetary policy. That is not to say that the surge of prosperity in these years was just or even mainly the result of an artificial consumer boom. It was more soundly based than that. The current account deficit which became a real problem must not obscure – indeed to some degree it reflected – the fact that industry was investing in the future during these years: in the 1980s British business investment grew faster than in any other major industrial country, with the exception of Japan. Profitability rose, and so did productivity. The improvement in British manufacturing industry's productivity in the 1980s was greater than in any other major industrial economy. New firms grew and expanded. New jobs followed – 3,320,000 of them created between March 1983 and March 1990.

It is, therefore, as important to understand what went right in these years as what went wrong. Provided that the benefits are not reversed by a combination of imprudent management of the public finances and Euro-regulation, the fundamental improvements in the British economy in the 1980s will endure. Where the problem arose was on the 'demand side' as money and credit expanded too rapidly and sent the prices of assets soaring, particularly non-internationally traded goods like houses. This spiral was clearly unsustainable and had to break or be broken. By contrast the 'supply side' reforms were highly successful. These were the changes which made for greater efficiency and flexibility and so enabled British business to meet the demands of foreign and domestic markets. Without them, the economy would not have been able to grow so fast and deliver such improvements in profits, living standards and employment: in short, the country would have been poorer.

Trade union reform was crucial. The most important changes were those made between 1982 and 1984, which have already been described in some detail. But the process continued right up to the time I left office. The 1988 Employment Act, based on our manifesto pledges, strengthened rights of individual trade unionists against industrial action organized by their unions without a ballot and against the unions' attempts to 'discipline' them if they refused to go out on strike. It also instituted a special commissioner to help individual union members exercise their rights and opened up trade union accounts for inspection. The 1990 Employment Act concluded the long process of whittling away at the closed shop, which had held so many in its vicious thrall in the 1970s. It now became unlawful to deny someone a job because they were – or were not – a member of a trade union. These reductions in trade union power, together with the reinforcements of individual trade unionist's rights and responsibilities, were crucial to a properly functioning labour market, in which restrictive practices were overcome and unit labour costs kept down below the levels they would otherwise have reached. The abolition of that monument to modern Luddism – the National Dock Labour Scheme* – was another blow to restrictive practices.

Such reforms had a continuing and beneficial effect. It was not just that they allowed management once more to manage and so ensured that investment was once again regarded as the first call on profits rather than the last; they also helped change the attitudes of employees to the businesses for which they worked, and in which they increasingly held shares. So in my last year in office there were fewer industrial stoppages than in any year since 1935: under two million working days were lost in this way, compared with approaching thirteen million a year on average during the 1970s. Still too many, by the way.

But there were other changes aimed at improving the quality of the workforce by helping people to obtain the right qualifications and experience for the jobs now available. In my last year as Prime

* See p. 355.

Minister some two and a half times as much – in real terms – was being spent by government on training as under the last Labour Government. Of course, there is always a danger that 'training' becomes an end in itself, with its own bureaucracy and momentum, particularly when public funds on this scale are involved. So I was keen that as much as possible of the administration and decision-taking in these great state-funded programmes should be decentralized. Training and Enterprise Councils (TECs) were set up from 1988 to take over responsibility for the delivery of these programmes. They consisted of groups of local employers, who knew more than any 'expert' what skills were actually going to be needed.

Another innovation in which I took a keen interest was the use of Training Vouchers – which because of the corporatist sensibilities of the training establishment I was always being urged to describe as 'Credits'. Under this scheme, school leavers were given the choice of where they would use their voucher to purchase a certain amount of training from an employer, a local further education college or other approved body. The basic psychology was that of any voucher: when someone can exercise power over his own future he will take a closer interest in it than under any system of central direction. And there is absolutely no reason why those who are in receipt of state funding should be deprived of choice or responsibility. This idea was at the heart of the 'empowerment' approach of our 1987 manifesto reforms and is, perhaps, of even more pressing relevance today when the threat of welfare dependency is widely recognized.

Housing is vital to a properly working labour market.* If people cannot move to regions where there are jobs – 'getting on their bike', to quote Norman Tebbit's immortal phrase – there will remain pockets of intractable unemployment. And the less willing or able they are to move, the greater call there will be for state intervention to force or bribe firms to go to commercially unsuitable locations to provide the jobs. The private rented sector of housing would be the ideal source of cheap, often temporary, accommodation of the sort that those seeking work are likely to want. After decades of rent control, however, private landlordism – almost uniquely in Britain – is popularly associated with exploitation and bad conditions. This meant that it was never possible to take the radical action needed to reverse the shrinkage in rented housing which has got steadily worse since the First World War.

In our 1987 manifesto we promised – and subsequently in our 1988

* See also Chapter 20.

Housing Act introduced – some measures to revive the private rented sector. We further developed the two schemes – originally introduced in 1980 – of the shorthold tenancy (short lets at market rents, after which the landlord can regain possession) and the assured tenancy (also market rents but with security of tenure). These measures had some effect, at least halting the shrinkage in private rented housing; but there will need to be a sea change in attitudes if it is ever to grow to make a major contribution to labour mobility.

By contrast, council housing is the worst source of immobility. Many large council estates bring together people who are out of work but enjoy security of tenure at subsidized rents. They not only have every incentive to stay where they are: they mutually reinforce each other's passivity and undermine each other's initiative. Thus a culture grows up in which the unemployed are content to remain living mainly on the state with little will to move and find work.

So the great increase in private home ownership in my years as Prime Minister and the corresponding reduction of the public sector's share of the housing stock was an important benefit to the economy. Attempts were made to deny this on narrow financial grounds. In particular, it was said that through mortgage tax relief too much of the nation's saving has been channelled into bricks and mortar, too little into industry. This I never found convincing. First, it overlooks the fact that many people whose main means of saving is by buying their house on a mortgage would probably not otherwise invest their money in shares or set up businesses: however pervasive an enterprise culture is, most people are not born entrepreneurs. Indeed, buying a house *is* for many people the gateway to other investments. Second, the idea that British industry has fallen behind in recent decades because of a lack of investment is at best a half-truth. The fact is that much of the investment has been of the wrong sort and wrongly directed. What Britain lacked in the past was the right opportunities to make use of the investment available – because of low productivity, poor labour relations, low profits and bad management. What is true is that a high level of home ownership does need to be complemented by a sufficiently large private rented sector, as ours is not. On this score we were only half successful and the private rented sector is an area in which, given time, I would have liked to do more.

It was a different story with deregulation of business. Year after year – and with a further boost from David Young when he went to the Department of Trade and Industry in June 1987 – unnecessary regulations on business were identified and duly scrapped. David Young also shifted the emphasis of the assistance received from the

DTI towards job creation, small firms and innovation. It was not just a piece of gimmickry when what had principally been a sponsoring Department for state-owned industries and heavy manufacturing was rechristened the 'Department for Enterprise'. The importance of a continuing drive for deregulation is that otherwise reregulation is never far behind. All the pressures of modern living (or at least of modern politics) are for more controls – to protect consumers, to protect investors, to protect the environment and, increasingly, to protect powerful lobbies in the European Community. But the general truth gets lost that more regulation means higher costs, less competitiveness, fewer jobs and thus less wealth to raise the real quality of life in the long run.

All of these areas – trade union power, training, housing and business regulation – were ones in which in varying degrees we made progress in strengthening the 'supply side' of the economy. But the most important and far-reaching changes were in tax reform and privatization. Tax cuts increased incentives for the shop floor as well as the board room. Privatization shifted the balance away from the less efficient state to more efficient private business. They were the pillars on which the rest of our economic policy rested.

TAX CUTS AND TAX REFORMS

Nigel Lawson's tax reforms mark him out as a Chancellor of rare technical grasp and constructive imagination. We had some differences – not least about mortgage tax relief which he would probably have liked to abolish and whose threshold I would certainly have liked to raise. But Nigel did not generally like to seek or take advice. Doubtless he felt he did not need to. His was precisely the opposite of the collegiate style which Geoffrey Howe before him practised. Nigel preferred to take me through his budget proposals when he already had them well worked out and without any private secretary present to take notes. He liked to do this over dinner at No. 11 one Sunday towards the end of January. Had I restricted informing myself of his plans to these formal occasions it would have been difficult for me to have any real influence; for to digest issues of such complexity over after-dinner coffee would put a strain on anyone's system. But in fact, Treasury spies, realizing that this was an impossibly secretive way of proceeding with someone who after all was 'First Lord of the Treasury', furtively filled me in – with the strictest instructions not to divulge what I knew

– before Nigel proudly announced to me his budget strategy. This at least put me in a better position to question the proposed fiscal stance or to object to individual measures.

But the fact remains that Nigel's budgets were essentially his. And just as I hold him largely responsible for the errors of policy which threw away our success on inflation, so I have no hesitation in giving him the lion's share of the credit for the ingenious measures in his budgets.

The distinctive marks of Nigel's budgets were clarity and cleverness. Whereas Geoffrey Howe was instinctively a Chancellor who liked well-balanced packages of measures, Nigel Lawson liked a budget with everything based on one central theme and purpose. Geoffrey was always one to go for the prudent course, even if the effect was undramatic, whereas Nigel's search for the brilliant solution to a fiscal problem could lead him to risk all on a winning streak. He was, indeed, a natural gambler.

But the 1984 budget showed Nigel at his brilliant best. He abolished the Investment Income Surcharge, which was a grossly unfair charge on often elderly savers, and finally got rid of the National Insurance Surcharge, which Geoffrey had already cut. But his most important reform was the phasing out of tax reliefs for business at the same time as he cut Corporation Tax rates, so improving the direction and quality of business investment and greatly increasing incentives for business success. Nineteen eighty-five was a less remarkable budget, but like that of 1984 raised personal income tax allowances well above inflation. In 1986 he made what I considered just the right political judgement by cutting the basic rate of income tax by one penny, which was in effect a statement that we would not ignore the basic rate in future budgets when there was more fiscal leeway. He also introduced Personal Equity Plans (PEPs) to encourage personal investment in shares as a way of encouraging popular capitalism. In 1987 he cut two pence more off the basic rate, but balanced what might have seemed a pre-election 'give away' with the incorporation within the MTFS of the objective of a PSBR of 1 per cent of GDP, as a standard of fiscal prudence.

More controversial was Nigel's 1988 budget. I certainly had my doubts at the time. I felt – rightly – that the overall financial conditions had become too loose. Although it is monetary not fiscal policy which has the decisive role in controlling inflation it is right to look at taxes and borrowing too. Not only does the level of government borrowing influence the level of interest rates needed to exert monetary control; there is also an argument that if the private sector is borrowing too much and saving too little – which is what happened in 1988 and 1989 as the savings ratio fell to 5.6 and 6.6 per cent – you should make up for this by raising taxes and cutting government borrowing (or increasing government debt repayment).

I began by questioning the size – though not the kind – of tax cuts Nigel now proposed, partly for these reasons and partly because I felt – again rightly – that big income tax cuts in a climate of excessive consumer and business confidence may have a psychological effect, not directly predictable by the dubious science of economics, but real nonetheless. They might fire up what already seemed to be overheating. In fact, the figures which I saw on the eve of the budget for the very large public sector debt repayment (PSDR) or budget surplus – forecast in the budget at £3 billion (though the figure was distorted by privatization proceeds) – considerably reassured me. Moreover the budget surplus out-turn for 1988–9 was some £14 billion. I therefore believe that – with one apparently technical but in fact significant qualification – Nigel's 1988 budget was a success. The cuts in the basic rate of income tax to 25 pence and the top rates to 40 pence provided a huge boost to incentives, particularly for those talented, internationally mobile people so essential to economic success.

The technical point which had such practical consequences was a change in the system of mortgage tax relief, by which the £30,000 limit would no longer apply to each individual purchasing a property but rather to the house itself. This removed the discrimination in favour of unmarried cohabiting couples. Though announced in April, however, it only took effect from August. This gave a huge immediate boost to the housing market as people took out mortgages before the loophole ended, and it happened at just the wrong time, when the housing market was already overheating. That said, the overall tax changes in the 1988 budget were of the right size and direction. If they had not been accompanied by a loose monetary policy, all would have been well.

By 1989 even Nigel's usual apparently limitless confidence about our economic prospects had become dented. Monetary policy had been tightened sharply to cut back inflation. But what about fiscal policy? It was clear that the budget surplus was a reflection at least as much of the runaway pace of economic growth raising tax revenues as of underlying financial soundness; even so it was difficult to argue that such a large budget surplus should be increased still further.

And indeed when I saw Nigel for our usual discussion on Sunday 12 February, I found less difficulty than usual in persuading him to see things my way. I urged him to revise his Cabinet paper, to be less complacent, to drop the idea of a further one-penny cut in income tax (which I said would look wrong psychologically), to forget his proposal to remove the tax on the basic retirement pensions and to scrap the earnings rule instead.* I also said that there must be no loosening of monetary policy. He went along with all this: he then used some of the revenue in hand to make sensible changes in the structure of employees' national insurance contributions.

But Nigel decided not to raise the excise duties with inflation, giving an artificial downward twist to the inflation figure, which enabled him to predict that inflation would rise to about 8 per cent before falling back in the second half of the year to 5.5 per cent and perhaps 4.5 per cent in the second quarter of 1990. However, by the second quarter of 1990 it was to reach not 4.5 per cent but approaching 10 per cent. The degree of inflation that shadowing the deutschmark had injected into the system was greater than anyone, including Nigel, had realized. But by 1990 Mr 10 per cent had departed and others were left to deal with the consequences.**

John Major was in some ways all too different from Nigel Lawson as Chancellor. It seemed strange to me that, having been a competent Chief Secretary, he did not feel more at home with tackling the difficult issues he now faced when he returned to the Treasury. But probably Nigel had made all the important decisions and John had not had much of a look in. As preparation for the 1990 budget, we had a seminar attended by John and me, Richard Ryder, the Economic Secretary to the Treasury, and officials. (Nigel would never have dreamed of such a thing before a budget.) It did not get us very far, which was not John's fault: the problem was that by now none of us had any faith in the forecasts. I found myself in disagreement with John on only one issue: I stopped consideration being given to a new tax on credit. I had a good deal of sympathy with the proposition that banks and building societies had made credit too easily available and that this was leading feckless or just inexperienced borrowers into debt. But I never doubted that if we once tried to stop this by imposing a tax on it, all that general support which puritanical policies evoke in principle would soon turn into a hedonistic outcry as video recorders, expensive lunches, sports cars and foreign holidays moved out of financial reach. The tax would also have put up the RPI, though this would have been a once-and-for-all effect only. In fact, within the little

* The earnings rule limited in the early years of retirement the amount a pensioner could earn without reducing his pension.

** For Nigel Lawson's resignation see pp. 715–18.

room for manoeuvre available in these circumstances, John Major's only budget was a modest success, containing several eye-catching proposals to boost the woefully low level of savings. But by then it would take more than a sound budget – more even than a Prime Minister and Chancellor who subscribed to the same policies – to avert the political and economic consequences of allowing inflation to rise.

The fact that the return of inflation and then recession obscured the benefits of the tax changes Nigel Lawson's budgets made does not mean that those benefits had evaporated. Inflation distorts; but, once tamed again, it turns out not to have destroyed the improvements in economic performance which lower and simpler taxes bring. Only one thing can undermine these supply side benefits: that is letting public expenditure get out of control, which puts up borrowing and which eventually requires tax increases that destroy incentives. When I left office both public spending and borrowing were under tight control. Indeed, we were still budgeting for a surplus. And during my period of office public spending fell as a share of GDP from 44 per cent in 1979–80 to 40.5 per cent in 1990–91. It has since risen to 45.5 per cent of GDP (1993–4) and public sector borrowing to around £50 billion, some 8 per cent of GDP. These figures bring strange echoes of the past. In politics there are no final victories.

PRIVATIZATION

Privatization, no less than the tax structure, was fundamental to improving Britain's economic performance. But for me it was also far more than that: it was one of the central means of reversing the corrosive and corrupting effects of socialism. Ownership by the state is just that – ownership by an impersonal legal entity: it amounts to control by politicians and civil servants; and it is a misnomer to describe nationalization, as the Labour Party did, as 'public ownership'. But through privatization – particularly the kind of privatization which leads to the widest possible share ownership by members of the public – the state's power is reduced and the power of the people enhanced. Just as nationalization was at the heart of the collectivist programme by which Labour Governments sought to remodel British society, so privatization is at the centre of any programme of reclaiming territory for freedom. Whatever arguments there may – and should – be about means of sale, the competitive structures or the regulatory frameworks adopted in different cases, this fundamental purpose of privatization must not be overlooked. That consideration was of practical relevance. For it meant that in some cases if it was a choice between having the ideal circumstances for privatization, which might take years to achieve, and going for a sale within a particular politically determined timescale, the second was the preferable option.

But, of course, the narrower economic arguments for privatization were also overwhelming. The state should not be in business. State ownership effectively removes – or at least radically reduces – the threat of bankruptcy which is a discipline on privately owned firms. Investment in state-owned industries is regarded as just another call on the Exchequer, competing for money with schools or roads. As a result, decisions about investment are made according to criteria quite different from those which would apply to a business in the private sector. Nor, in spite of valiant attempts to do so (not least under Conservative governments) can one find an even moderately satisfactory framework for making decisions about the future of state-owned industries. Targets can be set; warnings given; performance monitored; new chairmen appointed. These things help. But state-owned businesses can never function as proper businesses. The very fact that the state is ultimately accountable for them to Parliament rather than management to the shareholders means that they cannot be. The spur is just not there.

Privatization itself does not solve every problem; though, as I shall show, it certainly exposed hidden problems which could thus be tackled. Monopolies or quasi-monopolies which are transferred to the private sector need careful regulation to ensure against abuses of market power, whether at the expense of competitors (if there are such) or of customers. But on regulatory grounds there are good arguments for private ownership as well: regulation which had, when in the public sector, been covert now had to be overt and specific. This provides a clearer and better discipline. And more generally, of course, the evidence of the lamentable performance of government in running any business – or indeed administering any service – is so overwhelming that the onus should always be on statists to demonstrate why government should perform a particular function rather than why the private sector should not.

Now that almost universal lip service is paid to the case for privatization it is difficult to recall just how revolutionary – how all but unthinkable – it seemed at the end of the 1970s. Our 1979 manifesto had been quite cautious on the subject, promising: 'to sell back to private ownership the recently nationalized aerospace and shipbuilding concerns, giving their employees the opportunity to purchase shares' and selling 'shares in the National Freight Corporation to the general public'.

The depth of the recession meant that there was not much prospect of successful privatization in the early years, due to low market confidence and large nationalized industry losses. But, for all that, by the time of the 1983 election British Aerospace and the (now) National Freight Consortium were flourishing in the private sector, the latter after a spectacularly successful management and worker buy-out; Cable and Wireless, Associated British Ports, Britoil (a nationalized North Sea oil exploration and production company set up by Labour in 1975), British Rail Hotels and Amersham International (which manufactured radioactive materials for industrial, medical and research uses) had also in whole or in part been moved back to private ownership.

The huge losses of British Shipbuilding and the massive restructuring required of British Airways prevented their sale for the moment; though in both cases the prospect of privatization was an important factor in asserting tighter financial discipline and attracting good management. The British Telecom Bill – to privatize BT – had only fallen with the old Parliament and would be introduced with the new. The 1983 manifesto mentioned all of these as candidates for privatization as well as Rolls-Royce, substantial parts of British Steel and of British Leyland and Britain's airports. Substantial private capital would also be introduced into the National Bus Company. And there was the repeated promise of shares offered to employees in the companies concerned. Perhaps the most far-reaching pledge, though, was that we would seek to 'increase competition in, and [attract] private capital into the gas and electricity industries'. Gas was indeed privatized in 1986. The more complicated and ambitious privatization of electricity had to wait for the next Parliament.* In the 1987 manifesto both electricity and the water industry were the main candidates for privatization. So over these years privatization had leapt from fairly low down to somewhere near the top of our political and economic agenda. This continued to be so for the rest of my time in office. Why?

One reason I have already touched upon. Economic conditions improved and the prospects for privatization improved with them. But there is a further reason. Our privatization programme was constantly breaking new ground. Each industry posed its own special problems. Each flotation or trade sale raised separate issues. It is one of the

* On both of which, see pp. 681–5.

disadvantages of being in the vanguard of reform – as the British who pioneered the industrial revolution know well – that the only experience you can learn from is your own. Gradually, the general emphasis switched from privatization of industries whose nationalization was justified only by socialist dogma, to that of public utilities where the arguments were more complex.

I was always especially pleased to see businesses which had absorbed huge sums of taxpayers' money and been regarded as synonyms for Britain's industrial failure pass out of state ownership and thrive in the private sector. The very prospect of privatization compelled such companies to make themselves competitive and profitable. Lord King turned round British Airways by a bold policy of slimming it down, improving its service to the customer and giving its employees a stake in success. It was sold as a thriving concern in 1987. British Steel, which had absorbed vast subsidies in the 1970s and early '80s, re-entered the private sector as a profitable company in 1988. But it was perhaps BL (now known as the Rover Group) whose return to private ownership caused me most satisfaction – in spite of the almost endless arguments about how much its private sector purchaser, the once state-owned British Aerospace, had received.

Rover had by now a superb Chairman in Graham Day who had been making great efforts to do what I had always hoped would be done – dispose of surplus assets and increase the drive for higher productivity. But that did not mean that I was happy with the sort of figures the company's Corporate Plans contained. It retained an apparently insatiable appetite for cash – it had absorbed £2.9 billion of public money in total since we came to office in 1979 – and the Government's liabilities under the Varley-Marshall assurances remained at some £1.6 billion. The earlier anti-American hysteria about takeovers by foreign companies of our British car production meant that the prospects for sale of the main car business did not look promising,* though both Ford and Volkswagen continued to express some interest.

This was the position when, just before Christmas 1987, there were signs that British Aerospace might be interested in acquiring Rover. I was not immediately clear that British Aerospace's was a serious offer. But it soon turned out that it was. There was an industrial logic in the acquisition, for the car business – if relieved of its burden of debt and provided with a substantial injection of new investment – would complement the rest of BAe's business. Aerospace depends on

* See pp. 437–41.

gaining a few huge contracts at inevitably irregular intervals; cars satisfy a steadier market. And, of course, the sale to BAe would have one marked political advantage: the company would stay British.

David Young was subsequently heavily criticized for the way in which the deal was struck. In fact, he played a difficult hand with great aplomb. The special financial provisions of the deal only reflected the poor state of BL after years of state ownership and wasted investment. That the terms had to be revised reflected the new interest of the European Commission in probing the details of state aid to industry, rather than being a reflection on the basic soundness of the deal itself.

Only satisfied customers can ultimately guarantee the future of a business or the jobs depending on it and Rover could not be an exception to that rule. But the effects of the disastrous socialist experiment to which the company had been subject had now been overcome; and Rover was back in the private sector where it belonged.

PRIVATIZATION OF PUBLIC UTILITIES

British Telecom was the first utility to be privatized. Its sale did more than anything else to lay the basis for a share-owning popular capitalism in Britain. Some two million people bought shares, about half of whom had never been shareholders before. But the relationship between privatization and liberalization – that is opening up telecommunications to wider competition – was a complex one. The first steps of liberalization had begun under Keith Joseph who split British Telecom from the Post Office, removed its monopoly over telephone sales and licensed Mercury to provide a competing network. Further liberalization took place at the time of privatization.

But if we had wanted to go further and break up BT into separate businesses, which would have been better on competition grounds, we would have had to wait many years before privatization could take place. This was because its accounting and management sytems were, by modern standards, almost nonexistent. There was no way in which the sort of figures which investors would want to see could have been speedily or reliably produced. So I was well satisfied when, after the delay which had been caused by the need to withdraw the original bill with the advent of the 1983 general election, British Telecom was eventually successfully privatized in November 1984.

At the same time, a system of regulation was established under the control of an Office of Telecommunications (OFTEL) with the result that BT had to keep its price increases at a fixed level below the rate of inflation for a number of years. This was a quite new and – as it has turned out – influential departure. Not only did the 'RPI minus x' formula become the model for dealing with public utility privatizations in Britain: it has since been adopted overseas, for example in the United States.

The consequences of privatization for BT were seen in a doubling of its level of investment, now no longer constrained by the Treasury rules applying in the public sector. The consequences for customers were just as good. Prices fell sharply in real terms, the waiting list for telephones shrank and the number of telephone boxes in operation at any particular time increased. It was a convincing demonstration that utilities were better run in the private sector.

Many of the same issues arose in the privatization of British Gas, which had been a nationalized industry for nearly forty years. BGC had five main businesses. These were: the purchase of gas from the oil companies which produced it; the supply of gas, involving the transmission and distribution of gas from the beach-head landing points to the customer; its own exploration for and production of gas, mostly from offshore fields; the sale of gas appliances through its showrooms; and the installation and servicing of those appliances. Of these functions only the second – the supply of gas to consumers – could be described as a natural monopoly. But there were a number of considerations which argued against fundamentally restructuring or breaking up the business. The most important of these, curiously enough, was lack of parliamentary time. Consideration of privatization had inevitably been held up by the miners' strike of 1984–5. Both the BGC and Energy Secretary, Peter Walker, were determined to privatize BGC as a whole and their full co-operation was essential if it were to be achieved as I wanted during our second term. There was much to be said for using the model of British Telecom rather than trying to come up with a fundamentally different one under these conditions.

Accordingly, at a meeting I held with Peter Walker, Nigel Lawson and John Moore on Tuesday 26 March 1985 I agreed that we should go for a sale of the whole business. The formula for regulation and the issue of liberalizing imports and exports of gas became the focus of much argument between Peter Walker who was prepared to accept a degree of monopoly as the price of early privatization on the one hand, and the Treasury and the DTI on the other who would have preferred stronger competition from the first. We were able to liberalize gas exports but I went along with most of Peter Walker's arguments in order to achieve privatization in the available timescale. I still think I was right to do so because the privatization was a resounding success. (The problems of the monopoly power of British Gas are now being investigated by the Monopolies and Mergers Commission.) Four and a half million people invested in the shares, including almost all of the company's 130,000 employees.

The privatization of the water industry was a more politically sensitive issue. Much emotive nonsense was talked along the lines of, 'look, she's even privatizing the rain which falls from the heavens.' I used to retort that the rain may come from the Almighty but he did not send the pipes, plumbing and engineering to go with it. The Opposition's case was even weaker than this, for about a quarter of the water industry in England and Wales had long been in the private sector. Of more significance was the fact that the water authorities did not just supply water: they also safeguarded the quality of rivers, controlled water pollution and had important responsibilities for fisheries, conservation, recreation and navigation. It was Nick Ridley – a countryman with a natural feel for environmental issues – who, when he became Environment Secretary, grasped that what was wrong was that the water authorities combined both regulatory and supply functions. It made no sense that those who were responsible for the treatment and disposal of sewage, for example, should also be responsible for regulating pollution. So the bill which Nick introduced also established a new National Rivers Authority. Privatization also meant that the companies would be able to raise money from capital markets for the investment needed to improve the water quality.

The most technically and politically difficult privatization – and the one which went furthest in combining transfer of a public utility to the private sector with radical restructuring – was that of the Electricity Supply Industry. The industry had two main components. First, there was the Central Electricity Generating Board (CEGB) which ran the power stations and the National Grid (the transmission system). Second, there were the twelve Area Boards which distributed the power to customers. (In Scotland there were two companies running the industry – the South of Scotland Electricity Board and the North of Scotland Hydro Board.) Some attempt had been made in Nigel Lawson's 1983 Energy Act to introduce competition into the system. But it had had no practical effect. As a result the whole of the industry was based on monopoly. The CEGB had a monopoly nationally and the Area Boards monopolies regionally. The challenge for us would be to privatize as much as possible of the industry while introducing the maximum amount of competition.

I had an initial discussion about electricity privatization with Peter Walker and Nigel Lawson on the eve of the 1987 general election. I did not intend to keep Peter at Energy so there was no point in going into detail. But we did agree that the pledge of privatization should be included in the manifesto and be given effect in the next Parliament.

When Cecil Parkinson took over as Energy Secretary after the election he found that the department's thinking had been strongly influenced by Peter Walker's corporatist instincts – and by their recognition that Walter Marshall would be passionately opposed to the break-up of the CEGB of which he was chairman. The prevailing idea seemed to be that the CEGB and the National Grid would be floated as one company and the twelve Area Boards would be combined into another. This would have done no more than change a monopoly into a duopoly; but Cecil changed all this. He was subsequently the butt of much malicious and unjust criticism because of the changes which his successor, John Wakeham, had to make in his original privatization strategy, particularly in connection with the nuclear power stations. In fact, it was Cecil who took the bold and right decision to reject both corporatist thinking and vested interests by breaking up the CEGB and – most crucially – removing from its control the National Grid. The grid would now be owned jointly by the twelve distribution companies created from the old Area Boards rather than by the CEGB. Whereas under the old system the controller of the grid was also its near monopoly supplier, control would now be with those who had the strongest interest in ensuring that as much competition as possible be allowed to develop in power generation. These two decisions meant that competition became effective.

Cecil Parkinson was working towards this model over the summer of 1987 and in September we had a seminar at Chequers to look at the options. At this stage none was ruled out, but I insisted that all the legislation must be enacted before the end of that Parliament. Cecil continued to work up the plans and discussed them again with me and other ministers in mid-December. No one was attracted by solutions which retained a monopoly of generation for the CEGB or its continued ownership of the grid. The real question was whether the CEGB should be divided up into just two or as many as four or five competing generating companies. Nigel Lawson favoured the more radical option. The trouble was that it was difficult to see any of these companies being large enough to keep up the very costly development of nuclear power, which I regarded as essential both in order to ensure security of power supply and for environmental reasons.

There was also Walter Marshall to consider. Not only did I like and admire him. I also felt that we all owed him a great debt for having kept the power stations working during the miners' strike. He was opposed to any break-up of the CEGB, but he might just be willing to go along with a two-way split in which the larger company retained the nuclear power stations. There was no way in which he would have stayed on if the CEGB had been split into four. I could not, of course, allow his views to be decisive: nor did I do so. But I hoped to obtain his and his colleagues' co-operation in the difficult transition to the new privatized and competitive system. So at a meeting in mid-January I came down on the side of the solution that Cecil favoured. But I added that this did not preclude moving at some future time to the more competitive model which Nigel Lawson would have preferred.

Later that month I agreed that the split in capacity between the two new proposed generating companies should be 70/30. This was the plan which I tried to sell to Walter Marshall when he came in with Cecil Parkinson for a long talk one February evening. Walter – never averse to blunt speaking – did not conceal his disagreement with the approach we favoured. I agreed with him – as he knew I did – about the great importance of nuclear power. But I did not think that its prospects would be damaged by our plans. Again and again I insisted that whatever structure we created must provide genuine competition. I often found that straight talking pays dividends. On further consideration and after further discussions with Cecil, Walter Marshall said that though the CEGB would express regret at what we had decided he was prepared to make the system work. Cecil Parkinson's plans were also strongly opposed by Peter Walker who suggested that it would take at least eight years before there was any chance of completing this competitive model of privatization. None of us was convinced by this. So on Thursday 25 February Cecil could make his statement to the House of Commons setting out how we intended to privatize electricity.

This, though, was by no means the end of the matter. As always, the prospect of privatization meant that the finances of the industry were subject to searching scrutiny, perhaps for the first time ever. And what came to light was extremely unwelcome. For environmental reasons and to ensure security of supply, I felt it was essential to keep up the development of nuclear power. The real cost of nuclear energy compared with other energy sources is often overrated. Coal-fired power stations pour out carbon dioxide into the atmosphere and no one has yet put a credible figure on what it will ultimately cost to deal with the resulting problem of global warming. But the fact remained that there would be an immediate extra cost from nuclear energy which consumers would have to bear. This was tolerable if not popular.

But in the autumn of 1988 the figures for the cost of decommissioning the now ageing power stations were suddenly revised sharply upwards by the Department of Energy. These had been consistently underestimated or perhaps even concealed. And the more closely the figures were scrutinized the higher they appeared. By the summer of 1989 the whole prospect for privatizing the main generating company which would have the nuclear power stations started to look in jeopardy. So I agreed that the older Magnox power stations should be taken out of the privatization and remain under government control. This was one of Cecil's last actions at Energy and it fell to his successor, John Wakeham, to deal with the rest of the nuclear problem.

Alan Walters had been urging from the previous autumn that all the nuclear power stations should be removed from the privatization. As so often, he turned out to be right. It was never a matter of safety, which could perfectly well have been ensured in the private sector, but rather of cost. The figures for decommissioning the other power stations started to look uncertain and then to escalate, just as those for Magnox had done. John Wakeham recommended and I agreed that all nuclear power in England and Wales should be retained in state control. One consequence of this was that Walter Marshall, who naturally wanted to retain the nuclear provinces in his empire, decided to resign, about which I was very sad. But the other consequence was that privatization could now proceed, as it did, with great success, to the benefit of customers, shareholders and the Exchequer.

The result of Cecil Parkinson's ingenious reorganization of that industry on competitive lines is that Britain now has perhaps the most efficient electricity supply industry in the world. And as a result of the transparency required by privatization we also became the first country in the world to investigate the full costs of nuclear power – and then to make proper financial provision for them.

PLANS FOR FURTHER PRIVATIZATION

I have already mentioned the impact electricity privatization would have on the coal industry. Clearly, a privately owned electricity industry would be much more demanding in the commercial terms it expected from the NCB than would a state-owned monopoly. But in any case I always wanted to have the coal industry return to the private sector. In November 1990, not long before I left Downing Street, John Wakeham and I discussed the prospects for coal privatization, though not the detailed means. I felt that a combination of trade sales to companies with mining interests with special terms for the miners to buy shares would probably be the best way forward. How many of the pits had a long-term commercial future was unclear. We were still mining too much high-cost, deep-mined coal – a situation which had come about because of the protected and monopolistic market the nationalized coal industry had enjoyed. So there would have to be closures.

But – both when Cecil was Energy Secretary and when John succeeded him – I never had regard to the commercial aspects alone. The memories of the year-long coal strike were unforgettably etched on my mind. I kept in touch with Roy Lynk, the Nottinghamshire leader of the UDM, who knew that he could speak to me, if and when he needed, and I made sure that both Cecil and John understood my feelings about the need to protect the interests of his members. First, I felt a strong sense of obligation and loyalty to the Nottinghamshire miners who had stayed at work in spite of all the violence the militants threw at them. And, second, I also knew we might have to face another strike. Where would we be if we had closed the pits at which moderate miners would have gone on working, and kept more profitable but more left-wing pits open?

I also refused to allow the NCB to sidestep the agreed procedure of referring closures to the independent colliery review body, which had been set up as part of the settlement of the miners' strike. I had learned from hard experience that you must never allow yourself to be manoeuvred into taking drastic action on pit closures when a steady, low-key approach will secure what is needed over a somewhat longer period. In dealing with the coal industry you must have the mentality of a general as much as that of an accountant. And the generalship must often be Fabian rather than Napoleonic.

The other privatization project which I was considering at this time was that of British Rail. BR's subsidiaries had already been sold. It was the main businesses we had now to consider. Cecil Parkinson and I considered how to proceed in October 1990. Cecil was keen to privatize the separate rail businesses – like Inter-City, Freight, Network South-East. I, for my part, saw attractions in the idea of a national Track Authority which would own all the track, signalling and stations and then private companies would compete to run services. But these were large questions which needed careful thought and economic analysis. So I agreed with Cecil that a working party involving the

Treasury and DTI as well as the Transport Department be set up to study the isuue and report back to me. That was as far as I could take the issue.

There was still much I would have liked to do. But Britain under my premiership was the first country to reverse the onward march of socialism. By the time I left office, the state-owned sector of industry had been reduced by some 60 per cent. Around one in four of the population owned shares. Over six hundred thousand jobs had passed from the public to the private sector. It constituted the greatest shift of ownership and power away from the state to individuals and their families in any country outside the former communist bloc. Indeed, Britain set a worldwide trend in privatization in countries as different as Czechoslovakia and New Zealand. Some £400 billion of assets have been or are being privatized worldwide. And privatization is not only one of Britain's most successful exports: it has re-established our reputation as a nation of innovators and entrepreneurs. Not a bad record for something we were constantly told was 'just not on'.

CHAPTER XXIV

Floaters and Fixers

Monetary policy, interest rates and the exchange rate

A correct economic policy depends crucially upon a correct judgement of what activities properly fall to the state and what to people. The state has to set a framework of laws, regulation and taxes in which businesses and individuals are then free to operate. But there also has to be a financial framework for policy. After a long struggle during my first term, from 1979 to 1983, like-minded ministers and I had largely converted the Cabinet, the Conservative Party and opinion in the worlds of finance, business and even the media to a more restrictive view of what the state's role in the economy should be. Moreover, as regards the regulatory framework within which business could run its affairs, there was a general understanding that lower taxes, fewer controls and less interference should be the goal. But as regards setting the overall financial framework, within which the real economy generates wealth, there was less common ground. Whereas Nigel Lawson and I agreed strongly about the role of the state in general, we came sharply to differ about monetary and exchange rate policy.

Our success in bringing down inflation in our first term from a rate of 10 per cent (and rising) to under 4 per cent (and falling) had been achieved by controlling the money supply. 'Monetarism' – or the belief that inflation is a monetary phenomenon, i.e., 'too much money chasing too few goods' – had been buttressed by a fiscal policy which reduced government borrowing, freeing resources for private investment and getting the interest rate down. This combined approach had been expressed through the Medium Term Financial Strategy (MTFS) – in large measure Nigel Lawson's brainchild.* Its implementation depended heavily on monitoring the monetary indicators. These, as I have noted, were often distorted, confusing and volatile. We needed other indicators as well. So, before the end of Geoffrey

* See pp. 96–7.

Howe's Chancellorship the value of the pound against other currencies – the exchange rate – was also being taken into account.

It is important to understand what the relationship between the exchange rate and the money supply is – and what it is not. First consider the effect of an increase in the exchange rate; that is, one pound sterling is worth more in foreign currency. Because most import and export prices are fixed in foreign currencies, the sterling prices of these tradeable goods will fall. But this only applies to goods and services which are readily imported and exported, like oil, grain or textiles. Many of the goods and services that comprise our national income are not of this sort: for example, we cannot export our houses or the services provided in our restaurants. The prices of these things are not directly affected by the exchange rate, and the indirect effect – passed on via wages – will be limited. What does more or less determine the prices of houses and other 'non-tradeables', however, is the money supply.

If the money supply rises too fast, the prices of non-tradeable domestic goods will rise accordingly, and a strong pound will not prevent that. But the interaction of a strong pound and a loose money supply causes the export sector to be depressed, resources to flow to houses, restaurants and the like. The balance of trade will then go into larger and larger deficits, which have to be financed by borrowing from foreigners. This kind of distortion just cannot last. Either the exchange rate has to come down, or monetary growth has to be curtailed, or both.

This result is of the utmost importance. Either one chooses to hold an exchange rate to a particular level, whatever monetary policy is needed to maintain that rate. Or one sets a monetary target, allowing the exchange rate to be determined by market forces. It is, therefore, quite impossible to control both the exchange rate *and* monetary policy.

A free exchange rate, however, is fundamentally *influenced* by monetary policy. The reason is simple. If a lot more pounds are put into circulation, then the value of the pound will tend to fall – just as a glut of strawberries will cause their value to go down. So a falling pound may indicate that monetary policy has been too loose.

But it may not. There are many factors other than the money supply which have a great influence on a free exchange rate. The most important of these are international capital flows. If a country reforms its tax, regulatory and trade union arrangements so that its after-tax rate of return on capital rises well above that of other countries, then there will be a net inflow of capital and its currency will be in considerable demand. Under a free exchange rate, it would appreciate. But this would not be a sign of monetary stringency: indeed, as in Britain in 1987 to mid-1988, a high exchange rate may well be associated with a considerable monetary expansion.

It follows from this that if the exchange rate becomes an objective in itself, as opposed to one indicator among others for monetary policy, 'monetarism' itself has been abandoned. It is worth repeating the point because it is of such importance to understanding the arguments which took place: you can either target the money supply or the exchange rate, but not both. It is an entirely practical issue. The only effective way to control inflation is by using interest rates to control the money supply. If, on the contrary, you set interest rates in order to stick at a particular exchange rate you are steering by a different and potentially more wayward star. As we have now seen twice – once when, during my time, Nigel shadowed the deutschmark outside the ERM and interest rates stayed too low; once when, under John Major, we tried to hold to an unrealistic parity inside the ERM and interest rates stayed too high – the result of plotting a course by this particular star is that you steer straight on to the reefs.

ECONOMIC AND MONETARY UNION (EMU)

These questions were not ones for the technicians alone: they went to the very heart of economic policy, which itself lies at the heart of democratic politics. But there was an even more important issue which was raised first by argument about whether sterling should join the ERM and then, in a more acute form, about whether we should accept European Community proposals for Economic and Monetary Union (EMU). This was the issue of sovereignty. Sterling's participation in the ERM was seen partly as proof that we were 'good Europeans' (a phrase which in fact increasingly meant bad Europeans, as the Community adopted a selfish, protectionist stance to liberated eastern Europe). But it was also seen as a way of abdicating control over our own monetary policy, in order to have it determined by the German Bundesbank. This was what was meant when people said we would gain credibility for our policies if we were – to adopt another Euro-metaphor – 'anchored' to the deutschmark. Actually, the metaphor is strangely appropriate: for if the tide changes and you are anchored, the only option to letting out more chain as your ship rises is to sink by the bows; and in an ERM where revaluations were ever more frowned upon there was no more chain to let out. Which leads on to EMU.

The ERM was seen by the European Commission and others as a path to EMU – and this subtly changed the former's purpose. But EMU itself – which involves the loss of the power to issue your own currency and acceptance of one European currency, one central bank and one set of interest rates – means the end of a country's economic independence and thus the increasing irrelevance of its parliamentary democracy. Control of its economy is transferred from the elected government, answerable to Parliament and the electorate, to unaccountable supra-national institutions. In our opposition to EMU, Nigel Lawson and I were at one. Indeed, perhaps the most powerful critique of the whole concept was that contained in Nigel's lecture at Chatham House in January 1989 when he said:

> It is clear that economic and monetary union implies nothing less than European government – albeit a federal one – and political union: the United States of Europe. That is simply not on the agenda now, nor will it be for the foreseeable future.

Alas, by his pursuit of a policy that allowed British inflation to rise, which itself almost certainly flowed from his passionate wish to take sterling into the ERM, Nigel so undermined confidence in my government that EMU was brought that much nearer.

EARLY DISCUSSION OF THE EXCHANGE RATE MECHANISM (ERM)

To trace the course of our arguments in government about the Exchange Rate Mechanism of the European Monetary System (EMS) it is necessary to go right back to our first year in office. The Foreign Office and the Treasury both had an interest; the former regarded it as a question of European relations, the latter – rightly – as an economic question. I decided early on to be closely involved in the issue and held an initial meeting to discuss the question in October 1979. In retrospect, the balance of opinion in the Cabinet is of some significance. Geoffrey Howe as Chancellor was against membership at present, partly because of uncertainty about the effects of abolishing exchange controls. The then Governor of the Bank of England, though he agreed, was more enthusiastically in favour. Keith Joseph and John

Nott were against. So was I. But since we had devised the formula that we would join when the 'time was right' (or 'ripe' as it was sometimes expressed) there seemed no need to change our basic position. The time was not 'right' and no one seriously thought it was. Geoffrey Howe gave no hint of his future position. Indeed, in December he came to see me to complain that in a speech he had made about the subject in Brussels Peter Carrington had been too positive about the EMS.

Even at this stage, the basic arguments for and against the ERM were known, though none of us had, of course, given as much thought to the subject as we would do later. Britain had already had an unhappy experience of trying to peg sterling in a European currency system. In 1972 Ted Heath's Government had ignominiously been forced to leave the European 'snake' – the forerunner of the ERM – after a mere six weeks. So any British Government would need to be cautious.

There were two other matters which bore on the decision. First, there was no disguising, for reasons I have explained, that there was always going to be potential for conflict between our domestic monetary policy and an exchange rate target – this was brought out clearly in Treasury papers prepared for us now. Second, we were conscious – perhaps over-conscious as Alan Walters would argue – of sterling's position as a 'petro-currency'. The pound's value was affected by the discovery and exploitation of huge quantities of North Sea oil. This had the apparently perverse result that whereas higher oil prices increased the value of the pound, they would generally reduce the value of other western European currencies. But the greatest destabilizing factor was the appalling condition of the British economy in 1979. Until inflation had been brought under control and the public finances restored, it was not, in my view, realistic to consider participation in the ERM.

But in early 1980 Helmut Schmidt was urging me to enter the ERM and I was anxious to be as co-operative as possible to the Germans because I needed their support on the question of our Community budget contributions. So I reopened the question. The more I looked at the papers and the facts they revealed, the more sceptical I became. The Treasury were firmly against our joining. They noted that if we had joined in September 1979 there would have had to be very heavy intervention in the exchange markets – selling pounds – to hold sterling down. I chaired a meeting on the subject in March 1980 at which I opened by saying that domestic monetary policy must remain paramount. After we had argued all the points through, we concluded that we should not join in the immediate future but stick to the line that we intended to join when conditions permitted.

There was further discussion in the autumn of 1981. It will be remembered that this was a difficult time when some of the gains of lower interest rates obtained through our tough 1981 budget looked as if they might be dissipated as a result of international pressures. United States interest rates rose as the Federal Reserve Bank attempted to restrain the inflationary pressure generated during the previous Carter presidency: throughout the world interest rates followed. I asked Geoffrey Howe to bring forward a paper looking once again at the question of whether we should join the ERM. Opinion among Treasury ministers was divided. But both Geoffrey Howe and Leon Brittan (then Chief Secretary) were against our joining. The position of Nigel Lawson, then Financial Secretary, was less clear.

I said that I would need to be convinced that there were positive arguments for joining, not just an insufficiency of arguments against. My caution was reinforced by powerful advice from Alan Walters. His view was that it was wrong to think of the ERM as a force for stability. It did not even have the – arguable – merits of a system of fixed exchange rates. The parities moved within a band. Then, after bumping along against the ceiling or the floor, they would go through a process of periodic realignments in which the rates moved in discrete jumps. These movements, moreover, were the subject of political horse-trading rather than the workings of the market – and the market does a better job.

After several postponements as a result of other pressures on my diary, I eventually chaired another meeting on the subject in January 1982. Geoffrey Howe's view was still that this was not the right time to join. I agreed. I said that I was not convinced that there would be solid advantage in joining the ERM. I did not believe that in practice it would provide an effective discipline on our economic management. Rather, it removed our freedom of manoeuvre. I accepted, however, that when our inflation and interest rates moved much closer to those of West Germany the case for joining would be more powerful. For the time being, we would maintain our existing position on the issue.

ARGUMENTS ABOUT THE ERM: 1985

There could be no question of our entering the ERM on the eve of a general election, so this was the situation which Nigel Lawson inherited when I made him Chancellor in 1983. At this time the exchange rate was just one factor being taken into account in order to assess monetary conditions. It was the monetary aggregates which were crucial. The wider measure of money – £M3 – which we had originally chosen in the MTFS had become heavily distorted. A large proportion of it was in reality a form of savings, invested for the interest it earned. In Nigel's first budget (1984) he set out different target ranges for narrow as well as broad money. The former – M0 – had been moving upward a good deal more slowly and this was taken into account in plotting the future course. But at this stage M3 and M0 were formally given equal importance in the conduct of policy. Other monetary indicators, including the exchange rate, were also taken into account. Our critics, who had until now denounced our policy as a rigid adherence to a statistical formula, began to denounce our rootless and arbitrary pragmatism. And indeed, sensible as this change was, it was to mark the beginning of a process by which the clarity of the MTFS became muddied. This in turn, I suspect, caused Nigel, as the years went by, to search with increasing desperation for an alternative standard – reliable in itself, convincing to the markets – which he finally thought he had found in the exchange rate.

Events in January 1985 brought the ERM back into discussion. The dollar was soaring and there was intense pressure on sterling, in spite of the soundness of Britain's finances. I agreed with Nigel that our interest rates should be raised sharply. I also agreed with Nigel's view that there should be co-ordinated international intervention in the exchange rates to achieve greater stability, and I sent a message to this effect to President Reagan. This policy was formalized by Nigel and other Finance ministers under the so-called 'Plaza Agreement' in September. In retrospect, I believe that this was a mistake. As Alan Walters would always argue, if intervention is 'sterilized', that is to say not allowed to affect the money supply and short-term interest rates, it will have only a fleeting effect; on the other hand, if it does promote monetary growth then it will be inflationary. The Plaza Agreement gave Finance ministers – Nigel above all perhaps – the mistaken idea that they had it in their power to defy the markets indefinitely. This was to have serious consequences for all of us.

Sterling's problems also prompted Nigel to raise with me in February the issue of the ERM. He said that in his view controlling inflation required acceptance of a financial discipline which could be provided either by monetary targets or by a fixed exchange rate. It was essentially a secondary matter which of these was chosen. But new factors, argued Nigel, favoured the ERM. First, it was proving difficult to get financial markets to understand what the Government's policy towards the exchange rate really was: the ERM would provide much clearer rules of the game. There was also a political consideration. Many Conservative MPs were in favour of joining. In arguments about additional spending and borrowing it would, he thought, be helpful to be faced with a discipline which MPs themselves accepted. Entry into the ERM would also move the focus of attention away from the value of the pound against the dollar – where, of course, the problem at this particular moment lay. Finally, £M3 was becoming increasingly suspect as a monetary indicator because its control depended increasingly on 'overfunding', with the resulting rise in the so-called 'bill mountain'.* I was not convinced on any of these counts, with the possible exception of the last. But I agreed that there should be a seminar involving the Treasury, the Bank of England and the Foreign Office to discuss it all.

Alan Walters could not attend the seminar and so he let me have his views separately. He put his finger on the key issue. Would membership of the ERM reduce the speculative pressure on sterling? In fact, it would probably make it worse. That was the lesson to be drawn from what had happened to other ERM currencies, like the franc. Moreover, in view of Britain's open capital and exchange markets and the international role of sterling, we would be subject to greater pressures than France.

At my seminar Nigel did not argue that it would be right to enter the ERM under current circumstances. But he repeated the general argument in favour of joining which he had put to me earlier. Perhaps the most significant intervention, however, was that of Geoffrey Howe who had now been converted to the Foreign Office's departmental enthusiasm for the ERM and thought that we should be looking for an appropriate opportunity to join – though he too did not think the circumstances at the moment were right. In the course of the discussion it became clear that we would need to build up foreign exchange reserves if we wanted to be in a position to enter. I agreed that the Treasury and the Bank of England should consider how this should be done. But since no one was arguing for immediate entry, there was no other decision to take. The meeting ended amicably enough.

During the summer of 1985 I started to become concerned about

* Overfunding was the practice by which the Government sought to reduce private bank deposits – and hence £M3 – by selling greater amounts of public debt than were required merely to finance its own deficit. The 'bill mountain' arose from the use of the proceeds to buy back treasury bills from the market.

the inflation prospect. I was uneasy for a number of reasons. £M3 was rising rather fast. Property prices were increasing, always a dangerous sign. The 'bill mountain' was worrying too – not because it suggested anything about inflation (indeed the overfunding which led to it was in part the result of the Bank's attempt to control £M3). Rather, since we had decided against a policy of overfunding as far back as 1981, the fact that it had been resumed on such a scale without authorization did not increase my confidence in the way policy in general was being implemented.

Even now it is unclear whether my misgivings were justified. Some analysts – notably the perceptive Tim Congdon – would argue that the rise in £M3 now and later did cause inflationary problems. By contrast, Alan Walters, who believed that M0 was the best indicator, reckoned that monetary policy was sufficiently tight, as did the rest of my advisers. Essentially, these tricky questions are always a matter of judgement. The important thing is that when clear evidence appears that things are slipping you take action fast. Certainly, I do not believe that monetary policy in 1985 – or 1986 – was the main cause of the problems we were later to face.

Nigel now returned to the charge on the ERM. I agreed to hold a further seminar at the end of September. The subject seemed to be becoming something of an *idée fixe*. Nigel even sent me a paper envisaging what would happen if we were in the ERM in the run-up to a general election which the financial markets thought that we might lose. In such circumstances, he argued, we would need to announce our temporary cessation from operating the system coupled with an undertaking that on our return to office after the election we would immediately resume at the same parity as before. In itself, of course, this was an example of the perils of committing oneself to fixed parities irrespective of outside events.

By now I was more convinced than ever of the disadvantages of the ERM. I could see no particular reason to allow British monetary policy to be determined largely by the Bundesbank rather than by the British Treasury, unless we had no confidence in our own ability to control inflation. I was extremely sceptical about whether the industrial lobby which was pressing us so hard to join the ERM would maintain its enthusiasm once they came to see that it was making their goods uncompetitive. I doubted whether the public would welcome what might turn out to be the huge cost of defending sterling within the ERM – which, indeed, might well prove to be impossible in the run-up to a general election and so be compounded by a forced devaluation. Looking back over the last few years it was clear that sterling had not tracked other European currencies in a stable way. In 1980, sterling rose 20 per cent against the European Currency Unit (ecu). In 1981 it fell by 15 per cent from peak to trough. In 1982 it did the same. In 1983 it rose by as much as 10 per cent. In 1984 it was somewhat more stable. But in 1985 it had risen by more than 10 per cent. To control such movements, we would have needed recourse to huge quantities of international reserves and to a very tough interest rate policy.

There was nothing secret about these facts. They were available to anyone who wanted to know them. But nothing is more obstinate than a fashionable consensus. Nor is it without influence on Cabinet committees. I had no support at the seminar at the end of September. Nor did my arguments budge Nigel and Geoffrey. There was no point in continuing the discussion. I said that I was not convinced that the balance of argument had shifted in favour of joining. I said that I would hold a further meeting to which other colleagues would be invited.

Before this took place I had a long list of questions drawn up about the implications of the ERM. I hoped that these would illuminate some of the points we would need to discuss. It would be more charitable than accurate to suggest that the answers provided by the Treasury did so. Yet the paper which Nigel presented at the meeting now seems strangely prophetic. He suggested that we had to convince people that inflation would continue to come down and stay down, adding that there was still a nagging fear that sooner or later we would succumb to the temptation of going for an easy inflationary option. He also suggested that after a period of some years sticking to the same policy, this now needed a shot in the arm, a touch of imagination and freshness to help the explanation and to ensure that our policies continued to carry conviction. Entry into the ERM was, of course, the answer. Since it was Nigel's policy of shadowing the deutschmark – an informal version of ERM entry – that was to lead to inflation and undermine confidence, there now seems a certain irony in these assertions.

It has to be said that the wider meeting which I held to discuss the ERM on the morning of Wednesday 13 November did not advance us any further than the earlier meetings. We went over the same ground and at the end I repeated that I had not been convinced by the arguments I had heard. However, I agreed that we should strictly maintain the line we had taken so far, namely that Britain would join the ERM 'when the time was right'.

The position was unsatisfactory. Most of the arguments which persuaded me that we should not now enter the ERM applied to the principle – not just the circumstances – of entry. I knew that I was in a very small minority within the Cabinet on this matter, though most of my colleagues were probably not overinterested in it anyway. Geoffrey and Nigel, by contrast, were fervent. For Geoffrey membership of the ERM would be a demonstration of our European credentials. For Nigel it would provide stability in the turbulent and confusing world in which decisions about interest rates and monetary policy had to be made. And there is no doubt that those decisions could on occasion be extremely difficult.

INTEREST RATES AND INFLATION: 1986

It is worth noting at this point where the difficulty lay – and where it did not. Until 1987 when Nigel made the exchange rate the overriding objective of policy, there was no fundamental difference between us, although Nigel apparently now thinks I was 'soft' on interest rates. Anyone who recalls our decisions from 1979 to 1981 will find that implausible. It would also surprise anyone who considers that one of the main arguments advanced for joining the ERM, which Nigel so passionately wanted, was that it would lead to *lower* interest rates. And, as I shall show subsequently, there were occasions when I thought that *he* was soft on interest rates and wanted to raise them more quickly.* The two of us were equally opposed to inflation. If anything, I was more concerned than he was. It was my constant refrain that much as I might admire his fiscal reforms, he had made no further progress in getting down the underlying inflation rate.

Nevertheless, Nigel and I did have rather different starting points when it came to these matters. I was always more sensitive to the political implications of interest rate rises – particularly their timing – than was Nigel. Prime Ministers have to be. I was also acutely conscious of what interest rate changes meant for those with mortgages. Although there are several times as many savers as borrowers from building societies, it is the borrowers whose prospects – even lives – can be shattered overnight by higher interest rates. My economic policy was also intended to be a social policy. It was a way to a property-owning democracy. And so the needs of home owners must never be forgotten. Other things being equal, on every ground

* See p. 706.

a low interest rate economy is far healthier than a high interest rate economy.

High real interest rates* do ensure that there is a high real reward for saving. But they discourage risk-taking and self-improvement. In the long run, they are a force for stagnation rather than enterprise. For these reasons I was cautious about putting up interest rates unless it was necessary.

Another reason for caution was the difficulty of judging precisely what the monetary and fiscal position was. The M0 figures were volatile from month to month. The other aggregates were worse. We were given figures which underrated economic growth and so caused us to exaggerate the likely size of the PSBR. In these circumstances, making the right judgement about when and whether to cut or raise interest rates was indeed difficult. So at the meetings I had with Nigel, the Bank and Treasury officials to decide on what must be done I would generally cross-examine those involved, give my own reaction and then – when I was sure all the factors had been considered – go along with what Nigel wanted. There were exceptions. But they were very few.

SHADOWING THE DEUTSCHMARK: 1987–1988

It was only from March 1987 – though I did not know it at the time – that Nigel began to follow a new policy, different from mine, different from that to which the Cabinet had agreed, and different from that to which the Government was publicly committed. Its origins lay in the ambitious policy of international exchange rate stabilization. In February Nigel and other Finance ministers agreed on intervention to stabilize the dollar against the deutschmark and the yen by the 'Louvre Accord' agreed in Paris. I received reports of the massive intervention this required which made me uneasy. And it was not clear how long this would last.

In July Nigel raised again with me the question of whether sterling

* In all this, it is always necessary to distinguish between nominal and real interest rates. High money interest rates are predominantly a consequence of the market's expectations of high inflation. If inflation is expected to be high, say at 10 per cent, then, even if one ignores taxes, interest rates of 10 per cent are required just to offset the inflationary erosion of a family's savings. In fact it is real interest rates – the excess of the percentage interest rate above the expected inflation – which affects the thrift and investment of families and businesses.

should join the ERM. He felt that the first year of a new Parliament would be the right time to join. Membership would give us as much exchange rate stability as it was possible to achieve and help business confidence. I was not unprepared for this and had earlier talked the subject through with Alan Walters and Brian Griffiths, the head of my Policy Unit who in an earlier incarnation had been Director of the Centre for Banking and International Finance at the City University. I said to Nigel that the Government had built up over the last eight years a well-founded reputation for prudence. By joining the ERM we would in effect be saying that we could not discipline ourselves and needed the restraint provided by Germany and the deutschmark. ERM membership would reduce the room for manoeuvre on interest rates which would, at times of pressure, be higher than they would be if we were outside. I had heard the arguments about external discipline before. I recalled that Ted Heath had claimed in the early 1970s that European Community membership would help discipline the trade unions. But this had not happened; and the attempt to use ERM membership to influence the expectations of management and work-forces would be an equal failure. Overall, when things were going smoothly membership of the ERM would add nothing to our economic policy-making, and when things were going badly membership would make things worse. Nigel completely rejected this. He said he would want to discuss it all again with me in the autumn. I said that was much too soon: I would not wish to hold a further discussion on the subject until the New Year.

By now there was some evidence that the economy might be growing at a rate too strong to be sustainable. The monetary figures were ambiguous, but the PSBR looked as if it would turn out much lower than expected at the time of the budget. In August 1987 Nigel proposed a 1 per cent rise in interest rates on the grounds that this was required to defeat inflation by the next election. I accepted the proposal. That was the position when on 'Black Monday' (19 October 1987) there was a sharp fall in the Stock Market, precipitated by a fall in Wall Street. These developments were, in retrospect, no more than a market correction of overvalued stocks, made worse by 'programmed selling'. But they raised the question of whether, far from overheating, we might now be facing a recession as people spent less and saved more in order to make up for the decline in the value of their shares.

I was in the United States when I learnt about the Stock Market collapse. I had flown from the Commonwealth Conference at Vancouver to Dallas, where I was to stay with Mark and the family. As it happens I dined that evening with some of America's leading businessmen and they put what had happened in perspective, saying that, contrary to some of the more alarmist reports, we were not about to see a meltdown of the world economy. Still, I thought it best to make assurance doubly sure, and I agreed to Nigel's request for two successive half percentage point cuts in interest rates in response to help restore business confidence.

What I did not know was that Nigel was setting interest rates according to the exchange rate so as to keep the pound at or below DM3. It may be asked how he could have pursued this policy since March without it becoming clear to me. But the fact that sterling tracks the deutschmark (or the dollar) over a particular period does not necessarily mean that the pursuit of a particular exchange rate is determining policy. The same effect can have several causes. There are so many factors involved in making judgements about interest rates and intervention that it is almost impossible at any particular time to know which factor has been decisive for whoever is in day-to-day charge.

Of course, as the months pass and people look back at what has been happening questions begin to be asked. Nigel, who is nobody's fool, must have recognized that this would happen. Indeed, he presumably intended it. Had all gone well, it would have been taken as proof that we could enter the ERM at about DM3 with no adverse consequences. He would have been able to overturn my veto on entry under circumstances in which it was almost impossible for me to reimpose it. To some extent, indeed, this is what happened, though he did not actually force us into the ERM. Once the financial markets have become convinced that a particular policy – in this case shadowing the deutschmark at a particular parity – is the central guarantee of financial stability, the effect of moving away from this approach is profoundly destabilizing. That is why, when I discovered what was happening, I found we had already forfeited some of our freedom of action.

Extraordinarily enough, I only learnt that Nigel had been shadowing the deutschmark when I was interviewed by journalists from the *Financial Times* on Friday 20 November 1987. They asked me why we were shadowing the deutschmark at 3 to the pound. I vigorously denied it. But there was no getting away from the fact that the chart they brought with them bore out what they said. The implications of this were, of course, very serious at several levels. First, Nigel had pursued a personal economic policy without reference to the rest of the Government. How could I possibly trust him again? Second, our heavy intervention in the exchange markets might well have inflationary consequences. Third, perhaps I had allowed interest rates to be taken too low in order that Nigel's undisclosed policy of keeping the pound below DM3 should continue.

I did not want to raise this matter with Nigel until I was absolutely sure of my ground. So I brought together as much information as I could about what had been happening to sterling and the extent of intervention. Then I tackled him. At our meeting on Tuesday 8 December I expressed very strong concern about the size of the intervention needed to hold sterling below DM3. Nigel argued that the intervention had been 'sterilized' by the usual market operations and that it would not lead to inflation. I understood sterilization to mean that the Bank sold treasury bills and gilts to ensure that the intervention funds did not affect short-term interest rates. But the large inflow of capital, even if sterilized in this sense, had its own effect, on the one hand in increasing monetary growth and on the other in putting additional downward pressure on market interest rates. This was an environment where Nigel superficially could justify lower base rates than domestic pressures warranted. As a result, inflation was stoked up.

In the early months of 1988 my relations with Nigel worsened. I sought to discourage too much exchange rate intervention, but without much success. It seemed to me contradictory to raise interest rates – as we did by half a percentage point in February – while at the same time intervening to hold down sterling. But, equally, I knew that once I exerted my authority to forbid intervention on this scale it would be at the cost of my already damaged working relationship with Nigel. He had boxed himself into a situation where his own standing as Chancellor would be weakened if the pound went above DM3. It was a convincing if unwelcome demonstration of the folly of regarding a particular exchange rate parity as the criterion for political and economic success.

By the beginning of March, however, I had no option. On 2 and 3 March 1988 over £1 billion of intervention took place. The Bank of England, which is traditionally all for a managed exchange rate, was deeply anxious about the policy. So, I knew, were senior Treasury officials, though of course they could not say so openly.

I had the matter out with Nigel at two meetings on Friday 4 March. I again complained about the level of exchange rate intervention. For his part, Nigel said it would be sterilized. But he did accept that intervention at the present rate could not continue indefinitely. I asked him to consult the Bank of England and report back later that day on whether the DM3 'cap' should be removed and, if so, when. When he returned he accepted that if on Monday there was still strong demand for sterling the rate should be allowed to go above DM3. He was keen to have some further intervention to break the speed at which the exchange rate might rise. I expressed my concern about this and said that my strong preference would be to allow time for the rate to find its own level without any intervention. But I was prepared to go along with some limited intervention if necessary. The pound accordingly rose through the DM3 limit.

Immediately, the Opposition and the media sought to make capital out of divisions between Nigel and me. I set out the policy accurately and the thinking behind it in the House of Commons on Thursday 10 March at Prime Minister's Questions:

> My Rt. Hon. Friend the Chancellor and I are absolutely agreed that the paramount objective is to keep inflation down. The Chancellor never said that aiming for greater exchange rate stability meant total immobility. Adjustments are needed, as we learnt when we had a Bretton Woods system, as those in the EMS have learnt that they must have revaluation and devaluation from time to time. There is no way in which one can buck the market.

This last remark however provoked a flurry of press comment to which truth was no defence. The trouble was that it appeared to contrast with Nigel's continuing public statements that he did not want to see the exchange rate appreciate further. From now on it would be increasingly difficult to convince the markets that my Chancellor and I were at one. And, of course, the perception they had was basically an accurate one.

The question arises whether at some point now or later I should have sacked Nigel. I would have been fully justified in doing so. He had pursued a policy without my knowledge or consent and he continued to adopt a different approach from that which he knew I wanted. On the other hand, he was widely – and rightly – credited with helping us win the 1987 election. He had complete intellectual mastery of his brief. He had the strong support of Conservative back-benchers and much of the Conservative press who had convinced themselves that I was in the wrong and that only pettiness or pig-headedness could explain the different line I took. Whatever had happened, I felt that if Nigel and I – supported by the rest of the Cabinet – pulled together we could avert or at least overcome the consequences of past mistakes and get the economy back on course for the next general election.

But this was not to be. Whatever I said in the House in answer to questions about interest rates and the exchange rate was given a construction to suggest that either I was not endorsing Nigel's views or that I was protesting too much – and so unconvincingly – my adherence to them. In these situations you just cannot win. Nigel was extremely upset over my remarks at Prime Minister's Questions on Thursday 12 May. Though I warmly supported him and his public statements I had not repeated Nigel's view that further exchange rate appreciation would be 'unsustainable'.

Geoffrey Howe was now also making mischief. From this time on it became clear to me that Nigel and he – by no means on friendly terms in earlier years when there was a good deal of jealousy between them – were in cahoots, and that of the two Geoffrey was the more ill-disposed to me personally. Earlier – in March – Geoffrey had made a speech in Zurich which was widely taken as siding with Nigel against me on the question of the exchange rate. Then on Friday 13 May he quite gratuitously slipped into his speech to the Scottish Party Conference in Perth the remark, apropos of our commitment to join the ERM 'when the time is right', that: 'We cannot forever go on adding that qualification to the underlying commitment.' This led the press to widen the perceived rift between me and Nigel over the ERM once more. I was not best pleased. When Geoffrey imprudently telephoned me the morning after his speech to ask for a meeting at which he and the Chancellor should come to see me later in the day to 'settle the semi-public dispute', I told him that I would be seeing Nigel later in the day to discuss the markets – which Geoffrey's own remarks had unsettled. But I was not seeing them together. I told him three times – since he did not seem to take it in and persisted in his attempt to contrive a meeting at which he and Nigel could get their way – that the best thing he could do now was to keep quiet. We were not going into the ERM at present and that was that.

I spent Sunday at Chequers working on a speech I was to deliver to the General Assembly of the Church of Scotland: there was some mirth when my speech writers and I were discovered down on our knees in an appropriate posture, though drawing on the resources of sellotape rather than the Holy Spirit. But, following the news reports during the day, I was also aware of just how damaging the constant media reports of splits and disagreements on the exchange rate were becoming.

Nigel arranged to see me on the Monday. He wanted to agree a detailed formulation for use by me in the House to describe our policy. I had been told by the Treasury in advance of the meeting that Nigel wanted a further interest rate cut. For my part, I had become appalled at the size of our intervention in the money markets which was clearly still failing to hold sterling at the level Nigel wanted and which, in spite of assurances from Nigel, I feared might prove inflationary. But I had got part of what I wanted – which would ideally have been a pound which found its own level in the markets – in that sterling had been allowed to rise to DM3.18. So I was not unhappy to have the suggested interest rate cut I knew he wanted. I was also aware that the speculators were beginning to consider sterling a one-way bet and that allowing them to burn their fingers a little would do no end of good.

Above all, however, this reduction of the interest rate on Tuesday 17 May by half a point to 7.5 per cent was the price of tolerable relations with my Chancellor, who believed that his whole standing was at stake if the pound appreciated outside any 'band' to which he might have semi-publicly consigned it. If I had refused both intervention and an interest rate cut and sterling had drifted up to find its proper level there was little doubt in my mind that Nigel would have resigned – and done so at a time when both the majority of the Parliamentary Party and the press supported his line rather than mine. Yet the economic price of accepting this political constraint now seems to me to have been too high. For the whole of this period the interest rate was too low. It should have been a good deal higher, whatever the effect on the level of sterling – or the level of the Chancellor's blood pressure.

I also agreed to use in the House a detailed endorsement of the line which Nigel and I had agreed at our Monday meeting on the place of the exchange rate as an element in economic policy. I had to go further than I would have liked, saying:

> We have taken interest rates down three times in the last two months. That was clearly intended to affect the exchange rate. We use the available levers, both interest rates and intervention as seems right in the circumstances and . . . it would be a great mistake for any speculator to think at any time that sterling was a one-way bet.

ECONOMIC PROBLEMS MOUNT

In fact from June 1988 onwards interest rates rose steadily. Nigel insisted on raising them only half a per cent at a time. I would have preferred something sharper to convince the markets how seriously we took the latest indicator that the economy was growing too fast and that monetary policy had been too lax – namely the balance of payments figures. Nigel took a more laid-back view of these than I did. He thought that the current account balance of payments deficit, which was growing ever larger, was more important as an indicator that other things were going wrong than in its own right. But the deficit worried me because it confirmed that as a nation we were living beyond our means – as well as suggesting that higher inflation was on the way.

House prices were rising sharply. M0 was still growing too fast – outside its target range. The forecasts of inflation were constantly being revised upwards, though they still turned out to be too low. For example, in the September 1988 monthly Treasury Monetary Assessment inflation in March 1989 was forecast at 5.4 per cent. In October's note the forecast was 7 per cent. (In fact it turned out to be 7.9 per cent.) So as 1988 drew to a close – and although unemployment was down and growth and incomes were well up – there was trouble ahead.

It is on the face of it extraordinary that at such a time – November 1988 – Nigel should have sent me a paper proposing an independent Bank of England. My reaction was dismissive. Here we were wrestling with the consequences of his diversion from our tried and tested strategy which had worked so well in the first Parliament; and now we were expected to turn our policy upside down again. I did not believe, as Nigel argued, that it would boost the credibility of the fight against inflation. In fact, as I minuted, 'it would be seen as an abdication by the Chancellor when he is at his most vulnerable.' I added that 'it would be an admission of a failure of resolve on our part.' I also doubted whether we had people of the right calibre to run such an institution. As I told Nigel when he came in to discuss his paper, I had thought in the late 1970s about having an independent central bank but had come down against it. I considered it more appropriate for federal states. But in any case there could be no question of setting up such a bank now. Inflation would have had to be well down – to say 2 per cent – for two or three years before it could be contemplated.

In fact, I do not believe that changing well-tried institutional arrangements generally provides solutions to underlying political problems – and the control of inflation is ultimately a political problem. It can be kept down if you have the will to do so, as the Germans do because of their bitter experience of hyperinflation. We too could have kept it down if we had pursued a sufficiently tight monetary policy – without an independent central bank. What perhaps I should have taken more notice of, however, was that this proposal of Nigel's showed his attitude to the economic difficulties now clearly visible on the horizon. He wanted to pass the responsibility for them to something – or someone – else.

The year 1989 – Nigel's last as Chancellor – was a time of increasing political difficulty for me. It was the tenth anniversary of my becoming Prime Minister – an anniversary which I insisted should be kept as low-key as possible but which was inevitably the occasion for unflattering reviews in the press designed to leave the reader with the strong feeling that ten years of me was quite enough. It was also a time of very high interest rates – 13 per cent in January, 14 per cent from May and 15 per cent from October – and with inflation still rising and the forecast figures apparently inexorably rising too. The trade figures continued to be bad, especially July's, which undermined confidence and weakened the pound. Alan Walters's view was that there was now too tight a monetary squeeze which would push the economy into a serious recession. In particular, he strongly advised against raising interest rates to 15 per cent, as Nigel wanted in response to a rise in interest rates in Germany. Alan was right. But I went along with Nigel's judgement and up went interest rates again. It is perhaps sufficient comment on the later allegation that I was undermining the Chancellor's position by not dismissing Alan Walters, that I backed Nigel against Alan's advice and against my own instincts just days before Nigel walked out.

THE DELORS REPORT ON EMU

Apart from the conduct of monetary policy, there were two economic issues of substance which concerned us during this period. On the first – the ERM – Nigel and I were sharply at odds. On the second – European Economic and Monetary Union (EMU) – we were in complete agreement.

As a result of the Hanover European Council in June 1988 a

Committee of European Community central bank heads – serving in a personal capacity – had been set up under the chairmanship of Jacques Delors to report on EMU.* Nigel and I hoped that together Robin Leigh-Pemberton, Governor of the Bank of England, and Karl Otto Pöhl, President of the Bundesbank, would prevent the emergence of a report which would give momentum to EMU. Herr Pöhl we considered strongly hostile to any serious loss of monetary autonomy for the Bundesbank and Robin Leigh-Pemberton was in no doubt about the strength of our views – and indeed those (at this stage) of the great majority of the Parliamentary Conservative Party and of the House of Commons. Our line was that the report should be limited to a descriptive not a prescriptive document. But we hoped that paragraphs would be inserted which would make it clear that EMU was in no way necessary to the completion of the Single Market and which would enlarge upon the full implications of EMU for the transfer of power and authority from national institutions to a central bureaucracy.

Nigel and I had met the Governor on the evening of Wednesday 14 December 1988 and urged him to make all these points in the discussions on the text which ensued. We saw the Governor again on the afternoon of Wednesday 15 February. What we had seen of the draft report seemed thoroughly unsatisfactory, along lines known to be favoured by M. Delors who was clearly making the running. Nigel and I wanted the Governor to circulate his own document; but when this appeared it was something of a mouse. Most damaging of all was that Herr Pöhl's known opposition to the Delors approach simply was not expressed.

Whatever the Governor may have done proved ineffective. When the Delors Report finally appeared in April 1989 it confirmed our worst fears. From the beginning there had been discussion of a 'three-stage' approach, which might at least have allowed us to slow the pace and refuse to 'advance' further than the first or second stage. But the report now insisted that by embarking on the first stage the Community committed itself irrevocably to the eventual achievement of full economic and monetary union. There was a requirement for a new treaty and for work on it to start immediately. There was also plenty of material in the treaty about regional and social policy – costly, Delorsian socialism on a continental scale. None of these was acceptable to me.

* For this and for the Madrid European Council see pp. 740–2, 750–2.

THE AMBUSH BEFORE MADRID

Whatever problems the Delors Report raised, it won few friends at home. However, Nigel and then Geoffrey used it to reopen the argument about the ERM. Nigel argued at our meeting on the afternoon of Wednesday 3 May that we should now enter the ERM. I replied that the overriding priority must be to get down the rate of inflation and it would be quite wrong to adopt the objective of exchange rate stability. This is what we had done when we had been trying to shadow the deutschmark, and it had compromised our battle against inflation. I did not believe that the Delors Report on EMU altered the balance of argument on the ERM. On the contrary, we should certainly not be drawn further into a European system that would almost certainly change following the Delors Report. I did not accept the premise that it was necessary to join the ERM in order to prevent developments in the Community which we did not like. I thought that the idea of setting a target date for joining some time in the future would be particularly damaging. Nigel disagreed. But I said that I did not want the issue of UK membership of the ERM to be raised at this stage.

This did not mean that I was giving no thought to it. Indeed, a few days later Alan Walters sent me a paper entitled 'When the time will be ripe', spelling out the conditions which must be met before we would join. He suggested that all the constituent countries must have abolished all foreign exchange controls and the legal machinery through which they were imposed. All domestic banking systems and financial and capital markets must be deregulated and open to competitive entry from EC countries. Any institution, corporation, partnership or individual must be free to enter any banking or financial business, subject only to minimum prudential conditions.

These were bold suggestions. On the one hand, they would certainly give our position a much more positive aspect. The moves against corporatism in France, Germany and Italy would be valuable in their own right. Whether the ERM could for long stand the removal of all these controls, which helped give it a false stability, was to be seen. The difficulty of Alan's approach, of course, was that it did not remove the fundamental objections which both he and I had to the system of semi-fixed exchange rates which the ERM constituted. But in the end I knew that Alan's ingenious suggestion might be the only way in which I could resist the pressure from Nigel, Geoffrey and the European Community for early entry.

Leon Brittan – now Vice-President of the European Commission – came to see me soon afterwards to try to persuade me of the benefits of ERM membership. He argued that it would give us an important say in the next steps of economic and monetary co-operation. Indeed, he said that it would enable Britain to dictate the pace and course of further progress in this area. He had apparently been reinforced in this view by a remark made to him by M. Delors over dinner to the effect that 'if she joins, she wins.' I was not, however, overimpressed by the European Commission President's table-talk. I said that I did not believe that those who wanted to advance along the route mapped out by the Delors Committee on EMU would be deterred from pressing ahead by British membership of the ERM. And so, of course, it proved.

My relations with Nigel went through another difficult patch in May when an interview I gave to the World Service came indiscreetly close to admitting that the reason why our inflation rate had increased was because we had been shadowing the deutschmark. This, of course, was true, but it was a departure from the convenient answer that it was because we cut interest rates in the wake of the 'Black Monday' Stock Market crash and held them down too long that inflation had begun to rise. Nigel was at a European Finance ministers' meeting in Spain and became very upset. So I authorized a line for the press which reverted to the less accurate but more mutually acceptable explanation. But I did at this time ask the Treasury to provide me with a paper giving their explanation as to why inflation had risen. I was subsequently interested to learn that Nigel had asked that the first draft of this paper, which had focused almost exclusively on the shadowing of the ERM, should be revised to extend the analysis to cover the earlier 1985–6 period as well.* Not surprisingly under these circumstances, I found the finished product less sharp and persuasive than some other Treasury papers.

There was worse to come. On Wednesday 14 June 1989, just twelve days before the European Council in Madrid, Geoffrey Howe and Nigel Lawson mounted an ambush. Geoffrey, I soon learnt, was the moving force. They sent me a joint minute arguing that in order to strike an acceptable compromise on the Delors EMU proposals –

* The suggestion that the inflation which began at the end of 1988 and lasted until mid-1991 could be explained by decisions on interest rates and monetary policy in 1985 assumed almost a four-year lag in the effect of monetary expansion on inflation. We know that lags, in Milton Friedman's words, are 'long and variable' with an average of about eighteen months. So three to four years is possible, but hardly plausible.

agreeing to Stage 1 but with no commitment to Stages 2 and 3 or an Inter-Governmental Conference (IGC) – I should say that I would accept a 'non-legally binding reference' to sterling joining the ERM by the end of 1992, provided that certain conditions were fulfilled by then. The alternative was – as usual – 'isolation'. It was a typical Foreign Office paper which Nigel Lawson in his better days would have scornfully eviscerated.

I had myself, since reading Alan's earlier paper on the conditions for entry into the ERM, been giving a great deal of thought to this subject. It was not clear to me whether spelling out these conditions at this stage would help deflect the other Community countries and the Commission from the course towards EMU on which they seemed set. I was not convinced about the alleged political advantages. I was deeply concerned about the consequences of setting a specified date for the currency markets. However, I saw Nigel and Geoffrey on the evening of Tuesday 20 June to discuss their minute and its contents. At the end I said that I would reflect further on the way in which this issue should be handled at Madrid. I remained sceptical whether a concession on membership of the ERM would really achieve our agreed aim of blocking an IGC and Stages 2 and 3 of Delors. But this could only be judged on the spot at Madrid. In any event I remained very wary of setting a date for sterling's membership.

I had not liked this way of proceeding – by joint minutes, pressure and cabals. But I was more than angry about what happened next. I received a further joint minute. In this Nigel and Geoffrey said that just spelling out in greater detail the conditions which would have to be fulfilled before we joined – widening these to include for example Single Market measures – would be 'counter-productive'. There must be a date. And they wanted another meeting before Madrid.

I read their minute on Saturday morning at Chequers and almost immediately received a telephone call from my office to ask about the time for a meeting. This was extremely inconvenient. On Sunday afternoon I was due in Madrid. But they could not be deterred. I could have seen them late on Saturday night or early on Sunday morning at No. 10. They chose the latter.

I knew that Geoffrey had put Nigel up to this. He had been in a great state about the European election campaign which had not gone well for us. I knew that he had always thought that he might one day become Leader of the Conservative Party and Prime Minister – an ambition which became more passionate as it was slipping away from him. He considered himself – with some justice – as an important contributor to our past successes. This quiet, gentle, but deeply ambitious man – with whom my relations had become progressively worse as my exasperation at his insatiable appetite for compromise led me sometimes to lash out at him in front of others – was now out to make trouble for me if he possibly could. Above all, I suspect, he thought that he had become indispensable – a dangerous illusion for a politician. There is no other explanation for what he now did and put Nigel up to doing.

Geoffrey and Nigel came to see me at 8.15 on Sunday morning, as arranged. They were shown into my study and sat down facing me on the other side of the fireplace. They had clearly worked out precisely what they were to say. Geoffrey began. He urged that I should speak first at the Madrid Council setting out the conditions on which I would have sterling join and announcing a date for entry into the ERM. He and Nigel even insisted on the precise formula, which I took down: 'It is our firm intention to join not later than –' (a date to be specified). They said that if I did this I would stop the whole Delors process from going to Stages 2 and 3. And if I did not agree to their terms and their formulation they would both resign.

Whether I could have withstood the loss of both my Foreign Secretary and my Chancellor at the same time in this way I am not sure. But three things jostled together in my mind. First, I was not prepared to be blackmailed into a policy which I felt was wrong. Second, I must keep them on board if I could, at least for the moment. Third, I would never, never allow this to happen again. But this third reflection I pushed for the moment to the back of my mind. I told them that I already had a paragraph spelling out in more detail the conditions under which sterling could enter the ERM and I would be using this in my opening speech. But I refused to give them any undertaking that I would set a date. Indeed, I told them that I could not believe that a Chancellor and a former Chancellor could seriously argue that I should set a date in advance: it would be a field day for the speculators, as they should have known. I said that I would reflect further on what to say at Madrid. They left, Geoffrey looking insufferably smug. And so the nasty little meeting ended.

I shall explain shortly the rest of what happened at the Madrid Council. Suffice it to say here that on the basis of what Alan had already suggested and with some modification I spelt out what became known as the 'Madrid conditions' for sterling's entry into the ERM. I reaffirmed our intention to join once inflation was down and there was satisfactory implementation of the first phase of the Delors Report, including free movement of capital and abolition of foreign exchange controls. But I did not set a date for entry, nor was I put under any pressure at Madrid to do so.

I do not believe that spelling out the Madrid conditions significantly modified the pace, let alone the direction, of discussions on the Delors report on EMU. Only someone with a peculiarly naïve view of the world – the sort cultivated by British Euro-enthusiasts but without any equivalent among hard-headed continental Euro-opportunists – could have imagined that it would. In fact, though, the Madrid conditions did allow me to rally the Conservative Party around our negotiating position and got us away from the tired and faintly ridiculous formula of 'when the time was right'. The outcome of Madrid was widely praised back at home. Unfortunately, in a sense the time would never be 'right' – because the ERM, particularly now that the Delors objective of EMU had come out into the open, would never be 'right'. But that was something I could do little about.

Back home, Cabinet began as usual at 10.30 on Thursday 29 June. Normally, I would sit at my place with my back to the door as Cabinet ministers trooped in. This time, however, I stood in the doorway – waiting. But there were no resignations. The condition that there must be a date for our joining the ERM might never have been mentioned. Nigel Lawson even managed the remark that Madrid had gone rather well, hadn't it. He certainly had a nerve, I thought: but then Nigel always did. That was one of his engaging characteristics.

MORE TENSION WITH NIGEL LAWSON

It was from this time that tension between myself and Nigel Lawson arose over the independent economic advice that I was receiving from Alan Walters. Alan had returned to No. 10 in May 1989. I have already described his contribution to the 'Madrid conditions' for ERM entry. While the Treasury, thoroughly alarmed by the inflationary effects of Nigel's policy of shadowing the ERM, kept urging ever higher interest rates, Alan now drew my attention to the danger that excessively high interest rates might drive the economy into recession.* He was, in short, doing precisely what a prime minister's adviser should. He also had the merit of being right.

However, during his five-year absence from No. 10, he had been

* Interest rates had gone up to 13 per cent in November 1988 and to 14 per cent in May 1989.

asked to give his views in all sorts of different fora; and Alan's views were always trenchant. Various reports, articles and lectures containing his thoughts about economic policy issues in general and the ERM in particular kept on surfacing. Partly because these were exploited by the press to point up divisions between Nigel and me and partly because Nigel himself, knowing that he was being blamed for the return of inflation, was becoming hypersensitive, they became a major problem.

The important point, however, was that all this press speculation reflected an underlying reality. This was that Nigel and I no longer had that broad identity of views or mutual trust which a Chancellor and prime minister should. Nor was there any way – short of a full and totally uncharacteristic *mea culpa* on his part – that commentators were not going to hold Nigel to blame for the worsening economic outlook.

All of this was evident at the 1989 Party Conference – for which with greater optimism than caution the new Party Chairman, Ken Baker, had chosen the theme 'the Right Team'. A German rise in interest rates had led us to follow suit and we took the unpalatable decision to raise them to 15 per cent on the eve of the conference. The *Daily Mail* duly savaged Nigel as 'this bankrupt Chancellor' and demanded that he go. Nigel, who never lacked courage, gave a robust and successful speech. But even now the two of us had to negotiate the wording of his and my references to the exchange rate. There was a clear difference of emphasis – if no open contradiction – between his formulation:

> The Conservative Party never has been, and never will be, the party of devaluation.

– a statement which implied that it was in our hands what the ultimate value of the pound in the exchange markets would be, and my own:

> As Nigel Lawson made clear yesterday, industry must not expect to find refuge in a perpetually depreciating currency.

– a rather different point, based on a quite different economic analysis.

We survived the conference without mishap. But there was a general feeling in the press that with more unpleasant economic news to come it would be difficult for Nigel to continue. If he sought to do so, he would have my backing and indeed protection, as he always had. However convenient it might have been, I was not going to throw him to the wolves. Perhaps slightly less charitably, I felt that since he had got us into this inflation he should face up to the unpopular requirements for getting us out of it. It would, after all, be a highly unpalatable prospect for a new, incoming Chancellor. In any case – for reasons and in circumstances I shall describe shortly – I had made what I intended to be the last major reshuffle of this Parliament, moving Geoffrey Howe from the Foreign Office to be Leader of the House. I had decided – rightly or wrongly – that Nigel should stay. But what had Nigel himself decided?

NIGEL LAWSON'S RESIGNATION

I have already mentioned the stir which Alan Walters's comments, dragged out of the past and often torn out of context, created. Moreover, since the timing was quite unpredictable – it depended on how quickly journalists tracked down and republished past comments – there was very little my staff or Alan could do about it. The *Financial Times* published on 18 October an article in which Alan was quoted, among other things, as describing the ERM as 'half-baked'. This article was based on an essay to be published in the *American Economist*. But what the *FT* did not say was that the latter was written by Alan in 1988, long before he returned as my economic adviser. I felt that he had nothing to apologize for and minuted:

> As the article was written well before Madrid (in which Alan also advised), I don't see the difficulty. Moreover, advisers ADVISE, ministers decide policy.

At 4.30 in the morning on Wednesday 25 October the VC10 which brought me back from the Commonwealth Conference at Kuala Lumpur arrived at Heathrow. Back at No. 10 I sorted out my personal belongings, discussed my diary with Amanda Ponsonby (my indispensable diary secretary), had lunch in the flat and then saw Nigel Lawson for one of our regular bilaterals. He was exercised about Alan Walters, having been repeatedly questioned in interviews about whether Alan should be sacked. But there were many other things we had to think about. In particular, we had to agree the line which Nigel would take at the forthcoming meeting of European Community

Finance ministers on EMU. Nigel had devised an ingenious alternative approach, based on Friedrich Hayek's idea of competing currencies, in which the market rather than governments would provide the momentum for monetary union. (Unfortunately, this proposal did not in fact get very far, not least because it was not at all in the statist, centralist model which our European Community partners preferred.) After seeing Nigel, I held a wider discussion of EMU which also included John Major (Foreign Secretary) and Nick Ridley (Trade and Industry Secretary) at which we endorsed Nigel's proposed approach in his paper, while accepting that its purpose was mainly tactical in order to slow down discussion of EMU within the Community.

The next day, Thursday, was bound to hold its difficulties. But I did not know at this stage how many. Not only were there Prime Minister's Questions: I also had to make a statement and answer questions on the outcome of the Kuala Lumpur CHOGM and, inevitably, on South Africa. I was under the hairdryer shortly after 8 o'clock in the morning when I received a message from my Private Office via Crawfie that Nigel Lawson wanted to see me at 8.50, that is just before I began my regular briefing session for Parliamentary Questions. Crawfie said something to me about it all being quite serious and that Nigel might be going to resign. But I said: 'Oh no dear, you've got it all wrong. He's going to Germany this afternoon for a meeting and I expect he wants to see me about that.' So when I came downstairs to see Nigel in my study I was quite unprepared for what he had to say. He told me that either Alan Walters must go or he – Nigel – would resign. He wanted me to agree there and then to his demand.

At first I could hardly take him seriously. I told him not to be ridiculous. He was holder of a great office of state. He was demeaning himself even by talking in such terms. As for Alan, he was a devoted and loyal member of my staff who had given me frank and good advice but had always acted within the proprieties. If others, including the media, had attempted to exploit and exaggerate legitimate differences of opinion, that was no responsibility of his. There was no question of my sacking him. The meeting ended inconclusively. I asked Nigel to think again. I thought he accepted this advice. But there was little time to talk since I had to discuss the briefing for Parliamentary Questions and my statement at a meeting due to begin at 9.00 a.m.

An hour later Nigel came into a meeting with other ministers on the future of the Atomic Weapons Establishment at Aldermaston. He seemed on good form and made several acute interventions in the discussion. I hoped and believed that the storm had blown over. Then we met again – this time at Cabinet. I opened Cabinet by saying that we must be business-like and get through the agenda promptly because two ministers had to leave for meetings in Europe. Nigel was one of them.

I was, therefore doubly surprised when I was told over the light lunch – soup and fruit – I used to have on Parliamentary Questions days that Nigel again wanted to see me. I had thought he was not even in the country. We again met in my study where he repeated his demand and said that he wanted to resign. There was nothing much new I could say and not much time to say it since I had soon to be in the House of Commons. But I made it clear that Alan Walters was not going and hoped that Nigel would reflect further. I said that I would see him after I had finished with Questions and my statement.

Over in my room in the House of Commons I was having a last look through my briefing when at 3.05 p.m. – a bare ten minutes before I was due to answer Questions in the House – Andrew Turnbull, my private secretary, came in to tell me that Nigel Lawson had decided to resign and that he wanted an announcement out by 3.30 p.m. This was out of the question. We had not told the Queen. We had no successor arranged. The London financial markets would still be open. I myself was about to face an hour on my feet answering questions and making a statement on the Commonwealth Conference. I repeated that I would see Nigel some time between 5.00 p.m. and 5.30 p.m. back in No. 10.

I only got through Questions and the Statement by relegating the crisis of Nigel's departure to the back of my mind. About an hour later, on my way out of the Chamber, I asked John Major, who as Foreign Secretary had been sitting beside me for my Statement, to follow me to my room: 'I have a problem.'

Ideally, I would have liked to make Nick Ridley Chancellor. But, particularly under these difficult circumstances, Nick's scorn for presentational niceties might well have compounded the problem. John Major, who knew the Treasury from his days as Chief Secretary, looked the obvious choice. I had already thought that John might succeed me. But I would have liked him to gain more experience. He had only been at the Foreign Office for a few weeks and had not yet fully mastered this department, so very different from the Treasury where he had been an effective and competent Chief Secretary. He would have liked to stay as Foreign Secretary rather than return to pick up the pieces after Nigel. When he expressed some reluctance to go from the Foreign Office to the Treasury, I told him that we all have to accept second best occasionally. That applied to me just as much as to him. So he agreed with good grace.

I dashed back to No. 10 to see Nigel, who was still insisting that his resignation should be announced immediately. On reflection there seems to me just one explanation for Nigel's indecent haste. I think that he feared that I might telephone Alan Walters, who was in America and quite oblivious to what was happening, and that Alan would resign. This would have deprived him of the excuse he wanted. I now told Nigel that John Major was succeeding him. There was nothing left to discuss and it was a short meeting. I was sorry that our long and generally fruitful association should end in that way. I then telephoned Alan to tell him what happened. He told me that Nigel's resignation had put him in an impossible situation and so he insisted, against all my attempts to persuade him, on resigning too.

JOHN MAJOR AS CHANCELLOR

Nigel's departure was a blow to me – and one which Geoffrey Howe used to stir up more trouble when, the following weekend, in a speech of calculated malice, he praised Nigel as a Chancellor of great courage and insisted on entry into the ERM on the terms outlined at Madrid. But Nigel's going was also a boon in one respect. At least in John Major I had a Chancellor who, though he lacked Nigel's grasp of economics, had not got personal capital sunk in past policy errors. He was psychologically more able to deal with their consequences.

The three main tasks we faced were: first, to bring inflation under control, though it was important to moderate the pressure in time to avoid recession; second, to deal with the thorny issue of the ERM, which had done so much damage to the Government's unity and standing; and third, to avoid being sucked into European Economic and Monetary Union. On the first of these – inflation – it was mainly a matter of applying the continuing and unpalatable medicine of high interest rates. It may be that interest rates were kept rather too high for too long: they had already been 13 per cent or above for a year and had risen to 15 per cent the previous month. Yet as each month the forecast inflation figures kept on being revised upwards there was a general air of uncertainty about what precisely the underlying position was. We therefore thought it right to err on the side of financial prudence. John and I had no serious disagreements on this policy. By October 1990, when I insisted on a 1 per cent cut on entering the ERM, this was justified on the grounds that the money supply had turned sharply downwards: the RPI figure too was just on the turn, after reaching almost 11 per cent – a figure I had never believed would be reached again while I was Prime Minister

On the questions of the ERM and EMU, I was increasingly conscious of dealing with a very different sort of Chancellor than Nigel. John Major – perhaps because he had made his name as a whip, or perhaps because he is unexcited by the sort of concepts which people like Nigel and I saw as central to politics – had one great objective: this was to keep the Party together. To him that meant that we must enter the ERM as soon as possible to relieve the political strains. This primacy of politics over economics – an odd attribute in a Treasury minister – also meant that John was attracted by a fudge on EMU which would assuage the anxieties of the timorous Europhiles in the Party that we would otherwise be 'isolated'. On ERM, much as I continued to dislike the system and distrust its purpose, I had agreed the principle at Madrid subject to the conditions expressed. Eventually, I was to go along with what John wanted. On EMU, which for me went to the very heart not just of the debate about Europe's future but about Britain's future as a democratic, sovereign state, I was not prepared to compromise.

DISCUSSIONS ABOUT ERM AND EMU: 1990

From the spring of 1990 I discussed the ERM with John Major on a fairly regular basis. When I saw him on the morning of Thursday 29 March I said that I did not believe that the conditions for our membership had yet been met. Although the issue of the timing of membership would need to be considered in the run-up to the next election it would in any event be out of the question to publish a precise date by which the UK would join. I was glad to find that John agreed with me. Unlike Geoffrey and Nigel, he realized that to set an advance date for joining would leave us at the mercy of the markets. But it was increasingly clear that he still wanted us to join soon. He said that bearing in mind the likely favourable impact of entry into the ERM on political sentiment and in turn on sentiment in the markets, it would be easier to bring interest rates down and maintain a firm exchange rate if we were inside rather than outside the ERM. That sounded all too like Nigel's cracked record to the effect that you should steer by the exchange rate rather than by the money supply. Alas, that policy had steered us into inflation. John's approach was that if the Party and the Government united around the policy and we looked like winning the next election, the economic prospect would improve as well. But I knew full well that whenever you take economic decisions for political purposes, you run considerable risks.

A few days later I discussed EMU and the Delors Report with John. He said that he would be minuting me with his conclusions on the best way forward. He said that the strategy must be to slow down the advance towards Stages 2 and 3 of Delors and the erosion of national sovereignty they entailed, but to ensure all the while that the UK was not excluded from the negotiating process. This had an indiarubber feel to it. So I said that there were serious dangers if we adopted a posture which implied that moves beyond ERM membership towards further economic and monetary integration could be contemplated. If other member states wanted to take such steps that was up to them. But the UK would not participate in that process. If we made that absolutely clear, I thought it was likely that, under pressure from the Bundesbank, Germany would also decline to move to the next stages of EMU. I sought to get John to view all this in a wider context and talked to him about the need to develop free trade relations with the USA and other countries, pointing out that centrally controlled blocs of countries – such as a federal Europe looked like being – must not be allowed to stand in the way of this.

John Major became increasingly worked up about both ERM membership and EMU. On 9 April 1990 he minuted me that he had been startled by the determination of other European Community Finance ministers to agree a treaty for full EMU. He had found little support for our new alternative approach – a 'hard ecu' circulating alongside existing currencies, managed by a European Monetary Fund – which we had advanced as an 'evolutionary approach' to EMU.* He therefore set out a number of options as to how we might proceed. Of these the option which he recommended – and which was ultimately to be developed further at Maastricht – was to work for a treaty which gave a full definition of EMU and the institutions necessary for its final stage (together with any transitional stage, if agreed) but then allowed an 'opting-in' mechanism for member states. This would allow them to join in the new Stage 3 arrangements – that is the single currency – at their own pace. He believed that this should be the goal we should work for as the outcome to the IGC. At a meeting with me

* Following the negative reception accorded to our original proposal for competing currencies, we began to develop this new hard ecu approach based on the suggestions made by Sir Michael Butler, Britain's former Ambassador to the Community, now working in the City.

on Wednesday 18 April, John rehearsed the arguments of his paper, emphasizing that the goal of full EMU as described by Delors was shared by all except the United Kingdom.

I agreed neither with John's analysis nor his conclusion. I said that the Government could not subscribe to a treaty amendment containing the full Delors definition of EMU. Further work should be done to develop our proposal for a European Monetary Fund which we could put forward as the most that it was necessary for the Community to agree upon for now. I was extremely disturbed to find that the Chancellor had swallowed so quickly the slogans of the European lobby. At this point, however, I felt that I should hold my fire. John was new to the job. He was right to be searching for a way forward which would attract allies in Europe as well as convince Conservative MPs of our reasonableness. But it was already clear that he was thinking in terms of compromises which would not be acceptable to me and that intellectually he was drifting with the tide.

ENTRY OF STERLING INTO THE ERM

In tandem with consideration of tactics for EMU went consideration of timing for the ERM. The Treasury drew up a note for me about the best time for sterling to join, bearing in mind economic circumstances and political events. Although the other countries and central banks were pressing for our membership there would still be an established procedure to go through. So it was assumed that we would announce our intentions on a Friday so as to leave the weekend for the details to be settled before markets opened on Monday. There would have to be an initial discussion of the details between Finance Ministry and Central Bank representatives in the EC Monetary Committee: the possibility of a full meeting of EC Finance ministers and governors in person had also to be allowed for, though in practice this proved unnecessary. After timing, the two most important questions were with what width of 'band' (that is how much leeway would there be above and below the central parity chosen) and at what rate sterling should join. Of course, both these points received very close attention from me and the Treasury. Earlier hypothetical discussions had taken place on the basis of a narrow (+ or −2.25 per cent) band; but John and I now believed that the wider (+ or −6 per cent) band would be better, giving greater room for manoeuvre.

As for the central rate of sterling against the deutschmark, this was influenced by several factors. First, the rate chosen had to be credible in the light of recent exchange rate movements. Second, it should not be so low that it weakened the fight against inflation, by requiring imprudently low interest rates to keep sterling down. Third, and by contrast, it must not be so high that it imposed unnecessary pressure on industry, both through high interest rates which made borrowing expensive and a high exchange rate which made our goods uncompetitive.

It would, of course, test the wisdom of Solomon to settle on the 'right' rate: indeed, I doubt if Solomon in his wisdom would ever have set himself such a task. This is because ultimately there can be no 'right' level of sterling apart from what the market says it is. To search for such a thing is in a sense to fall into the trap of believing in the old precapitalist concept of a 'just price'. Had Nigel Lawson managed to persuade me to have sterling enter the ERM in November 1985 the sterling/deutschmark rate would have been about DM3.75. A year later the pound was down to DM2.88. In November 1987 it was up to DM2.98. In November 1988 it was right up to DM3.16. In November 1989 it was back down to DM2.87. When we entered it was at a central parity of DM2.95, which was the rate at which the London market closed that day. What this shows on even a cursory glance is that revaluations and/or heavy intervention and very large shifts in interest rates would have been necessary to keep sterling in the mechanism throughout this period. It is, in fact, a demonstration that Alan Walters had been right all along in his view that the ERM ensured not stability, but rather the kind of instability which comes from movement in large leaps rather than by the more gradual accommodation of the market.

Only at my meeting with John Major on Wednesday 13 June did I eventually say that I would not resist sterling joining the ERM. But the timing was for debate. Although the terms I had laid down had not been fully met, I had too few allies to continue to resist and win the day. There are limits to the ability of even the most determined democratic leader to stand out against what the Cabinet, the Parliamentary Party, the industrial lobby and the press demand – particularly when you have lived for so long, as I had, with a thoroughly unsatisfactory form of words ('joining when the time is right'), since qualified further by the Madrid conditions. By this stage all my advisers were telling me – though on political rather than economic grounds – that I should have sterling enter. Almost my only ally in the Cabinet was Nick Ridley – who was shortly to resign: together we were not a strong enough combination to have done what we would have had to do – that is to state that on grounds of principle we would not have sterling enter the ERM now or in the future.

But my willingness to join the ERM was qualified by a crucial condition. I was not prepared to keep to any particular parity at the expense of domestic monetary conditions. I insisted that we enter the wide band – 6 per cent on either side. Even then I made it very clear to John Major that if sterling came under pressure, I was not going to use massive intervention, either pouring in pounds and cutting interest rates to keep sterling down or raising interest rates to damaging levels and using precious reserves to keep sterling up. For me, willingness to realign within the ERM – as other countries had done – if circumstances warranted it, was the essential condition for entry. This makes nonsense of the claim, sometimes heard from ERM proponents justifying the subsequent collapse, that we were right to go in, but wrong to do so at that rate. In fact, a rate that is right today can be wrong tomorrow and vice versa. Until now, the ERM had never been a rigid system. I did not need to spell this out to our European partners because, whatever the fine points of detail, a country which wished to realign had always been able to do so in practice. Now that the UK was inside the ERM, other countries would have been so anxious to keep us in that they would have made little or no difficulty about realignment.

With the publication of the Delors Report, however, the Europeans began to regard the ERM as part of the move towards locking currencies, leading to a single currency. Accordingly, devaluations were more frowned upon than they had been. But they still occurred and would have to occur as long as we insisted on them. It was only when my successor went along with the objective of EMU as spelt out in the Maastricht Treaty and made it clear that sterling would enter the narrow band of the ERM that the pressure never to revalue 'growed and growed' until it became an overriding dogma. I had not the slightest doubt that if the ERM ever developed in the rigid way in which I knew many other European governments and the Commission would have liked, it would prove unworkable and would break up. I never envisaged that a Conservative government would talk itself into the trap of regarding a particular parity for sterling as the touchstone of its economic policy and indeed its political credibility.

I resisted John Major's wish to go into the ERM in July. The monetary signals, indicating that inflation was starting to turn down so that we could enter the ERM with some confidence that the parity could be sustained, were not yet in place.

By the autumn, however, the high interest rates were clearly doing their work. The money supply fell sharply. It was clear that interest rates should now be reduced, quite apart from the question of the ERM. As regards ERM entry, the Madrid conditions had not been fully met. But the most important consideration was inflation. It was not till the end of the year that inflation as measured by the RPI (heavily distorted by mortgage interest rates and the way the community charge figured in it) began to fall. Other indicators, however, – CBI surveys, car sales, retail sales and above all the money supply – showed that we were getting on top of inflation. I insisted against the Treasury and the Bank on a simultaneous announcement of a 1 per cent cut in interest rates. They had not disputed that the monetary and other figures warranted this; but they had wanted to delay. But I for my part was determined to demonstrate that we would be looking more to monetary conditions than to the exchange rate in setting interest rates. So on Friday 5 October we announced that we were seeking entry into the ERM, and I placed heavy emphasis on the interest rate cut and the reasons for it in presenting that day's decision.

NO COMPROMISE WITH EMU

As I have explained, the attitude taken by Britain and the rest of the Community to EMU had a bearing on the operation and development of the ERM. But, of course, EMU was a far greater question. The sense that I had had at my meeting with John Major in April that he was going wobbly on this increased when I received a further paper from him a little later, at the end of May. John's paper contained all the now familiar phrases about the prospect of a 'two-tier Europe' – on which I noted 'What's wrong with that if the other tier is going in the wrong direction?' – and the awful possibility of the other eleven negotiating a separate treaty for EMU – on which I wrote, 'So be it. Germany and France would have to pay all the regional subventions – OR there would be NONE in which case the poorer nations could NOT agree.' Quite apart from this tendency to be defeated by platitudes, which I found disturbing, it did not seem to me that John, who prided himself on his tactical political sense, had thought through the implications for the rest of the Community countries if they had to go ahead without us.

So at our meeting on the evening of Thursday 31 May I tried to stiffen John's resolve and widen his vision. He reiterated his concern that we would find ourselves 'isolated' in the run up to a general election. He argued that to avoid this we should agree to a treaty amendment establishing the aim of full EMU, but insist on an 'opting-in' provision which left it to individual member states whether and when to join. I rejected this. I said that it was psychologically wrong to put ourselves in a frame of mind in which we accepted the inevitability of moves towards EMU rather than attacking the whole concept. We had arguments which might persuade both the Germans – who would be worried about the weakening of anti-inflation policies – and the poorer countries – who must be told that they would not be bailed out of the consequences of a single currency, which would therefore devastate their inefficient economies. I said that I did not regard John's proposed 'opting-in' mechanism as an adequate defence against being drawn into full EMU. The same reasoning which led him now to argue that we had no alternative but to accept the treaty objective of full EMU would be employed later to concede that we could not afford to be left out of the move to a single currency either. So accepting the opting-in mechanism now would be tantamount to joining eventually and I was not prepared to make that commitment.

We had to use the time between now and the IGC in December to try to undermine the will of the other states to move to Stage 3 of the Delors Report and to develop a wider vision of the way ahead. I rehearsed once again my objection to the establishment of tight blocs of countries which stood in the way of a wider internationalism. I said that we must build on the American proposals for strengthening the political aspects of NATO, by suggesting a trade dimension to the alliance which would join Europe to a North American (US and Canada) Free Trade Area. I saw this as a way of averting the dangerous prospect of a world divided into three protectionist trading blocs, based on the European Community, Japan and the United States, which over time could become seriously unstable. I also suggested that we look at an idea on which Alan Walters had been working – a system of linking currencies to an objective reference standard, such as a commodity index, which would work automatically, without the bureaucratic paraphernalia and the intrusive federalism of the Delors proposals. Such a system might include both the dollar and the yen. I said that we had to set out our ideas boldly at international summits, emphasizing that we were going beyond the narrow European goals and were much more in tune with wider political developments. I was aware that this was visionary stuff: but if there was ever a time for vision this was it. So I had the Treasury and the Foreign Office work up these ideas, which without noticeable enthusiasm they did.

I felt that, much as I liked John Major and valued his loyalty, we had to bring others who were more at ease with large ideas and strategies into the discussion. So – as well as Douglas Hurd, who as Foreign Secretary was necessarily involved, for EMU was by now at the centre of debate in the European Council – I brought in Nick Ridley. I asked Nick to prepare a paper on EMU and the alternatives and he attended my meeting with John and Douglas on the morning of Tuesday 19 June before the forthcoming Dublin European Council. Nick made two contributions of great importance to the concept of an alternative Europe, going in a direction different from that of the inward-looking, statist and protectionist Europe with which we were faced. The first was to stress that the Delors-style Europe with a single currency would obstruct the enlargement of the Community. Our own vision of a wider, freer, more flexible Europe would be much more accommodating to the countries of the post-communist world. The second observation Nick made was to point out that we should not be alarmed by some countries going ahead with EMU and leaving us out: indeed, this was a model we should encourage – a wider Community in which different countries came together for different purposes on different occasions.

At this point it makes sense to consider how matters had been developing within the European Community itself and the stance we took in the face of the drive for federalism which was underway. But if there is one lesson which is to be learnt from the economic developments of the period of 1987 to 1990 – confirmed since by the circumstances preceding Britain's undignified departure from the ERM in 1992 – it is that contained in the phrase I used in the House of Commons, which so infuriated Nigel and summed up the difference between us: 'there is no way in which one can buck the market.' I might add that if you try to do so, the market will buck you. The belief that the laws of economics and the judgements of the markets can be suspended by clever people – and Nigel Lawson was one of the cleverest people in British politics – is a perpetual temptation to folly. That folly cost us dear. But then the idea that other clever people – and Jacques Delors was one of the cleverest people I met in European politics – can build their Tower of Babel on the uneven foundation of ancient nations, different languages and diverse economies is still more dangerous. Work on that shaky construction is still proceeding.

CHAPTER XXV

The Babel Express

Relations with the European Community – 1987–1990

I have already described how during my second term of office as Prime Minister certain harmful features and tendencies in the European Community started to become evident. Against the notable gains constituted by the securing of Britain's budget rebate and progress towards a real Common – or 'Single' – Market had to be set a more powerful Commission ambitious for power, an inclination towards bureaucratic rather than market solutions to economic problems and the re-emergence of a Franco-German axis with its own covert federalist and protectionist agenda. As yet, however, the full implications of all this were unclear – even to me, distrustful as I always was of that un-British combination of high-flown rhetoric and pork-barrel politics which passed for European statesmanship.

Indeed, the first three European Councils of my second term were very much of the traditional mould, dominated by finance and agriculture: and their outcome was equally traditional – a British victory on points. But from then on the Community environment in which I had to operate became increasingly alien and frequently poisonous. The disputes were no longer about tactical or temporary issues but about the whole future direction of the Community and its relations with the wider world changing so fast outside it. The Franco-German axis became more evident; and with the unification of Germany that relationship became still more lop-sided, with German dominance increasingly pronounced.

The Franco-German federalist project was wholeheartedly supported by a variety of different elements within the Community – by poorer southern countries who expected a substantial pay-off in exchange for its accomplishment; by northern businesses which hoped to foist their own high costs on to their competitors; by socialists because of the scope it offered for state intervention; by Christian Democrats whose political tradition was firmly corporatist; and, of course, by the Commission which saw itself as the nucleus of a supranational government. In the face of these powerful forces I sought for allies within the Community and sometimes found them; and so my strategic retreat in the face of majorities I could not block was also punctuated by tactical victories.

Ultimately, however, there was no option but to stake out a radically different position from the direction in which most of the Community seemed intent on going, to raise the flag of national sovereignty, free trade and free enterprise – and fight. Isolated I might be in the European Community – but taking the wider perspective, the federalists were the real isolationists, clinging grimly to a half-Europe when Europe as a whole was being liberated; toying with protectionism when truly global markets were emerging; obsessed with schemes of centralization when the greatest attempt at centralization – the Soviet Union – was on the point of collapse. If there was ever an idea whose time had come and gone it was surely that of the artificial mega-state. I was, therefore, convinced not just that I was right about the way forward for Europe, but confident that if the Government and Party I led kept their nerve we would be vindicated by intellectual developments and international events.

FINANCE AND FARMING

After the 1987 general election I was in just the mood to force the Community to live up to its previous protestations of virtue. For all the talk of financial rectitude at and since the Fontainebleau Council of 1984, there had still been no effective budget discipline and no binding limits on spending under the CAP. The rebate I had won had limited our net contribution from rising to a totally unacceptable level; but several of our Community partners now wanted to cut or eliminate it. There was a large Community budget deficit which was starting to concentrate minds. But from the Commission it had provoked the traditional answer to any financial problem – an increase in the Community's 'own resources'. They wanted to increase that sum not just to the 1.6 per cent of VAT which we had agreed at Fontainebleau might happen in 1988, but to 1.4 per cent of Community countries' GNP (equivalent to 2.2 per cent of VAT receipts). There was also on the table a pretty blatantly protectionist proposal, strongly supported by the French, for an Oils and Fats tax. This was, it is true, to be matched by measures to control spending on agriculture where huge sums were going on storing and disposing of surpluses, and to improve budget discipline. But these were not tough enough. Moreover, the Commission was still trying to whittle away at what I had secured at Fontainebleau by proposing to change our rebate mechanism. And M. Delors also wanted to double the structural funds (that is, spending on Community regional and social policy). This last proposal was, naturally, more than welcome to the southern member states and Ireland which expected to gain most from it.

Who were my allies? However unreliable the French and Germans would be when it came to cutting agricultural spending on which their politically influential farmers depended, I knew that at least I could look to them for support in trying to resist the huge increase in structural funds. I also had in M. Chirac, the Gaullist French Prime Minister, an ally in resisting the large increase proposed in 'own resources'. But my main allies – though inclined to be critical of our rebate – were the Dutch. Such then was the technically and politically complicated scene which I knew confronted me when I went to Brussels for the European Council meeting on Tuesday 29 and Wednesday 30 June 1987.

It was an intensely hot, humid day when I arrived. On the way from the airport, my car was pelted with water balloons by the less dangerous Euro-fanatics outside the Council. Inside, the possibilities of bad-tempered disagreement were maximized by the weak chairmanship of M. Martens, the Belgian Prime Minister and Council President. He allowed no less than four hours of discussion of the proposed Oils and Fats tax, which the Germans, the Dutch and I had not the slightest intention of accepting.

Generally, I was among the best briefed heads of government on these occasions – partly because I always did my homework and partly because I had a truly superb official team to help me. Perhaps the mainstay of this was David Williamson, who came from the Ministry of Agriculture to the key European policy role in the Cabinet Office and finally – and deservedly – became Secretary-General of the Commission. The intricacies of European Community policy, particularly finance, really test one's intellectual ability and capacity for clear thinking. With the exception of those of the presidency, the different delegations' officials were not present during the proceedings themselves; so the Foreign Secretary of the day wrote manuscript notes which were passed out to our people, against which the conclusions recorded by the presidency would be checked.

On this occasion (and at Copenhagen later) the complexity of some of the matters under discussion was absurd. They should have been dealt with by Agriculture or Finance or Foreign ministers: but there never seemed the will to take real decisions at this level and so heads of government would be left discussing matters which would boggle the mind of the City's top accountants.

The general view was that this first Brussels Council was a 'failure' and that I was responsible for it. There was only a little truth in either proposition. It was in any case unreasonable to think that with such a large number of contentious and complicated matters on the agenda agreement would be reached on the first serious attempt. Moreover, a good deal of progress was made on the key questions of finance and agriculture. It was accepted that budget discipline should be 'binding and effective', that it should apply to 'commitments' (that is basically what the Agriculture ministers agreed to spend) as well as actual payments, and that additional regulations (that is Community 'laws') would be adopted to keep the level of spending within the budget. The worst aspect – unacceptable to me – was that they wanted to build into the 'agricultural guideline' – that is the total permitted spending on agriculture – the present level of overspending. The package as a whole was not sufficiently tight for me to agree to an increase in 'own resources'. So the other heads of government left Brussels aware that I had lost none of my willingness to say no.

I met two of the key players in Berlin in September, where I was attending the IDU Conference. I had a working breakfast with M. Chirac at the British Ambassador's residence. Not for nothing was he known by his compatriots as '*le bulldozer*': and on more than one occasion I had to make it clear that the lady was not for bulldozing. He was a marked contrast to President Mitterrand. M. Chirac was blunt, direct, forceful, argumentative, had a sure grasp of detail and a profound interest in economics. The President was quieter, more urbane, a self-conscious French intellectual, fascinated by foreign policy, bored by detail, possibly contemptuous of economics. Oddly enough I liked both of them.

M. Chirac had apparently chastised me as a 'housewife' in Brussels in June 1987 and was to make an unprintable remark about me in a heated exchange at Brussels in February 1988. But I generally found him somewhat easier to deal with than President Mitterrand, because he said what he thought and because his public actions bore a greater similarity to his privately expressed views. I was, as M. Chirac knew, none too happy about the arrangements which led to the release of French hostages from the Lebanon and which were widely considered to have overstepped the mark as regards the principle of refusal to deal with terrorists. (M. Chirac furiously reproached me at a reception at the Copenhagen Council for allegedly leaking criticism of what the French had done: in fact I could lay my hand on my heart and assure him that we had done no such thing.) To be fair, the French had been of great assistance to us in the matter of intercepting the arms shipment from the *Eksund*.* And of course M. Chirac and I were very much on the same wave-length politically. He had done much to make the Gaullists (the RPR – *Rassemblement pour la République*) into a modern right-of-centre party, committed to free enterprise. This was of great significance not just to France but in the long term to Europe and the western alliance. I was disappointed, though not very surprised, at the way in which the wily President Mitterrand managed to turn the process of 'cohabitation' against the Right. At this time, though, it was the imminence of the French elections rather than their likely outcome which was the problem. For it was clear to me that neither M. Chirac nor President Mitterrand would be anxious to be seen taking tough action on agriculture when French farmers' votes would soon be needed.

Nor for that matter would Chancellor Kohl whom I saw for tea that afternoon in the German government guesthouse. He confessed to me that he too had had his domestic political difficulties. His farming supporters had stayed away from the polls in two recent Land elections which had led to bad results for the CDU. The small farmer was, he said, a great element of stability in Germany. He said he was prepared to make some sacrifices but it would take four or five years to 'get over the hill'. I retorted that we did not have four or five years. We must act on agricultural overspending now. But I did not come away from the meeting any more optimistic about the likely outcome of the next Council.

It was too much to expect, when I landed at an icy Copenhagen on Thursday 4 December, that the papers would not be full of allusions to the famous battle of Copenhagen, when Nelson, ignoring signalled orders by the device of holding a telescope to his blind eye, attacked and blew the opposing fleet out of the water. In fact, as at Brussels earlier, it was a magnifying glass – or perhaps a pocket calculator – which were most in order on this occasion, such was the complexity of the matters under discussion. At least we had the amiable Poul Schluter, the Conservative Danish Prime Minister, in the chair. The Danes were anxious to continue receiving as much as possible from the CAP. But of all the other Community countries they were the

* See pp. 405–6.

most anti-federalist. So there was a basic sympathy between us, even if not always a meeting of minds.

Discussions of the ideas put forward at Brussels had been continuing in the Agriculture Council and between officials and the Commission. But since then the pressure had increased to cut back our rebate. The Danes had unhelpfully brought it back into the limelight in their 'bidding letter' inviting heads of government to the Council. There was also continuing discussion about what should constitute the Community's 'own resources'. But for me everything really hinged – everything that is apart from the maintenance of our rebate on which I would not compromise – on the measures to control agriculture spending. The position here was far from satisfactory. I was still unhappy about the 'agricultural guideline' being proposed. But even more important was the way in which the Commission's idea of applying 'stabilizers' was to be put into effect. There were basically two possible ways of cutting agricultural subsidies. One was to tax overproduction by means of what – in another piece of Community jargon – was described as a 'coresponsibility levy'. This might have a place, but it was not the best method. The other way was to apply automatic and cumulative price cuts once a certain level of production was breached. This was the 'stabilizer' mechanism. It then fell to be discussed what the 'minimum quantity' of any particular commodity would be before the mechanism began to operate – for different agricultural products would require different formulae according to the market in which they were being produced – and what the price cuts should be.

It is also worth adding, however, one other possibility which I never actually advanced as an alternative to either of these routes but which from time to time I considered. This was to revert to a national system of subsidy for agriculture, thus bypassing the whole cumbersome Community apparatus altogether. It would, of course, have required a complete rethink of the regime imposed by the Community and could only have been possible if other countries had wanted to pursue the same approach. The disadvantage would have been that individual countries would have been competing in subsidy and probably our farmers would have lost out in that race to the French and Germans. It would only have been desirable if agriculture had been brought effectively under the GATT – and the difficulty of doing that was to become increasingly evident. But I was definitely attracted to a scheme by which each nation took financial responsibility for writing off surplus agricultural stocks and proposed this, without much success. I also raised with Helmut Kohl, when I saw him just before the Copenhagen Council, whether it might not be better if Germany used nationally financed aids to assist her small farmers – though these must not be used to finance increased production. (I recalled, of course, how he had essentially adopted this approach at an earlier Council.)* But though he took the point nothing came of it. I realized that the only immediate way to rein in Community spending on agriculture was within a Community framework.

My pre-Council meeting with Chancellor Kohl also revealed him to be even more preoccupied than before with his farming vote. He wanted a Community-financed 'set-aside' scheme, by which farmers would essentially be paid not to farm efficiently – something which ultimately demonstrated the Mad Hatter economics of the CAP. I was prepared to agree to this, as I told him, as long as we got effective stabilizers as well. I was also very tough with him about the prospect of increases in the Community's 'own resources', on which I knew Chancellor Kohl was willing to see a large increase (ultimately at the expense of the German taxpayer) in order to keep his farmers happy. So by the time the Council opened we knew where we stood.

Once it was clear that the French – principally for electoral reasons – were prepared to back the Germans on a formula for stabilizers which could not conceivably contain agriculture spending, it was evident that no satisfactory conclusion could be reached. Neither I nor Mr Lubbers of the Netherlands would agree to anything on these lines. The Commission added another split by pressing hard for a doubling of the structural funds, which pitted the northern against the southern Europeans. But it was not an acrimonious occasion. It was agreed that a special European Council would be held in Brussels the following February.

There were a number of long faces at the end of the Copenhagen Council. But mine was not among them. I knew that little by little I was winning the argument inside and outside the Council for the kind of solution I wanted. I told the other heads of government to cheer up and reminded them – with a little irony, for I suspected that some of them needed no reminding – of how difficult things had been at Brussels on the eve of the Fontainebleau summit and then how at the next moment what was insoluble suddenly seemed easy. Why should it not happen again in Brussels? President Mitterrand observed wryly that he was really not quite sure whether it was easier to deal with Madame Thatcher when she was difficult or when she was cheerful. Evidently he did remember.

But it was by no means certain that we would reach agreement at

* At Fontainebleau – see pp. 541–5.

the forthcoming special European Council. I was prepared to make some compromises; after all, the question of precisely when and how agricultural stabilizers would bite was the sort of matter even people intent on checking agricultural spending could legitimately disagree about. But far more difficult to gauge was whether Messrs Mitterrand and Chirac and Herr Kohl would think it worth their while achieving a settlement on terms which some of their farmers would find unpalatable.

By now the French election campaigns were in full swing and the rivalry between President and Prime Minister was intense, with 'cohabitation' nothing more than a fiction. Accordingly, when they arrived in London for an Anglo-French summit on Friday 29 January 1988, the important discussions I had with President Mitterrand and Prime Minister Chirac had to be at separate meetings. The contrast between their respective styles was once again evident. President Mitterrand was not in good form and had a heavy cold, which I hoped he would not pass on to me: I seem to have an unfailing ability to attract any passing cold germ. Nor was he properly briefed about the difficult European Community matters on which I wanted to concentrate and he had to break off half way through to receive explanations from Jacques Attali, his adviser. He was obviously relieved when the conversation turned to defence and foreign affairs. I was not sure that I had got very far by the end of the discussion, though as always it had been agreeable enough.

The same could not, however, be said of my meeting with M. Chirac, who was in robust form. He began very frankly, saying that with the presidential elections just three months away he had a real political problem with the forthcoming Council. His own interest, he said, lay in a failure at Brussels. But for wider international reasons he was prepared to work for success. Lest I conclude that this meant he was going to be a push-over, he spelt out for me precisely what his strategy was. He said that we could either settle at Brussels or wait until the financial pressure built up on the Community because of its lack of money. But in that case we would be under the Greek presidency, which he was certainly right in describing as offering an 'uncertain prospect'. If the British continued to block the settlement on agriculture at Brussels which the rest of the Community – by which he meant the French and the Germans – wanted we would be isolated and attention would focus on our rebate. I replied that this was evidently no time for diplomatic language. If he thought that ganging up with the Germans to 'isolate Mrs T' was going to work, he was sadly mistaken. I had no fear at all of being isolated because I was demanding that agricultural surpluses be brought under control. M. Chirac again insisted that if there was to be a row it would turn out not to be about surpluses but about Britain's rebate. I advised him not to threaten me and promised that if there was no satisfactory solution on agricultural spending and our rebate, there would be no increase in 'own resources'. But he continued to insist then and over lunch that the present German presidency's proposals were the furthest France was prepared to go.

How much of this was Gallic bluff I could not know. But it certainly made it all the more important to gauge precisely what the German position was. The fact that the Germans had the presidency meant, as always, that they had less scope for openly advocating their own interests, but this was more than made up for by the extra influence it would give them behind the scenes.

On the morning of Tuesday 2 February I had three hours of talks with Chancellor Kohl at No. 10. This was a business-like and quite successful meeting. Both of us had come with detailed proposals on each of the main elements of the package which would be on the table at Brussels. There were still large differences between us on the agricultural guideline and the stabilizers. He was also minded to be more accommodating to the southerners and the Commission over the structural funds than I was. But I was glad to find that he did not press me at all hard on the British rebate. We ended by discussing what the French attitude would really turn out to be. With some prescience (or perhaps knowledge) Chancellor Kohl thought that though it would be very difficult they might prefer a reasonable settlement now to postponement.

I flew into Brussels some time after midnight on Wednesday 10 February after having spoken at a Conservative Party National Union dinner. My first appointment the next day was a breakfast meeting with Mr Lubbers to agree tactics for the Council. In my speech later that day I warned against any temptation to run away from the problem of food surpluses which we all knew had now to be tackled. The battle lines formed much as could have been predicted. The Dutch and we were up against the French and the Danes over the agricultural guideline. The German presidency put forward proposals for the new 'own resources' ceiling, which were attacked as too high by the Dutch, the French and us and as too low by everybody else. M. Chirac argued passionately for a higher threshold on cereals before the stabilizer started to work than I and others were prepared to accept. He also tried, as he had threatened in our earlier conversation, to link Britain's budget rebate with the issue of stabilizers. But it was quickly apparent that this was not going to work. Throughout there was an odd, slightly theatrical air to his performance which was clearly designed to impress a domestic audience. President Mitterrand sat in complete silence throughout these proceedings, restricting himself to a lengthy speech at dinner about future European developments. Not much progress was made that day.

Overnight the Commission came up with a compromise package. But this was rejected by the Germans and the Council broke up for bilateral meetings without any paper as a basis for discussion. Chancellor Kohl was now the key, both as President of the Council and because if the Germans were prepared to do a deal on agricultural spending the French were unlikely to stand out against it. So late that afternoon Ruud Lubbers, Hans van den Broek, Jacques Delors, Geoffrey Howe and I went in to see Chancellor Kohl who was accompanied by Herr Genscher and several other officials. Chancellor Kohl's style of diplomacy is even more direct than mine. He was never above banging the table and on this occasion he spoke in a parade-ground bellow throughout. He said that Germany was making sacrifices, particularly the German farmers. I replied that British farmers were facing sacrifices too and that I was being asked to accept too large an increase in structural funds and too high a ceiling – 1.3 per cent of GNP – for Community 'own resources'. The argument went back and forth. M. Delors now proposed a 1.2 per cent ceiling. This prompted alarmed protests from Chancellor Kohl who thought that it might jeopardize his farmers' set-aside scheme. But I said that I would think further about what had been proposed. I was aware that the Dutch were becoming restive and would probably not be prepared to stand out against what was now on offer. In any case, it was necessary to discuss with my officials precisely what the package would mean and I could only do this in private. What I did insist upon, however, was that it should all be set out clearly on paper. As it turned out this was one of my better decisions.

I had a long discussion with Geoffrey Howe and my officials. We argued through each element. It seemed to me that the discipline was going to prove tighter and more effective than I had earlier thought – and perhaps than others had really understood. So when the full Council reconvened I was able to join in giving broad support to the proposals in the paper which was now circulated.

Anyone who imagined that it would now all be plain sailing underrated the French. The agreement we had reached covered the main agricultural products at issue. But it assumed that the other products for which stabilizers had been agreed at Copenhagen would also be covered. To everyone's surprise President Mitterrand and M. Chirac would not agree to this. A heated argument erupted which lasted more than four hours about their proposal to have the stabilizers for 'other products' referred to the Agriculture Council. In the end a Danish suggestion that it should go to a Foreign ministers' meeting in ten days' time was agreed. Ruud Lubbers and I insisted that our agreement to the overall package was conditional on the Foreign ministers not reopening the Copenhagen agreement on 'other products'. In fact, the French had to concede the issue when the Foreign ministers met.

I was right to settle when I did. I had secured my basic aims: effective and legally binding controls on expenditure, measures to reduce agricultural surpluses in which automatic price cuts were the principal weapon, no Oils and Fats tax, and Britain's rebate which had saved us some £3 billion in the past three years secure. I had had to concede a little on the threshold at which stabilizers began to work. I had had to compromise over the structural funds. I had reluctantly agreed a new 1.2 per cent of GNP ceiling for Community 'own resources'. But it was much better than a draw. Agricultural surpluses started to fall quite sharply and the new measures to enforce budget discipline were successful. None of that, of course, changed the fundamental direction or defects of the Community. The CAP was still wasteful and costly. Britain was still making a financial contribution which I considered too high. The bureaucratic and centralizing tendencies remained. But within its limits the February 1988 Brussels Agreement was not at all bad.

FREE TRADE V. PROTECTION

It is fair to say that from about this point onwards – early 1988 – the agenda in Europe began to take an increasingly unwelcome shape. It also began to deviate sharply from that being pursued in the wider international community. That does not mean, however, that my own relations with other European heads of government worsened at a personal level; far from it. I was sorry – though not surprised – to see the Right beaten in the French presidential elections. But I sent a message of congratulations to President Mitterrand and went to see him in Paris that June to talk about the international scene in general and the forthcoming Toronto G7 summit and Hanover European Council in particular.

I found him in understandably good humour now that he had been freed from the domestic torment of 'cohabitation' with the Right. He was pressing a scheme – not dissimilar to one advanced by Nigel Lawson – to tackle the crippling level of Third World debt. I would have had more sympathy with his ideas if France had not been so determinedly protectionist, an approach which did far more harm to poorer countries than any amount of overseas aid did good. The French line was expressed – or rather concealed – in a splendid piece of Euro-jargon: the concept of 'globality'. That is to say progress must be made on all the issues before the GATT at roughly the same pace, a transparent device for avoiding concentration on the thorniest issue – that of agricultural subsidies and protection. He was also keen to have a committee of 'wise men' set up to report on how to achieve economic and monetary union; he specifically hankered after a European Central Bank. I roundly rejected this. I said that the proposal for such a bank was motivated by political not technical considerations and that this was not an area for playing games. The President smiled and said that it was nice to be reminded that I knew how to say no. But I had no illusion that he was going to desist because of that.

I also met M. Rocard, the new Socialist Prime Minister. I had met him before but did not know him well. He spoke disarmingly and I felt sincerely about his affection for Britain and the special understanding – inherited from wartime – between the two countries. As French Socialists go, he was moderate, pragmatic and sensible and I warmed to him. I hoped that he might come to exercise some moderating influence on France's flirtation with European federalism.

On Saturday 18 June 1988 I flew to Toronto for the G7 economic summit. President Mitterrand had suggested optimistically to me in Paris that this being President Reagan's last summit there might be an inclination to put off difficult decisions. I had replied that I did not think this likely and, for my part, I was determined to ensure that we used this occasion to get to grips with agriculture and the GATT. By the time I reached Toronto I had done my homework on the subject. In particular, we had devised a mythical beast known informally as 'Howe's Cow' or more precisely as a 'Producer Subsidy Equivalent'. This was the calculation of how much agricultural support, whether in direct subsidy or from protection, each country provided, divided by the number of cows. The greediest cow turned out to be Japan's – so not surprisingly, the Japanese, with some support from the Americans, disputed our statistical approach.

I was, therefore, well armed with useful facts and figures when Brian Mulroney, the summit chairman, asked me to open the economic discussion on the Sunday afternoon. I drew attention to the success of the current second cycle of summits, now ending, compared with the first. We had seen economic growth, low inflation and more jobs in the years since the Montebello summit in 1981, because we had stuck to getting the fundamentals right rather than concentrating on demand management. But there was more to do. Above all, we must fight down protectionism. I strongly urged – and repeated in a further intervention the following day – that all of us should honour the commitments made at the start of the GATT Uruguay round in September 1986 by coming up with firm proposals at the forthcoming 'Medium Term Review' meeting of the GATT.

As the dispute over measuring agricultural subsidies exemplified, free trade is something which almost everyone subscribes to in principle and finds politically painful in practice. Britain always had everything to gain from a global open trading system. The United States too traditionally believed in free trade. But Britain's own trade policy was now in the hands of the Community, which contained a majority of countries with a tradition of cartels and corporatism and a politically influential agricultural sector. We were in a minority in Europe when it came to deciding trade policy. As for the United States, its huge trade deficit had given a protectionist turn to policy which President Reagan, a convinced free trader, found difficulty resisting. For its part, Japan not only subsidized and protected its agriculture more than anyone else; it also continued to place obstacles in the way of foreign imports of nonagricultural goods and services. Consequently, I increasingly had to look to the 'Cairns Group' of fourteen countries (which includes Canada, Australia, and Argentina) and to Third World countries, anxious to export their agriculture and textiles, to bring pressure on this wealthy western protection racket. I always regarded free trade as far more important than all the other ambitious and often counter-productive strategies of global economic policy – for example the policies of 'co-ordinated growth' which led principally to inflation. Free trade provided a means not only for poorer countries to earn foreign currency and increase their peoples' standards of living. It was also a force for peace, freedom and political decentralization: peace, because economic links between nations reinforce mutual understanding with mutual interest; freedom, because trade between individuals bypasses the apparatus of the state and disperses power to customers not planners; political decentralization, because the size of the political unit is not dictated by the size of the market and vice versa.

After some two and a half hours of discussion on this subject at Toronto we achieved a broadly satisfactory communiqué. It reaffirmed the Uruguay round commitments and underlined the importance of its 'Medium Term Meeting', while avoiding inclusion of what seemed to me the unrealistic United States objective of no agricultural subsidies by the year 2000. What remained to be seen was how the GATT negotiations now actually evolved. Had I been an optimist I might have drawn comfort from the fact that Toronto was the first time that M. Delors praised one of my speeches. But I kept my optimism in check.

DISCUSSION OF EMU

At Toronto I had an hour's meeting with Chancellor Kohl. Much of it focused on the forthcoming Hanover summit. Chancellor Kohl, supported by the German Finance Ministry and the Bundesbank, seemed ready now to plump for a committee of central bankers rather than academic experts – as the French and Hans-Dietrich Genscher wanted – to report on EMU. This I welcomed. But I restated my unbending hostility to setting up a European Central Bank. By now I was having to recognize that the chance of stopping the committee being set up at all was ebbing away; but I was determined to try to minimize the harm it would do. I also had to recognize that we were saddled with M. Delors as President of the Commission for another two years, since my own favoured candidate, Ruud Lubbers, was not going to stand and the French and Germans supported M. Delors. (In the end I bit the bullet and seconded M. Delors's reappointment myself.)

The Hanover Council turned out to be a fairly good-humoured if disputatious affair. The most important discussion took place on the first evening over dinner. Jacques Delors introduced the discussion of EMU. Chancellor Kohl suggested that a committee of Central Bank governors with a few outsiders be set up under M. Delors's chairmanship. In the ensuing discussion most of the heads of government wanted the report to centre on a European Central Bank. Poul Schluter opposed this and I supported him strongly, quoting from an excellent article by Karl Otto Pöhl, the President of the Bundesbank, to illustrate all the difficulties in the way of such an institution. We succeeded in getting mention of the Central Bank removed. But otherwise there was nothing I could do to stop the committee being set up. The Delors Group was to report back to the June 1989 European Council – that is in a year's time. I hoped that the Governor of the Bank of England

and the sceptical Herr Pöhl would manage to put a spoke in the wheel of this particular vehicle of European integration; unfortunately, as I have already explained, that was not to be.

My problem throughout these discussions of EMU was twofold. First, of course, was the fact that I had so few allies; only Denmark, a small country with plenty of spirit but less weight, was with me. But I was fighting with one hand tied behind my back for another reason. As a 'future member' of the EEC, the UK had agreed a communiqué in Paris following a conference of heads of government in October 1972. This reaffirmed 'the resolve of the member states of the enlarged Community to move irrevocably [towards] Economic and Monetary Union, by confirming all the details of the acts passed by the Council and by the member states' representatives on 22 March 1971 and 21 March 1972'. Such language may have reflected Ted Heath's wishes. It certainly did not reflect mine. But there was no point in picking a quarrel which we would have lost. So I preferred to let sleeping dogs lie.

Then, of course, they woke up and started barking in the course of the negotiation of the Single European Act of 1985–6. I had not wanted any reference to EMU in at all. The Germans failed to support me and so the reference to EMU was inserted. But I had Article 20 of the Single European Act give my interpretation of what EMU meant; its title read: 'Co-operation in Economic and Monetary Policy (Economic and Monetary Union)'. This enabled me to claim at subsequent forums that EMU now meant economic and monetary co-operation, not moving towards a single currency. There was a studied ambiguity about all this. Councils at Hanover in June 1988 and then at Madrid in 1989 referred back to the Single European Act's 'objective of progressive realization of economic and monetary union'. I was more or less happy with this, because it meant no more than co-operation. The rest of the European heads of government were equally happy, because they interpreted it as progress towards a European Central Bank and a single currency. But at some point, of course, these two interpretations would clash. And when they did I was bound to be fighting on ground not of my choosing.

For the fact was that the more I saw of how the Community operated the less I was attracted by any further steps on the road towards monetary integration. We advanced our proposals for a 'hard ecu'. We issued Treasury bills denominated in ecu terms. And (though this was done because it was in our own interests, not in order to please our European partners) we had swept away exchange controls before anyone else. All this was very *communautaire* in its way, as I never ceased to point out when criticized for resisting entry into the ERM. But my own preference was always for open markets, floating exchange rates and strong political and economic transatlantic links. In arguing for that alternative approach I was bound to be handicapped by the formal commitment to European 'economic and monetary union' – or indeed that of 'ever closer union' contained in the preamble to the original Treaty of Rome. These phrases predetermined many decisions which we thought we had reserved for future consideration. This gave a psychological advantage to my opponents, who never let an opportunity go by of making use of it.

THE BRUGES SPEECH

Not the least of those opponents was Jacques Delors. By the summer of 1988 he had altogether slipped his leash as a *fonctionnaire* and become a fully fledged political spokesman for federalism. The blurring of the roles of civil servants and elected representatives was more in the continental tradition than in ours. It proceeded from the widespread distrust which their voters had for politicians in countries like France and Italy. That same distrust also fuelled the federalist express. If you have no real confidence in the political system or political leaders of your own country you are bound to be more tolerant of foreigners of manifest intelligence, ability and integrity like M. Delors telling you how to run your affairs. Or to put it more bluntly, if I were an Italian I might prefer rule from Brussels too. But the mood in Britain was different. I sensed it. More than that, I shared it and I decided that the time had come to strike out against what I saw as the erosion of democracy by centralization and bureaucracy, and to set out an alternative view of Europe's future.

It was high time. It was clear that the momentum towards full blooded EMU, which I always recognized must mean political union too, was building. In July M. Delors told the European Parliament that 'we are not going to manage to take all the decisions needed between now and 1995 unless we see the beginnings of European government in one form or another,' and predicted that within ten years the Community would be the source of '80 per cent of our economic legislation and perhaps even our fiscal and social legislation as well'. In September he addressed the TUC in Bournemouth calling for measures to be taken on collective bargaining at the European level.

But there were also more subtle, less easily detectable, but perhaps even more important signs of the way things were going. That summer I commissioned a paper from officials which spelt out in precise detail how the Commission was pushing forward the frontiers of its 'competence' into new areas – culture, education, health and social security. It used a whole range of techniques. It set up 'advisory committees' whose membership was neither appointed by, nor answerable to, member states and which tended therefore to reach *communautaire* decisions. It carefully built up a library of declaratory language, largely drawn from the sort of vacuous nonsense which found its way into Council conclusions, in order to justify subsequent proposals. It used a special budgetary procedure, known as '*actions ponctuelles*' which enabled it to finance new projects without a legal base for doing so. But, most seriously of all, it consistently misemployed treaty articles requiring only a qualified majority to issue directives which it could not pass under articles which required unanimity.

Often, as over the environment, or later on health and hours of work, it was difficult to explain to the general public precisely why we opposed the specific measure the Commission wanted. When commissioners issued directives outside their competence they were careful to choose popular causes which had support among pressure groups in member countries, thus presenting themselves as the true friends of the British worker, pensioner and environmentalist. This made it politically difficult to resist the creeping expansion of the Commission's authority. In theory, it would have been possible to fight all this in the courts; for time after time the Commission were twisting the words and intentions of the European Council to its own ends. We did indeed fight, and won a number of cases on these grounds before the European Court of Justice (ECJ). But the advice from the lawyers was that in relation to questions of Community and Commission competence the ECJ would favour 'dynamic and expansive' interpretations of the treaty over restrictive ones. The dice were loaded against us.

The more I considered all this, the greater my frustration and the deeper my anger became. Were British democracy, parliamentary sovereignty, the common law, our traditional sense of fairness, our ability to run our own affairs in our own way to be subordinated to the demands of a remote European bureaucracy, resting on very different traditions? I had by now heard about as much of the European 'ideal' as I could take; I suspected that many others had too. In the name of this ideal, waste, corruption and abuse of power were reaching levels which no one who supported, as I had done, entry to the European Economic Community could have foreseen. Because Britain was the most stable and developed democracy in Europe we had perhaps most to lose from these developments. But Frenchmen who wanted to see France free to decide her own destiny would be losers too. So would Germans, who wished to retain their own currency, the deutschmark, which they had made the most credible in the world.

I was no less conscious of those millions of eastern Europeans living under communism. How could a tightly centralized, highly regulated, supra-national European Community meet their aspirations and needs? Arguably, it was the Czechs, Poles and Hungarians who were the real – indeed the last – European 'idealists'; for to them Europe represented a precommunist past, an idea which symbolized the liberal values and national cultures that Marxism had sought unsuccessfully to snuff out.

This wider Europe, stretching perhaps to the Urals and certainly to include that New Europe across the Atlantic, was an entity which made at least historical and cultural sense. And in economic terms, only a truly global approach would do. This then was my thinking as I turned my mind to what would be the 'Bruges Speech'.

The hall in which I made my speech was oddly arranged. The platform from which I spoke was placed in the middle of the long side so that the audience stretched far to my left and right, with only a few rows in front of me. But the message got across well enough. And it was not only my hosts at the College of Europe in Bruges who got more than they bargained for. The Foreign Office had been pressing me for several years to accept an invitation to speak there to set out our European credentials.

I began by doing what the Foreign Office wished. I pointed out just how much Britain had contributed to Europe over the centuries and how much we still contributed, with 70,000 British servicemen stationed there. But what was Europe? I went on to remind my audience that, contrary to the pretensions of the European Community, it was not the only manifestation of European identity. 'We shall always look on Warsaw, Prague and Budapest as great European cities.' Indeed I went on to argue that western Europe had something to learn from the admittedly dreadful experience of its eastern neighbours and their strong and principled reaction to it:

> It is ironic that just when those countries, such as the Soviet Union, which have tried to run everything from the centre, are learning that success depends on dispersing power and decisions away from the centre, some in the Community seem to want to move in the opposite direction. We have not successfully rolled

back the frontiers of the state in Britain only to see them reimposed at a European level, with a European super-state exercising a new dominance from Brussels.

There were, moreover, powerful non-economic reasons for the retention of sovereignty and, as far as possible, of power, by nation-states. Not only were such nations functioning democracies, but they also represented intractable political realities which it would be folly to seek to override or suppress in favour of a wider but as yet theoretical European nationhood. I pointed out:

> Willing and active co-operation between independent sovereign states is the best way to build a successful European Community . . . Europe will be stronger precisely because it has France as France, Spain as Spain, Britain as Britain, each with its own customs, traditions and identity. It would be folly to try to fit them into some sort of identikit European personality.

I set out other guidelines for the future. Problems must be tackled practically: and there was plenty in the CAP which still needed tackling. We must have a European Single Market with the minimum of regulations – a Europe of enterprise. Europe must not be protectionist: and that must be reflected in our approach to the GATT. Finally, I stressed the great importance of NATO and warned against any development (as a result of Franco-German initiatives) of the Western European Union as an alternative to it.*

I ended on a high note, which was far from 'anti-European':

> Let Europe be a family of nations, understanding each other better, appreciating each other more, doing more together, but relishing our national identity no less than our common European endeavour. Let us have a Europe which plays its full part in the wider world, which looks outward not inward, and which preserves that Atlantic Community – that Europe on both sides of the Atlantic – which is our noblest inheritance and our greatest strength.

* The WEU was formed in 1948, principally for the purpose of military co-operation between Britain, France and the Benelux countries. Germany and Italy joined it in the 1950s. The WEU predated NATO, which has entirely overshadowed it.

Not even I would have predicted the furore the Bruges speech unleashed. In Britain, to the horror of the Euro-enthusiasts who believed that principled opposition to federalism had been ridiculed or browbeaten into silence, there was a great wave of popular support for what I had said. It was to become noisily apparent when I addressed the Conservative Party Conference the following month in much the same vein.

But the reaction in polite European circles – or at least the official reaction – was one of stunned outrage. The evening of my speech I had a vigorous argument over dinner in Brussels with M. Martens, his Deputy Prime Minister and Foreign minister. But perhaps that was only to be expected from a small country which thought it could wield more power inside a federal Europe than outside it.

From Brussels I flew to Spain on an official visit – the first by a British Prime Minister – with the press in hot pursuit, as the story rumbled on. My host, Felipe González, was as always the model of courtesy and charm. He prudently, if ambiguously, told me that 'careful study' of my Bruges speech 'could lead to some useful conclusions'. But most of our conversations concentrated on defence and on Gibraltar. Though relations had much improved since the Brussels Agreement of 1984 which reopened the Spanish-Gibraltar border, there was tension over the use of the airport. Spain was, I knew, doing so well out of the Community that I would never get a Socialist Spanish Prime Minister to challenge the arrangements that his country found so lucrative. Equally, I had no doubt that in the long term a proud, ancient nation like Spain would baulk at continued loss of national self-determination in exchange for German-financed subsidies. But that time had not yet arrived.

VISIT TO DEIDESHEIM

The Rhodes European Council in early December of 1988 was something of a non-event in Community terms, though it was enlivened for the press by my forthright recriminations against the Belgians and the Irish for their shabby part in the Ryan affair.* The Community was – unusually – conscious that with the Delors Report on EMU in the making it had enough to be getting along with. Nor was the Greek presidency in a mood to press new initiatives: Mr Papandreou was in

* See pp. 413–4.

fragile health and his Government's political prospects were highly uncertain as a result of financial scandals which had caught up with it.

Nonetheless something productive did come out of Rhodes. I had one of my bilaterals with Helmut Kohl who was more sensitive than I was to the stories which by now regularly appeared in the press about our bad personal relations. Indeed, he had acquired the habit of beginning our discussions by stressing the importance of giving the public impression of being on good terms. In fact, we did not get on at all badly. The problem was that on certain economic and social questions we thought along different lines. At Rhodes he pressed again the invitation he had first made at Chequers in July for me to meet him at his home near Ludwigshafen in the Rhineland-Palatinate in the spring: I accepted with the greatest pleasure.

As always on these occasions, I was accompanied by Charles Powell. Charles was my private secretary on foreign affairs from 1984 until I left office. He worked tirelessly and fast; he was a uniquely gifted draftsman who invariably in his minutes got both flavour and substance precisely right; he managed always to be charming and diplomatic – yet recognized, as I did, that there was more to foreign policy than diplomacy. He was, in all respects, simply outstanding.

So it was that on Sunday 30 April we arrived in the charming village of Deidesheim to be met by a beaming Federal Chancellor on his home soil. In fact, there was not a great deal for him to beam about. He was in domestic political difficulties. West Germany had been rocked by the strange phenomenon of 'Gorby-mania' and, under intense pressure from an always instinctively neutralist German public opinion, the staunchly pro-NATO Chancellor Kohl had begun to shift his ground on the subject of short-range nuclear weapons (SNF). I took him to task on this, deploying all the arguments for a credible short-range nuclear deterrent and for sticking by previously agreed NATO decisions.* The discussion on this subject lasted two hours and became quite heated. Chancellor Kohl was, I thought, deeply uncomfortable, as any politician will be whose instincts and principles push him one way while his short-term political interests push him the other. But we both made an effort to live up to what our diplomats rather than the press – out as ever for a story of Anglo-German 'hand-bagging' – wanted.

And indeed the atmosphere at Deidesheim was otherwise amicable. It was jolly, quaint, sentimental and slightly overdone – *gemütlich* is,

* For a full discussion of this issue, see pp. 786–7.

I think, the German word. Lunch consisted of potato soup, pig's stomach (which the German Chancellor clearly enjoyed), sausage, liver dumplings and sauerkraut.

Then we drove to the great cathedral of Speyer nearby, in whose crypt are to be found the tombs of at least four Holy Roman Emperors. As we entered the cathedral the organ struck up a Bach fugue. Chancellor Kohl, knowing how much I love church music, had thoughtfully arranged this gesture. Outside, a large crowd had gathered which I understood was telling the Chancellor how right he was to get British and American tanks off German soil and stop the low-level flying.

Only afterwards did I learn that Helmut Kohl had taken Charles Powell aside behind a tomb in the cathedral crypt to say that now I had seen him on his home ground, on the borders of France, surely I would understand that he – Helmut Kohl – was as much European as German. I understood what Helmut meant and I rather liked him for it. But I had to doubt his reasoning.

This desire among modern German politicians to merge their national identity in a wider European one is understandable enough, but it presents great difficulties to self-conscious nation-states in Europe. In effect, the Germans, because they are nervous of governing themselves, want to establish a European system in which no nation will govern itself. Such a system could only be unstable in the long term and, because of Germany's size and preponderance, is bound to be lop-sided. Obsession with a European Germany risks producing a German Europe. In fact this approach to the German problem is a delusion: it is also a distraction from the real task of German statesmanship, which must be to strengthen and deepen the post-1945 traditions of West German democracy under the new and admittedly challenging conditions of unification. That would both benefit Germany and reassure her neighbours.

EUROPEAN ELECTIONS

By now attention in British politics was turning to two issues which, much as I sought to disentangle them, became entwined: the elections to the European Parliament and the occasion of my tenth anniversary. On the second of these, I had given strict instructions to Central Office and the Party that it should be handled with as little fuss as possible. I gave one or two interviews; I received a commemorative vase from the National Union; and a rather attractive publication was issued by the Party, which was a modest success without being exactly a best-seller. But, of course, there were plenty of journalists anxious to write 'reflective' pieces on ten years of Thatcher and to conclude, as I knew they would, that a decade of this woman was quite enough.

In such an atmosphere it was natural that the Labour Party would claim that the 1989 European elections were a 'referendum' on Thatcherism in general and the Bruges approach in particular. I might have accepted that the European elections were a sort of judgement on Bruges if we had had European candidates who were Brugesist rather than federalist. With a few notable exceptions that was not the case.

As every advertising expert or political strategist will tell you, perhaps the most important requirement in any campaign is to have one clear message. But the Conservative Party now seemed to have two quite contradictory messages which Peter Brooke, as Party Chairman, and Christopher Prout, as leader of the European Democratic Group (EDG – the Conservative MEPs from Denmark, Spain and the UK) struggled to try to reconcile. Many leading members of the EDG had gone into the European Parliament because their views were out of sympathy with the rest of the party: they were a residue of Heathism. Their criticisms of the campaign strategy, of our general policy towards Europe and – whenever they thought they could get away with it – of me too rebounded directly on themselves. For, by undermining the Party's credibility on European matters they destroyed their own political prospects.

I had put Geoffrey Howe in charge of preparing the manifesto. He tried to reach a consensus and consequently it was an unexciting document, although nicely written by Chris Patten. The advertising by contrast was sharp but not very good. I was shown the last proposed advertisement of the campaign when I was at Central Office after one of my few press conferences of the elections and was not at all happy with it. So, with various astonished creative experts standing around, I designed my own which read: 'Conservatives have created a strong Britain. Vote Conservative today for a strong Europe.' Uninspired, perhaps, but direct and a good deal more effective than the frivolous and obscure advertisements we had used earlier.

The overall strategy was simple. It was to bring Conservative voters – so many of whom were thoroughly disillusioned with the Community – out to vote. Perhaps it might have worked if the message had been got across with greater conviction and vigour by the candidates themselves and if we had been free of highly publicized attacks from Ted

Heath and others. In fact, at the very last moment – as the regular polling information which I received subsequently confirmed – there was a late surge to the Green Party which undercut our vote. People had treated the European elections rather as they would a by-election, voting not to effect real changes in their lives but to make a protest against the sitting government. Labour were the beneficiaries and gained thirteen seats from us. For all the mitigating factors, I was not happy. The result would encourage all those who were out to undermine me and my approach to Europe.

THE MADRID EUROPEAN COUNCIL

This did not take long to occur. I have already described how Geoffrey Howe and Nigel Lawson tried to hustle me into setting a date for sterling's entry into the ERM and how I avoided this at the Madrid Council in June 1989.* In fact, as I had expected, the ERM was something of an irrelevance at Madrid. The two real issues were the handling of the Delors Report on EMU and the question of whether the Community should have its own Social Charter.

I was, of course, opposed root and branch to the whole approach of the Delors Report. But I was not in a position to prevent some kind of action being taken upon it. Consequently, I decided to stress three points. First, the Delors Report must not be the only basis for further work on EMU. It must be possible to introduce other ideas, such as our own of a hard ecu and a European Monetary Fund. Second, there must be nothing automatic about the process of moving towards EMU either as regards timing or content. In particular, we would not be bound now to what might be in Stage 2 or when it would be implemented. Third, there should be no decision now to go ahead with an Inter-Governmental Conference on the Report. A fall-back position would be that any such IGC must receive proper – and as lengthy as possible – preparation.

As regards the Social Charter, the issue was simpler. I considered it quite inappropriate for rules and regulations about working practices or welfare benefits to be set at Community level. The Social Charter was quite simply a socialist charter – devised by socialists in the Commission and favoured predominantly by socialist member states. I had been prepared to go along (with some misgivings) with the

* See pp. 709–13.

assertion in Council communiqués of the importance of the 'social dimension' of the Single Market. But I always considered that this meant the advantages in terms of jobs and living standards which would flow from freer trade.

The Foreign Office would probably have liked me to soften my stance. They liked to remind me of how Keith Joseph in Opposition had written a pamphlet on 'Why Britain Needs a Social Market Economy'. But the sort of 'social market' Keith and I advocated had precious little similarity with the way the term '*Sozialmarktwirtschaft*' had come to be used in Germany. There it had become a kind of corporatist, highly collectivized, 'consensus'-based economic system, which pushed up costs, suffered increasingly from market rigidities and relied on qualities of teutonic self-discipline to work at all. The extension of such a system throughout the Community would, of course, serve Germany well, in the short term at least, because it would impose German wage costs and overheads on poorer European countries which would otherwise have competed all too successfully with German goods and services. The fact that the cost of extending this system to the poorer countries would also be financed by huge transnational subsidies paid by the German taxpayer seemed to be overlooked by German politicians. But that is what happens when producer cartels rather than customer demands become dominant in any system, whether it is formally described as socialist or not.

When I went to Madrid I took with me a document setting out all the benefits enjoyed by British citizens – the Health Service, health and safety at work, pensions and benefits for the disabled, training provisions and so on. I also advanced the argument that the voluntary Council of Europe Social Charter was quite sufficient and that we did not need a Community document which would, I knew, be the basis of directives aimed at introducing the Delors brand of socialism by the back door.

Most of the first day's discussions in Madrid were taken up with EMU. Late in the afternoon we turned to the Single Market and the 'social dimension'. I have already described how I used my first speech to spell out my conditions for entering the ERM. But I also backed Poul Schluter who challenged paragraph 39 of the Delors Report, which essentially spelt out the 'in for a penny, in for a pound approach' which the federalists favoured. The other extreme was represented by France. President Mitterrand insisted on setting deadlines for an IGC and for completion of Stages 2 and 3, which at one point he suggested should be 31 December 1992.

The argument then turned to the Social Charter. I was sitting next to Sr. Cavaco Silva, the rather sound Portuguese Prime Minister who would doubtless have been sounder still if his country was not so poor and the Germans quite so rich.

'Don't you see', I said, 'that the Social Charter is intended to stop Portugal attracting investment from Germany because of your lower wage costs? This is German protectionism. There will be directives based on it and your jobs will be lost.' But he seemed unconvinced that the charter would be anything other than a general declaration. And perhaps he thought that if the Germans were prepared to pay enough in 'cohesion' money the deal would not be too bad. So I was alone in opposing the charter.

Ironically, when – on the second day of the Council – it came to the drafting of the section of the communiqué which dealt with EMU it was France who was the odd man out. Insofar as there could be an acceptable text which advanced us towards an unacceptable objective I felt that I had got it. All my requirements were satisfied by it. We could not stop an IGC because all it needed was a simple majority vote, but its outcome had been left open and its timing was unclear. President Mitterrand's attempt to have a deadline for Stages 2 and 3 inserted in the text was unsuccessful. To the irritation of Sr. González, who had hoped to avoid more discussion, I made what I described as a 'unilateral declaration'. It ran:

> The United Kingdom notes that there is no automaticity about the move to nor the timing or content of Stage 2. The UK will take its decisions on these matters in the light of the progress which has by then been made in Stage 1, in particular over the completion of all measures agreed as being necessary to complete.

The phrasing was unpoetic but the meaning clear. This prompted President Mitterrand to make his own declaration to the effect that the IGC should meet as soon as possible after 1 July 1990. And so the Madrid Council came to an end not with a bang but two whimpers.

THE FRENCH REVOLUTION BICENTENNIAL

My disagreements with the French never led to ill-feeling. This was lucky for I was shortly to attend the G7 in Paris which had largely been overtaken by the hugely expensive – and for Parisians wildly inconvenient – celebrations of the Bicentennial of the French Revolution. The French Revolution is one of the few real watersheds in the history of political ideas. For most – though not all – Frenchmen it is nowadays accepted as the basis of the French state, so that even the most conservative Frenchman seems to sing 'the Marseillaise' with enthusiasm. For most other Europeans it is regarded with mixed feelings because it led to French armies devastating Europe, but it also stimulated movements which led eventually to national independence.

For me as a British Conservative, with Edmund Burke the father of Conservatism and first great perceptive critic of the Revolution as my ideological mentor, the events of 1789 represent a perennial illusion in politics. The French Revolution was a Utopian attempt to overthrow a traditional order – one with many imperfections, certainly – in the name of abstract ideas, formulated by vain intellectuals, which lapsed, not by chance but through weakness and wickedness, into purges, mass murder and war. In so many ways it anticipated the still more terrible Bolshevik Revolution of 1917. The English tradition of liberty, however, grew over the centuries: its most marked features are continuity, respect for law and a sense of balance, as demonstrated by the Glorious Revolution of 1688. When I was questioned about what the French Revolution had done for human rights by journalists from *Le Monde* on the eve of my visit I felt I ought to point out some of this. I said:

> Human rights did not begin with the French Revolution . . . [they] really stem from a mixture of Judaism and Christianity . . . [we English] had 1688, our quiet revolution, where Parliament exerted its will over the King . . . it was not the sort of Revolution that France's was . . . 'Liberty, equality, fraternity' – they forgot obligations and duties I think. And then of course the fraternity went missing for a long time.

The headline over my remarks in *Le Monde* ran '"Les droits de l'homme n'ont pas commencé en France," nous déclare Mme Thatcher.'

It was on this note that I arrived in Paris for the Bicentennial. I brought with me for President Mitterrand a first edition of Charles Dickens's *A Tale of Two Cities,* which he, a connoisseur of such things, loved, but which also made somewhat more elegantly the same point as my interview. The celebrations themselves were on the scale which only a Hollywood studio – or France – could manage: an almost endless procession, a military parade, an opera with pride of place in the set being given to a huge guillotine.

The G7 summit itself definitely took second place to this pageantry. Indeed, this posed a potential problem. A large number of Third World heads of government had been invited to Paris to the celebrations and there seemed some prospect of President Mitterrand suddenly seeking to relaunch another 'North-South' dialogue of the sort we had thankfully left behind at Cancún.* I alerted President Bush – arriving for his first G7 – to this when I had a bilateral meeting with him at the US Embassy before the summit. He said that he thought there was a problem in blocking such a move without appearing a 'parsimonious bunch of don't cares'. I said that this did not seem to me to be much of a problem. Nor did it prove to be. The French in the end thought better of introducing this controversial idea, preferring to rest on the level of generalities.

George Bush and I made the familiar pleas for free trade under the GATT. President Mitterrand – with some help from me – got the text of his Declaration on Human Rights (with its obvious revolutionary symbolism) accepted almost word for word. There were discussions of the environment and drugs. In fact, everyone left happy and little of note was achieved. It was the sort of occasion which in earlier years had given international summitry a bad name. But President Mitterrand's final dinner for heads of government held in the new pyramid in the forecourt of the Louvre was one of the best I have ever eaten. Some traditions are too important for even the French to overthrow.

CABINET RESHUFFLE

I returned to London conscious of unfinished business. The European election results had no particular significance in themselves. But they had revealed a groundswell of discontent which could not be ignored. That discontent was most in evidence in the Parliamentary Party. A minority of Conservative MPs were uneasy about the line I was taking on Europe. But more important was the fact that there was a widespread restlessness because avenues of promotion into the ranks of the Government seemed blocked. I too felt that changes were required. When a prime minister has been in power for ten years he or she must

* See pp. 168–71.

be that much more aware of the dangers of the government as a whole appearing to be tired or stale. Since I hardly ever felt seriously tired and never felt stale I had no intention of giving that impression. I decided to make some changes in the Cabinet to free up posts at every level and bring on some new faces.

I had also been thinking about my own future. I knew that I had a good few more years of active service left in me and I intended to see through to the end the restoration of our economic strength, the fulfilment of our radical social reforms and that remodelling of Europe on which I had embarked with the Bruges speech. I wanted to leave behind me when I went, perhaps half way into the next Parliament, several candidates with proven character and experience from whom the choice of my successor could be made. For various reasons I did not believe that any of my own political generation were suitable. 'Of course, she would say that, wouldn't she,' may be the obvious retort. But closer consideration will, I hope, show I had good reasons. If one considers the possibilities – first among those who were of my own way of thinking: Norman Tebbit was now concentrating on looking after Margaret and on his business interests; Nick Ridley who never suffered fools gladly would not have been acceptable to Tory MPs; Cecil Parkinson had been damaged in the eyes of the old guard. Geoffrey Howe I shall come to shortly. Nigel Lawson had no interest in the job – and I had no interest in encouraging him. Michael Heseltine was not a team player and certainly not a team captain. Anyway, I saw no reason to hand over to anyone of roughly my age while I was fit and active. In the next generation, by contrast, there was a variety of possible candidates who ought to be tested in high office: John Major, Douglas Hurd, Ken Baker, Ken Clarke, Chris Patten and perhaps Norman Lamont and Michael Howard. I felt it was not for me to select my successor. But I did have the obligation to see that there were several proven candidates from whom to choose.

I was, however, wrong on one important matter. Of course, I understood that some of my Cabinet colleagues and other ministers were more to the left, some more to the right. But I believed that they had generally become convinced of the rightness of the basic principles as I had. Orthodox finance, low levels of regulation and taxation, a minimal bureaucracy, strong defence, a willingness to stand up for British interests wherever and whenever threatened – I did not believe that I had to open windows into men's souls on these matters. The arguments for them seemed to me to have been won. I now know that such arguments are never finally won.

A little earlier I left aside Geoffrey Howe from my discussion of possible leadership candidates. Something had happened to Geoffrey. His enormous capacity for work remained, but his clarity of purpose and analysis had dimmed. I did not think he was any longer a possible leader. But worse than that, I could not have him as Foreign Secretary – at least while Nigel Lawson was Chancellor – after his behaviour on the eve of the Madrid Council. Perhaps if I had known that Nigel was about to resign I would have kept Geoffrey at the Foreign Office for at least a little longer. As it was, I was determined to move him aside for a younger man.

I decided that two ministers should leave the Cabinet altogether. Paul Channon was loyal and likeable. But Transport was becoming a very important department in which public presentation was at a premium – what with the appalling disasters which seemed to plague us at this time and in the light of the traffic congestion which Britain's new prosperity brought with it. I asked Paul to leave and he did so with perfect good humour. I appointed Cecil Parkinson to his place. Deciding to ask John Moore to go was even more of a wrench. He was of my way of thinking. At Health it was he – rather than his successor Ken Clarke – who had really got the Health review under way. At Social Security, after I split the DHSS into two departments, he had been courageous and radical in his thinking about dependency and poverty. But, as I have explained, John had never fully recovered, at least psychologically, from the debilitating illness he suffered while Secretary of State at the old combined DHSS. So I asked him to make way and appointed Tony Newton, a stolid, left-inclining figure but one with a good command of the House and of his brief. I also brought into the Cabinet Peter Brooke who had been a much loved and utterly dependable Party Chairman. He wanted to be Ulster Secretary and I gave him the job, moving Tom King to the Defence Ministry, vacated by George Younger who wanted to leave the Government to concentrate on his business interests. George's departure was something of a blow. I valued his common sense, trusted his judgement and relied on his loyalty. His career is proof of the fact that, contrary to myth, gentlemen still have a place in politics.

But there were three main changes which determined the shape of the reshuffle and the reception it received. In reverse order of importance: I moved Chris Patten to the Environment Department to succeed Nick Ridley, who went to the DTI (David Young left the Cabinet at his request and became Deputy Chairman of the Party); I moved Ken Baker to become Party Chairman from the Department of Education, where he was succeeded by John MacGregor. And John was succeeded by John Gummer who entered the Cabinet as Minister for Agriculture.

But first, and crucially, I called in Geoffrey Howe and said that I wanted him to leave the Foreign Office, where I intended to put John Major. It was predictable that Geoffrey would be displeased. He had come to enjoy the trappings of his office and his two houses, in Carlton Gardens in London and Chevening in Kent. I offered him the Leadership of the House of Commons at a time when the House was shortly to be televised for the first time. It was a big job and I hoped he would recognize the fact. But he just looked rather sullen and said that he would have to talk to Elspeth first. This, of course, held up the whole process. I could see no other ministers until this matter was decided. Geoffrey also, I believe, saw David Waddington, the Chief Whip, who had advised me to keep Geoffrey in the Cabinet in some capacity. David meant well by this advice, but perhaps I should have asked Geoffrey to go altogether, for he clearly never forgave me. Back and forth to Downing Street messages passed in the course of which I offered Geoffrey the Home Office – knowing in advance that he would almost certainly not accept – then, after conferring with Nigel Lawson, Dorneywood, the Chancellor's country house which I rightly thought that he would accept, and finally, with some reluctance and at his insistence, the title of Deputy Prime Minister which I had held in reserve as a final sweetener. This is a title with no constitutional significance but which Willie Whitelaw (until his stroke in December 1987 and subsequent resignation the following month) had almost made his own because of his stature and seniority. But because Geoffrey had bargained for the job, it never conferred the status which he hoped. In practical terms it just meant that Geoffrey sat on my immediate left at Cabinet meetings – a position he may well have come to regret.

The delay in concluding the reshuffle was bound to prompt speculation. But it was, I am told, Geoffrey's partisans who leaked the content of our discussions in a singularly inept attempt to damage me. As a result he received a very bad press about the houses, which was not unmerited, but which he doubtless blamed on me.

John Major was not at first very keen on becoming Foreign Secretary. A modest man, aware of his inexperience, he would probably have preferred a less grand appointment. But I knew that if he was to have a hope of becoming Party leader, it would be better if he had held one of the three great offices of state. I should add that I had not, contrary to much speculation, reached a firm decision that John was my preferred successor. I had simply concluded that he must be given wider public recognition and greater experience if he was to compete with the talented self-publicists who would be among his rivals. Unfortunately, because of Nigel Lawson's resignation, he had no opportunity to show what he was made of at the Foreign Office before returning to the Treasury.

In moving Nick Ridley to the DTI I was generally seen to be responding to the criticisms of him by the environmental lobby. This was not so. I knew he wanted a change. I was, of course, quite aware of the fact that the romantics and cranks of the movement did not like it when he insisted on basing policy on science rather than prejudice. I also suspected that from Chris Patten they would get a more emollient approach. Certainly, I subsequently found myself repeatedly at odds with Chris, for with him presentation on environmental matters always seemed to be at the expense of substance. But I also wanted Nick in the second most important economic department because of the need to have his support on the key issues of industry and Europe.

Ken Baker's appointment as Party Chairman was an attempt to improve the Government's presentation. Ken – like Chris Patten – had started off on the left of the Party. But unlike Chris, Ken had genuinely moved to the centre. In any case his great skills were in publicity. And I never forgot that for every few Thatchers, Josephs and Ridleys you need at least one Ken Baker to concentrate on communicating the message. I was also happy now to appoint John MacGregor with his Scottish devotion to Education as the right person to deal with the nuts and bolts of making our education reforms work. My appointment of Ken Baker to the chairmanship was a success. He served me with vigour and enthusiasm right to the end, however hot the political kitchen became. We had never been close political allies, so I was doubly indebted to him for this.

The immediate impact of the reshuffle was much worse than I had expected because of the stories of what Geoffrey had or had not been offered and demanded. Once the initial reaction had passed, it was clear that we benefited from the new look the Government had acquired. More seriously, though, Geoffrey was still well placed to make trouble for me and the balance of the Cabinet had slipped slightly further to the left with the promotion of Chris Patten and John Gummer and the departure of John Moore more than compensating for the arrival of Norman Lamont, who was on the right. Of course, none of this mattered as long as crises which threatened my authority could be avoided.

THE FRANCO-GERMAN AXIS – AND 'POLITICAL UNION'

In fact they came not in single spies but in battalions. The winter of 1989 saw those revolutionary changes which led to the collapse of communism in eastern Europe. In the longer term the emergence of free, independent and anti-socialist governments in the region would provide me with potential allies in my crusade for a wider, looser Europe. But the immediate effect, through the prospect and then the reality of German reunification, was to strengthen the hand of Chancellor Kohl and fuel the desire of President Mitterrand and M. Delors for a federal Europe which would 'bind in' the new Germany to a structure within which its preponderance would be checked. Although these matters are best dealt with later in the context of East-West relations, they formed the background to the ever more intense battles on monetary and political union in which I henceforth found myself engaged.

After Spain the European Community presidency passed to France. Partly in order to ensure that eastern Europe did not dominate the European Council scheduled for December at Strasbourg, President Mitterrand called a special Council in November in Paris specifically to discuss the consequences of events in the East and the fall of the Berlin Wall. He was also pressing hard for the creation of a European Bank of Reconstruction and Development (EBRD) in order to channel investment and assistance to the emerging democracies. I was sceptical about whether such an institution was really necessary. The case had not been made that aid of this dimension had to go through a European institution, as opposed to national or wider international ones. I conceded the point in Strasbourg; but my wishes were eventually met because the EBRD now sensibly involves the Americans and Japanese, not just the Europeans. President Mitterrand and I finally put together a deal in 1990: I agreed that his protégé Jacques Attali would be EBRD President and he agreed that the bank would be situated in London.

To some extent the French strategy of holding an 'unofficial' Paris Council on East-West relations worked because the Strasbourg Council concentrated – at least in its official sessions – heavily on the more narrowly European matters of EMU and the Social Charter. I was as strongly opposed to the holding of an IGC on economic and monetary union as ever. Equally, I had little hope of blocking it altogether. The

French aim was to set a date for the IGC and this I still hoped to stave off. Until a few days before the start of the Council we were optimistic that the Germans would support us in calling for 'further preparation' before the IGC met. But in a classic demonstration of the way in which the Franco-German axis always seemed to re-form in time to dominate the proceedings, Chancellor Kohl went along with President Mitterrand's wishes. By the time I arrived in Strasbourg I knew that I would be more or less on my own. I decided to be sweetly reasonable throughout, since there was no point in causing gratuitous offence when I could not secure what I really wanted. It was agreed that the IGC would meet under the Italian presidency before the end of 1990, but after the German elections. As for the Social Charter at which I had directed my fire at Madrid, I reaffirmed that I was not prepared to endorse the text, my determination having been if anything strengthened by the fact that the Commission was now proposing to bring forward no fewer than forty-three separate proposals, including seventeen legally binding directives, in the areas which the charter covered. That effectively ended the discussion of the charter from our point of view. On EMU I would return to the fray in Rome.

In the first half of 1990, however, there was the Irish presidency to contend with. The unwelcome habit of calling extra 'informal' Councils proved catching. Charles Haughey decided that another one was needed in order to consider events in eastern Europe and the implications for the Community of German unification. Perhaps that is what Mr Haughey really envisaged, but for others this was just an opportunity to keep up the federalist momentum.

'Political union' was now envisaged alongside 'monetary union'. In a sense, of course, this was only logical. A single currency and a single economic policy ultimately imply a single government. But behind the concept of 'political union' there lay a special Franco-German agenda. The French wanted to curb German power. To this end, they envisaged a stronger European Council with more majority voting: but they did not want to see the powers of the Commission or the European Parliament increased. The French were federalists on grounds of tactics rather than conviction. The Germans wanted 'political union' for different reasons and by different means. For them it was partly the price of achieving quick reunification with East Germany on their own terms and with all the benefits which would come from Community membership, partly a demonstration that the new Germany would not behave like the old Germany from Bismarck to Hitler. In this cause, the Germans were prepared to see more powers for the Commission and they gave special importance to increasing the power and authority of the European Parliament. So the Germans were federalists by conviction. The French pushed harder for political union: but it was the agenda of the Germans, who were increasingly the senior partner of the Franco-German axis, which was dominant.

For my part I was opposed to political union of either kind. But the only way that I could hope to stop it was by getting away from the standard Community approach whereby a combination of high-flown statements of principle and various procedural devices prevented substantive discussion of what was at stake until it was too late. Within the Community I must aim to open up the divisions between the French and the Germans. At home I must point out in striking language just what 'political union' would and would not mean if it was taken at all seriously. Far too much of the Community's history had consisted of including nebulous phrases in treaties and communiqués, then later clothing them with federal meaning which we had been assured they never possessed. Consequently, I decided that I would go to Dublin with a speech which would set out what political union was not and should never be. This seemed the best way of having all concerned define – and disagree about – what it was.

There was no doubt about how determined the French and Germans were in their federalist intentions. Shortly before the Council met in Dublin at the end of April President Mitterrand and Chancellor Kohl issued a joint public statement calling for the Dublin Council to 'initiate preparations for an Inter-Governmental Conference on political union'. They also called on the Community to 'define and implement a common foreign and security policy'. President Mitterrand and Chancellor Kohl chose at about the same time to send a joint letter to the President of Lithuania urging temporary suspension of that country's declaration of independence in order to ease the way for talks with Moscow. As I took some pleasure in pointing out in my subsequent speech at the Council, this was done without any consultation with the rest of the Community, let alone NATO – it demonstrated that the likelihood of a common 'foreign and security policy' was somewhat remote.

I made my speech early on in the proceedings over a working lunch. I said that the way to dispel fears was to make clear what we did not mean when we were talking about political union. We did not mean that there would be a loss of national identity. Nor did we mean giving up separate heads of state, either the monarchies to which six of us were devoted or the presidencies which the other six member states favoured. We did not intend to suppress national parliaments; the

European Parliament must have no role at the expense of national parliaments. We did not intend to change countries' electoral systems. We would not be altering the role of the Council of Ministers. Political union must not mean any greater centralization of powers in Europe at the expense of national governments and parliaments. There must be no weakening of the role of NATO and no attempt to turn foreign policy co-operation into a restriction on the rights of states to conduct their own foreign policy.

To deliver a ten-minute speech with one's tongue in one's cheek is as much a physical as a rhetorical achievement. For of course this was precisely the route which political union, if taken seriously, would go. Perhaps only my remarks about heads of state – which were widely reported – added a new element to the barely hidden agenda of the European Commission and those who thought like it. My speech did also have some immediate effect, for it rapidly became clear in the discussion that heads of government were either unable – or perhaps at this stage unwilling – to spell out precisely what political union meant for them. Top marks for calculated ambiguity, however, must surely have gone to Sig. Andreotti, who suggested that although we must set up an IGC on political union, it would be dangerous to try to reach a clear-cut definition of what political union was. Mr Haughey wound up the discussion by announcing blandly that almost all the points I had mentioned in my remarks would be excluded from political union. And perhaps that was said with tongue in cheek as well.

At the end of June we were back in Dublin again. The Community Foreign ministers had been told to go away and produce a paper on political union for the European Council's consideration. I hoped that I had at least put down a marker against the sort of proposals which were likely to come before us at some future stage. But I was in no position to stop an IGC being called. I spent more time elaborating on our latest thinking on the hard ecu proposal. Anything that I could do to influence the discussions in the IGC on EMU which would run in parallel with that on political union was of value. I took most satisfaction, however, at this Council from stopping the Franco-German juggernaut in its tracks on the question of financial credits to the Soviet Union. I was not generally convinced that allowing former communist countries in eastern Europe – let alone the communist USSR – to build up more debt would do them any favours. Above all, any assistance must be properly targeted and must be intended to reward and promote practical reform rather than – as I was to put it in discussion at the G7 in Houston the following month – 'providing an oxygen tent for the survival of much of the old system'.

President Mitterrand and Chancellor Kohl, however, were more interested in power politics and grand gestures. Shortly before the Dublin Council opened they had agreed to propose a multi-billion dollar loan to the Soviets and over dinner on the second day they tried to bounce the rest of us into endorsing this. I said that this was quite unacceptable. No board of directors of a company would ever behave in such an unbusiness-like way. We should not do so either. There must be a proper study done before any such decision was made. After much argument, which continued the following morning, my approach prevailed.

EMU AND THE GATT

Of the two, it was EMU rather than political union which posed the more immediate threat. What was so frustrating was that others who shared my views had a variety of reasons for not expressing them and preferring to let me receive the criticism for doing so. The weaker economies would have been devastated by a single currency, but they hoped to receive sufficient subsidies to make their acquiescence worthwhile. The classic case was that of Greece. I became all too used to a Greek chorus of support for whatever ambitious proposals Germany made.

Nor were the Germans at one on the move towards European economic and monetary union. From time to time Karl Otto Pöhl had been outspokenly critical of the concept. As I understood it, the pressure for EMU was coming from France which found it unacceptable to have monetary policy dominated by the deutschmark and the Bundesbank. The Bundesbank would not have had any problem sticking with the ERM rather than going further, but the political pressure for EMU was now very strong. I always had the highest respect for the Bundesbank and its record of keeping down inflation in Germany and I found it significant that those who contributed most to this achievement often had least time for a single European currency which would, of course, have meant the end of the deutschmark.

To get away from the often parochial atmosphere of the over-frequent European Councils to a meeting of the G7 was always a relief. That at Houston in July was the first chaired by President Bush, who was by now imposing very much his own style on the US Administration. These economic summits were by no means just 'economic' any longer: nor could they be when the economic and political world order was changing so radically and rapidly. In the forefront of all our minds was what needed to happen to ensure order, stability and tolerable prosperity in the lands of the crumbling USSR. But no less important was that at the G7 I could argue much more effectively for free trade and recruit allies for my cause than I could within the narrower framework of the Community.

It was scorching hot in Houston – so hot indeed that as heads of government stood watching the opening ceremonies the ever thoughtful and technology conscious Americans arranged for us to have special air conditioning around our feet, blowing up from the ground. President Bush asked me to open the discussion on the economy and, after noting the implications of the collapse of communism, I concentrated on the imminent danger of the collapse of free trade unless the GATT round was successfully completed. I said that it was vital that the world did not relapse into blocs, particularly in trade and monetary matters. That would be a step backwards with damaging economic and political consequences, particularly for the countries which were excluded. We should, in fact, be looking beyond the present GATT round to see how the process of freeing up world trade in goods and services could be continued.

The discussion returned to trade the following day. I now strongly supported Brian Mulroney who argued that the biggest losers if the GATT failed would be the less developed countries (LDCs). I also reminded those present of the huge amounts still being spent by the European Community, the United States and Japan on agricultural support. In fact, the section of the Houston communiqué which dealt with trade constituted the best and toughest statement ever made by the major economies on the subject. The tragedy was that the European Community's commitment to trade liberalization was only skin deep, as subsequent events were to show.

THE ROME EUROPEAN COUNCIL

I flew into Rome at midday on Saturday 27 October knowing full well that this would be a difficult occasion. But I still did not realize how difficult. This time the excuse for holding an 'informal' Council before the formal Council in December was even more transparent than in Paris or Dublin. The idea was allegedly to take stock of preparations for the forthcoming CSCE summit and to discuss relations with the

Soviet Union.* In fact, the Italians wanted to pre-empt the outcome of the two IGCs on EMU and political union. Nobody bothered to explain why a special Council was necessary before the IGCs reported.

As always with the Italians, it was difficult throughout to distinguish confusion from guile: but plenty of both was evident. In his 'bidding letter' to the Council Sig. Andreotti made no mention of the need to discuss the GATT Uruguay round. I wrote back insisting that if the Community Trade and Agriculture ministers had not reached agreement on the Community offer on agriculture beforehand we must discuss the matter at Rome because time was running out.

More of a clue to the Italians' intentions was perhaps given by the Italian Foreign minister's letter which went so far as to suggest a provision for future transfer of powers from member states to the Community without treaty amendment. The Italians gave out – and it was well reported in the press – that they would be taking a moderate line, not pressing for a specific date for the start of Stage 2 of EMU and noting that Britain's hard ecu proposal must be taken seriously. A long and often contradictory list of proposals on political union had been drawn up by the presidency, including plans for a common foreign policy, extended Community competence, more majority voting, greater powers for the European Parliament and other matters. The precise purpose of this paper remained unclear. What I did not know was that behind the scenes the Italians had agreed with a proposal emanating from Germany and endorsed by Christian Democrat leaders from several European countries at an earlier caucus meeting that the GATT should not be discussed at the Council. Had there been such a discussion, of course, they would have found it more difficult to portray me as the odd one out and themselves as sea-green internationalists.

Chancellor Kohl had spoken publicly of the need to set deadlines for the work of the IGCs and for Stage 2 of EMU. But on the eve of the Rome Council he took a surprisingly soft line with Douglas Hurd, now Foreign Secretary, about his intentions. Herr Kohl suggested that perhaps the conclusions of the special Council could say something about a 'consensus building around the idea' of a specified starting date for Stage 2. But Douglas recorded his impression that the German Chancellor was not set on seeking even this much, and that he might be open to persuasion to drop references to any date. Moreover, Chancellor Kohl said that he did not oppose discussion of GATT in Rome. What he would not get into was negotiation of the Community position. He said that he recognized the importance of the

* See pp. 799–800, 842–6.

Community's offer on agriculture in the GATT and accepted that December was a real deadline for the Uruguay round. He also recognized that Germany would have to compromise. He would be prepared to say tough things to the German farmers in due course – but not yet. Apparently he implied to Douglas that there could be a trade-off. If I was prepared to help him during the discussion of the GATT, he might be able to help me during the discussion on the EMU IGC. This, of course, turned out to be far from his real position.

I myself lunched with President Mitterrand at our embassy residence in Rome on the Saturday. He could not have been more friendly or amenable. I said that I was very disturbed at the Community's failure to agree a negotiating position on agriculture for the GATT negotiations. I understood that agreement had very nearly been reached after some sixteen hours of negotiations at the meeting of Agriculture and Trade ministers the previous day but had been blocked by the French. President Mitterrand said that this was all very difficult, that agriculture must not be looked at in isolation and that Europe – or more exactly France – should not be expected to make all the concessions at the GATT talks. He asked me when I proposed to raise the issue at the Council. I said that I would bring it up right at the beginning. I would demand that the Council make clear that the Community would table proposals within the next few days. Failure to do so would be a signal to the world that Europe was protectionist. President Mitterrand interjected that of course the Community was protectionist: that was the point of it. Clearly, there was not much to be gained by continuing this particular argument.

The French President did, however, agree with me – or so he claimed – about the political union proposals. Indeed, he was highly critical of some of M. Delors's remarks and had no time at all for the European Parliament. Somewhat more surprisingly, President Mitterrand claimed that France, like Britain, wanted a common currency, not a single currency. This was not true. But let me be charitable – there may have been some confusion in translation. In any case, I detected no hostility or wish to force me into a corner.

I was too well versed in the ways of the Community to take all this *bonhomie* at face value. But even I was unprepared for the way things went once the Council formally opened. Sig. Andreotti made clear right at the beginning that there was no intention of discussing the GATT. I spoke briefly and took them to task for ignoring this crucial issue at such a time. I had hoped that someone other than me would intervene. But only Ruud Lubbers did and he raised a mild protest. Although something found its way into the communiqué, no one else was prepared to speak up for these imminent and crucial negotiations.

Then M. Delors reported on his recent meeting with Mr Gorbachev. To my surprise, he proposed that the Council should issue a statement saying that the outer border of the Soviet Union must remain intact. Again I waited. But no one spoke. I just could not leave matters like this. I said that this was not for us in the Community to decide but for the peoples and Government of the Soviet Union. I pointed out that the Baltic States had in any case been illegally seized and incorporated in the USSR. In effect, we were denying them their claim to independence. M. Delors said that he had received an assurance from Mr Gorbachev that the Baltic States would be freed, so we should not become alarmed on that point. I came back at him, saying that we had heard this sort of reassurance before from the Soviets; and, in any case, what about the other nations of the Soviet Union who might wish to leave it as well? At this point first Sr. González, then President Mitterrand and finally Chancellor Kohl intervened on my side and this ill-judged initiative foundered.

But the atmosphere went from bad to worse. The others were determined to insert in the communiqué provisions on political union, none of which I was prepared to accept. I said that I would not pre-empt the debate in the IGC and had a unilateral observation to this effect incorporated in the text. They also insisted on following the German proposal that Stage 2 of monetary union should begin on 1 January 1994. I would not accept this either. I had inserted in the communiqué the sentence:

> The United Kingdom, while ready to move beyond Stage 1 through the creation of a new monetary institution and a common Community currency, believes that decisions on the substance of that move should precede decisions on its timing.

They were not interested in compromise. My objections were heard in stony silence. I now had no support. I just had to say no.

In three years the European Community had gone from practical discussions about restoring order to the Community's finances to grandiose schemes of monetary and political union with firm timetables but no agreed substance – all without open, principled public debate on these questions either nationally or in European fora. Now at Rome the ultimate battle for the future of the Community had been joined. But I would have to return to London to win another battle on which the outcome in Europe would depend – that for the soul of the Parliamentary Conservative Party.

CHAPTER XXVI

The World Turned Right Side Up

The fall of communism in eastern Europe, the reunification of Germany and the debate about the future of NATO – 1987–1990

OVERVIEW

The international scene in 1987 and 1988 was not so very different to that before the general election. President Reagan was in the White House, continuing the defence policies which time and again had forced the Soviets to the negotiating table. Mr Gorbachev was proceeding with increasingly far-reaching reforms in the Soviet Union which, whether he liked it or not, would eventually open the floodgates of democracy, if not prosperity. The West's strategy of defeating communism while ensuring our peace and security – a strategy in which I believed with a passionate intensity and that I sought to communicate when I went to eastern Europe – was working. Its very success would mean that new questions about Britain's foreign relations and NATO's defences would arise.

Yet even before this happened the familiar landscape changed in another way I did not foresee. I had breathed a sigh of relief when George Bush defeated his Democrat opponent in the US presidential election, for I felt that it ensured continuity. But with the new team's arrival in the White House I found myself dealing with an Administration which saw Germany as its main European partner in leadership, which encouraged the integration of Europe without seeming to understand fully what it meant and which sometimes seemed to underestimate the need for a strong nuclear defence. I felt I could not always rely as before on American co-operation. This was of great importance at such a time. For by now – 1989 – the cracks in the eastern European communist system were widening into crevices and soon, wing by wing, the whole edifice fell away.

This welcome revolution of freedom which swept eastern Europe raised great strategic issues, above all in the West's relations with the Soviet Union. (Indeed, what now was 'the West'?) But I also saw at once that it had profound implications for the balance of power in Europe, where a reunified Germany would be dominant. There was a new and different kind of 'German Question' which had to be addressed openly and formally: I did so.

History teaches that dangers are never greater than when empires break up and so I favoured caution in our defence and security policy. Decisions about our security must, I argued, be made only after careful reflection and analysis of the nature and direction of future threats. Above all, they must be determined not by the desire to make a political impression by arms control 'initiatives' but by the need credibly to deter aggression.

For thinking and speaking like this I was mocked as the last Cold Warrior – and an unreconstructed Germano-phobe to boot. In fact, they said, I was a tiresome woman who might once have served a purpose but who just could not or would not move with the times. I could live with this caricature; there had been worse; but I also had no doubt that I was right, that the unexpected did happen and that sooner or later events would prove it. And, without claiming any foresight about the precise timing of the fall of communism, I did find my basic approach vindicated as 1990 wore on. This occurred in several ways.

First, Anglo-American relations suddenly lost their chill; indeed by the end they had hardly been warmer. The protectionism of that 'integrated' Europe, dominated by Germany, which the Americans had cheerfully accepted, even encouraged, suddenly started to arouse American fears and threaten to cost American jobs. But this change of heart was confirmed by the aggression of Saddam Hussein against Kuwait which shattered any illusion that tyranny had been everywhere defeated. The UN might pass its resolutions; but there would soon be a full-scale war to fight. Suddenly a Britain with armed forces which had the skills, and a government which had the resolve, to fight alongside America, seemed to be the real European 'partner in leadership'.

Then again the full significance of the changes in eastern Europe began to be better understood. Having democratic states with market economies, which were just as 'European' as those of the existing Community, lining up as potential EC members made my vision of a looser, more open Community seem timely rather than backward. It also became clear that the courageous reforming leaders in eastern Europe looked to Britain – and to me because of my anti-socialist credentials – as a friend who genuinely wanted to help them, rather than exclude them from markets (like the French) or seek economic domination (like the Germans). These eastern European states were – and are – Britain's natural allies.

Further east in the USSR more disturbing developments made for a reassessment of earlier euphoric judgements about the prospects for the peaceful, orderly entrenchment of democracy and free enterprise. In the Soviet Union I had won the respect both of the embattled Mr Gorbachev and of his anti-communist opponents. I never underestimated the fragility of the movement for reform; that was why I spoke up for it – and for Mr Gorbachev – so forcefully in the West. Events now increasingly suggested that a far-reaching political crisis in the USSR might soon be reached. The implications of this for control over nuclear weapons and indeed the whole arsenal which the Soviet military machine had accumulated could not be ignored even by the most enthusiastic western disarmers. In short, the world of the 'new world order' was turning out to be a dangerous and uncertain place in which the conservative virtues of hardened Cold Warriors were again in demand. And so it was that in those last months and weeks of my premiership, while domestic political pressures mounted, I found myself once more at the centre of great international events with renewed ability to influence them in Britain's interests and in accord with my beliefs.

VISIT TO WASHINGTON IN JULY 1987

On Thursday 16 July 1987 I flew into Washington to see President Reagan. Our political fortunes at this time could not have been more different. I had just won an election with a decisive majority, enhancing my authority in international affairs. By contrast my old friend and his Administration were reeling under the continuing 'Irangate' revelations. I found the President hurt and bemused by what was happening. Nancy was spending her time listening to the cruel and contemptuous remarks pouring out from the liberal media commentators and telling him what was being said, which made him still more depressed. Nothing wounds a man of integrity more than to find his basic honesty questioned. It made me very angry. I was determined to do what I could to help President Reagan ride out the storm. It was not just a matter of personal loyalty – though it was that too, of course: he also had eighteen months to serve as leader of the most

Presenting the *Daily Star* Gold Awards for children of courage in 1985

Visiting a 'Guide Dogs for the Blind' centre in Devon during the 1987 general election

ABOVE: Launching the 1987 general election manifesto with Willie Whitelaw and Norman Tebbit, Party Chairman, at Central Office

LEFT: Meeting children and well-wishers during the campaign

"CLAIMED YOUR PENSION BONUS YET?"
First aider
First aid kit location
Authorised Plant
Operators: Dumper
Hoist
Forklift
Teleporter
Excavators
Disc cutters
No Go Areas &
Dangerous Operations
Protective gear issued by

With members of the Cabinet and Denis at the Carlton Club for a dinner to mark my tenth anniversary as Prime Minister, May 1989

With the Finchley team at a dinner to mark my thirtieth anniversary as their MP, December 1989

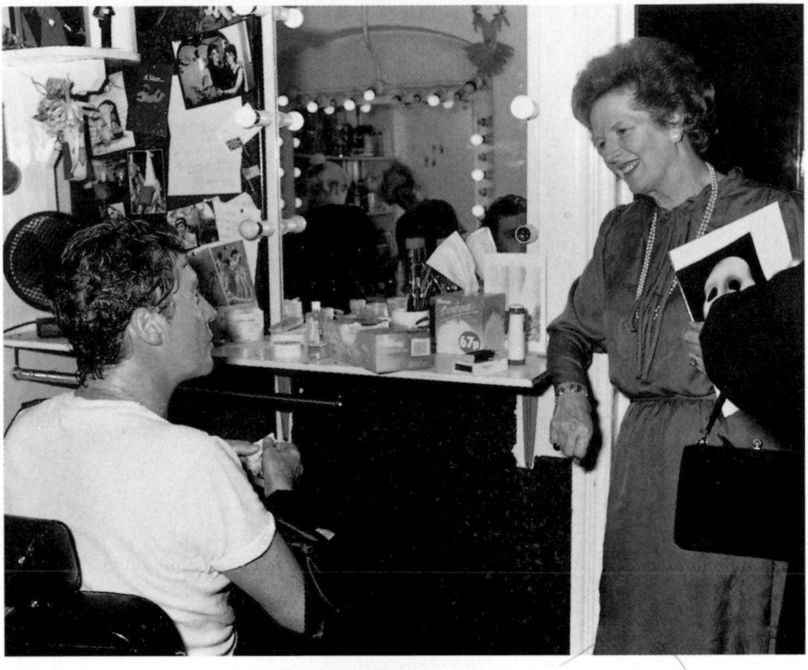

ABOVE: Talking to Michael Crawford after watching a perfomance of *Phantom of the Opera*

LEFT: With Peter Palumbo, chairman of the Arts Council, in March 1990

With Denis in the walled garden at Chequers in summer 1986

With Mark, Diane and Michael outside Number Ten, in May 1989

OPPOSITE ABOVE: Meeting building workers in Torquay during a regional tour, February 1990

OPPOSITE BELOW: Talking to workmen during the refurbishment of Number Ten in the summer of 1989

RIGHT: In my study at Number Ten with Charles Powell in 1989

BELOW: My last speech in the House of Commons as Prime Minister, 22 November 1990

LEFT: Leaving Number Ten for the last time, 28 November 1990

BELOW: Driving away from Buckingham Palace having handed over the seals of office, 28 November 1990

powerful country in the world and it was in all our interests that his authority be undiminished. So I set about using my interviews and public statements in Washington to get across this message. For example, I told the interviewer on CBS's *Face the Nation*:

> Cheer up. Cheer up. Be more upbeat. America is a strong country with a great president, a great people and a great future.

Our embassy was besieged by telephone calls of congratulation. My remarks also touched another grateful audience. On Monday evening – after I arrived back in London – I received a telephone call from the President who wanted to thank me for what I had said. He was in a Cabinet meeting and at one point he put down the receiver and told me to listen. I heard loud and long applause from the Cabinet members.

My main business in Washington, though, had been to discuss the implications for our future defence of the INF treaty which would be signed by Presidents Reagan and Gorbachev in December. I had always had mixed feelings about the INF 'zero option'. On the one hand, it was a great success to have forced the Soviets to withdraw their SS-20 missiles by deploying our Cruise and Pershing. But, on the other, the removal of our intermediate-range land-based missiles would have two undesirable effects. First, it threatened precisely what Helmut Schmidt had wanted to avoid when he originally urged NATO to deploy them: namely the decoupling of Europe from NATO. It could then be argued, as in the 1970s, that in the last resort the United States would not use nuclear weapons to deter a conventional Warsaw Pact attack on Europe. This argument would boost the always-present tendency to German neutralism – a tendency which it had been the long-standing Soviet objective to magnify wherever possible. Second, the INF 'zero option' also cast doubt on – though as I always argued it did not in fact undermine – the NATO strategy of 'flexible response'. That strategy depended on the ability of the West to escalate its response to Soviet aggression through each stage of conventional and nuclear weapons. The removal of the intermediate-range missiles might be argued to create a gap in that capability. It followed that NATO must have other nuclear weapons, stationed on German soil, which would be a credible deterrent and that those weapons be modernized and strengthened where necessary. It was this question – the avoidance of another 'zero' on Short-Range Nuclear Forces (SNF) – which was to divide the alliance so seriously in 1988–9.

The main points I now made to the President in Washington were the need to allocate submarine-launched Cruise missiles and additional F1-11 aircraft to the Supreme Allied Commander in Europe to compensate for the withdrawal of Cruise and Pershing and the need to resist pressure from the Germans for early discussion of reductions of SNF in Europe. I also wanted to see an upgraded and longer-range Follow-On to LANCE missile (FOTL) developed by the Americans and deployed by the mid-1990s, and a Tactical Air to Surface Missile (TASM) to replace our free-fall bombs. On these matters relating to the strengthening of our SNF the President and I saw eye to eye. Where I did agree with the Germans – but found myself unable to convince the Americans – was that I would have liked to retain the old German Pershing 1A ballistic missiles for the rest of their natural life (a few years), not including them as part of the INF package. But it was the future of SNF that to my mind was the most crucial element in our nuclear deterrence; and it certainly proved the most controversial.

DISCUSSIONS WITH MR GORBACHEV IN DECEMBER 1987

Britain's own security interests were closely bound up with US-Soviet arms negotiations. As regards SNF, these weapons were a vital protection for our troops stationed in Germany. Discussions between the two great powers about strategic nuclear weapons were also of direct interest to us insofar as they affected the position of our Trident nuclear deterrent. More generally, I never ceased to believe in the importance of nuclear weapons as a means of deterring conventional, not just nuclear, war – the one issue on which I knew I could not take the Reagan Administration's soundness for granted.

So although I had no intention of allowing myself to become a kind of broker between the Americans and the Soviets, I was delighted when Mr Gorbachev accepted my invitation to stop over at Brize Norton on his way to the United States to sign the INF Treaty. This would give me an opportunity to gauge his thinking before his meeting with President Reagan and to tackle him on other issues, such as human rights and regional conflicts, on which I thought I could exert beneficial influence. The Americans had specifically asked me to press Mr Gorbachev on Afghanistan, where it was clear he was trying to find a way of pulling Soviet forces out of that disastrous venture.

Within the Soviet Union there were mixed signs. Mr Gorbachev had brought his ally Mr Yakovlev into the Politburo; but – in a move which was to have enormous long-term consequences – his one-time protégé, Boris Yeltsin, who had been brought in as head of the Moscow Party as an incorruptible radical reformer, had been publicly humiliated. Within the Soviet leadership, apart from Mr Gorbachev himself, it still seemed that probably only Foreign minister Shevardnadze and Mr Yakovlev were fully committed to the Gorbachev reforms.

At the start of our talks I brought out my copy of Mr Gorbachev's book, *Perestroika*, which seemed to please him. It prompted a long description of the difficulties he was facing in bringing about the changes he wanted. In the language of the Soviets – faithfully reflected in the language of the western media – the opponents of *perestroika* were usually called 'conservatives'. I told him how irritating I found this and said that I wanted nothing to do with Mr Gorbachev's 'conservatives': they could hardly be more different from mine. Then we got down to the detailed discussions on arms control. There was not much to say now about INF and it was the projected START Agreement,* which would lead to cuts in strategic nuclear weapons, on which we focused. There were still large differences between the two sides as regards definition and verification. I also repeated my determination to keep nuclear weapons, which Mr Gorbachev described as my preferring to 'sit on a powder keg rather than an easy chair'. I countered by reminding him of the large superiority which the Soviets enjoyed in conventional and chemical forces. Then I raised Soviet withdrawal from Afghanistan and the human rights issue, suggesting that any action he took on these would be likely to assist the US Administration in overcoming opposition in the Senate to the INF Treaty. But I made no headway: he said that a solution in Afghanistan would be easier if we stopped supplying the rebels with arms and that human rights was a matter for the particular country involved. (It was this sort of attitude which had already created a very bad impression in the United States as a result of Mr Gorbachev's remarks about human rights in an interview with NBC.) There was nothing I could do on this occasion to change his mind.

I ended our discussion by saying that I hoped that the Gorbachevs would return for a full visit next year and he said that he was keen to accept. In spite of his tetchiness over human rights, it was a vigorous, enjoyable and even rather jolly occasion. We had lunch in the officers' mess at which we were joined by Ken Baker and Raisa Gorbachev who had been visiting a local school, meeting the children and teachers

* The US-Soviet Strategic Arms Reduction Talks, which had begun in the first year of the Reagan Administration.

and watching a Nativity play. On one particular matter, however, the Christmas spirit did not prevail. Biding my time and waiting until the Soviet interpreter was out of earshot, I asked Mr Gorbachev, who had been reciting for me a Russian folk-song in front of the Christmas tree in the foyer, whether he would let Oleg Gordievsky's family out of the Soviet Union to join him in Britain. He pursed his lips and said nothing: the answer was all too clear.

When I got back to London I telephoned President Reagan to let him know about our discussions. I told him what I had said on Afghanistan and arms control. I also said that though the President must be prepared to tackle Mr Gorbachev on human rights he should also be prepared for a sharp reaction. President Reagan said that he expected some tough sessions with Mr Gorbachev but that I had clearly softened him up. He also asked me if I thought that he should try to get on first name terms with the Soviet leader. I advised him to go carefully on this, because although I found Mr Gorbachev friendly and open he was also quite formal, something which the whole rigid Soviet system encouraged.

NATO SUMMIT IN BRUSSELS, MARCH 1988

In fact, the Reagan-Gorbachev summit in Washington was a success. The INF Treaty was agreed and a further summit in Moscow in the first half of 1988 was arranged in principle at which the treaty would be signed and possibly agreement reached on a START Treaty as well. In February 1988 Mr Gorbachev announced that Soviet withdrawal from Afghanistan would begin in May. We were clearly moving into new territory and it seemed to me the right time to take our bearings at a NATO summit. The first NATO heads of government summit for six years – incidentally, the first attended by a French president for twenty-two years – was scheduled for March in Brussels.

It was clear from the start that the West Germans were likely to be the main source of difficulty. Mr Gorbachev had launched a very successful propaganda drive to win over German opinion to a denuclearized Germany. Within the Federal German Government, I knew that Chancellor Kohl was still fundamentally sound on the need to avoid a 'third zero' and denuclearization. Herr Genscher, the Federal Foreign minister, by contrast, was not. Chancellor Kohl insisted on NATO adherence to what was called its 'comprehensive concept' – that is, regarding the different elements of defence strategy, of which

SNF was one, as a whole. Within this 'comprehensive concept' he was prepared to support measures agreed, after proper study by the alliance as necessary, to maintain flexible response; but he had said publicly in Washington that there was no present need to make a decision on SNF modernization. It was possible for the Americans and us to take account of German sensitivities in the NATO communiqué while still maintaining the right stance both on the military doctrine and modernization of nuclear weapons. Consequently, I was not at all displeased by the wording which resulted. The heads of government agreed on: 'a strategy of deterrence based on an appropriate mix of adequate and effective nuclear and conventional forces which will continue to be kept up to date where necessary'. That was enough.

After the Brussels summit officially broke up I met President Reagan to discuss the outcome. I told him that I thought the summit had been a great success because Britain and the United States had stood together. This demonstration of NATO's unity would be helpful to him when he went to Moscow to meet Mr Gorbachev in May. I regretted that it had not proved possible to get the Germans to accept explicitly that negotiations to reduce shorter-range nuclear weapons in Europe should only take place after parity on conventional weapons and a ban on chemical weapons had been achieved. But I said that it was quite clear to me that these were in fact the only circumstances in which NATO should negotiate on short-range systems. President Reagan said that he entirely agreed and that NATO could not go any further down this road until these conditions had been met. We were equally in accord on the approach to a START Agreement. I said that though I supported START as a goal it was more important to get the right agreement than to have it quickly. The President said that he too was being cautious in his public comments. He did not want people to say that the Moscow summit was a failure if no START Agreement could be signed. He also recognized that the START negotiations would be far more complex than those on INF, particularly as regards verification. I left Brussels reassured that the President and I were at one as we faced up to all the difficult and complicated arms control negotiations which would now ensue.

PRESIDENT REAGAN'S VISIT TO LONDON, JUNE 1988

President Reagan was as good as his word when he went to Moscow. Although the INF Treaty was signed there was tough negotiation and no compromise on START, where the Soviets wanted the United States to have Sea-Launched Cruise Missiles (SLCMs) included in the agreement. But, as with my own visit in 1987, it was the opportunity for President Reagan and the Russian people to meet one another face to face which was probably of greatest importance. He told me when he came to London on Thursday 2 June, on his way back from Moscow, how moved he had been by the huge, welcoming crowds there. The only thing which had upset him was the brutal way in which the KGB had dealt with the people who wanted to approach him. I told him that now the Russians had seen for themselves the sort of person he was it would be that much more difficult for the Soviet authorities to convince them that the United States was a dangerous enemy. He had given high prominence to human rights matters – particularly to freedom of worship – when he was in the Soviet Union and I said how right I thought he had been to do this. The President also told me about the difficult arms control talks. He said he had been determined not to give an inch on SDI and he was not going to be rushed on START. In the meantime, NATO must move ahead with modernization of its short-range nuclear forces and the West Germans must be persuaded to approach this in a positive way. He would continue to insist that a balance had to be achieved in conventional forces in Europe before there could be negotiations to remove short-range nuclear weapons.

The President spoke to a large City and diplomatic audience at Guildhall the next day. It was a vintage performance and one of some significance in the light of later events. He harked back to the speech he had made to Members of Parliament in 1982 in which he had enunciated what came to be called the 'Reagan Doctrine'.* Neither he nor I knew how close we were to its triumphant vindication; but what was clear was that great advances had been made in the 'crusade for freedom' we had been fighting. It was now time to restate the cause, which was as much spiritual as political or economic. As the President put it:

* See p. 258.

Our faith is in a higher law . . . we hold that humanity was meant, not to be dishonoured by the all-powerful state, but to live in the image and likeness of Him who made us.

VISIT TO POLAND, NOVEMBER 1988

Just five months later – in November 1988 – I visited Poland. If anyone had wanted a demonstration of the value of President Reagan's vision he would have found it in that country, where Catholic faith, national consciousness and economic frustration had come together to expose the empty sterility of Marxism and shake the foundations of communist rule. I was determined to accept the invitation I had earlier received from General Jaruzelski to go to Poland. I always felt the greatest affection and admiration for this nation of indomitable patriots, whose traditions and distinctive identity the Prussians, Austrians and Russians (in the eighteenth and nineteenth centuries) and the Nazis and communists (in the twentieth century) had sought vainly to extinguish. I could not forget the Polish airmen who had fought with the RAF against Nazism, and how a war begun over the freedom of Poland had ended leaving them trapped under tyranny. But, for all that, these were diplomatically treacherous waters I was entering; and I knew it.

My aim in going to Poland was to continue that strategy towards the eastern bloc countries which I had first begun in Hungary in 1984. I wanted to open up these countries – their governments and peoples – to western influence and to exert pressure for respect for human rights and for political and economic reform. But Poland's recent past demonstrated how dependent events in such countries were on the intentions of the Soviet Union. Whether one regarded General Jaruzelski as a patriot stepping in to prevent worse things befalling his fellow countrymen or just as a Soviet puppet, the circumstances under which martial law was imposed and Solidarity crushed in 1981 were an unforgettable lesson in the reality of power politics. Now the political and economic bankruptcy of the Jaruzelski Government was again apparent and its authority challenged by a revived Solidarity. The role of the West – above all of a visiting western leader – was to give heart to the anti-communists, while urging on them a carefully calculated response to the opportunities they had to improve conditions and increase their influence; and in dealings with the Government it must be to combine straight talking about the need for change with an attitude which avoided outright and counterproductive conflict. It would not be an easy task.

For their part, the authorities were determined to make it harder still. On the eve of my visit the Government announced their intention to close the Lenin Shipyard at Gdansk, the home of Solidarity. It was a trap and one no less dangerous for being clumsy. The communists hoped that I would be forced to welcome the closure of uneconomic plant and to condemn Solidarity's resistance to it on the grounds of 'Thatcherite' economics. Some commentators fully expected me to fall for this. For example, a leader in *The Times* on the eve of my visit noted:

> The Prime Minister sets out today on a visit many will say she should not be making. Her trip to Poland was always a questionable proposition, capable of being interpreted as a gesture of succour to the Jaruzelski regime. Now it is doubly so.

In fact, even the official published figures suggested that although the Lenin Shipyard was in a very weak economic position it was not making the greatest 'losses', which clearly implied that the decision to single it out had been politically not economically motivated. Anyway, since 90 per cent of the work at the shipyard was done for the Soviet Union its viability depended on little more than the exchange rate between the rouble and the zloty. Where there is no real market there can be no real estimates of 'profit' and 'loss'. But there was far more to it than that. I was convinced that you cannot expect people to shoulder the kind of economic responsibility which would be expected in a western economy unless they are granted the freedoms we expect in a western society.

In the light of these manoeuvrings I was glad that from the beginning I had insisted that there should be an unofficial as well as an official side to my visit. I was not prepared to be prevented from meeting Lech Walesa and the leading opponents of the regime. To his credit, I felt, General Jaruzelski did not raise objections to my doing so. Otherwise, of course, I would indeed have run the risk of unwittingly serving the cause of communist propaganda.

In planning my visit I had consulted the Pope whose own visit there in June 1987 had provided the main impetus for the revival of Solidarity and the pressure for reform. It was clear that the Vatican thought my visit could do good but also that the Church was proceeding with great caution – a caution which was even more evident when on the first day of my visit I had a meeting with Cardinal Glemp.

In preparing my Polish trip there was another matter on which I felt I must consult a wise authority and that was what I should wear. A Polish lady who served me at Aquascutum said that green was the colour which represented hope in Poland. So green was the colour of the suit I chose.

My first official meeting in Warsaw on the evening of Wednesday 2 November was with the recently appointed Polish Prime Minister, Mr Rakowski. He was not an impressive or persuasive advocate of the line the Polish Government was taking about the Lenin Shipyard, though he did his best. He said how much he agreed with my public statements about the need for economic reform and portrayed closure of the shipyard as part of this process. In somewhat forced 'Thatcherite' tones he told me that rationalization was the only way to extricate Poland from its crisis and that Poland's great weakness historically had been lack of consistency, which was something he was determined to change. I replied that going from a centralized economy to one based on private enterprise and competition was immensely difficult. But it was not just a matter of changing economic policies. There had to be personal, political and spiritual change. Under communism, people were like birds in a cage: even when you opened the door, they were afraid to go out. The vital task facing his Government, I said, was to take the Polish people with it in making the changes; and the problem was that there was no political mechanism for consulting them and allowing them to express their views. The difference between the situation I had faced in 1979 and that which confronted Mr Rakowski was that I had been democratically elected – and twice re-elected – to carry out the changes required.

Later that evening I met a number of opponents of the regime and learnt a little more about its shortcomings. I knew that the communists had never managed to achieve the scale of collectivization of agriculture in Poland which they had elsewhere and that this – alongside the influence of the Catholic Church – had given the Poles a degree of independence which was unique in a communist country. I said to those present that since they at least had the land they must be doing quite well. No, they said, this was not so. Did I not realize that the state directed most of the seed, fertilizer, tractors and other equipment – not least spare parts – to the collective farming sector? The authorities also controlled prices and distribution. Under these circumstances the benefits of ownership were limited. In effect, socialism, which is only a less developed form of communism, was doing its usual work of impoverishment and demoralization. I later raised the subject with Mr Rakowski, who did not seriously dispute the facts.

On Thursday afternoon I had my first real taste of Poland – the Poland which the communists had tried and failed to destroy. I visited the church of St Stanislaw Kostka in the north of Warsaw where Father Jerzy Popieluszko had preached his anti-communist sermons until in 1984 he was abducted and murdered by members of the Polish Security Services. (I also went to talk in their home to Father Popieluszko's parents, who were grief stricken but immensely proud of their son.) The church itself was overflowing with people of every age who had come out to see me and on my arrival they broke into a Polish hymn. In Father Popieluszko they had evidently found a martyr, and I came away in little doubt that it was his creed rather than that of his murderers which would prevail in Poland.

I said as much to General Jaruzelski when I met him for talks later. The General had spoken for one and three-quarter hours without interruption about his plans for Poland. In this, at least, he was a typical communist. He even said that he admired the trade union reforms I had put through in Britain. When he finished I pointed out that people in Britain did not have to rely on trade unions as a means of expressing their political views because we had free elections. I had just experienced the power of the Solidarity movement in that church in northern Warsaw. I said that, as a politician, all my instincts told me that this was far more than a trade union – it was a political movement whose power could not be denied. The Government was right to recognize that it had to talk to Solidarity and I hoped that the Solidarity leaders would accept its invitation.

The next day, Friday, was one I shall never forget. I flew up to Gdansk in the early morning to join General Jaruzelski in laying a wreath at the Westerplatte, which saw the first fighting between the Poles and the invading Germans in 1939. It was a bleak peninsula above the bay of Gdansk and the wind was bitter; the ceremony lasted half an hour. I was pleased to get aboard and into the cabin of the small naval ship which was to take me down the river to Gdansk itself. I changed out of my black hat and coat into emerald green and then went back up on deck. The scenes at the arrival of our boat at Gdansk shipyard were unbelievable. Every inch of it seemed taken up with shipyard workers waving and cheering.

After a walkabout in old Gdansk itself I was driven to the hotel where Lech Walesa and his colleagues came up to see me in my room. He had a somewhat ambiguous status at this time, being under a sort of liberal house arrest, and had been brought to the hotel, ironically enough, by Polish Security Police. I gave him the present I had brought with me – some fishing tackle, for he was a great fisherman

– and we departed again for the shipyard. Again there were thousands of shipyard workers waiting for me, cheering and waving Solidarity banners. I laid flowers on the memorial to shipyard workers shot by the police and army in 1970, and then went to the house of Father Jankowski, Mr Walesa's confessor and adviser, for a meeting followed by lunch.

The Solidarity leaders were a mixture of workers and intellectuals. Mr Walesa was in the former group, but he had a large physical presence as well as a symbolic importance which allowed him to dominate. He told me that Solidarity was disinclined to accept the Government's invitation to join in round-table talks, believing – probably rightly – that the purpose was to divide and if possible discredit the opposition. Solidarity's goal he described as 'pluralism', that is a state of affairs in which the Communist Party was not the sole legitimate authority. What struck me, though, was that they did not have a specific plan of action with immediate practical objectives. Indeed, when I said that I thought that Solidarity should attend the talks and submit its own proposals in the form of a detailed agenda with supporting papers my hosts looked quite astonished.

Over lunch – one of the best game stews I have ever tasted – we argued through together what their negotiating stance might be and how in my final discussions with the Polish Government I could help. We decided that the most important point I could make to General Jaruzelski was that Solidarity must be legalized. *De facto* recognition was not enough. Throughout I was repeatedly impressed by the moderation and eloquence of Mr Walesa and his colleagues. At one point I said: 'you really must see that the Government hears all this.' 'No problem', replied Mr Walesa, pointing up to the ceiling; 'our meetings are bugged anyway.'

After lunch it was suggested that I might like to look around the nearby church of St Brygida. To my delighted astonishment, when Mr Walesa and I entered I found the whole church packed with Polish families who rose and sang the Solidarity anthem 'God give us back our free Poland.' I could not keep the tears from my eyes. I seemed to have shaken hundreds of hands as I walked around the church. I gave a short emotional speech and Lech Walesa spoke too. As I left there were people in the streets crying with emotion and shouting 'thank you, thank you' over and over again. I returned to Warsaw with greater determination than ever to do battle with the communist authorities.

In my final meeting with General Jaruzelski that afternoon I kept my word to Solidarity. I told him that I was grateful that he had put no obstacle in the way of my visit to Gdansk – though it has to be said that the authorities had put on a total news black-out about it both before and afterwards. I said how impressed I had been by Solidarity's moderation. If they were good enough to attend round-table discussions they were also good enough to be legalized. General Jaruzelski gave no impression of being prepared to budge. I repeated that I did not believe that Solidarity could be ignored, indeed any attempt to ignore them would court disaster. It was a chilly though good-tempered discussion. General Jaruzelski was in any case a slightly awkward interlocutor until you got to know him: his dark glasses and his oddly rigid posture (the result of back trouble) made him seem rather remote. But I did not underrate his intelligence – nor his connections, for I knew that he was close to Mr Gorbachev. The proof that the General was a Pole and not just a communist was that just before my aeroplane was about to leave, in an unscheduled appearance his car screamed to a halt beside the aircraft and the General leapt out with a huge bouquet of flowers. Not even Marxism could suppress Polish gallantry.

THE BUSH ADMINISTRATION

A fortnight later I was back in Washington as President Reagan's last official guest. This gave me the chance of discussions with President-elect Bush. Mr Bush was slowly putting his Administration team together. On this occasion I also met Dan Quayle, the Vice-President-elect – who for all the cruel mockery to which he was subject I always found very well briefed and with a good political sense – and also future Secretary of State Jim Baker, whose views I shall mention shortly. Both the outgoing President and the President-elect spoke of the importance of dealing with the US budget deficit which had fallen for four years but which was still a problem. This inevitably raised a question mark over defence, so I was keen to restate to Mr Bush my views about SNF and the great significance I attached to the continuation of the SDI programme.

I had always found Vice-President Bush easy to get on with and I felt that he had performed good service to America in keeping the Reagan Administration in touch with European thinking. He was one of the most decent, honest and patriotic Americans I have met. He had great personal courage, as his past record and his resilience in campaigning showed. But he had never had to think through his beliefs and fight for them when they were hopelessly unfashionable as Ronald Reagan and I had had to do. This meant that much of his time now was taken up with reaching for answers to problems which to me came quite spontaneously, because they sprang from my basic convictions.

I later learned that President Bush was sometimes exasperated by my habit of talking nonstop about issues which fascinated me and felt that he ought to have been leading the discussion. More important than all of this perhaps was the fact that, as President, George Bush felt the need to distance himself from his predecessor: turning his back fairly publicly on the special position I had enjoyed in the Reagan Administration's counsels and confidence was a way of doing that. This was understandable; and by the time of my last year in office we had established a better relationship. By then I had learned that I had to defer to him in conversation and not to stint the praise. If that was what was necessary to secure Britain's interests and influence I had no hesitation in eating a little humble pie.

Unfortunately, even then the US State Department continued to put out briefing against me and my policies – particularly on Europe – until the onset of the Gulf crisis made them hastily change their stance. To some extent the relative tilt of American foreign policy against Britain in this period may have been the result of the influence of Secretary of State James Baker. Although he was always very courteous to me, we were not close as the admirable George Schultz and I had been. Yet that was not crucial. Rather, it was the fact that Jim Baker's many abilities lay in the area of 'fixing'. He had had a mixed record of this, having as US Treasury Secretary been responsible for the ill-judged Plaza and Louvre Accords which brought 'exchange rate stability' back to the centre of the West's economic policies with highly deleterious effects. Now at the State Department Jim Baker and his team brought a similar, allegedly 'pragmatic' problem-solving approach to bear on US foreign policy.

The main results of this approach as far as I was concerned were to put the relationship with Germany – rather than the 'special relationship' with Britain – at the centre. I would be the first to argue that if one chose to ignore history and the loyalties it engenders such an approach might appear quite rational. After all, there was some danger that Germany – first under the spell of Mr Gorbachev and later with the lure of reunification – might have moved away from the western alliance towards neutralism. Once Germany was reunified there was another argument – propagated by the French, but swallowed by the US State Department too – that only a 'united Europe' could keep German power responsibly in check and, more positively, that a German-led 'united Europe' would allow the Americans to cut back on the amount they spent on Europe's defence.

Each of these arguments – the sort I could imagine being generated by our own British foreign policy establishment – was false. The risk of Germany loosening its attachment to the West was greatly exaggerated. A 'united Europe' would augment, not check, the power of a united Germany. Germany would pursue its interests inside or outside such a Europe – while a Europe built on the corporatist and protectionist lines implicit in the Franco-German alliance would certainly be more antipathetic to the Americans than the looser Europe I preferred. Finally, the idea that the Europeans – with the exception of the British and possibly the French – could be relied on to defend themselves or anyone else for that matter was frankly laughable. In fact, the ties of blood, language, culture and values which bound Britain and America were the only firm basis for US policy in the West; only a very clever person could fail to appreciate something so obvious. But this was the range of personal and political considerations which affected US policy towards Britain as I tried to pursue my threefold objectives of keeping NATO's defences strong, of ensuring that the Soviet Union did not feel so threatened as to march into eastern Europe and of managing the effects of German reunification.

NATO SPLIT ON SHORT-RANGE NUCLEAR FORCES (SNF)

At the end of 1988 I could foresee neither the way in which Anglo-American relations would develop nor the scale of the difficulties with the Germans over SNF. My basic position on Short-Range Nuclear Weapons was that they were essential to NATO's strategy of flexible response. Any potential aggressor must know that if he were to cross the NATO line he might be met with a nuclear response. If that fear was removed he might calculate that he could mount a conventional attack that would reach the Atlantic seaboard within a few days. And this, of course, was the existing position. But once land-based intermediate-range nuclear weapons were removed, as the INF Treaty signed in Washington in December 1987 took effect, the land-based short-range missiles became all the more vital. So, of course, did the sea-based intermediate missiles.

At the Rhodes European Council in early December 1988 I discussed arms control with Chancellor Kohl. I found him quite robust.

He was keen for an early NATO summit which would help him push through agreement within his Government on the 'comprehensive concept' for arms control. I agreed that the sooner the better. We must take decisions on the modernization of NATO's nuclear weapons by the middle of the year, in particular on the replacement of LANCE. Chancellor Kohl said that he wanted both of these questions out of the way before the June 1989 European elections.

By the time of the next Anglo-German summit in Frankfurt the political pressure on the German Chancellor had increased further and he had begun to argue that a decision on SNF was not really necessary until 1991–2.

A week before I went to Frankfurt I had talked through the problem with Jim Baker over lunch at Chequers. I told him that I still considered that Chancellor Kohl was a courageous man and a strong supporter of the United States: the problem was Hans-Dietrich Genscher, who normally favoured a softer, more accommodating approach to the Soviets. I predicted that a number of other governments would be inclined to waver on SNF, because the opinion polls showed that people no longer believed in the Soviet threat. It was therefore vital that the United States and Britain should stand firm. Jim Baker said he very much agreed with my line. The Administration needed an assurance on deployment or it would not get funding from Congress to develop a successor to LANCE. But he wondered whether the price of German agreement would have to be the acceptance of vague language on negotiations on SNF. I replied that though there was scope for NATO to make unilateral reductions in its holdings of nuclear artillery, we could not negotiate on SNF without getting trapped into another 'zero'. Jim Baker was clearly more anxious about handling German sensitivities than I was, but I still believed that we saw things in the same way.

Consequently, when I met Chancellor Kohl in Frankfurt I was quite direct. I said that in putting the case for SNF to his people he should simply ask the fundamental question whether they valued their freedom. Freedom for the German people had started on the day the Second World War had ended and NATO had preserved it for forty years. The Soviet Union continued to represent a military threat. Britain, Germany and the United States represented the real strength of NATO. I understood his difficulties in dealing with German public opinion but I believed that he and I were fundamentally in agreement. NATO had to modernize its weapons, otherwise the United States would sooner or later start to withdraw its troops from Germany. Britain and Germany together should give a lead. In spite of the pressure the Federal Chancellor was under, I came away from Frankfurt feeling that the agreed line on SNF might still hold.

Certainly, the Soviets were in no doubt about the strategic importance of the decisions which would have to be made about SNF. Mr and Mrs Gorbachev arrived at 11 o'clock at night on Wednesday 5 April in London for the visit which had had to be postponed the previous December as a result of an earthquake in Armenia. I met them at the airport and returned to the Soviet Embassy where the number of toasts drunk suggested that the Soviet leader's early crackdown on vodka was not universally applicable. In my talks with Mr Gorbachev I found him frustrated by – and surprisingly suspicious of – the Bush Administration. I defended the new President's performance and stressed the continuity with the Reagan Administration. But the real substance of our discussions related to arms control. I raised directly with Mr Gorbachev the evidence which we had that the Soviets had not been telling us the truth about the quantity and types of chemical weapons which they held. He stoutly maintained that they had. He then brought up the issue of SNF modernization. I said that obsolete weapons did not deter and that NATO's SNF would certainly have to be modernized. The forthcoming NATO summit would confirm this intention. Mr Gorbachev returned to the subject in his speech at Guildhall which contained a somewhat menacing section about the effect on East-West relations and arms control talks more generally if NATO went ahead with SNF modernization.

All this pressure was by now having an effect. In particular, Chancellor Kohl was retreating. In April a new German position on SNF modernization and negotiation was extensively leaked before any of the allies – other than the Americans – were informed. The German position paper did not rule out a 'third zero', did not call on the Soviet Union unilaterally to reduce its SNF levels to those of NATO and cast doubt on SNF modernization.

I had acrimonious discussions with Chancellor Kohl behind the stage-managed friendliness of our meeting at Deidesheim at the end of April.* Chancellor Kohl gave a lengthy justification for Germany's recent conduct. He wanted NATO to discuss a mandate for negotiations on SNF, though he said he was absolutely opposed to a 'third zero'. He said that it was simply not sustainable politically in Germany to argue that those nuclear weapons which most directly affected Germany should be the only category not subject to negotiation.

I said that I would begin by reminding Chancellor Kohl of some

* For this meeting see pp. 746–8.

of the background. He had been the one who had originally proposed that there should be an early NATO summit to take the decision on modernization and I had supported him. I read out to him the joint statement which we had issued at Frankfurt. We had not been informed of the German Government's new position until several days after it had been leaked to the press. NATO had to have SNF and they must be modernized, as he himself had agreed recently. We could not become embroiled in SNF negotiations which would lead inexorably to a 'third zero'. I told Chancellor Kohl about the reports we had been getting of the Soviet Union's real views and intentions. They were delighted that they had gained an advantage with the modernization of their own SNF and that we were delaying ours. They were also confident that they could influence opinion in West Germany in favour of SNF negotiations. I repeated that Britain and the United States were absolutely opposed to negotiations on SNF and would remain so. Our present forces were an irreducible minimum if we were to sustain the strategy of flexible response and they would in due course have to be modernized. Even if a decision to deploy the Follow-On to LANCE (FOTL) were postponed, there must be clear evidence at the forthcoming summit of NATO support for the US development programme. In fact, the German Government's actions had put NATO under severe strain.

Chancellor Kohl began to get agitated. He said he did not need any lectures about NATO, that he believed in flexible response and repeated his opposition to a 'third zero'. But the fact was that Germany was more affected than anyone else by SNF and that therefore German interests should be given priority. I retorted that, contrary to what he said, SNF did not affect only Germany. Our troops were on German soil. It had never been possible to rely on all the NATO allies; there were always weak links. But hitherto the United States, Britain and Germany had constituted the real strength of NATO.

At this Chancellor Kohl became still more worked up. He said that for years he had been attacked as the vassal of the Americans. Now he was suddenly being branded a traitor. He repeated that he did not believe that once the INF agreement had been reached you could resist negotiations on SNF. But he would think again about what I had said and would be in touch with the Americans about it. I reported on our discussion in a message to President Bush, concluding that 'provided Britain and the United States remain absolutely firm, we can still achieve a satisfactory outcome at the [NATO] summit'.

In the run up to the NATO summit the newspapers continued to focus on splits in the alliance. This was particularly galling because we should have been celebrating NATO's fortieth anniversary and highlighting the success of our strategy of securing peace through strength. Apart from the Americans only the French fully agreed with my line on SNF and in any case, not being part of the NATO integrated command structure, they would not be of great importance in the final decision. I minuted on Tuesday 16 May: 'if we get a "no negotiations" SNF section this will be reasonable, combined with a supportive piece on SNF research.' I was still quite optimistic.

Then on Friday 19 May I suddenly learnt that the American line had shifted. They were now prepared to concede the principle of negotiations on SNF. Jim Baker claimed in public that we had been consulted about this US change of tack, but in fact we had not. Without in any way endorsing the American text, which I considered wrong-headed, I sent two main comments to the Americans. It should be amended to make the opening of SNF negotiations dependent upon a decision to deploy a successor to LANCE. It should include a requirement of substantial reductions in Soviet SNF towards NATO levels. Jim Baker replied that he doubted whether the Germans would accept this. The attitude of Brent Scowcroft – the President's National Security Adviser – was sounder. But I could not tell what the President's own view would be. In any case, I now found myself going to Brussels as the odd man out. Everyone else accepted the principle of SNF negotiations, and the differences between them existed only on the conditions to be met before these were held. I did not want any negotiations at all. And, if there had to be any, I wanted tougher conditions than those in the American text. Above all there must be no fudged language on the 'third zero'.

This was not like a European Council: it was important that we demonstrated the unity of NATO if it was to be effective and so I felt that compromise in some circumstances was a moral duty rather than a matter of weakness. However, I put my case very strongly in the speech I made. I said that I was profoundly sceptical whether negotiations on SNF could possibly be to NATO's benefit. I was prepared to consider a text which would envisage such negotiations, but only after an agreement for the reduction of conventional forces had been reached and partially implemented. This, moreover, could only be on the basis that another 'zero' was excluded.

In fact, at the last minute the Americans brought forward proposals calling for conventional forces reductions and for not just further deep cuts but accelerated progress in the CFE talks in Vienna, so that those reductions could be accomplished by 1992 or 1993. This sleight of hand permitted a compromise on SNF by enabling the Germans to argue that the prospect of 'early' SNF negotiations was preserved. However, I emphasized in my subsequent statement to the House of Commons the fact that only after agreement had been reached on conventional force reductions, and implementation of that agreement was under way, would the United States be authorized to enter into negotiations to achieve partial reductions in Short-Range Missiles. No reductions would be made in NATO's SNF until after the agreement on conventional force reductions had been fully implemented.

I felt that I had done as much as was humanly possible – without firm support from the United States for the line I really wanted – to stop our sliding into another 'zero'. I could live with the text which resulted from the tough negotiations which took place in Brussels. But I had seen for myself that the new American approach was to subordinate clear statements of intention about the alliance's defence to the political sensibilities of the Germans. I did not think that this boded well.

President Bush's remarks in his speech in Mainz on 31 May 1989 about the Germans as 'partners in leadership' confirmed the way American thinking about Europe was going. When the President came to London he sought to deal with the problems those remarks had caused by saying that we too were partners in leadership. But the damage had been done. Now, as 1989 wore on, the march of events in eastern Europe and the prospect of German reunification added a new element, inclining the United States to take German issues still more seriously.

THE FALL OF COMMUNISM IN EASTERN EUROPE IN 1989 AND ITS IMPLICATIONS

In the late summer of 1989 the first signs appeared of the imminent collapse of communism in eastern Europe. Solidarity won the elections in early June in Poland and General Jaruzelski accepted the result: I congratulated him on this when he came to London a few days later. Liberalization proceeded in Hungary, which opened its borders to Austria in September across which flooded East German refugees. The haemorrhage of population from East Germany and demonstrations at the beginning of October in Leipzig led to the fall of Erich Honecker. The demolition of the Berlin Wall began on 10 November. The following month it was the turn of Czechoslovakia. By the end of the year Václav Havel, the dissident playwright who had been gaoled in

February, had been elected President of Czechoslovakia and the evil Ceauşescus had been overthrown in Romania.

These events marked the most welcome political change of my lifetime. But no matter how much I rejoiced at the overthrow of communism in eastern and central Europe I was not going to allow euphoria to extinguish either reason or prudence. I did not believe that it would be easy or painless to entrench democracy and free enterprise. Some of the liberalizing and liberated countries had stronger traditions of freedom to draw upon than others. But it was too soon to be sure precisely what sort of regimes would emerge. Moreover, central and eastern Europe – still more the Soviet Union – was a complicated patchwork of nations. Political freedom would also bring ethnic disputes and challenges to frontiers, which might have moved several times in living memory. War could not be ruled out.

The welcome changes which were happening had come about because the West had remained strong and resolute – but also because Mr Gorbachev and the Soviet Union had renounced the Brezhnev doctrine. On the continued survival of a moderate, reforming Government in the USSR would depend the future of the new democracies. We had seen in the past – in 1956 in Hungary and 1968 in Czechoslovakia – what happened when democrats took to the streets believing that the West would ultimately step in to help them against the Soviets and then found themselves abandoned. It was too early to assume that the captive nations were permanently free from captivity: their Soviet captors could still turn ugly. It was therefore essential to go carefully and avoid actions which would be deemed provocative by either the Soviet political leadership or the military.

This led directly on to the third consideration – the future of Germany. For nothing was more likely to stir up old fears in the Soviet Union – fears which the hardliners would be anxious to exploit – than the prospect of a reunited, powerful Germany, possibly with renewed ambitions on its eastern flank.

THE GERMAN PROBLEM AND THE BALANCE OF POWER

There was – and still is – a tendency to regard the 'German problem' as something too delicate for well-brought-up politicians to discuss. This always seemed to me a mistake. The problem had several elements which could only be addressed if non-Germans considered them openly and constructively. I do not believe in collective guilt: it is individuals who are morally accountable for their actions. But I do believe in national character, which is moulded by a range of complex factors: the fact that national caricatures are often absurd and inaccurate does not detract from that. Since the unification of Germany under Bismarck – perhaps partly because national unification came so late – Germany has veered unpredictably between aggression and self-doubt. Germany's immediate neighbours, such as the French and the Poles, are more deeply aware of this than the British, let alone the Americans; though the same concern often leads Germany's immediate neighbours to refrain from comments which might appear insensitive. The Russians are acutely conscious of all this too, though in their case the need for German credit and investment has so far had a quiescent effect. But perhaps the first people to recognize the 'German problem' are the modern Germans, the vast majority of whom are determined that Germany should not be a great power able to exert itself at others' expense. The true origin of German *angst* is the agony of self-knowledge.

As I have already argued, that is one reason why so many Germans genuinely – I believe wrongly – want to see Germany locked in to a federal Europe. In fact, Germany is more rather than less likely to dominate within that framework; for a reunited Germany is simply too big and powerful to be just another player within Europe. Moreover, Germany has always looked east as well as west, though it is economic expansion rather than territorial aggression which is the modern manifestation of this tendency. Germany is thus by its very nature a destabilizing rather than a stabilizing force in Europe. Only the military and political engagement of the United States in Europe and close relations between the other two strongest sovereign states in Europe – Britain and France – are sufficient to balance German power: and nothing of the sort would be possible within a European super-state.

One obstacle to achieving such a balance of power when I was in office was the refusal of France under President Mitterrand to follow his and French instincts and challenge German interests. This would have required abandoning the Franco-German axis on which he had been relying and, as I shall describe, the wrench proved just too difficult for him.

GERMAN REUNIFICATION

Initially, it also seemed likely that the Soviets would be strongly opposed to the re-emergence of a powerful Germany, particularly one reunited on the West's terms and accompanied by the discrediting of communism. Of course, the Soviets might have calculated that a reunited Germany would return a left-of-centre government which would achieve their long-term objective of neutralizing and de-nuclearizing West Germany. (As it turned out – and perhaps with a clearer idea than we had of the true feelings of the East German people – the Soviets were prepared to sell reunification for a modest financial boost from Germany to their crumbling economy.)

These matters were at the forefront of my mind when I decided to arrange a stop-over visit in Moscow for talks with Mr Gorbachev on my way back from the IDU Conference in Tokyo in September 1989. In fact, my VC10 stopped first for refuelling in the Siberian town of Bratsk. I had two hours of conversation with the local Communist Party leaders over coffee in a chilly barn-like building. They seemed enthusiastic about *perestroika*, but I found the conversation flagging after an hour had been spent on the subject of the local beetroot crop. Stardom came to the rescue. John Whittingdale came in to ask if Oleg, the KGB guard outside the door, could have a signed photograph. I at once obliged. My hosts conferred in rapid Russian and then said that they too wanted signed photographs. The ice was broken.

In Moscow the following morning and over lunch Mr Gorbachev and I talked frankly about Germany. I explained to him that although NATO had traditionally made statements supporting Germany's aspiration to be reunited, in practice we were rather apprehensive. Nor was I speaking for myself alone – I had discussed it with at least one other western leader, meaning but not mentioning President Mitterrand. Mr Gorbachev confirmed that the Soviet Union did not want German reunification either. This reinforced me in my resolve to slow up the already heady pace of developments. Of course, I did not want East Germans – any more than I would have wanted anyone else – to have to live under communism. But it seemed to me that a truly democratic East Germany would soon emerge and that the question of reunification was a separate one, on which the wishes and interests of Germany's neighbours and other powers must be fully taken into account.

To begin with the West Germans seemed to be willing to do this.

Chancellor Kohl telephoned me on the evening of Friday 10 November after his visit to Berlin and as demolition of the Berlin Wall began. He was clearly buoyed up by the scenes he had witnessed: what German would not have been? I advised him to keep in touch with Mr Gorbachev who would obviously be very concerned with what was happening. He promised to do so. Later that night the Soviet Ambassador came to see me with a message from Mr Gorbachev who was worried that there might occur some incident – perhaps an attack on Soviet soldiers in East Germany or Berlin – which could have momentous consequences.

However, instead of seeking to rein back expectations, Chancellor Kohl was soon busily raising them. In a statement to the Bundestag he said that the core of the German question was freedom and that the people of East Germany must be given the chance to decide their own future and needed no advice from others. That went for the 'question of reunification and for German unity too'. The tone had already begun to change and it would change further – though in private Foreign minister Genscher was still assuring Douglas Hurd that the Germans wanted to avoid talk of reunification.

This was the background to President Mitterrand's calling a special meeting of Community heads of government in Paris* to consider what was happening in Germany – where Egon Krenz, the new East German leader who was, the Soviets had told me, a protégé of Mr Gorbachev, was looking precarious. Before I went I sent a message to President Bush reiterating my view that the priority should be to see genuine democracy established in East Germany and that German reunification was not something to be addressed at present. The President later telephoned me to thank me for my message with which he agreed and to say how much he was looking forward to the two of us 'putting our feet up at Camp David for a really good talk'.

Almost equally amiable was the Paris meeting on the evening of Saturday 18 November. President Mitterrand opened by posing a number of questions, including whether the issue of borders in Europe should be open for discussion. Then Chancellor Kohl began. He said that people wanted 'to hear Europe's voice'. He then obliged by speaking for forty minutes. He concluded by saying that there should be no discussion of borders but that the people of Germany must be allowed to decide their future for themselves and that self-determination was paramount. After Sr. González had intervened to no great effect, I spoke.

I said that though the changes taking place were historic we must

* For other discussions at this meeting see p. 759.

not succumb to euphoria. The changes were only just beginning and it would take several years to get genuine democracy and economic reform in eastern Europe. There must be no question of changing borders. The Helsinki Final Act must apply.* Any attempt to talk about either border changes or German reunification would undermine Mr Gorbachev and also open up a Pandora's box of border claims right through central Europe. I said that we must keep both NATO and the Warsaw Pact intact to create a background of stability. Whatever reservations Chancellor Kohl may have had were not voiced. Whether he had already decided on his next move to accelerate the process of reunification I do not know.

The following Friday – 24 November – I was discussing the same issues at Camp David with President Bush – though not exactly 'with my feet up'. Although friendly enough, the President seemed distracted and uneasy. I was very keen to persuade him of the rightness of my approach to what was happening in the crumbling communist bloc. I reiterated much of what I had said in Paris about borders and reunification and of the need to support the Soviet leader on whose continuance in power so much depended. The President did not challenge what I said directly but he asked me pointedly whether my line had given rise to difficulties with Chancellor Kohl and about my attitude to the European Community. It was also clear that we differed on the priority which still needed to be given to defence spending. The President told me about the budgetary difficulties he faced and argued that if conditions in eastern Europe and the Soviet Union had really changed, there must surely be scope for the West to cut its defence spending. I said that there would always remain the unknown threat which must be guarded against. Defence spending was like home insurance in this respect. You did not stop paying the premiums because your street was free from burglaries for a time. I thought that the US defence budget should be driven not by Mr Gorbachev and his initiatives but by the United States' defence interests. Perhaps I was insensitive to his difficulties with Congress. In any case, the atmosphere did not improve as a result of our discussions.

* The Helsinki Final Act of 1975 contained the following commitment: 'The participating States regard as inviolable all one another's frontiers as well as the frontiers of all States in Europe and therefore they will refrain now and in the future from assaulting these frontiers. Accordingly, they will also refrain from any demand for, or act of, seizure and usurpation of part or all of the territory of any participating State.' However, the Final Act also provided that 'frontiers can be changed, in accordance with international law, by peaceful means and by agreement'.

Shortly after my return to Britain I learned that without any previous consultation with his allies and in clear breach of at least the spirit of the Paris summit Chancellor Kohl had set out in a speech to the Bundestag a 'ten-point' plan about Germany's future. The fifth point was the proposal of the development of 'confederative structures between the two states in Germany with the goal of creating a federation'. The tenth point was that his Government was working towards 'unity, reunification, the reattainment of German state unity'.

The real question now was how the Americans would react. I did not have to wait long to find out. In a press conference briefing Jim Baker spelt out the American approach to German reunification which, he said, would be based on four principles. Self-determination would be pursued 'without prejudice to its outcome'. Another element was that Germany should not only remain in NATO – with which I heartily agreed – but that it should be part of 'an increasingly integrated European Community' – with which I did not. The third point was that moves to unification should be peaceful, gradual and part of a step-by-step process, which was fair enough. I entirely agreed with the final point – that the principles of the Helsinki Final Act particularly as they related to borders must be supported. What remained to be seen, however, was whether the Americans were going to give most weight to the notion of Germany's future in an 'integrated' Europe or to the thought that reunification must only come about slowly and gradually.

It was left to President Bush himself to provide the answer in his speech at the NATO heads of government meeting staged at Brussels in early December to hear his report on his talks with Mr Gorbachev in Malta. He made an obviously carefully prepared statement on Europe's 'future architecture', calling for a 'new, more mature relationship' with Europe. He also restated the principles Jim Baker had laid out as regards reunification. But the fact that the President placed such emphasis on 'European integration' at a predominantly European meeting in Brussels was immediately taken as a signal – which was perhaps not far from the truth – that he was aligning America with the federalist rather than my 'Bruges' goal of European development. There was no reason for journalists, who knew perfectly well of the direction of State Department background briefing, to take the President's remarks otherwise. The President telephoned me to explain his remarks and say that they just related to the Single Market rather than wider political integration. I hoped that they did – or that at least from now on they would. The fact remained that there was nothing I could expect from the Americans as regards slowing down

German reunification – and possibly much I would wish to avoid as regards the drive towards European unity.

AN ANGLO-FRENCH AXIS?

If there was any hope now of stopping or slowing down reunification it would only come from an Anglo-French initiative. Yet even were President Mitterrand to try to give practical effect to what I knew were his secret fears, we would not find many ways open to us. Once it was decided that East Germany could join the European Community without detailed negotiations – and I was resisting for my own reasons treaty amendment and any European Community aid – there was little we could do to slow down reunification via the Community's institutions. I placed some hopes in the framework offered by the 'Four Powers' – Britain, France, the United States and the Soviet Union – which were responsible for the security of Berlin. But with the United States – and soon the Soviets too – ceasing to regard this as anything other than a talking shop for discussion of the details of reunification, this framework too was of limited use. The CSCE – on which I was to develop my ideas the following year – would provide a basis for restricting any unwelcome attempts to change borders in eastern Europe as a whole; but it would not stand in the way of German reunification. So the last and best hope seemed the creation of a solid Anglo-French political axis which would ensure that at each stage of reunification – and in future economic and political developments – the Germans did not have things all their own way.

At the Strasbourg European Council in December 1989 President Mitterrand and I – at his suggestion – had two private meetings to discuss the German problem and our reaction to it. He was still more concerned than I was. He was very critical of Chancellor Kohl's 'ten-point' plan. He observed that in history the Germans were a people in constant movement and flux. At this I produced from my handbag a map showing the various configurations of Germany in the past, which were not altogether reassuring about the future. We talked through what precisely we might do. I said that at the meeting he had chaired in Paris we had come up with the right answer on borders and reunification. But President Mitterrand observed that Chancellor Kohl had already gone far beyond that. He said that at moments of great danger in the past France had always established special relations with Britain and he felt that such a time had come again. We must draw together and stay in touch. It seemed to me that although we had not discovered the means, at least we both had the will to check the German juggernaut. That was a start.

Discussion at the official meetings of the Strasbourg Council was of course very different in tone, although the Dutch Prime Minister Mr Lubbers said at the heads of government dinner that he thought Chancellor Kohl's 'ten-point' plan would encourage reunification, that there were dangers in talking about self-determination and that it was better not to refer to one 'German people'. This required some courage. But it hardly deflected Chancellor Kohl, who said that Germany had paid for the last war by losing one-third of its territory. He was vague about the question of borders – too vague for my liking – arguing that the Oder-Neisse line, which marked the border with Poland, should not become a legal issue. He did not seem now or later to understand the Polish fears and sensitivities.

I was due to meet President Mitterrand in January 1990 and I asked for papers to be drawn up showing ways in which we could strengthen Anglo-French co-operation. The French President had been to East Berlin shortly before Christmas in order to assert France's interests in the future of Germany. But his public attitude hardly betrayed his private thoughts and at his press conference there he claimed that he was not 'one of those who were putting on the brakes'. I hoped that my forthcoming meeting with him might overcome this tendency to schizophrenia.

Almost all the discussion I had with President Mitterrand at the Elysée Palace on Saturday 20 January concerned Germany. Picking up the President's remarks in the margins of Strasbourg I said that it was very important for Britain and France to work out jointly how to handle what was happening in Germany. East Germany seemed close to collapse and it was by no means impossible that we would be confronted in the course of this year with the decision in principle in favour of reunification. The President was clearly irked by German attitudes and behaviour. He accepted that the Germans had the right to self-determination but they did not have the right to upset the political realities of Europe; nor could he accept that German reunification should take priority over everything else. He complained that the Germans treated any talk of caution as criticism of themselves. Unless you were whole-heartedly for reunification, you were described as an enemy of Germany. The trouble was that in reality there was no force in Europe which could stop reunification happening. He agreed with my analysis of the problems but he said he was at a loss as to what we could do. I was not so pessimistic. I argued that we should at least make use of all the means available to slow down reunification. The trouble was that other governments were not ready to speak up openly – nor, I might have added but did not, were the French. President Mitterrand went on to say that he shared my worries about the Germans' so-called 'mission' in central Europe. The Czechs, Poles and Hungarians would not want to be under Germany's exclusive influence, but they would need German aid and investment. I said that we must not just accept that the Germans had a particular hold over these countries, but rather do everything possible to expand our own links there. At the end of the meeting we agreed that our Foreign and Defence ministers should get together to talk over the issue of reunification and also examine the scope for closer Franco-British defence co-operation.

The fact that little or nothing in practical terms came of these discussions between me and President Mitterrand about the German problem reflected his basic unwillingness to change the direction of his whole foreign policy. Essentially, he had a choice between moving ahead faster towards a federal Europe in order to tie down the German giant or to abandon this approach and return to that associated with General de Gaulle – the defence of French sovereignty and the striking up of alliances to secure French interests. He made the wrong decision for France. Moreover, his failure to match private words with public deeds also increased my difficulties. But it must be said that his judgement that there was nothing we could do to halt German reunification turned out to be right.

In February Chancellor Kohl – again without any consultation with his allies – went to Moscow and won from Mr Gorbachev agreement that 'the unity of the German nation must be decided by the Germans themselves.' (The *quid pro quo* would soon become clear. In July at a meeting in the Crimea the West German Chancellor agreed to provide what must have seemed to the Soviets a huge sum, though they could in fact have extracted much more, to cover the costs of providing for the Soviet troops who would be withdrawn from East Germany. For his part, Mr Gorbachev now finally agreed in public that the reunified Germany should be part of NATO.)

On Saturday 24 February I had a three-quarters-of-an-hour telephone conversation with President Bush. I broke with my usual habit of trying to avoid detailed factual discussions over the telephone and tried to explain to the President how I thought we should be thinking about the future of a western alliance and a Europe which contained a reunified Germany. I stressed the importance of ensuring that a united Germany stayed within NATO and that United States troops remained there. However, if all Soviet forces had to leave East Germany that would cause difficulties for Mr Gorbachev and I thought it best to allow some to stay for a transitional period without any specific terminal date. I also said that we must strengthen the CSCE framework, which would not only help avoid Soviet isolation but would help balance German dominance in Europe. One had to remember that Germany was surrounded by countries most of which it had attacked or occupied on mainland Europe in the course of this century. Looking well into the future, only the Soviet Union – or its successor – could provide such a balance. President Bush, as I afterwards learnt, failed to understand that I was discussing a long-term balance of power in Europe rather than proposing an alternative alliance to NATO. It was the last time that I relied on a telephone conversation to explain such matters.

Chancellor Kohl had managed to convey the worst possible impression by his unwillingness to have a proper treaty to settle Germany's border with Poland. Prime Minister Tadeusz Mazowiecki, whom I had first met in very different circumstances in Gdansk in November 1988, discussed his fears with me when he came to London in February 1990. I pressed the matter – though I received no real response – when I met Chancellor Kohl at the start of an Anglo-German summit in London at the end of March. I also ensured that the Poles received special status at the talks of the 'two-plus-four' (or as I preferred to call it the 'four-plus-two' – that is the Berlin Four Powers and the Two Germanies). Finally, and after much pressure, Chancellor Kohl did agree to settle Germany's border with Poland by a special treaty signed in November 1990.

THE CSCE AND THE 'ALLIANCE FOR DEMOCRACY'

One minor benefit which did come out of the saga of German reunification was an enhanced role for the CSCE (Conference on Security and Co-operation in Europe). I had begun by being very sceptical of the whole Helsinki process. But whatever its shortcomings at the height of the Cold War, it now provided a useful framework within which at least some of the problems arising in the new democratic Europe might be tackled. It could never take the place of NATO which must remain the basis of our defence, whatever changes in its strategy and priorities were required; though it did provide the framework for the Conventional Forces in Europe (CFE) arms negotiations between NATO and the Warsaw Pact which would lead to the CFE agreement, signed at what turned out to be my final summit in Paris in November 1990. The CSCE could not give the new democracies the assurance of security which they wanted: they continued to hanker after some sort of association agreement with NATO.

But the CSCE did have three important advantages. First, it involved both the Americans and the Soviet Union in Europe's future. Europe could never be stable without an American presence and commitment. Second, the CSCE was well suited to be the forum for any discussions of border disputes, although it would not be able to go beyond conciliation to enforcement. (Enforcement should be a matter for NATO, the UN or if necessary one or more countries under the inevitable lead of the United States.) Third, I envisaged that, building on the human rights content of the Helsinki principles, we should add the complementary principles of private property and free markets. We should use the CSCE summit in November to create the basis of a 'great alliance for democracy [stretching] from the Atlantic to the Urals and beyond' – as I described it in my speech to the Anglo-German Königswinter Conference in Cambridge in March.

I returned to the theme in my speech at Aspen, Colorado on Sunday 5 August. At Aspen I set out what I described as the 'fundamental tenets of true democracy'. These were not just related to suffrage: I pointed out that Britain was free long before a majority of the population had the vote. Democracy, I contended, required the limitation of the powers of government, a market economy, private property – and the sense of personal responsibility without which no such system could be sustained. I called for the CSCE summit to agree on what I called a 'European Magna Carta' which would enshrine all these basic rights, including the right to maintain one's nationhood. I urged closer association between east and west Europe. I also called for the Soviet Union to be brought into the western economic system. (These ideas were the basis of the Charter of Paris which I signed the morning after I learned that I had failed to secure the size of majority I needed in the first round of the Conservative Party leadership election.)

THE SOVIET UNION – 1989–90

Throughout my last year in office doubts were increasingly raised about the wisdom of supporting Mr Gorbachev in his reforms. But I continued to do so and have no regrets. First, I am not by instinct someone who throws over those I like and have shown themselves my friends simply because their fortunes change. And though this may have immediate disadvantages, in my experience it increases the respect in which one is held by those with whom one has to do business: respect is a powerful asset, as those in politics who fail to inspire it might secretly agree. But second, and more important, it did not seem to me that at the time anyone was better able than Mr Gorbachev to push ahead with reform. I wanted to see the fall of communism – indeed I wanted to see it not just in eastern Europe and the Soviet Union but in every corner of the globe – but I wanted to see this achieved peacefully. The two obvious threats to peace were a takeover – covert or overt – by hardliners in the Soviet military or the violent break-up of the Soviet Union. Throughout the summer of 1990 there were disturbing reports of possible rebellious activities within the Soviet military. Their authenticity was never certain but they carried some credibility. But it was the nationalities question – that is the future of the Soviet Union itself – which was most difficult for outsiders to assess.

I now believe that all of us in the West overestimated the degree to which a Soviet Empire whose core was provided by Marxist ideology and a communist *nomenklatura* – an empire constructed and bound together by force – could survive the onset of political liberty. Perhaps we listened too much to the diplomats and western experts and too little to the emigrés. That said, I did not go along with much of the thinking which characterized the British Foreign Office and US State Department on the issue of nationalities or nationhood.

We were all quite clear, as it happens, about the special legal status of the Baltic States: it was not a question of whether but of when they must be allowed to go free. (I had a long-standing interest in their future, having voted in 1967 against an agreement between the then Labour Government and the Soviet Union to use the Baltic States' gold reserves – frozen in the Bank of England since the Soviets invaded them in 1940 – to settle outstanding financial claims.) I warned the Soviets about the severe consequences of the use of force against the Baltic States when I saw Mr Gorbachev in June. But I urged the greatest caution on President Landsbergis (of Lithuania) when I saw him in London in November. And I pressed both sides to negotiate throughout – though only on the clear understanding that the final destination of the Baltic States was freedom.

The case of the other republics was less clear cut. Ukraine and Byelorussia – by an ill-judged concession to Stalin in 1945 – were actually members of the United Nations so they could perhaps claim a somewhat different status too. I did not share the apparently hard-headed but in fact economically illiterate view that a state had to have a certain population, or GDP, or range of natural resources to be 'viable': it was the spirit of the people and the general economic framework created in order to harness it which would determine such matters. Nor, in general, was I happy with the argument that it was for us in the West to determine the future shape – or even existence – of the USSR. Our duty lay in thinking about the consequences of future developments there upon our own security. And it was this last consideration which led me to go very cautiously. It is one thing to expect a military super-power – even a sickly one like the Soviet Union – to change its internal and external policies in order to survive: it is quite another to expect it peacefully to commit hara-kiri. When I was in Paris in November for the CSCE summit at a lunch for heads of government I had been saying to President Iliescu of Romania that in working out a negotiating position you must always be clear on the stopping point – the point you would never concede. Mr Gorbachev, who had been listening, leant across the table and said that he agreed: his stopping point was the external perimeter of the Soviet Union. I did not accept this – and, as I have mentioned, had challenged the same view when relayed by M. Delors in Rome* – but I took it seriously all the same.

The whole question of the future of the republics within the Soviet Union had by 1990 become the main source of controversy in Soviet political affairs. It was one of the subjects I had discussed with Mr Gorbachev on my stop-over visit in Moscow the previous September. He had just held a plenum on the nationalities question. There had also been some significant changes in the Politburo. The long-time communist leader in Ukraine, Mr Shcherbitsky, had left its ranks. Mr Pugo, previously the Latvian Party Chief – and one of the future coup leaders of 1991 – had been promoted to candidate membership of the Politburo. Mr Kryuchkov, Chairman of the KGB – also a coup leader – had been promoted to full membership. Mr Ryzhkov, with whom Mr Gorbachev was on close personal terms but who was quite out of his depth in dealing with the economy, remained as Prime Minister. Over lunch in the Kremlin Mr Gorbachev had recalled how General de Gaulle had once complained about the difficulties of ruling a country which had 200 cheeses: how much more difficult it was to rule one with 120 nationalities. 'Especially when there is a shortage of cheese,' chipped in Mr Albakin, the Deputy Prime Minister. And

* See p. 767.

indeed frustrations at the failure of economic reform were increasingly expressed in national dissent as the months went by.

The emergence of Boris Yeltsin as a radical proponent of reform – both political and economic – ought perhaps to have strengthened Mr Gorbachev's position. If the two of them had been able to sink their differences and if Mr Gorbachev had been prepared to cut his links with the Communist Party perhaps the impetus of reform might have been renewed. But these were two 'ifs' too many. Their relations remained bad and Mr Gorbachev remained a communist to the end.

There was a strong tendency in western circles to write off Mr Yeltsin as nothing more than a buffoon. I could not believe that this judgement – if such it can be called – was correct. But I wanted to see for myself. Consequently, although I was careful to notify Mr Gorbachev in advance and to make it clear that I was receiving Mr Yeltsin in the way that I would a Leader of the Opposition, I enthusiastically agreed to meet him when he came to London on the morning of Friday 27 April 1990. The briefing I had received about Mr Yeltsin sums up the attitude which was then prevalent. In this he was described as 'a controversial figure' because he had been the only member of the Party Central Committee to vote against the Draft Platform, arguing that it was the Communist Party's long monopoly of power which had brought the USSR to its present crisis and driven tens of millions into poverty. He had said that democratic centralism should be rejected and replaced by genuine democracy and had called for a law on parties ending the Communist Party's special status. Three cheers, I thought. My briefing went on to say – with less than complete perspicacity – that 'some pundits even suggest that if [Mr Yeltsin] is elected as President of the Russian Federation he may end up with a more important job than Gorbachev's presidency of a crumbling Union. This is an exaggeration.'

I only spoke with Mr Yeltsin for three-quarters of an hour. At first I was not quite sure what to make of him. He was far more my idea of the typical Russian than was Mr Gorbachev – tall, burly, square Slavic face and shock of white hair. He was self-confident without being self-assertive, courteous, with a smile full of good humour and a touch of self-mockery. But what impressed me most was that he had obviously thought through some of the fundamental problems much more clearly than had Mr Gorbachev. I began by saying that I supported Mr Gorbachev and wanted that to be clear from the outset. Mr Yeltsin replied that he knew I supported the Soviet leader and *perestroika* and on some of these matters our opinions differed, but basically he too supported Mr Gorbachev and the cause of reform.

Mr Gorbachev should, though, have paid more attention to some of the things being said by the supporters of reform three or four years earlier. *Perestroika* had originally been intended to make communism more efficient. But that was impossible. The only serious option was for far-reaching political and economic reform, including the introduction of a market economy. But it was all getting very late.

I totally agreed with this. What struck me was that Mr Yeltsin, unlike President Gorbachev, had escaped from the communist mindset and language. He it was who also first alerted me to the relationship between economic reform and the question of what powers should be devolved to the individual republics. He explained just how little autonomy the governments of the republics really had. They were essentially agents – though frequently incompetent and corrupt agents – of central decisions. He said that they must now be given proper budgets and the power to decide how to spend them. Each republic should have its own laws and constitution. He argued that it was the failure to grapple with the issue of decentralization which had led to the present troubles. With so vast a country it was simply not possible to run everything from the centre. As a result of this discussion I looked not just at Boris Yeltsin but at the fundamental problems of the Soviet Union in a new light. When I reported later in Bermuda to President Bush on my favourable impressions of Mr Yeltsin he made it clear that the Americans did not share them. This was a serious mistake.

VISIT TO THE SOVIET UNION, JUNE 1990

On my visit to the Soviet Union in June 1990 I was to encounter all the different elements which constituted Soviet politics at this time – not just President Gorbachev, but also more radical reformers, nationalists and those who posed the greatest potential threat to reform, that is the military. I flew into Moscow on the night of Thursday 7 June to be met by Prime Minister Ryzhkov. The following morning I met the reforming Mayor of Moscow, Mr Gavriil Popov. I had never met a Russian like Mr Popov. He was the complete opposite of the staid Soviet bureaucrat – informal, slightly scruffy and (as I was subsequently told) probably wearing a tie for the very first time, in honour of my visit.

I found him a devotee of Milton Friedman and the Chicago School of Economics. He had grasped the crucial point that you could not create a market economy in Moscow – or anywhere else for that matter – without both private property and a clear framework of law. It was the fact that the distribution of property was lagging far behind the other reforms which he saw as at the root of the current political turmoil. So he wanted people to be encouraged to own their own flats and shops and he wanted the service industries to be transferred to private ownership.

I went on to talks and a working lunch with President Gorbachev. I found him rather less ebullient than usual but equable and good-humoured. I took the opportunity to tell him that I continued to believe passionately in what he was trying to achieve in the Soviet Union. Many commentators and journalists had become blasé about how much had already changed. I assured him that he would have my full support both privately and publicly. As regards the changes which were taking place in central and eastern Europe, I tried to convince him that it was in the Soviet Union's own interests that a unified Germany should be part of NATO, because otherwise there would be no justification for the presence of US forces in Europe. It was this presence which was the crucial condition for European peace and stability. I also described to him my ideas about the development of the CSCE. Slightly to my surprise, I noted that at no stage did he say that a united Germany in NATO was unacceptable; so I felt on this matter at least I was making progress. The only significant differences between us were over Lithuania – as I have mentioned earlier – and my decision to raise with him the evidence which we had gleaned that the Soviet Union was doing research into biological weapons – something which he emphatically denied, but nonetheless promised to investigate.

That afternoon I had an hour's discussion with the Soviet military leadership. I had decided that I wanted to see how they were thinking and also let them know precisely what my own views were. Marshal Yazov, the Soviet Defence minister, was very much in charge and the others – including Marshal Moiseev, whose interventions and demeanour marked him out as someone of unusual intelligence and strength of character, only spoke when the Defence minister had nothing to say. This was a pity because what Marshal Yazov did say was conventional and predictable. I quickly turned the conversation to the subject of East-West relations. I said that it was good that we were entering a new period of better relations but that we should each of us understand the need for strong defence. There was scope for reducing conventional forces and nuclear weapons and for modifying our strategy to new circumstances. But we would continue to need some nuclear weapons which were the only effective deterrent. Marshal Yazov took up the line that I had heard so many times from the Soviets before about the need to do away with nuclear weapons altogether. I said that I took leave to doubt whether the views of Marshal Yazov and his colleagues on nuclear weapons were really very different from mine. After all, they did have an awful lot of them and presumably for some purpose. Unlike President Gorbachev, Marshal Yazov stated that the Soviets would simply not accept a united Germany in NATO. But whether this was because his views were genuinely different from the Soviet leadership or because he expressed them less subtly I could not fathom.

The following morning I flew to Kiev. My main purpose was to attend the 'British Days' Exhibition which was the return leg of an exchange which had opened with a 'Soviet Month' in Birmingham in 1988. When the idea of my going had first been mooted I had made enquiries with the Foreign Office about how much was being spent on the exhibition and – as usual – found that it had been subject to some penny pinching. Partly as a result of my pressure, the Kiev Exhibition turned out to be very good indeed. The intention was to portray a typical street in a typical British northern town showing shops and, in particular, the house of an ordinary working-class British family. When the local people looked around at the hi-fi and other domestic gadgets and luxuries and the car standing in the garage at first they could not believe their eyes. As I went round, they asked me whether this could really be true; did ordinary British people really live like this? I said that indeed they did. Well, came the reply, all we have been told was a lie and this proves it. In fact, everything in that house was typical, even down to the teenager's bedroom which – like most teenagers' bedrooms – had clothes and other possessions strewn about it. My immediate reaction was that it should all have been tidied up, but I was eventually persuaded that this was more authentic.

But if the Ukrainians had not been prepared for what life was like in Britain, I found that I had not been properly briefed on the situation in Ukraine. Everywhere I went I found blue and yellow bunting and flags (the colours of pre-Soviet Ukraine) and signs demanding Ukrainian independence. This put me into something of a quandary. Much as I admired General de Gaulle, I was not going to outrage my Soviet hosts by proclaiming the Ukrainian equivalent of 'Vive le Quebec Libre'. It was not just that I was convinced that Mr Gorbachev was never going to let Ukraine out of the Soviet Union without a struggle. That not just the USSR but even Russia would be threatened by the emergence of a separate Ukraine was a view that non-communist Russians as well as communists held. (In fact, since the break-up of the USSR, the emergence of an independent Ukraine has proved to be strategically advantageous for Europe and the West and much still rides on its economic and political stability and success.)

Any hope that I could avoid saying something which would be misinterpreted by one side or the other quickly evaporated. The recently appointed First Secretary of the Ukrainian Communist Party, Mr Ivashko, said that it was a pity that I had made no time in my schedule to meet members of the newly elected Ukrainian Supreme Soviet. Would I be prepared to do so? I agreed. I imagined that this would be a modest and informal reception. I entered the Parliament building and then went through the door into the Chamber to find, to my horror, that the whole hemi-cycle was full. I had no prepared speech and it was clear that they were expecting one. I thought that at least I would be able to think up something to say while I was being introduced. But Mr Ivashko simply welcomed me and then asked me to speak. I managed well enough, as I always do. But then came questions. One of the questioners told me that there were ten deputies present who used to be political prisoners. He said that he knew that it was due to my efforts and the efforts of President Reagan that he was there as a deputy able to see me today and not still a prisoner. But what I could not do was to agree to set up an embassy in Kiev; nor could I put Ukraine in the same category as the Baltic States. I felt that I disappointed them. But I went away understanding just how fundamental the whole problem of nationality was becoming and doubtful about whether the Soviet Union could – or should – ultimately be kept together.

The final leg of my visit to the USSR was Leninakan in Armenia, where I was to open a school built with British aid after the earthquake of 1988. It was another politically sensitive occasion for there had been fierce fighting between Armenia and Azerbaijan over the enclave of Nagorno-Karabakh and the Soviets were very jittery about security. The school itself was one of the few buildings which had been reconstructed: the general Soviet performance of rebuilding the area had been lamentable. I found myself engulfed in huge, enthusiastic crowds – to such an extent, indeed, that I was turned back by the security people from my original route. Though I had to cut short my visit I came away with no more doubt than in the Ukraine of the immense national fervour of the people around me.

VISIT TO CZECHOSLOVAKIA AND HUNGARY IN SEPTEMBER 1990

I shall always be glad that I was able to visit two former communist countries while I was still Prime Minister. In Czechoslovakia and Hungary in September 1990 I found myself speaking with people who not long before had been totally excluded from power by the communists and who were coming to grips with the communist legacy of economic failure, pollution and despondency.

I had been greatly impressed by the inaugural speech of President Havel of Czechoslovakia. He had spoken of 'living in a decayed moral environment . . . [in which] notions such as love, friendship, compassion, humility and forgiveness have lost their depth and dimension'. He had described the demoralization which communism brought about, how 'the previous regime, armed with its arrogant and intolerant ideology, demeaned man into a production force and nature into a production tool. In this way they attacked their very essence and the mutual relationship between them.'

Czechoslovakia was lucky to have President Havel as an inspiration, but no less lucky to have Václav Klaus as a dynamic, convinced free enterprise economist for its Finance minister (now Czech Prime Minister). Together they were rebuilding the social and economic foundations of the country. Apart from the obvious problems which confronted them, there was also the tension between the Czech and Slovak elements of the Federal Republic. I spent most of my time in Prague – a city which I did not know but where all my surroundings reminded me that I was genuinely at the heart of Europe. But I also visited Bratislava, whose economy and built environment bore many more scars of communist vandalism. The Slovakian Prime Minister, Mr Meciar, assured me that Czechoslovakia would remain a federal state and this seemed to me sensible until more economic progress had been made. But it was not to be.

Back in Prague I had discussions with President Havel. I had met him before when he came to Britain and though his politics were to the left of mine it was impossible to avoid liking and admiring him. He for his part shared my views about the need to have the eastern European countries in the Community as soon as that was practically possible. He also liked my ideas about a European Magna Carta and the development of the CSCE. I felt that he would be an ally in the course on which I had embarked in Europe.

Then I went on to Hungary. Among the eastern European countries Hungary had three important advantages. First, substantial economic and a large amount of political reform had occurred under the previous communist regime. So the transition was less difficult and painful. Second, in Jozsef Antall, the Hungarian Prime Minister, the country was in the safe hands of a genuine Conservative. I had met Mr Antall on several previous occasions and he and I shared very much the same political approach. Third, the Hungarians had held together their governing coalition rather than splitting up in divisions on minor points. Mr Antall had the skills and was quickly developing the authority to give Hungary the leadership and continuity it needed.

Yet the task of economic reform was still daunting. The Hungarians were tackling the key questions relating to property – both the ownership of land, which exiles and their families wanted back, and the privatization of industry. There was also a wider strategic issue. Even more than Czechoslovakia and Poland, the Hungarians were keen to break free once and for all from Soviet influence. Mr Antall had announced that Hungary would leave the Warsaw Pact and wanted closer relations with NATO or at least the Western European Union (WEU). Poland and Czechoslovakia were toying with the same idea. He assured me that the Warsaw Pact was indeed on its last legs. When it finally expired I favoured a special associate membership of NATO being offered to the eastern Europeans.

Another problem which the Hungarians, Czechs and Poles faced was that their security services were deeply penetrated by the KGB and this was a major obstacle to their taking a full role in intelligence co-operation with the West. In Czechoslovakia the Government had expelled Communist Party members from the old Intelligence Service altogether. My discussion with Mr Antall in his office in the Parliament building – which I was delighted now to see used for its intended purpose, unlike the time of my visit in 1984 – illustrated just how careful they had to be. At one point he pointed across to a statue presented to his liberal communist predecessor, Mr Nemeth, by the Soviet Prime Minister, Mr Ryzhkov. Apparently, on close examination it had turned out to be bugged. I said that I hoped it was still being monitored. On further inspection it seemed so ugly that I suggested he throw it away altogether. If only disposing of the rest of communism's legacy were so easy.

RESHAPING NATO

However fascinated I was by events in the Soviet Union and eastern Europe, I could not forget that the strength and security of the West ultimately depended upon the Anglo-American relationship. For reasons I have explained – partly personal chemistry and partly genuine differences of policy – that relationship had become somewhat strained. I regarded it, therefore, as essential that the talks I was due to have with President Bush in Bermuda in April 1990 should be a success. This would be as much a matter of tone as substance. Generally speaking, I now waited for the President to set out his views before explaining mine. In Bermuda we deliberately sought to create the kind of relaxed atmosphere which I now knew he preferred. It was almost a 'family' affair and concluded with the President and Denis playing eighteen holes of golf in the pouring rain – a very British occasion.

It was the future of NATO and decisions about the defence of Europe which were in the forefront of my and the President's minds. I sought to leave him in no doubt about my strong commitment to NATO which my earlier telephone conversation about the CSCE and the reasons for retaining the Warsaw Pact had apparently somewhat scrambled. The President was keen to have an early NATO summit. So, it seemed, was the NATO Secretary-General, Dr Woerner. I would have preferred one in the autumn in order to allow for more preparation. But it was clear that the President wanted a June summit and would like Britain to host it. (In fact it took place in early July.) He had also concluded that Congress was going to withhold funds for the development of a Follow-On to LANCE. He therefore wanted to announce its cancellation. I accepted that there was very little which could be done about this, but I thought it crucial to secure firm assurances about the future stationing of nuclear weapons in Germany, in particular TASM. The real question was how we were most likely to achieve this. In fact, this approach turned out to be a key to the Americans' thinking in the run-up to the NATO summit. Their aim was to make it a public relations success, so that we could win German support for SNF and Soviet acceptance that Germany should remain in NATO. When I got back to London I set in hand the arrangements for us to host a NATO summit. There was only one complication, which was that a meeting of the North Atlantic Council – that is NATO Foreign ministers – was scheduled for June at Turnberry, a few miles south of Ayr on the west coast of Scotland. I wanted this to go ahead because it was where the more significant decisions were likely to be made about how NATO's forces might be reshaped.

Not for the first time, I found myself at odds with the Americans and indeed with the NATO Secretary-General about how we should approach the NATO summit. The Americans were keen to announce a range of initiatives, proposing deep cuts in conventional forces and still deeper cuts in the nuclear stockpile. Messages flew back and forth between me and President Bush and some of the more eye-catching and less considered proposals were dropped. Not that I disagreed with everything the Americans wanted from the summit. In particular, I was strongly in favour of Jim Baker's ideas about strengthening political consultation, as opposed to just military planning, as one of the functions of NATO. I believed – as did the Americans – that the importance of NATO as a means of avoiding friction between America and Europe was greater than ever.

What I was unhappy about was the American proposal formally to change in the communiqué the traditional NATO strategy of flexible response. They were insistent on the insertion of the phrase that nuclear weapons were 'weapons of last resort'. This, I felt, would undermine the credibility of NATO's SNF. We should continue to resist any qualification of the role of nuclear weapons in NATO, just as we had always done. We were slipping towards – though we had not reached – that fatal position of undertaking that there would be 'no first use of nuclear weapons', on which Soviet propaganda had always insisted. Such an undertaking would leave our conventional forces vulnerable to attack by their superior numbers. In the end the first phrase did appear hedged around in the following form:

> Finally, with the total withdrawal of Soviet-stationed forces and the implementation of a CFE Agreement, the allies concerned can reduce their reliance on nuclear weapons. These will continue to fulfil an essential role in the overall strategy of the alliance to prevent war by ensuring that there are no circumstances in which nuclear retaliation in response to military action might be discounted. However, in the transformed Europe, they will be able to adopt *a new NATO strategy making nuclear forces truly weapons of last resort.* [my italics]

I cannot say that I was satisfied with this unwieldy compromise. But in the end military strategy is not dependent upon pieces of paper but on the commitment of resources to practical military objectives. The review which was begun at Turnberry and which in Britain's case would be put into effect through the 'Options for Change' exercise that Tom King conducted as Defence Secretary had to concentrate on where the priorities for inevitably decreased expenditure would now be.

A month before the NATO summit I set out in my speech to the North Atlantic Council my own views on the matter. The stress I placed on preservation of the United States' military presence in Europe and the continuing role of updated nuclear weapons would not have surprised my audience. But I also emphasized that NATO must consider an 'out of area' role. I asked the question:

> Ought NATO to give more thought to possible threats to our security from other directions? There is no guarantee that threats to our security will stop at some imaginary line across the mid-Atlantic. It is not long since some of us had to go to the Arabian Gulf to keep oil supplies flowing. We shall become very heavily dependent on Middle Eastern oil once again in the next century. With the spread of sophisticated weapons and military technology to areas like the Middle East, potential threats to NATO territory may originate more from outside Europe. Against that background, it would be only prudent for NATO countries to retain a capacity to carry out multiple roles, with more flexible and versatile forces.

This passage reflected my thinking over a number of years. I had seen for myself how important a western presence could be in securing western interests in far-flung areas of the world, not least the Middle East. I did not believe that even if the military threat from the Soviets had diminished, that from other dictators would not arise. But of course I could not know that within two months we would be confronted by an explosive crisis in the Gulf.

REFLECTIONS

As I look back on the international developments of the late 1980s, they seem to be overwhelmingly positive. Communism was defeated, freedom restored to the former satellites, the cruel division of Europe ended, the Soviet Union launched onto the path of reform, democracy and national rights and the West, in particular the United States, left in possession of the field as its political values and economic system were embraced both by its former adversaries and, increasingly, by the countries of the Third World.

The credit for these historic achievements must go principally to the United States and in particular to President Reagan, whose policies of military and economic competition with the Soviet Union forced the Soviet leaders, in particular Mr Gorbachev, to abandon their ambitions of hegemony and to embark on the process of reform which in the end brought the entire communist system crashing down. But this would never have been accomplished without the long and courageous resistance of the peoples of the Soviet Union and central and eastern Europe. We will never know the names of all who suffered and perished in that struggle but we can celebrate their leaders from Vladimir Bukovsky to Václav Havel, from Alexander Solzhenitsyn to Cardinal Mindszenty, and the four young heroes who gave their lives defending the Russian White House in the last dying days of the old regime.

As that old order crumbled and its people emerged blinking into the light, President Bush managed the dangerous and volatile transformation with great diplomatic skill. Nor should credit be withheld from the steadfast European allies of America who resisted both Soviet pressure and Soviet blandishments to maintain a strong western defence: in particular, Helmut Schmidt, Helmut Kohl, François Mitterrand and . . . but modesty forbids.

The world is a better place. But in some ways it is an old-fashioned place. The Europe that has emerged from behind the Iron Curtain has many of the features of the Europes of 1914 and 1939: ethnic strife, contested borders, political extremism, nationalist passions and economic backwardness. And there is another familiar bogey from the past – the German Question.

If there is one instance in which a foreign policy I pursued met with unambiguous failure, it was my policy on German reunification. This policy was to encourage democracy in East Germany while slowing down the country's reunification with West Germany. With the first half of that policy no one disagrees. Nor at the time did everyone disagree with the second, to which indeed frequent lip service was paid. Most observers were unaware of the nationalist passion for German unity that burned in the East. Indeed, even the dissident leaders of the East German demonstrations that led to freedom were themselves unaware of it, being in favour of a free, reformed, independent East Germany, rather than a larger Federal Republic. And Germany's neighbours all hoped to avoid this latter outcome because they saw it as destabilizing an already unsettled continent.

In the event, the desire for unity among Germans on both sides of the Elbe proved irresistible. So the policy failed.

But was the policy wrong? That is a more complex question requiring a more nuanced reply. Look first at the consequences of the rapid reunification as they worked themselves out. West Germany's absorption of its next-door relation has been economically disastrous, and that disaster has spread to the rest of the European Community via the Bundesbank's high interest rates and the ERM. We have all paid the price in unemployment and recession. East German political immaturity has affected the whole country in the form of a revived (though containable) neo-Nazi and xenophobic extremism. Internationally, it has created a German state so large and dominant that it cannot be easily fitted into the new architecture of Europe.

Look also at the incidental benefits that the policy brought about. It forced the German Government to clarify the border question with its eastern neighbours. More generally, it provided the occasion whereby the CSCE framework was established to ensure that existing borders would not be changed by unilateral action or without general agreement. It strengthened the relationship between Britain and the other countries of central and eastern Europe who now, to some extent, see us as attentive guardians of their interests. But the fundamental argument for slowing German reunification was to create a breathing space in which a new architecture of Europe could be devised where a united Germany would not be a destabilizing influence/over-mighty subject/bull in a china shop. Arriving prematurely as it did, a united Germany has tended to encourage three unwelcome developments: the rush to European federalism as a way of tying down Gulliver; the maintenance of a Franco-German bloc for the same purpose; and the gradual withdrawal of the US from Europe on the assumption that a German-led federal Europe will be both stable and capable of looking after its own defence.

I will not reiterate here all the reasons I have given earlier for believing these developments to be damaging. But I will hazard the forecast that a federal Europe would be both unstable internally and an obstacle to harmonious arrangements – in trade, politics and defence – with America externally; that the Franco-German bloc would increasingly mean a German bloc (in economics, a deutschmark bloc) with France as very much a junior partner; and that as a result America would, first bring its legions home, and subsequently find itself at odds with the new European player in world politics.

These developments are not inevitable. One revelation that emerged from the failure of Britain's German policy was the evident anxiety of France in relation to German power and ambition. It should not be beyond the capacity of a future British prime minister to rebuild an Anglo-French entente as a counter-balance to German influence. Nor, as part of this policy, to shift the emphasis in Europe back towards the original Gaullist idea of a *Europe des Patries*. What these new approaches will require, however, is a recognition from the French political élite that any stable European balance of power will require the more or less permanent presence of the United States in Europe. And that is a recognition that so far French presidents have been prepared to grant only in private.

CHAPTER XXVII

No Time to Go Wobbly

The response to Iraq's invasion of Kuwait in 1990

EVENTS AT ASPEN

On the morning of Wednesday 1 August 1990 the VC10 left Heathrow with me and my party aboard bound for Aspen, Colorado. The President was due to open the Aspen Institute Conference on the Thursday and I was to close it on the Sunday. I had gone out early in order to be present for his speech. At the time I left I already knew that the Iraqis were sending troops down to the border with Kuwait. The negotiations between Iraq and Kuwait which had been taking place in Jeddah had broken for the day but we understood that they were to be resumed. It therefore seemed that the Iraqi military action was a case of sabre rattling. We soon learnt that it was not. At 2 a.m. Kuwaiti time on Thursday 2 August Iraq carried out a full-scale military invasion – though claiming that it was an internal coup – and assumed total control.

An hour later – early evening on Wednesday, Colorado time – Charles Powell telephoned me from his hotel to tell me the news and I decided at once to instruct two ships in Penang and Mombasa, both about a week's sailing time away, to make for the Gulf while the situation developed. We already had one ship of the Armilla patrol in the Gulf – HMS *York*, at Dubai. First thing the following morning I learnt in a note from Charles about the latest situation. Other Arab governments had evidently been caught off balance. The Arab League of Foreign Ministers meeting in Cairo had failed to agree a statement. King Hussein was trying to excuse the Iraqi action on the grounds that the Kuwaitis had been unnecessarily difficult. The ruling families in the Gulf were alarmed. With strong British support the UN Security Council had passed a resolution condemning Iraq for its action and calling for total withdrawal and immediate negotiations. Back in London, Douglas Hurd – competent professional that he was – had ordered the freezing of Kuwaiti assets in Britain, the Iraqis unfortunately having only debts. An immediate question now was whether Saddam Hussein would go over the border and seize Saudi Arabia's oil fields. (This was indeed important: but I was convinced from the start that it must not divert us from the need to get Saddam Hussein out of the territory he had *already* seized by an act of illegal aggression.)

I was staying at the guesthouse to Ambassador Henry Catto's ranch while all this was going on. I read Charles's note, listened to the news and then went for a walk to sort things out in my own mind. By the time I got back Charles and Sir Antony Acland, our ambassador, were waiting for me. We established from the White House that President Bush was still coming to Aspen and would arrive later that morning. As is my wont, I set about arguing through the whole problem with them and by the end had defined the two main points. By the time I was due to meet him at the main ranch I was quite clear what we must do.

Fortunately, the President began by asking me what I thought. I told him my conclusions in the clearest and most straightforward terms. First, aggressors must never be appeased. We learned that to our cost in the 1930s. Second, if Saddam Hussein were to cross the border into Saudi Arabia he could go right down the Gulf in a matter of days. He would then control 65 per cent of the world's oil reserves and could blackmail us all. Not only did we have to move to stop the aggression, therefore, we had to stop it quickly.

In making these two points I felt that experience as well as instinct enabled me to trust my judgement. There was, of course, the enormously valuable experience of having been Prime Minister through the Falklands War. My visits to the Gulf had also allowed me to establish bonds of trust with the rulers of many of these states, who often had closer links with Britain than with America. I understood their problems and could gauge their reactions.

President Bush listened to what I had to say. He then told me that he had been speaking to President Mubarak and King Hussein. The message he had received was that the United States should stay calm and give an Arab solution a chance. He had said that that was fine but that it must involve Iraqi withdrawal and the restoration of the lawful Government of Kuwait. He had meanwhile authorized a boycott of Iraqi goods, termination of credits and the freezing of Iraqi and Kuwaiti assets. He had also instructed ships of the American fleet to move north from the Indian Ocean into the Gulf, although they were currently being hampered by heavy seas.

We then got down to discussing what must be done next. I said that if Saddam Hussein did not withdraw, the Security Council would need to impose a full trade embargo. That, however, would only be effective if everybody implemented it. It would be necessary to close down the pipelines across both Turkey and Saudi Arabia through which Iraq exported the greater part of its oil. Those would not be easy decisions. Saudi Arabia, especially, might fear that Iraq would use such action as an excuse to attack her. We could send troops to protect Saudi Arabia; but only at the specific request of the king. (In fact, a few days later the US Defence Secretary, Dick Cheney, flew to Saudi Arabia to talk to the king about precisely this.)

At this point President Bush was told that the President of Yemen wanted to speak to him on the telephone. Before the President left to take the call, I reminded him that Yemen, a temporary member of the Security Council, had not voted on the resolution demanding the withdrawal of Iraqi forces from Kuwait. It turned out that the President of Yemen too wanted time to come up with an Arab solution. President Bush told him that such a 'solution' must involve the withdrawal of Iraqi forces and return of the proper Government of Kuwait if it was to be accepted. The President of Yemen then apparently compared what had happened in Kuwait to US intervention in Grenada at which George Bush rightly bridled. When he returned President Bush and I agreed that all this did not seem very encouraging. We then went out to give a press conference. The President was asked if he ruled out the use of force. He replied that he did not – a statement the press took to be a strengthening of his position against Saddam Hussein. But I had never found any weakness in it from the first.

By now I was receiving a flood of telegrams reporting on reactions to the invasion. The Cabinet Office assessment of Iraq's plans noted that an attack against Saudi Arabia did not seem imminent, because it would probably take a week to assemble the required forces. To my mind this reinforced rather than diminished the need for immediate tough action.

Understandably, I now had only half my mind on the programme of events which had been arranged for me. That said, I was fascinated by what I saw. Friday was a day of presentations and discussions about science, environment and defence – punctuated by news about what was happening in the crisis which now gripped the international community. I was talking to the young scientists working at the SDI National Test Facility at Falcon when I was called away to speak to

President Bush on the telephone. He gave me the good news that President Ozal of Turkey had said he would take action to cut off the Iraqi oil which was going through the Turkish pipeline. I was not surprised. In my two visits to Turkey I had been very impressed with the President's toughness. I had also been struck by the country's strategic significance. As a secular but predominantly Muslim state with a large army, looking westwards to Europe but also on the fringe of the Middle East, Turkey would be a vital bulwark against aggressive Islamic fundamentalism or other brands of revolutionary Arab nationalism like that of Saddam Hussein.

After lunch I went by helicopter to the Strategic Air Defence Monitoring Centre at Cheyenne Mountain which keeps a watch on every satellite launched. Again I felt awed by the sophistication of America's scientific and technological achievement. From within this hollowed-out mountain the United States could observe deep into space for military and scientific purposes. Two days later I was told by the general in charge of the operation that they had observed that the Soviets had now put up two satellites over the northern end of the Gulf. It was a useful indication of their concern.

On Saturday morning I spoke with President Mitterrand on the telephone. As over the Falklands, he was taking a robust position: in spite of a misconceived speech at the United Nations which tried to link a solution of the Gulf crisis with other Middle Eastern issues, President Mitterrand and France showed throughout the crisis that the French were the only European country, apart from ourselves, with the stomach for a fight.

I have already described the speech I gave on Sunday morning to the Aspen Institute.* Though it addressed broader international issues, I inserted a section on the Gulf. It read:

> Iraq's invasion of Kuwait defies every principle for which the United Nations stands. If we let it succeed, no small country can ever feel safe again. The law of the jungle would take over from the rule of law.
>
> The United Nations must assert its authority and apply a total economic embargo unless Iraq withdraws without delay. The United States and Europe both support this. But to be fully effective it will need the collective support of all the United Nations' members. They must stand up and be counted because

* See p. 800.

a vital principle is at stake: an aggressor must never be allowed to get his way.

My mind was now turning to the next practical steps we could take to exert pressure on Iraq. The European Community countries had agreed to support a complete economic and trade embargo of Iraq. But it was the Iraqi oil exports and the willingness of Turkey and Saudi Arabia to block them which would be crucial. The Americans had some lingering doubts about whether Turkey and Saudi Arabia would act. I was more confident. But these doubts increased the importance of enforcing all other measures still more effectively. I instructed the Foreign Office to prepare plans to implement a naval blockade in the north-east Mediterranean, the Red Sea and the north of the Gulf to intercept shipments of Iraqi and Kuwaiti oil. I also asked that more thought be given to precise military guarantees for Saudi Arabia and for details of what aircraft we could send to the Gulf area immediately.

I had planned to take a few days' holiday with my family after the Aspen speech, but after an invitation from the White House decided instead to fly to Washington and resume my talks with the President. For all the friendship and co-operation I had had from President Reagan, I was never taken into the Americans' confidence more than I was during the two hours or so I spent that afternoon at the White House. The meeting began in a very restricted session with just the President, Brent Scowcroft, myself and Charles Powell. Half an hour later we were joined by Dan Quayle, Jim Baker and John Sununu. The last twenty minutes of discussion was attended by the Secretary-General of NATO.

The President that day was an altogether more confident George Bush than the man with whom I had had earlier dealings. He was firm, cool, showing the decisive qualities which the Commander-in-Chief of the greatest world power must possess. Any hesitation fell away. I had always liked George Bush. Now my respect for him soared.

The President began by reporting what was known about the situation and US plans to deal with it. Saddam Hussein had sworn that if American forces moved into Saudi Arabia he would liberate the kingdom from the Saudi royal family. There were now clear photographs – which the President passed around to us – showing that Iraqi tanks had moved right up to the border with Saudi Arabia. I said that it was vital to bolster the Saudis. The main danger was that Iraq would attack Saudi Arabia before the king formally asked the United States for help.

In fact, part of the way through our discussions, Dick Cheney telephoned the President from Saudi Arabia. He reported that King Fahd was fully behind the United States plan to move the 82nd Airborne Division together with forty-eight F-15 fighters to Saudi Arabia. The king's only condition was that there should be no announcement until the forces were actually in place. This was excellent news. But how would we be able to conceal all this from the world media and the Iraqis who, if they knew about it, might well decide to go into Saudi Arabia at once? In fact, we were helped by the fact that all eyes were on the United Nations which was discussing Security Council Resolution 661, that imposed a ban on trade with Iraq and Kuwait, though making no explicit provision for its enforcement. American aircraft were eight hours into flight by the time the press discovered they had left.

This meeting also saw the beginning of an almost interminable argument between the Americans – particularly Jim Baker – and me about whether and in what form United Nations authority was needed for measures against Saddam Hussein. I felt that the Security Council Resolution which had already been passed, combined with our ability to invoke Article 51 of the UN Charter on self-defence, was sufficient. Although I did not spell this out on the present occasion – there were too many other pressing matters to decide – my attitude, which had been reinforced as a result of our difficulties with the UN over the Falklands, was based on two considerations. First, there was no certainty that the wording of a resolution, which was always open to amendment, would finish up by being satisfactory. If not, it might tie our hands unacceptably. Of course, with the end of the Cold War the Soviet Union was likely to be more co-operative. Communist China, fearful of isolation, was also disinclined to create too many problems. But the fact remained that if one could achieve an objective without UN authority there was no point in running the risks attached to seeking it.

Second, although I am a strong believer in international law, I did not like unnecessary resort to the UN, because it suggested that sovereign states lacked the moral authority to act on their own behalf. If it became accepted that force could only be used – even in self-defence – when the United Nations approved, neither Britain's interests nor those of international justice and order would be served. The UN was a useful – for some matters vital – forum. But it was hardly the nucleus of a new world order. And there was still no substitute for the leadership of the United States.

The discussion between President Bush and myself in Washington continued. I emphasized the importance of preparing to respond to any Iraqi use of chemical weapons. I also stressed that we should fight the propaganda war with vigour. This was a defensive action by the West to preserve Saudi Arabia's integrity and anything which complicated or obscured that must be avoided. So, for example, we had to do everything to keep the Israelis out of the conflict. I also promised to use my contacts with Middle Eastern rulers to try to increase support for American action in defence of Saudi Arabia and to heighten the pressure on Iraq.

I returned to London on the Tuesday. The following day I had an hour's telephone conversation with King Fahd to receive his formal request for our own 'planes and (if necessary) armed forces to be stationed in Saudi Arabia. He expressed incredulity that King Hussein should have sided with Saddam Hussein, whose party had murdered King Hussein's relatives. But King Fahd was as strong as ever in his determination to stand up against aggression.

Later that day I also had the sad duty of attending Ian Gow's funeral. One of my most loyal and candid advisers, there were to be many times when I missed his shrewd counsel and his deadpan wit.

THE BUILD-UP TO WAR

I was not allowed by the Conservative Party to see through the campaign to throw Saddam Hussein out of Kuwait. But in the months which now followed – and in spite of the other difficulties I faced – my attention was rarely away from the Gulf for long. I set up a small Cabinet sub-committee – Douglas Hurd (Foreign Secretary), Tom King (Defence Secretary), John Wakeham (Energy Secretary), Patrick Mayhew (Attorney-General), William Waldegrave (Minister of State at the Foreign Office), Archie Hamilton (Minister of State for the Armed Forces) and the Chief of the Defence Staff. It was this group, which met regularly, rather than the wider Cabinet Committee OD, which took the main decisions.

One of our first tasks was to provide the promised support for Saudi Arabia. On Thursday 9 August Tom King announced the despatch of two squadrons of aircraft – one made up of Tornado F3 air defence fighters and the other of Jaguar ground attack 'planes, 24 aircraft in all. They were in place and operational two days later. Nimrod maritime reconnaissance and VC10 tanker aircraft were also sent. We reinforced them at the end of August with a further squadron of Tornados – but this time the GR1 ground-attack version – which were sent to Bahrain to provide a day-and-night anti-armour capability. Rapier air defence detachments were deployed in support.

Of course, I kept in frequent touch with President Bush over the telephone. I ensured that he was abreast of the military dispositions we were making and that we responded to American requests. We also regularly discussed the latest information about Saddam Hussein's intentions. The general view seemed to be that whatever he had originally planned, he would not attack Saudi Arabia, once American forces were there. But it seemed to me that the important lesson for us was that Saddam Hussein was simply not predictable. As I put it in a minute to the Ministry of Defence on Sunday 12 August:

> We thought that Iraq would not move into Kuwait, although their forces were massing on the border. Let us not make the same mistake again. They may move into Saudi Arabia. We must be ready.

These were weeks of vigorous telephone diplomacy. I encouraged Turkey in its steadfast opposition to Iraq. The Turkish economy was badly hit because – unlike Jordan – Turkey was applying UN sanctions effectively. I spoke to President Ozal about this over the telephone on Friday 24 August. He commiserated with me about what he described as Saddam Hussein's disgraceful exploitation of British hostages on television. He thought that this exhibition had in fact worked against him and shown what sort of person he really was. I never failed to remind the Saudis and the governments of the Gulf States how much they owed to Turkey and urged them to offer generous financial compensation.

A less savoury ally against Saddam Hussein was Syria, with which we still had no formal diplomatic relations. I disliked the regime and had no illusion about its continued willingness to employ terrorism and violence if they suited its purposes. But the fact remained that the rivalry between Syria and Iraq gave us an opportunity which must not be missed. Moreover, it made no sense to have our forces fighting alongside the Syrians if we still had no diplomatic channels for discussion. Reluctantly, therefore, I agreed to the reopening of diplomatic relations, though the formal announcement came a few days after I left office in November.

In the evening of 26 August President Bush telephoned me from Kennebunkport. I told him how pleased I was with Security Council Resolution 665 which had been passed the day before, enabling us to enforce the embargo. We must use our powers to stop Iraqi shipping. This was no time to go wobbly. Information we had gleaned from secret sources must be published to show up sanctions busting. The President agreed. I told him that the only area in which I thought we were not doing well was in the propaganda battle. We were now probably going into a longish period to see whether sanctions would work and we must not let the faint hearts grow in strength. The President was worried also about the use of the port of Aqaba in Jordan to evade sanctions and I told him that I would raise the question when I saw King Hussein in a few days' time.

In the case of Syria, my enemy's enemy had to become my friend. But I was saddened that one of Britain's most long-standing friends appeared to be siding with the enemy. I had been on the friendliest of terms with King Hussein of Jordan but there could be no question of just allowing him to continue to flout sanctions and justify the Iraqi invasion. So when he came to see me for lunch on Friday 31 August I could not conceal my feelings.

He was clearly very uneasy about the line he was taking. He began by making a forty-minute statement which yet again justified what the Iraqis had done. I said that I was amazed at his account of what was in fact a blatant act of aggression. Iraq was a country which had used chemical weapons – not just in war but against its own people. Saddam Hussein was not only an international brigand, he was also a loser who had done immense damage both to the Palestinian cause and to the Arabs and who over eight years had vainly thrown wave after wave of young Iraqis into the war against Iran. I said that the king should not be attempting to negotiate on Iraq's behalf but rather to implement sanctions against it. I could not have been more direct. But no amount of pressure was likely to alter the calculation which the king had made: that he could not come out openly against Saddam Hussein and survive.

On Thursday 6 September the House of Commons was recalled to debate the position in the Gulf. Unlike the US Congress, Parliament firmly supported the stance taken by the Government: the voting when the debate ended the following day was 437:35. I was also turning my mind to the military campaign which I believed would have to be fought. Later that same afternoon I discussed the situation with Douglas Hurd. I said that I was ever more certain that Saddam Hussein would not leave Kuwait unless he was thrown out. Douglas was more inclined to be optimistic, believing that sanctions might succeed if we could convince Saddam Hussein that he would be militarily beaten if he stayed. I agreed that sanctions must be given some more time to work. But we must not lose sight of the danger of leaving our forces too long in the desert and of the Arab and wider international front against Saddam Hussein crumbling. I did not want to see a firm deadline but we must start to look at the dates which would narrow the options for military action. I also said that we must not be under any illusion: if the sanctions against Iraq did not work, and the Americans and the Multi-National Force failed to take action, Israel would strike.

It was very difficult to know how effective the Iraqi army would be. I had some doubts about their soldiers' spirit, based on the assessment of their preference for high-level bombing and chemical weapons over infantry fighting in the war against Iran. But the Republican Guard was thought to be more formidable. The Americans were extremely cautious, wanting very large amounts of armour in the Gulf before they would be prepared to move. By contrast, some of Iraq's neighbours thought that the Iraqis would crumble quickly; and as it turned out they were proved right.

In any case, as with the Falklands, I was determined to ensure that our forces had the best possible equipment and plenty of it. The Americans wanted us to reinforce our troops in the Gulf and had suggested that we should send an armoured brigade equipped with Challenger I tanks to join the Allied Forces there. I knew that the Challenger had a good reputation for manoeuvrability, but a bad one for reliability. So on Thursday 13 September I called a meeting with Tom King, the Chief of the Defence Staff, the Chief of the General Staff and representatives of Vickers. I cross-questioned them about all the possible weaknesses. I could not forget the way in which the earlier American attempt under President Jimmy Carter to rescue the Iranian hostages had failed because the helicopters used had been unable to cope with the desert conditions. After much discussion they convinced me. But I said that they must take all the spare parts they could possibly need with them, not wait for more to be sent out, and I also insisted upon receiving a written guarantee of 80 per cent availability – several times better than Challenger had achieved in Germany.

I also wanted the commander of our forces to be someone in whom I – and they – would have complete confidence. The MoD came up with several names but only one man seemed to be right for the job – Sir Peter de la Billière. Tom King was reluctant to see him appointed: Peter de la Billière was within a week of retiring and the other candidates clearly had much to be said for them. But I wanted a fighting general. I knew the qualities of Sir Peter from his command of the

SAS operation at the time of the 1980 Iranian Embassy siege* and from the Falklands. I also knew that he spoke Arabic – of some importance when part of a large multi-national force with a crucial Arab element. So I told Tom King that Sir Peter was not retiring now if I had anything to do with it: and if he did not go to command our forces in the Gulf, he would be coming as personal adviser on the conduct of the war to Downing Street. He went to the Gulf.

I telephoned George Bush the next morning to tell him that I was about to announce the decision to send the 7th Armoured Brigade to the Gulf, comprising two armoured regiments with 120 tanks, a regiment of Field Artillery, a battalion of armoured infantry, anti-tank helicopters and all the necessary support. It would be a completely self-supporting force, numbering up to 7,500. They were the successors to the 'Desert Rats' of Alamein. The President was pleased. 'My heavens, a marvellous commitment; this is really something,' he said.

I met the President again in New York on the evening of Sunday 30 September. We were officially there to attend the 'UN Children's Summit', an occasion at which the only high point was an inspiring speech from President Havel of Czechoslovakia. President Bush was very tired, having flown back to Washington from New York to complete negotiations with Congress on the fateful 1990 budget compromise, which was to undermine him politically, before returning for this meeting. But he was in good spirits. We discussed Jim Baker's wish for another UN Security Council Resolution specifically to endorse the use of force to bring about Iraq's withdrawal from Kuwait. As always, I was dubious, preferring to rely on Article 51. But what was clear to all of us was that the time for using force was now rapidly approaching. There was no evidence that sanctions were having any real effect on Iraq's decisions – and that was what counted. I was clearer than ever in my mind that there could be no weakening in our resolve to defeat – and be seen to defeat – Saddam Hussein's aggression.

As so often over these months I found myself reliving in an only slightly different form my experiences of the build-up to the battle for the Falklands. There is never any lack of people anxious to avoid the use of force. No matter how little chance there is of negotiation succeeding – and no matter how many difficulties are created for the troops who are trying to prepare themselves for war – the case is always made for yet another piece of last-ditch diplomacy.

On this occasion it fell to Mr Yevgeny Primakov, Mr Gorbachev's special emissary on the Gulf, to make all the standard arguments. He

* See pp. 89–90.

came to see me at Chequers on the afternoon of Saturday 20 October, having just returned from Baghdad. He argued for some 'flexible linkage' between the crisis in the Gulf and the Arab-Israeli problem to save Saddam Hussein's face and to give 'some room for manoeuvre'. I said that Saddam Hussein was a dictator, that we should look at his actions rather than listen to his words, and that there could be no deals with such a man. Of course, we all had a duty to return with greater determination to resolve the Arab-Israeli problem; but that duty obtained quite independent of Saddam Hussein's invasion of Kuwait. He must not be appeased. We learned later that Mr Primakov had reported back to Moscow that Mrs Thatcher was quite the most difficult and determined of them all.

On the evening of Tuesday 23 October I had a meeting with Tom King and Douglas Hurd. The main purpose was to give guidance to the Chief of the Defence Staff at his meetings with General Colin Powell, chairman of the US Joint Chiefs of Staff, in the United States over the next two days. I began by listing our strategic objectives. These were to provide the guidelines according to which British policy in the forthcoming war should be determined. Saddam Hussein must leave Kuwait and the latter's legitimate Government must be restored. All hostages must be released. Iraq must pay compensation. Those responsible for atrocities must be brought to account before an international court. Iraq's nuclear, biological and chemical capability must be eliminated in the event of hostilities and dismantled in the event of a peaceful withdrawal of Iraqi troops. To do this the widest possible alliance of Arab governments against Iraq must be maintained and Israeli involvement must be avoided. A regional security system must be established to constrain Iraq in the future.

As for Saddam Hussein himself, it would not be a specific objective to bring about his downfall, though that might be a desirable side-effect of our actions. We must aim for a situation in which Saddam Hussein had to face his own people as a beaten leader of a beaten army. I said that further work on targets in Iraq was needed. Purely civilian targets must be avoided. But it was for consideration whether power stations and dams should be regarded as legitimate targets. There was no intention that our forces should occupy any part of Iraqi territory, but they might need to enter Iraq in hot pursuit of Iraqi forces. I said that it was necessary to get the Americans to accept that military action would in all likelihood have to be initiated before the end of the year. I also said that we must try to continue to wean them away from seeking prior authorization for the use of force from the UN and to rely instead on Article 51.

I argued this last point through with Jim Baker when he came to see me on the evening of Friday 9 November. But I was not able to sway him. He said that UN authority was crucial to sustain the support of American public opinion for military action. I also raised my worries about delaying the military option until the extra American forces now being sent had arrived in the Gulf. I said that it was vital not to miss the window of opportunity which would close in early March. He was able to reassure me on this point. But by now time was running out for me as well as for Saddam Hussein.

In response to Jim Baker's request and at my last Cabinet on Thursday 22 November – to which I announced my resignation as Prime Minister – the decision was made to double Britain's military commitment and to deploy an extra brigade to the Gulf. We would send the 4th Brigade from Germany, comprising a regiment of Challenger tanks, two armoured infantry battalions and a regiment of Royal Artillery, with reconnaissance and supporting services. Together the two brigades would form the 1st Armoured Division. The total number of UK forces committed would amount to more than 30,000.

Since the morning of Thursday 2 August hardly a day had passed without my involvement in diplomatic and military moves to isolate and defeat Iraq. One of my very few abiding regrets is that I was not there to see the issue through. The failure to disarm Saddam Hussein and to follow through the victory so that he was publicly humiliated in the eyes of his subjects and Islamic neighbours was a mistake which stemmed from the excessive emphasis placed right from the start on international consensus. The opinion of the UN counted for too much and the military objective of defeat for too little. And so Saddam Hussein was left with the standing and the means to terrorize his people and foment more trouble. In war there is much to be said for magnanimity in victory. But not before victory.

CHAPTER XXVIII

Men in Lifeboats

The background to and course of the 1990 Conservative Party leadership campaign – and resignation

BACKGROUND TO THE 1990 LEADERSHIP CAMPAIGN

In 1975 I was the first candidate for the leadership of the Conservative Party to challenge an existing leader under the rules which had been instituted by Sir Alec Douglas-Home a decade earlier. Having entered the field as a rank outsider, I won the leadership in an open contest. So I am the last person to complain about having to meet a challenge to my own leadership. But the circumstances of 1990, when Michael Heseltine challenged me, were very different. I had won three general elections and lost none, whereas Ted Heath had lost three out of four. I was a sitting prime minister of eleven and a half years in office, whereas Ted was a newly-defeated Opposition leader. The beliefs and policies which I had pioneered in Britain were helping to remould world affairs. And our country was at that moment on the verge of war in the Gulf.

Of course, democracy is no respecter of persons, as my great predecessor, Winston Churchill, learned when having led Britain through her supreme struggle against the Nazi tyranny and in the midst of negotiations crucial to the post-war world order, he was defeated in the 1945 general election. At least, however, it was the British people who dismissed him from office. I was not given the opportunity to meet the voters – and they were not able to pronounce on my final term of office, except by proxy.

The 1965 procedure for electing the Tory leader was, by unwritten convention, not intended for use when the Party was in office. Theoretically, I had to be re-elected every year; but since no one else stood, this was a formality. Ever since Michael Heseltine flounced out of the Cabinet in January 1986, however, he had kept up a constant if unavowed campaign to replace me. Inevitably, as problems mounted in late 1988 and 1989, closer attention was paid to the precise details of the system.

I have already described the growth of political discontent in the summer and autumn of 1989. Of its causes, the most important was the economy, as high interest rates had to be applied to curb the inflation which Nigel Lawson's policy of shadowing the deutschmark had generated. This aggravated what would otherwise have been more manageable problems, such as the agitation over the community charge – a running sore which would get much worse the following year. There was also a hard core of opposition to my approach to the European Community, though this was very much a minority view. And there was, of course, a range of back-benchers who for various idiosyncratic reasons, or because they had been denied or removed from office, would be happy to line up against me. There was even talk of one of them putting up for the leadership as a 'stalking horse' for the real contender, Michael Heseltine, lurking in the wings.

In fact, Sir Anthony Meyer decided to mount a challenge for reasons of his own in 1989, and there had to be a contest. Mark Lennox-Boyd, my PPS, George Younger, Ian Gow, Tristan Garel-Jones (a Foreign Office Minister of State), Richard Ryder (Economic Secretary) and Bill Shelton constituted my campaign team who quietly identified supporters, waverers and opponents. They did their job well. I did not myself campaign and no one seriously thought that I should. The results were by no means unsatisfactory. I won 314 votes, Sir Anthony Meyer 33. There were 24 spoilt ballots and 3 abstentions. But the contest had revealed, as George Younger told me, a certain amount of discontent.

Accordingly, I increased the amount of time set aside in my diary for meeting back-benchers. I made more frequent visits to that fount of gossip, the Commons tea-room. I also began regular meetings with groups of back-benchers, usually recruited according to region so as to ensure a wide spectrum of views. At these meetings, which usually took place in my room in the House, I would ask everyone around the table to speak their mind and then come in at the end to answer point by point. There was frank speaking on both sides – on one occasion a back-bencher told me it was time for me to go. I may not have complied, but I did listen.

But no amount of discussion or attention to personal sensitivities could compensate for the political situation in the summer of 1990. High community charge bills made Conservative MPs anxious about their seats. Inflation and interest rates were still high. Divisions in the

Parliamentary Party and the Government over Europe sharpened as the pace of the federalist programme accelerated. The rank and file of the Party was still with me, as they would show at the 1990 Party Conference, indeed perhaps stronger than ever in their support. But too many of my colleagues had an unspoken contempt for the party faithful whom they regarded as organization fodder with no real right to hold political opinions. And in the event, no one would seriously listen to them – though they were formally consulted and pronounced heavily in my favour – when it came for my fate to be decided.

For my part, I remained confident that we could ride out these difficulties and win the next election. High interest rates were already doing their work in bringing down inflation, whatever the headline RPI figures showed. I was only waiting for signs that the money supply was firmly under control before cutting interest rates – and continuing to cut them even if that would entail a changed parity in the ERM. At the end of April I had my first serious discussion with the Policy Unit about policies that might be in the next manifesto. And that summer I had discussions with colleagues on setting up manifesto policy groups. My Party Conference speech in October 1990 raised the curtain on just a little of this, outlining proposals for privatization, training vouchers (and hinting at education vouchers), and increasing the number of grant-maintained schools. I had not decided when we would go to the country. But I wanted to be ready for the summer of 1991.

I had also been thinking about my future beyond the next election. There was still much that I wanted to do. Most immediately, we had to defeat Saddam Hussein and establish a durable security framework for the Gulf. The economy was fundamentally strong, but I wanted to overcome inflation and recession and restore a stable framework for growth. I thought there was a good prospect of mopping up communism in central and eastern Europe and establishing limited government under law in the new democracies. Above all I hoped to win the battle for my kind of European Community – one in which a free and enterprising nation-state like Britain could comfortably flourish. But I also knew that the wider framework of international relations which was needed in the post-Cold War world – one in which international bodies like the UN, the GATT, the IMF, the World Bank, NATO and the CSCE held the ring, while nation-states and international commerce were left to their own proper spheres of activity – would not be built in a day. This was a substantial long-term programme.

My problem was the lack of a successor whom I could trust both to keep my legacy secure and to build on it. I liked John Major and thought that he genuinely shared my approach. But he was relatively untested and his tendency to accept the conventional wisdom had given me pause for thought. For reasons I have explained, however, no other candidate found greater favour with me.* Given time, John might grow in stature, or someone else might emerge. So, both because of the scale of the challenges and my uncertainty over the succession, I did not wish to step down before the next election.

Nor, however, did I seriously intend to go 'on and on'. I thought that about two years into the next Parliament would be the right time to leave. Of course, even then it would be a wrench. I felt as full of energy as ever. But I accepted that one day it would be my duty to leave No. 10, whether the electorate had demanded it or not.

What would not persuade me to depart, however, was the kind of argument put to me by Peter Carrington over dinner at his house one Sunday evening in April 1990. Denis was not there: he was away for the weekend. Peter argued that the Party wanted me to leave office both with dignity and at a time of my own choosing. I took this to be a coded message: dignity might suggest a rather earlier departure than I would otherwise choose. Peter was, I suspect, speaking on behalf of at least a section of the Tory establishment. My own feeling was that I would go 'when the time was ripe'. I reflected that if the great and the good of the Tory Party had had their way, I would never have become Party leader, let alone Prime Minister. Nor had I the slightest interest in appearances nor in the trappings of office. I would fight – and, if necessary, go down fighting – for my beliefs as long as I could. 'Dignity' did not come into it.

GEOFFREY HOWE'S RESIGNATION

The restiveness of Tory back-benchers was transformed into open panic by the Eastbourne by-election later in October. Ian Gow's old seat went to the Liberals with a swing of 20 per cent. The opinion polls also looked bad. Labour had a substantial lead. This was not a happy background to the Rome summit which I attended over the weekend of 27–28 October.** Yet even as I was fighting a lone battle in Rome, Geoffrey Howe went on television and told Brian Walden that we did not in fact oppose the principle of a single currency,

* See pp. 755–6.
** See pp. 764–7.

implying that I would probably be won round. This was either disloyal or remarkably stupid. At the first Prime Minister's Questions on my return, I was inevitably asked about his remarks. I countered Opposition taunts by saying that Geoffrey was 'too big a man to need a little man like [Neil Kinnock] to stand up for him'. But I could not endorse what he had said.

And my difficulties were just beginning. I now had to stand up in the House and make my statement on the outcome of the Rome summit. I duly stressed that 'a single currency is not the policy of this Government'. But this assertion – which I considered essential – had two important qualifications. The first was that our own proposal for a parallel or 'common' currency in the form of the hard ecu might evolve *towards* a single currency. The second was a form of words, which ministers had come to use, that we would not have a single currency 'imposed upon us'. And, inevitably, there were differing interpretations of precisely what that delphic expression meant. Such hypothetical qualifications could be used by someone like Geoffrey to keep open the possibility that we would at some point end up with a single currency. That was not our intention, and I felt there was a basic dishonesty in this interpretation. It was the removal of this camouflage which – if any single policy difference mattered – probably provided the reason for Geoffrey's resignation.

I said in reply to questions that 'in my view [the hard ecu] would not become widely used throughout the Community – possibly most widely used for commercial transactions. Many people would continue to prefer their own currency.' I also expressed firm agreement with Norman Tebbit when he made the vital point that 'the mark of a single currency is not only that all other currencies must be extinguished but that the capacity of other institutions to issue currencies must also be extinguished.' My reply was: 'This Government believes in the pound sterling.' And I vigorously rejected the Delors concept of a federal Europe in which the European Parliament would be the Community's House of Representatives, the Commission its Executive, and the Council of Ministers its Senate. 'No, no, no,' I said.

This performance set Geoffrey on the road to resignation. Exactly why is still unclear, perhaps to him, certainly to me. I do not know whether he actually wanted a single currency. Neither now or later, as far as I am aware, did he ever say where he stood – only where I should not stand. Perhaps the enthusiastic – indeed uproarious – support I received from the back-benchers convinced him that he had to strike at once, or I would win round the Parliamentary Party to the platform I earlier set out in Bruges.

No matter what I had said, however, Geoffrey would sooner or later have objected and gone. By this time the gap between us, unlike the rows I had with Nigel Lawson, was as much a matter of personal antipathy as of policy difference. I have explained how Geoffrey reacted when I asked him to leave the Foreign Office.* He never put his heart into the Leadership of the House. In the Cabinet he was now a force for obstruction, in the Party a focus of resentment, in the country a source of division. On top of all that, we found each other's company almost intolerable. I was surprised at the immediate grounds of his resignation. But in some ways it is more surprising that he remained so long in a position which he clearly disliked and resented.

I heard nothing of Geoffrey on Wednesday (31 October). On Thursday morning at Cabinet I took him to task, probably too sharply, about the preparation of the legislative programme. I was slightly curious at the time that he had so little to say for himself. Afterwards, I had lunch in the flat, worked on my speech for the debate on the Loyal Address, had a short meeting with Douglas Hurd about the situation in the Gulf, and then went off to Marsham Street where, in the cellars beneath the DoE/Department of Transport complex, the Gulf Embargo Surveillance unit was operating. I had not been there long when a message came through that Geoffrey wanted urgently to see me back at No. 10. He intended to resign.

I was back there at 5.50 p.m. for what turned out to be almost a rerun of Nigel Lawson's resignation. I asked Geoffrey to postpone his decision till the following morning: I already had so much to think about – surely a little more time was possible. But he insisted. He said that he had already cancelled the speech he was due to give that evening at the Royal Overseas League, and the news was bound to get out. So the letters were prepared and his resignation was announced.

In a sense it was a relief he had gone. But I had no doubt of the political damage it would do. All the talk of a leadership bid by Michael Heseltine would start again. Apart from myself, Geoffrey was the last survivor of the 1979 Cabinet. The press were bound to draw disparaging attention to my longevity. It was impossible to know what Geoffrey himself planned to do. But presumably he would not remain silent. It was vital that the Cabinet reshuffle, made necessary by his departure, should reassert my authority and unite the Party. That would not be easy, and indeed the two objectives might by now be in conflict.

I could not discuss all this with my advisers immediately, however,

* See p. 757.

because I had to host a reception at No. 10 for the Lord's Taverners, the charitable organization with which Denis was involved. But, as soon as I could, I broke away and went to my study where Ken Baker, John Wakeham and Alastair Goodlad, the Deputy Chief Whip, who was standing in for Tim Renton, got down to discussing what must be done.

I already knew my ideal solution: Norman Tebbit back in the Cabinet as Education Secretary. Norman shared my views on Europe – as on so much else; he was tough, articulate and trustworthy. He would have made a superb Education Secretary who could sell his programme to the country and wrong-foot the Labour Party. We could not reach him that night but made contact the following morning (Friday 2 November), and he agreed to come in and discuss it. As I feared, he would not be persuaded. He had left the Cabinet to look after his wife and that duty took precedence over all else. He would give me all the support he could from outside, but he could not come back into Government.

When Norman left, Tim Renton, the Chief Whip, now back in London, came in. He had undoubtedly breathed a sigh of relief that Norman was not coming back. He now argued strongly that William Waldegrave – who was on the left of the Party – should join the Cabinet. William was slim, cerebral and aloof – a sort of Norman St John Stevas without jokes – and he seemed likely to be even less of an ally. But I had never kept talented people out of my Cabinets just because they were not of my way of thinking, and I was not going to start even now. I asked him to take on the Department of Health.

But I still wanted a new face at Education, where John MacGregor's limitations as a public spokesman were costing us dear in an area of great importance. So I appointed Ken Clarke – again not someone on my wing of the Party, but an energetic and persuasive bruiser, very useful in a brawl or an election. John MacGregor I moved to Geoffrey's old post as Leader of the House. The appointments were well received. Although my preferred strategy of bringing back Norman had failed, my objective of uniting the Party seemed to be succeeding.

Any prospect of a return to business as usual, however, was quickly dispelled. I spent Saturday 3 November at Chequers working with my advisers on my speech on the Address, which had, of course, now assumed a new importance in the light of Geoffrey's resignation. That evening Bernard Ingham rang through to read me an open letter Michael Heseltine had written to his constituency chairman. It was ostensibly about the need for the Government to chart a new course on Europe. In fact, it was the first tentative public step in the Heseltine leadership bid. Sunday's papers (4 November) were accordingly full of stories about the leadership. They also contained the first opinion poll findings taken after Geoffrey's departure. Unsurprisingly, they were very bad. Labour was shown in one to be 21 per cent ahead. I spent the day working on another speech – on the environment – which I was to deliver on Tuesday in Geneva.

On as many Monday mornings as possible I used to meet Ken Baker and the Central Office team to look through the diary for the week ahead. Over lunch I would also discuss the political situation with Ken, the business managers and some other Cabinet colleagues. That Monday we talked about almost everything except what was on everyone's mind – whether or not there would be a leadership contest.

This was still far from certain. A feeling was now evident in the British press that Michael had perhaps overplayed his hand in his open letter. If he did not now stand, he would be accused of cowardice. If he did stand, he would probably lose – despite the tremors over Geoffrey's departure. Most people felt that he would have been better chancing his luck after a general election, which my enemies hoped and expected I would lose.

This was the background to the discussion I had with Peter Morrison, my PPS, and Cranley Onslow, Chairman of the '22, on Tuesday afternoon (6 November) after a short visit to Geneva to address the World Climate Conference. We were all concerned that the speculation about the leadership was doing the Party and the Government great harm. It seemed best to try to bring matters to a head and get the leadership campaign – if there was to be one – out of the way quickly. The contest had to take place within twenty-eight days of the opening of the new parliamentary session, but it was up to the leader of the Party in consultation with the Chairman of the '22 to name the precise date. Accordingly, we agreed to bring forward the date for the closing of nominations to Thursday 15 November, with the first ballot on Tuesday 20 November. This meant that I would be away in Paris for the CSCE summit when the first ballot – if there was one – occurred. The disadvantage, of course, would be that I would not be at Westminster to rally support. But Peter Morrison and I did not in any case envisage that I would canvass on my own behalf. As things turned out, this may have been a wrong judgement. But it is important to understand why it was made.

First, it would have been absurd for a prime minister of eleven and a half years' standing – leader of the Party for over fifteen years – to behave as if she were entering the lists for the first time. Tory MPs knew me, my record and my beliefs. If they were not already persuaded, there was not much left for me to persuade them with. Prime ministers can seek to charm and be sure to listen: I had been listening week after week to MPs' grumbles; but I could not now credibly tell an MP worried about the community charge that I had been convinced by what he said and intended to scrap the whole scheme. Nor would I have dreamt of doing so. Thus there were strict limits on any canvassing I could usefully do to maximize my vote. A challenger like Michael, however, could promise promotion to those out of office as well as security for those already in it; he would be the beneficiary of all the resentments of the back-benchers.

Second, I felt that, as in 1989, the most effective campaign would be carried out by others on my behalf. In Peter Morrison I considered that I had an experienced House of Commons man who could put together a good team to work for me. Peter and I had been friends ever since he entered the House. He had been one of the first back-benchers to urge me to stand in 1975. I knew that I could rely on his loyalty. Unfortunately, the same quality of serene optimism which made Peter so effective at cheering us all up was not necessarily so suitable for calculating the intentions of that most slippery of electorates – Conservative MPs. I also envisaged, of course, that Peter would have other heavyweights in my team, including George Younger who had done such a good job in 1989.

The debate on the Address would give me an opportunity to renew my authority and the Government's momentum. So I put extra effort into work on the speech. On the day itself (Wednesday 7 November), I was helped by yet another feeble attack from Neil Kinnock whose latest metamorphosis as a market socialist I mocked in the line: 'The Leader of the Opposition is fond of talking about supply-side socialism. We know what that means: whatever the unions demand, Labour will supply.' But I also had to deal with the more delicate issue of Geoffrey's resignation. And that had hidden traps.

In his resignation letter Geoffrey had not spelt out any significant policy differences between us. Instead, he had concentrated on what he described as 'the mood I had struck . . . in Rome last weekend and in the House of Commons this Tuesday'. I therefore felt entitled to point out in my speech that 'if the Leader of the Opposition reads my Rt. Hon. and learned friend's letter, he will be very pressed indeed to find any significant policy difference on Europe between my Rt. Hon. and learned friend and the rest of us on this side.'

That was true as far as it went, and it supplied my immediate needs. The debate went quite well. But it soon became clear that Geoffrey was furious about what I had said. He apparently felt that there were substantial points of difference on policy between us, even if he had not so far managed to articulate what they were. We had reached nothing more than a lull before a political storm that was to rage ever more strongly.

At the end of Thursday's Cabinet (8 November), we took the unusual step of adjourning for a political session, civil servants leaving the Cabinet Room. Ken Baker warned of the likelihood of extremely bad results at the Bootle and Bradford North by-elections. Things turned out as he feared. The worst result was in Bradford, where we slumped to third place. Early the next morning (Friday 9 November), Ken telephoned me to discuss these results which I had, as usual, stayed up to see. I put on a brave face, saying it was no worse than I expected. But it was bad enough, and at the wrong time.

What really set the political commentators talking, however, was a statement that day by Geoffrey that he would 'be seeking an opportunity in the course of the next few days to explain in the House of Commons the reasons – of substance as well as style – which prompted [his] difficult decision'. The speculation that Michael Heseltine would stand naturally increased over the weekend. Indeed, politics entered one of those febrile nervous phases in which events seem to be moving towards some momentous but unknowable climax almost independent of the wishes of the actors. And there was little I could do about any of this. I soldiered on with my arranged programme in the constituency on Saturday (10 November) and at the Cenotaph Remembrance Day Service on Sunday (11 November).

On Monday (12 November), as the previous week, there was only one subject on our minds at my morning 'Week Ahead' meeting with Ken Baker and at the subsequent lunch with colleagues – and again, significantly, none of us really wished to talk about it. No one knew as yet what Geoffrey would say, or even when he would say it. But never had a speech by Geoffrey been so eagerly awaited.

I delivered my own speech at the Lord Mayor's Banquet in Guildhall that evening, striking a deliberately defiant note. But words now began to fail me. I employed a cricketing metaphor which that evening drew warm applause but which would later be turned to my disadvantage:

> I am still at the crease, though the bowling has been pretty hostile of late. And in case anyone doubted it, can I assure you there will be no ducking bouncers, no stonewalling, no playing for time. The bowling's going to get hit all round the ground.

THE LEADERSHIP CAMPAIGN OPENS

I had now learned that Geoffrey would speak in the House the following day, Tuesday 13 November, about his resignation. I would, of course, stay on after Questions to hear him.

Geoffrey's speech was a powerful Commons performance – the most powerful of his career. If it failed in its ostensible purpose of explaining the policy differences that had provoked his resignation, it succeeded in its real purpose which was to damage me. It was cool, forensic, light at points, and poisonous. His long suppressed rancour gave Geoffrey's words more force than he had ever managed before. He turned the cricketing metaphor against me with a QC's skill, claiming that my earlier remarks about the hard ecu undermined the Chancellor and the Governor of the Bank of England: 'It is rather like sending your opening batsmen to the crease only for them to find, the moment the first balls are bowled, that their bats have been broken before the game by the team captain.' He persuasively caricatured my arguments of principle against Europe's drift to federalism as mere tics of temperamental obstinacy. And his final line – 'the time has come for others to consider their own response to the tragic conflict of loyalties with which I have myself wrestled for perhaps too long' – was an open invitation to Michael Heseltine to stand against me that electrified the House of Commons.

It was a peculiar experience listening to this bill of particulars, rather like being the accused during a prosecutor's summing up in a capital case. For I was as much the focus of attention as was Geoffrey. If the world was listening to him, it was watching me. And underneath the mask of composure, my emotions were turbulent. I had not the slightest doubt that the speech was deeply damaging to me. One part of my mind was making the usual political calculations of how I and my colleagues should react to it in the lobbies. Michael Heseltine had been handed more than an invitation to enter the lists; he had been given a weapon as well. How would we blunt it?

At a deeper level than calculation, however, I was hurt and shocked. Perhaps in view of the irritability that had been the coin of my relations with Geoffrey in recent years, I was foolish to be so pierced. But any ill-feeling between us had been expressed behind closed doors, even if news of it had sometimes leaked into political gossip columns. In public, I had been strongly supportive of him both as Chancellor and as Foreign Secretary. Indeed, the memory of the battles we had fought alongside each other in Opposition and in the early 1980s had persuaded me to keep him in the Cabinet as Deputy Prime Minister when a closer attention to my own political interests on Europe, exchange rates, and a host of other issues would have led me to replace him with someone more of my way of thinking.

Yet he had not been similarly swayed by those memories. After living through so many difficult times and sharing so many policy successes, he had deliberately set out to bring down a colleague in this brutal and public way. And with what result? It was not yet certain what would happen to me. Whatever it was, however, Geoffrey Howe from this point on would be remembered not for his staunchness as Chancellor, nor for his skilful diplomacy as Foreign Secretary, but for this final act of bile and treachery. The very brilliance with which he wielded the dagger ensured that the character he assassinated was in the end his own.

The following morning (Wednesday 14 November) Cranley Onslow telephoned to say that he had received formal notification of Michael Heseltine's intention to stand for the leadership. Douglas Hurd now proposed my nomination; John Major seconded it; this was intended as a demonstration of the Cabinet's united support for me. Peter Morrison quickly had my own leadership team up and running, though some people subsequently suggested that this was too energetic a metaphor. The key figures were to be George Younger, Michael Jopling, John Moore, Norman Tebbit and Gerry Neale. MPs would be discreetly asked their views so that we knew who were supporters, waverers and opponents. Michael Neubert was to keep the tally. Opponents would not be approached again, but waverers were to be called on by whichever member of the team seemed most likely to be persuasive.

It was agreed that I would use press interviews as the main platform for me to set out my case. So on Thursday evening (15 November) I was interviewed by Michael Jones of the *Sunday Times* and Charles Moore of the *Sunday Telegraph*. Nor did I back away from the European issue which Geoffrey's speech had reopened. Indeed, I said that a referendum would be necessary before there was any question of our having a single currency. This was a constitutional issue, not just an economic one, and it would be wrong not to consult the people directly.

When the nuts and bolts of my campaign were explained to me, they sounded fine. Unfortunately, it was not clear how much time some of the main members of my team could give to the campaign. Norman Fowler had been approached by Peter and agreed to be part of it, but then dropped out immediately, claiming past friendship with Geoffrey Howe. George Younger, about to become Chairman of the Royal Bank of Scotland, was heavily involved in his business affairs. Michael Jopling too bowed out. John Moore was not always in the country. Subsequently, a number of my younger supporters in the 'No Turning Back Group' of MPs, alarmed at the way my campaign was going, drafted themselves as helpers and pulled out every stop. Their help was welcome; but why had it become necessary? This should have been a warning sign. But the campaign played on, and I carried on with the arrangements already in my diary, spending Friday 16 November on a visit to Northern Ireland.

Meanwhile, Michael Heseltine's campaign was in full swing. He had promised a fundamental review of the community charge and was talking about transferring the cost of services like education to central taxation. I had already noted in the House that this could mean an extra 5 pence on income tax or large cuts in other public spending – or a budget deficit just when we had enjoyed four years of surplus and had redeemed debt.

I now pressed home the attack on Michael's approach in a *Times* interview with Simon Jenkins where I drew attention to Michael's long-standing corporatist and interventionist views. This appeared on Monday and was promptly criticized in some circles as being too aggressive. But there was nothing remotely personal about it. Michael Heseltine and I disagreed fundamentally about all that is at the heart of politics. MPs should be reminded that this was a contest between two philosophies as well as between two personalities. It was a sign of the funk and frivolity of the whole exercise that they did not want to think anything was at stake apart from their seats.

On Saturday evening 17 November Denis and I had friends and advisers to dinner at Chequers – Peter Morrison, the Bakers, the Wakehams, Alistair McAlpine, Gordon Reece, the Bells, the Neuberts, the Neales, John Whittingdale and of course Mark and Carol. (George Younger could not attend because he had another engagement in Norfolk.) We had an enjoyable dinner, and then got down to business. My team gave me a run down on the figures which seemed quite favourable. Peter Morrison told me he thought he had 220 votes for, 110 against and 40 abstentions, which would be an easy win. (To win in the first round I would need a majority of at least 15 per cent of those entitled to vote.) Even allowing for a 'lie factor', then, I would be all right. But I was not convinced, telling Peter: 'I remember Ted thought the same thing. Don't trust our figures – some people are on the books of both sides.' Everybody else seemed to be far more confident, and indeed spent their time discussing what should be done to unite the Party after my victory. I hoped they were right. Some instinct told me otherwise.

AT THE CSCE SUMMIT IN PARIS

The next day (Sunday 18 November) I departed for the CSCE summit in Paris. It marked the formal – though sadly not the actual – beginning of that new era which was termed by President Bush a 'new world order'. In Paris far-reaching decisions were taken to shape the post-Cold War Europe which had emerged from the peaceful defeat of communism. These included deep mutual cuts in conventional armed forces within the CFE framework, a European 'Magna Carta' guaranteeing political rights and economic freedom (an idea I had particularly championed), and the establishment of CSCE mechanisms to promote conciliation, to prevent conflict, to facilitate free elections, and to encourage consultations between governments and parliamentarians.

As usual, I had a series of bilateral meetings with heads of government. The Gulf was almost always at the forefront of our discussions, though my mind kept turning to what was happening back in Westminster. On Monday (19 November) I had breakfast with President Bush, signed on behalf of the United Kingdom the historic agreement to reduce conventional forces in Europe, attended the first plenary session of the CSCE, and lunched with the other leaders at the Elysée Palace. In the afternoon I made my own speech to the summit, looking back over the long-term benefits of the Helsinki process, emphasizing the continued importance of human rights and the rule of law, pointing to their connection with economic freedom, and warning against any attempt to downgrade NATO which was 'the core of western defence'. I later talked with the UN Secretary-General about the situation in the Gulf before entertaining Chancellor Kohl to dinner at the British Embassy.

It was characteristic of Helmut Kohl that, unlike the other leaders I had met, he came straight to the point, namely the leadership election. He said it was good to talk about these difficult issues rather than bottle them up. He had been determined to devote this evening to me as a way of demonstrating his complete support. It was unimaginable that I should be deprived of office.

Given that the Chancellor and I had strong differences on the future course of the European Community and that my departure would remove an obstacle to his plans – as, indeed, proved to be the case – this was big-hearted of him. With a more serpentine politician, I would have assumed this to be merely insurance against my victory. But Chancellor Kohl, whether as ally or opponent, was never devious. So I was very moved by his words, and by the real warmth of his feeling. I tried to overcome my confusion by explaining the peculiarities of the Tory leadership electoral system, but he said that my account only confirmed his suspicion that the system was quite mad. By now I had concluded he had a point. Then, somewhat to my relief, the conversation turned to the prospects for the IGCs and economic and monetary union, where Chancellor Kohl seemed willing to make compromises, at least on timing. Whether anything more would have come of it than from earlier assurances I cannot say; but I like to think it would have done.

The following day I would know the results of the first ballot. Peter had spoken to me on the telephone on Monday evening, and he was still radiating confidence. It had already been arranged that he would come out to Paris to be there to give me 'the good news', which would be telephoned through to him from the Whips' Office. It had also been agreed precisely what I would do and say in the event of various eventualities – ranging from an overwhelming victory to a defeat on the first round. Knowing there was nothing more I could do, I threw all my energies on Tuesday into more meetings with heads of government and the CSCE proceedings. In the morning (Tuesday 20 November) I had talks with President Gorbachev, President Mitterrand and President Ozal, and lunch with the Dutch Prime Minister, Ruud Lubbers. After lunch I had a talk with President Zhelev of Bulgaria who said that President Reagan and I shared the responsibility for delivering freedom to eastern Europe and no one would ever forget that. Perhaps it took the leader of a country which had been crushed for decades under communist terror to understand just what had happened in the world and why.

The afternoon's session of the CSCE closed at 4.30. After tea and some discussion with my advisers of the day's events, I went upstairs to my room at the residence to have my hair done. Just after 6 o'clock I went up to a room set aside for me to await the results. Bernard Ingham, Charles Powell, our ambassador Sir Ewen Fergusson, Crawfie and Peter were there. Peter had a line open to the Chief Whip, and Charles had another to John Whittingdale back in London. I sat at a desk with my back to the room and got on with some work.

Although I did not realize it then, Charles received the results first. Out of my sight, he gave a sad thumbs down to people in the room, but waited for Peter to get the news officially. Then I heard Peter Morrison receive the information from the Whips' Office. He read out the figures: I had 204 votes, Michael Heseltine 152, and there were 16 abstentions.

'Not quite as good as we had hoped,' said Peter, for once a master of understatement, and handed a note of the results to me. I quickly did the sums in my head. I had beaten Michael Heseltine and achieved a clear majority of the Parliamentary Party (indeed, I got more votes in defeat than John Major later won in victory); but I had not won by a margin sufficient to avoid a second ballot. If I had held two votes that in the event had gone to Michael, I would have beaten him by the required amount. But there was little point now in making precise calculations on the consequences of the want of a nail. A short silence followed.

It was broken by Peter Morrison's trying to telephone Douglas Hurd's room in the residence but finding that Douglas was on the line to John Major in Great Stukeley, where the Chancellor was recovering from an operation to remove his wisdom teeth. A few minutes later we got through to Douglas who at once came along to see me. I did not need to ask for his continued support. He declared that I should stand in the second ballot and promised his own, and John Major's, support. He proved as good as his word, and I was glad to have such a staunch friend by my side. Having thanked him and after a little more discussion I went down, as previously planned, to meet the press and make my statement:

> Good evening gentlemen. I am naturally very pleased that I got more than half the Parliamentary Party and disappointed that it is not quite enough to win on the first ballot, so I confirm it is my intention to let my name go forward for the second ballot.

Douglas followed me and said:

> I would just like to make a brief comment on the ballot result. The Prime Minister continues to have my full support, and I am sorry that this destructive, unnecessary contest should be prolonged in this way.

I went back upstairs to my room and made a number of telephone calls, including one to Denis. There was little to be said. The dangers were all too obvious, and the telephone was not right for a heart-to-heart discussion of what to do. Anyway, everyone in London knew from my statement that I would carry on.

I changed out of the black wool suit with its tan and black collar which I was wearing when the bad news came through. Although somewhat stunned, I was perhaps less distressed than I might have expected. The evidence is that whereas other outfits which evoke sad memories never see the light of day again, I still wear that black wool suit with the tan and black collar. But now I had to be in evening dress for dinner at the Palace of Versailles, before which a ballet was to be performed. I sent ahead to President Mitterrand warning him that I would be late and asking that they start without me.

Before leaving for Versailles, I went in to see my old friend Eleanor (the late Lady) Glover at whose Swiss home I had spent so many enjoyable hours on holiday and who had come round from her Paris flat to comfort me. We talked for just a few minutes in the ambassador's sitting-room. Her maid, Marta, who was with her, had 'seen it in the cards'. I thought it might be useful to get Marta on the campaign team.

At 8 o'clock I left the embassy with Peter Morrison to be driven at break-neck speed in a big black Citroën with outriders through the empty Paris streets, cleared for Presidents Bush and Gorbachev. But my mind was in London. I knew that our only chance was if the campaign were to go into high gear and every potential supporter pressed to fight for my cause. Again and again, I stressed this to Peter: 'We have got to fight.' Some twenty minutes later we arrived at Versailles where President Mitterrand was waiting for me. 'Of course we would never have started without you,' the President said, and with the considerable charm at his command, he accompanied me inside as if I had just won an election instead of half-losing one.

It will be imagined that I could not give the whole of my attention to the ballet. Even the dinner afterwards, always a memorable event at President Mitterrand's table, was something of a strain. The press and photographers were waiting for us as we left, and they showed a special interest in me. Realizing this, George and Barbara Bush, who were just about to leave, swept me up to come out with them. It was one of those little acts of kindness which remind us that even power politics is not just about power.

From Paris the arrangements were now being made for my return to London. I would attend the signing ceremony for the Final

Document of the summit but cut out the previously planned press conference so as to get back to London early. A meeting had been arranged with Norman Tebbit and John Wakeham immediately on my return, and they would be joined later by Ken Baker, John MacGregor, Tim Renton and Cranley Onslow. Meanwhile, three trawls of opinion were being made. For my campaign team Norman Tebbit would assess my support in the Parliamentary Party; Tim Renton would do the same for the whips; and the Cabinet would be canvassed by John MacGregor. This last task was, in fact, meant to be the responsibility of John Wakeham, whom I had decided to involve much more closely in my campaign; but because he was preparing for an announcement on electricity privatization, he delegated it to John MacGregor.

I now know that this was the time when other ministers back in London were preparing to abandon my cause. But I knew nothing of that when I went to bed late that Tuesday night. My first inkling of what was taking place came the next morning when my Private Office told me that in accordance with my request they had telephoned Peter Lilley – a card-carrying Thatcherite whom I had appointed to succeed Nick Ridley at Trade and Industry in July 1990 – to ask him to help with the drafting of my speech for that Thursday's No Confidence debate. Peter had apparently replied that he saw no point in this because I was finished. Coming from such a source, this upset me more than I can say. It was going to be even more difficult than I had imagined in my worst nightmares.

CONSULTATIONS ON RETURN TO DOWNING STREET

I arrived at No. 10 just before midday (Wednesday 21 November). At Peter Morrison's suggestion, I had agreed that I should see members of the Cabinet one by one on my return. The arrangements were made as soon as I got back to London where first appearances were deceptive. The staff of No. 10 clapped and cheered as I arrived; a thousand red roses had arrived from one supporter; and as the long day wore on a constantly increasing flow of other bouquets lined every corridor and staircase.

I went straight up to the flat to see Denis. Affection never blunted honesty between us. His advice was that I should withdraw. 'Don't go on, love,' he said. But I felt in my bones that I should fight on.

My friends and supporters expected me to fight, and I owed it to them to do so as long as there was a chance of victory. But was there?

After a few minutes I went down to the study with Peter Morrison where Norman Tebbit and John Wakeham soon joined us. Norman gave me his assessment. He said that it was very difficult to know how my vote stood with MPs, but many would fight every inch of the way for me. My biggest area of weakness was among Cabinet ministers. The objective must be to stop Michael Heseltine, and Norman thought I had the best chance of doing so. I was quite frank with him in return. I said that if I could see the Gulf crisis through and inflation brought down, I would be able to choose the time of my departure. In retrospect, I can see this was a kind of code assuring them that I would resign not long after the next election.

But we had to consider other possibilities. If Michael Heseltine was unthinkable, who could best stop him? Neither Norman nor I believed that Douglas could beat Michael. Moreover, much though I admired Douglas's character and ability, and grateful as I was to him for his loyalty, I doubted whether he would carry on the policies in which I believed. And that was a vital consideration to me – it was, indeed, the consideration that prompted me to look favourably on John Major. What of *him*? If I withdrew, would he be able to win? His prospects were, at best, still uncertain. So I concluded that the right option was for me to stay in the fight.

John Wakeham said that we should think about the wider meeting just about to start. I should prepare myself for the argument that I would be humiliated if I fought. It was the first time I was to hear the argument that day; but not the last. John, himself, was inclined to reject this logic – he said that one was never humiliated by fighting for what one believed in – at least while it was still hypothetical.

Norman, John, Peter and I then went down to the Cabinet Room where we were joined by Ken Baker, John MacGregor, Tim Renton, Cranley Onslow and John Moore. Ken opened the discussion by saying that the key issue was how to stop Michael Heseltine. In his view, I was the only person who could do this. Douglas Hurd did not want the job badly enough, and in any case he represented the old wing of the Party. John Major would attract more support: he was closer to my views and had few enemies, but he was short of experience. Ken said that two things were needed for my victory: my campaign needed a major overhaul and I must give an undertaking to look radically at the community charge. He advised against a high-profile media campaign.

John MacGregor then spoke. He said that he had done his trawl of Cabinet ministers who in turn had consulted their junior ministers. He said that there were very few who were proposing to shift their allegiance, but the underlying problem was that they had no faith in my ultimate success. They were concerned that my support was eroding. In fact, I subsequently learnt that this was not the full picture. John MacGregor had found a large minority of Cabinet ministers whose support was shaky – either because they actually wanted me out, or because they genuinely believed that I could not beat Michael Heseltine, or because they favoured an alternative candidate. He did not feel able to convey this information frankly in front of Tim Renton, or indeed of Cranley Onslow, and he had not managed to contact me with this information in advance. This was important because if we had known the true picture earlier in the day, we might have thought twice about asking Cabinet ministers individually for their support.

The discussion continued. Tim Renton gave a characteristically dispiriting assessment. He said that the Whips' Office had received many messages from back-benchers and ministers saying that I should withdraw from the contest. They doubted if I could beat Michael Heseltine and they wanted a candidate around whom the Party could unite. He said that the trend was worsening, but conceded that with the vote five days away support could be won back by a better focused campaign fought by the younger members.

But then came the rest of his message. He said that Willie Whitelaw had asked to see him. Willie was worried that I might be humiliated in the second ballot – it was touching that so many people seemed to be worried about my humiliation – and feared that even if I won by a small margin, it would be difficult for me to unite the Party. He did not want to be cast in the role of a 'man in a grey suit'. But, if asked, he would come in and see me 'as a friend'.

Cranley Onslow then gave his assessment. He said that he brought no message from the committee that I should stand down – the reverse, if anything, was true; but nor did they wish to convey any message to Michael Heseltine. In effect, with the ballot going ahead and the result uncertain, the '22 was declaring its neutrality. Cranley gave his own view that the quality of a Heseltine administration would be inferior to one led by me. As for issues, he did not believe that Europe was the main one: it would not be crucial in a general election. Most people were worried about the community charge and he hoped that something substantial could be done about that. I intervened to say that I could not pull rabbits out of a hat in five days. John MacGregor supported me: I could not now credibly promise a radical overhaul of the community charge, no matter how convenient it seemed.

John Wakeham said that the big issue was whether there was a candidate with a better chance of beating Michael Heseltine. He saw no sign of this. Everything, therefore, hung on strengthening my campaign which could only succeed if all my colleagues fought hard for me. Both Ken Baker and John Moore gave their views about the people I needed to win over. Ken noted that those who feared that I could not win were my strongest supporters – people like Norman Lamont, John Gummer, Michael Howard and Peter Lilley. John Moore stressed that I needed complete commitment from ministers, particularly junior ministers, in order to succeed. Norman Tebbit came in at the end. Like Cranley, he believed that Europe had faded as an issue in the leadership campaign: the only other major policy issue was the community charge where Michael's promise of action was proving particularly attractive to MPs from the North-West. In spite of this, however, Norman declared firmly that I could carry more votes against Michael, provided that most of my senior colleagues swung behind me.

The message of the meeting, even from those urging me to fight on, was implicitly demoralizing. Though I had never been defeated in a general election, retained the support of the Party in the country, and had just won the support of a majority of the Party in Parliament, the best thing to be said for me, apparently, was that I was better placed than other candidates to beat Michael Heseltine. But even this was uncertain since my strongest supporters doubted I could win, and others believed that even if I succeeded in that, I would be unable to unite the Party afterwards for the general election. And hanging over all this was the dread much-invoked spectre of 'humiliation' if I were to fight and lose. I drew the meeting to a close, saying I would reflect on what I had heard. In retrospect, I can see that my resolve had been weakened by these meetings. As yet I was still inclined to fight on. But I felt that the decision would really be made at the meetings with my Cabinet colleagues that evening.

Before then I had to make my statement in the House on the outcome of the Paris summit. Leaving No. 10 I called out to the assembled journalists in Downing Street: 'I fight on, I fight to win,' and was interested to see later on the news that I looked a good deal more confident than I felt.

The statement was not an easy occasion, except for the Opposition. People were more interested in my intentions than in my words. Afterwards, I went back to my room in the House where I was met by

Norman Tebbit. It was time – perhaps high time – for me to seek support for my leadership personally. Norman and I began to go round the tea-room. I had never experienced such an atmosphere before. Repeatedly I heard: 'Michael has asked me two or three times for my vote already. This is the first time we have seen you.' Members whom I had known well for many years seemed to have been bewitched by Michael's flattery and promises. That at least was my first reaction. Then I realized that many of these were supporters complaining that my campaign did not seem to be really fighting. They were in a kind of despair because we had apparently given up the ghost.

I returned to my room. I now had no illusion as to how bad the position was. If there was to be any hope, I had to put my whole campaign on a new footing even at this late stage. I therefore asked John Wakeham, whom I believed had the authority and knowledge to do this, to take charge. He agreed but said that he needed people to help him: physically, he had never entirely recovered from the Brighton bomb. So he went off to ask Tristan Garel-Jones and Richard Ryder – both of whom had been closely involved in the 1989 leadership campaign – to be his chief lieutenants.

I now saw Douglas Hurd and asked him formally to nominate me for the second ballot. This he agreed to do at once and with good grace. Then I telephoned John Major at home outside Huntingdon. I told him that I had decided to stand again and that Douglas was going to propose me. I asked John to second my nomination. There was a moment's silence. The hesitation was palpable. No doubt the operation on John's wisdom teeth was giving him trouble. Then he said that if that was what I wanted, yes. Later, when urging my supporters to vote for John for the leadership, I made play of the fact that he did not hesitate. But both of us knew otherwise.

I now went to the Palace for an audience with the Queen at which I informed her that I would stand in the second ballot, as indeed I still intended to do. Then I returned to my room in the House to see the Cabinet one by one.

THE VIEWS OF THE CABINET

I could, of course, have concentrated my efforts for the second ballot on winning over the back-benchers directly. Perhaps I should have done. But the earlier meetings had persuaded me that it was essential to mobilize Cabinet ministers not just to give formal support, but also to go out and persuade junior ministers and back-benchers to back me. In asking for their support, however, I was also putting myself at their mercy. If a substantial number of Cabinet colleagues refused their backing, there could be no disguising the fact afterwards. I recalled a complaint from Churchill, then Prime Minister, to his Chief Whip that talk of his resignation in the Parliamentary Party – he would shortly be succeeded by Anthony Eden – was undermining his authority. Without that authority, he could not be an effective prime minister. Similarly, a prime minister who knows that his or her Cabinet has withheld its support is fatally weakened. I knew – and I am sure they knew – that I would not willingly remain an hour in 10 Downing Street without real authority to govern.

As I have said, I had spoken to Douglas Hurd and John Major already, though I had not directly sought their views about what I should do. I had already seen Cecil Parkinson after returning from the tea-room. He told me that I should remain in the race, that I could count on his unequivocal support and that it would be a hard struggle but that I could win. Nick Ridley, no longer in the Cabinet but a figure of more than equivalent weight, also assured me of his complete support. Ken Baker had made clear his total commitment to me. The Lord Chancellor and Lord Belstead, Leader of the Lords, were not really significant players in the game. And John Wakeham was my campaign manager. But all the others I would see in my room in the House of Commons.

Over the next two hours or so, each Cabinet minister came in, sat down on the sofa in front of me and gave me his views. Almost to a man they used the same formula. This was that they themselves would back me, of course, but that regretfully they did not believe I could win.

In fact, as I well realized, they had been feverishly discussing what they should say in the rooms off the Commons Cabinet corridor above my room. Like all politicians in a quandary, they had sorted out their 'line to take' and they would cling to it through thick and thin. After three or four interviews, I felt I could almost join in the chorus. Whatever the monotony of the song, however, the tone and human reactions of those who came into my room that evening offered dramatic contrasts.

My first ministerial visitor was not a member of the Cabinet at all. Francis Maude, Angus's son and Minister of State at the Foreign Office, whom I regarded as a reliable ally, told me that he passionately supported the things I believed in, that he would back me as long as

I went on, but that he did not believe I could win. He left in a state of some distress; nor had he cheered me up noticeably.

Ken Clarke now entered. His manner was robust in the brutalist style he has cultivated: the candid friend. He said that this method of changing prime ministers was farcical, and that he personally would be happy to support me for another five or ten years. Most of the Cabinet, however, thought that I should stand down. Otherwise, not only would I lose; I would 'lose big'. If that were to happen, the Party would go to Michael Heseltine and end up split. So Douglas and John should be released from their obligation to me and allowed to stand, since either had a better chance than I did. Then the solid part of the Party could get back together. Contrary to persistent rumours, Ken Clarke at no point threatened to resign.

Peter Lilley, obviously ill at ease, came in next. From the message I had received in Paris, I knew roughly what to expect from him. He duly announced that he would support me if I stood but that it was inconceivable that I would win. Michael Heseltine must not be allowed to get the leadership or all my achievements would be threatened. The only way to prevent this was to make way for John Major.

Of course, I had not been optimistic about Ken Clarke and Peter Lilley for quite different reasons. But I had written off my next visitor, Malcolm Rifkind, in advance. After Geoffrey's departure, Malcolm was probably my sharpest personal critic in the Cabinet and he did not soften his criticism on this occasion. He said bluntly that I could not win, and that either John or Douglas would do better. Still, even Malcolm did not declare against me. When I asked him whether I would have his support if I did stand, he said that he would have to think about it. Indeed, he gave the assurance that he would never campaign against me. Silently, I thanked God for small mercies.

After so much commiseration, it was a relief to talk to Peter Brooke. He was, as always, charming, thoughtful and loyal. He said he would fully support me whatever I chose to do. Being in Northern Ireland, he was not closely in touch with parliamentary opinion and could not himself offer an authoritative view of my prospects. But he believed I could win if I went ahead with all guns blazing. Could I win if all guns did *not* blaze? That was something I was myself beginning to doubt.

My next visitor was Michael Howard, another rising star who shared my convictions. Michael's version of the Cabinet theme was altogether stronger and more encouraging. Although he doubted my prospects, he himself would not only support me but would campaign vigorously for me.

William Waldegrave, my most recent Cabinet appointment, arrived next. William was very formal. I could hardly expect more from someone who did not share my political views. But he declared very straightforwardly that it would be dishonourable for someone to accept a place in my Cabinet one week and not support me three weeks later. He would vote for me as long as I was a candidate. But he had a sense of foreboding about the result. It would be a catastrophe if corporatist policies took over, which, of course, was another way of saying that Michael Heseltine should be held at bay.

At this point I received a note from John Wakeham who wanted an urgent word with me. Apparently, the position was much worse than he had thought. I was not surprised. It was hardly any better from where I was sitting.

John Gummer bounced in next. His position was, on the face of it, not easy to predict. He was a passionate European, but he apparently shared the same general philosophy of government as I did. In fact I was mildly curious as to how he would resolve this tension. But he reeled off the standard formula that he would support me if I decided to stand, but as a friend he should warn me that I could not win, and so I should move aside and let John and Douglas stand.

John Gummer was followed by Chris Patten. Chris and I had worked together for many years from the time when he was Director of the Conservative Research Department until I brought him into the Cabinet in 1989. He had a way with words, and perhaps this had too easily convinced me that he and I always put the same construction upon them. But he was a man of the Left. So I could hardly complain when he told me that he would support me but that I could not win, and so on.

Even melodramas have intervals, even *Macbeth* has the porter's scene. I now had a short talk with Alan Clark, Minister of State at the Ministry of Defence, and a gallant friend, who came round to lift my spirits with the encouraging advice that I should fight on at all costs. Unfortunately, he went on to argue that I should fight on even though I was bound to lose because it was better to go out in a blaze of glorious defeat than to go gentle into that good night. Since I had no particular fondness for Wagnerian endings, this lifted my spirits only briefly. But I was glad to have someone unambiguously on my side even in defeat.

By now John Wakeham and Ken Baker had turned up to speak to me, and their news was not good. John said that he now doubted whether I could get the support of the Cabinet. What I had been hearing did not suggest that he was wrong. He added that he had tried to put together a campaign team but was not succeeding even at that. I had realized by now that I was not dealing with Polish cavalrymen; but I was surprised that neither Tristan Garel-Jones nor Richard Ryder were prepared to serve as John's lieutenants because they believed I could not win.

Tristan Garel-Jones had, of course, served on my campaign team the previous year when my position was not seriously under threat. Nonetheless, I could not find it in my heart to be really disappointed in him now. His view of Conservative politics had always been that the line of least resistance is the best course, and I suppose he was only being consistent. But it was a personal as well as a political blow to learn that Richard, who had come with me to No. 10 all those years ago as my political secretary and whom I had moved up the ladder as quickly as I decently could, was deserting at the first whiff of grapeshot.

Ken Baker went on to report that the position had deteriorated since we had spoken that morning. He had found between ten and twelve members of the Cabinet who did not think I could win. And if they thought that, there would not be enough enthusiasm to carry the day. Even so he believed that I should carry on. But he floated Tom King's suggestion – which I was myself to hear from Tom a little later – that I should promise to stand down after Christmas if I won. The idea was that this would allow me to see through the Gulf War. I could not accept this: I would have no authority in the meantime and I would need all I could muster for the forthcoming battles in the European Community.

After John and Ken had left, Norman Lamont came in and repeated the formula. The position, he said, was beyond repair. Everything we had achieved on industry and Europe would be jeopardized by a victory for Michael Heseltine. Everything but Robertson Hare's 'Oh Calamity.'

John MacGregor now appeared and somewhat belatedly gave me the news that I lacked support in the Cabinet which he had felt unable to convey to me earlier in the day. He too eschewed any originality and stuck by the formula. Tom King said the usual things, though more warmly than most. He added the suggestion trailed by Ken Baker that I should offer to stand down at a specific date in the future. I rejected this suggestion, but I was grateful for the diversion.

In all the circumtances, it was a relief to see David Waddington enter and sit down on the sofa. Here was a steadfast friend but, as I quickly saw, one in the deepest distress. All David's instincts were to fight on. For him the argument that battle should not be joined because defeat was likely had none of the attraction that it did for some of his colleagues. It was not an evasion, nor a disguised threat, nor a way of abandoning my cause without admitting the fact. It was a reluctant recognition of reality. But as a former Chief Whip – and how often in recent days had I wished that he still held that office – he knew that support for me in the Cabinet had collapsed. David said that he wanted me to win and would support me but could not guarantee a victory. He left my room with tears in his eyes.

The last meeting was with Tony Newton who, though clearly nervous, just about managed to get out the agreed line. He did not think I could win, etc., etc. Nor, by now, did I. John Wakeham came in again and elaborated further on what he had earlier told me. I had lost the Cabinet's support. I could not even muster a credible campaign team. It was the end.

I was sick at heart. I could have resisted the opposition of opponents and potential rivals and even respected them for it; but what grieved me was the desertion of those I had always considered friends and allies and the weasel words whereby they had transmuted their betrayal into frank advice and concern for my fate. I dictated a brief statement of my resignation to be read out at Cabinet the following morning. But I said that I would return to No. 10 to talk to Denis before finally taking my decision.

I was preparing to return when Norman Tebbit arrived with Michael Portillo. Michael was Minister of State at the DoE with responsibility for local government and the community charge. He was beyond any questioning a passionate supporter of everything we stood for. He tried to convince me that the Cabinet were misreading the situation, that I was being misled and that with a vigorous campaign it would still be possible to turn things round. With even a drop of this spirit in higher places, it might indeed have been possible. But that was just not there. Then another group of loyalists from the 92 Group of MPs arrived in my room – George Gardiner, John Townend, Edward Leigh, Chris Chope and a number of others. They had a similar message to Michael. I was immensely grateful for their support and warmth, and said that I would think about what to do. Then at last I returned to No. 10.

RESIGNATION

I went up to see Denis on my return. There was not much to say, but he comforted me. He had given me his own verdict earlier and it had turned out to be right. After a few minutes I went down to the Cabinet Room to start work on the speech I was to deliver in the following day's No Confidence debate. My Private Office had already prepared a first draft, conceived under very different circumstances. Norman Tebbit and – for some reason – John Gummer came in to help. It was a mournful occasion. Every now and again I found I had to wipe away a tear as the enormity of what had happened crowded in.

While we worked on into the night, Michael Portillo returned with two other last-ditchers, Michael Forsyth and Michael Fallon. They were not allowed to see me as I was engrossed in the speech. But when I was told that they had been sent away, I said that I would naturally see them, and they were summoned back. They arrived about midnight and tried in vain to convince me that all was not lost.

Before I went to bed that night I stressed how important it was to ensure that John Major's own nomination papers were ready to be submitted before the tight deadline if indeed I stood down. I said that I would sleep on my own resignation, as I always did with important matters, before making my final decision; but it would be very difficult to prevail if the Cabinet did not have their hearts in the campaign.

At 7.30 the next morning – Thursday 22 November – I telephoned down to Andrew Turnbull that I had finally resolved to resign. The private office put into action the plan already agreed for an Audience with the Queen. Peter Morrison telephoned Douglas Hurd and John Major to inform them of my decision. John Wakeham and Ken Baker were also told. I cleared the text of the press statement due to be issued later in the morning, spent half an hour of rather desultory briefing with Bernard, Charles and John for Questions in the House, and then just before 9 o'clock, went down to chair my last Cabinet.

Normally, in the Cabinet anteroom ministers would be standing around in groups, arguing and joking. On this occasion there was silence. They stood with their backs against the wall looking in every direction except mine. There was a short delay: John MacGregor had been held up in the traffic. Then the Cabinet filed, still in silence, into the Cabinet Room.

I said that I had a statement to make. Then I read it out:

> Having consulted widely among my colleagues, I have concluded that the unity of the Party and the prospects of victory in a general election would be better served if I stood down to enable Cabinet colleagues to enter the ballot for the leadership. I should like to thank all those in the Cabinet and outside who have given me such dedicated support.

The Lord Chancellor then read out a statement of tribute to me, which ministers agreed should be written into the Cabinet minutes. Most of that day and the next few days, I felt as if I were sleepwalking rather than experiencing and feeling everything that happened. Every now and then, however, I would be overcome by the emotion of the occasion and give way to tears. The Lord Chancellor's reading of this tribute was just such a difficult moment. When he had finished and I had regained my composure, I said that it was vital that the Cabinet should stand together to safeguard all that we believed in. That was why I was standing down. The Cabinet should unite to back the person most likely to beat Michael Heseltine. By standing down I had enabled others to come forward who were not burdened by a legacy of bitterness from ex-ministers who had been sacked. Party unity was vital. Whether one, two or three colleagues stood, it was essential that Cabinet should remain united and support their favourites in that spirit.

Ken Baker on behalf of the Party and then Douglas Hurd as the senior member of the Cabinet made their own short tributes. I could bear no more of this, fearing I would lose my composure entirely, and concluded the discussion with the hope that I would be able to offer the new leader total and devoted support. There was then a ten-minute break for courtesy calls to be made to the offices of the Speaker, the Leader of the Opposition and the Leader of the Liberal Party (Jim Molyneaux of the Unionists could not be contacted) and a statement was accordingly issued at 9.25 a.m.

The Cabinet meeting then resumed. It was almost business as usual. This ranged from matters of the utmost triviality – an unsuccessful Fisheries Council ruined by incompetent Italian chairmanship – to matters of the greatest importance, the decision to increase our forces in the Gulf by sending a second armoured brigade. Somehow I got through it by concentrating on details, and the formal Cabinet ended at about 10.15 a.m. But I invited ministers to stay on. It was a relief to have more or less normal conversation on what was uppermost in our minds, namely the likely outcome of the second ballot, over coffee.

After Cabinet I signed personal messages to Presidents Bush and

Gorbachev, European Community and G7 heads of government, and a number of Gulf leaders. Douglas and John were by now busily organizing their campaigns, both of them having decided to stand.

Later I worked on my speech for the afternoon debate. By this time I was beginning to feel that a great weight had been lifted from me. A No Confidence debate would have been a taxing ordeal if I had been fighting on with so many of the Cabinet, junior ministers and back-benchers against me. Now that I had announced my departure, however, I would again enjoy the united support of the Tory Party. Now it would be roses, roses, all the way. And since this would be my last major parliamentary performance as Prime Minister, I determined to defend the achievements of the last eleven years in the same spirit as I had fought for them.

After a brief Audience with the Queen I returned to No. 10 for lunch. I had a quick drink with members of my staff in the study. I was suddenly conscious that they too had their futures to think about, and I found myself now and later comforting them almost as much as they sought to comfort me. Crawfie had begun the packing. Joy was sorting out outstanding constituency business. Denis was clearing his desk. But I had more public duties to perform. I held my normal briefing meeting for Questions and then left for the House at just before 2.30 p.m.

GRAND FINALE

No one will ever understand British politics who does not understand the House of Commons. The House is not just another legislative body. On special occasions it becomes in some almost mystical way the focus of national feeling. As newspaper comments and the reflections of those who were present will testify, I was not alone in sensing the concentrated emotion of that afternoon. And it seemed as if this very intensity, mingled with the feelings of relief that my great struggle against mounting odds had ended, lent wings to my words. As I answered Questions my confidence gradually rose.

Then I sat down to draw breath and listen to Neil Kinnock make his opening speech in the No Confidence Debate. Mr Kinnock, in all his years as Opposition leader, never let me down. Right to the end, he struck every wrong note. On this occasion he delivered a speech that might have served if I had announced my intention to stand for the second ballot. It was a standard, partisan rant. One concession to the generosity that the House feels on such occasions (and that his own back-bencher, Dennis Skinner, no moderate and an old sparring partner of mine, was about to express in a memorable intervention) might have exploited the discomfiture that was palpably growing on the Tory benches. It might have disarmed me and eroded the control that was barely keeping my emotions in check. Instead, however, he managed to fill me and the benches behind me with his own partisan indignation and therefore intensified the newfound Tory unity – in the circumstances a remarkable, if perverse, achievement.

The speech which I then rose to deliver does not read in Hansard as a particularly eloquent one. It is a fighting defence of the Government's record which replies point by point to the Opposition's attack, and which owes more to the Conservative Research Department than to Burke. For me at that moment, however, each sentence was my testimony at the bar of History. It was as if I were speaking for the last time, rather than merely for the last time as Prime Minister. And that power of conviction came through and impressed itself on the House.

After the usual partisan banter with Opposition hecklers, I restated my convictions on Europe and reflected on the great changes which had taken place in the world since I had entered No. 10. I said:

> Ten years ago, the eastern part of Europe lay under totalitarian rule, its people knowing neither rights nor liberties. Today, we have a Europe in which democracy, the rule of law and basic human rights are spreading ever more widely; where the threat to our security from the overwhelming conventional forces of the Warsaw Pact has been removed; where the Berlin Wall has been torn down and the Cold War is at an end.
>
> These immense changes did not come about by chance. They have been achieved by strength and resolution in defence, and by a refusal ever to be intimidated. No one in eastern Europe believes that their countries would be free had it not been for those western governments who were prepared to defend liberty, and who kept alive their hope that one day eastern Europe too would enjoy freedom.

My final reflection was on the Falklands and Gulf Wars, the second of which we were just then gearing up to fight.

> There is something else which one feels. That is a sense of this country's destiny: the centuries of history and experience which ensure that, when principles have to be defended, when good

> has to be upheld and when evil has to be overcome, Britain will take up arms. It is because we on this side have never flinched from difficult decisions that this House and this country can have confidence in this Government today.

Such was my defence of the record of the Government which I had headed for eleven and a half years, which I had led to victory in three elections, which had pioneered the new wave of economic freedom that was transforming countries from eastern Europe to Australasia, which had restored Britain's reputation as a force to be reckoned with in the world, and which at the very moment when our historic victory in the Cold War was being ratified at the Paris conference had decided to dispense with my services. I sat down with the cheers of my colleagues, wets and dries, allies and opponents, stalwarts and fainthearts, ringing in my ears, and began to think of what I would do next.

BOWING OUT

But there was one more duty I had to perform, and that was to ensure that John Major was my successor. I wanted – perhaps I needed – to believe that he was the man to secure and safeguard my legacy and to take our policies forward. So it was with disquiet that I learnt a number of my friends were thinking of voting for Michael Heseltine. They distrusted the role which John Major's supporters like Richard Ryder, Peter Lilley, Francis Maude and Norman Lamont had played in my downfall. They also felt that Michael Heseltine, for all his faults, was a heavyweight who could fill a room in the way a leader should. I did all I could to argue them out of this, not only in personal conversation but also at the lunch to which I invited my supporters on Monday. In most cases I was successful.

Before then, however, I was to spend my last weekend at Chequers. I arrived there on Saturday evening, travelling down after quite a jolly little lunch with the family and friends at No. 10. On Sunday morning Denis and I went to church, while Crawfie filled a Range Rover with hats, books and a huge variety of personal odds and ends which were to be delivered to our house in Dulwich. Gersons took away our larger items. Denis and I entertained the Chequers staff for drinks before lunch to say farewell and thank you for all their kindness over the years. I had loved Chequers and I knew I would miss it. I decided that I would like to walk round the rooms one last time and did so with Denis as the light faded on that winter afternoon.

From the time that I had announced my resignation, the focus of public interest naturally switched to the question of who would be my successor. As I have said, I did all that I could to rally support for John without publicly stating that I wanted him to win. From about this time, however, I became conscious that there was a certain ambiguity in his stance. On the one hand, he was understandably anxious to attract my supporters. On the other, his campaign wanted to emphasize that John was 'his own man'. A joke – made in the context of remarks on the Gulf – about my skills as a 'back-seat driver' provoked a flurry of anxiety in the Major camp. It was, unfortunately, the shape of things to come.

However, I was truly delighted when the results came through – John Major 185 votes, Michael Heseltine 131 and Douglas Hurd 56. Officially, John was two votes short; but within minutes Douglas and Michael had announced that they would support him in the third ballot. He was effectively the new prime minister. I congratulated him and joined in the celebrations at No. 11. But I did not stay long: this was his night not mine.

Wednesday 28 November was my last day in office. The packing was now all but complete. Early that morning I went down from the flat to my study for the last time to check that nothing had been left behind. It was a shock to find that I could not get in because the key had already been taken off my key-ring. At 9.10 I came down to the front hallway. (I was due shortly at the Palace for my final Audience with the Queen.) As on the day of my arrival, all the staff of No. 10 were there. I shook hands with my private secretaries and others whom I had come to know so well over the years. Some were in tears. I tried to hold back mine but they flowed freely as I walked down the hall past those applauding me on my way out of office, just as eleven and a half years earlier they had greeted me as I entered it.

Before going outside and with Denis and Mark beside me, I paused to collect my thoughts. Crawfie wiped a trace of mascara off my cheek, evidence of a tear which I had been unable to check. The door opened onto press and photographers. I went out to the bank of microphones and read out a short statement which concluded:

> Now it is time for a new chapter to open and I wish John Major all the luck in the world. He will be splendidly served and he has the makings of a great prime minister, which I am sure he will be in a very short time.

I waved and got into the car with Denis beside me, as he has always been; and the car took us past press, policemen and the tall black gates of Downing Street, away from red boxes and parliamentary questions, summits and party conferences, budgets and communiqués, situation rooms and scrambler telephones, out to whatever the future held.

Chronology

1979

May 3	General election.
June 7	European elections.
June 12	1979 Budget. Standard rate of income tax cut to 30 per cent, top rate to 60 per cent.
June 28	Tokyo G7 summit.
August 1–8	Lusaka CHOGM.
August 27	Assassination of Lord Mountbatten / Warrenpoint bomb.
October 23	Geoffrey Howe announced abolition of remaining exchange controls.
November 29–30	Dublin European Council: budget arguments.
December 16	PM and Lord Carrington arrived in Washington for two-day visit.
December 25	Afghanistan: USSR began invasion.

1980

January 2	Steel strike began. Ended 3 April.
May 5	SAS stormed Iranian Embassy.
June 2	Cabinet endorsed EC budget agreement.
June 22	Venice G7 summit.
September 22	Iran-Iraq War began.
October 10	PM addressed Conservative Conference, Brighton: 'The lady's not for turning.'
October 27	First Maze hunger strike began. Ended 18 December.

November 4	USA: Ronald Reagan elected President.
December 8	Anglo-Irish summit in Dublin.

1981

January 5	Norman St John Stevas and Angus Maude left the Government. Francis Pym became Leader of House of Commons, John Nott to Defence, Leon Brittan joined Cabinet as Chief Secretary.
February 10	NCB announced pit closures. Government announced NCB plan withdrawn on 18 February.
March 1	Second IRA hunger strike begun by Bobby Sands. Ended 3 October after 10 deaths; then Chelsea Barracks bomb.
March 10	1981 Budget.
March 26	SDP formed. Alliance formed on 16 June.
March 30	364 economists' letter criticizing economic policy.
April 11–14	Brixton riots.
May 10	François Mitterrand elected French President.
July 3	Southall riot. Toxteth and Moss Side riots 4–8 July.
July 20	Ottawa G7 summit opened.
July 23	Argument at public spending cabinet.
September 14	Reshuffle: Ian Gilmour, Mark Carlisle and Lord Soames left the Government. Nigel Lawson, Norman Tebbit and Cecil Parkinson joined the Cabinet. Jim Prior appointed to Northern Ireland.
September 30	Melbourne CHOGM opened.
December 13	Poland: Martial law declared.

1982

March 25	Roy Jenkins won Glasgow, Hillhead by-election.
April 2	Argentina invaded Falkland Islands.
April 3	Saturday Commons debate on Falklands. Passage of UN SCR502.

April 5	First naval units left Portsmouth. Lord Carrington and other Foreign Office ministers resigned. Francis Pym became Foreign Secretary, John Biffen Leader HC.
April 25	South Georgia recaptured.
May 2	*General Belgrano* sunk by HMS *Conqueror*.
May 4	HMS *Sheffield* hit by an Exocet.
May 21	British troops landed at San Carlos.
June 5	Versailles G7 summit opened.
June 14	Capture of Port Stanley. Argentinian surrender.
July 20	Hyde Park, then Regent's Park bombs.
July 26	St Paul's Thanksgiving Service.
September 17	West Germany: fall of Helmut Schmidt's Government. Helmut Kohl succeeded him as Chancellor.
September 20	PM began visit to Japan/China/Hong Kong.

1983

January 6	Reshuffle: John Nott resigned. Michael Heseltine to Defence; Tom King to Environment.
March 23	USA: President Reagan announced SDI.
May 28	Williamsburg G7 summit opened.
June 9	General election.
June 11	New Government formed: Nigel Lawson Chancellor; Leon Brittan Home Secretary; Geoffrey Howe Foreign Secretary; Francis Pym dropped.
October 14	Cecil Parkinson resigned.
October 25	US invasion of Grenada.
November 14	Cruise missiles arrived at Greenham.
December 4	Athens European Council.
December 17	Harrods bomb.

1984

February 9	USSR: death of Andropov. PM attended funeral.
March 8	Miners' strike began.
June 25	Fontainebleau European Council: budget settlement.
July 10	National dock strike (ended 20 July).
August 24	Second national dock strike (ended 18 September).
October 12	Brighton bomb.
October 25	High Court ordered sequestration of NUM.
October 31	India: Mrs Gandhi assassinated.
November 6	USA: President Reagan re-elected.
November 20	British Telecom flotation.
December 15	Mr and Mrs Gorbachev visited Chequers.
December 19	China: PM signed Hong Kong agreement in Peking.

1985

February 20	PM visited Washington and addressed a joint session of Congress.
March 5	Miners returned to work.
March 11	USSR: Mr Gorbachev new Soviet leader. PM visited Moscow for Chernenko's funeral.
April 4	PM began eleven-day tour of Far East.
May 2	Bonn G7 summit opened.
September 2	Reshuffle. Peter Rees, Patrick Jenkin and Lord Gowrie left the Government. Norman Tebbit new party chairman. Leon Brittan to DTI. Douglas Hurd to Home Office. Kenneth Clarke, John MacGregor and Kenneth Baker all joined the Cabinet.
September 9	Handsworth riots (continued 10 September). Brixton 28 September.
September 16–19	PM toured Egypt and Jordan.
September 25	Plaza Accord to reduce value of the dollar.

October 6–7	Broadwater Farm riot.
October 16–23	Nassau CHOGM: arguments about South Africa.
October 24	PM and President Reagan addressed UN General Assembly.
November 15	PM signed Anglo-Irish Agreement at Hillsborough.
December 3	Luxemburg European Council.

1986

January 9	Westland: Michael Heseltine resigned.
January 24	Westland: Leon Brittan resigned.
January 28	Publication of Community Charge Green Paper.
April 15	US raid on Libya.
May 3–6	PM visited South Korea and attended Tokyo G7 summit.
May 21	Reshuffle. Keith Joseph resigned. Kenneth Baker replaced him as Education Secretary.
May 24–27	PM visited Israel.
August 3	Special London Commonwealth summit on South Africa.
October 24	Britain broke off diplomatic relations with Syria following Hindawi affair.
November 15–16	PM visited Camp David, following Reykjavik summit.
December 5	London European Council.

1987

February 22	Louvre Accord to stabilize the dollar.
March 28	USSR: PM began five-day tour of USSR (ended 2 April).
June 8	Venice G7 summit opened.
June 11	General election.
July 17	USA: PM visited President Reagan in Washington.

October 6	Conservative Conference: led to abandonment of decision to phase in community charge (dual running).
October 13	Vancouver CHOGM.
October 19	'Black Monday'.
November 8	Enniskillen bomb killed 11, injured 60.
December 7	PM held talks with Mr Gorbachev at Brize Norton.
December 8	INF Treaty signed in Washington.

1988

January 4–8	PM toured Africa.
January 10	Lord Whitelaw resigned due to ill-health.
March 7	Sterling 'uncapped'.
March 15	1988 Budget. Standard rate of income tax cut to 25 per cent, top rate to 40 per cent.
March	NATO summit in Brussels.
April 6–8	PM visited Turkey.
April 18	Michael Mates's amendment to band community charge defeated.
May 21	PM spoke to General Assembly of Church of Scotland.
June 2	Interest rates increased from low of 7.5 per cent to 8 per cent.
June 19–21	Toronto G7 summit.
July 17	Alan Walters's return as economic adviser to PM announced.
July 25	Reshuffle. DHSS split between Kenneth Clarke and John Moore.
July 30	PM began eleven-day tour of the Far East and Australia.
August 20	IRA bomb at Ballygawley, Co. Tyrone. PM cut short Cornish holiday.
September 20	Bruges speech.
November 2	PM began three-day visit to Poland.

November 8	USA: George Bush elected President.
November 17	PM visited Washington: farewell to President Reagan and talks with President Bush.
December 21	Lockerbie bombing.

1989

January 31	Publication of NHS White Paper.
March 27	PM began six-day visit to Africa.
April 1	PM visited Namibia.
April 5	Mr Gorbachev began a three-day visit to UK.
May 29–30	NATO fortieth anniversary summit in Brussels.
June 3	China: Tiananmen Square massacre.
June 26	Madrid European Council.
July 14–16	French Revolution Bicentennial and Paris G7 summit.
July 24	Reshuffle: John Moore, Paul Channon, Lord Young and George Younger left the Government. Geoffrey Howe from FCO to Lord President and Leader HC. John Major succeeded him at FCO.
September 19–22	PM visited Japan.
October 18–24	Kuala Lumpur CHOGM.
October 26	Nigel Lawson resigned. John Major replaced him as Chancellor and Douglas Hurd became Foreign Secretary.
November 9	East Germany: announced opening of its border with West Germany. Demolition of Berlin Wall began 10 November.
December 5	PM defeated Sir Anthony Meyer in leadership election 314:33. Twenty-seven abstained.
December 10	Czechoslovakia: end of communist rule.
December 22	Romania: Ceauşescu overthrown.

1990

February 2	South Africa: President de Klerk announced unbanning of ANC. Nelson Mandela released February 11.
March 31	Trafalgar Square riot.
April 24–25	PM visited Turkey on seventy-fifth anniversary of Gallipoli landings.
July 6	NATO summit in London.
July 9	Houston G7 summit.
July 14	Nick Ridley resigned.
July 30	IRA murdered Ian Gow.
August 2	Gulf: Iraq invaded Kuwait. PM held talks in Aspen, Colorado with President Bush.
September 17–19	PM visited Czechoslovakia and Hungary.
October 3	German reunification.
October 27–28	Rome European Council.
November 1	Geoffrey Howe resigned.
November 19–21	CSCE summit in Paris.
November 20	Conservative leadership first ballot: MT 204, Heseltine 152, 16 abstentions.
November 22	PM announced decision not to contest second ballot. Final speech to the Commons as PM.
November 28	MT resigned as PM.

The Cabinet and other important offices

Names marked with an asterisk denote ministers changing jobs or entering the Cabinet for the first time at the beginning of the defined period.

Names in italics denote ministers who left the Government at the end of the defined period.

Names in bold denote Cabinet members. Others in roman.

List of Offices	*May 1979 – January 1981*	*January – September 1981*
PM	**MRS THATCHER**	**MRS THATCHER**
Chllr Exchequer	**HOWE**	**HOWE**
Chief Secretary	**BIFFEN**	***BRITTAN**
Foreign Secretary	**CARRINGTON**	**CARRINGTON**
Home Secretary	**WHITELAW**	**WHITELAW**
Leader H/ Commons	***STEVAS***	***PYM**
Leader H/Lords	**SOAMES**	***SOAMES***
Ld Chllr	**HAILSHAM**	**HAILSHAM**
Ld President	**SOAMES**	***SOAMES***
Ld Privy Seal	**GILMOUR**	***GILMOUR***
Chllr of the Duchy	***STEVAS***	***PYM**
Agriculture	**WALKER**	**WALKER**
Defence	**PYM**	***NOTT**
Education	**CARLISLE**	***CARLISLE***
Employment	**PRIOR**	**PRIOR**
Energy	**HOWELL**	**HOWELL**
Environment	**HESELTINE**	**HESELTINE**
DHSS	**JENKIN**	**JENKIN**
Industry	**JOSEPH**	**JOSEPH**
Northern Ireland	**ATKINS**	**ATKINS**
Paymaster-General	***MAUDE***	***PYM**
Scotland	**YOUNGER**	**YOUNGER**

Trade	NOTT	*BIFFEN
Transport	(non-cabinet)	*FOWLER
Without portfolio	–	–
Wales	EDWARDS	EDWARDS
Attorney-General	HAVERS	HAVERS
Solicitor-General	PERCIVAL	PERCIVAL
Chmn Party	THORNEYCROFT	THORNEYCROFT
Chief Whip	JOPLING	JOPLING
Chmn 1922 Cttee	DU CANN	DU CANN

	September 1981 – April 1982	*April 1982 – January 1983*
PM	MRS THATCHER	MRS THATCHER
Chllr Exchequer	HOWE	HOWE
Chief Secretary	BRITTAN	BRITTAN
Foreign Secretary	CARRINGTON	*PYM
Home Secretary	WHITELAW	WHITELAW
Leader H/Commons	PYM	*BIFFEN
Leader H/Lords	*LADY YOUNG	LADY YOUNG
Ld Chllr	HAILSHAM	HAILSHAM
Ld President	*PYM	*BIFFEN
Ld Privy Seal	*ATKINS	*LADY YOUNG
Chllr of the Duchy	*PYM	*PARKINSON
Agriculture	WALKER	WALKER
Defence	NOTT	NOTT
Education	*JOSEPH	JOSEPH
Employment	*TEBBIT	TEBBIT
Energy	*LAWSON	LAWSON
Environment	HESELTINE	HESELTINE
DHSS	*FOWLER	FOWLER
Industry	*JENKIN	JENKIN
Northern Ireland	*PRIOR	PRIOR
Paymaster-General	*PARKINSON	PARKINSON
Scotland	YOUNGER	YOUNGER
Trade	BIFFEN	*COCKFIELD
Transport	*HOWELL	HOWELL
Without portfolio	–	–
Wales	EDWARDS	EDWARDS
Attorney-General	HAVERS	HAVERS
Solicitor-General	PERCIVAL	PERCIVAL
Chmn Party	*PARKINSON	PARKINSON

Ch Whip	JOPLING	JOPLING
Chmn 1922 Cttee	DU CANN	DU CANN

	January – June 1983	*June – October 1983*
PM	**MRS THATCHER**	**MRS THATCHER**
Chllr Exchequer	**HOWE**	***LAWSON**
Chief Secretary	**BRITTAN**	***REES**
Foreign Secretary	**PYM**	***HOWE**
Home Secretary	**WHITELAW**	***BRITTAN**
Leader H/ Commons	**BIFFEN**	**BIFFEN**
Leader H/Lords	**LADY YOUNG**	***WHITELAW**
Ld Chllr	**HAILSHAM**	**HAILSHAM**
Ld President	**BIFFEN**	***WHITELAW**
Ld Privy Seal	**LADY YOUNG**	***BIFFEN**
Chllr of the Duchy	**PARKINSON**	***COCKFIELD**
Agriculture	**WALKER**	***JOPLING**
Defence	***HESELTINE**	**HESELTINE**
Education	**JOSEPH**	**JOSEPH**
Employment	**TEBBIT**	**TEBBIT**
Energy	**LAWSON**	***WALKER**
Environment	**HESELTINE**	***KING**
DHSS	**FOWLER**	**FOWLER**
Industry/DTI	**JENKIN**	***PARKINSON**
Northern Ireland	**PRIOR**	**PRIOR**
Paymaster-General	**PARKINSON**	VACANT
Scotland	**YOUNGER**	**YOUNGER**
Trade	**COCKFIELD**	SEE DTI
Transport	**HOWELL**	***RIDLEY**
Without portfolio	–	–
Wales	**EDWARDS**	**EDWARDS**
Attorney General	HAVERS	HAVERS
Solicitor-General	PERCIVAL	*PERCIVAL*
Chmn Party	**PARKINSON**	**PARKINSON**/GUMMER
Ch Whip	JOPLING	WAKEHAM
Chmn 1922 Cttee	DU CANN	DU CANN

	October 1983 – September 1984	*September 1984 – September 1985*
PM	**MRS THATCHER**	**MRS THATCHER**
Chllr Exchequer	**LAWSON**	**LAWSON**
Chief Secretary	**REES**	***REES***
Foreign Secretary	**HOWE**	**HOWE**
Home Secretary	**BRITTAN**	**BRITTAN**
Leader H/ Commons	**BIFFEN**	**BIFFEN**
Leader H/Lords	**WHITELAW**	**WHITELAW**
Ld Chllr	**HAILSHAM**	**HAILSHAM**
Ld President	**WHITELAW**	**WHITELAW**
Ld Privy Seal	**BIFFEN**	**BIFFEN**
Chllr of the Duchy	***COCKFIELD***	****GOWRIE***
Agriculture	**JOPLING**	**JOPLING**
Defence	**HESELTINE**	**HESELTINE**
Education	**JOSEPH**	**JOSEPH**
Employment	***KING**	**KING**
Energy	**WALKER**	**WALKER**
Environment	***JENKIN**	**JENKIN**
DHSS	**FOWLER**	**FOWLER**
DTI	***TEBBIT**	**TEBBIT**
Northern Ireland	***PRIOR***	***HURD**
Paymaster-General	VACANT	GUMMER (non-cabinet)
Scotland	**YOUNGER**	**YOUNGER**
Transport	**RIDLEY**	**RIDLEY**
Without portfolio	–	***YOUNG**
Wales	**EDWARDS**	**EDWARDS**
Attorney-General	HAVERS	HAVERS
Solicitor-General	*MAYHEW	MAYHEW
Chmn Party	GUMMER	GUMMER
Ch Whip	WAKEHAM	WAKEHAM
Chmn 1922 Cttee	DU CANN	ONSLOW

	September 1985 – January 1986	*January 1986 – May 1986*
PM	**MRS THATCHER**	**MRS THATCHER**
Chllr Exchequer	**LAWSON**	**LAWSON**
Chief Secretary	***MACGREGOR**	**MACGREGOR**
Foreign Secretary	**HOWE**	**HOWE**
Home Secretary	***HURD**	**HURD**
Leader H/ Commons	**BIFFEN**	**BIFFEN**

Leader H/Lords	**WHITELAW**	**WHITELAW**
Ld Chllr	**HAILSHAM**	**HAILSHAM**
Ld President	**WHITELAW**	**WHITELAW**
Ld Privy Seal	**BIFFEN**	**BIFFEN**
Chllr of the Duchy	**TEBBIT**	**TEBBIT**
Agriculture	**JOPLING**	**JOPLING**
Defence	**HESELTINE**	******YOUNGER*
Education	**JOSEPH**	**JOSEPH**
Employment	***YOUNG**	**YOUNG**
Energy	**WALKER**	**WALKER**
Environment	***BAKER**	**BAKER**
DHSS	**FOWLER**	**FOWLER**
Industry/DTI	***BRITTAN**	***CHANNON**
Northern Ireland	***KING**	**KING**
Paymaster-General	***CLARKE**	**CLARKE**
Scotland	***YOUNGER**	***RIFKIND**
Transport	**RIDLEY**	**RIDLEY**
Without portfolio	–	–
Wales	**EDWARDS**	**EDWARDS**
Attorney-General	HAVERS	**HAVERS**
Solicitor-General	MAYHEW	MAYHEW
Chmn Party	**TEBBIT**	**TEBBIT**
Chief Whip	WAKEHAM	WAKEHAM
Chmn 1922 Cttee	ONSLOW	ONSLOW

	May 1986 – June 1987	*June 1987 – October 1987*
PM	**MRS THATCHER**	**MRS THATCHER**
Chllr Exchequer	**LAWSON**	**LAWSON**
Chief Secretary	**MACGREGOR**	***MAJOR**
Foreign Secretary	**HOWE**	**HOWE**
Home Secretary	**HURD**	**HURD**
Leader H/ Commons	**BIFFEN**	***WAKEHAM**
Leader H/Lords	**WHITELAW**	**WHITELAW**
LdChllr	**HAILSHAM**	***HAVERS**
Ld President	**WHITELAW**	**WHITELAW**
Ld Privy Seal	**BIFFEN**	***WAKEHAM**
Chllr of the Duchy	**TEBBIT**	***CLARKE**
Agriculture	**JOPLING**	***MACGREGOR**
Defence	**YOUNGER**	**YOUNGER**
Education	***BAKER**	**BAKER**

Employment	**YOUNG**	***FOWLER**
Energy	**WALKER**	***PARKINSON**
Environment	***RIDLEY**	**RIDLEY**
DHSS	**FOWLER**	***MOORE**
Industry/DTI	**CHANNON**	***YOUNG**
Northern Ireland	**KING**	**KING**
Paymaster-General	**CLARKE**	*BROOKE (non-cabinet)
Scotland	**RIFKIND**	**RIFKIND**
Transport	***MOORE**	***CHANNON**
Without portfolio	–	–
Wales	**EDWARDS**	***WALKER**
Attorney-General	MAYHEW	MAYHEW
Solicitor-General	LYELL	LYELL
Chmn Party	***TEBBIT***	BROOKE
Chief Whip	WAKEHAM	WADDINGTON
Chmn 1922 Cttee	ONSLOW	ONSLOW

	October 1987 – January 1988	*January – July 1988*
PM	**MRS THATCHER**	**MRS THATCHER**
Chllr Exchequer	**LAWSON**	**LAWSON**
Chief Secretary	**MAJOR**	**MAJOR**
Foreign Secretary	**HOWE**	**HOWE**
Home Secretary	**HURD**	**HURD**
Leader H/ Commons	**WAKEHAM**	**WAKEHAM**
LeaderH/Lords	**WHITELAW**	***BELSTEAD**
Ld Chllr	***MACKAY**	**MACKAY**
LdPresident	**WHITELAW**	***WAKEHAM**
Ld Privy Seal	**WAKEHAM**	***BELSTEAD**
Chllr of the Duchy	**CLARKE**	**CLARKE**
Agriculture	**MACGREGOR**	**MACGREGOR**
Defence	**YOUNGER**	**YOUNGER**
Education	**BAKER**	**BAKER**
Employment	**FOWLER**	**FOWLER**
Energy	**PARKINSON**	**PARKINSON**
Environment	**RIDLEY**	**RIDLEY**
DHSS	**MOORE**	**MOORE**
Industry/DTI	**YOUNG**	**YOUNG**
Northern Ireland	**KING**	**KING**
Paymaster-General	BROOKE(non-cabinet)	BROOKE

Scotland	**RIFKIND**	**RIFKIND**
Transport	**CHANNON**	**CHANNON**
Without portfolio	–	–
Wales	**WALKER**	**WALKER**
Attorney-General	MAYHEW	MAYHEW
Solicitor-General	LYELL	LYELL
Chmn Party	BROOKE	BROOKE
Chief Whip	WADDINGTON	WADDINGTON
Chmn 1922 Cttee	ONSLOW	ONSLOW

	July 1988 – July 1989	*July – October 1989*
PM	**MRS THATCHER**	**MRS THATCHER**
Chllr Exchequer	**LAWSON**	**LAWSON**
Chief Secretary	**MAJOR**	***LAMONT**
Foreign Secretary	**HOWE**	**MAJOR**
Home Secretary	**HURD**	**HURD**
Leader H/ Commons	**WAKEHAM**	***HOWE**
Leader H/Lords	**BELSTEAD**	**BELSTEAD**
Ld Chllr	**MACKAY**	**MACKAY**
Ld President	**WAKEHAM**	***HOWE**
Ld Privy Seal	**BELSTEAD**	**BELSTEAD**
Chllr of the Duchy	***NEWTON**	***BAKER**
Agriculture	**MACGREGOR**	***GUMMER**
Defence	***YOUNGER***	***KING**
Education	**BAKER**	***MACGREGOR**
Employment	**FOWLER**	**FOWLER**
Energy	**PARKINSON**	***WAKEHAM**
Environment	**RIDLEY**	***PATTEN**
DSS	***MOORE***	***NEWTON**
DH	***CLARKE**	**CLARKE**
DTI	**YOUNG**	***RIDLEY**
Northern Ireland	**KING**	***BROOKE**
Paymaster-General	BROOKE (non-cabinet)	***CAITHNESS**
Scotland	**RIFKIND**	**RIFKIND**
Transport	***CHANNON***	***PARKINSON**
Without portfolio	–	–
Wales	**WALKER**	**WALKER**
Attorney-General	MAYHEW	MAYHEW
Solicitor-General	LYELL	LYELL

Chmn Party	BROOKE	***BAKER**
Chief Whip	WADDINGTON	WADDINGTON
Chmn 1922 Cttee	ONSLOW	ONSLOW

	October 1989 – January 1990	*January 1990 – May 1990*
PM	**MRS THATCHER**	**MRS THATCHER**
Chllr Exchequer	***MAJOR**	**MAJOR**
Chief Secretary	**LAMONT**	**LAMONT**
Foreign Secretary	***HURD**	**HURD**
Home Secretary	***WADDINGTON**	**WADDINGTON**
Leader H/ Commons	**HOWE**	**HOWE**
Leader H/Lords	**BELSTEAD**	**BELSTEAD**
Ld Chllr	**MACKAY**	**MACKAY**
Ld President	**HOWE**	**HOWE**
Ld Privy Seal	**BELSTEAD**	**BELSTEAD**
Chllr of the Duchy	**BAKER**	**BAKER**
Agriculture	**GUMMER**	**GUMMER**
Defence	**KING**	**KING**
Education	**MACGREGOR**	**MACGREGOR**
Employment	**FOWLER**	***HOWARD**
Energy	**WAKEHAM**	**WAKEHAM**
Environment	**PATTEN**	**PATTEN**
DSS	**NEWTON**	**NEWTON**
DH	**CLARKE**	**CLARKE**
Industry/DTI	**RIDLEY**	**RIDLEY**
Northern Ireland	**BROOKE**	**BROOKE**
Paymaster-General	*RYDER	RYDER
Scotland	**RIFKIND**	**RIFKIND**
Transport	**PARKINSON**	**PARKINSON**
Without portfolio	–	–
Wales	**WALKER**	**WALKER**
Attorney-General	MAYHEW	MAYHEW
Solicitor-General	LYELL	LYELL
Chmn Party	BROOKE	***BAKER**
Chief Whip	*RENTON	RENTON
Chmn 1922 Cttee	ONSLOW	ONSLOW

	May – July 1990	*July – November 1990*
PM	**MRS THATCHER**	**MRS THATCHER**
Chllr Exchequer	**MAJOR**	**MAJOR**
Chief Secretary	**LAMONT**	**LAMONT**
Foreign Secretary	**HURD**	**HURD**
Home Secretary	**WADDINGTON**	**WADDINGTON**
Leader H/ Commons	**HOWE**	**HOWE**
Leader H/Lords	**BELSTEAD**	**BELSTEAD**
Ld Chllr	**MACKAY**	**MACKAY**
Ld President	**HOWE**	**HOWE**
Ld Privy Seal	**BELSTEAD**	**BELSTEAD**
Chllr of the Duchy	**BAKER**	**BAKER**
Agriculture	**GUMMER**	**GUMMER**
Defence	**KING**	**KING**
Education	**MACGREGOR**	**MACGREGOR**
Employment	**HOWARD**	**HOWARD**
Energy	**WAKEHAM**	**WAKEHAM**
Environment	**PATTEN**	**PATTEN**
DSS	**NEWTON**	**NEWTON**
DH	**CLARKE**	**CLARKE**
Industry/DTI	**RIDLEY**	***LILLEY**
Northern Ireland	**BROOKE**	**BROOKE**
Paymaster-General	RYDER	RYDER
Scotland	**RIFKIND**	**RIFKIND**
Transport	**PARKINSON**	**PARKINSON**
Without portfolio	–	–
Wales	***HUNT**	**HUNT**
Attorney-General	MAYHEW	MAYHEW
Solicitor-General	LYELL	LYELL
Chmn Party	BAKER	**BAKER**
Chief Whip	RENTON	RENTON
Chmn 1922 Cttee	ONSLOW	ONSLOW

	November 1990
PM	**MRS THATCHER**
Chllr Exchequer	**MAJOR**
Chief Secretary	**LAMONT**
Foreign Secretary	**HURD**
Home Secretary	**WADDINGTON**

Leader H/ Commons	***MACGREGOR**
Leader H/Lords	**BELSTEAD**
Ld Chllr	**MACKAY**
Ld President	***MACGREGOR**
Ld Privy Seal	**BELSTEAD**
Chllr of the Duchy	**BAKER**
Agriculture	**GUMMER**
Defence	**KING**
Education	***CLARKE**
Employment	**HOWARD**
Energy	**WAKEHAM**
Environment	**PATTEN**
DSS	**NEWTON**
DH	***WALDEGRAVE**
Industry/DTI	**LILLEY**
Northern Ireland	**BROOKE**
Paymaster-General	RYDER
Scotland	**RIFKIND**
Transport	**PARKINSON**
Without portfolio	–
Wales	**HUNT**
Attorney-General	MAYHEW
Solicitor-General	LYELL
Chmn Party	**BAKER**
Chief Whip	*RENTON*
Chmn 1922 Cttee	ONSLOW

List of Abbreviations

ABM	Anti-Ballistic Missile
ACAS	Advisory, Conciliation and Arbitration Service
AGR	Advanced Gas-cooled Reactor
ALCM	Air-launched Cruise Missile
ANC	African National Congress
AUEW	Amalgamated Union of Engineering Workers
BL	British Leyland (later Rover Group)
BMA	British Medical Association
BMD	Ballistic Missile Defence
BR	British Rail
BSC	British Steel Corporation
CAP	Common Agricultural Policy
CBI	Confederation of British Industry
CDU	German Christian Democrat Party
CEGB	Central Electricity Generating Board
CFCs	Chlorofluorocarbons
CFE	Conventional Forces in Europe
CHOGM	Commonwealth Heads of Government Meeting
CND	Campaign for Nuclear Disarmament
CPRS	Central Policy Review Staff
CPS	Centre for Policy Studies
CSCE	Conference on Security and Co-operation in Europe
DES	Department of Education and Science
DHA	District Health Authority
DHSS	Department of Health and Social Security (divided from 1988)
DoE	Department of the Environment
DTI	Department of Trade and Industry
DUP	Democratic Unionist Party

E	Economic Committee of the Cabinet
E(A)	Principal sub-committee of E
EBRD	European Bank for Reconstruction and Development
EC	European Community
ECJ	European Court of Justice
ECOFIN	Economic and Financial Affairs Council of the EC
ECST	European Convention on the Suppression of Terrorism
Ecu	European Currency Unit
EDG	European Democratic Group
EDU	European Democratic Union
EFL	External Financing Limit
EFTA	European Free Trade Association
EMS	European Monetary System
EMU	Economic and Monetary Union
EPG	Eminent Persons Group (sent to South Africa)
ERM	Exchange Rate Mechanism (of the EMS)
EXCO	Executive Council (Hong Kong)
FCO	Foreign and Commonwealth Office
FRG	Federal Republic of Germany
FSBR	Financial Statement and Budget Report ('the Red Book')
G7	Group of Seven
GATT	General Agreement on Tariffs and Trade
GDP	Gross Domestic Product
GLC	Greater London Council
GLCM	Ground-launched Cruise Missile
GM	General Motors
GM school	Grant-Maintained school
GNP	Gross National Product
GP	General Practitioner
H	Home Affairs Committee of the Cabinet
HAT	Housing Action Trust
HMI	Her Majesty's Inspectorate (of schools)
IDU	International Democratic Union
IEA	Institute of Economic Affairs
IGC	Inter-Governmental Conference
ILEA	Inner London Education Authority

IMF	International Monetary Fund
INF	Intermediate-range Nuclear Forces
INLA	Irish National Liberation Army
IRA	Irish Republican Army
ISTC	Iron and Steel Trades Confederation
ITC	Independent Television Commission
L	Legislation Committee of the Cabinet
LEA	Local Education Authority
MCAs	Monetary compensation amounts
MEZ	Maritime Exclusion Zone
MIRVs	Multiple independently targetable re-entry vehicles
MLR	Minimum Lending Rate
MNF	Multi-National Force
MoD	Ministry of Defence
MSC	Manpower Services Commission
MTFS	Medium Term Financial Strategy
M0	Monetary base
£M3	Sterling M3
NACODS	National Association of Colliery Overmen, Deputies and Shotfirers
NADs	National Armaments Directors
NATO	North Atlantic Treaty Organization
NCB	National Coal Board (later British Coal)
NCC	National Curriculum Council
NDLS	National Dock Labour Scheme
NEB	National Enterprise Board
NEDC	National Economic Development Council ('Neddy')
NGA	National Graphical Association
NHS	National Health Service
NICs	National Insurance contributions
NIO	Northern Ireland Office
NIS	National Insurance Surcharge
NRC	National Reporting Centre
NUM	National Union of Mineworkers
OAS	Organization of American States
OD	Overseas and Defence Committee of the Cabinet
OD(SA)	Sub-Committee of OD which ran the Falklands War
ODA	Overseas Development Administration

OECD	Organization for Economic Co-operation and Development
OECS	Organization of Eastern Caribbean States
OPEC	Organization of Petroleum Exporting Countries
OUP	Official Unionist Party
PLO	Palestine Liberation Organization
PPS	Parliamentary Private Secretary
PSBR	Public Sector Borrowing Requirement
PSDR	Public Sector Debt Repayment
QL	Queen's Speeches and Future Legislation Committee of the Cabinet
QUANGO	Quasi-autonomous non-governmental organization
RHA	Regional Health Authority
RPI	Retail Price Index
RUC	Royal Ulster Constabulary
SALT	Strategic Arms Limitation Treaty
SAS	Special Air Service
SDLP	Social Democratic and Labour Party
SDP	Social Democratic Party
SDI	Strategic Defence Initiative
SLCM	Sea-launched Cruise Missile
SNF	Short-range Nuclear Forces
SSA	Standard Spending Assessment
START	Strategic Arms Reduction Treaty
SWAPO	South West Africa People's Organization
TASM	Tactical Air-to-Surface Missile
TEZ	Total Exclusion Zone
TGWU	Transport and General Workers' Union
TSRB	Top Salaries Review Board
TUC	Trades Union Congress
UAE	United Arab Emirates
UDM	Union of Democratic Miners
UDR	Ulster Defence Regiment
UNSCR	United Nations Security Council Resolution
VAT	Value Added Tax
WEU	Western European Union

Index

NOTE: Government Departments and Ministries are grouped together under the heading **Departments and Ministries**